Electrodermal Activity

Wolfram Boucsein

Electrodermal Activity

Second Edition

 Springer

Wolfram Boucsein
University of Wuppertal
Wuppertal
Germany
boucsein@uni-wuppertal.de

ISBN 978-1-4614-1125-3   e-ISBN 978-1-4614-1126-0
DOI 10.1007/978-1-4614-1126-0
Springer New York Dordrecht Heidelberg London

Library of Congress Control Number: 2011939059

Printed on acid-free paper

Springer is part of Springer Science+Business Media (www.springer.com)

Foreword to the Second Edition

As noted by David Lykken in the foreword to the first edition of this book, electrodermal activity was observed for the first time in Germany. A quarter-century later the scientific study of psychology also originated in Germany. Over time, however, the focus of psychological research, including the then new field of psychophysiology, shifted to the United States and Great Britain. This trend to the dominance of the United States and Great Britain was prolonged by the devastation of World War II and its aftermath in Germany (and elsewhere in continental Europe). Slowly at first and then more rapidly, German psychological science, including psychophysiology, recovered. For several decades German psychophysiologists have been a major force in psychophysiology. With the publication of the first English edition of this book in 1992, it became essential for electrodermal researchers worldwide again to learn from our German colleagues.

When I came into psychophysiology in the mid-1960s, electrodermal activity was the most common system studied. Because of its popularity, a large literature had emerged on the physiological mechanisms producing these changes in the electrical properties of the skin and on the best methodology for recording them. Major reviews and/or chapters had been published or soon were to be published by Peter Venables and Irene Martin, Robert Edelberg, and David Lykken. Later reviews and articles were published by Venables and Margaret Christie, and by me. A chapter in 1990 by Michael Dawson, Anne Schell, and Diane Filion was especially noteworthy for its coverage of the psychological applications of electrodermal measures.

Note that all these publications were journal articles and chapters and that most of them focused almost entirely on mechanisms and methodology. The publication of this book, first in German and then in English, provided the first *book* on electrodermal activity, and one that extensively covers psychological applications as well as mechanisms and methodology. Again to quote David Lykken back in 1992, "The return of German scholarship to what I shall loftily call the high table of psychophysiology is exemplified by this fine book, the most comprehensive treatise on the electrodermal system to appear in any language . . ." I completely agree with that evaluation. Professor Boucsein's outstanding scholarship has produced a book of such breadth of coverage and depth of knowledge that it stands in a class by itself as *the* standard reference source on electrodermal activity. Even without a second edition the book would still constitute the definitive coverage of the topic. With the incorporation of new developments and addition of some new areas, the second edition is of even greater value. Professor Boucsein has provided a great service to the field by bringing all of this literature together in one comprehensive review.

Wolfram Boucsein was educated at the University of Giessen and later became Professor of Physiological Psychology at the University of Wuppertal. He has published extensively in the area of psychophysiology.

Iowa City, USA   Don C. Fowles

Preface to the Second Edition

After being now 20 years old, the present handbook needed an update, mainly because of new developments in electrodermal recording and scoring, but also because a great number of scientific papers on the application of EDA in various fields appeared. Not only emerged new possibilities such as recording EDA within a fMRI setting, but in addition new applications such as in decision making, biofeedback, and ergonomics, have been enlarged since the first edition appeared back in 1992. Hundreds of original papers and reviews were scrutinized and incorporated if applicable.

The general structure of the book has been retained, in order to allow the reader who is familiar with the first edition an easy detection of additional material. The following sections are entirely newly written: ambulatory monitoring (Sect. 2.2.3.4), recently proposed mathematical solutions for evaluating overlapping responses (Sect. 2.3.1.5), the use of EDA in decision making (Sect. 3.1.3.3), in human-computer interaction (Sect. 3.5.1.1), in marketing and product evaluation (Sect. 3.5.1.3), and in certain neurological diseases (Sects. 3.5.4.2 and 3.5.4.3). Other Sections were substantially updated and/or rewritten: central origins (Sect. 1.3.4.1), electrode arrangements (Sect. 2.2.6.4), significance of the orienting response (Sect. 3.1.1.1), classical conditioning (Sect. 3.1.2.1), biofeedback (Sect. 3.1.2.3), lateralization and hemispherical asymmetry (Sect. 3.1.4), multidimensional arousal modeling (Sect. 3.2.1.2), diurnal variations and sleep (Sect. 3.2.1.3), the use of EDA in emotion and stress (Sect. 3.2.2), in anxiety, psychopathy and depression (Sect. 3.4.1), in traffic and automation (Sect. 3.5.1.2), and in the detection of deception (Sect. 3.5.2), just mentioning the major ones.

The author thanks the following persons who helped him editing the book, with respect to both language and content: Mark Handler, John J. Furedy, John A. Stern, Andrew Munn, Florian Schaefer, Nathalie Fritsch, and Peter Kirsch. Appreciation for technical support is given first and above all to Janine Gronewold, but also to Sabine Hackenberg and Marie Drüge. I am very grateful to my wife Lilo who supported and encouraged me in the years during which I worked on the present book.

Wuppertal, Germany   Wolfram Boucsein

Foreword to the First Edition in 1992

Electrodermal activity was observed for the first time more than 150 years ago in Germany where, a quarter-century later, the scientific study of psychology also originated. Well into the twentieth century, English-speaking psychologists all read German and, if they could, made pilgrimages to Leipzig and Heidelberg and other seats of German scholarship. Then gradually the focus of psychological research, including the new field of psychophysiology, shifted to the United States and Britain. Studies of electrodermal activity, in particular, originated mainly in North America. As a student in the early 1950s, I learned about what we then called the Galvanic Skin Response or GSR by reading C.W. Darrow, G.L. Freeman, R.A. Haggard, R.A. McCleary, and H.G. McCurdy, all in American English.

The current renaissance of German science has made it necessary for psychologists, once again, to attend to and learn from the work of their Teutonic colleagues. Fortunately for us monolingual Americans, English has become the lingua franca of our field; German scholars speak our language fluently when they visit the United States and understand us when we go to them. The return of German scholarship to what I shall loftily call the high table of psychophysiology is exemplified by this fine book, the most comprehensive treatise on the electrodermal system to appear in any language and now available in English.

In 1971, in the eighth volume of the journal *Psychophysiology*, Lykken and Venables commented, "Of all psychophysiological variables, the GSR can lay reasonable claim to being the most popular in current use. In spite of years of searching study, we are still surprisingly uncertain about the function, not to say the mechanism of this phenomenon. ... Nevertheless, the GSR seems to be a robust sort of variable since, in hundreds of experiments, it continues stoutly to provide useful data in spite of being frequently abused by measurement techniques which range from the arbitrary to the positively weird." Now, more than 20 years later, the findings collected and integrated by Professor Boucsein should make it possible for future investigators to address this "robust sort of variable" with standardized technique and the respect that it deserves.

Wolf Boucsein was educated at the University of Giessen and is now Professor of Physiological Psychology at the University of Wuppertal. He has published extensively in the areas of psychophysiology and differential psychology. In the present volume, he has provided what should become the standard reference on the topic of electrodermal activity.

Minneapolis, USA   David T. Lykken

Preface to the First Edition

Since the discovery of the galvanic skin response over 100 years ago, recording of electrodermal phenomena has become one of the most widely used methods of measurement in various fields of psychophysiology. This book provides, for the first time, a comprehensive summary of perspectives and histories from different scientific disciplines as well as a complete outline of methodological issues, and a review of results from different areas of electrodermal research.

The book is divided into three parts. Part I (Chaps. 1.1–1.5) focuses on the anatomical, physiological, and biophysical origins of electrodermal phenomena. Peripheral and central nervous system mechanisms are discussed, and fundamental biophysical principles are provided together with an extensive discussion of the current electrical models of electrodermal activity.

Part II (Chaps. 2.1–2.6) outlines principles and methods of electrodermal recording, scoring techniques, and the action of internal and external influences on the signal, and describes statistical properties of the different electrodermal parameters. It ends with a summary of recent discussions on the advantages and disadvantages of the different methods.

Part III (Chaps. 3.1–3.6) reviews applications of electrodermal recording techniques within psychophysiology, personality research, clinical and applied psychology, and medical disciplines, for example, dermatology and neurology. Areas such as orienting and habituation, classical and instrumental conditioning, information processing and storage, multidimensional arousal, sleep, and stress research are considered with respect to the theoretical modeling of vegetative concomitants of central nervous system phenomena. Aspects of specific validity of electrodermal measures are discussed within the framework of neurophysiological and psychophysiological systems.

The present volume is conceptualized as a handbook. A reader who is not especially interested in the signal's origin may start with Part II, after having read the introductory Sect. 1.1.1 and the summary in Chap. 1.5. Readers having fundamental knowledge in electrophysics may skip Sect. 1.4.1, and also Sects. 2.1.1 and 2.1.2. Since the book contains numerous cross-references to the different sections, starting from any point is possible without loss of content. Several chapters and sections end with summaries that provide the appropriate highlights (Chaps. 1.5 and 3.6, and Sects. 2.1.6, 2.2.7, and 2.3.5).

Appreciation for adding to the book's content is given to my coworkers Rüdiger Baltissen, Jörn Grabke, Peter Kirsch, and Florian Schaefer as well as to Mike Dawson, Bob Edelberg, and John Furedy. I would also like to thank Ulrike Hillmann, Marlies Knodel, Brigitte Kapanke, and Boris Damke for doing the text editing, and Sebastian Boucsein, Katrin Boucsein, Martina Promeuschel, and Timothy Skellett for helping with figures, references, and language editing. In addition, I would like to thank Cecilia Secor, Judith Ray, and especially Alex Vincent, who helped tremendously to improve my English, the latter one also for making several proposals that added to the content. Finally, appreciation is given to the series editor, Bill Ray, who performed a great job getting the present volume published.

Wuppertal, Germany   Wolfram Boucsein

Contents

Chapter 1
Principles of Electrodermal Phenomena

Since the 1880s, when psychological factors related to electrodermal phenomena were first observed, electrodermal recording has become one of the most frequently used biosignals in psychophysiology. The major reason for its popularity is the ease of obtaining a distinct electrodermal response (EDR), the intensity of which seems apparently related to stimulus intensity and/or its psychological significance. Electrodermal recording is possible with rather inexpensive equipment, not only in the laboratory but also under less controlled field conditions.

In spite of the widespread use of electrodermal recording in research and application, electrodermal phenomena are not yet fully understood. Originating in neurology and physiology, electrodermal phenomena became a domain of psychophysiology. Only in the last four or five decades, basic research in mechanisms underlying electrodermal phenomena has intensified. However, a tradition of joint research is lacking in the related disciplines of anatomy, physiology, physics, and psychology. Moreover, scientific papers and reviews concerning electrodermal recording are spread over a wide variety of journals and books, and a comprehensive handbook dealing only with electrodermal activity (EDA) has not been available until the first edition of the present book in 1992.

After a general introduction, the first chapter of the present book combines anatomical, physiological, and biophysical aspects of electrodermal research, which will provide users from different backgrounds a general description of the many aspects of electrodermal phenomena without troublesome study of the large number of original papers on the subject.

1.1 Terminology and History

This section outlines terminology and gives basic definitions of the different electrodermal phenomena (Sect. 1.1.1). An introduction to electrodermal methodology and research is given in the mainly historically oriented Sect. 1.1.2, and finally a brief overview of more recent basic electrodermal research is provided in Sect. 1.1.3.

W. Boucsein, *Electrodermal Activity*, DOI 10.1007/978-1-4614-1126-0_1,
© Springer Science+Business Media, LLC 2012

Table 1.1 Methods of electrodermal recording, units of measurement, and abbreviations in the corresponding classes of units

Methods of recording	Endosomatic	Exosomatic			
Applied current		Direct current		Alternating current	
Units	Skin potential	Skin resistance	Skin conductance	Skin impedence	Skin admittance
Abbreviations					
In general	SP	SR	SC	SZ	SY
Tonic (level)	SPL	SRL	SCL	SZL	SYL
Phasic (response)	SPR	SRR	SCR	SZR	SYR
Supplementary abbreviations					
nonspecific response	NS.SPR	NS.SRR	NS.SCR	NS.SZR	NS.SYR
frequency	SPR freq.	SRR freq.	SCR freq.	SZR freq.	SYR freq.
amplitude	SPR amp.	SRR amp.	SCR amp.	SZR amp.	SYR amp.
latency	SPR lat.	SRR lat.	SCR lat.	SZR lat.	SYR lat.
rise time	SPR ris.t.	SRR ris.t.	SCR ris.t.	SZR ris.t.	SYR ris.t.
Recovery time					
63% recovery	SPR rec.tc	SRR rec.tc	SCR rec.tc	SZR rec.tc	SYR rec.tc
50% recovery	SPR rec.t/2	SRR rec.t/2	SCR rec.t/2	SZR rec.t/2	SYR rec.t/2

Reasons for the omission of the phase angle measure $S\varphi R$ are given in Sect. 2.3.1.2 under "Amplitudes of Exosomatic Responses Recorded with Alternating Current."

1.1.1 Definitions and Terminology

EDA was first introduced by Johnson and Lubin (1966) as a common term for all electrical phenomena in skin,[1] including all active and passive electrical properties which can be traced back to the skin and its appendages. One year later, a proposal for standardization made by a terminology commission of the Society of Psychophysiological Research had been published (Brown, 1967), which is now generally accepted (Table 1.1).[2] Electrodermal recordings which do not use an external current are called *endosomatic*, since only potential differences originating in the skin itself are recorded. Methods of *exosomatic* recording apply either *direct current* (DC) or *alternating current* (AC) to the skin. In DC measurement, if voltage is kept constant, EDA is recorded directly in skin conductance (SC) units, while skin resistance (SR) units are obtained when current is kept constant (Sect. 2.1.1). Accordingly, if effective voltage is kept constant in AC measurement, EDA is

---

[1] Dermal stems from Latin: *derma* = true skin, see Table 1.2, Sect. 1.2.1.1.

[2] Abbreviations are determined by the first letter of the words: skin, potential, resistance, and conductance. Unfortunately, the commission overlooked that the abbreviation C is already reserved in physics for capacitance, and G is used for conductance, according to SI units (Sect. 1.4.1.1). The terminology used in AC methodology is somewhat more complicated. Edelberg (1972a) proposed A for admittance, and Z – the last letter in the alphabet – for the reciprocal unit, impedance. While the latter abbreviation was kept, admittance is abbreviated today by Y, the penultimate letter of the alphabet.

recorded directly as skin admittance (SY), while the appliance of constant effective current results in skin impedance (SZ) recordings (Sect. 2.1.5). The third letters in electrodermal units refer to either level (L) or response (R). Accordingly, EDA is divided into *tonic* (EDL = electrodermal level) and *phasic* phenomena (EDR = electrodermal response or reaction). Typical forms of EDRs are shown in Figs. 2.13 and 2.14 (Sect. 2.3.1.2). Tonic electrodermal measures are obtained either as EDLs in response-free recording intervals or as the number of non-stimulus-specific EDRs in a given time window (Sect. 2.3.2).

The use of the term "response" for phasic electrodermal phenomena suggests that there is a distinct relationship to a stimulus producing an EDR. However, there are often phasic parts of EDA which cannot be traced to any specific stimulation. Hence, they are called "spontaneous" or "nonspecific" EDRs (Sect. 2.3.2.2), which are characterized by the prefix "NS" (e.g., NS.SCR is used as an abbreviation for nonspecific skin conductance response).

In addition, various suffixes are added to the abbreviations of EDRs as shown in the lower part of Table 1.1, indicating the parameter which is obtained from the phasic component: frequency (e.g., SCR freq.) which means number of EDRs in a given time window; amplitude (e.g., SCR amp.) which refers to the height of a single response; latency (e.g., SCR lat.) which is the time from stimulus onset to response onset in case of a specific EDR; rise time (e.g., SCR ris.t.) which is the time from the onset of a response to its maximum; and recovery time, indicating the time that is needed to recover either 50% (i.e., SCR rec.t/2) or 63% (i.e., SCR rec.tc) of the amplitude. All those parameters are described in detail in Sect. 2.3.1.

An older notation persisting in the literature is "galvanic skin response" or "galvanic skin reflex" (GSR). It is no longer recommended to use this term for several reasons. First, it suggests that skin can be regarded as a galvanic element, which does not correspond to the multiplicity and complexity of electrodermal phenomena (Sects. 1.4.2 and 1.4.3). Second, it suggests that EDRs are elicited as a kind of reflex, which would neither comprise spontaneous EDRs nor psychologically elicited electrodermal changes. Finally, the term GSR has been used to cover not only phasic EDRs but also electrodermal phenomena in general, including tonic EDA, which gives rise to its ambiguity.

There are also some tendencies in neighboring disciplines to use other terms and abbreviations, for example, the introduction of "peripheral autonomic surface potential" (PASP) in neurology (Knezevic & Bajada, 1985) instead of skin potential (SP). For the sake of interdisciplinary clarity, the sole use of terms and abbreviations given in Table 1.1 is recommended.

1.1.2 Early History of Electrodermal Research

The history of research into EDA, which has been thoroughly reviewed by Neumann and Blanton (1970), dates back to experiments performed in 1849 by DuBois-Reymond in Germany. He had the participants in his study put either hands or feet into a zinc sulfate solution and observed an electrical current going from the limb at rest to the other one that was voluntarily contracted (Veraguth, 1909). However, in accordance with the opinion shared by most scientists at that time, DuBois-Reymond considered the observed phenomenon as being due to muscle action potentials.

The first experiment that showed a connection between sweat gland activity and current flow in skin was performed in Switzerland by Hermann and Luchsinger (1878), who observed that an electrical stimulation of the sciatic nerve in the curarized cat resulted in sweat secretion as well as an electric current in the footpad on the same body side. Injections of atropine sulfate increased the latency of the current, decreased its intensity, and finally stopped both the electrical current and sweat secretion. Three years later, Hermann repeated the voluntary movement experiment performed more than 30 years earlier by DuBois-Reymond. He found that areas with stronger sweating such as palms and fingers showed greater skin current than other body sites such as the wrist and elbow regions, which pointed to the importance of human sweat glands in electrodermal phenomena (Neumann & Blanton, 1970).

The observation which first related psychological factors to EDA is attributed to Vigouroux (1879), an electrotherapist working in France. He measured SR changes that paralleled changes in the amount of anesthesia in hysterical patients and supposed that both phenomena were dependent upon central processes. However, he did not believe that the sudden changes in SR he observed could be produced by local processes in the skin itself. Instead, he presumed a change in vascular conductivity, which was in line with the developing research on autonomic nervous control of blood flow at that time.

The essential discovery of electrodermal phenomena is, however, attributed to two researchers who might not have been aware of each other, the French neurologist Féré (1888) and the Russian physiologist Tarchanoff (1889). Féré used an external direct current and observed a decrease in SR following sensory or emotional stimulation in hysterical patients. Since his paper on SR was a brief and informal report, it was not cited during the rest of the nineteenth century, and it is possible that Tarchanoff did not notice the work of Féré before publishing his own results on EDA in the same French journal (Veraguth, 1909). However, Neumann and Blanton (1970) suggested that international tensions between France and Germany, where Tarchanoff published his results again in 1890, were the cause of both researchers ignoring the other's results. Tarchanoff himself did not use the exosomatic method as Féré did. Instead, he used endosomatic, i.e., SP recording in his observations of electrodermal changes following sensory stimulation, imagination, mental arithmetic, expectation, and voluntary muscle contractions.

Tarchanoff (1890), in his German paper, clearly presumed that the electrodermal phenomena observed by him were a result of sweat gland activity dependent on the action of the secretory nerves, which were not well known at that time. He observed a current flow, even at rest, from areas rich in sweat glands to those poor in them. This result seems to be in line with the Swiss/German tradition mentioned above.

On the contrary, Féré – more in the French tradition – presumed the decrease of SR following stimulation being an effect of a decrease in skin blood flow, i.e., caused by partial displacement of the peripheral resistance of blood by the lower resistance of interstitial fluidity. The interpretation of the SRR as a vasomotor phenomenon, which had been defended for the last time in 1933 by McDowall (Edelberg, 1972a), is no longer pursued seriously, because the EDR showed independence from plethysmographic changes, and relationships between EDA and skin blood flow remain more or less contradictory (Sect. 2.4.2.1). Another hypothesis stated in 1902 by Sommer, suggesting the EDR was a result of involuntary muscle activity, could also not be proven, since a correlation between EDR and finger tremor is lacking (Venables & Christie, 1973).

In 1904, the engineer Müller demonstrated the electrodermal phenomenon to the Swiss neurologist Veraguth, claiming to have discovered it independently (Neumann & Blanton, 1970). Veraguth's monograph entitled "Das psychogalvanische Reflexphänomen" (*The psychogalvanic reflex phenomenon*), which was published in 1909, for the first time gave rise to a broader interest from psychiatrists and psychologists, because it focused on the suggested psychophysiological origin of electrodermal phenomena. Since then, the number of articles on basic electrodermal research as well as on various applications has increased.

In spite of the insufficient methods for biosignal recording and amplification at that time, physiologists pushed forward with the investigation of the origins of EDA. In 1921, Ebbecke observed a local EDR which could be elicited by rubbing or pressing skin sites, even several hours postmortem (Keller, 1963), and these results directed attention to the polarizational properties of skin (Sect. 1.4.2.3). In 1923, Gildemeister applied high-frequency alternating currents to skin and found very small, or even an absence of, EDRs. His conclusion that SR was possibly only an impedance phenomenon resulting from membrane polarizations (Sect. 1.4.2) is no longer regarded as valid (Edelberg, 1971). Additionally, AC measurement, the use of which is quite common in investigations of electrical properties of tissues, was not used very much in electrodermal recordings.

In 1928 and 1929, Gildemeister and Rein made a decisive contribution to the investigation of the origins of endosomatic EDA. For the first time they restricted the locus of SP origin to only one of two recording sites by injuring the skin below the other electrode, where no SP of its own could develop (Keller, 1963). In 1929, Richter was the first to state the hypothesis of a causal mechanism for EDA including both epidermal and sweat gland mechanisms, which is still regarded as valid (Edelberg, 1972a; Fowles, 1986a). Thus, by the end of the 1920s, the early phase of electrodermal research was completed. In the 1930s, Darrow (1933, 1937a, 1937b) worked as a pioneer in various fields of electrodermal research. Extensive reviews of early electrodermal methodology and its significance in physiological research on arousal and emotion (Sects. 3.2.1 and 3.2.2) were provided by Wechsler (1925) and by Woodworth and Schlosberg (1954) in their book on experimental psychology.

1.1.3   Recent Developments in Electrodermal Research

Improvements in equipment for physiological and psychophysiological research, such as the invention of the oscilloscope, the polygraph and especially highly integrated amplifier and computer technology, considerably contributed to the increase not only in the amount of basic electrodermal research but also in applications during the second half of the last century. Both Bloch (1952), working with humans, and Ladpli and Wang (1960), investigating EDA in cats, were equipped to take polygraphic recordings simultaneously from different limbs. Wang (1964) added much to the knowledge of central mechanisms eliciting EDA by using appropriate methods with cats, performing lesion experiments at different levels in the CNS (Sect. 1.3.4.1). Although these animal results cannot fully be generalized to humans (Footnote 10, Sect. 1.2.3), much of our knowledge concerning the central origin of EDA is based on research with cats (Sequeira & Roy, 1997), since investigations of EDA in nonhuman primates are sparse (e.g., Kimble, Bagshaw & Pribram, 1965).

Basic electrodermal research with humans as performed in the previous decades concentrated on the peripheral mechanisms (Sect. 1.5) as well as on the influence of different methods of measurement on recordings (Sect. 2.6). As a result, Darrow (1964) as well as Lykken and Venables (1971) strongly supported skin conductance units as being adequate with respect to physiological models of the peripheral EDA mechanisms (Sect. 2.6.5). Edelberg (1971), after having performed electrodermal research for more than a decade, proposed an electrical model of the skin which takes into account the presence of polarization capacitances (Sect. 1.4.3.2). Using this background, Edelberg (1972a) for the first time established the different psychophysiological aspects of various EDA components in detail, including parameters which were subsequently focused on, for example, rise times and recovery times of EDRs (Sect. 2.3.1.3). In addition, there are continuing attempts to improve electrodermal recording and signal evaluation, such as developing new measures for AC recording of EDA (Sects. 1.4.3.3 and 2.2.3.3) or finding better solutions for handling overlapping EDRs (Sect. 2.3.1.2 "Amplitudes of Exosomatic Responses Recorded with Direct Current").

With few exceptions, EDA methodology is nowadays regarded as being well established (see Chap. 2). Earlier comprehensive reviews of EDA methodology were given by Edelberg (1967) in Brown's book on psychophysiological methods, and – enriched with more empirical results – by Edelberg (1972a) in the *Handbook of Psychophysiology* edited by Greenfield and Sternbach. In the only book solely concerned with EDA that has been published up to the appearance of the present volume's first edition – an edited book by Prokasy and Raskin (1973) – the methodological section of which was written by Venables and Christie, who also wrote the EDA chapter in the Martin and Venables (1980) volume on *Techniques in Psychophysiology*. In that chapter, Venables also reported the results of his extensive cross-sectional survey on EDA performed in Mauritius as a follow-up study during the 1970s. During the beginning of the 1980s, the development of EDA methodology came to a standstill. As a consequence, Fowles' (1986a) chapter on EDA in the Coles, Donchin, and Porges *Handbook of Psychophysiology* contained only an appendix concerning methodology and focused instead on research into basic electrodermal mechanisms and the psychological significance of electrodermal measures.

The widespread use of EDA as a tool in basic as well as in applied psychophysiological research has resulted in a great variety of publications on EDA. Edelberg (1972a) estimated the number of these publications as exceeding 1,500 in 1972, and a first attempt to summarize EDA research in the different fields occurred in the book edited by Prokasy and Raskin (1973). Since then, a wealth of studies have been published (see Chap. 3), giving evidence that EDA measurement is nowadays regarded as "one of the most widely used ... response systems in the history of psychophysiology" (Dawson, Schell, & Filion, 2007, p. 159). Also, the areas for application of EDA have been steadily widened during the last decades, e.g., in the field of engineering psychophysiology (Sect. 3.5.1) and in neurology (Sect. 3.5.4). Such applications require that electrodermal recording techniques being robust enough for the use in various field settings outside the laboratory, including ambulatory monitoring techniques (Sect. 2.2.3.4).

Psychophysiological measures in general have often been used without sound theoretical background (Boucsein & Backs, 2000). In the first edition of this book, the present author suggested a neurophysiologically based multidimensional arousal model to fill this gap for some electrodermal and cardiovascular measures. Since then, this model has been continuously extended (Sect. 3.2.1.2).

Shortly after the appearance of the first edition of the present book, a conference on EDA was held in Lille, France, the results of which were published by Roy, Boucsein, Fowles, and Gruzelier (1993). Various methodological issues were addressed, starting with a critique of the widely accepted twofold origin of electrodermal phenomena in the sweat glands and in an active epidermal layer (Sect. 1.4.2.3), followed by a suggestion to replace the two-effector hypothesis by a hydraulic pressure-oriented poral valve model, requiring only a single effector (Edelberg, 1993, see Sect. 1.4.3.2). An intriguing new area for basic research into electrodermal phenomena was reviewed by Raine and Lencz (1993), i.e., recording EDA during functional magnetic resonance brain imaging (fMRI, see Sect. 2.2.3.5). This technique allows testing hypotheses about central origins of EDA from animal research by a direct observation of brain activity in humans (Sect. 1.3.4.1 "Subcortical Control of EDA"). Finally, several applied areas were considered, such as psychopathology (Sect. 3.4) and hemispheric asymmetry (Sect. 3.1.4.3), which covered some of the widespread application of EDA as reviewed in the third chapter of the present book.

Despite the progress in electrodermal research made until 1993 and further on, much work remains to be performed concerning basic electrodermal phenomena, since EDA is a rather complex phenomenon with respect to its central and peripheral causal mechanisms. Future basic electrodermal research should be encouraged by the integrative view of anatomical, physiological, and physical principles of EDA, as outlined in the first chapter of this book.

1.2   Anatomy of Skin and Sweat Glands

It is far beyond the scope of this chapter to give an exhaustive description of the skin's complex features. Only those parts of the skin and its appendages that are necessary to understand the mechanisms of EDA – the epidermis and the sweat glands – are discussed in detail. The reader who is particularly interested in this topic is referred to the textbook by Millington and Wilkinson (1983), to the multivolume series edited by Jarrett (1973a, 1973b, 1980), or to the handbook of dermatology and venerology which is in part German and in part English (e.g., the volumes edited by Marchionini & Spier, 1963; or by Schwarz, Spier, & Stüttgen, 1979). For age-related changes in the skin, see Sect. 2.4.3.1.

The skin consists of a complex set of organs that provide protective and sense functions. Skin protects the body from environmental threats such as temperature, chemical, mechanical and infectious agents by acting as a selective barrier. From a sensory standpoint, skin houses various receptors to provide afferent information related to touch (mechanoreceptors), pain (nociceptors), and temperature (thermoreceptors). The skin's role in the regulation of perspiration is twofold. On the one hand, the skin prevents the body from drying out; on the other hand, with the aid of the sweat glands, the skin enables a controlled emission of body fluid.

1.2.1   Vertical Structure of the Skin

The skin is composed of different layers which can be easily distinguished from each other by means of a light microscope. These layers show characteristic differences at different body sites. Thus, the layers described in Fig. 1.1 and Table 1.2 do not appear in the same way and are not clearly recognizable at all sites.

Figure 1.1 depicts a typical cross section of glabrous (hairless) skin, as it appears on the palms of the hands (palmar) and the soles of the feet (plantar or volar). On these strongly mechanically stressed surfaces, which are especially significant for EDA measurements because of their specificity for emotional sweating (Sect. 1.3.2.4), the epidermis has an unusual thickness of approximately 1 mm; ordinarily it is only 50–200 μm.

The skin (cutis) is composed of two markedly distinguishable layers, the dermis and the epidermis[3]. The epidermis is located on the skin surface and consists of epithelial tissue, which becomes progressively hornier closer to the surface.

---

[3] Note that the dermis is also known as the *corium* (Latin for tauter skin) and that sometimes the term *cutis* is used only for the dermal part of skin (*cutis vera*, see Table 1.2).

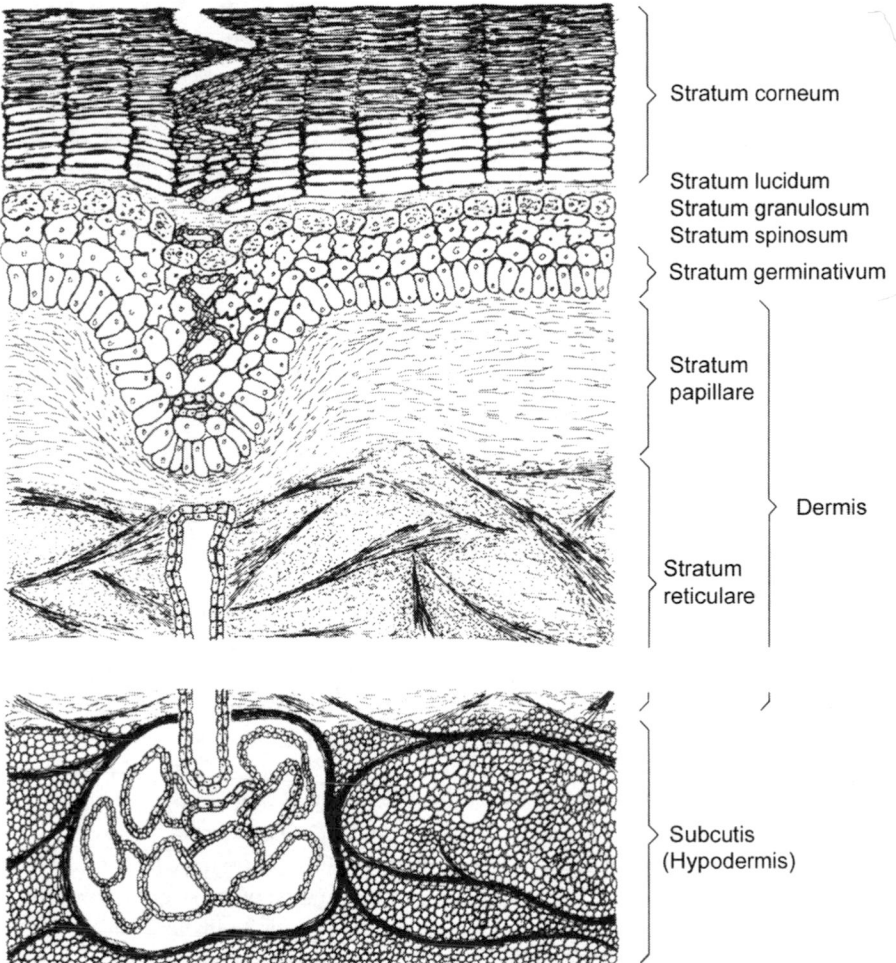

Epi
Dermis

Stratum corneum

Stratum lucidum
Stratum granulosum
Stratum spinosum
Stratum germinativum

Stratum
papillare

Dermis

Stratum
reticulare

Subcutis
(Hypodermis)

Fig. 1.1 Layered composition of the glabrous human skin. An eccrine sweat gland, encircled by its glomerulus, together with its straight dermal and irregularly coiled (helical) epidermal duct (labeled acrosyringium), is shown in cross section. A part of the reticular layer has been omitted due to its size in relation to the rest of the skin

The deeper-lying dermis consists of taut, fibrous connective tissue. The epidermis is relatively thin in comparison with the dermis.[4]

The hypodermis (subcutis) is composed of loose connective tissue which forms the transitional layer between the skin and the deeper-lying tissue. It contains the secretory part of the sweat glands, appearing as a glomerulus (Fig. 1.1), as well as fatty tissue, and the larger vessels which supply the body surface.

---

[4] For example, Birgersson et al. (2011) performed a literature review on the skin thickness at the female volar forearm, revealing a stratum corneum thickness of 14 ± 3 μm compared to $1.2 \pm .2$ mm for the subcutis.

Table 1.2 Layers of the skin. The zonal layering is not so distinct in every region of the skin. The *stratum lucidum* is only clearly recognizable on palmar and plantar skin areas

Cutis (skin)	Epidermis	Stratum corneum	upper zone
			middle zone
			lower zone
		Stratum lucidum	Stratum intermedium
		Stratum granulosum (granular layer)	
		Stratum spinosum (prickle cell layer)	Stratum Malpighii
		Stratum germinativum (basal layer)	
	Dermis (cutis vera = true skin)	Stratum papillare (papillary layer)	
		Stratum reticulare (reticular layer)	
Subcutis (hypodermis)			

1.2.1.1 The Epidermis

The most common division of the epidermis is into five different layers (Jarrett, 1973a; Klaschka, 1979).[5] The lowest layer, in which the epidermal cells generate, is the *stratum germinativum* (from Latin *germino*) or germinating layer; it lies on top of the basal lamina (which belongs to the dermis) and is sometimes named after the basal lamina as the basal layer (see Table 1.2). This layer produces mainly *keratinocytes*, which are cells that can store keratin and later become horny; it also produces *melanocytes*, which supply the skin pigment melanin, as well as Langerhans and Merkel cells. Within a period of around 30 days, the keratinocytes reach the skin surface and are exfoliated there in the form of horny (keratinized) plates. The characteristic form changes which these cells undergo as they migrate have been used in part to characterize the corresponding epidermal layers.

Figure 1.1 shows the basal cells in the stratum germinativum, which are at first columnar and later rounded. They shrink during the course of their migration, which enlarges the intercellular spaces. Since the shrunken cells, with their cytoplasmic extensions, come to appear as having spines, sometimes the term *stratum spinosum*, or prickle cell layer, is applied as a special name for this particular stage. The stratum germinativum and the stratum spinosum are labeled together as the Malpighian layer (*stratum Malpighii*) as shown in Table 1.2.

The *stratum intermedium* represents a transitional zone[6] between the cells of the stratum Malpighii, which are not yet horny, and the horny cells of the outer epidermal layer, forming the *stratum corneum* (Table 1.2).

---

[5] Some authors (e.g., Orfanos, 1972) proposed a division into three layers, which may have been dependent upon different microscopic technology.

[6] This transitional layer, with an overall thickness of around 1 µm, is unusually thin in comparison with the underlying Malpighian layer and the overlying part of the epidermis. Orfanos (1972) has hence suggested that this layer should not be subdivided, but should be named on the whole as the stratum intermedium (i.e., intermediate) instead. However, sometimes only the granular layer is distinguished as the transitional zone (Jarrett, 1973a).

In the lower stratum intermedium the keratinocytes contain keratohyaline granules, giving this layer the name granular layer (*stratum granulosum*). During their upward migration, the cells may be soaked with an oily substance called eleidin. Due to their ability to strongly refract light, they appear as a homogenous layer, named the *stratum lucidum*. The stratum lucidum, however, is visible only on some body sites, especially on the palms and the soles, upon successful removal of the whole horny layer (Sect. 2.2.1.2).

The outer epidermal layer is called the *stratum corneum* (from Latin *cornu* for horn) or, since its cells are fully keratinized,[7] the keratin-layer zone. In accordance with both the form of its cells and the width of its intercellular spaces, the horny layer can be subdivided into a lower, middle, and upper zone (Table 1.2). However, this subdivision is not as clear in other sites as it is in the palmar and plantar ones. Therefore, the layers of the corneum can sometimes only be distinguished as a taut layer called the *stratum compactum* or *stratum conjunctum*, and the *stratum disjunctum*, a loose surface layer. According to Tregear (1966), the stratum conjunctum forms the epidermal part which cannot be removed by the stripping technique (Sect. 1.3.4.2 "The Role of the Epidermal Barrier Layer").

In the corneum, the fully keratinized cell acts at first as a direct barrier between the body and its environment. After a while, the horny cell desquamates like a withered leaf, curling up from its margin. An adult's skin surface area, which is approximately 1.7 m^2, loses about 0.5–1 g of such horny material every day. At the same time, an appropriate amount of keratinocytes is replaced through cell proliferation (mitosis) of the basal epidermal cells in a kind of continuous molting.

In the stratum germinativum, cells are meshed together like a zipper. Sometimes a total melting of cell membranes appears, together with a reduction of intercellular spaces. Some of these contact areas of adjacent membranes remain visible in the stratum corneum as membrane-like lines. They probably work as electrical contact areas for transmission of action potentials from cell to cell (Sect. 1.3.4.2 "The Role of Skin Components and of Membrane Processes"). The keratinized epidermal cells are kept in their formation by desmosomes (see Footnote 7) until they fall away from the skin surface.

As shown in Fig. 1.1, the keratinocytes undergo a typical metamorphosis of their form and position while moving from the basal layer to the corneum, probably caused by the growing pressure of the cells pushing from inside out. The basal cells change their form from upright spheric or elliptic cell bodies to flat, keratinized

---

[7] The process of keratinization begins during mitosis via forming of the so-called *tonofilaments*, which are thin intraplasmatic fibers. In the upper layers, they are transformed into bundles of *tonofibrillas* having a greater density. With the keratohyaline generated in the lower stratum intermedium, these fibrillas merge to form complexes, which are converted in the upper stratum intermedium from one cell layer to another into epidermal keratin through changes in the cellular milieu. The tonofilaments are approximately parallel to the surfaces of the flattened cells, but are not in contact with the *desmosomes*, which are the intercellular contact zones of the keratinocytes. In the prickle cell layer, the number of desmosomes decreases and the intercellular spaces enlarge. This enables other cells, e.g., the melanocytes, to change their positions through movements.

cells lying parallel to the skin's surface. In the formation of the horny layer, each cell forms a hexagonal sheet approximately 30–50 μm in diameter, interlocking precisely into ramifications of adjacent cells above and beneath like a zipper. If the epidermis is not influenced by irritation, single cell layers may be visible, stacking up from the basal to the upper horny layer like boxes.

The epidermis, whose layering is of great importance to EDA, consists of a regularly arranged cell formation, which becomes dryer toward its outside layer as the cells become less tightly packed and look more like slide-shaped parallel structures. The completely horny outer layer, the stratum corneum, is especially thick on palmar and plantar sites, which are preferred for electrodermal recording (Sect. 2.2.1.1). The role of the stratum corneum in producing changes of the skin's resistance is discussed in Sect. 1.4.2.1.

1.2.1.2 Dermis and Hypodermis

The dermis, also labeled the *corium* (which means leather, since leather is the tanned corium of animals), is much thicker than the epidermis. However, it consists of only two dermal layers (Table 1.2), which can be distinguished according to their density and the arrangement of their collagen fibers (Fig. 1.1).

The dermal layer next to the epidermis is called the *papillary layer* (stratum papillare). It is named after fingerlike projections, the *dermal papillae*, which fit into cavities in the underside of the epidermis. Thus the two main parts of the cutis are intimately intermeshed at the epidermal-dermal junction. Apart from the possible adhesive effects of this gearing, there is also a great increase of the basal-layer area, and hence an enlargement of the area for producing new epidermal cells (Montagna & Parakkal, 1974). The epidermal-dermal boundary is formed by a so-called basal membrane zone, which is an adhesive layer in which the epidermal basal cells are inserted with projections. In the papillar layer, arterial and venous blood vessels end in a capillary net (Fig. 1.2), and receptor organs, melanocytes, as well as free collagen are included in this layer. The inner dermal layer is called the *reticular layer* (stratum reticulare) because of its texture, made by strong collagenous fibers, giving the skin a high resistance against rupture. Thus, the reticular layer, sometimes called the *fibrous stratum*, forms the leathery skin in its true sense.

The *hypodermis* (subcutis) consists of loose connective tissue. It connects the skin with the connective tissue covering the muscles, and it allows for good horizontal mobility of the skin across its surface. The hypodermis has the ability to store fat, thus working as a thermal as well as a mechanical insulation layer. It contains the nerves and vessels which supply the skin, also the hair follicles and glands (e.g., the secretory part of the sweat gland; Fig. 1.1). According to some authors (e.g., Millington & Wilkinson, 1983), the secretory parts of some sweat glands are located in the dermis and not in the hypodermis. These sweat glands then are surrounded by fatty tissue instead of collagen fiber bundles (Fig. 1.2).

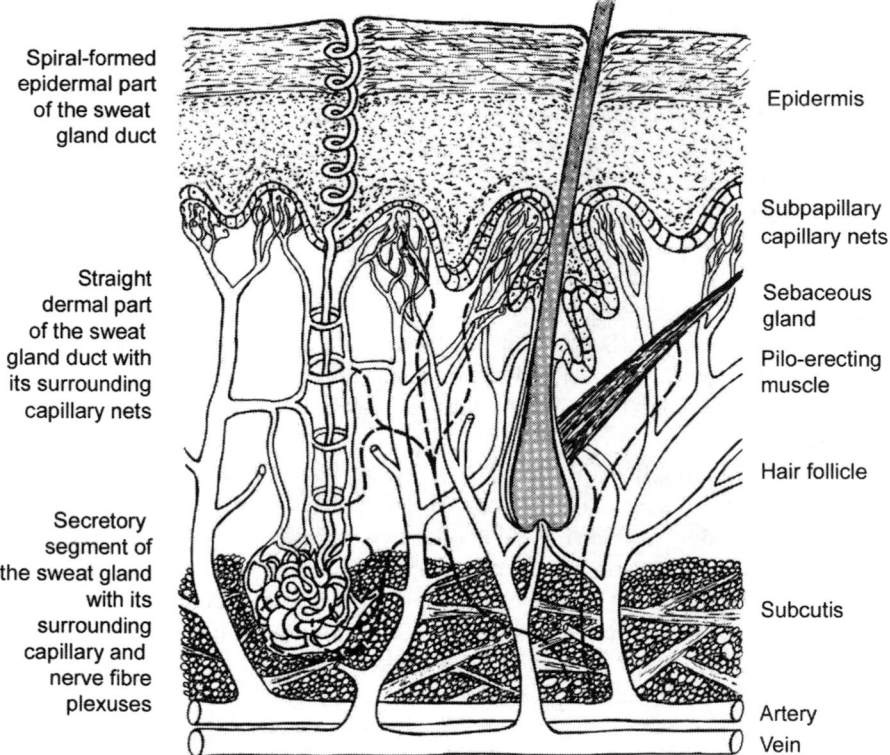

Spiral-formed epidermal part of the sweat gland duct

Epidermis

Subpapillary capillary nets

Straight dermal part of the sweat gland duct with its surrounding capillary nets

Sebaceous gland

Pilo-erecting muscle

Hair follicle

Secretory segment of the sweat gland with its surrounding capillary and nerve fibre plexuses

Subcutis

Artery

Vein

Fig. 1.2 Schematic vertical section of the skin that artificially combines a sweat gland in ridged skin (*left*) together with a hair and a sebaceous gland in polygonal skin (*right*). In addition to the supply with blood vessels, the efferent sympathetic innervation is indicated by *dashed lines* (Sect. 1.3.2)

1.2.1.3   Vascular System of the Skin

As pointed out in the preceding section, the bigger vessels supplying the body surface are located in the hypodermis. From there, smaller ramifications supply the sweat glands, the hair follicles, and the subpapillary capillary nets. The arterioles located there are surrounded by small muscles which are innervated adrenergic and regulate the cutaneous blood flow (Sect. 1.3.3.2). Arteriovenous anastomoses, which form bypasses of the capillary nets (Stüttgen & Forssmann, 1981), and also glomeruli (similar to those located in the kidney) in some body parts which jut outward, such as fingertips, are also controlled by these adrenergic muscle fibers.

The lymphatics form nets in the dermis and in the hypodermis. The main portion of the lymph flows away via subcutaneous lymph vessels. In the same way as the blood and the interstitial fluid (Sect. 1.4.2.1), the lymph contributes to the relatively high electrical conductivity of the inner skin layers.

1.2.2 Horizontal Structure of the Skin

There are regional differences not only in the skin's vertical layering, as outlined in Sect. 1.2.1.1, but also in its horizontal structure. In the early stages of embryonic development, different patterns of skin are formed by either ridge formation or folding into polygonal structures (Millington & Wilkinson, 1983). Thus, the different types of skin are referred to as ridged skin and polygonal skin.

Ridged skin is seen only on the palms and soles, including the flexor side of fingers and toes. At these sites, the skin surface is covered with ridges and furrows, the pattern of which is genetically fixed and corresponds to the pattern of the papillary layer (Sect. 1.2.1.2). Two papillary ridges project into each epidermal ridge. The sweat gland ducts usually enter the epidermis at the nadir of the ridges. The ridged skin is glabrous (hairless) and has no sebaceous nor scent glands.

The rest of the body is covered by polygonal skin patterns. *Polygonal skin* is divided by thin channels into numerous polygons, the pattern of which also corresponds to the pattern of the papillary layer. Both the number of polygons and the depth of channels are dependent on the degree of elasticity necessary, e.g., for body movements. At some sites the channels may even disappear. Unlike ridged skin, the ducts of sweat and scent glands enter the epidermis at the higher parts of the skin. Hairs and sebaceous glands, however, are located in the channels of the polygonal skin.

1.2.3 Distribution and Structure of Sweat Glands

The sweat glands are considered to be exocrine glands because they secrete directly onto the skin's surface. The human body has about three million sweat glands, the greatest density being found on the palms, soles, and forehead, and the least density on the arms, legs, and trunk (Kuno, 1956). They are totally missing on the lips and in the inner ear channel (Pinkus, 1971), on the glans penis and clitoris, on the labia minora, and on the inner surface of the prepuce (Montagna & Parakkal, 1974). The following mean numbers of sweat gland per cm^2 of the adult's skin are taken from Millington and Wilkinson (1983): 233 on the palms, 620 on the soles, 360 on the forehead, and only 120 on the thighs.[8] However, not all of these glands are active. Children may have much greater sweat gland densities, since their density decreases from fetal stage ($3,000/cm^2$ in the 24th week of pregnancy) to adulthood (Sect. 2.4.3.1). This is because the total number of sweat glands is fixed at birth, yet the total body surface area increases by a factor of 7 from birth to adulthood

---

[8] Sato et al. (1989) give slightly different numbers for the eccrine sweat glands: 1.6–4.0 million glands in total, with densities per cm^2 of 64 on the back, 108 on the forearm, 181 on the forehead, and 600–700 on the palms and soles. For age, gender, and ethnic differences, see Sect. 2.4.3.

(Montagna & Parakkal, 1974). There are also some ethnic differences in the distribution and activity of sweat glands (Sect. 2.4.3.3).

The majority of human sweat glands are regarded as *eccrine,* which means that their secretions do not contain noticeable amounts of cytoplasm from the glandular cells. In addition, a major number of the large sweat glands, mainly found in the areola region of the breast, the axillary, the circumanal, and the genital regions, are *apocrine* (Millington & Wilkinson, 1983; Sato, 1977).[9] Apocrine means that the secretion is formed when the apical (distal) part of the glandular cell is tied off, and the cytoplasm which is lost via secretion has to be replaced. Apocrine glands open into hair follicles, and their secretory functions do not begin until puberty (Sato, 1977). However, apocrine sweat glands play only a negligible role with respect to the total amount of sweating (Herrmann, Ippen, Schaefer, & Stüttgen, 1973).[10]

The eccrine sweat gland can be subdivided into the secretory segment and the duct. The secretory segment is located in the hypodermis or in the dermis (Sect. 1.2.1.2). It consists of a tube which is irregularly coiled into a rounded mass approximately 0.4 mm in diameter (Fig. 1.2). From it comes the duct, following an undulating course through the dermis (called, however, the straight duct) and then a spiral (helical) course through the epidermis (Ellis, 1968). The dermal part of the duct also contains secretory cells (Odland, 1983).

Both the secretory and the ductal segments are formed by double or triple cell layers surrounding a lumen of 5–10 μm in diameter. The cells of the outer layer are called basal cells, those of the inner layer luminal cells. The wall of the epidermal part of the duct, i.e., of the acrosyringium, has no cells of its own in the part which passes through the stratum corneum (Fig. 1.1). The duct opens onto the skin surface through a little pore.

According to Hashimoto (1978), a part of the duct between the secretory segment and the beginning of the undulating dermal duct has walls composed of only single cell layers and is not surrounded by myoepithelial cells (Sect. 1.3.2). On the other hand, a cross section of the secretory segment shows that it is surrounded by a thin sheet, the basal lamina, or basement membrane. Above it, a layer of myoepithelial cells, the form of which resembles that of smooth muscle cells, lines the outermost portion of the secretory tubule.

---

[9] Some authors (e.g., Thiele, 1981a) use the term "atrichial" (from Greek: τρίχα = hair) for the eccrine glands, referring to these glands being not associated with hair follicles, which most apocrine glands are (Venables & Christie, 1973, p. 19).

[10] Sweat glands are found in the footpads of many species (Edelberg, 1972a, p. 378). Wang (1964) presumes that the cat's sweat glands are apocrine instead of eccrine, but this view remains controversial (Edelberg, 1972a). Sato (1977) found it unlikely that the cat's or the rat's sweat glands had the capability to reabsorb ductal NaCl (Sect. 1.3.3.1), while those from the monkey's paw closely resemble human eccrine sweat glands. Thus, generalization from primate results to human species is more tenable than from cats or rats (Roy, Sequeira, & Delerm, 1993). Types and distributions of sweat glands in different species are summed up in a description by Fowles (1986a, p. 54); more details are given by Weiner and Hellmann (1960).

The secretory cells are subdivided into either clear, serous cells or dark, mucous cells (Sect. 1.3.3.1). The clear cells are noteworthy for their glycogen content and abundant mitochondria (Sato, 1977), which is suggestive of the high rate of metabolic activity necessary for active sweat secretion by these serous cells. The other secretory cells show a dark color under the light microscope, resulting from abundant mucous granules and ribosomes, which are responsible for the secretion of mucous substances (mucopolysaccharides).

There are two kinds of intercellular spaces in the secretory segment of the sweat gland: the intercellular channels, which open into the basal interface, and the intercellular canaliculi, which may be regarded as extensions of the lumen (Sato, 1977). While the intercellular channels allow absorption of material from the interstitium, the canaliculi permit the secretion of sweat into the lumen.

While the coiled part of the dermal duct, which cannot be clearly distinguished visually from the secretory part of the sweat gland, shows very tight junctions of its luminal cells, the cells in the so-called straight dermal duct show interspaces. According to Hashimoto (1978), these interspaces may function to increase the surface area available for reabsorption of sodium from the precursor sweat (Sect. 1.3.3.1). The acrosyringial luminal cells (Fig. 1.1) also show those interspaces, which – more prominent in the human embryo than in the adult – seem to contain lysosomes. Hashimoto assumes that materials and fluid absorbed by the epidermal duct must be digested within these lysosomes. It is assumed that the acrosyringium produces its own keratinocytes (Sect. 1.2.1.1), and that its keratinization is more advanced than that in the surrounding epidermis. Thus the sweat gland pore opening onto the skin surface is of the same type as epidermal cells, making its wall indistinguishable from its surrounding and allowing the sweat to pour out easily onto the stratum corneum.

1.2.4   Other Effector and Sensor Organs in the Skin

Besides sweat glands, the dermis contains other glands: the scent glands, which are present only at some sites (the axillae, the genital, and perianal area, as well as in the external ear canal); the sebaceous glands, which are – with a few exceptions – linked to the hair follicles (Fig. 1.2); and the mammary glands. The hairs are likely to have efferent and afferent functions as well. They mount diagonally to the body surface out of their roots, which are infundibular insertions into the skin into which the sebaceous glands discharge. Below the sebaceous gland pore, originating from the side to which the hair is inclined, a small bundle of smooth muscle cells is located, the pilo-erecting muscle, which runs diagonally up to beneath the epidermis. The muscle can erect the hair and can also retract the skin (forming goose pimples), at which the sebaceous glands are compressed between the muscle and the hair-root sheath. Hair is found only on polygonal skin and not in the regions normally used for EDA measurement, i.e., the palmar and plantar areas (Sect. 2.2.1).

The hair roots reach into the upper hypodermis. Each root is surrounded by a dense nerve net which possibly serves a perceptual role. Other receptors of skin sensory organs appear in all layers of the hypodermis (subcutis) and cutis in large numbers. Parts of them are free-ending sensitive nerves, i.e., they do not end in recognizable specific receptor structures. The endings can, however, also be encapsulated in connective tissue (e.g., Pacinian corpuscles).

Some of the sensory nerves reach into the epidermis, such as nerve endings observed in the stratum germinativum, and these possibly serve as tactile receptors (Sect. 1.3.5). There is also an indication of an efferent system which sensitizes such peripheral receptors (Edelberg, 1971).

1.3 Physiology of the Electrodermal System

As in the preceding section dealing with anatomical aspects, this section will outline only those physiological mechanisms required for understanding electro-dermal mechanisms. However, the appropriate restrictions cannot be made as easily as in anatomy, because the innervations of skin and sweat glands are embedded in the context of the autonomic nervous system (ANS), the functioning of which is highly complex. In particular, sweat gland activity takes part in the homeostatic process of thermoregulation, together with other organs of the skin, the various physiological mechanisms of which are involved in thermoregulatory aspects of the ANS. Thus, the description of mechanisms having rather indirect influences on EDA (e.g., peripheral vascularization) will be restricted here to their peripheral parts localized in the skin.

In humans, thermoregulation constitutes a phylogenetically highly developed autonomic system with impacts on kidney and cardiovascular functions (Thews, Mutschler, & Vaupel, 1985). The power of this system is illustrated by its reaction to stress (Sect. 3.2.2.2), where under extreme circumstances secretion rates up to 2 L sweat per hour can be observed, which may lead to a loss of up to one quarter of the whole body fluid during a single day under continuously experienced stress (Sargent, 1962).

1.3.1 Efferent Innervation of the Skin

Human skin is reached by numerous efferent vegetative fibers, including sympa-thetic fibers for innervation of the eccrine sweat gland's secretory segment[11] and of the pilo-erecting muscles (Fig. 1.2), as well as exerting vasoconstrictory effects on

---

[11] Only few human apocrine glands possess an ANS innervation (e.g., those in the axilla); they may be partly or even mainly under the control of circulating adrenaline (Weiner & Hellmann, 1960).

the blood vessels.[12] As they are intermingled with each other, it is not possible by means of a light microscope to differentiate nerve fibers going to the sweat glands from those supplying the blood vessels. Whether there is an additional parasympathetic innervation of the skin's blood vessels, which could be analogous to the regulation of the blood flow in skeletal muscles, or whether the dilatatory responses of the skin's blood flow are only due to a central inhibition of the sympathetic vasoconstrictory fibers, remains debatable (Jänig, Sundlöf, & Wallin, 1983).[13]

The postganglionic sympathetic fibers leave the sympathetic trunk via the gray communicating ramus, being included in the so-called mixed spinal nerve, which also contains all motor as well as sensory fibers traveling into and from the periphery (Fig. 1.3). At their peripheral end, the sympathetic fibers travel close to the somatosensory fibers for surface sensibility and form characteristic plexuses in the subcutis (Fig. 1.2).

Separation of human sudomotor[14] from vasoconstrictory fibers is only possible in the periphery, namely, via stimulation and blocking procedures, but not at the spinal cord level, where sudomotor efferents cannot be differentiated from other sympathetic fibers (Schliack & Schiffter, 1979). The spinal sympathetic nerves, which descend in the anterolateral part of the spinal cord near the pyramidal tract (Sect. 1.3.2.2), are switched over in the lateral horn and leave the spinal cord via its ventral root together with the motoric fibers, traveling via the white communicating ramus to the sympathetic trunk (Fig. 1.3). Here the neuronal activity is distributed by numerous collaterals to different levels of the sympathetic trunk, so that one preganglionic fiber may reach up to 16 postganglionic neurons. The collaterals of fibers originating in the upper thoracic part are mainly cranial oriented, whereas those from fibers originating in the lower thoracic, as well as in the lumbar part of the spinal cord, are mainly caudal oriented (Schliack & Schiffter, 1979).

In spite of the fact that neuronal activity is widely distributed, which is typical for the sympathetic as compared to the parasympathetic system, the organization within the sympathetic nervous system is mainly segment-oriented. This can be shown with segmental reflexes elicited by electrical stimulation of the ventral root, which are most pronounced when the same segment is stimulated (Jänig, 1979).

However, skin reflexes can also be elicited without inclusion of the spinal cord, as can be shown with the so-called axon reflexes. These reflexes are dependent on the peripheral organization of the vegetative fibers in a certain region of the skin, which all stem from a distribution point within the inner half of the dermis. If one of the efferent collaterals originating there is mechanically stimulated, an impulse is transmitted backward to that distribution point, which is acting like a ganglion,

---

[12] It is still unclear whether specific vasodilative fibers exist in the human skin (which are known from cats), or if vasodilatation is secondary to sweating (Wallin, 1992).

[13] The search for origins of the skin's vegetative activity is further complicated by the fact that transmitters such as noradrenaline, which acts vasoconstrictory on the peripheral blood vessels (Sect. 1.2.1.3), are also circulating freely in the blood.

[14] Sometimes also called sudorisecretory (sweat secretion eliciting) fibers.

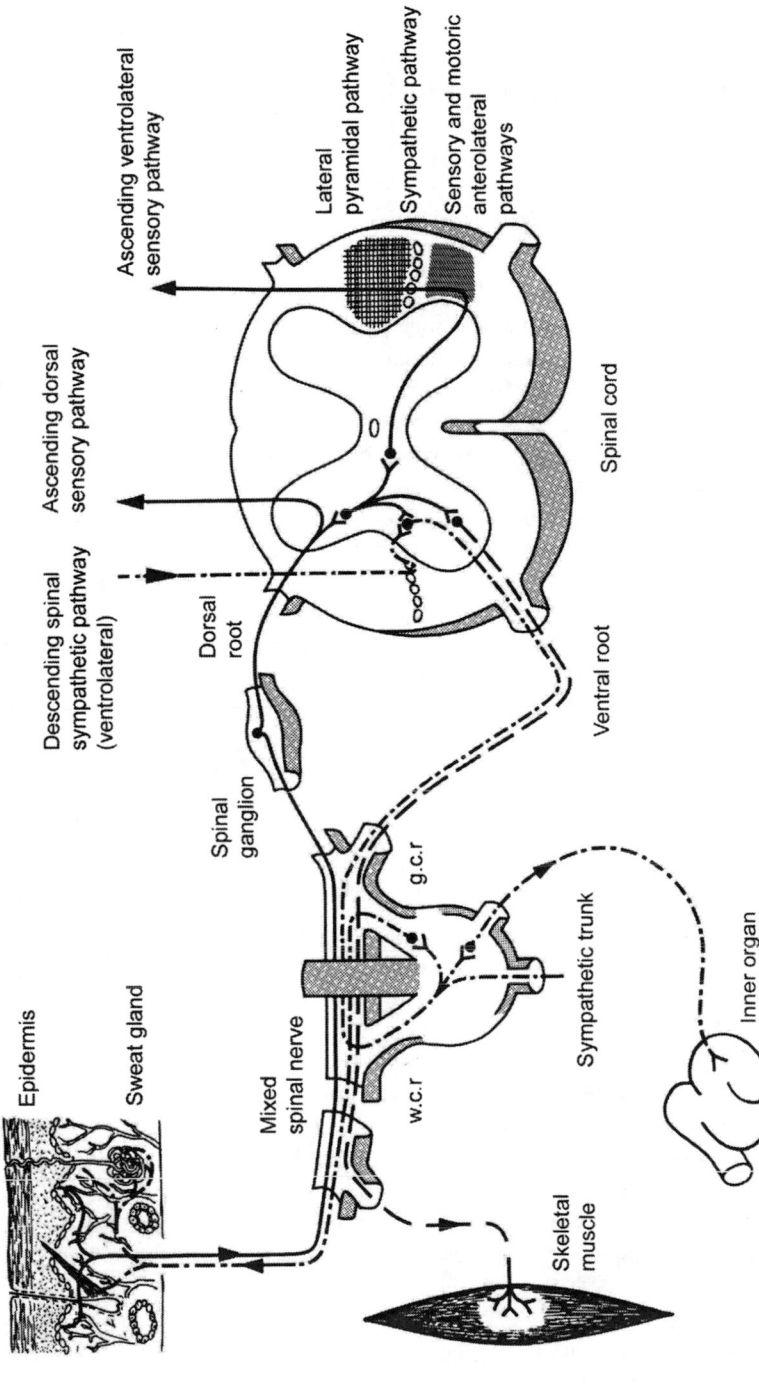

Fig. 1.3 Traveling of skin afferents and efferents at spinal cord level and their connections with ascending and descending pathway. *dashed line*: motoric pathway to the skeletal muscle, – · – : sympathetic efferents, *solid line*: skin afferents. *w.c.r.* white communicating ramus, *g.c.r.* gray communicating ramus

sending efferent "sympathetic" signals via the other collaterals into the periphery, thereby causing a local sweat secretion (Schliack & Schiffter, 1979). Another kind of axon reflex is elicited by nociceptive afferents, which cause vasodilatation in the corresponding skin area via a hitherto unknown pathway.

1.3.2   Innervation of Sweat Glands

Of all vegetative efferent innervations, those of the sweat glands have been investigated most thoroughly. The secretory part of the sweat gland is supplied by widely ramified sympathetic postganglionic nerve fibers, which consist of nonmyelinated class C fibers (Sato et al., 1989), some of which also reach the dermal part of the duct (Sinclair, 1973). Though postganglionic sympathetic transmission is normally adrenergic, using noradrenaline (norepinephrine) as a transmitter, sudomotor transmission is cholinergic, which means that acetylcholine acts as a synaptic transmitter. This has given rise to discussions of a possible parasympathetic innervation of sweat glands (Tharp, 1983); in contrast to the more generally adopted view of sympathetic sweat gland innervation. There has always been some question concerning reasons for the cholinergic transmission in the postganglionic sympathetic system. With respect to this, Fowles (1986a) pointed to the fact that the sweat glands have exocrine functions, and that cholinergic innervation is common in exocrine glands.

Nevertheless, there are also adrenergic fibers that travel to sweat glands via the peripheral nerve supplying the skin.[15] Previously, the additional adrenergic supply had been thought to be related to the specific reactivity of sweat glands on palmar and plantar sites to emotional changes (Sect. 1.3.2.4). However, because an adrenergic innervation has also been found in eccrine sweat glands within other regions (Shields, MacDowell, Fairchild, & Campbell, 1987), this is no longer accepted as true.

Weiner and Hellmann (1960) demonstrated that adrenaline (epinephrine) acts on apocrine glands by bringing about myoepithelial contractions. Thus, there had been some speculation that adrenergic fibers may also supply the myoepithelial cells surrounding the secretory segment as well as the dermal part of the eccrine sweat gland, the function of which is described in Sect. 1.3.3.1. However, Sato (1977) showed that those myoepithelial cells react to cholinergic stimulation only.

There is some evidence for adrenergic supply of the apocrine sweat glands, as mentioned in Sect. 1.2.3 (Millington & Wilkinson, 1983). Since a general neural innervation of human apocrine sweat glands is lacking (Footnote 11, Sect. 1.3.1), Grice and Verbov (1977) suggested that the adrenergic influence on these glands may be exerted via sympathetic nerve fibers ending near the blood vessels and/or via

---

[15] Sato and Sato (1981) used an in vitro preparation of single monkey palm eccrine sweat glands to demonstrate its reactivity to both cholinergic and andrenergic agents. They found that the maximum sweat rate was highest after cholinergic stimulation.

Table 1.3 Correspondence of the sudomotor fibers, leaving the ventral roots of the spinal cord, to sensory dermatomes, according to Klaschka (1979)

Anterior root of spinal nerve	Dermatomes of skin which are influenced by the corresponding sudomotor neurons
Th3–4	Trigeminus region and C2–C4
Th5–7	C5–Th9
Th8	Th5–L11
Th9	Th6–L1
Th10	Th7–L5
Th11	Th9–S5
Th12	Th10–S5
L1	Th11–S5
L2	Th12–S5

C cervical; *Th* thoracic; *L* lumbar; *S* sacral segments

freely circulating noradrenaline stemming from the adrenergic medulla. As a whole, the contribution of adrenergic stimulation to sweat secretion is poorly understood. In any case, its action on eccrine sweat glands plays a minor role as compared to the role of cholinergic innervation (Millington & Wilkinson, 1983; Sato, 1983).

1.3.2.1 Peripheral Aspects of Sweat Gland Innervation

As previously mentioned, the preganglionic sudomotor neurons travel into the periphery, together with the other sympathetic nerve fibers, going from the lateral horn of the spinal cord ipsilaterally via the sympathetic trunk, in which they are switched to the postganglionic neurons. According to Jänig et al. (1983), their transmission velocity is 1.2–1.4 m/s.

The cell bodies of the preganglionic sympathetic neurons are not present in all segments of the spinal cord, only from C8 to L2. The origins of sudomotor efferents must be even more restricted, since no important sudomotor fibers leave rostral to T3. Thus, the sudomotor innervation of dermatomes is deviant from their sensory innervation (Table 1.3). As can be further inferred from Table 1.3, it is not always possible to establish an unambiguous correspondence between the sudomotor cell bodies within specific segments of the spinal cord and certain dermatomes. This is also due to the distribution of neuronal activity by collaterals to the different levels of the sympathetic trunk (Sect. 1.3.1).

However, even the correspondences outlined in Table 1.3 have to be regarded with caution. They are mainly based on observations made in patients with lesions of the sympathetic trunk (Sect. 3.5.4). It is not easy to describe or produce precisely localized lesions in sympathetic pathways, because often collaterals are not completely degenerated and therefore remain able to transmit neuronal activity. Additionally, it is presumed that microscopically small single cells and cell units in the neighborhood of autonomic nerve fibers, located between the sympathetic trunk and the periphery, may serve as relay stations of the sympathetic system. They may even function as ganglia, which would serve as an explanation of the sometimes surprising residual sweat gland activity after sympathectomy (Schliack & Schiffter, 1979).

The investigation of the peripheral sympathetic activity's neuronal basis in humans is further complicated, because the effector organs respond relatively slowly to sympathetic neuronal impulses, and also react to various other stimuli such as hormonal, local chemical, and mechanical ones (Wallin, 1992). Therefore, microneurography[16] has been applied to establish a relationship between the discharge amplitude of the sympathetic part of the median nerve, which innervates part of the palms, and the appropriate EDR amp. (Wallin, 1981).[17]

The secretory part of the sweat gland is surrounded by a very dense plexus of sympathetic fibers which allows a wide distribution of ANS activity. It is not yet fully clear how the cholinergic transmission of nerve impulses to the sweat gland cells works. It has not been possible to establish real synaptic clefts, nor have nerve endings been observed penetrating into the secretory cells. Ellis (1968) suggested these cells were being stimulated via neurohumoral substances poured out by nerve endings nearby. Presumably it is the transmitter itself which empties from sympathetic nerve endings into the immediate neighborhood of the secretory cells. Edelberg (1967) pointed to the dependency of acetylcholine transportation velocity upon body temperature together with the temperature dependency of the EDR lat. (Sect. 2.4.2.1), stating that 25–50% of the latency is due to the mechanism of acetylcholine transportation.[18]

1.3.2.2   Central Aspects of Sweat Gland Innervation

The sympathetic pathway forms a narrow bundle between the lateral pyramidal tract and the anterolateral tract (Fig. 1.3). Within this pathway, the sudomotor fibers, which end at the preganglionic sudomotor neurons, are in close proximity with other sympathetic fibers (e.g., those for vasomotor or pupilomotor efferences). Schliack and Schiffter (1979) presumed that there is no compact pathway for sweat gland activity. Instead, the sudomotor fibers are diffusely intermingled with the surrounding sympathetic fibers.

At the spinal cord level, the sudomotor fibers are in close contact with afferent pathways, located in the anterolateral tract and belonging to the nonspecific

---

[16] Recording of action potentials from nerves with tungsten microelectrodes having tip diameters of a few µm, which are inserted through the intact skin into an underlying nerve, with a reference electrode placed subcutaneously in 1–2 cm distance (Wallin, 1992).

[17] Microneurography from the tibial nerve has been used by Nishiyama et al. (2001), together with videomicroscopy for recording sweat secretion of individual glands on the sole of four male individuals. Only 46% of the suprathreshold sudomotor nerve bursts elicited sweat secretion, but the number of sweat glands recruited was linearly related to the amplitude of sudomotor bursts. Hence, sweat secretion is primarily dependent on the intensity of sudomotor neural activity; however, the microenvironment of sweat glands may also play a role.

[18] Nishiyama et al. (2001), in their study described in the previous footnote, also recorded SPRs, finding that sudomotor bursts were followed by SPRs with latencies of $1.33 \pm .33$ s. The latency of sweat secretion was $2.29 \pm .03$ s, and the sweat expulsion latency was $3.22 \pm .03$ s.

(extralemniscal) somatosensory system. These are regarded as classical pathways for the perception of temperature as well as pain, contributing to the affective tone of perception, to the degree of consciousness, and to the elicitation of the defensive response (Sect. 3.1.1.2). Despite no direct reports are available on synaptic connections of thermosensitive afferents with sudomotor efferents in the spinal cord, influences of somatosensory afferents on vegetative efferents at the spinal level are generally well known.

The sympathetic part of the ANS is represented widespread and manifold throughout the brain. In general, the hypothalamus is regarded as the control center for all vegetative functions, including those for vasomotor activity and sweat secretion. Electrical stimulation in the "sympathetic" (ergotropic) hypothalamic area, especially in the paraventricular and posterior nuclei, is always followed by sympathetic reactions such as vasoconstriction, piloerection (Sect. 1.2.4), and sweat secretion. Since knowledge of the neuronal organization in this phylogenetically primordial structure is still incomplete, the functioning of hypothalamic elicitation of sweat gland activity cannot be pursued in detail.

Figure 1.4 shows the origin and course of the most important descending sympathetic pathway from the hypothalamus to the spinal cord. It originates in the weakly myelinated part of the hypothalamus (darkly shaded in Fig. 1.4) and, according to results available up to now, runs via the tegmentum and ventrolateral reticular formation (RF) to the ventrolateral spinal sympathetic tract (mentioned above). For a long time, there has been controversy as to whether the course of this hypothalamic-reticular-spinal sympathetic pathway is ipsilateral or, partly or wholly, contralateral. However, Schliack and Schiffter (1979) were convinced that its course is mainly ipsilateral (see Fig. 1.6, Sect. 1.3.4.1).

Hypothalamic sympathetic activity can be elicited or modified by higher-level cerebral structures. Various influences from the limbic system,[19] especially from the amygdala and the hippocampus, on thermoregulatory hypothalamic functions have been verified (Edelberg, 1973a). There is also close proximity of the so-called Papez circuit (Papez, 1937) with the nuclei in which the hypothalamic-reticular-spinal sympathetic pathway originates (Fig. 1.4). Additionally, other structures like the ventro-oral internal thalamic nucleus, extrapyramidal nuclei, and various cortical areas are connected with the hypothalamus.

As a result of stimulation and lesion experiments, the basal ganglia, the thalamus, and the Brodmann area 6 of the frontal lobe, which is adjacent to the precentral motor area, can be regarded as taking part in eliciting sweat gland activity (Schliack & Schiffter, 1979). Other than the sudomotor fibers originating in the hypothalamus, the pathways stemming from these structures cross in the medulla oblongata to the contralateral side (Fig. 1.6).

---

[19] Recently, the existence of the limbic system has been much debated (e.g., LeDoux, 1996). However, since most of the literature on CNS elicitation of electrodermal phenomena used this expression (see Sect 1.3.4.1 "Subcortical Control of EDA"), it will be used in the present book as well.

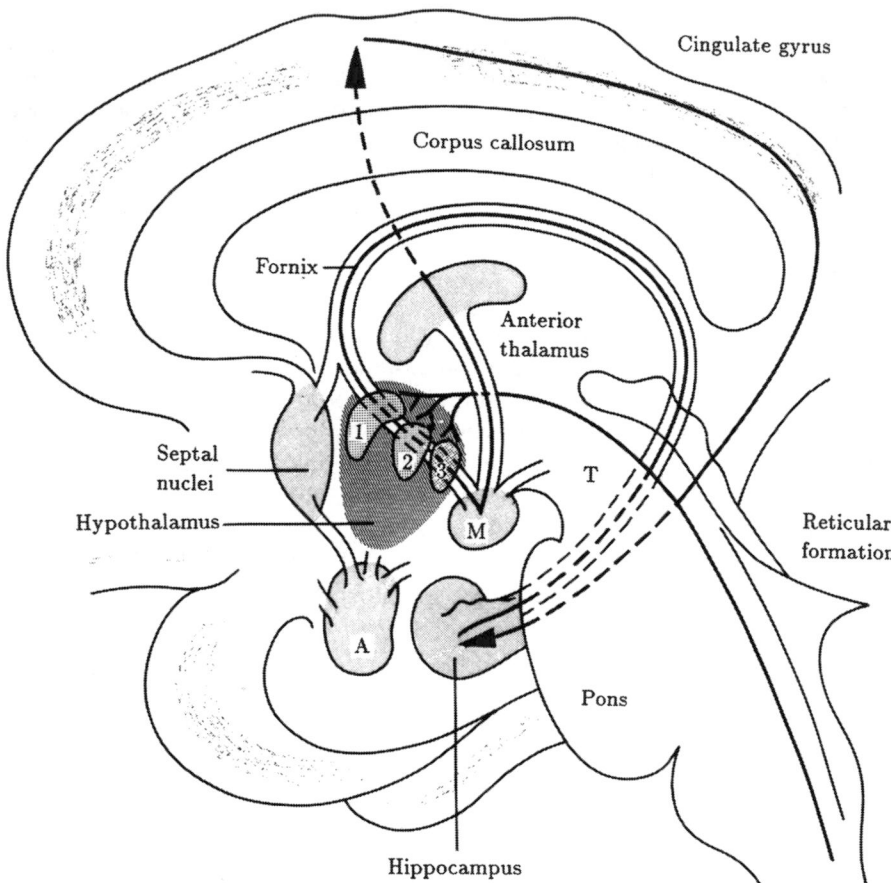

Fig. 1.4 The limbic system in medial section. The hypothalamic-reticular-spinal sympathetic pathway stems from the paraventricular (1), posterior (2), and supramamillary (3) nuclei of hypothalamus (weakly myelinated part). The Papez circuit (which is partly dashed because of its spatial course) goes from the hippocampus via the fornix to the mamillary body (M), to the anterior thalamus, to the cingulate gyrus, and back to the hippocampus. *T* Tegmental midbrain area; *A* Amygdala. Adapted from Schliack and Schiffter (1979), Fig. 1.4d. Vol. 1/4A. Copyright 1979 by Springer. Used by permission of the publisher

All existing findings concerning the central innervation of sweat gland activity point to several centers for the origin of sweating, being located at different levels of the CNS and partly independent of each other. Sympathetic activity can be elicited from the cortex, the basal ganglia, diencephalic structures like the thalamus and the hypothalamus, the limbic system, and from brain stem areas. Accordingly, there are not only specific cerebro-efferent pathways to the sudomotor neurons, which reach the spinal cord either directly or after synaptic transmission, but also nerve fibers connecting the various areas with one another which are involved in the elicitation of sweat (Fig. 1.5, Sect. 1.3.4.1).

In spite of the existence of other cerebro-efferent pathways to the sudomotor neurons in the spinal cord, the hypothalamus should be regarded as the main region which governs sweat secretion (Schiffter & Pohl, 1972; Schliack & Schiffter, 1979). Since the hypothalamus is also the main center for thermoregulation, an older view provided by Kuno (1956) restricted hypothalamic elicitation of sweat secretion to thermal sweating, which appears on the whole body surface except for palms and soles (Sect. 1.3.2.4). In contrast, the so-called emotional sweating (Sect. 1.3.3.3), which appears on palmar, plantar, and axillary areas, had been regarded by Kuno as being mostly under cortical control. Critical to this position is the influence of limbic structures on hypothalamic sweating as outlined by Schliack and Schiffter (1979) which probably also contributes to emotional sweating. The possibility of different CNS influences on sweat gland activity which are in part independent from one another will be further discussed with respect to CNS elicitation of electrodermal phenomena in Sect. 1.3.4.1.

1.3.2.3   Questions of Double Innervation and Resting Activity in Sweat Glands

Present understanding is that sweat glands receive only excitatory sympathetic nerve impulses. Inhibitory effects on EDA elicited by CNS stimulation as obtained by Wang (1964) are supposedly already set off against excitatory effects at the CNS level (Fig. 1.5). In the past, an additional peripherally inhibitory parasympathetic innervation of sweat glands had been discussed (Braus & Elze, 1960). In particular, the active reabsorption of sweat in the ducts (Sect. 1.3.3.1) was assumed to be controlled via parasympathetic fibers that reach the peripheral cutaneous nerve from the spinal cord's dorsal root. This, along with the existence of vasodilative neuronal influences on the skin's blood vessels (see Footnote 12, Sect. 1.3.1), could never be proved to exist. There is no need to assume the existence of a sweat inhibiting innervation, since the sweat normally vaporizes so quickly in the absence of sudomotor impulses, that additional sweat inhibition would not reduce the amount of sweat significantly.

As Sato et al. (1989) pointed out, speculative debates about the possibility of dual cholinergic and adrenergic innervation of the sweat glands were around for decades until Uno (1977) directly demonstrated catecholamine fluorescence in the periglandular nerves of both human and macaque eccrine sweat glands, thus settling the issue.

Whether the stimulation of the myoepithelia around the ductal walls is mediated by freely circulating transmitters, or whether it requires a separate orthosympathetic innervation stemming from the sympathetic trunk, is yet to be resolved. Adrenergic transmission to the myoepithelia, formerly assumed to be responsible for the sweat secretion stimulated by adrenaline or noradrenaline, is no longer believed likely (Sect. 1.3.2). However, a possible cholinergic parasympathetic innervation of the ductal walls or, alternatively, the possible action of freely circulating acetylcholine is discussed (Sect. 1.3.4.2).

The problem of the sweat gland's resting activity still remains unresolved. Schliack and Schiffter (1979) regarded spontaneous sweating as the expression of an appropriate resting tonus (Sect. 1.3.3.3), whereas Jänig et al. (1983) could not find spontaneous sweat gland activity, at least at temperatures below the thermoregulatory neutral zone (Sect. 1.3.3.2).

1.3.2.4 Specific Innervations of Sweat Glands in Different Regions of the Skin

Regional specificities in the innervation of sweat glands are found especially in the face as well as at palmar and plantar sites, the latter also being morphologically different from the rest of the body's skin (Sects. 1.2.1 and 1.2.2).

The sweat gland innervation in the face, where measurement of EDA is uncommon, has been thoroughly investigated. In contrast to all other regions of the skin, there is a dual path of distal sympathetic efferent fibers to the regions innervated by the trigeminal nerve. This is indicated by the remission of sweat gland activity in those regions after an irreversible trigeminal lesion.[20] Since the trigeminus is a cranial nerve and not a spinal nerve, the sudomotor fibers originating in the cranial sympathetic trunk leading to the trigeminal nerve (Sect. 1.3.2.1) first have to follow the common carotid artery. Subsequently, the main part of sudomotor neurons follows the internal carotid to the trigeminal branches, while the rest of them directly follow the external carotid to the facial sweat glands.

Facial sweat secretion is especially active on the upper and lower lips, the bridge of the nose, the nasolabial folds, and the forehead, where it is most pronounced on the frontal bald area. Above the radix of the nose there is sometimes a small circular region in the medial line which is totally anhydrous. There has been some discussion of trigeminal fibers having the ability to inhibit sweat. These fibers are supposedly independent of the sympathetic trunk. In addition, a second possible parasympathetic "bulbar" pathway within the facial nerve has been discussed as acting either excitatory or inhibitory on sweat secretion. However, both of these possibilities lack convincing evidence (Sect. 1.3.2.2).

Most interesting with respect to electrodermal recording is the innervation of sweat glands at palmar and plantar sites, which probably differs from the sweat gland innervation in the rest of the body. It is controversial whether the sweat glands at palmar and plantar sites take part in thermal perspiration at all (Kuno, 1956). Jänig et al. (1983) reported palms and soles taking part in thermal sweating only at high ambient temperatures. Whereas Wilcott (1963) observed palmar and plantar sweat production following thermal stimulation, Schliack and Schiffter (1979) reported that palms and soles remained dry while the rest of the body was vigorously sweating, for example, when they were held out of a hot bath. In a study performed with 34 participants, Kerassidis (1994) demonstrated that in

---

[20] An appropriate double innervation may exist in the region of the mouth floor which corresponds to dermatome C3 (Table 1.3, Sect. 1.3.2.1).

ambient temperatures up to 60°C the amount of palmar and plantar thermal sweating is negligible compared to that on the thorax and the forehead. Only if additional stress was induced by bicycle ergometer riding or mathematical calculations, substantial palmar and plantar sweating could be observed. A peculiarity of these sites is also observed under psychological stress, where palmar and plantar sweating may appear together with vasoconstriction, which is paradoxical with respect to thermoregulation. In general, there is ample evidence that these sites are linked to emotional rather than thermoregulatory sweat gland activity, though other parts of the body can also take part in emotional sweating (Sect. 1.3.3.3). However, Conklin (1951), in a study described in Sect. 2.4.1.1, could not find differential temperature dependency of SCL at the palms as compared with the wrist and the forehead.

There is also some evidence for at least two different kinds of sweat gland receptors at palmar sites, since emotional sweating is completely abolished by atropine blockade, while both adrenaline-induced and spontaneous palmar sweating remain unaffected (Millington & Wilkinson, 1983). The specialization of sweat gland activity at palmar and plantar sites, together with the possibility of its unique innervation, has given rise to considerations concerning the biological significance of palmar and plantar sweat glands (Sect. 1.3.5) and stimulated psychophysiological investigations of the so-called palmar/dorsal effect (Sects. 3.1.1.2 and 3.4.1.1). Some authors discuss an intermediate position of palmar and plantar sweat glands between apocrine glands and the phylogenetically younger eccrine glands. Since apocrine sweat glands (Sect. 1.2.3) play no role in EDA measurement, idiosyncrasies in their innervation can be disregarded at this point.

1.3.3   Functions of Sweat Gland Activity

While the preceding section focused on sweat gland innervation, the following sections will describe the functional aspects of sweat gland activity. These are the mechanisms of sweat production and the embedding of sweating in thermoregulatory activity and in other functional relationships. An extensive review of the regulation of sweat secretion and the mechanism of sweat production has been provided by Fowles (1986a, pp. 62–72).

1.3.3.1   Mechanism of Sweat Secretion and Contents of Sweat

The secretory segment of the sweat gland, which is surrounded by a layer of myoepithelial cells, consists of clear and dark secretory cells (Sect. 1.2.3). The clear cells produce the liquid part of secretion, while the mucin produced by the dark cells may have protecting functions within the lumen. According to Ellis (1968), the serous cells act like a filter through which water and specific ions pass from plasma into the lumen. Since the so-called precursor sweat in the sweat gland's secretory segment is more hypertonic than blood, Fowles (1974) suggested an active transport mechanism for sodium chloride from the interstitial fluid into the lumen, producing an osmotic gradient which the water follows.

The human precursor sweat contains approximately 147–151 mM Na (sodium), 123–124 mM Cl (chloride), 5 mM K (potassium), probably 10–15 mM HCO_3 (bicarbonate), and 15–20 mM lactic anion (Sato, 1977, p. 103). Sweat also contains small amounts of other ions and urea, as well as traces of biogenic amines and vitamins. The precursor sweat is modified as it passes through the ductal part of the sweat gland. In surface sweat, Na varies from 10 to 104 mM, paralleled by the Cl concentration ranging from 10 to 30 mM (Sato, 1977). These lower concentrations gave rise to the hypothesis of an active NaCl reabsorption mechanism in the ductal wall, comparable to the one in the renal tubules, which is regarded as being well established (Bijman, 1987; Fowles, 1986a). The NaCl concentration at the skin surface, which falls within the range of 0.015–0.06 M (Rothman, 1954), becomes higher with an increased rate of perspiration, which presumably reflects a limited reabsorption capacity of the duct. Since the NaCl concentration has been reduced by the time the sweat reaches the epidermal duct, most of the reabsorption is likely to having taken place in the dermal duct (Schulz et al., 1965), although there is possibly an additional NaCl absorption mechanism in the epidermal ductal walls (Sect. 1.4.2.3, Fig. 1.14). The reabsorption as a whole may prevent the body from excessive NaCl loss through sweating in high ambient temperatures (Fowles, 1974).

NaCl can be regarded as playing a mediator function in sweat production, since it is actively transported into the lumen within the secretory segment of the sweat gland to produce an osmotic gradient, which draws water into the lumen, and is subsequently actively reabsorbed within the duct.[21] Reddy and Quinton (1994) demonstrated in human sweat glands that a similar molecular mechanism in the Cl channel is responsible for sweat secretion and for sweat reabsorption in the duct wall.

Sweat does not flow continuously through the duct to the skin surface, but rather in a pulsatile manner with pulsations of 12–21 Hz, as Nicolaidis and Sivadjian (1972) showed by applying a fast-moving humidity sensitive film. Rhythmic contractions of the myoepithelia, surrounding not only the secretory but also the ductal part of the sweat gland like a helix, are regarded as the source of the pulse (Ellis, 1968). Although an adrenergic influence on these myoepithelia has been discussed, they might be innervated cholinergically as well, since adrenergic receptors play a minor role, if any, in eccrine sweat secretion (Sect. 1.3.2).[22]

---

[21] It is also important for cardiac functions related to blood pressure. The metabolic processes that take place during sweat secretion, including the possible role of Ca as a second messenger in cholinergic sweating, are discussed in detail by Sato (1977) and summed up by Fowles (1986a).

[22] Sato (1977) generally questions the hypothesis of expulsion of already existing sweat by adrenergic stimulation. In his in vitro studies with isolated monkey sweat glands, he found so little preformed sweat in the lumen that an initial myoepithelial contraction could not expel an appreciable amount of sweat. Furthermore, Nicolaidis and Sivadjian (1972) used forehead sites for recording, so their observations may not be generalized to palmar sweat secretion.

According to Sato (1977), sweat can be observed rising and falling in a micropipette brought into the lumen at a frequency of 0.5–2 Hz during low sweating rates. He followed Kuno (1956) in arguing that this phenomenon should be due to neural stimulation rather than to myoepithelial contraction. However, the nature of an appropriate innervation remains unclear (Sect. 1.3.2.3).

1.3.3.2   Thermoregulatory Function of Sweating and Skin Blood Flow

Vaporization from the skin is mainly considered with respect to its thermoregulatory function. It is divided into visible, or the so-called sensible perspiration, and invisible, or the so-called insensible perspiration.

The thermoregulatory functions of vaporization from the skin and of blood flow in the skin are closely related to each other. With respect to thermoregulation in the so-called neutral zone (ambient temperature 28–30°C, 50% relative humidity and calm wind, for an unclothed resting adult), heat loss can be controlled solely by vasomotor activities. Below this zone, water vaporizes through insensible perspiration (Thews et al., 1985). Above the neutral zone, visible thermal sweating appears, and water loss through sweating reaches a significant amount above 34°C (Thiele, 1981a).

One-half to two-thirds of the total insensible water loss is through the skin, while the rest is through the lungs, but the skin's portion is not all conducted by sweat glands, since anhydrotics lose as much water as normals (Tregear, 1966). However, atropinization, which blocks the cholinergic sweat gland innervation, reduces the amount of insensible perspiration to 50% (Herrmann et al., 1973).[23] Thus, a considerable part of insensible perspiration is controlled by sweat gland activity (Jeje & Koon, 1989), using at least the whole peripheral apparatus including the efferents from the sympathetic ganglia (Schliack & Schiffter, 1979).

The regulation of skin blood flow is deliberately described by Houdas and Ring (1982). It consists of two distinct mechanisms which show regional differences. The skin sites located distal to the trunk, such as palms, soles, and ears, are rich in sympathetic adrenergic fibers, which act in a vasoconstrictory manner and show strong tonic activity even under temperature-indifferent resting conditions. Peripheral vasodilatation is a result of inhibiting their activity. Contrarily, the resting activity of those sympathetic adrenergic fibers is low at the proximal parts of extremities, as well as at the trunk itself, while its increase leads to vasoconstriction. In the latter skin areas, vasodilatation is a direct consequence of sweat gland activity, since bradykinin, which is released when sudomotor fibers are stimulated, has a strong vasodilative action upon the skin's capillaries. With regard to these

---

[23] In deviation from the classical dermatological hypothesis, Tregear (1966) presumed that the sweat gland ducts, as well as the hair follicles, were of no importance for the amount of the body's water loss. He referred to observations that the palmar skin, having three times the density of sweat glands compared to the rest of the body, is not very permeable to fluids, and that individuals without any sweat glands show as much insensible perspiration in a cool environment as normal individuals.

mechanisms, Edelberg (1972a) considered the possibility of reflex sweating being nothing more than a handmaiden of the cardiovascular system.

Of great importance for skin blood flow and thermoregulation is the microcirculation in the skin, which accounts for 9% of the total blood flow during resting conditions. As described in Sect. 1.2.1, the larger vessels which supply the body surface are located in the hypodermis, from where smaller branches ascend to the sweat glands, the hair roots, and up to the dermal papillae (Fig. 1.2). They form a widespread subpapillary net of capillaries, the arterioles of which show an unusual thick wall of 2–3 µm (compared to 0.1 µm in the rest of the body), being covered with small alpha-adrenergic innervated muscles, which govern the amount of vasoconstriction. Such kind of muscles is also found at the arteriovenous anastomoses (Sect. 1.2.1.3), the opening of which is responsible for the increase of skin blood flow during increasing temperature, constituting a major mechanism for releasing heat from the skin (Houdas & Ring, 1982). Whether the decrease of skin blood flow is governed by parasympathetically innervated vasodilative fibers (analogous to the blood flow in the skeletal muscles) or whether peripheral vasodilatation is a result of the central inhibition of the sympathetic vasoconstrictory fibers remains debatable (Jänig et al., 1983).

Based on a mathematical model, Love (1980) suggested that skin blood flow should be regarded as the major determinant for skin temperature. This was, however, doubted by Brown, Bygrave, Robinson, and Henderson (1980), who – using a thermal clearance method (van de Staak, 1966) – determined the skin's thermal conductivity as the major factor eliciting changes in skin temperature. Furthermore, Houdas and Ring (1982) obtained a nonlinear relationship between skin blood flow and skin temperature. On the other hand, local changes in blood circulation as elicited by pressure on the skin are paralleled by decreases in skin temperature. After 20 min, when a normal unclothed person with a core temperature of 37°C is adapted to an ambient temperature of 23°C, skin temperature ranges from 32.2°C at the soles of the feet to 34.2°C at the center of the abdomen (Millington & Wilkinson, 1983, Table 1.1). A similar range can be observed during an ambient temperature of 32°C, whereas during ambient temperatures between 10 and 20°C local differences in skin temperature may be observed.

The local skin temperature has the ability of changing the action of sweat glands and skin blood vessels in the appropriate regions (Jänig, 1990). Therefore, reduced sweating and hence reduced EDA can result in cooled skin areas, despite a high amount of sudomotor impulses from the CNS. In turn, a local warming of skin can increase sweating and EDA.

The efferent CNS control of the skin's thermoregulatory function does not only include the sympathetic part of the ANS. Since voluntary as well as involuntary muscle activity takes part in thermal balance, the somatic sensory system is also included. The afferent limb is formed by peripheral thermoreceptors, mainly by receptors for cold and heat in the skin, and by a centrally located receptor which belongs anatomically to the medial hypothalamus, the firing rate of which is primarily determined by the internal body temperature (Kupfermann, 1985). Temperature control, including thermal sweating, is modulated by hypothalamic structures (Sect. 1.3.2.2).

1.3.3.3 Other Functions and Special Features of Sweating

Besides the thermal sweating described in the previous section, Schliack and Schiffter (1979) gave evidence for an additional five kinds of sweating which are classified according to the stimuli eliciting them.[24] Every type uses the postganglionic sympathetic neuron, which has its origin in the sympathetic trunk and travels via the peripheral cutaneous nerve to the sweat gland as a final common terminal path (Sect. 1.3.2.1). However, their mechanisms of CNS elicitation differ in part.

1. "Emotional sweating" means increased sweat gland activity as a concomitant of psychological and, especially, emotional states which appear, for example, in high arousal or under stress (Sect. 3.2.1). It is likely to be elicited via hypothalamic-limbic connections as described in Sect. 1.3.2.2. Emotional sweating is observed mainly on palmar and plantar sites (Sect. 1.3.2.4), but also in the axillary and genital regions (Millington & Wilkinson, 1983), as well as on the forehead (Schliack & Schiffter, 1979). However, Allen, Armstrong, and Roddie (1973) reported increased sweating at other body sites during emotional strain (see Footnote 180, Sect. 3.2.2.2) induced by arithmetic exercises. They observed the amount of sweating as being directly proportional to the number of sweat glands per region, thus indicating no regional differences in emotional sweating. Shields et al. (1987) also considered the possibility of the specific reactivity of palmar and plantar sweating to psychological stimulation as being dependent on the greater sweat gland density on these sites. Thus, the specific role of palms and soles in emotional sweating remains to be considered further.
2. Gustatory sweating appears when food is consumed which is especially sour, highly salted, or spicy. There are marked interindividual differences with respect to the sites included. Gustatory sweating mainly appears on the face (e.g., on the forehead and the upper lip; Schliack & Schiffter, 1979) and on the wings or the top of the nose. Its intensity can be irritating without being pathological. However, pathological gustatory sweating may appear after sympathetic nerve lesions. It can also be elicited in the absence of gustatory stimuli – it does not even require intact gustatory sensation – via chewing and olfactory as well as psychological stimulation. It is probably elicited via an irritation or partial blocking of sudomotor pathways from the sympathetic trunk or its peripheral ramifications, which lead to a local disinhibition of an otherwise subliminal physiological reflex (Schiffter & Schliack, 1968).
3. Ubiquitous spontaneous sweating can be observed on palmar and plantar sites, even by a simple magnifying glass. It may be regarded as an expression of a resting tonus, comparable to the resting muscle tonus of motor units. However, the existence of such a resting tonus in sweat glands remains debatable (Sect. 1.3.2.3).

---

[24] The specific meaning of these different kinds of sweating for EDA is as yet unexplored, except those of the so-called emotional-sweating type. They are reported here for the sake of completion and with respect to possible future electrodermal research.

4. Reflex sweating is an expression that describes sweat gland activity at sites which are innervated from spinal cord segments distal to the locus of certain damage (e.g., paraplegia). The expression is also used for a confined, local sweating following stimulation of an area with radiation, heat, needle punctures, or electricity. It is assumed to be mediated through the so-called axon reflexes (Sect. 1.3.1) instead of possible spinal connections between sympathico-efferents and pain afferents.
5. Pharmacologically produced sweating is a local sweat secretion elicited through either subcutaneous or intracutaneous injection, as well as through iontophoresis with cholinergic substances (e.g., nicotine or pilocarpine).

There is also a special mechanism of sweating which underlies the so-called cold sweat. Startle responses (Sect. 3.1.1.2) and other strong emotionally tinted responses, as well as deep breathing and coughs – all situations associated with a sudden elicitation of adrenaline – also lead to sweat secretion. Free circulating adrenaline, however, acts in a vasoconstrictory manner similar to a cold stimulus. At the same time, sweat secretion may be activated via hypothalamic centers. Both responses result in cold sweat, which seems to be paradoxical with respect to thermoregulation. However, Ebbecke (1951) was convinced that expulsion of so-called cold sweat is not a result of the secretory part of the sweat gland's innervation. Instead, he adopted an adrenergic stimulation of the myoepithelia around the duct as a source of expulsion of sweat already produced in this case, a hypothesis also held by Kuno (1956) but which is no longer regarded as valid (Sects. 1.3.2. and 1.3.3.1).

1.3.4   Specific Physiological Mechanisms Underlying Electrodermal Activity

The following two sections investigate CNS mechanisms (Sect. 1.3.4.1), epidermal features, and sweat gland features (Sect. 1.3.4.2) with respect to their contributions to electrodermal phenomena. For the time being, these descriptions are incomplete, since the central origin of sweat gland activity is not fully understood in detail (Sect. 1.3.2.2). Additionally, most findings are taken from animal preparations and so generalization to humans may not be conclusive (see Footnote 10, Sect. 1.2.3).

1.3.4.1   Central Origins of Electrodermal Activity

Electrodermal phenomena are not only influenced by parts of the CNS involved in the classical sympathetic elicitation of sweat secretion (Sect. 1.3.2.2). Various subcortical and cortical regions contribute, forming a complex system, the role of which is far from being fully understood. A thorough review of the evidence with regard to different brain levels existing at that time had been rendered by Venables and Christie (1973). In the 1992 edition of this book, the present author added some more recent results and provided an integrative view on the origin of electrodermal phenomena in the CNS, which will be amended here with more recent results.

Much of what was known in the early 1990s about the central origins of electrodermal phenomena came from studying the effects of lesions and stimulations in the cat's brain, sometimes under the influence of heavy narcotics (for a summary of research with cats into the CNS influences on EDA, see Sequeira & Roy, 1997). Evidence from humans and from nonhuman primates was sparse at that time.[25] Therefore, the first version of the schematic overview depicted in Fig. 1.5 (see Boucsein, 1992, Fig. 5) was originally based on the knowledge of Wang (1964), who summarized results from various studies with anesthetized and nonanesthetized cats. The excitatory and inhibitory sweat centers from which the cat's EDA originates provide the basis for the present edition's Fig. 1.5. However, the picture has become more complicated, since various areas have been detected by brain imaging studies that could be connected to electrodermal phenomena (for a review, see Critchley, 2002). Unfortunately, this kind of research has not yet converged to a systematic view similar to the one provided by Wang (1964).

Subcortical Control of EDA

There is no doubt that the *hypothalamic areas* which exercise thermoregulatory control play a major role in the elicitation of EDA (Fig. 1.4, Sect. 1.3.2.2). Interestingly, not only posterior but also medial and anterior hypothalamic regions exert excitatory influences on the cat's EDA (Sequeira & Roy, 1993). In particular, EDRs could be elicited in some animal preparations by stimulation of anterior hypothalamic regions (for summaries see Edelberg, 1972a; Venables & Christie, 1973), which are regarded as belonging to the trophotropic (parasympathetic) system. This gave rise to the hypothesis that at least part of CNS elicitation of EDA could be under parasympathetic control (Venables & Christie, 1973, p. 30). However, as Bard (1960) pointed out, no mechanism which parallels the representation of the sympathetic system exists for the parasympathetic system in the hypothalamus or in any other part of the CNS. Furthermore, evidence is lacking for influences of anterior hypothalamic regions on sweat gland activity in humans (Sect. 1.3.2.2). Hence, in the updated Fig. 1.5, Wang's (1964) notion of the anterior hypothalamus was put in brackets and amended by the hypothalamic regions shown in Fig. 1.4.

As previously outlined in Sect. 1.3.2.2, the sudomotor hypothalamic areas are under control of the *limbic system* (see Footnote 19 in Sect. 1.3.2.2), which has also been regarded as the neurophysiological basis for emotional and partly for motivational phenomena (Sects. 3.2.1.2 and 3.2.2.1). Subcortical limbic influences mainly stem from the *hippocampus* (which is involved in the Papez circuit) and from the

---

[25] One major difference between sweating in cats and humans may be that there is probably no thermal sweating in the cat (Jänig et al., 1983). Therefore, Roy, Sequeira, and Delerm (1993), hypothesized that the sweating of the cat's footpad could be analogous to "emotional sweating" in humans (Sects. 1.3.2.4 and 1.3.3.3).

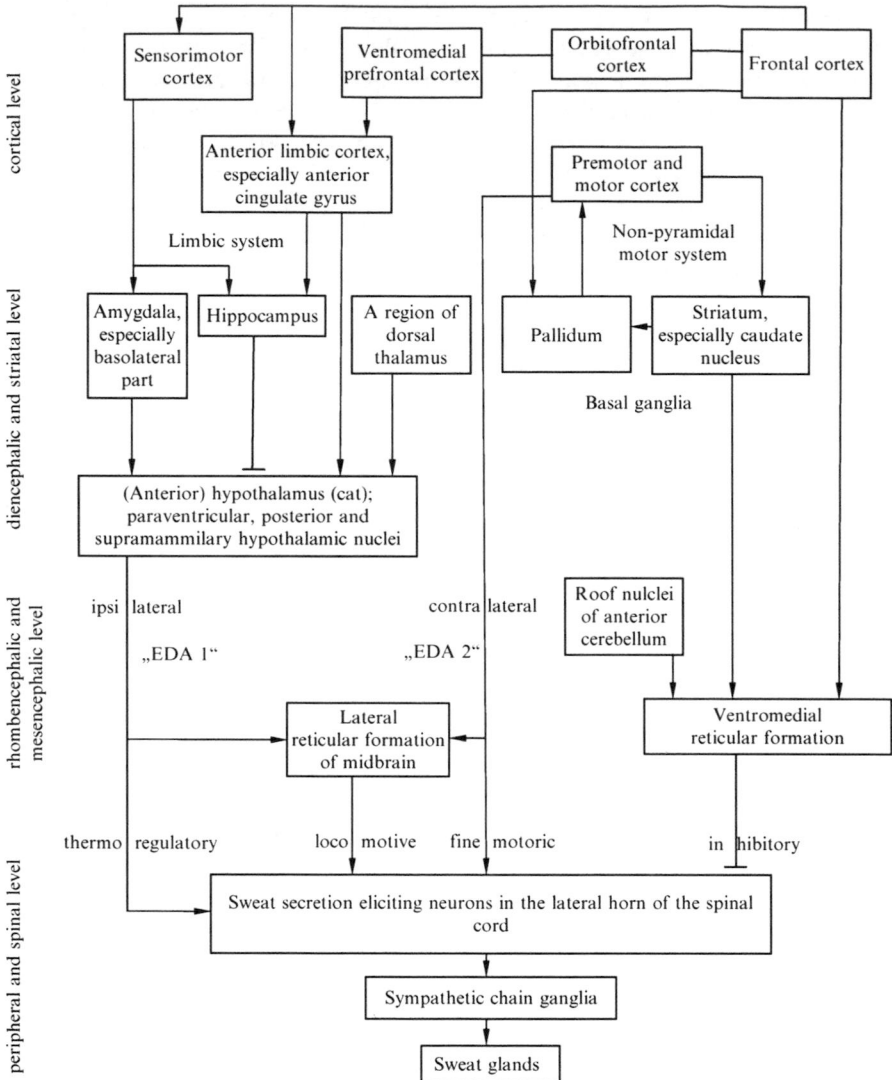

Fig. 1.5 Block diagram showing brain regions at different levels (see left margin) which may constitute or influence sweat centers and their common efferent pathway to sweat glands. For explanations of "EDA1" and "EDA2," see Fig. 1.6. The figure was originally based on Wang (1964), Fig. 8.1. Copyright 1964 by the Regents of the University of Wisconsin. Used by permission of the publisher

amygdala (Edelberg, 1972a; see also Sect. 3.4.2). Stimulation of the basolateral amygdala could evoke a single EDR with its typical recovery (Lang, Tuovinen, & Valleala, 1964), and amygdalectomy in monkeys produced a marked impairment of EDRs following acoustic stimulation (Bagshaw, Kimble, & Pribram, 1965). This gave rise to the hypothesis that the amygdala might be responsible for the elicitation of the electrodermal orienting response (ED-OR; see Sect. 3.1.1.1). However, Tranel and Damasio (1989) obtained regular ED-ORs in a 60-year-old patient whose entire amygdalar complex had been destroyed bilaterally by encephalitis. There seems to be some laterality, since Raine, Reynolds, and Sheard (1991), who used a magnetic resonance imaging (MRI) technique for relating individual differences in the size of selected brain areas to electrodermal phenomena in 17 normal participants (9 females, 8 males), obtained significant correlations between the size of the left temporal area (including the amygdala) and the frequency of ED-ORs, but not for the right temporal area.[26]

Findings with respect to *hippocampal* influences on EDA are mixed (Sequeira & Roy, 1993). Some results from animal studies gave rise to the hypothesis that the hippocampus has an inhibiting effect on EDA. Yokota, Sato, and Fujimori (1963) and Yokota and Fujimori (1964) found an inhibiting influence when stimulating the hippocampus in nonanesthetized curarized cats. However, such an influence could not be confirmed in monkeys, in which Bagshaw et al. (1965) did not find any influence on EDRs when bilateral hippocampus lesions existed. Furthermore, a possible EDA inhibiting center in the hippocampus was omitted by Wang (1964) from his Fig. 8.1, because he could not form any simple notion concerning its descending pathway. In humans, hippocampal stimulation can also elicit EDRs. Mangina and Beuzeron-Mangina (1996) elicited EDRs (recorded bilaterally with standard methodology; see Sect. 2.2.7) in five young adult surgical patients with direct stimulation via intracerebral electrodes from various brain regions. Stimulation of both amygdalae yielded the highest EDRs, followed by anterior and posterior hippocampi, and left and right anterior cingulate gyri, which incidentally play an important role in the cortical control of EDA (see section "Cortical Control of EDA"). However, these authors found that SCRs elicited by limbic structures were of considerably higher amplitude than those elicited from cortical areas. Amygdala and hippocampus exert differential influences on EDA measures in conjunction with information processing (Table 3.1, Sect. 3.1.3.1).

Excitatory centers for EDA in cats are also located in a region of the dorsal thalamus (Isamat, 1961). The *ventromedial part of the RF* at the rhombencephalic level was regarded by Wang (1964) as the most powerful inhibitory center for EDA in the cat's brain. Presumably, there is not much influence from the *cerebellum*, although Wang located some facilitation of the ventromedial RF in the roof nuclei in the anterior lobe of the cerebellum, which, however, only inhibit autonomic functions during strong muscular movement. Additionally, removal of the

---

[26] Skin conductance was recorded bilaterally with 0.5 V constant voltage from the medial phalanges, using Ag/AgCl electrodes filled with 0.5% KCl in an agar medium (Sect. 2.2.2.5). A series of six 75 dB tones (1.311 Hz, 1 s, ISI randomized between 35 and 50 s) and four reorienting stimuli for probing OR reinstatement after habituation (Sect. 3.1.1) were applied. Left and right hand SC-OR was significantly related to left and right prefrontal areas ($r = 0.44$–0.60), area of the pons ($r = 0.43$–0.54) and left but not right temporal/amygdalar area ($r = 0.47$–0.53). No significant correlations were found with the area of the cerebellum, nonfrontal cortical areas, and the medial prefrontal cortex.

cerebellum had no observable effect on EDRs of cats. Corresponding results for humans were obtained by Raine et al. (1991), who could not find relationships between amplitudes of EDRs and the size of the cerebellum, and from Critchley's (2002) review on brain imaging and EDA, who reported that the area of the cerebellum was not related to the EDR amp.

The *basal ganglia* seem to play an important role in the control of EDA. Wang (1964) located an important inhibitory center for EDA in the cat's *caudate nucleus*, which is part of the striatum. Since synchronization of spontaneous SPRs in the cat's four footpads was present in the striatal but not in the hypothalamic nonanesthetized cat, he assumed a regulatory center for EDA being located in some part of the *pallidum* (see Fig. 1.6), exerting influences on both excitatory and inhibitory centers (Wang, 1964, Fig. 8.1; see also Boucsein, 1992, Fig. 5).

Cortical Control of EDA

Besides influences from subcortical structures, *cortical* limbic structures have also been found to be involved in the generation of electrodermal phenomena, and a diversity of extralimbic cortical areas was shown to influence EDA.[27] In the cat's brain, excitatory centers for EDA were located in anterior limbic and infralimbic areas (Isamat, 1961) and in *sensorimotor* cortical areas (Wang, 1964). Wang and Brown (1956) were able to demonstrate inhibitory influences from large *frontal* cortical areas acting on excitatory cortical sweating centers of the sensorimotor and the anterior limbic cortex.[28] However, not only inhibitory but also excitatory areas were located in the cat's frontal cortex (Wang & Lu, 1930; Wilcott, 1969; Wilcott & Bradley, 1970; see also Langworthy & Richter, 1930). In humans, indirect evidence for inhibiting effects of cortical regions (however, more central than frontal in location) on EDA was inferred by Weitkunat, Bührer, and Sparrer (1990) from analyzing grand average EEG waveforms preceding spontaneous EDRs in 12 healthy participants (5 females, 7 males).

Cortical areas that putatively interact with the limbic system were also found to influence EDA in humans and in nonhuman primates. SCRs were not diminished in monkeys with medial frontal lesions (Kimble et al., 1965), but were completely absent in monkeys with bilateral removal of the dorsolateral cortex (Grueninger, Kimble, Grueninger, & Levine, 1965). Luria and Homskaya (1970) observed reduced ED-ORs in human patients with frontal lesions as compared to those with lesions in other cortical areas. Raine et al. (1991) observed a strong relationship between spontaneous and elicited EDA and their MRI measure of the *prefrontal* area size. In his review, Critchley (2002) regarded cortical areas as being responsible for eliciting EDRs as

---

[27] Animal research on hypothalamo-limbic and cortical control of EDA has been summarized by Sequeira and Roy (1993) in their Table 1.1, pp. 97–99.

[28] In general, the question of ipsi- or contralaterality of inhibitory vs. excitatory influences on electrodermal phenomena remains unresolved (Sect. 3.1.4.2).

concomitants of cognitive and anticipatory behavior, while the amygdala seems to mainly contribute to the generation of EDRs to salient stimuli with acquired emotional meaning. In their combined SCR/fMRI study with six participants, Critchley, Elliott, Mathias, and Dolan (2000) investigated regional brain activity preceding SCR peaks and subsequent to them (Sect. 2.2.3.5). Significant activity preceding SCRs was observed bilaterally in the cerebellum and in extrastriate visual cortices (the task was visual in nature, i.e., making decisions on playing cards) as well as in the left medial prefrontal lobe. Subsequent to SCRs there was significant activation in the right medial prefrontal cortex, being presumably associated with representations of peripheral states of arousal (i.e., reflecting afferent feedback of ANS arousal).[29]

During the last two decades, much regard has been given to the possible role of the *ventromedial prefrontal cortex* (VMPFC) in eliciting electrodermal concomitants of decision making (Sect. 3.1.3.3). Tranel and Damasio (1994), in a study with 36 patients with MRI-diagnosed well-defined brain lesions, observed reduced ED-ORs subsequent to lesions of the VMPFC, of the right inferior parietal cortex and of the anterior cingulate gyrus.[30] In a study with seven patients having bilateral damage in the ventromedial sector, Bechara, Tranel, Damasio, and Damasio (1996) observed that anticipatory SCRs prior to choices in a decision task (see Sect. 3.1.3.3) were entirely missing, but were observable in 12 matched controls. Ten patients with lesions in the VMPFC, as diagnosed by MRI (Tranel, 2000), showed impaired SCRs[31] to psychological stimuli (i.e., affective laden slides) but not to physical stimuli (i.e., loud noise or taking a deep breath), the SCRs being even more reduced when the anterior cingulate gyrus was also damaged. Extensive damage of the anterior cingulate gyrus was associated with impairments in SCRs to both kinds of stimuli. No relationships were observed between EDA and nonfrontal cortical areas. Bechara, Damasio, Damasio, and Lee (1999) used a computerized version of the decision task applied by Bechara et al. (1996) in five patients with amygdala lesions and five patients with VMPFC lesions. Both groups were unable to develop anticipatory SCRs as a sign for impairment in decision making, but patients with lesions in the VMPFC were able to produce SCRs as a consequence of reward or punishment, while amygdala-lesioned patients could not. Differences in the role of the VMPFC and the amygdala in eliciting cognitively determined EDRs are discussed in more detail in Sect. 3.1.3.3.

However, both brain areas exert their influence on EDA via sympathetic hypothalamic areas (see left side of Fig. 1.6; see also Fig. 3.4, Sect. 3.2.1.2). The VMPFC has also been discussed as being responsible for SCRs in restful, but

---

[29] The bilateral medial prefrontal cortex is subsumed by the VMPFC, an area that is most consistently associated with missing SCR in patients with appropriate lesions. The possible role of brain areas for EDA biofeedback is discussed in Sect. 3.1.2.3.

[30] In the studies of this group, patients were diagnosed by MRI or X-ray computerized tomography, and SC was recorded with standard methodology (Sect. 2.2.7) from thenar/hypothenar sites.

[31] Recorded with standard methodology from 36 brain-damaged (15 females, 21 males) compared to 20 matched normal participants (7 females, 13 males).

mentally alert states (Raichle et al., 2001), while SCRs during fear and threat stimuli are more likely to be elicited by amygdalar activity (Williams et al., 2001). In an fMRI study with eight healthy volunteers who performed SC[32] biofeedback (Sect. 3.1.2.3), Nagai, Critchley, Featherstone, Trimble, and Dolan (2004) obtained significant negative correlations between orbitofrontal cortical and VMPFC activity and SCL, while SCRs were concomitantly elicited with lateral prefrontal, anterior cingulate, insular, thalamic, and hypothalamic activity.

There is also evidence for cerebral influences on EDA from regions outside of cortical areas related to the limbic system. Langworthy and Richter (1930) as well as Spiegel and Hunsicker (1936) already emphasized the role of *premotor cortical* regions (Brodmann area 6, see Fig. 1.6) in eliciting EDA, since a close connection between the pyramidal fibers for the transmission of skeletal muscle impulses and sudomotor fibers has been found in degeneration studies. As Darrow (1937a) pointed out, those pathways cannot be identical, because pyramidal stimulations did not elicit responses in the skin.[33] He suggested that the sudomotor fibers were corticopontine, rather than corticospinal like the pyramidal fibers. Thus, the neurophysiological basis for electrodermal changes which accompany changes in posture should be influenced from tegmental or pontine areas in which the premotor fibers end. Since it is widely accepted that subcortical structures such as the basal ganglia participate in motoric integration or programming (Marsden, 1982), the combined striatal and premotor cortical origins of EDA can be viewed together as a single premotor electrodermal component and a concomitant of nonpyramidal motor system activity (see upper right of Figs. 1.5 and 1.6).[34]

When premotor cortical areas are electrically stimulated or are removed, excessive sweating is observed, which points to both excitatory and inhibitory influences from this region. The role of EDRs as concomitants of motor actions is well established in humans (Edelberg & Wright, 1964; Pugh, Oldroyd, Ray, & Clark, 1966). Bilateral electrodermal recordings at palmar sites following strong acoustic stimuli sometimes showed noticeable lateral differences, which, however, never exceeded a ratio of 1:1.5 (Fisher, 1958; Obrist, 1963). However, if study participants were asked to move one foot as a response to the acoustic stimulation, the lateralization increased in favor of the EDR amp. as measured at the ipsilateral hand (Culp & Edelberg, 1966).

---

[32] Measured with a biofeedback system via silver electrodes and KCl electrolyte cream from the palmar surface of the left hand. Their method of recording SC within an fMRI was described by Critchley et al. (2000), see Sect. 2.2.3.5.

[33] However, Langworthy and Richter (1930) could elicit EDRs and other autonomic responses by stimulating the pyramidal tract in cats. Roy, Sequeira-Martinho, and Brochard (1984) suggested this was due to the collaterals from the pyramidal tract reaching the RF, by which reticular elicitation of EDA has been mediated.

[34] Sequeira and Roy (1993) managed to elicit EDRs in cats by stimulating both motor and premotor cortical areas electrically, even in a "pyramidal preparation," where all descending pathways except the pyramidal tracts were interrupted at bulbar level.

In a positron emission tomography (PET) brain imaging study which related regional cerebral blood flow to NS.SCRs during aversive and nonaversive stimulation,[35] Fredrikson et al. (1998) correlated the activity in cortical areas with the presence of considerable EDRs. While the anterior and posterior cingulate cortices were active in connection with bilateral EDRs, a laterality effect was observed in the primary motor cortex (Brodmann area 4). Activities in other brain regions such as the secondary visual, the inferior parietal, and the insular cortices showed negative relations to the appearance of EDRs. The authors suggested a complicated and distributed neuronal system in the human brain that governs elicitation and inhibition of EDRs.

Three Different CNS Originating Pathways for EDA

Taking all these human and animal results together, CNS elicitation of EDA can be allocated to two major pathways above the RF and one within it. First, there are *ipsilateral hypothalamic influences* on sweat secretion that are controlled by limbic structures (Fig. 1.4) with facilitating influences stemming mainly from the amygdala (e.g., in the case of orienting and defensive responses) and inhibitory influences stemming mainly from the hippocampus (e.g., in the case of behavioral inhibition, see Sect. 3.2.1.2). The *basal ganglia* together with *premotor cortical areas* form a second system with separate and mainly *contralateral influences* on sweat secretion and hence on EDA (Sect. 1.3.2.2). These influences were not only found in animal lesions studies but also in stimulation and lesion studies in human neurological patients (Schliack & Schiffter, 1979). According to the present author's suggestion (Boucsein, 1988, 1992), the limbic-hypothalamic electrodermal source is labeled here as "EDA1" and the premotor source as "EDA2" (sources 1 and 2 in Fig. 1.6; see also Fig. 3.4, Sect. 3.2.1.2).

In cats, the laterality of EDA seems to disappear at the *reticular level* and/or below, since unilateral cortical and pyramidal stimulation elicited bilateral SPRs with comparable amplitudes (Sequeira-Martinho, Roy, & Ba-M'hamed, 1986) and reticular stimulation in the cat was always followed by bilateral responses (Ba-M'hamed-Bennis, Sequeira-Martinho, Freixa i Baqué & Roy 1985; see also Sequeira & Roy, 1993). However, the laterality may sustain in humans, since Mangina and Beuzeron-Mangina (1996) observed ipsilateral SCRs much higher than contralateral ones after electric stimulation of limbic structures in neurosurgical patients. As to these authors, the disparity between cats and humans can be explained by direct pathways connecting the left and right limbic structures in cats, which are very limited in humans and in nonhuman primates.

---

[35] White noise and videos of snakes with or without electric shocks delivered to the right hand. Laterality could not be evaluated since EDA was only measured on the left hand. SC was recorded with standard methodology (Sect. 2.2.7); the amplitude criterion was set to 0.05 µS.

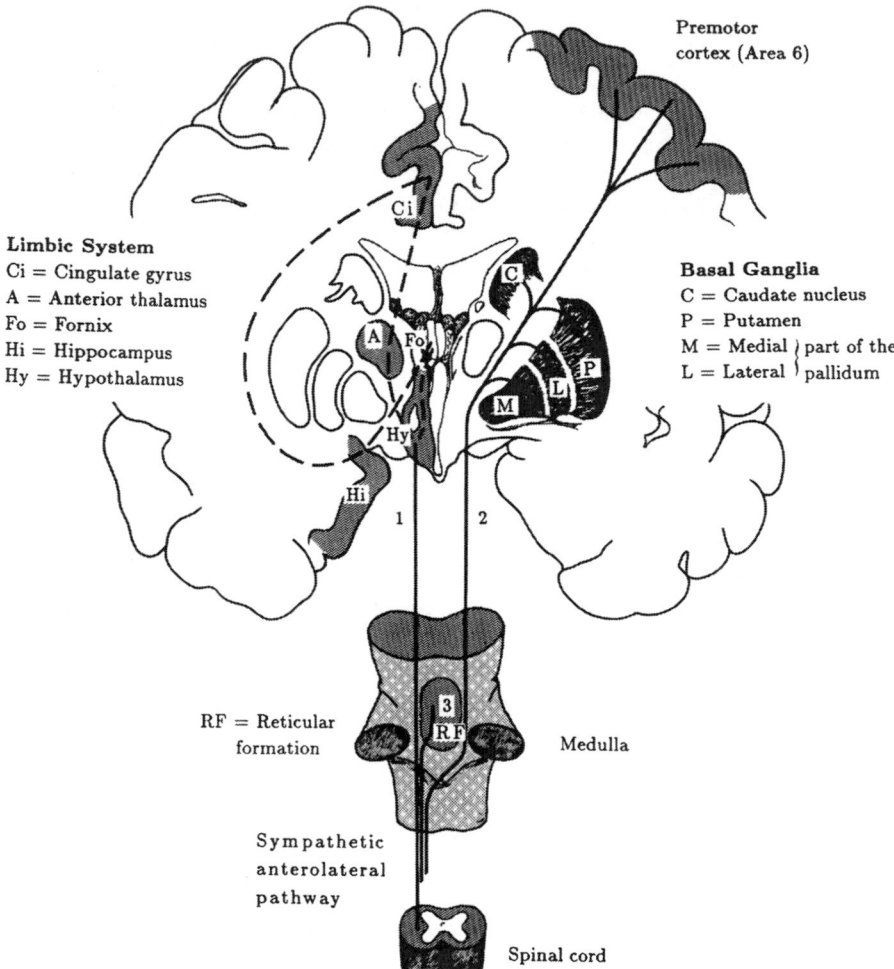

Premotor
cortex (Area 6)

Limbic System
Ci = Cingulate gyrus
A = Anterior thalamus
Fo = Fornix
Hi = Hippocampus
Hy = Hypothalamus

Basal Ganglia
C = Caudate nucleus
P = Putamen
M = Medial ⎞ part of the
L = Lateral ⎠ pallidum

RF = Reticular
        formation

Medulla

Sympathetic
anterolateral
pathway

Spinal cord

Fig. 1.6 Central nervous system elicitation of EDA in humans. *1*: ipsilateral influences from the limbic system via hypothalamic thermoregulatory areas (EDA1); *2*: contralateral influences from premotor cortical and basal ganglia areas (EDA2); *3*: reticular influences. Dashed: Connections within the limbic system (Fig. 1.4, Sect. 1.3.2.2). Adapted from Schliack and Schiffter (1979), Fig. 1.4c. Copyright 1979 by Springer. Used by permission of the publisher

The RF itself can have eliciting as well as modulating influences on EDA (Roy, Sequeira-Martinho & Brochard et al., 1984, Roy, Sequeira, and Delerm 1993). Bloch (1965) pointed to EDA as a reflection of central activation which is controlled by excitatory as well as inhibitory areas in the RF. These areas are regarded as mainly influenced by inhibitory corticofugal neurons. An inhibitory reticular center could be located in the ventromedial RF (Roy, Delerm, & Granger, 1974; Wang & Brown, 1956), whereas the lateral portion of the midbrain RF and portions of the diencephalic RF have excitatory effects on EDA (Edelberg, 1972a). Venables and Christie (1973) provided evidence that stimulation of appropriate mesencephalic excitatory regions facilitates motor activity via the action of the RAS (Sect. 3.2.1.1). Since the RF is connected with the striopallidum as well as the cerebellum, and is known to strongly influence skeletal muscle tone as well as muscle contractions via the gamma-efferent system, there is likely to be a close connection between the reticular modulation of sweat gland activity and skeletal muscle activity (Roberts & Young, 1971). Thus, while influences on EDA stemming from EDA2 have to be regarded as concomitants of preparing to activate distinct motor units, reticular influences on EDA (source 3 in Fig. 1.6) are more likely to be connected with a general increased muscular tone due to an increased general arousal (Footnote 113, Sect. 3.2.1.1). Reticular-mediated EDRs should likely be concomitants of locomotive changes, which may appear in emergency situations, and not of distinct or even fine manipulative motor actions which require a stronger cortical participation. Whether electrodermal changes that appear as concomitants of inspiration, and which are mainly regarded as artifacts in electrodermal recording (Sect. 2.2.5.2), are more cortically or more reticularly influenced remains unanswered.

In summary, the experimental as well as clinical evidence concerning the CNS elicitation of EDA points to the existence of two different origins above reticular level, which were already suggested by Edelberg (1972a): a *limbic–hypothalamic source* labeled EDA1, being thermoregulatory and also emotionally influenced, and a *premotor-basal ganglia source* labeled EDA2, eliciting electrodermal concomitants of the preparation of specific motor actions. In addition, there may be a *reticular modulating system* which mediates EDA changes that appear with variations of general arousal (source 3 in Fig. 1.6). The reticular modulating system is also likely to be responsible for inhibitory influences on EDA (Fig. 1.5), which may be either ipsi- or contralateral. However, under conditions of diffuse sweat gland activation with generalized EDA, the specificity of those neuronal systems may at least partly disappear.[36]

The three-sources model of EDA as proposed by Boucsein (1988, 1992) was probed in the above-mentioned PET study by Fredrikson et al. (1998), who grossly confirmed the bilateral emotional (EDA1) and the contralateral preparatory (EDA2) sources, whereas their data remained silent on the possible reticular source because they did not sample blood flow in the RF. The ipsilaterality hypothesis of EDA1 was confirmed by Kubota et al. (2000) in a study with six epileptic patients who underwent unilateral temporal lobectomy. They were presented ten slides with negative emotional valence and ten neutral slides subliminal by means of a masking procedure, while SPR was recorded thenar/hypothenar from both hands with Ag/AgCl electrodes. SPR amp. following negative stimuli compared to the neutral ones were significantly greater from the intact-side hand than those from the lesion side, indicating that amygdalectomy (which comes with temporal lobectomy) results in damage of the ipsilateral EDA1 concomitant of subliminal emotional processing.

---

[36] Wilcott (1963) showed that nonpalmar areas of skin that are normally regarded as thermoregulatory also took part in emotional sweating during a stressful situation (Sect. 3.2.2.2).

1.3.4.2 Properties of Skin and Sweat Glands Influencing Electrodermal Activity

While the dermis and also the hypodermis are well supplied with blood and interstitial fluid, at least the upper epidermal layers consist of relatively dry and horny cell structures and are not necessarily surrounded by much fluid. Hence, both kinds of skin structure will have different electrical properties, which is of great importance for EDA. The intact skin shows little permeability for water and soluble agents, which is also seen in epidermal tissue taken apart from skin. On the other hand, skin from which the epidermis has been removed shows very high permeability (Tregear, 1966). Therefore, an epidermal barrier layer is assumed, which is penetrated by skin appendages (see section "The Role of Skin Components and of Membrane Processes"). These structures show not only resistive but also membrane-dependent polarization properties.

The Role of the Epidermal Barrier Layer

There has been much discussion concerning the localization of an epidermal diffusional barrier, which is reviewed in detail by Fowles (1986a). Though it is not possible to give an exact localization of this barrier (Thiele, 1981b), there are some researchers who suggest a gradient of increasing resistance from the outer to the inner parts of the horny layer (e.g., Montagna & Parakkal, 1974), pointing to the inner stratum corneum as the main portion of the barrier layer (Table 1.2, Sect. 1.2.1.1). However, most findings provide evidence that the entire stratum corneum forms the barrier, with the exception of its desquamating surface cells (Jarrett, 1980).

Attempts to localize this barrier layer were mainly performed using the so-called "stripping" technique. With this technique, epidermal layers down to the stratum lucidum are successively pulled off by means of an adhesive cellophane-tape, which makes 4–40 successive trials necessary, depending on the method used (Klaschka, 1979).[37] With the stripping technique, only the fully keratinized dry epidermal layers can be removed, because the adhesive tape does not adhere to the inner humid layers such as the stratum intermedium. It has been shown that after complete removal of the corneum, there remains only a low diffusional resistance (Tregear, 1966) and also a low electrical resistance in the epidermis (Lykken, 1968). However, since stripping also results in erythema (inflammation stemming from hyperemia), these results cannot exclude the existence of another barrier layer located in the deeper layers of the intact corneum (Tregear, 1966). Van der Valk and Maibach (1990) recorded the transepidermal water loss with an evaporimeter during adhesive cellophane-tape stripping on the volar forearm of six participants.

---

[37] More recently, Lademann, Jacobi, Surber, Weighman, and Fluhr (2008) showed that up to around 80 strippings may be required to fully remove the stratum corneum.

The increase of water loss was found to be proportional to the decrease in thickness of the horny layer, demonstrating that not only the inner but also the outer layers are important in forming the epidermal barrier.

Since the stratum corneum consists of dead cell material, the nature of the epidermal barrier is likely to be that of a passive membrane. This was shown by in vitro experiments using epidermal preparations, which yielded the same estimates for permeability to water, electrolytes, nonelectrolytes of low molecular weight (such as alcohols), and steroids (Fowles, 1986a). The barrier properties stem from lipids and essential fatty acids like linoleic acid but not from the keratin in the cells of the corneum. This is evident because strongly keratinized structures like nails are permeable to water, but de-lipidization of the corneum or diets deficient in essential fatty acids causes a marked increase in transepidermal diffusion of water.

A factor influencing the epidermal barrier function under normal physiological conditions is skin temperature. As Fowles (1986a) pointed out, the permeability for water increases exponentially with an increase in skin temperature. For example, within the range of 25–39°C, which corresponds to the normal variations in palmar skin temperature, water permeability doubles if skin temperature is raised 7–8°C. Thus, temperature effects on water permeability may significantly influence EDA (Sect. 2.4.2.1).

In spite of the diffusional barrier, and independent of whether sweat glands are active or not, there is a continuous transmission of water, from the dermis via the epidermis, out of the body by insensible perspiration (Sect. 1.3.3.2). Thus, the corneum, which is extremely hydrophilic, is always partially hydrated under physiological conditions. Its hydration is, however, dependent on external as well as internal factors. There is a linear relationship between the increase of environmental relative humidity (Sect. 2.4.1.2) and corneal hydration up to humidity of about 60–70%. At higher levels, the increase of hydration is exponential up to a relative humidity of 95% (Fowles, 1986a). Thiele (1981b) showed that the thickness of the corneum is halved when the air's relative humidity is halved.

Sweat gland activity in which the ducts are filled up to the epidermis results also in corneal hydration. Since the acrosyringium has no wall cells of its own (Sect. 1.2.3), sweat penetrates unimpeded into the corneum as a result of high pressure in the duct and/or diffusion. As a consequence, the corneum soaks sweat like a sponge. If the sweating rate increases, the corneum gets even more soaked with sweat from the skin surface, which has been poured out by sweat glands. Adams (1966) demonstrated in cats, the footpads of which were dried out, that repeated stimulation of plantar nerves resulted in an outpouring of sweat after a certain temporal delay, which varied inversely with stimulation frequency. This shows that the corneum becomes hydrated first, before sweat reaches the surface. If the corneum is already hydrated, adequate nerve stimulation results in the appearance of visible sweat immediately.

Since sweat contains numerous ions (Sect. 1.3.3.1), the electrical conductance of the corneum increases when being soaked with sweat, thus being dependent on sweat gland activity (Sect. 1.4.2.1). However, as compared to the ducts filled with sweat, the stratum corneum provides a relatively weak conducting path. In their in vitro studies, Campbell, Kraning, Schibli, and Momii (1977) obtained an unequivocal relationship between the hydration of the plantar stratum corneum and its electrical resistance. According to Tregear (1966), it is uncertain which part of the corneum adds more to its electrical conductivity: the hydrated keratinocytes themselves or the fluid within the intercellular spaces. However, Fowles (1986a) argues that water-soluble molecules follow a transcellular route as a pathway through the barrier.

The Role of Skin Components and of Membrane Processes

It is unlikely that the sebaceous glands' outlets form shunt conductances through the stratum corneum as do the sweat gland ducts, since lipids act as electrical isolators. The same is true for hair, since their sites are always connected to sebaceous glands (Sect. 1.4.2).

On the other hand, there is only little doubt (Footnote 23, Sect. 1.3.3.2) that the sweat glands aggregate quantitatively as pathways for water loss under some conditions and at some body sites (Fowles, 1986a), thus acting as diffusional shunts, a topic which had been treated systematically by Scheuplein (1978). The cross-sectional area of the stratum corneum is by a factor of 1,000–100,000 greater than the area covered by sweat glands. Therefore, under steady state conditions of diffusion, the corneum more than balances its lower diffusivity for water, so that the possible contribution of the diffusional shunt function of sweat glands may become nonsignificant. However, out of such a steady state, the sweat glands' role as diffusional shunts may be quite important, because water loss occurs via the sweat glands sooner than it does through the corneum. Since the time lag gets more pronounced with an increasing thickness of the corneum (Scheuplein, 1978), water loss through sweat glands should make a significant contribution to the total water loss for a much longer time at palmar and plantar sites, where the stratum corneum is especially thick (Sect. 1.2.1.1), compared to other sites of the body (Fowles, 1986a). However, this effect may in part be annihilated by the fact that the coefficient of diffusion (i.e., the rate of penetration of a given solute through the tissue) is much greater on palms and soles than on other body sites (Scheuplein, 1978).

Unfortunately, appropriate comparisons were made only for various solutions but not for electrolytes by Scheuplein (1978), who also stated that the permeability of the intact stratum corneum for electrolytes is extremely low. Edelberg (1971), on the other hand, provided some evidence that an at least moderately hydrated corneum will allow ions to diffuse through. He also suggested that the electrical current employed through skin during exosomatic electrodermal recording may facilitate epidermal diffusion.

Though the relative contributions of the epidermis and sweat gland ducts to total diffusion of electrolytes are unclear, the sweat gland ducts on palms and soles may play a more important role as electrical shunts than those on the rest of the body. So the possibility of site-specific time courses of the electrodermal signal on palmar and plantar sites, which are preferred for electrodermal recordings (Sect. 1.2.1.1), has to be considered.

With respect to its electrical resistance, the skin has an inner humid, conductive layer, formed by the dermis together with the nonhorny epidermal layers (Sect. 1.2.1), and an outer less humid layer which contains a barrier for water and ions which is therefore less conductive (Campbell et al., 1977). The sweat gland ducts break this barrier, act as electrical shunts, and allow an additional path for diffusion.

Besides these purely resistive properties, living tissue also has capacitive or polarization features which stem from its active membranes (see Sect. 1.4). All living cell membranes, such as present in the noncorneal part of the skin, can build up polarization capacities (Sect. 1.4.2) via an active ion transportation mechanism through their semipermeable structures. These active membranes are also present in the wall cells of the sweat gland, as well as in the myoepithelial cells surrounding them. It is not likely that active membrane processes are present in the stratum corneum, since fully keratinized cells behave electrophysiologically like plant cells. It is possible that the membrane-like lines between corneal cells (Sect. 1.2.1.1) still act as contact zones for the transmission of action potentials (Klaschka, 1979); however, they do not have any capability to form polarization capacities.

Tissue conductivity can be held responsible for tonic EDA and perhaps also contributes to phasic electrodermal phenomena with slow recovery, while the active membrane processes elicited by sudomotor nerve impulses may be responsible for EDRs with fast recovery. Polarization features of membranes may also be influenced by humoral factors. Various hormones like adrenaline, noradrenaline, and bradykinin act directly on biological membranes. Detailed descriptions of pharmacological actions of those substances on sweat glands in vitro are given by Sato (1977, 1983).

1.3.5 Suggested Biological Relevance of Electrodermal Phenomena

Apart from the psychophysiological relevance of EDA, which is the subject of the third part of this book, there have been several hypotheses concerning its biological significance, especially that of palmar and plantar sites. There is some evidence that those sites do not take part in thermal sweating (Sect. 1.3.2.4). However, Edelberg (1972a) discussed the possibility of palms and soles being an allostatic part of a sweat secretion thermoregulatory functioning, which may serve the following biologically adaptive response. Heat loss due to peripheral vasodilatation together with increased "emotional" sweating may constitute preparatory adaptations to the increase of body core temperature as a result of enhanced metabolic activity in states of high arousal or stress (Sects. 3.2.1.1 and 3.2.2.2).

Another hypothesis concerning the biological significance of the EDA focuses on the role of the sweat glands in regulating the hydration of the palmar and plantar stratum corneum. Darrow (1933) has argued that hydration provides optimal frictional contact with objects being manipulated and increases tactile sensitivity. However, it is questionable whether tactile sensitivity is really dependent on corneal hydration, or whether EDA is to be regarded as a concomitant of CNS activity leading to a sensitization of cutaneous receptors (Sect. 1.2.4). Edelberg (1971), who investigated the relationship between the degree of ANS activity on the one hand, as measured by SRR and finger pulse volume, and the tactile sensitivity using 250-Hz vibratory stimuli on the other hand, found evidence for a central activation process, providing an explanation of the high correlation between ANS and sensitivity threshold shift. During resting, the correlations between spontaneous EDRs and tactile sensitivity were low, whereas these correlations increased rapidly during recording periods following a startling stimulus. The lowering of sensation thresholds was paralleled by an increase in central activation, which was in turn already regarded by Edelberg (1961) as a source for autonomic activity as well as for the sensitivity threshold shift.

The relationship between EDA and tactile sensitivity is further enlightened by pharmacological evidence. Arthur and Shelley (1959) and Fitzgerald (1961) suggested that free nerve endings that extend into the epidermis (Sect. 1.2.4) serve as sensory afferents. However, those fibers may also serve as autonomic efferents which may take part in the origin of SP (Niebauer, 1957). Additionally, there is evidence for a direct influence of a cholinergic agent on cutaneous sensitivity. Bing and Skouby (1950) showed that the number of active cold receptors at the volar surface of the lower arm increased, following injections of acetylcholine, mecholyl, or prostigmine. Injections of atropine had the opposite effect. Wilcott (1966) observed that intracutaneous mecholyl injections into the forearm resulted in changes of sensory thresholds. He also showed that lowering of pain threshold following a needle prick was associated with a negative SP wave, whereas a rise of this threshold was associated with a positive SP wave (Sect. 1.4.2.3). Another experiment reported by Wilcott (1966) investigated the relationship between palmar SP and changes in pain threshold elicited by electrical stimulation. Wilcott found a lowering of thresholds that was accompanied by either positive or negative SPRs. These results may suggest that changes in sensitivity thresholds are influenced by cholinergic agents, which also produce the EDA changes being observed as concomitants of threshold shifts. Earlier, Löwenstein (1956) observed that the stimulation of sympathetic fibers traveling to the frog's skin resulted in lowered tactile receptor thresholds and a delay of their adaptation. However, sympathetic influences in the frog are transmitted adrenergic and not cholinergic.

The possible association between EDA and improvement of frictional contact may be illustrated by everyday behavior, which also optimizes the wetness of palmar epidermal sites, such as moistening the finger with the lips before turning pages and rubbing one's palms before grasping a tennis racket.[38] In the latter case, there is an inverted-U-shaped relationship between the degree of moistening of the skin and the frictional contact with the rugged synthetic surface of the racket (Adams & Hunter, 1969). Since the frictional properties of skin reach their maximum at an intermediate level of surface moisture, Edelberg (1972a) presumed the existence of a control mechanism, which has the ability to prevent excessive moistening of the skin. Edelberg (1973a) suggested this being the role of an absorption reflex, which is connected with the positive SP wave. Hence, the positive SP component could be interpreted as an indication of task-oriented, finely coordinated motor activity (Edelberg, 1972a).

Additional evidence for the friction improvement hypothesis came from Edelberg (1967), who showed that EDRs could be recorded on those sites of the soles – the heel and the ball of the foot – that are in direct contact with the ground. Another plantar site showing considerable EDA is on the inner side of the foot between the big toe and the ankle (Sect. 2.2.1.1). This region is especially stressed in tree-climbing primates. Edelberg (1967) also observed that the amplitudes of the negative SPRs on palmar and dorsal surfaces of the fingers were nearly identical, however, by far lower than those at thenar and hypothenar sites or at the foot. On the other hand, the positive SPRs were particularly high on palmar sites of the fingers and the hand. Hence, positive SPRs are prominent on those sites which are needed for tactile manipulation, while sites that are included in gross body movements, such as on the feet, show predominantly negative SPRs. However, it remains open as to what degree the different thicknesses of stratum corneum at different sites contributed to these results.

Besides the biological significances of EDA previously discussed, moisturizing of skin following subsequent EDRs may also have protective properties in cases of injury, since it increases the resistance of the corneum against cutting or rubbing (Adams & Hunter, 1969). Wilcott (1966) observed that skin treated with atropine, which abolishes sweat gland activity, can be more easily abraded with a dental drill than untreated skin or skin soaked with distilled water. Having a defensive orientation, this kind of adaptation could serve as an explanation for the observation that threatening situations are strong eliciting stimuli for EDRs.

A somewhat speculative interpretation of the "emotional" sweating occurring at palmar and plantar sites (Sect. 1.3.3.3) is given by Edelberg (1972a): because sweat is not simply a solution of electrolytes but additionally contains organic substances (Sect. 1.3.3.1), sweating at those sites could serve as a tracking aid in certain species. It is possible that the olfactory action of organic agents in sweat would help, for example, a child to identify her/his mother's scent, or act as a signal for a threatening situation. This would, however, require a CNS-guided secretion mechanism for emotion-specific organic sweat components, for which evidence is missing.

---

[38] From their lesion and stimulation research with cats, Sequeira and Roy (1993) concluded that a direct corticospinal sudomotor pathway may exist, contributing to the corticospinal control of final autonomic adjustments, in particular during grasping.

1.4 Biophysics of Electrodermal Measurement

Electrodermal phenomena are spontaneous as well as elicited changes of a complex system with elements showing different electrophysical properties. All electrodermal models described in Sect. 1.4.3 consider fixed as well as variable resistors and capacitors. In addition, some of them comprise voltage sources localized in the skin or the sweat glands, which represent polarized membranes. Electrophysiologically, these can be regarded as capacitors which are already charged. Therefore, the following introduction focuses mainly on the electrophysical properties of resistances and capacitors.

From a system-theoretical view point, methods of electrodermal recording can be assigned to the following three groups:

1. *Endosomatic recording* (Sect. 2.2.3.1). In this method, only those properties of the electrodermal system which result from active changes of the system are considered. The electrical energy is presumed to originate in the polarized membranes in the skin as mentioned above.
2. *Exosomatic recording with direct current* (Sects. 2.1.1, 2.1.2, and 2.2.3.2). Here, the electrodermal system is supported with electrical energy from an external source, using either a constant voltage or a constant current. The appropriate models mainly focus on passive properties of a system, in which capacitors are charged and changes in the signal are mainly due to resistive changes.
3. *Exosomatic recording using alternating current* (Sects. 2.1.5 and 2.2.3.3). This method is infrequently used. In addition to the system properties mentioned under (2), responses of the electrodermal system to oscillatory signals are investigated, which also include changes in capacitors or charged membranes in the skin.

Prior to the description of electrophysical properties of the skin and the sweat glands, some fundamental principles of electrophysics and systems theory will be discussed below.

1.4.1 Resistor- and Capacitor-Based Systems

In this section, some fundamentals of electrophysics are described in using an illustrative and clear manner, which are considered necessary for the comprehension of electrodermal phenomena and the corresponding models. Readers who already have knowledge of electrophysics may find Sect. 1.4.1.1 and the beginning of Sect. 1.4.1.2 somewhat elementary. However, they address researchers who do not possess such prior knowledge.

1.4.1.1 Some Fundamental Electrical Properties

Between two bodies with electrical charges Q of different sizes (e.g., between the two poles of a battery) there exists a potential difference, which is described as the voltage U and is measured in volts (V). When the two bodies are connected by a conductor, an electrical current will flow through the conductor until the potential difference is equalized and voltage becomes zero; this current I is measured in amperes (A), 1 A being defined as the amount of current that flows with a charge of one coulomb for 1 s.

In the simplest case, voltage and current are proportional, that is, the quotient of voltage and current is constant. This constant is defined as the electrical resistance R, the relationship between the three dimensions being set out in the following equation:

$$U = RI \qquad (1.1)$$

This equation is known as Ohm's law. Electrical conductors which obey this law are called ohmic resistances. Their strength is given in ohms (Ω) which is defined as follows: when, by a voltage of 1 V, a current of 1 A flows, there exists a resistance of 1 Ω.

Equation (1.1) states that the proportionality between applied voltage and flowing current is dependent upon the resistance R. It also illustrates the reversed proportionality between resistance and current flow with constant voltage; the greater the resistance, the less current can flow. This dependence can also be formulated using the reciprocal of resistance, that is conductance G as follows:

$$G = \frac{1}{R} \qquad (1.2a)$$

G (Footnote 2, Sect. 1.1.1) is measured in siemens (S).[39] The reverse is also true:

$$R = \frac{1}{G} \qquad (1.2b)$$

When the reciprocal conductance value from (1.2b) is inserted in place of R in (1.1), it follows

$$U = \frac{I}{G} \qquad (1.3)$$

Hence, the strength of the current I flowing through the resistance is directly proportional to the conductance G if the voltage U is constant.

---

[39] In Anglo-American papers, there was a widespread custom for using the unit "mho," i.e., the mirror image of "ohm," instead. Meanwhile, S was introduced as the SI unit for conductance. Despite Venables and Christie (1980) argued for the continued usage of mho, in the last 20–30 years most researchers have used the unit S for conductance. The unit mho corresponds 1:1 to the unit μS.

In biological processes, resistances appear commonly in the range of several thousand ohms, therefore kiloohm (kΩ) is used as the denotation symbol for resistance in electrodermal measurement. Correspondingly, it is common to use microsiemens (μS) for conductance. Resistance and conductance can be converted into each other as shown by the following two equations:

$$G[\mu S] = \frac{1,000}{R[k\Omega]} \tag{1.4a}$$

and

$$R[k\Omega] = \frac{1,000}{G[\mu S]} \tag{1.4b}$$

Equations (1.4a) and (1.4b) can only be used for converting resistance and conductance values into each other, which were recorded at a specific point in time. If the resistance and conductance changes (i.e., ΔR and ΔG) shall be converted, which is rather common in the recording of EDA, the simple relationships of (1.4a) and (1.4b) do not apply anymore. Given $\Delta R = R_2 - R_1$ and $\Delta G = G_2 - G_1$, then the following equation applies:

$$\Delta G = \frac{1}{R_2} - \frac{1}{R_1} = \frac{R_1}{R_1 R_2} - \frac{R_2}{R_1 R_2} = -\frac{\Delta R}{R_1 R_2} \tag{1.5a}$$

The minus sign shows that an increase in resistance leads to a decrease in conductance. Correspondingly, the reverse, following (1.2b), also applies:

$$\Delta R = \frac{1}{G_2} - \frac{1}{G_1} = \frac{G_1}{G_1 G_2} - \frac{G_2}{G_1 G_2} = -\frac{\Delta G}{G_1 G_2} \tag{1.5b}$$

When converting changes in resistance and conductance into each other, levels for both the conductance and resistance must be taken into account. This means that they must also be recorded. In practice, R_1^2 is normally used in the denominator of (1.5a) instead of the product of R_1 and R_2, because the error is small when ΔR is relatively small in comparison to R (Sect. 2.3.3.2). Correspondingly, G_1^2 can be substituted in (1.5b) when ΔG is small in comparison to G_1.

1.4.1.2 Application of Direct Current to RC Circuits

An electrical circuit in which a capacitor (C) is charged and discharged through a resistor (R) is labeled "RC circuit."

An ohmic resistor to which direct current is applied will transform electrical energy into heat. Voltage is said to "drop" across the resistor. Basically, there are

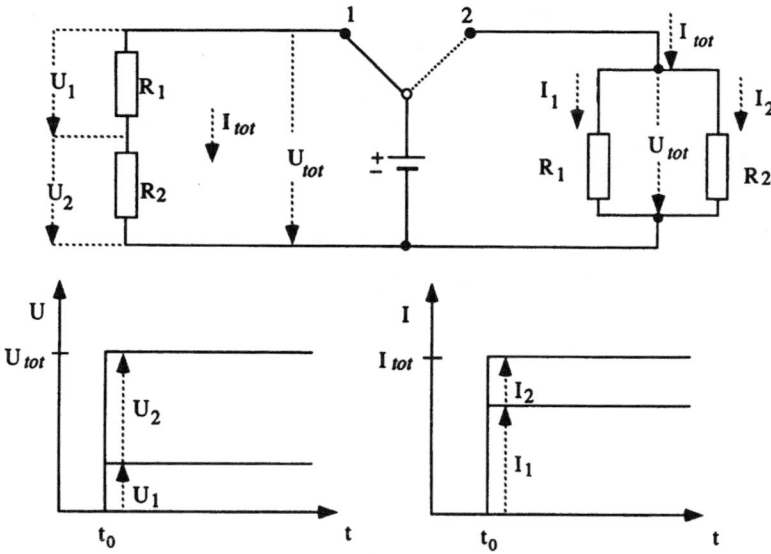

Fig. 1.7 Resistors connected serially (left, switch position 1) and in parallel (right, switch position 2) and the resulting subdivisions of the total voltage U_{tot} and total current I_{tot}

two ways to connect resistors in a circuit: either in series with each other or in parallel.[40]

On the left-hand side of Fig. 1.7, two resistors connected in series are depicted. Over each resistor, the voltage U_{tot} applied to the circuit as a whole drops and the partial voltages U_1 and U_2 add up to the original U_{tot}. The current I_{tot} is the same in both resistors. Hence, resistors connected in series behave additively.

When the resistors are not connected serially but in parallel, as depicted on the right-hand side of Fig. 1.7, another effect results: the same voltage U_{tot} lies on each resistor independent of its size, since they are all directly connected to the full voltage. The current is subdivided according to the size of each resistor, in which case Ohm's law must be applied to each resistor. The currents I_1 and I_2 add up to the current I_{tot} which flows through the circuit.

The size of an insertable resistance R_{tot} through which the same current flows by the same voltages as by the parallel resistances R_1 and R_2 can be calculated by Ohm's law which was shown in (1.1):

$$R_{tot} = \frac{U}{I_{tot}} = \frac{U}{I_1 + I_2} \qquad (1.6a)$$

---

[40] During the following considerations, the inner resistance of the voltage source should always be negligible for the reason of simplification.

Again following Ohm's law:

$$I_{tot} = \frac{U}{R_{tot}} \quad \text{and} \quad I_1 = \frac{U}{R_1} \quad \text{and} \quad I_2 = \frac{U}{R_2} \tag{1.6b}$$

By dividing the right- and left-hand sides of (1.6a) by U, inverting them, and inserting the values of I_1 and I_2 from (1.6b), the following relationship results:

$$\frac{U}{R_{tot}} = \frac{U}{R_1} + \frac{U}{R_2} \tag{1.6c}$$

Dividing both sides of (1.6c) by U results in

$$\frac{1}{R_{tot}} = \frac{1}{R_1} + \frac{1}{R_2} = \frac{R_1 + R_2}{R_1 R_2} \tag{1.6d}$$

From that follows directly

$$R_{tot} = \frac{R_1 R_2}{R_1 + R_2} \tag{1.6e}$$

Equation (1.6e) illustrates that the replacement resistance for a parallel circuit is smaller than the sum of single resistances. This can be easily seen by using numerical examples.

In contrast to resistors which use up electrical energy, capacitors store it. Technical capacitors consist of two parallel, electrically conductive plates separated by an isolating dielectric (an electrical insulator which can be polarized by an applied electric field). When voltage is applied to these plates, they become charged and build up an electrical field. Upon becoming fully charged, no more charging current will flow. If the voltage source is removed, the full voltage remains between the plates until they are short circuited through a load. During the discharge process, a current flows in the direction opposite to the charging current, until the voltage between the plates reaches zero.

The capacitance of a capacitor indicates its ability to store an electrical charge. The larger the capacitance is, the more charge can be stored, given a fixed voltage. The relationship between the charge Q, the capacitance C, and the voltage U is linear, as shown in (1.7):

$$Q = CU \tag{1.7}$$

The capacity of a capacitor is expressed in farads (F) and is defined as follows: a capacitor in which the voltage reaches 1 V in 1 s by a charge current of 1 A has a capacity of 1 F. In practice, the usual values are much smaller, as in the case of conductance (Sect. 1.4.1.1). Therefore, capacitance is given in μF, nF, or pF (microfarad, nanofarad, or picofarad).

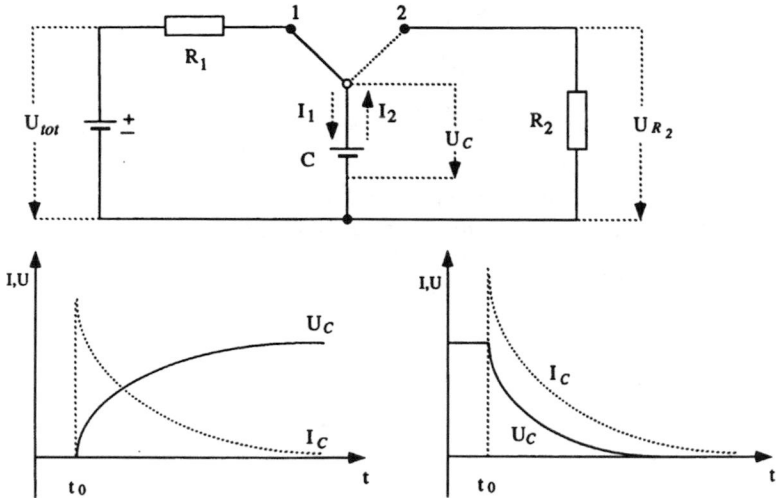

Fig. 1.8 The charging (left, switch position 1) and discharging (right, switch position 2) of a capacitor in an RC circuit, with the corresponding current and voltage graphs

Figure 1.8 presents the temporal relationship between voltage and current from charging and discharging a capacitor. In circuit position 1 the capacitor is charged. Voltage U_C, measured on the capacitor C, rises exponentially until the value U is reached, while the charge current I drops exponentially to zero, which is dependent upon the serially connected resistor R_1 and the capacitor C. When the fully charged capacitor is connected as in position 2, the capacitor discharges through R_2, (i.e., it is short-circuited). Thus, voltage and current drop exponentially to zero, whereas the strength of the discharge current I_2 as a temporal alteration of the capacitor charge is defined by

$$I_2 = \frac{dQ}{dt} \tag{1.8}$$

In the short-circuited system, the voltage U_{R2} that drops across the resistor R_2 is in the opposite polarization to the voltage U_C and shows the same temporal course as I_2; therefore

$$U_C + U_{R2} = 0 \tag{1.9a}$$

Following Ohm's law, $U_{R2} = R_2 I_2$, and transformation of (1.7) results in $U_C = Q/C$. Therefore

$$(R_2 I_2) + \frac{Q}{C} = 0 \tag{1.9b}$$

Dividing by R_2 and insertion from (1.8) gives:

$$\frac{dQ}{dt} = -\frac{Q}{CR_2} \tag{1.9c}$$

If the change of a value is in proportion to that value, the value will show an exponential course over time, as seen in the differential equation (1.9c) for the charge Q of the capacitor. As can be shown through insertion, the exponential course is described by (1.10a):

$$Q = Q_0\, e^{-t/RC} \tag{1.10a}$$

at which Q_0 is the initial charge value and Q is the charge value at a particular point in time t. The product of resistance and capacitance, RC, is labeled time constant τ and indicates how fast the exponential curve declines:

$$\tau = CR \tag{1.10b}$$

In (1.10b), capacitance must be given in F and resistance in Ω. A capacitor, when being charged, reaches 63% of its full charge at τ s. If it is discharged, then 37% of its charge is left after τ s (Sect. 2.3.1.3 "Recovery Parameters"). Increasing the capacitance n times results in a time constant of $n\tau$, as does an increase of the resistance n times.

When several capacitors are connected in series and are fully charged, the charge is the same in each capacitor and corresponds to the total charge Q_{tot}. In the case of two serially connected capacitors, this means

$$Q_1 = Q_2 = Q_{tot} \tag{1.11a}$$

If (1.7) is solved for U for each capacitor, Q_1 and Q_2 can be replaced by Q_{tot} following (1.11a):

$$U_1 = \frac{Q_{tot}}{C_1} \quad \text{and} \quad U_2 = \frac{Q_{tot}}{C_2} \tag{1.11b}$$

As depicted on the left-hand side of Fig. 1.7, the voltages U_1 and U_2 add up to the voltage U_{tot}; the same goes for U_{tot} as for the single voltages (1.11b), and the following results:

$$\frac{Q_{tot}}{C_{tot}} = \frac{Q_{tot}}{C_1} + \frac{Q_{tot}}{C_2} \tag{1.11c}$$

When both sides of (1.11c) are divided by Q_{tot}, the following results:

$$\frac{1}{C_{tot}} = \frac{1}{C_1} + \frac{1}{C_2} \tag{1.11d}$$

Therefore, in the case of serially connected capacitors, the reciprocal value of the replacement capacitor is determined by addition of the reciprocal values of the single capacitors, in opposition to serially connected resistors which are added to each other.

When two capacitors are connected in parallel, the full voltage U_{tot} lies across both capacitors simultaneously. The charges of the capacitors are calculated using (1.7) as follows:

$$Q_1 = C_1 U_{tot} \qquad\qquad (1.12a)$$

and

$$Q_2 = C_2 U_{tot} \qquad\qquad (1.12b)$$

Since the adjacent plates of the single capacitors can be regarded as one big capacitive plate, the total charge is calculated as follows:

$$Q_{tot} = Q_1 + Q_2 = C_1 U_{tot} + C_2 U_{tot} \qquad\qquad (1.13a)$$

Isolating U_{tot} and dividing the left- and right-hand sides of (1.13a) by U_{tot} results in

$$\frac{Q_{tot}}{U_{tot}} = C_1 + C_2 \qquad\qquad (1.13b)$$

If (1.7) is transformed and the result is applied to (1.13b), it can be seen that the left-hand side of (1.13b) equals C_{tot}. Thus

$$C_{tot} = C_1 + C_2 \qquad\qquad (1.13c)$$

Therefore, capacitors connected in parallel behave as if added to each other, in contrast to the replacement resistance for parallel resistors, which is smaller than the sum of the single resistors, as shown in (1.6e).

Figure 1.8 depicts an RC circuit in which a resistor and a capacitor are connected in series (i.e., the capacitor C is charged through the resistor R_1 and discharged through R_2). It is also possible to build networks of resistors and capacitors connected in parallel. The charging and discharging processes are similar to those shown in Fig. 1.8; however, the voltage rise time will be delayed.

1.4.1.3   Application of Alternating Current to RC Circuits

Once the capacitor in an RC circuit is fully charged following the application of a DC, only the resistive properties of the circuit are measurable. Should the capacitive properties of RC circuits also continually be determined, as in the course of possible variations in polarization capacities during an EDR (Sects. 2.1.5 and 2.2.3.3), either the direct current must be continually switched on and off (pulsed DC, Sect. 1.4.1.4) or, for example, a sinusoidal alternating voltage must be applied for the measurement of the system's electrical properties.

Alternating voltages are characterized by changing their strength and direction periodically. The most commonly used alternating voltage is sinusoidal. Here, the voltage amplitude is calculated by the sinus of the angle of a circle, whose radius is the maximum amplitude and is passed once during a period, as shown in the following equation:

$$U(t) = U_0 \sin(2\pi f t) \tag{1.14}$$

at which f is the frequency of the alternating voltage, $U(t)$ is the amplitude at time t, and U_0 is the maximum amplitude of the voltage. In an AC circuit when only ohmic resistances are involved, the voltage drops as in a DC circuit. Furthermore, the effect of serially connected resistors as voltage dividers and of parallel-connected resistors as current dividers is the same as in a DC circuit (Fig. 1.7). Current and voltage in the presence of purely ohmic resistances are always "in phase."

This is no longer the case when a capacitor is put into an AC circuit. In DC, following the finish of charging, no more current can flow through the capacitor branch and the full voltage is measurable across the capacitor (Fig. 1.8), but the electrically conductive plates in an AC circuit charge up alternatingly positive and negative, so that a standing alternating charge and discharge current flows.

In a circuit with only one capacitor, an AC is measurable, the strength of which varies with the rise and fall of the alternating voltage. When the voltage and current of a capacitor are measured, the phase of the current will lag behind that of the voltage. The reason for this is as follows: before a voltage can build up on the capacitor's plates, a current must flow. This current is at its maximum when the voltage is zero and is itself at zero when the full voltage is reached (Fig. 1.8, lower left). This is true for the positive and negative phases (i.e., the current's maximum is reached a quarter period before the maximum of the positive and negative voltage amplitude). This phase displacement is described by the phase angle φ through which the current flow precedes the voltage course.

The AC resistance of a capacitor is frequency dependent. With a lower frequency the capacitor will be charged and discharged less often during a certain period; the average strength of the current is therefore smaller with a lower than with a higher frequency, by which the capacitor would be charged and discharged more often. The rising current indicates a higher transmission factor for AC, which means that the AC resistance of the capacitor decreases with rising frequency.

This can be inferred mathematically from (1.7), (1.8), and (1.14). The transformation and differentiation of (1.7) with t gives

$$\frac{dQ}{dt} = C\frac{dU}{dt} \tag{1.15a}$$

For sinusoidal alternating voltage, differentiation of (1.14) with t gives

$$\frac{dU}{dt} = (2\pi f U_0)\cos(2\pi f t) \tag{1.15b}$$

If (1.15b) is inserted in (1.15a), and it is noted from (1.8) that $I = dQ/dt$, then

$$I(t) = (2\pi C f U_0)\cos(2\pi f t) \tag{1.16a}$$

The product $2\pi C f U_0$ is a constant and gives the maximum value of the current I_0 by a certain frequency f:

$$I(t) = I_0 \cos(2\pi f t) \tag{1.16b}$$

Figure 1.9 refers to a system composed of just one capacitor, where the inner resistance of the voltage source is negligible. In this case, the phase displacement φ will be 90° as shown in the vector diagram in the lower part of Fig. 1.9. In this diagram, the current I, whose strength is calculated by (1.16b), has a value of

$$|I| = 2\pi C f U_0 \tag{1.16c}$$

The value of the impedance $Z(f)$ for the frequency f is given as the quotient of the values of U and I from (1.14) and (1.16c):

$$|Z(f)| = \left|\frac{U}{I}\right| = \frac{U_0}{2\pi C f U_0} = \frac{1}{2\pi f C} \tag{1.17}$$

It can be seen in (1.17) that the impedance Z behaves as the reciprocal of the frequency f, given a constant capacity C (i.e., by increasing frequency, the AC resistance decreases).

Since an ohmic resistance transforms electrical energy into heat (Sect. 1.4.1.2) it is described as an active resistance. By contrast, a capacitor in a circuit does not transform electrical energy but stores it. Despite this, the capacitor limits the current dependent upon the frequency f of the applied alternating voltage. This effect is described as blind resistance or as reactance X:

$$X(f) = Z(f)\sin\varphi(f) \tag{1.18a}$$

Since the phase angle φ is 90° in a system composed of only one capacitor as shown above (which can, however, be only theoretically true in case of a so-called ideal capacitor), $X(f) = Z(f)$ in that case (i.e., reactance equals impedance).

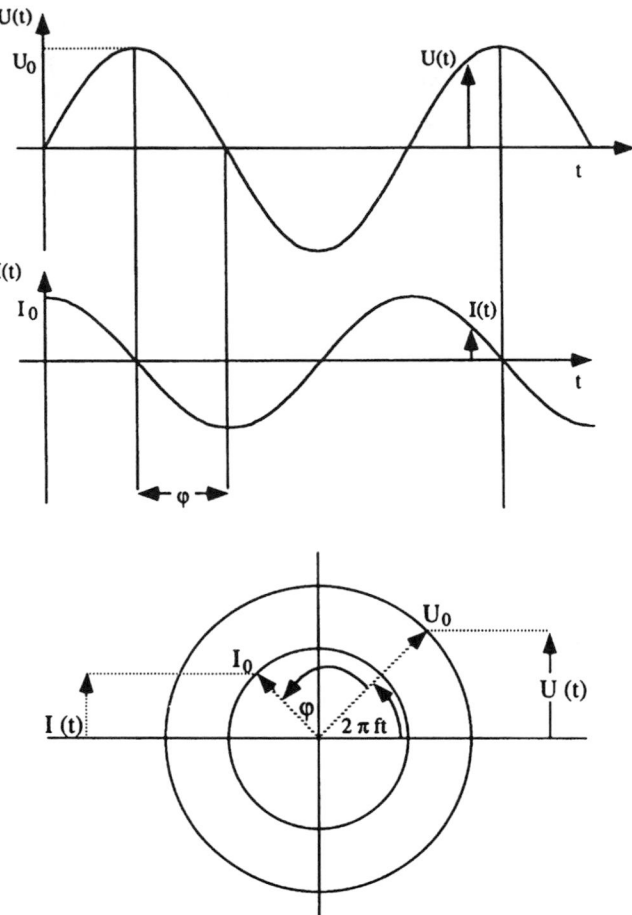

Fig. 1.9 Phase displacement of voltage and current by application of alternating voltage to a capacitor (upper part) together with the corresponding vector diagram (lower part). See text for explanations

Through incorporation of an active (ohmic) resistance in such a circuit, the phase angle φ is changed, in relation to the frequency f of the alternating voltage, between 0 and 90°. Using the impedance $Z(f)$ and the phase angle $\varphi(f)$, the reactance (blind resistance) $X(f)$ can be calculated from (1.18a). The ohmic resistance $R(f)$ is calculated as follows:

$$R(f) = Z(f)\cos\varphi(f) \qquad (1.18b)$$

In a graph made up from $R(f)$ as the abscissa and $X(f)$ as the ordinate, a characteristic curve for $Z(f)$ can be plotted (Fig. 1.10). This curve, or locus as it

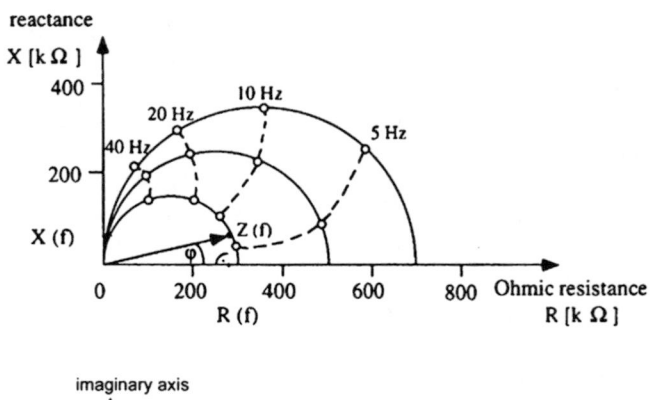

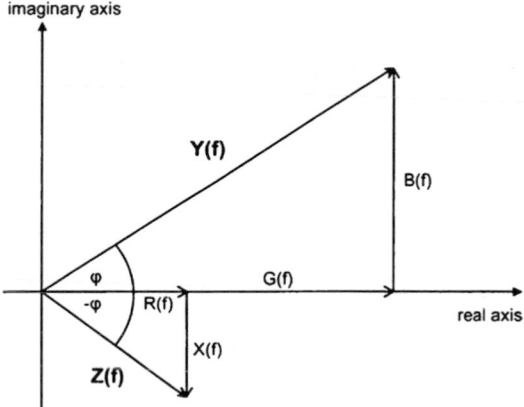

Fig. 1.10 Upper part: Three different loci. The innermost curve results from an impedance vector Z (f) of around $f = 7\,Hz$ with its projections $X(f)$ and $R(f)$ drawn to the respective axes. Lower part: The admittance vector $Y(f)$ with its components: conductance $G(f)$ and susceptance $B(f)$, and the impedance vector $Z(f)$ with its components: resistance $R(f)$ and reactance $X(f)$, being represented in the complex plane. The phase angle φ has the same absolute value in both cases but differs in sign. Reprinted from Schaefer and Boucsein (2000), Fig. 1.2. Copyright 2000 by the Society for Psychophysiological Research. Reprinted by permission of the publisher and the first author

is called, fully describes the transmission behavior of the RC system and can be used for its characterization.[41]

In the upper part of Fig. 1.10, three differing loci are plotted, through which the responses of three different systems to the applied alternating voltage can be described. The curves shown in the diagram apply to a system with a parallel circuit comprising a resistor and a capacitor.

---

[41] These connections can also be elucidated through a depiction with complex numbers. There $R(f)$ is taken as the real part and $X(f)$ as the imaginary part of a complex function. This depiction, which is preferred in electrophysics and in systems theory, is shown in the lower part of Fig. 1.10.

Such a locus materializes as follows: when the frequency f of the alternating voltage has the value 0, the system is virtually on direct voltage. In this case, the resistance of the capacitor C would be infinite (Sect. 1.4.1.2) and the impedance Z would be determined solely by the ohmic resistance; therefore $Z(0)$ would equal $R(0)$. The vector Z would therefore lie on the R axis at $f = 0$. When f is raised by an applied alternating voltage, then C would, so to speak, allow current flow through it (i.e., the Z vector becomes shorter as the total impedance of the system decreases). With increasing f, the angle of the vector Z to the X axis increases, that is, the blind resistance part of the impedance increases. The total impedance decreases constantly with rising frequency (i.e., the Z vector becomes constantly shorter) until it achieves 0 by $f \rightarrow \infty$, and then the capacitor practically short-circuits the resistor.

From the projection of the impedance vector $Z(f)$ to the R- and X-axes, the relationship between Z, R, and X can clearly be shown. Following Pythagoras' theorem, (1.19a) holds for each frequency, and therefore being independent of the phase angle:

$$Z(f) = \sqrt{R(f)^2 + X(f)^2} \tag{1.19a}$$

The AC conductance, which corresponds to the AC resistance (i.e., impedance $Z(f)$), is labeled admittance and symbolized by Y (Table 1.1, Sect. 1.1.1):

$$Y(f) = \frac{1}{Z(f)} \tag{1.19b}$$

$Y(f)$ can be subdivided into its real part, the conductance $G(f)$, and its imaginary part, the susceptance $B(f)$ (see Footnote 41). With application of (1.19a) and (1.19b), susceptance $B(f)$ can be calculated as follows from reactance X and the ohmic resistance R:

$$B(f) = \frac{X(f)}{X(f)^2 + R(f)^2} \tag{1.20a}$$

The conductance G is calculated as follows:

$$G(f) = \frac{R(f)}{R(f)^2 + X(f)^2} \tag{1.20b}$$

By using (1.18a) and (1.18b), B and G can be determined from the impedance Z and also the phase angle φ. The locus determination of conductance and susceptance ensues correspondingly from the upper part of Fig. 1.10, and the equivalent of (1.19a) also applies to the relationship between $Y(f)$, $G(f)$, and $B(f)$. Examples of loci in the conductance-susceptance graph are given in Sect. 1.4.3.3.

The lower part of Fig. 1.10 depicts the relationships between admittance and impedance and their components in the plane made up by the real and the imaginary axis. As can be seen, the phase angle φ has the same absolute value for admittance and conductance, differing only in its sign, provided that a specific AC frequency is applied and under the assumption of constant imaginary components (see Boucsein, Schaefer, & Neijenhuisen, 1989; cf. also Sect. 2.3.1.2 "Amplitudes of Exosomatic Responses Recorded with Alternating Current"). Hence, the phase angle φ can be used as a measure for EDA which is independent of the measurement technique applied (Sect. 2.5.3.1).

The processes which occur by application of alternating voltage to biological tissues with the ability to build up polarization capacities (Sect. 1.4.2.2) are comparable to technical capacitors. However, they are complicated by the fact that tissues must be, electrophysically, regarded as circuits of higher complexity than the simple RC circuits discussed here. This is partly because more capacitors and also more resistors, both in series and in parallel, are involved (Sect. 1.4.3.2). By the use of these types of additional elements, the current and voltage processes through time are further affected. In principle, however, the resistive and capacitive properties of such complex systems can be simulated by relatively simple substitute circuits (Sect. 1.4.3.3).

The various measurement procedures for determining the phase angle φ, the impedance Z, and the admittance Y are described in Sect. 2.1.5.

1.4.1.4 Determining System Properties of Unknown RC Systems

The consequences of application of sinusoidal alternating voltage to circuits comprising resistors and capacitors (as described in the previous section) can be regarded from the systems theory perspective as the deformation of a defined input signal by a system. In systems theory, such processes are used to investigate the properties of unknown systems.

By using an oscilloscope which allows replacing the time basis by an amplifier, a depiction of phase displacement and amplitude relationship between the input and output signal can be obtained. Figure 1.11 depicts an example of the resulting so-called Lissajous figure, which shows how the combination of an input signal possessing the maximum amplitude E_0 and an output signal with the maximum amplitude A_0 creates an elliptical figure whose main axial incline is dependent upon the A_0/E_0 relationship. The length of the short axis is dependent upon the phase displacement; it reaches its maximum at $\varphi = 90°$ and disappears at $\varphi = 0°$.

The system properties of an RC circuit with known resistors and capacitors in series and in parallel can be determined through the application of a single alternating voltage frequency. However, to investigate unknown systems such as the skin, recording must be repeated with a number of different frequencies. The disadvantage of such a process is the long time needed for measurement, especially with the inclusion of low frequencies. This is because in the low-frequency area the system becomes stabilized only after around five full periods. Therefore, techniques

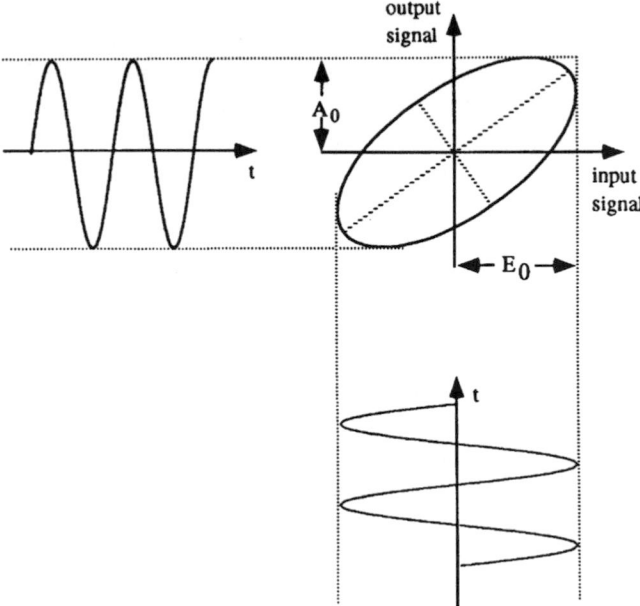

Fig. 1.11 Lissajous figure. E_0: maximum amplitude of the input signal. A_0: maximum amplitude of the output signal. t: time axis. Dotted: the axes of the ellipse

using successive impulses with differing alternating voltage frequencies have been developed to date only for the recording of the tonic parts of EDA and not for those of a phasic EDR (Sect. 2.1.5).

However, it is theoretically possible to stimulate a system such as the skin with all frequencies of a defined spectrum at the same time (known technically as "noise"). The system's response is divided into its spectral components by using Fourier analysis. This allows phase and amplitude spectrums to be obtained from the system's response to the differing frequencies of the given input noise. Such a process requires a very high temporal resolution and – depending on the narrow phasic variations in comparison to the possible tonic values of the EDA signal (Sect. 2.1.3) – necessitates, not only in the temporal but also in the amplitude area, high resolution analog/digital (A/D) converters, and laboratory computers which make a correspondingly fast data transfer possible.

A further possibility is offered by the so-called pulse spectrum analysis for simultaneously recording the system's response to all frequencies of a spectrum. The responses to pulse-formed signals, which begin at zero, return to zero, and will remain there until the next signal, are described in systems theory as "transients." The unknown system is stimulated by a sequence of periodic DC impulses (the so-called pulsed DC). Each sequence of square wave impulses can be conceived as a result of superimposed sine waves of different frequencies. Figure 1.12 highlights how a certain spectrum of sine waves can be summarized, forming needle impulses (a process that can be regarded as opposed to Fourier analysis). The resulting

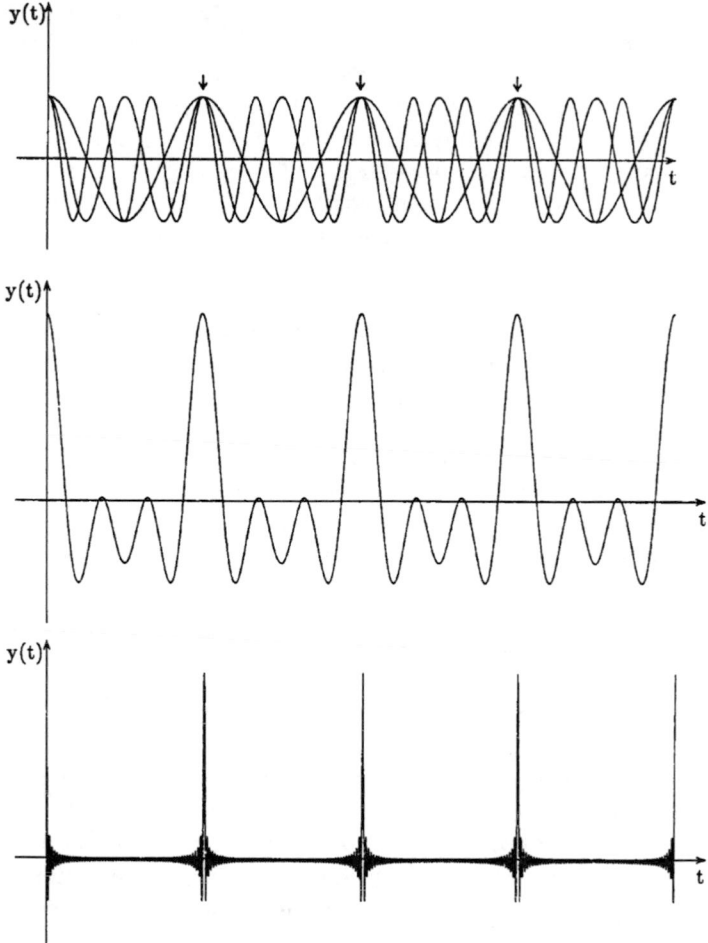

Fig. 1.12 Three superimposed sine curves (above), their summation curve (middle), and a corresponding summation curve of 60 basic sine frequencies. The arrows indicate the temporal points, where all waves are in phase

value y at a given time t is calculated as the sum of the amplitudes from n superimposed sine waves according to (1.21), where $\pi/2$ is brought in to obtain a maximum at the beginning:

$$y(t) = \sum_{t=1}^{n} \sin\left(2\pi f i t + \frac{\pi}{2}\right) \tag{1.21}$$

In the upper part of Fig. 1.12, due to the need for transparency, only $n = 3$ superimposed sine waves have been displayed. It can be seen that at particular points in time, when all single sine waves are in phase (see arrows), constructive interference occurs. In the middle section of Fig. 1.12, the summation curve of three sine waves, as determined by (1.21), is shown. Here, an enlargement of the resulting amplitude at all the time points at which the single waves are in phase can be seen. From the summation of sine waves by $n = 60$ frequencies, peaked square wave impulses will result, as shown in the lower part of Fig. 1.12. When the number of such superimposed frequencies is very large, spikes are created, the so-called Dirac impulses or delta surges, which are preferred in systems theory applications because of their ideal properties (i.e., theoretically infinitely peaked and containing all frequencies). Dependent on the system's recovery time, they can be applied in very fast sequences, thus making a continuous recording of the system's properties possible. This is only limited by the scanning rate and the repetition rate of the impulses. The system's response to the impulse of a delta surge, which consists of all stimulation frequencies, can be calculated by Fourier analysis, which again requires fast data handling.

Theoretically, the electrical properties of the unknown skin/sweat gland system may be continuously analyzed by using transient analysis, for example, with delta surges (see also Footnote 53, Sect. 2.1.5) or by using noise as a probe signal, instead of using various successive frequencies. However, these techniques will create specific problems in electrodermal recording that will be discussed in Sect. 2.1.5.

1.4.2 Electrophysical Properties of Skin and Sweat Glands

When an external current is applied to biological tissues such as skin, they act like electrical networks built of resistors and capacitors. Electrical modeling of the skin using the elements described in Sect. 1.4.3 does not require the skin to be built of elements having discrete resistive or capacitive properties. However, there are parts of the skin and sweat glands that are likely to act electrophysically similar to resistive or capacitive elements and may thus be included in appropriate models.

Blood, ductal sweat, and interstitial fluid have differing conductivities, dependent on their ionic concentration. Therefore, they act as variable resistors (Sect. 1.4.2.1). In contrast, the cellular boundaries formed by membranes appear to have more capacitor-like characteristics (Sect. 1.4.2.2), since their selective permeability forms an obstacle for the ions involved in the current flow. As a result, storage of ions at these boundaries is followed by the buildup of a potential difference across the cell membrane, the direction of which is opposite to the applied voltage – hence called "counter electromotive force" or "back electromotive force" (back e.m.f.).

Membranes that have the ability to store electrical energy like capacitors can act as a polarization capacity (Fricke, 1932). These become potential sources, which are included in some models of EDA (Sect. 1.4.3.2). Membranes having polarization capacity and hence capacitor-like or potential-like properties are presumed to be located at the sweat gland membranes, at the dermal-epidermal boundary membrane and in the epidermis (Sect. 1.3.4.2 "The Role of Skin Components and of Membrane Processes"). All those properties together form the active sources for electrodermal phenomena (Sect. 1.4.2.3).

1.4.2.1 Resistive Properties of Skin and Sweat Glands

The dermis and the hypodermis, being well supplied with blood and interstitial fluids (Sect. 1.2.1.3), possess good electrical conductivity, which may vary to some extent, depending on changes in blood flow. Additionally, the epidermal Malpighian layer and the stratum intermedium (Table 1.2, Sect. 1.2.1.1) may be regarded as relatively conductive structures, thus not adding much to the skin's resistance. Therefore, the lower corneal zone, which is relatively impermeable to water and solutions, is thought to be mainly responsible for the skin's resistance (Fowles, 1974). However, as outlined in Sect. 1.3.4.2 "The Role of the Epidermal Barrier Layer," an exact localization of such an epidermal barrier is not possible, and the whole stratum corneum is regarded as being a variable resistor, depending on its degree of hydration.

The stratum corneum, with its keratinized cells, does not contain living membranes, which maintain a diffusional balance between the inner and outer cellular milieu. Instead, the whole corneum acts like a sponge, taking up water and solutions from inside and outside the body, which are released when the corneum becomes dry. Under normal physiological conditions the corneum is always partially hydrated, the degree of its hydration being dependent on the environment's relative humidity. With an increase in sweating, corneal hydration also increases, leading to tonic and/or slow phasic changes in skin resistance. If the corneum becomes dry, for example, as a result of aging (Sect. 2.4.3.1), and probably by spontaneous reabsorption of water into the underlying dermis (Edelberg, 1973a), tonic skin resistance increases.

However, it is more likely that the conductivity of the stratum corneum depends on its electrolyte content than on its humidity (Sect. 1.3.4.2 "The Role of the Epidermal Barrier Layer"). As outlined by Fowles (1986a), corneal permeability for electrolytes is much less thoroughly investigated than that for water. Edelberg (1971) alluded to some more or less contradictory results, stating that most ions will be able to penetrate the main part of the stratum corneum, where lots of intercellular spaces are present, at least to the barrier layer as mentioned above. He also presumed that the corneal permeability for the electrolytes is the same as water, since an active ionic transport seems to be improbable in fully keratinized cells (Sect. 1.3.4.2 "The Role of Skin Components and of Membrane Processes"). Thus, moistening of the corneum by sweat through the acrosyringium and/or via the skin surface will add more to its conductance than insensible perspiration, which penetrates the epidermal barrier layer (Sect. 1.3.3.2).

As previously mentioned in Sect. 1.3.4.2 "The Role of Skin Components and of Membrane Processes," sweat gland ducts act as a sort of electrical shunt through the stratum corneum. This is especially important with respect to palmar and plantar sites which are preferred for electrodermal recording, because of their great sweat gland density (Sect. 1.2.3). It is generally supposed that skin conductance increases with the height of the ductal sweat column (e.g., Edelberg, 1968). Accordingly, the slow decline in SCL which appears in the absence of EDRs may reflect a gradual

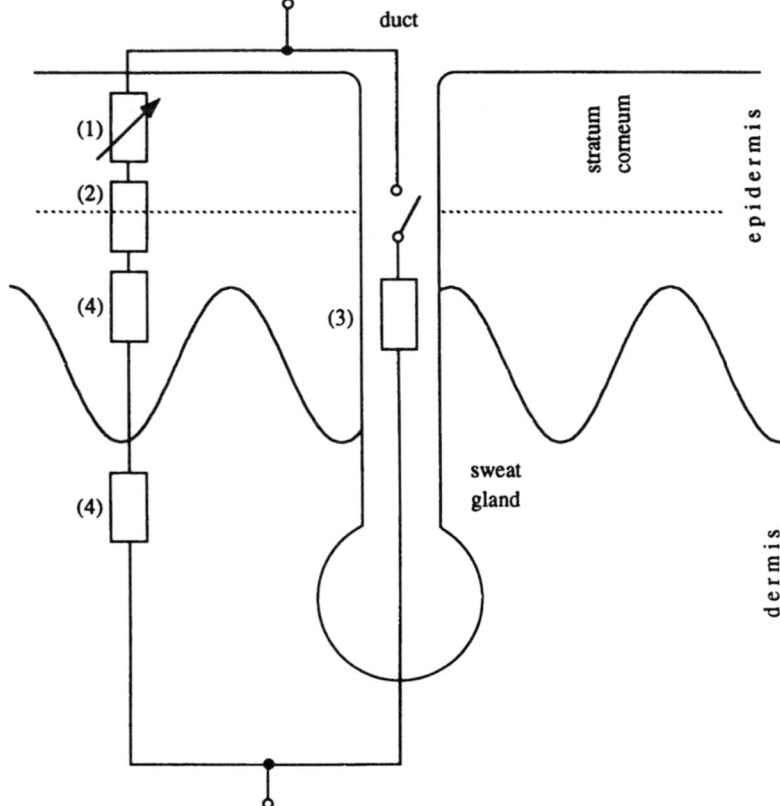

Fig. 1.13 Schematic illustration of resistive pathways through the skin and the sweat gland. An explanation of the numbering is provided in the text

dissipation of sweat in the ducts. This is possibly attributable to the reabsorption mechanism mentioned in Sect. 1.3.3.1 (e.g., Rothman, 1954). However, electrical models of skin that focus on its resistive properties (e.g., Montagu & Coles, 1966) regard each sweat gland as a single resistor with a more or less fixed value that can be switched on or off (Fig. 1.15, Sect. 1.4.3.1). This kind of modeling will be adequate in the case of a fast rise and fall of ductal sweat, leaving the gradual changes of conductance owing to the corneal moistening.

In summary, resistive properties of the skin/sweat gland system may be described as several serial- and parallel-connected resistors, as illustrated in Fig. 1.13:

(1) A variable resistor formed by the stratum corneum
(2) A fixed resistor formed by the epidermal barrier as mentioned in Sect. 1.3.4.2 "The Role of the Epidermal Barrier Layer"
(3) Resistances of sweat gland ducts that are switched either into or out of the circuit
(4) A fixed but relatively low resistance of the lower epidermis, the dermis, and probably the hypodermis

In addition to these resistive pathways which are vertical to the skin surface, various horizontal resistances can be assumed in all layers of the skin, especially in the lower epidermis and in the dermis, depending on the tissue's conductivity. However, the majority of electrodermal models do not consider those resistances, except for the model given by Fowles (1974), which is shown in Fig. 1.17 (Sect. 1.4.3.2).

1.4.2.2 Capacitive Properties of Skin and Sweat Glands

When an external current is applied to the skin, the cell membranes exhibit their polarization capacities, storing electric potentials like technical capacitors (Sect. 1.4.1.3). However, the selective permeability for ions, which is the basis of these capacitive properties, is not only linked to single membranes (Sect. 1.3.4.2 "The Role of the Epidermal Barrier Layer"). In addition, according to Edelberg (1971), whole cell assemblages such as epidermal layers may act selectively to some degree on the influx of ions of different sizes because of the cell structures extending into the intercellular spaces (e.g., in the stratum spinosum; Sect. 1.2.1.1). Therefore, the whole epidermis will react to an external current like a network built from RC links connected in parallel and in series.

As previously outlined in Sect. 1.3.4.2 "The Role of Skin Components and of Membrane Processes," the membrane-like properties of the keratinized epidermal layers have to be regarded as passive, compared to those of living tissue. However, skin also contains active membranes (e.g., those of nerve, muscle, and glandular cells). These membranes have a resting charge which becomes reversed when stimulated. In addition, they also show capacitive properties when an external current is applied. Active membranes that act as capacitors with respect to EDA are located mainly in the secretory part of the sweat gland. Edelberg (1972a) presumed an active epidermal membrane with a fixed negative charge, making it selectively permeable to cations.[42] He postulated a phasic increase in permeability, which can be detected using surface electrodes as an EDR. It is probably located either in the stratum granulosum, at the dermal/epidermal boundary, or in the epidermal wall of the sweat gland duct.[43] Other capacitive properties may stem from membrane polarizations and depolarizations in the blood capillaries, the pilo-erecting muscles (Sect. 1.2.4), and the myoepithelia surrounding the sweat glands (Sect. 1.2.3).

---

[42] Edelberg (1971) reported microelectrode recordings which provide evidence for the existence of an electrical barrier layer in the deeper layers of the epidermis. The SRL measured via a microelectrode, which had been slowly pushed into the epidermis, showed a slow continuous decrease at the beginning. If a certain point had been passed at which the participant first reported weak pain, SRL suddenly decreased until only the electrode resistance itself was present. The depth of the appropriate layer is 350 µm at the palm and 50 µm at the forearm.

[43] Edelberg (1971) first suggested a second barrier membrane at the dermal/epidermal boundary. According to Fowles (1974), he later preferred the ductal wall at the height of the stratum germinativum as the locus of this second membrane.

Edelberg (1971) regarded any contribution by myoepithelial potentials to the endosomatic EDA as unlikely. This is because potentials arising there would be shunted by the freely conducting dermal tissue. According to Edelberg's view, this cannot be generalized to the influence of capacitive properties of the sweat gland as well, since potential changes at its secretory membrane are transmitted immediately to the skin surface when sweat gland ducts are filled. There is also a possibility of epidermal reabsorption processes in the ductal walls, found up to the stratum germinativum (Sect. 1.3.3.1), to form membrane-like capacitors which have an influence on EDA. However, it is not certain that the appropriate charges are big enough to be measurable with relatively large electrodes at the skin surface.

The capacitive properties of skin and sweat glands have been much less investigated than the resistive ones. Those investigations require measurement with AC, which is far less common than DC measurement (Sect. 1.4.3.3).

1.4.2.3 Origins of Active Electrical Properties in the Skin and in Sweat Glands

While the previous two sections focused on passive electrical properties of the skin/sweat gland system, the active electrodermal phenomena stemming from the active membranes previously mentioned will be discussed in this section. The method of choice for investigating these active properties is endosomatic EDA measurement (i.e., without applying external current), the result of which is skin potential.

Exosomatic EDRs have a simpler form than endosomatic ones, since they are always unidirectional. SPRs, on the contrary, can appear as monophasic negative responses, as biphasic responses, where an initial negative component is followed by a positive one, or as triphasic responses, where the positive limb of the biphasic response achieves a greater negativity than the initial negative wave (see Sect. 2.3.1.2 "Amplitudes of Endosomatic Responses"). Under certain circumstances it is also possible that only a positive SPR is recorded showing either no initial negativity or an extremely small one (Fowles, 1986a). This variety of responses has generated various explanations that have combined active membrane properties together with resistive properties of corneal hydration and duct filling, as discussed in Sect. 1.4.2.1. A major portion of the appropriate research was performed with the cat's footpads,[44] and based on these results hypotheses were formed by Lloyd (1961), Darrow (1964), and Adams (1966), which were comprehensively reviewed by Edelberg (1972a).

Lloyd (1961) observed that each single sympathetic nerve stimulation was followed by a negative SPR, which he called "presecretory." Repeated stimulation

---

[44] The SPRs in cats differ from those seen in humans in that they show only a monophasic negative SPR (Edelberg, 1973a), which reaches its peak amplitude very quickly (for differences between species, see also Footnote 10, Sect. 1.2.3).

resulted in a very slow positive SPR wave of several minutes duration, which was accompanied by duct filling, and thus labeled secretory potential. When ducts were already filled, further stimulation led to presecretory potentials with an increase in amplitude. Hence, the rise of sweat in the ducts is likely to enable better electrical contact to the generator of the presecretory SPR.

Darrow (1964) and additionally Darrow and Gullickson (1970) regarded the sweat gland as the source of changes in SP, both negative and positive. They further assumed that neural impulses may cause increases in permeability of the epidermis, including the corneum. They regarded the intraluminal potential of the sweat gland as being positive with respect to the surrounding tissue, leading to negative SPRs on the surface resulting from the extraluminal tissue when ducts are empty, and to positive lumen-generated surface potentials when the ducts are filled. However, positive SPRs could not be obtained from the cat's footpad, even when the ducts were full (Wilcott, 1965; see also Footnote 44). Additionally, with direct micro-electrode recordings, Schulz et al. (1965) found that the lumen of the human sweat gland duct is highly negative with respect to the surrounding tissue.

Therefore, Edelberg (1968, 1971), in his model outlined in Sect. 1.4.3.2, presupposed a negative intraluminal potential, together with a relatively steady tonic sweat gland activity, which results in the sweat column normally reaching up to the Malpighian layer. Outpouring of sweat onto the surface may result from either increased sweat gland activity or a contraction of the myoepithelial tissue surrounding the duct (Sect. 1.3.3.1). This causes an increase in surface negativity (a negative SPR with long rise time and slow recovery) which is due to the sweat reabsorption in the ductal walls.

However, Edelberg (1972a) pointed to the fact that this duct-filling component explains neither the mostly short SPR recovery times, nor the observation that EDRs appear with heavily sweating persons whose ducts should always be completely filled. Therefore, he suggested a short-lasting increase of the permeability for cations in the active epidermal membrane (previously mentioned in Sect. 1.4.2.2) as the appropriate source for EDRs with fast rise times and quick recoveries. He assumed the appropriate mechanism is connected with the control of evaporation (Sect. 1.3.3.2), either with the control of corneal moistening or with the reabsorption of sweat in the ductal walls. However, the independence of such a reabsorption component from sweat gland secretion, as assumed by Edelberg, was questioned by Bundy and Fitzgerald (1975), who found a dependency of the EDR recovery on the previous phasic EDA (Sect. 2.5.2.5).

Edelberg explained, in his model, that the biphasic and triphasic SPRs (Fig. 2.14, Sect. 2.3.1.2) are composed of a positive membrane component with short recovery time and a negative duct-filling component with long recovery. Whether the SPR begins with a negative or positive component is, according to Edelberg (1971), dependent on the degree of duct filling at the onset of the EDR. If ducts are relatively empty, the rise of sweat will establish a connection between skin surface and the negative lumen potential, thus leading to an initial negative SP wave. On the other hand, if ducts are already full, an additional sweat secretion will result in corneal hydration, thus producing the epidermal potential, which is less negative than the ductal one (Fig. 1.16, Sect. 1.4.3.2) and is observable at the surface as a

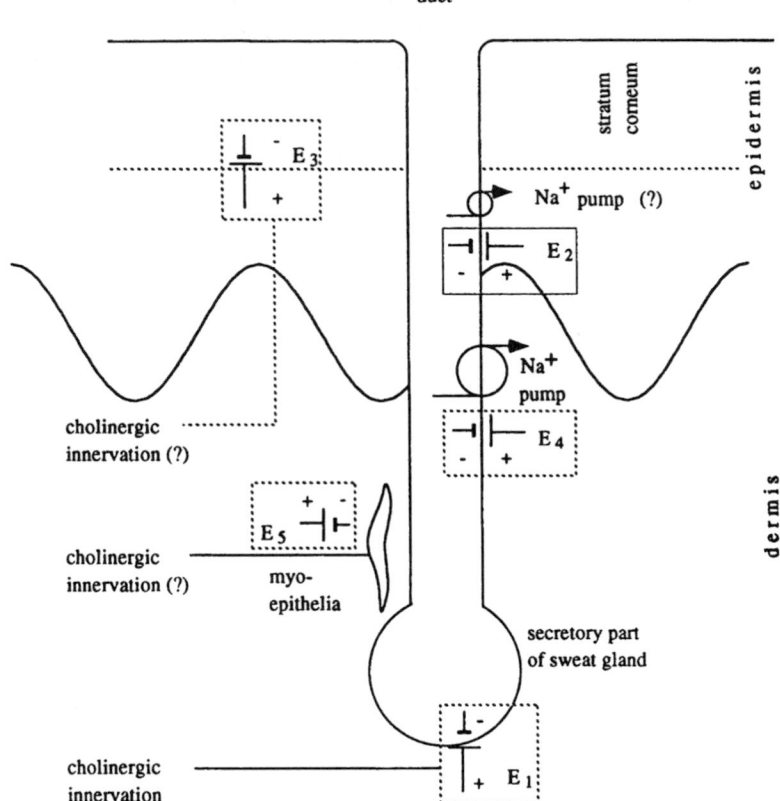

Fig. 1.14 Schematic illustration of the localization of active electrical properties in the skin and sweat gland. E_1, E_2, and E_3: see explanations for Fig. 1.17 in the text of Sect. 1.4.3.2; E_4 and E_5: see text for explanations. Adapted from Muthny (1984), Fig. 17.4. Copyright 1984 by the author. Used by his permission

positive SP shift. Since hydration would occur too slowly to explain fast, positive SPRs, Edelberg (1972a) assumed an epidermal or ductal membrane response as the source of the positive SPR with fast recovery.

Empirical evidence is available for both an active sweat gland and an active epidermal component of SP. Fowles and Johnson (1973) as well as Fowles and Rosenberry (1973) showed that the amplitudes of positive and negative SPRs markedly decrease when the stratum corneum becomes moistened. They assume that this is caused by a mechanical closure of sweat pores and additionally take these observations as evidence that positive as well as negative SPRs are due to changes in sweat gland potentials. Experiments with parallel recordings from the fingertip and the nail bed (which does not contain sweat glands) performed by Edelberg (1973b) and repeated by Burbank and Webster (1978) gave evidence for additional sources of skin potential, probably being located in the epidermis.

Figure 1.14 schematically depicts the localization of all hitherto discussed active electrodermal components. The depicted potential sources also act as capacitors in case of an applied external current (Sect. 1.4.2.2). They mainly correspond to the potential sources as assumed in the Fowles model (Fig. 1.17, Sect. 1.4.3.2): E_1 is located in the secretory part of the sweat gland, E_2 corresponds to the potential source in the epidermal duct at the level of the stratum germinativum, and E_3 is the membrane potential stemming from the inner corneal zones. E_2 and E_4 correspond to the membrane potentials mentioned in Sect. 1.4.2.2, which relate to the sodium reabsorption mechanism in the dermal and possibly also in the epidermal part of the duct (Sect. 1.3.3.1). E_5 stems from the myoepithelia and is probably cholinergically supported (Sect. 1.3.2).

It remains questionable if an active epidermal membrane E_3 should be included, since evidence for its innervation is lacking. Fowles (1974) pointed to authors such as Lykken (1968), who – contrary to Edelberg's view – located the above-mentioned active membrane responsible for fast SPR components not in the epidermis but in the secretory part of the sweat gland. Therefore, those electrodermal components could also be regarded as a result of an increased permeability of the secretory cells during secretion. Like all active membranes, secretory cell membranes have a high polarization capacity at rest, which is diminished during depolarization. However, Fowles (1974) objected to this hypothesis, stating that this active membrane is easily reached by solutions on the skin surface which have the capacity to change its properties. It is not clear whether the active membrane, which is probably responsible for a main portion of the EDR, is really cholinergically innervated. Muthny (1984), in his experiments described in Sect. 2.4.2.2, could not abolish all palmar EDRs after an intradermal application of atropine; a finding contrary to all previous research. So the nature and the localization of this active membrane component remain unclear (Edelberg, 1983).

1.4.3   Models of the Electrodermal System

To assist in the depiction of the electrophysiological properties of the skin/sweat gland system, a succession of electrical equivalent circuits of varying complexity which simulate the electrodermal system is sketched out below. Discussions of the various models can also be found in Edelberg (1971, 1993) and Fowles (1974), as well as in Millington and Wilkinson (1983).

As our knowledge of the electrical properties of the skin is still rather limited, all attempts to develop electrical equivalent circuits for the involved physiological structures have been tentative (Venables & Christie, 1980). It must also be pointed out that although the skin may display the same systematic properties as an electrophysical model, it still cannot be assumed that the skin is built in the same manner as the model. The following section describes the most important electrical circuits discussed in the literature, together with perspectives for the future research into the electrodermal system, and for further modeling by means of the application of AC technology.

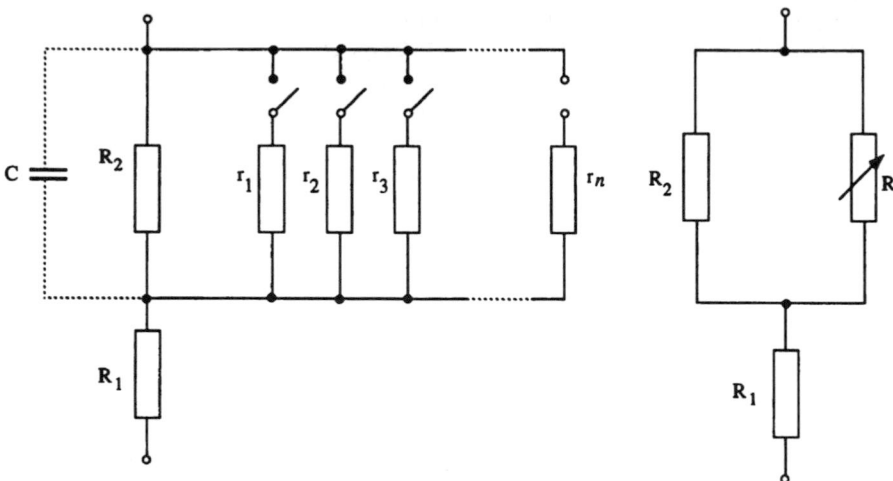

Fig. 1.15 *Left-hand panel*: Electrical equivalent circuit for the skin, according to Montagu and Coles (1966). R_1: resistance of the dermis and the body core. R_2: resistance of the stratum corneum. $r_1, \ldots, r_n$: connectable resistances of the sweat gland ducts. C: capacitive element. *Right-hand panel*: Simplified Montagu-Coles model. R: variable resistance resulting from sweat gland ducts. *Left-hand panel* from Montagu and Coles (1966), Fig. 1.1. Copyright 1966 by the American Psychological Association. Reprinted by permission of the publisher

1.4.3.1 Models Based Exclusively on Resistive Properties

Although there is no doubt that the electrodermal system also contains capacitive properties, models built exclusively of resistive elements have at least a heuristic value for DC measurements. In such an approach, capacitors play a role for only a short period, that is, after switching current on or off (Sect. 1.4.1.2).

The left-hand panel of Fig. 1.15 shows such a model, which has been suggested by Montagu and Coles (1966). The model displays, but does not further discuss, an additional capacitive element C. Resistor R_1 represents a series resistance located in the dermis and body core. R_2 represents the resistive value of the stratum corneum, which is in parallel to resistors $r_1, \ldots, r_n$ of the sweat gland ducts. These single ductal resistors can be switched either into or out of the circuit, depending on the respective sweat gland activity, thereby altering the parallel resistance (Sect. 1.4.1.2).

The right-hand panel of Fig. 1.15 shows a simplified Montagu-Coles model set up by Boucsein, Baltissen, and Euler (1984), who have formally substituted a variable resistor R in place of the single parallel resistances of the sweat glands and who also left out the capacitor C, which was not considered further in the original publication. Adopting a constant value for the resistance of the corneum by Montagu and Coles (1966) is a simplification (Sect. 1.4.2.1). However, it may be taken as an initial approximation that R_2 is relatively constant in comparison to R, since the keratinized layer has a considerably narrower range of resistive changes than do the sweat gland ducts. The total resistance R_{tot} of the equivalent circuit on the right-hand panel of Fig. 1.15 is calculated as follows (Sect. 1.4.1.2, (1.6e)):

$$R_{\text{tot}} = R_1 + \frac{R_2 R}{R_2 + R} \tag{1.22}$$

Fluctuations of the total resistance, which depend upon small variations of the resistance R, are calculated according to the following differential equation[45]:

$$dR_{\text{tot}} = \frac{R_2{}^2}{(R_2 + R)^2} dR \tag{1.23}$$

It can be inferred from (1.23) that, in case the keratinized layer resistance (R_2) is not considered constant, differentiation using a second variable is necessitated, which would considerably complicate the equation system. However, the more serious limitation of the Montagu-Coles model stems from being a solely resistive model, which can only take resistance changes into account. Therefore, the application of that model is limited to DC measurements of EDA. As on the one hand, the greatest number of EDA investigations has used external DC, and on the other hand, the introduction of capacitive elements significantly complicates the mathematical formulation for models, the heuristic value of this simple model remains undiminished.

1.4.3.2 Models Going Beyond Single Resistive Properties

While the Montagu and Coles (1966) model described in the preceding section focuses mainly on the resistive properties of the skin,[46] the models proposed by Edelberg (1971) and Fowles (1974) additionally took into account potential sources. These were regarded as sources of endosomatic EDA. In the case of exosomatic EDA AC measurement (Sect. 1.4.3.3), these potential sources primarily display capacitive properties of the electrodermal system.

To account for the active electrical processes which are the basis for the origins of skin potentials, Edelberg (1971) incorporated inner potential sources into his model, which is depicted in Fig. 1.16. He inferred from results obtained by means of microelectrode measurements that the epidermis features a negative potential with

---

[45] Taking into consideration that $R_1 = $ constant and with application of the quotient rule for differentiation. The corresponding conductance equation is given in Boucsein, Baltissen, and Euler (1984).

[46] As shown in the left-hand panel of Fig. 1.15, Montagu and Coles (1966) in principle acknowledged the necessity of including capacitive elements into electrodermal modeling.

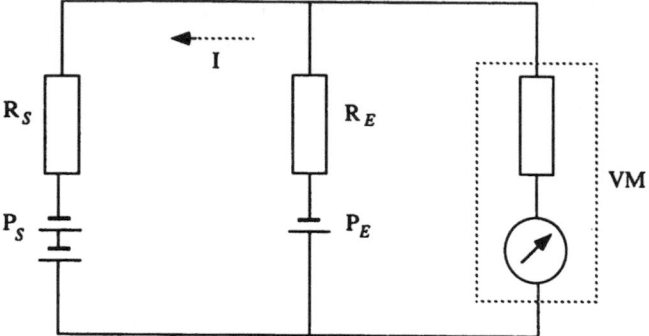

Fig. 1.16 Equivalent circuit for the generation of the inner potential compensative current I in the skin. R_S: sweat gland resistance and the inner resistance of the generator of the sweat gland potential P_S. R_E: epidermal resistance and inner resistance of the generator for the epidermal potential P_E. VM: voltmeter with its internal resistance. From R. Edelberg (1971), Fig. 15.3. Copyright 1971 by the New York Academy of Sciences. Reprinted by permission of the publisher and the author

reference to the body core, and that the lumen of the sweat gland duct shows an even greater negative potential (Sect. 1.4.2.3). Edelberg viewed a current flow in the skin as being a major factor determining the potential difference at the surface, which depends on strongly differing polarization capacities (Sect. 1.4.2) in the epidermis and the sweat glands (Fig. 1.16). Hence, the current I flows from the less negative pole P_E (epidermis) to the more negative pole P_S (sweat glands). The potential, measured with the voltmeter (VM) on the surface of the skin, is additionally a function of the resistances of the epidermis R_E and of the sweat gland duct R_S.

The model proposed by Edelberg (1971) is suitable for an explanation of skin potentials but does not account for the processes involved in exosomatic EDA measurements using DC, since no connecting, resistive pathway between the electrodes is taken into account. Therefore, once the capacitive elements (as which the potential sources act, in case an external current is applied) are fully charged, no further current can flow through the system (Sect. 1.4.1.2).[47]

Figure 1.17 shows the electrical model of the skin/sweat gland system proposed by Fowles (1974), in which three potential sources from Fig. 1.14 (Sect. 1.4.2.3) were combined with three major conductance paths[48] as follows:

1. The lumen negative potential E_1, which originates in the ductal wall in the dermis, and is determined primarily by the sodium ionic concentration in the lumen,

---

[47] However, since all the potential sources are "leaky" capacitors (see comments on Fig. 1.17 below), the parallel resistive component can conduct DC even when the capacitive component is fully charged.

[48] For the sake of simplification, Fowles omitted a fourth pathway in which the current flows into the duct from the corneum and then along the two sweat gland pathways.

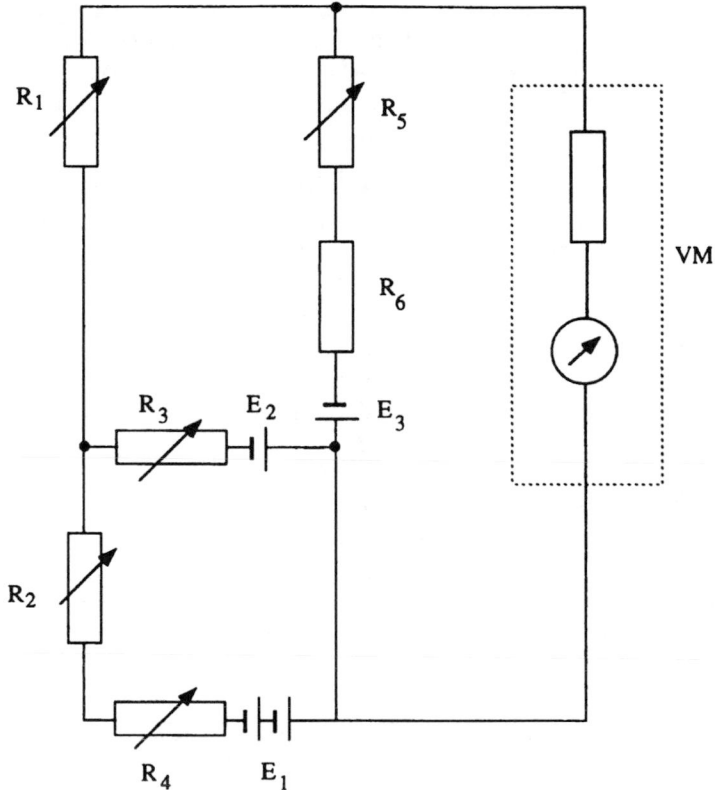

Fig. 1.17 Equivalent circuit for the skin/sweat gland system. VM: voltmeter with its internal resistance. See text for explanations of the other elements. From Fowles (1974), Fig. 9/5. Copyright 1974 by Academic Press. Reprinted by permission of the publisher and the author

together with the possible variable resistance R_4 of the dermal duct wall, and the variable resistance R_2 of the dermal section of the duct which depends upon duct filling (E_1 and R_4 in Fig. 1.17 correspond in part to P_S and R_S in Fig. 1.16).

2. The potential E_2, which is also a lumen negative potential, is generated across the epidermal duct wall at the stratum germinativum level. It is dependent on the concentration of sodium and chloride ions in the lumen. Due to the capacitive properties of the ductal wall (Sect. 1.4.2.2), the membrane in this part of the duct is less selective. Hence, E_2 is likely to be smaller than E_1 during sweat gland activity. R_3 represents the variable resistor of the duct wall, and R_1 is the resistive value of the epidermal part of the duct, depending on the duct filling.

3. According to Fowles' suggestion, E_3 represents the localized membrane potential, located in the lower zone of the stratum corneum (Table 1.2, Sect. 1.2.1) and is a function of the potassium ionic concentration in the interstitial fluid as well as of the applied electrolyte in the electrode cream (Sect. 2.2.2.5). It will be

surface negative as long as the outer potassium ionic concentration is greater than that of the interstitial fluid. Resistive values in this pathway are the relatively constant resistance R_6 of the compact keratinized layer zone and the variable resistance R_5 of the upper layers of the corneum, varying with their hydration (E_3 and R_6 in Fig. 1.17 correspond in part to P_E and R_E in Fig. 1.16).

Under complete resting conditions, reabsorption predominates over secretion, whereby the resistances R_1, R_2, and R_3 maintain high values, while the potentials E_1 and E_2 are minimal. The potential E_3 is then the most important factor for measurement of the potential at rest and reflects the potassium ionic concentration in the interstitial fluid. A small or moderate sweat secretion lowers the resistance of R_2 and probably also of R_1, producing an SCR with slow recovery. At the same time, the sodium ionic concentration of the lumen rises, thereby increasing E_1. The increase of this potential together with the decrease of the resistance in the duct leads to a negative SPR with slow recovery.

These reactions cause an increase in both the SCL and the SPL. Larger sweat gland responses or those occurring in ducts which are partially filled with sweat will further decrease R_1 and R_2. If the hydrostatic pressure (or the sodium ionic concentration) is high enough to depolarize the epidermal duct membrane, a response in the epidermal duct occurs, whereby R_3 is decreased and a small lumen negative potential originates at E_2. This membrane response produces a SCR with short recovery time, and at the same time a positive SPR appears, because of a shunting effect on E_1. However, in most cases there will be a small initial negative component of the SPR since the negative wave begins earlier than the increase in permeability. Once the ducts are filled to their maximum, further sweat gland secretions will produce only membrane responses.

In this model, most of the presumed origins of electrodermal phenomena are taken into account (Sect. 1.4.2.3). According to Edelberg (1971), negative SPRs as well as SCRs with longer recovery times appear as a result of the duct filling, while the membrane responses cause SCRs with shorter recovery times, positive SPRs, and possibly negative SPRs with short rise time, which appear either alone or as the initial portion of many biphasic SPRs. The modification of Edelberg's model by Fowles (1974) was that positive SPRs were not regarded as originating in a positive potential of the epidermal duct's wall. Instead, their origin was supposed to be a breakthrough of the potential from the dermal part of the duct to the surface. Furthermore, it had been presumed that the membrane response might be triggered through hydrostatic pressure and not through a cholinergically transmitted neuronal response. Edelberg's model was further revised by relating the duct potentials to the sodium transport mechanism, and attributing the epidermal membrane potential, which is independent of sweat gland responses, to the potassium ionic concentration in the interstitial fluid and in the applied electrolyte.

Contrary to the purely resistive model in Sect. 1.4.3.1, the models presented in Figs. 1.16 and 1.17 also allow the depiction of active electrical properties of the skin and sweat glands, which go beyond simple variations in the ohmic resistances. However, in a strict sense, not only the model proposed by Edelberg (1971) but also the Fowles (1974) model is limited to the explanation of skin potentials, because both models do not include a resistor pathway between the electrodes which is not in series with a capacitive element. Furthermore, biological membrane potentials are usually designated as "leaky" capacitors, that is the capacitor is in parallel with a resistor, and not in series as shown in Fig. 1.17. In any case, the heuristic value of such a complicated system remains questionable, since clearly defined anatomical and physiological structures of the skin have not yet been successfully identified with respect to their postulated electrical elements. Consequently, the Japanese team of Yamamoto and Yamamoto, in their investigations based on AC measurements (Sect. 1.4.3.3), used a simplified model (Fig. 1.18) which corresponds more closely to the Montagu-Coles model (Fig. 1.15) than to the Fowles model depicted in Fig. 1.17.

More recently, Edelberg (1993) challenged the membrane-based electrical models and proposed that intraductal hydraulic pressure could be responsible for some of the hitherto unexplained phasic changes in SP and SC. Edelberg called his model "poral valve model" because the intraductal pressure has the ability to open the sweat pores like valves and thus raising skin conductance sharply. Edelberg's (1993) model will be shortly summarized here:

1. When the ducts are relatively empty and the upper corneum is sufficiently hydrated, it is likely that some or most of the pores on the skin surface are closed, since the acrosyringium will be collapsed due to the pressure exerted by the hydrated corneal tissue surrounding the pore (Sarkany, Shuster, & Stammers, 1965). In this case, changes in membrane potential or conductance in the sweat gland's secretory segment will not be observable as EDRs at the skin surface (Shaver, Brusilow, & Cooke, 1965). As a consequence of continued sweat gland response to sudomotor impulses, the ducts will be filled with sweat and will finally provide a more conductive path through the relatively high-resistive corneum, thus increasing both skin conductance and the negative surface potential. The latter may be a result of the sodium reabsorption mechanism (see Fig. 1.14, Sect. 1.4.2.3).

2. In case the ducts are completely filled, subsequent sweat gland responses will build up an intraductal pressure, causing a hydraulic-driven penetration of sweat from the ducts into the lower zone of the corneum (see Fig. 1.1 and Table 1.2). This will result in a further increase of conductance and may contribute to a positive SPR.

3. If the intraductal pressure increases further, it will exceed the tissue pressure of the duct-surrounding corneum. In that case, the collapsed terminal portion of the acrosyringium will be filled with sweat and the pore opens like a valve. Sweat

will pour out on the skin surface, which will rapidly augment skin conductance and also increase the rapidly developing positive SPR.

4. As sweat pours out on the surface, the intraductal pressure drops, and unless the secretory rate can keep up with this loss of volume, the corneum will collapse the acrosyringium and close the pore once again. Together with the closure of the pore, this will cause a rapid fall in conductance – measurable as accelerated recovery – and a positive shift in the surface potential. The sudden increase in the horizontal resistance near the skin surface may appear as a "reabsorption" response. Diffusion of sweat from the area around the duct will cause slower but still relatively rapid recovery of the SCR and the positive SPR.

Tonic reabsorption of sweat into the dermis or outward diffusion into the electrode cream, which slowly dehydrates the corneum and causes a slow emptying of the ducts, will result in slow SC and SP drift. If the pores are already open when sweat secretion starts, which can be artificially achieved by using a dehydrating electrolyte medium, no dilatation and collapse of the acrosyringium will occur, and no accelerated recovery and reabsorption will be observed. However, if the sudomotor activity becomes very strong, the emptying capacity of the open sweat pores may be exceeded, resulting in a high ductal pressure, rapid positive SPRs and an acceleration of recovery at hydrated recording sites as observed by Fowles and Schneider (1974).

Edelberg's "poral valve model" has been able to explain a variety of electro-dermal phenomena, including rapid phasic changes, without the assumption of an active reabsorption membrane (Sect. 1.3.3.1), which has never been anatomically confirmed (Hugdahl, 1995). Edelberg's model has been partially supported by Yamazaki, Okamura, and Takasawa (2001), who could not observe overt sweat-ing responses when the SPR showed negative waves.[49] On the other hand, when overt sweating responses were recorded, SPRs exhibited monophasic positive or biphasic waves (see Fig. 2.14, Sect. 2.3.1.2 "Amplitudes of Endosomatic Responses"). Their results indicated that negative SPRs represent electric phe-nomena deep within the sweat gland, whereas positive SPR waves or components point to electrodermal phenomena closely associated with surface sweating. The "poral valve model" has recently also been used for modeling the recovery limb of the SCR (Benedek & Kaernbach, 2010, see Sect. 2.3.1.5). Unfortunately, there has not yet been much empirical support for the model, so that further experimen-tation will be necessary to test its predictions against those derived from purely electrical models.

---

[49] Observed in 10 healthy male participants who were subjected to handclaps and bursts of 85 dB white noise. Palmar sweating was recorded with a capacitance hygrometry technique, using a capsule mounted on the left hypothenar eminence close to the active SP electrode. The capsule was ventilated with dry nitrogen. For SP recording, Ag/AgCl electrodes filled with isotonic electrode cream made from Unibase were used, the neutral electrode being attached to a lightly abraded ventral site of the left forearm.

1.4.3.3   Specific Advantages of AC Methods in Model Building

The models portrayed in the two previous sections are based on the preponderance of DC measurement and SP recording of EDA. Although Lykken, Miller, and Strahan (1966) already demonstrated, using pulsed DC measurements, that only a small portion of conductance or resistance changes recorded during an EDR can be explained by ohmic changes in the tissue, investigations of the electrodermal system, which used AC technology or transients, were sparse (summarized by Edelberg, 1971), and systematic sequences of studies in this area are still missing, especially on the intact human skin (Sects. 2.5.3 and 2.6.3).

Results obtained by AC measurements on such a complex system as the skin are not easily interpretable (Millington & Wilkinson, 1983). Therefore, simpler substitute circuits are applied to modeling with AC measurements, as compared to the Fowles model presented in the preceding section (Fig. 1.17). In the simplest case, such depictions represent a fixed polarization capacity being connected in parallel with a resistor, together with a resistor in series with both of them (e.g., Edelberg, 1971). The serial resistance is necessary for the description of AC properties of the skin, since the impedance of the system decreases by using very high frequencies, due to the decrease of the resistive properties of the capacitor (Sect. 1.4.1.3), but does not fully disappear. From the value of this residual impedance the purely ohmic components of the skin resistance, which are not connected in parallel with the capacitor, can be determined.

The same holds for the Montagu and Coles (1966) model (Fig. 1.15), in which a variable resistance R (replacing the single resistors $r_1, \ldots, r_n$) is connected in parallel with the fixed resistor R_2. Yamamoto et al. (1978) based the interpretations of their results using AC measurement upon such a model which closely resembles the one proposed by Tregear (1966), adding a capacitor in parallel (Fig. 1.18). Yamamoto et al. (1978) regard the resistance R_1 as negligible, thus only specifying values for R_2, R, and C (Sect. 2.5.3.1). The model proposed by Lykken (1971, Fig. 1.2), based upon pulsed DC measurements, unites R and R_2 into a single variable resistor and thereby presents the simplest depiction of a circuit composed of a capacitor and resistors connected in series and in parallel. The capacitor and the parallel resistors are localized in the stratum corneum, while the serial resistor represents the deeper dermal and epidermal skin layers, including the stratum granulosum.

By using AC measurements, the quantification of variations in the different elements of this simple electrical equivalent circuit will now be explained by means of their loci (Sect. 1.4.3.1). Following the presently dominating preference of conductance units over resistance units (Sect. 2.6.5), conductance (C) and susceptance (B) are used here instead of ohmic resistance (R) and reactance (X), respectively, and admittance instead of impedance as well. Therefore, opposed to what is shown in the upper part of Fig. 1.10 (Sect. 1.4.1.3), the vector moves to the right on the locus with increasing AC frequency. Figure 1.19 shows the change of the admittance vector $Y(f)$ as a function of the frequency of the applied

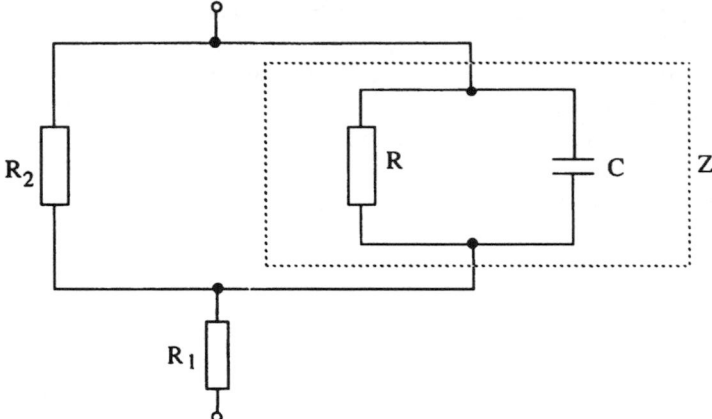

Fig. 1.18 Equivalent circuit for the skin, according to Yamamoto et al. (1978). R_1: resistance of the dermis. R_2: constant resistance of the epidermis. Z: variable impedance, composed of the ohmic section R and the capacitive section C. Adapted from Yamamoto et al. (1978), Fig. 1.1. Copyright 1978 by Peter Peregrinus. Used by permission of the publisher

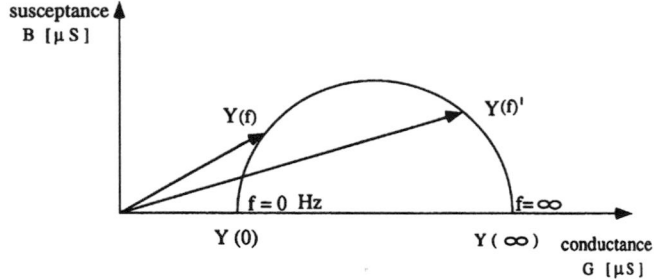

Fig. 1.19 Alternation fluctuation of the admittance vector $Y(f)$ in dependence upon the frequency of the applied measurement voltage

measurement voltage as used in the electrical equivalent circuit of Fig. 1.18, where, for the sake of simplicity, R and R_2 are combined as a single resistor, R_2 (Lykken, 1971), as both circuits are electrically equivalent.

When $f = 0$ Hz (i.e., if DC is applied), the admittance is determined by the conductance of the ohmic resistors R_1 and R_2 alone, since no more current flows once the capacitor C is fully charged (Sect. 1.4.1.2), the phase displacement is zero, and the vector Y lies on the real axis (Footnote 41, Sect. 1.4.1.3). The length of the vector $Y(0)$ (i.e., the conductance of the entire system by $f = 0$) corresponds to the conductance G_{tot} for DC and is calculated, as derived from (1.2a), by

$$Y(0) = G_{tot} = \frac{1}{R_{tot}} = \frac{1}{R_1 + R_2} \qquad (1.24a)$$

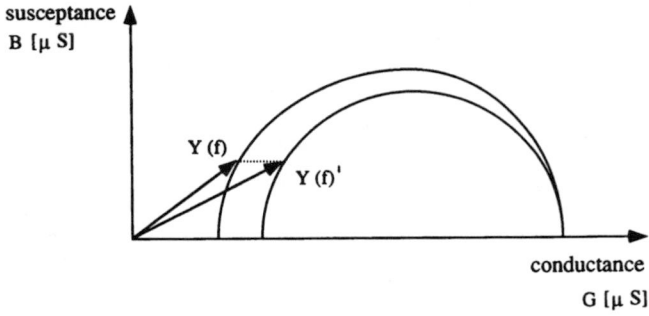

Fig. 1.20 Alternation of the locus and the admittance vector $Y(f)$ by an increase of the parallel resistance R_2

Inserting the values for R_1 and R_2, in the form of $1/G_1$ and $1/G_2$, into (1.24a) according to (1.2b) will result in a common denominator G_1G_2 by which (1.24a) is expanded, resulting in the following equation:

$$Y(0) = \frac{G_1G_2}{G_1 + G_2} \tag{1.24b}$$

If a DC voltage is applied in the circuit shown in Fig. 1.18, the admittance $Y(0)$ corresponds to the harmonic mean of the conductances of both the series (R_1) and parallel $(R_2$, including $R)$ resistors. When f is increased, the capacitor begins to conduct (Sect. 1.4.1.3 for apparent conductance) and increasingly short-circuits the parallel resistor R_2. This lengthens the admittance vector, which describes a circle in the conductance/susceptance plane (cf. vectors in Fig. 1.19) forming the locus (see upper part of Fig. 1.10, Sect. 1.4.1.3). At infinitely high values of f on the end of the curve, the apparent conductance becomes so high that ultimately admittance is determined by the series resistor R_1 alone and is composed of only the real conductance component G_1; that means $Y(\infty) = G_1$.

The course of such a locus depends upon the construction of the circuit. Empirical loci for skin admittance (Yamamoto & Yamamoto, 1976, 1981) show good congruity with a semicircle; therefore, the underlying electrical model of the skin (Fig. 1.18) can be regarded as quite adequate.

Fluctuations of the resistive (or conductive) and capacitive values of single elements of this model can be quantitatively described through alterations of the locus. As shown in Fig. 1.20, an increase in the parallel resistance R_2 will displace the starting point of the locus along the G-axis to the right, thus diminishing the radius, since the end point remains stationary on the G-axis. For the admittance at a specified frequency f, an increase occurs only in the conductance but not in the susceptance (compare the displacement between $Y(f)$ and $Y(f)'$ in Fig. 1.20).

In contrast, if the serial resistance R_1 is increased, there will be only a small displacement of the curve's starting point, since R_1 is very small in comparison to R_2 (Sect. 2.5.3.1). Therefore the end point of the semicircle on the G-axis is

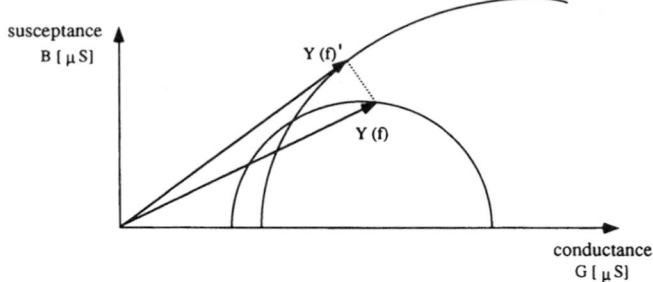

Fig. 1.21 Alteration of the locus and the admittance vector $Y(f)$ by an increase of the serial resistance R_1

displaced to the right, thus increasing the radius (Fig. 1.21). The manner in which these changes act upon the components of the admittance at a specific frequency f is therefore dependent upon which point on the locus is regarded. However, alteration of R_1 affects, above all, the susceptance (cf. the displacement between $Y(f)$ and $Y(f)'$ in Fig. 1.21).

An isolated fluctuation of the capacitor C at a specified frequency f will have an effect in the same manner as a frequency fluctuation at a fixed value of C (and the other elements); the admittance vector proceeds along the locus. With small and high values of f, an alteration of C will result mainly in an increase and decrease, respectively, of the susceptance, while average values of f will cause an alteration in the conductance. It is therefore necessary to determine, within a range of measurements with the widest possible frequency spectrum, the form and position of the locus, so as to be able to correctly interpret results obtained from a single measurement frequency.

Although the loci and parameters of the single elements from the electrical equivalent circuits resulting from AC measurements can be used for representing the frequency-dependent system properties (Sect. 3.5.3), it must be kept in mind that these are not ideal RC circuits which are being considered but, on the contrary, real and very complex systems. While AC measurements in these systems give results that are compatible with the properties of the respective models, the same measurements can, however, result from different physical processes (Millington & Wilkinson, 1983). To date the dependence of these systems upon the current density, as upon possible nonlinear elements, has been considered only in an extremely small number of cases (e.g., Yamamoto et al. 1978), as is the case with implications of system properties of electrical equivalent circuits that include a variable capacitor C (e.g., Tregear, 1966).

Models trying to simulate the anatomical features of the skin in different ways are hardly testable with conventional EDA measurement techniques. Tregear (1966) described the stratum corneum alone as a system of about 12 parallel-connected pairs of a resistor and a capacitor, a model that can only be empirically approximated through the aid of the stripping technique (Sect. 1.3.4.2 "The Role of the Epidermal Barrier Layer").

Yamamoto and Yamamoto (1976) have determined the dielectrical and resistive values of five places in the corneum with this technique (Sect. 3.5.3).[50] Thiele (1981a) stated in his considerations about modeling that the electrodermal system is composed of several closely spaced interconnected single systems. Lykken (1971, Fig. 1.6) has also suggested a model comprising several sequential, parallel-connected RC networks lying in series with additional potential generators. As a result of his measurements with pulsed DC (Sect. 1.4.1.4), he doubted that polarization capacity in the sense of a frequency-dependent capacitance is present (Sect. 1.4.2.2). In any case, it is possible to use, as simulations, parallel polarized capacitors, connected in series with resistors, such as the RC networks proposed by Lykken (1971). Salter (1979) has shown that for real physiological systems, polarized capacitances cannot be the only elements in electrical equivalent circuits. Additional elements have to be taken into account, such as ideal capacitors being in series and/or parallel in material that is mainly built up dielectrically, or ideal resistors in parallel and in series in material that is composed of conductors and semiconductors, respectively. As an alternative, the AC properties of the skin (with the inclusion of the sweat glands) can be depicted through nonlinear electronic components, such as Zener diodes and capacitive diodes (Thiele, 1981a) or transistors (Salter, 1981). It remains to be seen whether or not the dynamics of these nonlinear systems will better fit the EDA signal than those of the RC models.

In summary, investigating the AC properties of the skin and sweat glands is more complex than investigating the DC properties. However, due to the capacitive properties of the electrodermal system, such AC investigations are indispensable for modeling. By means of studies using a wide spectrum of AC frequencies and/or the use of transients (Sect. 1.4.1.4), it should be possible to quantitatively compre-hend the electrical properties of single components of the electrodermal system, to

---

[50] Recently, Birgersson et al. (2011) refined the AC-recording technique as used by the Yamamoto group by means of electrical impedance spectroscopy. They also proposed a mathematical three-layer model of the skin, comprising (1) the stratum corneum, (2) the viable skin, which includes the other epidermal layers and the dermis, and (3) the fatty tissue of the hypodermis (Sect. 1.2.1.2). A noninvasive gold-plated probe, featuring two voltage injection electrodes, one current detector and a circular guard electrode (for diminishing the impact of surface leaking currents) was designed for carrying out two-point measurements with sinusoidal AC of varying frequencies. Recordings were taking from the volar forearm of a homogenous group of 60 young females. The skin site was soaked with a physiological saline solution (0.9% NaCl) for 1 min before the first recording was performed. Subsequent recordings were carried out at 5 min intervals up until 30 min in an ambient temperature of 21.7°C (±3°C) and a relative humidity of 36% (±7%). Impedance magnitudes (in kΩ) and the phase angle φ (in degrees) were measured at five different current penetration depths (by varying the voltage at the second current injection electrode from 5 to 50 mV) at 35 frequencies logarithmically distributed between 1.0 kHz and 2.5 MHz. In addition, the impact of NaCl concentration (0.9–18% NaCl) and soaking time was investigated in ten participants. Preliminary results revealed that – in the frequency range – the amount of current passing through the hypodermis (subcutis) can be regarded as negligible. As to be expected, the measured SZ varied considerably with the saline concentration and soaking time.

sketch out electrical equivalent circuits, and to describe the tonic as well as the phasic components of EDA in connection with their origins and interaction.

Especially with respect to the phasic EDA components, pioneer research is still needed, as the temporal relationship of the single components of skin impedance and admittance (Sect. 1.4.1.3) during EDRs has hardly been investigated. In a pilot study aided by a specially developed phase voltmeter (Sect. 2.2.3.3), Boucsein et al. (1989) showed that the phasic variations during an EDR are found in the parallel resistors R and/or R_2 (as shown in the simple models in Figs. 1.15 and 1.18) and not in the serial resistor R_1 or the capacitive part C, or only to an extremely small degree (Sect. 2.5.3.1).

1.5 Summary of Electrodermal Phenomena

EDA results from an interaction of sympathetic nervous system activity and local processes in the skin. There are at least two different CNS sources of sudomotor activity leading to electrodermal changes (Fig. 1.6, Sect. 1.3.4.1). However, they use the same peripheral sudomotor efferents to the sweat glands as a common final pathway (Sect. 1.3.2.1). Specific central sudomotor pathways are not well established (Sect. 1.3.2.2), and even with the aid of brain imaging, no final breakthrough has been reached in clarifying the central elicitation or inhibition of electrodermal phenomena (Sect. 1.3.4.1). Hence, there is still need for future research into the central origins of EDA.

In contrast to the CNS phenomena, local processes in the skin underlying EDA are much better known. It is now generally supposed that sweat gland innervation is cholinergic, which is an exception within the postganglionic sympathetic system (Sect. 1.3.2). Sometimes, additional adrenergic influences on myoepithelia surrounding the sweat gland are discussed (Sect. 1.2.3), which could have the capacity to squeeze preformed sweat out of the duct. However, this plays a minor role, if any (Sect. 1.3.3.1). Another possible cholinergic innervation, which could influence the permeability of a suggested epidermal membrane, remains uncertain, as does the existence of such an active membrane in general (Sect. 1.4.2.3).

There is ample empirical evidence that electrodermal phenomena are generated by sweat gland activity in conjunction with epidermal membrane processes. When sweat gland activity is abolished in humans, either as a result of congenital absence, by sympathectomy, by peripheral sudomotor nerve discharge, or by pharmacological blocking, SCRs and SPRs are normally eliminated and SCL is considerably reduced (Fowles, 1986a). Martin and Venables (1966) observed the SCR freq. being highest in skin areas with the greatest density of sweat glands. Thomas and Korr (1957) reported a median intrasubject product moment coefficient of $r = 0.91$ (with a range from 0.44 to 0.96) between counts of active sweat glands and the SCL measured with dry electrodes, being held only a few seconds to the skin, so that the corneum beneath the electrode remained dry (Sect. 2.6.5). Since EDA is normally recorded using electrolytes and thus from a moistened stratum corneum, these high correlations cannot be generalized to EDA recording as a whole. Thus, Edelberg (1971), using his microelectrode technique, found that sweat glands are only responsible for less than 50% of the SCL in case of a moistened corneum.

Sweat secretion does not only lead to duct filling but also to moistening of the relatively dry upper epidermal layer, the stratum corneum (Sect. 1.3.4.2). Both processes cause changes in skin conductance: the ducts form electrical shunts through the epidermal barrier, thus connecting the skin surface with the highly conductive dermal tissue, and moistening of the corneum with the salty sweat generally increases skin conductivity (Sect. 1.4.2.1). Those purely resistive properties of the electrodermal system can be depicted in relatively simple electrical models (Fig. 1.15, Sect. 1.4.3.1).

In addition to these rather slow-going processes, active electrical properties of the skin and the sweat glands have to be taken into account, acting as potential sources in endosomatic recording (Sect. 1.4.2.3) or as capacitors in exosomatic recording (Sect. 1.4.2.2). These electrical properties are formed by the secretory activity of the sweat gland, the sodium reabsorption mechanism in the dermal and perhaps also in the epidermal part of the duct (Sect. 1.3.3.1), by a suggested epidermal barrier membrane, and by the electrical activity of the myoepithelia surrounding the duct.

Sources of electrical potentials taking part in the occurrence of an EDR could be shown not only for endosomatic but also for exosomatic recordings. It is widely accepted that the effects of electrical potentials on the form of the EDR depend on both duct filling and corneal hydration, which are, however, not independent of each other (Sect. 1.4.2.1). Edelberg (1971) as well as Fowles (1974) argued that the duct filling and the hydration components themselves, together with the ductal reabsorption, represent relatively slow processes, and hence can only influence recovery time but not rise time, which is generally shorter than recovery time (Sects. 2.5.2.3 and 2.5.2.4). The fast EDR components were presumed to be caused by membrane polarizations and depolarizations, as described in Sect. 1.4.2.3, which take place in one of the potential sources mentioned above (e.g., Edelberg, 1972a).

However, electrical models which additionally take into account those various sources of electrical potentials remain of questionable heuristic value, at least for modeling exosomatic EDA, since there are no appropriate methods available to experimentally investigate the behavior of their elements (Sect. 1.4.3.2). Consequently, for an explanation of exosomatic electrodermal changes, Edelberg (1983, Fig. 1.1) proposed a resistive model of EDA, which resembles the simplified form of the Montagu-Coles model as depicted in the right-hand part of Fig. 1.15 (Sect. 1.4.3.1). He regarded the corneum and the sweat duct as resistors in parallel, connected in series with a resistor which includes some corneal and all subcorneal structures, except the sweat gland lumen. Edelberg (1983) also did not include the frequently discussed active epidermal membrane (Sect. 1.4.2.3), because of its hitherto uncertain role in contributing to conductance changes (see Boucsein et al., 1989). In case of exosomatic recording, such a membrane would act as a capacitor lying in parallel to the resistors of the corneum and the sweat duct.

Edelberg's (1983) simplified modeling of EDA leaves aside several of the rather complicated interrelationships of various peripheral elements which may actually contribute to the generation of electrodermal phenomena. If the corneum is very dry – which is normally not the case in EDA recordings using electrolytes – an increase of SRL should rely upon the sweat duct filling. However, the hydrated corneum will act as a shunt around the sweat duct, thus reducing the ductal contribution to the SRL. In his experiments using cats, in which the central sympathetic component was interrupted, Edelberg (1983) observed that sympathetic nerve stimulations at intervals of approximately 30 s produce EDRs of much higher amplitudes if preparations with a dry corneum were used, compared to those with a moistened corneum. So there is ample evidence that under a solely resistive perspective, corneal hydration is mostly responsible for EDL, while the exosomatic EDR relies on a secretory membrane component together with a duct-filling component. As an alternative to the hitherto existing electrical models, Edelberg (1993) proposed his "poral valve model" (see end of Sect. 1.4.3.2), which requires, however, additional verification by empirical studies.

For most applications of electrodermal recording, a simple resistive model will be sufficient to explain the phenomena observed. However, capacitive elements certainly play an important role in tonic EDA (e.g., in dermatological applications; Sect. 3.5.3). Their possible contribution to EDRs is not well known and should therefore be investigated further. An appropriate electrical modeling of EDA has to take into account, at minimum, one capacitor in parallel to the resistors of the corneum and the sweat duct (Fig. 1.18, Sect. 1.4.3.3), and EDA recording has to be performed using high-resolution AC instead of DC methods of measurement (Sect. 2.2.3.3).

The utilization of AC based models and recording techniques is valuable, therefore, for research into the causal mechanism of EDA. It will also be able to supplement and correct some speculative conceptions which were developed on the basis of DC and potential measurements. An intensified teamwork among physicists, engineers, dermatologists, and psychophysiologists will be necessary to overcome the sustaining problems of measurement using AC techniques.

Chapter 2
Methods of Electrodermal Recording

The second chapter of the book discusses the different methods used for electrodermal recording. As mentioned in the introduction to Chap. 1, the observation of electrodermal phenomena requires only relatively basic equipment. As a consequence, a variety of recording methods have been proposed.

During the 1970s and 1980s, there have been several attempts to standardize techniques of electrodermal recording (e.g., Fowles et al., 1981; Lykken & Venables, 1971). However, because their basis was not always empirically wide-ranging, these recommendations do not provide sufficient information on what will result as a consequence of their violation. Therefore, Sect. 2.6 comprehensively reviews the current state of discussions concerning the use of various concepts in recording and evaluating EDA.

As a supplement to the electrophysical and system-theoretical fundamentals provided in Sect. 1.4.1, Sect. 2.1 outlines the basic principles of measurement techniques for electrodermal recording. Even for those experienced in the recording of biosignals, specific problems may arise in EDA measurement, which are discussed in Sects. 2.1.3 and 2.1.4.

Section 2.2 describes recording techniques and data analysis, followed by methods of parameterization in Sect. 2.3. Section 2.4 discusses the various influences of physical and nonelectrodermal physiological influences, including age, gender, ethnic differences, and heritability. Data concerning distributions of, reliabilities of, and interrelationships between the various electrodermal parameters are given separately for the different measurement techniques in Sect. 2.5.

The reader who is only interested in basic knowledge of the most important principles of measurement and evaluation techniques is referred to Sects. 2.1–2.3, which provide short summaries of the appropriate standards together with cross-references for more details.

W. Boucsein, *Electrodermal Activity*, DOI 10.1007/978-1-4614-1126-0_2,
© Springer Science+Business Media, LLC 2012

2.1 Introduction to Electrodermal Measurement

The fundamentals of measurement techniques reported here are restricted to problems which emerge in circuitry for measuring EDA. Since endosomatic EDA recording does not require specific circuitry (Sect. 2.2.3.1), except for obtaining phasic responses with higher resolution (Sect. 2.1.3), the following descriptions refer mainly to exosomatic EDA recording techniques.

The electrical current necessary to measure exosomatic EDA can be delivered to the skin by either DC or AC. Since AC is seldom used in electrodermal recording, Sects. 2.1.1–2.1.3 refer to DC measurement only, while Sect. 2.1.5 discusses AC measurement separately. This section includes techniques for pulse spectrum or transient analyses (Sect. 1.4.1.4), which can be regarded as a special case of AC measurement, since the current does not flow continuously in one direction but switches on and off. Section 2.1.4 outlines specific problems of coupling, amplification, and filtering in electrodermal measurement devices. Disregarding these features is likely to produce considerable inaccuracy of measurement and corruption of the signal.

The measurement techniques described in this section should enable users to form their own opinions concerning the quality of various EDA measurement devices, to localize possible sources of measurement error in their own device and to eliminate those errors. Since not every polygraph system provides EDA recording facilities, it will sometimes be necessary to construct the appropriate circuitry. In this case, even an experienced engineer should be aware of the specific problems discussed in Sects. 2.1.3 and 2.1.4 that arise from the dynamics of the electrodermal signal. An electric circuitry for an EDA coupler to be used with a high-quality biosignal amplifier is given in Fig. 2.12 (Sect. 2.2.3.2).

2.1.1 Measuring Electrodermal Activity with Voltage Dividers

In this form of exosomatic measurement, two electrodes are attached to the subject's skin and connected in series with a system reference resistor, as shown in Fig. 2.1. A voltage source is applied, providing a constant voltage U_{tot}. The fluctuations in the electrodermal system can be read through the variations of the partial voltages (Sect. 1.4.1.2). With the aid of such a voltage divider, two different methods of measurement can be applied:

1. The *quasi-constant current method* (see beginning of Sect. 2.1.2): The voltage is measured on R_1, which is the resistance of the skin (left-hand side of Fig. 2.1). The measured voltage U_1 is in the same proportion to U_{tot} as R_1 is to R_{tot}, R_{tot} being $R_1 + R_2$ combined:

$$\frac{U_1}{U_{tot}} = \frac{R_1}{R_1 + R_2} \tag{2.1a}$$

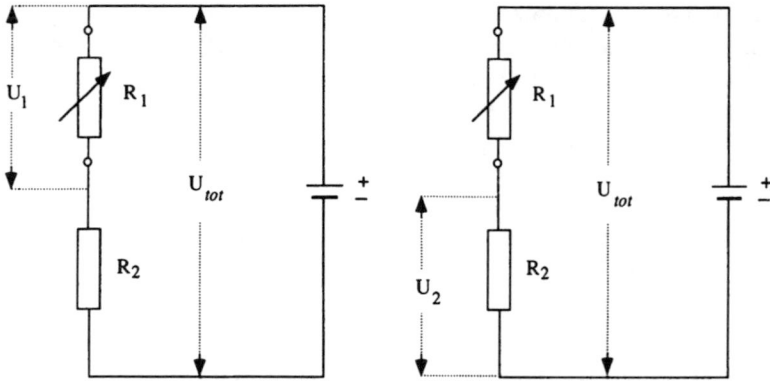

Fig. 2.1 The quasi-constant current method (*left*) and the quasi-constant voltage method (*right*) of exosomatic EDA measurement. U_{tot} is the source voltage applied to the system, and U_1 and U_2 are the measured partial voltages in the measurement of the variation of the resistance R_1 of the skin. R_2 is a fixed reference resistor

Multiplying both sides by U_{tot} gives:

$$U_1 = U_{tot} \frac{R_1}{R_1 + R_2} \tag{2.1b}$$

Following Ohm's law, and with regard to $R_{tot} = R_1 + R_2$, gives:

$$I_{tot} = \frac{U_{tot}}{R_{tot}} = \frac{U_{tot}}{R_1 + R_2} \tag{2.1c}$$

When the system is calibrated so that the fixed reference resistor R_2 is much larger than the variable skin resistance R_1, I_{tot} can be regarded as largely determined through R_2. Fluctuations of the skin resistance R_1 hardly affect the strength of the flowing current I_{tot}. Therefore, a "constant current system" will result. When R_2 is much higher than R_1, the denominator of (2.1c) can be regarded as being almost constant. The voltage U_1, taken from the skin, is then almost totally proportional to variations of the skin resistance R_1.

2. The *quasi-constant voltage method*: The voltage is measured on R_2, the fixed resistor (right-hand side of Fig. 2.1). The measured voltage U_2 is in the same proportion to the applied total voltage U_{tot} as R_2 is to R_{tot}, being $R_1 + R_2$ combined:

$$\frac{U_2}{U_{tot}} = \frac{R_2}{R_1 + R_2} \tag{2.2a}$$

Multiplying both sides by U_{tot} gives:

$$U_2 = U_{tot} \frac{R_2}{R_1 + R_2} \tag{2.2b}$$

When a system is calibrated so that the fixed reference resistor R_2 is much smaller than the variable skin resistance R_1, then the current I_{tot} flowing through the system, according to (2.1c), is no longer constant: as R_2 is negligible in comparison to R_1, the current increases as the skin resistance R_1 decreases and vice versa. As the voltage dropping on R_2 is negligible in comparison to that on R_1, practically the whole voltage U_{tot} is applied to the skin. Therefore, a "constant voltage system" will result. When R_1 is much larger than R_2, the numerator of (2.2b) can be regarded as negligibly small in comparison to the denominator. The voltage U_2 measured on the reference resistor is then almost wholly proportional to variations in the reciprocal conductance value G_1 of the skin resistance R_1.

Higher signal amplification is needed for the quasi-constant voltage method than for the quasi-constant current method, which can be explained with the following example. If skin resistance decreases from 100 to 90 kΩ, then, under the quasi-constant current method following (2.1b), with a reference resistor of $R_2 = 10$ MΩ, and an applied voltage of $U_{tot} = 0.5$ V, the recorded voltage U_1 changes from 4.950 to 4.459 mV (i.e., a change of around 491 μV). Under the quasi-constant voltage method with $U_{tot} = 0.5$ V and a reference resistor of $R_2 = 100$ Ω, following (2.2b), the recorded voltage U_2 changes from 0.499 to 0.555 mV. This is a change of 56 μV, which is about one tenth of the difference obtained by the quasi-constant current method.

Every voltage measurement in such a circuit, whether by voltmeter, oscilloscope, or with another amplifier system, causes a change of the phenomenon under investigation. This change is dependent upon the properties of the measuring instrument. A decisive influence is caused by the internal resistance of the recording instrument and the input resistance of the amplifier. When measuring voltages, this resistance and the input impedance should be as high as possible, commonly known as "high-impedance" amplification.

The necessity of using a high-impedance voltmeter in case of measuring voltage can be illustrated with the help of the right-hand side of Fig. 1.7 (Sect. 1.4.1.2). When R_2 is regarded as the internal resistance of the meter which is used to measure the voltage that drops over R_1, the total resistance of this parallel circuit is calculated according to (1.6e). As a result, the total resistance of the circuit and voltmeter system will be smaller than the resistance of the circuit alone, as represented through the resistor R_1 in the right-hand side of Fig. 1.7. Hence, the voltage which drops over the entire system and is shown on the meter is smaller than the voltage which drops over R_1 alone. As can be inferred from (1.6e), the measurement error produced by the use of the voltmeter is smaller, the higher R_2 (the internal resistance of the meter) is in comparison to R_1.

Even with the use of a high-input impedance of, for example, $R_2 = 10$ MΩ, a clearly perceptible measurement error remains. If, for example, skin resistance drops 10 kΩ from 100 to 90 kΩ, the insertion of 100 kΩ for R_1 in (1.6e) results in a measurement of 99.0 kΩ for R_{tot}; whereas the insertion of 90 kΩ for R_1 results in 89.2 kΩ. The measured difference is 9.8 kΩ, which – in comparison to the actual change of 10 kΩ – is an error of 2%.

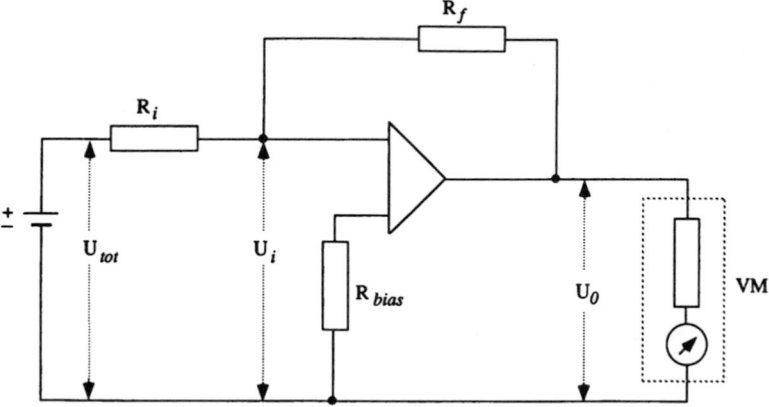

Fig. 2.2 Operational amplifier for measuring electrodermal activity. U_i input voltage; U_0 output voltage; R_i input impedance; R_f feedback resistor; R_{bias} reference resistor; VM voltmeter with its internal resistance (from Lowry (1977), Fig. 2. Copyright © 1977 by the Society for Psychophysiological Research. Reprinted by permission of the publisher)

2.1.2 Measuring Electrodermal Activity with Operational Amplifiers

The methods of measurement described in Sect. 2.1.1 which use voltage dividers have been referred to as quasi-constant current and quasi-constant voltage methods. For example, the voltage U_1 applied to the skin when using the quasi-constant current method (not shown for the sake of simplicity in the right-hand side of Fig. 2.1) is not fully constant, but is a result of the difference between the voltage U_{tot} from the voltage source and the voltage U_2 used for measurement, and varies in accordance with this difference. The greater fluctuations in EDA are, the more the voltage applied to the skin electrodes will oscillate. The respective measurement error of both methods is also determined by the dependence upon the relationship between the resistance values of R_1 and R_2.

To avoid possible measurement errors caused by voltage divider-based circuits, Lowry (1977) suggested an active circuitry for measurement of EDA (as opposed to the use of a passive voltage divider), based upon an operational amplifier as shown in Fig. 2.2.

The amplification factor k of an operational amplifier is determined through the relationship of its input impedance R_i to the feedback resistor R_f (which is necessary for stabilization), as follows:

$$k = \frac{R_f}{R_i} \tag{2.3}$$

The output voltage U_0 results from the product of the voltage U_{tot} on R_i and the amplification factor k. U_0 is inverted in comparison to U_{tot}, as shown with a minus sign in (2.4):

$$U_0 = -kU_{tot} = -\frac{R_f}{R_i}U_{tot} \tag{2.4}$$

Since the internal resistance of today's operational amplifiers is in the range of GΩ, the voltage U_i impressed on the active input of the operational amplifier is practically determined by the relationship of R_i and R_f of the so formed voltage divider. As the current flow is the same through both these resistors, Ohm's law can be applied, so that:

$$U_{tot} - U_i = R_i I \tag{2.5a}$$

and

$$U_i - U_0 = R_f I \tag{2.5b}$$

Solving (2.5a) and (2.5b) for I results in:

$$\frac{U_{tot} - U_i}{R_i} = \frac{U_i - U_0}{R_f} \tag{2.6a}$$

Multiplying out (2.6a) gives:

$$(R_f U_{tot}) - (R_f U_i) = (R_i U_i) - (R_i U_0) \tag{2.6b}$$

Inserting U_0 according to (2.4) and solving for U_i results in:

$$U_i = \frac{(R_f U_{tot}) - (R_f U_{tot})}{R_f + R_i} = \frac{0}{R_f + R_i} = 0 \tag{2.7}$$

The voltage U_i impressed on the operational amplifier input is therefore always set to 0 by the amplifier. This enables a genuine constancy of current and/or voltage. U_{tot} is thereby taken from a constant voltage source (a stabilized power supply). Two different methods of measurement are possible with the use of this circuit:

1. The *constant current method*: The skin is used as the feedback resistor R_f in the system. The current which flows through R_i and the skin is determined following Ohm's law as the quotient of the voltage drop $U_{tot} - U_0$ over both resistors and the sum of both resistors:

$$I = \frac{U_{tot} - U_0}{R_i + R_f} \tag{2.8a}$$

Inserting U_0 as taken from (2.4) results in:

$$I = \frac{U_{tot} + (U_{tot}(R_f/R_i))}{R_i + R_f} \tag{2.8b}$$

U_{tot} is bracketed in the numerator and $R_i + R_f$ can be shortened as follows:

$$I = \frac{U_{tot}((R_i + R_f)/R_i)}{R_i + R_f} = \frac{U_{tot}}{R_i} \tag{2.8c}$$

Since R_i is a fixed value and U_{tot} is stabilized, the current I that flows through the skin will be constant. The current flow can be determined by the choice of appropriate values for U_{tot} and R_i. The voltage U_0, measurable on the output of the operational amplifier, is proportional to the skin resistance R_f following (2.4), but with inverted polarity.

2. The *constant voltage method*: The subject's skin is used as the input impedance R_i of the system. The voltage impressed on the skin electrodes results from the difference between U_{tot} and U_i following Fig. 2.2. The input voltage U_i is, however, always set to 0 following (2.7), so that a constant, because well stabilized, voltage U_{tot} lies on the skin. The voltage U_0, measurable on the output of the operational amplifier, is proportional to the reciprocal of the skin resistance R_i (i.e., the conductance value) but with inverted polarity.

Measurement of the voltage on the output of the operational amplifier can be performed at a relatively low-impedance level, as the measurement errors, which result from the insertion of a meter in a voltage divider, and the resulting parallel connection of the meter's internal resistance and the system's resistance (Sect. 2.1.1), do not occur here. The reference resistor R_{bias} (Fig. 2.2) is introduced to set the measurement error caused by bias currents at minimum.

Today's physiological equipment commonly utilizes differential amplifiers. These amplifiers function in the way shown in Fig. 2.2, but they do not amplify the potential variations of a single input signal with respect to a floating reference wire (formerly referred to as the ground, see Sect. 2.1.4) which is common to output and input. Instead, they amplify the difference between two input voltages impressed on two respective inputs of the operational amplifier. This voltage difference is independent from a reference point. Therefore, the problematic endosomatic contamination of exosomatic measurement values (according to Edelberg, 1967, p. 27 f.) no longer exists.

2.1.3   Circuitries for Separating Electrodermal Responses from Levels

Electrodermal responses normally constitute small variations compared to the total range of measurement (i.e., the possible tonic range). If the measurement system is set up in a way that level variations in their fullest possible range can be recorded

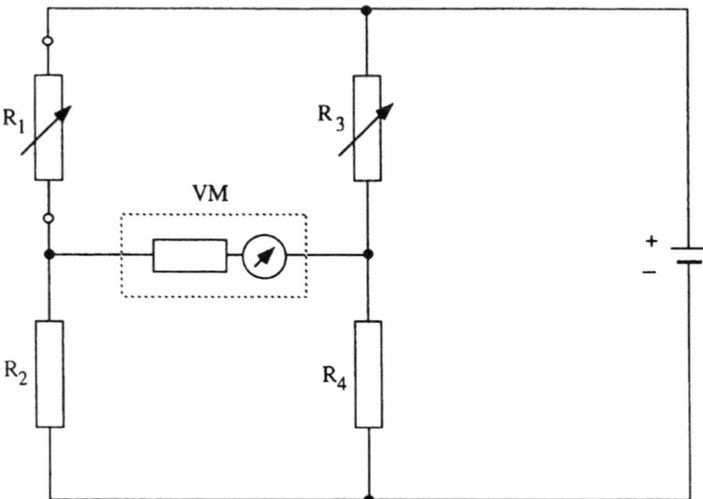

Fig. 2.3 Wheatstone bridge circuitry. R_1 resistance of skin; R_3 variable resistor for alignment of the level value; R_2 and R_4 fixed reference resistors; *VM* voltmeter with its internal resistance

without altering the amplification, EDRs to single stimuli and spontaneous fluctuations can only be recorded with a very small resolution and are therefore subject to a high measurement error (Sect. 2.1.4).

An easy compensation for the EDL is featured by the Wheatstone bridge circuitry, composed of two voltage dividers connected in parallel, as shown in Fig. 2.3. The potential difference between the central points of both voltage dividers is measured by a voltmeter, or over both inputs of an operational amplifier. One of the voltage dividers uses the subject's skin as resistor R_1 and a fixed resistor R_2; the other uses a variable resistor (a potentiometer) R_3 and a fixed resistor R_4. At the beginning of measurement the bridge is calibrated. In place of the unknown skin resistance R_1, a defined resistor must be inserted. R_3 is adjusted so that the potential difference between the two voltage dividers will be 0. When an EDR occurs, this balance is disturbed and the potential difference can be read on the meter. As the corresponding variations are small compared to the possible range of EDL values, a significantly higher amplification can be used as for the EDL, which leads to an enhanced resolution of the EDR. Since the EDL will drift as a rule during the course of a measurement, it is necessary to adjust R_3 from time to time to prevent the recorded potential difference from exceeding the range of measurement.

Nowadays, this method of suppressing the baseline component of EDA during recording is replaced by the use of an AC amplifier (AC-coupled amplifier). Here, a capacitor is inserted prior to the input resistor R_i in an operational amplifier circuit (Fig. 2.2). The voltage time curve on the operational amplifier output runs in a similar manner to that in Fig. 1.8 (Sect. 1.4.1.2); thus, the recorded signal shows only the variations in voltage. The amplifier reacts to a variation in the input voltage, as evoked through an EDR, resulting in a variation in the output signal. The new baseline level is not being transmitted but instead drops back down to

0 after a certain amount of time. With the use of an AC-coupled amplifier, the range of measurement is small in comparison to the possible range of level variations, thereby enabling a higher amplification and a higher resolution of the EDR. The transmission properties of the operational amplifier are characterized by its time constant (see (1.10b)). Fowles et al. (1981) considered a 6 s time constant as being long enough to accurately measure EDRs while maintaining a fairly stable baseline. The special problems of amplification which apply here are discussed in Sect. 2.1.4. It should also be noted that the amplitude and the course of an EDR signal as recorded by an AC-coupled amplifier differ from the corresponding parameters of the original EDR.

The EDR can be regarded electrophysically as the alternating voltage component of the EDA signal, whereas the EDL can be regarded as its direct voltage component. Since the AC resistance of a capacitor is frequency dependent, as shown in Sect. 1.4.1.3, the EDR signal is changed in shape at the output of the operational amplifier. As this becomes critical only when the phase duration of the EDR signal approaches the time constant τ of the amplifier, the resulting measurement error can be minimized through an appropriate choice of τ. The time constant of the AC amplifier plays a significant role in the evaluation of the rise and recovery times of the EDR (Sect. 2.3.1.3). It should be at least 3 s in case of exosomatic recording. Fowles et al. (1981) recommended time constants of over 6 s to avoid distortion of the EDR amp. Following Edelberg (1967), time constants of 15 s and above should be chosen for endosomatic recordings.

Elimination of the level component of the EDA is also enabled by "backing-off" circuits. Here, the direct voltage component is actively suppressed, similar to the adjustment of the input voltage U_i to 0 in the operational amplifier (Fig. 2.2), however, not by the input amplifier but at a later time. An appropriate circuitry is depicted in Fig. 2.10 (Sect. 2.2.3.2). With such a system, to avoid loss of data, it is necessary that the experimenter observes the recording curve and changes the backing-off voltage before the curve proceeds out of the measurement range. Therefore, additional circuitries are in use which automatically adjust and record the backing-off voltage (Fig. 2.11, Sect. 2.2.3.2).

Special problems of amplification which occur with AC-coupled amplifiers and "backing-off" circuits are discussed in Sect. 2.1.4. With time constants being large enough, AC-coupling will result only in a small EDR change; despite that, some authors recommended that this change should be eliminated by transforming to a very large time constant, which can be done during computer analysis (Sect. 2.2.4.2; Thom, 1988). It must be noted that, in the use of all decoupling methods for electrodermal response values described in this section, a new type of measurement scale is introduced for the EDA signal during the process.[1]

---

[1] Although the respective EDL is built up of physical units with ratio scales, it is sometimes recommended that the EDL signal – like most psychophysiological variables – be treated as based only on interval scales (Levey, 1980; Stemmler, 1984), which would naturally also affect the performance of transformations (Sect. 2.3.3). However, EDR amp. obtained by the AC-coupled amplification cannot be treated as based on a ratio scale anyway.

When resistance values are to be transformed into conductance values (Sect. 2.3.3.2), and such a transformation cannot be performed prior to the stage of data collection, the recording of tonic values will be required, since transformations with change values alone are not calculable without knowledge of the base levels (Sect. 2.3.3.2). It is therefore sometimes recommended to record the EDL on a parallel channel to the EDR, though with correspondingly smaller amplification.[2] Since polygraph recording instruments are often very limited in the number of channels available, special measurement procedures for the simultaneous recording of the EDL and the highly resolved EDR on a single channel have been developed. The EDA coupler of such a polygraph system enables the recording of the EDL as a sequence of impulses which overlie the AC signal of the EDR and whose spacing is proportional to the EDL. These impulses must in any case undergo a special treatment through subsequent automated processing of the EDR (Sect. 2.2.4.2).

Since high-resolution A/D converters with subsequent computer storage of biosignals came into use (Sect. 2.2.4.2), separate channels for EDL and EDR recording are no longer required, since the whole EDA signal can be displayed on a computer screen with sufficient resolution.

2.1.4 Specific Problems of Electrodermal Measurement

With the technology available nowadays, a relatively distortion-free high amplification of biosignals existing as voltages in the range of μV to mV can be obtained. However, some specific problems can arise in coupling, amplification, and filtering of the EDA signal, which will be discussed below.

In contrast to other biosignals, where all input amplifiers are connected with each other through the electric floating reference wire (mostly replacing the formerly used ground, since patients are no longer recommended being connected to the electric ground, i.e., the protective earth; see Grimnes & Martinsen, 2008, pp. 233 f.), the input section of an EDA coupler for exosomatic measurement must be fully electrically separated from all other amplifier inputs. Otherwise, the application of a reference or ground electrode for another signal (e.g., ECG, EEG, etc.) will short-circuit the EDA measurement voltage applied to the skin and will thereby significantly reduce the EDA signal. The smaller the resistance between the ground (i.e., the floating reference) electrode and the skin in comparison to that of the EDA electrodes would be in such a case, the greater such a reduction would become. Furthermore, if simultaneous recordings with several EDA couplers from the same subject are attempted, the input sections of the different EDA couplers must be fully electrically separated; as otherwise cross currents will appear.

---

[2] The reading off and manual recording of the placement of the potentiometer R_3 in Fig. 2.3 cannot be recommended because of its error proneness.

Problems for the amplification of the EDA signal mainly result from its wide range, since the many possible inter- and intraindividual differences in EDLs result in a large recording range. In comparison, the fluctuations appearing as EDRs are relatively small. When, for example, a SC-recording device covers a range from 0 to 100 μS, and fluctuations with amplitudes of 0.05 μS, or greater, should be scored as SCRs (Sect. 2.3.1.2 "Choice of Amplitude Criteria"), the resolution in the analysis must be better than 0.0005. This, however, is not obtainable with paper analysis (Sect. 2.2.4.1); for even if a 25-cm recording width is available for the EDA channel, which covers the whole bandwidth (recording range) of 100 μS, SCR amp. of 0.125 mm would be required being recognizable, which is not possible even with a magnifying glass. With a computer analysis using A/D conversion with 12-bit accuracy, such resolution would only just be achievable; i.e., possible 4,096 digital scores would lead to a resolution of 0.025 μS/bit, and the minimum amplitude of 0.05 μS would be converted into 2 bits. Therefore, 16-bit A/D conversion rates are nowadays used for computerized storage and analysis of EDA signals, allowing for resolutions of 0.0015 μS/bit (Sect. 2.2.4.2).

Sufficiently high resolution of SCRs can be also achieved by uncoupling the EDR component of the EDA signal from the measured EDL and amplifying it with a higher gain (Sect. 2.1.3). When such an uncoupling during recording results from electrical compensation of the baseline component using a Wheatstone bridge (Fig. 2.3), the entire amplification range is available for the EDR. However, in this case the SCL is lost during recording.

If an additional recording of the EDL is also attempted, then the entire EDL range must be covered through preamplification, and the EDR component must be uncoupled through a second amplification by using an AC amplifier, as described in Sect. 2.1.3. This leads to a problem with amplification, since only a very small part of the entire recorded EDL is of interest and, therefore, will be amplified. In the previous example, the minimum SCR of 0.05 μS takes up only 0.05% of the entire amplification range, if the first amplifier is set for an SCL range from 0 to 100 μS. This requires an excellent signal-to-noise ratio.

All amplifiers produce noise, but good amplifiers have only 0.01% noise on average. The signal-to-noise ratio is measured in dB = 20 log (signal voltage/noise voltage). A noise ratio of 0.01% corresponds therefore to 20 log (100/0.01) dB = 20 log 10,000 dB = 80 dB. If as in the previous example, the signal takes up only 0.05% of the amplifier's working range, the signal-to-noise ratio is only 5:1 = 0.2. This corresponds to a signal-to-noise ratio level of 20 log 5 dB = 14 dB. In this case, the signal-to-noise ratio of an 80 dB amplifier may drop to 14 dB. Furthermore, the above taken 0.01% noise ratio of the amplifier relates to the average noise amplitude; at particular times the voltage peaks, varying at random, can reach higher noise amplitudes, so that the noise component may sporadically appear in the range of the EDR signal. Since the high-frequency noise components are normally eliminated through the use of low-pass filtering; only a noise component in the frequency range of the EDA signal remains and thus can simulate small EDRs. It is therefore necessary for the preamplification of the EDA signal to use an amplifier with a signal-to-noise ratio of at least 80 dB.

Another problem may appear during the filtering process in connection with the EDA signal amplification. As shown in Sect. 2.1.1, the amplitude of the EDR signal in exosomatic measurement can be in the μV range. Therefore, it is in the same range as noise picked up by the skin, electrodes, and electrode wires (Sect. 2.2.5.1). It is not possible to totally eliminate all such noise from the input signal. Therefore in general, filtering is combined with amplification. As in the case of the EDR signal and especially the EDL signal, when slow fluctuations are in question, low-pass filters are inserted in EDA amplifiers.

The use of a low-pass filter can be explained with the help of Fig. 2.2 in Sect. 2.1.2. When a capacitor C is connected in parallel with the feedback resistor R_f and the direct voltage is replaced by alternating voltage with a variable frequency f, the amplification factor, as calculated following (2.3), changes in dependence upon f. This is because the AC resistance of the capacitor C decreases with a rise in frequency (Sect. 1.4.1.3). As the resistance of this parallel circuit becomes smaller with the resistance of C (Sect. 1.4.1.2), the feedback resistance of the operational amplifier becomes smaller with increasing frequency f. When the input resistor R_i remains constant, the amplification factor is directly proportional to the feedback resistance (i.e., it decreases when R_f decreases).

Through an appropriate selection of the values for R_f and C, the low-pass filter can be constructed with differing limiting frequencies f_{lim}, following the equation $f_{lim} = 1/(2\pi R_f C)$, which, according to the construction of each filter, more or less steeply cuts off frequencies above the limit. Often, instead of the limiting frequencies, the time constant is given, $\tau = R_f C$ (see (1.10b) in Sect. 1.4.1.2). Accordingly, time constants of 0.25, 0.5, 1, and 2 s correspond to limiting frequencies of 0.64, 0.32, 0.16, and 0.08 Hz. Such low-pass filters eliminate a large part of possible noise in EDA recording and might also be used for a simple artifact removal (Sect. 2.3.4.1). By contrast, the EDRs with small time constants (i.e., with short recovery times) may be changed, both with respect to amplitudes and response shapes (Sect. 2.3.1.3). How much such a RC-circuit may distort an input signal is shown in Fig. 1.9 (Sect. 1.4.1.3).

Though these filtering problems are more easily controlled in exosomatic DC measurement than in AC measurement, significant errors of measurement can arise in apparently simple EDA measurements with DC when the above problems are ignored. These errors are normally not noticed by the experimenter, because a characteristic-looking EDA signal can be obtained with below-standard equipment. Therefore, the standards described in this section should be especially noted when procuring an EDA measurement apparatus.

2.1.5 Measuring Electrodermal Activity with Alternating Current

In the simplest case, arrangements of measurement of the skin impedance and admittance (Sect. 1.4.1.3) differ from DC measurement in that an alternating voltage source is used instead of a direct voltage one. AC measurement devices

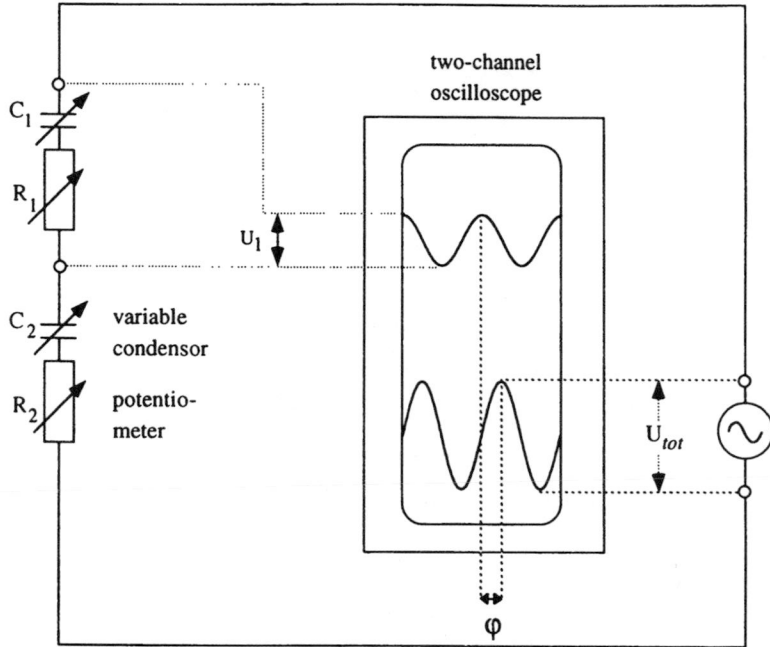

Fig. 2.4 Circuitry for demonstrating the principle of AC measurement of EDA. C_1 and R_1 serve as a simplified simulation of the skin; C_2 and R_2 are variable components of the measurement circuit; φ is the angle of the phase displacement between U_{tot} and U_1

can be constructed with a voltage divider (Sect. 2.1.1, Fig. 2.1) or by using an operational amplifier (Sect. 2.1.2, Fig. 2.2). The measured voltage is rectified and amplified; it can also be used to separate EDR and EDL components with a "backing-off" circuit (Edelberg, 1967; see Sect. 2.1.3). Devices for exosomatic AC measurement provide values for admittance or impedance but do not necessarily release information concerning the phase angle φ, from which the capacitive properties of the skin could be determined.

However, the most significant gain by using AC instead of DC measurement in electrodermal recording is the possibility to split impedance into its ohmic part R and the reactance X, or to split conductance into its ohmic part G and susceptance B, respectively. This can be performed when the phase angle φ is recorded as well (Sect. 1.4.1.3). In the first instance, as previously discussed in Sect. 1.4.1.3 and later in Sect. 2.2.3.3, the principle of impedance measurement is focused on here, because Salter (1979) stated a preference for the constant current method, which implies impedance measurement, in biomedical applications of AC measurement. He argued that with the use of the constant voltage method, uncontrolled fluctuations in the current density can lead to nonlinearity in transmission behavior (Sect. 2.6.2). The equivalent admittance values can be calculated through the respective transformations (Sects. 1.4.1.3, 1.4.3.3, and 2.3.1.2 "Amplitudes of

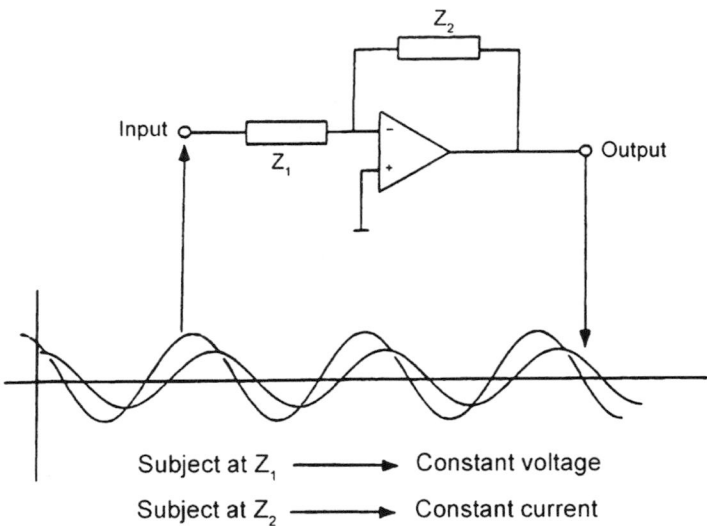

Fig. 2.5 Measurement of electrodermal activity with AC, using a sinusoidal probe signal, either with constant voltage or constant current, depending on the subject's placement in the circuitry (reprinted from Schaefer and Boucsein (2000), Fig. 3. Copyright © 2000 by the Society for Psychophysiological Research. Reprinted by permission of the publisher and the first author)

Exosomatic Responses Recorded with Alternating Current"). A device that is capable of both CC and CV measurement with AC is shown in Fig. 2.5.

One method described by Tregear (1966) to simultaneously determine X and R is shown in Fig. 2.4. The figure depicts a modification of the measurement principle shown in the left-hand side of Fig. 2.1 (Sect. 2.1.1). For AC measurement, the direct voltage source is replaced with an alternating voltage source, the resistor R_1 is complemented by a capacitor C_1 and a variable capacitor and a potentiometer are inserted in place of R_2. For demonstration purpose, the temporal course of the input voltage U_{tot} and the measured voltage U_1 can be displayed together on a two-channel oscilloscope. Then the values of the variable resistor R_2 and the serially connected capacitor C_2 are changed until the voltage course of U_1 is in phase with U_{tot} and has half the amplitude. In this case, not only is the skin impedance the same as the impedances of the equivalent RC-circuit, but it is also composed of the ohmic resistance and the reactance in the same manner. The ohmic component R is directly readable from the placement of the potentiometer, while the reactance X is calculable from the set value of the variable capacitor and the frequency of the AC according to the following formula:

$$X(f) = \frac{1}{2(\pi f c)} \tag{2.9}$$

Such an arrangement for measurement is only conditionally suitable for continuous recording of EDA. This is because every change in the weighting circuit requires a certain amount of time, as variations in the AC circuit resistance and capacitance influence each other (Sect. 1.4.1.3), so that the courses of short-period changes either in impedance and phase angle, or in reactance and the ohmic component of the resistance, cannot be reliably recorded with this method. Moreover, when a more complicated electrical model of the skin is applied (Sect. 1.4.3.2), further resistors and/or capacitors must be included in the compensatory branch of the voltage divider, which considerably lengthens the time necessary for trimming, i.e., adapting R_2 and C_2 as described above. It is also apparent that the accuracy of all these methods is dependent upon the accuracy of the manual trimming (Edelberg, 1967).

For a more exact and also continuous recording of EDA with AC, methods using analog computer components have been applied. With these, reactance and the ohmic resistance, with the use of a given frequency, can be directly calculated and constantly recorded from a comparison between an alternating voltage applied to the skin and the output voltage of the EDA measurement system. Such a system had been applied by Yamamoto and Yamamoto (1979, Fig. 2). An operational amplifier is fed by the output voltage $U(f)$, which corresponds to the output voltage U_0 according to Fig. 2.2 (Sect. 2.1.2), with an alternating voltage source oscillating with the frequency f used instead of a direct voltage source. The output of a sine wave oscillator, which is in the same phase with the frequency f, is both directly and through a differentiator (which shifts the phase by 90°, thus calculating $\cos 2\pi f$) multiplied by the output signal of an operational amplifier. On one output, $X(f) = Z(f) \sin \varphi(f)$ can be measured, as can $R(f) = Z(f) \cos \varphi(f)$ on the other output. With these two results, the AC characteristics of RC systems with a single given frequency f can be described (Sect. 1.4.1.3). In contrast to the method of photographic recording of Lissajous figures (Fig. 1.11, Sect. 1.4.1.4) every 0.8 s, as used by Yokota and Fujimori (1962, Fig. 5), such a continuous recording of $R(f)$ and $X(f)$ has the advantage of better quantification and control of the parameters of the electrodermal system. The phase voltmeter for EDA measurement described in Sect. 2.2.3.3 operates according to this principle. Through the appropriate transformations (Sect. 1.4.1.3), susceptance $B(f)$ and conductance $G(f)$ can be continually calculated in place of reactance and resistance.

Constant voltage and constant current methods can be applied in AC measurement analog to their use in DC measurement, following the logic of Fig. 2.2 in Sect. 2.1.2, as depicted in Fig. 2.5. If the subject's skin is used as input impedance Z_1, a constant peak-to-peak alternating voltage will flow through the skin. If, however, the subject's skin is used as feedback impedance Z_2, a constant alternating current will be applied to the skin. The two sinusoidal curves below the circuitry illustrate the phase shift between alternating current and voltage (see Fig. 1.9, Sect. 1.4.1.3).

For successive stimulation of the skin with varying alternating voltage frequencies (Sect. 1.4.1.4), it will be necessary to go through a certain frequency range of the input voltage $U(f)$, using a voltage-dependent oscillator's directing voltage, which is recorded and calculated as well. Particularly suitable here is a "lock-in amplifier," by means of which the single frequencies of a certain range are given in succession in very small bandwidths to the system under investigation, and the responses are selectively amplified. With the use of a single lock-in amplifier,

EDR courses can be recorded only if the measurement is repeated with all frequencies in question – several times during an EDR – which is hardly feasible with lower frequencies due to the attenuative behavior of the electrodermal system itself and the low-pass filter used (Sect. 1.4.1.4). Therefore, Morkrid and Qiao (1988, Fig. 2) used two lock-in amplifiers in parallel, together with a three-electrode arrangement, to measure skin admittance with two frequencies simultaneously.

Spectral analysis methods also allow continuous monitoring of the electrodermal system's responses to stimulation by several alternating voltage frequencies. Here, the direct voltage circuit shown in Fig. 2.2 can be used to illustrate the principle (Sect. 2.1.2), in which case, according to Faber (1980), the constant voltage method should be preferred because of its faster regulability. Instead of continuously flowing DC, a test signal composed from a base frequency and its harmonics (Sect. 1.4.1.4) is applied to the skin (i.e., a square wave signal or sequences of Dirac impulses).[3] Noise which is composed of all frequencies could also be used. The amplitude and phase angle can be determined for the entire spectrum from the output signal by means of Fourier analysis. This avoids problems with temporal requirements created by the lock-in technique, as the temporal resolution is only limited by the lowest frequency component used in the spectrum. In any case, a very high temporal resolution of the output signal is necessary with digitalization. Experience with such methods of EDA analysis is lacking.

Special technological problems that also exist for the recording of EDRs by means of AC are due to the highly selective amplification of the EDR, which is necessary because of the signal range (Sect. 2.1.4). In order to separate electrodermal level and response values, Wheatstone bridges can be used for single frequencies – either that given by Edelberg (1967, p. 33), which corresponds to the one shown in Fig. 2.3 (Sect. 2.1.3) with a variable capacitor connected in parallel with variable resistor R_3, or that given by Schwan (1963, p. 367), in which the resistors R_2 and R_4 are supplemented by capacitors connected in parallel. Once the bridge is trimmed by the proper setting of the variable resistors and capacitors, fluctuations of X and R can be displayed in high-resolution as deviations from the respective baselines.

When "backing-off" circuits are used to separate responses from baseline levels with AC measurements, the resistive and capacitive components of the signal must be actively suppressed (Sect. 2.2.3.3). A technical solution for a continuous adjustment of "backing-off" circuits during an EDR has not yet been developed.

A basic problem in the AC measurement of EDA appears during amplification through the filtering techniques usually used for noise reduction (Sect. 2.1.4). As the skin's response to applied alternating voltage or impulses can also fall in the noise range, a simple filtering of the EDA signal leads to a suppression of possibly relevant components of the output signal. Therefore, special care must be taken to

---

[3] Dirac impulses only exist in theory; in practice, a very narrow bandwidth square wave impulse with high amplitude is used. There may be danger of developing pain and erythema.

thoroughly avoid noise from foreign alternating voltage sources, such as hum produced by power lines (Sect. 2.2.5.1), while using as little filtering as possible.

The development of methods for recording phasic electrodermal phenomena by means of AC measurement is still in its beginning (Boucsein, Schaefer, & Neijenhuisen, 1989; Schaefer & Boucsein, 2000). In contrast, AC measurement of tonic EDA in some applied areas such as dermatology (Sect. 3.5.3) is well developed and realizable at little technical expense (Sect. 2.2.3.3).

2.1.6 Summary of Measurement Principles

EDA can be measured either without externally applied voltage (i.e., the endosomatic method) or with application of DC or AC (i.e., the exosomatic method). Exosomatic DC recording is by far the most commonly used method.

With the application of direct voltage, skin resistance measurements will result when current is kept constant, while skin conductance measurements will result when voltage is kept constant. Correspondingly, in the application of alternating voltage, if constant effective current is used, the result measured is the impedance, whereas the use of constant effective voltage will result in the admittance. Advantages and disadvantages of constant voltage and constant current methods are discussed together in Sect. 2.6.2.

Older principles of measurement based on the voltage divider (Sect. 2.1.1) have been mostly replaced by those based upon operational and differential amplifiers (Sect. 2.1.2), which not only guarantee genuinely constant voltage or current, but also enable minimization of measurement errors, owing to the avoidance of problems that otherwise stem from the internal resistance of the measurement device.

A problematic feature of EDA measurement, in deviation from other biosignals, is the relationship between the total width of the recording range and the usually small variation of the signal during an EDR. To cover the total range of the EDA signal, EDRs may be separated from the EDL by using a Wheatstone bridge, "backing-off" circuits, or AC-coupling (Sect. 2.1.3). Other specific measurement problems resulting from amplification, especially from the amplifier's signal-to-noise ratio, and from the danger of signal distortion through filtering, were discussed in Sect. 2.1.3.

In summary, if the factors mentioned in this section are considered, adequate and disturbance-free EDA measurement systems can be built with the measurement and amplification technology available today. New developments in the area of AC measurement (Sect. 2.1.5), especially for recording appropriate phasic fluctuations, need to be expanded further. Specifications for exosomatic EDA measurement with DC and AC are provided in Sect. 2.2.3.1.

2.2   Recording Techniques

Based on the principles of electrodermal measurement as described in Sect. 2.1, the following section gives detailed information on how to perform recordings of EDA. As far as possible, the methodology proposed by Venables and Christie (1980) and recommendations by a commission of the Society for Psychophysiological Research (Fowles et al., 1981), which are currently in the process of being updated (Boucsein, Fowles, Grimnes, Ben-Shakhar, Roth, Dawson, & Filion 2012), will be used. Although the use of constant voltage methodology for exosomatic EDA recording was generally preferred by the authors of the two decisive publications from the 1980s, not all researchers adhered to that particular recommendation, as can be inferred from Chap. 3 of the present book. This is not unjustified, since the general preference for CV can be questioned, because both the constant voltage and constant current methods have advantages and disadvantages (Sect. 2.6.2). Therefore, as far as exosomatic EDA measurement is concerned, the following section will include constant current recording as a standard methodology as well (Sect. 2.2.7).

2.2.1   Recording Sites

Although some special techniques use up to four electrodes (Sect. 2.2.6.4), electrodermal recording is usually performed with two electrodes. As a rule, exosomatic techniques use two active sites, while endosomatic recording requires an active and an inactive site. Several proposals have been made concerning the choice and a possible pretreatment of EDA recording sites. However, attempts for standardization have not yet been fully successful.

2.2.1.1   Choice of Sites

Most researchers make use of the palms or the volar surfaces of the fingers as active sites for electrodermal recording. The following reasons for this are given by Venables and Christie (1980):

1. Electrodes can be fixed easily, and those sites are not susceptible to disturbance by movement.
2. The size of available area is sufficient.
3. Those sites are relatively free from scarring.
4. Palmar sites show distinguished electrodermal activity (see Sect. 1.3.5).

Figure 2.6 depicts the preferred palmar recording areas for exosomatic and endosomatic EDA recording. Following Edelberg (1967), Venables and Christie (1980) recommended the medial phalanges of the index and middle fingers for bipolar recordings (sites A and B). These medial phalanges are less prone to

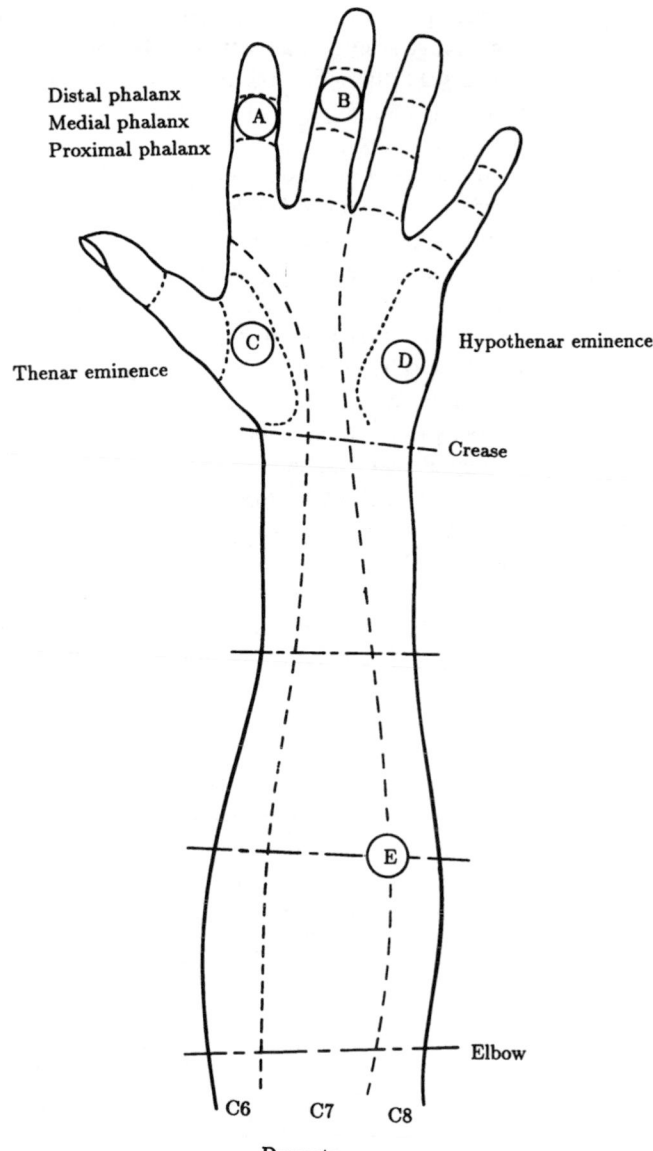

Distal phalanx
Medial phalanx
Proximal phalanx

Thenar eminence

Hypothenar eminence

Crease

Elbow

C6   C7   C8

Dermatomes

Fig. 2.6 Preferred palmar or volar electrode sites (*A–D*), recommended position for the inactive electrode (*E*) used in endosomatic recording, and their relationship to dermatomes C6–C8 (from Venables and Christie (1980), Fig. 1.7. Copyright © 1980 by Wiley. Reprinted by permission of the publisher and the first author)

scarring and to movement effects than the proximal ones, and the distal phalanges as well as the phalanges of other fingers provide smaller areas for electrode fixing. However, recordings from distal sites may have an advantage since Scerbo, Freedman, Raine, Dawson, and Venables (1992) found SCR amp. recorded from the distal phalanges of 12 participants of each gender being 3.5 times higher than those from medial phalanges, and SCLs being 2.08 times larger at distal compared to medial phalanges. Furthermore, the distal sites were more sensitive to habituation in a series of ten orienting- and probably defensive-responses eliciting stimuli (Sect. 3.1.1.2).

If both electrodes are fixed to recording sites belonging to the same dermatome (Table 1.3), which is the case for the index- and middle finger sites A and B as shown in Fig. 2.6, it might have the additional advantage of avoiding EDA asynchrony, which has been observed in some individuals by Christie and Venables (1972). However, the significance of possible differences between adjacent dermatomes remains questionable, given the yet unexplained organization of the sudomotor cell bodies in certain segments of the spinal cord (Sect. 1.3.2.1).

In case of difficulties to appear with fixing the electrodes to the fingers (e.g., if fingers are too slim or electrodes with a large surface are used; Sect. 2.2.2.1), bipolar recordings from thenar and hypothenar eminences (sites C and D) is a solution which became very common. According to Edelberg (1967), both the SCL and the SCRs are even slightly higher at these sites compared to appropriate signals from the fingers. The two electrodes can also be fixed on either the thenar or hypothenar eminence, as long as no direct electrical contact will be established between them by a possible outpouring of electrode cream. The center of the palm is not recommended because of the difficulty of fixing electrodes firmly and its proneness to movements as the hand flexes (Venables & Christie, 1980). Also, the nondominant hand should be preferred, since it tends to be less callous, the probability of the appearance of movement artifacts is lower (Sect. 2.2.5.2), and the dominant hand is free for writing or other motor activities. Electrode placements should be kept on the same hand to avoid ECG artifacts (Venables & Christie, 1973).[4]

Systematic investigations comparing the SCL on various body sites have revealed that the scalp possesses almost 4½ times as much conductance as the palmar sites of the fingers (Edelberg, 1967), presumably due to the numerous hair follicles.[5] However, comparisons of SRRs at corresponding sites (Rickles & Day, 1968) yielded that all nonpalmar sites, except the feet, display long periods of electrodermal inactivity, whereas at the same time spontaneous and evoked EDRs can be obtained from palmar sites. The special suitability of the palmar and plantar

---

[4] In a recently performed study for comparison of electrode creams for electrodermal recording, Tronstad, Johnsen, Grimnes, and Martinsen (2010; see also Sect. 2.2.2.5) applied constant voltage AC to contralateral palmar and abdominal sites. They observed an inverse EDR at abdominal sites which they interpreted as being due to an easier penetration of the hydrous components of the electrode gel into the sweat ducts, being facilitated by the thinner stratum corneum compared to palmar sites. They presumed that the mechanism of sweat reabsorption during recovery from sudomotor activity facilitates relatively moist and low-viscosity creams such as TD-246 (see Footnote 22 in Sect. 2.2.2.5) to penetrate into the ducts, thereby changing EDRs.

[5] A comparison of different recording sites with SZL applied had been performed by Grimnes (1983; see Sect. 2.5.3.1).

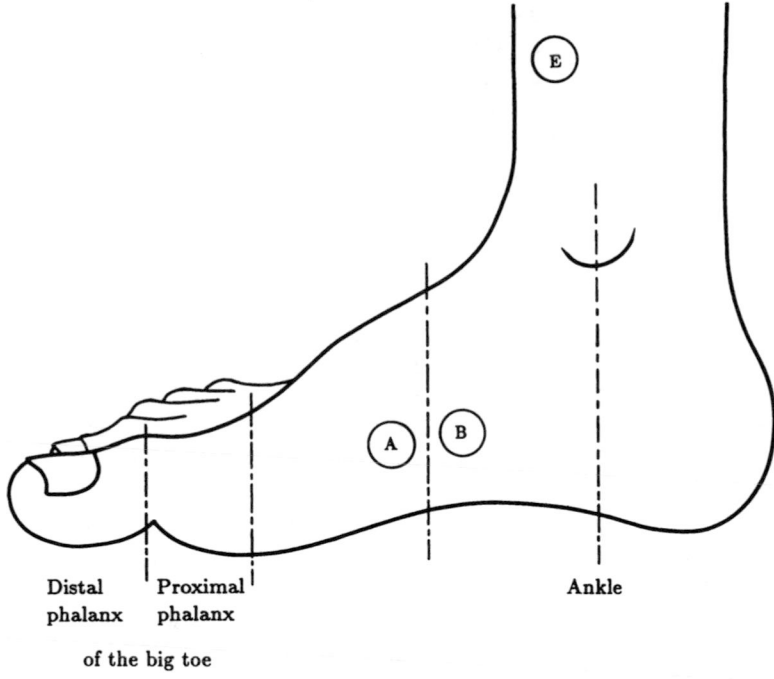

Distal   Proximal   Ankle
phalanx   phalanx

of the big toe

Fig. 2.7 Medial side of the right foot with the recommended recording sites *A* and *B* for exosomatic recording, and position *E* of the inactive electrode for endosomatic recording

skin surfaces for EDA recording is probably due to the different innervation of the respective sweat glands and their role in "emotional" sweating (Sect. 1.3.2.4).[6]

Therefore, in the case where both hands are needed for manipulation during EDA recording, the next best recording sites would be the plantar ones (i.e., the soles of the feet). As the soles are normally subjected to pressure during standing or walking, Edelberg (1967) recommended a medial site on the inner side of the foot instead, over the abductor hallucis muscle (the extensor of the big toe's base joint) adjacent to the foot sole, and midway between the proximal phalanx of the big toe and a point directly beneath the ankle (A and B in Fig. 2.7).

According to Edelberg (1967), these sites display the highest SCRs in the foot area, and almost as high an SCL as the plantar surface. Rickles and Day (1968) also

---

[6] Toyokura (1999) recorded SPRs following electric stimulation of the left median nerve at the wrist from 41 participants (9 females, 32 males; aged 22–60 years) from palmar and plantar sites in parallel, using reference electrodes on the nail of the index finger and the big toe. In general, SPRs at the soles had longer latencies and smaller amplitudes than those at the palms. These differences were larger than those between left- and right-recording sites. Furthermore, SPR waveforms (Sect. 2.3.1.2 "Amplitudes of Endosomatic Responses") yielded not always congruent patterns on the palms and soles. However, these regional differences were not always reproducible.

found that evoked SRRs recorded from below the ankle joint appeared in parallel to those taken from plantar sites. The sites shown in Fig. 2.7 have further advantages over the soles of the feet, since the socks may not need to be removed for fixing the electrodes but only pulled down, and that recordings can be performed during both resting and movement (e.g., in field studies, see Boucsein & Thum, 1997; Sect. 3.5.1.1). In any case, artifacts from muscle tension beneath and mechanical pressure on the electrode should be avoided if possible (Sect. 2.2.5.2).

The inactive electrode being necessary for endosomatic recording (Sect. 2.2.3.1) should be placed on a site that has the smallest potential difference between the skin surface and the body core and being essentially inactive in terms of SPRs. According to Edelberg (1967), the inner aspect of the ear lobe is the most inactive reference site, but its use may introduce ECG artifacts when recording SP from the hands or the feet (Sect. 2.2.5.2). In addition, when physiological variables other than skin potentials are to be recorded, the subject is usually grounded (i.e., connected to the floating reference wire; see Sect. 2.1.4) on one site only, in which case the ground electrode should be placed as near as possible to the recording site for the biosignal showing the lowest voltage. Therefore, one has no choice but to place the ground electrode on the head when, for example, both EEG and SP are being measured. In this case, an amplifier uncoupled from the floating reference wire is necessary for the SP measurement (Venables & Christie, 1980) otherwise scattering from ECG would appear in the SP recordings (Sect. 2.1.4).

For palmar SP recordings, Venables and Christie (1980) recommended fixing the inactive electrode to a slightly abraded site (Sect. 2.2.1.2) on the volar surface of the forearm (site E in Fig. 2.6), about two thirds of the distance from the wrist to the elbow. This site is even more likely to be electrically inactive than the site recommended by Edelberg (1967) on the ulnar bone about 4 cm underneath the elbow. In case of SP recordings from the feet, Edelberg suggested an inactive site about 3 cm above the ankle (site E in Fig. 2.7), which should be prepared in the same way as the forearm site.

More recently, nonstandard electrode sites came into use, especially for avoiding obtrusiveness of electrodermal recording during ambulatory monitoring (Sect. 2.2.3.4). For example, Westerink et al. (2009) constructed a wristband for SC-recording to be worn like a wristwatch, using a Bluetooth-like wireless communication with a digital recorder at some distant place of the body. Two metal skin contacts (10.5 mm in diameter) were placed side by side (3 mm apart) for contacting the volar surface of the wrist, since it does not contain hairs.[7] The device has been worn by 16 participants of each gender for 4 h at work and 4 h during

---

[7] No further specifications were provided for SC-recording in the paper. The electrodes were made from nickel plated brass and a stable 1.2 V reference was applied to the skin (Ouwerkerk, May 2011, personal communication). The device is also capable of storing data on onboard flash memory in off-line mode (de Vries, May 2011, personal communication). The data were sampled at 2 Hz, but actually, low-pass filtering was attained by taking eight samples in a row at 16 Hz which were then averaged (moving average). SCL and SCRs were evaluated, the latter by using the SCRGAUGE parameterization program from Kohlisch, published in the Appendix of Boucsein (1992). Because of the low quality of the SC signal, additional filtering was necessary.

leisure time. Compared to other recording utilities, the wristband seemed to be accepted by the participants as rather "natural."[8]

A different type of wristband recording device was applied by Poh, Swenson, and Picard (2010), who compared EDA recordings from the volar side of the distal forearm with those taken from standard sites at the palmar areas of the medial phalanges (A and B in Fig. 2.6). For recordings from the forearm site, dry Ag/AgCl or conductive stretch fabric electrodes[9] were sewn into a wristband. Mean correlations between standard and forearm sites from 26 participants were in the range of $r = 0.57$ to 0.96 for a baseline and various stimulation conditions, which is only partly satisfying. It should be further kept in mind that electrode positions at the volar surface of the forearm may not yield the same reactivity as palmar or plantar sites (Edelberg, 1967).

2.2.1.2 Pretreatment of Sites

Various recommendations have been made concerning pretreatment of the active electrodermal recording sites. Both the degree of hydration and the electrolyte concentration on the skin surface undoubtedly influence EDA. If the electrode cream is allowed to penetrate the skin for a certain time following the fixation of the electrodes (see end of Sect. 2.2.2.5), effects such as the decrease of NaCl concentration following washing with soap – as recommended for standardization by Venables and Christie (1980) – are neutralized. However, washing with soap may also cause a swelling of the epidermis and thereby lowering of the SCL. Walschburger (1976) recommended washing with lukewarm water without soap and a final cleaning with a 70% solution of ethanol. According to the present author's experience, there is normally no need for a pretreatment of sites used for exosomatic recording. In cases of extremely oily skin, cleaning of skin surface with alcohol may be advisable in order to enable fixation of the adhesive tape to keep the electrodes in position (Sect. 2.2.2.1).

By contrast, the site used for the inactive electrode in endosomatic recording must be pretreated. The stratum corneum has to be removed to diminish the potential difference between the site and the body core underneath the electrode. This can be done by light rubbing with fine sandpaper until a small, shiny pit can be seen on the skin by transverse illumination (Venables & Christie, 1980), which ensures that the stratum lucidum has been reached (Sect. 1.2.1.1).

Abrasion should never be carried to the point where the skin is injured, because a wound may create a potential of its own (Venables & Christie, 1980). Therefore, great caution has to be exerted and some training is required, during which the experimenter might practice abrasion on her/his own forearm skin first. Even with great precaution, pain can result from contact of the electrode cream with the pretreated site, and following removal of the electrode an erythema and/or light

---

[8] At present, the use of such non-standard electrode sites cannot be recommended, since thorough comparisons of their electrodermal reactivity with the one of standard sites are still missing.

[9] Silver plated 92%, nylon 8%, surface resistance $<1\Omega$/sq and contact area of 3.5 cm^2.

swelling may appear. Therefore, an experimenter should always weigh a reduction of pretreatment, which bears the potential risk of reduced SPLs and SPR amp. against possible unpleasantness from abrasion for the study participant.[10]

Some authors used a dentist's drill to remove the stratum corneum (e.g., Shackel, 1959). Pasquali and Roveri (1971) described a method (later automated by Zipp, 1983) by which the decrease of SRL can be measured during skin drilling, thereby avoiding too deep abrasion. Instead of the surface excision, Burbank and Webster (1978) used a micropuncture technique for lowering the resistance of the stratum corneum. Given the danger of transmitting diseases such as HIV or hepatitis, abrasion, is no longer recommended.

2.2.2 Electrodes and Electrolytes

In comparison with localization and pretreatment of recording sites, a more extensive standardization has been implemented in EDA recording with respect to the choice of electrodes and electrolytes. Problems with the described arrangements can, however, arise with recordings over longer periods than a couple of hours. Possible solutions are described in detail in Sect. 2.2.6.1. Electrodes and electrolytes for special purposes are described in Sects. 2.2.6.3 and 2.2.6.4.

2.2.2.1 Forms of Electrodes and Their Attachment

The EDA electrodes predominantly used today are disc electrodes having the electrode surface on the bottom of a cylindrical plastic chamber. The space between the electrode surface and the bottom of the ring is filled with the electrode cream containing the electrolyte (Sect. 2.2.2.5). Figure 2.8 depicts such an electrode in cross-section. It consists of a round silver plate about 6 mm in diameter, on which a sintered silver/silver chloride (Ag/AgCl) layer has been deposited (Sect. 2.2.2.3).

The electrodes are usually attached to the skin with appropriately sized double-sided adhesive collars. One adhesive surface of the collar is fitted to the electrode rim. Thereafter, the chamber is held upside down[11] and filled with electrode cream, at which air bubbles should be avoided if possible. Finally, the surplus cream is removed with a spatula or the rim of a paper, while the protective cover still remains in place on the outer side of the adhesive collar. This cover is then removed and the electrode fixed on the skin, thus providing a precisely defined area of contact

---

[10] According to Venables and Christie (1980), no differences of skin potentials between abraded and non-abraded forearm sites were observable with children, so when children are used as participants, pretreatment will not be necessary.

[11] For an improved handling, the overlaying rim of the adhesive collar can be attached horizontally to the rim of a table, to allow the experimenter using both hands for the electrode cream insertion.

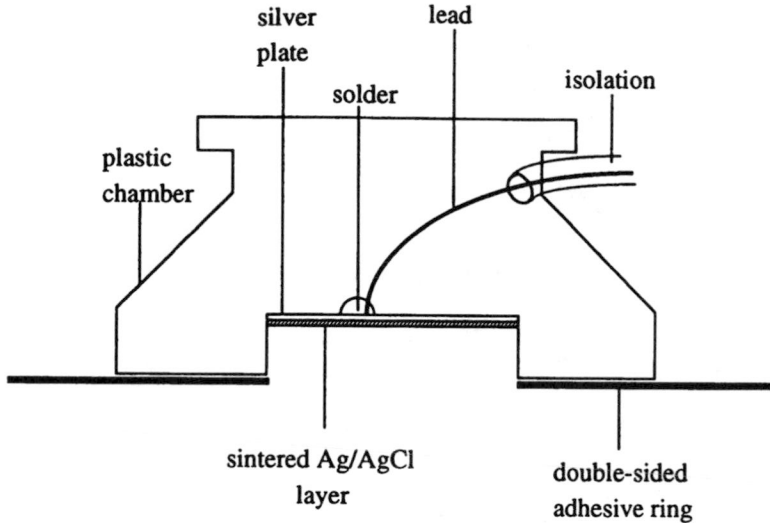

silver
plate

lead

solder

isolation

plastic
chamber

sintered Ag/AgCl
layer

double-sided
adhesive ring

Fig. 2.8 Cross-section of an Ag/AgCl electrode. The electrode surface consists of a silver plate which is covered by a sintered Ag/AgCl layer. It is soldered to an insulated lead and enclosed by a cylindrical plastic chamber which is attached to the skin with a double-sided adhesive collar

between the skin and the electrolyte. This is in particular necessary if the constant current recording method is used (Sect. 2.2.3.2). However, a precise contact area will be lost if electrode cream gets between the adhesive collar and the skin,[12] which can easily happen, especially when electrodes are attached to the fingers (Sect. 2.2.1.1).

An alternative method of electrode attachment was proposed by Venables and Christie (1980): fixing an adhesive collar on the skin first, thereafter fastening the electrode, which was previously filled with an electrode cream, to the other side of the adhesive collar. Some preliminary practice is indicated for using this method, since the electrode rim must not come into contact with the cream, as this can lead to detachment of the electrode.[13] Avoiding any contact of the electrode rim with the cream may be attained through the sacrifice of a second adhesive collar. The electrode is prepared with an adhesive collar as described above, the latter being removed along with any surplus cream. Then, the filled electrode is fastened to the second adhesive collar which was already fixed on the skin.

---

[12] The relative error due to seepage is dependent on electrode diameter. One millimeter of seepage increases the contact area to 2.25 times of its original size with 4 mm diameter miniature electrodes, but to only 1.13 times in case of 1 cm diameter electrodes are used (Venables & Christie, 1980).

[13] Furthermore, to the present author's experience, removing the second cover from the adhesive collar which is already fixed on the skin exerts some tension on the collar, which may lead to its detachment from the skin.

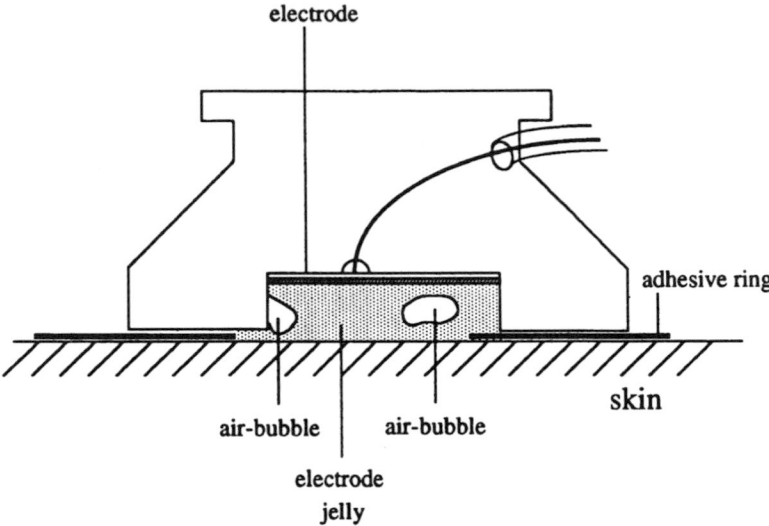

Fig. 2.9 The effects of displacement of the electrode chamber on the adhesive collar attached to the skin, and of air bubbles in the electrode cream (see text for explanations)

When this method is applied, it may happen that the surface area of the cream-filled electrode chamber does not exactly match the aperture in the adhesive collar. However, if the skin/electrolyte contact surface and the electrolyte/electrode contact surface will remain constant, as shown in Fig. 2.9, no corruption of measurement results has to be expected. The same holds for smaller air bubbles, which can result from incompletely filled electrode chambers, since the conductance of the electrode cream in the remaining cream bridges is so high that a somewhat reduced cross-sectional area in comparison to the total area does not matter (Fig. 2.9).

An electrode fixed by means of an adhesive collar may detach quickly in case of a strongly sweating individual. One possible solution for preventing this may be an additional wrapping of the fingers and electrodes with adhesive tape, which had been recommended, for example, by Venables and Christie (1980), in case of hand movement being expected. However, such a wrapping contains the danger of mechanical pressure being exerted on the skin. Edelberg (1967) pointed out that changes in pressure may act as local stimuli producing Ebbecke waves, which must be regarded as artifacts (Sects. 1.4.2.3 and 2.2.5.2). In addition, pressure on the electrode might elicit variations in local blood circulation, thereby causing reductions of EDR amp., especially of the positive component of the SPR. Therefore, the pressure which the electrode may exert on the skin should be held as small as possible. Alternatively, the electrodes can be attached with histoacryl glue and later removed with acetone.[14]

---

[14] Histoacryl glue must be refrigerated. Experimenters must be also seriously cautioned, since careless use of histoacryl can result in eye damage. Also, acetone (which is also a cancer-causing suspect) might attack the rim of the electrode's plastic chamber, thus roughen it and eventually damage its surface which is needed for the adherence to the collar.

If this method is used, an adhesive collar should be attached to the electrode first, then the electrode be filled with cream and the overflow removed together with the ring, after which the electrode is fixed onto the skin using the histoacryl glue. An alternative technique is to fix the empty electrode to the skin with the glue first, then to fill the electrode with cream using a syringe. To apply this technique, two holes must be drilled through the electrode's plastic chamber on opposite sides, roughly 1–1.5 mm in diameter; one for the syringe and the other for the air to escape. The syringe must be completely filled with cream to completely rid the chamber of air (Andresen, 1987). In case of long-term recordings (Sect. 2.2.6.1) collodium has also been successfully used for electrode attachment (Turpin, Shine, & Lader, 1983).

A much easier-to-handle method for increasing the durability of electrode attachment has been used by Boucsein and Thum (1996, 1997) in their ambulatory monitoring study (Sects. 2.2.3.4 and 3.5.1.1). First, the recording sites are cleaned by alcohol to improve adhesiveness and marked with a felt-tip pen by using the protection ring of an adhesive collar as a mask. A skin-friendly glue (Mastic adhesive[15]) as used by actors is put on the skin area which surrounds the electrode site, avoiding contaminating the electrode site itself, and given the opportunity to dry for 5–10 min until the glue becomes thread-like by touch. Thereafter, the adhesive collar of the electrode is fixed on the prepared site. This technique can be improved by using an additional but larger double-sided adhesive collar (40 mm inside and 50 mm outside diameter). The protection ring is removed from one side and the adhesive area is coated with Mastic adhesive. After the time period which allows the glue to become dry to the touch, the big collar is attached to the previously marked skin sites, and the protection ring on its other side is removed. The smaller collar is attached to the electrode, which is then filled with cream and the protection of the attached collar is removed. Finally, the adhesive collar attached to the electrode is centered on the adhesive side of the big collar already sitting on the skin site. Afterwards, the collars can be supplementally fixed laterally from the electrode with a skin-friendly adhesive tape. This technique has also been successfully used in a study performed by Koglbauer, Kallus, Braunstingl, and Boucsein (2011) in pilots during aerobatic maneuvers (Sect. 3.5.1.2). Recently, disposable EDA electrodes came into use as well (see Footnote 21, Sect. 2.2.2.5).

In order to avoid strain on the electrode, the electrode wire should be fixed to the skin at a distance of 2–3 cm from the electrode, using a strip of adhesive tape. During the whole recording, full contact of the electrode to the skin including a constant contact area between the skin and the electrolyte must be ensured. The hand with the electrodes should be placed in a lightly bent, resting position, with the palm either up or down. In the latter case, one may use a soft, thermally conductive underlay on which palm may rest (Walschburger, 1975).

---

[15] Mastic adhesive is made from the Mastic pistachio tree. The German name is Mastix.

2.2.2.2 Bias Potentials and Polarization of Electrodes

Edelberg (1967) and Fowles et al. (1981) pointed out the following requirements for EDA electrodes:

1. They should show a minimum bias potential (between pairs of electrodes).
2. They should display as little tendency as possible toward polarization upon the passage of current, even when large current densities are applied.

Bias potentials are defined as potential differences existing between two electrodes immersed in the same electrolyte without application of any voltage. The development of a bias potential is often incorrectly labeled "polarization" (Edelberg, 1967, p. 6). The bias potential can be measured by joining two electrodes filled with electrode cream together in full surface contact. For endosomatic EDA measurement, the bias potential should be smaller than 1 mV (Venables & Christie, 1980; Fowles et al., 1981). As a rule, electrodes with smaller bias potentials also display a smaller drift over a period of time (Sect. 2.3.4.3). Fowles et al. recommended checking the bias potentials every 2 or 3 days, for which an amplifier system is required that can reliably perform measurements between 100 µV and 10 mV.

Bias potentials influence both exosomatic and endosomatic EDA recordings, although they play a significantly greater role in the latter, in which they can easily amount to an error of 100% in SPL readings (Edelberg, 1967). Electrodes which are used for endosomatic recording should be checked every 3 days; they should be replaced if displaying bias potential of more than 3 mV (Fowles et al., 1981). For exosomatic recordings, bias potentials between 3 and 5 mV can be tolerated.

Polarization refers to the development of a counter electromotive force (or back e.m.f., the direction of which is opposed to the applied voltage; see Sect. 1.4.2) in biological membranes and at the interface between the electrode and electrolyte, if an external voltage is applied (Fowles et al., 1981). It is a result of either energy barriers on the electrode surface created by oxidation-reduction interaction or of ion transport over these borders being limited by the ion-diffusion rate (Venables & Christie, 1980). Polarization voltages influence exosomatic measurements by counteracting the applied voltage. According to the results from Barry's (1981) investigation, polarizable electrodes hardly influence the SRR, but a possible influence on the SRL cannot be ruled out.

Polarization effects can be checked both in vitro and in vivo. An in vitro method of measuring polarizability of electrodes has been described by Edelberg (1967) as follows: two electrodes, each with a surface area of 1 cm^2, are placed 1 cm apart in a 0.1 N NaCl solution[16] whose specific resistance is around 100 Ω/cm. The voltage appearing between both electrodes should be 1 mV at most, since higher potential differences are due to polarization effects. Fowles et al. (1981) recommended a

---

[16] This corresponds to a 0.1 M solution of the monovalent NaCl (i.e., 0.58 g NaCl dissolved in 100 mL water).

method which can be used in vivo during EDA recording with DC: the polarity of the electrodes is reversed, and the time necessary to reach the original SCL or SRL is noted. After some practice, the shape of the corresponding transients can be judged as being either due to polarization of the electrodes or due to normal polarization of skin membranes. However, quantifiable results are hardly obtainable with this method.

A systematic reversal of polarity during recording may additionally ensure a better comparability of the electrodes over long times, since in case of DC being used together with Cl containing electrolytes, one electrode will become chlorinated and the other one dechlorinated during EDA recording. Though there is some probability that simply the effect of random placement of the electrodes during repeated use will prevent systematic polarization effects, reversing their polarity will be a safe measure. As already pointed to by Montagu (1973), electrode polarization effects are negligible in case of AC recording (Sect. 2.1.5).

2.2.2.3 Choice or Assembling of Electrodes

Today sintered silver/silver chloride (Ag/AgCl) electrodes are practically the only standard EDA electrodes in use. These are so-called *reversible electrodes* which are made from a metal in contact with a solution of its own ions (Fowles et al., 1981). Such electrodes display the smallest possible bias potentials and are nonpolarizable to a high degree (Sect. 2.2.2.2).[17] According to Edelberg (1967), as compared to the zinc/zinc chloride and zinc/zinc sulfate electrodes, Ag/AgCl electrodes require only a NaCl electrolyte solution that is tolerable to the skin (Sect. 2.2.2.5). Fowles et al. (1981, footnote 3) reported that zinc/zinc sulfate electrodes are also "nonpolarizable". They are simple to construct but are not commercially available. However, because of problems with the exact composition for an adequate electrode cream as well as with their maintenance, these electrodes were not recommended by Fowles et al.

The contact surface area of the electrolyte with the skin should be 1 cm^2 according to Fowles et al. (1981), as long as the recording site permits this, because with smaller areas proportional error increases with possible seepage of the electrode cream (see Footnote 12, Sect. 2.2.2.1), and problems of linearity may appear

---

[17] The Beckman biopotential electrodes (see Footnote 18) show bias potentials of less than 250 μV and polarization potentials of less than 5 μV (Venables & Christie, 1980). Ag/AgCl electrodes can also be homemade, albeit unsintered (cf. Venables & Christie, 1973, p. 107), and good results are obtainable, but the manufacturing process is rather expensive, since pure silver (99.99%) would be necessary. Therefore, buying commercially available Ag/AgCl electrodes should be preferred. It should be noted that even with the use of so-called nonpolarizable electrodes there is still the possibility of counter e.m.f generation at the electrodes (Sect. 2.2.2.2).

with the use of the constant current method (Sect. 2.6.2). However, the commercially available standard electrodes[18] have a surface area being only around 0.6 cm^2.

The effect of variation in contact surface area has been a matter of discussion. Mitchell and Venables (1980) provided evidence from their systematic investigations of the relationship between electrode contact areas of 0.017–0.786 cm^2 and SCL as well as SCR amp. They found that the electrode/skin contact area had a minimal effect, at least within the range tested by them. The authors recommended that for finger recording the electrode area should be around 0.8 cm in diameter (approximately 0.503 cm^2), but they stated that the influence of the area size upon measurement results is so small that electrodes of other sizes could also be used (Sect. 2.2.3.2). However, results reported by Mahon and Iacono (1987) indicated a marked linear dependence of the SCL and the SCR amp. upon the skin/electrolyte contact area (Sect. 2.3.3.1), so that a standardization of the electrode area appears desirable. In the case of endosomatic EDA recording, the electrode size plays a subordinate role (Sect. 2.2.3.1).

2.2.2.4   Cleaning, Maintenance, and Storage of Electrodes

Electrodes have to be cleaned very carefully to prevent damage of the Ag/AgCl layer. EDA electrodes should *not* be *mechanically* cleaned or dried under any circumstances. The electrodes must be thoroughly rinsed under flowing water immediately after their use, for which a water-pik can be helpful. In order to avoid calcium deposits from tap water, electrodes should be subsequently rinsed with distilled water. Air drying should follow, for which a fan might be used.

If electrodes are not continuously used, they should be *stored* in dry conditions. Venables and Christie (1980) recommended that prior to EDA recording, electrodes should be short-circuited and soaked for at least 24 h in a solution of electrolyte of the type and concentration which is used in the electrode cream, allowing local responses to take place before the beginning of recording. Tassinary, Geen, Cacioppo, and Edelberg (1990) compared different storage conditions for several types of Ag/AgCl electrodes. They recommended storing sintered metallic Ag/AgCl electrodes non-short-circuited in a 0.9% NaCl solution, which they found being superior to having their wires short-circuited via a carbon rod or non-short-circuited dry storage.[19]

Despite the greatest care, a black deposit of AgCl may appear on top of the gray Ag/AgCl layer after some time, which is a result of chlorinization (Sect. 2.2.2.2).

---

[18] The standard biopotential electrodes from Beckman Instruments have a contact area of 0.636 cm^2. In Vivo-Metric-Systems electrodes, which are also sold alternatively together with a plug connection between the electrode and its wire, are of approximately the same size.

[19] As to the present author's experience, relatively long fluid storage may enable the saline penetrating into the plastic electrode chamber, which could result in corrosion of the contact between electrode and lead.

As long as bias potentials and polarizational tendencies do not increase too much, the functioning of the electrode will remain unimpaired. Under no circumstances should mechanical removal of deposits be attempted.[20] If a layer of bright silver appears, the electrode can be re-chlorinated (Sect. 2.2.2.3), but then the electrode coverage is no longer completely composed of a sintered Ag/AgCl layer.

2.2.2.5 Electrolytes and Electrolyte Media

In general, hypertonic electrode gels as used for other biosignals such as the ECG, the EEG, and the EMG are not suitable for EDA recording. Hypertonic gels have a higher conductivity than the epidermis, which is instrumental in some other biosignals to transmit potentials created in the body core underneath the skin to the electrodes with minimal loss of voltage.

In contrast, during EDA recording the electrolyte-skin system should be disturbed as little as possible, since an interaction between skin and electrolytes can have a marked effect on variations in EDA. Barry (1981, footnote 1) showed that additional lowering of the skin resistance with hypertonic electrode cream invalidated the transformation of resistance into conductance units (Sect. 2.3.3.2). Edelberg, Greiner, and Burch (1960) also found that many gels contain multivalent ions such as calcium, zinc, and aluminum which may potentiate the skin conductance and lower the skin potential. Since both NaCl and KCl appear as salts with monovalent ions in the stratum corneum (Sect. 1.3.4.2 "The Role of the Epidermal Barrier Layer"), these two are suitable to use for electrolytes in EDA measurement. Since NaCl ions are preponderant in sweat, the use of a NaCl-based electrolyte can be expected to disturb the electrodermal system least.

As the NaCl concentration in sweat varies between 0.015 and 0.06 M dependent upon the amount of sweating (Sect. 1.3.3.1), it is not possible to determine precisely the optimal electrolytic concentration in the electrode cream. Fowles et al. (1981) were convinced that if the NaCl concentration of the electrolyte is between 0.05 and 0.075 M it is unlikely that NaCl will transfer out of the sweat into the cream, and thereby alter the electrolytic concentration significantly. Edelberg (1967) recommended a 0.05 M concentration, which can be made by dissolving 0.29 g of pure NaCl in 100 mL of distilled water. Hygge and Hugdahl (1985) found no difference in size among SCRs with four electrode creams differing in NaCl concentration, showing that small deviations from the recommended NaCl concentration can be tolerated.[21]

---

[20] Sensor Medics recommended removing the deposit with dilute ammonium hydroxide. A five-to-one dilution with distilled water has been used with success (Vincent, July 1990, personal communication).

[21] Recently, disposable EDA snap electrodes came into use, being distributed by BIOPAC Systems Inc. (http://www.biopac.com) and in Germany by med-NATIC (http://www.med-natic.de). These are Ag/AgCl electrodes of 2.5 × 4.5 cm size, filled with a 0.5% NaCl cream, with a foam backing and a stainless steel snap for electrode wires.

Some authors use the monovalent KCl instead of NaCl (cf. Fowles & Schneider, 1978). Venables and Christie (1980) recommended, on the basis of their own laboratory experiments, 0.05 M NaCl creams for exosomatic and 0.067 M KCl creams for endosomatic EDA measurements. Schneider and Fowles (1978) suggested KCl as electrolyte for SP measurement (see the end of this section). Fowles et al. (1981) pointed out that KCl, above all, should be used for SPL measurement so that results published in the literature are comparable, especially with those from the Venables group, while NaCl is adequate for SPR measurement. Since the contents of commercially available gels – including the so-called isotonic ones – are not provided by the manufacturers,[22] investigators have the choice of either trusting them or produce their own electrode cream.

As a base for the electrolytes, a number of hydrophilic and widely ion-free electrolyte media are suitable (Edelberg, 1967), for example, agar (a type of gelatine made from algae), starch, or methylcellulose (the base of wallpaper glue but also used in food).[23] However, these media may cause problems, since their manufacture and storage require a controlled temperature. Furthermore, when agar is used, the SCL and SCR decrease with time, which is probably due to hydration of the corneum following blocking of the sweat gland ducts by the agar (Fowles & Schneider, 1974). Those types of electrode creams are also very susceptible to bacterial degradation. Glycol, used by Edelberg, escapes from under the adhesive tape with which the electrode is fixed (Venables & Christie, 1980) and thereby builds up conductive bridges on the skin.

During the 1980s, Unibase became the standard electrolyte medium for EDA. Unibase is an ethylene polymer which requires an emulgator due to its hydrophobic properties. This white, smooth ointment base can take up to 30% of its own weight in water. In their committee report, Fowles et al. (1981) advised that for manufacturing an EDA cream, 1 lb (i.e., 453.6 g) of Unibase should be mixed with 230 mL of physiological NaCl solution. Such a 0.15 M, or 0.9% of NaCl solution, which can be bought commercially, can also be produced by immersing 2.0 g of chemically pure NaCl in 230 mL of distilled water. To remove lumps, Unibase and NaCl solution have to be well mixed using an electric mixer and allowed to stand

---

[22] This is also true of the electrode cream "Synapse" made by Beckman Instruments which has been frequently used in EDA measurements. An analysis of this and other gels was made by Zipp, Hennemann, Grunwald, and Rohmert (1980), who found in "Synapse" a significant quantity of K and Cl ions in addition to Na ions. Grey and Smith (1984) reported that the Beckman cream has a NaCl concentration of 4.1 M, and contains glycerol, gum tragacanth, and 0.5% benzyl alcohol (as preservative). Beckman does no longer offer "Synapse," and Unibase is also no longer available. The TD-246 electrode paste, which contains 0.5% saline in a neutral base, can be bought from Discount Disposables: http://www.discountdisposables.com/. According to the manufacturer, this cream "meets all the recommended specifications." The cream is also distributed by Grass Technologies under the brand name EC33: http://www.grasstechnologies.com/ and as TD-246 in Germany by PAR Medizintechnik (http://www.PAR-Berlin.com).

[23] Grey and Smith (1984) used a custom-made cream of 0.05 M NaCl solution in methylcellulose. However, they did not provide the correct formula of the ingredients they used (Clements, 1989).

for 24 h. The resulting electrode cream has an approximately 0.05 M NaCl concentration.[24] The cream should be kept cool (in the refrigerator), otherwise it degrades and can leak from the tube.

Tronstad et al. (2010) compared four types of electrodes, all with similar Ag/AgCl parts but with different composition of the creams. Skin admittance was recorded with a special three-electrode arrangement (Sect. 2.2.6.4) in 18 participants (4 females, 14 males) during resting, a startling noise (breaking glass; 82 dB) and thermal sweating (induced by performing squats for 2 min). The creams induced large SYL changes over time, dependent on the water content and viscosity of the electrolyte media. Solid creams yielded a better recovery of the SYL to the baseline 15 min after thermal sweating than the more moist creams including the TD-246 (see Footnote 22, Sect. 2.2.2.5), which the authors tried to explain by a possible penetration of the latter into the sweat gland ducts. Furthermore, SYL and SCL values were more affected by the differences in electrolyte media than the NS.EDR freq. (Sect. 2.3.2.2).

Despite all efforts to match electrolytes to the skin electrolyte concentration and control of other factors such as the cream's consistency, the electrolytes can still affect the skin over time. Therefore, the time lag between electrode placement and recording should be considered as a possible source of error in EDA measurement. Since destabilizing effects such as drift can be expected at the initial phase of recording, the electrodes should be placed at least 10 min, preferably 15–20 min before the beginning of recording, so that the skin-electrolyte interface can stabilize. According to results from Campbell, Kraning, Schibli, and Momii (1977), who used microelectrode recording in vitro (Sect. 2.2.6.4), the water concentration of the stratum corneum had matched that of the electrolytes and had stabilized after approximately 16 min.

Problems that arise with long-term recordings, where the electrodes stay attached to the skin for several hours, are discussed in Sect. 2.2.6.1. Here, it appears that electrode creams based on polyethylene glycol have an advantage over the standard ointment-based creams, due to their lesser propensity to hydrate the epidermis. Schneider and Fowles (1978) recommended a mixture of 100 mL polyethylene glycol and 100 g Unibase, to which 0.76 g KCl are added for SP measurements.

---

[24] Grey and Smith (1984) have published the following as being the ingredients of Unibase: cetyl and stearyl alcohols, soft paraffin, glycerol, and, as preservatives; 0.0015% propyl hydroxybenzoate, sodium citrate, and sodium lauryl sulfate. The relative quantities are not provided. The water content is 63.4%. According to Grey and Smith, Unibase contains 0.028 mol/L Na ions. Back in the 1980s, the present author had this recipe chemically analyzed; the results were 0.07 mol/L Na and 0.045 mol/L Cl, the increased sodium being due to the Unibase itself (see Footnote 23). The cream is free from K and Ca ions (less than 0.01 g/kg) and has a nearly neutral pH value of 6.5. The analysis was performed by B. Neidhart, Institute for Industrial Physiology at the University of Dortmund, Germany.

2.2.3   Recording Devices

The following three sections provide details for the methodology used in EDA recording with the three different methods outlined in Sect. 1.4: Endosomatic recording (Sect. 2.2.3.1), exosomatic recording with DC (Sect. 2.2.3.2), and exosomatic recording with AC (Sect. 2.2.3.3). Since the reader probably already has access to equipment for EDA recording, the following sections will give examples of appropriate devices, the features of which may be compared with the equipment being available in the reader's laboratory.

2.2.3.1   Endosomatic Recording

In contrast to the exosomatic recording techniques, endosomatic EDA recording does not require an external voltage applied to the skin, since only potential differences are recorded. However, it is recommended that one active and one inactive site should be used, as previously mentioned in Sect. 2.2.1.1. With the use of two active sites, SPL will be rather low and SPRs will look similar at both sites; that is, there will be no marked shift in potential differences between them. The appropriate inactive sites for SP recordings taken from the palms of the hands and from the feet are marked by E in Figs. 2.6 and 2.7. Although these sites are already relatively inactive, interindividual and intraindividual comparability of SP recordings is only given if the corneum is extensively abraded (Edelberg, 1967). However, skin-drilling methods for preparing an inactive site, which would be able to reduce skin resistance from about 1 MΩ to as low as 100 kΩ (Venables & Christie, 1980), are no longer recommended nowadays (Sect. 2.2.1.2).

Endosomatic recording of EDA requires an amplifier with at minimum 1 MΩ input impedance; however, Venables and Sayer (1963) recommended 5 MΩ. The necessity for a high-impedance amplifier can be shown using the left-hand side of Fig. 1.7 (Sect. 1.4.1.2). If the skin is regarded as a voltage source with its internal resistance R_2, and if R_1 is regarded as the amplifier's input impedance over which the voltage changes being produced by the skin are read off, R_1 and R_2 form a voltage divider (Sect. 2.1.1). Hence, R_1 should be as large as possible compared to R_2, to ensure that the greatest proportion of the measured voltage descends over R_1, thus enabling it to be available for recording and amplifying. Today, recording equipment with very high-input impedances is the rule, so there is no need to provide a specific circuitry diagram for an SP amplifier.[25]

However, several problems may arise while using standard amplifier techniques for SP recording. First, there may be no way to lower the amplifier gain enough for SPL recording, which may require a range down to 500 mV/division. Thus, the

---

[25] Skin potential can be recorded with any EEG or EMG channel, which is a standard technique in neurology (Sect. 3.5.4).

possibility of attenuating the amplification should be taken into consideration. Second, based on the reasons given in Sect. 2.2.1.1, an SP amplifier should be used, the floating reference wire ("ground") of which is separated from the one of amplifiers recording other low voltage biopotentials (e.g., EEG). If the individual is not connected to a floating reference wire otherwise (e.g., by the use of simultaneous ECG or EEG recordings), she/he must be additionally connected to the floating reference wire in the amplifier box to prevent power-line noise (Sects. 2.1.4 and 2.2.5.1). Third, because SPRs are of small size compared to the whole range of the SP signal, a backing-off circuit might be considered for recording SPRs with satisfyingly high-resolution (Sect. 2.1.3). Bridge circuits cannot be used here because an external voltage is not available. Therefore, backing-off has to be performed by adding a potential of equal value but of opposite sign to the SPL, so that SPR is amplified at a higher gain around an arbitrary zero point. Another effect of this backing-off procedure is to reduce the current flow in the circuit and hence lessen the proportion of voltage being dropped across R_2, which will drive the apparent input impedance of the amplifier up to 10 MΩ and reduce measurement error to 1% (Venables & Christie, 1980). A "backing-off" circuit that allows compensation as well as simultaneous recording of the SCL has been recommended by Venables and Martin (1967a). If the SCL is not being recorded, an AC-coupled amplifier may be used, which must, however, have a rather high time constant with a minimum of 30 s, to prevent deformation of the signal. Since no external voltage is applied, there is no danger of polarization effects on the boundary between electrode and electrolyte (Sect. 2.2.2.2). However, due to its small bandwidth of 0–3 Hz, the signal is inseparably superimposed by possible electrode drifts (Sect. 2.2.2.5). Therefore, for SP recording, the use of bias potential free electrodes is essential (Sect. 2.2.2.2).

The electrode diameter and the delimitation of the contact area between skin and electrolyte play a subordinate role in SP recording. By contrast, differences in skin temperature between recording sites may result in error potentials up to 2 mV (Venables & Christie, 1980), because they exclusively influence the active site (Venables & Sayer, 1963). Temperature differences are likely to occur between sites with large distances from each other, such as the distance between the palm and the upper forearm. Additionally, an increase of electrode temperature may result in error potentials up to 450 μV/°C. Venables and Sayer (1963) proposed an electric circuitry for the compensation of temperature effects in SP recording.

Problems with bias potentials can be minimized by careful selection and maintenance of electrodes for SP recording (Sect. 2.2.2.2). The possibility of using KCl cream instead of NaCl cream, especially in SPL recording, has been previously mentioned in Sect. 2.2.2.5.

2.2.3.2   Exosomatic Recording with Direct Current

DC recording of EDA is the most frequently used method for obtaining electrodermal measures. Its physical principles, as well as the advantages and disadvantages of the various recording techniques, were already discussed in Sect. 2.1. A

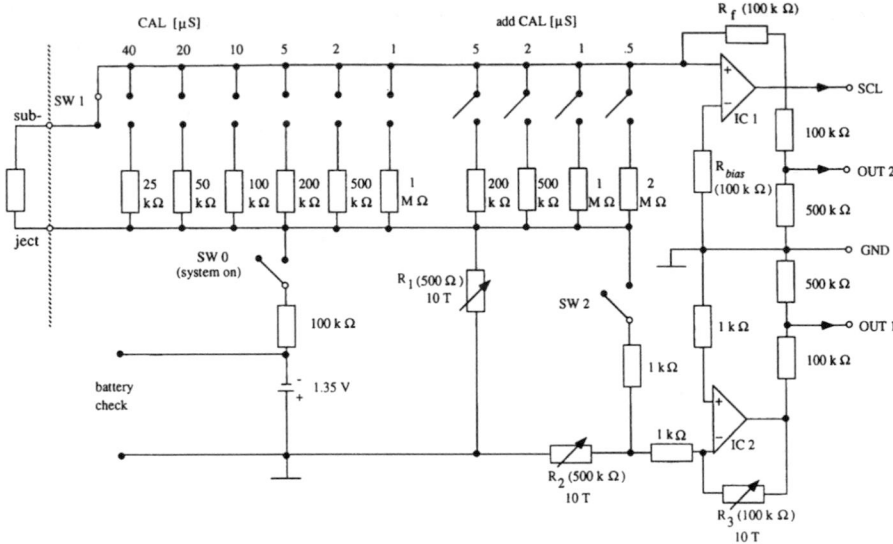

Fig. 2.10 Active skin conductance coupler (see text for explanations) (reprinted from Venables and Christie (1980), Fig. 1.13. Copyright © 1980 by Wiley. Reprinted by permission of the publisher and the first author)

description of a skin conductance coupler which uses appropriate methodology – with the exception of filter characteristics (Sect. 2.1.4) – was provided by Venables and Christie (1980, Fig. 1.13). The circuitry for this active coupler, being depicted in Fig. 2.10, is derived from a circuitry proposed by Lowry (1977), which incorporated some of the operating features of the passive circuitry described by Venables and Christie (1973).

The circuitry shown in Fig. 2.10 enables continuous DC recording of SCL and SCR with high-resolution, using a constant voltage source.[26] SW 0 (system on) connects a 1.35 V mercury cell battery to the circuitry, whereas SW 1 switches between calibration (CAL) or subject to be operated. The switches "CAL" (on the left upper side of Fig. 2.10) allow for dummy loads of 1, 2, 5, 10, 20, and 40 µS to be connected in place of an actual subject. Additionally, the press-button switches "add CAL" (on the upper middle part of Fig. 2.10) allow conductance values of 0.5, 1, 2, and 5 µS to be added during the course of recording. Figure 2.2 (Sect. 2.1.2) will be referred to for an explanation of the action in an operational amplifier circuitry: the resistor provided by either the actual subject or a dummy load conductance (respectively the sum of both in case of the "add CAL" option)

---

[26] Since Lykken and Venables (1971) recommended that skin conductance should be used as the appropriate unit for EDA measurement, constant current recording went out of use in most psychophysiological laboratories. However, because of the lower amplifier gain required, constant current methods are sometimes preferred in field applications (Sects. 2.1.1 and 2.6.2).

is equivalent to R_i. The operation amplifier IC 1 is fed back by R_f and is referenced by R_{bias} to ground. The upper right part of Fig. 2.10 shows that the differential amplifier of the recording system for SCL is connected to outputs SCL and GND.

The lower right part of the circuitry depicted in Fig. 2.10 enables additional simultaneous recording of SCR with higher resolution between OUT 1 and OUT 2. The ten-turn potentiometers R_2 and R_3, together with the network around the amplifier IC 2, provide a manually operated backing-off system, which can be switched on by SW 2. Instead of a manually operated suppression, an automatic high-resolution evaluation of SCR may be obtained with the use of an AC-coupled amplifier or a digital operating auto-suppression device that will be described later (Fig. 2.11), which is connected to outputs SCL and GND.

The 1.35 V mercury cell together with the 100 Ω resistor and the ten-turn potentiometer R_1 enable the voltage applied across the subject to be set at 0.5 V. The use of constant 0.5 V for DC recording of SC dates back to a recommendation made by Edelberg (1967, p. 19), who observed the voltage/current curves being linear below an impressed voltage of 0.8 V across a single recording site. Since bipolar recording is predominant in exosomatic DC recording of EDA, the applied voltage is cut in half according to the principle of a voltage divider (Sect. 2.2.1). Hence, across each single recording site, only half of the applied voltage is dropped, provided that that the sites' resistances are approximately equal. In spite of these considerations, a total voltage of 0.5 V had been introduced as a standard for constant voltage DC recording (Lykken & Venables, 1971). Fowles et al. (1981) stated that in this case both sites will show a 0.25 V potential difference, given the same SRL at the sites.[27]

The calibration procedure of the SC coupler depicted in Fig. 2.10 has been described by Venables and Christie (1980, p. 58) as follows[28]:

1. Set sensitivity of the recording instrument (e.g., a polygraph) to 5 mV/cm.
2. Select a dummy load value (CAL) of 20 µS with SW 1.
3. Switch on the coupler with SW 0 and adjust R_1 to achieve a pen deflection of 1 cm. Then, the voltage across the dummy load will be 0.5 V and the current 10 µA.
4. Set the dummy load to 40 µS, switch on suppression circuit with SW 2, and turn the zero suppression R_3 potentiometer to its maximum. Return the pen to zero deflection by adjusting the suppression calibration control potentiometer R_2.
5. Select subject with SW 1, with an unconnected subject (i.e., with an open circuit). Return zero suppression potentiometer R_3 to zero and check that the pen gives zero deflection.

---

[27] Though Venables and Christie (1980, p. 40) argued for the application of 0.5 V across each active site, following a suggestion by Edelberg (1967), their circuitry which underlies Fig. 2.10 provides a total of 0.5 V.

[28] Note that this description is oriented towards paper recording (Sect. 2.2.4.1) which has come widely out of use. However, it is worth pondering such a procedure for a complete understanding of SC-recording, even if it is performed with A/D conversion of the recorded signal and subsequent computer evaluation (Sect. 2.2.4.2).

Steps (4) and (5) calibrate the zero suppression control R_3 to provide 4 μS/turn of the potentiometer. If other values are selected during step (4), the potentiometer R_3 may be calibrated with other values (e.g., if the dummy load is set to 10 μS, R_3 calibration would be in terms of 1 μS/turn). The polygraph indicates 20 μS/cm with the sensitivity of 5 mV/cm selected in step (1). If the polygraph amplifier gain is increased to, for example, 0.05 mV/cm, an increase of sensitivity to 0.2 μS/cm will result. Thus, as a consequence of the restricted width of the recording channel (normally 4–5 cm), the SCR output with zero suppression and higher resolution (Fig. 2.10) has to be used for recording with higher polygraph amplifier gain (Sect. 2.1.3).

In addition to the coupler circuitry depicted in Fig. 2.10, Venables and Christie (1980, Fig. 1.11) provided a block diagram of a complete SC-recording system with automatic suppression of the SCL and the elimination of temperature effects (Sect. 2.4.2.1), additionally providing calibration pulses for computer analysis (Sect. 2.2.6.2). In their diagram, the output SCL is fed into the automatic SCL suppression system developed by Simon and Homoth (1978), which is schematically depicted in Fig. 2.11.

The automatic voltage suppressor shown in Fig. 2.11 can be used together with the active skin conductance coupler depicted in Fig. 2.10. The voltage that corresponds to the total SC (which appears between SCL and GND on the output side of the SC coupler depicted in Fig. 2.10) is fed into a voltage-to-frequency converter (VF converter) with a dynamic range from 0.01 to 10 V. It is thereby transformed into a pulse rate which is fed into the counter during a time interval of 20 ms. Those 20 ms pulses are deduced from the 50 Hz AC power frequency. The rise of the pulses are triggering the storage in memory, the contents of which are converted by a digital/analog (D/A) converter to an analog voltage, which is available until the next pulse from the control unit arrives. Additionally, a digital output of SC is provided (see upper right in Fig. 2.11).

The output of the D/A converter is reduced by an adjustable reserve voltage (RV) within the amplifier A1 and is subtracted from the input signal by means of the amplifier A2. The resulting voltage is amplified in A3 by a factor of 100, thus providing a high-resolution SCR in output 1. The compensation voltage which comes from A1 is available at the output 2 and can be recorded and processed separately. After adjustment of the RV, the compensation voltage varies in discrete and reproducible steps. Thus, the original signal of the SC can be exactly reproduced by adding output 2 to output 1.[29]

An easy-to-construct coupler for exosomatic DC recording which can be used in combination with a high-quality biosignal amplifier (e.g., for EEG recording) is depicted in Fig. 2.12. The coupler uses a special integrated circuit (LM 10) to obtain a highly constant voltage $U_{ref} = 0.5$ V. By means of an operational

---

[29] Simon and Homoth (1978) stated an error of 0.4% of the D/A converter's output voltage. A circuit diagram of their voltage suppressor is given in their Fig. 1.2, together with a list of components in their Table 1.1.

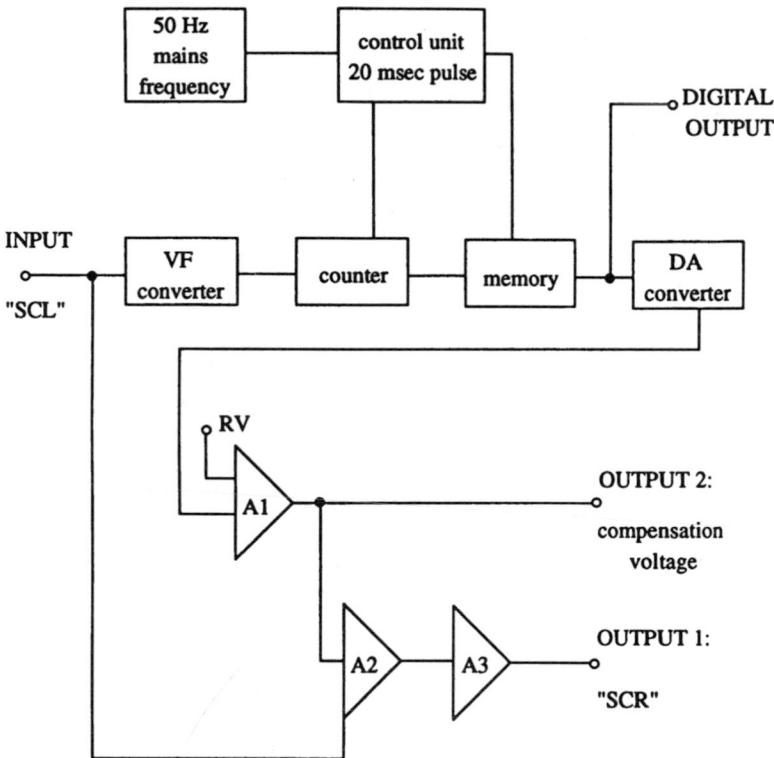

Fig. 2.11 Block diagram of the automatic voltage suppressor (adapted from Simon and Homoth (1978), Fig. 1. Copyright © 1978 by the Society for Psychophysiological Research. Used with permission of the publisher)

amplifier circuitry OP 1 (see Fig. 2.2, Sect. 2.1.2), the current through the subject is converted to a negative voltage $-U_{SCL}$, which is proportional to the SCL, showing a sensitivity of 0.5 mV/µS. This output voltage is further amplified and inverted by means of another operational amplifier OP 2, resulting in $U_{out} = VU_{SCL}$, with $V = R_1/R_2$. If the biosignal amplifier's time constant τ is not large enough (e.g., 10 s, see Sect. 2.1.4), OP 3 can be used together with the amplifier's DC mode output voltage U_{SCR}, which has the sensitivity $S = (R_4/R_3)$ [0.5 mV/µS] and the time constant $\tau = R_3C$. To guarantee a maximum of security, the device should be battery operated, and the bioamplifier's input should be galvanically separated.

Because constant voltage recording had been recommended (Fowles, 1986a; Fowles et al., 1981; Venables & Christie, 1980) and is predominantly used, there is no additional need to depict and describe circuitry for constant current recording. However, some remarks on the CC method should be made here. According to Edelberg et al. (1960) and Edelberg (1967), the current density should not exceed 10 µA/cm² since above this value the SRL and SRRs decrease markedly, temporal measures of SRRs will be changed, and sweat gland damage may result in extreme

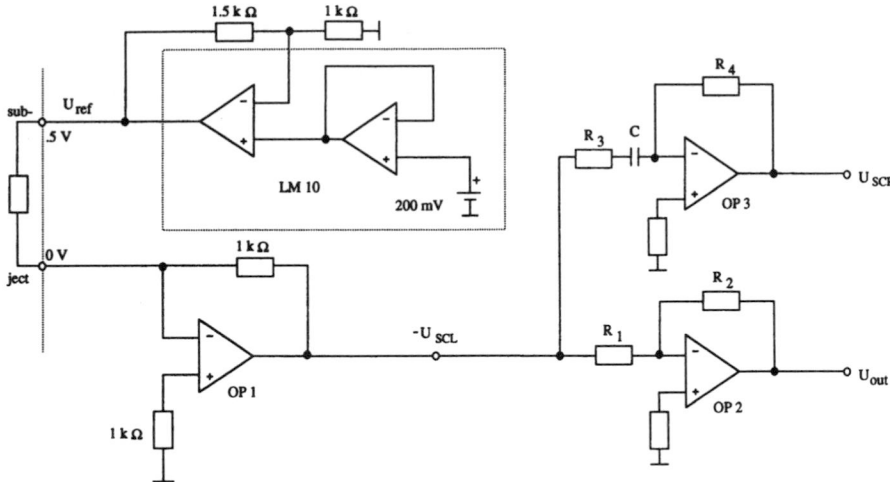

Fig. 2.12 Coupler for DC recording of SCL and SCR, to be used with a high-quality amplifier system (designed in the present author's laboratory by Dipl.-Ing. Jörn Grabke, University of Wuppertal, Germany)

cases (Sect. 2.6.2). Hence, Venables and Martin (1967a) and Edelberg (1972a) recommended the use of 8 μA/cm^2 current density for constant current recording. Since the contact area of the electrode forms a circle, the current I that has to be applied with a given electrode diameter d is: $I = 2\pi d^2$ (Venables & Martin, 1967a).

Since the standard electrodes described in Sect. 2.2.2.3 have a contact area of 0.6 cm^2, an appropriate current density between 4.8 and 6 μA should be applied, leading to current density values between 8 and 10 μA/cm^2. Since the values for current densities should be kept constant, the limitation of the contact area between skin and electrolyte has to be adhered to. In turn, such a restriction of the contact area is not necessary if constant voltage recording is used (Sect. 2.2.2.1). If results obtained with constant current recording are reported – independent from the use of SR or SC units – the size of the electrode area should additionally be specified. This will enable the reader to calculate the specific resistance for making subsequent comparisons with other results (Sect. 2.3.3.1). However, Mitchell and Venables (1980) regarded – contrary to the older hypothesis – the influences of the contact area as negligible (Sect. 2.2.2.3).

2.2.3.3 Exosomatic Recording with Alternating Current

Until now, the hitherto nearly exclusive use of DC methods in exosomatic EDA recording prevented the development of a widely accepted technique of AC recording. However, at least several recommendations concerning the appropriate frequencies might be derived from the literature. Montagu and Coles (1968) observed that the lead electrodes they used showed the smallest amount of polarization if a 5 Hz recording frequency was applied. Edelberg (1967) pointed to the impossibility of obtaining EDRs with sufficient reliability using high AC frequencies, because the polarization capacities of skin would become too low. According to Brown (1972), the biological membrane looses its changeability for polarization between 5 and 10 kHz, and its capacitive properties will become negligible above 20 kHz. Faber (1980), who continuously varied the AC frequency between 5 Hz and 10 kHz, yielded the largest differences in frequency locus (see Fig. 1.10, Sect. 1.4.1.3) with the lower frequencies when measuring EDA in three participants during different tasks. Thus, the use of AC frequencies between 5 and 100 Hz can be recommended.

One possible application of AC recording for EDA is to prevent polarization effects (Sect. 2.2.2.2). Instead of DC, an appropriate AC may be used as an exosomatic electricity source, together with a subsequent rectification of the signal. However, the phase angle must also be determined if capacitive properties of the skin are under investigation (Sect. 2.1.5). Devices for measuring the frequency locus are available for cardiac surgery, but the specific problems of filtering as well as separating phasic and tonic parts of EDA (Sects. 2.1.3 and 2.1.4) require the construction of specific instruments for EDA-AC recording.

A device for AC recording of EDA used by Boucsein et al. (1989) will be described here, which was a further development of a phase voltmeter suggested by Neijenhuisen and de Jongh (1981) for use in dermatology. Despite the fact that constant voltage is generally preferred for DC measurement of EDA (Sect. 2.2.3.2), recording was performed here with a constant current source, since Salter (1979) pointed out that this method is preferred for medical applications to prevent non-linearities that may result from uncontrolled current densities when using a constant effective voltage source. Impedance and phase angle are obtained as analog output signals; a digital laboratory computer is used to transform these values into reactance and resistance as well as susceptance and conductance (Sect. 1.4.1.3).

A block diagram of the phase voltmeter for AC recording is given in Fig. 2.13. A sine wave voltage generated by an oscillator being continuously adjustable between 1 Hz and 1 kHz is converted by a voltage-to-current converter into a constant current, being adjustable between 0 and 10 µA peak value, which is delivered to the subject's skin. The terminal voltage from the skin site is pre-amplified and processed in two ways:

1. To evaluate *impedance*, the voltage is submitted to a voltage amplifier, the sensitivity of which is adjustable between 1 mV and 10 V in steps of decades, and the output signal is rectified and low-pass filtered with either 0.1 or 1 Hz. After subtracting a manually adjusted offset, the signal is delivered to output 1 and to a digital display.
2. For measuring the *phase angle*, the preamplified signal is multiplied in a phase sensitive detector with the oscillator signal – which has been phase shifted with the possibility of adjusting the phase angle continuously – acting as a zero-offset for the phase signal. The output signal of the phase sensitive detector is also rectified, low-pass filtered with the same frequency limit as the impedance signal, and delivered to output 2 and to a second digital display.

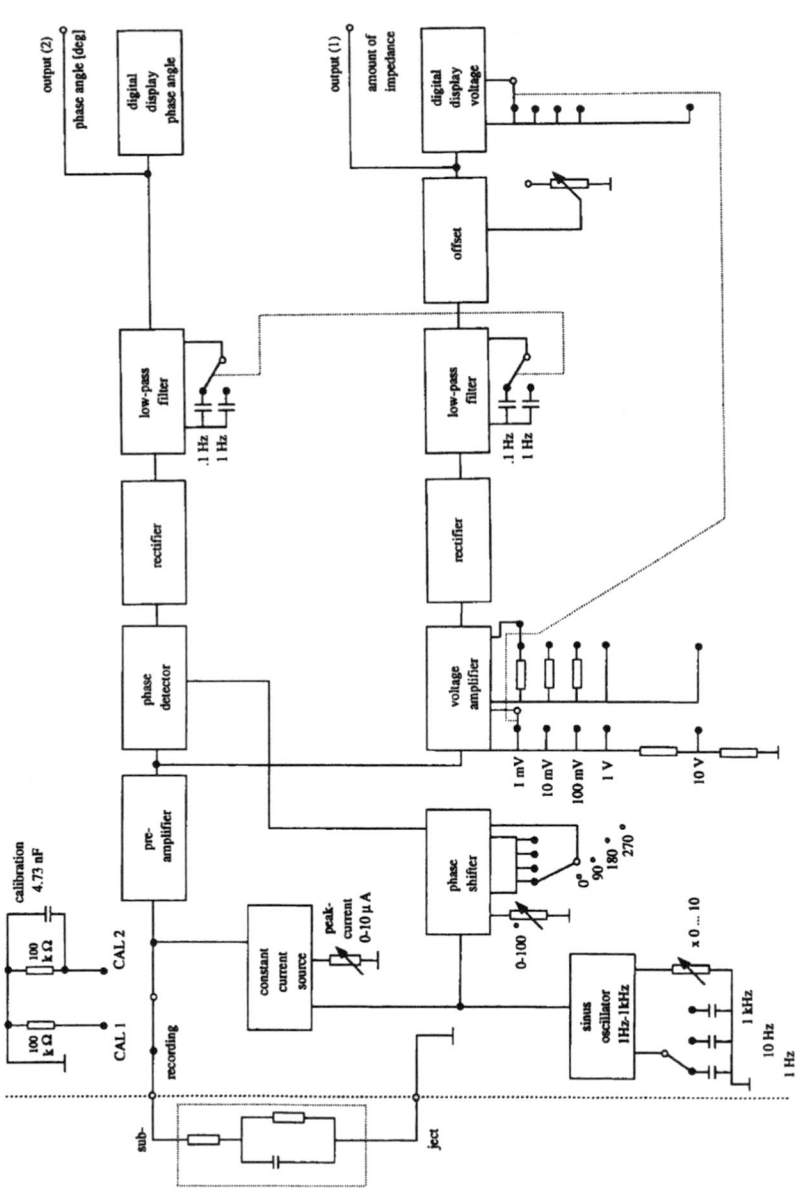

Fig. 2.13 Block diagram of a phase voltmeter for simultaneous recording of impedance and phase angle (see text for explanations) (from Boucsein et al. (1989), Fig. 3. Copyright © 1989 by the Society for Psychophysiological Research. Redrawn with permission of the publisher)

Outputs 1 and 2 are digitized using two channels of a 12 bit A/D converter with 16 Hz. The resolution for impedance is about 10 Ω/bit and for the phase angle 0.008°/bit. $X(f)$ and $R(f)$ are calculated from impedance $Z(f)$ and $\varphi(f)$ at the given AC frequency f, according to (1.18a) and (1.18b), through the use of a digital computer. In addition, susceptance $B(f)$ and conductance $G(f)$ can be calculated at each sampled data point.

Calibration is enabled by the recording device in Fig. 2.13 in two positions: CAL 1 for impedance uses a 100 kΩ resistor as a substitute, whereas CAL 2 for the phase angle adds an additional 4.73 nF capacitance in parallel. The input impedance is 10 MΩ, the signal-to-noise ratio for impedance as well as for the phase angle is better than 98 dB.

Based on theoretical considerations and empirical evidence, Schaefer and Boucsein (2000) recommended using the phase angle φ as a measure for the EDR amp. which is independent of the method applied (constant alternating voltage vs. constant alternating current). It also makes EDR amp. comparable without computations according to (1.5a) and (1.5b), which would require information about the EDL (Sect. 1.4.1.1), since φ values obtained with constant current and constant voltage technique do not differ in their magnitude but only in their sign (Sect. 1.4.1.3). Thereafter, the phasic changes in φ can be treated in the same manner as traditional phasic EDA measures (Sect. 2.3.1.2 "Amplitudes of Exosomatic Responses Recorded with Alternating Current").

Another attempt to continuously measure reactance as well as the ohmic part of impedance was performed by Almasi and Schmitt (1974) using Lissajous figures for signal control (Fig. 1.11, Sect. 1.4.1.4). These authors presumed that only three periods of the applied AC current would be sufficient for determining EDA with a single frequency, enabling them to obtain several measuring points even with low frequencies within relatively short periods (e.g., with the use of $f = 1$ Hz every 3 s). Nevertheless, they stated that an experienced experimenter would need approximately 1 min to determine the impedance locus from three discrete frequencies between 500 Hz and 1 kHz.

Salter (1979) described the development of a continuous AC recording technique based on a 16 bit microprocessor. In his concept, the sine wave AC frequency used for exosomatic EDA recording was created in the central processor and given, via a D/A converter, to the analog part of the measuring device. The advantage was that the whole calculating procedure could be performed on a digital basis, using the originally generated digital sine wave signal. This also made all manual changes during recording (e.g., frequency changes) superfluous, because all adjustments could be performed by the software. Unfortunately, Salter did not pursue this concept further, and details about it are difficult to obtain.

Lykken (1971) used pulsed DC, instead of the usual sine wave AC method, for EDA recording, but only with one participant (Sect. 2.5.3.2). The use of pulsed DC current may be regarded as equivalent to sine wave AC recording, since Faber (1980) found an intraindividual correlation of $r = 0.93$ between SCLs obtained with 10 Hz sinusoidal recording and a pulsed DC recording, with a 10 ms pulse and an interval of 250 ms duration. Thus, further development and validation studies will be desirable for AC recording of exosomatic EDA.

2.2.3.4 Ambulatory Monitoring of Electrodermal Activity

Due to the availability of small but potent electronic devices for psychophysiological recording, ambulatory monitoring has come into use more frequently during
the last two decades (for an overview, see Fahrenberg & Myrtek, 1996, 2001).
Low-volume digital mass storage has widely replaced portable cassette recorders as
used in the 1980s (e.g., Simpson & Turpin, 1983). Today's ambulatory monitoring
systems such as the Vitaport[30] or Varioport[31] are capable of collecting data from
multivariate recordings over more than 24 h, depending on the actual storage capacity
and the chosen sampling rates. To keep the latter low, an onboard parameterization of
relatively high frequent signals (such as ECG, EEG or EMG) is normally performed
on-line during recording. Sampling rates of 20 Hz as recommended for EDA
(Sect. 2.2.4.2) do not constitute a problem for long-term mass storage. In cases
where only EDL information is to be stored, sampling rates as low as 1 Hz might
be sufficient. However, if separation of phasic and tonic parts of the signal is required,
the default sampling rates of ambulatory monitoring devices may need to be
increased, e.g., from 4 to 8 Hz, as performed by Boucsein and Thum (1996) when
using the Vitaport together with the semiautomatized off-line computer analysis
program described in the Appendix of this book, which allows also for detecting
and removing recording artifacts in the EDA signal (Sect. 2.2.5.1).

However, the duration of ambulatory EDA monitoring can be seriously limited
by the problems with long-term recording of electrodermal phenomena, especially
when electrode cream is used as recommended (Sect. 2.2.6.1). Therefore, some
researchers preferred using dry electrodes in ambulatory recording of EDA
(Sect. 2.2.6.3). For comparsion with standard recording Poh, Swenson, and
Picard (2010) performed parallel recordings from palmar finger sites (A and B in
Fig. 2.6, Sect. 2.2.1.1) and from two electrodes attached to the volar side of the
distal forearm. In addition, they probed different kinds of dry electrodes, i.e.,
standard Ag/AgCl electrodes vs. stretch conductive fabric, both sewn into a wristband (Sect. 2.2.1.1). Ambulatory monitoring was performed by a custom-made
modular device delivering 3.3 V DC to the skin. The analog EDA signal was
sampled at 32 Hz via a 12-bit A/D converter and stored in a 2 GB flash memory
card, providing enough capacity for up to 28 days storage of continuous recording
with a 32 Hz sampling rate. A triple-axis accelerometer was also onboard for
recording physical activity, and an optional radio transceiver could be mounted
on top of the device which in total was not much bigger than a quarter coin
($20 \times 30 \times 8$ mm). Comparisons with a traditional stationary recording system
were performed in the laboratory with 26 participants of both genders during
physical (bicycle ergometer), cognitive (subtracting of seven backwards), and
emotional (watching a horror movie) tasks, each consisting of a 10 min baseline,
a 3–5 min task period, and a 10 min recovery period. Raw data were filtered with a

---

[30] The Vitaport ambulatory monitoring system is now distributed by TEMEC Instruments in
Kerkrade, The Netherlands.

[31] The Varioport ambulatory monitoring system is distributed by Becker Meditec in Karlsruhe,
Germany.

low-pass filter (cutoff frequency 3 Hz) and analyzed by customized software. Pearson correlations revealed very good correspondences between both measurement devices from standard palmar sites during all phases of the laboratory experiment ($r = 0.93$–0.99). The conductive fabric electrodes produced lower SCLs than all other recording methods in about 80% of the participants during cognitive and emotional tasks, but highest SCLs toward the end of the physical task and during the subsequent recovery period in 46% of participants.

One 19-year-old male participant volunteered for wearing the ambulatory monitoring device with dry Ag/AgCl electrodes on his left volar distal forearm for a whole week during daily activities. After periods between 24 and 30 h, the participant temporarily removed the flash memory card for downloading the data and also replaced the 3.7 V battery. The recordings revealed a consistent peak in SCL between midnight and 3 a.m. during sleep (see Sect. 3.2.1.3). No SCL drift was observable and the recordings were – as the authors stated – relatively artifact-free. However, when using dry electrodes, instabilities have to be considered for an unknown amount of time following their attachment (see Footnote 39, Sect. 2.2.6.3).

Boucsein, Schaefer, and Sommer (2001) compared ambulatory monitoring with traditional recording of SC from the nondominant hand in 24 female participants using standard methodology (Sect. 2.2.7), using Ag/AgCl electrodes and isotonic electrolyte cream in both instances,[32] together with skin temperature taken from the same hand, ECG from a chest lead and vertical arm movements by means of a Piezo-electric sensor from the same side where EDA recordings were taken. Ambulatory monitoring was performed by the Vitaport 2 system worn in the pocket of a waist belt. First, laboratory recordings were made during a 2 min baseline, during a habituation series (Sect. 3.1.1) of eight 90 dB A, 1 s white noise stimuli with a variable interstimulus interval (ISI) of average 22.5 s, and during 16 subsequently presented different meaningful auditory stimuli (e.g., broken glass, barking dog, shriek) with a mean duration of 1 s, an intensity of 90 dB A, and the same variable ISI as in the habituation series. The mean correlation between SCR amp. from parallel recordings with the ambulatory monitoring and the traditional recording device calculated over three participants and applying Fisher's z-transformation was $r = 0.95$. When using another traditional laboratory device instead of the Vitaport 2 at the same recording sites, the mean correlation between the two traditional laboratory devices over two participants was $r = 0.99$, which was only slightly higher than the correlation between the ambulatory monitoring and the traditional recording device.

After the first laboratory session, the participants were released being wired to the Vitaport 2 and equipped with a synchronized pocket computer. Their task was simply to carry on with their everyday activities, which should be marked on the ambulatory computer, serving also for presentation of short questionnaires. Additionally, they were given a tape recorder, with a horror story for half of the participants and a rather boring description of a landscape for the other half, which

---

[32] Two pairs of standard Ag/AgCl electrodes were fixed on the same hand, one at standard thenar/hypothenar sites, the other one in 2–2.5 cm distance distal from the first ones (C and D in Fig. 2.6, Sect. 2.2.1.1).

they should listen to immediately before going to sleep. The stories (between 15 and 20 min each) had been rated significantly different with respect to excitement. The participants returned 24 h after the first session for a second laboratory test, comprising three habituation series with ten white noise stimuli as used in the first session. For the traditional recording, two fresh EDA electrodes were attached, while the Vitaport 2 electrodes stayed in position. Between the first and the second habituation series, the Vitaport 2 electrodes were replaced by fresh electrodes. Unfortunately, only 12 out of the original 24 participants could be evaluated for this part of the study, since 10 of them had at least one of the EDA electrodes detached on the morning of the second day, one participant forgot to listen to the tape and one participant did not go to sleep after listening to the tape but left her home for personal reasons.

For the 24-h recordings, 5-min intervals were evaluated with respect to the mean EDL, the NS.SCR freq. and the mean NS.SCR amp. Group comparisons were performed for the 3 h before listening to the tape, for the listening period itself and for the 3 h thereafter. The same evaluation periods were applied to the other three measures recorded by the ambulatory monitoring system. The two groups did not differ significantly in EDL which showed a continuous decline over time, being only reversed during listening to the tapes, during which both NS.SCR freq. and mean amplitudes were significantly higher in the group listening to the horror story compared to participants listening to the landscape description. No correspondence to arm movements, heart rate (HR), or skin temperature was observed. Despite the huge amount of data loss mostly due to spontaneous electrode detachment, ambulatory monitoring of EDA figured out being a viable method for determining differences in emotional states (Sect. 3.2.2.1) in everyday life. Furthermore, there was some indication of the EDL rising during the first rapid eye movement (REM) phase and of NS.SCR freq. being higher during the first slow wave sleep (SWS) period after listening to the horror story, which corresponds to the phenomenon of EDA "storming" during the night described in Sect. 3.2.1.3. However, the sleeping phases could only be roughly estimated since no EEG data were available.

The mean correlation over three participants between the SCR amp., being recorded by the electrodes of the Vitaport 2 which had been 24 h in place, and the freshly attached electrodes for the traditional device during the first series of ten stimuli in the second laboratory session was $r = 0.85$. The correlation between the two recording sites was increased to $r = 0.96$ when fresh electrodes were used for the Vitaport 2 as well. This difference points to the possibility of changes in the closed electrode/electrolyte system during the 24-h ambulatory monitoring, which is typical for long-term recording (Sect. 2.2.6.1). For this reason and because of the high probability of electrode detachment, standard recording methodology, i.e., electrodes with plastic chambers filled with isotonic paste and being attached by double-sided adhesive rings to the palmar sites as described in Sects. 2.2.1 and 2.2.2, may not be the best choice for long-term ambulatory monitoring of EDA.

Therefore, using either dry electrodes at the wrist as probed by Poh, Swenson, and Picard (2010) in one participant (see above) or attaching standard electrodes to foot sites (see Fig. 2.7) with a special technique that increases the durability of attachment, which has been described in Sect. 2.2.2.1 and successfully used in 11 participants by Boucsein and Thum (1997) in their ambulatory monitoring study reported in Sect. 3.5.1.1, could serve as suitable alternatives in ambulatory monitoring of EDA. In addition, the application of a nonhydrating electrode paste as used by Turpin et al. (1983) for electrodes staying a week in position might be considered (Sect. 2.2.6.1).

Doberenz, Roth, Wollburg, Maslowski, and Kim (2011) investigated the influence of physical activity, ambient temperature and corneal hydration on the results of 24-hour ambulatory SC recording, obtained from 48 participants (32 females, 16 males). Skin conductance was recorded with standard methodology by means of an ambulatory device from the middle or lower phalanges of digits 2 and 3 of the nondominant hand. Electrodes were pre-filled with isotonic gel, which was supplemented by additional humid gel of the same kind brought to the center of the electrode before attachment. To control for the effects of corneal hydration, fresh electrodes were attached after the 24-hour period to adjacent sites either on the same or different phalanges. Ambient temperature was recorded by means of a sensor close to the recorder with an accuracy of 0.1 °C, general body movements were registered by an accelerometer and the participants used an event marker for indicating beginning and end of sleep. All SC parameters yielded higher values during physical activity compared to sleep, but little effects of temperature variations were observed. However, electrode sensitivity declined significantly by an average of 20% over the 24 hours, pointing to an important influence of corneal hydration on the results of long-term recording (Sect. 2.2.6.1).

In conclusion, the use of dry electrodes instead of those with humid or even liquid gels (Sect. 2.2.6.3) for ambulatory monitoring needs further research to determine advantages and disadvantages of either method.

2.2.3.5   Recording of EDA Within a Magnetic Field

During the last two decades, the use of EDA recording together with brain imaging techniques such as computer tomography (CT), MRI, and PET scanning has become an opportunity for combining CNS and ANS measures directly (Raine & Lencz, 1993). More recently, recording of EDA within the fMRI has been used in several studies. Anticipated problems have been resolved, since the artifacts produced by the magnetic resonance tomography (MRT) are in a much higher frequency band than changes in the EDA signal and can be easily removed by low-pass filtering. However, sampling EDA in a MRT environment requires taking some precautionary actions in the setup of measurement devices, their connection to the electrodes, and in the treatment of EDA data.

Positioning of metal objects in such a strong magnetic field as induced by fMRI is a general problem. The magnetic field might impact upon the measurement device which generates the voltage for EDA recording, and in turn this device may also impact the quality of the MRT recording by influencing the homogeneity of the magnetic field or the application of the gradients used for MRT measures. To avoid such influences and appropriately amplify the recorded signal, the circuitry for EDA measurement could be taken out of the magnetic field to an adjacent room. However, this requires very long electrode cables, and it is of paramount importance that they are not moved during EDA recording. This is because moving a conductor within a magnetic field has the potential to change this field; a process which in turn may induce a voltage on the electrode cables, thus distorting the EDA signal. Furthermore, long electrode cables serve as antennas for the high-frequency gradients used for the image acquisition, which could result in signal loss due to EDA amplifier limitations. Therefore, one possible solution is using a custom-made nonmagnetic recording device that can be placed in the magnetic field, thus allowing the electrode cables to be kept short (see below).

Researchers who used standard EDA recording devices (Sect. 2.2.3.2) made special arrangements for avoiding the high-frequency pulses used for fMRI recording to overly interfere with the electrodermal signal. For example, Critchley, Elliott, Mathias, and Dolan (2000) used a commercially available biofeedback system for continuously monitoring SC during a decision-making task in an fMRI[33] study using six participants (three of each gender). Off-line postprocessing of the A/D converted SC signal (sample rate 100 Hz) was performed to remove the repetitive signal contamination which resulted from the high-frequency noise which came with the fMRI volume acquisition. Further filtering and smoothing was applied to remove nonrepetitive noise. Two types of analysis were performed to determine CNS correlates of SCRs: a covariance analysis with statistical regressors derived from the filtered SCR trace, excluding the first 20 scans acquired during task performance to avoid including NS.SCRs that were observable during the beginning of the task; and an event-related analysis based on those SCR amp. being at least two standard deviations above the background EDA. According to Williams et al. (2001), such a conventional SC-recording with subsequent postprocessing of SCR data in fMRI studies may result in restricting the recording to larger SCRs which may not be directly linked to discrete stimuli.

Therefore, Williams et al. (2000) in their study on neuronal correlates of SC-OR (SC-orienting response; see Sect. 3.1.1) connected conventional Ag/AgCl electrodes, filled with 0.05 M NaCl electrode cream (Sect. 2.2.2.5) and attached to the distal phalanges of the ring and middle finger of the left hand, by means of a custom-made fiber-optic system to the EDA recording device located out of the fMRI scanner[34] room. The system reduced the possibility of inducing currents in the scanner by inclusion of resistors in all wires, the reduction of loop area in the wires and by the use of an optical signal that was converted back to an electric

---

[33] Siemens 2-T VISION system for acquiring gradient-echo, echo-planar T*-weighted images with BOLD (blood oxygenation level dependent) contrast. Each volume comprised 48×3 mm axial scans with 3 mm inplane resolution, continuously acquired every 4.2 s. SC was recorded with Ag electrodes taped to the palmar surface of the left index and middle fingers, presumably without electrode cream.

[34] Participants were scanned using a Siemens 1.5-T Magnetom VISION Plus system to acquire 64 T2*-weighted images depicting BOLD contrast for each stimulus of 3 s duration at 18 axial noncontinuous 6 mm thick planes (slices), parallel to the intracommissural line; sampling rate for the BOLD response (TR) = 3 s, TE = 40 ms, 128×128 matrix, interslice gap 0.6 mm.

signal once relayed outside the scanner. Thereby, SCR recording was protected against interference from radio frequency pulses in the fMRI environment. This system produced noise-free data that did not require filtering or smoothing. Eight male participants were repeatedly presented flashing checkerboard stimuli (four blocks of eight stimuli of 3 s duration; ISI 0.75 s) alternated with four equally structured blocks of control stimuli (blank screens). Contrasting the checkerboard with the control stimuli and checkerboards with and without SC-ORs did not only reveal neuronal correlates of visual processing but also brain regions which were especially active when ORs occurred (see Sect. 3.1.1).

A different methodological approach has been performed by Blecker, Kirsch, Schaefer, and Vaitl (2001) who used a custom-made nonmagnetic version of a standard battery-operated SC coupler (Fig. 2.10, Sect. 2.2.3.2) which was placed very close to the individual to be recorded. Therefore, electrode cable lengths of 20 cm were sufficient for the standard Ag/AgCl electrodes, thus avoiding the above-mentioned induction problems that may result from the use of long wires in a magnetic field. The output signal of the coupler was low-pass filtered with 9 Hz (Sects. 2.1.4 and 2.2.5.1) to rid the EDA signal of the noise, which is produced by the application of high-frequency gradients during fMRI acquisition and possible low-frequent contaminations. Thereafter, the EDA signal was A/D converted (Sects. 2.1.4 and 2.2.4.2) with a sampling rate of 1 kHz to obtain a high-resolution of the gradient artifacts. For the subsequent off-line computer analysis of SCRs (Sect. 2.2.4.2), the original sampling rate was reduced by the factor 100. Using this methodology, it was possible to obtain high-resolution artifact-free SC-ORs in the fMRI from three male participants.[35]

Patterson, Ungerleider, and Bandettini (2002) used SC-recording during a sequence of task- and resting periods from two female and four male participants being tested in an fMRI.[36] Two tasks were performed in counterbalanced order with resting periods before, after and in between: a modification of the gambling task described in Sect. 3.1.3.3, and a rather similar working memory task which, however, lacked the reward-based decision-making component of the gambling task. The SC

---

[35] The functional imaging data were acquired by a 1.5-T Siemens Symphony MRI-scanner with a Quantum gradient system. To measure the BOLD contrast, a T2*-weighted EPI (echo-planar imaging) sequence (TR = 2.5 s, TE = 60 ms, 64 × 64 matrix) was used. The volume contained 16 slices with a 5-mm slice thickness (no gap). The slices were acquired interleaved in ascending order. Artifacts stemming from recording (Sect. 2.2.5.1) were reduced with automatic 1D denoising using wavelets. The threshold selection rule was a heuristic variant of Stein's Unbiased Risk (Matlab R12).

[36] Functional and structural MRI scans were obtained using a GE Signa 1.5-T scanner. The participant's neck and head were stabilized within foam padding within a brain-specific RF head coil. An EPI pulse sequence was used for collecting functional data (TR = 2.5 s, TE = 30 ms, FOV = 24 cm, 64 × 64 matrix). The entire brain was covered in 20 or 21 slices in the sagittal plane, resulting in voxel dimensions of 3.75 × 3.75 × 7 mm. Additionally, a high-resolution fast 3D T1-weighted structural image (TE = 6 ms, FOV = 24 cm, 256 × 256 × 124 voxels of 1.9 × 1.9 × 2 mm) was obtained as anatomical reference. SC was recorded by AgCl electrodes from the index and middle fingers of the participant's left hand by means of a commercially available recording system which was placed outside the magnet room. Analog SC signals were recorded at 10 Hz and passed to an A/D converter. No more SC-recording details were provided.

data were processed by means of a 5-point moving average filter to remove high-frequency artifacts that could have been induced by the scanner. AC-coupling (Sect. 2.1.3) was applied to obtain SCRs being free from SCL drifts (Sect. 2.3.4.3). The SCR waveform was resampled by interpolation, in order to match the repetition time of the measure (TR, 2.5 s) resulting in one SC value per measured fMRI volume. The waveform was also time-shifted (± 1 TR) to account for the hemodynamic variability across the brain. No convolution with a standard hemodynamic response was necessary, since the SCR (the authors referred to Fig. 2.15, Sect. 2.3.1.2 "Amplitudes of Exosomatic Responses") is nearly identical in latency and shape to that of the hemodynamic impulse response. NS.SCR freq. was calculated using an amplitude criterion of 0.05 µS (Sect. 2.3.1.2 "Choice of Amplitude Criteria"). Correlations between the fMRI time series data and the simultaneously collected SCR time series data were obtained on a voxel-wise basis. During both kinds of task and during the resting periods, activity in a specific group of brain regions was significantly correlated with SCR changes. These included the VMPFC, the posterior cingulate gyrus, the right anterior superior temporal cortex, the bilateral inferior parietal cortex, the supplementary motor cortex, the cingulate cortex adjacent to the supplementary motor area, the bilateral cerebellum, and the thalamus. In addition, SCRs correlated with cognitive activity during the tasks in several bilateral visual cortical areas and in the left primary motor cortex (see Sect. 1.3.4.1 "Cortical Control of EDA"). The authors interpreted the total absence of amygdalar activity with the lack of penalty for failures in both tasks. The study showed that even complicated tasks could be used in the fMRI to reveal correlations between moment-to-moment changes in mental activity and phasic EDA.

An additional problem with the fMRI is the loud noise generated by switching the magnetic field on and off. This constitutes an obstacle for designing experiments with acoustic stimuli, but also an additional source for orienting responses (Sect. 3.1.1), arousal (Sect. 3.2.1.1) and stress (Sect. 3.2.2.2), which has to be taken care of during the interpretation of results.

2.2.4   Methods of Storage and Evaluation of the Electrodermal Signal

2.2.4.1   Paper Recording and Evaluation by Hand

Although the majority of EDA recording is now performed with subsequent A/D conversion and digital storage, the conventional method of recording EDA on polygraph paper and evaluating the recording by hand is still in use in some applications. Since the changes in the EDA signal which form a single EDR are relatively small as compared to the whole range of the signal, polygraph recording may be performed as a continuous recording of the EDL on one channel and the EDRs with higher resolution on a second channel (Sect. 2.1.3). An alternative method would be using only one polygraph channel for high-resolution EDRs, on which impulses are superimposed, the distances of which are proportional to the current EDL.

In any case, the extremely wide range of the EDA signal is likely to cause problems with recording and evaluation. If the normal polygraph recording width of 40–50 mm is used, and the AC-coupled EDR signal is recorded with a high amplifier gain, unexpectedly large EDRs will exceed the boundaries of the recording channel, which will result in loss of data (Fig. 2.22, Sect. 2.3.4.1). If the amplification is reduced to avoid this, small EDRs will no longer be identifiable. Therefore, compensation recorders which allow 20 or 25 cm recording range for each channel are recommended for paper recording of EDA (Table 2.1, Sect. 2.3.1.2 "Choice of Amplitude Criteria").

For the evaluation of parameters like EDR amp. or NS.EDR freq., a paper speed of 5–10 mm/s will be sufficient. However, if temporal measures such as latencies, rise times, or recovery times are to be obtained from the recording chart (Sects. 2.3.1.1 and 2.3.1.3), paper speeds below 10 mm/s will result in unreliable scoring. The curvilinear pen deflections of some polygraphs may also cause marked distortions of rise times and recovery times, especially in EDRs with high amplitudes. However, the attenuation of frequency caused by technical features of the galvanometer system plays practically no role in the recording of the relatively low-frequency EDA signal.

It is highly recommended that the experimenter will note the paper speed as well as the amplifier gain and every change made during the recording on the chart paper. This includes possible changes in signal range and calibration marks, which should be applied in phases of relative EDR inactivity. Those calibration marks, which can be obtained using the "add CAL" switches in Fig. 2.10 (Sect. 2.2.3.2), will be helpful for the subsequent evaluation, and will ensure unambiguity, even if the recording has been calibrated in absolute values.

As a convention for graphical representations, Venables and Christie (1980) recommended taking over the neurophysiologist's tradition of recording "negative up." This makes sense especially for SPL, where an increase of negativity indicates increasing general arousal (Sect. 3.2.1.1), and the initial SPR component, which is also likely to be negative in most cases (Sect. 1.4.3.2), will also show upward deflection. Using exosomatic methods, "negativity" makes no direct sense. Therefore, "negative up" should be replaced by "EDR up." Hence, the convention is to display increasing skin conductance values (including SCRs), which indicate an increase of arousal, as upward deflection. Their reciprocal, i.e., increases of SR, should be recorded as upward deflection as well, because they indicate a decrease of skin resistance, which is also an indicator of increased arousal. Thus, in tonic exosomatic recording, an increase of SCL and a decrease in SRL will deflect upward on the paper output.

Evaluation of the EDA signal requires marking the appropriate time windows on the paper. These windows may refer either to the evaluation of the response to a single stimulus, or they may indicate periods for which the NS.EDR freq. will be evaluated (Sect. 2.3.2.2). Before single EDR amp. can be evaluated, an amplitude criterion should be defined (Sect. 2.3.1.2 "Choice of Amplitude Criteria"). Using a ruler and perhaps a magnifying glass, amplitudes can be obtained in millimeters or even in fractions of millimeters, and may be either listed in millimeters or transformed into appropriate units (i.e., mV, µS, or kΩ).

To obtain EDR ris.t., EDR rec.t/2 or EDR rec.tc, it will be helpful to mark the previous level from which the EDR deflected with a horizontal line, using pencil and ruler, and to draw in a vertical line at the maximum peak as well as another horizontal line at the height of either half or 63% amplitude recovery (see Fig. 2.15, Sect. 2.3.1.2). However, these pencil lines will prevent an independent additional evaluation to be performed by another experimenter, which could be useful for reliability testing. Additionally, curve-matching techniques using transparent templates may be applied as described in Sect. 2.3.1.3 "Recovery Parameters."

2.2.4.2 Off-Line Computer Analysis

Since psychophysiological laboratories are nowadays equipped with personal computers, the evaluation of electrodermal recordings is normally no longer performed by hand but by computer analysis. Since most computer programs do not allow a fully automated treatment of the various possible artifacts (Sect. 2.2.3.3), it is advisable to conduct a careful inspection of the raw signal during the computer analysis of the EDA. Therefore, the entire analog/digital (A/D) converted original EDA signal should be recorded in a form that enables its reconstruction for a subsequent artifact control during an off-line computer evaluation. Storage is normally performed digitally on a hard disk or memory card with a sampling rate of approximately 20 Hz.[37] A flow diagram for a computer analysis system was given by Venables and Christie (1980, Fig. 1.16), and programs have been made available in BASIC (e.g., Spinks, Dow, & Chiu, 1983) and in FORTRAN (e.g., Foerster, 1984). More recently, custom-made solutions are used is some laboratories based on computing environments such as MATLAB. A program for the detection and parameterization of SCRs, written by F. Schaefer according to recommendations given by the present author and extensively probed in our laboratory, is described in the Appendix of this book.

The analysis of an EDA signal that has been recorded with high-resolution A/D converters may generate a problem never seen in hand scoring from paper recordings. The system will probably quantitatively evaluate very small changes that look like EDRs but stem from filtered artifacts generated by the measurement device. If the A/D conversion is performed with 16 bits, (Sect. 2.1.4), $2^{16} = 65,536$ steps will be available. If for the AC-coupled SCR, a recording range of 20 µS is chosen, the A/D conversion will result in 0.001 µS being represented as three steps of digital information stored in the computer, which can be reliably determined by the evaluation program. However, such a resolution is far beyond the widely accepted amplitude criteria of 0.05 or 0.01 µS (Sect. 2.3.1.2 "Choice of Amplitude Criteria"). Therefore, additional methods for separating real EDRs from possible artifacts (e.g., resulting from amplifier characteristics; see Sect. 2.1.4) have to be evaluated. As a possible solution for such a distinction, Foerster (1984) and Thom (1988) used a minimal ascent of 0.08 µS/s (Sect. 2.3.1.3) as an additional criterion for the identification of an EDR, in addition to an amplitude criterion of 0.01 µS.

---

[37] The conversion rate depends on the A/D converter used in the computer system. Thus, Venables and Christie (1980) recommend 20 Hz, while Foerster (1984) used 16 Hz, which makes no difference in accuracy with respect to the phasic changes that occur in the electrodermal signal.

Because of the above-mentioned high-resolution performed by A/D conversion, separate recording of the AC-coupled EDR in addition to the EDL is no longer necessary. Given 16 bit A/D conversion and 100 µS recording range, which would cover all SCLs that appear under normal circumstances (Sect. 2.5.2.1 "Tonic Skin Conductance Measures"), a change of 0.01 µS would result in six steps of the stored digital information and could be reliably detected. However, for the sake of visual inspection during recording, and since some EDA couplers provide AC-coupling of the signal as an option for recording EDRs, uncoupling of EDR from EDL as described in Sect. 2.1.3 (e.g., by a "backing-off" circuit) is still in use. In this case, the EDL might get lost if only one EDA channel is stored. A subsequent reconstruction of the EDL from the AC-coupled signal stored in the computer requires the following steps:

1. The short time constant used during recording may be replaced by transforming it to a longer one (e.g., 10–100 s), which eliminates the deformation of the signal that resulted from AC-coupling (Foerster, 1984; Thom, 1988).
2. The appropriate EDL values are added to the retransformed EDR curve. If the EDL is not recorded as a continuous curve, but as a sequence of pulses (Sect. 2.2.4.1), a higher conversion rate of, for example, 250 Hz, must be applied to obtain the exact pulses. The EDL curve may then be restored from these pulses (Foerster, 1984).

Since those calculation procedures may result in some inaccuracies, Foerster (1984) preferred the AC-coupled EDR signal for the parameterization procedure. However, if transformations are to be performed later – which requires level information (Sect. 2.3.3.2) – a reconstruction of the EDL curve will be necessary. It should be noted that nowadays several recording systems provide an autoscale function which ensures an optimal range for observing EDRs.

For a thorough control of artifacts (Sect. 2.2.3.3), an interactive computer evaluation of EDA has been proposed by Thom (1988). During the computer analysis of the EDR signal, as many "EDRs" as possible are detected which fulfill the above-mentioned amplitude and minimal ascent criteria, and those being artifact prone are shown on a high-resolution video display. In these critical cases, the experimenter's decision is required whether or not this is an EDR (following a recommendation by Venables & Christie, 1980), and artifact-correcting procedures are offered by the program. The computer program in the Appendix of this book allows identifying and excluding artifact prone responses during its interactive evaluation procedure. A precursor of this program had been applied by Schneider, Schmidt, Binder, Schaefer, and Walach (2003) who developed a rule-based guideline for identifying potential respiratory artifacts, using a feature which allows for parallel display of EDA and respiration during interactive EDR evaluation (see Sect. 2.3.4.1).

As possible solutions for the nagging problem of evaluating overlapping EDRs (Sect. 2.3.1.2 "Amplitudes of Exosomatic Responses Recorded with Direct Current"), several mathematical procedures to be applied during off-line computer analysis have been suggested lately (e.g., Lim et al., 1997), which will be described in Sect. 2.3.1.5.

2.2.4.3   On-Line Computer Analysis

An on-line computer analysis of all information which the EDA signal contains requires a great amount of run time for data collection, analysis and storage of this single signal. Therefore, in most applications, a subsequent off-line analysis is preferred, as described in the previous section. Additionally, an interactive evaluation as strongly recommended by the present author may hardly be performed on-line, since it would require the complete attention of an experimenter. However, an immediate signal evaluation is inevitable for applications like biofeedback (Sect. 3.1.2.3). If the information used for biofeedback should go beyond the plain EDL, which shows only slow changes, an on-line evaluation of each EDR would have to be performed. This would require an intermediate storage of a certain time window in a data buffer, which might lead to additional temporal delays in feedback. Also, a quick decision of whether or not a recorded change is due to an artifact would be required. Similar problems have been dealt with when using on-line EDA evaluation during the interaction with computers or even virtual agents (Sect. 3.5.1.1) and in adaptive automation (Sect. 3.5.1.2).

Fried (1982) used time series analysis as proposed by Lathrop (1964) for an on-line analysis of the EDA. He was able to show a very good correlation between the measures obtained and the EDR amp. An on-line procedure for the evaluation of skin impedance developed by Almasi and Schmitt (1974) is described in Sect. 2.2.3.3.

A further development of these methods of on-line computer analysis should take into account the considerations concerning the *Gestalt* of an EDR. This has been discussed in Sect. 2.3.1.3 "Recovery Parameters" with respect to modeling the recovery limb. In addition, the minimal ascent criterion mentioned in the previous section is not sufficient to make the on-line computer evaluation of the EDR similar to eyeball detection, which is normally performed by the experimenter.

2.2.5   Sources of Artifacts

Previous sections have already mentioned several possible sources of artifacts and made suggestions how to avoid them. The following sections will provide a more thorough discussion of artifacts in EDA recording. Artifacts are defined as changes in the recorded biosignal which do not stem from the signal source in question. Instead, they may result from the recording procedure (Sect. 2.2.5.1) or from physiological responses in systems other than the electrodermal one (Sect. 2.2.5.2).

2.2.5.1   Artifacts Stemming from Recording

As in any biosignal which is directly recorded as electrical activity from the body surface, a main source for artifacts is the power line noise resulting from the AC frequency input for non-battery operated recording devices, which – depending on the country – can be either 50 or 60 Hz. This kind of noise may be reduced to a great extent by means of shielding and/or connecting to the floating reference wire (Sect. 2.1.4). Sometimes, twisting of electrode cables is recommended to prevent their differential antenna effects. Another way to reduce high-frequency noise is low-pass filtering prior to amplification, which may be performed with different time constants (e.g., between 0.25 and 2 s; equivalent to frequency limits between 0.64 and 0.08 Hz, respectively). However, this may lead to a visible deformation of fast-recovering EDRs, as described in Sect. 2.1.4. Some amplifiers also provide so-called "notch" filters, which selectively block a narrow frequency band around 50 or 60 Hz, which frees electrodermal recording from most power-line noise. Recording artifacts may also arise if EDA is measured in a magnetic field (Sect. 2.2.3.5) or in field studies outside the laboratory, as frequently conducted in engineering psychophysiology (Sect. 3.5.1).

Since the influence of noise increases with amplification, constant voltage recordings are more artifact prone compared to constant current recordings, since they require higher amplification (Sects. 2.1.1 and 2.6.2). Special problems with filtering may also arise in the AC recording of EDA (Sect. 2.1.5).

In endosomatic EDA recording (Sect. 2.2.3.1), additional noise may result from insufficient connection to a floating reference wire (Sect. 2.2.3.1) or from increased transient resistance between skin and the reference electrode (Sect. 2.2.1.2). This can be improved by an additional treatment of the electrode site with subsequent reattachment of the electrode. Similar artifacts may result when electrodes detach from the skin or when there are problems stemming from cable contacts.

Additional sources of artifacts, most likely in endosomatic EDA recording, are drifts caused by bias potentials (Sect. 2.2.2.2), which inseparably superimpose themselves on the SP signal. Drifts that may result from electrode polarization can be eliminated by changing the polarity during recording (Sects. 2.2.2.2 and 2.2.3.2). Section 2.2.6.1 outlines how drifts that arise during long-term recordings can be prevented. Post-hoc removal of drifts by means of high-pass filtering is not uncritical, since it will also eliminate slow EDL changes that might be psychophysiologically relevant.

2.2.5.2 Physiologically Based Artifacts

The most important physiological source of artifacts in EDA recording is movement. This includes not only skin movements beneath the electrodes, but also muscular activity being exerted not directly underneath electrodermal recording sites.

Therefore, to provide an optimal artifact-free EDA recording, gross body movements should be avoided during recording. It is best to tell the study participant to sit or lie quietly, to relax and to try to avoid movements, especially those of the limbs from which EDA is recorded. Thus, artifacts which arise from pressure or stretching of the skin at the recording site and from changes in skin blood flow can be prevented (Sect. 2.4.2.1). Fixating the electrode wires with tape at some distance from the electrode, allowing slack in the connection, can prevent artifacts resulting from the wires being pulled. Edelberg (1967, p. 38) pointed to the following four main sources of movement artifacts:

1. Disturbance of the electrolyte concentration near the solid-liquid electrode interface.
2. Change in the intimacy of contact between electrode and skin.
3. Pressure-induced local changes in SR (Ebbecke-waves, Sect. 1.1.2).
4. Movement of the appendage across an electromagnetic field.

Quantitative relationships between skin stretching at the volar side of the forearm and elicited EDA artifacts have been established by Burbank and Webster (1978). Whereas mechanical skin tension reached a plateau during stretching, SP continued to increase with an increase of stretching. However, SZ, which had been simultaneously measured with 10 Hz AC, showed no change with stretching. Ödman (1981) used a similar arrangement for investigating the immediate consequence of a reduction of skin stretching in one individual. He also observed different courses of SP and SZ, with SP being more prone to stretching artifacts than SZ. Hence, endosomatic recordings are likely to be more influenced by stretching than exosomatic ones.

Millington and Wilkinson (1983) found a reduction of both sweat rate and salt loss (both sodium and potassium) when pressure was applied to the skin, which might have been due to an increased ductal reabsorption while sweat gland activity continues. It is likely that these processes also influence EDA (Sect. 1.3.4.2).

Apart from peripherally elicited artifacts, body movements may directly lead to EDRs via the premotor cortical and basal ganglia CNS pathway (EDA2 in Fig. 1.6; Sect. 1.3.4.1 "Three Different CNS Originating Pathways for EDA"). Thus, an increase of the NS.EDR freq. is to be expected during periods of work (Sect. 3.5.1) and also during speech activity (Sect. 2.2.5.2). Tongue-biting, which is used as a method to "beat the test" in lie-detection (Sect. 3.5.2), will elicit an EDR. Additionally, study participants may elicit voluntary EDRs by a deep inhalation and subsequent holding of their breath (e.g., Hygge & Hugdahl, 1985). Stern and Anschel (1968) investigated the action of different respiratory patterns on the SRR amp. and on cardiovascular measures in 20 study participants. They observed increasing electrodermal changes with more frequent and/or deeper inspiration. Therefore, the respiration curve should be recorded in addition to EDA recording, to enable a later elimination of artifacts caused by irregular respiratory activity (Fig. 2.23, Sect. 2.3.4.1; see also the computer program in the Appendix).

Whether EDRs as concomitants of motor actions and respiration have to be regarded as artifacts, or whether changes in the latter physiological variables and in EDA can be interpreted as covarying indicators of a psychophysiological phenomenon under investigation, depends mainly on the question being investigated (see also Schneider et al., 2003). Such a covariation of measures may be present, for example, in orienting- and defensive-responses (Sect. 3.1.1.2), where both an EDR and a deep inspiration might be reactions to a high-intense stimulus. In such a case, regarding the EDR as being merely a respiratory artifact would be not appropriate. A similar consideration might apply in case of strong emotion-eliciting or stress-inducing stimuli (Sect. 3.2.2). However, in case of low-intensity stimulation and during stimulus-free recording periods such as baselines, study participants should be instructed to avoid not only body movements but also irregular respiratory activity, in order to enable an artifact-free electrodermal recording. Needless to say that speech activity should be avoided during electrodermal recording whenever possible.

Another source of physiological artifacts is the influence of temperature on EDA recording, which will be discussed in Sect. 2.4.2.1. A special case of physio-logically-based artifacts is the possible interference from ECG which may appear in SP recordings, if electrodes are attached to sites with a relatively large distance, or if common ground electrodes are used (i.e., those connected to a floating reference wire; Sect. 2.2.1.1).

2.2.6 Techniques of Electrodermal Recording in Specific Contexts

The EDA recording methods described in Sects. 2.2.1–2.2.3.3 constitute standard techniques. However, some relatively seldom-treated questions require specific EDA recording techniques, which will be described in the following sections.

2.2.6.1 Long-Term Recording

Several types of psychophysiological investigations – for example, studies of extended sensory isolation, circadian rhythms including sleep (Sect. 3.2.1.3), and long-haul traffic operations (Sect. 3.5.1.2) with and without ambulatory monitoring (Sect. 2.2.3.4) – require that EDA electrodes be left in place undisturbed for an extended period, up to several days.

A major problem in long-term recordings is that electrodes may fall off. This can be prevented by additional fixing of electrodes being attached with adhesive tape rings (Sect. 2.2.2.1) by means of rubber bands or adhesive tapes (Sect. 2.2.1.2). Normally, such an additional fixation should be avoided because of the pressure artifacts which may result (Sect. 2.2.5). However, such a risk must be balanced against the risk of electrode detachment, which will result in total data loss. Further-more, the electrode cream should be prevented from leaking from the electrode. However, the electrode cream may also get lost while being completely absorbed by the skin, especially in case of relatively moist electrolyte media, which has been observed by Tronstad et al. (2010) after 24 h in their study described in Sect. 2.2.2.5.

Edelberg (1967) pointed to the following additional problems in long-term recordings:

1. If a closed electrode/electrolyte system as described in Sect. 2.2.2 is applied, a gradual buildup of osmotic pressure results from the use of hypertonic electrode cream. The use of an unsealed system leads to a progressive drying out of the electrode cream.

2. Inflammations may occur, especially along the edge of the electrode.[38]
3. Discomfort will result if electrodes are fixed by rubber bands or adhesive tape to the limbs, because of pressure or blood constriction.
4. Maceration of skin may occur after long exposure to an aqueous electrode cream.
5. In long-term exosomatic DC recording, a progressive de-anodization of the cathodal electrode and a progressive depression of SR have been observed.

Edelberg (1967, p. 40) described a recording method which allows EDA electrodes to be left in place for more than 10 days and avoids the problems mentioned above. He used silver cloth electrodes forming a partially closed system, held in place with a nonadhesive elastic bandage. The cloth was soaked with a solution of 78% glycerol having a total concentration of 0.6% NaCl (which is 0.1 M) or 1 of 90% polyethylene glycol-400 with the same NaCl concentration. That electrolyte had been found to be in vapor equilibrium with ambient air at 65% relative humidity.

Using this method (i.e., replenishment of the electrolyte) in seven participants for 12–14 days, Edelberg (1967) found in only 2 of his 16 test sites problems with inflammation and minor skin eruptions along the edge of the electrodes. However, compared to freshly attached electrodes, the EDR amp. decreased from an average of 96% at the beginning to 74% at the end of the long-term recording period. Furthermore, if replenishment of the cream was not possible at least every 48 h, the constant current methodology appeared to be superior to constant voltage recording (Sect. 2.6.2). Finally, if sites had been in place for 9 through 11 days in another five participants, they showed only slight activity during recording with constant voltage. However, when switched over to a constant current system, their response amplitude increased from 15 to 60% of the respective control site responses. Therefore, in cases where daily or 48-h replenishment of the electrolyte is not possible, constant current should be preferred during long-term recordings.

Zipp et al. (1980) investigated the effect of different NaCl concentrations in long-term AC measurements from sites on the back of 12 participants. An increase of the NaCl content led to a faster stabilization of the system (after 30 min), as compared to a decrease of SZL which lasted hours when lower NaCl concentrations were applied. However, the authors observed more severe skin irritations with higher NaCl concentrations.

According to Venables and Christie (1973), skin macerations will constitute a more severe problem in endosomatic compared to exosomatic recording, since in the latter case the different effects of corneal hydration may neutralize each other: on one hand, SCL will increase because of increased humidity, while on the other hand, a decrease in SCL will result from mechanical pore closure (Sect. 1.4.2.3). Using 5% KCl cream for SP recordings in five participants, Venables and Christie

---

[38] After gentle removal of their electrodes being for 24 h in place, Tronstad et al. (2010) took photographs of the skin areas that were blindly assessed by a dermatologist for skin irritation by different electrode creams. Only some signs of very faint erythema were observed, the degree of which was always lower than on the skin areas under the adhesive tape.

(p. 58) observed a marked reduction in SPR amp. during recordings of less than 1 h duration compared to freshly prepared control sites. The low-basal skin potential level (BSPL) (Sect. 2.3.2.1), however, appeared relatively uninfluenced by hydration. As a consequence, Schneider and Fowles (1978) recommended using a less hydrating mixture made from Unibase and glycol for endosomatic recording, and Unibase without glycol for exosomatic recording (Sect. 2.2.2.5). A mixture of Unibase and glycol was also held suitable for long-term recordings. However, Unibase is no longer available (see Footnote 22 in Sect. 2.2.2.5).

Turpin et al. (1983) continuously recorded SC from 12 participants for 7 h, evaluating three periods of resting and RT task performance of 10 min duration each. With a week's distance, they compared two electrolytes in counterbalanced order: (1) a nonhydrating polyethylene glycol cream and (2) a hydrating methylcellulose cream. As a control for daytime effects, fresh electrodes were attached to two fingers of the same hand which were not used for long-term recordings and differences between these and the probe sites were investigated. The hydrating cream yielded significant reductions in NS.SCR freq. and in SCR amp. as compared to the nonhydrating polyethylene glycol cream.

Whether or not a problem of polarization will appear in exosomatic DC recording depends on the actual recording time. Thus, intermittent recording may be performed, even when electrodes are left in place during the entire course of an experiment. However, if continuous recording is a requirement (e.g., during sleep studies; Sect. 3.2.1.3), either AC recording should be used (Sect. 2.2.3.3), or the polarization of DC should be changed regularly during recording (Sect. 2.2.2.2).

During sleep, a marked increase in SRL is likely to occur (Sect. 3.2.1.3). This may lead to additional problems if constant current is used, because relatively high voltages will be necessary to maintain the intended current density, which can possibly lead to tissue damage (Sect. 2.6.2). Edelberg (1967, p. 42) proposed a solution which utilizes the endosomatic potential produced by the skin to measure its own resistance. If two SP electrodes, between which an initial potential U_0 is measured, are suddenly shunted by means of an external resistor R_S, the potential U_0 recorded with a high-impedance amplifier will drop to U_S. The internal resistance R_0 of the SP generator in the skin can be calculated according to (2.10a):

$$R_0 = \frac{U_0 - U_S}{U_S} R_S \qquad (2.10a)$$

However, considerable switching artifacts may arise if SP measurement is performed in conjunction with EEG recordings. Therefore, Edelberg (1967) described an alternative technique that couples SP with SY measurement. Because of its more general usability, the appropriate method is described separately in the next section.

It should be pointed out that an application of procedures for correction of drifts, which occur during long-term recordings, will require the recording of control values by using additional freshly prepared control sites (Sect. 2.3.4.3).

2.2.6.2 Recording Simultaneously with Different Techniques

Some scientific questions (e.g., direct comparisons of different EDA recording techniques; Sects. 2.6.1–2.6.3) may require simultaneous recording of EDA using different methods. In these cases, the inputs of the amplifiers used must be galvanically separated to avoid cross currents (Sect. 2.1.4).

A method of simultaneous recording of skin potential and skin admittance had been described by Edelberg (1967, p. 42). Between one of two SP electrodes and the amplifier, a low-impedance source of low-level and low-frequency AC (e.g., 10 mV at 20 Hz) is interposed. This voltage will divide itself between the subject and the amplifier in proportion to their impedances (Sect. 2.1.1). If an AC-coupled amplifier (Sect. 2.1.3) whose output is rectified is used with a time constant of 0.05 s, the SPL part of the signal will be blocked and the SCL part can be calculated according to (2.10b):

$$ \mathrm{SCL} = \frac{Y_S}{Y_T - Y_S} C_A \tag{2.10b} $$

where at C_A is the amplifier input conductance, Y_T is the deflection produced by the AC source when the subject leads are short-circuited, and Y_S is the deflection with the subject in series. According to the present author's experience, it is not easy to obtain artifact-free recordings using AC and DC measurement techniques simultaneously, since the AC signal which is applied to the skin at one site superimposes the DC-recorded signal, even contralaterally. One technique to overcome this problem is continuously switching between these recording methods, which also allows the same site to be used for both methods. The disadvantage is that switching skin to a different EDA coupler will always result in an adaptation of the gain process, dependent on the filter characteristics of the amplifier system, which constitutes a time consuming procedure. Parallel recordings of SP and exosomatic DC measurements on contralateral sites are possible without such problems.

To ensure that different measurement techniques do not influence each other, they should be used together with a substitute circuitry formed either by resistors alone (e.g., Boucsein & Hoffmann, 1979), or by resistors together with capacitors, according to the electrical model of skin as depicted in Fig. 1.18 (Sect. 1.4.3.3). Also, possible influences stemming from other physiological variables recorded at the same time should be carefully controlled (Sect. 2.2.5.2).

Recently, Grimnes, Jabbari, Martinsen, and Tronstad (2011) used a special recording method for combining SY with SP recordings from an active electrode at a palmar site together with a large indifferent electrode connected to a physiological NaCl bath in which the forearm was immersed. Their recording system used a small AC current, enabling the DC potential and SY to be recorded simultaneously at the same site. They found SPRs with diphasic sharp edges which did not appear in the SYR waveforms. Furthermore, the SPRs were more robust with respect to movement artifacts than the SYRs.

2.2.6.3 Recording with Dry Electrodes or Liquid Electrolytes

Today's standard technique of electrodermal recording, i.e., using electrodes together with humid electrolytes as described in Sect. 2.2.2, may cause the following problems, as pointed out by Muthny (1984):

1. The moistening of skin by the electrolyte cream may lead to an EDL drift over time and additionally make the system less sensitive to EDRs (Sect. 2.2.6.1).
2. Polarization which appears at the boundaries of the electrode/skin system may be reduced to some extent when appropriate electrodes and electrolytes are used (Sect. 2.2.2.2). However, since polarization can never be totally eliminated, an oscillation of the electrode/skin system may appear which may last even for hours.
3. There might be uncontrolled and as yet unexplored interactions between electrodes, electrolytes and skin, which may influence the measurement in an uncontrolled manner.

Fowles (1974) suggested the swelling of the stratum corneum being the main reason for the effects observed with skin moistening, as outlined under (1). On one side, moistening leads to an increase in SCL, while on the other hand ductal pores are mechanically closed, causing a decrease in EDR amp., since the ducts are no longer in use as electrical shunts between skin surface and sweat gland membranes (Sects. 1.4.2.3 and 2.2.6.1).

To prevent changes in EDA which may arise from moistening of the skin, dry electrodes have been used by several authors. However, Millington and Wilkinson (1983) point to the existence of mechanisms for ionic transport in dry corneum (Sect. 1.4.2.1). Additionally, sweat will act as an electrolyte between dry electrodes and the skin surface, which makes recording conditions even more uncontrollable (Muthny, 1984). Thomas and Korr (1957) artificially dried out the skin with heat to prevent against this effect.[39]

Dry electrodes have to be used in case of parallel recordings of EDA and skin vaporization. Thus in an appropriate investigation described in Sect. 2.4.1.1, Rutenfranz and Wenzel (1958) used dry electrodes made from V2A-steel nets, which appeared, however, to be polarizable. Hence, Zipp and Faber (1979) developed a dry electrode made from platinum/platinum-Mohr, which has low polarization proneness, similar to that of Ag/AgCl electrodes. The electrode was provided in a ventilated chamber and attached with a constant pressure of 0.5 kPa to the skin. In recordings performed with one participant, these authors found no marked differences in the amplitudes of the oscillations over time of the SYL between their dry electrode and a conventional humid Ag/AgCl electrode. However, their comparisons of EDRs obtained with the different methods were not stringent, so the asserted advantage of their dry electrode method remains somewhat doubtful.

---

[39] Recently, omitting of an electrode cream became rather common in EDA recording devices for applications outside the laboratory (Sects. 2.2.3.4 and 2.2.6.3). However, it must be kept in mind that such a system will be unstable for an unknown period of time, since the humidity built up by sweat under dry electrodes will cause a drift towards an increase of skin conductance.

EDA recording with liquid electrolytes had been used, for example, in determining the influence of locally acting drugs or cosmetics on the peripheral mechanism of EDA (Sect. 3.5.3). Edelberg (1967, p. 12) described such a method, which had been used in a similar manner by Lykken and Rose (1959) for measuring EDA in rats, which Edelberg combined with a special masking technique. First, the recording site on the finger was covered with a disc of pressure-sensitive tape. Second, the entire finger, including the nail, was covered with rubber paper cement, whereat two thin coatings were more effective than a single thick layer. Third, when the cement was almost dry, the covering of the recording site was removed. Two fingers prepared like this were immersed in separate baths, each of which was connected via an agar-KCl salt bridge (Sect. 2.2.2.5) to a chamber with an Ag/AgCl electrode in 1 M KCl solution. The salt bridge's end was immersed into a perforated plastic tube forming a barrier, thus preventing contamination of the contact electrolyte with the KCl.

Another method to measure EDA using liquid electrolytes has been used at forearm sites by the Yamamoto group (cf. Yamamoto et al., 1978, Fig. 5). They applied a plastic tube with two open ends vertically to the skin, which had been filled with an electrolyte made of 91.6% polyethylene glycol, 0.9% NaCl, and 7.5% water (by weight), in which an Ag/AgCl electrode was immersed. Because of the negative effects on EDA elicited by impeded blood circulation, the tube was not fixed with the use of adhesive tape or rubber bands, but instead through the use of histoacrylic glue (Sect. 2.2.2.1).

2.2.6.4 Other Specific Electrode Arrangements

This section outlines several infrequently employed recording techniques, using more than two electrodes or unusual types of electrodes. In addition to the construction of Ag/AgCl chamber electrodes, Venables and Martin (1967a) gave a description of how to manufacture sponge electrodes, which should be less prone to error potentials and to electrode drift (Sects. 2.2.2.2 and 2.2.5.1). Therefore, their use might be appropriate for endosomatic rather than exosomatic EDA recording (Grings, 1974).

A two-element electrode had been described by Lykken (1959a), consisting of an inner circle surrounded by a concentric ring, both made from zinc, and isulated against each other. Two of these electrodes were applied, and the measurement current was brought to the skin via the outer rings, while the inner rings were used for recording. Since the current flow through the inner rings was rather low, no polarization occured. Edelberg (1967), Montagu and Coles (1968), and Grings (1974) suggested not to transfer the principle of the two-element electrode to constant current measurement. The latter might be performed by the use of comparator circuitry.

A similar principle of measurement was used by the four-line microelectrode, proposed by Campbell et al. (1977), which has a total width of 0.11 mm. The two outer electrode lines were connected with the voltage source, while recording was performed via the two inner electrode lines (cf. also Millington & Wilkinson, 1983, p. 129). These microelectrodes allow recording from a very small single site and may be used to investigate resistivity at any point in the stratum corneum (Footnote 42, Sect. 1.4.2.2).

More than two electrodes have been used for AC measurement of EDA with higher frequencies: Edelberg (1971) and Yamamoto et al. (1978) used a three-electrode technique, while Salter (1979) and Thiele (1981a) used four electrodes in AC recording. Grimnes (1983) and Tronstad et al. (2010) applied a three-electrode configuration for SY recording, to obtain unipolar measurements of the skin surface conductance density below the active electrode. The AC injecting electrode was connected via an additional operational amplifier to a remote reference electrode, thereby providing a potential below the reference electrode which balances the applied AC voltage and thus eliminates the contribution from the AC injecting electrode and the underlying SY to the measurement. Further discussions of the technical implications for multielectrode recordings are given by Schwan (1963) and by Salter (1979, pp. 36 ff.).[40]

2.2.7 Summary of Recording Techniques

EDA recording is normally performed at palmar sites, with the use of an inactive reference electrode on the upper forearm in endosomatic recording (Fig. 2.6, Sect. 2.2.1.1). While the reference site has to be pretreated to reduce the electrical resistance between surface and inner tissue, no such treatment is necessary for the active recording sites, both in endosomatic and exosomatic measurement, although some authors recommended such a procedure (Sect. 2.2.1.2).

The following recording techniques will be referred to as "standard methodology" in the present book: DC recording with constant voltage of 0.5 V (Sect. 2.6.2) or constant current not exceeding 10 $\mu A/cm^2$ (Sect. 2.2.3.2), using Ag/AgCl chamber electrodes with 0.5–1 cm^2 area (Sect. 2.2.2.3), filled with an isotonic NaCl cream, based on a neutral medium (Sect. 2.2.2.5) and fixed by means of double-sided adhesive collars (Sect. 2.2.2.1) on skin sites, which should be neither pretreated (except for the inactive site in SP recording, see Sect. 2.2.1.2) nor washed with water and soap.[41] After being used, electrodes are rinsed carefully with distilled water to avoid damage of the Ag/AgCl layer. When not in use, electrodes may be short-circuited and stored in NaCl solution, but dry storage will do in most cases as well (Sect. 2.2.2.4). No such standard technique for exosomatic recording

---

[40] For a multiple-electrode recording technique using electrical impedance spectroscopy, see Footnote 50, Sect. 1.4.3.3.

[41] Small deviations from this standard methodology will be mentioned in the text, larger ones in footnotes.

using AC has been established as yet, however, the use of φ values (i.e., phase angles) instead of EDR amp. obtained with DC constant current or constant voltage technique might be a direction to go for the future (Sects. 2.2.3.3 and Sect. 2.3.1.2 "Amplitudes of Exosomatic Responses Recorded with Alternating Current").

There are specific features of the EDA signal to be considered for obtaining a reliable and artifact-free recording (see Sect. 2.1). Experimenters should be aware of these problems, comparing the features of their own equipment with those of the apparatus described in Sect. 2.2.3.1.

Recording methods, whether they use paper or electronic storage, should take the wide range of the electrodermal signal into consideration (Sect. 2.2.4.1). Recording of EDRs requires a high resolution, and care must be taken not to lose data by exceeding the boundaries of the recording channel. Computerized systems for recording and for data evaluation are available now (Sects. 2.2.4.2 and 2.2.4.3, see also the Appendix of the present book). Ambulatory monitoring and EDA recording within a magnetic field have made great progress now but still require special precautions (Sects. 2.2.3.4 and 2.2.3.5).

In the most frequently applied exosomatic DC recording of EDA, interference with power-line noise is less problematic than for other biosignals (Sect. 2.2.5.1). However, physiologically produced artifacts, especially those from movements and respiratory activity during recording, have to be considered (Sect. 2.2.5.2). Artifact-correcting procedures in computer evaluation of EDA are time consuming (Sect. 2.2.4.2). Therefore, artifact-free recordings should be attempted whenever possible.

2.3 Analytic Procedures

As usual for biosignals, parameters have to be extracted from electrodermal recordings prior to statistical evaluation. In comparison with higher frequent signals like ECG, EMG or EEG, recording of EDA is based on relatively slow-changing physiological processes. The evaluation of phasic changes focuses mainly on irregularly appearing single events, rather than on patterns that may be characterized by changes in frequency and/or amplitude. Hence, there is no point in applying procedures like power spectrum or Fourier analyses for obtaining parameters from electrodermal recordings.

The first stage of parameterization is the extraction of phasic and tonic values from the recorded signal. Since the evaluation of one kind of tonic parameter, i.e., the NS.EDR freq., requires knowledge of how to obtain phasic parameters, the latter ones will be treated first (Sect. 2.3.1) and thereafter tonic parameters (Sect. 2.3.2). Two successive subsections in the present section outline further possibilities of data treatment prior to statistical evaluation: transformations and artifact removal (Sects. 2.3.3 and 2.3.4).

2.3.1 Parameters of Phasic Electrodermal Activity

The phasic fraction of the EDA signal is labeled "response," although there is not always a distinct relationship between a stimulus and an EDR (Sect. 1.1.1). However, most phasic changes of EDA show a rather characteristic course or *Gestalt* (Sect. 2.3.1.3 "Recovery Parameters"), which enables the experimenter to separate them from artifacts with sufficient reliability. Unfortunately, algorithms for the detection of an EDR *Gestalt* are not simply obtainable for computer analysis (Sect. 2.2.4.3). Therefore, visual control of the signal during an interactive evalua-tion is highly recommended (Sect. 2.2.4.2).

2.3.1.1 Latency Times and Windows

Electrodermal responses have relatively long latencies compared to other biosignals, for example event related potentials (ERPs) or changes in HR. Latencies of exosomatic EDRs (EDR lat.) are normally between 1 and 2 s, but may be prolonged up to 5 s in cases of skin cooling (Edelberg, 1967).

The latency of the first SPR component is about 300 ms shorter than the SCR lat. (Venables & Christie, 1980).[42] There are many discussions of the appropriate time window for an EDR following a distinct stimulus and hence for the possible range of latencies. Edelberg (1972a) suggested a window between 1.2 and 4 s, regarding 1.8 s as a characteristic value in comfortable ambient temperature. Venables and Christie (1980), who considered EDR lat. exceeding 4 s being too long, proposed a window between 1 and 3 s as being rather conservative but suitable in most cases (Fig. 2.21, Sect. 2.3.2.2).

Levinson and Edelberg (1985, Table 4) reported a synopsis of all EDR latencies published in the journal *Psychophysiology* between 1977 and 1982. According to this synopsis, windows between 1 and 4 s and between 1 and 5 s were the most frequently used ones. These authors recommended the calculation of a specific time window for each experiment, taken from the range of the EDR lat. of all participants to the first applied stimulus. They reported windows between 1.0 and 2.4 s from their own laboratory.

Stern and Walrath (1977) proposed an individual standardization of the time window, using the individual modal value, and limiting the window to ±0.5 s of this value. Venables and Christie (1980) also recommend this kind of standardization, however, only in cases of atypical EDRs, for example, those obtained from older study participants (Sect. 2.4.3.1) or from patients (Sect. 3.4).

---

[42] Nishiyama, Sugenoya, Matsumoto, Iwase, and Mano (2001), in their study described in Foot-note 17, Sect. 1.3.2.1, observed that sudomotor bursts as recorded by microneurography were followed by SPRs with latencies of 1.33 ± 0.33 s.

In some individuals, it is difficult to obtain stimulus-dependent EDRs and hence EDR latencies at all, since they display such a high frequency of nonspecific phasic electrodermal changes (Sect. 2.3.2.2). Also, in many cases the lack of exact criteria for appropriate windows or their inadequate application may have led to a mis-interpretation of nonspecific EDRs as specific EDRs (Levinson & Edelberg, 1985).

Other authors (e.g., Thom, 1988) used the point of the EDR maximum to calculate the EDR lat. instead of the EDR onset. In this case, the rise time (Sect. 2.3.1.3 "Parameters of Ascent") has to be subtracted for comparison with common latency values.

Another problem that arises in the evaluation of EDR lat. is the often indistinct onset of an EDR. In this case, calculating the first derivative may be helpful (Sect. 2.3.1.3 "Parameters of Ascent"), which, however, presupposes data being electronically recorded. If paper recording is used, latencies can only be obtained in a reliable manner if the paper speed is at minimum of 10 mm/s.

Additionally, skin temperature should be recorded if it is intended to compare EDR latencies from different investigations (Sects. 2.4.2.1 and 2.5.2.3), since 20–50% of the EDR lat. is dependent on the acetylcholine transport in the periphery, which in turn varies with temperature (Sect. 1.3.2.1).

2.3.1.2 Amplitudes

The amplitude is the most frequently used measure to describe a single EDR. Evaluation of amplitudes (EDR amp.) should be performed using certain criteria for their minimum value (section "Choice of Amplitude Criteria") and for the correct treatment of superimposed EDRs (Fig. 2.16).

A further complication may arise from the inconsistently use of the term "EDR magnitude." Unfortunately, several authors, i.e., Venables and Christie (1980), recommended the use of the term *magnitude* instead of *amplitude*. However, for the sake of unambiguity, "magnitude" should be restricted to a special kind of missing data treatment, being described in Sect. 2.3.4.2, which takes into account zero response to stimuli which is included in averaging, thus leading to a *mean magnitude* which is different from the mean EDR amp., being calculated as arithmetic mean of all observed EDR amp.

Amplitudes of Endosomatic Responses

While the exosomatic EDR is always monophasic, as pointed out in the next section, endosomatic EDRs may be mono- , bi- or even triphasic, for reasons which were previously discussed in Sect. 1.4.2.3.

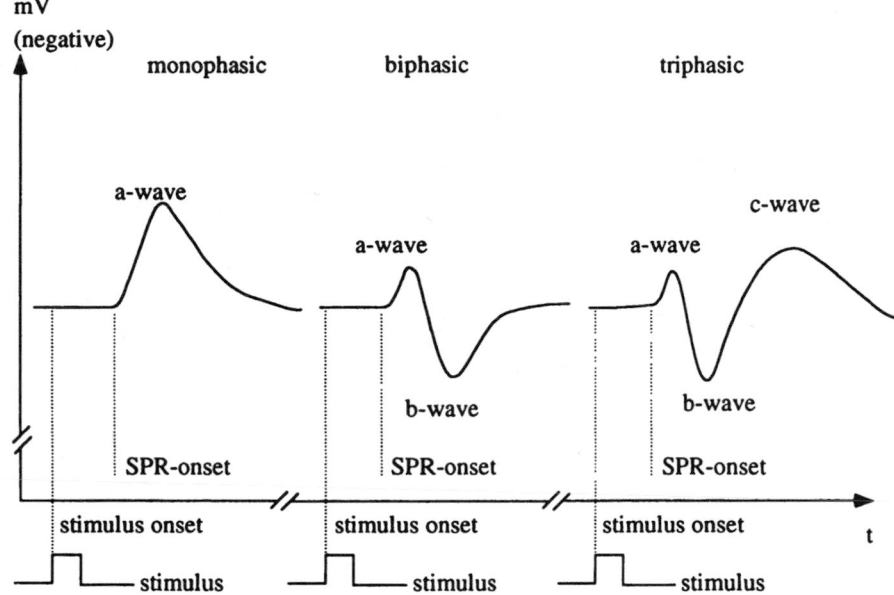

Fig. 2.14 Different types of SPRs: mono- , bi- , and triphasic forms. Higher values mean greater negativity of the active with respect to the passive recording site (Sect. 2.2.1.1)

Figure 2.14 shows examples of different kinds of SPRs. As proposed by Forbes (1964), the first negative deflection is labeled a-wave, the positive deflection b-wave, and the second negative deflection c-wave or γ-wave.[43] Monophasic SPRs may also be positive instead of being negative as usual. Since the observed SPR is always composed of two underlying processes, the evaluation of SPR amp. remains problematic (Venables & Christie, 1980; for a further discussion see Edelberg, 1967, p. 48). In biphasic SPRs, some authors prefer an amplitude evaluation from the negative to the positive peak instead of evaluating a negative and a positive deflection from the prestimulus level; however, there is not enough evidence that this constitutes an appropriate evaluation (Venables & Christie, 1973).

SPR amp. are recorded in mV. Results from several experiments which made use of SPR amp. evaluations are given in Sect. 2.5.1.1. The advantage of endosomatic recording, which incurs from being free from any external current applied to the system, is outweighed by the ambiguity of the endosomatic EDR amp. evaluation.

---

[43] The convention for graphical representation is, as in the neurophysiological tradition of EEG recording, "negative up" (Venables & Christie, 1980).

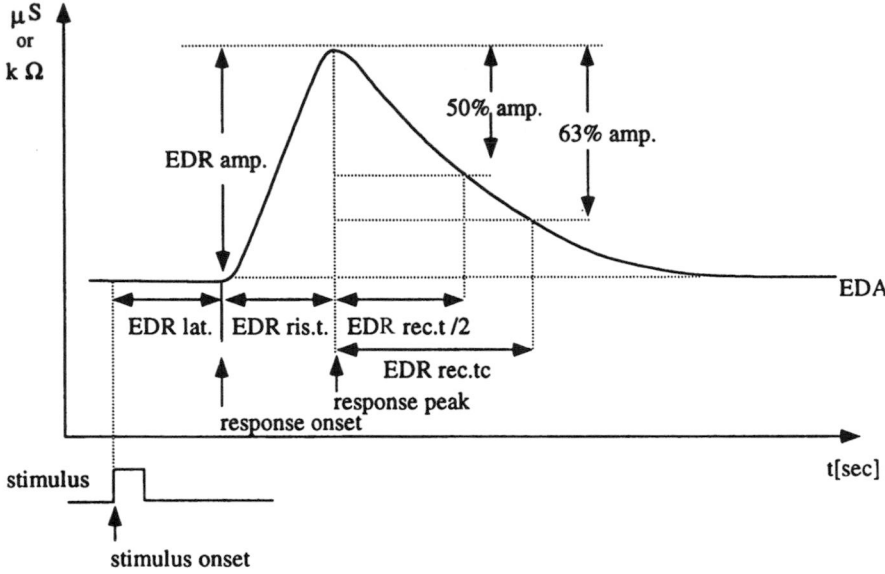

Fig. 2.15 An ideal type-1 DC recorded exosomatic EDR and the parameters to be obtained from it (see text for explanations)

Amplitudes of Exosomatic Responses Recorded with Direct Current

Exosomatic EDRs are always monophasic as shown in Fig. 2.15. A given stimulus will – after a certain latency (Sect. 2.3.1.1) – lead to a deflection which constitutes an increase in SC or a decrease in SR, depending on the recording technique (Sects. 2.1.1 and 2.1.2). The SCR amp. is measured in µS, whereas the SRR amp. is measured in kΩ (Sect. 1.4.1.1). The *Gestalt* of an exosomatic EDR shows a relatively steep onset and a flatter recovery, i.e., the rise time of an EDR is shorter than its recovery time (Sect. 2.3.1.3 "Recovery Parameters").

The evaluation of a single EDR amp. may become problematic in case of overlapping (i.e., superimposed) EDRs. These are typical for states of high arousal (Sect. 3.2.1.1), in individuals being high in electrodermal lability (Sect. 3.3.2.2), during EDA conditioning (Sect. 3.1.2.1) or during parallel recordings of EDRs and ERPs (Sect. 2.3.1.5). The degree to which a subsequent EDR is distorted depends on the amplitude and proximity of a preceding EDR (Grings & Schell, 1969). Figure 2.16 shows two examples of superimposed EDRs. They are labeled – in opposition to the ideal "type 1" in Fig. 2.15 – as "type 2" and "type 3." In cases of superimposed responses, where there is evidence for an incomplete response (i.e., if the recovery of the first EDR does not fall beyond at least half of EDR amp.), evaluation method "A" in Fig. 2.15 can be used to

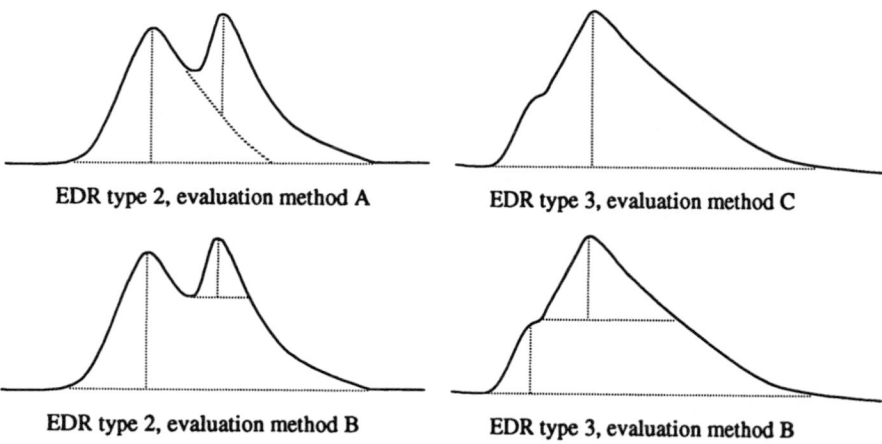

EDR type 2, evaluation method A   EDR type 3, evaluation method C

EDR type 2, evaluation method B   EDR type 3, evaluation method B

Fig. 2.16 Examples of overlapping (superimposed) exosomatic EDRs of type 2 and 3, and methods of evaluating the appropriate amplitudes (see text for explanations)

extrapolate the first EDR.[44] The amplitude of the second EDR is then obtained by measuring the vertical distance from its peak to the extrapolated recovery line of the first response (Hagfors, 1964).

Evaluation method "B" in Fig. 2.16 is much easier to perform and has been widely regarded as standard (see the evaluation method used in the Appendix). Edelberg (1967, p. 46), who electrically stimulated the distal stump of the cat's plantar nerve, demonstrated that such an evaluation will lead to sufficiently exact results in most cases.

While in type-2 recordings there are always two distinct EDRs to be detected, this is not the case in type-3 overlaps, especially if there is no return subsequent to the first peak of the curve, but instead another ascent. To avoid any bias, one has to fix appropriate criteria before starting the evaluation, i.e., whether an EDR course is to be regarded as a single EDR (evaluation method "C" in Fig. 2.16) or as two superimposed EDRs (evaluation method "B"), being recommended by Edelberg (1967, Fig. 1.16d). It is also possible to evaluate the three types of EDRs separately (Thom, 1988).

Foerster (1984), in his computer evaluation program (Sect. 2.2.4.2), used a criterion of distance to the secant line to distinguish between a hump that is formed by superimposed EDRs and another one that might be due to artificial deflections. A formalized hump detection procedure is used by the computer program in the Appendix of this book for identifying superimposed EDRs. Mathematical solutions for evaluating superimposed EDRs will be described in Sect. 2.3.1.5.

---

[44] An illustration of two subsequent EDRs, from both of which all EDR parameters can be obtained without extrapolation because the recovery of the first EDR goes beyond half of its amplitude is shown in Fig. 18.3 of Boucsein (2005).

Table 2.1 Dependency of the minimum amplitude criterion on amplification and channel width in paper recording

| Method | Expected values | | Resolution | |
| | Upper and lower limit | Range | Corresponding value to 1 mm deflection, given a channel width of: | |
			40 mm	200 mm
SC	10–30 µS	20 µS	0.5 µS	0.1 µS
	10–20 µS	10 µS	0.25 µS	0.05 µS
SR	100–500 kΩ	400 kΩ	10 kΩ	2 kΩ
	20–100 kΩ	80 kΩ	2 kΩ	0.4 kΩ

Choice of Amplitude Criteria

Before starting with the evaluation of the electrodermal signal, a *criterion* should be fixed concerning the *minimum deflection* in µS or kΩ, which has to appear to register an EDR. Such a criterion is largely dependent on the resolution of the recording, which in turn depends on the signal's expected range and its amplification. Table 2.1 provides examples of the amplification's dependency on the amplitude criterion. Given that 1 mm is the minimum deflection being reliably detectable by hand evaluation and the normal polygraph recording channel width is 40 mm, a range for recording of SC between 10 and 30 µS will restrict the possible amplitude criterion to values being not smaller than 0.5 µS. However, if electrodermal reactivity is so low that the range may be restricted to values between 10 and 20 µS without the danger of SCRs exceeding this range (Sect. 2.2.4.1), an increase of amplification may occur and, in turn, the amplitude criterion can be lowered to 0.25 µS. If a compensation recorder with 20 cm channel width is in use instead of the above-mentioned polygraph, the resolution will become 5 times as high, which – with a 20 µS range – will lead to a minimum amplitude criterion of 0.1 µS, and with a 10 µS range to a 0.05 µS criterion. An appropriate example for SR recording is given in the lower part of Table 2.1.

As already pointed out in Sect. 2.2.4.2, an A/D conversion with subsequent computer parameterization of the electrodermal signal may allow for much higher resolution than paper recording and hand evaluation. If it is attempted to make these different evaluations comparable, the same amplitude criterion should be chosen for both hand- and computer evaluation. This may lead to disregarding very small EDRs, which could be evaluated with computer parameterization instead of using traditional hand scoring.

In some scientific contexts, e.g., in schizophrenia research, electrodermal non-reactivity has to be defined, which requires a fixed amplitude criterion (Sect. 3.4.2.2). As can be inferred from Table 2.1, values recommended in these contexts (e.g., 0.05 µS by Gruzelier & Venables, 1972; or 0.4 kΩ by Zahn, 1976) require relatively high amplification, and hence might not be attained by electrodermal recording devices using paper output (Sect. 2.2.4.1).

Moreover, the question of whether or not a specific amplitude criterion makes sense cannot be answered without knowledge and inclusion of the signal-to-noise ratio of the recording system.[45] As pointed out in Sect. 2.1.4, the frequently used decoupling of EDR with higher amplification may lead to effective signal-to-noise ratios below 20 dB. Given a total range of 20 μS, as in line 1 of Table 2.1, and a signal-to-noise ratio of 20 dB, it is possible that changes produced by noise reach values of 2 μS. This can be calculated using a transformation of the equation provided in the sixth paragraph of Sect. 2.1.4. Thus, it might not make sense in this case to lower the amplitude criterion below the appropriate value.

Because of the possible level dependency of the EDR (Sect. 2.5.4.2), Edelberg (1972a) proposed a *relative amplitude criterion* of 0.1% of the initial SRL for counting SRRs. He also recommended resetting the amplitude criterion again, if changes in SRL exceed 10%. However, it has become more common to prefer an amplitude criterion which remains constant throughout the whole recording time. For such a case, Edelberg recommended a 0.1 μS criterion for SCRs, whereas Venables and Christie (1980) chose the above-mentioned criteria of 0.05 μS for SCRs and 0.4 kΩ for SRRs. Given today's A/D converter resolutions (Sect. 2.2.4.2), it is possible to lower the amplitude criterion to 0.01 μS.

While the SCR is independent from the contact area between skin and electrode, this area plays an important role in SRR because of its influence on current density (Sect. 2.2.3.2). Therefore, several authors provide their SR results related to the electrode area as *specific resistances* in kΩ-cm^2 (Sect. 2.3.3.1).

Edelberg (1972a) pointed to a method of EDR evaluation which might be used if a signal cannot be unambiguously defined, using the difference between a prestimulus and a poststimulus EDL. Those EDLs are obtained either as mean or as minimum-to-maximum values of a certain period, e.g., 15 s before and after stimulus onset.

Amplitudes of Exosomatic Responses Recorded with Alternating Current

Since the output signal of AC-recorded EDA is rectified (Sect. 2.1.5), the appropriate EDRs can be evaluated in the same manner as shown for DC-recorded EDRs in Fig. 2.15 (section "Amplitudes of Exosomatic Responses Recorded with Direct Current"). Due to the recording technique and/or subsequent transformations used, evaluations are performed in kΩ in case of a SZR or in μS in case of a SYR. If the phase angle φ is recorded continuously in addition to impedance or admittance, it is possible to analyze the phase angle's course in time in a similar manner to the courses of R and X or B and G, respectively, which are computed according to the appropriate equations given in Sect. 1.4.1.3.

---

[45] A declaration of the signal-to-noise ratio, which is obvious in audio devices, is often lacking in descriptions of polygraph amplifiers.

An example of evaluating an AC-recorded EDR is given by Boucsein et al. (1989, Fig. 4) using the recording device described in Fig. 2.13 (Sect. 2.2.3.3). The authors found very similar, though mirror-imaged, courses of Z and φ. This similarity remained after a transformation into values of R and X. However, if a transformation into values of G and B was performed, EDR-like changes of the signal could only be observed in conductance but not in susceptance, even with high resolution. This provides evidence for the hypothesis that the major changes during an EDR take place in the parallel resistance R_2 (Fig. 1.18, Sect. 1.4.3.3), which can be inferred from Fig. 1.20 (Sect. 1.4.3.3).

The use of the phase angle φ as phasic EDA-AC measure has been suggested by Schaefer and Boucsein (2000), since φ is independent of both the measurement technique applied and the existing EDL (Sects. 2.1.5 and 2.2.3.3). In terms of the nomenclature employed in Table 1.1 (Sect. 1.1.1), the phasic response could be labeled SφR, and all the appropriate supplementary abbreviations in Table 1.1 would be applicable as well. For example, SφR amp. would be the amplitude of a deflection, SφR lat. would be the latency from stimulus onset to the point of time when the deflection started, SφR ris.t. and SφR rec.tc or SφR rec.t/2 would correspond to rise time, 63% recovery or 50% recovery. The frequency of the nonspecific SφRs could be labeled NS.SφR freq. However, Table 1.1 was not amended accordingly, since SφR has not yet been used in that way outside of the present author's laboratory.

If a continuous recording of EDA using more than one AC frequency is attempted, as described in Sect. 2.1.5, the depiction of the course of an EDR could be plotted in the form of loci (Fig. 1.10, Sect. 1.4.1.3), which might be extended for incorporating the time dimension, parallel to what is used in 3D EEG recordings.

2.3.1.3 Shape of Electrodermal Responses

The major electrodermal parameters which describe the shape of an EDR were depicted in Fig. 2.15 (Sect. 2.3.1.2). The following sections describe how to obtain those as well as additional parameters of ascent (section "Parameters of Ascent") and descent (section "Recovery Parameters") for an EDR.

Parameters of Ascent

To obtain reliable values for EDR rise times (EDR ris.t.), it is necessary to unambiguously define its onset and its peak, since EDR ris.t. is defined as the time span between response onset and response peak (e.g., Venables & Christie, 1980). The point of response onset, which separates EDR lat. from EDR ris.t., is much less reliably obtainable than the time point of an EDR peak, especially if the EDR begins to ascend as a flat curve. Edelberg (1967) recommended the use of a

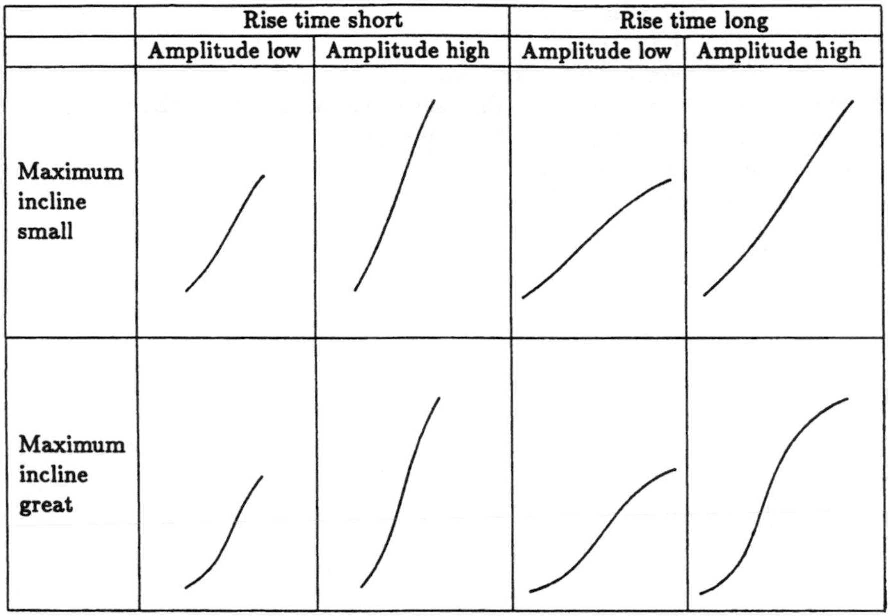

	Rise time short		Rise time long	
	Amplitude low	Amplitude high	Amplitude low	Amplitude high
Maximum incline small				
Maximum incline great				

Fig. 2.17 Examples of different forms of an EDR ascent, which have different rise times and maxima of their incline, depending on the EDR amplitude

first derivate, which passes the zero line if the curve shows maxima or minima.[46] Unfortunately, this method provides only unambiguous values for the peak of an EDR, since its onset is normally not a minimum in the EDA curve, but an upward deflection from a more or less steady line. Hence, Foerster (1984), in his computer program for EDA analysis (Sect. 2.2.4.2), detected the turning point of the ascent as a first step, going back to the point where the incline goes under 1% of its maximum value, and defined this point as EDR onset.[47] Instead, the computer program described in the Appendix of this book uses the gradient of incline to decide when to start an EDR evaluation. This may become problematic if an EDR is less ideally formed than the curve depicted in Fig. 2.15. To avoid such a problem, Thom (1988) recommended defining rise time as the time the curve needs to pass between 10 and 90% of the amplitude.

When hand evaluation of paper-recorded EDA is performed, response onset and peak are obtained with the aid of graphical methods (Sect. 2.2.4.1). As with the

---

[46] The first derivate has been used by Biro and Stukovsy (1993) in an evaluation of paper-recorded SRRs to 1 kHz, 100 dB, 550 ms tones from 300 male participants. Besides the SRR amp. evaluated from the original curve, several amplitude, time, and reaction shape parameters were exploited from the first derivate. A factor analysis of all parameters revealed a response shape factor, an amplitude factor and a latency factor, which altogether accounted for 84.6% of the total variance.

[47] Thom (1988) used a criterion of 10% instead, because the application of the 1% criterion is difficult if numerous electrodermal fluctuations appear.

evaluation of latency times, the accuracy of EDR ris.t. is dependent on recording paper speed (Sect. 2.3.1.1).

An additional measure of ascent, which can, however, only be obtained with sufficient reliability by means of computer evaluation, is the EDR's maximum incline (e.g., Foerster, 1984; Thom, 1988). Figure 2.17 shows hypothetical forms of an EDR ascent, combining characteristics of amplitude, rise time and maximum incline. The maximum incline can be used to describe the *Gestalt* of an EDR ascent, which becomes more S-shaped as the maximum incline increases. Figure 2.17 also shows that – given the same amplitude – a negative correlation between rise time and maximum incline of an EDR ascent is to be expected.

Recovery Parameters

In most cases it will not be possible to determine the exact point in time when an EDR is terminated. As depicted in Fig. 2.15 (Sect. 2.3.1.2), the decline may end more or less asymptotically. Additionally, due to EDL shifts that might occur during an EDR, the end point is very likely not to reach the pre-response level of the EDL in cases of DC coupling or when time constants in AC-coupled systems are long (Sect. 2.1.3).

In order to obtain measures for EDR recovery, Darrow (1937b) used the half-life concept as applied to radioactive matter. Half-life indicates the time span after which one-half of the available amount of a radioactive substance decays. Transferring this concept to an EDR, its amplitude is regarded as the "total amount," and its half-life, or EDR rec.t/2, is the time from response peak to the point where the curve falls below one-half of the EDR amp. (Fig. 2.15).

In the following equation, the height of the EDR amp. is indicated by A,[48] and the velocity of an EDR recovery can be calculated – according to the appropriate function in a radioactive matter – as follows:

$$\frac{dA}{dT} = -\tau A \qquad (2.11a)$$

at which τ is the time constant, and the minus sign indicates that the EDR is recovering. If a quantity is proportional to its own change, as is the case for A in (2.11a), this always indicates an exponential course of the quantity with respect to time (Sect. 1.4.1.2). Such a time course can be described in terms of electrophysiology as a capacitor's discharge within a RC-circuit (see (1.10a), Sect. 1.4.1.2):

$$A = A_0 \, e^{(-t/\tau)} \qquad (2.11b)$$

A_0 is the initial value of A (i.e., the EDA at the response peak) which can be shown when substituting $t = 0$, because $e_0 = 1$.

---

[48] A is measured in mV for SP, in μS for SC and SY, and in kΩ for SR and SZ.

To obtain the time constant τ in s, t must be substituted by τ in (2.11b). This leads to an exponent of -1, and because $e^{-1} = 1/e$, it follows:

$$A = \frac{A_0}{e} = \frac{A_0}{2.7182\ldots} = 0.3678\ldots A_0 \tag{2.11c}$$

The time, which corresponds to the time constant τ, is reached when the EDR has descended to about 0.37 of its maximum value A_0 (i.e., the EDR has recovered by about 63%). Thus, calculating the EDR rec.tc leads directly to the time constant for EDR recovery (Sect. 1.4.1.2).

The half recovery time, EDR rec.t/2, in the following indicated by A_0, is calculated using (2.11b), in which t is substituted by λ and A by $A_0/2$ (i.e., half of the maximum amplitude A_0):

$$\frac{A_0}{2} = A_0\, e^{-\lambda/\tau} \tag{2.11d}$$

Dividing both sides of (2.11d) by A_0 and forming the reciprocal values leads to:

$$e^{\lambda/\tau} = 2 \tag{2.12}$$

At both sides of (2.12), natural logarithms are formed, which results in:

$$\frac{\lambda}{\tau} = \ln 2 \tag{2.13}$$

Multiplying both sides by τ gives:

$$\lambda = \ln 2\tau = (0.6931\ldots\tau) \tag{2.14}$$

Venables and Christie (1973, p. 96) recommended to use 0.7 as an approximate value in their equation for calculating EDR rec.t/2 out of the time constant τ, corresponding to (2.14): $\lambda = 0.7\tau$.

However, the form of the decline of an EDR curve, as depicted in Fig. 2.15 (Sect. 2.3.1.2), cannot sufficiently be approximated through a simple e-function as in (2.11b). This has been demonstrated by Stephens (1963) who performed a comparison of empirically determined SRR decline curves with theoretical courses. He too came to the conclusion that, especially with high initial values, a simple exponential curve does not correspond to but only approximates the SRR decline curves. Instead, a superposition of several e-functions with different time constants will be necessary, as exemplified in Fig. 2.18.[49]

The determination of the time constants for the three e-functions used in Fig. 2.18 was performed empirically from several SC and SP curves of an experimental subject. The displayed curve shows the response to a square pulse of 1.4 s

---

[49] The curve was kindly made available by F. Foerster, University of Freiburg, Germany.

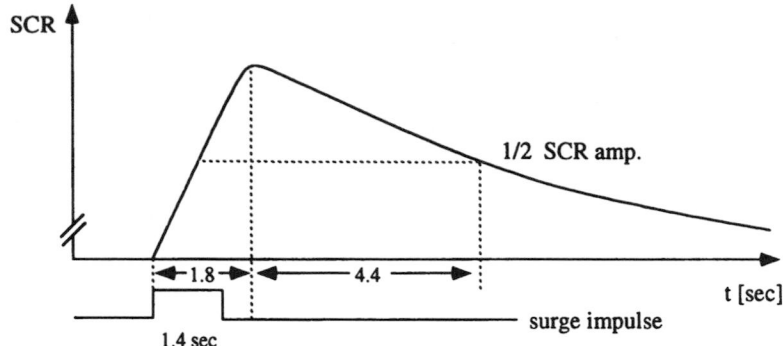

Fig. 2.18 Simulated SCR curve which results from the summation of three *e*-functions (see text for explanations)

duration (Sect. 1.4.1.4), where a combination of two *e*-functions with time constants of 0.2 and 6.0 s was used for the decline, and an *e*-function with $\tau = 0.1$ s was used for the incline. The simulated SCR curve in Fig. 2.18 gives a SCR ris.t. of 1.8 s and a SCR rec.t/2 of 4.4 s, which is a good approximation of a typical SCR course such as shown in Fig. 2.15.[50]

The incomplete approximation of EDR decline curves through a single *e*-function with a negative exponent questions the value of the approximation of the inexactly determined recovery time by means of the parameter EDR rec.tc. Furthermore, the relationship between the recovery time calculated like this and the EDR rec.t/2 remains equivocal, as the necessary preconditions are only approximate. This problem is also present in Edelberg's (1970) proposed use of graphic matching methods, so-called curve matching, as an alternative to the EDR rec.tc calculation. Through the insertion of resistors of differing resistances in a simple RC-circuit, a group of comparison curves can be produced, which the steepest point on the measured EDR decline curve should be compared with. The time constant of the RC-circuit that most closely approximates the EDR decline curve should then serve as estimation for the EDR rec.tc. The comparison may be performed using transparent templates. This method can also produce a form parameter for decline in those cases where the recorded EDA curve only attains 20–30% recovery. Edelberg (1971) identified a range from 1 to 15 s, with typical values between 4 and 6 s, for the time constants of the EDR decline curve (Sect. 2.5.2.4).

---

[50] Refined mathematical modeling of EDR curves had been performed by Hunt (1977), who developed an equation based on overlapping Gaussian distributions to fit the course of SRRs, and by Schneider (1987). Schneider fitted a three-compartment model to the recorded SC curve (personal communication) which includes the physical properties of the duct filling, the active membrane response in the duct walls, and the corneal hydration (Sect. 1.4.2). Schneider could show that a typical SCR can be modeled by assuming a roughly triangular input signal and choosing as an impulse response a sum of two exponentials with time constants of approximately 2 and 20 s, respectively. More recently, several authors came forward with similar proposals for the mathematical modeling of overlapping SCRs which are generated by short ISIs (Sect. 2.3.1.5).

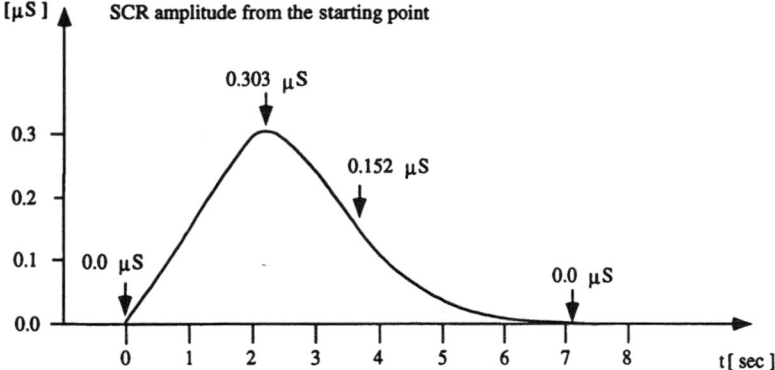

Fig. 2.19 Simulated SCR curve, as obtained by the interpolation between four empirically determined points of an SCR by using cubical splines (see text for explanations)

However, it is not a prerequisite for the calculation of EDA recovery measures, e.g., for the EDR rec.t/2, that the decline forms a base for a recovery process which can be described with one or more *e*-functions. Such characteristic decline values can be built for steadily falling curves as long as the curve declines. For example, a good approximation of the SCR can be obtained by an interpolation from the EDR onset point, the maximum and half-way decline points, and the extrapolated total decline point, with the use of cubical splines (Ahlberg, Nilson, & Walsh, 1967). The problem here is the definition of the starting point, because the interpolation method cannot simulate naturally occurring steep slopes. Using cubical spline interpolation would lead to a subzero deflection following the start of the response, which was calculated, but not depicted, for the curve displayed in Fig. 2.19.

The simulated SCR curve depicted in Fig. 2.19 is based upon the empirical values of an experimental subject, calculated by the aid computer analysis (Sect. 2.2.4.2; see also Thom, 1988). The SCR amp. equals 0.303 μS, the distance between the point of onset and the calculated peak point is 2.125 s, and the SCR rec. t/2 is 3.602 s. The point of time for the theoretical termination of the SCR is defined as approximately the triple of the SCR rec.t/2. The curve shown in Fig. 2.19 is an empirical interpolation by means of a third-grade function group in relation to the decline.

As long as systematic comparisons of the different methods of determining the EDR decline measures and more exact mathematical functions for the observed EDR decline forms are lacking, the evaluation might be supported by considerations of practicality. Undoubtedly, for the paper evaluation, the determination of EDR rec.t/2 is easier than that of the EDR rec.tc. Furthermore, the half point is more easily obtained than the 63% recovery point. Since the decay of radioactive matter which in fact follows an *e*-function is nevertheless expressed in half-life time, the present author does not see a convincing reason for using EDR rec.tc instead of EDR rec.t/2 (see also the computer program in the Appendix). In case of curvilinear writing, as used in some polygraph systems, it must be noted that

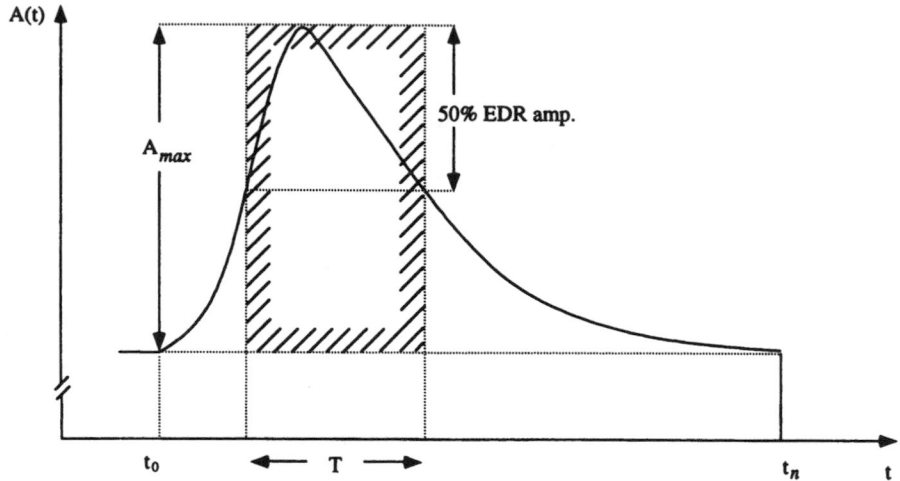

Fig. 2.20 Approximated area (*shaded*) under the EDR curve (see text for explanations)

the recording itself distorts the form parameter especially when its range exceeds the middle third of the writing channel's width (Edelberg, 1970).

The incompleteness of matching negatively accelerated e-functions to observed EDR curve declines has implications for discussions in later sections. It is partly the independence of the time constant τ from the initial value of such a decay process that provides the basis for the assumption of independence between EDR rec.tc and EDR amp. (Sect. 2.5.2.5). The arguments used by Sagberg (1980) for the differing recovery of SC and SR values (Sect. 2.6.2) are also based on an assumption that the decline forms of SCR and SRR are well enough approximated through a single e-function.

Frequently neither EDR rec.tc nor EDR rec.t/2 can be determined, because another EDR has already started before a corresponding recovery point is reached (Fig. 2.16 in Sect. 2.3.1.2 "Amplitudes of Exosomatic Responses recorded with Direct Current," EDR type 2). In that case, Fletcher, Venables, and Mitchell (1982) recommended calculating the EDR rec.t/4 instead of EDR rec.t/2. Using samples of more than 1,000 participants in total, correlations between SCR rec.t/2 estimated from the log SCR rec.t/4, and the actually measured log SCR rec.t/2 were around $r = 0.90$. Using SCR rec.t/4 instead of SCR rec.t/2, these authors were able to obtain a 23% increase in the number of SCRs for which decline measures could be calculated. Waid (1974) used the SRR rec.t/3 and also significantly increased the number of SRRs with calculable recovery values.

If the EDR rec.t/2 was not obtainable, Foerster (1984) determined the tangent in the turning point of the decline of the curve. The intersection point of this tangent with the parallels of the time axis at half amplitude can be used for the extrapolation of the fall times for the turning point, which however must be evaluated separately from the other recovery times (see also the computer program in the Appendix).

It has yet to be demonstrated that such an evaluation of the recovery of relatively rapidly overlapping EDRs provides homogeneous, reliable, and valid information. It should at least be attempted to ensure that the forms of the calculated EDRs are in fair concordance with that of an individual normative EDR, which is obtained within a recording period without any overlaps. Since ascent and descent times show a clear correlative connection (Sect. 2.5.2.4), Venables and Christie (1980) considered the replacement of calculating the EDR recovery by an alternative calculation of the EDR ris.t. as a measure of response shape (section "Parameters of Ascent"). Mathematical solutions for the treatment of overlapping (superimposed) EDRs have been recently proposed, thus opening the possibility for a treatment of missing recovery times as part of the deconvolution techniques (Sect. 2.3.1.5).

Several authors prefer the use of *recovery rate* instead of recovery time (see Sect. 2.3.3.3). Recovery rate is expressed as Ω gained per second during EDR rec.t/2 (Mednick & Schulsinger, 1968).

2.3.1.4   Area Measurements

Traxel (1957) suggested using an extended concept of electrodermal recovery for a further description of the EDR. He assumed that not only the peak amplitude but also the EDA recorded at each point during the course of an EDR might be regarded as a value for the "strength of affect" (Sect. 3.2.2.1). Consequently, he proposed the calculation of an integral which corresponds to the area under the curve between the starting and end points of the EDR, which could serve as measure for the entire "quantity of affect" as follows:

$$F = \int_{t_0}^{t_n} A(t)\,\mathrm{d}t \tag{2.15a}$$

where F represents the area under the curve between t_0 (starting point) and t_n (end point), and $A(t)$ represents the EDR amp. at the time point t (Fig. 2.20).

Since it is practically impossible to determine t_n exactly (Sect. 2.3.1.3 "Recovery Parameters"), Traxel recommended approximating the area under the curve by multiplying the EDR amp. by the time T the curve exceeds half of the amplitude (see the shaded rectangle in Fig. 2.20):

$$\hat{F} = A_{\max}T \tag{2.15b}$$

where $\hat{F}$ is the approximate area and $A_{\max}$ the maximum deflection, i.e., the EDR amp. According to Traxel (1957), the correlation between this approximation and the area measured with a planimeter was $r = 0.91$ for 50 SRRs. Schönpflug,

Deusinger, and Nitsch (1966) generally questioned the validity of area measures because of the dependency between amplitudes and temporal measures of the EDR (Sect. 2.5.2.5). In contrast, Lüer and Neufeldt (1967, 1968) demonstrated that a moderate correlation between the EDR amp. and the half-life period[51] does not lead to a decrease in the validity of the area measures, since it may have even more validity than each of them alone. In general, area measures for evaluating EDRs were not much used the international psychophysiological literature.

Recently, Bach, Friston, and Dolan (2010) proposed an area evaluation based on a convolution model of how sudomotor bursts may cause fluctuations in SC (see Sect. 2.3.1.5). They regarded the SCL-corrected time integral, or the area under the curve, as reflecting the number and strength of sudomotor nerve discharges, thus reflecting the status of the sympathetic branch of the ANS.[52] To provide an as much as possible assumption-free approach, the area under the SC curve (AUC) was calculated according to (2.15c):

$$\text{AUC} = \int_{t_0}^{t_n} \text{SC}(t)\, dt - \text{SCL} = cn\bar{a} + e \qquad (2.15c)$$

at which c is a constant, n is the number of responses with their mean amplitude $\bar{a}$, and e is an error term that absorbs random fluctuations and any violations of time-invariance and linearity assumptions. Bach et al. (2010) analyzed a data set with 1,153 NS.SCRs taken from an experiment with 40 males who anticipated a public speech (Sect. 3.2.2.2), obtaining rather high correlations of their AUC measure with the NS.SCR freq. ($r = 0.71$) and the mean NS.SCR amp. ($r = 0.81$), which were both scored by an independent, conventional evaluation method. If number and mean amplitudes of NS.SCRs were multiplied, their correlation with the AUC reached $r = 0.94$, coming close to short-term reliabilities of tonic SC measures (Sect. 2.5.2.1 "Tonic Skin Conductance Measures"). The authors performed an additional analysis, demonstrating that their AUC measure rendered somewhat superior to the product of number and mean amplitudes with respect to differentiating speech anticipation from baseline conditions. They concluded that the time integral may provide a better quantification of the underlying autonomic

---

[51] The half-life period is defined by these authors – in contrast to the nomenclature used in section 2.3.1.3 under "Recovery Parameters" – as the time the curve remains over the half amplitude ($T/2$) in Fig. 2.20. It therefore includes the time characteristics of the ascent as well.

[52] In their mathematical model, sudomotor nerve discharges were regarded as Dirac impulses (see Sect. 1.4.1.4). According to the convolution theorem, the Fourier transformed SC – SCL signal time series equals the product of the Fourier transformed nerve discharges with the Fourier transformed response function (see equation (3) in Bach et al., 2010). This means that the sudomotor nerve discharge frequency will have its greatest impact on the SC spectral power if it matches the peak frequencies of the response function. If the spectral power of the response function is known, it will be possible to recover the sudomotor nerve firing frequency according to equation (5) in Bach et al. However, unknown noise and response variability may prevent such an approach.

arousal (Sect. 3.2.1.1) than the NS.SCR freq. and its mean amplitude alone or
their product.

Due to a rather small data basis, the specific validity of measures reflecting the
area under the EDR curve cannot yet be unambiguously determined but will need
further research.

2.3.1.5 Mathematical Solutions for Overlapping EDRs

Since EDA has been increasingly recorded together with ERPs or even during fMRI
recordings (Sect. 2.2.3.5), mathematical solutions have been provided for determining characteristics of overlapping (superimposed) EDRs (see Fig. 2.16, Sect.
2.3.1.2 "Amplitudes of Exosomatic Responses Recorded with Direct Current")
which result from stimulus sequences with rather short ISIs. A possible solution
for a computer-based treatment of overlapping SCRs has been suggested by Lim
et al. (1997). Their modeling was based on the assumption of the stereotypical
nature of the SCR waveform within each subject.[53] They proposed a curve-fitting
four- to eight-parameters model for decomposing skin conductance into its tonic
and phasic components, the aim of which is to obtain the "pure" SCR (excluding the
SCLs and the residuals from a previous SCR if present). This "pure" SCR waveform can be mathematically described by combining two distinct functions – a
sigmoid function and an exponential decay function – in a sigmoid-exponential
four-parameter model as follows:

$$f_{s1} = \frac{g_1^{-((t-T_{os1})/t_d)}}{\{1 + [(t-T_{os1})/t_r)]^{-2}\}^2} \tag{2.16a}$$

in which the four parameters are: $g_1 = $ gain; $T_{os1} = $ response onset time; $t_r = $ rise
time constant; and $t_d = $ decay time constant. For $t \leq T_{os1}$, the value of f_{s1} will be 0.
Different terms have to be added if a single SCR is superimposed on a fixed SCL; or if
a SCR occurs on a decaying limb of a previous response (EDR type 2 in Fig. 2.16); or
if two overlapping SCRs occur on a decaying slope (see Lim et al., 1997, p. 107).

A computer program is used to automatically scan the entire date file (Sect. 2.2.4.2)
and to detect SC trough- and peak-latencies and their amplitudes for a rough estimate
of the initial model parameters. Thereafter, the waveforms are visually inspected,
providing the opportunity to accept or modify the automatically generated initial
values before curve-fitting is committed. After 10–30 iterations, success of the fit
should be apparent by visual inspection. If not, the initial values may be modified

---

[53] The appropriateness of this assumption is questionable. In general, mathematical models have
not yet overcome the general problem that EDRs reveal so different shapes. Even if the model fits
the majority of the empirically observed EDR recoveries, there is still a remainder of forms which
differ so much from the identified standard that models may fail in evaluating them adequately.

again until a satisfactory fit is achieved. The fitted curves were demonstrated to be almost indistinguishable from their respective raw response complexes.

Finally, the SCRs being free of the complication of an overlap can be quantified. The method was applied by Lim et al. (1997) to more than 60 SC segments, each containing one SCR or two overlapping SCRs on a sloping baseline elicited by 80 dB tones with ISIs as short as to 1.32 s, obtained from 20 normal participants and recorded with standard methodology, following evaluation method B for EDR type 2 in Fig. 2.16. In comparison with a standard evaluation method, their decomposition methodology yielded a significant mean amplitude increase of 14% and an increase in peak latencies of 140 ms. The reason for the enlargement of amplitudes becomes obvious from comparing the two alternatives in the left-hand side of Fig. 2.16, since evaluation method A, which was used by the algorithm of Lim et al.'s model, will automatically result in higher amplitudes than evaluation method B. The latency increase can be regarded as a consequence of removing the disguising effect of the preceding SCR's tail on the onset of the subsequent SCR.

The method was applied by Lim et al. (1999a) to SCR recordings (obtained with standard methodology) from 50 participants (25 of each gender) during an auditory odd-ball paradigm with constant ISIs of 1.32 s. All 10-s epochs which contained an SCR within 1–3 s following each of the 40 targets were evaluated for each participant. Epochs containing composite SC signals and/or overlapping SCRs were decomposed into phasic and tonic components by the curve-fitting computer program developed by Lim et al. (1997). For each target stimulus, the SCL and the "pure" peak amplitude and peak latency of the first SCR associated with a certain stimulus were mathematically determined. The resulting parameter values of all SCRs were grouped into bins for the 40 target stimuli and subaveraged, leaving missing values out. Finally, a SCR waveform was constructed from the parameter values for each target. A total of 1,421 SCRs (or 71% of the targets) were obtained from all 50 participants. A clear habituation of the SCR amp. emerged during repeated presentation of the target stimuli, showing an exponential decline with time (Sect. 3.1.1.3). The authors observed highly significant negative correlations between log SCR amp. and EEG-alpha activity ($r = -0.64$), EEG-beta activity ($r = -0.61$), and the N200 amplitude ($r = -0.50$). Lim et al. (1999a) suggested that the N200 component may have reflected the progressive consolidation of Sokolov's (1963a, 1963b) "neuronal model" (Sect. 3.1.1), the peripheral correlate of which was the diminishing of the SCR amp. It should be noted that such a direct comparison of SCR amp. with an ERP parameter would barely have been possible with the use of traditional SCR evaluation methodology.

The Lim et al. (1997) evaluation method has been successfully applied by Williams et al. (2004) in a study with 22 participants (7 females, 15 males) viewing four blocks of fearful alternated with four blocks of emotional neutral faces in an fMRI. All stimuli were presented with ISIs of 0.75 s SC data were acquired with standard methodology simultaneously with fMRI data, an amplitude criterion of 0.05 μS was used for the detection of SCRs, and a time window between 1 and 3 s after stimulus onset for the beginning of a stimulus related SCR was applied. Despite the rather short ISIs, fear and neutral stimuli could be significantly differentiated by means of SCR amp., which gives some hint on the validity of this evaluation method.

To overcome the problem arising from the necessity of a visual curve inspection and the linked subjective choices being inherent in Lim et al.'s (1997) method, Alexander et al. (2005) proposed an automated scoring for individual SCRs which converts the SC signal into a time series with a shorter time constant. Their rationale was that sweat gland activity results from discrete bursting episodes of the sudomotor nerves, and that the time constant of these bursting episodes is much shorter than the recorded SCR. The authors used a biexponential function to model this relationship. They considered the SC time series to be governed by the following differential equation:

$$q(t) = (\tau_0 \tau_1) \frac{d^2 y}{dt^2} + (\tau_0 + \tau_1) \frac{dy}{dt} + y(t) \qquad (2.16b)$$

where $y(t)$ is the measured SC, and $q(t)$ is the driver function, which the authors consider to reflect the activity of the sudomotor nerve. The larger time constant τ_0 is descriptive for the decaying tails of SCRs, whereas the shorter time constant τ_1 governs the rise time in response to a peak in the driver. In case τ_0 approaches zero, i.e., a SCR does not originate during the recovery of a previous SCR, equation (2.16b) approximates the formula for an RC-circuit (cf., (1.8) in Sect. 1.4.1.2).

The SCR is suggested to be generated by a nerve impulse at $t = 0$. Equation (2.16b) defines the SC signal $y(t)$ as the convolution of the driver function $q(t)$ with the biexponential function rendered in (2.16c):

$$y(t) = e^{-(t/\tau_0)} - e^{-(t/\tau_1)} \qquad (2.16c)$$

In terms of electrophysiology, the time course of each of the two exponential functions resembles the discharge of a capacitor within a RC-circuit (cf., equations (1.10a) and (2.11b)).[54]

The evaluation method of Alexander et al. (2005) consists of three steps: (1) performing a deconvolution of the SC signal in order to obtain the driver function, (2) isolating single peaks in the driver function, and (3) convolution of the peaks identified in the driver function with the biexponential function (2.16c) for reconstructing the individual SCRs. For a minority of SCRs, i.e., where the driver does not conform to the standard function as depicted in figure 1 of Alexander et al., or where the driver signal contains overlapping peaks, an iterative procedure is applied to the sequence of potential peak intervals, until no further changes occur. Alexander et al. applied their evaluation method to a large data set obtained from 735 participants from various countries, aged between 6 and 82 years. They were presented auditory stimuli with ISIs of 1 s in an odd-ball paradigm designed for ERP recording. Skin conductance was measured with standard methodology and sampled at 2 ms intervals. They found their method being not overly sensitive to the values of parameters which affect the apparent time constant of the driver signal.

---

[54] As already demonstrated by Boucsein (1988, 1992), a sufficient approximation of a typical SCR can be attained by a combination of two e-functions for the descent and another e-function for the ascent (see Fig. 2.18, Sect. 2.3.1.3).

For τ_0 and τ_1, optimal values of 2.0 and 0.75 were obtained, which worked well for all SC time series in the database.

The Alexander et al. (2005) method was further applied in a study on a rule-plus-exception category learning task by Davis, Love, and Maddox (2009). Forty-four participants viewed pictures of beetles, the features of which had to be classified according to a complicated set of category structures. The duration from stimulus onset to the response prompt varied randomly between 2 and 6 s. Recording techniques were not reported, except the amplitude criterion for SCRs, which was set to 0.05 µS. Participants who performed better in the learning task exhibited a large difference in anticipatory SCRs between rule-following and exception responses, as compared to poorly performing participants. The authors concluded that anticipatory SCRs were governed by the response type instead of being strictly stimulus bound. In general, the Alexander et al. (2005) evaluation method was shown to be useful in an experimental setting in which multiple stimuli were presented in tight sequences.

Another proposal for computer-aided analyses of overlapping SCRs resulting from short ISIs has been published by Bach, Flandin, Friston, and Dolan (2009), who criticized the not fully described and hence not testable implicit assumptions about the shape of the SCR in the above-described models and their restriction to SCR amp., its peak latency, and the area under the curve (Sect. 2.3.1.4). They suggested an alternative approach which compared the observed SCR time series as a whole to predicted time series, derived from a general linear time-invariant convolution model, which is akin to the analysis of event-related BOLD responses from fMRI data (see Sect. 2.2.3.5). Bach et al. regarded the SCR at a given time point t as the output of a finite linear time-invariant filter. Their assumptions about the nature of the SCR were:

1. The shape of SCRs can be described by an impulse response function, which is regarded as constant within an individual and level of an experimental factor,[55] whereas the SCR amp. varies as a function of the input.
2. The amplitude of two overlapping SCRs constitutes the sum of two single SCR amp., i.e., the SCR at a given time elicited by two (or more) stimuli is the sum of SCRs which would have been elicited by each stimulus individually.
3. The SC signal turns to zero at some time point after each SCR as a consequence of the finite property of the filter, which can be approximated by high-pass filtering the SC signal that removes slow SCL changes.[56]

---

[55] This is an assumption which is not in line with the variability in SCR shape observed by various researchers (cf. Benedek & Kaernbach, 2010) (see also Footnote 53).

[56] In the present author's view, this assumption does not meet what can be observed in the majority of EDRs, which do not return to the SCL prior to their onset, even in case of nonsuperimposed SCRs (Sect. 2.3.1.3 "Recovery Parameters"). Bach et al. (2009) artificially attained such a return to zero by applying high-pass filtering, thus removing slow components of the SCR which may reflect important processes resulting from moistening the corneum (Sect. 1.4.2.3).

The input function of the model has been regarded as a series of impulses which correspond to the onsets of specified experimental events. The authors presented data from three experiments for demonstrating the robustness of their assumptions. Their conclusion was that their method was capable of de-convolving SCRs to loud noise bursts with ISIs as short as 3 s, and of testing a priori hypotheses about parametric trial-to-trial effects of adaptation, thus being viable for analyzing SCRs in both long and short ISI paradigms.

The most recently published approach on the decomposition of superimposed SCRs by Benedek and Kaernbach (2010) was not only based on mathematical modeling but also took into account a particular model of the electrodermal system, i.e., the "poral valve model" (Edelberg, 1993) which has been described in Sect. 1.4.3.2. Benedek and Kaernbach proposed that the SCR shape could be ascribed to two different underlying physiological processes: (1) an unconditional diffusion process which would cause a rather flat SCR, and (2) a pore-opening process, having the property to add a steep peak to this basic SCR shape. Therefore, the Benedek and Kaernbach model allows for taking the empirically observed variability of SCR shapes into account, which constitutes an apparent advantage over the Bach et al. (2009) evaluation method (cf. their assumption (1)).

Benedek and Kaernbach's quantitative approach to the slow process (1) is based on a diffusional model of the dynamics of sweat concentration in the corneum, which is assumed being governed by the laws of diffusion (Edelberg, 1993; Schneider, 1987). The model dynamics is described by the so-called "Bateman function" being well known from pharmacokinetics, where a biexponential function as rendered in (2.16c) has been used to quantitatively describe the course of the drug concentration observed in a body compartment, being a result of its first-order invasion into and its first-order evasion out of this compartment. No comparable clear assumptions for the pore-opening component (2) could be made. Based on their mathematically formulated two-compartment diffusion model, Benedek and Kaernbach decomposed the SC signal into a tonic and a number of separate phasic components. However, their systematic analyses of empirically obtained SC data with standard 1D deterministic deconvolution as already used by Alexander et al. (2005), employing the biexponential function of (2.16c) with varying parameters for the two τ-values was not able to deal with varying SCR shapes. In particular, such a standard deconvolution for peaked SCR shapes showed a negative bend after the main deflection (i.e., going beyond the SCL before the beginning of the SCR), thus violating the assumption of nonnegativity.

Therefore, Benedek and Kaernbach (2010) suggested applying a mathematically derived nonnegative deconvolution procedure, the results of which do not differ from those of the standard deconvolution in case of flat SCRs. Notwithstanding, in case of peaked SCRs, their nonnegative deconvolution results in a compact positive SCR, followed by a smaller positive remainder (see the bottom of their Fig. 2). They interpreted the compact part as being due to the diffusional processes in the corneum, whereas the remainder has been attributed to the pore-opening process (see the description of Edelberg's, 1993 model in Sect. 1.4.3.2). The authors applied their evaluation procedure to SC[57] data gathered from 48 participants (29 females, 19 males) who were subjected to 13 noise bursts (95 dB, 140 ms with 20 ms linear ramps, ISIs between 4 and 32 s) delivered over earphones. Seven participants who failed to show significant SCRs to at least 50% of the stimuli were excluded from evaluation. The procedures for estimation of tonic SC components, nonnegative deconvolution process, segmentation of compact parts and remainders of the SCRs, and the recomposition of the original SC curve from these components were deliberately described by the authors.

All data were evaluated automatically and successfully decomposed into a slowly varying SCL component superimposed by sequences of SCRs. SCR amp. were found to increase with increasing ISI length.[58] As could have been expected, short ISIs resulted in stronger superposition of SCRs. Even with ISIs as short as 4 s, the event-related driver impulses (see (2.16b)) resulting from the nonnegative deconvolution did not show any overlap or distortion caused by the preceding SCR. However, the authors acknowledge that comparisons with standard SCR evaluations have still to be performed.

In summary, the various mathematically based deconvolution methods offer considerable progress in the evaluation of overlapping SCRs which are very common to stimulus sequences with short ISIs. However, they all have in common that – once the basic evaluation procedure has been determined – EDA data are parameterized fully automatically. This surely saves evaluation time compared with the traditional evaluation of superimposed EDRs, but it also bears the disadvantage of losing the contact to the original EDA signal, thus overlooking critical events such as types of artifacts which cannot be automatically detected (Sect. 2.2.5). Therefore, for the time being, semiautomatic interactive evaluation procedures should be at least applied in parallel to highly automated evaluation procedures.

2.3.2   *Parameters of Tonic Electrodermal Activity*

There are two reasons for discussing tonic EDA values after the description of phasic parameters. First, the tonic parameters discussed in Sect. 2.3.2.2 are derived from phasic ones; therefore, the phasic parameters must be known beforehand. Second, the level values discussed in Sect. 2.3.2.1 are, at least for the most widely used exosomatic measurement, of less practical significance than the specific and

---

[57] A nonstandard recording method has been applied, using a 10 V source in series with a 13.2 MΩ resistor over dry Ag/AgCl electrodes of 10 mm diameter. SC data were sampled at 32 Hz and 24 bit A/D conversion. As an amplitude criterion, 0.01 μS was applied. To improve distributional characteristics, data were logarithmically transformed (Sect. 2.3.3.3).

[58] An increase of SCR amp. with increasing ISI length was also found by Breska, Maoz, and Ben-Shakhar (2011), who compared ISIs ranging from 16 to 24 s (mean 20 s) with ISIs shortened by 50% in a within-subjects design with 36 participants (19 females, 17 males).

nonspecific EDRs, as they are less reactive to variations of experimental conditions. Therefore, many investigators did not perform an evaluation of the EDL.

2.3.2.1 Electrodermal Level

The determination of genuine EDLs is not as easy as it might appear at first glance. Although an EDL score can be determined at any given time point, a true level score can only be obtained in case no EDR being in progress. While the usual time constants for the ascent of the EDR are around 0.5 s and for the descent of the EDR around 4–6 s (Sect. 2.3.1.3 "Recovery Parameters"), time constants between 10 and 30 s must be considered for changes in EDL. If the chosen evaluation point turns out falling within the range of an EDR, this point may be shifted in time without significantly affecting the reliability of the obtained EDL. Such a temporal displacement is easy to perform during an evaluation of paper recordings (Sect. 2.2.4.1). However, this is not the case if computer analysis is automatically performed (Sects. 2.2.4.2 and 2.2.4.3). In such a case, a distortion of EDL scores by ongoing EDRs can be avoided with the use of averaging techniques. This is done by forming the average EDL of all artifact-free scanning points within a sufficient interval (e.g., 10 s). However, the inferred EDL is likely to be overestimated in states of high arousal (Sect. 3.2.1.1), due to the increased number of EDRs.[59] To avoid this overestimation of the EDL, the minimum EDL during a certain time interval might be identified during an automatic, noninteractive computer analysis. However, such an automatic evaluation method cannot be fully recommended, since bogus minima may be caused by movement artifacts (Sect. 2.2.5.2).

More exact values are provided by averaging all EDL scores measured immediately before the beginning of each EDR. These are available from the calculation of the EDR amp. (Sect. 2.3.1.2 "Amplitudes of Exosomatic Responses Recorded with Direct Current," Fig. 2.15), whereupon the EDLs at the beginning of overlapping (superimposed) EDRs (Fig. 2.16) must be excluded. Sufficiently reliable data can be expected from such a process only if enough EDRs appear during the interval in question.

Christie and Venables (1971) proposed another EDL score for endosomatic EDA evaluation, which they called low-BSPL (Sect. 2.2.6.1). Lykken, Rose, Luther, and Maley (1966) observed interindividual differences for the minimum SPL even in fully relaxed individuals; Venables and Christie (1980) conjectured, on the basis of theoretical considerations and investigations from their research group, that the BSPL corresponds to the membrane potential E_3 in the Fowles model (Fig. 1.17 in Sect. 1.4.3.2). This BSPL, which is obtainable after a long resting period from fully habituated individuals, can be regarded as the individual minimum score of

---

[59] The same is true for the EDL values which are calculated from the decoupled AC curve of overlapping impulses (Sects. 2.1.3 and 2.2.4.2).

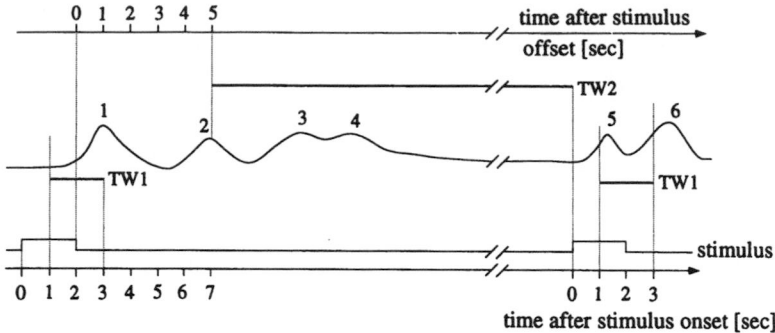

Fig. 2.21 Separation of specific and nonspecific EDRs. *TW1* Time window for specific EDRs; *TW2* time window for the NS.EDRs. *1* and *6* are specific EDRs following prior stimulation, *3* and *4* are NS.EDRs in the interval between both stimuli, *2* and *5* could not be evaluated as either specific or nonspecific EDRs

the SPL and can be used for setting the time point in the recording for obtaining the minimum SCL for range correction (Sect. 2.3.3.4 "Range Corrections").

2.3.2.2 Tonic Parameters Derived from Phasic Changes

As mentioned in Sect. 1.1.1, electrodermal recording yields phasic changes which are not traceable to specific stimuli and therefore are known as "electrodermal spontaneous fluctuations" or "nonspecific EDRs." If internal or external stimuli cannot be ascertained, any emerging EDRs are regarded as being an expression of tonic EDA. Thus, the frequency of the nonspecific EDRs (*NS.EDR freq.*) with respect to a fixed time interval, usually 1 min, constitutes an additional tonic EDA measure, which plays an important role in research into arousal, stress, and emotions (Sects. 3.2.1.1 and 3.2.2).[60]

There are ample reasons for assuming that the EDL (Sect. 2.3.2.1) and the NS. EDR freq. constitute autonomous parameters of tonic EDA. Venables and Christie (1980) summarized the hitherto published investigations comparing the SRL and NS.SCR freq. and concluded that – although these two tonic measures are correlated – each of them can still feature differential validity; an aspect which will be discussed in Sect. 3.2.1.1 in greater detail.

If NS.EDRs are to be determined during a recording phase in which defined stimuli appear, EDRs being traceable to specific stimuli must not be considered for evaluating NS.EDRs. As a conservative rule, EDRs which appear up to 5 s after the beginning of an intentional or unintentional stimulus should not be regarded as NS. EDRs. Additionally, the termination of a stimulus can act as a trigger for a specific EDR as well. Therefore, as Fig. 2.21 shows, only EDRs beginning later than 5 s

---

[60] Edelberg (1967) proposed using the frequency of changes in the EDL within a certain time span instead of the NS.EDR freq. as an indicator of arousal, a method which has not yet been applied to the present author's knowledge.

after the termination of a stimulus should be evaluated as nonspecific to avoid the inclusion of specific EDRs.

Another method of determining NS.EDRs being free of specific EDRs and artifacts was described by O'Gorman and Horneman (1979). They recommended dividing the EDA recording into 10 s segments. Subsequently, all segments in which movement and breathing artifacts are detected (Sect. 2.2.5.2), together with all segments which directly follow these segments, should be excluded from further evaluation. The remaining artifact-free 10 s segments are divided into those in which "large" NS.EDRs appear (i.e., EDR amp. higher than 1% of the EDL), and those in which "small" NS.EDRs appear (i.e., EDR amp. smaller than 1% of the EDL). Thereafter, the number of both types of segments is related to the total number of artifact-free intervals. However, the possibility of discovering small NS.EDRs is highly dependent upon amplification (Sect. 2.3.1.2 "Choice of Amplitude Criteria").

A particular problem in determining the NS.SPR freq. from endosomatic recordings is that they may contain biphasic and triphasic SPRs (Sect. 2.3.1.2 "Amplitudes of Endosomatic Responses"). Therefore, SPRs quickly following each other as under high arousal cannot be separated with certainty (Venables & Christie, 1980).

Depending on the experimental conditions under which data are obtained, correlations between NS.EDR freq. and mean NS.EDR amp. may vary considerably. Zimmer (2000) found these measures being highly correlated under resting conditions ($r = 0.80$) but significantly less correlated during an imagination phase ($r = 0.58$).

In addition to the frequency measures, the mean of all NS.EDR amp. (*mean NS. EDR amp.*) can be computed as an additional parameter of tonic EDA. For certain interpretations, the mean NS.EDR amp. which allows for determining the total amount of nonspecific changes in EDA, constitutes an indicator with its own differential validity (cf. Table 3.2, Sect. 3.5.1). The *standard deviation* of NS. EDR amp. could be used as an additional tonic parameter as well; however, to the present author's knowledge, no specific validity aspect has been yet determined for it. Besthorn, Schellberg, Pfleger, and Gasser (1989) used the *variance* of the SCR amp. over the whole stimulation time as a tonic EDA measure in continuous audiovisual stimulations lasting from 1.5 to 3 min.

One measure that also principally falls into the category of tonic EDA parameters is the so-called EDA *magnitude*, which is, however – due to the inclusion of zero responses is discussed in connection with the missing data handling – discussed in Sect. 2.3.4.2.

2.3.3   Transformation of Electrodermal Parameters

In general, the usefulness of data transformation has been treated controversial in the literature on statistics and methodology. Levey (1980), who gave a comprehensive discussion of this topic, stated that the necessity for transformations should be ideally backed up by known or assumed properties of the system under investigation. However, the transformations that are commonly used in EDA research are seldom based on physiological or system-theoretical considerations. Instead, transformations of EDA raw data are normally based on statistical considerations (e.g., Edelberg, 1972a; Venables & Christie, 1980).

The adequateness of transformational procedures should be assessed by an analysis of whether or not the particular transformation results in improving the validity compared to the original EDA parameter, the criterion for which should be an improved representation of the underlying psychophysiological processes. Since there is no rationale for generalizations beyond specific experimental contexts (Levey, 1980), the question of whether statistical analysis should be carried out with transformed data or with raw data still cannot be answered in general.

2.3.3.1 Taking the Electrode Area into Account

A transformation that is especially useful in the application of the constant current technique is the calculation of scores related to the electrode area, called specific EDA scores (Sect. 2.2.3.2). As a result of the reciprocal relationship between resistance and conductance, the specific resistance is expressed in $k\Omega$ cm^2, while the specific conductance is expressed in $\mu S/cm^2$ (Edelberg, 1967).[61] On the basis of the differing principles of measurement as outlined in Sect. 2.1.1, it can be shown that the calculation of *specific resistance* is of greater importance than the calculation of specific conductance. If the constant current method is used and a model of parallel resistances/conductances is adopted, an increase of the electrode area would imply that the current is divided by an increasing number of pathways (Sect. 1.4.3.1). Although the current is limited in total, the current per pathway decreases, since the effect of the applied constant current is dependent upon the current density and thereby upon the electrode area. In case of the constant voltage method, by contrast, the electrode area plays no such role, since with an increase in the number of parallel pathways the voltage applied on any pathway remains constant (Sect. 2.6.2).

In spite of this, Lykken and Venables (1971) supported reporting SC scores as *specific conductance* as well, because they have empirically found a linear relationship between the electrode area and the SC. However, Venables and Christie (1980), relying on data reported by Mitchell and Venables (1980), concluded that no such linearity exists between the SCL or SCR amp. and the electrode area, because an increase of the electrode area above 0.8 cm^2 does not appear to increase conductance (Sect. 2.2.2.3). Therefore, they do not endorse relating SC scores to the electrode area. Instead of calculating the specific conductance, the size of the electrodes should be provided for purposes of comparison. In contrast, Mahon and Iacono

---

[61] Following the same rationale, impedance and admittance values might be related to the electrode area. Such kind of transformation is not common in endosomatic recording.

(1987) found a linear relationship between electrolyte/skin contact areas, which they varied in size in six steps from 0.131 to 0.786 cm^2, and the SCL/SCR amp. Thus, they also supported reporting the specific conductance. No data are available concerning a possible dependency of the form parameters of EDA upon the electrode area.

2.3.3.2 Transforming Resistance into Conductance Units

In an attempt to follow the recommendation of Lykken and Venables (1971) for preferring the constant voltage method in exosomatic EDA recording, many authors who continued to use the constant current method felt obliged to transform their obtained SR units into SC units prior to further statistical evaluation. During computerized EDA evaluation (Sects. 2.2.4.2 and 2.2.4.3), this can be easily performed by transforming the SRL into the SCL for each point sampled, using (1.4a) in Sect. 1.4.1.1. However, if the parameterization has already been performed based on the SR recording, transformation into conductance units becomes more complicated. According to (1.5a) in Sect. 1.4.1.1, the SRL scores at the onset of the respective responses must be known in order to convert the SRR amp. into a SCR amp. For simplification, the square of the SRL score at the onset of the response is used as the denominator instead of the product from the SRL scores of the response onset and its maximum. This is possible because the difference between both SRL scores is usually small compared to the absolute SRL values. This conversion follows (2.18a) in Sect. 2.3.3.4 "Evaluating EDR with Respect to EDL."

Hagfors (1964) pointed to the possibility of alterations in the ranking of the amplitudes which may result from transforming the SRR amp. into the SCR amp., in case of the corresponding EDRs are based on differing EDLs. Moreover, the conversion of SR into SC units can also lead to different results with respect to the EDR amp. However, within the range of stimulation usually applied in psychophysiological experiments, SCR amp. being calculated from SRR amp. obtained by constant current recording can be expected to yield results comparable to SCR amp. being recorded directly by using constant voltage.[62]

On the other hand, form parameters may not show the same kind of invariance to resistance-conductance transformations. Sagberg (1980) has empirically and theoretically demonstrated that the SCR rec.tc must be shorter than the corresponding SRR rec.tc. However, he used a single e-function for modeling EDR recovery, the rationale for which remains questionable (Sect. 2.3.1.3 "Recovery Parameters").

---

[62] This has been demonstrated by Boucsein, Baltissen, and Euler (1984) using both recording methods in parallel during the application of 2-s white noise stimuli with intensities between 60 and 110 dB.

2.3.3.3 Improving Distributional Characteristics

In order to improve the distributional characteristics of EDA data, especially with respect to skewness, *logarithmic transformations* are primarily used. While Edelberg (1972a) and Venables and Christie (1973) regarded log transformations of SC scores as unnecessary because of their relatively normal distributions, Venables and Christie (1980) advocated a different point of view based on voluminous data sets from three large-sample investigations. They found clear improvements in both skewness and slope through the log transformations of the SCL scores. These improvements were also seen for SCR amp. if the log transformations were performed following the determination of the amplitudes, but not if the amplitudes were calculated based on log transformed raw scores (i.e., as the difference between the log SCL at the peak response and the log SCL at the response onset). Venables and Christie also investigated the unusual log transformations of latency, rise time, and recovery measures of the SCR. They found clear improvements in the distributional characteristics by means of these transformations for SCR rec.t/2 but not for SCR lat. and SCR ris.t. Why just a log transformation leads to a normalization of the EDA data cannot be statistically determined (Levey, 1980).

Two mathematical considerations with respect to the problem of using log transformations should be made:

1. If stimulus-dependent EDRs are evaluated and, as in experiments on habituation (Sect. 3.1.1.3), zero responses are to be expected, it should be taken into consideration that the log SCR amp. of a zero response is mathematically not defined. Venables and Christie (1980) suggested that in this case a 1 should be added to all SCR amp. scores before the log transformation is performed.
2. To transform SR scores which have already been logarithmically transformed into SC scores, the following transformation should be used (Edelberg, 1967): $\log G = -\log R$, which follows from $G = 1/R$. Since G is expressed in μS and R in kΩ (Sect. 1.4.1.1), and $\log 1{,}000 = 3$, then according to (1.4a):

$$\log G\,[\mu S] = 3 - \log R\,[k\Omega] \tag{2.17}$$

Another method being widely used for the improvement of distributional characteristics is the *square root transformation* (Grings, 1974). Such a transformation is capable to normalize a Poisson distribution for rare events, which has been observed in many physiological processes (Levey, 1980). Within EDA evaluation, it has been mostly applied to SCR amp. scores.

Both square root and log transformations are sometimes used in addition to other transformations (e.g., relating EDA to the electrode area; see Sect. 2.3.3.1). A distributional normalization of the EDR amp. can also be attained through a *standardization* to z scores (Sect. 2.3.3.4 "Transformation into Standard Values").

Several authors subjected EDR recovery times to a reciprocal transformation for obtaining the recovery speed (Sect. 2.3.1.3). This so-called *recovery rate* results in a stronger deviation from the normal distribution compared to the recovery measures, so that a reciprocal transformation of the recovery times cannot be recommended taking this distributional argument into account (Sect. 2.5.2.4).

2.3.3.4 Reduction of Interindividual Variance

Several transformations, which can be performed prior to further statistical treatment of EDR data stemming from different individuals, lead to a reduction of the interindividual variance. Among the reasons for their use are: (1) the supposed baseline dependence of the EDR data (Sect. 2.5.4.2), (2) the aim of expressing the respective EDR in terms of the individual response range, and (3) matching the distribution of the EDRs from various individuals in order to achieve better preconditions for a group analysis.

The methodological and statistical implications of these transformations are discussed here only insofar as they can be regarded as being specific for EDA. For further discussion, the reader is referred to the respective statistical literature.

Evaluating EDR with Respect to EDL

A simple rationale for calculating EDR scores which take the respective EDL into account is forming a quotient from the EDR amp. and the EDL immediately before the beginning of an EDR. This quotient can also be expressed as percentage: EDR amp./EDL.100% (Traxel, 1957). Edelberg (1967, p. 47) purported that such a transformation would be unnecessary in case of SC-recordings, because according to (1.5a) in Sect. 1.4.1.1, ΔG (i.e., the SCR amp.) already takes regard of the resistance level in the denominator. However, Edelberg's claim – being based on the assumption that SC is to be regarded as the sole adequate measurement unit (Sect. 2.6.5) – does not acknowledge that the same is applicable to ΔR, since the conductance level is already represented in the denominator, as can be seen in (1.5b).

A further relationship can be derived from (1.5a), as suggested by Edelberg (1967): since the difference between R_1 and R_2 is relatively small in comparison to the absolute values of R_1 and R_2 themselves, R_2^2 can be used as an approximation instead of the product of both values in the denominator of (1.5a) in Sect. 1.4.1.1. The relatively small difference between R_1 and R_2 justifies replacing R_2 by R for the sake for simplicity, which yields:

$$\Delta G = -\frac{\Delta R}{R^2} \qquad (2.18a)$$

Both sides of (2.18a) are multiplied by R, and on the left-hand side R is replaced by $1/G$, according to (1.2b):

$$\frac{\Delta G}{G} = -\frac{\Delta R}{R} \tag{2.18b}$$

Equation (2.18b) shows that the relative variations of the conductance and resistance are approximately equal in their absolute values. Therefore, the corresponding transformations lead to the same data independent of whether the raw scores were recorded as conductance or resistance values.

Range Corrections

Transformations which reduce interindividual variance so that each value is set in proportion to the intraindividual range are known as range correction procedures. The "correction" is based on the assumption that the part of interindividual physiological differences which does not relate directly to the psychophysiological processes can be eliminated (Levey, 1980). A precondition for this procedure is the calculation of the intraindividual range of maximum reactivity. Paintal (1951) determined the maximum possible EDR amp. by applying a strong electrical stimulus and dividing each single EDR amp. by the so obtained maximum amplitude (*Paintal index*, cf. Edelberg, 1972a). Lykken and Venables (1971) recommended inflating a balloon until it bursts in order to determine the maximum SCL. It remains, however, questionable whether these two techniques approximate the ideal of recording the maximum physiological reactivity free from psychological influences. Lykken, Rose, Luther, and Maley (1966) provided the following formula for range correction:

$$SCL'_i = \frac{SCL_i - SCL_{min}}{SCL_{max} - SCL_{min}} \tag{2.19a}$$

in which SCL_i is the uncorrected level value and SCL'_i the range corrected level value at the time point i, while SCL_{max} is the highest possible value and SCL_{min} the lowest possible value for the particular individual. The determination of the minimum value is much more difficult than that of the maximum value. Venables and Christie (1973) suggest using the SCL obtained as BSPL (Sect. 2.3.2.1), which, however, requires simultaneous recordings with both exosomatic and endosomatic techniques (Sect. 2.2.6.2).

The determination of a minimum value appears not to be a problem, at least in theory, for the EDR amp., as the minimum EDR can be regarded as a nonexistent EDR. Accordingly, Lykken and Venables (1971) derive the range correction for the SCR amp. from (2.19a), in which $SCL_{min} = 0$ has been inserted as follows:

$$SCR'_i = \frac{SCR_i}{SCR_{max}} \tag{2.19b}$$

In Equation (2.19b), SCR'_i is the corrected and SCR_i the uncorrected skin conductance response, while SCR_{max} is the maximum possible SCR amp. Following the method proposed by Venables and Christie (1973), the maximum SCR amp. can be determined during the experiment by means of an application of loud tones or electrical stimuli, or by taking a deep breath. In addition, the OR to the first stimulation of a habituation procedure will also usually emerge the maximum EDR of the experiment (Sect. 3.1.1.3).

Additional problems have been anticipated for the use of range corrections. Grings (1974) demonstrated that the range, especially in small samples, is usually an unreliable value which is highly dependent upon the situational conditions of the respective experiment. Sagberg (1980) has shown that range correction is not invariant throughout transformations of SR into SC values and vice versa. Ben-Shakhar (1985) demurred that the greatly extended resting period necessary for the determination of the minimum EDL, together with manipulations for the determination of the maximum EDR amp. and/or the highest EDL, may invalidate the whole experiment.

Transformation into Standard Values

The problem of determining individual EDR maxima being a prerequisite for range correction as described in the previous subsection can be bypassed, if standardization is based upon the individual mean and standard deviation of EDRs instead of their range. The raw scores can then be turned into standard values by means of an appropriate transformation.

For a transformation of the EDR amp. into z scores (e.g., Ben-Shakhar, Lieblich, & Kugelmass, 1975), means and standard deviations of the recorded EDRs are calculated for each particular individual. Then a standard value is calculated for each EDR amp. as follows:

$$z_{ik} = \frac{X_{ik} - \bar{x}_i}{s_i} \tag{2.20a}$$

where X_{ik} is the raw score and z_{ik} the standard value of the individual i for the EDR_k; with the mean $\bar{x}$ and the standard deviation s_i of all EDRs of the individual i.

The z scores are normally distributed with an average of 0 and a standard deviation of 1. It is common to transform z scores into T scores as follows:

$$T_{ik} = 50 + 10z_{ik} \tag{2.20b}$$

The T scores are normally distributed with a mean of 50 and a standard deviation of 10; therefore, minus signs drop out.

Using data from 147 participants, Ben-Shakhar (1985) performed systematic comparisons between SCRs in raw score form calculated from SRRs and range-corrected as well as z-transformed electrodermal response scores. He observed that the response scores obtained through standard transformations differentiated most clearly between meaningful and neutral stimulus conditions, a finding which he ascribed to the z-transformed average individual reactivity being more representative than the rather unreliable maximum individual reactivity which was used for calculating range-corrected scores. However, in a study using simulated EDA data, Stemmler (1987) showed that the design applied by Ben-Shakhar, together with the z-score calculation and the inferential statistics used for the determination of the differences between experimental conditions, resulted in a positive bias for the method of standard transformation. Therefore, the generalizability of Ben-Shakhar's argument remains questionable.

Using Autonomic Lability Scores

Lacey (1956) suggested a method of standardization for psychophysiological response scores which considers the respective baseline values (section "Evaluating EDR with Respect to EDL") and undertook a standard transformation (section "Transformation into Standard Values"). These so-called autonomic lability scores (ALS) form response scores, where the component, which is predictable by means of linear regression from the level score, is ruled out. Thus, they can be regarded in principle as scores adjusted by covariance analysis (Grings, 1974).

In order to calculate the ALS scores, all n EDRs obtained from an individual i in a sequence $k = 1,...,n$ are collected together, as in the standard transformation described in the previous subsection. However, instead of using the EDR amp., the EDL at the response onset, i.e., X_{ik}, and the EDL at its maximum, i.e., Y_{ik}, are determined for each single EDR (i.e., $Y_{ik} - X_{ik} = $ EDR amp_{ik}). According to Lacey, the score sequence X_{ik} constitutes the baseline values, while the sequence Y_{ik} constitutes the response scores. Between both score sequences, the correlation $(r_{xy})_i$ is calculated for each individual i. The values X_{ik} and Y_{ik} are transformed into standard values $(z_x)_{ik}$ and $(z_y)_{ik}$ using their respective means, i.e., $\bar{x}$ and $\bar{y}$, and their standard deviations $(s_x)_i$ and $(s_y)_i$, according to (2.20a). An ALS score is calculated for each EDR k of an individual i as follows:

$$\text{ALS}_{ik} = 50 + \left(10 \left[\frac{(z_y)_{ik} - (r_{xy})_i (z_x)_{ik}}{\sqrt{1 - (r_{xy})_i^2}} \right] \right) \tag{2.21}$$

These ALS scores are, like the T scores in (2.20b), normally distributed with a mean of 50 and a standard deviation of 10, and are linearly independent from the baseline values of the respective individual.

The calculation of ALS scores presupposes a large number of EDLs per individual, since a correlation between baseline and response scores must be determined for each participant in a study.[63] In addition, Johnson and Lubin (1972) pointed out that ALS scores have an advantage over raw scores with respect to reliability and validity only if the so-called Law of Initial Values (LIV) holds true, which will be discussed in Sect. 2.5.4.1.

Levey's (1980, p. 621) opinion on the application of ALS scores to SCRs may serve as an example of the problems which are raised by transformations in general (see the introductory remarks in Sect. 2.3.3) and of the problems of ALS transformations in particular. Levey reappraised the results of an investigation published by Germana (1968) showing that ALS and log EDR amp. transformations differ from each other in nearly the same way as both differ from the EDR amp. raw scores. Levey (1980) argued against the ALS correction, as it only corrected the baseline effects, and recommended log transformation instead, which he regarded as being derivable from theoretical considerations and modeling.

2.3.4   Removing Artifacts and Treatment of Missing Data

In spite of exact control of measurement techniques, the behavior of individuals and/or the environmental conditions during EDA measurement can lead to the recording of artifacts (Sect. 2.2.5) in the EDA data, which must be eliminated before further statistical treatment. Therefore, identification of artifacts, as described in Sect. 2.3.4.1, plays a significant role after the parameterization of the EDA signal, because the experimenter must choose between correcting or discarding such data which might have been a result of an artifact or not.

The gaps created by missing data (e.g., if the electrodes are detached; Sects. 2.2.2.1 and 2.2.5.1) necessitate subsequent treatment (Sect. 2.3.4.2). A formal missing data treatment may be necessary in the EDA evaluation, even if the stretch of data in question does not need to be deleted, e.g., in case of expected EDRs fail to appear due to genuine zero responses, as during advanced habituation (Sect. 3.1.1.3), in extinction (Sect. 3.1.3.1), or with electrodermal nonresponders (Sect. 3.4.2.2).

2.3.4.1   Identification of Artifacts During Recording

The detection of artifacts in the EDA signal necessitates a visual inspection of the data sequence by the experimenter, even if an automatic parameterization is performed by means of laboratory computers (Sect. 2.2.4.2). To facilitate this

---

[63] ALS scores can be standardized not only intraindividually over the different EDRs, but also interindividually for each response over all participants. In the latter case, both score sequences X and Y are calculated using the EDRs of all participants to the same stimulus.

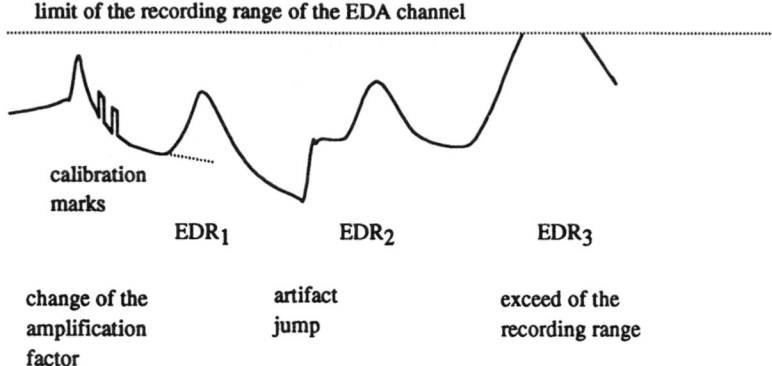

Fig. 2.22 Examples of artifacts in an EDA recording sequence (see text for explanations)

procedure, all artifacts created by changes of amplification factors and/or calibration as well as movement (insofar as they can be identified from the record) should be noted during the recording.

Figure 2.22 shows some typical artifacts in an EDA recording   segment. A change of the amplification factor causes a transient response which appears as a jump in the recording, followed by an exponential adaptation to a new baseline. This process might not be terminated until the occurrence of the following EDR, thus obscuring its course (as indicated by the dashed line in Fig. 2.22). Jumps in the EDA curve can also result from movements of the electrodes or the area to which they are attached (Sect. 2.2.5.2), shown as an artifact jump in Fig. 2.22. Since these usually do not result from an exponential adjustment, the EDR_2 in Fig. 2.22 can be unequivocally evaluated, in contrast to the EDR_1. Computer programs can automatically recognize and correct such jumps (Foerster, 1984) or enable correction during the interactive work with the video screen display (Thom, 1988). Andresen (1987), having used an interactive artifact correction with a large data series, advocated its use in spite of being time consuming. The present author prefers a semiautomatically method for artifact removal as suggested by the computer program in the Appendix of this book. Calibration marks can influence evaluability, especially if they are produced during the rise time or the response maximum of an EDR. They must be eliminated before automatic evaluation can be performed.

EDRs which exceed the recording range, such as the EDR_3 in Fig. 2.22, have to be excluded from evaluation. They can appear, for example, as part of an orienting- or defensive-response to an unexpected, strong stimulus (Sect. 3.1.1.2). Although in this particular case they are not artifacts with respect to the goal of the investigation (Sect. 2.2.5.2), the questionable recording sequence must be excluded from parameterization. Such EDRs also appear subsequent to strong respiratory activity (e.g., sighing) or gross physical movement. Escapes from the recording range can be avoided either by choosing a larger recording range (e.g., through less amplification) or by using automatic reset procedures (e.g., Thom, 1988).

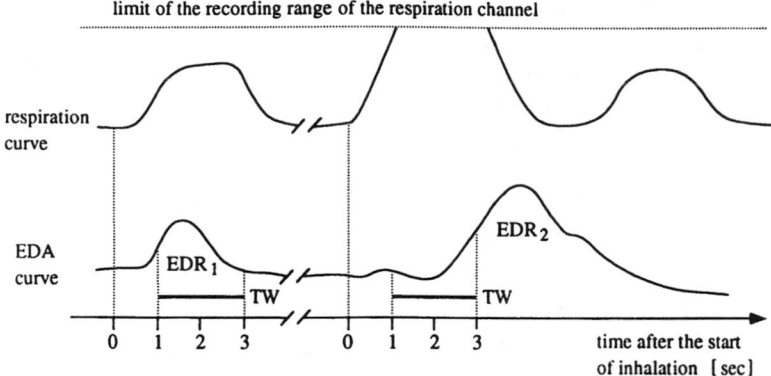

Fig. 2.23 EDA artifact identification by using the respiration curve. *TW* Time window of a respiratory artifact, suggested 1–3 s after the start of an inspiration. As the EDR₁ does not begin within the time window, it does not result from a respiratory artifact, while the EDR₂ does

An EDA artifact can be detected by visually inspecting both EDA and respiratory curves, as shown in Fig. 2.23.[64] No connection with inspiration can be seen with the EDR_1 in Fig. 2.23. However, the EDR_2, which follows a sufficiently long latency period in the time window after an exceptional deep breath, has to be treated most probably as a respiratory artifact. Problems of interpretation arise, if the inspiration and the EDR in a corresponding time window can be regarded as covariant indicators of an orienting- or defensive-response (Sect. 3.1.1.2). In such a case, the EDR cannot be regarded merely as an artifact, but it is also not really independent from breathing. But even in case of non-stimulus conditions, EDRs correlated with respiratory irregularities constitute a problem (Sect. 2.2.5.2). Artifacts resulting from the study participant's speech activity cannot be easily determined, since the relationship of speech activity to single EDRs is less clearly detectable than in respiratory activity.

Low-pass filtering (Sect. 2.1.4) can be used as an easy-to-apply method of artifact removal from EDA recordings, since the EDR constitutes a rather slow-changing signal. By means of low-pass filtering, unusual steep rises stemming from artifacts such as pressure exerted on the electrodes (Sect. 2.2.2.1) will be automatically eliminated; however, an appropriate choice of the filter characteristics will be critical here.

A more refined method had been proposed by Wilhelm and Roth (1996) for EDA recordings from ambulatory monitoring (Sect. 2.2.3.4). They developed a computerized evaluation method for the detection of SCR artifacts resulting from changes in electrode/skin contact due to the movement of fingers to which the electrodes were attached. The detection of artifacts based on their unusual steep rise times.

---

[64] The computer program described in the Appendix of this book allows for a display of the respiratory signal together with the EDA curve to be evaluated.

The authors plotted bivariate distributions of SCR ris.t. with both SCR amp. and SCR rec.t/2 to identify outliers falling outside a range of 20% change in slope of the regression. These outliers were regarded as artifacts and were removed from the raw data before their further evaluation.

Unfortunately, an automatic removal of respiration-based artifacts is not so easy to perform. Schneider et al. (2003) analyzed 26 EDA recordings of 25 min length each, taken from an earlier study, by means of the computer program described in the Appendix of the present book, which allows for simultaneous display of EDA and respiration recordings. Respiration-related EDRs were independently rated by three experimenters. They used a criterion catalog for detecting respiration-based artifacts in the EDA recordings, which referred to features of typical EDRs as shown in Fig. 2.15 (Sect. 2.3.1.2 "Amplitudes of Exosomatic Responses Recorded with Direct Current") and Fig. 2.21 (Sect. 2.3.2.2). For the criteria in the catalog, interrater reliabilities were calculated from two experiments with 14 and 12 participants of both genders under resting conditions. The reliabilities were between $r = 0.82$ and 0.95, thus being sufficiently high. After discarding the respiration-related EDRs from the material, frequencies and mean amplitudes of NS.SCR dropped to about 50% of the originally detected amounts. This pointed to a substantial common variance of EDRs and respiratory activity. In any case, removal of possible respiratory artifacts from EDA recordings remains a rather time-consuming venture, because of complex inter- and intraindividual differences in the link between both measures.

2.3.4.2 Missing Data Treatment and EDR Magnitude

Missing data can be handled during EDA parameterization in the same way as in other biosignals. If the statistical package to be used does not feature missing data procedures, appropriate supplements of the data sets with missing data should be implemented subsequently to the procedure of parameterization.

For missing data treatment, a time window grid could be applied to the data, thereby defining the smallest window for the statistical evaluation. Depending on the experimental design, this window can range from 5 s to 1 min. For obtaining the NS.EDR freq., EDRs in each interval have to be counted (Sect. 2.3.2.2). If no EDRs appear within a certain window, it is normally a case of zero responses (see below) and not of missing data. If only a part of the window under evaluation is so error-prone that it is impossible to parameterize it, a weighted mean may be calculated, taking the ratio of an estimable time span to the total window into consideration. If too big a part of the window has to be excluded from evaluation, the score of either the preceding or the subsequent window may be inserted, as long as no clear change of the situational condition has occurred between those.

While such corrections as a rule can be usefully made in the case of lost EDL scores, their application in case of lost NS.EDRs is more equivocal because the appearance of spontaneous EDRs is an unpredictable event. Therefore, it is not possible to act from the assumption of an approximately equal distribution of EDRs in neighboring time windows of the same length. Thus, records of a particular study participant containing large portions of missing data should be totally excluded from the statistical evaluation of NS.EDRs.

Missing data corrections for stimulus-dependent EDRs cannot be recommended, neither being performed intraindividually, due to the possible appearance of habituation (Sect. 3.1.1.3), nor across individuals in a group, due to the large interindividual differences.

A parameter that is often calculated for the description of electrodermal habituation processes, taking into account expected stimulus-dependent EDRs which did not emerge, is the *EDR magnitude*.[65] The inclusion of such "zero responses" presupposes that it is possible to clearly define when EDRs are to be expected within the course of an experiment, which also requires exactly defined and recorded stimuli. The EDR magnitude is normally used in an interindividual averaging procedure (e.g., to determine the average response strength to a certain stimulus in a habituation series), but it might also be used as an intraindividual measure as well (e.g., to obtain the total reactivity of an individual to a series of stimuli).

Which measure, mean amplitude or mean magnitude, will be the more adequate one for determining the average strength of EDRs, remains debatable. Using the EDR magnitude avoids the difficulty of defining zero responses (e.g., see Sect. 3.4.2.2), and will create the same sample size in each ANOVA cell for further statistical analysis (Venables & Christie, 1980). On the other hand, the magnitude measure confounds frequency of response and response strength which are not necessarily covarying (Prokasy & Kumpfer, 1973). Both methods of missing data treatment may produce considerably differing results. For example, if habituators and nonhabituators are combined, different habituation courses will be obtained when using the interindividual mean EDR amplitude instead of the more commonly used mean magnitude, since the mean magnitude will yield an overall habituation, while calculating the mean amplitude will result in a habituation followed by an increase of response strength in later trials.[66]

2.3.4.3 Correction for EDL Drift

The retroactive correction for drift in the EDA signal is only possible if control scores are obtained during data recording. One possibility is performing a regular setting of calibration marks (Sect. 2.2.4.1). A drift has appeared if the signal curve alters when the same calibration resistance is repeatedly applied while amplification is held constant. All kinds of drift correction are costly in terms of calculation and

---

[65] Several authors used the term "EDR magnitude" instead of "EDR amplitude" (Sect. 2.3.1.2). Therefore, care should be taken in ascertaining just which method of evaluation was used in the respective publications.

[66] Mathematically this is a type of missing data treatment, as nonappearing EDRs, or EDRs which remain below an amplitude criterion (Sect. 2.3.1.2 "Choice of Amplitude Criteria") are taken into account in evaluation. The EDR magnitude (more precisely, the mean EDA magnitude) is calculated by dividing the sum of the evaluated EDR amp. by the number of occasions in which EDRs might have been expected.

prone to high uncertainty. However, in the case of long-term runs (Sect. 2.2.6.1), such corrections are usually indispensable.

Drift resulting from electrode polarization during exosomatic DC recording can be detected by changing the polarization during long-term recording phases. For endosomatic recording, drift correction is impossible (Sect. 2.2.5.1).

Both body temperature and ambient temperature can be used for EDL drift correction. In this case, Grings' (1974) empirically determined value of 3% SRR increase/°C decrease can be used. In case the temperature drift results from the recording device used, the amplifier can be allowed to run free of an input signal for the same length of time as the experiment's recording period, and the resulting recorded SCL "signal" is used for correcting the drift in the recorded EDA data.

A pragmatic reduction of drift due to any cause can be made using the trend validation methods proposed by Stemmler (1984). Here, EDL differences to reference phases of identical structure (e.g., simple resting periods), which shortly precede or follow the experimental conditions under investigation, are obtained, and a linear interpolation in real time is calculated.

2.3.5 Summary of Analytic Procedures

Depending on the problem under investigation, different parameters of phasic and tonic EDA can be extracted from the recorded signal. The most commonly used phasic measure is the EDR amp. (Sect. 2.3.1.2), for which an amplitude criterion must be defined, because of possible individual differences in the amplification factors used (Sect. 2.3.1.2 "Choice of Amplitude Criteria"). The next most commonly extracted phasic measures are form parameters of recovery, predominantly the half recovery time (Sect. 2.3.1.3 "Recovery Parameters"). Parameters of ascent are less frequently used (Sect. 2.3.1.3 "Parameters of Ascent"). If the EDRs are elicited by defined stimuli, latency times can be determined, as long as the temporal resolution is high enough (Sect. 2.3.1.1). Several mathematical solutions for the deconvolution of overlapping (superimposed) EDRs because of tight stimulus sequences have been recently proposed (Sect. 2.3.1.5). As a tonic measure, the frequency of non-stimulus-specific EDRs (Sect. 2.3.2.2) is preferred over recordings of the EDL (Sect. 2.3.2.1). Evaluating the NS.EDR freq. requires a separation of nonspecific from specific EDRs, by using an adequate time window (see Fig. 2.21).

Transforming resistance into conductance units, following the suggestion for standardization made by Fowles et al. (1981), is overwhelmingly the most common transformation practice in use. Additionally, a range correction recommended by Lykken and Venables (1971) is also frequently used for the reduction of interindividual variance. In all cases, it should be determined whether the intended transformations are really necessary and helpful with respect to possible improvements of reliability and validity.

Identification and elimination of artifacts and drifts should be treated with diligence, for which records of other biosignals can be helpful (Sects. 2.3.4.1 and

2.3.4.3). If missing data problems or genuine zero responses are present, the mean EDR magnitude can be calculated instead of the mean EDR amp. (Sect. 2.3.4.2). Unfortunately, some authors continue to use the term "EDR magnitude" instead of mean EDR amp., which adds ambiguity to publishing EDR analyses.

In summary, a variety of EDA parameters can be extracted, and their number may be increased through possible transformations. Suggestions for the choice of parameters in each context are given in Sect. 2.5 and in the corresponding passages in Chap. 3 of the present book. In most cases, only a small range of parameters are used in applied EDA recording, whereas an abundance of parameters might be used for research purposes.

2.4 External and Internal Influences on Recordings

This section deals with factors that should be controlled as possible sources of variance in EDA recording. These include environmental conditions (Sect. 2.4.1) and influences from other physiological factors (Sect. 2.4.2), such as age, gender, heredity, and ethnic differences (Sect. 2.4.3).

Potential confounding factors that arise in the following two sections as well as in Chap. 3 of this book are the variety of recording techniques used by different investigators. Technical details will be reported in footnotes, except for studies using the standard methodology as summarized in Sect. 2.2.7. This will allow the reader to make her/his own judgment on the generalizability of results from the studies reported in the present book.

2.4.1 Climatic Conditions

Investigations into the influence of climatic factors on EDA are mostly concerned with ambient air temperature, while recordings of other factors which determine climatic effects (e.g., humidity) are sparse. A person feels comfortable in what is known as the thermoneutral zone, in which neither shivering nor evaporative heat loss through sweating occurs (Thews, Mutschler, & Vaupel, 1985). For a sitting and lightly dressed person, the comfortable temperature is between 25 and 26°C, if the wall and air temperatures are equal and the relative humidity is 50%. The comfortable temperature drops to 22°C during the performance of office work. Venables and Christie (1973) allowed a range of the laboratory temperature between 20 and 30°C, at which the vasomotor control of body temperature is fully functioning. However, they recommended that a low temperature should not be preferred, since participants in psychophysiological experiments are mostly inactive and become more quickly cool than active participants in a field study. The resulting lower body temperature is very likely to cause a reduction in electrodermal reactivity

(Sect. 2.4.1.1). Therefore, they suggested covering inactive study participants with a light sheet, even in summer.[67]

2.4.1.1 Ambient Temperature

Investigations into the dependence of EDA upon ambient temperature have either taken the outside air temperature (e.g., seasonal differences) or the laboratory temperature into account. Temperature influences on EDA were demonstrated by Venables and Christie (1980) in their Mauritian study with 640 participants aged between 5 and 25 years. Positive correlations between $r = 0.20$ and 0.40 were obtained between ambient temperature and SCL, as well as negative correlations in the same range between temperature on the one hand and SCR amp., SCR lat., and SCR rec.t/2 on the other hand.[68] However, those correlations only appeared in participants that were older than 5 years. Such a lack of correlations had been also found in an investigation performed simultaneously with 1,800 three-year old children.

Several older studies reviewed by Rutenfranz and Wenzel (1958) and Venables and Christie (1973) point to clear differences between EDA in summer and in winter months. Venables and Christie suggest that the cause of this yearly swing is a hormonal change in reaction to heat effects, since pituitary adrenocortical hormones may influence both eccrine sweating and the electrolytic structure of epidermal tissue.[69]

An interaction between seasonal and room temperature effects on EDA[70] had been observed by Neumann (1968). In three experiments with 11 adults and 26 children (aged between 6 and 11 years), using different sites on the hand and the forearm, she investigated the connection between log SRL and room temperature variations of between 18.3 and 40°C at different times throughout the year. She observed differing SRL patterns from the recording sites in winter and summer, as well as during an extended heat spell. In particular, the palmar SRL was relatively low in winter, intermediate in early summer and high during the heat spell. Experimental heating

---

[67] This is understandable if one notes that Venables and Christie give 21°C as the correct temperature for a European laboratory, which is in the present author's experience somewhat too low. Instead, in his own laboratory, the present author maintained a constant temperature of 23°C and 50% relative humidity.

[68] The authors reported that they had to raise the laboratory temperature to an unusually high 30°C, since at lower temperatures the Mauritians displayed hardly any EDRs.

[69] In addition, functional and morphological changes in eccrine sweat glands have been observed in vitro and in vivo during heat acclimatization in three patas monkeys by Sato, Owen, Matthes, Sato, and Gisolfi (1990).

[70] Recorded as SR by means of a modified Wheatstone bridge (Fig. 2.3, Sect. 2.1.3), converted into log resistance values (Sect. 2.3.3.3). The recording device allowed for up to 20 active electrodes being connected in rapid succession. Recording sites were: fingertips, middle and proximal phalanges of the fingers, several palmar (including thenar and hypothenar) sites, the dorsal side of the hand, the wrist, several volar, and one dorsal point on the forearm.

and cooling led only partly to the expected effects of increase and decrease of the SRL, which differed dependent on both the recording site and the season. In any case, the SRL was lowest when the temperature – independent of all other conditions – was raised to an average of 35°C. Children showed less differentiated patterns than the adults.

In a repeated-measurement design with seven participants, Conklin (1951) investigated the relationship between three different room temperatures (21.9, 26.9, and 29.5°C) and the SCL measured at three different sites (wrist, forehead, and palm).[71] He observed that, as temperature decreases, the SCL decreased significantly. No significant differences between the recording sites were observed.

Rutenfranz and Wenzel (1958) also reported a clear connection between temperature increase and SRL decrease. They studied five participants for several weeks on a treadmill in a climate chamber in which the relative humidity was 60–65% and the wind speed at constant 0.5 m/s, whereas air temperature and the radiation temperature of the walls varied simultaneously between 15 and 36°C. By means of AC recording, they found that the SZL increased with lowering the temperature, while the skin capacitance decreased. Interindividual differences were more pronounced at lower temperatures than at higher ones.

Significant correlations between the SCL measured with dry electrodes and the effective room temperature were also found by Venables (1955), however, only with a sample of neurotic individuals ($N = 52$) but not with their healthy controls ($N = 210$), and only with temperatures exceeding 20°C. The direction of the correlations changed from $r = -0.48$ during motor exercise to $r = 0.51$ during a resting period.

Wenger and Cullen (1962) summarized the results of three investigations, reporting correlation coefficients between the palmar log SCL and the room temperature of $r = 0.22$ for female participants and of $r = -0.09$ and –0.15 for male participants. They took this as an indication of a gender-specific temperature effect. However, corresponding recordings from the forearm gave the same positive correlations between SCL and temperature for female and male participants (Sect. 2.4.3.2).

In a study with 21 participants, Wilcott (1963) observed a SRL decrease during an increase of the room temperature up to 65.5°C. Additional variations of the SRRs in amplitude and shape which he observed were not conclusive, as his stimulus conditions under different temperatures were not comparable. Grings (1974) reported a SRL decrease of 3%/°C; a value which had also been reported for skin temperature variations by Edelberg (1972a). While the SRR amp. may rise with decreasing temperature, it clearly decays when lower temperatures (e.g., 20°C) are present over longer periods of time.

Effects of temperature on the SPL differ according to the type of electrode and electrolyte concentration (Grings, 1974). Positive and negative components of the

---

[71] This study was performed with electrodes that were mechanically pressed to the skin.

SPR are influenced in different ways by room temperature, since the positive SPR decreases together with the temperature, while in turn the negative SPR component emerges more clearly.

In a habituation experiment with 96 participants, Fisher and Winkel (1979) obtained significant correlations between the outside temperature and the SCR amp. as well as the NS.SCR freq., however, they regarded these influence as small enough to decide against performing an accordant correction of their data. Waters, Koresko, Rossie, and Hackley (1979), who were in particular interested in middle- and long-term covariations between EDA and meteorological variables (Sect. 2.4.1.2), found in their 336 participants only a significant connection between temperature and SCL with long-term observations (1 week or a month) but not with phasic EDA measures. In their study described in Sect. 2.2.6.1, Turpin et al. (1983) recorded SC together with room temperature in 12 participants during 7 h working days, determining inter- and intraindividual correlations with hourly intervals. They obtained a significant correlation of $r = 0.61$ between room temperature and NS.SCR freq. and almost as high a correlation of $r = 0.53$ between room temperature and SCL, but only as interindividual correlations. The corresponding intraindividual correlations were between $r = 0.81$ and -0.50, being on average not significant. The authors traced this to differing climatic conditions on different days of their investigation.

Since there is an overall clear dependency of EDA upon the room temperature and the seasonal temperature, these variables should at least be recorded. Furthermore, the ambient temperature should be held as close as possible to a constant 23°C. Keeping an EDA investigation within seasonal limits is also definitely recommended.

2.4.1.2   Other Environmental Conditions

Negative correlations between both SCL and SCR and relative humidity were reported by Venables and Martin (1967a) and by Grings (1974). In the Venables (1955) study mentioned in the previous section, negative correlations between SCL and relative humidity were found when the latter was between 54 and 66%. Contrarily, both higher and lower values of relative humidity resulted in positive correlations.[72]

Results from Wenger and Cullen's (1962) study pointed to gender-specific differences in the correlations between humidity and SCL (as with temperature; see previous section). However, these differences were relatively small, as were the correlations between SCL and humidity ($r = -0.23$ for females and $r = -0.11$ for males).

Fisher and Winkel (1979) could not determine any significant connection between EDA and humidity. Waters et al. (1979) observed significant connections

---

[72] The dry electrodes used in this study may have contributed to this inconsistency.

between humidity and SCL, in their short- and middle-term study, and between humidity and the square root of the SCR amp. as well as a habituation index, in their middle- and long-term study (for more details of both studies, see previous section).

Venables and Christie (1980) obtained several positive correlations between relative humidity and SC with the 5- to 20 year-olds (from $r = 0.20$ to 0.40) in their Mauritius study (Sect. 2.4.1.1). No such correlations appeared with the older adults. However, these correlations were found for their different age groups in different SC parameters (SCL, SCR amp., SCR lat. and SCR rec.t/2), which complicates possible conclusions about the influence of humidity on SC. The same held for the connection between air pressure and SC parameters (cf. Venables & Christie, Table 1.7). Altogether, air pressure does not appear to influence EDA significantly. Only Wenger and Cullen (1962) obtained significant correlations of $r = 0.27$ between air pressure and SCL for their male participants, and Waters et al. (1979) found a corresponding effect in their long-term study. Fisher and Winkel (1979) could not confirm correlations between EDA and air pressure.

On the other side, Waters et al. (1979) who calculated multiple correlations between their EDA parameters and three meteorological variables (i.e., outside temperature, air humidity and pressure) came to the conclusion that EDA was influenced by these variables over short-, middle- and long-term periods. Within one-half of their participants ($N = 169$) they calculated predictors of EDA parameters by means of meteorological variables. Those were positively correlated with the measured SCL scores and the square-root transformed SCR amp. scores within the other half of the participants in middle- and long-term observation. However, the percentage of EDA variance explained by meteorological conditions was only 6–9%.

In general, possible influences of meteorological variables on EDA are difficult to demonstrate, since these variables cannot be easily experimentally manipulated. If marked climatic changes can be expected during the course of an experiment, meteorological variables should be recorded for control purposes.

2.4.2 Physiological Influences

In the following sections, influences of physiological processes that are intimately related to sweat gland activity and hence may influence EDA will be described. They are also connected with thermoregulation, whose contribution to elicitation of the EDA has already been discussed in Sect. 1.3. A systematic treatment of relationships between EDA and various other physiological measures is beyond the scope of the present book. Where those will be of particular interest, those relationships will be reported in the appropriate sections of Chap. 3.[73]

As all physiological processes being under ANS control, EDA is subject to a circadian influence (Sect. 3.2.1.3). Therefore, for example, the relationship between EDA and temperature parameters may be obscured by circadian factors. Venables and Christie (1973) have shown that the daily courses of SC and body core temperature show a similar progress, while the circadian rhythm of the finger temperature progresses, with its lowest point in the afternoon, mirror-inverted to that of the body core temperature. Rutenfranz (1958) observed with two participants, using both DC and AC recordings over 24 and 29 days, not only one but two SC minima, occurring around 10 a.m. and 7 p.m.

Infradian rhythms may also influence EDA, such as body temperature fluctuations associated with the menstrual cycle. With ovulation, the basal body temperature (measured in the morning under basal metabolic rate conditions) suddenly rises by about $0.5°C$ and remains at this level until next menstruation, due to an effect of progesterone on the temperature regulation (Thews et al., 1985). Hot flushes which appear as the most widely reported menopausal women symptom in Western culture may also be at least partly dependent on changes in the production of sex hormones and their action upon skin (Sect. 2.4.3.1).

2.4.2.1   Skin Temperature and Skin Blood Flow

Skin temperature can be recorded by means of thermistors (i.e., thermosensitive elements) attached to the skin or by measuring the heat radiation via infrared sensors. Compared to the EDA signal, changes in skin temperature are relatively slow (Boucsein, 2001).

All temporal measures of EDA show reciprocal relationships to skin temperature, i.e., EDA lat. as well as EDR ris.t. increase if skin temperature decreases (Maulsby & Edelberg, 1960), which can be explained by the temperature dependency of the acetylcholine transport mechanism (Sect. 1.3.2.1). Venables and Christie (1980, Table 1.8), investigating 260 eleven-year old children, obtained also negative correlations between skin temperature and SCR latency, risetime, and recovery parameters. However, these correlations where small, ranging from $r = -0.19$ to -0.30. While neither SCL nor SCR amp. were correlated with skin temperature in this study, Maulsby and Edelberg (1960) found a 3% increase of SRL for each

---

[73] One interesting result should be mentioned here: Christie and Venables (1971) observed negative correlations between the BSPL (Sect. 2.3.2.1) and the T-wave amplitude (TWA) in the ECG, from investigating 21 male participants lying down ($r = -0.70$) and from another 15 participants in a sitting position ($r = -0.61$). The authors suggest the extracellular potassium ionic concentration as being the cause for both an increased TWA and an increased negativity of the BSPL. Furedy and Heslegrave (1983) suggested that the TWA constitutes an index of excitatory sympathetic activity. Since the EDA is a valid index of sympathetic excitation, a high correlation between TWA and EDA could have been expected.

degree decrease in finger temperature between 40 and 20°C (see Edelberg, 1972a; also Sect. 2.4.1.1). In addition, the relationship between log SRL and skin temperature was found to be linear. With another sample of seven participants, Maulsby and Edelberg obtained inverse relationships between SRR amp. and skin temperature in the range of 5%/°C as a result of abrupt temperature changes. The observed changes in electrodermal reactivity recovered within 2–8 min after the temperature change, and thereafter actually displayed a reverse trend in several participants. While recommending a correction of the SRL according to skin temperature, Maulsby and Edelberg (1960) advised against a corresponding correction of SRR parameters due to heterogeneity and instability of the observed effects.

Lobstein and Cort (1978) investigated the effects of variation in skin temperature over the entire body on the SCR. They enveloped each of their 14 supine participants in a plastic suit, except for the face and one hand, and warmed the air inside, until the average skin temperature recorded from six sites increased from 26.0 to 37.1°C. Under each temperature condition, SCR parameters in response to three tones with signal characteristics were obtained and averaged. The authors found a significant increase of SCR amp. and a significant decrease of SCR lat. with increasing temperature, but could not demonstrate an influence on SCR rec.t/2. From their results, which were obtained under much better controlled conditions than those of Maulsby and Edelberg (1960), the necessity for correcting the EDR amp. with respect to changes in skin temperature can be derived even for small temperature variations.

The possible significance of skin temperature for SP recording was also pointed to by Venables and Sayer (1963). Due to the distance between recording sites (Sect. 2.2.1.1), the skin areas for the active and inactive electrodes may display different temperatures, leading theoretically to deviations of 1 mV/5°C in the range from 20 to 35°C. However the authors could not statistically demonstrate such a relation in an empirical study. Deltombe, Hanson, Jamart, and Clérin (1998) recorded skin temperature by using a digital infrared thermometer immediately before and after a series of electric stimulations given for eliciting SPRs (so-called sympathetic skin responses (SSRs); see Sect. 3.5.4) in ten participants (four females, six males). Mean SPR lat. and peak-to-peak amplitudes (Sect. 2.3.1.2 "Amplitudes of Endosomatic Responses") were obtained from al four limbs. After a baseline recording at a mean room temperature of 26°C, the right arm was immersed for 10 min in 14°C water. Thereafter, six series of four electric stimuli were applied. The test was repeated 1 week later with cooling the right hand only. The SPR lat. decreased at a rate of 0.088 s/°C within a temperature range of 26–35°C. This rate was higher in the whole arm cooling than in hand cooling only. The SPR amp. decreased with skin cooling. The authors concluded that skin temperature should be recorded as a control measure during SPR recording.

Simultaneous recording of SYL (with a three-electrode lock-in amplifier system), skin blood flow (using laser Doppler flowmetry), and skin temperature (with the aid of a thermistor) by means of a combined probe from a single palmar site has been developed and probed in 12 participants by Quiao, Morkrid, and Grimnes (1987). During the decrease of blood flow, corresponding changes in conductance and capacitance (Sect. 1.4.1.3) were observed. Skin temperature varied so slowly that hardly any correspondence between stimulation (i.e., deep inspirations, sound stimuli of 1 kHz, 80 dB, and 80 dB white noise pulses) and temperature changes was observable.

Summarizing, the rather few systematic studies on the relationship between EDA and skin temperature indicate that EDA parameters can be considerably influenced by increases or decreases in skin temperature, thus suggesting possible corrections of EDA results.

In the majority of psychophysiological investigations, skin blood flow has been recorded by means of photoplethysmograpy, the results of which are mostly expressed in pulse volume amplitude changes (Boucsein, 2001). Skin blood flow is predominantly determined by vasoconstrictory influences from the sympathetic branch of the ANS. Additional vasodilatatory influences were also discussed (Jänig, 1990). Pulse volume amplitude responses have been used as standard measures in research on orienting- and defensive-responses (Sect. 3.1.1.2). It should be noted that skin blood flow is a major determinant of skin temperature. Both measures are substantially correlated but not linearly related to each other (Boucsein, 2001).

Only a very small number of investigations of the influence of skin blood flow on EDA have been performed. Summarizing the hitherto available results, Muthny (1984) concluded that in a few cases excessively high or low blood flow to specific areas could affect both endosomatic and exosomatic EDA, whereas in other investigations no dependence of EDA upon skin blood flow could be found. Thus, not least because of these unexplained contradictions, vasomotor activity is no longer regarded as a significant factor of influence for EDA today (Sect. 1.1.2). Possibly, the sometimes observed connection between the skin blood flow and EDA can be traced to the relationship between vasomotor activity and sweat gland activity in thermoregulation (Sects. 1.3.3.2 and 1.3.5). Although the connection between skin blood flow and electrodermal phenomena appears to be rather unsystematic, disturbances of the blood flow should be avoided in all cases, therefore, wrapping of the electrode with adhesive tape to recording limbs such as fingers for fastening the electrode should be avoided if possible (Sect. 2.2.2.1).

2.4.2.2 Evaporative Water Loss and Skin Moisture

Although sweat gland activity is for sure one of the most important factors in the origin of electrodermal phenomena (Sect. 1.4.2.3), there is no perfect correlation between EDA and sweating, so that they must be treated as two separate biosignals.

Edelberg (1972a, Table 9.2) summarized the results from eight older studies which have measured both sweat secretion and EDA with a variety of methods. While as a rule between-subjects correlations were below $r = 0.50$, within-subjects correlations exceeded $r = 0.85$. However, in a study performed by Edelberg (1964) with 12 participants, intraindividual correlations between amplitudes of SRR or SCR and skin vaporization as measured by resistance hygrometry (i.e., directing a stream of dry air over a skin area of 1 cm^2) showed medium-size correlations of $r = 0.24$ and 0.30.

An independence of EDA and sweat gland activity was also reported by Wilcott (1964) as a general result from three studies with a total of 26 participants. During mental strain, the water vapor content of a dry nitrogen current blown across the skin was recorded, together with alternating SP and SR readings. In addition, atropine (an anticholinergic agent) was applied iontophoretically to the skin of five participants. The differences in recovery to this procedure, between both exo- and endosomatic EDA on one hand and skin evaporation on the other hand, was an indicator for independence of electrodermal and sweat gland activity measures.

Muthny (1984) performed a series of three studies on the covariation between EDA and sweat gland activity with a total of 70 participants. Blowing a dry air current with a constant 2 mL/s across a 5 cm^2 palmar skin area, vapor release was recorded with an evaporimeter (Muthny, Foerster, Hoeppner, Mueller, & Walschburger, 1983). SP- and SC-recordings were taken simultaneously from adjacent skin sites. Different habituation series and stress tasks (i.e., cold pressor test, arithmetic performance under noise, anticipation of giving a speech, and taking a blood sample) were investigated. In addition, the direct effects of locally applied (either injected or iontophoretically inserted) atropine as well as neostig- mine (a parasympathomimetic agent which facilitates cholinergic transmission) on EDA and sweat gland activity, as measured by skin vapor release, were investigated. The latency of the so-recorded phasic sweat gland activity was on average 1.1 s longer than the SCR lat. This result demonstrated that no outpouring of sweat on the skin surface is necessary for eliciting an SCR (Sect. 1.4.2.3). Consistent with previous reports (Edelberg, 1972a), within-subjects correlations were much higher (median $r = 0.88$) than those between-subjects (from $r = 0.23$ to 0.64), indicating marked differences of interindividual variances in both biosignals (Muthny, 1984).

Various methods have been used to determine the amount of sweat secretion (Boucsein, 2001), e.g., gravimetric methods, where a humidity-sensitive film is attached to the skin, the ninhydrin test, during which sweating areas are colored by means of an agent that reacts with the amines in the sweat (Schliack & Schiffter, 1979), or other colorimetric techniques such as so-called finger-sweat prints (Silverman & Powell, 1944). By means of the latter method and the aid of a magnifying glass, the number of active (i.e., completely filled) sweat glands per skin area can be estimated (Malmo, 1965).[74] Thomas and Korr (1957), studying six participants, obtained within- subjects correlations ranging from $r = 0.44$ to 0.96 between sweat gland counts, which were recorded photographically, and the SCL. Johnson and Landon (1965), in their study described in Sect. 2.4.3.3, used a technique developed by Thomson and Thomson (1952), in which a plastic ink impression of the skin is transferred to cellophane-tape and studied microscopically with a magnification of

---

[74] In this preparation, the active sweat glands appear as holes, since the plastic film does not attach to water (i.e., sweat on top of the open pore), which can be counted. This method had been discussed as a cheap alternative to recording tonic EDA, labeled "palmar sweat index" (Turpin & Clements, 1993) but was rather seldom used to date.

25 or more.[75] Their intraindividual correlations between SCL[76] and the number of active glands varied between $r = 0.29$ and 0.79, thus being on average not as high as those reported by Thomas and Korr (1957). Köhler, Vögele, and Weber (1989) used a fixation solution containing polyvinyl formaldehyde being removed with a cellophane-tape strip from the finger to count the active sweat glands under a microscope. They obtained with 20 participants a correlation between the occurrence of palmar sweating and the SCL change during a stress-inducing film of $r = 0.71$; all other correlations were not significant.

There is some evidence that tonic measures of skin moisture such as sweat gland counts yield a consistent relationship to tonic EDA parameters. However, the phasic sweat gland activity cannot be reliably obtained with the hitherto available methods for measuring skin moisture. For this purpose, refined methods to quantify evaporative water loss would be necessary.

2.4.3 Demographic Characteristics

From the demographically determined individual differences which can contribute to differing behavior of the electrodermal system, age- and gender-differences are the most carefully investigated ones (Sects. 2.4.3.1 and 2.4.3.2), whereas possible influences of ethnic factors and heredity on EDA were more infrequently studied (Sect. 2.4.3.3).

2.4.3.1 Age Differences

The first unambiguously *age-related changes* in the adult human *skin* appear between the third and fourth decade of life. However, influences from physical aging processes are frequently outweighed by those stemming from long lasting exogenous factors such as weather and climatic conditions (e.g., solar radiation; see Fenske & Lober, 1986). In the fourth decade, a decrease in skin thickness and elasticity is likely to occur. In addition, insensible perspiration (Sect. 1.3.3.2) diminishes relatively suddenly after the 60th year of life, presumably due to decreasing skin blood flow (Leveque, Corcuff, de Rigal, & Agache, 1984). Potts, Buras and Chrisman (1984) inferred from changing effects of mechanical strain imposed on the dorsal skin of the left hand of 16 male participants aged between 24 and 63 years, that aged skin has lower water content in the stratum corneum than younger skin.

---

[75] EDA was measured as SRL with a 2.54 cm² dry silver disk electrode and transformed into SCLs.

[76] EDA was measured as SR through Ag/AgCl sponge electrodes of 1 cm diameter with an "inert" electrolyte using 40 μA current and a Wheatstone bridge, being transformed to SC values.

While the epidermis and dermis are still firmly interlocked in young people (Sect. 1.2.1.2), this binding loosens with age, both the epidermis and the dermal-epidermal interface flatten and the barrier function of the epidermis can be reduced. Furthermore, decreases in the number of active eccrine sweat glands and the sweat quantity per gland occur (Fenske & Lober, 1986; Balin & Pratt, 1989), as well as a reduction of the sweat's salt content (Pollack, 1985). The epidermal ridges on the palmar and plantar surfaces of the ridged skin (Sect. 1.2.2) get partly lost, whereby the area for the mitosis of the basal epidermal cells decreases in relationship to the area of the horny cell layer (Sect. 1.2.1.1). There-fore, a higher mitosis rate per square centimeter would be required to compensate the loss of keratinocytes (Steigleder, 1983).

A diminishing amount of sweating per gland with increased age was reported for males but not for females by Morimoto (1978),[77] while Silver, Montagna, and Karacan (1965) found a decrease in both the number of active glands and in the output per gland with aging for both genders. Millington and Wilkinson (1983) mentioned two possible changes in old age that may influence sweat gland activity: the deterioration of an intrinsic glandular condition resulting in a limitation of responses to all kinds of stimuli, and an extrinsic factor affecting the sensitivity to cholinergic stimulation in general.

Dependencies of *tonic EDA* parameters on age have been demonstrated in several studies. Barontini, Lazzari, Levin, Armando, and Basso (1997) recorded SCL from 60 participants of both genders, who were divided into three age groups of 20 participants each (21 – 40, 41 – 60, and 61 – 80 years), during supine resting, standing and hyperventilation. SCLs were significantly lower in older than in younger participants during resting ($r = -0.42$) and hyperventilation ($r = -0.41$). Decreased sympathetic activity could not have accounted for these results, since blood samples of norepinephrine yielded opposed age effects. In general, a decrease of SCL is observed in old age, the reason for which is not well understood. Edelberg (1972a) held that the epidermal changes in aged skin would be too small to explain the observed increase in skin resistance. However, considerable changes in relationships between electrodermal phenomena and EDA-related properties of skin appear during aging. With 12 young participants of both genders (mean age 25.3 years), Catania, Thompson, Michalewski, and Bowman (1980) obtained a correlation of $r = 0.74$ between the number of active sweat glands as measured by means of finger-sweat prints (Sect. 2.4.2.2) and the SCL during resting, recorded with standard methodology and Beckman cream from the preferred hand. On the contrary, a group of 12 older participants (mean age 69.5 years) showed a much lower correlation of $r = 0.22$.

To investigate the effects of age on corneal hydration, Garwood, Engel, and Quilter (1979) recorded SC and SP in 12 young and 12 old participants (mean ages 30.8 and 75.5 years), applying KCl electrolytes with varying moisture. The induced

---

[77] In their comparison of eight postmenopausal older females (52–62 years) with eight younger females (20–30 years) during exercise under dry heat, Anderson and Kenney (1987) observed a lower sweating rate in the older group, which reflected a diminished output per heat-activated sweat gland rather than a decrease in the number of sweat glands recruited.

change in corneal hydration did not affect the SCL in both young and old participants, but affected the SPL. Whereas, a monotonic relationship between SPL and hydration existed in the young participants, so that the most negative SP appeared with the smallest hydration, the old participants displayed an increase of negativity of the SP together with increasing hydration instead. The authors explained their results with an increase in the epidermal potential component and a decrease in sweat gland potential in old age, which is a consequence of the sweat gland ducts' decay during aging. These findings were confirmed in another investigation by Garwood, Engel, and Kusterer (1981) with 25 young and 37 old male participants.

Surwillo (1969), recording SP in 58 young (23–53 years) and 64 old (54–85 years) males during 15 min of an attention demanding task, revealed that mean SPLs were in the same range in both groups, fitting the normal distribution better in old as compared to young males. However, Surwillo (1965) reported a low but significant correlation of $r = -0.23$ between age and SPL from the same set of data. A significant decrease of NS.SPR freq.[78] with age had been found by Surwillo and Quilter (1965) in 132 males between the ages of 22 and 85.

Investigations of *phasic EDA* parameters yielded a general decrease of electro-dermal reactivity in old age. This may be partly due to pronounced age-related changes in the hypothalamus (Andrew & Winston-Salem, 1966), leading to additional differences in the central triggering of ANS reactions which may interact with peripheral physiological differences of old as compared to young individuals (Edelberg, 1971). Botwinick and Kornetsky (1960), Shmavonian, Yarmat, and Cohen (1965), and Shmavonian, Miller, and Cohen (1968) obtained a decrease of electrodermal reactivity during classical conditioning (Sect. 3.1.2.1) with elderly individuals. In addition, Zelinski, Walsh, and Thompson (1978) observed a decrease of the SCR amp. in a group of very old participants, in contrast to young and less old participants, during a memory test. However, conflicting results have also been reported. Furchtgott and Busemeyer (1979) could not find differences in the change of SC[79] during mathematical exercises and memory tests with 67 male participants (23–87 years), divided into four age groups. Eisdorfer (1978) summarized several studies performed by his group, reporting more electrodermal reactivity in older individuals if they were emotionally challenged, but not during learning tasks or under relatively nonthreatening conditions. Garwood et al. (1979) could also not demonstrate an influence of age on the SCR in various reaction time (RT) tasks in their above-mentioned investigation.[80]

---

[78] Recorded with pure silver spiral electrodes that were chlorided electrolytically.

[79] Recorded as SR with 46 μA from palm vs. forearm with 1 cm^2 Ag/AgCl electrodes held in place by an elastic band, using cellulose sponge holders soaked with saline as electrolyte.

[80] To the present author's experience, electrodermal nonreactivity in elderly study participants may be a result of too low ambient temperatures and hence generally reduced sweat gland activity (Sect. 2.4.1.1). Therefore, care should be taken for creating comfortable climatic conditions for elderly participants, e.g., by raising the laboratory temperature several degrees or covering their body with a light blanket.

Plouffe and Stelmack (1984) compared ED-ORs (Sect. 3.1.1) to pictures of simple objects with either familiar or unfamiliar word names from 30 young (17–24 years) and 30 elderly (60–88 years) females. The young group showed a higher SCL during a baseline period as well as larger SCRs (recorded with standard methodology, but using K–Y gel) as compared with the old group. Furthermore, the older females displayed larger SCR amp. to items which they recalled in a subsequent recognition memory test, particularly to recalled unfamiliar-named items. This points to a differential sensitivity of the SCR to information processing (Sect. 3.1.3.1) in young and old people, whose nature remains unexplored (i.e., whether being more CNS or more peripherally determined).

No differences between young and old age groups of the ED-OR on the first two of a series of 1 kHz tones as well as in the trial-to-habituation criterion (Sect. 3.1.1.3) were observed by Catania et al. (1980). These authors claim that the method of recording might account for the failure to obtain age differences in phasic EDA, since studies having used constant current (e.g., Botwinick & Kornetsky, 1960; Shmavonian et al., 1965, 1968) obtained differences, whereas other studies using constant voltage (e.g., Eisdorfer, 1978; Catania et al., 1980) did not. Such an effect could have been due to the susceptibility of the constant current method to the decrease of the number of active sweat glands (Sect. 2.6.2). McDowd and Filion (1992) showed that 40 older adults (alumni) exhibit a smaller SC-OR[81] to irrelevant (i.e., to-be-ignored) auditory stimuli compared to 38 students. Furthermore, habituation speed was much faster in younger than in older individuals. Similar results have been obtained by Eisenstein, Bonheim, and Eisenstein (1995) with 49 male participants aged between 18 and 39 years. EDA[82] was recorded in a classical conditioning paradigm, in which an electric shock served as UCS and a tone as CS (Sect. 3.1.2.1). Participants were assigned to three arbitrary age groups. There was no correlation between age and habituation to the tone-alone trials. However, younger participants showed faster initial habituation to the electric shock. Weisz and Czigler (2006) compared SCR amp. (recorded with standard methodology) from ten young (eight females, two males; 18–26 years) with those from ten elderly (four females, six males; 64–84 years) adults during the repeated presentation of novel but neutral visual stimuli (i.e., letters on a computer screen). While the younger participants habituated to novel stimuli, older individuals showed hardly any habituation. However, no age differences were seen in SCR amp. to stimuli serving as target in the design used for recording of ERPs.

The appearance of differences in reactivity between young and old individuals in a particular study may also depend on the experimental context and the character of the stimuli, such as their emotional meaningfulness. Silverman, Cohen, and

---

[81] Recorded with standard methodology with the use of a Wheatstone bridge from the volar surfaces of the distal phalanges of the first and second fingers of the nonpreferred hand. The recording interval was 1–5 s after stimulus onset (1 kHz, 75 dB tones at irregular intervals between 30 and 90 s); the amplitude criterion was 0.05 μS.

[82] Using 2 cm diameter zinc electrodes, embedded in a plastic cup, which was filled with 1% zinc sulfate in agar paste. A 40 μA current was applied to measure SR, the SRR amp was determined and transformed to log SC change.

Shmavonian (1958) and Shmavonian and Busse (1963) showed that old individuals responded with a marked increase of the EDR amp. to words having specific emotional significance to them, in comparison to neutral stimuli. Baltissen (1983), who recorded SR with standard methodology, also found no lesser electrodermal reactivity in his study with 20 male participants, aged between 65 and 75 years, in comparison to 20 young male controls, aged between 25 and 35 years, when using nonage-specific emotion-inducing material. In contrast, the elderly participants yielded even higher values in both SRR amp. and NS.SPR freq. during the presentation of pictures showing children, varying in emotional quality and intensity. Gavazzeni, Wiens, and Fischer (2008) reported that older healthy individuals (70–80 years) showed diminished SCR amp. to neutral and negatively tuned pictures than younger individuals (20–30 years), which was in contrast to their increased subjective intensity ratings.

There is some inconsistency with respect to EDA in *infants* and *children* (Edelberg, 1972a). An increased SRL was observed in 24 seven- to 8 year old children by Corah and Stern (1963), as compared to SRLs obtained from adults (Sect. 2.5.2.2 "Tonic Skin Resistance Measures"). Kaye (1964) who recorded EDA from 112 neonates, observed a marked increase of the SCL[83] on palmar and plantar skin surfaces during the first 4 days of life, being interpreted by the author as a consequence of an increasing sweat gland activity. Mize, Vila-Coro, and Prager (1989) confirmed the increase in sweat gland activity during the first year in life, which resulted in an increased skin hydration being quantified by a significant drop in skin impedance recordings from 36 full term infants. Spontaneous and evoked EDRs had been observed in babies being only a few days old (for further references see Edelberg, 1972a, p. 408). Using the finger-sweat print method (Sect. 2.4.2.2), Jorgenson, Salinas, Dowben, and St. John (1988) counted the number of active sweat glands per 1/4 cm on the left hypothenar eminence in altogether 549 individuals. The mean number of sweat glands increased from about 500 in newborns to about 640 in children of mean age 7–8 years, decreasing again in adults of about 25 years on average to 400–500.[84]

Considerable age differences in younger children have been revealed with respect to orienting and habituation of the SCR amp. (Sect. 3.1.1). Gao, Raine, Dawson, Venables, and Mednick (2007) analyzed data from 100 female and 100 male children (mostly Indians and Africans) which had been collected in Mauritius at ages 3, 4, 5, 6, and 8 years. They consisted of 37 electrodermal nonresponders, 99 hyperresponders, 11 children with long SCR recovery plus 53 with modal values of SCR amp. and recovery (for further details, see Venables, 1978). At each point of age, six 75 dB tones of 1 s duration were presented over headphones, i.e., three 1,000 Hz tones, followed by three 1,311 Hz tones. SC was recorded using standard methodology but with 0.5% KCl in 2% agar-agar as electrolyte medium from the

---

[83] Recorded with silver electrodes covered with an AgCl layer attached by means of flexible wires to palmar, plantar, and calf regions, using a constant voltage of 1.35 V.

[84] In their study on seasonal effects on the SRL described in Sect. 2.2.1.1, Neumann (1968) revealed a less differentiated pattern in children between 6 and 11 years compared to adults.

medial phalanges of the left hand's index and middle fingers. Response criteria were SCR onset within 1 and 3 s poststimulus and a minimum SCR amp. of 0.05 μS (Sect. 2.3.1.2 "Choice of Amplitude Criteria"). Different mathematical growth models were applied to the development of the initial SC-OR, to habituation (calculated as the difference between trials 3 and 1) and to OR reinstatement (calculated as the difference between trials 4 and 3; see Sect. 3.1.1). Initial SC-ORs gradually increased between age 3 and 4 and increased more quickly from age 5 to 6, leveling off thereafter. Habituation was absent at age 3 but increased linearly from 4 years on, whereas OR reinstatement could not be observed at all in children aged between 3 and 8 years. The authors were critical about the last result, because the difference in tone frequency between the third and fourth stimulus was relatively small. They were also concerned about the generalizability of their results because of their culturally and ethnically somewhat unique sample. Furthermore, using CV recording was probably less sensitive than CC recording would have been for detecting age-related differences in SCRs, which had been pointed out by Catania et al. (1980) as mentioned above. In general, if EDA is recorded in children, it has to be kept in mind as well that the number of sweat glands is fixed at birth, but the skin surface increases by a factor of 7 from birth to adulthood (Sect. 1.2.3), which will result in a considerable change of sweat gland density.

Fowles, Kochanska, and Murray (2000) recorded SC[85] from 99 children (49 girls, 50 boys) at the age of 2 and subsequently when they were 4 years old, using a test battery made up from deep exhalation, turning off the room lights for "seeing planets," popping a paper bag, pointing to body parts, and other stimulus conditions made interesting for young children. Both stimulus-elicited SCRs and the SCL were evaluated. Large SCRs (>50 μS) were observed following all stimulations of abrupt onset. Smaller SCRs were elicited by mildly positive and mildly negative stimulation but not by emotional conflicts. Most experimental conditions did not elicit increases in SCL. The authors concluded that SCRs at this early age are fully elicited by physical stimulation, but psychologically meaningful stimuli or situations elicit SCRs to a much lesser extent. Unexpectedly, motor activity per se did not elicit SCRs that would have been considered as artifacts (Sect. 2.2.5.2).

El-Sheikh (2007) recorded SC (with standard methodology, however attaching the electrodes with Velcro bands to the fingers) from 64 children of each gender (6–13 years at the time of the first investigation) under 3-min baseline, during listening to a stressful interaction between adults and during a mirror-image drawing test. The experiment was repeated after 2 years. A median split was applied to designate the children in the age groups 6–8 and 9–13 years at the time of the first investigation. Averaged across the two investigations, younger children showed significantly higher mean SCLs than older ones.

Curzi-Dascalova, Pajot, and Dreyfus-Brisac (1973) investigated the appearance of spontaneous SPRs in 29 *children during sleep*. The sample consisted of both full term and of premature infants, their age being calculated between 23 and 41 weeks

---

[85] With 1.0 V CC, using a Wheatstone bridge, 7.5 mm diameter Ag/AgCl electrodes thenar/hypothenar from the nondominant hand.

from the estimated date of conception. SPRs[86] first appeared in the premature infants from the 28th week of life. After this time, the triggering mechanism of phasic electrodermal activity appeared to be fully functional. The authors observed an increased appearance of SPRs during REM sleep, while in contrast to adults, the NS.EDR freq. was higher during SWS than in REM sleep (Sect. 3.2.1.3), and in total the frequency of nonspecific EDRs during sleep was lower for children than for adults.

In summary, age-related physiological and psychological changes have to be considered as possible causes for both decreases of SCL and of SCR amp. in older study participants. In addition, the method of recording may interact with peripheral changes appearing in older individuals. In infancy and childhood, electrodermal behavior is also different from that of adults, but the results are not so consistent. Characteristic values for EDA parameters within several age groups are also reported in Sects. 2.5.2.1 and 2.5.2.2.

2.4.3.2 Gender Differences

Differences between females and males have been studied for both sweating and EDA. Females have a greater sweat gland density than males but display more delayed and, in total, less sweating (Morimoto, 1978; Edelberg, 1971). Interestingly, Jorgenson et al. (1988) in their study described in the previous section, revealed by using the finger-sweat print method (Sect. 2.4.2.2) that the number of active sweat glands, which was considerably lower in female compared to male newborns, reported this difference being reversed in children of mean age 7–8 years and in adults of about 25 years.

The observed gender-related differences in both sweating and EDA can presumably be ascribed to endocrine influences (Venables & Christie, 1973). Females have (not significantly) more active sweat glands than males, but males show a greater gland flow (Fowles, 1986a). A number of studies have also reported gender-based differences in electrodermal activity and reactivity. Kimmel and Kimmel (1965) obtained a significantly lower mean SCR amp.[87] in eight female participants than in eight male participants as reaction to the presentation of simple visual stimuli. Purohit (1966) observed that the SRR amp.[88] was significantly lower in 64 female participants than in 64 male participants during both an acquisition phase and an extinction phase of a light/tone conditioning procedure (Sect. 3.1.2.1).

In contrast, an increase of EDA had been found in females during the presence of threatening stimuli. Kopacz and Smith (1971) observed a lowered SRL[89] and an

---

[86] Unipolar recording taken from the palm and the sole with Ag/AgCl electrodes of 7 mm diameter, filled with Beckman electrode cream enriched with additional salt. The inactive electrode was attached to the dorsum of the respective hand and foot, and another one on the forearm as control site.

[87] Recorded by zinc/zinc sulfate saline electrodes from palmar sites, transformed to log values.

[88] Method not reported in detail, presumably unipolar.

[89] With zinc electrodes and zinc sulfate electrode cream from palmar sites.

increased NS.SRR freq. among 30 female in comparison to 30 male participants during anticipation of an electric shock, where a faster rise of the NS.SRR freq. was especially noticeable among the female participants in the first of several anticipation phases.

Ketterer and Smith (1977), using standard methodology, studied 32 females and 27 males under different experimental conditions and found a significant interaction between gender and condition. The NS.SCR freq. was highest among the female participants under verbal stimulation and under resting conditions, and highest among the male participants during the presentation of music. By contrast, Hare, Wood, Britain, and Frazelle (1971), comparing 25 females and 25 males, observed both increased tonic EDA and higher electrodermal reactivity[90] among the male participants. In the initial 10 min resting phase, the male participants showed a significantly higher SCL. Furthermore, subsequent to the announcement of the presentation of stimuli, males showed a significantly greater number of NS.SCRs per minute than the female participants. In response to the 30 slides presented afterwards, which included neutral, sexual, and forensic material, males compared to females displayed a significantly higher SCR amp. at the beginning, and in total a slower SCR recovery with the sexual material.

An investigation by Neufeld and Davidson (1974) yielded significantly lower averaged SCL maxima[91] for 30 females compared with 30 males during presentation of accident and control slides. Maltzman, Gould, Barnett, Raskin, and Wolff (1979) also observed higher electrodermal reactivity among males in comparison with females in two experimental studies from a series comprising 440 participants of both genders. The studies included initial habituation as well as classical conditioning and extinction of verbal stimuli. In particular, participants with smaller SC-ORs at the beginning and towards the end of the conditioning and extinction phases, observed considerably higher SRR amp. in males than in females.[92]

In contrast, Eisdorfer, Doerr, and Follette (1980) using a valsalva maneuver[93] observed significantly higher SCR amp., being recorded with standard

---

[90] Recorded with standard methodology, however using Beckman cream, as SR and transformed to SC. Differences appeared in both SCL and NS.SCR freq.

[91] Maximum SCL reached during the presentation of five slides, recorded with K–Y gel, the type of electrodes not being mentioned.

[92] Gender differences in electrodermal conditioning have also be observed in dependence of the person's gender who expressed emotions on slides used as CSs. Mazurski, Bond, Siddle, and Lovibond (1996) presented to 52 females and 35 males angry faces as CS+ and neutral faces as CS− in a picture-shock conditioning paradigm, crossing the expressing person's gender with the gender of participants. Male participants showed larger SCR amp. (recorded with standard methodology) to expressions of males than did female participants, whereas the respective SCR amp. did not differ in female participants. Therefore, the "preparedness" hypothesis of conditioning (Sect. 3.1.2.1 "UCR Diminution, Preception and Preparedness") could only be confirmed for male participants.

[93] Increasing thoracic pressure through trying an exhalation with mouth and nose shut, following deep breathing.

methodology, among 20 female (20–29 years old) in comparison to male participants. Contrarily, in the age groups of 40–49, and 65–75, no gender differences were displayed in reactivity. However, before starting the experiment, the SCLs of the male participants of all age groups were higher than those of the females, which might have influenced the observed SCR differences (Sect. 2.5.4.2). Generally higher ED-ORs to neutral auditory stimuli and slower habituation in 16 males compared to 16 females were observed by Martínez-Selva, Gómez-Amor, Olmos, Navarro, and Román (1987).

Román, García-Sánchez, Martínez-Selva, Gómez-Amor, and Carrillo (1989) presented a verbal and spatial performance task to 22 participants of each gender. They could not reveal gender differences in both SCR amp. and NS.SCR freq.[94] after the participants were grouped according to their preferred body side of response. The authors supposed this might have partly invalidated previous findings of their group, in which no control for EDR lateralization had been performed (Sect. 3.1.4.2).[95]

El-Sheikh (2007), in her study described in Sect. 2.4.3.1, found 6–13 year old girls having higher SCLs than boys in the same age group. Furthermore, the mean SCL declined significantly for younger girls (6–8 years of age) during the 2-year follow-up period but not for younger boys.

Gender differences have also been observed with respect to SP. Edelberg (1972a) reported opposed SP variations among female and male participants in his laboratory studies. Gaviria, Coyne, and Thetford (1969) found marked differences between 20 females and 20 males in the correlations between SPL and SRL scores (Sect. 2.6.1) immediately before presentation of acoustic (in particular verbal) stimuli. The tonic endosomatic and exosomatic EDA of the male participants did not significantly correlate, whereas those of the female ones yielded correlations between $r = -0.48$ and -0.59. Corresponding gender-based differences did not show up in the correlations between the phasic measures. Presumably, the differences among the correlations may partly stem from the greater variance of SPL and SRL scores among female in comparison to male participants.

The *menstrual cycle* may contribute to gender differences in EDA as well (Edelberg, 1972a). This was shown by Asso and Braier (1982) in 36 females (not using contraceptive pills) who were divided in those being tested in their premenstrual and those tested in their intermenstrual phase. In the latter group, SCL[96] increases during the experiment were significantly higher as compared to the

---

[94] Recorded with 7 mm diameter Ag/AgCl electrodes, 0.068 M NaCl cream and two 0.2 V constant voltage amplifiers on both hands simultaneously.

[95] Gender differences have also been observed in EDA recordings during the presentation of emotion-inducing films (Kring & Gordon, 1998; see Footnote 158 in Sect. 3.2.2.1) and in pictures with emotional content (Bradley, Codispoti, Sabatinelli, & Lang, 2001). In the first study of the latter authors performed with 50 females and 45 males, a marginal gender main effect was obtained for the SC peak, indicating that larger SC changes were observed when males viewed opposite-sex erotic pictures, compared with females.

[96] Recorded with CV from 10 mm diameter Ag/AgCl electrodes, filled with 17% NaCl gel; no further specifications provided.

premenstrual group, whereas the mean resting SCL did not yield such a difference. Martínez-Selva et al. (1987) who divided their female participants according to being in preovulatory and postovulatory phases found support for the hypothesis that the autonomic arousal level increases in the preovulatory and decreases in the postovulatory phases. Gómez-Amor, Martínez-Selva, Román, Zamora, and Sastre (1990) grouped 62 females into different phases of the menstrual cycle, based on self-report measures and basal body temperature recordings. All participants were presented 15 tones (1 kHz, 80 dB, 4 s), while SC was recorded.[97] Compared with the luteal and premenstrual phases, significant increases of SCR amp., NS.SCR freq., SCL and a decrease in habituation rate were observed in the ovulatory phase. Hence, care should be taken for at least asking female study participants about the presumed phase in their menstrual cycle when measuring EDA.

Goldstein et al. (2005) recorded EDA[98] in an fMRI (Sect. 2.2.3.5) from 12 females twice in counterbalanced order during different times of their menstrual cycle, i.e., during the early follicular and during the late follicular/midcycle phase. The participants viewed pictures of different arousal and valence (Sect. 3.2.2.1). EDA correlated positively with brain regions involved in the CNS response to stress such as the amygdalae during the midcycle but not during the follicular period. This was attributed by the authors to a diminished cortical control of the amydgdala during the early follicular period. Goldstein, Jerram, Abbs, Whitfield-Gabrieli, and Makris (2010) extended the earlier study comparing 12 females in the same different stages of their menstrual cycle with 12 males. Unfortunately, EDA was not recorded in the fMRI while the participants viewed negative valence/high arousal vs. neutral visual stimuli. There were few significant differences in BOLD signal changes between females in the early follicular stage and males, but significantly lower changes in the BOLD signal in females during the late follicular/midcycle phase compared with males. The results support the existence of gender-based hormonal differences in the stress response (Sect. 3.2.2.2), which is modified in females by their menstrual cycle.

Hot flushes – a symptom which appears frequently in postmenopausal females – were demonstrated by Swartzman, Edelberg, and Kemmann (1990) being paralleled by marked increases in palmar and sternal SCL (2.05 and 1.34 μS, respectively).[99] The correlation between sternal SC changes during hot flushes and subjective flush severity ratings was $r = 0.592$. The authors suggested that influences of hormonal changes on peripheral and central thermoregulatory processes may contribute to EDA being a suitable objective indicator of hot flushes, which constitute a noticeable age-related symptom in females (Sect. 2.4.3.1). The

---

[97] Recordings were performed with 0.2 V "constant current" from 7 mm diameter Ag/AgCl electrodes filled with 0.068 M NaCl gel, attached to the thenar/hypothenar eminences of the right hand.

[98] Described only as taken from the fingers and expressed in μS.

[99] For more information on sweat gland activity in postmenopausal females, see Footnote 77 in Sect. 2.4.3.1.

usability of sternal SC-recording for detecting hot flushes has been confirmed by Freedman, Woodward, and Norton (1992) who compared 18 postmenopausal females with and eight menopausal females without suffering under hot flushes during a 1 h supine resting period and a subsequent 45 min heat induction period in the laboratory and during 24 h of ambulatory monitoring (Sect. 2.2.3.4). They recorded finger temperature and HR together with sternal SC[100] and used any SCL increase of 2 μS and more in 30 s as indicator for a hot flush. These were only very seldom detected in the control females, whereas females who reported having hot flushes in everyday life frequently showed those under all three recording conditions. The hot flushes were subjectively registered by the participants in 77–84%. Skin temperature showed an increase of 0.5°C from 4 min before to 4 min after the SCL peak, revealing its slow-changing nature (Sect. 2.4.2.1). HR showed an increase of about 8 bpm after the SCL peak compared to 4 min before. Hence, both laboratory and ambulatory SC-recording might be used for detecting hot flushes, both being highly correlated with in the affected females.

In summary, females in general display higher SCLs, while males tend to show a greater electrodermal reactivity under conditions of stimulation. However, these results may be influenced by the menstrual cycle and postmenopausal hot flushes. Furthermore, the observed gender differences cannot be generalized to clinical applications. In their studies described in Sect. 3.4.1.3, Ward, Doerr, and Storrie (1983) and Ward and Doerr (1986) observed significantly lower SCLs among depressed female patients in comparison to depressed male patients, and therefore applied different diagnostic criteria along gender lines. Also generally observed was that females show smaller electrodermal lateralization effects (Sect. 3.1.4.2) than males. Additional gender differences were observed in correlations between EDA and temperature (Wenger & Cullen, 1962; Sect. 2.4.1.1), season (Venables & Mitchell, 1996), relative humidity (Sect. 2.4.1.2), as well as with respect to age effects as described in the previous section.

2.4.3.3   Ethnic Differences and Heritability

Compared with age and gender issues, *ethnic differences* were not often investigated in the literature on EDA. It is very likely that the difference in the number of active sweat glands between dark- and light-skinned individuals (cf. Millington & Wilkinson, 1983, Table 3), which is presumably attributable to an increase in the sweat gland density along a temperature gradient (Morimoto, 1978; Muthny, 1984), is related to observed ethnic differences in EDA. Thompson (1954, Table 3) gave normative values for Europeans and Africans for the regional distribution of sweat glands and outputs per gland, unfortunately only for dorsal areas of hand and feet. Venables and Christie (1973) reported that Japanese individuals have more eccrine sweat glands on their extremities as compared to Europeans. Weigand, Haygood,

---

[100] Using a 0.5 V constant voltage and 1.5 cm diameter Ag/AgCl ambulatory monitoring electrodes, filed with 0.05 M KCl Unibase-glycol paste. Ambulatory recording was performed with a Medilog tape recorder.

and Gaylor (1974) observed that African-Americans had significant more cell layers in the stratum corneum as compared with Caucasians. Berardesca, de Rigal, Leveque, and Maibach (1991) observed marked differences between skin thickness, transepidermal water loss (Sect. 1.3.4.2 "The Role of the Epidermal Barrier Layer"), and water content of the stratum corneum between Caucasians, Latinos, and African-Americans, which seemed to be correlated with the different melanin content of the skin (Sect. 1.2.1.1). Fowles (1986a) pointed to the difficulty of studying different ethnic groups under precisely the same conditions, and to the minimal differences in sweating between Caucasians, African-Americans, and Japanese obtained in the few studies fulfilling these requirements.[101] Consequently, Venables and Christie (1980) reported normative values for EDA without further consideration of ethnic differences, though those were obtained from their Mauritian sample (Sect. 2.5.2.1).

Several studies compared EDA of Caucasian and African-American individuals living in North America under comparable environmental conditions. Johnson and Corah (1963) found reliably higher base levels of skin resistance in African-Americans than in Caucasians, and Bernstein (1965) reported the same for skin impedance levels,[102] both in schizophrenic patients and normal controls, independent from the examiner being of either ethnic group. An increased SRL in African-Americans which is independent from the experimenter's skin color was also confirmed by Fisher and Kotses (1973).[103] No differences in NS.SRR freq.[104] were seen during a resting phase, but the study participants examined by experimenters with opposite ethnic affiliation showed significantly more NS.SRR freq. during the presentation of the first half of 14 white noise stimuli (75 dB, 5 s), which the authors explained as being due to novelty effects.[105]

Using finger-sweat prints (Sect. 2.4.2.2) and SR recording in 31 African-American and 32 Caucasian males during resting and during the presentation of 10 tones (1 kHz, 55 dB, 5 s), Johnson and Landon (1965)[106] could not confirm the hypothesis that African-Americans have a lower SCL being due to their smaller number of active sweat glands. They found Caucasians being more reactive during the first four tones, which seemed to be contradictory to common concepts of level dependency (Sect. 2.5.4.2). In addition, rank-order correlations between both variables were consistently smaller in Caucasians than in African-Americans.

---

[101] It is sometimes said that Chinese people do not have sweat glands. This erroneous statement may result from sweat gland activity being normally lower in Asiatic people, due to their sweat glands being smaller as compared to those of Caucasians.

[102] Recorded with stainless steel disc electrodes of 9.5 mm diameter, filled with so-called Cambridge cream, by means of a tissue resistance monitor providing 8 Hz square wave and a constant current of 20 µA.

[103] For further discussion of experimenter's ethnic group on participant's physiological reactions, see Venables and Christie (1973).

[104] Measured palmar/dorsal at the dominant hand by Ag/AgCl electrodes and Beckman electrode cream, using "a constant direct current of 20 µV" (which should be presumably µA).

[105] Barabasz (1970) observed significant more EDA changes during an imagination task in 19 African-Americans compared to 20 Caucasians.

[106] Method of EDA measurement as used by the Johnson group (see Footnote 131, Sect. 3.2.1.3).

Sweat gland counts and SR measures[107] were also recorded in parallel by Juniper and Dykman (1967) from different clinical groups of both genders. They confirmed lower SRLs and lower sweat gland counts in African-Americans as compared to Caucasians for both females and males. Using variable numbers of participants (from 2 to 27 in each group), they also observed an increase in SRL and a decrease of active sweat glands with increasing age (Sect. 2.4.3.1). In addition, they reported that African-American females aged 20 to 39 years had fewer active sweat glands than Caucasian females in the same age range.

Korol and Kane (1978) compared SRLs[108] during a resting period, and SRRs to a 1 kHz 60 dB tone of 10 s duration, taken from 26 Caucasians, 25 African-Americans, and 25 Indians. The latter ones were anthropologically more Caucasians but in skin color more akin to the African-Americans. They observed a significant correlation of $r = -0.34$ between the skin color as measured with a pigmentometer and the resting SRL in the total sample, the SRL of Indians being intermediate to that obtained in African-American and Caucasian participants. However, they observed no differences in SRRs. Their conclusion was that skin color may have a greater influence on SRL than ethnic affiliation itself, which had not been clear from the data of a previous investigation by Korol, Bergfeld, and McLaughlin (1975) using a very similar procedure with 25 Caucasians and 25 African-Americans.[109]

Lieblich, Kugelmass, and Ben-Shakhar (1973) obtained SCLs[110] under baseline conditions from groups in Israel, differing in ethnic and cultural origin, and compared their data with those from other groups in previous studies. As a confirmation of earlier results, Caucasians showed significantly higher SCLs than colored individuals. In addition, Caucasian Bedouins yielded the highest SCLs, while the SCLs of the Negroid Bedouins were lowest, which was interpreted by the authors as ethnic origin being an important factor influencing SC within individuals of the same cultural and geographical environment.[111]

Janes, Hesselbrock, and Stern (1978) investigated the influence of ethnic group and parental psychopathology in a total of 206 African-American and Caucasian children with a mean age of 9.6 years on SP (measured with standard methodology).

---

[107] Obtained with a so-called Fels Dermohmeter and zinc electrodes from the palms, and in one group from the plantar arch.

[108] Recorded with standard methodology, using constant current of 10 µA/cm^2.

[109] Jorgenson et al. (1988) in their study described in the Sect. 2.4.3.1, revealed by using the finger-sweat print method that the number of active hypothenar sweat glands per 1/4 cm was considerably higher in African-American compared to White newborns, being reversed in children of mean age 7–8 years and in adults of about 25 years, with some gender differences as well (cf., Jorgenson et al., Table 3).

[110] Measured with standard methodology (using Beckman cream) as skin resistance (but with 20 µA constant current), transformed to SC.

[111] These results are not really convincing, since the Caucasian Bedouin sample participants were partly gathered by the police and were being moved, both actions may raise SCL markedly. In another study, Kugelmass and Lieblich (1968) observed higher SCL and lower electrodermal reactivity in Bedouin samples as compared to Israeli samples.

A factor analysis of 18 SP and two movement-artifact variables obtained from a habituation series to 10 cool-air stimuli and a conditioning and extinction series (20 and 5 trials with cool air as CS and warm air as UCS; Sect. 3.1.2.1) yielded five factors. In none of these, children stemming from schizophrenic, manic depressive, physically ill and normal parents differed from each other. However, children of psychotics showed more movements during the experimental session than control children, thus exhibiting greater artifact proneness (Sect. 2.2.5.2). Caucasian children showed significantly more nonspecific EDA as compared to African-Americans, but most ethnic differences were not significant. In an earlier study using the same methodology, Janes, Worland, and Stern (1976) also observed an increased SP reactivity in 42 Caucasian as compared to 64 African-American children, while vasomotor responsiveness as measured by finger pulse volume was greater in African-American as compared to Caucasian children.

Fredrikson (1986) investigated 21 Caucasian and 15 African-American participants of both genders during resting as well as during a stress task.[112] Resting SCLs recorded with standard methodology were greater in Caucasian as compared to African-American hypertensives (Sect. 3.5.5). However, the difference was not significant in normotensive individuals, and also disappeared during the stress task. The NS.SCR freq. showed a very similar pattern. Cardiovascular activity revealed an opposite pattern, yielding no ethnic differences under resting conditions and a greater increase in Caucasian as compared to African-American participants under stress. SCR amp. to the stimuli were also higher in Caucasian than in African-American participants.

Sternbach and Tursky (1965) studied ethnic differences in SPRs[113] to 29 repetitive electrical stimulations of 1 s duration each applied to the left forearm of 15 female participants of the following groups: "Old Americans" (i.e., whose parents and grandparents were born in the U.S.), as well as Jewish, Italian and Irish immigrants. The "Old Americans" showed a faster and more complete habituation of the SPR compared to the other groups, which correlated with their more matter-of-fact orientation towards pain as verbalized in an interview.

There are also several studies, the results of which suggest a *genetic determination* of EDA. For example, Lobstein and Cort (1978, Table 4) reported results from an earlier study performed with a small sample of fraternal and identical twins, in particular correlations between the rating of genetic fitness and different EDA parameters. Raine and Venables (1984) came to the conclusion that the majority of the hitherto existing studies could not demonstrate a genetic influence on the SCR amp. of the OR (Sect. 3.1.1). However, Lykken (1982) provided data for 63 pairs of monozygotic twins, as compared to 18 pairs of dizygotic twins, which were presented 17 tones (110 dB, 0.5 s). The mean SCR amp. over the first four trials yielded an intraclass correlation of $r = 0.55$ for monozygotic compared with

---

[112] Presentation of 16 combinations of a tone (1 kHz, 68 dB, 35 s) with a 110 dB white noise of 0.5 s duration, the length of which could be shortened by pressing a button.

[113] Measured by Ag/AgCl sponge electrodes from the right palm.

$r = -0.13$ for dizygotic twins. After applying a range correction, correlations increased to $r = 0.65$ for monozygotic and to $r = 0.37$ for dizygotic twins. Lykken interpreted these results being due to the removal of interaction effects between genetically determined ANS responses to the stimuli and peripheral factors, like density and reactivity of the sweat glands, by means of the range correction (Sect. 2.3.3.4 "Range Corrections"). Lykken, Iacono, Haroian, McGue, and Bouchard (1988) investigated SCR amp. (recorded bilateral with standard methodology, but from soap-washed sites on the index and third fingers) to a balloon burst, a 110 dB blast of pink noise and a series of to-be-ignored loud tones (1 kHz, 105 dB, 0.5 s, with pseudorandom ISIs of average 60 s) in 121 pairs of adult twins. A total of 53 pairs were reared together and 68 pairs were reared apart. Comparison of the combined 79 pairs of monozygotic and 42 pairs of dizygotic twins revealed that the initial electrodermal reactivity is strongly genetically determined. Furthermore, stable individual differences in not range corrected SCR amp. and in habituation slope (Sect. 3.1.1.3) are primarily determined by non-additive genetic factors. Also, about 40% of the total variance in the number of trials needed for habituation appeared genetically determined. Monozygotic twins tended to be similar in electrodermal nonresponsivity, which dizygotic twins did not.

Hettema, Annas, Neale, Kendler, and Fredrikson (2003) performed a classical differential fear conditioning study (Sect. 3.1.2.1) with 173 same-gender twin pairs (90 monozygotic and 83 dizygotic; 111 female-female and 62 male-male pairs; age range 25–38 years). Sequences of either evolutionary fear-relevant (snakes, spiders) or fear-irrelevant (circles, triangles) slides were used as conditional stimuli, and a mild electric shock served as UCS (Sect. 3.1.2.1). SCR amp.[114] were recorded for habituation prior to conditioning, during conditioning and during extinction. For all components of the fear conditioning process, intraclass correlations were considerably higher for monozygotic twins ($r = 0.26$–0.54) than for dizygotic twins ($r = 0.00$–0.26). Univariate structural equation modeling yielded that additive genetic effects accounted for between 34 and 43% of the total variance, thus demonstrating moderate heritability.

El-Sheikh (2007), in her study described in Sect. 2.4.3.1, found among 6–13 year olds significantly higher electrodermal responses to stressful tasks (calculated as differences between mean SCLs during stress and baseline) in their Caucasians compared to African-Americans. In addition, there was an increase in responsiveness during the 2-year follow-up only for Caucasian but not for African-American children.

Summarizing, it seems well established that African-Americans tend to have higher SRLs or lower SCLs than Caucasians under resting conditions. This is presumably dependent upon the decreasing number of active sweat glands with increasing darkness of skin. Additionally, differences in sweat electrolytes concentrations have been suggested as a possible cause of these differences (Johnson & Landon, 1965). Caucasians are also more electrodermal reactive during

---

[114] Recorded with CV, 8 mm diameter Ag/AgCl electrodes with an isotonic NaCl paste from the participant's left index and middle fingers, scoring the maximum SCR during 1–4 s after stimulus onset.

presentation of tones or noises. Thus, ethnic differences have to be carefully controlled in EDA studies. Hereditary influences are also rather likely being present in electrodermal activity and reactivity.

2.5   Statistical Properties of Electrodermal Parameters

This section provides characteristic values of EDA parameters, in the sequence of endosomatic recording (Sect. 2.5.1), of exosomatic recording with direct current (Sect. 2.5.2) – where SC and SR measures are treated separately – and of exosomatic recording with alternating current (Sect. 2.5.3). In addition, Sect. 2.5.4 presents the level dependence of the different EDA parameters.

In trying to cope with the numerous publications on EDA (Sect. 1.1.3), only studies that were methodologically oriented were included. In cases where such studies or appropriate review articles were not available, results from other studies will be reported. The present author prefers reporting results within the body of the text rather than providing tables because of the wide variety of methods used to obtain those results (see introductory remarks of Sect. 2.4). In addition to means and standard deviations, reliabilities for and correlations between various EDA parameters are provided.[115] The aspects of validity of electrodermal recordings are treated in Chap. 3.

2.5.1   Characteristics of Endosomatic Measures

Skin potential measurement poses problems for both recording and evaluation (Sect. 2.6.1). Therefore, only a relatively small number of studies have made use of endosomatic methods, especially among those who have extracted phasic parameters (Sect. 2.5.1.1). In a number of studies, connections between endosomatic and exosomatic EDA parameters have been investigated, these are reported in Sect. 2.5.1.3.

2.5.1.1   Skin Potential Responses

The problem of evaluating endosomatic responses has been previously discussed in Sect. 2.3.1.2 "Amplitudes of Endosomatic Responses."[116] Since the SPR may not only be monophasic, but also biphasic or triphasic, a measure of the total amplitude is always questionable. The range of observed SPRs, yielding usually only a

---

[115] A review of reliabilities of different EDA parameters including various investigations was provided by Freixa i Baqué (1982).

[116] Since phasic SP measures are so much dependent upon experimental as well as recording conditions, reporting typical distribution parameters and reliabilities will not be attempted.

few mV, is between 0.1 and −20 mV (Venables & Christie, 1980). Relationships between the stimulus strength and the size of the SPR are hardly predictable, since even a markedly uniphasic response can be altered and thereby weakened by a latent polarity which counteracts the response. Disregarding this, several studies used the measure of the difference between the negative and positive SPR maxima, for example by Gaviria et al. (1969) in their correlation study (Sect. 2.5.1.3).

The separate evaluation of single components of the SPR also poses problems for parameterization. Thetford, Klemme, and Spohn (1968) determined both the negative amplitude, measured from the prestimulus level to the negative maximum, and the positive amplitude which was calculated either, in the case of a single positive SPR, from the prestimulus level, or, in the case of a biphasic SPR, from the preceding negative maximum. In addition, they calculated the number of biphasic responses. While a marked habituation was displayed with the positive SPRs, an inconsistent process appeared over the 20 trials with the negative SPRs.

In an investigation with 30 participants, Knezevic and Bajada (1985) calculated the average amplitude of the biphasic SPR from the negative to the positive maximum, following electrical stimulation of the median nerve in the wrist.[117] The mean SPR amp. recorded from palmar sites was 479 μV, with SD = 105 μV, while the mean for the plantar surface was 101 μV, with SD = 40 μV. The palmar mean latency time was 1.52 s, with SD = 0.13 s. The plantar mean latency time was 2.07 s, with SD = 0.16 s. Here it should be noted that the latency times of the first SPR waves can be expected being 300 ms on average shorter than the SCR latencies (Sect. 2.3.1.1).

The presumed reductions of both the negative and the positive SPR amp. caused by an increasing hydration of the recording sites were quantified by Fowles and Rosenberry (1973) with the data from 12 participants, using different sites. In the beginning, the negative SPR amp. at the hydrated sites was around 14 mV less than at the nonhydrated sites; after 20 min the difference decreased to 8 mV. The positive SPR amp. almost fully disappeared at the hydrated sites.

Francini, Zoppi, Maresca, and Procacci (1979) recorded SPL and SPR during repeated electrical stimulation in 32 participants of both genders. During this procedure, the SPL became more negative, and the SPR − which has been monophasic and positive at the beginning − adopted a biphasic-negative shape with an increasing negative and decreasing positive component. This result again showed the general problem of SPR amp. evaluation, being further complicated by level dependence.

Uncini, Pullman, Lovelace, and Gambi (1988) recorded the so-called "sympathetic skin response,"[118] which is a term used by neurologists instead of SPR

---

[117] They used tin electrodes with a contact surface area of 0.72 cm^2, probably without electrolytes.

[118] Recorded with disc electrodes of 10 mm in diameter from the volar and dorsal side of the hand and the foot. SPRs were evoked by various stimuli at irregular intervals: deep inspiration, single auditory clicks and electrical stimulation of the median nerve at the wrist, the tibial nerve at the ankle, and the supraorbital nerve at the forehead.

(Sect. 3.5.4), in 10 patients with peripheral neuropathy and 20 normal controls. In the controls, SPR lat. remained fairly constant over stimulation methods but were different for recording sites: about 1.5 s at the hand and 1.9–2.1 s at the foot. Toyokura (1999) recorded SPR amp. from the palmar skin of 50 normal individuals, which were elicited by electrical stimulation. He described the relationship between the different waveforms (see Fig. 2.14, Sect. 2.3.1.2) and habituation parameters. The waveform types were consistent across all stimulations in 23 of their participants, whereas the remaining 27 showed various waveforms. In another study with 40 male participants, Toyokura (2006) obtained a proportional relationship between the intensity of an electrical stimulus applied to the median nerve at the wrist and the SPR amp., being either positively or negatively directed (Sect. 2.3.1.2 "Amplitudes of Endosomatic Responses"). This relationship persisted after habituation.

2.5.1.2 Skin Potential Levels

The SPL may vary between 10 and -70 mV[119] (Venables & Christie, 1980), whereupon the skin surface normally displays a negative potential in contrast to the body core, being greatest on the palmar and plantar surfaces. Thus, the average transcutaneous potential on the palms is -39.9 mV, the corresponding value for the forearm being only -15.2 mV (Edelberg, 1971). The deviation appears greater on the palm than on the arm. The potential on the right hand has been found to be around 5–7 mV more negative than the one the left hand, this being true for both right- and left-handed people (Sect. 3.1.4). Edelberg suggested a connection between this difference and the higher conductance of the right hand. Positive SPL values represent an exception (Venables & Christie, 1980). Like the SPR, the SPL is dependent upon the degree of hydration. Fowles and Rosenberry (1973), in their study discussed in the previous section, observed a decrease of the SPL of around 25–30 mV through hydration of the recording sites.

Shapiro and Leiderman (1954) investigated connections between and distributional characteristics of various SP measures, which they obtained for two rest breaks and one simple response task with 53 student nurses as participants. They found that the average SPL, ranging between 0 and -55 mV, was approximately normally distributed, while the variance and the mean square of successive differences (a time series statistic) displayed a positive skew. The mean SPL showed the same significant correlation with both other measures ($r = 0.32$), and the correlation of the variance with the time series statistics was highly significant ($r = 0.78$). The rank correlations between the two rest breaks, being 1 min apart from each other, pointed to differing reliabilities of each measure used ($r = 0.71$ for the mean SPL, $r = 0.47$ for the SPL variance, and $r = 0.63$ for the time series statistics). Surwillo (1969) in

---

[119] The method of determining the BSPL as the minimal obtainable SPL has already been discussed in Sect. 2.3.2.1.

his study, described in Sect. 2.4.3.1, found palmar SPLs between -12.3 and -56.8 mV during attentive conditions, the mean SPLs being normally distributed only in the group of 54–85 year of individuals but not in the 23–53 year old group.

O'Connell, Tursky, and Evans (1967) recorded resting SPLs in 75 students (21 females, 44 males), in another sample of 54 participants (14 females, 40 males), and in a sample of 55 housewives. SP was recorded between an active electrode below the hypothenar eminence and an inactive one on the dorsum of the forearm. Three measurements at half-minute intervals were averaged for the first two samples, while the SPL average from 30 readings of 1 s each was obtained for the housewives. The range of scores for all three samples was from 0 to 60 mV, which was in good agreement with the range for SPLs obtained by Shapiro and Leiderman (1954). No gender differences emerged in the two mixed samples. Therefore, tests of normality of the distribution were performed on each total sample. Although most tests of normality did not reveal significant deviations in both skewness and kurtosis, the housewives sample showed a significant positive skewness. The authors discussed this as a possible effect of the lower mean SPL in this particular group or of its greater age, thus challenging the generalizability of results obtained from student samples to samples differing from them in age. Neither unilateral stimulation nor handedness affected the maximum SPR.

Wyatt and Tursky (1969) recorded bilateral SPs from palmar sites, using the dorsal forearms as inactive sites, with Ag/AgCl sponge electrodes, during the presentation of auditory, visual and tactile stimuli of 1 s duration presented on either side and bilaterally. Regardless of the stimulus condition, right-hand SPL changes were consistently higher than those recorded from the left hand (cf. Wyatt & Tursky, Table 1).

With 17 participants of each gender, Foulds and Barker (1983) determined the SPL on numerous sites around the entire body in contrast to a reference electrode in electrical contact with the forearm dermis.[120] They observed a mean SPL of -23 mV, with SD = 9 mV. Significantly higher negativity appeared on the palmar and plantar surfaces, and relationships to dermatomes were not displayed (Table 1.3, Sect. 1.3.2.1).

Use of the NS.SPR freq. as a tonic parameter (Sect. 2.3.2.2) can lead to ambiguous results because of the multiphasic structure of the SPLs (see previous section). However, Fowles et al. (1981) assumed a particularly sensitive parameter being in question here (Sect. 2.6.1). Crider and Lunn (1971), in their study described in Sect. 3.3.2.2, obtained a mean of 6.36 and SD = 5.42 for the NS. SPR freq. during 4 min of 72 dB white noise, with a reliability of $r = 0.70$ after 7 days. In summary, it can be seen that the tonic SP measures, and the phasic SP measures as described in the previous section, are dependent to a considerable extent upon recording and other environmental conditions. Both the SPL and the NS.SPR freq. also show relatively small reliabilities.

---

[120] They used liquid electrolytes (KCl/agar) and calomel (mercury chloride) electrodes.

2.5.1.3   Relationships Between Endosomatic and Exosomatic Measures

Burstein, Fenz, Bergeron, and Epstein (1965), who investigated SR and SP concurrently during a word association test, found that the correlations between the amplitude of the SP c-wave (Fig. 2.14, Sect. 2.3.1.2 "Amplitudes of Endosomatic Responses") and the SRR increased from $r = 0.63$ to 0.79 together with stimulus intensity. The a-wave yielded a significant correlation to the SRR only with stimuli of high emotional importance ($r = 0.62$).

Lykken, Miller, and Strahan (1968) studied simultaneous SC and SP recordings taken from 19 participants during a stress period and a following resting period, with different combinations of two active and two inactive (by skin drilling) palmar sites on the fingers. The mean intraindividual correlations between the SCR amp. and SPR amp. was between $r = -0.18$ and 0.96, with an average of $r = 0.69$. The largest connections appeared in case of the observed SPR could be regarded as the result of a superposition of an a-wave on a b-wave. The positive b-wave, which reduces the SPR, first appears with high arousal (i.e., with a high SCL).

Wilcott (1958) recorded SPR and SRR amp. alternatingly, using the same sites (palmar against forearm) from 25 participants performing word association and mental arithmetic tests. He obtained significant correlations between the SPR and the SRR amplitudes. The interindividual correlations were higher ($r = 0.75$–0.97, average $r = 0.90$) for monophasic, negative and positive SPRs than for biphasic SPRs ($r = 0.51$–0.95, average $r = 0.62$).

Gaviria et al. (1969) who studied simultaneous SP and SR recordings from 20 female and 20 male participants during two sessions being 2–9 days apart, each with five different acoustic stimuli, found very high intraindividual correlations between the amplitudes of the SRR and those of the SPR.[121] The SPR amplitudes were obtained as the difference between the negative and positive maxima, an evaluation which is at least controversial (Sect. 2.5.1.1).

Venables and Sayer (1963) reported results from two studies with a total of 93 schizophrenic patients (Sect. 3.4.2), in which the SP and the SR were taken in parallel. A curvilinear relationship between the SPL and the SRL was displayed. If the SRL scores were transformed into SCL scores, a linear relationship of these transformed scores to the SPL scores resulted, together with correlations between these two measures of $r = 0.60$ and 0.51.

Hupka and Levinger (1967) recorded palmar SC and SP simultaneously with nonpolarizing Ag/AgCl sponge electrodes, placed to the thenar eminence of the right and left palm and on the dorsal right or left forearm. SC and SP recordings from right and left sites were balanced between their 10 female participants, who solved a series of 15 problems of finding a correct light pattern, for which they operated two sets of four toggle switches (one for each hand). Intraindividual correlations between SPLs and SCLs during the initial resting condition yielded

---

[121] They used the earlobe as an inactive site for SP recordings, and dry silver electrodes with 3.8 cm^2 surfaces for SR recordings.

positive values between $r = 0.21$ and 0.90, whereas more variable correlations (between $r = -0.66$ and 0.54) were obtained during periods of motor activity. During the initial resting period, negative SPR deflections were matched by concurrent SCR deflections. The correspondence between SCRs and negative SPRs was generally lower during the tasks than during the resting periods. The authors discussed their results with respect to the possibility that an epidermal factor may contribute to the occurrence of both SPR and SCR.

2.5.2 Characteristics of Exosomatic Measures with Direct Current

Exosomatic direct voltage recordings are either performed with constant voltage or constant current methods (Sect. 2.2.3.2), resulting in different units of measurements (i.e., conductance or resistance units). Many authors transform values of resistance into values of conductance before statistical data processing (Sect. 2.3.3.2). The majority of published results obtained with exosomatic DC recordings are expressed in terms of conductance. As conductance values, transformed from resistance values obtained through the constant current method, are equivalent to conductance values obtained through the constant voltage method (Sect. 2.6.2), values of skin conductance obtained with either method are therefore given together in Sect. 2.5.2.1. Section 2.5.2.2 will provide results of skin resistance recordings that were not transformed. The results for the form parameters are displayed together, specifically with respect to the latencies and the ascent parameters in Sect. 2.5.2.3, and with respect to the recovery times in Sect. 2.5.2.4. In Sect. 2.5.2.5, the question of a possible dependence of electrodermal recovery and amplitude will be discussed.

2.5.2.1 Results of Skin Conductance Measures

Venables and Christie (1980) summarized the most important aspects of the distributional characteristics of skin conductance values. The authors noted especially, however, that both the SCL and the SCR amp. can vary with the concentration of electrolytes and with the size of electrodes.

Skin Conductance Responses

Venables and Christie (1980) reported that the maxima of the SCR amp. are between 2 and 3 μS if standard methodology is used as outlined in Sect. 2.2.7. When these values are logarithmized, maximum SCRs lie between 0.30 and 0.47 log μS. Corresponding values for minima cannot be given, naturally, as they are dependent upon the amplification and the definition of the amplitude criterion (Sect. 2.3.1.2 "Choice of Amplitude Criteria").

Venables and Christie (1980, Table 1.1) reported the distributional data from a Mauritian sample ($N = 539$; 5–25 years of age), divided into five age groups.[122] The mean SCR amp. was 0.518 µS and the corresponding values increased from 0.430 to 0.668 µS with increasing age of their participants. The standard deviation was 0.576 µS and increased with age from 0.475 to 0.734 µS. Distributions of the amplitudes were significantly positively skewed and leptokurtic as compared to the normal distribution. Through logarithmization of the SCR amp., the distributions could be normalized. After the log transformation, the total mean was −0.496 log µS and the variance was 0.200 log µS. Since logarithmization had been performed with the SCR amp. values, no differences appeared between logarithmized SCL values. Corresponding improvement of the distributional characteristics through log transformation was obtained with a sample of 1,761 three-year-old children (Venables & Christie, Table 1.3). In a further sample of 65 participants between 18 and 75 years of age, the distribution of the raw scores of the SCR amp. was similarly positively skewed, but markedly less leptokurtic, while both kurtosis and skewness deviated significantly from the normal distribution. This could possibly be due to the low-intensity of tones being only 75 dB, while results reported earlier were obtained with tones of 90 dB (Venables & Christie, Table 1.4).

Fahrenberg, Foerster, Schneider, Müller, and Myrtek (1984) recorded SCRs with standard methodology from 58 participants during resting and mental arithmetic performance conditions in the laboratory. They observed an average SCR amp. of between 0.46 and 0.54 µS (SD = 0.31–0.57 µS) under resting conditions, and between 0.72 and 0.89 µS (SD = 0.39–0.44 µS) during performance. The SCR amp., with the exception of one of the mental arithmetic exercises, were significantly positively skewed and leptokurtic. Sufficiently high short-term reliabilities emerged only during performance ($r = 0.72$), whereas values less than $r = 0.20$ were obtained for the resting condition. Iacono et al. (1984a), in their study described in Sect. 3.4.1.3, reported a 1-year retest reliability of the maximum SCR amp. during a series of tones of $r = 0.68$ in 23 normal study participants.

Much higher average SCR amp. were obtained in an additional evaluation of data in one of the studies performed by the present author. Boucsein and Hoffmann (1979) recorded SC and SR from the middle phalanges of the left hand in parallel using standard methodology. They presented 30 stimuli, consisting of 2 s white noise between 60 and 110 dB. The grand mean across all participants and stimuli for the SCR amp. was 1.152 µS with SD = 1.021 µS. The distribution of the SCR amp. was highly significantly positively skewed and leptokurtic in comparison to the normal distribution. Following a log transformation which eliminated the positive skewness, the mean SCR amp. was 1.033 log µS with SD = 0.535 log µS. The reliability, estimated according to Hoyt (1941), was $r = 0.971$ for the raw scores.

---

[122] Venables' team used KCl-based electrode cream. Although sweat contains by far more NaCl than KCl, the difference between the use of those monovalent ions is given little importance in the literature on methodology (Sect. 2.2.2.5).

El-Sheikh (2007), in her study with 6–8 year old children of both genders described in Sect. 2.4.3.1, reported stabilities within the same session for electrodermal responses to stressful tasks (calculated as differences between mean SCLs during stress and baseline) of $r = 0.64$ during the first experiment but only of $r = 0.48$ during the second one performed after 2 years. Reliabilities over the 2-year period were rather low, not exceeding $r = 0.20$. For reliabilities of SCRs and SCLs in schizophrenic patients compared to normal controls, see Footnote 245 in Sect. 3.4.2.2.

In summary, it can be expected that the SCR amp. is clearly positively skewed and leptokurtic, so that log transformations are an appropriate choice. The reliabilities are high in arousing conditions and low during resting conditions.

Tonic Skin Conductance Measures

In addition to the SCL scores, the frequencies of the nonspecific EDRs are used as tonic measures (Sect. 2.3.2.2). In a summary of the different studies in the respective literature, Venables and Christie (1980) came to the conclusion that SCL and NS. SCR freq. cannot be simply regarded as interchangeable parameters of tonic EDA. Silverman, Cohen, and Shmavonian (1959) could show in their study, discussed in Sect. 3.2.1.1, that the number of NS.SCRs can increase due to a decrease of SRL. Kimmel and Hill (1961) found that while the SCL was appropriate as a stress indicator, this was not true for the NS.SCR freq. Katkin (1965) and Miller and Shmavonian (1965) could also demonstrate that both measures diverge as indicators of tonic arousal. Martin and Rust (1976) found only low correlations between the two tonic measures for interindividual ($r = 0.27$) and for pooled intraindividual ($r = 0.15$) coefficients. However, Fahrenberg and Foerster (1982) observed with standard methodology in 125 participants markedly higher correlations between the SCL and the NS.SCR freq., which were $r = 0.55$ for interindividual and $r = 0.50$ for pooled intraindividual coefficients.

Minima and maxima of the SCL can hardly be reported, as they are dependent upon the electrode size. Venables and Christie (1980) have argued against a weighting of the SCL to the electrode area (Sect. 2.3.3.1) as they observed a nonlinear relationship between conductance and electrode area. They reported, for recordings with two active electrodes, a SCL range of 1–40 µS, and of 0–1.6 log µS.

In the table from Venables and Christie (1980) already cited in the previous section, the corresponding values for the SCLs and the log SCLs are given.[123] The average SCL of the total Mauritian sample yielded 3.040 µS. However, the course with aging was not linear: the mean for the 5 year olds was 3.597 µS, for the 10 year

---

[123] Since the SCL scores are also dependent upon the type and concentration of the electrolytes, the distribution data from the study of Venables' team cannot easily be generalized, as they used a KCl cream that is not commonly used for SC measurements.

olds 2.613 µS, and for the 25 year olds 3.223 µS. The standard deviations differed as well: 2.467 µS for the 5 year olds, 1.901 µS for the 10 year olds, and 2.539 µS for the 25 year olds, with a grand average SD = 2.238 µS. The distributions of the SCL scores were only slightly positively skewed, but significantly more leptokurtic than the normal distribution, however, not as pronounced as in case of the SCR amp. scores. It was also possible to eliminate the deviation from the normal distribution to a large extent through a log transformation. The results were based upon recordings from 635 participants. The SCL mean (2.383 µS) of the 3-year-olds ($N = 1,145$) was markedly lower than the one of the 5 year olds of the Mauritian sample; the standard deviation in the 3-year-olds was 1.564 µS. With respect to skewness and kurtosis, the distribution was more or less the same as in the Mauritian sample, whereas a log transformation was not fully able to eliminate the leptokurtic property of the distribution. In the third sample of 18- to 75 year-old adults ($N = 45$), the average SCL was 3.612 µS with SD = 2.470 µS, while the distribution was not skewed, but significantly more leptokurtic than the normal distribution, which was, however, eliminated through log transformation.

In the study by Fahrenberg et al. (1984), mentioned in the previous section, average SCLs between 9.1 and 16.58 µS were obtained, and the standard deviation was between 8.88 and 13.60 µS. The distribution deviated significantly from the normal distribution in skewness and kurtosis.

Walschburger (1976) found reliability coefficients of 0.95 and 0.98 for SCL over differing rest breaks of a laboratory experiment determined with standard methodology from 67 participants. The unusual high stability can be ascribed to the very small intraindividual variations in comparison to the interindividual variance. Fahrenberg and Foerster (1982) also report a short-term stability of 0.96 for their 125 participants.

Jones and Ayres (1966) recorded the SCL of 15 adult male postaddicts during therapeutic sessions over 5 weeks, each session lasting 25 min, beginning with an injection of a placebo and containing 12–15 electrical stimuli each. The reliabilities in the first 3 weeks lay between $r = 0.81$ and 0.94, but decreased thereafter (between 1 and 5 weeks) to $r = 0.60$. Iacono et al. (1984a) obtained a 1-year retest reliability of $r = 0.66$ for the mean SCL in 23 participants of their study described in section "Skin Conductance Responses."

Boucsein and Hoffmann (1979), in their study described in section "Skin Conductance Responses," reported that the mean SCL before application of their stimuli was 8.263 µS with SD = 4.646 µS, the distribution being significantly positively skewed and leptokurtic. Following the log transformation which only eliminated the positive skewness, the mean SCL was 2.139 log µS with SD = 0.214 log µS. The reliability of the raw data, calculated according to Hoyt (1941), yielded $r = 0.998$.

El-Sheikh (2007), in her study with 6–8 year old children of both genders described in Sect. 2.4.3.1, reported stabilities within the same session for mean SCLs of $r = 0.30$ for baseline recordings after 2 years.

Not many normative data have been published for the NS.SCR freq. Fahrenberg et al. (1984), in the above-mentioned study with 58 participants, found a mean number of 3.0–3.5 SCRs/min with standard deviations between 4.0 and 5.0

SCRs/min under resting conditions. Under performance conditions, they obtained mean values of between 13 and 13.5 SCRs/min with standard deviations of between 5.0 and 5.5 SCRs/min. The distribution was significantly positively skewed and leptokurtic during the resting conditions, whereas the normal distribution hypothesis could be retained under performance conditions.[124]

In a study with 49 female and 49 male participants, Zimmer (2000) obtained mean NS.SCR freq. between 4.9 and 5.4/min under resting conditions with standard deviations between 4.1 and 4.7, rising to values of between 6.1 and 7.7 SCRs/min under imagination conditions, with standard deviations between 4.6 and 5.6. Walschburger (1976) provided values for stability coefficients of $r = 0.80$–0.90 for the NS.SCR freq., determined in his above-mentioned experiment with 67 participants in different resting phases. Fahrenberg and Foerster (1982) reported a short-term stability of $r = 0.81$ for the NS.SCR freq., and Iacono et al. (1984a) yielded a 1-year retest reliability of $r = 0.62$.

Schulter and Papousek (1992) in their study with 54 participants of both genders described in Sect. 3.1.4.1, reported short- and long-term reliabilities for NS.SCR freq. and mean NS.SCR amp. from 15 min stimulation-free intervals with distances of 20, 40, and 60 min as well as 2–3 weeks. Reliabilities for NS.SCR freq. averaged across both hands were generally higher than those for NS.SCR amp., diminishing from $r = 0.84$ through $r = 0.73$ and $r = 0.70$ for the three short intervals to $r = 0.64$ for the 2–3 week period, compared to reliabilities of NS.SCR amp., which were $r = 0.69, 0.58, 0.52$, and 0.56, respectively.

The number of observed nonspecific EDRs is dependent upon the amplification factor and the amplitude criterion applied (Sect. 2.5.1.1). In the present author's experience, they can range between 0 and 10 SCRs/min during periods of relative quietness, whereas values of around 20 SCRs/min can be reached in periods of high arousal. However, in case of high NS.SCR freq., overlapping responses are very likely to appear, making the number of SCRs to be counted dependent upon additional evaluation criteria (see Sect. 2.3.1.2 "Amplitudes of Exosomatic Responses Recorded with Direct Current").[125]

In summary, SCL scores tend to be positively skewed and leptokurtic compared to the normal distribution, which can be eliminated through log transformations. Their reliability is very high but markedly decreases over periods of several weeks between recordings. A similar picture emerges for the frequency and mean amplitude of NS.SCRs. The correlations between both tonic SC parameters are middling high to low.

---

[124] Based on the same data set, Fahrenberg, Schneider, and Safian (1987) reported short-term stabilities between $r = 0.03$ and 0.27 under resting conditions and between $r = 0.05$ and 0.32 under performance conditions for the NS.SCR freq. (amplitude criterion $= 0.3$ μS). A short-term stability of $r = 0.57$ was reported within a 30-min session from initial to final resting.

[125] For mathematical solutions for overlapping EDRs, see Sect. 2.3.1.5.

2.5.2.2   Results of Skin Resistance Measures

Today, skin conductance recordings predominate, and since many authors who use the constant current method transform their results into conductance units (Sect. 2.3.3.2), relatively little data exists for resistance values. When comparing results from different studies, it must be noted that both the SRL and the SRR amp. can vary, depending on the electrode size (Sect. 2.2.3.2).

Skin Resistance Responses

Venables and Christie (1980) did not report any statistics for SRR data as they decided for using skin conductance measures in general. Instead, in their Table 1.5 they provide only a typical range for the SRR amp. between 0.1 and 16.6 kΩ, with an assumed SRL of 100 kΩ, and a range from 0.02 to 4.54 kΩ with a base resistance of 50 kΩ.

Kaelbling, King, Achenbach, Branson, and Pasamanick (1960) recorded from 12 participants the SRR values in response to acoustic, electric, and verbal stimuli, and obtained mean values between 3.0 and 16.3 kΩ with ranges up to 76.9 kΩ. The reliability was 0.76 after 2 days. Bull and Gale (1973, Table 1) presented 1 kHz tones of 90 dB to 12 participants and recorded SRR values at four time intervals.[126] They found values for SRR amp. between 1.5 and 33.5 kΩ for the first trial and between 0 and 11.5 kΩ for the fourth trial. The reliability, calculated as an intraclass correlation, was however not significant ($r = 0.42$).

Unpublished data taken from the study of Boucsein and Hoffmann (1979) with 60 participants (Sect. 2.5.2.1 "Skin Conductance Responses") yielded norm values of 21.01 kΩ for the mean SRR amp. with SD = 24.30 kΩ, the distribution deviated significantly in positive skewness and leptokurtosis from normality. After log transformation with a resulting mean of 1.057 log kΩ and SD = 0.522 log kΩ, the distribution was no longer skewed, but was still slightly leptokurtic. The reliability of the raw data, estimated as according to Hoyt's (1941) formula, was $r = 0.975$.

In summary, as with the SCR amp., a positively skewed and leptokurtic distribution is to be expected with the SRR amp., and a log transformation can lead to an improvement of skewness. The reliabilities are high for short-term periods but markedly decrease with time intervals in the range of weeks.

Tonic Skin Resistance Measures

As with the phasic values, Venables and Christie (1980, Table 1.5) provided only a possible range for SRLs between 25 and 1,000 kΩ, as being equivalent to SCLs from

---

[126] Three weeks being between the first and second recordings and between the third and fourth recordings, and 6 weeks being between the second and third recordings.

40 down to 1 μS. Edelberg (1967) reported values of between 10 and 500 kΩ/cm^2 for the specific resistances (Sect. 2.3.3.1).

An evaluation of the unpublished SCL data from the Boucsein and Hoffmann (1979) study with 60 participants (Sect. 2.5.2.1 "Skin Conductance Responses") resulted in mean SRLs of 167.2 kΩ, with SD = 74.88 kΩ. Following log transformation, the mean was 2.174 log kΩ, with SD = 0.205 log kΩ. Both the raw scores and the transformed values significantly deviated in kurtosis but not in skewness from the normal distribution. The reliability of the raw, calculated according to Hoyt's (1941) formula, data was $r = 0.997$.

On the other hand, retest reliabilities reported for SRLs were not always sufficient. Wieland and Mefferd (1970), who recorded the SRL from three participants during two resting periods within a stimulus series which were 120 days apart, obtained high reliabilities between $r = 0.95$ and 0.97 of the intraindividual differences. However, Galbrecht, Dykman, Reese, and Suzuki (1965) found with 20 participants concordance coefficients of only $r = 0.67$ for SRLs recorded a day apart under stimulation by 60 dB tones.

Arena, Blanchard, Andrasik, Cotch, and Myers (1983) reported even lower reliabilities in an investigation with 15 participants, where the SRL was recorded with palmar and dorsal electrodes under different resting- and stress-conditions. The recordings were made on the 1st, 2nd, 8th, and 28th day. Only the correlations between the 8th and the 28th day (average $r = 0.72$ for the resting conditions, and $r = 0.453–0.556$ for the stress conditions) and the 2nd and 8th day ($r = 0.482$ for resting conditions) were significantly different from zero. All other reliability coefficients were not significant, which let the authors conclude that the SRL would be an unreliable measure.

It might be expected that the NS.SRR freq., as another tonic measure (Sect. 2.3.2.2), can outnumber the NS.SCR freq. This is because less amplification is required when using the CC instead of the CV method (Sect. 2.6.2), which automatically results in SR instead of SC units (Sect. 2.6.5). Thus, in SR recordings, EDRs are more easily discovered and the amplitude criterion can be set correspondingly lower than in SC-recordings (Sect. 2.3.1.2 "Choice of Amplitude Criteria").

O'Gorman and Horneman (1979), in their study with 48 participants described in Sect. 2.3.2.2, investigated the stability of measures for "small" and "large" NS. EDRs whose number was determined under three experimental conditions 2 weeks apart.[127] The number of "large" NS.EDRs significantly decreased after 2 weeks, while a corresponding increase was observable with the "small" NS.EDRs. Unfortunately, reliability coefficients were not calculated.

Docter and Friedman (1966) investigated the reliability of NS.SRRs[128] while presenting 80 dB white noise to 23 participants. The average reliabilities computed from several single coefficients were $r = 0.54$ after 5 days, and $r = 0.30$ after 30 days.

---

[127] The authors used standard methodology, with electrodes of 12 mm in diameter, but transformed the SR scores into SC units before calculating nonspecific responses.

[128] In this study, an unusually high current of 70 μA was used.

The correlation between the two tonic measures, i.e., the SRL and the NS.SRRs, was in the predicted direction ($r = -0.34$), although being not significant. On different days, the medians of the NS.SRRs were between 10 and 15 during a 15 min recording period, while the ranges reached from 0 to 90 NS.SRRs per 15 min.

Using a sample of 24 seven- to 8 year old children being recorded during a 2 min resting period, Corah and Stern (1963) obtained average SRL values between 194.1 and 275.3 kΩ, with standard deviations between 74.8 and 97.4 kΩ, as well as mean NS.SRRs/min between 7.3 and 13.8, with standard deviations between 5.0 and 7.3. The correlation between both tonic measures was between $r = -0.33$ and -0.64. The average reliability for recordings being 1 day apart was $r = 0.86$ for the SRL and $r = 0.61$ for the NS.SRR freq.

With 48 pilots, Johnson (1963) obtained a reliability of $r = 0.69$ for the NS.SRR freq. recorded 1 day apart. Hustmyer and Burdick (1965) determined a reliability of $r = 0.75$ for the NS.SRR freq. recorded during 15 min resting periods from 14 participants 2–4 months apart. In their study mentioned in section "Skin Resistance Responses," Bull and Gale (1973) reported an intraclass reliability of $r = 0.91$ for the NS.SRR freq. recorded at four points of time. The respective reliability of the mean NS.SRR amp. was $r = 0.75$.

In summary, it has been observed that the distribution of SCLs are strongly positively skewed and more leptokurtic in comparison to the normal distribution. A log transformation may at least improve the skewness. The reliabilities for short periods are fairly high, but – as expected – decrease over intervals of several weeks. In contrast to the NS.SCR freq., enough data exists for the reliability of the NS.SRR freq. for inferring that – while it appears rather lower than that of the SRL values over short periods – it is still comparably high over long periods of weeks to months. While the correlations between both tonic SR measures are also relatively low, they are somewhat higher than those of the corresponding tonic SC measures (Sect. 2.5.2.1 "Tonic Skin Conductance Measures").

2.5.2.3   Latency and Rise Time Parameters

A general range for the latency times cannot be provided, since they are based on an a priori limited time window (Sect. 2.3.1.1). Maulsby and Edelberg (1960) found with seven participants SRR lat. (EDR evoked by sniffing) with a mean of 1.5 s at a room temperature of 30°C, rising to 4 s if the temperature was lowered by 5–10°C. Edelberg (1972a, p. 370) pointed out that the latency is dependent both on the temperature (Sect. 2.4.2.1) and the recording site.

Venables and Christie (1980, Table 1.2) reported distributional data for the latency times of SCRs in response to 4 s white noise of 90 dB with 559 participants in their Mauritian sample. The lowest mean (1.472 s) was observed in the 5 year olds, whereas the highest one was seen in the 15 year olds (1.822 s). Standard deviations were lowest in the 5 year olds (SD = 0.373 s), while the largest ones appeared in the 10 year olds (SD = 0.418 s). The deviations from the normal distribution were small in comparison to those of the SCL scores and the SCR amp.

Hence, the benefit from a log transformation of latencies would be lower than in the other measures.

Venables and Christie (1980) calculated reciprocal values for the latency times, in addition to other temporal measures of the EDR, since those had the advantage of being proportional to the response speed. Here, as with log transformation, small improvements of distributions towards normality were obtained (Sect. 2.3.3.3).

Under the same stimulus conditions as in their above-mentioned Mauritian study, Venables and Christie (1980) found that latency times for 1,161 three-year olds were on average 1.488 s, with SD = 0.714 s, and were significantly positively skewed as well as leptokurtic. Among 45 adults between 18 and 75 years of age, the latencies of the SCRs in response to 75 dB tones of 1 kHz and 1 s duration yielded a mean of 1.896 s and SD = 0.349 s, with no significant deviation from the normal distribution.

With 18 participants, Rachman (1960) observed average latency times of 2.94 s, with SD = 0.71 s, when evaluating EDRs in response to 35 loud buzzer tones of 2 s duration each. The retest reliability over 6–8 weeks was $r = 0.96$. Lockhart (1972) found, in a combined sample of 129 participants taken from five experiments, a mean latency time of 2.11 s with SD = 0.56 s.[129]

Levinson and Edelberg (1985, Table 5) reported means and standard deviations for the SCR lat. in response to differing strong acoustic stimuli for the first and subsequent stimulus presentations within habituation experiments performed with various groups of schizophrenics and controls (Sect. 3.4.2.2). No differences emerged between the first and subsequent presentations; however, the SCR lat. was shorter (1.44 s) in one data set using a response to white noise of presumably over 100 dB used as UCS than in response to tones of 78 dB (1.92 s).

In a sample of 42 participants, Surwillo (1967) obtained highly significant differences in the SPR lat. between conditions of simple and disjunctive acoustic stimuli. In the first case, the SPR lat. had a mean of 1.73 s with SD = 0.2 s, while in the second case a mean of 1.65 s with SD = 0.224 s was obtained.

The EDR rise time is relatively seldom studied. Grings (1974) reported a range between 0.5 and 5 s. Venables and Christie (1980) only determined the SCR ris.t. values for their sample of 65 eighteen- to 75-year-old participants, being 2.184 s on average, with a standard deviation of 0.643 s, the distribution being slightly positively skewed and platykurtic, but the deviation from normality was far from being significant. Lockhart (1972) in his study cited above obtained a mean SCR ris.t. of 2.8 s with a SD = 1.54 s.

Venables and Christie (1980), in the Tables 1.9–1.11 of their review, gave interindividual and intraindividual correlations between SCR lat., SCR ris.t. and other temporal, level and amplitude measures of the skin conductance from their own and other investigations. Their results revealed the relative independence of the latency time from other temporal measures as well as from both the SCR amp.

---

[129] Recorded by means of zinc electrodes with a contact surface area of 0.32 cm^2, zinc sulfate as electrolyte and a constant current method with 3.0 µA; results being transformed into conductance units, and the SCR amp. being square root transformed (Sect. 2.3.3.3).

and the SCL. The correlations were mostly negative and smaller than $r = -0.21$. In contrast, the correlations to the logarithmized SCL and SCR amplitude scores were higher, and an inverse relationship between the SCR lat. and the logarithmized amplitudes emerged ($r = -0.31$ to -0.58). That means, if the SCR amp. were logarithmized, shorter latency times were followed by higher amplitudes. The correlations between SCR lat. and SCR ris.t. were between $r = 0.17$ and 0.30, i.e., shorter rise times tended to appear after longer latencies.

Using intraindividual correlations within 13 participants, Bull and Gale (1971) also found connections between a low SRR amp. on one hand and long latency times and short rise times on the other hand. However, most of these connections failed to reach significance. In a further investigation with 12 participants, Bull and Gale (1973, Table 3) observed significant interindividual rank correlations between the SRR lat. and several other EDA parameters, ranging from $r = -0.44$ to -0.64. The reliabilities, calculated as intraclass correlations over four recording periods (Footnote 126 in Sect. 2.5.2.2), were $r = 0.84$ for the SRR lat., and $r = 0.67$ for the SRR ris.t.

Venables, Gartshore, and O'Riordan (1980) obtained, with 65 participants, a higher correlation between the SCR ris.t. and measures of attentiveness towards environment derived from the ECG, than between the SCR rec.t/2 and their ECG parameters used.

To date, few results are reported on the EDR's maximum incline (Sect. 2.3.1.3 "Parameters of Ascent"). Fahrenberg, Walschburger, Foerster, Myrtek, and Müller (1979) calculated the respective mean of the maximum incline of the NS.SCRs during a 2 min resting period and during a 2 min mental arithmetic exercise under noise with 125 participants. The scores, measured in 0.01 µS/s units, displayed a mean of 103.5 with SD $= 60.69$ during resting, and a mean of 133.6 with SD $= 67.25$ under the stress condition. The distributions under both conditions were significantly positively skewed and platykurtic. The maximum incline was uncorrelated with the SCR ris.t. ($r = 0.03$), and was slightly negatively correlated with the SCR rec.t/2 ($r = -0.29$). In contrast, a positive correlation with the SCR amp. emerged ($r = 0.66$), and also – though being somewhat lower – with the NS. SCR freq. ($r = 0.25$). During the mental arithmetic condition, the SCR amp. were overall higher than in the resting period, and the SCRs were of shorter duration, displaying a greater maximum incline.

In summary, only little distributional data exists for the parameters discussed in this section. Thereby, latency and rise times appear to satisfy criteria of normal distribution well (with the exception of children), while the maximum incline shows a rather positively skewed flatter distribution. The reliability of the latency tends to be somewhat higher than that of the rise time. The latency seems to constitute a relatively independent parameter with respect to the other temporal measures, but can display correlations with both the rise time and the EDR amp. The maximum incline appears to be an autonomic parameter of response shape, which, however, can be positively correlated with the EDR amp.

2.5.2.4 Measures of Recovery

Venables and Christie (1980) reported 50% recovery values for the 220 participants
from the Mauritian sample. The mean SCR rec.t/2 was 4.144 s (3.252 s for the 5 year
olds and 4.851 s for the 25 year olds) with a SD of 2.466 s (2.197 s for the 5 year olds
and 2.725 s for the 25 year olds), the distributions being slightly positively skewed and
leptokurtic. Deviations from the normal distribution markedly increased if reciprocal
scores of the recovery were calculated, while a logarithmic transformation only
increased the kurtosis. The SCR rec.t/2 was 4.113 s in mean with SD $= 3.217$ s for
678 three-year olds. The nonsignificant deviation in skewness from the normal
distribution became highly significant for both distributional characteristics once
reciprocally transformed. The SCR rec.t/2 was 3.971 s on average with SD $= 5.012$ s
for 42 participants from the adult sample. By means of the above-mentioned transformations, the positive skewness lost its significance, but the kurtosis still deviated
significantly from the normal distribution. Therefore, the authors recommended to
waive the use of reciprocal transformations of the rec.t/2 measure, and also pointed out
that the logarithmic transformation will not improve any distributional pitfalls.

In their study described in Sect. 3.4.1.2, Levander, Schalling, Lidberg, Bartfai, and
Lidberg (1980) found a significant negatively skewed distribution of the SCR rec.t/2 in
a habituation procedure using 25 male delinquents between 18 and 30 years of age.
Through logarithmic transformation the distribution was normalized. Hinton, O'Neill,
Dishman, and Webster (1979) performed a habituation experiment over 2 successive
days with 71 hospitalized male participants, obtaining a SRR rec.t/2 reliability of
$r = 0.63$.[130] As for the rise time (see previous section), Bull and Gale (1973) reported
only a nonsignificant ($r = 0.18$) reliability for their recovery time.[131]

Correlations with other SC measures, collected from various studies, were also
published for the SRC rec.t/2 by Venables and Christie (1980) in their
Tables 1.9–1.11. The data show high consistency over different stimulus
conditions, genders, and clinical groups. The correlations of the SCR rec.t/2 with
the other SC parameters were low throughout, although values around $r = 0.40$
also appeared. Correlations between SCR rec.t/2 and rise time, on the other hand,
lay between $r = 0.54$ and 0.80. The half-time recovery therefore appears to be
relatively independent from other components of the SCR, however, there is a
marked relationship to the rise time. These authors conclude that in case of recovery
will be difficult to measure (e.g., if a NS.SCR appears before half-time recovery is
reached; see Sect. 2.3.1.3 "Recovery Parameters"), the less difficult obtainable rise
time can be used as a form parameter instead.

In his 5 experiments with a total of 129 students (Sect. 2.5.2.3), Lockhart (1972)
also obtained a positive correlation of $r = 0.62$ between the rise time and the SCR

---

[130] Recording was performed with constant current using concentric electrodes with an internal
diameter of 5 mm and an external diameter of 0.6–1 cm, using 0.05 M KCl cream on an agar base,
from the index and middle fingers of the left hand.

[131] Recovery measured in percent of amplitude decrease 2 s after the point of maximum deflection.

rec.t/2. The correlations which he obtained between the amplitude and the three temporal measures – latency, rise time, and recovery – were rather small and nonsignificant ($r = -0.11$, 0.04, and -0.06). These correlations were somewhat higher for the rise time and recovery ($r = 0.39$ and 0.44) if the unexpected appearance of an electrical stimulus as UCS was evaluated separately. The correlation between the EDR amp. and the EDR rec.t/2, being dependent on the experimental conditions, was attributed by Lockhart to the action of a homeostatic mechanism under certain conditions, while the two measures remained independent from each other under the majority of other conditions. He obtained a mean of 4.8 s with SD = 2.92 s for of the SCR rec.t/2.

Becker-Carus and Schwarz (1981) studied 30 male soldiers during a series of short-term memory tasks and correlated the SRR amp. with the "half-life period," as defined by Lüer and Neufeldt (1968), which contained both the rise time and recovery characteristics (see Footnote 51 in Sect. 2.3.1.4). The correlations were positive and mostly significant, ranging from $r = 0.19$ to 0.63. Levander et al. (1980), in their above-mentioned study, obtained significant negative correlations in a habituation series between the mean SCR rec.t/2 on one hand and the mean SCL ($r = -0.55$) as well as the mean NS.SCR freq. ($r = -0.65$) on the other hand, while the correlation with the mean SCR amp. remained insignificant ($r = -0.14$).

In summary, the frequently used EDR recovery parameters, which also often cannot be objectively evaluated (Sect. 2.3.1.3 "Recovery Parameters"), yield measures of rather questionable reliability. Their possible dependency upon other EDA parameters remains also partly unexplained (Sect. 2.5.2.5). Transformations of the recovery times should be avoided as those tend to impair the distributional characteristics.

2.5.2.5 Relationship Between Measures of Amplitude and Shape

While little attention has been drawn to, and not many data were gathered on, the relationship between EDR amp. and ris.t. (Sect. 2.5.2.3), a possible autonomy of the recovery time has been the subject of numerous studies and controversy.

This controversy started with Edelberg's (1972a) hypothesis that sweating and sweat reabsorption have separate nervous controls, and that the SCR rec.t/2 is the best measure for the reabsorption processes (Sect. 1.4.2.3). The view of EDR recovery as having an independent indicator function (in contrast to other EDA parameters) is supported by the studies of Edelberg (1972b) and Janes (1982) described in Sect. 3.1.3.1. Recovery time could be used to differentiate between resting and stress conditions, and also between task performances of varying complexity. Stimulus significance may affect recovery to an even greater degree than amplitude. In addition, the EDR recovery has been shown to be an especially valid predictor in some risk studies on schizophrenia (Sect. 3.4.2.1). The hypothesis of the recovery time's autonomy has been supported by an argument of Venables and Christie (1973) that on the basis of an exponential drop of the EDA, the time constant must be mathematically independent from the amplitude per se. However, as shown in Sect. 2.3.1.3 "Recovery Parameters," the exponential function is only one possible description of the recovery process of the EDR.

A decisive empirical objection to the recovery's autonomy was made by Bundy and Fitzgerald (1975) who found that the time of descent was dependent upon the number and intensity of preceding SCRs (the so-called Bundy effect). Bundy and Fitzgerald proposed a measure "X," whereby the amplitudes of the two spontaneous SCRs immediately preceding a stimulus-dependent SCR were divided by the respective times (t_1 and t_2) between them and the stimulus-dependent SCR, the results then being added according to (2.22). This measure "X" displayed intraindividual correlations between $r = -0.51$ and -0.91 with the half-life of the stimulus-dependent SCR as obtained from five participants.

$$X = \frac{\text{SCR}_{\text{amp.1}}}{t_1} + \frac{\text{SCR}_{\text{amp.2}}}{t_2} \qquad (2.22)$$

This measure has also been used by Venables and Fletcher (1981), who studied the dependence of the SCR rec.t/2 upon the SCR amp. of foregoing EDRs among 65 participants of both genders, using the same techniques of recording as in the Mauritian study with the 3 year old children (Sect. 2.5.2.1 "Skin Conductance Responses"). The participants received 20 stimuli of 75 dB and 1 kHz, the sixth stimulus deviating in being 1,311 Hz. Intraindividual correlations were only calculated from those ten participants who fulfilled the criterion of showing two spontaneous SCRs before the stimulus-elicited SCR in at least 5 of altogether 20 trials. Apart from two correlations, which were $r = 0.47$ and 0.84, all other correlations between the SCR rec.t/2 and the measure "X" were negative (from $r = -0.15$ to -0.79), as would be expected according to Bundy and Fitzgerald (1975). However, those coefficients were only significant in two cases, which may partly depend on the low number of scores per participant (between 5 and 12).

Bundy and Fitzgerald also analyzed data from the Mauritian study, but found only 11 cases out of the almost 1,800 children in the study who showed two anticipatory SCRs (FAR and SAR, Sect. 3.1.2.1) in the CS–UCS interval of a conditioning procedure over more than half the trials. The intraindividual correlations between the SCR amp. of the UCS and the measure "X" displayed the total range of potentially positive and negative scores (cf. Venables & Fletcher, 1981, Table 3). This study is also an example of the data base being too narrow to either support or reject Bundy and Fitzgerald's (1975) hypothesis, since the number of participants from which appropriate data can be gathered is normally too small for providing the necessary data.

Large interindividual differences with respect to the relationship between recovery time and the amplitudes of preceding EDRs were also observed by Edelberg and Muller (1981). In an experiment with 20 participants, the authors correlated the SCR rec.t/2 (using standard methodology, however with K–Y gel) and the "X"-score during word association- and RT-tasks. The "X"-scores could only predict 14% of the recovery variance; the individual scores were between 0 and 70%. A reanalysis of the data from Edelberg (1972b) with "X" as a covariate resulted in no significant alteration of the differential indicator function of the recovery time. However, if the number of NS.SCRs which appeared in the last 15 s before the SCR, the recovery of which was evaluated, had been used as covariate, the differences in SCR recovery originally observed (as described at the beginning of this section) were no longer significant.

In a study with 55 participants of different races and both genders, which explored different motor responses to varying acoustic stimuli, Janes, Strock, Weeks, and Worland (1985) showed that the SCR rec.t/2 (using standard technique with KCl electrolyte) was independent from both the "X"-score according to Bundy and Fitzgerald (1975) and the NS.SCR freq. prior to the specific SCR as determined according to Edelberg and Muller (1981). In any case, significant intraindividual correlations with an average score of $r = 0.61$ appeared in 16 cases.

In summary, the question of a possible autonomy of recovery measures of the EDR cannot be totally settled based on existing data. However, there is some evidence that a possible dependence of the recovery time upon preceding sponta- neous electrodermal activity should be taken into account. Alternatively, this problem can be considered as a question of dependence of phasic upon tonic EDA, which is mostly discussed in the context of links between the EDR amp. and the directly preceding EDL (Sect. 2.5.4.2). However, this does not necessarily imply a dependency of recovery and amplitude of the EDR in question. Hence, recovery may be used as a relatively independent measure of a single response, given the low correlations between recovery and amplitude as reported in the previous section. The observation that the temporal measures are independent from electrode size and electrolyte type, as are the amplitude measures, implies a relative independence from temporal and amplitude measures of the EDR (Venables & Christie, 1980). Cort et al. (1978), who evaluated intraindividual correlations between the SCR amp. and SCR rec.t/2 stemming from 5 different studies with a total of 140 participants, observed different dependencies of both measures: in experiments using habituation of plain orienting responses (Sect. 3.1.1.1), significant connections between amplitude and recovery appeared within almost all participants. However, if motivational and emotional situational components were added, the number of significant correlations decreased to less than 50%.

2.5.3   Characteristics of Exosomatic Measures
with Alternating Current

A major application for alternating current recordings of EDA has been investigating system properties of the skin (Sect. 1.4.3.3). Outside these, only data from a small number of studies with AC recordings are available to date. Furthermore, most of these studies were performed for evaluation of AC techniques, with the consequence that small numbers of participants were investigated. Finally, the studies are hardly comparable which each other, due to the different concepts of measurement applied.

The following two sections will be devoted to two of these methods, i.e., sinusoidal AC and square wave current. A separation between level and response scores which had been performed for DC measures in the previous sections will not be introduced here, since almost only tonic AC measures were recorded. With respect to results from older studies, the reader is referred to reviews provided by Tregear (1966) and Edelberg (1971).

2.5.3.1 Recordings with Sinusoidal Current

In an experiment performed with 104 participants, Lawler, Davis, and Griffith (1960) used a Wheatstone Bridge (Sect. 2.1.5) with an oscilloscope; two variable capacitors were wired in parallel with the potentiometer. The authors used alternating voltage of 2 V and 0.1 mA with frequencies of 1, 4, 10, and 20 kHz.[132] The R and C values being necessary for the bridge were used to calculate the phase angle and the impedance. As expected, the impedance decreased with rising frequency, dropping from a mean of 6.487 kΩ (SD = 1.733 kΩ) at 1 kHz to a mean of 0.507 kΩ (SD = 0.111 kΩ) at 20 kHz. Thereafter, the authors decided to use 4 kHz for further recordings, which yielded an average impedance of 1.882 kΩ (SD = 0.468 kΩ) with approximately normally distributed scores. The phase angle decreased between 1 and 20 kHz from a mean of 75$°$ (SD = 5.0$°$) to a mean of 57$°$ (SD = 5.9$°$). A higher impedance and lower capacitance were observed; however, quantitative values were not reported. In addition, the authors removed the stratum corneum and stratum intermedium on certain sites with 23 of the participants by the skin-stripping technique (Sect. 1.2.1.1), after which the impedance fell and the phase angle increased as the frequency rose in contrast to the intact skin sites.

Plutchik and Hirsch (1963) performed AC recordings of 14–61 μA with 1, 10, 50, 100, and 1,000 Hz using two participants. The authors used dry silver electrodes of 1 cm diameter fastened to the palmar side of a finger. As the frequency rose, the impedance dropped from 130 to 30 kΩ, and the phase angle increased from $-2°$ to $-58°$. Both measures appeared to be invariant with respect to the applied current density. The interindividual differences were smaller with the phase angle than with the impedance. Faber (1977) observed – without giving more exact descriptions of the recording technique or the number of participants – a decrease of impedance from 152.6 to 14.6 kΩ with frequencies between 10 Hz and 1 kHz, which somewhat confirmed the results from Plutchick and Hirsch.

Burton, David, Portnoy, and Akers (1974) studied, with six participants, the palmar skin response to AC with 0.1–0.3 V effective voltage and 13 or 3 different frequencies of between 10 Hz and 100 kHz, using a frequency analysis suitable for passive electrical systems, and Ag/AgCl electrodes of 2 cm^2 area each, filled with isotonic cream. The results were displayed in their Table 1 in a much more

---

[132] They used stainless steel electrodes with 2 cm diameter, at a distance of 2 cm on the volar middle of the underarm, fastened with rubber bands to filter paper soaked with a NaCl solution.

differentiated manner; most importantly, they confirmed the decrease in impedance and the increase in the phase angle with rising frequency. The means over all frequencies for each participant were determined for the single parameters of the Montagu-Coles model (Fig. 1.15, left-hand side, Sect. 1.4.3.1). They observed (with respect to 1 cm^2 area of skin) scores that were between 470 Ω and 2.0 kΩ for the serial resistance R_1, between 159 and 212 kΩ for the parallel resistance R_2, and between 0.0075 and 0.013 µF for the capacitive element C; the phase angle varied between −8° and −63°.

Yamamoto et al. (1978) determined the single parameters of their equivalent circuit (Fig. 1.18 in Sect. 1.4.3.3). However, they set aside the resistance R_1 which represents the deeper skin layers, because they had found in an earlier study (Yamamoto & Yamamoto, 1976), which used the skin-stripping technique, that the skin impedance is mainly dependent on the resistive properties of the keratinized layers of the epidermis, while the deeper layers (including the granular layer; see Sect. 1.2.1.1) contribute less than 500 Ω/cm^2 of skin to the overall resistance. Recordings were made 3 times within 6 h on both forearms, using Ag/AgCl electrodes with liquid electrolytes (Sect. 2.2.6.3), having a skin contact area of 3.14 cm^2. A constant current of 10 µA was applied at frequencies from 10 Hz to 1 kHz. The value obtained for the conductance component which corresponds to the resistance R_2 varied between 1.84 and 4.17 µS, and the conductance component corresponding to the resistance R varied between 0.029 and 0.793 µS, while values for C were between 0.143 and 0.155 µF. In total, the variances were small and the distributions approximately normal, as previously described by Yamamoto and Yamamoto (1978) who covered the same data set.

De Jongh (1981) studied SZ, using an alternating voltage at 25 Hz and 32 µA with 263 participants. He used platinum electrodes of 1 cm^2 in area and a liquid electrolyte (0.015 M NaCl) with a contact surface of 6.2 cm^2. The average impedance from three equidistant sites on the volar side of the right underarm showed a mean over all participants of 51.211 kΩ (SD = 13.234 kΩ); the corresponding logarithmic value was on average 1.692 log kΩ (SD = 0.117 log kΩ). Both raw scores and logarithmized scores were normally distributed. Zipp et al. (1980), using frequencies between 7 Hz and 1 kHz at recording sites on the backs of 14 participants, found a markedly higher decrease of skin impedance after 30 min in the lower frequency range as opposed to higher frequencies.

Grimnes (1983) used an additional ground electrode for determining the impedance of different active electrode used in AC recording separately. He applied sinusoidal frequencies of 10 Hz and 1 kHz via a dry 1 cm plate electrode for the comparison of skin impedances at different recording sites, the with 1 kHz recorded SZLs being generally lower (by factor 10 or more) than those recorded with 10 Hz. The highest SZL was observed on the dorsal side of the upper arm (700 kΩ cm with 10 Hz and 33 kΩ cm with 1 kHz), whereas SZLs were lowest at the forehead (40 kΩ cm with 10 Hz and 7 kΩ cm with 1 kHz). The palm was in between these sites with 190 and 33 kΩ cm, respectively.

As previously noted in Sect. 1.4.3.3, hardly any data exists for the behavior of single components of skin impedance and admittance during the EDR. McClendon and Hemingway (1930) found both a variation in the impedance and a marked capacitive change during the EDR using a single participant. However, neither the underlying skin model nor the method used to calculate C were specified by him; the temporal trends also point to tonic rather than phasic variations. Forbes and Landis (1935) observed capacitive changes during the EDR, which however only were in the range of 0.5–1% of the tonic values.

These results of the capacitive component of EDRs could not be confirmed by Boucsein et al. (1989) who used 100 Hz alternating voltage with considerably better equipment (Sect. 2.2.3.3) and three participants; the EDR appeared being primarily due to changes in the parallel resistance R. With a similar arrangement of measurement based on a lock-in amplifier, Grimnes (1982) found marked capacitive changes at 20, 90, 500, and 1,000 kHz with EDRs provoked by movement together with holding the breath. However, since he used dry electrodes covered with AgCl, and since the EDRs had unusually long rise times and recovery times, it can be presumed that he might have recorded a polarization capacity build-up effect in the epidermis, rather than the suggested moistening effect on the walls of the sweat gland ducts, which would have been due to the rise of the sweat column during the EDR. Such an interpretation would be in line with Grimnes' result that the latency time was at least 2 s longer for susceptance than for conductance.

Thus, Edelberg's (1971) conclusion, that the electrical processes during an EDR are fully attributable to resistance variations in the parallel branch of the electrodermal skin model, owing to the 0.5–1% (at most) observed capacitive changes, could not be conclusively disproved to date. The results of corresponding studies, like those using constant voltage recording, show to a large degree a dependency upon ancillary conditions, such as the type of electrode, the electrolyte and the AC frequency used. Therefore, more systematic investigations are needed in order to resolve the question of what role the capacitive structures might play in the generation of an EDR.

A direct comparison of CV and CC techniques for AC measurement has been performed by Schaefer and Boucsein (2000). They developed a special EDA coupler enabling a quasi-simultaneous recording by multiplexing the two techniques. The circuitry was built according to Lowry (1977), using an operational amplifier with the study participant connected either between the inverting input and a CV source, resulting in CV recording, or in the negative feedback loop between output and the inverting input, resulting in CC recording (see Fig. 2.5, Sect. 2.1.5). The two different connections of the participant were switched 10 times/s. In addition, the probe voltage source could be switched between 500 mV constant (DC measurement) and a sinusoidal alternating voltage of 100 Hz with a constant peak-to-peak amplitude of 500 mV (AC measurement). The device allowed for quasi-simultaneous comparisons of CV vs. CC within both AC and DC recording separately. A similar sort of fast multiplexing between AC and DC, however, was not possible, because the operational amplifier needed about 10 s to become re-stabilized after such a switch. During AC measurement, a phase angle detector recorded the phase shift between output and input signals and converted it to the phase angle $S\varphi R$ (Sect. 2.3.1.2 "Amplitudes of Exosomatic Responses Recorded with Alternating Current"). The recording was performed with standard methodology in 40 participants during two sessions with habituation series of 20 tones (1 kHz, 85 dB, 1 s duration, ISIs varying between 30 and 60 s) in two sessions being 2 weeks apart. During the first session, the temperature in the air conditioned chamber was set to 23°C (73°F) for all participants. To induce considerable variations in EDLs, the temperature was raised for half of the participants to 26°C (80°F) in the second session, while the remaining participants were investigated under a lowered temperature of 19°C (66°F). Results from the CC and CV recordings with AC measurement were equivalent over a wide range of EDL variations, when EDRs were expressed as changes of $S\varphi Rs$ between voltage and current. This sort of equivalence cannot be observed when DC measurement is applied (e.g., Boucsein, Baltissen, & Euler 1984). Besides solving the nagging problem of the differential level dependencies of SCR and SRR amplitudes (Sect. 2.5.4), the use of AC also prevents both skin and electrode polarization (Sect. 2.2.2.2).

2.5.3.2   Recordings with Square Wave Current

Yokota and Fujimori (1962) studied the changes in the skin's system properties during the EDR in one participant, using square wave pulses of 50 ms in length, 10 μs in rise slope, with 20–100 mV and a repetitive frequency of 3–5 Hz. The authors applied unipolar recording by means of an active palmar Ag/AgCl electrode (using a physiological NaCl solution as electrolyte) and an inactive electrode placed on the forearm. In concordance with the model shown in Fig. 1.18 (Sect. 1.4.3.3) the values of the serial resistance R_1, the parallel resistance R_2 (including R), and the capacitance C were determined both before an EDR and during its maximum. The changes appearing during an EDR in the serial resistance R_1 were smaller than 0.1 kΩ, and in the capacitance smaller than 0.001 μF, while the change in imped-ance during the EDR were completely dertermined by the parallel resistance R_2, which decreased between 15 and 49%. The resting value for R_1 varied between 300 and 800 Ω, that for the R_2 being between 34 and 168 kΩ, and that for C being between 0.12 and 0.29 μF. Kryspin (1965) used pulses of 4 s duration with a current density of between 0.1 and 90 μA/cm^2. He found the average palmar impedance in 5 of his 14 participants to be 406 kΩ, using Ag/AgCl electrodes on both palmar and dorsal hand sites, as well as dorsal foot sites.

   Lykken (1971) performed a study using pulsed DC with unipolar recording from an active palmar electrode of 10 cm^2 area together with a reference electrode on a forearm site previously prepared by skin drilling. The pulse sequence was bipolar, being 50 ms positive and 50 ms negative with a 50 ms break in between at the active electrode. He used voltages between 0.2 and 10 V. Individual recordings from the six participants of the study were not provided; but Lykken reported that the serial resistance R_1 remained constant, which was also true for the parallel resistance R_2 if 2 V were used. However, R_2 decreased by 24% at 5 V and by 35% at 10 V. If an active recording site was previously prepared by skin drilling, the charging and discharging behavior of the skin changed, showing a behavior as if a parallel circuit composed of a number of very small resistors with a capacitor had been replaced by a solely capacitive circuit with a small serial resistance.

In his investigation of the linearity of the current voltage curves of the skin, Stephens (1963) used pulsed DC between 3 and 300 ms in length at 60 μA to 1 mA during 1 min rest breaks, performing unipolar recording with a 7 cm^2 sized liquid electrode on the underarm. He observed (although presumably with only one probe) a linear system behavior between −1 and +1 V and a skin impedance of 13 kΩ, which decreased to 4 kΩ at 400 μA. The voltage built up in the skin during the first 4 ms approximated an e-function until 300 μA, but deviated markedly from such functions at higher current (Sect. 2.3.1.3 "Recovery Parameters"). The decrease in voltage following switching-off was approximately exponential at 0.6 V, and significantly steeper at 1.4 and 4 V. Based on these observations, the author suggested that the behavior of the skin could be modeled by a nonlinear resistance together with a parallel capacitance in a circuit.

Van Boxtel (1977) used DC pulses of 1 ms length at different frequencies and at 1–10 mA, with both constant current and constant voltage, using Ni/Ag electrodes of 3.53 cm^2 contact area and an isotonic NaCl electrolyte cream at bipolar recording sites on the lateral and medial gastrocnemius muscles. The parallel resistance R_2 displayed a marked dependence upon the current, showing changes both over time and subsequent to stimulation, while in contrast R_1 showed only small changes. With these results, van Boxtel confirmed Lykken's (1971) findings, including the effects of skin drilling.

To date, pulsed DC has hardly been used in recording of the EDR. When he used this method with the aid of an oscilloscope, Lykken (1971) demonstrated changes during an EDR which could be attributed to capacitive influences; however, a similar picture emerged on the oscilloscope through proper changes in the parallel resistance R_2. As can be stated for recordings with sinusoidal AC, too few results exist here for safe assertions regarding the effects of variations of single components in an underlying skin model during the EDR.

2.5.4 Level Dependence

Level dependencies of psychophysiological data are frequently discussed with reference to the so-called Law of Initial Values (LIV) proposed by Wilder (1931), which states that response amplitude capabilities in ANS-controlled physiological systems should be reciprocal to their respective baseline. The LIV is physiologically based upon the antagonism between the sympathetic and parasympathetic branch of the ANS, which brings about homeostatic functioning by preventing preponderance of either branch. Such an antagonism does not apply to the EDA, since electrodermal phenomena can be regarded as being exclusively influenced by the sympathetic branch of the ANS (Sects. 1.3.2.3 and 1.3.4.1).

Based on these considerations, Hord, Johnson, and Lubin (1964, p. 86) considered the EDA as belonging to the "slow equilibrium variables," to which – owing to their missing parasympathetic counter regulation – the LIV is not applicable. Interestingly, a large number of studies investigating the validity of the LIV have been performed with the aid of electrodermal measures. The reason for this might be found with the following considerations: for most other physiological variables, the necessary baseline scores for probing the LIV can only be determined with specific sampling methods, taking into account their respective functional fluctuations (see, e.g., Malmstrom, 1968). In contrast, the EDA baseline value appears to be easily determined as the EDL recorded immediately prior to each single EDR.

However, from a psychophysiological conceptual point of view, investigations into the validity of the LIV with respect to EDA on one hand, and into the dependence of the EDR upon the momentarily preceding EDL on the other hand, should be clearly separated from each other. The major reason for such a separation is, that most probably different physiological mechanisms are to be held responsible for EDR and EDL (Sect. 1.4.2.3), whereas investigations into the baseline dependence as proposed by the LIV should make use of the same class of parameters as the basis for obtaining both baseline and response scores. Such a differentiation was also suggested by Levey (1980, p. 618), who proposed a separate treatment of the following two tonic EDA scores:

1. The resting EDL before commencing any stimulation and/or before introducing an experimental condition. This would correspond to the baseline as required by the LIV.
2. The EDL in the intervals between single EDRs during subsequent stimulation, e.g., during the ISIs of a habituation study (Sect. 3.1.1). Such a tonic value would be appropriate for investigating tonic-phasic relationships.

Therefore, the two following sections separately deal with the possible dependence of the EDR upon the resting EDL (Sect. 2.5.4.1) and the potential relationship of EDR to the directly preceding EDL (Sect. 2.5.4.2).

2.5.4.1 Dependence of Treatment Recordings on Baseline Recordings

The problem that psychophysiological response scores, being obtained under treatment conditions, might possibly be dependent on baseline recordings had been discussed during the 1950s in a number of publications. However, these discussions were not always based on sufficient empirical data bases, and did not carefully separate physiological from statistical concepts. There have been only few studies investigating a possible level dependency of the EDA which did not refer to the dependency of the EDR on the preceding EDL. This kind of level dependency will be discussed in the next section. One additional problem is that the question of baseline dependency of EDA (as with level dependency) had been too quickly coupled with the problem of making a choice between SC and SR units (Sect. 2.6.5), and the necessity of checking the $a(a - b)$ effect[133] remained widely unrecognized.

In their study which tested the validity of the LIV in EDA, Hord et al. (1964) recorded the SRL with 105 participants just before presentation of a 500 Hz, 73 dB tone, and recorded the lowest SRL[134] during the 5 s following the tone. After transforming resistance units into conductance units, they partially observed high positive correlations ($r = 0.35$–0.77) between the SCL prior to the stimulus and the rise of the SCL afterwards, which invalidated the LIV. However, the authors pointed out that owing to the reciprocal relationship between conductance and resistance, the LIV could be valid for SR if not for SC data. These considerations had been questioned by Benjamin (1967) who demonstrated, in a so-called Monte-Carlo study with a large number of randomly created correlations, that a reciprocal transformation may change the sign of the correlations between prestimulus- and difference scores; but this is not absolutely the case. Thus, Benjamin concluded that the considerations made by Hord et al. (1964) on the validness of the LIV for SR data but not for SC data were not valid themselves.

Myrtek, Foerster, and Wittmann (1977), after thoroughly discussing of the LIV's theoretical foundations, performed an empirical examination with a huge data set. In particular, these authors systematically studied the statistically important a $(a - b)$ effect with respect to baseline dependence. From a within-subjects probe of the LIV with 20 participants over 16 trials, and two between-subjects studies of baseline dependence (with 107 and 67 individuals), emerged only few negative correlations between baseline and response scores, which would have confirmed the LIV. Instead, twice as many positive correlations were obtained, being contrary to the predictions of the LIV in EDA. Thus, the authors could not confirm the LIV's role as an overall valid law, as was attempted by Wilder (1931) and in many other later publications. Instead, the functioning of the LIV might be regarded more as a rare exception than as a rule (Myrtek & Foerster, 1986).[135] Myrtek et al. (1977) recorded both the baseline and the mean SCL during each respective 5 min long recording phase where their 67 participants performed mental arithmetic exercises under noise stress. The authors obtained a nonsignificant correlation of $r = -0.19$ between the baseline and the SCL increase during the mental arithmetic.

---

[133] When a baseline score (a) and a response score (b) are uncorrelated, the correlation of the reactivity measure (a − b) and the baseline score (a) cannot equal zero because they have a common term (Myrtek & Foerster, 1986). For many physiological variables, (a) and (b) are not totally independent from each other, which leads to differently high correlations between (a) and (b), and therefore to a differently large $a(a - b)$ effect.

[134] Palmar recording with zinc sulfate cream, at 40 μA.

[135] As a consequence, one should rather use the term "concept of initial values" instead of the term "law."

In addition, a specific coefficient for the determination of the "true" baseline dependence that avoided the $a(a - b)$ effect, was also not significant.

The invalidity of the LIV has also been demonstrated wit endosomatic EDA measures. Shapiro and Leiderman (1954) performed an experiment during which they recorded SP from 53 participants (Sect. 2.5.1.2). They only obtained a correlation of $r = -0.09$ between the average baseline SPL and its rise during an easy reaction task. Gaviria et al. (1969) studied the baseline dependence of endosomatic and exosomatic EDA by simultaneously recording both SP and SR from 20 married couples (for the methodology, see Sect. 2.5.1.3). The correlations between the baseline scores and variations of the EDL during five different acoustic stimulus presentations varied between $r = 0.47$ and -0.47, being significant only for the SR in one case for each gender, i.e., in most cases the LIV appeared to be invalid. Venables and Christie (1980), taking the overwhelmingly negative results into regard, questioned the validity of the LIV for EDA, considering it doubtful anyway that the question of its validity could be answered in general.

However, an examination of possible baseline dependencies cannot be dispensed with when response scores must be calculated in the form of differences to baseline scores. When the LIV applies in such a case, evaluations of the individual reactivity using the differences to the baseline are subject to a systematic error as significantly entailed by each baseline score (Fahrenberg & Myrtek, 1967). The same holds for statistically significant positive correlations between response and baseline scores which contradict the LIV.

In order to avoid the problem by calculating bias free reactivity scores, many authors make use of ALS scores (Sect. 2.3.3.4 "Using Autonomic Lability Scores") as suggested by Lacey (1956). These are practically based upon the consideration that a covariance-analytical correction of response scores will make them independent from baseline influence by definition. However, assumptions such as the linearity of regression between response and baseline scores, a bivariate normal distribution or even homoscedasticity are often neither checked nor provided (Fahrenberg & Myrtek, 1967; Lykken & Venables, 1971). In addition, mostly no care is taken for making sure that the samples are not too small for the necessary standardization when the ALS scores should be calculated.

Fahrenberg et al. (1979), using a large data set, performed a systematic analysis of different baseline correction methods, ranging from simple difference scores to response scores based on principal component analysis. Their conclusion was that no particular method can be recommended. Instead, in each single case the question of baseline dependence should be checked using bivariate distribution of resting and response scores, together with their correlation; thereafter, the decision can be made whether or not to perform a correction. The question whether statistical corrections of response scores in relation to baseline scores are psychophysiological meaningful, or if baseline dependency should be only recorded as a system-specific response component by means of appropriate parameters, which should be additionally reported in a publication, cannot generally be answered. In addition, a possible answer to this question depends on which source of variance the experimenter will be interested in.

A baseline dependency which may appear in extreme ranges of tonic EDA is formed by so-called ceiling and bottom effects. When the SCL is already very high during the resting phase at the beginning of the experiment, SCL can only increase to a limited degree when activated by experimental conditions because of physiological reasons (constituting a ceiling effect), in contrast to changes from a SCL baseline being in an average range. The same but opposite effect holds for an extremely low initial SCL baseline, which cannot be lowered much further by deactivating experimental conditions, thus yielding a bottom effect. Such a baseline dependency may feign the LIV, however, without corresponding to the original concept, since it is not a consequence of a homeostatic regulation (Lykken & Venables, 1971).

A similar effect occurs in comparing groups which yielding generally differing EDLs, as for example anxious and non-anxious individuals (Edelberg, 1972a; see also Sect. 3.3.1.2). Therefore, if necessary, the baseline scores should be taken into consideration on an individual basis for the evaluation of electrodermal reactivity.

2.5.4.2 Dependence of Phasic on Tonic Electrodermal Measures

As outlined in the previous section, the majority of investigations into the baseline dependency of EDRs take the directly preceding EDL as a reference. There is not much of a point in referring to the existing literature on phasic-tonic correlations, since the results of the level dependency studies are extraordinarily inconsistent, which might result above all from huge differences in experimental settings. Various level dependencies may result from situational characteristics, e.g., if the experimental group is activated and thus the SCL increases steadily, whereas the control group shows deactivation instead, thus yielding a decrease in SCL. If under those circumstances SCRs to repeated single stimulation are taken into consideration, which are expected to habituate over trials (Sect. 3.1.1.3), a negative correlation between tonic and phasic parameters would result under the experimental condition, whereas a positive correlation between SCL and SCR amp. would more likely be observed in the control condition.

On the other hand, different level dependencies appear as a rule, contingent upon whether interindividual or intraindividual correlations are calculated. Thus, Martin and Rust (1976) found the relationships between the SCR amp. and the SCL, being dependent on the correlational methods used. In a habituation experiment with 84 twins as participants being presented with 21 tones of 1 kHz at 95 dB, the interindividual correlation of the mean scores for all stimuli was $r = -0.619$, while the pooled intraindividual correlation yielded only $r = 0.081$. Their interindividual correlation was in accordance with a result reported by Venables and Christie (1980) who reported a $r = 0.62$ between the SCR amp. to a single acoustic stimulus and the preceding SCL in a study with 123 participants.

In 60 participants, Boucsein, Baltissen, and Euler (1984) also observed positive mean interindividual correlations between the SCR amp. and the SCL, which however decreased with rising intensity of the applied stimuli (from $r = 0.613$ at 60 dB A to $r = 0.315$ at 110 dB A white noise). The corresponding intraindividual correlations, calculated over all 30 stimuli including all levels of intensity, were only $r = 0.06$ on average and covered a large range. Block and Bridger (1962), in an experiment with 18 participants who were presented 32 electrical stimuli of four different intensities, had already found that the form of the interindividually determined regression of the SRR amp. to the preceding SRL was not predictable from the regression among the single participants over the trials. Thus, in addition to taking the level dependencies calculated from group statistics into consideration, intraindividual correlations between EDRs and the EDL should also be calculated and included in the interpretation. Many corrections of the EDR using the EDL are made with the aim of eliminating phasic dependencies upon tonic EDA. As with the baseline problem discussed in the previous section, the general usage of corrections with respect to possible level dependency cannot be recommended. If such corrections are applied without a careful scrutiny of individual data structures, important properties of EDA parameter may be getting lost and erroneous interpretations of the reactivity of the electrodermal system could be made. According to Grings (1974), two cases should be distinguished from each other if attempting to adjust the EDR with respect to the EDL:

1. Both scores can be regarded as correlating indicators of the phenomenon under investigation, both of them explain specific variance components. In this case no baseline correction should be made; instead, the information from both scores should be combined. An example here are canonical correlations between "electrodermal behavior" on one hand, and personality dimensions on the other (Sect. 3.3).
2. The investigation focuses on EDRs, whereupon the influence of differing EDLs is regarded as erroneous and thus should be eliminated. An example is the use of the EDR as an indicator for an orienting (Sect. 3.1.1) or for a conditional response (Sect. 3.1.2). In this case corrections taking regard of varying EDLs may be applied (Sect. 2.3.3.4). However, it should be carefully ensured that the differing EDLs do not appear as a consequence of the experimental manipulation (Edelberg, 1972a).[136]

It is both theoretically and practically important that the level dependency of the EDR is influenced by a transformation of SR into SC data and vice versa (Johnson & Lubin, 1972; see also Sect. 2.3.3.2). Boucsein, Baltissen, and Euler (1984) demonstrated that the correlations between SRR and SRL increased with stimulus intensity, while the correlations between the simultaneously recorded SCR and SCL showed an inverse relationship. Therefore, the intraindividual tonic-phasic correlations for the SR, as determined across the different stimulus intensities, were significantly higher than those for SC, and a high standard deviation of the correlations pointed to large interindividual variations in the level dependence of the EDR.

---

[136] A thorough discussion of such corrections which are based either on the use of transformations or on regression techniques is found in Levey (1980, p. 619 ff.).

One possible explanation of the level dependency being different with the use of either SC or SR can be provided by the simplified Montagu-Coles model (see the right-hand side of Fig. 1.15 in Sect. 1.4.3.1): if R_1 and R_2 (the resistances of the dermis and of the stratum corneum) are held as being predominantly responsible for the EDL, and a variable resistance x (which can be traced back to sweat gland activity) is regarded being responsible for the EDR, the total resistance R of the system can be calculated by using the rule for adding two resistors in parallel for the addition of R and x, and adding R_1 according to the more simple rule for resistors in series:[137]

$$R = R_1 + \frac{R_2\,x}{R_2 + x} \tag{2.23}$$

The conductance values G (corresponding to R), G_1 (corresponding to R_1), G_2 (corresponding to R_2), and y (corresponding to x) are given according to (1.2a) in Sect. 1.4.1.1 as follows:

$$\frac{1}{G} = \frac{1}{G_1} + \frac{(1/G_2)\,(1/y)}{(1/G_2) + (1/y)} \tag{2.24a}$$

When the sums in the denominator of the right-hand fraction of (2.24a) are added, $1/G_2 \cdot 1/y$ can be shortened, resulting in:

$$\frac{1}{G} = \frac{1}{G_1} + \frac{1}{G_2 + y} \tag{2.24b}$$

Further addition leads to:

$$G = \frac{G_1 + G_2 + y}{G_1(G_2 + y)} \tag{2.24c}$$

When (2.24c) is inverted, then an equation for the total conductance equivalent to (2.23) is given as follows:

$$G = \frac{G_1(G_2 + y)}{G_1 + G_2 + y} \tag{2.24d}$$

In order to calculate the variation dR of the total resistance due to small variations dx, (2.23) is differentiated whereby R_1 disappears since it is a constant:

---

[137] See (1.6e) in Sect. 1.4.1.2. To avoid confusion, the parameter x is used instead of R in (1.22) in Sect. 1.4.3.1.

$$dR = d\frac{R_2\,x}{R_2 + x} \tag{2.25a}$$

As during an SRR, R_2 can also be regarded as being constant, following the rules for differentiation of constants produces, $d(R_2\,x) = R_2\,dx$ and $d(R_2 + x) = dx$. According to the quotient rule, (2.25a) then produces:

$$dR = \frac{(R_2 + x)R_2\,dx - R_2\,xdx}{(R_2 + x)^2} \tag{2.25b}$$

which once multiplied out results in:

$$dR = \frac{R_2{}^2}{(R_2 + x)^2}\,dx \tag{2.25c}$$

Correspondingly, differentiation of dG as for dy from (2.24d) when taking G_1 and G_2 as constants, produces:

$$dG = d\frac{G_1(G_2 + y)}{G_1 + G_2 + y} \tag{2.26a}$$

Multiplying out the numerator in (2.26a) gives: $G_1\,(G_2 + y) = (G_1G_2) + (G_1y)$. When this is differentiated since G_1G_2 is constant, the following results: $d((G_1G_2) + (G_1y)) = G_1dy$. Differentiation of the denominator in (2.26a) produces: $d(G_1 + G_2 + y) = dy$. Following the quotient rule results in:

$$dG = \frac{(G_1 + G_2 + y)G_1dy - ((G_1G_2) + (G_1y))dy}{(G_1 + G_2 + y)^2} \tag{2.26b}$$

Multiplying this out results in:

$$dG = \frac{G_1^2}{(G_1 + G_2 + y)^2}\,dy \tag{2.26c}$$

As can be inferred from the equivalent (2.25c) and (2.26c), the SRR and the SCR are not only dependent upon the "true" resistance and conductance variations dx and dy but are also influenced in different ways through the various branches of the base resistances or conductance of the model which result in a nonlinear dependence of response on level (Boucsein, Baltissen, & Euler 1984).[138] Thus,

---

[138] When the resistance R_2 (or the conductance G_2) of the epidermis are also regarded as variable, Equations (2.25c), respectively (2.26c) become more complicated as they must be differentiated for a second variable. However, in this case, different level dependencies will also result.

Table 2.2 Fictitious examples of generating correlative dependencies between formerly independent EDRs and EDLs after transformation from SC into SR and vice versa

Example A					Example B				
Trial	SCL (μS)	SCR (μS)	SRL (kΩ)	SRR (kΩ)	Trial	SRL (kΩ)	SRR (kΩ)	SCL (μS)	SCR (μS)
1	10	1	100	9.09	1	100	10	10	0.11
2	11	1	91	7.57	2	90	10	11	0.13
3	12	1	83	6.41	3	80	10	13	0.18
4	13	1	77	5.49	4	70	10	14	0.24
5	14	1	71	4.76	5	60	10	17	0.33
6	15	1	67	4.17	6	50	10	20	0.50
7	16	1	62	3.68	7	40	10	25	0.83
Correlation EDR/EDL	0.0		0.998			0.0		0.985	

Example A: From Lykken and Venables (1971, p. 669)
Example B: Contrary example from SR. Equations (1.5a) and (1.5b) were used in the transformation (Sect. 1.4.1.1)

dependencies of phasic upon tonic EDA as found in many studies can be also theoretically verified in the model. Additionally, a differential level dependence appears when regarding SC and SR data, which – in addition to the above-mentioned individual influences – can lead to different and partly contrary results when SC or SR methods are used.

How cautious one should be with pure statistical treatment of tonic-phasic dependencies can be shown with the help of the following two examples. Lykken and Venables (1971, p. 669), using fictitious data, showed that uncorrelated tonic and phasic SC scores may show a completely positive correlation after being transformed into SR units. Their example is repeated in the left-hand side of Table 2.2. In addition, in the right-hand side, uncorrelated SRL and SRR scores are produced in the same manner and are transformed into SC units, which then display almost the same positive correlation owing to the reciprocal relationship between SC and SR. Thus, it cannot be inferred from that particular example that SC units are to be preferred over SR units due to the presumed nonexistent dependence of the EDR upon the EDL.

Another example can be taken from Bull and Gale (1974). Their aim was to avoid habituation effects while recording the EDR in response to only one single stimulus on 10 different days; which, however, only worked with 7 out of their 15 participants. Use of the standard constant current method (but without the necessary adaptation time for the electrode/skin system) displayed a clear inverse relationship between the SRR and the immediately preceding SRL. This was interpreted by the authors as an unwanted action of the LIV (Sect. 2.5.4.1) when using SR scores. This tonic-phasic relationship got lost after a transformation into SC scores, even revealing a trend to the opposite interrelation. However, this can be easily inferred from the transformation used. It cannot – also with regard to the narrow database provided – be used as general argument for the skin conductance being the more adequate unit of measurement than skin resistance (Sect. 2.6.5).

In summary, an empirical explanation of the relationship between tonic and phasic EDA has not yet been provided, and the application of baseline corrections on the EDR using the EDL remains problematic. Furthermore, intermingling questions of level dependency with those in regard to an adequate unit of measurement for exosomatic EDA is not justified on the basis of the hitherto existing data.

2.6 Summary of Conceptual Discussions

Out of the three basic approaches to EDA – (1) endosomatic, (2) exosomatic DC, and (3) exosomatic AC recordings (see introductory remarks to Sects. 1.4 and 2.5) – exosomatic DC has been used in the majority of investigations. Although endosomatic recordings have acknowledged advantages owing to the fact that no current is applied, exosomatic recordings can be obtained and interpreted more easily, as described more detailed in Sect. 2.6.1. AC measurement is more complicated in both recording and evaluation but can provide more information about the electrodermal system than DC recording. However, it has been used to date only by few authors. Section 2.6.3 is devoted to the comparison of AC and DC methods.

In addition to the other advantages of AC recording, the controversy regarding the preference for either constant current or constant voltage DC recording methods, which will be discussed in Sect. 2.6.2,[139] could be set aside if the phase angle φ would be used from AC recording, instead of measuring the pure SRRs or SCRs (Sect. 2.2.3.3).

Separating the EDR from the EDA signal by means of an AC-coupled amplifier, which has been previously described in Sect. 2.1.3, will be discussed in terms of its advantages and disadvantages in Sect. 2.6.4. Another problem which did not recuperate much attention in EDA methodology – the choice between electrodes combined with an electrolyte on one hand and dry electrodes on the other hand – has already been discussed in Sect. 2.2.6.3. Section 2.6.5 will be devoted to the choice between expressing one's results in either resistance or conductance units. Finally, Sect. 2.6.6 gives an outlook on emerging issues in EDA methodology, which might determine the future of electrodermal research.

The comparisons made in this section between the differing methodological concepts will provide readers with the ability to plan for an optimal EDA recording in their own investigations. In addition, the discussions in the following sections will show that – despite all necessary attempts for standardization – various

---

[139] In spite of Lykken and Venables gave a clear recommendation for constant voltage methods as early as in 1971 and the SPR Publication recommendations adhered to this 10 years later (Fowles et al., 1981), both types of methods are still in use as can be inferred from various studies cited in the present book.

approaches towards recording of EDA often maintain a methodological value of their own.

2.6.1   Endosomatic vs. Exosomatic Recording

Although advantages and disadvantages of using an external current in electrodermal recording had been thoroughly discussed in the literature (e.g., Grings, 1974, p. 277), the majority of EDA studies have been performed with exosomatic methods. One of the main reasons for this is presumably the problems arising from parameterization and interpretation of the SPR amp. (Sect. 2.3.1.2 "Amplitudes of Endosomatic Responses" and Sect. 2.5.1.1). Therefore, Fowles et al. (1981) took up the recommendation already made by Lykken and Venables (1971) that skin conductance should be preferred over skin potential recording, unless researchers have a definite interest in comparing their work with the relevant literature on SP. Nevertheless, either technique has its own advantages and disadvantages as summarized below.

Exosomatic EDA recording has the following technical advantages over endosomatic recording (Edelberg, 1967):

1. Exosomatic measures are always unidirectional and therefore easier to analyze. This is particularly not the case for biphasic or triphasic SPRs which are inseparably composed of negative and positive waves (Sect. 2.3.1.2 "Amplitudes of Endosomatic Responses").
2. Exosomatic recording is less affected by electrode artifacts such as bias potentials or drift (Sect. 2.2.2.2).
3. When constant current is used in exosomatic recording, considerably less amplifier gain is required as compared to endosomatic recording (Sects. 2.1.1 and 3.4.2.2).
4. No inactive reference electrode is required at an abraded site (Sect. 2.2.3.1). Abrasion may cause pain and bear the danger of infections (Sect. 2.2.1.2).
   Fowles et al. (1981) mentioned two additional advantages of exomatic measurement:
5. The sensitivity of SPL to hydration effects is probably greater than that of SCL.
6. Much more is known about the psychological correlates of exosomatic EDA recordings, since the majority of studies have used this method.

By contrast, according to Edelberg (1967), *endosomatic* methods have the following advantages over exosomatic ones:

1. Endosomatic recording is regarded as being more "physiological," since the skin system is not influenced by an application of an external current. This is especially an advantage in long-term recordings (Sect. 2.2.6.1).
2. Electrode polarization is prevented since no external current is applied.
3. No special circuits are needed, as endosomatic EDA measurement can be performed with sufficiently sensitive high-ohmic amplifiers (except when

baseline and response scores shall be separated; Sect. 2.1.3). Therefore, no special EDA coupler is needed in case of using a general-purpose biosignal amplification system.

Fowles et al. (1981) added two further advantages of endosomatic methods:

4. The simple counting of NS.EDRs (Sect. 2.3.2.2) without regard to amplitude may be more sensitive in SP measurement than in SC measurement, according to a personal note of Edelberg to Fowles et al. (1981).

5. Endosomatic recordings will not be affected by variations in contact area, as long as skin areas with different potentials are not connected with each other.

Hardly any systematic methodological comparison studies with large samples using simultaneous endosomatic and exosomatic EDA recording (e.g., taking them in parallel from different sites) have been performed. Burstein et al. (1965) reported a high correspondence between the occurrence of SRRs and SPRs in reaction to emotionally significant stimuli with 20 participants (Sect. 2.5.1.3). Lykken et al. (1968) attempted to find a method to estimate SC parameters from SP scores, using parallel recordings from 19 participants. Montagu (1958) compared SP scores with SZ scores from 24 participants and found differing baseline dependencies for both. Gaviria et al. (1969), investigating 20 female and 20 male participants, obtained large interindividual and gender-based differences in simultaneously measured SP and SR raw scores (Sect. 2.4.3.2), but they also obtained high correlations between SP and SR change scores throughout. Venables and Martin (1967b) studied the effects of denervation and pharmacologically blocking the sweat glands upon SP and SC, however only with very few participants. The differentiated relationships between SPR and SRR amplitudes observed by Wilcott (1958) with 25 participants have previously been reported in Sect. 2.5.1.3.

The particular relevance of the SPL for determining the minimal state of activation of an individual (i.e., the BSPL) has been previously discussed in Sect. 2.3.2.1. Neurologists predominantly use SPR recordings, which they call the "sympathetic skin response (SSR)" (Sect. 3.5.4). In addition, endosomatic EDA recording might be a valuable tool for basic research, since the interpretation of single positive and negative components of an endosomatic EDR in response to a stimulus may give rise to interpretations beyond pure response strength, probably with respect to their different psychological meaning (Edelberg, 1967).

2.6.2   Constant Current vs. Constant Voltage Recording

The quality of the discussion on the pros and cons of constant current vs. constant voltage methods has suffered from lacking a clear separation between the questions of recording methods and of measurement units (Boucsein, Baltissen, & Euler 1984; Sagberg, 1980). As derived in Sect. 2.1.1, the results from constant current methods are proportional to SR, while those from constant voltage methods are proportional to SC. As long as the corresponding EDL has also been recorded (Sect. 2.1.3), SR and SC scores can be transformed into each other (Sect. 2.3.3.2). Such transformed results obtained from either constant current or constant voltage recordings can also be regarded as being equivalent (Boucsein & Hoffmann, 1979; Sagberg, 1980), since all apparent differences can be ascribed to the unit of measurement (conductance vs. resistance) and not to the method of recording (constant voltage vs. constant current; see Boucsein, Baltissen, & Euler 1984). The argument that conductance recording is more suitable to the physiological model of the skin (e.g., Lykken & Venables, 1971) must be regarded as misleading, since it relates to the method and not to the unit of measurement, and will be discussed under this aspect below. A discussion of the appropriate units will follow in Sect. 2.6.5.

The first thorough comparison of constant current vs. constant voltage systems had been performed by Edelberg (1967). According to his view, the use of constant current method has several disadvantages. Practically all models of EDA state that the sweat gland ducts represent conductance paths through the epidermis, which alter their resistance or conductance according to the degree to which they are filled with sweat; single paths can therefore drop to practically zero in conductance (Sect. 1.4.2.1). If the resistance of the epidermis increases, these sweat-filled conductors must carry larger currents when the total current remains constant. Since the electrode area is precisely limited (Sect. 2.2.2.3), the current density will remain constant. Hence, the current which flows through a single duct is inversely proportional to the number of ducts filled with sweat. Edelberg was assuming an extreme case, where most ducts no longer carry current, so that the total current is divided by a few ducts. This situation can lead to nonlinearities in the current/voltage curve.[140] Such nonlinearities that appear in dependence upon the EDL were demonstrated by Edelberg with the use of the constant current method. Individuals with low skin resistances could tolerate current densities up to 75 μA/cm^2 without the current/ voltage curve displaying nonlinearities, which otherwise appeared already at 4 μA/cm^2 within individuals with high SRLs. Based on these and other similar observations, the recommendation had been made that with constant current recordings the current density should be limited to 10 μA/cm^2 (Sect. 2.2.3.2) and electrodes with the greatest possible area should be used (Sect. 2.2.2.1).

The above-mentioned extreme case, which may lead to damage or destruction of the affected sweat glands, cannot appear when constant voltage methods are used, since the same voltage drops over each duct and the current alters in accordance with Ohm's law in proportion to the resistance of each duct. However, with the constant voltage method, the total current is dependent upon the number of "switched on" ducts (this was not discussed by Edelberg). In an extreme case, with a high epidermal resistance and only a few filled ducts, only a very low current

---

[140] This discussion has been taken up by Catania et al. (1980) to explain the dependency of finding age-related differences in electrodermal reactivity upon the method of measurement (Sect. 2.4.3.1).

can flow through the whole system, and as the SR approaches the value of the inner resistance of the voltmeter, there is a greater probability for measurement errors (Sect. 2.1.1).

According to Edelberg (1967), the constant voltage method has also its problems, since the relevant electrical models of EDA include a resistance in series with the variable resistances of the epidermis and ducts (Sect. 1.4.3.1). In the extreme case of a dry stratum corneum (which may only appear if no electrode cream is used), the EDR can be traced for its predominant part back to the membrane component of the sweat gland activity (R_E in Fig. 1.16; Sect. 1.4.3.2). In this case, the ohmic or impedance parts (Sect. 2.1.4) of the epidermis and the dermal structures form a voltage divider (Sect. 2.1.1), in which practically the total voltage drops on the epidermis. In such an extreme case, changes in the membrane components will more likely be in the range of measurement errors, if the constant voltage method is applied, as compared to the use of the constant current method. In the latter case, the absolute fluctuations of the resistance in dependence upon the membrane components will remain independent from the size of the serially connected epidermal resistance (Edelberg, p. 24). In addition, very high currents (up to 100 $\mu A/cm^2$) can also flow if SRs are low, even when voltages as low as 0.5 V are applied.

The following comparison of both recording methods has been given by Edelberg (1967).[141] *Constant current* techniques have the following advantages:

1. They need less amplification than constant voltage techniques, by about a factor of 10 (Sects. 2.1.1 and 2.2.4). This is especially useful in field recordings.
2. The density of the current flow through the electrodes is limited and therefore the danger of electrode polarization is reduced (Sect. 2.2.2.2).
3. An unknown series resistance (e.g., a dry corneum) has a less serious effect in a constant current as compared to constant voltage system.

By contrast, *constant voltage* methods have the following advantages:

1. High voltages over single sweat glands resulting from current concentration on a few ducts are avoided, thus eliminating the danger of sweat gland damage.
2. In a certain sense, the system is self-correcting with respect to the peripheral influence of the EDL upon the EDR amp.
3. The reference resistance, over which the amplifier measures the voltage, is low and constant (Sect. 2.1.1 and Fig. 2.1), which leads to a good, constant relationship of the electrodermal system's impedance and the input impedance of the amplifier.
4. The currents flowing through both electrodes are independent from each other.
5. When electrodes of different sizes are used (which is not usual), no matching of the current density to the electrode area must be made.

---

[141] The points raised by Edelberg (1967, p. 25 f.) on technical control of the current density with constant voltage systems are not further discussed here since they are taken care of in modern equipment (Sect. 2.2.4).

An apparent advantage of constant voltage methods is that EDA measurement results are immediately expressed in conductance units and do not have to be transformed if one prefers conductance values.

What was decisive for the preference of the constant voltage technique (Fowles et al., 1981; Lykken & Venables, 1971; Venables & Christie, 1980) was the above-mentioned observation made by Edelberg (1967) concerning a possible nonlinearity when using constant current. However, this had only been substantiated through a few trials with a small number of participants. The concentration of the current on only a few paths of conductance in those extreme cases may hardly ever appear in normal recording with electrodes of 0.6 cm^2 area (Sect. 2.2.2.1) and with a sweat gland count of over 200 sweat glands/cm^2 (Sect. 1.2.3). Whereas the recommendation for using constant voltage is to be welcomed as a proposal for standardization, it is not really convincing in a technical sense.

Furthermore, in electronic engineering the constant current technique is generally preferred, as with the equipment now available, constant current sources are more easily stabilized and show much smaller tolerances than constant voltage sources. The recommendation here is to choose either technique according to the device available, but generally prefer the constant voltage method on behalf of standardization. One area in which the constant current method had been preferred for a long time is the application of EDA recording in so-called lie detection, but this is no longer the case (Sect. 3.5.2).

Direct empirical comparisons of EDA recordings with constant current and constant voltage methods have rarely been made. Wilcott and Hammond (1965) performed recordings of 1 min duration alternately with either technique using 66 participants, where the applied voltage was varied.[142] SRL scores were calculated from the results of both methods; these were in good accordance at low voltage levels, but differed more and more as the voltage increased. Wilcott and Hammond concluded from this that – at least with SRL scores in a medium range – both methods can be regarded as being equivalent. However, they recommended the use of constant voltage methods when SRL scores were high.[143]

Boucsein and Hoffmann (1979) conducted a direct comparison study of EDRs obtained from both methods with 60 participants. Using standard methodology, they measured EDA from both hands of each participant simultaneously with constant current and constant voltage methods.[144] The data from this study were

---

[142] Zinc electrodes of 21 mm diameter together with zinc sulfate as electrode cream were used.

[143] Constant current recordings might have an advantage over constant voltage ones during long-term recordings, as Edelberg (1967) revealed (Sect. 2.2.6.1).

[144] With 0.6 cm^2 Beckman Ag/AgCl electrodes, Hellige isotonic electrode cream (Sect. 2.2.2.5), 0.5 V constant voltage and 10 μA/cm^2 constant current. The participants received 30 acoustic stimuli at intensities varying between 60 and 110 dB.

reanalyzed by Boucsein, Baltissen, and Euler (1984); the EDR scores, obtained with constant current, were transformed into SCRs, while the results from constant voltage recordings were transformed into SRRs (Sect. 2.6.5). Responses to stimuli with intensities exceeding 90 dB were found differing from each other in SR and SC units, regardless of whatever method of recording – constant current or constant voltage – had been used.

Barry (1981)[145] could demonstrate that such differences may not appear if stimuli of lower intensities are used, presenting both acoustic (ten tones of 50 dB intensity) and visual stimuli (white rectangles). Measures of orienting responses and their habituation appeared to be very robust, no matter whether constant current or constant voltage recording had been used. The general conclusion here is that the unit of measurement is more important for results than the recording method with which results are obtained (Sect. 2.6.5).

2.6.3   The Use of Direct vs. Alternating Current

As mentioned at the beginning of Sect. 2.6, exosomatic EDA recordings are mainly performed using direct current. Even the elementary use of the alternating current recording method (i.e., without recording information from the phase angle; Sect. 2.1.5) has only been realized in a small number of studies to date.

Both advantages and disadvantages exist in using either method. With AC recording, electrode polarization and error potentials are ruled out (Sect. 2.2.2.2). These may play a role despite using to a high degree nonpolarizable electrodes being nowadays available (Sect. 2.2.2.3). Difficulties may arise in AC recording from amplification and filtering (Sects. 2.1.4 and 2.1.5): if the EDA signal itself contains higher frequency AC components, the elimination of possible noise during recording and amplification is more complicated than in DC recording, since the noise may be within the same frequency range as the to-be-recorded signal.

AC recording has also advantages for studying electrical models of the skin and sweat glands, as outlined in Sect. 1.4.3.3. Unfortunately, studies concerning the electrical properties of the skin with inclusion of the phase angle are sparse (Sects. 2.1.5 and 2.2.3.3). A series of older results with AC recording were summarized by Tregear (1966). Additionally, studies were performed by Rutenfranz (1955) and Rutenfranz and Wenzel (1958, see Sect. 2.4.1.1) within the area of work physiology, during which both impedance and capacitance of the skin at frequencies between 500 Hz to 10 kHz were measured. Most of the systematic investigations into AC recording since the mid 1970s have been

---

[145] In a study where 20 participants were presented 10 tones of 50 dB each, and additionally white quadrangles as stimuli. With the constant current measurements, Barry (1981) used polarizable electrodes and non-isotonic cream, while the constant voltage measurements were performed using standard methodology.

performed by the Yamamoto group (Sect. 1.4.3.3). These authors estimated values for the single resistances and capacitances in a simple model of the skin (Fig. 1.18, Sect. 1.4.3.3) using mathematical derivations (Sects. 2.5.3.1 and 3.5.3; see also Millington & Wilkinson, 1983, p. 135 f.). Additional studies performed by Salter (1979), Faber (1980), Thiele (1981a) and Boucsein et al. (1989) complement the paradigmatic methodological investigations.

Common to most of these studies is that they could not directly compare their results with those of DC studies, because they did not use standard methodology. For example, Yamamoto et al. (1978) did not record from the palmar or plantar areas, but instead used forearm skin sites with electrodes of 3.14 cm^2 in area at 10 μA effective current. This method of recording has presumably developed from these authors' interest in examining changes in skin impedance under the influences of cosmetics (Sect. 3.5.3). Since the technology necessary for recording and evaluation with AC measurement is mostly custom-made and therefore relatively expensive (Sect. 2.1.5), a widespread application of AC recording cannot be expected in the very near future.

Thus, to date EDA recording by means of AC represents a very interesting and promising theoretical area, but has not been investigated enough as a concept of measurement in practical application yet. In particular, systematic comparisons between AC and DC recordings are lacking, such as had been performed within the DC method with constant current vs. constant voltage (Sect. 2.6.2). Systematic investigations of the theoretically interesting frequency dependency of the phasic components (i.e., SZR und SYR) are also still to be performed. Examples of the time courses of single scores of R, X, G and B calculated from the impedance and phase angle at a frequency of 100 Hz were given by Boucsein et al. (1989, Fig. 4).

A major advantage of AC measurement is the possibility of recording SφR instead of SZR or SYR. As Schaefer and Boucsein (2000) demonstrated, phasic changes of the phase angle φ are independent both of recording techniques (CC vs. CV) and of different electrodermal levels (Sect. 2.6.5).

2.6.4   The Use of DC vs. AC-Coupling

When using an AC-coupled amplifier (Sect. 2.1.3), it must be kept in mind that the raw signal undergoes a mathematical differentiation. This means that the recorded EDA signal corresponds to the first derivation of the original signal. The distortion of the original signal becomes more prominent if the value of the applied time constant becomes smaller (Edelberg, 1967). In an extreme case, a biphasic EDR could be created from an originally monophasic one by the use of AC-coupling.

Obscuring the form of the EDR is especially noticeable at the rise times and recovery times (Sect. 2.3.1.3), but may also lead to decreasing amplitudes. Edelberg (1967, Fig. 1.13) showed that a linear relationship between the original EDR amp. and those of the AC amplified EDR exists, even when their correlations are as low as $r = 0.05$. AC-coupling has the following *advantages*:

1. A much lower resolution is necessitated for EDR recognition as compared to DC coupling.
2. Therefore, the required amplification factors and/or the recording ranges are smaller (see Table 2.1, Sect. 2.3.1.2 "Choice of Amplitude Criteria").
3. Owing to the self regulating artificial zero line, continuous regulation by the experimenter is not needed, except when using a Wheatstone bridge circuit (Fig. 2.3, Sect. 2.1.3). This is especially advantageous for long-term recordings.

By contrast, AC amplification has the following *disadvantages*:

1. The data only have interval scale levels (Sect. 2.1.3).
2. The form parameters (Sect. 2.3.1.3) can only be evaluated when using special back calculation methods (Thom, 1988).
3. When the EDL is not additionally recorded, no transformations of SR into SC units and vice versa are possible (Sects. 2.3.3.2 and 2.6.5).
4. Special amplification problems can appear with performing a high amplification of a small section of the original signal (Sect. 2.1.4).

Barry (1981) pointed out that to date no systematic studies into the influence of AC-coupling upon relationships between stimulus and response under differing amplification conditions do exist.

2.6.5 Resistance vs. Conductance Units

The controversy on an adequate unit of measurement for exosomatic EDA dates back to the 1950s and is still not settled. As pointed out in Sect. 2.6.2, unfortunately this discussion is often confounded with the question of the choice of the recording method, i.e., constant current or constant voltage.

According to Grings (1974), the question of the unit of measurement should be focused on for mainly three reasons:

1. An attempt on theoretical considerations to find the most appropriate electrical unit, especially with taking concepts of the electrical model of the skin into regard.
2. The statistically founded choice of units with respect to desirable distributional characteristics for further treatment of the data, e.g., normal distribution, and independence of means and variances from each other.
3. The search for relatively baseline-independent EDR units, i.e., such units where the EDR (as a measure of change) is not dependent upon the directly preceding EDL (Sect. 2.5.4.2).

It appears that the question of the adequate unit of measurement cannot be discussed separately from the underlying model concepts. To date, most discussion are based on simple resistance models, as Montagu-Coles model shown in Fig. 1.15 (Sect. 1.4.3.1), using parallel resistors connected in series with another resistor. In essence, the parallel resistors represent single sweat gland ducts, which can be turned on or off according to the duct-filling activities of the sweat glands. If a voltage is applied to such parallel connected resistors, the total resistance cannot simply be calculated by adding the sum of the individual resistors (see (1.6e)). The reciprocal values of the single resistors (i.e., their conductance values) are added according to (1.6d), resulting in the reciprocal value of the total resistance (Sect. 1.4.1.2). The total conductance can therefore be calculated from the sum of the single elements' conductance values. During an EDR, the change of the total conductance would in this case be proportional to the sum of the elements' conductances, which does not hold for the respective change in resistance.

The results from a study by Thomas and Korr (1957) are often used as evidence for a linear relationship between the conductance and the number of active sweat glands (Sect. 1.5). However, the experiment in question was performed with dry electrodes and heated skin, so that the upper layers of the stratum corneum had been dried out, and no contact existed between the filled sweat gland ducts and the electrode. Therefore, no plain use can be made of these results for usual EDA recordings, during which the skin is not artificially dried and moistening electrode cream is used. Blank and Finesinger (1946) could already show that the sweat glands display graded responses to neural impulses of differing frequencies. In normal cases, the skin surface and thereby the electrode will come into electrical contact with not totally filled sweat gland ducts (e.g., through the fully moisturized corneum). Therefore, the simple supposition of the all-or-nothing principle of connected parallel resistances is no longer applicable. Instead, the resistance resulting from sweat gland activity depends much more upon the degree of duct filling. Since in this case the relationship between the decrease of the resistance and the height of the duct filling would be linear, resistance and not conductance would be the adequate measure.

As discussed in Sect. 1.4.2.3, the secretion processes of the sweat glands are far too slow as being the only cause of the relatively fast changing EDR signal. Therefore, Edelberg (1971) presumed that only the slow fluctuations of EDA may be attributed to duct filling, while EDRs with shorter recovery times should be attributed to changes in permeability of the sweat gland membranes. Hence, the discussion on resistances as held above might not be of basic importance for the EDR. However, for parallel connected membranes which behave similarly to capacitors, a simple addition of the single capacitances would be again valid (Sect. 1.4.1.2), thus fostering conductance being an adequate measure for the EDR. Hence, contrary demands exist for the measurement unit of choice for the slow and fast components of EDRs. In addition, the differential dependence from the respective EDL must be taken into account for comparison between SCR and SRR (Sect. 2.5.4.1).

To date, modeling electrodermal phenomena does not allow a theoretical answer to the question of adequate units of measurement. In case of the argument that conductance is more "physiological" (which in fact relates to the method and not to the unit of measurement; Sect. 2.6.2) being not considered, the question of the adequate unit of measurement can only be answered empirically. Distributional characteristics and level dependencies may serve as criteria here, and the validity of the different units of the parameters obtained should also be taken into consideration.

Although a conversion of resistance units into conductance units and vice versa is easily made when EDL scores are available (Sect. 2.3.3.2), only a few empirical studies which empirically compared different units of measurement for EDA have been performed to date. Lader (1970) blocked the sweat glands on the fingers with iontophoretic application of atropine, and directly thereafter recorded SRRs in response to a series of stimuli. It could be shown that it took up to 40 min before the effect of the atropine had advanced so far that no more SRRs were observed. When the SRRs were transformed into SCRs, an exponential decrease in the amplitudes was observable. In contrast, the increasing atropinization effect showed an irregular influence on the non-transformed SRR amp. This study is often cited as empirical proof for the preponderance of conductance units instead of resistance units.

Using SC data obtained from 28 participants, Hölzl, Wilhelm, Lutzenberger, and Schandry (1975) showed that a transformation of SCR and SCL scores into units of resistance (i.e., into SRR and SRL units) resulted in a better matching to a normal distribution compared with the original SC data. According to these results, transformations of resistance scores to conductance scores for normalization (Sect. 2.3.3.3) do not need to be performed.

Boucsein, Baltissen, and Euler (1984) undertook a systematic comparison of SCR and SRR amplitudes which were obtained from 60 participants through parallel constant voltage and constant current recordings (Sect. 2.6.2); these scores were additionally transformed into each other while taking the respective EDLs into account. It was observed that with high levels of stimulus intensity (i.e., with white noise exceeding 90 dB) the SRR and SCR amplitudes clearly differed from each other in the course of their habituation, whereby the direction of the results (habituation or sensitization, Sect. 3.1.1.3) was dependent upon the respective unit of measurement and not upon the method of recording which had been originally applied. Through the proper transformation of the amplitudes of both units with the use of mean level changes throughout the experiment, the differing courses could be made congruent. Thus, the equivalence of both recording methods could be shown, and the authors abandoned the option of recommending one or the other method because of a missing validity criterion.

Bitterman and Holtzman (1952) had already reported a differential level dependency of SRR and SCR amplitudes similar to that observed by Boucsein, Baltissen, and Euler (1984). These authors recorded the EDA from 40 participants with a constant current technique and investigated both SR score and then transformed SC score data with respect to their level dependency. For the first stimulus in the extinction phase, they obtained a significant negative correlation between the SCL and conductance units, whereas a corresponding level dependency for resistance units did not appear. Therefore, Bitterman and Holtzman decided to report their results in resistance units.

The question of choice between units of conductance or resistance for exosomatic EDA appears to be mostly an academic one. On one hand, the use of conductance units provides a standardization, while on the other hand, not enough empirical proof exists yet to fulfill the above-mentioned three criteria as outlined by Grings (1974) and therefore to settle the issue. Although the whole matter can be solved at best pragmatically in favor of conductance units as an attempt for standardization, theoretical as well as empirical questions still remain to be resolved with respect to the adequate unit of electrodermal measurement.

Furthermore, there has always been a potential confounding between discussing recording techniques (i.e., CC vs. CV) and response units (i.e., SR vs. SC). Schaefer (1993) suggested an approach to EDR recording for circumventing this persisting problem. He recommended AC measurement and utilizing the phase angle between current and voltage as the unit for EDRs. The skin-phase-angle response ($S\varphi R$, Sect. 2.3.1.2 "Amplitudes of Exosomatic Responses Recorded with Alternating Current") can be recorded directly by using either CC or CV. It has been theoretically derived by Schaefer and empirically demonstrated by Schaefer and Boucsein (2000) that the results obtained can be expected to be independent from the recording techniques applied. Thus, EDRs obtained by different recording techniques (i.e., CC or CV) should become comparable without any transformation which requires information about levels, if $S\varphi R$ is used as dependent variable. In addition, level dependencies revealed by $S\varphi R$ are independent of the recording technique, and thus may be regarded as reflecting the physiological properties of the electrodermal system.

2.6.6 Emerging Methodological Issues

Since the present book first appeared in 1992, attempts have been made in various areas for improving EDA methodology. Considerable progress of research into the CNS correlates of EDA emerged from the development of techniques for recording EDA concomitantly with brain imaging. For example, Raine, Reynolds, and Sheard (1991) recorded EDA together with MRI, finding the size of the left but not right temporal area (including the amygdala) being correlated with the frequency of ED-ORs. Furthermore, the use of EDA concomitantly with a PET scan technique by Fredrikson et al. (1998) confirmed the existence of different CNS sources for eliciting bilateral vs. contralateral EDRs as postulated in Fig. 1.6 (Sect. 1.3.4.1 "Cortical Control of EDA"), which had been inferred from neurological research performed in the 1970s. More recently, artifact-free EDA recording has become feasible within the magnetic field (Sect. 2.2.3.5). Given the high temporal resolution of the fMRI, fine-grained research into brain structures being active during EDRs has been performed.

A second accomplishment for EDA research is the progress in ambulatory monitoring (Sect. 2.2.3.4). Until the first edition of the present book appeared, long-term recordings had been rarely performed outside the laboratory (Sect. 2.2.6.1), mainly because of the limited storage capacity of the hitherto used tape recorders. However, with digital mass storage becoming available and recording devices becoming much smaller since the beginning of the 1990s, ambulatory recording in the real world outside the psychophysiological laboratory became an easy-to-accomplish option, for example in research on diurnal variation and sleep (Sect. 3.2.1.3) or engineering psychophysiology (Sect. 3.5.1). Although the technical possibilities for long-term EDA recording exist now, precautions should be taken to avoid problems with the attachments of EDA electrodes over long periods, as discussed in Sect. 2.2.6.1.

In the wake of ambulatory monitoring, so-called "life-shirts" (Wilhelm, Roth, & Sackner, 2003) or "wearable sensors" (Poh, Swenson, & Picard, 2010) have recently come into use (Sect. 3.5.1.1). Special prepared clothing such as wristbands, gloves, or shirts have been equipped with electrodes and connected to an ambulatory monitoring device, which is not only capable of EDA measurement but also allows for various psychophysiological recordings. It should, however, be kept in mind that these recording devices use nonstandard electrodes and sites. Thus, their introduction requires a direct comparison with standard recording techniques as had been performed by Poh, Swenson, and Picard (2010; see Sect. 2.2.1.1).

Another methodological progress in EDA measurement would emerge from switching DC- to AC recording, which had been already available for a long time (Sect. 2.1.5). From a physiological view, recording the electrical properties of tissue such as the skin by means of alternating current would be highly preferable to the widely used recording of skin conductance with the aid of direct current. Most electrical models of the skin contain elements behaving like capacitors (Sect. 1.4.3.2), the behavior of which cannot be registered by DC recording. The use of AC recording is, however, not only more "physiological"; it also provides solutions for pending problems. In particular, using the phase angle φ as dependent-variable measure (Sects. 1.4.1.3, 2.1.5, 2.2.3.3 and Sect. 2.3.1.2 "Amplitudes of Exosomatic Responses Recorded with Alternating Current") has been demonstrated by Schaefer and Boucsein (2000) to be a recording method which has the property to overcome the nagging problems of how to decide between recording with CC and CV (Sect. 2.6.2) and between SR and SC units (Sect. 2.6.5), which remain still unresolved if DC recording is used. Unfortunately, so far there are almost no devices on the market which allow for EDA recording with alternating current.

Finally, the fast development in computerization facilitated the use of mathematical procedures for evaluating the EDA signal. Various parameters can be obtained automatically, however, for the time being, it is highly recommended to perform such an evaluation under visual control as enabled by the computer program developed by F. Schaefer (see the Appendix of this book), since not all kinds of irregularities such as resulting from artifacts can be automatically detected (Sect. 2.3.4). This also holds for refined mathematical modeling for the evaluation of overlapping EDRs, which started with Lim et al.'s (1997) work, principally providing the opportunity to enable a theory-based analysis of responses to stimuli which follow each other in a tight sequence (Sect. 2.3.1.5). The most striking advantage of these mathematical methods is that they allow for the conjoint evaluation of EDRs together with event related potentials (ERPs) (Sect. 2.3.1.2 "Amplitudes of Exosomatic Responses Recorded with Direct Current") or stimulus-locked results from the fMRI, where fast stimulus sequences constitute a prerequisite for obtaining measures for rapidly changing CNS activity (Sect. 2.2.3.5).[146] The danger that comes with the availability of highly sophisticated computerized evaluation procedures for electrodermal phenomena is that the experimenter might lose the contact with the signal, the visual inspection of which still constitutes the basis for the soundest inferences about the underlying psychophysiological processes.

---

[146] In the present author's view, other attempts which take advantage of computerized EDR evaluation have not as yet demonstrated their superiority to traditional procedures within a theoretically underpinned context, such as discarding the theoretically founded FIR/SIR evaluation of EDRs within classical conditioning (Sect. 3.1.2.1 "Recent Developments in EDR Conditioning"). At least, all attempts to modify standard EDA evaluation procedures should include a diligent empirical comparison with traditional evaluation methods.

Chapter 3
Applications of Electrodermal Recording

The third part of this book is dedicated to various applications of EDA recording. The aim is to provide a theoretical framework for the use of the different EDA parameters described in Chap. 2 as psychophysiological indicators in the appropriate fields. Since there are thousands of articles reporting EDA results (Sect. 1.1.3), their comprehensive description would go far beyond the limits of the present book. Instead, the focus will be on giving more detailed information especially for studies which enlighten either methodological issues or provide support for interpretation of results in the light of psychophysiological theories related to EDA. The scope of applications will be mainly restricted to those areas where considerable developments in the use of EDA measurement have taken place since the 1970s.[1]

As in Chap. 2 of the present book, the term "standard methodology" will be used for EDA recordings in accordance with the standards as outlined in Sect. 2.2.7. Methodology seems a most crucial point in fields of application outside laboratory psychophysiology. It is the present author's hope that this book will stimulate the use of these standards in different fields of applied research within psychology as well as outside of it.

3.1 Stimulus-Related Psychophysiological Paradigms

With respect to the preponderance of either phasic or tonic parameters, the scope of psychophysiology may be divided into parts, focusing either on responses to distinct stimuli or on physiological parameters as indicators of changes in more general states. While the second kind of paradigm is dealt with in Sect. 3.2, the present chapter's focus is on electrodermal concomitants that appear during stimulation and information processing.

---

[1] For summaries of older results, see Prokasy and Raskin (1973) and Edelberg (1972a). More recent reviews will be referred to within the appropriate sections.

W. Boucsein, *Electrodermal Activity*, DOI 10.1007/978-1-4614-1126-0_3,
© Springer Science+Business Media, LLC 2012

As a consequence of the widespread use of EDA parameters in orienting, habituation, and conditioning research, the respective results have been summed up by different authors (see the appropriate contributions in the books edited by Gale & Edwards, 1983; Kimmel, van Olst, & Orlebeke, 1979; Prokasy & Raskin, 1973; Siddle, 1983). Therefore, Sects. 3.1.1 and 3.1.2 will focus on the extraction and use of appropriate EDA parameters and only report a small number of studies as typical examples of parameterization in the different contexts. Another focus will be on the role of EDA in information processing, as outlined in Sect. 3.1.3.

3.1.1 Electrodermal Indices of Orienting and Habituation

The concepts of orienting and habituation are widespread used in psychophysiology. A short outline of the most important theories, for example, Sokolov's (1963a, 1963b) "neuronal model," the dual-process theory proposed by Groves and Thompson (1970), and Wagner's (1976) so-called "priming theory," was given by Stephenson and Siddle (1983).

The orienting response (OR) was first discovered by Pavlov (1927) as a reflex elicited by environmental change. Its biological aim had been proposed to let the organism turn toward the source of stimulation to analyze its content or meaning. The components of an OR are lowering of sensory thresholds, pupillary dilatation, eye and gross body movements, alpha-blockade in the EEG, and various vegetative changes, the most prominent of which are the EDR and a deceleration-acceleration pattern in HR. In addition, cephalic vasodilatation and peripheral vasoconstriction will be observed (Sect. 2.4.2.1).

Because of its connections with the neuronally based arousal model proposed in Sect. 3.2.1.2, Sokolov's (1963b) comparator theory will be briefly outlined here. Certain features of stimulus information are stored in neuronal networks in the cortex, forming a "neuronal model." The information is also forwarded via collaterals to novelty detectors in the hippocampus, which execute a comparator function between already stored and newly incoming stimulus patterns. In case of mismatch, subcortical structures will be activated, and both central and peripheral components of the OR will be elicited. Repeatedly presented identical stimuli will continue to be cortically analyzed, but elicit less and less activity in the hippocampal novelty detectors, thus leading to habituation of the OR.[2]

---

[2] During the 1970s, in the wake of the cognitive "paradigm shift" (Sect. 3.1.2.1 "Cognitive vs. Noncognitive View of EDR Conditioning"), comparator theories of OR have been partly rephrased in terms of resource allocation in a system with limited capacity (Sect. 3.1.2.1 "Components of EDR Conditioning"). A brief description of Öhman's (1979) and his own model is provided by Hugdahl (1995, pp. 135–138). The possible role of the SC-OR being a potential indicator of resource allocation will be discussed in Sects. 3.1.3.1 and 3.1.3.4. For more information on SC-OR and resource allocation see, for example, Siddle (1991), Siddle, Lipp, and Dall (1996) and Filion, Dawson, Schell, and Hazlett (1991), described in Sect. 3.1.3.2; critical results were reported by Niepel (2001).

With the advent of the possibility of combining EDA with brain imaging techniques (Sect. 2.2.3.5), the presumed role of the hippocampus in the generation of ORs could be more directly investigated. In their MRI study with 17 participants of both genders described in Sect. 1.3.4.1 "Subcortical Control of EDA", Raine, Reynolds, and Sheard (1991) found the skin conductance OR (SC-OR) being significantly related to left and right prefrontal areas, an area of the pons and left but not right temporal/amygdalar areas. No significant correlations were obtained with nonfrontal cortical areas and the medial prefrontal cortex. Unfortunately, the hippocampus was not among the areas observed by Raine and coworkers. Williams et al. (2000) in their study described in Sect. 2.2.3.5 recorded SC-ORs in parallel with fMRI recordings from 8 healthy males during a repeated presentation of various checkerboard stimuli compared to a blank screen. The fMRI data set provided full coverage of the temporal (including amygdala and hippocampus), frontal, occipital, and parietal lobes. Their results evidenced that the hippocampus, the anterior cingulate gyrus and the VMPFC are associated with the generation of ORs. Thus, the hippocampus may well play a key role in generating SC-ORs as supposed by Sokolov in the 1960s.

Since the OR is regarded being unspecific, it should be elicited by both an increase and a decrease of stimulus intensity. Hence, an OR can be expected as a response not only to the stimulus onset but also to the end of stimulation. Furthermore, different kinds of ORs have been distinguished:

1. Generalized vs. localized OR (Lynn, 1966; Sokolov, 1960). A generalized OR is characterized by a general activation of the sensory cortex as well as by an increase of sensitivity in various sensory systems. On the contrary, a localized OR is restricted to the stimulation of a specific system, and therefore does not fully meet the criterion of nonspecificity typical of the OR. Despite this lacuna, it is classified as an OR by Sokolov (1963b) because of its nonspecificity with respect to the direction of change. There are also noticeable differences in habituation speed: the generalized OR typically habituates within 2–5 trials, while the localized OR needs 20 or more trials to habituate (Sect. 3.1.1.3). Examples of localized ORs are long-lasting EDRs following tactile stimuli and the occipital blockade due to visual stimulation.

2. Phasic vs. tonic OR (Sokolov, 1963b, 1966). A phasic OR can be traced back to a transient increase of sensitivity of the different receptor systems. The term *receptor system* is used here as an equivalent to Sokolov's (1963b) "analyzer," which is an integrating system of peripheral as well as central mechanisms fundamental for transmission and processing of stimulus properties. Within the electrodermal system, the stimulus-related EDR is regarded as the phasic OR component. By contrast, the tonic OR consists of a kind of level-shift in the background sensitivity of the receptor systems which may even continue after the end of a habituation series. It is presumed to be dependent on the overall cortical arousal level (Sect. 3.2.1.1) whether a phasic or tonic OR appears. According to Sokolov (1963b), the increase in general arousal which causes a tonic OR may

have the property to amplify the phasic OR produced by the comparator mechanism. A novel stimulus could elicit a tonic OR lasting up to an hour in a drowsy person, while eliciting only a phasic OR in a person being awake.

According to Sokolov (1963b), the increase of tonic EDA is a typical indicator for a tonic OR, which may be observed as an increase in SCL and/or in NS.EDR freq. (Sect. 2.3.2). Whereas EDR components have been in the focus of research into the phasic SC-OR, investigations aiming at the usability of EDA measures for tonic SC-OR components are sparse. Barry and Sokolov (1993) examined the role of tonic SC-OR in modulating the phasic SC-OR in an elementary habituation procedure (Sect. 3.1.1.3). Twelve participants were presented 12 white rectangles on a black screen. Prestimulus SCLs were regarded as tonic SC-ORs, while SCR amp. were evaluated to obtain phasic SC-OR components. The SCL showed an initial increase after the first stimulus, and thereafter a systematic decline with stimulus repetition. The SCR amp. displayed typical habituation, which persisted if the SCL effects were removed by means of linear within-subjects regression. The authors interpreted their results as supporting Sokolov's notion of the tonic OR having amplifying properties for the phasic OR. The initial increase of tonic EDA was interpreted by Barry (2004) as indicating sensitization such as proposed by the dual process theory of Groves and Thompson (1970).[3] He performed an additional study with 40 participants (21 females, 19 males), using the same 12 stimuli as in the experiment together with Sokolov and recorded SC with standard methodology from the medial phalanges of the right hand's ring and middle fingers. However, an initial SCL increase emerged only in the half of participants having not received an additional instruction to silently count the stimuli. In the other half that received such an instruction, no habituation of the tonic SC-OR component could be observed. The nonhabituation of the tonic component was interpreted as an indication of enhanced arousal, which was induced by the significance given to the stimuli by instruction. Furthermore, the phasic SC-OR to the stimuli without instruction habituated faster than those following the stimuli to be counted. This closely resembles a differentiation between "voluntary" and "involuntary" ORs, which has been made by Maltzman (1979a, 1979b) who regarded "voluntary" ORs as being cognitively mediated, e.g., by instructions or by the cortical processes underlying thinking (Sect. 3.1.1.1). In turn, "involuntary" ORs are thought to be solely elicited by stimulus characteristics, which makes them habituating faster. In addition, Barry and O'Gorman (1987) pointed to EDR lat. being significantly longer with voluntary ORs (e.g., following stimulus omission) as compared to involuntary ORs.

After a habituation took place, *OR reinstatement* can be observed following changes in stimulus intensity, modality, duration, frequency, sequence (i.e., duration and variability of the ISIs), complexity, information content, or stimulus significance,

---

[3] The Groves-Thompson theory had been developed based on research on spinal cats. Since the proposed sensitization process has not been unambiguously demonstrated in studies with humans, such a conclusion is barely justified (see Sect. 3.1.1.3).

the latter of which may also be acquired during classical conditioning (Sokolov, 1960; see Sect. 3.1.2.1). OR reinstatement appears during below-zero habituation[4] and also during dishabituation. After the habituation process has been interrupted by a stimulus change which leads to an OR reinstatement, resuming the presentation of the first stimulus will result in an increase in EDR amp. compared to the one seen before the interruption, which is called *dishabituation*. Thompson and Spencer (1966) regarded increasing stimulus intensities as a prerequisite for eliciting dishabituation. However, this phenomenon may also be elicited by changes in stimulus modality, by frequency changes of acoustic stimuli, and even by stimulus omission (Edwards & Siddle, 1976; Magliero, Gatchel, & Lojewski, 1981; Martin & Rust, 1976; McCubbin & Katkin, 1971; Siddle, 1985; Siddle, Remington, Kuiack, & Haines, 1983). Responding to the omission of a stimulus suggests that there has been an anticipation of the stimulus which, however, did not appear (Sokolov, 1963b). One procedure that has been used by Siddle and colleagues to investigate the effect of stimulus omission on the SCR amp. involved the presentation of two paired but different stimuli (tone, light, or vibration) of moderate intensity. As summarized by Siddle (1991, Fig. 3), omission of the second stimulus resulted in a marked increase of the already habituated SCR amp., and dishabituation was also demonstrated by a further increase of SCR amp. after subsequent continuation of pairing the two stimuli.

The influence of phasic and tonic SC-OR components on dishabituation has been investigated by Rushby and Barry (2007) who also examined putative CNS correlates of phasic and tonic ED-ORs. Thirty-six participants (30 females, 6 males; aged 19–43 years) underwent three consecutive series with 30 s intertrial intervals (ITIs) of 7 stimuli each (ISI fixed at 8 s) with a stimulus change at position 6 and presentation of the original stimulus at position 7. The series alternated between high-intense (80 dB) and low-intense (50 dB) 1,000 Hz tones (50, 15 ms rise/fall times) presented over headphones, with the mutual other stimulus intensity used as dishabituation stimulus in position 6. The sequence of series was counterbalanced over two groups, each one made up from half of the participants. EDA was recorded with standard methodology from the distal phalanges of the index and middle fingers of the nondominant hand. EEG was recorded from 19 sites and EOG was used as artifact control. An increase of the tonic SC-OR (i.e., the SCL) as reported in Barry's earlier work (Barry & Sokolov, 1993; Barry, 2004) was only observed in the series starting with five 80 dB stimuli, but OR reinstatement of the tonic SC-OR was much more pronounced when the dishabituation stimulus was a high-intense one presented within a series of low-intensity stimuli. Phasic SC-ORs showed marked habituation under both conditions, but a much more pronounced dishabituation if the appropriate stimulus was low intense being presented within the high-intense series compared to the opposed condition, whereas comparable reinstatement of the phasic OR appeared in both kinds of series. There was some evidence for the contingent

---

[4] Below-zero habituation represents a continuation of stimulus presentation after reaching an individual habituation criterion, e.g., two successive "zero-responses" (Sect. 3.1.1.3).

negative variation (CNV) prior to stimulation across frontal sites paralleling SCL, while SCR amp. following stimulus onset showed some relationship to the P300 across parietal sites. Thus, the tonic SC-OR may represent an anticipatory component, whereas the phasic SC-OR may relatively independently reflect the amount of stimulus information processing (Sect. 3.1.3.1).

Another stimulus modality, the dishabituating effect of which had been stressed by Berlyne (1961), is conflict or the possibility of choice between several reactions. In addition, during the 1970s there was a controversy concerning the role of stimulus significance between Bernstein (1979) and Maltzman (1979a) on one side and O'Gorman (1979) on the other side (see Sect. 3.1.1.1). They discussed the role of personality characteristics, individual experience, mood, motivation, state of arousal, and various other contextual conditions. However, the main issue was the importance of cognitive factors in explaining individual differences in the OR. These factors have been especially stressed by Bernstein who regarded the OR mainly as a consequence of the stimulus input's cortical evaluation, including the paticipant's above-mentioned individual characteristics. On the contrary, O'Gorman regarded individual OR differences as being mainly due to different degrees of readiness in the peripheral physiological systems, for which the dependence of the electrodermal OR upon the spontaneous EDA (Sect. 2.5.4.2) served as a typical example.

In comparison with other physiological indicators of an OR, the phasic EDA component emerges as the most suitable correlate of stimulus intensity. For example, a linear relationship between SCR amp. and the intensity of 2 s white noise stimuli between 70 and 100 dB[5] has been found in 12 participants by Uno and Grings (1965). Jackson (1974) also reported a monotonous increase of the SCR amp., averaged over the first four as well as over all ten trials, during an increase in intensity of a 1 kHz tone,[6] while the phasic HR showed a nonlinear increase-decrease-increase change with increasing stimulus intensity. Barry (1975), varying the intensity of a 1 kHz tone between 20 and 50 dB in 10 dB steps, all of which were presented in counterbalanced order to 24 participants, also observed an approximately linear increase of the SRR amp. with the increase of stimulus intensity.[7] In a study using the same experimental conditions, EEG power remained nearly constant up to an intensity of 40 dB, only showing an increase under the 50 dB condition (Barry, 1976). A positive linear relationship between stimulus intensity and the EDR amp. has been reported by Turpin and Siddle (1979) in their study described in the next section and by Boucsein

---

[5] In steps of 10 dB, each stimulus applied five times in a balanced design, SR recording with 50 μA constant current using 2 cm^2 Ag electrodes from two fingers of the right hand, transformed to SC.

[6] In steps of 20 dB; SCR recorded with standard electrodes and voltage, however unipolar thenar against a neutral forearm side and with K–Y gel (Experiment 3).

[7] Recorded AC coupled (Sect. 2.1.3) with a 5 s time constant volar from the left hand's fingers.

and Hoffmann (1979) in their habituation experiment already mentioned in Sect. 2.5.2.1 "Skin Conductance Responses".[8]

There might also be developmental aspects of the SC-OR amp., its habituation, and OR reinstatement, as obtained by Gao, Raine, Dawson, Venables, and Mednick (2007) in their study with children at the ages 3, 4, 5, 6, and 8 years, described in Sect. 2.4.3.1. They found – in their, albeit somewhat unusual, sample – a nonlinear increase of the initial SC-OR amp., habituation not occurring before the age of 4, and 3–8-year-old children not showing any OR reinstatement.

3.1.1.1 Differential Influences of Novelty and Significance on the OR

A number of investigations have been performed with respect to the influence of the *stimulus significance* or "salience" on the electrodermal OR's strength and course of habituation. It can be regarded as a widely accepted result that the OR following a certain stimulus or a class of stimuli can be enlarged if those stimuli are given signal value for a cognitive or a motor response (Maltzman & Langdon, 1982; Spinks & Siddle, 1983).[9] Maltzman and Langdon (1982) attempted to separate the influences of novelty and significance on the electrodermal OR. One hundred twelve participants of both genders were presented 0.5 s 1 kHz 70 dB tones. The ISIs between the tones were 12 s during the presentation of the initial 16 training stimuli and varied between 5.5 and 260 s in logarithmic steps during successive test series. Half of the participants served as experimental group and were instructed to lift their foot as fast as possible from a pedal, thus imposing significance on the stimuli, while the control group was instructed to sit quietly and listen. The experimental group showed significantly higher EDR amp.,[10] while the control group showed faster habituation. The latter one reacted only to the 26 s interval with a significant increase of the EDR amp. compared to the training phase. On the other hand, in the experimental group which was overall more reactive, only the difference between the 5.5 s ISI and the training interval approached significance. The authors concluded that stimulus significance is not a necessary condition for the occurrence of an OR. Instead, it may predetermine the effects of novelty to some degree. Without referring to a specific theoretical model, the authors offered global

---

[8] As already described at the end of Sect. 2.5.1.1, Toyokura (2006) obtained a directly proportional relationship between the intensity of an electrical stimulus applied to the median nerve at the wrist and SPR amp., being either positively or negatively directed (Sect. 2.3.1.2 "Amplitudes of Endosomatic Responses") in 40 male participants. This relationship persisted even after habituation. Furthermore, OR reinstatement was clearly observable if the electric stimulation was switched to magnetic stimulation.

[9] Rotenberg and Vedenyapin (1985) in a study with 15 participants being presented a series of tones, a subset of whom had to react to the tone, found some evidence of SPR amp. to the tones being more dependent on decision making than on motor preparation.

[10] Recorded as SRR palmar, 0.5–5.0 s after stimulus onset and subjected to a logarithmic SCR transformation.

concepts like "dominant focus" or "cortical set" as already stated by Maltzman (1979a) for an explanation of their results, however not making any predictions for further research into this area.

The same question was investigated by Barry (1982) in two experiments; he introduced stimulus significance by cognitive demands instead of requiring motor responses. In the first experiment, two groups of 10 participants (of both genders) were given a series of seven stimulus pairs (capital letters A and B in random order). The experimental group had to count the Bs which gave them significance, while the controls counted every letter. There was a significantly enhanced mean SCR amp.[11] in the experimental group. In the second experiment, the procedure was repeated with the same number of participants. Thereafter, another seven stimuli with different relations of As to Bs were presented to induce novelty. Unfortunately, these were different in both groups which confounded task difficulty and group effects, thus invalidating partly the interpretation of the significant increase of SRR amp. observed during the eighth trial as a consequence of novelty. Altogether, the EDR amp. appeared to be influenced by both stimulus characteristics and additional cognitive processes. However, among all psychophysiological variables recorded, only EDA reflected manipulations of significance.

Ben-Shakhar, Asher, Poznansky-Levy, Asherowitz, and Lieblich (1989) reported results from three experiments investigating the effects of stimulus novelty and significance on the OR. In the first experiment with a total of 108 participants of both genders, nonsignificant test stimuli were introduced at different positions within a complex eight-stimulus series.[12] The test stimuli did not evoke any enhanced SCR amp. (recorded with standard methodology) under either condition. In the second experiment performed with a total of 128 participants, test stimuli were introduced at the same positions, however within a sequence of simple standard stimuli, yielding greater SCRs to the test stimuli, thus being at odds with the "neuronal model" (Sokolov, 1963a, 1963b). The goal of the third experiment using 128 participants was to directly compare the response to a nonsignificant stimulus change with that to a similar stimulus change including a significant element. Therefore, the test stimulus was made relevant prior to its presentation in one condition by the use of the so-called Guilty Knowledge Technique (Sect. 3.5.2). However, the attempted effect of significance had been probably

---

[11] Measured with stainless steel 2×3 cm electrodes from the volar surface of the left hand's fingers with Biocom Inc. Biogel as contact medium; 1–5 s following stimulus onset was used as time window.

[12] Stimuli were one-word (name of an occupation) or two-word stimuli (occupation name combined with name of a hobby), both kinds mutually used as standard and as test stimuli. The participants had to recall as many words as possible. Receiver operating characteristic (ROC) curves were generated by comparing the distributions of standardized responses to test stimuli vs. standard stimuli.

obscured by the nature of the test stimulus,[13] therefore, effects of novelty and significance could not be clearly separated. Both factors were regarded as nonadditive by the authors, and instead of regarding significance as a necessary condition for an OR, it was suggested that stimulus significance is only necessary when the contrast between test and standard stimuli is small (i.e., when the test stimulus follows a complex sequence of stimuli).

In his examination of the by then published investigations into the roles of stimulus novelty and significance in determining OR strength, Ben-Shakhar (1994) suggested the inconsistency of results being partly due to the incongruence in definitions of both significance and novelty. For example, the degree of novelty was defined by several authors as the amount of change in physical stimulus characteristics (e.g., Siddle, O'Gorman, & Wood, 1979); in other instances, the presentation frequency was used for varying the degree of novelty (e.g., Ben-Shakhar, Lieblich, & Kugelmass, 1982), whereas other authors defined novelty in terms of the amount of common vs. distinctive stimulus components (e.g., Gati & Ben-Shakhar, 1990). In two successive experiments with different kinds of stimuli – meaningless geometrical figures vs. meaningful verbal stimuli – Ben-Shakhar (1994) attempted to independently vary stimulus novelty and significance. In the first experiment, 156 participants were randomly allocated to 16 conditions, made up by four orthogonal factors: (1) significance vs. neutrality of the test stimulus, (2) early vs. late position of the test stimulus in a row of 16 trials, (3) complexity of the stimulus sequence preceding the test stimulus (a single stimulus repeatedly presented vs. a different stimulus on each trial of the sequence), and (4) similarity between the preceding stimuli and the test stimulus (differing only in one feature vs. differing in color, shape, and number of figures shown on the screen). ISIs varied between 16 and 24 s (mean 20 s). In the first phase of the experiment, one stimulus was made significant by the participant's choice. Thereafter, SCRs were recorded with standard methodology, scored as the maximum change in SC between 1 and 5 s after stimulus onset and standardized (Sect. 2.3.3.4 "Transformation into Standard Values"). Since the position factor did not yield a difference between early and late test stimulus position, Ben-Shakhar challenged Sokolov's (1963b) notion that forming a stable "neuronal model" would be a prerequisite for an OR following a stimulus change. In contrast to the hypothesis of Ben-Shakhar et al. (1989) that ORs are products of an interaction between novelty and significance, no such interaction was observed here. The second experiment was performed with 196 participants to investigate the generalizability of these results, using words of two categories (names of cities and animals) as stimuli that were displayed on a computer screen. Results were consistent with those of the first experiment. Since none of the three factors used for manipulating novelty showed an interaction with stimulus significance in either experiment, Ben-Shakhar (1994) concluded that the OR magnitude is determined by novelty and significance in an additive but not in an interactive manner.

---

[13] A name of a hobby instead of a certain number, as used in an earlier experiment (Ben-Shakhar & Lieblich 1982), had a clear common component shared with the standard stimuli (which were also numbers).

Based on their previous research with giving stimuli significance by means of a modified Guilty Knowledge Technique, Gati and Ben-Shakhar (1990) proposed their so-called *"feature-matching theory,"* which was not meant to replace but rather to expand Sokolov's (1963b) comparator theory (Sect. 3.1.1) in two directions. First, it specified the comparator (or matching) mechanism insofar that the comparison between input and the "neuronal model" (i.e., the representation of past stimulation) is based on contrasting common and distinctive features of both stimulus input and stored stimulus information. Second, they proposed two separate feature-matching mechanisms: one for assessing significance and one for assessing novelty, both of them being based on feature-matching algorithms for assessing stimulus significance and novelty, which were demonstrated later by Ben-Shakhar (1994) to be independent of each other. They also considered the OR strength being a nonnegative monotonic function of both the degree of significance and the degree of novelty. In their theoretical approach, significance is based on matching the features of a test stimulus for eliciting the OR and a stimulus made relevant by the context (e.g., by a conditioning process or an instruction for paying special attention to it). The stimulus match is a function of common features and two sets of distinct features (i.e., features of each stimulus that do not belong to the respective other stimulus). The match becomes better with an increasing amount of common features and a decreasing amount of distinctive features. On the other hand, stimulus novelty takes into account the set of all stimuli that precede the test stimulus in a sequence. Gati and Ben-Shakhar (1990) proposed that the degree of novelty is positively related to the amount of its unique features and negatively related to the common features which the test stimulus shares with at least one of the preceding stimuli, following a linear function. It can be manipulated by adding, deleting, or substituting stimulus components.

To probe their "feature-matching theory," Ben-Shakhar, Gati, and Salamon (1995) investigated the effect of common and distinctive stimulus components on the OR generalization to similar stimuli (Maltzman, 1977). Two hundred forty participants (101 females, 139 males) were randomly allocated to ten experimental conditions, made up from combinations of different numbers of common and distinctive components of a relevant and a test stimulus (both schematic drawings of faces). Common and distinctive features were independently manipulated. First, one of six basic faces was presented as "murder victim" (the relevant stimulus) to be memorized by the participant. During the subsequent test phase, where SCRs were recorded from two fingers of the left hand with standard methodology, a sequence of 13 facial stimuli was presented (ISIs 16–24 s) for 5 s each. Test stimuli were always located at trials 4 and 8. Participants who failed to identify the relevant face from a set of six faces were not included in the data evaluation (less than 3%). Consistent with the authors' theoretical view, OR generalization was independently affected by common and distinctive features, since no interaction effect was found between the two kinds of features. However, contrary to the authors' expectations, similar OR generalization was observed regardless of whether the test stimuli were derived from the relevant stimulus by deleting or by adding components to that stimulus. Since the latter manipulation is likely to elicit novelty in addition to a possible stimulus significance, Ben-Shakhar et al. (1995) concluded that novelty may not necessarily be a prerequisite for the elicitation of an OR as postulated by Sokolov (1963b). However, since the appropriate results remained statistically nonsignificant, such a general conclusion from this rather complicated study may be regarded only as preliminary.

Additional factors that might affect the novelty of a test stimulus were investigated by Ben-Shakhar and Gati (2003) in a study with 256 participants (208 females, 48 males). The authors systematically manipulated the frequency for the appearance of features common to a schematic face stimulus, which was made relevant for the participants, and a set of preceding schematic face stimuli. The features consisted of the following five components: basic frame (including eyes, nose, and mouth), glasses, a hat with an ornament, a beard and a mustache, and a pipe with smoke. They also manipulated the serial position of these features. A similar experimental setting was performed with verbal descriptions of persons (i.e., occupation, personality, hobby, appearance, and city of residence) and applied in counterbalanced order with the face setting. Each test stimulus was preceded by 12 control stimuli and followed by two additional control stimuli. It was composed of three novel components not included in any of the control stimuli and two components that were included in a control stimulus type that shared no components with the test stimulus, which was made relevant during the first part of the experiment by declaring this being the face or description of a "murder victim" in a mock-crime setting (Sect. 3.5.2). SCRs were recorded with standard methodology, evaluated as the maximum SC change in the interval 1–5 s after stimulus onset and transformed into relative within-subjects scores, which were defined as the SCR amp. following the test stimulus minus the mean SCR amp. to all preceding control stimuli (Sect. 2.3.3.4 "Transformation into Standard Values"). To examine whether or not OR reinstatement to the test stimulus occurred, the SCR elicited by that stimulus was compared to the SCR elicited by the immediately preceding stimulus. Although the SCR amp. following the test stimulus was always higher than the one elicited by the preceding control stimulus, thus confirming OR reinstatement, the appropriate difference was significantly influenced by the serial position of the stimulus components common to test and control stimuli. No statistically significant dishabituation effects were observed. As a result of the study, only the serial position of common components had the property to affect OR reinstatement, however also only under the conditions of low frequency of appearance of features common to the test stimulus and the set of preceding stimuli, which might have limited the generalizability of the findings. The authors concluded that "neuronal models" decay very quickly, and they proposed a partial reformulation of their "feature-matching theory" (Ben-Shakhar & Gati, 2003, p. 144). In the present author's view, comparator theory explanations of the OR may be still far from being elaborated enough to explain all kinds of observations made under various experimental manipulations.

Another investigation into the relevance of significance of verbal stimuli for the SC-OR was performed by Dindo and Fowles (2008). In a first experiment with

43 participants (21 females, 22 males) SCRs[14] were obtained during the presentation of 20 words rated as highly significant, low arousal and negatively valenced, in counterbalanced order with 20 low-significant words that were matched on arousal and valence. Results showed that significant nonarousing words were associated with significantly higher SCR amp. compared to nonsignificant, nonarousing words. A second experiment was performed with 44 participants (22 of each gender), using the same recording technique but a more complicated design. For each combination of self-referent vs. non self-referent and negative vs. positive valenced rated words, eight highly significant stimuli were presented, together with eight control words being rated as neutral in valence and low in significance. Again, all words were rated as low arousing. Each of the group of experimental words elicited higher SCR amp. than the control words. Highly significant, nonarousing words were associated with significantly higher SCR amp. compared to nonsignificant, nonarousing words, regardless of their valence. Their results suggest that significance alone can be regarded as a critical stimulus feature for eliciting an OR, regardless of the general arousal level, emotional valence, or self-reference stimulus properties.

Since most authors confined themselves to use the EDR amp. as a measure of OR strength, further progress may result from a multiparameter or even multivariate approach to determining factors that may influence the strength of the OR. For example, Janes (1982) reported some evidence for electrodermal recovery being a valid indicator of stimulus significance, as suggested by Edelberg (1970). Ten participants of both genders were delivered 76 tones (800 Hz, 75 dB) after 16 habituation trials in a within-subjects design. Combinations of delivering the tone to the right or left ear in a distinct sequence were used to induce stimulus meaning (they either prepared to press a foot pedal, or did not, at the onset of the next tone) with identical stimulation. As a result, SCR amp.[15] were higher and SCR rec.t/2 were longer when stimulus meaning increased, both measures being significantly correlated in 9 out of 10 participants.[16] However, the recovery time increase held up under two types of amplitude correction, based on both an individual regression procedure and an inspection of amplitude-matched trial pairs. Therefore, Janes (1982) concluded that stimulus significance may affect EDR recovery to an even higher degree than EDR amplitude, and that peripheral and central mechanisms are involved in determining both parameters (Sect. 1.4.2.3).

---

[14] Recorded with 12.55 mm diameter Ag/AgCl electrodes filled with K–Y jelly from thenar/hypothenar sites of the nondominant hand, using 1.0 V DC and a Wheatstone bridge. Two separate channels were used for SCL and SCR to enable a full range of 5 µS for the response channel (Sects. 2.1.3 and 2.2.4.1). SCR amp. were scored as changes in SC from the prestimulus level to the response peak within a 3–7 s window after the presentation of words.

[15] Recorded bilaterally from the hypothenar eminence with standard methodology, using Beckman miniature electrodes, logarithmically transformed.

[16] Bundy's "X" (Sect. 2.5.2.5, (2.22)) and SCR rec.t/2 yielded significant correlations for 3 of the 10 participants.

A differentiated view concerning the role of EDR as an indicator of OR was provided within the multiprocess OR model proposed by Barry (1987). This model assumed different registers or systems interacting during an OR, which are represented in various physiological measures. These are: a stimulus register, as indicated by HR deceleration and cerebral pulse volume; an intensity register, the indicators of which are EDR and peripheral pulse volume; a novelty register, being indicated by EDR, pronounced respiratory activity, and EEG alpha; and the response system, the activation of which is accompanied by HR acceleration. To the present author's knowledge, this model has not yet been empirically probed.

3.1.1.2   Differentiation Between Orienting, Defensive, and Startle Responses

It is presumed that the OR has an important survival function, since it shifts the organism to a state in which its resources are mobilized for an adequate response to changed or new stimulation. If stimuli which are nonthreatening or even unimportant to the organism are repeated, the OR amplitude decreases as a sign of an adaptation process, which manifests as habituation of the OR. However, highly intense or even aversive stimulation requires a different response pattern, which indicates a continuous readiness for response.

Pavlov (1927) already distinguished between the OR and the *defensive response* (DR), insofar as the biological aim of the latter is to protect the organism against harm. As a consequence, the DR does not show considerable habituation. In addition, a DR never appears following the termination of a stimulus as may the OR. According to Sokolov (1963b), OR and DR can be distinguished by their vasomotor components: peripheral vasoconstriction and cephalic (forehead) vasodilatation in cases of an OR vs. constriction at both sites during a DR. In addition, Lacey (1967) described differentiating HR patterns: a biphasic deceleration-acceleration pattern being typical of an OR vs. a monophasic acceleration pattern which indicates a DR.

Dykman, Reese, Galbrecht, and Thomasson (1959) made a distinction between OR and another response type labeled *startle response*, which was based on their concomitant body movements: those that are supposed being directed toward the stimulus in case of an OR but not in case of a startle response. Also, the latency time was presumed being shorter for the startle response. However, EDR latencies cannot fall below a threshold of 0.5 s as reported previously (Sect. 2.3.1.1). According to Graham (1979), the startle response habituates quickly, as opposed to the DR. On the other hand, Turpin (1986) described the startle as being an early component of a DR elicited by stimuli with short rise times.[17]

---

[17] During the last 2 decades, SC-OR has been frequently used to determine the OR component of a so-called prepulse, which has been applied to modify the human startle eyeblink reflex (Filion, Dawson, & Schell, 1998). Such a stimulus either terminates before, or continues up to, and sometimes beyond the startle stimulus (Wynn, Dawson, & Schell, 2000). It was hypothesized that a prolonged prepulse may elicit a generalized OR (Sect. 3.1.1).

Several EDA parameters have also been used to distinguish between OR and DR. As Uno and Grings (1965) have shown in their study mentioned in the previous section, the number of biphasic SPRs[18] increased when stimulus intensity approached 100 dB. In addition, the amplitudes as well as the rise times of the SPRs and the SCRs recorded in parallel increased with stimulus intensity. Raskin, Kotses, and Bever (1969), using a broader range of stimulus intensities,[19] revealed only small differences in SPR and SCR amp. when comparing the different intensities. However, they found the positive SPR component increasing markedly with stimulus intensity. Therefore, they interpreted the positive SPR component as being an indicator for DR and in turn the negative SPR component as being an indicator for OR.[20] Edelberg (1970) questioned their conclusion, since he revealed a connection between the positive SPR component and a prolonged SCR rec.t/2, which he later proposed as an index of aversive stimulation (Edelberg, 1972a).

As could be inferred from Edelberg's (1973a) considerations, the prolongation of SCR recovery may possibly function as a differential indicator between DR and OR, independently from being recorded at palmar or dorsal sites. However, this has not yet been unambiguously demonstrated. Turpin and Siddle (1979) presented series of twelve 1 kHz tones with five different intensities between 45 and 105 dB[21] in a between-subjects design with 15 participants for each intensity. When they evaluated the responses to the first tone of each series, the authors observed a linear increase of SCR amp. with increasing tone intensity. However, there was no unequivocal relationship between the inverse of SCR rec.t/2 following the first tone and its intensity. It was only in the seventh and ninth trial of the 15 trial habituation series that the recovery time that followed the 105 dB stimuli was markedly longer than those following the lower intensity stimuli (cf. Turpin & Siddle, 1979, Fig. 1). There was also no systematic relationship between SCR ris.t.

---

[18] Recorded between an active palmar and an inactive wrist site with Ag electrodes being 2.6 cm in diameter.

[19] Between 40 and 120 dB in steps of 20 dB, however with independent groups of 25 participants each. Endosomatic EDA was recorded from left thenar against pretreated forearm sites, while exosomatic measures were taken as SR from the right hand palmar vs. dorsal with 40 µA, being transformed to SC values, using Beckman Ag/AgCl electrodes with NaCl paste for both measures.

[20] Although not aiming at the OR/DR distinction, Toyokura (2006) demonstrated in 40 healthy participants that a positive SPR component was more likely to be observed in high-intensity compared to low-intensity median nerve electrical stimulation. In the second out of four consecutive sessions, the predominant SPR component switched from positivity to negativity, which the author interpreted as an effect of habituation. However, the stimulation sequence was not suitable for investigating habituation as described in Sect. 3.1.1.3. A sort of OR reinstatement was observed when introducing a magnetic stimulation to the neck, which also showed no habituation of the SPR. SP (labeled SSR, see Sect. 3.5.4) was recorded from the right midpalm against the forearm.

[21] In 15 dB steps, 30 ms stimulus rise time and 2 s duration. EDA was recorded with standard methodology, however using K–Y gel.

and stimulus intensity. One reason for the absence of differentiation between DR and OR by means of EDR parameters in this study might have been that the 30 ms stimulus rise times used could have been too long for eliciting a DR. In his study described in Sect. 3.4.1.2, Hare (1978a) found SCR rec.t/2 increasing with stimulus intensity only with 10 ms but not with 25 ms stimulus rise times[22] especially when using intensities of 100 dB and above. Since he obtained this relationship mainly in left-hand recordings, the question of a possible lateralization of electrodermal temporal measures with respect to DR could be raised here (Sect. 3.1.4.2). Boucsein and Hoffmann (1979), in their study already described in Sect. 2.5.1.1, reported significant main effects of stimulus intensities in logarithmized SCR rec.t/2 and SRR rec.t/2. The recovery times were markedly prolonged following 100 and 110 dB white noise stimulation of 2 s duration with instantaneous rise time, compared to lower stimulus intensities. In the same study, differences between courses of habituation for ORs and DRs were observed, which will be discussed in the following section.

Another attempt to differentiate OR from DR by means of EDA made use of the difference between palmar and dorsal recording. Older studies performed by Darrow (1933) and by the Edelberg group (for a review see Edelberg, 1972a) had pointed to differences in reactivity between these sites, the dorsal being more likely to reflect OR while the palmar EDA seemed to be more closely linked to DR or anxiety responses (Sect. 3.4.1.1). Possible sources of the so-called palmar/dorsal effect were seen in the palmar and plantar surfaces being different from others with respect to sweating (Sect. 1.3.2.4), as well as simply in the greater sweat gland density in the palmar ridged skin as compared to the dorsal polygonal skin (Sects. 1.2.2 and 1.2.3). Based on his two-component model of EDA (Sect. 1.4.2.3), Edelberg (1973a) suggested that the predominance of the sweat gland component over the epidermal component is responsible for the observations of higher SCR amp. and prolonged SCR rec.t/2 at palmar as compared to dorsal sites during aversive stimulation. This is because it is suggested that only the membrane component, which has a short recovery time, plays a considerable role in the dorsal EDR (Sect. 1.4.3.2).

Support for the presumably greater complexity of the palmar as compared to the dorsal EDR comes from a study performed by Sorgatz (1978) whose 80 participants underwent a monotonous task with relatively low requirement for muscular activity. The crossproduct matrix of the SZRs[23] from all 24 trials was factor analyzed. Eighty percent of the dorsal SZR variance could be explained by one component, while two components were necessary to explain the same proportion of the palmar SZR variance. Using the same technique, Sorgatz and Pufe (1978)

---

[22] Presenting 1 kHz tones between 80 and 120 dB intensity, in steps of 10 dB.

[23] Recorded with 32 Hz and 8 µA via 1 cm² Ag electrodes, using paper soaked with 0.5% NaCl as an electrolyte, dorsal from the first and third finger, and palmar from the second and fourth finger of the nondominant hand.

recorded palmar and dorsal SZR from 36 participants during aversive and neutral stimulation. Electric shocks and slides displaying skin diseases served as aversive stimuli, while light flashes and cartoon slides were used as neutral stimuli, all of them being presented in counterbalanced sequence with ISIs of either 10 or 20 s. Under the electric shock condition, palmar SZR amp. were increased as compared to light flashes during anticipation, while dorsal SZR amp. were higher following the shocks. Inverse palmar/dorsal relationships appeared under the slide conditions, thus rendering a simple interpretation in terms of OR vs. DR not very likely.

Turpin, Schaefer, and Boucsein (1999) systematically investigated effects of stimulus intensity, duration, and rise time on ANS and behavioral components of ORs, DRs, and startle responses. Sixty participants (27 females, 33 males) were randomly assigned to one of six experimental groups. Each participant received 15 presentations of a white noise stimulus over loudspeakers placed 1.5 m in front of the participants (mean ISIs 45 s, range 30–60 s). Stimulus intensity was either 60 or 100 dB against a background noise level of 20 dB. An incomplete factorial design was applied with stimulus durations of 1 vs. 5 s with 5 vs. 200 ms rise time each for the 100 dB intensity groups, and the same rise times but only 1 s duration for the 60 dB intensity groups. In each group, a 100 Hz tone with corresponding intensity, duration, and rise time was presented as dishabituation stimulus 30 s after the last stimulus in the series. Heart rate and SC[24] were recorded and behavioral correlates of ORs, DRs, and startle responses were obtained by blind ratings from a videotape, based loosely on the notion of primary and secondary startle responses (Landis & Hunt, 1939) together with behavior categories identified by Ekman, Friesen, and Simons (1985). Results from the manipulation of stimulus intensity and rise time endorsed several classical distinctions between OR on one side and DR and startle response, respectively, on the other side. The transition from 60 to 100 dB not only enhanced SCR amp. but also resulted in a HR shift from deceleration to acceleration, in greater frequencies of eyeblinks and in more head and body movements. Faster stimulus rise times elicited higher SCR amp., larger initial accelerative HR response components and greater frequencies of eyeblinks as well as head and body movements, while slow rise times tended to demonstrate faster response habituation, particularly within the 60 dB conditions. Rise time effects were more likely to be observed when intensity was increased from 60 to 100 dB and duration fixed at 1 s, than when rise times were manipulated across the different durations (1 vs. 5 s) within the 100 dB groups. These effects were explained by Turpin et al. (1999) with regard to the influence of stimulus rise time on the transition from OR to startle response: as rise time is shortened together with increases in stimulus intensity, such a transition is reflected in larger EDRs, a shift toward HR

---

[24] Recorded with standard methodology from the middle phalanges of the index and middle finger of the left hand. SCR amp. with latencies between 1 and 5 s after stimulus onset and an amplitude exceeding 0.02 μS were evaluated and log-transformed (Sect. 2.3.3.3).

acceleration and an overall increase in behavioral responding. Furthermore, effects of intensity and rise time tended to be additive because of the very few interactions obtained between these manipulations. Interestingly, fast rise times had the property to elicit startle responses even within the 60 dB conditions, and both ORs and startle responses could be observed at 100 dB, their relative presence being determined by stimulus rise time. The increase of stimulus duration from 1 to 5 s, which was only probed in the 100 dB condition, resulted in relatively fewer significant effects than either the rise time or intensity manipulations. There was only a trend for longer duration stimuli to elicit higher mean SCR amp. A dishabituation effect in EDRs could be observed as expected but was not significant. In general, EDR amp. can be expected to increase from OR-like to DR-like and startling stimuli, but differentiation between these types of responses might not be successful based on EDA recordings alone. Additional inspection of HR responses is advisable, which allows to distinguish between biphasic (OR) and monophasic (DR or startle) response pattern types, thus facilitating a multivariate approach which may also include recordings of finger pulse and cephalic pulse volume.

For an explanation of their observations, Turpin et al. (1999) considered the existence of two attentional systems as parsimonious: orienting which indicates engagement vs. startle which indicates disengagement. They hypothesized that orienting is concerned with such stimulus characteristics as novelty and moderate changes in stimulus intensities, whereas startle is elicited by stimuli with rapid rise times. As stimulus energy increases (i.e., the product of intensity and duration), stimuli with rapid rise times are more likely to elicit startle responses as opposed to ORs. In deviation to classical views, the authors did not regard it necessary to identify a third phasic component such as the DR at high stimulus intensities. As a matter of fact, startle has played a much more important role in recent contributions to the field as the traditional notion of the DR as postulated by Sokolov (1963b).

3.1.1.3 Electrodermal Indices of Habituation

According to the classical definition given by Humphrey (1933) and Harris (1943), *habituation* is characterized by decreasing response intensity with repeated stimulation. Habituation has also been regarded as the most elementary form of learning (e.g., Thorpe, 1969; Petrinovich, 1973) which may be reflected in different ways in various measures and/or parameters (Siddle, Stephenson, & Spinks, 1983). However, the OR cannot be regarded as an outcome of a learning process (Sokolov, 1963b). Therefore, a conceptual distinction has to be made between habituation and extinction (Sect. 3.1.2.1).

In experiments with humans, the EDR is the psychophysiological indicator of habituation most frequently used. This may be partly ascribed to the fact that a stimulus dependent EDR is easily detectable, and that the decrease of its amplitude over trials can be easily tracked by simple visual inspection. At first glance, it seems to be similarly easy to visually determine the time point at which the response is completely habituated as indicated by a total disappearance of the EDR.

However, criteria for "zero-responses" depend on properties of the recording device (e.g., the amplifier's signal-to-noise ratio; see Sect. 2.1.4) and on the resolution chosen for EDA recording, thus an a priori definition of an appropriate minimum amplitude criterion will be required (Sect. 2.3.1.2 "Choice of Amplitude Criteria").[25]

As already pointed out in the previous section, a repeated presentation of stimuli which elicit a DR should not result in habituation. In their dual-process theory, Groves and Thompson (1970) proposed a hypothetical *sensitization* process, which is held responsible for the appearance of a delayed or missing decrease of response strength with repeated stimulus presentation. The observed amplitude of the phasic OR is a result of two underlying hypothetical tonic processes, i.e., habituation and sensitization. The observable course of response amplitudes over trials is regarded being a result of the interaction of these processes. Thus, if sensitization prevails, an increase over trials will result, while a decrease of amplitude over trials reflects the preponderance of habituation. To avoid any reference to unknown hypothetical neuronal processes, Siddle, Stephenson, and Spinks (1983) proposed to prefer the term dishabituation over sensitization.[26] However, since the term dishabituation is already assigned to an increase in EDR amp. in response to the presentation of an already habituated stimulus after a OR reinstatement (Sect. 3.1.1), it should not be used for describing the process of increasing EDR amp. over trails as opposed to habituation as well.

Empirical evidence for nonhabituation of the electrodermal DR component comes from a study performed by Boucsein, Baltissen, and Euler (1984, Fig. 3), in which data taken from the Boucsein and Hoffmann (1979) experiment (Sect. 2.5.2.1 "Skin Conductance Responses") were reanalyzed. SCR amp. as well as level-dependency-corrected SRR amp. following 110 dB white noise stimuli yielded a marked sensitization effect.[27] Sensitization effects could also be unambiguously demonstrated in the Baltissen and Boucsein (1986) study which will be described in detail in Sect. 3.1.2.1 "UCR Diminution, Preception and Preparedness", where a group of participants received a series of 110 dB white noise stimuli of 2 s duration without warning.

---

[25] Providing such an amplitude criterion is also of fundamental significance for investigations into the so-called "below-zero" habituation (Thompson & Spencer, 1966), which also requires taking into account the sensitivity of the physiological system in question (Stephenson & Siddle, 1976). However, there is only weak evidence from studies with humans for an influence of the duration of "below-zero" habituation on the spontaneous recovery of an OR after being habituated (i.e., OR reinstatement; Siddle, Remington, Kuiack, & Haines 1983).

[26] Hölzl, Wilhelm, Lutzenberger, and Schandry (1975, Fig. 12) in their study described in Sect. 2.6.5 observed three types of SCR courses in their 28 participants. Most of them showed an exponential decrease over trials, a few "sensitizers" exhibited a slight increase, and some other "initial sensitizers" showed an increase followed by a considerable decrease.

[27] This result gives rise to the hitherto unanswered question of the adequate unit of measurement in EDR habituation studies (Sect. 2.6.5). However, the habituation effects in this study may have been obscured by the fact that a counterbalanced presentation of different stimulus intensities had been applied. This is different from standard habituation series, which may have contributed to the marked dishabituation effects observed with the high-intensity stimuli.

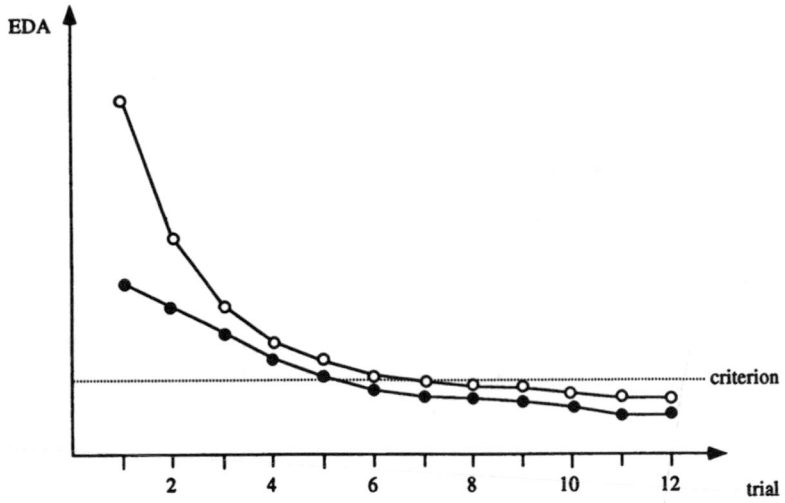

Fig. 3.1 Results of using different habituation indices. Parameters of the habituation course yield a fast habituation for the *empty dots* and a slow one for the *solid ones*. Parameters which determine the end of the habituation process by applying a minimum amplitude criterion would result in contrary results. From Schandry (1978), Fig. 3. Copyright 1978 by the author. Reprinted by his permission

Turpin and Siddle (1979), in their study described in the previous section, also observed an initial delay of habituation to their 105 dB white noise stimuli, though altogether the SCR amp. habituated over trials. Because of the differences observed in courses over trials, Walrath and Stern (1980) considered a quantitative differentiation between the courses of habituation for ORs and DRs being more adequate than the frequently claimed distinction between habituating and nonhabituating responses. Turpin et al. (1999), in their study described in the previous section, did not observe any nonhabituation even with their starling stimuli. In general, evidence for EDR amp. sensitization or nonhabituation from studies with humans is sparse.

It has already been mentioned that quantification of EDR habituation is less unequivocal as it seems at first glance. Figure 3.1 shows how the use of different habituation indices may lead to divergent results. In particular, the two concepts of habituation mentioned in the beginning of this section will have different implications for an appropriate quantification (Schandry, 1978):

1. If habituation is regarded as change (i.e., decrease in response over time), the parameter of interest will be the course of habituation, which is for example quantified by the steepness of the decrease of the habituation curve.
2. On the other hand, if habituation is regarded as a learning process (i.e., "learning not to respond," researchers will be interested in determining the completion of a habituation process, and the time (or number of trials) which is needed before no response can be observed any more will have to be ascertained as criterion.

Figure 3.1 illustrates how both forms of quantification may lead to contrary results, despite utilizing the same data set. Below, the most frequently used EDA parameters for determining either course or end of the habituation process will be discussed. Additional electrodermal habituation indices were described by Ben-Shakhar (1980) as well as by Hiroshige and Iwahara (1978). In principle, there are three different types of indices for describing the process of habituation:

1. Regression indices using the gradient of a curve that fits the empirical data, which is either a straight line or an exponential function of the habituation rate, the most well known of which is Lader and Wing's (1966) H score (see (3.1)).
2. Amplitude scores using the EDR amp. at a given point of the habituation curve for an ANOVA procedure (Siddle, Stephenson, & Spinks 1983). Alternatively, mean amplitudes or magnitudes (Sect. 2.3.4.2) of the whole habituation series are used as amplitude scores (O'Gorman, 1977).
3. Difference scores describing differences between the EDR amp. at two or more points within a habituation series, for example, the difference between the mean EDR amp. of the first and the last trial block[28] (Koriat, Averill, & Malmstrom, 1973). Frequently, those difference scores are formed by using interaction terms from the ANOVA (O'Gorman, 1977).

Since the course of habituation can be normally described by a negative exponential function of the response strength with increasing trial number (Thompson & Spencer, 1966), a decadic log transformation of the abscissa should be performed before forming regression indices as mentioned under (1), to obtain a linear relationship between number of trials and EDR amp. Afterwards, a regression of the EDR amp. on the log trial number is calculated starting from trial number 2. There are two indices that can be formed from this regression equation (Montagu, 1963): the gradient of the regression line b, and the y-intercept a. Normally, high negative correlations are obtained between a and b; individuals having larger EDRs during the first trials usually show a higher absolute value of the slope b which is used as a habituation index.

To obtain a habituation index independently of the initial EDR, the gradient b has to be corrected with respect to the ordinate value a, which is performed by the use of a regression (3.1), the result of which was labeled as b' by Montagu (1963) and as H by Lader and Wing (1966):

$$H = b - c(a - \bar{a}) \tag{3.1}$$

Here, b is the individual gradient of the regression from the response strength to the trial number, a is the individual ordinate value, $\bar{a}$ is the mean of the ordinate values across all individuals, and c is the regression of the gradient coefficient b on the values of a. The index H is an estimation of the absolute rate of habituation,

---

[28] Many authors combine two or more trials forming a trial block when reporting habituation courses.

assuming that the y-intercept is a constant (e.g., comparable to a sample mean). Therefore, the appropriate calculation corresponds to the use of covariance analytic techniques in inferential statistics.

Koriat et al. (1973) pointed out that the calculation of b' (i.e., H) values is only justified if different processes can be assumed underlying a and b, which implies that their interrelation can be regarded as being artificial. An additional problem arises if the procedure is applied to experimental groups differing a priori in their y-(ordinate-)intercept a, such as groups formed by an organismic variable like age or sex. In that case, the regression measure according to (3.1) may be obscured. Overall and Woodward (1977) deliberately precluded applying analysis of covariance procedures in cases where a significant correlation between an experimental condition and the covariate (in this case, the y-intercept a) is to be expected.[29]

If the course of habituation is described using amplitude scores as mentioned under (2), differences in habituation speed or in habituation rate are determined by means of the interaction between experimental condition and trial number. Therefore, individual measures of habituation speed cannot be obtained by this type of index. Instead, it enables the comparison of effects for different experimental conditions on the course of EDR amp. over trials. However, that particular technique becomes insensitive with an increasing number of trials, since all experimental groups will reach stable low EDR amp. with a large number of trials. Hence, this problem may be circumvented by including only the first part of trials in ANOVA, which however requires an a priori formulation of reasons for that particular choice. An amplitude measure sometimes used to quantify the amount of habituation is the mean EDR amp. or – if "zero responses" are included – the mean EDR magnitude (Sect. 2.3.4.2), averaged over all trials (Siddle & Heron, 1976; Vossel & Roßmann, 1982). Such a measure does not provide any specific information concerning the change of EDR amp. over time. It is simply assumed that responses showing a lower EDR amp. or "zero responses" during late trials contribute to an overall lower mean amplitude or magnitude. However, individuals showing rather low EDR amp. already during the first trials will also yield a strong habituation index, even if they showed an increase in EDR amp. over trials. Therefore, an overall mean amplitude or magnitude has to be questioned seriously as being a valid index of habituation. This is also pointed out by Siddle, Stephenson, and Spinks (1983), stating that the average magnitude measure confounds individual differences in amplitudes and habituation course.

---

[29] For example, if significantly smaller values for a as well as for b are observed in a group with older participants as compared to a younger group, and if the age effects on the ordinate value a and on the gradient b are independent of each other as well as of the correlation between a and b, the correction of the gradient b according to (3.1), taking into account the ordinate value a, will lead to a reduction of the "independent" age effect on gradient b. In general, it must be regarded as difficult to determine the relative influence of experimental conditions or somatic variables like age and gender on values of a and b. Therefore, if those conditions have a significant influence on a, corrections according to (3.1) should be avoided.

Calculating mean amplitude scores is further questioned by results of several studies. Siddle and Heron (1976) obtained only relatively low 3–5 month reliabilities (between $r = 0.26$ and $r = 0.66$) of mean amplitude scores, and correlations to a criterion measure of habituation were as low as $r = -0.06$ and $r = -0.23$, those to the H-score being also not higher than $r = 0.08$ to $r = 0.47$.[30] In turn, high positive correlations between $r = 0.63$ and $r = 0.76$ were obtained with the ordinate value a of the regression curve. Vossel and Roßmann (1982) also reported a correlation of $r = 0.86$ between a and the mean EDR magnitude. As opposed to Siddle and Heron (1976), they obtained a positive correlation of $r = 0.32$ to a habituation criterion measure, but a similar correlation of $r = 0.46$ to the H-score. The relatively high correlations between the mean EDR magnitude and the EDR amp. following the first stimulus as obtained by these authors point to the mean amplitudes being considerably determined by the initial OR. Thus, neither adding valuable information nor really describing the course of habituation properly, mean EDR amp. or magnitude measures cannot be recommended.

Difference scores of type (3) describing the habituation process are also dependent on the value of the initial OR, especially if the amplitudes of the first and last trial are included. Individuals or groups showing a high initial EDR amp. would yield a higher habituation rate, even if their responses to the other trials showed no differences to participants having lower initial ORs.

According to O'Gorman (1977), difference scores are mainly used to compare groups of participants. In that sense, the interaction term as mentioned above under (2), taken from ANOVA using repeated measures over trials, is comparable to the interaction term in an ANCOVA using difference scores (Huck & McLean, 1975).

Difference indices can also be obtained as an individual characteristic (Koriat et al., 1973; Lader, 1964; Vossel & Roßmann, 1982). Correlations between H-scores and these difference scores have been found to be negative (between $r = -0.21$ and -0.51). Difference scores correlate negatively with the regression slope b ($r = -0.90$ to -0.94) and positively with the ordinate values a ($r = 0.80–0.90$). This leads to the conclusion that difference scores do not provide essential information beyond the regression indices mentioned under (1); however, they may as well be used as an alternative to those measures of the habituation process.

A special difference index to be applied to each individual participant of a study has been proposed by Gruzelier (1973). He used only the first section of a habituation series in which the decrease in amplitude approximates an exponential curve, dropping the second part in which a visual inspection yields a more random individual course. The first section was divided into two halves and the mean EDR amp. of each one was calculated. The difference between both served as an index of the individual habituation course. Gruzelier (1973) as well as Gruzelier and Venables (1972) applied that index to obtain differential habituation in

---

[30] SCR recorded with standard methodology during the presentation of 1 kHz tones (70 or 90 dB). The signs from Siddle and Heron's (1976) Table 2 were inverted to make the directions of correlations comparable to each other.

schizophrenics and normal controls (Sect. 3.4.2.2) as well as in EDR lateralization studies (Sect. 3.1.4.2).

Instead of giving a description of its course, habituation is more frequently ascertained in terms of its duration. Determining the end of the process requires a criterion for "zero responses" (Fig. 2.23, Sect. 2.3.4.1). In this case, two different habituation measures can be formed:

1. One method is the use of *criterion measures*. The number of trials necessary or the time elapsed to reach the end of the habituation process (O'Gorman, 1977) is taken as a measure of habituation. Usually, the criterion consists of two or three consecutive trials eliciting "zero responses" (Siddle, Stephenson, & Spinks 1983).
2. A second method is to form a *frequency index*. Here, the number of trials which exceed the "zero response" is used as criterion. When this method is used, OR reinstatement which occurs after several trials of "zero responses" is accounted for, which is not the case when using the criterion method. Thompson, Groves, Teyler, and Roemer (1973) claimed that this procedure provides a more precise analysis of the underlying habituation process. They considered it being superior to the method of inspecting the amplitude changes over trials (see, however, O'Gorman, 1977 for a contrary position on this matter).

The overall high correlations between criterion and frequency measures of habituation seem to point to the possibility that both may be describing a similar aspect of the habituation phenomenon (i.e., trials to habituation). For example, Coles, Gale, and Kline (1971) presented 60 participants with a series of 20 stimuli[31] and obtained a correlation of $r = 0.92$ between both types of measures. A similar correlation of $r = 0.94$ was reported by Vossel and Roßmann (1982). However, in some instances, criterion and frequency measures may generate different results as shown by Zahn, Carpenter, and McGlashan (1981a) in schizophrenic samples (Sect. 3.4.2.2).

Both measures seem to be influenced by individual differences in tonic EDA, since several studies reported significant positive correlations to NS.EDR freq. between $r = 0.44$ and $r = 0.75$ (e.g., Coles et al., 1971; Crider & Lunn, 1971; Martin & Rust, 1976; Siddle & Heron, 1976; Vossel & Roßmann, 1982). Therefore, Crider and Lunn (1971) suggested that speed of habituation (as indicated by either measure) and spontaneous fluctuations of EDA should be treated as interchangeable, which is however not justified since the mean common variance explained over studies is only approximately 36%.

In addition, the criterion measure is likely not to be independent of the initial amplitude in the series, which seems obvious since the decline of a large response is likely to require more trials than the decline of a small initial response. For example, Nebylitsyn (1973) reported a correlation of $r = 0.68$ between the EDR amp. within the first trial and the number of trials until the habituation criterion was reached.

---

[31] 1 KHz, 65 dB, 5 s duration tone. EDA was recorded as SR with 1 cm^2 Ag/AgCl electrodes and NaCl paste, using 11 μA current, transformed into log SC units.

Furthermore, Coles et al. (1971) in their above-mentioned study observed inverse relationships between SCR lat. following the first stimulus and the criterion measure ($r = -0.58$) as well as the frequency measure of habituation ($r = -0.67$).

Reliabilities of the frequently used criterion measures are only moderately high. O'Gorman (1974) reported coefficients between $r = 0.55$ and $r = 0.75$ from several studies that used intervals between 1 week and 3 months. Similar coefficients were obtained by Siddle and Heron (1976) over 3–5 months from 37 participants, where their criterion index[32] yielded retest reliabilities between $r = 0.47$ and $r = 0.56$.

Electrodermal habituation indices referring to the end of the process seem to be relatively independent of indices of habituation course, thus indicating different aspects of the phenomenon. This could be demonstrated by Spinks (1977, after Siddle, Stephenson, & Spinks, 1983) in a factor-analytic study with 45 participants, where both types of parameters yielded their highest loadings in different factors. It would be desirable if one could refer to theories which allow precise selection of the appropriate measure (Koriat et al., 1973). However, the hitherto available theories do not explain the apparent dependency of EDA habituation on the initial EDR amp. (Siddle, Stephenson, & Spinks 1983). Therefore, range correction of EDRs in a habituation series should be taken into consideration using the initial OR as the maximum response (Sect. 2.3.3.4 "Range Corrections").

Levinson and Edelberg (1985) could show that the use of large time windows may result in a misclassification of spontaneous EDRs as being stimulus dependent (Sect. 2.3.2.2), thus invalidating habituation indices. Therefore, these authors proposed the application of relatively small windows (1.0–2.4 s after stimulus onset), probably using the latencies to the first stimulus taken from all study participants to determine the window's upper limit. They also recommended the use of not more than two "zero responses" in sequence as habituation criterion.

Barry (1990) in his investigation of the relationship between time windows and the end of habituation came to a similar conclusion. In comparing EDR magnitudes which were evaluated during time windows of 1–3 and 1–5 s after stimulus onset, he found only small differences in the course of the habituation process. Additional comparisons using criteria of two vs. three successive "zero responses" yielded the most pronounced habituation when combining the narrow time window with the low-number "zero response" criterion.

Evaluation of electrodermal habituation should consider significant correlations of various habituation indices to the NS.SCR freq. For criterion as well as frequency measures, those are between $r = 0.52$ and $r = 0.67$ (Martin & Rust, 1976; Siddle & Heron, 1976; Vossel & Roßmann, 1982); for the index of mean amplitude between $r = 0.41$ and $r = 0.56$ (Bull & Gale, 1973; Martin & Rust, 1976); and for the H-score between $r = 0.47$ and $r = 0.77$ (Lader, 1964; Lader & Wing, 1966; Siddle & Heron, 1976). Correlations between the regression coefficient b and NS.SCR freq. are

---

[32] Three successive SCRs recorded with standard methodology, showing SCR amp. below 0.02 µS.

considerably lower ($r = 0.19$–0.32; Martin & Rust, 1976; Siddle & Heron, 1976), and the y-intercept is uncorrelated with spontaneous EDA (Siddle & Heron, 1976).

Because of the relatively close interrelations between spontaneous EDA and various habituation parameters, Crider and Lunn (1971) suggested habituation speed (as obtained by criterion measures) and NS.SCR freq. being indices of a common dimension of "electrodermal lability" (Sect. 3.3.2.2). However, the mean common variance has been found not exceeding 55% (Vossel & Roßmann, 1982). On the other hand, Martin and Rust (1976), as a result of a factor-analytic study that used various EDA parameters including several habituation indices, pointed to the possible existence of a common factor which could be labeled "general reactivity."

When taking into consideration concepts like "general reactivity" or "electro-dermal lability" in the discussion of habituation processes, there is a noticeable missing link based on possible structural, physiological, and biochemical factors. Therefore, correlations may be simply determined by peripheral factors, the influence of which has been discussed in detail by Lykken, Miller, and Strahan (1966) as well as Lykken and Venables (1971). These authors recommended a range correction (Sect. 2.3.3.4 "Range Corrections"), as already mentioned above, the advantages and disadvantages of which for habituation studies were discussed by Siddle, Turpin, Spinks, and Stephenson (1980). In general, theories which try to explain the habituation phenomenon do not specifically address the idiosyncratic characteristics of the electrodermal system. Attempts to model the habituation of ORs along more cognitive lines (Sect. 3.1.3.2) have not yet been proved sufficiently.

3.1.2   Conditioning of Electrodermal Responses

Though integrated in most learning instances, the two forms of classical and instrumental (or "operant") conditioning are presented separately for theoretical and experimental purposes. With respect to EDA, that distinction parallels the one between stimulus specific EDRs (Sect. 2.3.1) and NS.EDRs, which cannot be easily separated in each case (Fig. 2.20, Sect. 2.3.2.2). Hence, separating EDR components with respect to the specific vs. nonspecific distinction is focused on within the following sections. A special application of EDA measures that emerged from instrumental conditioning (Sect. 3.1.2.2) is the use of EDA in biofeedback (Sect. 3.1.2.3).

3.1.2.1   Classical Conditioning of Electrodermal Responses in Humans

In this experimental paradigm (that has been employed by experimental psychologists since the 1930s), humans are presented with repeated pairings of a conditional stimulus (CS) like a weak light or tone with an unconditional stimulus (UCS) like an electric shock or noise loud enough (over 100 dB) to be aversive. Because of ethical restrictions the UCSs, although aversive, are so lacking in intensity or impact that for many individuals these repeated CS–UCS acquisition trials can result in decrease of general arousal due to boredom. Habituation (i.e., decrease in responding over repeated stimulus trials) can occur even to the "aversive" shock or loud-noise UCS.[33]

To demonstrate that the conditional response (CR) is really dependent on the CS–UCS coupling, two different approaches may be used. The between-subjects design compares two groups of participants, one receiving contingent CS–UCS pairings, while the other group is exposed to the same stimuli in random order. This random-order control is used if one accepts that the cognitive contingency account (e.g., Rescorla, 1967) applies to the electrodermal conditional response (ED-CR). Otherwise, in the control group, the CS and UCS are "explicitly unpaired," with a time of at least 20 s between the CS and the next UCS.

In a within-subjects design each participant serves as her/his own control, insofar as responses to the solely presented neutral stimuli (CS–) are compared to responses to conditional stimuli (CS+) which are followed by an UCS. Differential conditioning is said to have occurred only if the CR following the CS+ is significantly higher than to the CS– during the extinction period.[34]

Cognitive vs. Noncognitive View of EDR Conditioning

The classical conditioning of (human) electrodermal responses (EDRs) has been significantly affected by the "paradigm shift" (Segal & Lachman, 1972) to what is known as the "cognitive" approach, or a shift from "the learning of a response" to "the processing of propositional information" (Furedy & Riley, 1987, p. 1). Good examples of how this shift has affected the currently dominant interpretation of classical (or Pavlovian) EDR conditioning are provided by widely cited papers by Grings and Dawson (1973) and by Prokasy and Kumpfer (1973).

According to these authors, the conditional EDR reflects only the human learning of the (propositional) relationship or, in the terms Tolman would have used,

---

[33] The author thanks Professor John J. Furedy for his contributions to this section, especially to its historical part.

[34] The problems with this design, from the perspective of the cognitive contingency paradigm, are discussed in detail by Grings, Givens, and Carey (1979), Rescorla (1967), and Seligman (1969). However, from a consideration of the first fact regarding EDR conditioning, noted below, these methodological problems do not apply to the within-subjects, differential conditioning design. The practical advantage of this design is its greater sensitivity, which is important for the EDR conditioning phenomenon. If a between-subjects design is used, the conditioning/control difference requires about 20 or more participants just to obtain the basic conditioning phenomenon at the 0.05 level of significance within humans, partly because the aversive UCS (shock or noise) has to be kept at relatively mild levels for ethical reasons. This practical advantage is much less important in the older human eyelid conditioning preparation (for an account, see Kimble, 1961), which is more robust and allows observation of gradually increasing acquisition functions over as many as 100 trials; this preparation has mostly used the between-subjects design.

the "sign-significate relation" or *contingency* (Rescorla, 1967) relationship between the CS and the UCS. In other words, in this "relational learning" interpretation, the EDR conditional response is viewed as a CS–UCS contingency analyzer. As was detailed by Furedy and Riley (1987), an important feature of this cognitive approach is that what is learned is a *propositional* psychological function, and the distinction between truth and falsity can be meaningfully applied to it. This form of learning is thus rational in the sense that it is based on propositions the true value of which can be objectively assessed.

Before psychology's "cognitive revolution," the prevailing stimulus-response (S–R) paradigm for the CR was that what was learned was not the (propositional, rationally analyzable) relation between the CS and the UCS, but rather an irrational and nonpropositional *response* to the CS, a response which had previously been elicited (unconditionally) by the UCS. Irrational is an appropriate term because the true/false category is not applicable to responses to stimuli (whereas it is to propositional beliefs about the relation between stimuli). Moreover, given that the UCS in these human experiments has almost always been aversive (shock and loud noises) rather than appetitive (e.g., Furedy, 1967), EDR conditioning was often referred to as the conditioning of the emotional (irrational) response of fear, with fear being defined ("operationally") as the conditionable component of the UR of pain elicited by the UCS. What was learned during conditioning, moreover, was thought to be stimulus substitution, with the CS coming to elicit, through training, a component of the UR elicited by the UCS.

It will be noted that this irrational, fear-conditioning view of the ED-CR is consistent with the neurotic phenomenon of phobias (of which more in Sect. 3.4.1.1). Phobias are conceived of as irrational fear responses which are not justifiable in terms of the actual dangers. A laboratory analog of this sort of irrational or "neurotic" fear is the phenomenon of the CS-elicited EDR failing to extinguish when the UCS no longer follows the CS (known as Pavlovian extinction), even though humans participating in a study are clearly aware that this extinction period has begun (for a recent focus on extinction in EDR conditioning, see Furedy, Damke, & Boucsein, 2000).

Perhaps the most thoroughgoing application of the S–R paradigm to classical EDR conditioning was the contiguity-reinforcement theory (Jones, 1962). The so-called "backward" conditioning phenomenon (Champion & Jones, 1961; Furedy, Arabian, Thiels, & George, 1982) was considered the most important. In this phenomenon, there is evidence for conditioning with UCS onset *preceding* CS onset by 500 ms. Because of the EDR's relatively long onset latency (more than 1 s), UR onset *follows* CS onset. From an S–R perspective, this constitutes forward conditioning. From a cognitive paradigmatic perspective, however, no conditioning should occur, since the CS must *precede* the UCS in order to be a signal for it.

It is a feature of any paradigmatic approach that contrary facts are often ignored. As Furedy and Riley (1987) detailed, the ignoring of contrary, well established or "brute facts" (Maze, 1983) was just as much a feature of the era in psychology when the Hull-Spence S–R paradigm was dominant as it has been in the current "cognitive" era. The S–R equivalent of the Segal and Lachman (1972) paradigmatic defense of the current information-processing approach is a widely cited paper by Kendler (1952) which argued that what was then the central question for experimental psychologists ("what is learned") was not an empirical question but rather one of "modern methodology" or paradigm preference. The much less widely cited refutation of Kendler's position by Ritchie (1953), which ridiculed Kender's attempt to "circumnavigate" the fact of cognition, fell largely on deaf ears at a time when the dominant scientific paradigm was an S–R one.

The currently dominant paradigm (since the 1970s) in classical EDR conditioning has been the "cognitive" approach. The following review of the literature will reflect this dominance not only in terms of the interpretations offered but also in the choice of parameters chosen by experimenters who have employed this paradigm. One such choice is the lengthening of the CS–UCS interval from about 1 s to about 8 s. From a cognitive paradigmatic perspective, this lengthening should not matter much, given that what is learned is the propositional sign-significate relation between the CS (sign) and the UCS (significate). However, from an S–R perspective the shortness of the CS–UCS interval is critical for maximizing EDR conditioning (for the EDR, see, e.g., Jones, 1962; for the well-documented human eyelid conditioning procedure, the "short half second" was so critical that CS–UCS intervals of 2 s produced no conditioning and could be considered to be a control condition). This is empirically important because the EDR conditioning phenomenon itself is less than robust in humans with UCSs-like electric shocks having to be relatively weak[35] – the procedure requires at least 20 participants to reliably obtain significant differences between the CS associated with the UCS (CS+) and the control CS not so associated (CS–). On the other hand, the lengthening purportedly allows separation of components of the response elicited by the CS before UCS onset, components like the initial OR and the "true" conditional response (see, e.g., Stewart, Stern, Fredman, & Winokur, 1960; Prokasy & Kumpfer, 1973).

Nevertheless, there are certain facts concerning the actual behavior of the ED-CR which do not get much current attention, but which are both well established and which will remain relevant to those working with this procedure regardless of what paradigm enjoys current dominance. To use Maze's (1983) terminology, these are "brute facts" which are true and independent of current (expert) opinion. Before moving to a current review of the literature on human classical EDR conditioning, a literature that is almost exclusively dominated by the cognitive, information-processing paradigm (for an exception see Furedy et al., 2000), three of these facts will be briefly summarized.

---

[35] For ethical reasons, it came into use in the recent practice of aversive EDR conditioners to have participants set their own level of UCS intensity, rather than the older practice of the experimenter setting UCS intensity for all participants. This practice reduces the robustness of the ED-CR phenomenon, as well as making it more difficult to vary UCS intensity itself, which used to be one of the basic independent variables of human eyelid conditioning (Spence, Haggard, & Ross, 1958), seldom if ever appears in current human EDR conditioning papers.

The first fact is that the ED-CR (defined as a relative increase in CS-elicited responding that is due to the association of the CS with the UCS) is totally insensitive to an independent variable that Rescorla (1967, 1969, 1988), who is arguably the cognitive paradigm's most influential authority on classical conditioning, has identified as critical for the understanding of classical or Pavlovian conditioning. This variable is the difference between what Rescola called an "explicitly unpaired" CS (euCS) which he considered to produce conditioned inhibition and a "truly random" CS (trCS) which is considered to produce no conditioning, and is hence was claimed to be the "proper control" (Rescorla, 1967) for all classical conditioning. This euCS/trCS difference may emerge in many conditioning procedures and hence may also constitute evidence for conditioned inhibition (Rescorla, 1969). However, by the early 1970s a number of papers investigating the ED-CR preparation (Furedy & Schiffman, 1971, 1973, 1974; Schiffmann & Furedy, 1972) showed that the (human) ED-CR was totally insensitive to this euCS/trCS difference. These experiments ranged over a number of CS–UCS intervals, of which some were long enough to separate the so-called merely orienting ORs from "true" CRs (Stewart et al., 1960). The experiments also included both between-subjects designs (where CS+ and the control CSs were given to three separate groups of participants) and (the more sensitive and more frequently used procedure for EDR conditioning) within-subjects discrimination-conditioning designs, where each participant receives both the CS+ and either the random or unpaired control CS. In addition, these studies showed that the participants' (propositional) knowledge of the CS/UCS contingencies, as indexed by "subjective contingency," was highly sensitive to the contingency differences that the cognitive, contingency paradigm considers, following Rescorla (1967, 1969) and Prokasy and Kumpfer (1973), to be crucial for EDR conditioning. It is worth emphasis that subjective contingency measures what the participant *actually* knows about the CS/UCS contingencies, rather than modeling what the participant is *assumed* to know.

The second fact bears more directly on the cognitive paradigm's central claim concerning human EDR conditioning: that it is solely caused by the human participant's coming to learn a proposition about the contingency between the CS and the UCS. The very strong causal claim that A is the main cause of B requires, as an absolute minimum, evidence that A and B are strongly correlated. Yet the above-mentioned experiments of the 1970s (Furedy & Schiffman, 1971, 1973, 1974) indicate that the correlations between subjective contingency (purportedly the main cause) and the ED-CR (purportedly the effect) were not only not high (say $r = 0.80$ or above), but also failed consistently even to reach statistical significance.

The third fact concerns a feature of the EDR which differentiates it from other responses used to index conditioning such as the eyelid response or even the original Pavlovian salivary response. This feature is often referred to as the "neutrality" of the CS before conditioning occurs. The eyelid and salivary conditioning procedures do have such a "neutral" CS, inasmuch as there is no blinking (above spontaneous, "operant" levels) to the tone, or salivation to the bell, before these CSs have been associated with the loud noise or food UCS. In contrast, there are no such "neutral" stimuli for the EDR, which certainly is elicited by the tone or light CSs prior to the association of these CSs with the UCS. The existence of this third fact (that the ED-CR has no "neutral" CS before conditioning proceeds) means that the definition of classical EDR conditioning cannot include the restrictive and false requirement of CS neutrality. Rather, as stated above, definition must be in terms of a relative increase in responding to the CS due to its association with the UCS that is provided by the CS–UCS trials of classical conditioning.

Within the cognitive paradigm, the accepted view of classical EDR conditioning is nicely summarized in papers by Grings and Dawson (1973) and by Prokasy and Kumpfer (1973). One of the assumptions of this approach is that it is possible to assure that the CS is neutral (i.e., does not elicit an EDR) before conditioning. This assumption ignores what was referred to as the third fact above – that for the EDR, the CS is not "neutral." One way of trying to achieve this electrodermal "neutrality" has been to expose participating individuals to a CS series prior to the conditioning trials, to allow the OR following the CS to habituate. One problem with this procedure is that it requires total habituation (i.e., no responding) for real "neutrality," and this means that for the odd participant there may be a very large number of these preexposed CS-alone trials. In addition to practical difficulties, this would diminish the standardization of the procedure, which should be the same for all participants. Additionally, however, this preexposure to the CS is also a condition that should, in terms of the cognitive paradigm, produce a latent inhibition to the CS: a CS presented several times without being followed by the unconditioned stimulus (UCS) gains properties of a CS− (i.e., a stimulus that indicates that no UCS will follow). In this sense a CS− cannot be associated to an UCS as easily as a nonpresented CS could be. Although this inhibition could be demonstrated in several animal studies (e.g., Wagner, 1969), it has not been unambiguously seen in human classical conditioning studies (for a review, see Siddle & Remington, 1987). Of course, in the light of the first fact stated above and the evidence from the experiments reported in the early 1970s discussed above, one would not expect any of this sort of inhibition to occur in the human EDR, which has been shown to be insensitive to the conditioned inhibition (e.g., Rescorla, 1969) independent variable. The reason why animal studies have shown this evidence may be that these do reflect the human individual's learning of the propositional relationship between the CS (sign) and the UCS (significate) and is a form of what Gormezano & Kehoe (1975) have called a CS-IR (i.e., conditioned stimulus-instrumental response) rather than a CS-CR paradigm.

Components of EDR Conditioning

Since the 1960s, most researchers into human classical electrodermal conditioning have maintained that there are two separate EDR components in the CS–UCS interval (Stewart, Stern, Winokur, & Fredman, 1961). These researchers, instead of scoring a single peak EDR within this interval (e.g., Bitterman & Holtzman, 1952), have used

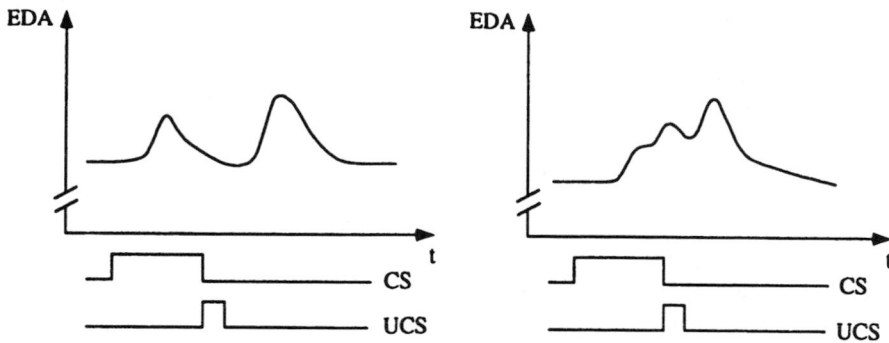

Fig. 3.2 Typical course of an EDR during classical conditioning in the first trial (*left-hand panel*) and after several CS–UCS pairings (*right-hand panel*). From Grings (1969), Fig. 1. Copyright 1969 by the Society for Psychophysiological Research. Reprinted by permission of the publisher and the author

an ISI between CS onset and UCS onset of at least 8 s and have identified two components that both occur before UCS onset.

Figure 3.2 shows a typical development of the EDR in the course of CS–UCS pairings, on the left-hand panel during the first CS–UCS presentation and on the right-hand panel after several trials. Nevertheless, most EDRs show an overlapping form in the CS–UCS interval as depicted in the right-hand panel of Fig. 3.2 (Grings, 1969). In the analysis and interpretation of those EDRs the question arises to what extent these single components may be separated (Sect. 2.3.1.2 "Amplitudes of Exosomatic Responses Recorded with Direct Current"). This is necessary to analyze how those components vary with experimental conditions. In addition there might be anticipatory responses to an expected UCS especially during long ISIs. To differentiate those components, Prokasy and Ebel (1967) ran a conditioning experiment with 121 participants. They presented an 8-s 1 kHz tone CS with an intensity of 75 or 100 dB, and a 0.2-s electric shock as UCS. The authors were able to distinguish three different kinds of EDRs[36] with respect to their latencies:

1. A first-interval anticipatory response (FIR), starting within 1.35–4.95 s after CS onset
2. A second-interval anticipatory response (SIR);[37] with a latency between 4.95 and 9.53 s after CS onset
3. A third-interval unconditioned response (TUR), which should be unambiguously elicited by the UCS, starting between 9.53 and 14.55 s after CS onset

   Since Prokasy and Ebel did not find correlations between FIR and SIR, they concluded that both were independent responses rather than two components of

---

[36] Electrodermal recording has been described as being taken from the left index finger and the right palm with a Fels dermohmeter.

[37] Formerly abbreviated as FAR and SAR, respectively.

a single response.[38] In addition to these three terms, Prokasy and Kumpfer (1973) introduced another term for EDRs appearing when the CS was presented without UCS (i.e., in the extinction phase, unless one employs a partial reinforcement schedule during acquisition, so that, even during acquisition, a few CS+ trials are presented without a following UCS):

4. A third-interval omission response (TOR); which appears in the same time window as the TUR to the omitted UCS.

Since the FIR appears within the time window for an EDR following the CS (Sect. 2.3.1.1), it is likely to be interpreted as an OR to the CS. This view is supported by the FIR amplitude often showing an exponential decrease over trials, which indicates habituation (Graham, 1973). On the other hand, the human EDR often habituates not only to the CS that is coupled with the UCS, but also to the UCS itself.

Still, sometimes an increase of the FIR during the first trials can be observed, the FIR amplitude reaching its maximum when the individual becomes aware of the CS–UCS contingency. This awareness occurs early during acquisition among normal humans, unless the CS–UCS contingency is masked. According to Zeiner (1970), this phenomenon may be traced back to the CS habituation series preceding the CS–UCS presentation as described above. Since normally only one or two stimuli are used as CS during classical conditioning, the CS–UCS contingency is recognized immediately, which explains the rapid decrease of FIR amplitudes during the early trials. If the trials are preceded by a CS habituation series, a delay in contingency recognition is likely to appear, and an initial change in expectation (CS alone vs. CS–UCS coupling) leads to an increase of FIR amplitudes (Maltzman, Raskin, & Wolff, 1979). Of course if one steps outside the cognitive, contingency paradigm, then this delay in contingency recognition may be a function of boredom with the experiment, where meaningless CS-alone trials are being presented at intervals of at least 30 s between CSs in the typical EDR conditioning experiment.

---

[38] This argument may be questioned, based on findings obtained by Furedy and Scull (1971). They observed what they called a "relative refractory period" of at least 20 s for an EDR. However, in the present author's view, this term could be misleading, since its physiological meaning refers to nerve discharge in time windows of millisecond duration. Instead, the observed phenomena might be discussed in terms of relationships between EDR amp. following each other in short sequence (Sects. 2.3.1.5 and 2.5.2.5). A decrease of SCR amp. with shortening the ISI of average 20 s length by 50% was recently observed by Breska, Maoz, and Ben-Shakhar (2011), in their study mentioned in Footnote 58, Sect. 2.3.1.5. Since the ISIs used in classical conditioning are even much shorter, the logical consequence would be that the larger the FIR, the smaller the following (by about 4 s) SIR, a factor which would contribute a negative correlation between FIR and SIR. On the other hand, in terms of trial-to-trial variation, one would expect a positive correlation between FIR and SIR. Accordingly, the sum of these two opposing factors may produce a zero correlation which does not necessarily indicate real independence between FIR and SIR. The eyelid conditioning case is different, as in this paradigm a clear independence between FIR (called alpha response) and SIR (called and scored as the true CR) is demonstrated inasmuch as the former *decreases* as a function of repeated CS–UCS trials (habituation), whereas the latter *increases* (CR acquisition).

Öhman (1971) demonstrated that the FIR also fulfills another important criterion of an OR; it is susceptible to novelty. In an aversive conditioning study, all 40 participants received a 70 dB tone with a frequency of 3 kHz during a training period. During the test period, tones with 200, 500, and 1,200 Hz were presented as CSs. In the conditioning and the control groups (without CS–UCS coupling), a direct association appeared between the FIR (measured as SCR using standard methodology) following the novel stimulus and the difference between frequencies of training and test stimuli.

As opposed to the FIR, the SIR shows only a small amplitude at the beginning of conditioning (Dengerink & Taylor, 1971). The SIR also remains uninfluenced by CS properties (Orlebeke & van Olst, 1968) or by training trials prior to conditioning (Surwit & Poser, 1974). Instead, the SIR depends on the UCS quality and on the probability of its occurrence. Many results indicate that the SIR is more frequently conditioned if electric shocks are used as UCS instead of acoustic stimuli (Dengerink & Taylor, 1971). Thus the SIR may be regarded as a preparatory response while expecting the UCS.

The appearance of a TOR instead of a TUR during CS-alone extinction trials after subsequent CS–UCS coupling can be regarded as an OR to a stimulus change, i.e., the omission of the UCS (Öhman, 1983) eliciting an OR reinstatement (Sects. 3.1.1 and 3.1.1.3).[39] In terms of cognitive psychology, the TOR can be traced back to the discrepancy between an expected and a real stimulus situation. After the participants have learned to expect a specific UCS, changes in UCS appearance will be followed by a marked EDR. These perceptual disparity responses (Grings, 1960) presuppose a learned expectation of the UCS following the CS, which implies that an associative learning process is necessary for the TOR to occur.

In his information processing model of the OR, Öhman (1979) provided a theoretical interpretation for the different kinds of EDR during classical conditioning. The core of his model is the so-called expectancy loop, which is depicted in the central part of Fig. 3.3. The expectancy loop has access to information about certain features of the CS–UCS contingency being stored in the short-term memory (STM), such as qualitative and quantitative properties of the UCS and temporal relations between CS and UCS (i.e., ISI duration and variability). With regard to the ISI properties, the UCS occurrence is continuously checked; a process which is

---

[39] A very strong version of this "reinstated" OR was used (e.g., Stewart et al., 1961) to reject the short-interval ISI preparation as a demonstration of EDR conditioning, a preparation that required CS-alone test trials during acquisition to assess conditioning. The argument was that the EDRs to such CS-alone test trials were not CRs, but were merely "reinstated" ORs to stimulus change, rather than to classical EDR conditioning. Now it is true that marked stimulus change does increase the EDR, as in a crossmodal change following 15 repetitions (Furedy, 1968), and this could be reasonably referred to as the phenomenon of OR reinstatement. However, this change effect requires far greater quantitative and qualitative changes from repetition to change than are involved in CS-alone test trials during acquisition (CS–UCS pairings), so that the empirical evidence that supports the reinstated OR interpretation on UCS-omission trials is quite weak (Furedy & Poulos, 1977).

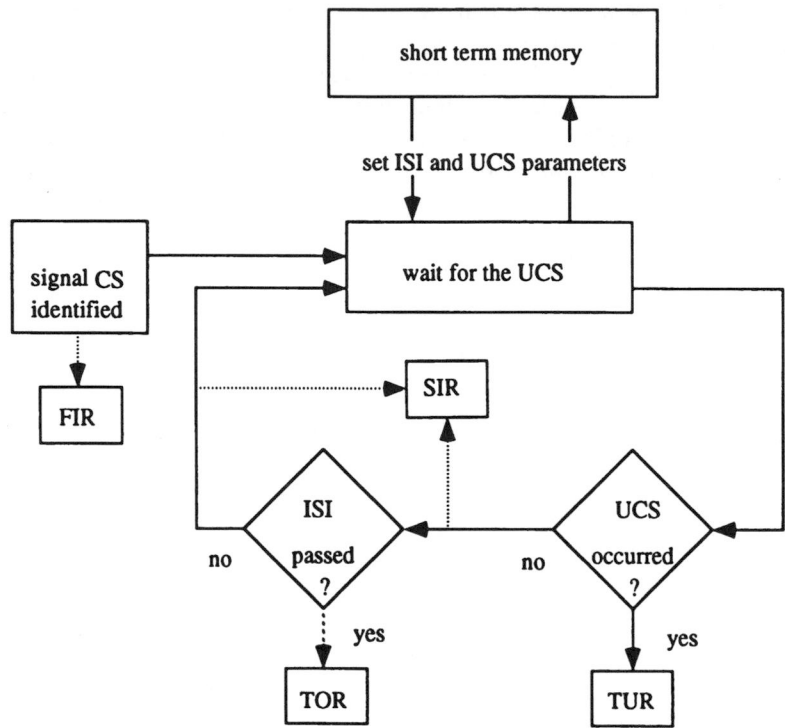

Fig. 3.3 Information processing model after Öhman (1979), Fig. 27.3. Copyright 1979 by the author. Used by his permission

indicated by the SIR. If the UCS does not occur in the expected time window (i.e., the learned ISI plus a psychophysically determined difference time threshold), a TOR is elicited. If an UCS occurs, a TUR is elicited. Although the differentiation between TOR and TUR looks theoretically sound, these terms fell out of use during recent decades. Instead, the term TIR (third-interval response), being proposed by Furedy and Schiffman (1971) as theoretically neutral, came widely to be used in the literature on classical conditioning.

The possibility that conscious cognitive processes are probably involved in classical conditioning was demonstrated by Dawson, Catania, Schell, and Grings (1979) in a study with 64 participants. They were presented different visual (colored lights) and auditory (tone) stimuli compounds during acquisition, and a certain stimulus combination served as CS+ for the subsequent shock-UCS pairings. All participants received information about the light-shock contingency, while half of them had additional information concerning the tone-shock combination.[40] Whereas the fully informed group exhibited conditioning to both visual and auditory CS+,

---

[40] EDRs were recorded as SRRs using standard methodology, however with K–Y gel.

the partially informed group showed conditioning only to the visual CS+ and to compounds which included the visual CS+. The authors concluded that classical conditioning is due to complex information processing comprising different stages. Among those enumerated were CS perception and recognition, memory of the UCS occurrence and encoding, along with the storage of this information at the end of each trial. The autonomic responses being observed in the classical conditioning procedure can be regarded as peripheral correlates of the outlined central cognitive processes.

In a subsequent experiment, Dawson, Schell, Beers, and Kelly (1982) demonstrated the importance of cognitive processes in classical conditioning, by using an RT task within the CS–UCS interval as an indicator of allocation of attentional resources. The CS was followed within 300–750 ms by a signal which the participants had to respond to. RT was significantly longer to the CS+ (signaling an electric shock) as compared to the CS–, which was interpreted by the authors as being due to the higher amount of attentional capacity used for CS+ processing (Sect. 3.1.3.2).

The hypothesis that cognitive processes are solely responsible for classical EDR conditioning (summarized by Dawson & Schell, 1987)[41] was questioned by Furedy and colleagues (Furedy & Schiffman, 1971, 1973; Furedy, Poulos, & Schiffman, 1975; for an overview see Furedy & Riley, 1987). Stimulated by the discussion on control groups within classical conditioning being elicited by Rescorla (1967), these authors investigated the connection between EDR and subjective awareness of CS–UCS contingency. They obtained a positive correlation between EDR amp. and the amount of awareness of the CS+ UCS contingency, which is in accordance with the hypothesis of Maltzman, Raskin, and Wolff (1979). However, significant differences between a randomly paired CS condition and a contingent nonreinforced (CS–) condition appeared exclusively in the expectation of the individuals (as measured by movement of a lever that indicated the individual's perception of the contingency relation between CS and UCS). In addition, there was a zero correlation between EDR and subjective contingency. Despite this, Furedy and Riley (1987) concluded from a large number of experiments that EDR conditioning is at least partly due to noncognitive response learning, even though knowledge of the CS–UCS contingency seems to be necessary for the acquisition

---

[41] The role of awareness in classical electrodermal conditioning has also been extensively discussed by Dawson and Schell (1985, pp. 107 f.). They compared the technique used in various studies of their own group and by other researchers, embedding CS–UCS pairings within a "masking task," with the method of CNS ablation studies, since the participant's attention and concern is effectively directed away from the learning task. During the 1970s, the Dawson group published seven separate experiments involving more than 300 participants using the same masking task (reporting colors of lights and position of tones). They all showed that CS–UCS pairings were not sufficient to establish differential autonomic conditioning unless participants were aware of the contingency, the most suitable measure of which was a short recognition post-conditioning questionnaire. Their conclusion was that controlled cognitive processes are necessary for human autonomic discrimination in classical conditioning (see also Sect. 3.1.3.2).

of EDR conditioning (Dawson & Furedy, 1976), although perhaps not for EDR extinction (Furedy et al., 2000).

For a quantitative investigation of the role of information processing in classical electrodermal conditioning, Kirsch, Boucsein, and Baltissen (1993) utilized conditional and non-aversive unconditional stimuli with varying amounts of information content. Their design was based on an investigation performed by Spinks, Blowers, and Shek (1985), which is described in Sect. 3.1.3.2 and closely resembles a classical conditioning procedure. To ensure differential conditioning, Kirsch et al. (1993) added a CS− condition to the warning stimulus conditions used by Spinks et al. (1985). The nonaversive UCS was a letter reproduction task. Either three or six letters were displayed on a computer screen; the letters had to be reproduced by the participants during CS+ trials. A black screen was presented during CS− trials instead. The amount of information about the nature of the UCS given by the CS was varied in three steps: no information in case of CS−, partial information by the CS+ (i.e., the number of letters in the UCS), and full information by the CS++ (i.e., the actual 3 or 6 letters in the subsequent UCS). For conditioning, 30 trials (10 of each CS type) were applied. Five seconds after UCS offset, the participants were asked to reproduce the letters seen before, by means of typing them into the computer keyboard. Their response was followed by a feedback (correct or false). The ITI varied between 25 and 45 s (mean = 35 s). SCRs were recorded with standard methodology from thenar/hypothenar sites of the nondominant hand (not used for typing). Significant main effects for CS information content and number of letters in the UCS emerged, reflecting increased SCR amp. with increasing amount of information. Furthermore, FIR amp. increased over trials for CS+ and CS++, whereas they tended to decrease for CS−. There was a significant TIR main effect for CS information content: their amplitudes were highest when the UCS was preceded by a CS+, while TIR amp. markedly decreased when the whole UCS information was already presented in the CS++. Moreover, TIR amp. increased with an increasing number of letters in the UCS. No significant results were obtained for SIR, pointing to FIR as a more sensitive indicator of the amount of information processing resources allocated during classical conditioning of EDRs.

Fredrikson, Annas, Georgiades, Hursti, and Tersman (1993) investigated the reliability and internal consistency of the different kinds of EDRs to be observed during classical conditioning. In a first experiment, 14 participants of each gender were subjected to the same differential conditioning procedure (i.e., circles and triangles serving as CSs and a 1 s 110 dB white noise over headphones as UCS) 20 days apart. SCRs were recorded with standard methodology, an amplitude criterion of 0.05 µS was used. The FIRs yielded significant reliabilities (from $r = 0.37$ to 0.85) during habituation, acquisition, and extinction, whereas SIRs were reliable ($r = 0.51$) only for the CS+ during acquisition and TIRs showed significant reliabilities both during acquisition ($r = 0.65$) and extinction ($r = 0.83$). The procedure for the second experiment performed with 223 participants (120 females, 103 males) was basically the same as in the first one, except for an unpleasant electric shock serving as UCS. Split-half reliability according to the Spearman-Brown formula was determined, yielding highly significant internal consistencies ($r = 0.77$ to $r = 0.96$) for all kinds of EDRs in all phases. Taken together, FIRs were the most reliable measures, followed by the TIRs, while the SIRs were less reliable than the other kinds of EDRs being observable during classical conditioning.[42]

UCR Diminution, Preception, and Preparedness

Another phenomenon which appears regularly in electrodermal conditioning is the so-called unconditional response (UCR) diminution during repeated CS–UCS combination. Some authors regard this as being due to the buildup of conditioned inhibition, whereby the CS gains inhibitory properties (e.g., Kimmel, 1966). An alternative view has been provided by Lykken (1968) formulating a so-called preception hypothesis which states that temporal predictability of an UCS reduces its aversiveness (Sect. 3.2.2.2). This is performed by a phasic and selective inhibition process reducing the arousal response to the UCS, which is cognitively mediated by the warning signal quality of the CS. However, this interpretation of UCR diminution remains questionable. On the one hand, the physiological (especially the electrodermal) responses to such an UCS paired with a warning CS decrease over trials as predicted (e.g., Furedy, 1970, 1975; Grings, 1960; Lykken, Macindoe, & Tellegen, 1972). On the other hand, most studies did not yield a decrease of subjective responses to the UCS over trials (Baltissen & Boucsein, 1986). An example of this is given by the study of Lykken et al. (1972) who continuously recorded HR and SCR with standard methodology in 48 male participants receiving 12 consecutive shocks under each of four conditions that were counterbalanced in order. Shocks were combined by presence of a warning signal vs. no warning and predictable vs. nonpredictable locus of shock (on which of the four limbs the next shock would occur). Range-corrected SCR amp. were consistently reduced when shock was preceded by a warning signal, while the appropriate effect of predictability of locus was weak. Neither aspect of predictability influenced shock magnitude estimates as performed by half of the participants.

Therefore, to explain UCR decline, additional concepts were employed, referring to habituation of the OR as well as to response interference. The observation of an EDR amp. following an unpredictable electric shock as being higher when compared to a predictable one has been interpreted as OR reinstatement by Grings (1969) as well as by Furedy and Klajner (1974), because the less predictable a stimulus the greater is its novelty (Sect. 3.1.1.1). Lykken and Tellegen (1974) proposed a so-called first-signal system which causes habituation without attentional or conscious processes being involved. An additional second-signal system which is responsible for the "preception" mechanism should have the ability to "short-circuit" the sluggish habituation process. This may lead to a weakening of

---

[42] There is also the possibility of a moderate heritability of electrodermal differential fear conditioning (Sect. 2.4.3.3).

the OR already during the first trials before the normal habituation process reduces the response strength. This hypothesis, which stated an interesting connection between habituation and classical conditioning was, however, not sufficiently supported by empirical evidence (Baltissen & Boucsein, 1986).

Another possible explanation for UCR decrease during classical conditioning was provided by Grings and Schell (1969), based on data from a within-subjects design ($N = 27$). They showed that the SCR amp., following a constant UCS, changed reciprocally to the intensity and proportionally to the duration of a preceding CS.[43] This allowed for the interpretation of UCR decrease as being dependent on CR–UCR interference. However, the interference hypothesis is contradicted by results showing a decline in the UCR elicited by a CS having the quality of a warning signal, even if possible interference effects are controlled for. Such an observation has been made by Peeke and Grings (1968), using 20 participants in each group, with constant (5 s) vs. variable (0.6–11 s) ISIs between a CS and an electric shock as UCS. They found lower SCR amp.[44] to shocks preceded by constant ISIs, comparing only those trials in which the ISIs for the variable condition were the same as for the constant condition.

Katz (1984) was able to show that the preception hypothesis can be confirmed if interference effects are controlled, if stimulus conditions are sufficiently aversive, and if the subjective impact is adequately assessed. Using 80 female participants, he observed a decrease of the electrodermal UCR[45] following a warning stimulus (Sect. 3.2.2.2). However, he presented a series of lights which were illuminated sequentially during the ISI instead of using a classical delay conditioning procedure, thus facilitating time estimation which can be assumed to be a critical factor with respect to preception (Furedy, 1975).

To test differential predictions based on a habituation vs. preception position, Baltissen and Boucsein (1986) subjected two groups of 20 male participants each to a series of thirty 110 dB, 2 s white noise UCSs, one group with and the other group without a CS as warning stimulus (i.e., dimming the ambient light 5 s prior to the UCS onset). A control group with 20 additional male participants received 30 nonsignaled 70 dB white noise stimuli. SCR amp. (recorded with standard methodology), following warned UCSs, habituated within 6–8 trials; however, they did not reach as low a level as the SCR amp. to 70 dB control stimuli. Instead, the SCRs following the nonsignaled 110 dB UCSs showed a marked tendency

---

[43] Recorded from the fingers as SR with 2 cm² Ag electrodes, NaCl paste, and 45 μA current strength, changed to SC values and square-root transformed. Two-second white noise of 100 dB served as UCS, while the CS was 80, 90, or 98 dB, varying between 2 and 10 s, in 2 s increments.

[44] Recorded from the fingers as SR with 2.5 cm² Ag electrodes, using 45 μA current, changed to SC and square-root transformed.

[45] Recorded as SR from the medial phalanges using standard methodology. SRRs exceeding an amplitude criterion of 0.05 kΩ were transformed to SCRs and additionally square-root transformed.

toward sensitization (Sect. 3.1.1.2). However, subjectively rated aversiveness,[46] which slightly decreased under all conditions, did not differentiate between signaled and nonsignaled 110 dB stimuli; it was only generally lower for 70 dB stimuli. The authors concluded that their data did not fit in a cognitive set or cognitive perceptual, nor in a response interference or a conditioned inhibition interpretation. They seemed to be in line with an OR reinstatement explanation taken from habituation (Sect. 3.1.1.3).

A subsequent study performed by Baltissen and Weimann (1989) varied both aversiveness (60 vs. 100 dB white noise) and predictability (6 s constant vs. 2–12 s variable ISIs) in a two-factorial design with 15 participants in each group. Within the total of 30 trials, only those 11 with a 6 s ISI in all conditions were evaluated. A significant interaction between aversiveness and predictability which could have confirmed the preception hypothesis appeared only as a tendency toward significance in the SCR magnitudes (Sect. 2.3.4.2) recorded with standard methodology, but not in subjective aversiveness. However, possible response interferences between FIR and/or SIR on one side and TUR on the other side cannot serve as an alternative explanation in this instance, since ISIs were comparable between groups differing with respect to predictability. Thus, for classical conditioning research in the electrodermal realm, a sufficient number of ISIs having equal length in each group will be necessary to control for possible interference effects. Furthermore, more simple explanations (like response interference) than cognitive hypotheses should be taken into account as well in this area of research.

Classical EDR conditioning has been widely used as a model for acquisition of fear and phobias (Sect. 3.4.1.1). Most of these empirical phobia-inducing studies in normal individuals are more or less explicitly based on Seligman's (1971) "preparedness" hypothesis. According to this concept, stimuli which gained fear-inducing properties during phylogenetic development should be more prone to be established as CS+ for phobic responses than those which did not. In case of previously neutral but "prepared" stimuli (e.g., snakes, spiders and angry human faces) paired with a potent UCS, an accelerated acquisition or even one-trial learning may take place. During the 1960s and 1970s, Öhman and colleagues have repeatedly demonstrated the preparedness effect (see Öhman, 1993). Deviating from his model depicted in Fig. 3.3, Öhman presumed that conditioning of prepared CSs appears without any need of being consciously processed, so that cognitive processes should not affect this form of EDR conditioning.

This was demonstrated by Öhman, Erixon, and Löfberg (1975) who presented 64 participants of both genders ten colored slides (snakes, houses, and faces) for 8 s each during an acquisition and an extinction phase. Half of their participants were conditioned by an uncomfortable electric shock to the potentially phobic stimuli (snakes), while in the other half the UCS was paired with supposedly neutral

---

[46] Recorded after each UCS presentation by means of a seven-point Likert scale via microkeys.

(unprepared) CSs. EDA was recorded with standard methodology from the left hand's first and second finger, and evaluated as logarithmized FIRs, SIRs, and TORs in slightly changed intervals (1–4, 4–9, and 9–13 s after CS onset). FIR amp. were significantly higher, and TORs showed more resistance to extinction in potentially phobic stimuli as compared to the neutral ones. As an additional experimental manipulation, half of the participants in each group were informed before the extinction phase that no more shocks would be given, while the other half were not. Surprisingly, the informed participants in the group who received the potentially phobic CSs showed more resistance to extinction as compared to the uninformed participants. This pointed to some resistance of potentially phobic stimuli to cognitive manipulations. No such effects of information were found in the group being conditioned to the neutral CSs.

A typical experimental design for probing the classical conditioning of "prepared" vs. neutral stimuli would compare differential conditioning in a group where both CS+ and CS− are fear-relevant stimuli with another group where both stimuli are neutral (i.e., fear-irrelevant) stimuli. However, since fear-relevant stimuli elicit larger CRs than fear-irrelevant ones even before the occurrence of conditioning, such a comparison does not unambiguously evidence the "preparedness" effect. An alternative hypothesis has been proposed by Lovibond, Siddle, and Bond (1993), based on Gray's (1987) notion that fear-relevant stimuli exert their potential only under particular conditions of anxiety or arousal (Sect. 3.2.1.2), since the pure threat of electric shock without any pairing between CSs and shock as UCS will increase electrodermal responding to fear-relevant but not to fear-irrelevant stimuli (Öhman, Eriksson, Fredrikson, Hugdahl, & Olofsson, 1974), a phenomenon which they called "selective sensitization." Lovibond et al. (1993) performed two subsequent experiments to demonstrate the possible influence of "selective sensitization" in classical conditioning with "prepared" UCSs. First, 87 participants (63 females, 24 males) were assigned to a preexposure group ($N = 40$), being confronted with a fear-relevant and a neutral stimulus before conditioning with the information that no shock would be delivered, or a control group ($N = 47$) without preexposure. The preexposure group showed an overall sensitization effect on the FIR (recorded as SCR with standard methodology) in the conditioning and a subsequent test phase. In addition, this group showed selective sensitization as well, since FIRs to the fear-relevant and to the fear-irrelevant stimuli were similar during preexposure but were higher to the fear-relevant stimuli during the test phase than to the fear-irrelevant ones.

It has been proposed that, in cognitive terms, "prepared" conditioning might use a nonconscious, automatic, and "parallel" information processing, while conditioning with unprepared CSs uses a different "serial" mechanism (Öhman, Erikson, & Olofsson, 1975). To test this hypothesis, Kirsch and Boucsein (1997) presented "prepared" stimuli of 8 s duration (pictures of a snake and a spider) as CSs to half of their 42 participants (22 females, 20 males), while the other half received flower pictures as unprepared CSs. A 100 Hz electric shock of 100 ms duration, varying between 140 and 150 V in strength, based on prior commitment, served as UCS at CS+ offset. For quantification of the amount of information processing capacity needed, eight RT probes were interspersed during the 40 acquisition trials and another 12 probes during the 40 extinction trials. The probes consisted of a red light in the center of the pictures being used as CSs, either 300 or 350 ms after stimulus onset. The participants were asked to respond as fast as possible to the probe by pressing a button to their right. SCRs were recorded with standard methodology from left palmar sites, and FIRs, SIRs, and TIRs were evaluated. The results showed significant differential conditioning effects but no differences between prepared and unprepared stimuli, neither in SCR amp. nor in RT. This points to "serial" processing in both cases, suggesting that the so-called "prepared" conditioning may not be different in underlying mechanism from classical autonomic conditioning.

Evidence for the existence of serial instead of parallel processing of the CS during extinction was provided by Furedy et al. (2000), whose 80 participants (44 females, 36 males) underwent a 20-trial acquisition phase with ten CS+ and CS−, during which the CS+ was followed by a 96-dB white noise UCS 8 s after CS onset. The material for the CSs consisted of pairs of two-syllable words belonging to one of the two semantic categories: buildings or animals, presented over headphones. The ITI varied unsystematically between 25 and 45 s. For each of four groups of 20 participants, one word from one CS category (e.g., station out of the category buildings) served as CS+, while two of the three words serving as CS− were taken from the other category (e.g., lion and zebra out of the category animals) and the third word was taken from the same category as the CS+ (e.g., barn). For the 20-trial extinction phase, participants were instructed to not attend the words presented on the side of the headphone where the CS words were again presented without UCS. Instead, they were asked to focus their attention on the other side where words from two other semantic categories (fruits and vegetables) were presented and to respond as quickly as possible to words from one of the categories by pressing a button. During early extinction, the SCR occurring at an interval of 9–15 s after CS onset (i. e., the TOR) showed reliable conditioning, which could have been interpreted as due to "parallel" processing, since the ear of presentation was unattended. However, the reaction time and a later memorial recognition test for the critical words presented on the attended ear revealed that the unattended CS+ required more processing capacity than the unattended CS−, thus indicating that the CSs were processed in a serial rather than in a parallel fashion. Therefore, the Furedy et al. (2000) results constitute a relatively unequivocal refutation of the information-processing approach to EDR conditioning in humans (section "Cognitive vs. Noncognitive View of EDR Conditioning").

Recent Developments in EDR Conditioning

Most of the recent research into classical EDR conditioning has focused on modeling the acquisition of fear and phobias in humans (Sect. 3.4.1.1). Conditioned fear is often not restricted to the presentation of the original CS+, since a more or less similar stimulus will have the ability to elicit some amount of the CR as well, even after successful extinction of the CR. However, successful extinction may be restricted to the original CS+. Vervliet, Vansteenwegen, Baeyens, Hermans, and Eelen (2005) assigned their 32 participants to either an extinction group or a generalization group. Geometric figures served as CS+ and CS−, with the CS+ followed by an electric shock as UCS. Differential SCR conditioning[47] emerged in both groups during the course of acquisition. During extinction, the generalization group was presented similar geometric figures instead of the original CSs. All stimulus conditions were counterbalanced whenever possible. During a final test phase, the CS+ and CS− were presented without UCS for both groups. Only the generalization group showed differential conditioning in the test phase, providing evidence for the return of fear with the original CS+ being presented after extinction of the CR to the similar generalization stimulus. Thus, extinction is likely to be restricted to the original CS+/CR coupling, instead of working with similar stimuli as well.

Flykt, Esteves, and Öhman (2007) challenged the hypothesis that evolutionary old fear-relevant stimuli have an advantage over threat stimuli of a more recent origin in fear conditioning with respect to nonconscious information processing during EDR conditioning, using a backward masking procedure for the extinction phase. In their first experiment, they assigned 64 participants (28 females, 36 males) randomly to four groups, made up from evolutionary old (snake) vs. more recent (firearm) and masked vs. unmasked extinction. Four pictures of snakes or firearms, directed toward the viewer, served as CS+, while four averted snakes or firearms, served as corresponding CS−. An unpleasant but not painful electric shock was applied as UCS for the evolutionary old fear stimuli, whereas a burst of broadband noise served as UCS for the threat stimuli of a more recent origin. SCRs were recorded with standard methodology from the distal phalanges of the first and second fingers of the left hand. After six habituation trials, a 20-trial acquisition phase was applied, followed by an extinction phase of 32 trials, during which the CSs were masked for half of the participants by pictures rephotographed from cut pieces. Afterwards, participants in the masking conditions were asked about having noticed the double exposures of stimuli, and a forced-choice recognition task was applied. Results showed that ED-CRs conditioned to evolutionary old fear stimuli (snakes) were not abolished by backward masking, but a similar effect was seen for the threat stimuli of a more recent origin (firearms). Since the authors presumed that directed firearms may be perceived as a more imminent threat than a directed snake, Flykt et al. (2007) performed a second experiment with 32 participants (16 of each gender), using the stimuli as CS+ that served as CS− in the first experiment, thus providing stimuli with less fear imminence. Pictures of spiders and hand grenades, respectively, were used as CS−. The procedure was very similar to the first experiment, except UCSs were delivered 0.5 s instead of 1 s after CS+ onset, and only four

---

[47] Recorded with constant 0.5 V across two sintered-pellet 8 mm diameter AgCl electrodes filled with K–Y jelly from the hypothenar left-hand palm. FIR amplitudes (starting 1–4 s after CS onset) were range-corrected (Sect. 2.3.3.4 "Range Corrections") using the largest UCR as the maximum range for each participant.

habituation trials were applied. Unexpectedly, differential ED-CR responding which was installed during acquisition did not only disappear during masked extinction when threat stimuli of a more recent origin (firearms) were used for CS+ but also in case of evolutionary old fear stimuli (snakes). Thus, evolutionary old fear-relevant stimuli seem not having an advantage over threat stimuli of a more recent origin with respect to nonconscious information processing. However, both stimulus types may need an additional component such as imminence of threat to become effective as prewired ED-CR stimuli.

Weike, Schupp, and Hamm (2007) performed a study with 64 participants (49 females, 15 males) to reveal the difference between trace vs. delay conditioning in the acquisition of fear. The authors referred to earlier conflicting results, i.e., that Hugdahl and Öhman (1980) managed to establish fear conditioning of EDRs in both paradigms, whereas Dawson & Schell (1987) regarded CS–UCS contingency as prerequisite for differential EDR conditioning, which is more likely for trace than for delay conditioning, and assigned their participants randomly to either a delay or a trace conditioning group. After each participant ranked 12 neutral male faces according to their likeability, the most neutral two faces were chosen as CSs individually for each participant. An electric shock (500 Hz monopolar DC pulse to the left forearm), being individually adjusted to a "highly annoying, but not painful" level, served as UCS, the mean physical intensity of which was comparable between the two groups. Startle eyeblink probes[48] were used to determine the amount of fear elicited by the presentation of the CSs. After a preconditioning period during which all stimuli except the UCS were repeatedly presented, nine presentations of CS+ and CS− each followed in the conditioning phase and the same number of stimuli in the extinction phase. For the delay conditioning participants, the CS+ of 6 s duration always coterminated with the presentation of the UCS. During trace conditioning, the CS+ was terminated after 2 s and followed by the UCS after 4 s. ITIs varied between 14 and 22 s. FIRs were scored as the largest increase in SC[49] between 0.9 and 4 s after CS onset, and preceded the

---

[48] During the last 3 decades, EDRs have been frequently obtained in the context of startle eyeblink modulation (e.g., Böhmelt, Vanman, Dawson, & Boucsein, 1983; Lipp, Siddle, & Dall, 1997). Earlier research in this area focused on facilitation or inhibition of the startle response by a nonstartling stimulus presented prior to the startling stimulus and the influence of attentional factors on the magnitude of the eyeblink responses. Based on the bidirectional nature of the valence dimension of emotions, Lang, Bradley, and Cuthbert (1990) proposed that not only attentional but also emotional processes should have the ability of modifying the startle eyeblink. Since the nature of the startle response is more DR- than OR-like (Sect. 3.1.1.2), a positive emotional foreground stimulus should diminish the startle eyeblink magnitude, whereas emotional negative foreground stimulation should enhance its magnitude. Because of its indicator function for the intensity of especially negatively tuned emotional states, EDRs have come into use for verifying the nature of emotional foreground stimulation (e.g., Lipp et al., 1997). Since the startle eyeblink research does not primarily aim at EDR conditioning, it will not be reviewed in this section.

[49] Recorded with standard methodology from the right hand's hypothenar eminence. The amplitude criterion was set to 0.05 μS.

presentation of the startle probes. Approximately 3% of the trials had to be rejected because of respiratory or recording artifacts (Sect. 2.2.5). Missing data were replaced by individual mean responses across CS+ and CS— presentations (Sect. 2.3.4.2). SC values were logarithmized to improve distribution characteristics (Sect. 2.3.3.3), and the log values were range-corrected (Sect. 2.3.3.4 "Range Corrections") by dividing each individual score by the participant's maximum response within all trials including the UCRs. Postexperimental interviews were performed to evaluate awareness of the CS–UCS contingencies. Neither the UCS intensity nor UCR amp. differed between aware and unaware participants, either in delay or trace conditioning, confirming that the UCS was equally aversive in participants being aware or unaware of the CS–UCS contingency. During the conditioning phase, only participants who figured out having correctly recognized the CS–UCS contingencies in the postexperimental interview showed differential conditioning under both delay and trace conditions. Discrimination between CS+ and CS— was maintained during the extinction phase in the aware participants of both groups, while no such discrimination could be observed in participants who were not aware of the CS–UCS contingencies. Moreover, the ED-CR was more readily extinguished in the trace conditioning than in the delay conditioning group. Correlations between the conditioned startle eyeblink potentiation (as a measure of the amount of fear elicited by the CS+), startle eyeblink discrimination (as a measure of the success of eyeblink conditioning), and the SCR discrimination (CS+ amp. – CS— amp.) revealed that startle parameters were clearly related to SCRs in the trace conditioning but not in the delay conditioning group, both during the conditioning and the postconditioning phases. The authors concluded that in trace conditioning, where UCS and CS+ overlap and normally coterminate, the acquisition of a fear response does not depend on explicit CS–UCS awareness. If the unconditioned stimuli does not directly follow the CS+ as in delay conditioning, explicit declarative knowledge (awareness) of their contingency might be a prerequisite for the acquisition of conditioned fear. Since conditioning of SC was a more robust phenomenon in aware than in unaware participants, irrespective of the trace vs. delay conditioning procedure, the ED-CR seems to be an index of cognitive learning of the circumstances under which a CS+ signals an aversive event, requiring a declarative and explicit memory.

Vansteenwegen, Iberico, Vervliet, Marescau, and Hermans (2008) investigated the influence of UCS predictability on electrodermal conditioning. Their investigation based on earlier results with fear-potentiated startle conditioning (e.g., Grillon & Davis, 1997), where UCS unpredictability was found being powerful in eliciting conditioned fear which closely resembled the sustained level of anxiety being characteristic of patients with anxiety disorders (Sect. 3.4.1.1). Vansteenwegen et al. (2008) introduced a continuous subjective estimation of the UCS predictability in a classical EDR conditioning paradigm. In addition, they modified the amount of UCS predictability by contrasting a CS1 which was reliably followed by the UCS with a CS2 which was presented explicitly unpaired with the UCS. For half of the participants (23 females, 26 males), presence of the central room lighting signaled the predictable context, while the unpredictable context was signaled by only a dimmed light being present. For the other half of participants, the conditions were reversed. A square and a triangle which served as CSs were balanced over participants, and the UCS was an electric shock of 2 ms duration delivered to the left wrist and being individually adjusted. By means of a dial operated by her/his right hand, the participants had to indicate continuously during the whole experiment on a scale from 0 to 100 to what extent they expected the UCS to appear. EDA was measured as SC,[50] and 100 dBA white noise bursts served as stimuli for the startle eyeblink. After a preconditioning phase, two blocks of CS1 and two blocks of CS2 were presented in alternating order across participants. Each block consisted of four trials, with 8-s CS presentations and ITIs varying between 8 and 16 s. SCR amp. to the CSs in the predictable context were higher than to the CSs in the unpredictable context, contrarily to what could have been expected. Since even the startle eyeblink responses yielded no difference between the predictability conditions but only a steady decline over trials, the general problem of packing too much into the experimental procedure, especially startle stimuli plus continuous subjective ratings of predictability, might have counteracted the possibility of conditioning effects to appear. Thus, the ED-CR might be a phenomenon that may be easily obscured by distracting stimuli.

Pineles, Orr, and Orr (2009) challenged the distinction between FIR and SIR in evaluating EDRs in the CS–UCS interval during differential fear conditioning. They performed a literature review of 66 studies with sufficiently long ISIs (7 s and above) in which the FIR/SIR distinction had been applied, contrasting the results with those from four studies of their own research group which had not used such a distinction. Their conclusion was that differential conditioning of both the FIR and SIR had been observed in the majority of studies with separate evaluation, which confirms earlier findings that both FIR and SIR are conditionable (e.g., Dengerink & Taylor, 1971; Prokasy & Ebel, 1967). This and their consideration that large ED-CRs may be diminished or obscured if their onset or peak occur close to the FIR-SIR boundary[51] let the authors propose a different evaluation method as used in their own studies. Data from 287 participants who underwent differential aversive conditioning of SC measured with standard methodology were reanalyzed in two ways: using the traditional FIR/SIR distinction and calculating a summary response from the entire CS–UCS interval. FIR was defined as a SCR, the deflection of which occurred within 1–4 sec and the peak of which occurred within 2–6 sec following CS onset. The response onset for the SIR needed to be within 2 and 4 sec and its peak

---

[50] With two 1 cm diameter Ag/AgCl electrodes filled with K–Y gel (which is hypertonic) attached to the hypothenar palm of the left hand, the signal was visually inspected and corrected for artifacts. SCRs were scored if their maximum increase appeared within 1–4 s after CS onset. Zero responses were included in all analyses, and a range correction was applied using the largest UCR peak (between 9 and 13 s after UCR) in the acquisition phase as maximum individual value. A square-root transformation was applied to the SCR amp. data to improve distributional characteristics (Sect. 2.3.3.3).

[51] This is a matter of evaluating superimposed EDRs (Fig. 2.16, Sect. 2.3.1.2 "Amplitudes of Exosomatic Responses Recorded with Direct Current") but is not necessarily an argument in favor of discarding the distinction between FIR and SIR, as proposed by Pineles et al. (2009).

between 5 and 9.5 s after CS onset. The summary response was obtained by subtracting the mean SCL for the 2 s immediately preceding CS onset from the highest SCL recorded during the 8-s CS–UCS interval. A subsequent averaging over all participants resulted in a single peak during the CS–UCS interval. Differential conditioning was observed in all three parameters, leading Pineles et al. (2009) to the conclusion that the easier-to-obtain summary response might be preferred over the traditional FIR and SIR measures. Since the authors acknowledge that different results could have been obtained with more conditioning trials or longer CS–UCS intervals, such a conclusion needs to be supported by more empirical data. Furthermore, the results from the literature review and the data provided by the authors provide evidence for the SIR being a weak but not necessarily negligible phenomenon. Therefore, for the time being, differentiation between FIR and SIR still constitutes a potentially valuable research tool in classical conditioning of EDRs.

An attempt to directly observe CNS correlates of electrodermal conditioning in humans was performed by Hugdahl (1998) in a study with 5 male participants using 1 kHz tones (5 s, 70 dB) as CSs and a brief electric shock as UCS. PET scans were performed during the habituation and extinction phases, whereas SCRs were recorded during acquisition with standard methodology. Classical conditioning significantly increased the cerebral blood flow in the right orbitofrontal cortex, dorsolateral prefrontal cortex, inferior and superior frontal cortices, as well as in inferior and middle temporal cortices. Hugdahl suggested this reflecting a shift from limbic structures during acquisition to cortical areas during extinction, thus strengthening the role of cortical control for EDA (Sect. 1.3.4.2 "The Role of Skin Components and of Membrane Processes").

3.1.2.2 Instrumental or Operant Conditioning of Electrodermal Responses

According to the dated view of Miller and Konorski (1928), classical conditioning should be restricted to ANS variables, while motor responses should be influenced only by instrumental conditioning. Meanwhile several ANS functions including the generation of EDA could be successfully modified by instrumental conditioning techniques as well. Kimmel (1967), and Miller and co-workers (e.g., DiCara & Miller, 1968; Miller, 1969, 1972) challenged the view that visceral functions could only be classically, not instrumentally, conditioned. In their experiments conducted with curarized rats, these authors showed conditioning of ANS functions (e.g., HR, peripheral vasomotor tonus, or gastrointestinal activity) as a result of stimulating "reward" areas in the brain (Sect. 3.2.1.2).

The question of whether instrumental conditioning of autonomic functions could also occur in humans had been determined to be equivocal, since it could not be ruled out that instrumental visceral conditioning effects may be mediated by motor responses (Beatty, 1983). However, in a study performed with 72 male participants, Rice (1966) measured EMG activity in the forearm muscles used to move the fingers from which EDA[52] was recorded, in an attempt to separate SCRs preceded by motor responses from those which were not. Participants were assigned to four groups of equal size. In one experimental group, all spontaneous SCRs were reinforced by a square of white light, while in its counterpart only SCRs preceded by EMG changes were reinforced. For each condition, yoked-control groups were formed, which significantly differed from their experimental counterparts during the reinforcement period. Further analyses including the SCRs preceded and not preceded by movements indicated that movement-related SCRs were not significantly responsible for the differences between experimental and control groups.

In general, a possible muscular mediation does not play an important role in discussing the elicitation of electrodermal phenomena, except for physiologically induced artifacts (Sect. 2.2.5.2) and possible supportive actions of myoepithelia surrounding the duct in squeezing sweat out of the pores (Sect. 1.3.3.1). On the other hand, a possible cognitive mediation of instrumentally conditioned EDRs has been widely discussed.

This topic was addressed by a study performed by Martin and Dean (1970) consisting of two experiments. In the first, 33 female participants were presented a light as a discriminative stimulus. An EDR[53] during the presentation of the red light switched the light off and elicited an electric shock of 1 s duration. A spontaneous EDR appearing during the blue light prevented the shock. Participants in the instrumental group were instructed with respect to this contingency and were told to elicit EDRs only through internal emotional processes and not by movement or respiration. Participants of a yoked-control group received the same instructions, but the shocks were given according to the reactions of their partner in the instrumental group. Another yoked-control group only received the instruction that both lights were followed by an electric shock in an irregular manner. The latter group showed, as compared to the others, smaller EDRs following the discriminative stimulus which announced the shock. The spontaneous EDR amp. in this group were higher than those in the other groups during the presentation of the light, which signaled that the EDR would allow a prevention of shock. This result points to a marked influence of the instruction on the instrumental modification of EDA. In their second experiment, it was shown that a response-contingent presentation of shock does not have an instrumental effect. It seems that the different responses to the discriminative stimuli observed in the first experiment had been cognitively mediated. It might be that those cognitive processes are even more important than the stimulus presentation being contingent upon responses, because even with noncontingent shock application as for the second group of the first experiment both stimuli elicited EDRs of different strength.

Various other studies being performed during the 1960s and 1970s showed successful instrumental conditioning of different EDA parameters with the use of different paradigms and types of reinforcers. Fowler and Kimmel (1962)

---

[52] Recorded as SC with a Fels dermohmeter and zinc electrodes, taped to the first and third fingers of the participant's right hand.

[53] Recorded from the first and second left-hand fingers with constant current.

demonstrated the usability of light as reinforcer for spontaneous SRRs[54] in a study performed with 40 participants. The response-contingent group maintained its initial level of SRR freq. while the noncontingent control group did not. Since both groups diverged during reinforcement and reconverged during extinction, the authors concluded that unelicited SRRs have been instrumentally conditioned.

Helmer and Furedy (1968) managed to elicit significantly higher EDR amp. in a group of 40 participants being reinforced with money for an amplitude increase[55] as compared to a control group of equal size with noncontingent reinforcement. Kotses, Rapaport, and Glaus (1978), with a total of 36 male participants, observed an SRL[56] increase induced by reinforcement via a flashing light, while SRL changes in a yoked-control group varied unsystematically. In his comprehensive review of studies using different forms of instrumental EDR conditioning (i.e., positive and negative reinforcement as well as avoidance conditioning), Kimmel (1973) concluded that enough evidence was available to support the existence of the phenomenon under investigation. However, the main problem is the lack of a generally accepted theoretical framework. Additionally, experimental procedures proposed to separate operantly conditioned from cognitively mediated ANS responses did not yield unequivocal results in electrodermal research.

Experiments using EDRs as only dependent measure do not allow for an unambiguous determination as to whether the results are solely mediated by instrumental conditioning. EDRs may be due to uncontrolled classical conditioning or to cognitive processes and might even be elicited by voluntary muscular contractions (contrary to instructions) leading to an artifactual EDR (Sect. 2.2.5.2). As a possible solution, Katkin and Murray (1968) proposed the use of curare which paralyzes the skeletal muscles, without influencing functions of the brain and of inner organs. Understandably, applications of curare in humans are sparse. Birk, Crider, Shapiro, and Tursky (1966) performed an appropriate study using only one participant. They could show a tendency toward conditioning, despite a decrease of EDR rate during application of curare.[57]

---

[54] Recorded palmar/dorsal with zinc electrodes, saline electrode cream and a constant current of 40 μA. SRRs which occurred within 5 s after the presentation of the light were not scored. The NS. SRR freq. was transformed to reduce skewness and expressed as percentage of the NS.SRR freq. obtained during an initial 2-min resting period.

[55] Measured as SR with a Fels dermohmeter, using 70 μA current, with zinc-manganese dioxide electrodes from the left palm and upper arm. Contact was made by a 5% saline-soaked cotton ball.

[56] Recorded with Ag/AgCl electrodes and Beckman cream from ethanol-cleaned volar finger sites using 20 μA constant current. Red and green lights were used to signal that either an increase or a decrease of SRL would be reinforced by a flashing white light.

[57] Roberts, Lacroix, and Wright (1974) could not observe instrumental conditioning of spontaneous SPRs in curarized rats. They used an electric shock as reinforcer which was applied when SPRs appeared exceeding either 10, 35, 60, or 75% of the greatest response during the baseline. As compared to a yoked-control group, no differences in SPR frequency appeared. Neither variation of shock intensity nor of curare dosage had an effect.

By recording respiration as well as EMG in addition to EDA, van Twyer and Kimmel (1966), in a study with 42 participants, tried to control muscle artifacts without the application of curare or of muscle relaxants.[58] A light was presented when EDRs deflected 1% or more from the EDL. Recordings of EMG and respiration did not yield significant differences between the contingent and the noncontingent reinforced groups. For further analyses only those EDRs were taken that were not accompanied by changes in respiratory or muscle activity. In the contingent reinforced group as compared to the noncontingent one, EDR frequency increased during acquisition and decreased during extinction, thus pointing to a conditioning effect.

EDRs cannot only be elicited by instrumental conditioning but also be suppressed. This was demonstrated by Johnson and Schwartz (1967) using an aversive loud tone (700 Hz, 3 s, 95 dB) as negative reinforcer. Sixteen female participants were tested in each of the following conditions. The experimental groups received aversive tones contingent with spontaneous SRRs,[59] while the control groups received the same number of negative reinforcers per minute, however during periods with no NS.SRRs. Experimental participants showed in the acquisition as well as in the extinction phase a significantly lower NS.SRR freq. as compared to the controls. An additional variation in instruction did dot yield significant differences. Using parallel measures of EMG, the authors found no evidence supporting a possible skeletal-muscle mediation explanation of their results with SRRs.

In a study on instrumental conditioning, Gomez and McLaren (1997) investigated the hypothesis that punishment should be related to behavioral inhibition system (BIS) activity, while reward should be related to BAS activity (Sect. 3.2.1.2). They randomly assigned 86 participants to a punishment group (27 females, 16 males) and a reward group (26 females, 17 males). The participants' task was learning to distinguish "bad" from "good" numbers, while punishment or reward was induced by monetary loss or gain. Contrary to the theoretical predictions, HR did not significantly differ between reward and punishment, whereas the hypothesis of higher SCLs[60] in the punishment group in comparison to the reward group was confirmed. There was, however, no support for Gray's (1970) notion that BIS is linked to trait anxiety and BAS to trait impulsivity (see Fig. 3.5, Sect. 3.3.1.1).

---

[58] Recorded palmar vs. dorsal with 2 cm^2 zinc electrodes filled with NaCl cream, transformed to log units.

[59] Two SR channels with different sensitivity were used to avoid loss of SRR data in the high sensitivity channel (Sect. 2.1.3) which allowed the detection of 500 Ω changes (amplitude criterion). Eight-millimeter diameter zinc electrodes together with a zinc sulfate cream were placed on the participants' fingers. Spontaneous EDRs were defined as not occuring within 6 s following any observable event which could give rise to an EDR (see Fig. 2.20, Sect. 2.3.2.2).

[60] Recorded by Ag/AgCl electrodes and presumably hypertonic cream from the first and third fingers of the participant's nondominant hand, voltage not reported.

Also in the context of EDRs indicating BIS activity, Latzman, Knutson, and Fowles (2006) performed two successive experiments with altogether 43 children of both genders, aged 8–12 years, probing the influence of interreinforcement intervals on the SCR.[61] The first experiment revealed that SCR amp. were significantly higher for long interreinforcement intervals of 60 s on average, compared to those from short intervals of 20 s on average. The task was to give either 10 or 20 correct responses in a row to letters appearing on a computer screen, and 25-cent coins served as reinforcers. The authors interpreted the height of SCR amp. as indicators for the amount of negative emotion elicited by the different reinforcement schedules. Surprisingly, SCR amp. following the first reinforcement after a 90-s extinction phase were significantly higher than those in both reinforcement schedules. Since this could have been simply elicited by the mere length of the interreinforcement interval from the last reinforcer before to the first one after extinction (which could vary between 110 and 150 s), an additional condition with an interreinforcement period of about 100 s was introduced in the second experiment. The results replicated and extended those of the first experiment, showing that the height of SCR amp. increased with the length of interreinforcement intervals. The authors concluded that their paradigm provides an effective and also fully acceptable method for eliciting aversive SCRs in children, which could be used as a model for basic research on the development of antisocial disorders (Sect. 3.4.1.2).

The investigation of instrumental (or operant) EDR conditioning was often connected with the use of electrodermal biofeedback, for example in the above-mentioned study by van Twyer and Kimmel (1966). Hence, studies of instrumental EDR conditioning were largely integrated in research on biofeedback during the 1970s (see Beatty & Legewie, 1977; Obrist, Black, Brener, & DiCara, 1974; Shapiro, 1977). In terms of learning theory, the operant response is the occurrence of the ANS change, and the information about the response serves as reinforcer (Shapiro, 1977). Since it has become an important area of application since, EDA biofeedback will be described separately in Sect. 3.1.2.3.

3.1.2.3   Biofeedback of Electrodermal Activity

The term *biofeedback* refers to the use of a wide variety of experimental procedures that present parameters obtained from biosignals to an organism as an exteroceptive feedback, with the aim of modifying the underlying physiological processes (Beatty & Legewie, 1977). It refers to "the feeding back of information to the individual about change in a physiological system" (Hugdahl, 1995, p. 39), with the aim of teaching individuals to gain control over their physiological processes (Martin &

---

[61] Recorded with standard methodology except for using K–Y gel and a 1.0 V constant current. A Wheatstone bridge was incorporated to allow for greater amplification of the signal being transformed to SC. SCR amp. was calculated as the difference between the maximum SCL during 2–5 s and the minimum SCL during 0–2 s following the reward.

Rief, 2009). This requires the system to be continuously monitored and analyzed, to provide as close to continuous feedback as possible (Sect. 2.2.4.3). Biofeedback techniques make use of operant control of involuntary responses, thus being related to instrumental conditioning (Sect. 3.1.2.2). This implies that the respective electrodermal changes are not stimulus-elicited, but spontaneous or nonspecific in nature. As with other biofeedback techniques, EDA biofeedback has been predominantly used as a therapeutic tool for psychopathological disorders (Sect. 3.4), often in combination with relaxation techniques.

Using EDA for the purpose of feedback is not as straightforward as performing such a function for HR, temperature, or EMG biofeedback. EDA biofeedback may use the occurrence of spontaneous EDRs (i.e., NS.EDRs) as an appropriate parameter, as most studies on instrumental conditioning of EDA did. However, to maintain a close temporal relationship between the underlying physiological processes and the feedback signal, the latter has to be evaluated online without noticeable delay. This requires a short time window for signal evaluation. An analog of phasic changes in EDA cannot be obtained as easily as with HR, where single interbeat intervals (IBIs) or averaging a few consecutive intervals may be used for feedback. First, spontaneous EDRs appear without regularity (see Fig. 2.20, Sect. 2.3.2.2), and a time window of 3–5 s is required to obtain at least one EDR, since even in states of high arousal, NS.EDR freq. is not expected to exceed 20 per minute (Sect. 2.5.2.1 "Tonic Skin Conductance Measures"). Second, the online detection of EDRs is all but easy to perform, as already discussed in Sect. 2.2.4.3. Therefore, EDA biofeedback had mostly used the EDL signal, which has the disadvantage of monitoring only slow changes.

In one of the earliest studies on EDA biofeedback, Steinberg and Schwartz (1976) demonstrated that an acoustic biofeedback signal could help 10 male primary psychopaths (Sect. 3.4.1.2) to influence their NS.SRR freq.[62] They were unable to achieve any control by means of a simple instruction, in comparison with 12 healthy controls who at least managed to increase their NS.SRR freq. After 16 min of auditory biofeedback training, both groups were able to lower or raise their NS.SRR freq. considerably as compared to the instruction alone condition. Interestingly, psychopaths showed reduced HR control concurrent with enhanced EDA control. This demonstrated the specificity of NS.SRR learning in this particular group, in contrast to a control group, in which the participants learnt to influence their autonomic arousal in a more general manner as reflected in both EDA and HR changes.

A study that used EDA biofeedback to counteract its natural decline in resting or drowsiness-inducing situations was performed by Volow, Erwin, and Cipolat (1979) with 10 healthy male participants. Half received 20 min of training in increasing SPL negativity (recorded with standard methodology), followed by 20 min of training in decreasing SPL negativity over 3 days. The order was reversed for the

---

[62] Recorded by means of a Wheatstone bridge, using 10 μA current, with a standard electrode/cream setting from the fingers. The amplitude criterion was 415 Ω for psychopaths and 376 Ω for controls.

other half of participants. During the last training day, a significant difference between increasing and decreasing conditions emerged, demonstrating that the participants were able to influence their SPL negativity in the instructed direction.

EDA biofeedback appears to require a certain amount of training time before becoming effective. Steptoe and Greer (1980) investigated SCL biofeedback[63] combined with taped relaxation instructions, compared to relaxation instructions alone in counterbalanced order on 2 consecutive days, using 8 participants of each gender. Six 5-min relaxation phases were inserted between two complex problem-solving tasks on each day. No significant differences in rated feelings of relaxation or in SCL emerged, only a tendency toward a lower SCL in the EDA feedback group during the later task trials. The authors concluded that the total duration of only 33 min of EDA biofeedback training might have been too short for inducing an enhanced relaxation effect supplemental to the taped instructions.

To replicate and enhance the results of Steptoe and Greer (1980), Falkowski and Steptoe (1983) performed a study with extended biofeedback training and a more suitable control group. In addition, they inserted 1 week between the initial presentation of a stressful cognitive task plus an anxiety-provoking industrial accident film and the first biofeedback and/or relaxation session. Furthermore, they matched their two groups of 5 females and males each by their electrodermal reactivity[64] during the initial day. After 24 min of relaxation with or without SCL biofeedback training with the same methodology as used by Steptoe and Greer (1980), another 20 min of relaxation training was conducted on a third day, followed by the same stressful tasks used on the initial day. On the final day, the group with additional SCL biofeedback showed lower SCLs compared to the relaxation-alone group, the difference being marginally significant during the relaxation period and highly significant during the stressful tasks.

EDA biofeedback may be principally used to change autonomic arousal in both directions. However, the main aim has been its therapeutic use (e.g., in the reduction of clinical anxiety; Sect. 3.4.1.1), where a decrease in arousal is attempted. In summarizing results from earlier studies, Holmes, Frost, Bennett, Nielsen, and Lutz (1981) found EDA biofeedback effective for increasing arousal in all of the five studies where this had been attempted. With respect to decreasing arousal levels, two of three experiments failed to show the effectiveness of biofeedback.

In their own study, Holmes et al. (1981) performed two experiments on the effect of instructions to increase as well to decrease SRL,[65] with or without the aid of

---

[63] Recorded with two-element lead electrodes, K–Y gel and 10 μA CC from the first and second fingers of the left hand, transformed to and stored as SCL, using a continuous tone pitch change as biofeedback signal.

[64] SC reactivity was the peak change in SCL during the accident film, calculated as change from the last minute of the resting period.

[65] These authors measured skin resistance with constant voltage (which normally gives conductance values) from the first and second fingers of the participant's nondominant hand, using 20 × 25 mm electrodes.

biofeedback in nonstressful and stressful conditions. In their first experiment with 48 participants of both genders, Holmes et al. observed that during six 3 min nonstressful recording periods, biofeedback generally increased SRL (i.e., decreased arousal), but biofeedback only helped those participants who followed the instruction to increase their arousal, and not those who tried to decrease it. Furthermore, participants who were not instructed to change their SR and were not given feedback showed the lowest levels of arousal. Holmes et al. (1981) performed a second experiment with 52 participants, based on Shapiro's (1977) suggestion that biofeedback training may be more effective when conducted in stressful situations during which participants show an increased arousal. They applied the following five conditions: stress induced by threat of electric shock alone; stress together with instructions to relax; stress with relax instructions plus biofeedback; stress with instruction to relax plus placebo; and a nonstress condition as control. SRL was decreased by stress, and instructions to relax increased SRL (i.e., decreased arousal), but neither SR biofeedback nor placebo were effective in reducing arousal levels.

Apart from the question of the therapeutic viability of biofeedback, this second experiment of Holmes et al. (1981) clearly shows the general control group problem in this research area. First, as discussed in Sect. 3.1.2.2 for the instrumental conditioning of EDA, various factors have to be carefully controlled, including possible cognitive processes as well as elicitation of EDRs by artifacts (e.g., muscular contractions or respiratory irregularities, see Sect. 2.2.5.2), which may influence EDL in an uncontrolled manner. Second, the necessity for a double-blind placebo control (as in the realm of psychopharmacology, see Sect. 3.4.3) has been largely neglected in biofeedback therapy, but also in biofeedback research in general (Furedy, 1987). While such a placebo control is not possible in most psychological treatment conditions, a noncontingent feedback condition can be easily administered in biofeedback research in such a way that participants serving as controls do not know whether they are getting accurate feedback or not. The lack of placebo controls means that the basic question of whether biofeedback has a specific beneficial effect on the ability to control a particular physiological function like SCL decrease (presumably indicative of relaxation) remains unanswered, quite aside from such more abstract theoretical issues as whether instrumental conditioning of autonomic responses is possible.

It is only after the basic placebo-control issue has been answered in the affirmative (i.e., that biofeedback does indeed have a specific beneficial effect on the ability to lower SCL or frequency of spontaneous SCRs) that other questions regarding the mechanisms involved in such a specific beneficial effect can be asked. These questions include that of how biofeedback is mediated and whether the control gained over the particular physiological function (here SCL or frequency of SCRs) is selective, or concerns general changes in the ANS (i.e., real psychological relaxation or even sympathetic withdrawal). These sorts of questions have been thoroughly discussed by Shapiro (1977), they remain "academic" until the specific beneficial effect of biofeedback on SCL control has been demonstrated through the placebo-control method.

An attempt to investigate the specificity issue was made by Roberts (1977), reporting data from an experiment that compared SCL and HR biofeedback, under either increase or decrease instruction, in four independent groups with 8 participants each. Control over EDA and HR was affected differently by various training variables. Simple instructions to change SCL in either direction without exteroceptive feedback resulted in substantial control over HR but not over SCL. On the other hand, with the aid of biofeedback it was possible to gain electrodermal control.[66] Roberts offered a neurophysiological explanation of these differences between both systems. While HR may be voluntarily changed by the use of different afferent sources (e.g., pressure receptors, auditory sensations, or mechanoreceptor stimulation by vascular changes), interoception that arises directly as a consequence of sudomotor effector action is questionable (Kuno, 1956), though tactile or thermal changes following sweat gland activity are known (Edelberg, 1961). Thus, some specificity of the EDA biofeedback may be given, but the overall effect seems to be rather weak (Roberts, 1977).

More recently, EDA biofeedback has been used in several studies aimed at the detection of CNS origins of electrodermal phenomena (Sect. 1.3.4.1). This new generation of biofeedback research made use of brain imaging techniques to identify brain mechanisms which influence the volitional control of ANS responses such as EDA. Critchley, Melmed, Featherstone, Mathias, and Dolan (2001) assessed the influence of cognitive intent to diminish peripheral sympathetic arousal and its interaction with SCL biofeedback[67] by means of PET scanning in 8 right-handed male participants. The four experimental conditions which were repeated three times in a pseudorandom order were a combination of contingent vs. random biofeedback and intended vs. no relaxation. No significant main effect of contingent vs. random feedback emerged. Intentional relaxation was associated with increased activity in the left anterior cingulate gyrus, in the pallidum and in the inferior parietal lobule. Relaxation-related CNS activity was modulated by contingent biofeedback in the cerebellar vermis, bilaterally in the anterior cingulate gyrus and in the medial prefrontal cortex. In the case of intended and successful relaxation, activity in the anterior cingulate gyrus was negatively correlated ($r = -0.81$) with the rate of SCL change during relaxation. This was not the case in the nonrelaxation condition. The authors concluded that activity in this particular area is related to the intention to relax, since activity in other areas such as the pallidum correlated with EDA changes during both relaxation and nonrelaxation.

---

[66] Stern (1972) showed that SRR biofeedback training had only a small effect on the participants' ability to detect whether or not they reacted electrodermally to a low-intensity sound. Furthermore, prior EDA biofeedback training was more effective for the detection of large as compared to small EDRs.

[67] Recorded with dry silver electrodes taped to the palmar surface of the left index and middle fingers with unreported voltage; the biofeedback signal was presented visually on a sort of thermometer.

In a further study in which these authors simultaneously recorded EDA and fMRI by means of the technique reported by Critchley, Elliott, Mathias, and Dolan (2000) as described in Sect. 2.2.3.5, Critchley, Melmed, Featherstone, Mathias, and Dolan (2002) probed four different modes of SCL biofeedback (using the same methods for recording and display as in their earlier study) with 17 healthy right-handed participants (7 females, 10 males). The four modes were combined by two degrees of feedback accuracy manipulation, i.e., adding noise to the feedback signal or not, and two degrees of sensitivity manipulation, i.e., doubling the amount of the feedback signal or not. Each of the resulting combinations was presented twice in a pseudorandom order with interspersed resting periods. Participants relaxed at a significantly slower rate in case of doubling the signal, and adding noise tended to decrease relaxation. No significant interactions between the two manipulations emerged. In comparison to a resting condition, various brain areas were active under the four biofeedback tasks, including those connected with attention and response selection (dorsolateral prefrontal cortex, anterior cingulate gyrus, inferior parietal lobe, and thalamus), areas representing somato-visceral bodily states (bilateral insulae, primary and secondary somatosensory cortices, and thalamus), and brain regions involved in the autoregulatory control of sympathetic ANS responses (substantia nigra, hypothalamic nuclei, and pons). The latter regions were not generally influenced by manipulations in accuracy and sensitivity of the biofeedback signal; however, activity in the hypothalamic/substantia nigra area was influenced by noise in the biofeedback signal. This was interpreted by the authors as identifying the lowest level on which autonomic regulation may be directly modulated by descending cognitive influences.

In their fMRI study previously mentioned in Sect. 1.3.4.1 "Cortical Control of EDA", Nagai, Critchley, Featherstone, Trimble, and Dolan (2004) aimed at identifying areas involved in relaxation and arousal responses during EDA biofeedback. Eight healthy volunteers (5 males, 3 females) participated in a biofeedback relaxation and a biofeedback arousal session of 6 min each in counterbalanced order. The SCL was displayed as a horizontal line that moved downward if changes were in the intended direction. Relaxation was more successful (only one participant failed) than arousal (3 participants showed an unintended SCL decrease). Diminished SCLs were related to increased VMPFC and orbitofrontal cortical activity, extending to the right medial temporal lobe. During successful performance (SCL changes in the intended direction) the left midorbitofrontal cortex, the medial occipitoparietal junction, and the cerebellar vermis were most active, while activity in the right frontal pole and the right superior temporal gyrus was correlated with failure to change the SCL signal in the intended direction. Transient arousal responses, i.e., SCRs, were found during activity in the anterior cingulate and insular cortices, thalamus, hypothalamus, and lateral regions of the prefrontal cortex. While these regions can be regarded as involved in the generation of changes in internal bodily states, regions such as the orbitofrontal cortex, which were active during successful biofeedback performance, are more prone to being activated by rewarding stimuli.

Although brain imaging techniques provide an interesting approach for determining CNS areas that may be involved in EDA biofeedback, the vast number of regions identified in each study does not allow us establishing a theoretical framework for how CNS mechanisms influence changes in different EDA parameters which have been used for biofeedback. Despite this lack in its theoretical background and the persisting methodological problems mentioned above, EDA biofeedback has demonstrated some utility in various clinical-therapeutic settings. These will be discussed in the appropriate sections of this book. In addition, a very special application of EDA biofeedback in the field of engineering psychophysiology will be described in Sect. 3.5.1.2: the use of the online evaluated NS.SCR freq. for adaptive automation.

3.1.3   Electrodermal Indices of Information Processing

In addition to the electrodermal concomitants of simple orienting and conditioning as outlined in the previous sections, there is also theoretical and empirical evidence for close connections between higher stages of information processing and certain EDA parameters. Aside from the mainstream focus on EEG variables (e.g., event-related components such as the P300) as suitable correlates of information uptake, decision and storage processes, a small but effective psychophysiological research area, is maintained using ANS parameters as indicators of cognitive processing (Sects. 3.1.3.1 and 3.1.3.2). Section 3.1.3.3 will describe the recently emerged use of the EDR as an indicator of decision making, whereas Sect. 3.1.3.4 will review the role of electrodermal indicators for memory consolidation. Another field in which EDA has been related to cognitive functioning is hemispheric specialization, which will be reviewed in Sect. 3.1.4.

Since the focus of the present chapter is on phasic EDA parameters, results which consistently show an improvement of performance (e.g., in vigilance and RT tasks) with higher levels of tonic EDA are not reported here.[68] These are supposedly due to a higher level of general arousal which may cause increased attention and motor readiness, together with higher tonic EDA values that typically come with high arousal (Sect. 3.2.1.1).

3.1.3.1   Neurophysiological Considerations on EDA and Information Processing

As previously seen while discussing Sokolov's (1963a, 1963b) model of the OR and its habituation (Sect. 3.1.1), subcortical structures are generally accepted as exerting an important influence on higher levels of information processing. A similar point is made by a model proposed by Pribram and McGuinness (1975) based on their

---

[68] The reader is referred to reviews given by Raskin (1973), Spinks and Siddle (1983), or Koelega (1990), as well as Sect. 3.3.2.2.

extensive review of studies of neuropsychological and psychophysiological research on attention performed with both monkeys and humans. They concluded that the following three neuronally distinct and separate attentional subcortical systems have the property to exert an impact on the information processing mechanism. These three systems closely resemble Posner's (1975) taxonomy for attentive processes and also include the main aspects of the two-arousal hypothesis as proposed by Routtenberg (1968):

1. An "affect arousal system" which centers on the amygdala as part of facilitatory and inhibitory serotonergic pathways. It regulates specialized "arousal" neurons and is organized around a "stop" or balancing mechanism as well. It also regulates focusing of attention (or selective attention in Posner's sense), elicits phasic physiological concomitants to sensory input, and is closely connected to the kind of arousal covered by Routtenberg's arousal system I (Fig. 3.4, Sect. 3.2.1.2).

2. A "preparatory activation system" centers on the basal ganglia, therefore being apparently dopaminergic in nature. It exerts control over the "go" mechanism in brain systems which elicit tonic physiological concomitants of increased perceptual and motor readiness, corresponding to alertness in Posner's terms, and closely resembling Routtenberg's arousal system II.

3. An "effort system" which comprises the hippocampus and the Papez circuit. It exerts control over the relationship between amygdalar "arousal" and basal ganglia "activation," leading to changes in central representation which may be conceived as changes of state, set, or "attitude." This process entails "effort," which is related to the degree of consciousness according to Posner (1975). The effort system has the ability to decouple the two other systems and thus coordinate tonic and phasic components of physiological responses.

Two years earlier, Kahneman (1973), after having reviewed various studies on problem-solving taken from the psychophysiological literature, identified the above-mentioned "arousal" component (1) as a possible indicator of a process, which he described as modifying the allocation of resources from an altogether limited-capacity attentional system to mental activities (Sect. 3.1.3.2). While Kahneman did not unambiguously distinguish between "arousal," "capacity," "effort," and "attention," Pribram and McGuinness (1975) restricted the amygdala-centered component of information processing to viscero-autonomic, mainly sympathetic "arousal," which often mirrors stimulus parameters such as novelty and complexity. Consequently, McGuinness and Pribram (1980) proposed a close association between "affect arousal" and the OR (Sect. 3.1.1). On the other hand, basal ganglia-centered "activation" was mostly identified by Pribram and his collaborator with somatomotor readiness, for which cardiovascular processes have been regarded as most adequate indicators. Finally, hippocampus-generated "effort," which is necessary to overcome established connections between stimulus and response characteristics, is indicated by its theta rhythm (which is, however, not directly recordable from the intact human brain). It may also be reflected in some aspects of the CNV in the EEG.

All CNS structures mentioned above can presumably influence EDA (Sect. 1.3.4.1 "Cortical Control of EDA"). As Bagshaw, Kimble, and Pribram (1965) demonstrated, the electrodermal component of the OR and its habituation is markedly impaired in amygdalectomized monkeys. The basal ganglia are involved in the origin of a premotor (locomotor) electrodermal component labeled EDA2 (Fig. 1.4, Sect. 1.3.4.1). The hippocampus has easy access to the origin of hypothalamically elicited electrodermal activity (EDA1) via its connections within the limbic system (see Fig. 1.4, Sect. 1.3.2.2), but has also inhibiting properties on EDA, which has been demonstrated in experiments with primates (Pribram & McGuinness, 1976).

Further evidence for a tight connection between hippocampal information processing and EDA is provided by Fowles' (1980) psychophysiological extension of Gray's (1973, 1982) septo-hippocampal system, which is outlined in Sect. 3.2.1.2. Based on this theoretical framework, an increased tonic EDA may be regarded as a concomitant of behavioral inhibition with increased selective attention and a thorough information content analysis. Combining those models with the one provided by Pribram and McGuinness, different components of EDA can be hypothetically related to three different stages of information processing:

1. A phasic electrodermal concomitant of sensory input, indicating an OR or a DR (Sect. 3.1.1.2), which is a result of an interaction between hippocampus and amygdala.
2. Another phasic or perhaps tonic electrodermal component,[69] indicating expectation or preparation, which is a result of an interaction between hippocampal and basal ganglia structures.
3. A tonic electrodermal concomitant of increased attention and arousal, being an indicator of hippocampal information processing.

Using the labels for the different origins of EDA as introduced in Sect. 1.3.4.1, the EDA1 pathway will be used for the above type (1) and (3) components, while the EDA2 pathway will be used solely for the type (2) component (see Fig. 3.4).

Considerations relating EDR recovery time to the range of attention made by Venables (1975) based upon animal as well as on human experimental and clinical research gave rise to an opposite action of the amygdala and hippocampal structures on electrodermal concomitants of information processing. Earlier, Bagshaw et al. (1965), relying on their research with hippocampus- and amygdala-lesioned monkeys, suggested that the duration of an EDR may be regarded as an index of the registration process for stimulus characteristics in a Sokolovian neuronal

---

[69] Despite this component labeled "tonic" by Pribram and McGuinness (1975), the preparatory EDA is often clearly phasic in nature, as in the case of the SIR (Sect. 3.1.2.1). Additionally, the CNV paradigm, which is regarded by Pribram and collaborator as appropriate for testing preparatory activation, is mostly tested within an S1–S2 paradigm with intervals of less than 6 s. "Tonic" cannot be used here in the sense of longer-lasting shifts of arousal level; therefore, "phasic" would be more suitable. Since the sudomotor pathway used here is clearly connected to CNS structures preparing distinct motor actions (see Fig. 1.6, Sect. 1.3.4.1), the label "phasic" for this component is preferred here.

model (Sect. 3.1.1). Thus, a faster recovery indicates a shorter duration of this registration process, which results in a slower buildup of the neuronal model, and hence a greater probability for reorientation together with a slower habituation. This view closely resembles Kahneman's (1973) report on pupillary as well as electrodermal concomitants of resource-allocation strategy. Venables (1975) combined this view with his own reinterpretation of results obtained by Edelberg (1972b), who recorded EDA[70] from 16 participants during a resting and a stress condition (cold pressor test), as well as during four tasks differing in complexity (counting forward and backward, reading aloud, and mirror drawing). EDR rec.tc was longest during resting and under stress and decreased with increasing task complexity. In another 14 participants, prolonged EDR recoveries were found under threat of electric shock while performing an RT task. Edelberg's conclusion was that acceleration of recovery indicates a mobilization for goal-directed behavior and that slow recovery may be an indicator of a DR (Sect. 3.1.1.2).

Deviant from this view, Venables (1975) offered the hypothesis of EDR recovery time being an indicator of readiness for information uptake. Accordingly, short recovery times will indicate an "open attentional gate" (i.e., a wide range of attention), for example during complex cognitive tasks. Instead, long recovery times are likely to occur under conditions of a "closed attentional gate" which occurs during resting and under stress conditions as well. Results obtained by Furedy (1972) provided additional evidence for a prolonged electrodermal recovery under increased anticipatory stress, using a tone-shock conditioning paradigm with 28 participants.[71] In this study a significant increase of electrodermal FIR rec.t/2 (Sect. 3.1.2.1) had been observed with an increase of the UCS intensity.

Clinical evidence for Venables' (1975) suggestion that EDR recovery is related to attention and information uptake comes from research with psychopaths and schizophrenic patients. It has been demonstrated that psychopaths show fast electrodermal habituation (Sect. 3.4.1.2) and also exhibit poor passive avoidance conditioning. They are assumed to constantly focus their attention, and their long electrodermal recovery times indicate what may be called a "closed gate" state of attention. It can be hypothesized then that psychopaths may have deficits in their septo-hippocampal system, which prevents them from effective conditioning to punishment, nonreward, and also to novel stimuli. As will be pointed out in Sect. 3.2.1.2, these conditions form the input of the septo-hippocampal BIS according to Gray (1982).

Schizophrenics, on the other hand, exhibit slow electrodermal habituation and short electrodermal recovery times (Sect. 3.4.2.1).[72] These can be regarded as signs

---

[70] Recorded as SR unipolar between a 2 cm^2 electrode at the middle finger and a 75 cm^2 electrode on the upper arm with starch cream and 8 μA/cm^2 constant current, transformed into SC scores.

[71] Performed as a reanalysis, in terms of electrodermal recovery, of data reported by Furedy and Klajner (1972) from a study with high vs. low intensity and signaled vs. nonsignaled UCS.

[72] This can be stated only for schizophrenic responders, since habituation cannot be measured in nonresponders (Sect. 3.4.2.2).

Table 3.1 Suggested relationships between subcortical activity, EDR recovery, habituation speed, attentional processes, and psychopathological groups (see text for explanations)

	Predominance of subcortical activity from	
	Amygdala	Hippocampus
Buildup of the neuronal model	Fast	Slow
Electrodermal habituation	Fast	Slow
Electrodermal recovery time	Long	Short
Range of attention	Narrow (focused)	Over-wide (distributed)
Attentional gate	Closed	Open
Clinical groups	Psychopaths	Schizophrenics

for a so-called open gate state of information processing, which may be due to a predominance of subcortical activity from the hippocampal area over neural impulses stemming from the amygdala. Table 3.1 combines the evidence for two different subcortical systems acting on the elicitation of EDA during information processing, including habituation and conditioning.

Differential influences of the subcortical structures mentioned in Table 3.1 on attention were suggested by Douglas and Pribram (1966) as well as by Pribram and McGuinness (1975). According to these authors, the amygdala's influence is predominantly on focusing of attention, while the hippocampus determines its direction.[73] However the connections between EDR recovery and cognitive processes outlined in Table 3.1 have to be treated as a working hypothesis, since most of the evidence comes from research with schizophrenics, and is controversial in some respects, which is also the case for the differences in habituation speed (Sect. 3.4.2.2). Furthermore, the discussion concerning recovery as being possibly dependent on EDR amp. has to be considered, though Janes (1982), in her study described below, and Janes, Strock, Weeks, and Worland (1985), in their study previously reported in Sect. 2.5.2.5, found ample evidence for electrodermal recovery showing enough independence of EDR amp. as well as of baseline EDA. On the other hand, results with respect to the role of EDR amp. as an indicator of cognitive processes seem confusing because of the wide variety in theoretical backgrounds and applied experimental settings. Extensive reviews of the appropriate literature have been provided by Spinks and Siddle (1983) with respect to cognitive influences on the OR and by Dawson and Schell (1985) focusing on cognitive control in classical autonomic conditioning (Sect. 3.1.2.1 "Cognitive vs. Noncognitive View of EDR Conditioning").

---

[73] For the general excitatory and inhibitory role of the amygdala and the hippocampus in controlling EDA, see Sect. 1.3.4.1 "Subcortical Control of EDA".

3.1.3.2   The EDR and Information Processing Capacity

One of the most widely discussed theoretical views of the autonomic response's role in cognitive processing is the Öhman (1979) model (see Fig. 3.3, Sect. 3.1.2.1), which suggests that an OR indicates a call for information processing resources (Sect. 3.1.1). In this model, an OR is elicited when an incoming stimulus fails to find a matching representation in STM,[74] which initiates a call for resources in a central processing channel with limited capacity, or initiates an unspecific response mobilization (Öhman, Dimberg, & Esteves, 1989). An opposing view has been advocated by Pribram and McGuinness (1975), who supposed the OR being a passive reflection of the amount of information being registered in the CNS. In a later paper, McGuinness and Pribram (1980) associated the OR with their "affect arousal system" which elicits phasic physiological concomitants of sensory input (Sect. 3.1.3.1). To test those different views of the OR's significance, Spinks et al. (1985) presented 76 participants of both genders a complex series of two-stimulus anticipation tasks. The imperative stimulus consisted of a slide with either one or six letters presented for either 100 or 1,000 ms, the content of which had to be reported not earlier than 8 s following stimulus offset. It was preceded 8 s earlier by a warning stimulus with three possible stages of information concerning the imperative stimulus (no, partial or full information). Similarly to the FIR-SIR differentiation being used in S1–S2 paradigms (Sect. 3.1.2.1), the authors applied a time window of 1–5 s following the warning stimulus' onset for the stimulus-registration component and a window of 5–9 s for the preparatory component of the EDR.[75] The amplitudes of both EDR components turned out to be more dependent on the anticipated amount of information within the imperative stimulus than of the warning stimulus' information content. Therefore, the authors concluded that the registration of information is neither a necessary determinant of the electrodermal OR's amplitude nor a parsimoniously useful part of OR theory. Instead, it is suggested to index an anticipatory activating process; this was also suggested by Sokolov (1966).

However, cognitive processes may not only influence electrodermal ORs to external stimulation. Internal cognitive processes (e.g., thoughts or expectations) may themselves elicit EDRs which has been demonstrated by Nikula (1991). In his study with 31 participants of both genders, Nikula used the onset of NS.SCRs[76] for triggering a 2 kHz tone upon which the participants had to speak out their ratings of thoughts they just had before the stimulus on seven Likert scales (e.g., how

---

[74] The autonomic OR component is regarded as being elicited by "preattentive" mechanisms in Neisser's (1967) sense.

[75] Recorded as SR with standard methodology, using an additional abraded forearm site for grounding, transformed to SCRs, range-corrected with respect to the EDR following a 1 s, 100 dB white noise stimulus at the end of the experiment (Sect. 2.3.3.4 "Range Corrections"), and finally square-root transformed.

[76] Recorded with standard methodology, detected by an analog computer using a slope criterion of 0.07 μS/s and an amplitude criterion of 0.3 μS.

surprising was the thought, how present were arousal and emotions, did they experience inner speech). As a within-subjects control, the same kind of rating was obtained during the absence of NS.SCRs. Negative emotion, subjective arousal, current concerns, and inner speech were significantly higher rated in intensity prior to the spontaneous occurrence of NS.SCRs compared to electrodermal "silent" periods.[77] The author concluded that cognitive processes seem to be concomitants of spontaneous EDRs. Those were labeled earlier as "voluntary" ORs by Maltzman (1979a) (Sect. 3.1.1). From a cognitive point of view, the use of NS.EDR freq. as a tonic EDA measure (Sect. 2.3.2.2) may reflect the general presence of highly arousing negatively tuned cognitive activity.

The TOR which follows stimulus omission (Sect. 3.1.2.1) can be regarded as another example of an EDR being not elicited by an external stimulus. This was demonstrated by Siddle and Packer (1987) who attempted to test the models of Wagner (1978) and Öhman (1979). With the use of an S1–S2 paradigm in several successive experiments, they demonstrated a reliably higher mean SCR amp. following S2 omission together with a dishabituation (Sect. 3.1.1) to re-presentation of S2 in the immediately following trial.[78] When using RT to auditory and visual probes in a similar experiment,[79] there was also some evidence of electrodermal omission responding and dishabituation, which was accompanied by slowing down of RT. The authors concluded that this might have been due to the fact that both omission and re-presentation of an expected stimulus demand information processing resources.

Similar results were obtained by Packer and Siddle (1989) who studied the effects of stimulus miscuing on the EDR. In their first experiment with 24 participants of both genders, the control groups received 33 S1–S2 pairings intermixed with presentations of a different stimulus S3.[80] The experimental group received 29 S1–S2 pairings intermixed with another 29 S3-alone presentations and four S3–S2 pairings. Miscuing (i.e., pairing CS– with UCS) in the experimental group increased SCR amp. as compared to appropriate trials in the control group. However, SCR amp. decreased across miscued trials, showing that miscuing became less surprising over time. Significant enhancement of SCR amp. appeared only in the first re-presentation trial. Both results were paralleled by those

---

[77] There was no relationship between the occurrence of NS.SCRs and positive emotions, which points to the specificity of NS.EDRs as indicator for negative emotional states (Sect. 3.2.2.1).

[78] Experiment 1 was performed with two independent groups (12 participants each of both genders), with vs. without omission in the 16th trial, either light-tone (1 kHz, 75 dB) or tone-light pairings as S1–S2. SCRs recorded with standard methodology were subjected to a range correction using a 100 dB stimulus at the end of the experiment to elicit a maximum SCR, and a square-root transformation.

[79] Experiment 3 was performed with 48 participants, presenting light circles or tones as RT probes 1,300 ms following S2 omission and S2 re-presentation.

[80] Similar stimulation and the same recording and evaluation techniques were applied as by Siddle and Packer (1987). A vibratory stimulus was used in addition to tone and light stimuli, all of them occurring equally often as S1, S2, and S3 in a Latin square design.

of continuously recorded S2 expectancy, being interpreted by the authors as consistent with Wagner's (1978) priming theory of STM. In the second experiment performed with another 24 participants of both genders, a RT stimulus probe (after the 300 ms S2 onset) was added, which yielded slower RTs following miscued and re-presented S2 trials in comparison to ordinary S1–S2 pairings within the control group. Thus, an enlarged EDR following unexpected omission or signaling of stimuli can be regarded as due to incongruencies in expectancy that appear during information processing within the central channel, with the aid of information stored in the STM (Fig. 3.3, Sect. 3.1.2.1).

The EDR has been used as an indicator for automatic processing of salient stimuli, which the participating individuals are instructed to ignore while taking part in experiments on selective attention.[81] Those studies use competing information, methods of distraction, shadowing or variations of attention via instructions. A frequently used paradigm is "dichotic shadowing," where the attended ear is presented with relevant information, while the other (unattended) ear is provided (masked) with irrelevant information.

Dawson and Schell (1982) confirmed results obtained earlier by Corteen and Wood (1972) as well as Corteen and Dunn (1974), demonstrating that even unnoticed information is processed to a level enabling semantic analysis. In addition, they found influences of shifts of attention as well as of lateralization (Sect. 3.1.3.4), since significant stimuli interspersed within irrelevant material were followed by an EDR only if they were presented to the left ear. During the first phase of the experiment, all 60 participants were subjected to a differential conditioning procedure (Sect. 3.1.2.1), in which animal words were associated with an electric shock while anatomical terms serving as control words were not. In the test phase, all words were repeated without shock. The critical words were presented embedded in the attended message to 20 participants and to 40 participants in the unattended one. Half of the latter group had to press a key when having perceived a critical word. The attended message was tape-recorded by a male experimenter while the unattended one was recorded by a female one. Both consisted of single-syllable high frequency words (every 750 ms). The ear for presentation was counterbalanced over participants. EDR amp.[82] were higher following shock-conditioned words as compared with neutral ones in the irrelevant material. However, this was only true in trials where participants temporarily shifted their attention to the unattended ear, which was indicated by masking errors, in postexperimental interviews, and by key presses in the appropriate group. Thus, a short-time attentional shift had been a

---

[81] The various filter and channel capacity theories are summarized elsewhere (e.g., Broadbent, 1971; Massaro, 1975).

[82] Recorded as SR (without reporting current density) with Beckman Ag/AgCl electrodes and K–Y gel from fingertips of the left hand, transformed to square-root conductance values. SCR amplitudes were evaluated quantitatively within 1–3 s following each critical word, contrarily to the Corteen group, which used an all-or-none amplitude criterion of 1 kΩ for an EDR appearing within a 13 s window.

prerequisite for detecting significant stimuli within unattended material being accompanied by an ANS response. This casts doubt on the earlier hypothesis of cognitive processing with unperceived sensory input, as stated by Davies (1983).

Spinks and Siddle (1983, p. 259), summarizing older studies performed by their own group, also concluded that electrodermal ORs to irrelevant stimuli redirect attention away from the attended channel to the unattended one. Presumably, a higher EDR amp. reflects a greater amount of redistribution of attention, while rapid habituation is an indicator of the speed at which processes develop that inhibit an analysis of the distracting stimulus.

By contrast, Frith and Allen (1983) came to the conclusion that the EDR amp. following irrelevant stimuli probably reflects the level of attention rather than its direction, which shows up in the habituation rate. In their first experiment, 41 participants performed different computer tasks (RT, vigilance, and arithmetic) while hearing irrelevant tones (1 kHz, 70 dB) which were also presented during work breaks. The SCR amp.[83] following irrelevant stimuli were significantly higher during task performance as compared to the breaks. In the second experiment with 39 outpatients suffering from minor neuroses, 16 participants heard the irrelevant tones while performing a forewarned RT task (as in the first experiment), while 23 participants were presented the same sequence of tones but had no task to perform. Habituation speed was significantly greater in participants given the tones during task performance. The authors suggested that a higher attentional level during the task would have been responsible for the greater OR to irrelevant stimuli as well as for their faster habituation.

One method being used for determining whether or not limited processing resources are shifted involves the use of a dual-task paradigm. Within this paradigm, slowing of RT to secondary task stimuli indicates the degree to which resources are allocated to a primary task. Such a paradigm was used by Dawson, Filion, and Schell (1989) in two experiments which examined the hypothesis that the larger a stimulus elicited electrodermal OR magnitude, the greater the resource allocation for the processing of that stimulus would be. In their first experiment, 75 participants of both genders performed a primary binaural auditory orienting task consisting of 48 trials. Participants were instructed to count the number of longer than usual tones (7 s instead of 5 s duration of 70 dB 1 kHz tones) on one ear (task-relevant tones) and simply to ignore the same kind of tones presented to the other ear (task-irrelevant tones). The last trial included an unexpected 1.5 kHz tone presented binaurally. The secondary task consisted of 248 visual RT probes being interspersed within the primary task in a way that could not directly affect the

---

[83] Recorded from the left hand's fingers with 1 cm^2 Ag/AgCl electrodes and K–Y gel, within 1–4 s following stimulus onset. Two successive intervals without an SCR exceeding 0.02 µS were used as the habituation criterion (Sect. 3.1.1.3).

expected ORs. SCR amp. obtained with standard methodology[84] from 12 "clear" presentations of the orienting stimuli[85] were higher following significant stimuli, those being longer as compared to nonsignificant stimuli. There was also a significant correlation ($r = 0.40$) between OR magnitude and the amount of resources allocated to the significant orienting stimuli, as determined by the RT in the secondary task. However, this was only true for RT probes presented either 300 or 600 ms following stimulus onset. Unexpectedly, at the 150 ms probe position the task-irrelevant orienting stimuli seemed to elicit the greatest amount of resource allocation.

To further enlighten this unexpected result of a directional dissociation between the OR magnitude and the amount of resource allocation, Dawson, Filion, and Schell (1989) performed a second experiment with 86 participants drawn from the same population, using a modified arrangement of tasks. In general, they replicated the findings of their first experiment. In addition, they revealed that manipulation of predictability and discriminability of significant vs. nonsignificant orienting stimuli affected the dissociation between OR magnitude and the probe RT-based resource allocation measure. An increase in predictability made the dissociation disappear because of the generally lowered requirement of resource allocation; an increase of difficulty of the discrimination also reduced the dissociation because there was large and equal resource allocation to both kinds of stimuli. The authors concluded that the relationship between ANS orienting response and resource allocation might be a more complex one as hitherto suggested. However, they also claimed that the theoretical framework provided by Kahneman (1973) and Öhman (1979) is consistent with their results and may be used in the planning of further research.

To further examine the dissociation effect with respect to its generality, i.e., the conditions under which it can be observed, Filion, Dawson, Schell, and Hazlett (1991) performed three subsequent experiments in which SCR amp. were recorded with standard methodology as measures for the OR strength and RT probes as indicators for the resource allocation. In the first experiment, a total of 72 participants who underwent a primary auditory and a secondary visual RT task were divided into an early probes group (20 females, 16 males) and a late probes group (24 females, 12 males). Two blocks of 24 primary tasks each were presented, 12 of which were task relevant and 12 task irrelevant.[86] Three of them were "clear" trials (see Footnote 85) for measuring autonomic responses without contamination of movement artifacts (Sect. 2.2.5.2). After all 48 trials, two additional novelty trials with 800 instead of the usual 1,000 Hz tones were added to measure resource

---

[84] Including a square-root transformation, using a time window within 1.0–3.05 s following stimulus onset, and an amplitude criterion of 0.008 μS.

[85] Clear trials were those without probes presented from 2 s before OR stimulus onset until 2 s after its offset.

[86] Auditory tasks were the same as in the first experiment of Dawson, Filion, and Schell (1989). All tones presented to the to-be-ignored ear were designated task-irrelevant stimuli, whereas all tones presented to the to-be-attended ear were designated task relevant, regardless of their length.

allocation during the processing of novel stimuli. For the early probes group, secondary RT probes were presented in a counterbalanced order 50, 100 or 150 ms after stimulus onset, whereas the delays were 150, 200 or 250 ms for the late probes group. Results were in general accordance with the Dawson, Filion, and Schell (1989) findings, supporting a general relationship between SC-OR amp. and resource allocation, but also replicating the dissociation effect. In addition, there was a significant correlation ($r = 0.59$ and 0.63) between the SC-OR amp. and resource allocation for the 150 ms probe position during the task-relevant stimuli, regardless of being presented in the early or late probes group, which was not found for all other probe positions. This was confirmed in a second experiment with 24 participants, in which low-pitched (800 Hz) and high-pitched (1,200 Hz) binaural tones were applied as task-relevant and task-irrelevant stimuli, with 50, 150, and 250 ms intervals for the probe RT tasks, and other slight procedural changes. Again, no significant correlations between SC-OR amp. and resource allocation were obtained during presentation of task-irrelevant tones. As in the first experiment, significant increases of resource allocation to novel tones presented at the end of the trials were only observed in the 150 ms condition. To further enlighten the special role of the 150 ms interval for the resource allocation hypothesis, Filion et al. (1991) performed a third experiment with 26 participants, in which they presented task-relevant and task-irrelevant stimuli in different sensory modalities, i.e., tones as used in the previous experiments vs. tactile vibration stimuli applied to the upper arm. The intervals for secondary RT probes were the same as in experiment 2. Presenting task-relevant and task-irrelevant stimuli to different sensory modalities, hence being not physically similar, eliminated the dissociation between SC-OR amp. and resource allocation as measured by slowing down the probe RT. Their interpretation was that the slower RT associated with the task-irrelevant stimuli as observed in the earlier studies might have been associated with an automatic switch of attention prompted by the physical similarity of task-relevant and task-irrelevant stimuli. The authors suggested that there is a general positive relationship between SC-OR amp. and resource allocation under selective attention conditions.

Melis and van Boxtel (2001) used SCL[87] together with other ANS measures (including ECG) from 52 right-handed participants (27 females, 25 males) during performance of a figural and a verbal inductive reasoning task. Participants were post hoc divided into good and poor inductive reasoners ($N = 26$ each). Weighted multidimensional scaling analysis of the psychophysiological responses revealed three dimensions, one of which was identified as mainly sympathetic, the other one mainly parasympathetic dominated. The SCL showed only slightly higher factor loadings in the sympathetic dimension, whereas heart rate variability (HRV) clearly

---

[87] Recorded with standard methodology from thenar/hypothenar left-hand sites; differences between mean SCLs during the task and the preceding baseline period were used as response measure which was logarithmically transformed (Sect. 2.3.3.3).

dominated the loadings of the parasympathetic dimension. Overall, the results suggested that sympathetic activity yielded relatively more importance for poor as compared to good reasoners, being interpreted by the authors as reflecting the higher cognitive activity level needed by the poor reasoners for solving the tasks. Although being rather indirect support for a possible role of EDA as indicator of information processing capacity required, the results somehow add to the empirical evidence for EDRs being a possible indicator of information processing, as proposed by Öhman (1979). However, the ED-OR seems to be rather sensitive to stimulus conditions and individual differences.

3.1.3.3 EDA and Decision Making

During the last 2 decades a specific use of EDA as an indicator for decision making emerged in the context of the somatic marker (SM) hypothesis. Damasio (1994) proposed the SM hypothesis to explain typical deficits in decision making observed in patients with VMPFC damage (Sect. 1.3.4.1 "Cortical Control of EDA"). Whereas VMPFC patients appear cognitively unimpaired (i.e., having no apparent deficits in working memory, attention, cognitive estimation, and cognitive flexibility), they exhibit a pronounced inability in decision making, especially in the social and personal domain and where decisions are ambiguous and require a quick response. They have great difficulties in experiencing and expressing emotions and exhibit increased impulsivity (Damasio, Tranel, & Damasio, 1991). The psychophysiological claim of the SM hypothesis is that VMPFC patients are unable to use physiological signals which normally assist cognitive processes such as decision making, particularly under conditions of uncertainty and complexity. The term SM suggests that the underlying somatic arousal works as a characteristic signal for both an emotional response to, or in anticipation of, a specific decision option. This in turn serves to assess its value and acts as a booster signal for working memory and attention (Bechara & Damasio, 2005; Damasio, 1994). Negative SMs are believed to act as bodily signal, which may help the individual to avoid negative outcomes. Conversely, positive SMs are thought to serve as trigger signals for attempting positive outcomes. Somatic markers can be generated either in the periphery or in the CNS itself, among others in the basal ganglia, the amygdala, the cingulate gyrus, and the VMPFC.

According to Damasio's theoretical view, SMs constitute special cases of the so-called secondary emotions, which are acquired during the association of certain event categories with corresponding evolutionary-based and universal primary emotions. Somatic markers have the ability to act through a so-called as-if loop in the CNS, without the individual becoming aware of their peripheral physiological concomitants. In case of damage to one of the involved brain structures, especially the VMPFC, the generation of SMs will fail, thus leading to decisions based solely on a logical cost-benefit analysis, without the SM's guidance toward advantageous choices and avoidance of nonadvantageous choices. The more complex and uncertain the situations are, the more an appropriate cost-benefit analysis may be replaced by a procrastination of the decision and/or by an impulsive and short-sighted behavior.

Bechara, Damasio, Damasio, and Anderson (1994) introduced a particular experimental setting called the Iowa gambling task (IGT) which was designed to ascertain risky and impulsive decision making, as well as for probing the effects of VMPFC lesions on decision making and impairments in the as-if loop. A key feature of the IGT is that test takers need to forgo short-term in favor of long-term benefits. They are required to select a card from one of four different card decks. Two of the decks are disadvantageous, because they are coupled with high gains but even higher losses. Over time, choosing these decks will lead to an overall negative balance. The other two decks are advantageous, because they are coupled with small gains but even smaller losses. Choosing cards from these decks will lead to a overall positive balance. In contrast to nonimpaired test takers, who begin to avoid disadvantageous decks rather quickly, bilateral VMPFC damaged patients continue to prefer selecting cards from disadvantageous decks.

Most studies investigating the SM hypothesis by comparing the IGT behavior of VMPFC patients and controls used the SCR amp. as psychophysiological concomitant of experiencing SMs. Bechara, Tranel, Damasio, and Damasio (1996) recorded SC with standard methodology from thenar/hypothenar sites in 7 patients with VMPFC lesions (3 females, 4 males) and 12 normal controls (7 females, 5 males) during their IGT performance. The authors confirmed the prevalence of a disadvantageous strategy among VMPFC patients which was not present in the controls. Both groups generated SCRs in response to gains and losses. However, while becoming experienced with the task, only the controls showed anticipatory SCRs prior to the card selections. The SCR amp. were significantly higher for the disadvantageous than for the advantageous card decks. No such discriminative anticipatory SCRs were observed in the group of VMPFC patients. Motor artifacts (Sect. 2.2.5.2) could not have been the cause for the anticipatory SCRs, since they appeared well ahead of moving the hand to pick up a card. In addition, EDA was recorded from the nonmoving hand. Bechara et al. concluded that the lack of anticipatory SCRs in VMPFC patients points to their insensitivity for future outcomes.

Bechara, Tranel, and Damasio (2000) addressed the question of whether the impairment of VMPFC patients in avoiding disadvantageous card decks is generated by hypersensitivity to reward, insensitivity to punishment, or insensitivity to future consequences in general. They used the original IGT and a modification, where the advantageous decks yielded high immediate punishment but even higher future reward, whereas the disadvantageous decks yielded low immediate punishment but even lower future reward. In the first experiment each task was performed by different samples of 10 patients (5 of each gender) and 20 control participants (12 females, 8 males), from which SCR amp.[88] were recorded as concomitants of

---

[88] Recorded with a method described by Bechara, Damasio, Damasio, and Lee (1999), though incompletely reported, from thenar/hypothenar sites. SCRs appearing between the end of the reward/punishment window and the next decisive mouse click (on average 10 s) were considered anticipatory, whereas SCRs being generated after turning cards were considered reward or punishment SCRs. After removing tonic SCL changes by a difference-based transformation, an area measurement (see Sect. 2.3.1.4) was calculated and expressed in microseconds per time interval.

SMs. The results of the modified IGT were comparable to those obtained with the original IGT, i.e., insensitivity for punishment or sensitivity for reward was unlikely to be the underlying mechanism for the patients' impairment.

The second experiment used another IGT variant. This was established to test whether the task performance within the VMPFC group could be improved by increasing the adversity of future consequences, using a stepwise increase of the immediate punishment and a decrease of the delayed reward. Even after increasing the amount of punishment and decreasing the reward on the "risky" decks, the 8 VMPFC patients (4 of each gender) were impaired on the task compared to the 17 control participants (9 females, 8 males). Additionally, the authors compared SCR amp. after punishment with those following reward. In both conditions, the authors observed that patients and controls did not significantly differ in their SCR amp., regardless of whether the consequences occurred immediately or with delay. Bechara et al. (2000) argued that only the insensitivity for future consequences could serve as an explanation for the impaired decision making of VMPFC patients. Unfortunately, the authors did not report anticipatory SCRs. Therefore, it remained unclear if the patients also failed to produce anticipatory SCRs as they did in earlier studies using the original IGT.

To enlighten the underlying psychological mechanisms of the VMPFC patients' failure in the IGT and corresponding lack of SCRs, several studies were conducted with normal individuals differing in IGT performance. For example, Crone, Somsen, van Beek, and van der Molen (2004) recorded anticipatory SCRs[89] and those in response to decision options for both reward and punishment during the performance of a computerized IGT version. Based on their IGT performance, 96 healthy participants were split into three groups: poor (8 males, 21 females), moderate (11 males, 23 females), and good performers (11 males, 22 females). Good and moderate performers showed larger anticipatory SCRs preceding disadvantageous selections, while the bad performing group did not seem to differentiate between the "good" and "bad" decks. The amplitude of anticipatory SCRs was highest for the good performers, followed by moderate and then poor performers. Differences between "good" and "bad" decisions were largest for the good performer group, followed by moderate and then poor performers. The relationship between performance and anticipatory EDA was confirmed by a positive correlation ($r = 0.49$) between the number of advantageous choices and the difference between the SCR amp. prior to advantageous and disadvantageous choices. Additionally, EDA following reward and punishment was independent of performance strategy. However, higher punishment SCR amp. were observed following disadvantageous compared to advantageous choices. Reward SCR amp. did not differentiate between advantageous and disadvantageous decks. The authors proposed that impairments in IGT

---

[89] Recorded with constant 0.5 V from 1 cm^2 Ag/AgCl electrodes attached to the medial phalanges of the nondominant hand's middle and index fingers. Artifacts stemming from gross respiratory maneuvers (Sect. 2.2.5.2) were eliminated by means of the respiration signal obtained from a temperature sensor placed under the nostrils.

performance of bad performers were more likely due to weak somatic responses (i.e., SMs) as opposed to being caused by reward and punishment.

To clarify the extent to which SMs guide decisions, Jenkinson, Baker, Edelstyn, and Ellis (2008) investigated if SC measures distinguish between good and bad decision makers. Forty-one healthy participants (30 females, 11 males) performed a computerized version of the IGT with either play money or real money as reinforcers. This condition was introduced to determine whether the use of real or play money may lead to differences in IGT performance and whether somatic activity is affected by the type of reinforcer, even if there is no real financial incentive. Based on their IGT performance, participants were classified as impaired and nonimpaired performers. Jenkinson et al. (2008) recorded SCL with standard methodology (except sites being cleaned with alcohol) continuously during the IGT, with electrodes attached to the distal phalanx of the index and ring finger of the nondominant hand. The extracted parameters were (1) punishment SCL and reward SCL, calculated as change between baseline score (average over the last 50 s prior to the experiment) and the average score over the 2 s immediately after each card selection; (2) anticipatory SCL changes calculated as above, except using the last 5 s prior to each card selection. Analysis of the physiological data revealed that first the increase of the anticipatory SCL was greater preceding selections from disadvantageous decks compared to advantageous decks. Similarly, the SCL rise following reward was higher for disadvantageous decks as opposed to advantageous decks. No differences between the deck types were found for punishment SCL changes. The comparison between impaired (bad) and nonimpaired (good) performers showed no difference, both for the anticipatory SCL and for the appraisal SCL data (SCLs following the outcomes of deck decisions, i.e., reward and punishment).

Taken together, the findings discussed so far support Damasio's claim that SMs influence decision making in terms of immediate choices on the IGT as reflected by electrodermal differentiation between good and bad options prior to a decision. However, the fact that impaired and unimpaired task performance cannot be physiologically distinguished suggests that SMs do not discriminate between good and bad decision makers, in terms of overall performance or long-term consequences, but instead reflect only immediate decisions. According to Jenkinson et al. (2008), the pattern of autonomic activity found in their study is consistent with the suggestion of Tomb, Hauser, Deldin, and Caramazza (2002) that the overall performance on the IGT is independent of somatic activity, which instead only reflects the magnitude of immediate reward or punishment. The differentiation between good and bad decision making ("good" and "bad" decks) and good and bad decision makers (impaired vs. nonimpaired performance) may provide some explanations for the conflicting evidence with respect to the SM hypothesis. According to Jenkinson et al. (2008), the finding of abnormal IGT performance despite normal SMs could be explained if SMs were independent of overall IGT performance and only reflected the immediate deck selection. In addition, the comparison of real money and play money condition showed a marginally greater SCL rise in anticipation of a selection from disadvantageous decks compared to the advantageous decks when play money was used but not when real money was used. In line with this, an SCL rise occurred following reward from disadvantageous decks when using play money, but not for real money. The same influences of play money were found for the IGT performance. There are, however, studies which indicate that real money leads to improved performance (Bowman & Turnbull, 2003; Carter & Smith-Pasqualini, 2004).

As people are getting older, their decision-making performance may become impaired, even in the absence of observable diseases. In an attempt to use EDA for enlightening the possible underlying mechanisms, Denburg, Recknor, Bechara, and Tranel (2006) applied the IGT to 80 older adults (56–85 years) and calculated an overall IGT impairment score for each participant. They determined 31 clearly unimpaired (16 females, 15 males) and 23 clearly impaired decision makers (14 females, 9 males). SCR was recorded from thenar/hypothenar sites with unreported methodology. Results showed that the older impaired participants failed to generate discriminatory SCRs, since their anticipatory SCRs did not differentiate between the advantageous and disadvantageous decks, although the impaired group produced anticipatory SCRs of similar magnitude as the unimpaired group. The older unimpaired participants generated discriminatory SCRs, but in contrast to younger healthy individuals, they produced significantly larger SCRs as response to the advantageous decks compared to the disadvantageous decks. The authors interpreted the reverse direction of discrimination among older, unimpaired individuals as an inverted marker signal. Unlike healthy young participants who produced negative SMs to avoid disadvantageous options and outcomes, a positive somatic state in elderly healthy individuals may promote approach behavior. This interpretation is supported by results of other developmental studies (e.g., Carstensen, Issacowitz, & Charles, 1999; Charles, Reynolds, & Gatz, 2001; Gross et al., 1997) which advocate that elderly people experience less negative affect than younger adults.

Additional support for the assumption that EDA distinguishes between "good" and "bad" decisions derives from studies with patients having no diagnosis of brain damage. Bechara and Damasio (2002) tested the hypothesis that some substance-dependent individuals suffer from decision-making deficits, which are comparable to those observable in patients with VMPFC lesions. They compared IGT performance and arousal as indexed by EDA[90] in 46 substance-dependent individuals,[91] 10 VMPFC patients (5 of each gender) and 49 healthy controls (28 females, 21 males). The results showed that a subgroup (63%) of substance-dependent participants used disadvantageous strategies in the IGT, which were preceded by impairments of anticipatory SCRs, whereas the remaining 27% were inconspicuous. The impaired subgroup generated lower SCR amp. compared to the controls, but higher anticipatory SCRs than the VMPFC patients. The differences between

---

[90] Recorded as stated in Footnote 88.

[91] Alcohol-, cocaine/crack-, or metamphetamine-dependent inpatients shortly before the completion of their rehabilitation; 25 females, 21 males.

substance-dependent and healthy participants reached significance only for the disadvantageous decks, whereas the difference for either group to the VMPFC patients remained significant for the advantageous decks. The behavioral data of the IGT revealed analog findings. A subgroup of their substance-dependent participants yielded normal SCRs to punishment, but an impairment of anticipatory SCRs. The authors presumed that this subgroup might have suffered from a similar dysfunction of the VMPFC as the patients. Hence, in some substance-dependent individuals, the "myopia" for the future resulting from a dysfunctional VMPFC may be one of the core mechanisms leading to compulsive and uncontrollable behavior.

In a subsequent study with the same participants, Bechara, Dolan, and Hindes (2002) tested the possibility that hypersensitivity to reward may account for the "myopia" for the future in this subgroup of substance-dependent individuals, using the IGT modification from the Bechara et al. (2000) study. Bechara et al. (2002) recorded SCRs (by means of the same method as the first study) after receiving a reward and anticipatory SCRs during the deck decision. A subgroup of 14 substance-dependent participants (6 females, 8 males), who performed normally in both IGT variants, generated SCRs which were not different from the control group. By contrast, a subgroup of 9 substance-dependent participants with impairments on both IGT variants, were indistinguishable from the VMPFC patients in all psychophysiological measures. A third subpopulation of 16 substance-dependent individuals was impaired during the original IGT, but not in the IGT modification. This subpopulation yielded several significant differences to VMPFC patients and controls: (1) they displayed abnormally high reward SCRs; (2) their anticipatory SCRs seemed more sensitive to the amount of reward, because their amplitudes became higher in relation to the advantageous decks as the reward increased; and (3) anticipatory SCRs became smaller in relation to the disadvantageous decks as the reward began to be reduced, relative to the reward of the "good" decks. In contrast, the anticipatory SCRs generated by the controls seemed more sensitive to the loss associated with each deck. According to the authors their results support the hypothesis that at least a subgroup of substance-dependent individuals is hypersensitive to reward, and the presence or the prospect of receiving a reward guides their choice and behavior. Additionally, the results of the Bechara and Damasio (2002) study imply that the same subgroup of substance-dependent participants might be hyposensitive to punishment, because this subgroup showed reduced punishment SCRs in comparison to nonimpaired groups. For this reason, their good performance in the reversed IGT variant could be an indirect consequence of their addiction, leading them to accept a greater amount of punishment for obtaining a larger reward.

The SM hypothesis and some of its predictions have come under criticism, particularly with respect to the interpretation of psychophysiological findings. For example, several researchers challenged the importance of anticipatory SMs for the guidance of future decisions, as proposed by the SM hypothesis (e.g., Jenkinson et al., 2008), emphasizing that future decision making is determined not only by anticipatory SMs but also by experienced outcomes of previous decisions, since developing an anticipatory marker is contingent with the perception of physiological responses that follow previous decisions. Tomb et al. (2002) further challenged the proposition that SMs mark the long-term consequences of decisions. Instead, they proposed that the anticipatory SCRs elicited during the selection of cards in the IGT occur because disadvantageous decks yield high amounts of reward and punishment relative to the advantageous decks. As a consequence, the larger anticipatory SCRs for "bad" decks may represent the magnitude of gains and losses rather than long-term outcomes. Consistent with the Tomb et al. criticism, Suzuki, Hirota, Takasawa, and Shigemasu (2003) observed that low appraisal SCRs in response to early IGT trials were related to persistence in selecting risky choices, despite the common observation of greater anticipatory SCRs prior to selecting "bad" compared to "good" decks. Suzuki et al. (2003) applied a Japanese IGT version to 40 healthy participants (13 females, 27 males) and found no relationship between anticipatory SCRs and task performance in contrast to Crone et al. (2004). Conversely, they revealed that SCRs in response to reward or punishment may be more important for mediating task performance, because participants who elicited greater SCRs tended to have a steeper learning curve on the task. Together with findings that a subgroup of healthy individuals who exhibit normal anticipatory SCRs but are indicative of impaired performance on the IGT (around 20%; e.g., Bechara and Damasio 2002; Bechara et al., 2000), the Crone et al. (2004) results challenge the importance of SMs for advantageous decisions especially with respect to long-term planning.

Another critical point concerns the crucial role of SMs in guiding decisions and how much of human decision making could be ascribed to their emotional influence. This question is related to whether the effect of the SMs is implicit or explicit. One claim of the SM hypothesis is that SMs evaluate the choice as good or bad before conscious knowledge is available. However, Maia and McClelland (2004) reported evidence that healthy individuals are able to demonstrate conscious knowledge about the IGT to behave advantageously. In response to the criticisms of Maia and McClelland (2004), Bechara, Damasio, Tranel, and Damasio (2005) described findings which denote that implicit learning was taking place prior to explicit understanding of the IGT procedure. Analysis of SCRs, performance and participant's reports on the matter, if they knew consciously what was going on, showed that individuals reach a conscious knowledge about the reward/punishment schedule before they have such an understanding. This means, they intuitively create a hypothesis on which were "good" and "bad" decks. Around 30% of the 10 healthy participants did not reach the conscious level, despite performing normally on the task. Additionally, anticipatory SCRs emerge and selections from the "good" decks increased at the intuitional level. However, Maia and McClelland conducted a more sensitive test which took the form of a structured interview, to indicate the awareness of the study participants in more detail than simple yes/no questions. They concluded that individuals begin to behave advantageously when they have conscious knowledge of the relative strengths and weaknesses of each deck, and that they can use this knowledge as the basis for judgments on which deck to select next. Bechara, Damasio, Tranel, and Damasio (2005) stated that the research of Maia and McClelland (2004) does not undermine the SM hypothesis. Whereas Maia and McClelland (2004) focused on the participant's level of conscious knowledge with respect to the task, Bechara and colleagues focused on the amount of SCR being present in relation to the beginning of advantageous decisions. Bechara et al. (2005) emphasized that the central feature of SMs is not that unconscious biases accomplish decisions in the absence of conscious knowledge in a given situation, but that emotion-related signals assist cognitive processes, even when being not conscious. Somatic markers are emotion-related signals which are either conscious or an unconscious processes.[92]

In summary, one might conclude that empirical studies of the SM hypothesis have emerged which both support and conflict findings for Damasio's claim that SMs are crucial for guiding decisions. The research of Bechara and colleagues was in favor of the assumption that somatic states are involved in decision making, and that the differentiation between "good" and "bad" decisions by means of anticipatory SCRs is a crucial finding in supporting the SM hypothesis. The role of SMs as indexed by physiological arousal has been reconfirmed in several studies. However, other researchers have failed to support the assumptions of Damasio and colleges. Possible explanations for these conflicting findings might depend on several methodological and conceptual points. For example, existing variations in the administration of the IGT, e.g., the use of play money vs. real money (e.g., Bowman & Turnbull 2003; Jenkinson et al., 2008) or variations in the frequency of reward and punishment (Chiu et al., 2008) might influence equivocal findings regarding the SM hypothesis (e.g., Colombetti, 2008; Dunn, Dalgleish, & Lawrence, 2006; Jenkinson et al., 2008). Another unexplained question is the contribution of SMs to immediate decisions and/or long-term consequences. Furthermore, it remains unclear to what extent SMs are unconscious or implicit to regulate decision making.

EDA has also been used in other settings as an unobtrusive measure for detecting the individuals' expectations, i.e., without asking them directly about their expectations, by Carbonnell, Vidal, Sequeira, and Caverni (2006) in a study on reasoning bias. In a first experiment, 10 participants (7 females, 3 males) performed a computerized task which required the detection of a set of rules in pairs of cards with geometric figures within a finite number of 8–12 trials. After each presentation, they were asked to respond, indicating whether the example fits the rule or not, followed by feedback. They were given a maximum of 20 s per card. In the second experiment with 16 participants (10 females, 6 males), SCRs were recorded with standard methodology from the medial phalanges of the index and middle fingers, with an amplitude criterion of 0.02 μS when elicited 1–6 s after feedback. To avoid anticipatory SCRs, feedback appeared variable between 6 and 8 s after the participant's response. Too much habituation was prevented by restricting the set of rules to four. After the key trial, during which the participants were expected to

---

[92] Abnormal EDRs in connection with poor IGT performance have also been observed in a variety of neurological and psychiatric conditions, e.g., substance and alcohol addiction (Bechara & Damasio, 2002; Bechara et al., 2001, 2002; Fishbein et al. 2005), Huntington's disease (Campbell, Stout, & Finn, 2004), multiple sclerosis, Parkinson's disease (Sect. 3.5.4.2), and anorexia nervosa (Tchanturia et al., 2007).

having correctly detected the rule, negative feedback evoked significantly higher SCR amp. compared to positive feedback. Such a difference could not be observed in the second trial which served as control. This points to a high probability that participants did not expect negative feedback at the key trial, since there was no difference between SCRs following positive and negative feedback in general.

Critchley et al. (2000) in their study, the method of which is described in Sect. 2.2.3.5, combined SC with fMRI recording from 3 participants of each gender during a playing-card guessing task with feedback of the cumulative financial gain or loss. Participants were unaware of gains and losses being predetermined randomly. For SCR analysis, peaks were identified being more than two standard deviations higher than the SC background activity and showing a typical waveform of an SCR. Significant SCR-related fMRI activity was observed in the right lateral orbitofrontal cortex, extending posteriorly into the anterior insula, in the left lingual gyrus, the right fusiform gyrus, and the left cerebellum. However, the SCR-related analysis did not allow distinguishing between anticipatory and feedback-elicited SCRs and their fMRI concomitants.

3.1.3.4 EDR and Memory Storage

Besides their role as concomitants for cognitive processes during information uptake, processing, and establishing learned relationships, EDRs are also discussed as potential indicators of information storage and retrieval. However, the results in this area of research were not unequivocal. Several studies reviewed by Raskin (1973) supported the view that stimuli being accompanied by a higher EDR amp. have a greater probability of being transferred to long-term memory (LTM). Since the stimuli used in these studies were often emotion eliciting in nature, it remained unclear whether the EDR evoked by their presentation had been determined by their concomitant arousal level as supposed.[93] Unexpectedly, an elicitation of large EDR by a stimulus did not facilitate its representation in the STM. This was demonstrated in a study performed by Corteen (1969) with 60 participants, which were divided into three groups. The first group had to recall 21 or 15 words immediately, the second group after 20 min and the third group after 2 weeks. The point-biserial correlation between the log SCR amp.[94] following the stimulus presentation during acquisition and the recall criterion increased from $r = 0.13$ to a range from $r = 0.23$ to $r = 0.40$ with the interval between learning and recall.

---

[93] A possible LTM-modulatory mechanism for emotion-eliciting events, which includes influences from the amygdala and from hormonal systems on hippocampus-dependent declarative memory storage, backed up by PET studies and discussions of ANS responses in general, was suggested by Cahill and McGaugh (1998).

[94] Recorded as SR by the use of a Wheatstone bridge, presumably using AC, transformed into log SCR. Ag/AgCl electrodes, saturated with 3% NaCl solution, were screwed into the arm-rest of the participant's chair, fitting to the palm of the right hand.

Corteen interpreted this result as showing the establishment of LTM traces for highly arousing stimuli, while autonomic arousal does not seem to influence STM, where stimuli differing with respect to the elicited arousal are recalled with about the same probability.

The information processing model suggested by Öhman (1979), which attempts to integrate the concepts of OR, learning, and attention, allows the derivation of a specific indicator function of the EDR for stimulus processing in STM and LTM. As previously mentioned in Sect. 3.1.2.1, the EDR components that appear during classical conditioning can be regarded as concomitants of specific cognitive processes within the Öhman model. A new and/or unexpected stimulus without STM representation will elicit an OR and begin concurrently with analyzing and processing its properties. This includes search and finally storage in LTM, which is connected with "cognitive effort" (Kahneman, 1973). Therefore, Stelmack, Plouffe, and Winogron (1983) concluded that the high recall rate of unusual stimuli is due to an increased amount of energy needed during their storage, which had been available as a result of the strong OR following those stimuli.

This hypothesis was tested by Stelmack, Plouffe, and Falkenberg (1983) in three experiments on the role of the OR in recognition memory for pictures and words, being presented for 3 s on slides. The stimuli had been dichotomized with respect to their frequency of recall. In the first experiment, 15 participants of both genders were assigned to one of the four groups of stimuli, made up by pictures vs. words and frequently vs. nonfrequently recalled. After ten stimulus presentations, a test stimulus of the alternate frequency-of-recall class was introduced. The SCR amp.[95] was significantly higher in the group which received high recognition memory pictures as opposed to the other groups. Thus, the connection between the electrodermal OR and the recall probability could only be shown for figures. In the subsequent experiment, 56 participants received 12 repetitions of a picture or word stimulus which they either recognized or failed to recognize. The initial SCR amp. was higher for the nonrecognized compared to the recognized stimuli. This finding was replicated in the third experiment with 40 participants. Stelmack, Plouffe, and Winogron (1983) interpreted these results as being due to a "priming" effect, indicated by a relative SCR decrement to stimuli which had been recognized.

The observation that stimuli which elicit high SCR amp. are memorized better than those which elicit smaller SCRs, may be more an arousal-elicited than a cognitive phenomenon. LaBar and Phelps (1998) performed a study with 10 left-temporal (7 females, 3 males) and 12 right-temporal (7 females, 5 males) lobectomized patients 2–8 years after their surgery, in comparison with 23 healthy controls (14 females, 9 males) matched for age and educational level. The participants were shown 20 arousing (e.g., sexually and taboo) and 20 neutral words in random sequence on a computer screen (4 s duration, ISIs between 12 and 16 s), buffered with two additional

---

[95] Recorded with standard methodology, but using Beckman miniature electrodes and K–Y gel, within 1–5 s following stimulus onset, using an amplitude criterion of 0.024 µS, and square-root transformed.

filler words at the beginning and at the end of the list. SCRs were recorded from the middle and ring finger of the participant's nondominant hand. After the disappearance of each word, participants rated its arousal-inducing property on a 4 point Likert scale and their familiarity on a 6 point Likert scale. In all groups, square-rooted SCR amp. (Sect. 2.3.3.3) were significantly higher for arousing than for neutral words. Recall for words was assessed immediately after their presentation and 1 h later. Only the controls exhibited an increase of memory for the arousing words after 1 h, pointing to the importance of medial temporal lobe structures for memory consolidation of arousing events.

An attempt to combine emotional properties of stimuli with the role of EDA during information processing had been made by Öhman et al. (1989). They exposed two groups of 20 participants each to pictures of angry and happy faces taken from the Ekman and Friesen set (Ekman, Friesen, & Ellsworth, 1972), while SCRs[96] were recorded. Participants were given the opportunity to habituate to unmasked as well as masked versions of these faces. An acquisition phase followed in which one group was shock-conditioned to angry faces and the other one to happy faces, which had a clear effect on the subsequent test trials. When the conditioned stimuli were masked with neutral faces, at least a portion of the differential responding survived backward masking in angry faces but not in happy ones. The authors concluded that responses conditioned to visual stimuli can be elicited very early in the informational chain of events, even if its access to awareness is blocked through backward masking. However, this effect appeared to be specific to biologically fear relevant stimuli like angry faces, since it did not show up in happy faces despite an equal amount of conditioning being evident for these pictures. Thus, emotional stimuli may be capable of evoking physiological responses after a very quick stimulus analysis, and even if the stimuli are blocked from entering consciousness. Investigating the specific role of emotional and cognitive factors in eliciting electrodermal concomitants to stimulation requires highly controlled experimental research, paralleled by neurophysiological modeling, such as proposed in Sect. 3.2.1.2.

3.1.4 Electrodermal Lateralization and Hemispheric Asymmetry

Despite reports on side differences in EDA appeared as early as in the 1920s, not much attention was given to this topic until the 1970s, since EDA was mainly considered a measure of nonspecific arousal under reticular control (Freixa i Baqué, Catteau, Miossec, & Roy, 1984). Meanwhile, research on electrodermal lateralization focused on two major topics: (1) the possible laterality of excitatory and inhibiting CNS influences on EDA (Sect. 1.3.4.1) and (2) using EDA as dependent

---

[96] Method of recording not reported. A range correction was performed.

measure in hemispheric specialization, either in the intact brain or after unilateral brain lesions (Sect. 3.5.4.1). In addition, specific interest was given to bilateral EDA recordings in affective disorders and in schizophrenia (Sect. 3.4.2.3). A review of more than 50 papers on hemispheric asymmetry and bilateral electrodermal recording was performed by Hugdahl (1984), which has been amended by Hugdahl (1988). More recently, the last five chapters in the proceedings on the progress in electrodermal research, edited by Roy, Boucsein, Fowles, and Gruzelier (1993), were devoted to issues of hemispheric asymmetry. Bilateral differences in EDA are relatively small and can be easily distorted, thus optimal experimental conditions are required to demonstrate them (Hugdahl, 1984, p. 389). Methodological problems involved in EDA lateralization research were extensively discussed by Miossec, Catteau, Freixa i Baqué, and Roy (1985). Since this area of research is highly sensitive to subtle changes in the methods applied, which is reflected in rather inconsistent results in this field, the first subsection will be devoted to methodology.

3.1.4.1 Methodological Considerations

The most important factor to be controlled in lateralization research is *handedness of participants*. Sinistral as compared with dextral persons show either an opposite lateralization or no left/right differences when given hemisphere-specific tasks (Annett, 1982; Bryden, 1965; Springer & Deutsch, 1981) but also smaller lateralization with higher overall activation and smaller left-hemisphere activation (Smith, Kline, & Meyers, 1990). Hécaen and Sauguet (1971) pointed out that only sinistrals having a familial history of left-handedness differ from dextral participants in lateralization experiments. Appropriate differences due to familial handedness were also demonstrated by Smith, Ketterer, and Concannon (1981). Connected with handedness, there may also be considerable individual differences in the lateralization of skin thickness and sweat gland activity. Since the skin of the dominant hand is more frequently physically stressed than the contralateral one, its stratum corneum is likely to be thicker thus increasing the SRL. This may have consequences for a differential level dependency of both hands (Sect. 2.5.4.2). Furthermore, dextral individuals show more sweat gland activity on their right arm as compared to the left one, which is however possibly a concomitant of its muscular activity being greater (Sect. 1.3.4.1), as supposed by Ogawa (1984). Such a lateral dominance of sweat gland activity could not be found with sinistrals (Dean, 1981), which may partly explain the weak relationship between handedness and electrodermal laterality (Miossec et al., 1985).

Another important factor is the *gender of participants* (Sect. 2.4.3.2). Kimmel and Kimmel (1965), Ketterer and Smith (1982), and Boyd and Maltzman (1983) reported smaller lateralization effects in male than in female participants. Contrarily, Kimura (1969), Rizzolatti and Buchtel (1977), Bryden (1979), and Rippon (1990) obtained smaller lateralization effects in female as compared to male participants, especially with nonverbal stimuli (Sect. 2.4.3.2). Based on these results, differential gender-specific cognitive mechanisms were assumed (e.g., female participants being more prone to use verbal strategies even when processing spatial stimuli). However, Román, García-Sánchez, Martínez-Selva, Gómez-Amor, and Carrillo (1989) showed that gender differences in EDA lateralization disappeared when participants were grouped into right-hand and left-hand responders. Since there had been a higher percentage of left-hand responders among males in two previous studies of these authors' group, results on gender differences in EDA lateralization may have been obscured by a gender-specific asymmetry in electrodermal reactivity.

Stimulus properties play also a crucial role in EDR laterality research. First, *stimulus duration* is of great importance, since it is generally accepted that transfer time between both hemispheres is below 1 s (summarized by McKeever & Gill, 1972). Nevertheless, several authors used presentations of 6 s (e.g., Williams, Parsons, & Strayer 1981), 10 s (Myslobodsky & Rattok, 1977), 15–25 s (Meyers & Smith, 1987; Smith et al., 1981), 1 min (Smith, Gatchel, Korman, & Satter, 1979), or even 5 min (Ketterer & Smith, 1977). Such prolonged stimulus durations clearly facilitate processing within both hemispheres, thus obscuring CNS-laterality interpretations of EDA results. As a possibility to avoid an exchange between hemispheres, the so-called visual half field (VHF) technique has been established to study asymmetries in the intact human brain (Beaumont, 1982; Kimura, 1973; Springer, 1977). This technique makes use of the CNS visual pathways being anatomically perfectly crossed, with the nasal part of the retinal image projected to the contralateral, and the temporal part to the ipsilateral visual cortex. Therefore, stimuli being flashed either briefly to the left or right of a central fixation point are transmitted only to the contralateral hemisphere. However, stimuli must be flashed before saccadic eye movements can interfere.

Stimulus complexity should be considered as well. The higher the information contents of a stimulus, the greater is the probability for the processing to occur in both hemispheres. Therefore, the use of abstract words (as, for example, by Prior, Cumming, & Hendy, 1984, in a dichotic listening paradigm) can be regarded as a suitable tool, and spatial stimuli should be reduced to their geometric elements.[97] Unfortunately, various studies on hemispheric specialization assumed spatial and verbal stimuli being hemispheric specific without assessing their possible differences in complexity as well.

Stimulus intensity may also be of importance for the investigation of bilateral EDRs. Brand, Millot, Saffaux, and Morand-Villeneuve (2002) presented two odorants to either only the left or the right or simultaneously to both nostrils of 37 dextral students (22 females, 15 males): a rose-like odorant eliciting a low intranasal trigeminal stimulation, and a mustard oil eliciting a strong trigeminal stimulation. EDA was recorded bilaterally with constant alternating current (22 mV

---

[97] It is, however, questionable whether geometric figures are really typical for right-hemisphere processing, since cognitive representation of abstract material may be more prone to left-hemisphere processing.

at 75 Hz) from the palmar surfaces of the middle phalanges of the first and second fingers.[98] An amplitude criterion of 0.02 µS was applied, bilateral EDRs were assumed when SZR onset times were within 0.5 and 4 s after stimulus onset and SZR rec.t/2 of the other hand's response, and the LC according to (3.2b) was calculated. The authors found a highly significant stimulus-by-presentation-mode interaction, with always higher left-hand SZR amp. for the low-intensity trigeminal stimulation and always higher right-hand amplitudes for the high-intensity trigeminal stimulation.

Another possibly important influence to be considered is the *laterality of a subsequent response task*. As Gruzelier (1993) pointed out, electrodermal lateralization effects may be reversed under active as compared to passive task conditions, since contralateral excitatory influences may prevail in case of motor preparation (Sect. 1.3.4.1 "Three Different CNS Originating Pathways for EDA"). In the last one of three consecutive experiments, Gruzelier, Sergeant, and Eves (1988) recorded the SC-OR with standard methodology bilaterally from 9 dextral participants (4 females, 5 males) with and without a requirement for subsequent muscular activity in either hand. They presented two tones, differing or not in pitch, with ISIs between 8 and 16 s, asking their participants to judge whether the tones were the same or different. After 15 s, a yellow light requested the participants to press a button with either the right or left hand if they thought the stimuli were the same. The OR was defined as SCR with minimum amplitude of 0.02 µS occurring between 0.8 and 5 s after the tone onset. SCR amp. following the second tone were significantly higher on the hand which prepared the motor response compared to the passive hand. This result demonstrates that the preparation of a response task may have the ability to overshadow the stimulus evaluation process reflected in the OR (Sects. 3.1.1.1 and 3.1.2.1).

To constitute the existence of bilateral EDRs, a *criterion* for their detection should be formed. A common criterion is that EDR onset times at both sides are within 0.5 and 4 s after stimulus onset and EDR rec.t/2 of the other side's response (e.g., Brand et al., 2002). For a subsequent quantitative evaluation of electrodermal lateralization, several lateralization coefficients (LCs) were proposed. Myslobodsky and Rattok (1975) suggested the following:

$$LC = \frac{EDR_{right} - EDR_{left}}{EDR_{max}} \qquad (3.2a)$$

To obtain this coefficient, right/left differences for each pair of EDR amp. are categorized as either higher on the right as compared to the left side (R > L) or vice versa (L > R), excluding differences which do not exceed a specific criterion.[99]

---

[98] Using dry, bright-plated electrodes attached to the fingers by means of Velcro strap.

[99] It is recommended using the same values as for the amplitude criterion (Sect. 2.3.1.2 "Choice of Amplitude Criteria").

Schulter and Papousek (1998) proposed an alternative LC for single responses, which included dividing the difference between right and left peak SCR amp. by the sum of both amplitudes:

$$LC = \frac{EDR_{right} - EDR_{left}}{EDR_{right} + EDR_{left}} \qquad (3.2b)$$

Freixa i Baqué and de Bonis (1983) suggested a laterality coefficient reflecting the percentage of cases in which the EDR observed on the right side shows a higher amplitude than the corresponding EDR on the left side:

$$LC\% = \frac{\%[EDR_{right} > EDR_{left}] - \%[EDR_{left} > EDR_{right}]}{\%[EDR_{right} > EDR_{left}] + \%[EDR_{left} > EDR_{right}]} \qquad (3.2c)$$

This coefficient may be used for both specific SCRs to repeated stimulation and for NS.SCRs during a prolonged observation period without distinct stimulation.

Naveteur and Sequeira-Martinho (1990) investigated the *reliability* of bilateral differences in EDA, using a sample of 11 male dextral participants (aged between 19 and 22 years). They recorded both SC and SP bilaterally with standard methodology during a series of 100 dB 1,000 Hz stimuli of 1 s duration, which were repeated with an average 30 s ISI, until ten simultaneous responses were obtained bilaterally (maximal 18 stimuli).[100] Four sessions were applied, with a week between each of them. Significantly higher left- compared to right-hand SCR amp. were observed in 60% of the participants, while the reverse effect appeared for SPR amp. However, the reliabilities for the observed lateral differences were low over sessions, because only 3 participants showed the same laterality pattern in all sessions. Since substantial correlations were obtained between the laterality effects in the SCR amp. and in the SCL for both hands ($r = 0.54$) and for the right hand ($r = 0.64$) alone (but not for the left hand alone), the authors suggest a level dependency of their laterality effects (see Sect. 2.5.4.2).

Schulter and Papousek (1992) performed a more sophisticated reliability study with 54 dextral participants (37 females, 17 males; aged between 18 and 33 years). SC was recorded thenar/hypothenar from both hands with standard methodology. Bilateral NS.SCRs were considered if their onset times were between onset and SCR rec.t/2 of the contralateral response, plus the NS.SCR amp. exceeded 0.02 μS. The LCs according to (3.2b) and (3.2c) were calculated for each of four successive stimulus-free 5-min periods, which were separated by 15 min periods during which the participants were given 30 verbal and 18 spatial tasks in counterbalanced order. The whole procedure was repeated 2–3 weeks later. By and large, reliabilities decreased with the time between trials and were generally higher for the LC

---

[100] Amplitude criteria were 0.02 μS for SCRs and 0.2 mV for SPRs (monophasic from the SPL or biphasic from peak to peak). Latencies for SCRs were 1–5 s, and for SPRs 700 ms to 5 s after stimulus onset.

(3.2b) compared to the LC% (3.2c), with a range from $r = 0.70$ for successive trials in the same session to $r = 0.12$ for the 2–3 weeks interval. Reliabilities for the bilateral peak latency differences, which were also calculated according to (3.2b) and (3.2c), were partly somewhat higher than those for amplitude differences, but did not exceed $r = 0.71$. In general, short-term reliabilities of EDA laterality were considered moderate to high, while long-term reliabilities were insufficient.

3.1.4.2   The Laterality of CNS Influences on EDA

The model depicted in Fig. 1.6 (Sect. 1.3.4.1) makes a clear distinction between ipsilateral limbic-hypothalamic and contralateral motor-activity related influences. However, the literature about the laterality of CNS influences on EDA is manifold and partly controversial. At least two competing hypotheses are discussed in the literature: a model of contralateral excitation (Myslobodsky & Rattok, 1977) and a model of contralateral inhibition (Lacroix & Comper, 1979).

Myslobodsky and Rattok (1977) recorded bilaterally tonic as well as phasic EDA[101] during four different tasks from 14 participants (12 dextral and two sinistral ones). They formed an asymmetry index according to (3.2a), which significantly differentiated between responses to the visual and to the verbal tasks in dextral participants. Myslobodsky and Rattok (1977) observed increases of SCR amp. contralateral to the stimulated hemisphere. However, they did not discuss their results on the basis of a contralateral excitatory control (as could have been expected). Instead, they claimed for an ipsilateral control mechanism with respect to the close association of EDA and OR (Sect. 3.1.1.1). This implies that the less informed (and perhaps competent) a system is, the higher the electrodermal OR generated by a stimulus is supposed to be. Thus, higher EDR amp. should be generated by the ipsilateral hemisphere which is not familiar with the kind of stimuli presented. However, this interpretation could only be retained if information processing would be strictly separated within the hemispheres, which is highly improbable.

In contrast to Myslobodsky and Rattok's (1977) view, Lacroix and Comper (1979) proposed a model of contralateral inhibition. They examined patterns of bilateral differences in SCR amp.[102] as a function of verbal vs. spatial tasks in three experiments, performed with a total of 40 female participants being dextral in the first two,

---

[101] Recorded as SR using standard methodology (except a current density as high as 20 $\mu A/cm^2$) from the distal phalanges of two fingers of each hand, transformed into SC values. Unfortunately, the EDA values reported in the results section remain ambiguous with respect to their unit and magnitude. The tasks were visual-imagery (15 slides, 9 of them with sexual content, with subsequent imaging); verbal-analytic (series of words, from which those denoting numbers had to be selected for calculation); auditory; and light stimulation.

[102] Recorded between the distal phalanges of two fingers from both hands using standard methodology.

and sinistral in the third experiment. Despite some differences in experimental techniques, EDA lateralization effects of both types of tasks were consistently found with dextral participants, i.e., significantly higher left-hand SCR amp. during verbal and significantly higher right-hand SCR amp. during spatial tasks. However, when using sinistral females or tasks activating both hemispheres (mental arithmetic or music), laterality effects disappeared. Since these authors observed lower SCR amp. in recordings contralateral to the activated hemisphere with their dextral participants, they identified the neurophysiological mechanism responsible for bilateral EDA differences being contralateral inhibitory in nature. This hypothesis is supported by earlier studies with unilateral brain lesions (Darrow, 1937a; Holloway & Parsons, 1969) as well as by animal experiments using brain stimulation techniques (Wilcott, 1969; Wilcott & Bradley, 1970).

Despite the vast literature on unilateral brain damage and EDA, the emerging picture is far from being consistent (Zoccolotti, Caltagirone, Pecchinenda, & Troisi, 1993). In their study previously mentioned in Sect. 1.3.4.1 "Cortical Control of EDA", Tranel and Damasio (1994) compared the effect of unilateral focal brain lesions on the SCR amp. (recorded with standard methodology) which followed either physical stimuli (e.g., taking a deep breath) or psychological stimuli (positive and negative affective and neutral pictures). In comparison to healthy controls, patients with right-hemisphere inferior parietal lesions yielded reduced SCR amp. for both stimulus classes, with smaller lesions only affecting the SCR following psychological stimuli. Thus, the right hemisphere might be more important for eliciting electrodermal concomitants to emotional stimuli than the left one. In their study with direct electrical stimulation of various subcortical brain areas in 5 surgical patients (2 females, 3 males) which was previously mentioned in Sect. 1.3.4.1 "Subcortical Control of EDA", Mangina and Beuzeron-Mangina (1996) recorded bilateral SC with standard methodology from the distal phalanges of the index and middle fingers. Following a stimulation of the left amygdala, the left anterior and posterior hippocampus, or the left cingulate gyrus, the left-hand SCR amp. was significantly higher than the right one. The reverse was found for the right-hand SCR amp. when the above mentioned structures were stimulated in the right hemisphere. The authors concluded that human bilateral EDR is ipsilaterally controlled as far as limbic structures are concerned.

Different lateralization effects appeared in tonic and phasic EDA parameters. Smith et al. (1981) presented 64 dextral and sinistral participants of both genders a counterbalanced series of 31 slides depicting objects spatially, and 31 slides describing the same objects verbally, while recording EDA[103] bilaterally. Stimulus-specific EDRs (within 1–4 s following stimulus onset) showed no laterality differences in amplitudes. Instead, the hand contralateral to the activated hemisphere yielded lower amplitudes of NS.EDRs which appeared outside the time window. Supposedly the contralateral inhibition of EDA acts as a contrasting

---

[103] Recorded from medial phalanges of both hands as SR with standard methodology, transformed to SC and square-root transformed.

phenomenon as follows: on the background of tonic EDA being reduced on the body side opposite to the activated hemisphere, phasic EDRs could yield higher amplitudes, thus displaying a true level dependency (Sect. 2.5.4.2).

Gruzelier, Eves, and Connolly (1981) investigated lateralization effects on electrodermal habituation in three experiments with a total of 109 participants (minor surgery patients, medical students, and hospital staff) of both genders, nine of whom were sinistrals. SCR amp. recorded from the left hand (with standard methodology using KCl cream) were higher at the beginning of a series of 1 kHz tones (70 or 90 dB with varying ISIs) as compared to those recorded from the right hand, and habituated faster than the latter ones, while a lower NS.SCR freq. appeared during this process. Contrarily, the slower habituation appeared together with a higher spontaneous EDA in the right hand. Therefore, inhibitory influences from the left hemisphere could have evoked both a lower NS.SCR freq. and a faster habituation ipsilaterally, as well as the reduction of SCR amp. on the contralateral body side. Thus, the hemispheres may differ in the polarity of their influences on EDA, the left one being predominantly inhibitory while the right one acts excitatory. Overall, empirical support for the hypothesis of contralateral excitation is less than for contralateral inhibition (Hugdahl, 1984, p. 389).

In addition, electrodermal lateralization may be influenced by the amount of general arousal (Sect. 3.2.1.1). Obrist (1963) suggested that low levels of arousal facilitate EDA asymmetry, whereas alerting or stressing the participating individual decreases the size of lateral differences in EDA.[104] Freixa i Baqué and de Bonis (1983) observed extremely high values of electrodermal asymmetry during sleep within 4 male participants[105] as compared to results from waking states obtained in other studies. To quantify asymmetry, they used the LC% according to (3.2c). The overall LC during sleep was 80% as compared to 9% during stress and 18% during nonstressful situations (de Bonis & Freixa i Baqué, 1980).

Davidson, Fedio, Smith, Aureille, and Martin (1992) demonstrated a mediating effect of arousal on bilateral EDA. They recorded SC bilaterally with standard methodology from the second and third fingers during habituation to 15 consecutive 64 dB 1,000 Hz tones (1 s duration, ISIs randomly between 30 and 60 s) and during a tone discrimination phase 20 min later in 8 unilateral left temporal lobectomy patients (5 females, 3 males), 10 unilateral right temporal lobectomy patients (3 females, 7 males), and 12 normal controls (6 of each gender). The right lobectomy group showed significantly lower SCR amp. and faster habituation

---

[104] Recorded from 5 male participants with two Fels dermohmeters using a constant current of 70 µA each, with zinc/zinc sulfate electrodes and electrode cream (unspecified). Electrode positions were the center of each palm and the midline of the chest. Separate measures of SRL and mean NS.SRR amp. were taken during resting and during a serial learning task (as an appreciable stressor) on each of 24 or 36 days.

[105] Recorded during three consecutive nights as NS.SPRs with standard methodology and Beckman cream, however with an unusually low time constant of 0.6 s (Sect. 2.1.4). Monophasic and diphasic SPRs (Sect. 2.2.3.1) exceeding 0.2 mV in at least one of the two hands were evaluated; differences less than 0.1 mV between both hands were not considered.

compared to the left lobectomy group, the controls falling in between. The authors suggested the interpretation of hypoarousability of the right temporal lobectomy group and hyperarousability of their left-hemisphere counterparts.

3.1.4.3 EDA as a Measure of Hemispheric Asymmetry

According to the traditional view, verbal stimuli should be mainly processed in the left hemisphere, while visual-spatial stimuli are regarded to be typically processed in the right hemisphere. However, this traditional verbal/nonverbal dichotomy has been questioned in several reviews (e.g., Bradshaw & Nettleton, 1981; Dimond & Beaumont, 1974). According to these authors' views, there seems to be more a quantitative rather than a qualitative difference between hemispheres, with a high degree of duplicated function, and with hemispheric specialization as an additional feature.

To establish relationships between habituation of the electrodermal OR and hemispheric asymmetry, Hugdahl, Broman, and Franzon (1983) used the VHF technique presenting 15 verbal and 15 spatial stimuli in randomized order to the left and right visual half field of 20 dextral participants of each gender. They recorded SCL as well as SCRs with standard methodology from the medial phalanges of the index and middle fingers at both hands. Results showed significantly higher mean SCR amp. (and slower habituation) to the verbal stimuli as compared to the spatial ones when presented in the left visual half field. This was reversed when stimuli were presented in the right visual half field. However, this was only true when stimuli were presented in a 6.0° angle of projection and not in an additional 2.5° condition. There were no differences between left- and right-hand recordings, and the SCL yielded no significant effects except a linear decrease over time. Thus, the electrodermal OR system had been influenced differentially by CNS laterality of stimulus processing. However, there was no direct connection with electrodermal lateralization. Despite a great number of positive and even partially replicated results, Hugdahl (1984) in his review of the appropriate literature concluded that bilateral electrodermal recordings cannot be unambiguously related to the phenomenon of hemispheric asymmetry.

Another factor that can exert influences on hemispheric asymmetry is the emotional significance of stimuli. There has been some debate concerning lateralization of processing emotions within the CNS. In general, there is a high probability of the right hemisphere playing an important role in mediating emotional processes (summarized by Gainotti, 1979). Dimond, Farrington, and Johnson (1976) advocated a more differentiated view, stating that each hemisphere has its own distinct emotional vision of the world, being more unpleasant and horrific in the right hemisphere as compared to the left one. However, this typical right-hemisphere world view is usually suppressed. This is only partly in accordance with Tucker's (1981) view that the left hemisphere exerts an inhibitory or at least a regulatory influence over the right hemisphere, which in turn is regarded as being primarily involved in processing emotional material.

Meyers and Smith (1987) investigated the dependence of electrodermal laterali-zation on emotional stimulus qualities. Twenty-eight dextral participants of each gender (all having two dextral biological parents) were presented two positive (a woman laughing and a baby cooing) and two negative (a woman crying and a woman screaming) emotional acoustic stimuli with 24 s duration each. Neutral control stimuli were created by integrating them and modifying the amplitude of a 1 kHz tone to match that of the emotional stimuli. They were presented before the emotional stimuli. Critical stimuli were given twice in randomized order: under an "affective" instruction (focus on the feelings) and under a "cognitive" instruction (think of how to react to the sound). A significant interaction between body side and instruction was observed in the analysis of the highest response SCR amp.,[106] yielding a greater relative activity in the "affective" condition on the right side and greater relative activity in the "cognitive" condition on the left side, regardless of stimulus kind and gender. These results point to the possibility that the request for affective stimulus processing may be more important for EDA lateralization than the emotional content of the stimulus material itself, which is at variance with Myslobodsky and Rattok's (1977) interpretation reported above.

Kayser (1995) performed a series of five studies, examining the hypothesis of the right hemisphere being more involved in emotional processing than the left one, probing also the laterality of the excitatory or inhibitory CNS influences on EDA. In all studies, SC was recorded bilaterally with standard methodology from thenar/hypothenar sites with two different EDA couplers, which were systematically counterbalanced over participants to prevent recording biases. Since rather complex stimuli were used, the time window for stimulus-elicited SCRs was fixed to 1–5 s after stimulus onset (Sect. 2.3.2.2), and SCRs were regarded as bilateral if the deflection point of at least one side's SCR was within that interval. Two parameters were formed: (1) a response frequency measure as the percentage of SCRs for each stimulus quality exceeding an amplitude criterion of 0.025 μS (Sect. 2.3.1.2 "Choice of Amplitude Criteria") and (2) a response intensity measure as the square-root transformed (Sect. 2.3.3.3.) maximum SCR amp. in each interval. The VHF technique was used in all studies for presenting 20 pictures of mutilated accident victims matched by color, brightness, and perspective with 20 neutral photos from pedestrians.

In his first study, Kayser (1995) presented these stimuli three times to 40 dextral females (19–34 years): once in the central field for 1,000 ms to make participants familiar with the stimuli, and once in each of the visual half fields for 200 ms. In the second study which was performed with another 40 dextral females in the same age range, stimuli were presented only in each of the VHFs for 1,500 ms. In both studies, significantly more and stronger SCRs were elicited by the emotional-negatively

---

[106] Recorded as SR (9.66 μA/cm^2) with Ag/AgCl cup electrodes and 0.05 molar NaCl cream from the pretreated (rubbing with isopropyl alcohol and drying) volar middle phalanges of the first and middle fingers of both hands, transformed to SC.

toned stimuli compared to the neutral ones, but the expected lateralization of the emotion-elicited SCR failed to reach significance, presumably because the complexity of the differences between the classes of stimuli were too high. To make the stimulus sets better comparable, Kayser (1995) chose a different set of stimuli for his third study with another sample of 40 dextral females of about the same age range, i.e., 20 pairs of pictures from patients with dermatological diseases before and after plastic surgery as emotional negative and neutral stimuli, presented for 1,000 ms in each of the visual half fields in randomized order. He obtained significantly more and higher SCRs to emotional stimuli compared to neutral ones, an effect which was strongest for the left hand and after right-hemisphere presentations. This effect reversed for left-hemisphere presentations but failed to reach significance. The results of the third study may have been obscured by the high percentage of participants (42.5%) who had to be rejected from the analysis because of lateral eye movements following the presentation of negative emotional stimuli to the right hemisphere, which is common for high-anxious participants. Therefore, in a fourth study with another 48 females (18–33 years), the same stimuli were used, but participants were trained to avoid lateral eye movements, and the presentation time for half of them was reduced to 250 ms. As a result, less than 1% lateral eye movements appeared, but only in the 250 ms condition the emotional stimuli presented to the right hemisphere elicited more frequent and higher SCRs in the left hand compared to neutral stimuli.

To investigate the influence of cognitive coping strategies on the SCR to emotional negative pictures, Kayser (1995) performed a fifth study with 32 females in the same age range, half of them being high anxious and the other half low anxious, half of each group using either a verbal or an imaginative coping strategy. A significant interaction between stimulus quality and coping strategy occurred, with SCRs being highest for the negative emotional stimuli under the imaginative strategy. Contrarily, the instruction to use a verbal strategy inhibited the SCR, especially when the emotional negative stimuli were presented to the right hemisphere. However, taken together, there were always more and higher SCRs contralateral to the stimulated hemisphere, which supports an interpretation of contralateral excitation. The general conclusion from this well-designed and controlled series of studies is that the lateralization of emotions seems to be an instable phenomenon, which is easily disturbed by changes in stimulus conditions.

In a thoroughly designed study, Peper and Karcher (2001) demonstrated the importance of the right hemisphere for controlling conditioned emotional responses to a negatively valenced CS (Sect. 3.1.2.1). They assigned 41 healthy dextral participants (19 females, 22 males) randomly to two experimental groups. With a 2-weeks interval, the groups were subjected to two conditions, differing only in the valence of the CS (facial expressions from the Ekman et al., 1972, pictures), paired with an UCS (a 3 s 95 dB baby cry presented binaurally over headphones). Each experiment consisted of a preconditioning (habituation), an acquisition, and an extinction phase. By using the VHF technique, four blocks of lateralization conditions were applied in the preconditioning phase, made up from positive or negative CSs in the left or right visual field. The same four conditions were applied in the extinction phase.

Each CS was followed by a mask (a puzzle made up from scrambled facial elements) appearing bilaterally in each VHF to avoid the conditioning effect being obscured by ORs to a shifting from unmasked foveal presented stimuli to masked and lateral presentations during extinction. All participants were tested under two conditions, with either preattentive or identifiable CSs during preconditioning and extinction. Bilateral SC was recorded with standard methodology from hypothenar sites, using two identical couplers counterbalanced over the participants' hands. SCRs were defined as FIRs (1–4 s after stimulus presentation, see Sect. 1.3.2.1) with a minimum amplitude of 0.05 µS, range-corrected and log-transformed to reduce skewness (Sect. 2.3.3.3). Both negative and positive facial expressions could be aversively conditioned. The difference between hands did not reach significance. Only preattentive but not consciously perceived negative CSs presented to the left VHF yielded a trend toward higher SCR amp. compared to presentation in the right VHF, thus confirming the important role of the right hemisphere for the control of conditioned emotional responses to negatively valenced CSs.

In cases of using hemispheric-specific tasks for investigating electrodermal lateralization, it would be useful to apply direct measures for their differential activation which are independent of EDA. While recordings of the usual spontaneous EEG frequency bands were of not much help for such a differentiation (e.g., Meyers & Smith, 1986), an analysis of beta-subbands and more refined brain imaging techniques revealed some parallels between task-related CNS activity differences and SCRs. Rippon (1990) recorded a total of 28 EEG channels from 8 dextral participants of each gender (aged 22–46 years) during the performance of a verbal and a visuospatial task. Concomitantly, SC was measured from the medial phalanges of the index and second fingers of both hands.[107] The first SCR exceeding 0.02 µS within 1–5 s after stimulus presentation was scored, and the LC according to (3.2b) was calculated for mean SCR amp. and each of the EEG bands. A significant rank correlation of $r = 0.48$ was obtained between the SCR amp. and the beta-2 band LCs for the verbal task. Since the author could not decide between the two possible interpretations, whether an increase of beta-2 power would be an index for an increase or decrease in cortical arousal, she was also not decisive with respect to being in favor of a contralateral excitation or inhibition model for EDRs.

More recently, hemisphere asymmetry of EDA has been brought into connection with frontal EEG asymmetry and the BIS/BAS concept (Sect. 3.2.1.2). Knygazev, Slobodskaya, and Wilson (2002) related the BIS and BAS scores from the Gray-Wilson Personality Questionnaire (Sect. 3.3.1.1) to bilateral frontal and parietal EEG activity, HR, and SC (measured with standard methodology from the distal phalanges of the index and second fingers of the nondominant hand) of 63 participants (53 females, 10 males, aged 18–37 years) during a baseline and arithmetic task of 2 min duration each. While individual BAS scores were negatively related to HR accelerations during mental arithmetic, no correlations between SCL

---

[107] Recorded with 1 cm diameter Ag/AgCl electrodes filled with 0.05% KCl solution in agar.

during the baseline or the difference between SCL during the mental task and baseline on the one hand and BIS scores on the other hand were found.

Various electrodermal lateralization effects appear in psychiatric disorders (for a short summary, see Flor-Henry, 1993). Studies of EDA lateralization being related to hemispheric dysfunctions in schizophrenia will be reported in Sect. 3.4.2.3. There are results pointing to endogenous depressives (Sect. 3.4.1.3) showing an inverse EDA lateralization pattern being due to a hyperactivity of their right hemisphere (Freixa i Baqué et al., 1984). Psychopaths (Sect. 3.4.1.2) and even patients suffering from cardiovascular disorders (Gruzelier, 1993) have also yielded specific electrodermal lateralization effects. Therefore, further research in this field should provide techniques not only for investigating hemispheric specialization in healthy individuals, but also for testing neuropsychological hypotheses within the area of psychopathological research (Sect. 3.4).

3.2 Generalized Psychophysiological States

In contrast to Sect. 3.1, where phasic EDA parameters as event-related concomitants within various psychophysiological paradigms were discussed, the present chapter is concerned with those paradigms in which EDA is an indicator of more general psychophysiological states. These are general and motivational arousal including sleep (Sect. 3.2.1) and states of emotion and stress (Sect. 3.2.2). The use of EDA in some of these fields has been previously reviewed in books edited by Prokasy and Raskin (1973) and Gale and Edwards (1983). Therefore, the present chapter's focus is on the theoretical background, including a comprehensive neurophysiological modeling of different kinds of EDA (Fig. 3.4, Sect. 3.2.1.2), providing some typical studies as examples of the use of EDA in different fields.

3.2.1 Electrodermal Indices of Arousal

Unitary (i.e., one-dimensional) arousal theories (e.g., Lindsley, Schreiner, Knowles, & Magoun, 1950) prevailed from the 1950s into the 1970s. They were based on the RF with its sensory inflow and its projections into cortical, hypothalamic, and thalamic areas. The RF hosts the so-called reticular activating system (RAS), being the neuroanatomical substrate of nonspecific arousal. If the RAS is stimulated through sensory input or by applying an electrical current directly to the RF, an arousal will result with typical EEG changes to be observed. The so-called EEG-alpha blockade, which comes with an increase of faster EEG components (i.e., beta activity), is regarded as the classic marker variable for general arousal processes.

One of the major theoretical notions which came with unitary arousal concepts was the inverted-U relationship between arousal and performance (Malmo, 1962), also identified as the so-called Yerkes-Dodson law. Its essence is that an increase from low to moderate arousal results in a performance increase, whereas a further heightening of arousal will result in performance decrement. This gave rise to the hypothesis of a task-specific, optimal arousal, which had been located in the middle of an assumed arousal continuum. Section 3.2.1.1 will deal with the use of EDA in the frame of unitary arousal theories, while a multidimensional arousal model will be proposed in Sect. 3.2.1.2, together with its implications for differential indicator functions of electrodermal and cardiovascular measures.

3.2.1.1   EDA as an Indicator of General Arousal

Following Duffy's (1951) energetic view of general arousal as an organic overall excitation, it should be possible to quantify arousal processes not only by means of CNS indicators but also by using parameters of the ANS and the endocrine system. Among the ANS measures, tonic EDA parameters have been for a long time the most frequently used indicator of arousal in psychophysiological research (Duffy, 1972).[108] Thus, the focus of the following discussion will be on the indicator functions of the different EDA parameters with respect to general arousal.

In several experiments which addressed the effects of physical strain on physiological and performance variables elicited by rotation, Silverman, Cohen, and Shmavonian (1959) showed that in a certain range of the presumed arousal continuum both tonic and phasic EDA parameters may have different indicator functions.[109] In a first gravitational experiment, 5 participants were given accelerations of 2.5 g-force and 4 g-force, respectively. In addition, another condition with an acceleration of 0.4 g-force prior to the loss of consciousness was applied. The average EDA variations revealed increasing arousal under higher acceleration; the stimulation of the participants with 2.5 g-force led to an increase of both the mean SRR amp. and the NS.SRR freq. Under 4 g-force, the mean SRR amp. was slowly reduced, while the NS.SRR freq. continued increasing. This progress was more clear under a gravitational condition of 4 g-force prior to the loss of consciousness, where the SRR amp. strongly decreased, while the NS.SRR freq. showed a further increase. In another experiment, 15 participants were given a tracking task under 2 and 4 g-force. In accordance with the above-mentioned hypothesis of an inverted-U-shaped relationship between arousal and performance, an improvement in psychomotor performance was observed in states of medium

---

[108] Older results in the area of EDA and arousal are reported by Duffy (1972) and Raskin (1973). More recent descriptions of activational, attentional, and cognitive phenomena with respect to their physiological concomitants can be found in the second volume of the series edited by Gale and Edwards (1983). A methodologically oriented, strongly generalized presentation of psychophysiological paradigms is given by Fahrenberg (1988).

[109] In these experiments, EDA was recorded as SR from the soles of the feet with 2 × 4 cm lead electrodes and K–Y gel from acetone cleaned sites.

arousal as defined by means of EDA parameters, while an increase in arousal above this level led to a performance decrement.

The results from Silverman et al. (1959) could be largely confirmed by Burch and Greiner (1960), who systematically varied arousal by pharmacological substances (Sect. 3.4.3), however with the use of only one participant. They obtained a sigmoid-formed relationship between the NS.SRR freq.[110] and the arousal level, while SRRs in response to an electrical stimulus followed an inverted-U function. The administration of sedatives led, in a dose-dependent manner, to a decrease in the NS.SRR freq. and to a lowering of the amplitudes of stimulus dependent SRRs. Simultaneously, a reduction of fast EEG components could be observed. The increasing arousal following an injection of a stimulant led to both an increase of the NS.SRR freq. and of the stimulus-dependent SRR amp. An increase of the dose or a chronic administration of the stimulant resulted in a dissociation of both EDA parameters, since the NS.SRR freq. increased further, while the amplitudes of the specific SRRs decreased. In the highest arousal state, the participant displayed very few responses to the standard stimulus.

Both Silverman et al. (1959) and Burch and Greiner (1960) deduced different courses of the indicator functions for tonic and phasic EDA parameters from their results. The number of NS.EDRs was assumed to show an approximately linear relationship to the arousal state in the CNS, while the observed curve of SRR amp., in contrast, had been found to correspond to the inverted-U function. Such a relationship has also been observed between arousal and performance. The lowering of the EDR amp. in the states of excitation (cf. Malmo, 1959, footnote 3) may reflect a breakdown in the adaptive, goal-oriented behavior as a result of a deficit in selective processing of environmental stimuli at the upper end of the assumed arousal continuum. Christie and Venables (1971) suggested the BSPL, which is the SPL reached after a long resting period (Sect. 2.3.2.1), as an appropriate electrodermal indicator for the other extreme of the arousal continuum, i.e., minimal arousal.

Empirical evidence for different tonic EDA parameters yielding some type of differential validity with respect to arousal processes was provided by Walschburger (1976) in his study described in Sect. 2.5.2.1 "Tonic Skin Conductance Measures". Walschburger observed that the SCL, being originally tonic in nature, showed only a slight increase as a result of arousal processes, which appeared clearly only in the moderate range of arousal, with a tendency toward a ceiling effect (Sect. 2.5.4.1). On the other hand, the NS.SCR freq., which is derived from phasic electrodermal phenomena, indicated a steady rise from resting values of practically near to zero over a wide range of the arousal continuum.

An attempt for taking into account general and localized aspects of arousal (Lindsley, 1951), as being reflected in psychophysiological measurement, was made by Haider (1969, 1970). In his hierarchical arousal model, different physiological

---

[110] Recorded with dry lead electrodes from palmar finger sites against the forearm. A bipolar parieto-occipital EEG was recorded in parallel to the SR measurement.

parameters taken from the CNS and ANS were assumed to be indicators for different levels of generality of arousal phenomena. For example, EDRs were regarded as an indicator of localized phasic arousal processes, while tonic electrodermal parameters were suggested to be useful for measuring more generalized arousal. This model provided an appropriate rationale for deriving tonic EDA parameters from phasic electrodermal changes (Sect. 2.3.2.2).[111] An appearance of nonspecific EDRs was advocated to indicate the existence of numerous phasic arousing processes which underlie an increased general tonic arousal.[112]

Above all, the discussion of physiological measures as indicators of arousal suffers from the general lack of clarity of the concept itself. Furthermore, one of the most consistent findings in arousal research seems to be an observable dissociation of psychophysiological parameters. Due to various methodological problems such as the specificity and covariation of peripheral physiological (and also subjective) arousal indicators, the focus of psychophysiological research moved away from a study type based on the assumption of a generalized unitary arousal concept to investigations of such conditions which were supposed to elicit certain arousal states and alterations, as well as to research in differential psychophysiology (summarized by Fahrenberg, 1988). Despite some progress in multivariate arousal research, no satisfactory predictions can yet be made with respect to the dependence of the differential strength and direction of arousal from possible predictors such as stable interindividual differences, so that – instead of sticking with global arousal concepts – the development of psychophysiological micro theories of activating processes should be attempted (Fahrenberg, Walschburger, Foerster, Myrtek, & Müller, 1983).

However, there exists one hypothesis, being more explicitly referred to in the next section, for which at least some support is given from psychophysiological arousal research. In general, electrodermal and cardiovascular measures seem to have different domains of validity with respect to their indicator function in different parts of an assumed arousal continuum. EDA is regarded as a sensitive and valid indicator for the lower arousal range, reflecting small, mostly cognitively determined, variations in arousal. By contrast, HR may suit better as an indicator for the higher arousal range and for pronounced and often somatically determined arousal processes (Epstein, Boudreau, & Kling, 1975; Miezejeski, 1978; Walschburger, 1986).

The possibly differentiated areas of validity of those different systems within the ANS do not have to be directly traced back to differences in their CNS control.

---

[111] However, Haider (1969) did not use the NS.EDR freq. but slow SP changes as an indicator of tonic EDA.

[112] Furthermore, considerations of a differentiated view of the role of the RF in the elicitation of EDA were made by Sharpless and Jasper (1956), which could complement the neurophysiological concepts of EDA origins described in Sect. 1.3.4.1, if confirmed empirically. Those authors regarded the caudal (deeper) structures as the neurophysiological correlates of tonic EDA, while the rostral (higher) components of the RF were regarded as mainly contributing to phasic EDA phenomena, which indicate orienting or attentional processes (Sects. 3.1.1.1 and 3.1.3).

Instead, the differing attenuative and regulative behavior of both systems can also play a role. So it is possible that the above-mentioned lower sensitivity of tonic EDA parameters in the upper range of arousal is brought about by the increasing moisturization of the stratum corneum following frequently appearing EDRs (Sect. 1.4.2.3). This may be supported by the decrease of the SRR amp. as found by Silverman et al. (1959), while the HR will be able to reflect rapid arousing and dearousing processes even during high arousal and motor activity. In contrast, the HR can easily become insensitive in a low overall arousal range dependent on system compensatory regulative processes, while the electrodermal system responds to each psychological variation with a clear-cut EDR, no matter how small the variation is.[113] Thus, concepts of differential indicator functions can be generated not only for various physiological systems; in addition, specific indicator functions may be found for different parameters obtainable within the same system. This seems to be at least a reasonable line of study to be followed in future arousal research.

3.2.1.2 EDA and Multidimensional Arousal Modeling

Since psychophysiological responses were not always in line with the hypothesis of a single arousal dimension, unitary arousal concepts which dominated the 1950s have been supplemented or replaced by more differentiated neurophysiological views of arousal processes. Questions arose as early as in the 1960s, when – contrary to the predictions of unitary arousal theories – Lacey (1967) demonstrated that the pattern of psychophysiological responses may vary with stimulus properties. In particular, HR and EDA sometimes changed in the same but in other instances in different directions, which was referred to by Lacey as "directional fractionation." The more general theoretical consideration of this approach was that different parts of the ANS may show opposite reactions with respect to general arousal. Consequently, unitary arousal theories were considered to be too simplistic for adequate neurophysiological modeling. Instead, arousal proved to be a complex and multidimensional phenomenon that can be best taken care of by considering different neurophysiological systems for different kinds of arousal. These will be in the focus of this section.

During the last four decades, there have been several attempts to replace the above-mentioned unitary arousal theories by more complex systems with regard to

---

[113] Fundamentally different neuronal trigger mechanisms of cardiovascular and electrodermal responses were also found in experiments with rats by Roberts and Young (summarized by Roberts, 1974). In a series of investigations into the effect of aversive stimuli upon approach behavior, consistent connections between HR and physical movement of rats were observed, which decreased over the trials, while both the SC and the negative SP component showed an ascending progress during the course of the trials. Roberts (1974) could exclude all possibilities of a somatic coupling of EDA, as in, for example, overall muscular tension or breathing, and he therefore presumed motivational and/or attentional processes (Sect. 3.1.3) as causative factors in the increase of EDA.

different sources and kinds of arousal. Routtenberg (1968, 1971) formulated his two-arousal hypothesis, taking into account the arousing properties of the limbic midbrain reward structures as found by the Olds group (e.g., Olds & Olds, 1965), in addition to the popular RAS (Sect. 3.2.1.1).

Though he could not give an unequivocal anatomical description of the two systems proposed, Routtenberg related his "Arousal System I" to the RAS, being responsible for drive-related response energy. On the other hand, his "Arousal System II" has been related to the medial forebrain bundle (MFB) which runs through hypothalamic and telencephalic structures, influencing positive incentive- or reward-related behavior.[114] The two-arousal system proposed by Routtenberg (1968, Fig. 2) is incorporated in the lower right part of Fig. 3.4, being indicated by dotted connections. His "Arousal I," which is more general in nature, inhibits – via negative incentive structures in the dorsal midbrain – the limbic system (see Footnote 19 in Sect. 1.3.2.2) and thus inhibits "Arousal II," which is more motivationally determined. In turn, System II inhibits System I via pathways from medial septal through hippocampal and lateral septal regions. Thus, both systems have the ability to suppress each other, while posterolateral hypothalamic stimulation can facilitate both of them. Since both systems can elicit EEG desynchronization, the only possibility of differentiating Arousal I and II electrophysiologically may be via the hippocampal theta as a concomitant of System II being active, which is not recordable via surface electrodes. Consequently, Routtenberg's theoretical notion did not have much impact on psychophysiology, especially with respect to ANS measures.

As previously outlined in Sect. 3.1.3.1, both arousal systems may be connected to Pribram and McGuinness' (1975) model of information processing: Routtenberg's "Arousal System I" resembles in some respects their "Affect Arousal" and/or "Effort" systems, while "Arousal System II" is tied to their "Preparatory Activation" system. According to McGuinness and Pribram (1980), the former is a phasic short-lived and more reflex-like response to input, while the latter is long lasting in preparation to respond.

Research into the function of brain neurotransmitters enlightened the nature and role of Routtenberg's motivationally determined "Arousal II." Both noradrenaline and dopamine facilitate self-stimulation at various sites in the MFB and also in the lateral hypothalamus, but the dopamine effect is the better established one (Panksepp, 1982, p. 418). On the other hand, the nigrostriatal dopamine fibers running through MFB and lateral hypothalamus also supply the basal ganglia, thus facilitating motor preparation via reciprocal connections to the premotor and motor cortex, as well as enhancing associational learning via a "complex loop" (DeLong, Georgopoulos, & Crutcher, 1983), which connects basal ganglia with

---

[114] In the 1971 revision of his theory, Routtenberg became more careful with respect to the neuroanatomical structures that may underlie his "System II," relating it closer to motor components of behavior.

(pre)frontal cortical areas.[115] The outcomes of this motivational arousal system are: directed cortical-driven motor actions on the one hand, being accompanied by the "preparatory" EDA2 (Fig. 1.6, Sect. 1.3.4.1) as concomitant ANS response; and hypothalamic action patterns which typically occur during exploration and self-stimulation on the other hand.

Figure 3.4 depicts a model of the four arousal systems and their neurophysiological underpinnings as proposed by the present author (Boucsein, 1988, 1992). This model integrates the two-arousal system of Routtenberg (1968), the three-arousal system of Pribram and McGuinness (1975), a three-arousal system proposed by Fowles (1980), Gray's (1982) BIS, and the circuits between basal ganglia and frontal cortex modeled by DeLong et al. (1983). The horizontal structure of Fig. 3.4 corresponds to the structural and functional hierarchy within the brain, whereas its vertical grouping follows a sequence from stimulation through information processing to response preparation, as previously outlined in Sect. 3.1.3.1:

1. Arousal System 1 (checkered background) is the "Affect Arousal System," centered on the amygdala, being responsible for focusing attention and for the elicitation of ORs and DRs (Sect. 3.1.1.2), but also other immediate reactions to stimulation such as fight/flight or startle vs. freezing, the patterns of which are available in the ventromedial hypothalamus (lower left in Fig. 3.4).
2. Arousal System 2 (vertically striped background) is the "Effort System," centered on the hippocampus, which has the ability to connect or disconnect CNS input and output. The physiological patterns generated by this system can be regarded as concomitants of central information processing. Arousal System 2 comprises the basic hippocampal circuit involved in the BIS proposed by Gray (1982).
3. Arousal System 3 (oblique striped background) is the "Preparatory Activation System," centered on the basal ganglia. Its activation results in an increased readiness of brain areas involved in somatomotor activity. It has close relationships to the behavioral activation system described by Fowles (1980).
   The three systems are supplemented by another arousal system previously described in Sect. 3.2.1.1:
4. Arousal System 4 (dotted background, below the effort system), which is an unspecific arousal system that can be located in the RF, therefore also labeled reticular activation system (RAS). It was not only postulated as early as in the 1950s but also again included by Fowles (1980) in his three-arousal system.

---

[115] To avoid making Fig. 3.4 more complicated, the thalamic parts of these loops are left out. Later, Alexander, Crutcher, and DeLong (1990) added another circuit which they identified as "limbic," since it connects certain portions of the basal ganglia with structures of the limbic system, including the hippocampus, the amygdala, and the entorhinal cortex, in a very similar manner as motor and premotor or (pre)frontal cortical areas in the other two loops (or circuits, as labeled by Alexander et al., 1990). Connections of these limbic structures with the basal ganglia were left out in Fig. 3.4, since their primary function is supposed to be coordinating somatomotor concomitants of emotion-related mimics and gestures.

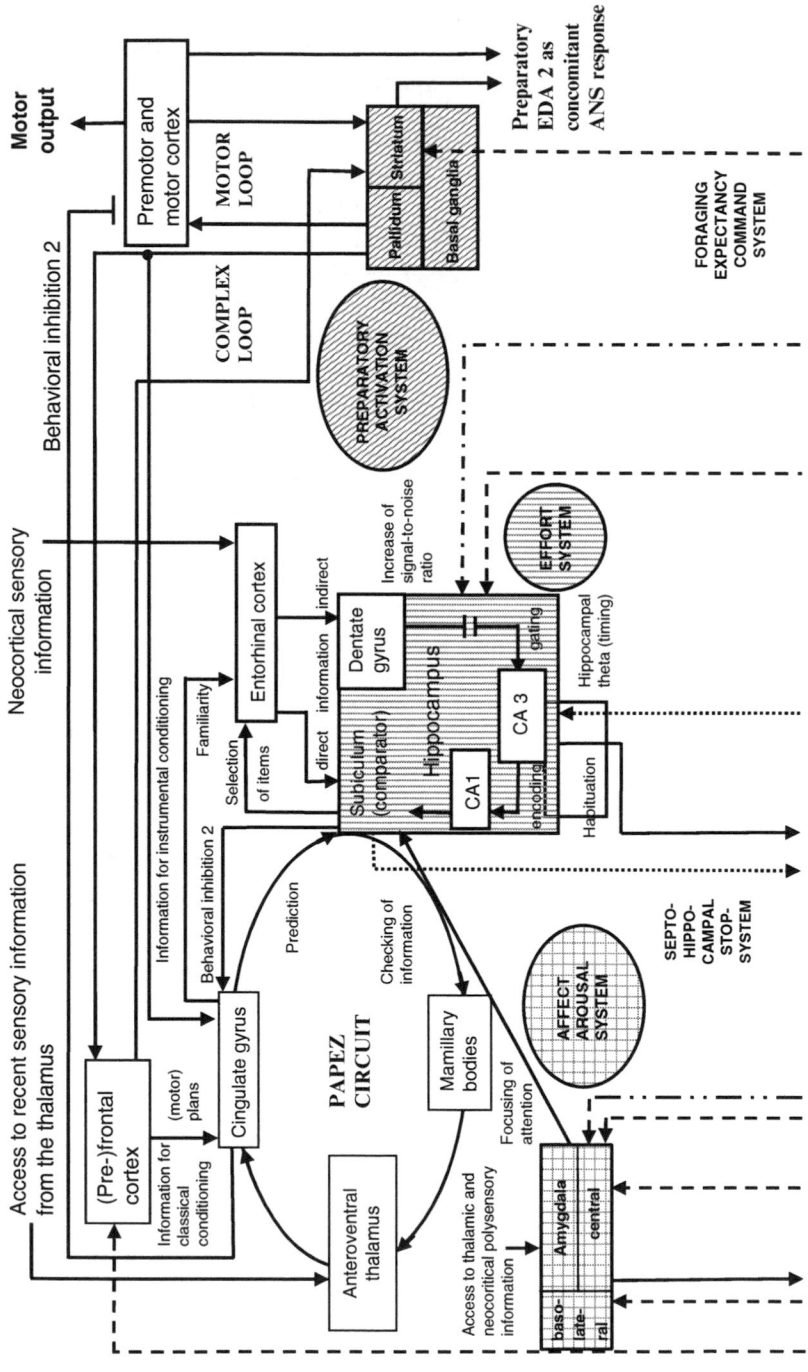

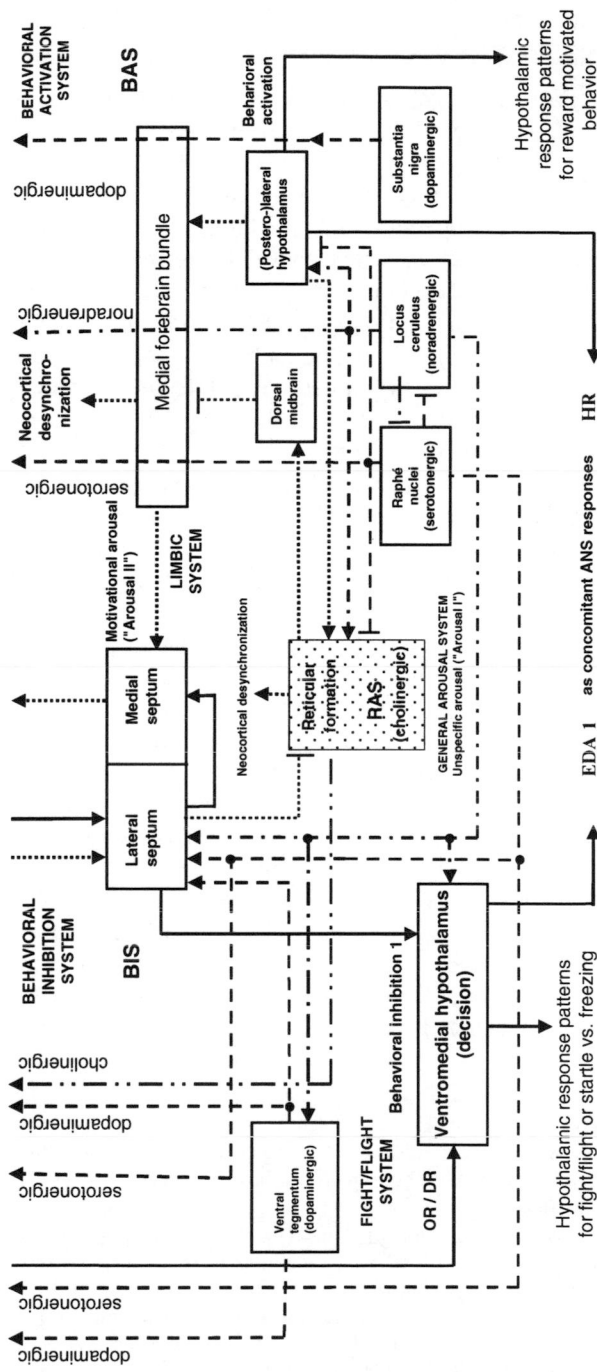

Fig. 3.4 An integrative model of multidimensional arousal systems, together with their electrodermal and cardiovascular concomitants. Transmitter systems: - - : dopaminergic, - • : noradrenergic, - - - : serotonergic, - • - • : cholinergic. The *dotted* connections represent Routtenberg's two-arousal system. *Arrows* indicate facilitation; *crossbars* indicate inhibition. See text for further explanations

It features reciprocal relationship to the "Arousal II" system proposed by Routtenberg (1968) as already described above and hence to Gray's (1982) septo-hippocampal stop-system described below.

The lower right part of Fig. 3.4 shows the nigrostriatal dopaminergic pathway from the substantia nigra to the striatal part of the basal ganglia (i.e., the striatum, consisting of caudate nucleus and putamen), which also plays a role in certain neurological movement disorders such as parkinsonism (Sect. 3.5.4.2). Together with the mesolimbic dopaminergic pathway, which originates in the ventral tegmentum (lower left in Fig. 3.4), this system may well be regarded as responsible not only for reward and self-stimulation in animals (Olds & Olds, 1965) but also as the neurochemical basis of Panksepp's (1982) "foraging expectancy command system." It partially coincides with Routtenberg's "Arousal System II."[116] The (postero) lateral hypothalamus, the output of which facilitates both arousal systems proposed by Routtenberg, elicits the so-called ergotropic responses, e.g., tonic increases in HR (see bottom of Fig. 3.4).

Acetylcholine is another neurotransmitter which plays an important role in CNS activation. Since there is strong evidence for EEG arousal being controlled by cholinergic pathways from the RF (Warburton, 1983), its major neurotransmission function is regarded here as being cholinergic. Furthermore, the noradrenergic system facilitates RF activity, thus increasing indirectly the neocortical desynchronization and hence the efficiency of cortical information processing. In turn, the serotonergic system inhibits not only RF activity but also the (postero)lateral hypothalamus, thus reducing cortical processing and diminishing probability of behavioral output as well. The general idea of brain noradrenaline acting excitatory in a nonspecific way and serotonin acting in a typically inhibitory way on motivated behaviors is generally consistent with existing evidence from both human and animal research (Panksepp, 1982, p. 419). Thus, the noradrenergic system and its interaction with cholinergic transmission may be regarded as the neurochemical basis for Routtenberg's "Arousal I."

As Fig. 3.4 further shows, serotonergic fibers from raphé nuclei stimulate the central and the basolateral amygdala, which have been regarded as a neurochemical basis for the "Affect Arousal" system by Pribram and McGuinness (1975).[117] The amygdala, which is facilitated by serotonergic fibers as already described and by

---

[116] The close connections of the nigrostriatal dopaminergic fibers to motor behavior via the basal ganglia matches well with the slightly changed view of Routtenberg (1971) concerning his "System II" (see Footnote 115).

[117] More recently, the basolateral amygdala has been identified as acting upon the the central amygdala to very rapidly eliciting fear responses via its projections to the hippocampus and the brain stem, whereas projections from the basolateral amygdala to the bed nucleus of the stria terminalis – together with those from the central amygdala – may be responsible for sustained fear responses, akin to anxiety (Heimer, Van Hoesen, Trimble, & Zahm, 2008). It is known from animal studies that the basolateral amygdala serves as input region, whereas the central amygdala plays a role in the mobilization of defensive behavior (Davis, 2000).

cholinergic input from the RF, receives thalamic and neocortical polysensory information, which may facilitate the elicitation of OR and DR together with their ventromedial-hypothalamic mediated behavioral action patterns being typical for fight/flight or startle vs. freezing responses (Sect. 3.1.1.2). Therefore, this amygdala-hypothalamus connection may be labeled "fight/flight" system. The amygdala does increase not only subcortical "Affect Arousal" but also the focusing of attention by exerting its influence on the subiculum (Sect. 3.1.4.1). With respect to Routtenberg's two-arousal hypothesis, this arousing mechanism may be regarded as belonging to his "Arousal System I."[118]

Besides the reticular structures that have general arousing properties and the limbic reward structures, the activation of which facilitates motivated behavior, Gray and Smith (1969) and later Gray (1973, 1982) proposed another arousal-related system which inhibits overt behavior and increases attention by means of mainly subcortical connections. According to Gray (1982), signals of nonreward or punishment as well as novel and fear stimuli serve as inputs for this "septo-hippocampal stop-system" or "behavioral inhibition system" (BIS). Gray (1973, Fig. 6) first regarded the observation of behavioral inhibition as a concomitant of the inhibiting influence of the medial septal area via the hippocampal formation on the RAS, which had also been described by Routtenberg (1968). However, in his later formulation, Gray (1982) proposed a highly complex system including the Papez circuit of the limbic system (Fig. 1.4 and Footnote 19 in Sect. 1.3.2.2), together with medial and lateral septal areas, and a highly differentiated view on hippocampal substructures, which can be identified as Pribram and McGuinness' (1975) "effort system" (Sect. 3.1.4.1), being depicted in the middle column of Fig. 3.4.

The effort system plays a central role in arousal, which can be best described starting from Gray's (1982) BIS, that is activated by noradrenergic and serotonergic pathways from the locus ceruleus and the raphé nuclei, respectively (see lower right in Fig. 3.4). In case of stress-relevant stimuli being present, these pathways increase the signal-to-noise ratio in the indirect information flow within the hippocampus. Although Gray primarily refers to anxiety and stress, this particular gating mechanism in the hippocampus may presumably be elicited by all kinds of negatively tuned emotions.

In Gray's view, neocortical sensory information is forwarded via the entorhinal cortex to the subicular area directly, as well as indirectly by means of a pathway via dentate gyrus, CA3, and CA1.[119] The direct information flow contains complete but

---

[118] This is in accordance with Sokolov's (1960) view of arousal within the OR (Sect. 3.1.1), insofar as an RF-mediated EEG desynchronization, together with hypothalamic ANS action patterns, being considered its concomitants.

[119] From Latin *cornu ammonis*, which is another name for hippocampus. The hippocampus theta which is generated in the medial septal area, as already outlined by Routtenberg (1968), is transmitted to the CA3 field in the hippocampus to provide exact temporal information to the system. Gray (1982) suggested a feedback loop from the subiculum to the medial septal area, the anatomical confirmation of which is, however, lacking. Therefore it is not included in Fig. 3.4.

unselected information, whereas the indirect path provides the subiculum with particular aspects of the current information flow, which gained importance by an increased signal-to-noise ratio in the gate, being under control of noradrenergic and serotonergic input. Encoding of information which has gained importance is elicited in the subiculum via the indirect pathway. In other words, this basic hippocampal circuit selects particular information which has to be compared with the past (stored regularities) as well as with the future (plans). The subicular area is regarded as the comparator, and the checking of information is performed by the Papez circuit (Sect. 3.2.2.1), which has direct access to recent sensory information via the anteroventral thalamus as well as to stored information via the cingulate gyrus. The latter receives information concerning classical conditioning as well as planning of (motor) behavior from the prefrontal cortex, and information of instrumental conditioning from the basal ganglia.

According to Gray (1982), this system is continuously monitoring what should occur next. If the system has the ability to predict what will happen next or to select an appropriate response from the sources mentioned, the subiculum will not impose an inhibition of behavior. If not, the BIS will be activated via the lateral septal area and the ventromedial hypothalamus ("behavioral inhibition 1") and/or via the cingulate gyrus and premotor/motor cortical areas ("behavioral inhibition 2"). In addition, the system increases attention by selecting items for entering the system via the entorhinal cortex. If the dentate gyrus-CA3 gate is closed as a consequence of increasing familiarity and unimportance of the stimulus, habituation is induced by CA3 via the lateral septum. This may be considered as the neuronal path in Sokolov's (1963b) comparator model (Sect. 3.1.1) that signals an increased familiarity to those subcortical structures from which otherwise ORs are elicited. As a consequence, the OR is likely to be directly influenced by the BIS, insofar as in Gray's system, habituation is mediated via inhibition of the ventromedial hypothalamus by lateral septal activity (Gray, 1987). The BIS has two major outcomes:

1. Inhibition of behavior, including instrumentally or classically conditioned ones, and even innate behavioral patterns. This is labeled "freezing" at the left bottom of Fig. 3.4, which is opposed to fight/flight or startle patterns.[120] However, behavioral inhibition is induced not only by preventing the elicitation of hypothalamic action patterns, but also by inhibiting cortically released motor activity via a pathway from the subiculum over the cingulate gyrus to the motor cortex (see top of Fig. 3.4).
2. Facilitation of a comprehensive and accurate analysis of environmental stimuli, especially those showing characteristics of novelty. The hippocampal system switches to an active mode, so that the subicular comparator acts upon the entorhinal cortex deliberately to select items to be processed within the basic hippocampal circuit. A connection can be made here to Sokolov's OR model,

---

[120] More recently, Gray and McNaughton (2000) made a distinction between fear, being mediated by the flight/fight freeze system, and anxiety, being mediated by the BAS.

where the hippocampus functions as a comparator between stored and newly incoming information (Sect. 3.1.1).

As shown in Fig. 3.4, ascending noradrenergic fibers from the locus ceruleus stimulate the septo-hippocampal and hypothalamic decision centers, and serotonergic fibers from the raphé nuclei do the same with the hippocampus. In the basic hippocampal circuit, both monoamines open the gate between the dentate gyrus and CA3 for specific sensory information to be checked by the subiculum (Gray, 1982). They also stimulate the lateral septal area. These monoaminergic pathways are stimulated in generalized states of stress and anxiety (Sects. 3.2.2.2 and 3.4.1.1) and are inhibited by the action of "anxiolytic drugs" (Sect. 3.4.3).[121] The dopaminergic pathway from the ventral tegmental area to the prefrontal cortex, in which activity is also increased during those states, was regarded as secondary by Gray, since the ventral tegmental area itself receives a noradrenergic input from the locus ceruleus (lower left in Fig. 3.4).

The initial model as proposed by Gray and Smith (1969) had been directed toward explaining approach vs. avoidance behavior, with an appropriate decision-making mechanism presumably located in the medial hypothalamic area, being preceded by a reward and a punishment system inhibiting each other, both facilitating general arousal. While Gray (1973, 1982) expanded the punishment system to the above-mentioned BIS, he did not further track an opposed behavioral activation system (BAS) as formulated earlier (Gray, 1970). However, he identified the BAS later on with the reward structures as described by Olds and Olds (1965) without giving as detailed a description of its action as he did for the BIS (Gray, 1973).

Consequently, Gray (1987, p. 225) distinguished between three separate mechanisms in his conceptual nervous system: a *reward system* which responds to signals of reward or nonpunishment by initiating approach behavior; the *BIS*, which responds to signals of punishment or nonreward by suppressing overt behavior; and a *fight/flight system* which responds to unconditioned punishment or nonreward by activating escape or aggressive behavior.[122] BIS activity inhibits not only the activity of the reward system (which could be performed by serotonergic inhibitory action on the lateral hypothalamus as depicted in the lower left of Fig. 3.4) but also the activity of the fight/flight system via serotonergic inhibition of an output from central-gray located fight/flight neurons.[123] This matches the well-established role of serotonin as a predominantly inhibiting transmitter.

---

[121] Gray (1982) explained the anxiolytic properties of tranquilizers as well as hypnotics via their facilitating properties on the inhibitory action of GABA (gamma-aminobutyric acid) on noradrenergic and serotonergic synaptic transmission. Tranquilizers of the benzodiazepine type act directly via a specific postsynaptic receptor, while hypnotics like barbiturates and alcohol act indirectly through a blockade of picrotoxine receptors, a substance which inhibits GABA.

[122] Gray (1987, p. 226) pointed to the difference between his own and Panksepp's (1982) view concerning fear and anxiety (Sect. 3.4.1.1), the latter identifying those largely with the activity of the fight/flight system, while Gray identified them with BAS activity.

[123] Those neurons, which are not depicted in Fig. 3.4, receive afferent impulses from the medial hypothalamic decision center (Gray, 1987, p. 265).

Gray (1982), focusing on observations of animal behavior, has always been cautious with respect to possible psychophysiological concomitants of BIS or BAS activity. An attempt to develop systematic hypotheses concerning psychophysiological concomitants of motivation-directed arousal processes was made by Fowles (1980, 1986b). Starting from the model of Gray and Smith (1969), Fowles (1980) explicitly formulated a "three arousal model," in which two mutually antagonistic systems determine the outcome of either behavioral activation or inhibition, while another system which receives input from both of them presumably increases behavioral vigor or intensity. While the latter system is identified with the RAS (Sect. 3.2.1.1), the BAS corresponds to Routtenberg's (1968) "Arousal System II," and the third type of arousal, which mediates the effects of aversive stimuli, has its neurophysiological substrate in the BIS as formulated by Gray (1973, 1982).

While Fowles (1980) did not explicitly deal with the problem of psychophysiological indicators for general arousal or "Arousal System I" – for which EEG activity may still serve as a major indicator (Sect. 3.2.1) – he integrated various animal as well as human psychophysiological studies with respect to presumed autonomic nervous system correlates of BIS and BAS activity. His conclusion was that HR can be regarded as an even more accurate index of BAS activity than overt behavior, and hence indicate positive emotional and motivational aspects of arousal. On the other hand, EDA appears to respond more to situations typically connected to BIS activity such as those characterized by the presence of fear- or punishment-relevant stimuli. Since the appropriate neural impulses for EDA are most likely to stem from hypothalamic areas in which sympathetic activity originates (Fig. 1.4, Sect. 1.3.2.2), they should be labeled EDA1 (Fig. 1.6, Sect. 1.3.4.1).

The elicitation of EDA1 is indicated at the bottom of Fig. 3.4, where the model of a medial hypothalamic decision structure as proposed by Gray and Smith (1969) is extended according to the results from hypothalamic lesion and stimulation studies on motivated behavior (see Stellar & Stellar, 1985, for a comprehensive summary). Another extension of the model concerns the possibility that the ventromedial hypothalamus is the output region for behavioral inhibition, and the (postero) lateral hypothalamus is more likely the output region for behavioral activation. Though there is no direct evidence for a corresponding selective action of these structures on EDA and HR, the appropriate hypothetical notion for these variables is that they may be concomitants of BIS and BAS activity according to Fowles (1980). These are depicted at the bottom of Fig. 3.4.

The specific indicator function of EDA, with respect to BIS activity as elaborated by Fowles (1980), relies on research in the field of conditioning and stress (Sects. 3.1.2 and 3.2.2). It is mainly focused on the appearance of stimulus dependent as well as spontaneous EDRs, but not on the EDL which is regarded as being more influenced by peripheral physiological states (e.g., corneal hydration, Sect. 1.3.4.2 "The Role of the Epidermal Barrier Layer") than by fear-evoking stimuli. Evidence for the suggested coupling of BIS and EDA is drawn indirectly from observations. It has been interpreted by Fowles as directional fractionation between EDA and HR during situations of nonreward (frustration) or punishment. The occurrence of such a directional fractionation is suggested to be dependent on response contingency. This means, in cases when a person expects that her/his responding will not result in avoidance or escape, but that the probability of punishment will be increased, the result will be an increase in EDA but no HR acceleration. The same response pattern is to be expected if the experimental demands are strong enough for the person to not consider active avoidance as an alternative.

The coupling of BAS and HR could be shown in a series of successive experiments (Fowles, Fisher, & Tranel, 1982; Tranel, 1983; Tranel, Fisher, & Fowles, 1982). A typical study which explicitly investigated the supposed BIS-EDA coupling was performed by Tranel (1983). Forty-eight participants of both genders underwent six trials of a choice-RT task. During trials 2–4 they received feedback tones indicating monetary reward for success, which had been set to 100% success. During the last two trials, no tones were given. Half of the participants were informed that this would happen, thereby being subjected to an expected no-feedback condition, the remaining participants were not informed. The latter, frustrated group showed a significant increase in NS.SCR freq. with respect to the no-feedback-expecting group, which only showed a further decline of EDA that normally occurs during successive trials. This was interpreted as conforming to Fowles' (1980) hypothesis of EDA indicating BIS activity during frustrative nonreward, while HR was not influenced by the change of experimental conditions. However, it remains questionable whether the increase of NS.EDR freq. could not be simply attributed to uncertainty or an increase of orienting activity that appeared as a consequence of the unannounced situational change.[124]

Fowles (1988) reviewed a series of studies, including the Tranel (1983) one, which evidence the specific indicator function of EDA for BIS activity. Therefore, the differential indicator function of EDA and HR[125] can be regarded as a sound working hypothesis: opposed to HR, which responds to positive hedonic

---

[124] Fowles (1988) reported data from a doctoral dissertation performed by Fisher in 1985, examining the effects of 10, 50, and 100% success using 20 participants per group. In contrast to a feedback-only condition, a monetary incentive condition, holding the amount of money earned constant across the different success groups, yielded significantly greater HRs regardless of the amount of success. On the other hand, NS.SCR freq. was significantly heightened in the 10% group as compared to the other ones, regardless of monetary incentive, which supports EDA not being influenced by appetitive motivational states during task performance. Sosnowski, Nurzynska, and Polec (1991) could not find an influence of manipulating monetary reinforcement on both HR and SCR amp. (recorded with standard methodology) in 60 student women randomly assigned to reward, frustration, and control groups performing a problem-solving task. Participants were run in pairs; the active participant solved the problem, being observed by the passive one. During the task, SCR amplitudes decreased significantly in active participants while being markedly increased in passive participants. The authors interpreted this result as being in accordance with Fowles' EDA-BIS hypothesis since EDA was increased in what they called passive coping.

[125] In her study comparing HR-reactive and HR-nonreactive participants under various stimulation conditions, Lawler (1980) found that HR reactivity being associated with minimal EDA, while HR nonreactive individuals showed more NS.SCRs.

motivational states but not to aversive stimuli, NS.EDR freq. does not increase during appetitive motivational activation.[126] Instead, increased nonspecific EDA is observable in arousing states accompanied by negative emotions, such as being elicited by aversive stimuli. However, multivariate psychophysiological research will still have to prove the existence of particular ANS variables exhibiting such a differential and specific indicator function (Sect. 3.2.2.1). Parameters of different systems tend to covary or dissociate dependent on stimulus properties and/or individual differences (Fahrenberg, 1988). Nevertheless, the development of psychophysiological hypotheses on the basis of a more differentiated neurophysiological model of arousal processes as depicted in Fig. 3.4 may help to enlighten the hitherto unexplained relationships between arousal-related changes in frequently measured variables like HR and EDA.[127]

More recently, the BAS/BIS concept has been brought into connection with Davidson's (1993) approach/withdrawal model of frontal EEG-alpha asymmetry in emotion (Sutton & Davidson, 1997). Relatively higher left frontal activity (measured as the inverse of EEG-alpha power) has been regarded as concomitant of both BAS activity and approach tendencies, whereas relatively higher right frontal EEG activity – or possibly less left frontal activity (Coan, Allen, & Harmon-Jones, 2001) – has been connected to BIS activity and withdrawal tendencies (Coan & Allen, 2003). In their review of 28 empirical studies, Coan & Allen (2004) came to the conclusion that the proposed relationship may be robust for the BAS, but not so robust for the BIS, presumably because Davidson's withdrawal concept refers to a more general predisposition to withdraw from sources of aversive stimulation, whereas the activation of Gray's BIS depends more on actual stimulus properties. This is in line with Knygazev et al.'s (2002) failure to relate frontal EEG asymmetry and BIS scores obtained by questionnaire data to EDA (see Sect. 3.1.4.3).

An adaption of the four arousal model shown in Fig. 3.4 for the field of engineering psychophysiology has been performed by Boucsein and Backs (2009) and will be presented in Sect. 3.5.1. Table 3.2 in that section will summarize the psychophysiological measures that typically reflect each type of arousal, including various EDA and HR parameters.

---

[126] Altogether, the BIS-EDA connection seems to be better established than the BAS-HR connection (see as an example, Gomez and McLaren's (1997) study described in Sect. 3.1.2.2).

[127] However, the postulated relationships were not always confirmed. Brenner, Beauchaine and Sylvers (2005) performed a study with 50 participants (28 females, 22 males) who were given different reward and nonreward conditions in sequence during a number-recognition task, while cardiovascular and electrodermal measures were recorded as markers for BIS/BAS activity. Unexpectedly, electrodermal reactivity was elevated not only during nonreward but also during reward. Furthermore, the proposed psychophysiological markers for BIS and BAS did not yield substantial correlations with a BIS/BAS questionnaire but only with subjective measures of affect.

3.2.1.3   Diurnal Variation and EDA in Different Sleep Stages

As already mentioned in Sect. 2.4.2, EDA belongs to the physiological processes being under ANS control, thus being subject to a circadian influence (Rutenfranz, 1955). Even though EDA effects of the time of day were reported from the Mauritius study (see Sect. 2.4.1.1), not too many publications on diurnal variations of EDA have been around. In two experiments, Hot, Naveteur, Leconte, and Sequeira (1999) revealed that SCL was higher in the evening than in the morning, regardless of the season.[128] In experiment 1, which was performed in summer, 6 participants (2 females, 4 males) spent 6 days under laboratory conditions. SCL was recorded bilaterally with standard methodology from the medial phalanges of the second and third fingers. In addition, hand temperature was recorded bilaterally from the middle phalanx of the ring finger. Recordings were taken in the morning, in the afternoon, and in the evening. Experiment 2 was performed in winter and spring with 12 participants (8 females, 4 males) on a single day. Participants adhered to their own activities while SCL was recorded in the morning and in the evening. In both experiments, skin temperature showed a pattern which was asynchronous with the SCL (Sect. 2.4.2.1).

Hot, Leconte, and Sequeira (2005) presented 12 participants (5 females, 7 males) neutral and emotion-evoking stimuli from the International Affective Picture System (IAPS; Lang, Bradley, & Cuthbert, 1999) during seven sessions in the course of 1 day (from 9:30 am to 9:30 pm) for 6 s each. SCL and SCRs were bilaterally recorded with standard methodology. The prestimulus SCL showed significant diurnal variation, with a peak at 3:30 pm and subsequent insignificant decline. This result corroborates the finding of Hot et al. (1999) reported above. Mean SCR amp. also peaked at 3:30 pm and ratings of emotional experience[129] yielded a steep increase between 1:30 and 3:30 pm. The authors point to the possible importance of their results for diurnal variations in depressive patients (Sect. 3.4.1.3).

In their ambulatory monitoring study described in Sect. 2.2.3.4, Boucsein, Schaefer, and Sommer (2001) averaged the NS.SCR freq. every 5 min for the last 3 h of the day, observing that the general decrease of tonic EDA seen during the course of the day became especially prominent when preparing for sleep.[130]

---

[128] This result is at variance with the Neumann (1968) findings described in Sect. 2.4.1.1 who obtained different SRL patterns in summer and in winter. There were also seasonal differences in EDA in the Mauritius study (Sect. 2.4.1.1), since Venables and Mitchell (1996) reported a significant interaction between gender and season, yielding a greater responsivity of females in hot weather.

[129] However, in their review on the indicator function of EDA for arousal and emotion, Sequeira, Hot, Silvert, and Delplanque (2009) came to the conclusion that EDA might be used as a valid indicator for diurnal variations in emotional reactivity, which is not necessarily represented in subjective emotionality.

[130] Unfortunately, for technical reasons such as electrode detachment, only 12 of the 24 participants (7 with the horror tape, 5 controls) could be included in the sleep evaluation. As could have been expected, tonic EDA increased during listening to the horror story compared to the boring story. No differences were found in HR.

These EDA results were not paralleled by recordings of skin temperature. However, ambient temperature and body movements exerted a more prominent influence on EDA than skin temperature. In summary, diurnal variations of EDA are far from being clarified and require further investigation.

Until the early 1960s, it had been generally accepted that spontaneous EDA would be practically disappearing during sleep, especially in stages of slow wave sleep (Kleitman, 1963). On the contrary, Johnson and Lubin (1966) observed the highest NS.EDR freq. in the deepest sleeping stages (III and IV). They recorded endosomatic and exosomatic EDA[131] during three consecutive nights from 6 epileptic patients of each gender and from 17 healthy male participants. The analyses were collapsed over groups since no differences in EDA were found between patients and controls. While the authors observed less than one SRR or two SPRs per minute on average during sleep stage I and during rapid eye movement (REM) sleep, an average of 2.2 NS.SRRs and 7.2 NS.SPRs per minute was observed in stages III and IV. There were marked intraindividual differences between the different nights of the study. However, similar patterns emerged in comparable sleep stages within a given night.

Johnson and Lubin interpreted their observed differences between frequencies of spontaneous SRRs and SPRs as demonstrating a dissociation between exosomatic and endosomatic EDA during sleep, but Edelberg (1972a) pointed to a potential confounding caused by local differences at different recording sites. This view was supported by Broughton, Poire, and Tassinari (1965). By recording SPR[132] at 6–8 sites from 25 participants during sleep, they observed an increase of spontaneous EDA during stages of deep sleep, but in addition a marked increase of SPR lat. in caudal and distal directions on the body surface.

The appearance of a maximum in spontaneous EDA during stage IV as well as its decrease during REM phases is regarded as a well-established result in sleep research (Edelberg, 1972a; Jovanovic, 1971). This had been shown for example by Freixa i Baqué et al. (1983, Table 1) who reviewed 12 studies published between 1962 and 1976. In addition, they reported results of their own, obtained from 8 male participants during three consecutive nights (following a habituation night). Differences in NS.SPR freq.[133] between the first and the three consecutive sleep cycles could be observed in a consistent manner during all nights. While total EDA

---

[131] Recorded with Ag/AgCl sponge electrodes from the fingers of the right hand with an "inert" electrolyte and 21 µA/cm² for SR, and from the left middle finger to the scrubbed left forearm with Redux cream, and 1 s time constant, for SP. Amplitude criteria: 50 Ω and 100 µV (positive or negative), respectively.

[132] Recorded with silver cup electrodes and an EEG electrode cream from acetone-cleaned sites, each pair having interelectrode distances of 5–6 cm. They were placed palmar/dorsal, at the dorsal forearm; and over the frontal, trapezius, deltoid, biceps, extensor digitorum, or other muscles, approximately along the neuraxis and peripheral nerves.

[133] Recorded with Beckman electrodes, time constant 0.6 s, low-pass filtered with 15 Hz, amplitude criterion 200 µV. Results were log-transformed.

(independent of sleep stages) and EDA during stage II were significantly lower in the first as compared to the following cycles, there was a significantly higher NS.SPR freq. during the REM phase in the last cycle as compared to the first three sleep cycles.

Kushniruk, Rustenburg, and Ogilvie (1985) awakened their 8 participants who spent two nights in a sleep laboratory four times from REM sleep: (1) in the presence of both eye movement and phasic EDA, (2) if phasic EDA was present without eye movements, (3) if eye movements were present without EDA, and (4) in the absence of both EDA and eye movements. SRRs were recorded with 10 μA CC between silver electrodes attached to the plantar surface of the right hand and the ventral surface of the right arm, while EOG and EEG were recorded as well. SRRs during REM sleep were associated with the report of bizarre dreams (containing distortion or discontinuity). Dreams from condition (1) were significantly more bizarre than those from the other conditions, but no relationship between EDA and emotion-related dream reports could be observed. The authors regarded this particular type of REM sleep as "activated" but not necessarily as emotional.[134]

In addition to frequently observed differences in EDA between sleep stages, attempts to differentiate these stages by means of EDA parameters remained unsatisfactorily. Koumans, Tursky, and Solomon (1968) recorded SP and SR[135] from 9 male participants during two nights of normal sleep, together with EEG and EOG. It was not possible to differentiate between sleep stages by means of SPL and SRL; there was only a significant change from the waking state to sleep in SPL (an increasing negativity). Instead, higher rates of NS.EDR freq. during stages III and IV were observed in both EDA recordings, plus lower spontaneous EDA rates during REM sleep as compared to the waking state. Though the authors were cautious with respect to identifying sleep stages by spontaneous EDA, they inferred from its decrease occurring consistently about 6 min before the onset of each REM period that it should be possible to use NS.EDRs to detect REM-phase onset (e.g., for the sake of REM deprivation). Johns, Cornell, and Masterton (1969) found similar results in a study with 12 healthy participants and 19 convalescent surgical patients of both genders, recording SR[136] together with EEG and EOG during sleep. By means of tonic EDA parameters (SRL as well as NS.SRR freq.) they could determine the time of sleep onset, disturbances during the night, and waking with a resolution of 1–2 min. Furthermore, they obtained a rough estimate of the amount of slow wave sleep.

---

[134] Pivik (1978) reported that individuals being asked to get more involved as usual in their own dreams showed an increase of EDA during sleep.

[135] Recorded from comparable unipolar right and left sites (thenar against forearm) with Ag/AgCl sponge electrodes; amplitude criteria 200 μV and 100 Ω, respectively.

[136] SRL and SRRs measured from different washed volar sites at two fingers, with Ag electrodes, 5 mm in diameter contact area. An AC-coupling circuit was used that resulted in biphasic SRRs.

In a study performed with 20 male participants, Hori (1982) showed that palmar but not dorsal SP[137] could be used as an indicator for the onset of sleep, since only the palmar SPL decreased between 3.5 min before and 1.5 min after onset of sleep stage I. Similar anticipatory changes were observed in palmar SPRs and slow eye movements, suggesting the existence of a common underlying CNS mechanism.

Several results indicate that nocturnal tonic EDA could be regarded as an indicator of stress-induced changes of sleep quality. Lester, Burch, and Dossett (1967) investigated the aftereffect of different stressors on EEG and SR measures.[138] After two habituation nights, participants were studied in the following sequence: three consecutive nights before, during, and after a time-interval anticipation test used as a mild stressor; three other consecutive nights clustered around a 1-day medical exam as a strong stressor; and a minimum of two nights after the end of the semester. During the initial nights, the overall mean NS.SRR freq. decreased, but increased again in nights after stressful experiences, being highest in the night following the exams. This effect was most prominent in stages III and IV and lowest during REM sleep. A maximum of nonspecific EDA was usually noted during the first and/or second period of slow wave sleep, and an average of 10–12 EDRs/min was not unusual, leading the authors to the use of the term "storming" to describe this unique electrodermal activity. However, nocturnal EDA was markedly reduced when following unexpected severe life stresses which appeared during the investigation, thus showing that a direct relationship between severity of stress and nocturnal EDA remains equivocal.

Boucsein and Ottmann (1996), investigating possible interactive effects of noise and shift work (Sect. 3.5.1), recorded SC with standard methodology from thenar/ hypothenar sites of the nondominant hand during 5 consecutive days and nights in the laboratory from 24 male participants, who performed a 10 h vigilance task daily at a simulated computer work place. Half of them worked on day shift, the other one on night shift, and half of the participants in each group worked under 80 dB white noise, the other half under 50 dB white noise. SC was recorded both during work and leisure time as well as during sleep. Differential effects of noise and shift work appeared during the subsequent sleep, i.e., a significant increase in NS.SCR freq. after working under noise, thus pointing to a prolonged stress unwinding process during sleep. Unfortunately, no EEG recordings were performed so that results differentiating sleep stages were not available.

In a series of three studies on spontaneous EDR "storming" in stages III–IV sleep, McDonald, Shallenberger, Koresko, and Kinzy (1976) investigated the influence of various factors on nocturnal EDA. In all studies, EEG, EOG, HR, finger

---

[137] DC-recorded thenar and dorsal against a skin-drilled forearm site with Ag/AgCl electrodes and 0.05 M NaCl agar-agar cream. Amplitude criterion for SPRs (negative, diphasic, and positive waves) was 250 μV.

[138] Recorded from the left middle finger by Ag/AgCl electrodes, NaCl cream, and 10 μA/cm^2 constant current. Amplitude criterion for NS.SRRs: 50 Ω.

plethysmogram, respiration rate, and exosomatic as well as endosomatic EDA[139] were continuously recorded. In their first study performed with 46 participants, the authors found significant correlations between spontaneous EDA during the 5-min period of waking prior to sleep onset and "storming" rates in stage IV sleep ($r = 0.41$ for NS.SRR freq. and $r = 0.37$ for NS.SPR freq.). Twenty-one participants were instructed to remain awake as long as possible, while the others were told to go to sleep as usual. In their subsequent sleep, the group who remained awake showed a highly significant greater NS.SPR freq. as compared to the other participants. In their second study, 21 male participants performed two nights of laboratory sleep. There was a significant decrease of NS.SPR freq. as recorded during stage IV from the first to the second night. McDonald et al. (1976) interpreted this as a habituation effect, though correlations with different indices of sleep quality could not be observed (e.g., amount of movement). In addition, participants were divided into subgroups of "stormers" and "nonstormers" (showing either more or less than one SPR per minute in stages III–IV). "Stormers" revealed significantly higher values in anxiety and ego-strength measures of the MMPI as compared with "nonstormers." During the third experiment, 23 male participants who slept two consecutive nights in the laboratory were awakened 3–7 times each night and asked if they had been dreaming. Affirmative reports of dreaming were given in 87.5% of the REM awakenings, and in 34.7% of the non-REM awakenings. However, dream reports from "storm" awakenings were reported in 54.0% of the time but only in 15.4% of "nonstorm" awakenings. There were no differences in the dream contents in phases with different amounts of EDA. HR and finger pulse differentiated only between REM and the other sleep stages and showed no relationships to the various sleep parameters as did EDA.

McDonald et al. (1976) interpreted their results and those of Lester et al. (1967) reported above as showing an increase in tonic EDA during stages III–IV sleep that is not a by-product of deep sleep. Instead, EDA "storming" seems to be highly related to some activities or events before sleep. Since EDRs were identified as concomitants of information processing during waking (Sect. 3.1.3.2), these authors suggested that "storming" during sleep may indicate releasing of information which had been stored during the day (see also Pivik, 2007, p. 649). These processes disturbed and shortened phases of deep sleep, as could be shown in the reported negative correlation between stage IV duration and EDA during sleep. A more careful interpretation of their results had already been provided by Lester et al. (1967). They suggested that EDA during slow wave sleep is a continuation of EDA during wakefulness, the reason for which could be cessation of cortical inhibition during those sleep stages.

---

[139] Recorded with Beckman Ag/AgCl electrodes as SR from the fingers of the right hand using 40 μA, and as SP between left index finger and forearm with 0.24 s time constant. A time window of 1–3 s following stimulus onset was used to determine EDR; SPR amp. measured as the total biphasic amplitude (Sect. 2.3.1.2 "Amplitudes of Endosomatic Responses"); SRR amp. being transformed to log SCR amp.

An aftereffect of information uptake during the day on EDA during sleep did also emerge in the Boucsein et al. (2001) study mentioned above. The authors observed increased SCLs and NS.SCR freq. during initial sleep in half of their 24 female participants who listened to a horror story immediately before going to sleep compared to the other half who listened to rather boring material. A less-prominent increase was found for the mean NS.SCR amp.

Several studies on EDA during sleep focused on orienting and habituation (Sect. 3.1.1) instead on spontaneous electrodermal activity. Johnson and Lubin (1967) reported additional data obtained from 12 healthy participants in their 1966 study described above. These participants received a series of tones[140] starting before going to sleep and continuing throughout the night. During sleep, the previously habituated ED-OR following tones appeared again. This was interpreted by the authors as indicating resistance to habituation of autonomic response not only at the upper but also at the lower end of the arousal level (Sect. 3.2.1.1). The decrease in SPR amp. observed after 3–4 h of stimulation (and after 380 or more stimuli) was interpreted as being more likely associated with diurnal patterns of physiological activity rather than being due to true habituation.

In contrast, Firth (1973) doubted the suggested incompatibility of sleep and habituation. He pointed to the former authors' method of averaging responses over hourly periods as well as to the fact that long irregular ISIs may have prevented the observation of short-term habituation. Therefore, in their own study with 3 participants, Firth compared the effect of six ISI conditions on the SPR[141] in a within-subjects design. The SPR amp. showed significant habituation in all sleep stages (II, IV, or REM) and under all ISI conditions, which also appeared in the HR response (except during REM sleep).

In an attempt to confirm the lack of habituation during sleep as revealed by their earlier research, Johnson, Townsend, and Wilson (1975) recorded SRRs to a series of 20 stimuli[142] presented during stage II and REM sleep. Data from 9 participants with complete recordings did not yield unambiguous stimulus-dependent SRRs in either sleep stage, due to the infrequency of responses during REM, and either no SRRs or too much spontaneous EDA during stage II. Therefore, an estimate of electrodermal habituation effects was unfeasible. In accordance with Firth's (1973) results, HR response habituation occurred during stage II but not during REM sleep.

---

[140] 1 kHz, 30 dB tones presented over a loudspeaker for 45 s. Amplitude criteria: 125 Ω for SRRs and 100 mV for SPRs, within a time window of 1–5 s after stimulus onset.

[141] Recorded between scrubbed volar forearm and thenar sites with a 0.3 s time constant. A 1 kHz, 1 s tone was presented over loudspeakers with 70 dB at the participant's head, using three regular (10, 20, and 30 s) and three randomized irregular ISI conditions (8, 10, or 12; 16, 20, or 24; and 24, 30, or 36 s).

[142] 800 Hz, 75 dB, 1 or 2 s duration, at 30, 45, and 60 s ISIs. SRRs were obtained by dividing the prestimulus SRL by the maximum poststimulus resistance change occurring within 7 s after stimulus onset, log-transformed.

McDonald and Carpenter (1975) did not find habituation of exosomatic or endosomatic EDRs in 46 participants during the presentation of 33 tones (500 Hz, 40 dB, ISIs at random 10, 15, or 20 s) during stage IV and REM sleep. By contrast, HR and finger plethysmographic responses showed marked habituation and also dishabituation to a tone of different frequency.

In summary, EDA during sleep may not be able to sufficiently contribute to the differentiation of sleep stages. However, an increased spontaneous EDA, especially during deep sleep phases, can be used to indicate continuous processing of information taken up during the day. This is confirmed by observations of a larger amount of EDA during those phases following stressful days. On the other hand, results concerning electrodermal orienting and habituation during sleep remained somewhat contradictory, which leads to ambiguity on the role of EDA for indicating a processing of information taken up while being asleep. In various sleep studies, the circadian periodicity of tonic EDA has to be taken into account, because it may show several maxima and minima (Sect. 2.4.2.1) as well as huge individual differences (Rutenfranz, 1958). Furthermore, problems of long-term recording must be dealt with, which were discussed in Sect. 2.2.6.1.

3.2.2   Electrodermal Indices of Emotion and Stress

Research areas of emotion and stress are closely related. Both distress and eustress, i.e., negatively and positively experienced stress, come with hefty emotional responses and manifest most prominently in ANS measures and especially in the EDA. In turn, laboratory research into emotional states might induce stress experience in participants in case of high-intense stimulation or the use of stimuli becoming very realistic for the participants (Sect. 3.2.2.1). Consequently, rather similar stimulus conditions had been sometimes used in both fields, such as presenting emotion-inducing (or stress-inducing) films. Nevertheless, distress has been a more unitary concept than negative emotion, the latter having always been a target for differentiating various emotional states from each other by means of psychophysiology. Section 3.2.2.2 will focus on a specific use of EDA in laboratory stress research, i.e., the temporal course of stress induced in laboratory settings and its modification by various instructional manipulations. For using EDA as stress indicator outside the laboratory, the reader may be referred to Sect. 3.5.1 where studies will be reported, the goal of which was to elucidate psychophysiological responses to stressful working conditions.[143]

---

[143] In a famous series of field studies, differences in time courses between electrodermal and subjective measures of stress had been obtained within nonlaboratory research with parachutists (for a summary, see Epstein, 1972). Whether or not psychophysiological dissociations during the course of anticipating stressful events will increase with the complexity of the stress situation should be further investigated. This requires combined laboratory/field studies in the area of stress research, which are also necessary to establish possible relationships between short-lasting psychophysiological stress effects and long-lasting changes.

3.2.2.1   EDA in Emotional States

The history of using ANS variables in research on emotions is a long and controversial one, starting with James and Lange who published their psychophysiological theories of emotion at the end of the nineteenth century. The basic theoretical issues that have been discussed in this field since then were summarized by Levenson (1988).[144] Among these were the specificity question of ANS patterns and the dimensionality issue, both of which will be referred to below. Attempts to include knowledge about the role of CNS structures in eliciting autonomic responses as concomitants of emotions have not gone beyond theories of general arousal for a very long time (Sect. 3.2.1.1). A closer theoretical connection has been established between neurophysiological mechanisms of information processing and motivational arousal (Sects. 3.1.3.1 and 3.2.1.2) on the one hand and the neurophysiologically oriented emotion theory of Papez on the other hand. These views have special implications for the use of EDA and thus will be briefly referred to below.

According to Papez (1937), emotional excitement is maintained via circulation of neuronal activity in a loop-like structure of the limbic system which carries his name – the so-called Papez circuit (Fig. 1.4, Sect. 1.3.2.2). In this proposed circuit, emotions are supposed to not only being checked against sensory information within thalamic areas but also having access to ANS programs which are stored in the hypothalamus, thereby eliciting autonomic concomitants of various emotional states. Gray (1982), in his neurophysiological model of anxiety, again used the Papez circuit for processing emotionally tinged information (Fig. 3.4, Sect. 3.2.1.2). Gray extended the ideas of Papez with respect to the central role of the subiculum (a part of the hippocampus) which uses the information check within the Papez circle to decide whether or not behavior should be inhibited via the septo-hippocampal stop-system or BIS. As outlined in Sect. 3.2.1.2, Fowles (1980) suggested that EDA has specific validity with respect to BIS activity, thus providing a theoretically founded but not yet empirically fully confirmed background for the use of EDA as a specific indicator of anxiety states and traits (Sect. 3.4.1.1).

As opposed to general arousal research, the psychophysiological investigation of emotional states requires not only physiological measures but also subjective reports. Therefore, even a neurophysiologically oriented inquiry into emotional processes must start with a taxonomy of emotional experience in humans (Panksepp, 1982). As already pointed out by Wundt (1896), the subjective experience of emotions should be regarded as multidimensional. Different emotions may elicit the same amount of general arousal, thus becoming possibly undistinguishable with respect to their ANS concomitants. Therefore, in classic psychophysiological emotion research, emotional quality is determined via subjective variables while their quantitative properties are measured by ANS parameters.

---

[144] With respect to the theories of the psychobiology of emotions in general, the reader is referred to appropriate comprehensive reviews (e.g., Grings & Dawson, 1978; Panksepp, 1986; Plutchik, 1980; Schwartz, 1986).

An attempt to quantify the strength of emotions by the use of EDA was made by Traxel (1960). Eighty male participants were visually presented 20 pairs of words in sequence for 7 s each while recording SZ.[145] After each pair they had to decide which word, if any, elicited a greater amount of emotional experience. The judgments were evaluated by paired comparisons, and the obtained strength of emotion was correlated with the differences between SZR amp. elicited by the particular words in a specially developed a posteriori paired-comparison technique. A linear relationship appeared between log SZR amp. and the strength of emotion determined by the method of psychophysics. After an additional square-root transformation (Sect. 2.3.3.3), the correlation between subjective and electrodermal measures of emotion strength increased slightly from $r = 0.94$ to an almost ideal $r = 0.99$.

Several attempts have been made to obtain emotion-specific patterns of physiological responses, since Ax (1953) tried to differentiate the effects of anger and fear by means of ANS variables. In his experiment, a total of 43 participants of both genders received two conditions in counterbalanced order. In one of these, participants were annoyed by means of an obnoxious experimenter. In the other condition they were frightened by having an electric shock applied to their finger, accompanied by sparkles close to the participant, and the experimenter exclaimed that this was a high voltage short-circuit. Differences between anger and fear appeared on seven of 14 psychophysiological measures recorded, whereas anger elicited a significant increase of NS.EDR freq.[146] as compared to fear. In turn, EDL was significantly higher under fear as compared to anger conditions. However, large individual differences were observed; for example, some of the fearful participants evidenced higher changes in EDA than in respiration while others showed the reverse pattern. Nevertheless, Ax attributed the observed ANS responses to specific underlying endocrine patterns as outlined in the next paragraph.[147]

Methodological issues in this kind of peripheral physiological differentiation of emotions have been discussed by Wagner (1989) who also summarized results on anger vs. fear and other emotions. A systematic comparison of results taken from eight multivariate studies attempting to differentiate experimentally induced anger and/or fear by means of ANS variables, including Ax's (1953) study, was performed by Stemmler (1984, 1989). In most of the studies, both emotions yielded higher cardiovascular output (increases in HR and blood pressure) as compared to resting conditions. An elevated NS.EDR freq. had been found for both emotions in

---

[145] Recorded with 600 Hz, 1 V, using an RC bridge (Sect. 2.1.5) and metal electrodes with 1 cm diameter. SZR amp. were subjected to log transformation with respect to a suggested validity of Fechner's law for EDR.

[146] Recorded by the use of a 60 Hz AC and a bridge from volar finger surfaces, evaluated as SY, using 1 μS as amplitude criterion.

[147] Uchiyama (1992) brought real-life situations in the laboratory for inducing the emotions fear, anger, and joy in 6 male participants. NS.SCR freq. (recorded with unreported methodology) was found to be higher in the fear situation (i.e., informing the participant that he would suffer from a heart disease) compared to the others.

one study, while not differing from a resting condition in another study. Four studies with a direct comparison of anger and fear yielded an elevated HR, two of them a decrease in diastolic blood pressure, lower tonic EMG values, and an increased SCL during fear. The two studies that directly compared NS.EDR freq. yielded opposite results. In summary, the so-called adrenaline-noradrenaline pattern under anger vs. adrenaline pattern under fear/anxiety as supposed by Ax could only partially, if at all, be confirmed.[148]

In his own experiment, Stemmler (1989) induced three emotions (fear, anger, and pleasure) to 42 female participants in a within-subjects design.[149] Various peripheral physiological measures including SC[150] were continuously recorded during the induction of emotions and also during interspersed resting phases. In addition, several standardized ratings of emotional states were applied. These subjective measures yielded their most pronounced results in the appropriate situational context. However, their specificity was less during fear and anger conditions as compared to the pleasure condition. Out of the 34 parameters that were extracted from the psychophysiological measures, the 14 which significantly differentiated between the reference phases for the three emotions were included in a discriminant analysis, which resulted in a highly significant rejection of the null hypothesis of profiles for the three emotions being parallel. Multivariate comparisons yielded low EMG values together with peripheral vasoconstriction, low skin temperature, and a low SCL taken from the hand, but an increase of forehead SCL during the fear state. During anger, the forearm EMG and the vasodilatation at the hand and the forehead were increased, and an increase of forehead SCL emerged as well. The NS.SCR freq. did not belong to the variables discriminating fear and anger. Though the observation that SCL recorded from the hand was lowered under fear showed some coincidence with Ax's findings, Stemmler's results did not really fit those of Ax (1953) with respect to EDA. The pleasure condition yielded an increase of the hand's skin temperature and a decrease of forehead SCL.

To obtain valuable information concerning the specific role of electrodermal parameters in further multivariate emotion research, experimental conditions have

---

[148] Ax (1953) did not obtain measures of catecholamines but concluded that the ANS pattern under anger resembled the expected response to adrenaline and noradrenaline injections, while the ANS pattern under fear resembled the response in case adrenaline would have been injected.

[149] Fear was induced by tape presentation of a fear-evoking short story being accompanied by an unannounced darkening of the room; anger was induced by presenting a series of anagrams developed by Boucsein and Frye (1974), most of which were unsolvable; however, the insoluble nature of the anagrams was not detected by the participants during their presentation; and pleasure was induced by positive reinforcement and the announcement of increased payment at the end of the study.

[150] Recorded with standard methodology from the left hand's fingers. To obtain an additional objective measure of the "forehead anxiety sweat," another EDA recording was taken from the forehead. Electrodes were fixed by means of histoacryl (Sect. 2.2.2.1); the evaluation of EDA followed Thom's (1988) method (Sect. 2.2.4.2).

to be chosen which enable a direct comparison of different emotions. The problem of how to parallel qualitatively different states of emotion with respect to their quantitative properties is central (Sokolov & Boucsein, 2000). In addition, marginal conditions of the experimental design such as counterbalancing of the sequence of different emotions may have a strong influence on results. Various response specificities as already observed by Ax (1953) and systematically treated by Engel (1972) and Fahrenberg (1988) further complicate psychophysiological research of emotional states.

Another potential specific indicator function of EDA for emotional states comes from research on emotional expression, which plays a role not only in normal individuals but also in psychopathology, especially in schizophrenia (Sect. 3.4.2.3).[151] The hypothesis that facial expression not only being a concomitant of emotion but also having a role in regulating the emotional experience itself dates back to Darwin and was again taken up by Gellhorn (1964) and Izard (1971). These authors suggested that the facial actions trigger central nervous circuits that elicit ANS changes as well as the emotional experience. Despite Pribram (1980), in his biologically oriented view of psychophysiological correlates of emotion, did not indicate that EDA has an emotion-specific indicator function, phasic electrodermal parameters have gained an important role in the research into this "facial feedback" hypothesis.

Lanzetta, Cartwright-Smith, and Kleck (1976) investigated the influence of an instruction to manipulate one's facial expression on EDRs during the anticipation and application of electric shocks of different intensities. They performed three successive experiments, the third being the most carefully controlled one. In this study, 10 participants of each gender received 2 s electric shocks of 33, 66, and 99% of a previously established individual tolerance limit. The shocks were announced 8 s prior to their presentation displaying the numbers 1, 2, and 3, respectively. During the 10 s following each of 15 baseline trials, the participants rated their discomfort caused by the shock on a scale from 0 to 100. The session was videotaped, and the discomfort experienced was rated afterwards by six judges (2 females, 4 males) who knew neither the shock intensity nor the participant's rating. The anticipatory EDR[152] as well as the EDR to the shock

---

[151] A further domain is animal research about which Panksepp (1982, p. 410) stated that brain research in this area seems to regard the study of emotional expression as the only credible scientific approach.

[152] As inferred from another article of the Lanzetta group (Kleck et al., 1976), EDA was probably recorded with 3.14 cm^2 zinc electrodes using a zinc sulfate electrode cream and a Fels dermohmeter with 70 μA constant current. SRL values recorded from palmar sites were transformed to SCL values. The anticipatory EDR was computed as an increase from the average SCL 2 min before and at the beginning of shock application to the average SCL from 2 min before and at the beginning of the slide projection. The latter SCL was used as a reference for the EDR to shock application, thus being subtracted from the average SCL 6 and 8 min after its application.

itself increased monotonically with shock intensity; as did the experienced discomfort obtained by self-ratings as well as the judges' ratings of observed discomfort. During another 26 trials with counterbalanced intensities, participants were instructed to either hide or amplify their experienced discomfort by means of their facial expression, dependent on different colors of the slides. These manipulations were successful with respect to influencing the judges appropriately; in addition, the EDR amp., especially the one following the shock, was significantly lower when participants tried to hide their discomfort as compared to extensive facial expression of pain.

Monotonic relationships between the degree of mimic expression of experienced pain and EDR strength have been confirmed in other studies of the Lanzetta group (Colby, Lanzetta, & Kleck, 1977; Kleck et al., 1976; Orr & Lanzetta, 1980).[153] In addition, Vaughan and Lanzetta (1981) investigated the effects of facial expression on vicarious emotional arousal. They presented three groups of 20 participants each a videotaped model, giving them either instructions to amplify or to inhibit their own facial muscles when the model appeared to be shocked, while the third group received no facial instructions. The effectiveness of these instructions was controlled by means of EMG recordings from three facial muscles (orbicularis oculi, masseter, and medial frontalis). The model appeared to undergo a word-shock classical conditioning paradigm with four practice, ten acquisition, and ten extinction trials, while the participant's electrodermal FIR, SIR, and TUR were recorded during the appropriate time windows (Sect. 3.1.2.1 "Components of EDR Conditioning").[154] All groups showed greater electrodermal responsivity on CS+ trials as compared to CS− trials. However, this difference was more pronounced for the group having received the "amplify" instruction in comparison to either the "inhibit" group or the uninstructed participants. Additionally, a tendency appeared in the extinction phase for the "amplify" participants to reveal a greater FIR to CS+ than to CS−, while the other groups did not. These results provided support for the "facial feedback" hypothesis with respect to autonomic reactivity in general, since HR recordings showed a similar pattern. Such a view is rather close to James' ideas incorporated within the so-called James-Lange theory, stating that different emotions are caused by muscular reafferents to the CNS (McFarland, 1981, p. 289). However, the results above did not unambiguously show whether EDRs in fact served as

---

[153] The relationships between voluntarily expressed facial emotions and EDA (among other ANS variables) have been studied in 20 elderly individuals (71–83 years) of both genders by Levenson, Carstensen, Friesen, and Ekman (1991). The magnitude of ANS changes was smaller compared to young individuals.

[154] EDA was recorded as SR via palmar Ag/AgCl electrodes, transformed into SC and individually standardized.

indicators for emotion, or were only an ANS correlate of increased facial muscle activity, which in that case could be regarded as an artifact (Sect. 2.2.5.2).[155]

In opposition to the results of the Lanzetta group, Buck and colleagues obtained inverse relationships between EDA and facial responses to emotion-inducing slides (summarized by Buck, 1980). Buck, Miller, and Caul (1974) investigated 32 participants of each gender in randomly chosen sender-observer pairs, while their facial responses to 25 slides were videotaped. Five slides of each of five categories (sexual, pleasant landscape, pleasant people, unpleasant injuries, and unusual photographic effects) were presented in randomized order. The observer rated the sender's mimic on a nine-point scale from pleasant to unpleasant, and the sender performed the same rating while watching the slides. Communication accuracy, measured by the correspondence between the sender's and observer's ratings, correlated significantly negative with the sender's EDA,[156] however only with male sender ($r = -0.74$). As found in a previous study by Buck, Savin, Miller, and Caul (1972), the correlation of communication accuracy with HR remained insignificant ($r = -0.27$ for male senders). However, during a postexperimental verbal description of the slide contents, the participants responded more explicitly with their cardiovascular than with their electrodermal system. Buck et al. (1974) interpreted this as being consistent with other findings (e.g., Campos & Johnson, 1967) which showed that emotional arousing visual stimuli affect EDA more than HR, while the requirement to make overt responses (including verbal ones) is more likely to elicit HR acceleration than EDRs. This also parallels the results of the Fowles group with respect to differential validity of these two ANS variables (Sect. 3.2.1.2).

---

[155] Gross and Levenson (1993) investigated the effect of suppressing emotional expression while watching a short disgusting film, using the SCL, various cardiovascular and respiratory measures, somatic activity, and eye blink frequency as psychophysiological indicators. Suppression reduced the expressive behavior in their 42 female and 43 male participants but did not reveal a clear-cut psychophysiological pattern. Interestingly, participants in the suppression condition showed significantly higher increases in SC than their nonsuppression counterparts, but also yielded significantly greater HR deceleration. This was interpreted by the authors as reflecting the possibility that voluntary suppression of facial disgust expressions may lead to greater physiological "disgust-like" responding (Gross & Levenson, 1993, p. 981). Gross (1998) proposed an antecedent- and response-focused model of emotion regulation based on the work of the Lazarus group reported in this section, which he supposed having beneficial consequences for health. For testing his model, Gross presented 120 participants (60 of each gender) stressful films. Among other measures, SCL was recorded during baseline, instructions, film presentation, and a postfilm period. After the first presentation of either a stress inducing or a neutral film, a second film was announced with the instruction to simply watch, reappraise, or suppress during the presentation (40 participants per group). As in the Gross and Levenson (1993) study, suppression increased SCL markedly, compared to both baseline recordings and the other two groups. The author concluded that the health-promoting mechanism suggested here might result from an increase of the classical sympathetic stress response which may in turn influence the course of immune responding.

[156] Unipolar recordings with zinc electrodes and a zinc sulfate electrode cream from palmar against forearm sites, using a "low" constant current, thereafter transformed into SC values.

Buck et al. (1974) offered a conditioning explanation for the negative correlation between facial expressiveness and electrodermal responding to stimuli, assuming a socially learned inhibition of overt affective responses. Inhibitory responses may become CSs which elicit similar autonomic responses as the former UCSs. Thus, together with a masked facial expression, a large ANS response will appear, which is more likely an electrodermal than a cardiovascular one because no action (including facial muscles) is elicited.[157] Following this line, Buck (1980, p. 821) concluded that facial expression is more likely to serve as a readout device than as a feedback device, and that our facial emotional expression reflects central processes, not the reverse.

Winton, Putnam, and Krauss (1984) tried to explain the opposite findings of the Buck group and the Lanzetta group by their different experimental manipulations of two dimensions of affective experience, consistent with two of the three dimensions proposed by Wundt (1896): the intensity (arousing) and the evaluative/valence (pleasant vs. unpleasant) aspect of emotion. Lanzetta and colleagues used expressiveness ratings as measures of shock painfulness, thus reflecting the intensity dimension of affective response, which is positively correlated with EDR. In the Buck studies, however, the slide stimuli presumably evoked affective changes not only on the intensity but also on the evaluative dimension, while the participant's as well as judge's ratings may have specifically reflected the evaluative dimension. As suggested by the Laceys (e.g., Lacey & Lacey, 1970), phasic HR would be the more appropriate measure for this dimension than phasic EDA.

To further test this hypothesis, Winton et al. (1984) performed an experiment with 24 male participants who viewed a series of 25 emotionally evocative slides in a procedure similar to that of Buck et al. (1972, 1974). Facial expressions were covertly videotaped and were later shown to 90 judges of both genders. HR and SCR (using standard methodology with K–Y gel) were continuously recorded, and participants rated the pleasantness of slides 10 s after stimulus onset on a seven-point Likert scale. While HR increased monotonically with increasing subjective pleasantness of the slides shown, SCR amp. (evaluated between 1 and 5 s following stimulus onset) showed a U-shaped course, being higher in highly pleasant and in unpleasant stimuli as compared to neutral ones. The HR results paralleled the judges' ratings of facial pleasantness, while ratings of facial intensity showed the same U-shaped relationship to slide pleasantness as the SCR amp. These results could be replicated in two successive slide rating studies of Putnam and co-workers (Winton et al., 1984).[158]

---

[157] This social learning should have appeared early during life, since Buck (1977) found comparable negative correlations between SCR and communication accuracy even in preschoolers, giving nonverbal messages via spontaneous facial expressions and gestures to their mothers.

[158] Gender differences in expressed emotions were observed by Kring and Gordon (1998) who presented 22 female and 21 male participants six brief emotion-inducing film clips (two of each: happy, sad, and fear), separated by neutral film segments. SC was recorded with standard methodology from the thenar eminence of the nondominant hand, and videotaped facial expressions were automatically coded. NS.SCR freq. was highest for fear in both genders, whereas females yielded higher values in the sad category than males, the reverse of which was found for happy film contents. The EDA results did not correspond to the evaluation of facial expressions.

The observed curvilinear relationship between SCR amp. and pleasantness could have been interpreted as supporting Schachter and Singer's (1962) theory of emotion. Their cognitively oriented theoretical view regarded physiological arousal as a necessary condition for the elicitation of an emotional state, the nature of which, however, would be determined by situational cues. SCR amp. being high in extreme self-report categories and low in moderate categories, as observed by Winton et al. (1984), would have aligned along those predictions, if one had regarded EDA as an index of general arousal. However, when HR results were considered together with those from EDA, the conclusion would be that different emotional states correspond to different patterns of autonomic activity (Sokolov & Boucsein, 2000).

Similar relationships between emotional valence and HR as well as between SCR and emotional arousal obtained by Winton et al. (1984) were found by Greenwald, Cook, and Lang (1989). Forty-eight participants of both genders were presented 21 slides for 6 s each, while facial EMG (zygomatic and corrugator), HR, and SC[159] were continuously recorded. Based on results from a previous validation study, valence and arousal dimensions of the slides were regarded as relatively independent ($r = -0.24$ for females and $r = -0.01$ for males). Subjective ratings were recorded by a computerized self-assessment technique. Larger SC changes were significantly related to increased arousal ratings, the effect being pronounced only for males. Valence ratings were related to changes in HR but not in SC. Thus, in this investigation, EDA appeared as a sensitive and specific measure of arousal, while phasic HR acceleration seemed to be a more sensitive and specific measure of emotional valence. A corresponding result was obtained by Johnsen, Thayer, and Hugdahl (1995) in a study with 28 female and 16 male participants, viewing 14 slides of facial emotional expression from the Ekman and Friesen series (see Sect. 3.1.3.4). HR and SC[160] were evaluated together with subjective ratings of pleasantness and arousal, which yielded that the latter were positively related to SCR amp. and valence ratings were associated with HR. In addition, SCR amp. were significantly higher in females than in males. Thus, this study seemed to emphasize a differential validity for EDA, indicating arousal, and HR, indicating the valence aspect of emotion.

However, contrary results had been obtained by Levenson, Ekman, and Friesen (1990). In three successive experiments performed with a total of 62 participants (35 females, 27 males; actors, emotional facial expressions researchers, students, and nonstudent adults), they studied subjective and autonomic concomitants of voluntary facial configurations for the negative emotions anger, fear, sadness, and

---

[159] With standard methodology, using K–Y gel. Mean SC change was calculated by subtracting the 1 s prestimulus average from the average between 2 and 7 s after stimulus onset.

[160] Recorded with standard methodology from distilled water-cleaned medial phalanges of the third and fourth fingers of the right hand. SCR amp. were obtained 1–4 s after stimulus onset with an amplitude criterion of 0.05 µS.

disgust, as well as for happiness and surprise[161] as positive emotions. EDA was recorded as SR (with standard methodology and transformed to SC), together with HR, finger temperature, and forearm flexor muscle tension. EDA clearly differentiated between positive and negative emotions, being higher in the latter ones (see footnote 77 in Sect. 3.1.3.2), while HR was lower in the disgust condition as compared to the other negative emotions, not clearly reflecting the emotional valence as in the Winton et al. (1984) study.[162]

Gross and Levenson (1997) demonstrated that an instruction to hide their feelings, i.e., trying their best not to let those feelings show, had differential effects on HR and EDA. Compared to a control group of 90 female participants, 90 other female participants who received the suppression instruction revealed less HR increase during viewing an amusing film and more HR increase during a sadness-inducing film, whereas suppression of feelings induced only a significantly lesser SCL decrease in the latter film.

In the present author's view, the repeatedly reported specificity of EDA for intensity and HR for valence could be an effect of the stimulus set used in the appropriate studies, i.e., pictures from the IAPS by Lang et al. (1999). More recently, a great deal of this research incorporated additional startle probes, which might have imposed another not emotion-specific influence on the ANS response to the potentially emotion-eliciting stimulus material.[163] The reader who is particularly interested in the startle-emotion issue is referred to reviews written by Cuthbert, Bradley, and Lang (1996) or Filion et al. (1998). A more recent example of this kind of research is the study performed by Bernat, Patrick, Benning, and Tellegen (2006) who presented 54 IAPS pictures to 58 male participants. Pictures from the positive valence (erotic, adventure) and the negative valence category (victims, threat) were individually subjectively rated with respect to low, medium, and high intensity, and compared to a neutral picture. Besides SC recorded with standard methodology from the hypothenar eminence of the nondominant hand, HR, three facial muscles (orbicularis oculi, zygomatic major, and corrugator

---

[161] It is not obvious that surprise does predominantly elicit positive emotions. If strong enough, it may as well elicit a DR which is normally negatively tuned (Sect. 3.1.1.2).

[162] Combining EDA with fMRI recordings, which has been recently available (Sect. 2.2.3.5), together with mathematical solutions for the evaluation of overlapping EDRs, constitutes an intriguing new possibility of research into CNS correlates of processing emotion-expressing faces. This had been demonstrated by Williams et al. (2004) in their study described in Sect. 2.3.1.5. Their fMRI data revealed that the U-shaped SCR pattern across early, middle, and late presentations of face stimuli expressing fear was paralleled by a temporal sequence of somatosensory insula, dorsomedial prefrontal cortical, and left amygdalar activation.

[163] Ekman et al. (1985) in an experiment on startle simulation and suppression revealed that startle should be considered a reflex rather than an emotion. To the present author's view, the widely used paradigm of startle response modification by manipulations of the emotional background might be regarded as a sideline in emotion research which concentrates on a single dependent measure. Revealing its contribution to the core of psychophysiological research into emotional states may require further theoretical integration.

supercilii), startle eyeblink, and (for half of the participants) EEG/ERP recordings were obtained. Individualized stimulus intensity was significantly linearly related to log SCR amp., suggesting that stimuli of higher intensity prompted increased SCR amp. regardless of stimulus qualities. However, more fine-grained analyses revealed that such a relationship was evident only for erotic and threat but not for adventure and victim picture categories.

Given the possible differential indicator functions of electrodermal and cardio-vascular measures,[164] the use of multivariate methodology in psychophysiological research into emotional states has to be strongly advocated, despite some inconsistencies between the appropriate studies as described at the beginning of this section. Different parameters could have different validities not only with respect to various emotional states, as observed by Stemmler (1989),[165] but also with respect to different experimental settings, as being apparent from the final part of this section. However, there is still no general theoretical framework available for using different tonic EDA measures (Sect. 2.3.2) and phasic measures of EDR amp. and shape (Sect. 2.3.1) which would explain different components of variance in various emotional contexts.

Replacing picture presentations with moving stimuli had been demonstrated having an increasing effect on arousal but little impact on valence. Simons, Detenber, Roedema, and Reiss (1999) presented 35 participants either a still or a moving version of the same image for 6 s, in counterbalanced order. The 27 images were extracted from movies and TV programs and selected according to categories used in the IAPS. SC recorded with standard methodology, HR, and facial EMG were sampled at 50 Hz. SC data were visually inspected and evaluated for each trial, identifying the largest peak with an onset latency of 0.5–4 s following stimulus onset as SCR. Both HR deceleration and SCR amp. were significantly related to valence and arousal, but only SCR amp. showed a distinct and significant effect of the movement factor.

Kreibig, Wilhelm, Roth, and Gross (2007) investigated various cardiovascular, electrodermal, and respiratory response parameters together with facial muscle activity (zygomatic and corrugator) during fear- and sadness-inducing films in 37 participants (19 females, 18 males). Six film clips (two of each category, a neutral category included) lasting about 10 min were counterbalanced according to a Latin

---

[164] An attempt to determine an individual's most reactive ANS channel (i.e., EDA or HR) was made by Levis and Smith (1987), using the balloon-burst test to preclassify their participants as high SC responders, high HR responders, high responders in both channels, or low responders in both channels. In a subsequent presentation of a fear-eliciting slide (a man who died in an accident), those participants found to be high responders on a given channel showed greater reactivity on that particular channel as compared to low responders.

[165] Seligman (1975), in an explorative study with 6 participants, obtained differential effects of pleasant and released vs. unpleasant and inhibited feelings (as reported on a Mood Adjective Check List) on negative vs. positive SPR waves, respectively, during ten counseling sessions of 50 min duration each. However, Edelberg (1972a) already pointed to results with respect to the emotional valence of different SP wave forms being equivocal in general.

square design, resulting in six sequences to which the participants were randomly assigned. SC was recorded with standard methodology from soap washed middle phalanges of the first and second finger of the nondominant hand. An amplitude criterion of 0.025 μS was applied for obtaining NS.SCR freq. and mean NS.SCR amp. Multivariate ANOVAs generally confirmed the presence of fight/flight response patterns during fear and also a single conservation/withdrawal response during sadness (HR deceleration). Among other results, SCL increased during fear-inducing and decreased during neutral films. The authors conclude that a multiresponse system model such as the above-mentioned one proposed by Fowles (1980) would fit their results better than a unitary construct of activation/arousal (Sect. 3.2.1.1).

Silvestrini and Gendolla (2007) attempted to induce negative, neutral, and positive mood states in 44 participants (36 females, 8 males) by means of film clips with 10 min duration each. Thereafter, participants performed a mood regulation task, for which they were instructed to try getting into a pleasant feeling state while listening to a depressing musical piece. SCL was recorded with standard methodology from the middle and index fingers of the nondominant hand, low-pass filtered at 10 Hz and sampled with 1 kHz, then averaged over 1 min intervals. HR, blood pressure, and facial EMG (zygomatic and corrugator) were recorded as well. Change scores calculated as differences between SCLs during stimulus presentations and baseline revealed a significantly stronger electrodermal reactivity during mood regulation than during the previous mood inductions. The SCL increase was significantly higher in the negative mood induction condition compared to the neutral and positive ones. Comparable results emerged for HR.

Kim, Bang, and Kim (2004) who attempted developing an automated recognition system for emotions in 125 five- to eight-year-old children also preferred using moving pictures over still images from the IAPS, which they considered not sufficient for emotion induction. Instead, they created a computer scenario in which a toy was telling a story to the children, the emotion-inducing property of which was primarily evaluated by their subjective reports and observations by an expert. The authors applied a multivariate psychophysiological approach that included SC recording (with Ag/AgCl electrodes attached to the index and middle fingers of the right hand, otherwise unreported methodology), HR, HRV, and skin temperature, calculated as differences to baseline recordings and fed into a support vector machine for automatically detecting the emotional status. After differentiation and smoothing of the SC curve, SCRs were detected as two subsequent zero crossings in different directions. Using an amplitude criterion (Sect. 2.3.1.2 "Choice of Amplitude Criteria") of 10% of the maximum SCR amp., the mean SCR amp. was determined within each 50-s segment. For a data set with 50 children, the percentage of correctly classified emotions was 78.4% for the combination of three (sadness, anger, and feeling stressed) and 61.8% for a four-emotions combination (sadness, anger, surprise, and feeling stressed), being much higher than chance probabilities.

Summarizing, the possible differential indicator functions of EDA and HR in the detection of emotions may need further clarification. There seems to be a strong dependency on both the kind of stimulus material (e.g., still vs. moving images) and instructions applied in laboratory studies. At present, psychophysiological patterns for different emotions as discussed earlier in this section do not seem easily attainable. For more comments on methodological problems within this kind of research, the reader is referred to Stemmler (2002).

3.2.2.2 EDA as an Indicator of the Course of Laboratory Stress Responses

The use of the term *stress* in psychology covers a wide range of phenomena, from simple over- or understimulation, via frustrative experience, to life-challenging situations. Therefore, it is not easy treating stress as a clearly unitary concept, especially when taking regard of arousal and/or emotional experience elicited. Most researchers operationally define the term stress for characterizing a distressing experience of high intensity (Lazarus, 1966), since only a minority of studies has been concerned with the concept of eustress (i.e., experience of stress in a positive emotional context). Despite this problem of delineation, stress can be defined as a state of high general arousal and negatively tuned but unspecific emotion, which appears as a consequence of stressors (i.e., stress-inducing stimuli or situations) acting upon individuals. Stressors can be defined as subjective and/or objective challenges exceeding a critical level with respect to intensity and/or duration.

Adequate stress reactions should attempt to reestablish homeostasis on both physiological and psychological levels. If this goal cannot be attained by an individual, fundamental psychophysiological changes might be expected. However, it remains debatable whether long-lasting neuroendocrine changes (as focused on in the stress concept of Selye, 1976) develop as a consequence of continuous short-lasting psychophysiological and endocrine responses, which are the only kinds of stress that can be expected to be elicited in laboratory situations. Experimental evidence for the possibility of such a generalizability comes from animal research (as in the development of ulcers, cf., McFarland, 1981), but appropriate experiments cannot be performed with humans for ethical reasons.

However, modeling stress in laboratory settings serves as a tool for observing the course of corresponding psychophysiological processes under experimentally controlled conditions. Therefore, the investigation of the characteristic course of psychophysiological parameters over time can be regarded as a major aim in this area of research (McGrath, 1982, p. 36). Since EDA is solely determined by the activity of the sympathetic branch of the ANS which is predominant in stress states, such an observation regularly included tonic electrodermal parameters, such as the EDL and the NS.EDR freq. (Sect. 2.3.2.2) as suitable measures to continuously monitor ANS activity elicited by stress.

Early research into the EDA recording (paralleled by HR recording) during stress and coping processes had been performed by the Lazarus group (summarized by Lazarus, 1966; Lazarus & Opton, 1966). In several experiments, they could demonstrate a marked SCL increase while watching stressful scenes of films. By presenting those films with coping-inducing sound tracks, the SCL could be markedly reduced. Following the concept of threat and appraisal as proposed by

Lazarus (1966), the subsequent laboratory experiments of his group focused on the role of anticipation of harmful events.

In one study performed by Nomikos, Opton, Averill, and Lazarus (1968), two groups with 26 participants of both genders viewed two versions of an industrial safety film portraying three wood-mill accidents. One group which viewed the short version, in which most of the anticipatory scenes preceding the accidents were taken out, yielded a lower increase of SCL[166] as compared to the group viewing the original version. In addition, for both treatment groups, most of the buildup of electrodermal stress responses occurred during the anticipation period immediately before the accident being shown. Interestingly, viewing the accident as opposed to its anticipation added comparatively little to the rise in sympathetic ANS activity. For HR, group differences were in the same direction as those for SC, but did not reach significance. The self-report measures also did not differentiate between the treatment conditions. The general finding that anticipating a stressful event could elicit electrodermal changes comparable to, or even greater than, those following the event itself, initiated various systematic studies on conditions that might influence anticipatory stress, such as the duration of the anticipation interval, temporal, and event uncertainty (i.e., predictability of time and probability of the appearance of the aversive event), settings with and without temporal feedback, and variation of controllability (i.e., having control over the aversive event by, e.g., terminating it by pressing a button). Most of these studies used tonic EDA parameters as measures of stress.

Folkins (1970) threatened 60 male participants (in independent groups of 10 each) with the announcement of repeating an electric shock which had been delivered at the beginning of six different anticipation intervals (5, 30 s, 1, 3, 5, and 20 min). Time cues were provided by a large clock; however, no more shocks were given. In a second run, the participants were reassigned on a separate random schedule (however, avoiding the application of the 20-min condition twice) to control conditions using the same intervals being terminated by a neutral stimulus (lightening of a lamp). During the anticipation intervals (a 1-min prewarning baseline and a 1-min poststimulus period) SCL[167] and HR were recorded every 10 s (except for the 5 s conditions where only one reading was performed). Each of the participants was interviewed post hoc. An additional 30 participants were run but were interrupted for on-the-spot reports with respect to their cognitive functioning during the anticipation of stress. The latter participants were assigned to the following three independent groups: interruption of a 1-min interval after 30 s, of a 20-min interval after 30 s, and of a 20-min interval after 3 min, respectively. Subjective stress was assessed by three self-report measures. SCL as well as HR steeply increased immediately after the shock announcement, with a continuing

---

[166] Recorded with a Fels dermohmeter and 70 μA current, by means of zinc/zinc sulfate electrodes (cream not mentioned), transformed into SC units.

[167] Bilateral thenar recording as SR with Beckman electrodes of 1 cm diameter, 10 μA constant current, transformed to SC values.

increase during anticipation periods up to 1 min, while there were no comparable changes in EDA or HR in control conditions.

Within the 3- and 5-min intervals, a plateau appeared in SCL with another rise immediately before the end of the interval period. Contrarily, during the 20-min intervals, a decrease to base levels appeared after 2 min, and another rise of SCL started in the 16th min. The greatest amount of subjective stress was induced with the 1-min anticipation interval. As could be inferred from the interviews that were performed after interruptions, the coping mechanisms started 1 min after shock announcement. The presence of coping mechanisms was used by the authors to explain the plateau or even a decrease observed in the course of SCLs. As opposed to SCL, HR showed inconsistent forms of progress and could not differentiate experimental from control groups in conditions with intervals exceeding 1 min.

By contrast, Monat, Averill, and Lazarus (1972) obtained a relatively good concordance between EDA, HR, and subjective measures in two experiments investigating the effects of temporal uncertainty and event uncertainty on anticipatory stress reactions to the threat of shock during a 3-min interval. Their first experiment was performed with 80 male participants who were assigned to four independent groups of 20 each: (1) 100% shock at time known, (2) 100% shock at time not known, (3) 50% probability of shock at time known, and (4) 50% probability of shock but no shock received. There were three trials under each condition. The second experiment with 40 male participants used a within-subjects design with the first three conditions as in the first study, but with an additional 5% event uncertainty condition. In both experiments, the mean SCR amp.[168] decreased continuously during the condition of temporal uncertainty (with 100% event certainty), while the different conditions (100, 50, and 5%) with temporal certainty (and temporal feedback) showed the same course of initial decrease of EDRs and again a steep increase during the last 30 s. The courses of HR and of the self-reported tension (obtained during first, middle, and last thirds of trial) showed similar results but figured out to be more susceptible to the repeated measurement design effects as compared to EDA. This might have resulted in a diminution of the differences between temporal certainty and uncertainty in these two measures at the end of the anticipation interval, which were probably due to learning effects.

Different courses of SCL[169] and HR in dependence of temporal feedback (by means of a clock) given or missed during a 6-min period of anticipating an electric shock were found by Gaebelein, Taylor, and Borden (1974) with a total of 20 male participants. In their feedback group, HR showed a slight decrease followed by a steep increase at the end of the interval, and a continuous HR decrease appeared in

---

[168] Recorded with 10 μA constant current from thenar/hypothenar sites, using Ag/AgCl electrodes of 1 cm diameter with K–Y gel, amplitude criterion 80 Ω. Responses in 10-s intervals were averaged and transformed to log SC.

[169] Recorded with Ag/AgCl sponge electrodes (other details of recording not reported) as SRL values, averaged for every 10 s and transformed to SCL values.

the group without temporal feedback. Different from the course of HR, the SCL markedly increased following instruction in the no-feedback group and remained at this level, while under the condition of temporal feedback a decrease in SCL subsequent to an initial increase emerged, followed by another increase during the last minute. The authors attributed the steep HR increase during the anticipation period to a covert preparation for shock delivery via increased muscular tension. Thus, HR was interpreted as reflecting somatic activity, while the SCL course was more likely reflecting the progress of psychophysiological stress reactions themselves. This interpretation remains, however, ambiguous, since EMG recordings were not available.

Niemelä (1975) investigated the preparatory effect of long-lasting anticipatory periods on EDRs to wood-shop accident scenes. Thirty male participants expected viewing the film 3 days after being presented with a subincision[170] film, followed by a detailed description of the film scenes that were to be expected. The stress films were shown either immediately or after 1 or 2 days. Participants from another study in the same laboratory who were shown the film at the time announced (from 0 to 3 days) served as controls. For each scene, the SCR was computed as mentioned in Footnote 169, and participants reported their expectations after the presentation. The shorter the interval was, the lower the SCRs to the accident scenes were, which was different from the results in the control group viewing the film at the announced time. This was interpreted by the author as a consequence of the participant's suppression of the stress-inducing material, which increases with the distance from the expected stressful event.[171]

Bankart and Elliot (1974) performed three experiments using electric shock anticipation with varying probabilities of occurrence (event uncertainty). In their first study which confounded shock probability and number of trials, all 40 male participants received eight electric shocks, 10 of them under each of the following conditions: within 8, 11, 16, or 32 trials (i.e., 100, 73, 50, or 25% probability). A verbal countdown from 10 to 0 was applied within the 30 s ITIs. A rise of SCL[172]

---

[170] Crude surgeries on the male genitals of a primitive native culture in Australia. EDA has been recorded from both hands as SR with zinc electrodes of 2 cm diameter, using an agar–zinc electrode cream and a 40 μA constant current. SR values were transformed to log SC changes (differences between pre- and postaccident SCLs).

[171] A phylogenetically oriented approach into the psychophysiological responses to film stimuli has been performed by Westbury and Neumann (2008) with 73 participants (37 females, 36 males). Four 10-min clips for each of five target groups (depicting humans, primates, quadruped mammals, and birds in victimized circumstances) were presented in randomized order. Participants were asked to rate their empathy, SC (recorded according to some of the standards, but with "surgicon" electrolyte paste), respiration and corrugator muscle activity were recorded. SCRs were obtained as trough-to-peak distance within 1–4 s after the film presentations and square-root transformed (Sect. 2.3.3.3). Both SCRs and empathy ratings increased with phylogenetic similarity to humans across animal groups, being highest in the films showing human victims.

[172] Recorded as SR with dry 2 cm² lead electrodes from previously acetone-cleaned finger sites, transformed to values of μS/cm².

during the session in general as well as during the anticipation periods could be observed, the latter one increasing in steepness with event certainty. In a second experiment, an equal number of participants were given either 5, 10, 15, or 20 shocks in 20 trials, which confounded event probability with the number of shocks. SCL did not discriminate among the groups since SCL increased in all groups both within and across trials. Because no habituation of EDA could be observed in the second study, a third experiment was performed using the same 25 and 100% probability conditions of the second study, however, with markedly reduced shock intensities. In the second experiment, a dependence of HR on the amount of threat had been observed, being reflected in HR which was a direct function of number and probability of shocks. This dependence disappeared in the third study as a consequence of reduced shock intensity. Again, no group differences in SCL appeared, only a slightly overall downward drift. The authors concluded that variations in event uncertainty do not exert an influence on the anticipatory proportion of the SCL. However, they suggested that other EDA parameters like the NS.EDR freq. might serve as more appropriate indicators of anticipatory stress than the EDL.

A possible specific indicator function of these two kinds of tonic EDA measures had already been revealed by Katkin (1965). He compared the course of SRL and of NS.SRR freq.[173] during the 10-min anticipation of an electric shock (which was not actually given) with a control condition (the experimenter announced to be back at the end of the time span), using 26 male students in each condition. NS.SRR freq. was significantly increased in the experimental as compared to the control group, while the SRL decreased in both groups during a postexperimental interview. The unequivocal effect of stress on spontaneous EDA was replicated in several successive studies performed by Katkin and coworkers (summarized by Katkin, 1975). Katkin's (1965) interpretation assumed that the EDL is more influenced by cognitive demands, while NS.EDR freq. is more prone to anticipatory stress. These hypotheses were supported by a study of Kilpatrick (1972) with 32 male participants, half of whom were given stressful (anticipating an intelligence test), while the other half received control instructions. NS.SRR freq. but not SRL[174] differentiated between conditions. However, the SRL markedly decreased during a subsequent performance test.

Boucsein and Wendt-Suhl (1976) introduced a 20-min anticipation period to test differential cardiovascular and electrodermal reactivity to announcements of different shock intensities. Thirty male participants in each group were announced a shock either two or five times as strong as compared to the one that had been previously experienced and rated as unpleasant, or expected only a questionnaire

---

[173] Measured unipolar from left middle finger against forearm sites with electrodes (metal not specified) of 0.32 cm^2 and 3 $\times$ 4 in., respectively, starch cream and 20 µA constant current. 100 Ω were used as amplitude criterion.

[174] Recorded unipolar thenar vs. forearm with 5 and 58 cm^2 Ag/AgCl electrodes, respectively, filled with 0.5 M NaCl (probably liquid) electrolyte, using a current of 10 µA/cm^2. Amplitude criterion for NS.SRRs was 100 Ω.

(control group). The NS.SRR freq. recorded with standard methodology decreased during the first 5 min and again significantly increased in the last 2 min of the anticipation interval in both stress groups (announcement of a twice or five times as strong shock) as compared to the control group. However, the increase in spontaneous EDA, which was paralleled in a subjective finger-span rating of emotional arousal, was not different in the groups that were announced different shock strength. HR did not parallel EDA or subjective measures, since only in the group anticipating a shock five times as strong did a significant increase in HR appear during the last minute.

A direct comparison of electrodermal and cardiovascular changes during 6 s anticipation of an aversive stimulus (a 1-s auditory signal of 100 dB) was performed by Sosnowski (1988). The stimuli were delivered in the first and the fourth of four trials, and the announcement was made by presenting two slides with circles each time. Eighteen participants were run under each of the following conditions: an unambiguous one with a clear announcement and another one with an ambiguous signal given by the circles. Changes in SCR[175] were more prominent in the latter condition, showing a similar course as during the unambiguous condition, with an increment during presentation of the message, a subsequent plateau, and another increase after delivery of the aversive stimulus. On the contrary, HR changes recorded were relatively small, except for a rise after message presentation, and the ambiguity factor did not significantly influence HR. However, the author's conclusion that EDA was a more suitable indicator of anticipatory stress, while HR is more likely to reflect cognitive elaboration of the message and/or coping with the stressor, remains preliminary with respect to the narrow database.

EDA is also influenced by the controllability of a stressor. Gatchel, McKinney, and Koebernick (1977), in a study on "learned helplessness," used 12 participants of both genders in each of three groups. The experimental participants could terminate nonsignaled tones (1 kHz, 95 dB) by pressing a microswitch four times, while the inescapable yoked-control group could not. A third group (also yoked) was used as control for separating the physiological effects of controllability from those of motor activity; therefore, they were instructed to press the switch when the tone came on. The tones were presented in five blocks of seven trials, during which the SCR amp.[176] following the tones habituated. SCR amp. were significantly higher in experimental participants and habituated more slowly compared to the other two groups, indicating that this was not a motor artifact (Sect. 2.2.5.2). Therefore, individuals with "learned helplessness" yielded less phasic EDA compared to those who were able to exert control.

---

[175] Measured with Ag/AgCl electrodes of 4 mm diameter, KCl cream (0.67 M) in agar, and 0.5 V, evaluated as log SC change from pretreatment level.

[176] Recorded as SR with 10 μA constant current, Beckman Ag/AgCl electrodes, and K–Y gel palmar/dorsal. Separate channels were used for SRL and SRRs (sensitivity 50 Ω). SRL values were transformed to SCL, and SCRs were computed as differences between logarithmized SCLs before and the maximum within 6 s after stimulus onset.

Even in situations where individuals did not really exert control over a stressor but believed they could, putative control yielded a reduction of EDA. Geer and Davison (1970) subjected 40 male participants to a RT task, during the first ten trials of which they were told to respond to the onset of a 6-s shock. For the next ten trials, half of the participants were made to believe that decreasing their RT would reduce the shock duration, while the remaining participants were simply informed that the shock duration would be reduced. Putative control over the shock significantly reduced the NS.SCR freq. obtained with standard methodology, and log SCR amp. following the shock onset showed a faster habituation as compared to the first part as well as to the control group.

To avoid confounding the effects of controllability and predictability, Geer and Maisel (1972) performed a study with 20 participants in each of the following three groups that were presented ten slides showing victims of violent death. In the controllability condition, participants were able to terminate the presentation by pressing a button; the predictability group was given the mean duration for a given yoked participant in the first group, the length of which they were informed about; both groups were warned 10 s prior to the slide by a 1 kHz, 60 dB tone, while the third group received random presentations of slides and tones of the same length as the second group. Predictability increased EDR amp.,[177] although a marked habituation occurred over trials. EDR amp. following the aversive stimuli were considerably increased in both the predictability and the group without any control, as compared to the group that exerted control over stimulus duration. These results pointed to a relative independence of the action of controllability and predictability of aversive events on the ANS.[178] However, the number of NS.EDRs occurring between stimulus presentations did not differentiate between the two experimental groups, being significantly higher in both of them as compared to the group without any control. Thus, nonspecific EDA seemed to serve as an indicator of generally increased cognitive activity (as already suggested by Katkin, 1965 and Kilpatrick, 1972), while stimulus qualities like its aversiveness or serving as a warning cue are reflected in specific phasic EDA components.

Studies testing the "preception" hypothesis can also be regarded as having an aspect of predictability of stressful events. Katz and Wykes (1985), in a further evaluation of the Katz (1984) study described in Sect. 3.1.2.1 "UCR Diminution, Preception and Preparedness", investigated the effect of temporal certainty in 80 female participants anticipating six predictable and six unpredictable electric shocks in a within-subjects design with counterbalanced order. During the anticipatory intervals (with 9, 12, or 15 s duration) the NS.SRR freq. was significantly

---

[177] Recorded as SR between palm and forearm with Beckman electrodes and cream, transformed to square-root SCR. Time window for SCRs: 0.5–3 s after stimulus onset; amplitude criterion for NS.SRR freq.: 200 Ω.

[178] This could be shown by Overmier (1985) with animals, using completely different experimental conditions and plasma cortisol as stress indicator.

higher under the condition of temporal uncertainty compared with knowledge of the duration of the anticipation period.

Phillips, Evans, and Fearn (1986), in a study with 12 participants of each gender, varied shock predictability by introducing different probabilities for warning signals (5, 20, or 50%) in three successive trials of .3 min duration. During each trial, participants could continuously choose between time monitoring and receiving distracting information by pressing appropriate keys. They were further assigned to three different controllability conditions (0, 50, or 100%) which allowed the termination of the shock by means of another key. While SCL[179] steadily increased during the experiment, NS.SCR freq. significantly increased with predictability (i.e., the probability of warning signals). In addition, there was a significant correlation between NS.SCR freq. and the average time spent with monitoring ($r = 0.37$). Again, NS.EDR freq. appeared to be a better indicator of anticipatory stress reactions than the EDL.

An increase of nonspecific EDA was also observed during the anticipation of public speaking which had been demonstrated being a very potent stressor in laboratory experiments. Erdmann, Janke, and Bisping (1984) applied four different stress conditions of 10 min duration each to 24 male participants in counterbalanced order. The conditions were: white noise (95 dB) presented discontinuously; anticipation of a painful electric shock; anticipation of public speaking; and a Charlie Chaplin film (as a "eustress" condition). The NS.SRR freq. (recorded with standard methodology, using an amplitude criterion of 300 Ω) was significantly higher during the anticipation of a public speech as compared to all other situations. The same was true for HR, blood pressure, and a subjective rating of emotional tension taken twice during the stress periods. Spontaneous EDA reached its peak during the first third of the anticipation period, except in the condition with anticipation of pain, where the time course could be monitored via a clock, which resulted in a biphasic course with another peak in the final third. However, the subjectively rated emotional tension did not parallel the course of NS.SR freq. in the anticipation of speech condition, since it increased throughout anticipation.

To determine a possible influence of mental strain[180] resulting from the preparation of a public speech on the emotional strain induced by its anticipation, Erdmann and Baumann (1996) divided their 48 female participants into four groups. Half of them had the topic for the speech announced immediately, while the other half received their topic prior to the second half of the altogether 14 min anticipation period. In a nonstress control condition, half of each group received an instruction to collect material for the same topic instead of preparing a public speech. During the first 3 min of the first and second half of the anticipation periods, NS.SCR freq. (recorded with standard methodology, using an amplitude

---

[179] Recorded palmar with Ag/AgCl electrodes and 10 µA constant current, transformed to SC. No information was provided concerning electrode size, cream, and amplitude criterion for SCRs.

[180] The term "strain" comes from physics, where strain is used for the response of a system being under stress.

criterion of 0.1 μS) and HR were obtained, with a subsequent blood pressure recording and a rating of mood and bodily symptoms. NS.SCR freq. was considerably (though only marginally significant) higher in the speech anticipation condition with immediate knowledge of the topic compared to all other conditions, whereas the appropriate HR differences reached significance. The authors concluded that at least an important portion of the stress response during the preparation of a public speech could be due to the mental strain induced by the knowledge of the topic to be prepared.

In a second experiment, Erdmann and Baumann varied the degree of stress induced by speech preparation in three steps: they used the two conditions from the first experiment plus a third condition with a "real" expert commission listening to the speech (almost as realistic as in Boucsein and Wendt-Suhl, 1982, study described in Sect. 3.4.3.1, but without the experimenter actually "entering" the room where the "expert" commission was seated). The time point for getting to know the topic was additionally varied as in the first experiment within each group. Twelve male participants were assigned to each of the six resulting experimental groups. The same dependent measures were recorded, with only slight differences to the first experiment. Unfortunately, the three conditions for the speech preparation-induced stress factor did not result in the expected psychophysiological responses. The strongest so-called speech anxiety condition emerged significant HR increases only if the topic was already known to the participants. No appropriate EDA results could be found. One explanation for the inconsistent results could be that the speech-preparation paradigm might be rather susceptible to subtle changes in experimental conditions, especially to those which tangle the credibility of the existence of a real public to which the speech has to be delivered. Another possibility is the existence of gender differences, since Erdmann and Baumann obtained conflicting results with female (first experiment) and male (second experiment) participants.

To enlighten possible gender differences in stress induced by public speaking, Carrillo et al. (2001) compared a group of 23 female with another group of 15 male participants who did not differ in trait anxiety (Sect. 3.3.1.2) and other relevant personality factors. After a 5-min baseline recording, the participants were instructed to prepare a speech on a highly relevant topic (i.e., aspects of their academic career) within 2.5 min to be presented to an academic teacher who would consider it for the participant's academic qualification. A video-recording procedure was used to enhance the situational stress during delivering the speech, which an experimenter listened to while taking notes. The session was terminated by a 5-min recovery period. HR, finger pulse volume, and SC[181] were recorded throughout. Artifact-free SC changes exceeding an amplitude criterion of 0.05 μS were evaluated for obtaining NS.SCR freq. and mean NS.SCR amp. No gender differences were observed for HR and NS.SCR freq. However, females showed overall significantly higher finger pulse

---

[181] Recorded with Ag/AgCl electrodes of 6 mm diameter from previously washed sites on the medial phalanges of the index finger and thumb of the nondominant hand with hypoallergenic gel and a CC below 0.5 V.

volumes in all periods except the task, during which their mean NS.SCR amp. was significantly higher compared to the males. Females, but not males, yielded a significant increase in state anxiety (Sect. 3.3.1.2) from the baseline to the recovery period. The authors' conclusion that "it is worth nothing that only amplitude, but not frequency, of NSRs was different" (Carrillo et al., 2001, p. 261) cannot be supported in the present author's view, since the mean NS.SCR amp. may well have a specific indicator function independent of the NS.SCR freq. (cf. Table 3.2, Sect. 3.5.1), indicating increased preparatory activation (cf. Fig. 3.4, Sect. 3.2.1.2). Such an interpretation also fits the decrease in finger pulse volume observed in females but not in males during the task of delivering the speech.

Recently, the activity of several regions in the prefrontal cortex when using reappraisal to decrease negative emotion has been demonstrated by means of fMRI recordings. In a study with 26 older participants (64–66 years; 14 females, 12 males) viewing unpleasant IAPS pictures, Urry, van Reekum, Johnstone, and Davidson (2009) used SCR recording with standard methodology by means of an isolated EDA coupler in an fMRI (Sect. 2.2.3.5), for probing the success of a reappraisal manipulation of emotional arousal. Participants were trained to comply with one of three following situation-focused reappraisal instructions during each picture presentation: increase, maintain, or decrease their negative emotion. Pictures were presented for 12 s, and the reappraisal instruction was delivered via headphones 4 s after stimulus onset, thus allowing for 8 s of active regulation. Reappraisal instructions were given counterbalanced across participants in a within-subjects design, featuring three blocks of 18 pictures each, ISIs being 5–10 s. A monotonic relationship between reappraisal instructions and NS.SCR freq. was observed, EDA being lowest under the decrease instruction, medium under the maintain instruction, and highest under the increase instruction, thus indicating the success of the reappraisal induction. Conversely, HR acceleration did not show such a linear relationship; instead, it was higher under both increase and decrease as compared to maintain instructions. These HR changes were correlated with reappraisal-related activation in two medial prefrontal regions (i. e., dorsal medial frontal gyrus and dorsal cingulated gyrus), indicating that these two regions were involved in the allocation of cognitive resources for the regulation of unpleasant emotions. Whereas HR reflected the effort component, EDA was clearly correlated with the strength of negative emotions, which is in accordance with the differential indicator functions of electrodermal and cardiovascular measures discussed in Sects. 3.2.1.2 and 3.2.2.1.

As in the case of emotions, EDA had been frequently used as a stress indicator during the presentation of all kinds of stressful stimuli, e.g., stressful interviews (Page & Robson, 2007), presentation of aversive words (Silvert, Delplanque, Bouwalerh, Veerpoort, & Sequeira, 2004)[182] and expressive suppression during acoustic startle (Hagemann, Levenson, & Gross, 2006), just to mention a few more recent examples. Summarizing, it can be concluded that both nonspecific and specific EDRs constitute a valuable tool to be used in the area of stress research.

---

[182] See also the Dindo and Fowles (2008) study which is described in Sect. 3.1.1.1.

3.3 Personality and Individual Differences

Psychophysiological research on individual differences has been comprehensively reviewed by Gale and Edwards (1986). Their general conclusion was that research in this area is still fragmented and lacks integration. One aspect of their criticism on research in this field having specific implications for the use of ANS measures like EDA, concerns the discrepancy between the personality theories' focus on behavior, while most studies examined participants in a merely passive nonbehaving state with only weak external stimulation. Furthermore, the present author's general impression is that only a few personality theories offer testable predictions for psychophysiological reactivity. The following section will focus both on broad and narrow personality dimensions with specific reference to electrodermal reactivity. From the beginning, various attempts to establish relationships between personality dimensions and electrodermal responses have adopted an implicit arousal model for their interpretation (Edelberg, 1972a). This was the case for both broad personality traits like extraversion/introversion or emotional lability (Sect. 3.3.1) and more specific traits like repression/sensitization or sensation seeking (Sect. 3.3.2). A special case in this area is electrodermal lability, constituting a personality characteristic based on EDA measurement itself (Sect. 3.3.2.2).

The concept of electrodermal reactivity as a relatively stable individual characteristic is also related to the problem of idiosyncratic ANS responses or individual specificity (Engel, 1972). An individual person who consistently tends to overreact in a specific physiological modality is commonly regarded to be prone to develop psychophysiological (psychosomatic) diseases related to that particular system (Sect. 3.5.5).

3.3.1 General Personality Traits

Psychophysiological correlates of general personality traits (i.e., those on the most general factor analytic level) have been most thoroughly investigated for extraversion/introversion and emotional lability ("neuroticism"). The reason is that Eysenck (1967) proposed a neurophysiological basis for these two major, independent second-order factors which caused a great number of empirical studies in this field. In general, Eysenck identified introversion with the existence of lower thresholds in the various parts of the RAS (Sect. 3.2.1.1) and emotional lability with lowered thresholds in the limbic system. According to this, emotionally labile individuals should be more ANS reactive than stable ones, and extraverts were suggested to have a tendency toward a lower resting arousal level than introverts (Eysenck, 1983). Since the appropriate literature has been thoroughly reviewed by Stelmack (1981), the following two sections can be restricted to conceptual and methodological considerations, providing results only from several representative studies.

3.3.1.1 EDA and Extraversion/Introversion

According to Eysenck (1967), introverts are characterized by being easier conditionable, since their supposed RAS-mediated general higher cortical activity (Sect. 3.2.1) is presumed to facilitate consolidation of learned material. On the other hand, introverts are supposed to elicit cortical inhibition faster, which provides a kind of protection against strong stimulation. This in turn brings their counterparts, i.e., extraverts, close to sensation seekers (Eysenck & Zuckerman, 1978; see Sect. 3.2.1). Eysenck's conclusion is that – provided the same objective stimulation – introverts should be more aroused than extraverts within an average intensity range, whereas the opposite is true for the upper intensity range, due to the increase of cortical inhibition in introverts.[183]

Higher reactivity of introverts to stimuli of moderate intensities, which has been demonstrated in various studies of the Eysenck group, was most consistently observed in the electrodermal system (Eysenck & Eysenck, 1985; Stelmack, 1981). Also in line with Eysenck's hypothesis, tonic EDA was higher in introverts than in extraverts, though appropriate differences in phasic EDA were not frequently reported (Eysenck, 1983). Unfortunately, other groups found it difficult to replicate the psychophysiological relationships observed in the original laboratories, which Eysenck (1994) explained as being due to other researchers neglecting the complexity of person/situation relationships.

In general, the following three different approaches may be used to establish relationships between EDA and personality characteristics such as extraversion/introversion:

1. An approach which correlates personality questionnaire data and EDA obtained under conditions of resting and stimulation.
2. An ANOVA approach using one or more traits as somatic factors. Groups are formed either by the use of median split or by selecting extreme groups. This allows an investigation of the main effects of personality characteristics as well as interactions of experimental conditions with personality factors.
3. A psychopharmacological approach (Sect. 3.4.3) that has been especially favored by Eysenck (1967), in which the cortical excitation/inhibition balance is adjusted by the use of specific drugs, thus providing an experimental manipulation of the neurophysiological correlate of extraversion/introversion.

---

[183] Eysenck discussed his inhibition concept with respect to Pavlov's "transmarginal inhibition" or "protective inhibition," the neurophysiology of which he regarded as unrealistic, though the phenomenon itself (which is also in accordance with the so-called Yerkes–Dodson law, and the inverted U-shaped relationship between arousal and performance; see Sect. 3.2.1.1) has been frequently observed (Eysenck, 1983, p. 18). However, Eysenck's attempt to include different aspects of inhibition into a unitary CNS inhibition concept may have contributed to various differences between theoretical concepts and experimental results (Nebylitsyn, 1972, p. 21; Strelau, 1983, p. 145), thus being in part responsible for pitfalls in establishing reliable psychophysiological correlates of extraversion/introversion.

For each of these three approaches, a typical investigation into the differences in EDA between extraverts and introverts will be summarized below.

Rajamanickam and Gnanaguru (1981) performed a study following approach (1) with 23 male participants, using the change in SRL[184] before and after the application of an electric shock. Significant correlations to extraversion ($r = -0.62$) as well as to emotional lability ($r = 0.52$) were obtained, which were interpreted by the authors as being due to an increase in ANS reactivity in introverts and in emotionally labile individuals (Sect. 3.3.1.2).

A more refined analysis with respect to extraversion was performed by Fowles, Roberts, and Nagel (1977) in a series of four experiments following approach (2). The authors also investigated emotional lability ("neuroticism") as a personality trait in addition to extraversion/introversion. However, they formed extreme groups by the use of lower and upper terciles, and they measured changes in SCL[185] during the presentation of twenty 1 kHz tone series with different intensities. In addition, general arousal level was manipulated by presenting solvable and unsolvable tasks performed prior to stimulation.

In their first experiment with 80 male participants (half introverts and half extraverts), as well as in their second study (a replication with 20 participants of each group), Fowles et al. (1977) reported a higher SCL increase in extraverts with high tone intensities (103 dB) as compared to a control condition (83 dB), independent of arousal manipulations (i.e., varying difficulty of previous task). In introverts, a corresponding difference appeared only when easily solvable tasks had been presented. Contrarily, in case of a previous increase of arousal induced by difficult tasks, the second study yielded smaller changes in SCL to high-intensity tones, supporting Eysenck's hypothesis of a protective cortical inhibition. This was more clearly shown in the third experiment with 80 female participants (half introverted and half extraverted) as well as in the fourth study with 10 female participants in each of four groups formed by a combination of extreme groups of extraversion/introversion and emotional lability. Since the last two experiments were performed without previous performance tasks for manipulating arousal, the base-level arousal was assumed to be relatively low in all participants. Under these conditions, introverts showed a marked SCL decrease with increasing stimulus intensity, whereas the SCL in extraverts increased or remained unchanged with higher intensity stimuli. Emotional lability did not exert an effect on SCL changes.

A study performed by Smith, Wilson, and Jones (1983) following approach (3) will serve as the third example here. Forty-eight extraverts and 48 introverts, half of whom belonged to each gender, were selected as extreme groups from a larger sample. To induce different levels of cortical arousal, they were randomly assigned to three caffeine doses (1.5, 3.0, and 4.5 mg/kg body weight) and a placebo condition. After 45 min, the participants received two series of six 1.5 kHz tones

---

[184] Recorded with zinc electrodes of 25 mm diameter and 1% zinc sulfate cream, current density not reported.

[185] Recorded with 2 cm^2 Ag/AgCl electrodes, 0.5% KCl in Unibase, and 1.0 V constant current.

with intensities varying between 60 and 110 dB, thereafter a test stimulus of 3 kHz of the same intensity was presented. This procedure was applied twice, either with or without a prewarning signal, in randomized order. Introverts showed generally higher SCLs[186] than extraverts. However, there was a steady increase of both SCL and SCR amp. in extraverts with increasing doses of caffeine regardless of the presence of a warning condition. Introverts, on the other side, showed a steady decrease of SCR amp. with increasing caffeine doses in case of no warning signals, as well as a decrease from placebo to the lowest caffeine condition and a further increase of SCR amp. with increasing doses under the warning condition. In addition, a significant interaction between stimulus intensity and personality trait emerged, whereas introverts responding to tones of lower intensities (up to 80 dB) with higher SCR amp. as compared to extraverts, while no such difference appeared with tones of high intensities. The higher-order interaction between personality, caffeine doses, and presence or absence of the warning signal also reached significance.

The results of Smith et al. (1983) can be regarded as supporting some of the hypotheses proposed by Eysenck (1957). First, a higher general arousal of introverts under conditions of low stimulation was observed throughout the study. Second, the introversion-inducing effect of stimulants, which is part of Eysenck's "drug postulate," could be demonstrated in the group of extraverts, since their arousal increased with the caffeine dose. The decrease of the SCR amp. with an increasing caffeine dose in the group of introverts was in accordance with the hypothesis of a protective cortical inhibition mechanism in this group if arousal is increased. On the other hand, anticipatory processes induced by the warning signal could have reduced the effects of an increased stimulation level, thus dropping the cortical arousal beyond the threshold for the elicitation of protective inhibition. This points to a possibly important role of attention as a moderator variable within Eysenck's postulated excitation-inhibition continuum. Indeed, introverts showed a generally better performance in vigilance tasks as compared to extraverts (Krupski, Raskin, & Bakan, 1971).

Nevertheless, in general, the empirical data on arousal of introverts vs. extraverts were equivocal. Therefore, Gray (1970, 1973) proposed a modification of Eysenck's original theory, starting from the existence of relatively independent reward and punishment systems in the brain (Sect. 3.2.1.2). According to Gray's (1970) view, introverts were no longer regarded as easier conditionable. Instead, he suggested that introverts were more susceptible to punishment and frustrative nonreward (Sect. 3.2.1.1). Extraverts, on the other hand, were regarded as being more susceptible to positive reward. Furthermore, according to Gray's view, the extraversion/introversion dimension should not be regarded as orthogonal to

---

[186] Recorded with Ag/AgCl electrodes of 1 cm diameter, 0.05M NaCl cream, and 9.55 µA/cm^2 current density; SR values transformed into SC values. SCLs and SCRs were obtained at the beginning and after each test stimulus. SCR amp. were square-root transformed and range-corrected.

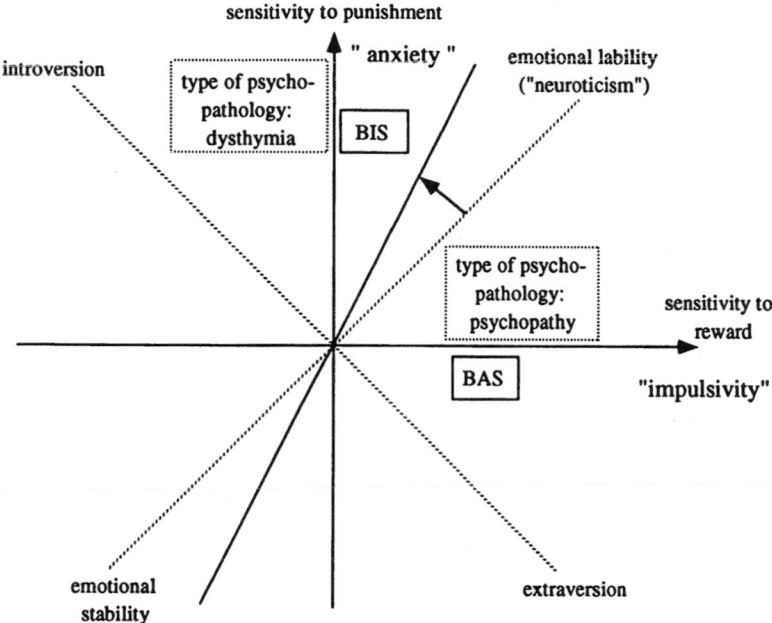

Fig. 3.5 Eysenck's (1967) C-level personality dimensions (*dotted lines*) extraversion/introversion and "neuroticism" (i.e., emotional lability vs. stability) as bisectors of angles in Gray's (1970) modified dimensional system (*solid lines*) formed by impulsivity and anxiety, together with their suggested behavioral (sensitivity to reward vs. punishment) and CNS correlates (BAS vs. BIS), further including the related types of psychopathology. The correlation between Eysenck's dimensions as found in questionnaire data is indicated by an additional axis which is rotated against the original lability/stability axis (see *arrow*)

emotionality or "neuroticism" in Eysenck's sense. Emotionality is treated as the degree of sensitivity to both reward and punishment, which is in accordance with repeatedly confirmed negative correlations between extraversion and emotional lability obtained from questionnaire data (Boucsein, 1973). The correlation is depicted in Fig. 3.5 by shifting Eysenck's original "neuroticism" axis out of orthogonality, as indicated by the arrow in the upper right. Later, Gray (1981) identified "sensitivity to reward" with the personality dimension "impulsivity," being orthogonal to an axis "sensitivity to punishment," which corresponds to the factor "anxiety" as measured by the Taylor (1953) Manifest Anxiety Scale (MAS).

As Fig. 3.5 shows, Eysenck's extraversion/introversion dimension is located as a bisector of the angles between impulsivity and anxiety. The aim of Gray's axis rotation was the establishment of a one-to-one relationship between C-level personality factors and their suggested behavioral concomitants and psychobiological sources. Increasing degrees in Gray's anxiety factor were regarded as being a correlate of an increasing sensitivity to signals of nonreward and novelty. On the other hand, an increase in impulsivity should go with an increasing susceptibility to signals of reward and absence of punishment.

In addition, Gray (1970, 1982, 1987) suggested that anxiety might reflect individual differences in the BIS (i.e., the septo-hippocampal stop-system), while individual differences in the approach system (the limbic reward system or BAS, Sect. 3.2.1.2) should be regarded as neurophysiological basis for impulsivity. The latter part of this hypothesis is in accordance with results concerning electrodermal and cardiovascular activity in psychopaths, who were regarded by Eysenck (1967) as neurotic extraverts, as opposed to dysthymics who are neurotic introverts (see Fig. 3.5). Hence, as Fowles (1980) stated, psychopaths should be prone to high BAS activity and a weak BIS, which is reflected in an increased HR and a decreased EDA in that particular clinical group (Sect. 3.4.1.2).

From this point of view, a differential validity of the electrodermal and the cardiovascular system for the two discussed broad personality dimensions might be suggested as follows. An increase in EDA may be regarded as a specific indicator of anxiety (or introverted emotional lability), while an increase of HR should specifically reflect impulsivity (or extraverted emotional lability).[187] Although the major evidence for a direct connection between BIS and anxiety as originally proposed by Gray (1982) stems from animal studies, the connection between EDA and BIS as suggested by Fowles (1980, 1988) constitutes a working hypothesis which is soundly based on data from humans (Sect. 3.2.1.2). However, it is not always possible to find the proposed connections between questionnaire-based personality traits and physiological measures. For example, Andresen (1987), in a multivariate study with 66 female participants, investigated possible interrelationships between personality and various psychophysiological responses to emotion-inducing situations (such as frightening acoustic and optic stimulation, preparing for a free speech, etc.). He reported that NS.SCR freq. (measured with standard methodology, using 0.01 µS as an amplitude criterion) was more an indicator of anxiety-related arousal but less so of behavioral inhibition. In addition, EDA yielded a connection with a decreased sensation seeking (Sect. 3.3.2.1). There is still no sound conclusion as to whether a single psychophysiological measure such as tonic EDA may really reflect differences in second-order personality factors. It is probably more likely that physiological measures are connected to specific traits or even states, both of which may be correlated with general personality dimensions.

3.3.1.2 EDA and Emotional Lability

According to Eysenck (1967), individuals scoring high on the personality dimension of emotional lability should exhibit a higher tonic level as well as hyperreactivity

---

[187] Indirect support comes from an investigation of Wilson (1990) with 61 male and 50 female participants who self-recorded their SCL throughout a whole working day. The recording device featured dry electrodes being not fixed to the skin which constituted a somehow instable methodology. By applying various questionnaire measures, Wilson came to the conclusion that sociability, rather than impulsivity, seemed to have been the component of extraversion responsible for individual variations in the diurnal SCL curve.

of the limbic system (Fig. 1.4, Sect. 1.3.2.2), especially under conditions of stress. In the early 1970s, a high correlation between this trait and EDA had been regarded as being one of the most established results in psychophysiological personality research (Stern & Janes, 1973), which was, however, questioned later (Katkin, 1975; Stelmack, 1981). In addition, Eysenck's identification of emotional lability with "neuroticism" does not provide a clear-cut separation of anxiousness in normal individuals from neurotic anxiety which is regarded as being psychopathological (Sect. 3.4.1.1). Furthermore, the localization of that particular personality dimension in the second-order factor space remains unclear. Gray's (1981) identification of Taylor's (1953) MAS anxiety with his own anxiety dimension which he proposed being a bisector in Eysenck's introversion/"neuroticism" quadrant had been criticized by Eysenck (1982). He pointed to the higher correlation between MAS scores and his "neuroticism" dimension ($r = 0.70$) as compared to their correlation with introversion ($r = 0.30$). This fits well to the shift of the emotional lability axis as indicated by the arrow in Fig. 3.5, which is, however, only one possible solution to this dilemma.

Of the three approaches outlined in the previous section, approach (2) has been most frequently used in research on EDA and emotional lability. As an example, a study performed by Rappaport and Katkin (1972) will be reported here. These authors used a short form of the MAS for classifying their participants in 24 high- and 24 low-anxious individuals by selecting the upper and lower 20% of a larger male student sample. Sixteen participants of each group were instructed after a resting period to report their own emotional responses by pressing a foot pedal, which had been previously shown to produce no movement artifacts in EDA (Sect. 2.2.5.2). The participants were told that electrodermal recording could be used to validate their subjective report. The additional 8 participants in each group served as a control group that underwent another resting period instead.

High- and low-anxious participants did not differ significantly in their NS.SRR freq.[188] during the initial resting condition. High-anxious participants responded to self-reporting their emotionality with a marked increase, and during the control condition with a less prominent decrease, of NS.SRR freq. as compared to low-anxious participants. Cognitive processes could be ruled out as a possible explanation, since there were no differences in self-reported reactions to the test situation between groups. On the other hand, the appearance of differences in EDA between high- and low-anxious participants seems to be connected to situations showing light stress character and including ego involvement, like the one used in that particular study. This is supported by the preponderant lack of correlations between trait anxiety and tonic EDA under resting (Stern & Janes, 1973), as well as under strong stress conditions such as receiving electric shocks (Katkin, 1975).

The lack of correlations reported by Stern and Janes (1973) was in essence confirmed in a literature review of studies connecting various EDA parameters to

---

[188] Recorded with standard Beckman Ag/AgCl electrodes and Beckman cream from the left palm, using 20 $\mu A/cm^2$ as current density and 100 Ω as an amplitude criterion.

both pathological and nonpathological anxiety performed by Naveteur and Freixa i Baqué (1987). Few significant correlations between tonic EDA and either trait or state anxiety have been reported from studies with nonpathological anxious individuals, which were somewhat higher in individuals with pathological anxiety. However, when participants were more relaxed, connections between tonic EDA and anxiety level disappeared. Significant relationships between spontaneous EDA and trait-anxiety measures in nonpathological anxious individuals were also rather rare, whereas individuals with pathological anxiety frequently showed a larger number of NS.EDRs than normal controls. Connections between high trait anxiety in nonpathological individuals and phasic EDA were seldom reported. In their own study with 22 high anxious and 22 nonanxious participants separated as extreme groups by means of a French adaptation of Cattell's anxiety questionnaire, Naveteur and Freixa i Baqué (1987) obtained results that even contradicted the hypothesis of EDA being increased in anxious individuals. All participants were presented eight negative emotional (disfigured babies, bloody faces, insects, etc.) and eight neutral (landscapes) slides in randomized order, while SC was bilaterally recorded with largely unreported methodology. Anxious participants showed significantly lower SCLs, a smaller amount of NS.SCRs during ISIs, lower SCR amp., and longer SCR lat. compared to their nonanxious counterparts. No significant results emerged from the analysis of a state anxiety measure.[189]

Attempts to investigate the influence of emotional lability on EDA according to approach (3) have been made by using tranquilizers as a tool to induce anxiolytic effects. These will be reported in detail in Sect. 3.4.3. However, influences of anxiolytic drugs were predominantly observed on state anxiety, which is not fully corresponding to the personality factor emotional stability vs. lability (e.g., Boucsein & Wendt-Suhl, 1982). To date, Stelmack's (1981) conclusion is still unrefuted, stating that relationships between emotional lability ("neuroticism" in Eysenck's sense) and EDA have not been demonstrated with sufficient consistency to infer the proposed ANS basis for this broad personality dimension. Instead, as already discussed at the end of the previous section, NS.EDR freq. may be used as an effective index of emotional response to anxiety and stress states (Sect. 3.2.2.2), a conclusion which is also in accordance with the findings of Katkin (1975).

Furthermore, as Fahrenberg (1987) pointed to, it can be regarded as doubtful that a single psychophysiological measure may be used as a valid indicator for a specific

---

[189] Such a contrary to classic expectation of greater electrodermal reactivity of low trait anxious compared to high trait anxious individuals has, under conditions of relatively low stress, been more recently confirmed by Wilken, Smith, Tola, and Mann (2000) and by Naveteur, Buisine, and Gruzelier (2005). Wilken et al. tried to explain their observation with the inverted-U-shaped relationship between general arousal and behavioral outcomes (Sect. 3.2.1.1). Trait anxious participants might have come to their experiment with higher arousal than their low anxious counterparts, thus reaching the peak of the inverted-U arousal curve earlier. It remains, however, unclear why EDA as a direct measure of general arousal should decrease with a further increase of arousal after this peak. Their alternative interpretation with respect to the LIV (Sect. 2.5.4) seems to be more appropriate here.

personality trait. Instead, he advocated a multivariate approach resulting in individual specific response patterns. These may show closer relationships to subfactors of the broad C-level personality dimensions than to general traits themselves. When following this line of research, the above-mentioned approach (1) may be of only limited value, because relationships between personality and psychophysiological patterns lack transsituational consistency. Instead, approach (2) should be preferred, since it allows studying main effects of situational factors and their interactions with personality traits under investigation as well. Approach (3), which would have the property of providing a rather tough test of the suggested CNS-ANS relationships underlying personality dimensions, would require drugs of highly specific and selective action within these systems, which are, however, not available for the use in human psychopharmacological studies (Sect. 3.4.3).

More recently Norris, Larsen, and Cacioppo (2007) successfully tried to increase the statistical power of approach (1) by treating emotional lability as a continuous between-subjects variable, together with two sessions separated by 2 weeks, valence (unpleasant, neutral, pleasant pictures), and point of time (during the early and late picture presentation and during the subsequent ISI) as between-subjects factors in a general linear model (GLM) approach. The 61 female participants viewed 66 slides from the IAPS (Sect. 3.2.2.1) in different orders during the two sessions (22 pictures from each valence category), while SC was continuously recorded using standard methodology and subsequent log transformation. A significant main effect of emotional lability (i.e., the inverse of the emotional stability subscale of the "Big Five" personality questionnaire; Goldberg, 1992) revealed that individuals higher in emotional lability showed overall higher SCR amp. No such result emerged for extraversion (Sect. 3.3.1.1). Significant interactions revealed that neurotics exhibit both greater electrodermal reactivity and more sustained SCRs to emotional stimuli than their stable counterparts. Only those individuals being high, but not those being low in emotional lability, responded with higher EDRs to unpleasant than to pleasant pictures. This result is consistent with Eysenck's (1967) above-mentioned hypothesis that emotional labiles have a hyperactivity of the limbic system, which results in lowered tolerance for aversive or stressful stimuli.

3.3.2   Specific Personality Traits

Establishing connections between long-lasting individual differences and electrodermal reactivity was also attempted by means of questionnaires focusing on traits below the second-order factorial level. Common to these traits is that they are supposed being connected to certain ANS features. As already mentioned, the amount of nonspecific EDA has been tried being established as a trait of its own, which will be treated separately in Sect. 3.3.2.2.

3.3.2.1 Traits Based on Questionnaire Data

In an attempt to find personality-related explanations for observed discrepancies between physiological and self-report indicators of stress, Weinstein, Averill, Opton, and Lazarus (1968) performed a reanalysis of six studies on film stress performed by the Lazarus group (Sect. 3.2.2.2). By using the *repression/sensitization* scale constructed by Byrne (1961) from MMPI items to detect opposed defense styles, the authors demonstrated that the discrepancy between self-report and psychophysiological responses to stress was greater in repressors than in sensitizers.[190] Their conclusion was that both groups were equally physiologically aroused, but repressors consistently claimed to be less distressed than sensitizers.

For testing this hypothesis in a specifically designed experiment, Boucsein and Frye (1974) classified 58 male participants as repressors, unspecific defenders, and sensitizers using the terciles of Byrne's scale. Each of these groups was divided into a stress group being blamed for failing to solve anagrams most of which were unsolvable, and a control group that was told they would not have been able to solve the task perfectly, because the experimenter was interested in response differences to difficult vs. easy anagrams. Skin resistance was recorded continuously with standard methodology using Beckman cream, and a subjective mood scale was applied twice during the anagram-solving task. ALS scores (Sect. 2.3.3.4 "Using Autonomic Lability Scores") were obtained for the mean NS.SRR amp. (Sect. 2.3.2.2) and for the subjective scales. ANOVA was performed with discrepancy scores that were formed as differences between standardized subjective and EDA scores. The only personality-stress interaction that reached statistical significance showed a greater subjective as compared to physiological reactivity of repressors. Furthermore, a correlation of $r = 0.78$ was obtained between the MAS (Sect. 3.3.1.2) and the Byrne scale. Therefore, the authors concluded that repression/sensitization may not be clearly separated from the second-order factor trait "anxiety," neither as a construct nor with respect to psychophysiological reactivity.

Weinberger, Schwartz, and Davidson (1979) also obtained a very high correlation ($r = 0.94$) between the MAS and the Byrne scale in their 40 male participants. To separate "true repressors" from purely low-anxious individuals, they used an ad hoc scale to measure subjectively reported repressive defensiveness. Fifteen low-anxious, 11 high-anxious, and 14 "true repressors" were selected from a total of 200 male participants. After an adaptation period they were subjected to a phrase association procedure as a mild stress condition. The "true repressors" showed a

---

[190] Individual ANS reactivity was obtained by using the higher of either HR or EDA standardized scores. However, since EDA was used in all six studies but not HR, individual reactivity might have been mainly expressed within the electrodermal system. EDA was recorded in all studies as SR by means of a Fels dermohmeter with a constant current of 70 µA across palmar zinc/zinc sulfate electrodes with 2 cm diameter.

significantly higher NS.SRR freq.[191] as compared to the other two groups under stress but not under resting conditions. Since their RT was also significantly longer, Weinberger et al. (1979) concluded that "true repressors" may not only have a higher trait anxiety as inferred from questionnaire data but also show ineffective coping with psychosocial stressors.

Gudjonsson (1981) further tried to clarify the observed discrepancy between subjective and electrodermal responses to social stress situations by means of a post hoc classification of his 36 male participants into repressors vs. sensitizers. He presented emotionally loaded questions, recorded NS.SCR freq.[192] between 1 and 5 s from the beginning of stimulus presentation, and obtained visual analog scale ratings of the disturbance by the questions. According to their subjective-physiological discrepancy, participants were classified into three groups: "repressors" who reported disturbance below the median but above-median elec-trodermal reactivity; "sensitizers" with disturbance scores above the median and below-median electrodermal reactivity; and "concomitants" who gave concomitant subjective and physiological scores. Repressors tended to have high defensiveness scores (taken from the Social Desirability Scale; Crowne & Marlowe, 1960) and low trait-anxiety scores (measured by Eysenck's neuroticism scale), while sensitizers showed low defensiveness and high trait anxiety. However, the two personality measures were significantly negatively correlated ($r = -0.47$), thus complicating possible conclusions with respect to repression/sensitization as an underlying personality dimension.

Another specific personality construct with a close relationship to psychophysio-logical reactivity is the *type A vs. type B* concept, measured by questionnaire as well as behavioral data, which has been related to risk for coronary heart disease (Rosenman et al., 1966). The coronary-prone type A has been characterized by time urgency, excessive activity, competitiveness, impatience, aggressiveness, and hostility, all of which are easily evoked under environmental challenges being due to an increased lability in the sympathetic-parasympathetic balance (Dembroski, MacDougall, & Shields, 1977). Whereas various studies in which cardiovascular measures were used ascertained a greater psychophysiological arousal in type A individuals, especially in interpersonal threatening situations (summarized by Houston, 1983), most investigations that used EDA as a typical measure for the suggested higher sympathetic reactivity of type A participants did not yield supporting results (Dembroski et al., 1977, Dembroski, MacDougall, Shields, Petitto, & Lushene, 1978, Dembroski, Weiss, Shields, Haynes, & Feinleib, 1978; Holmes, McGilley, & Houston, 1984; Krantz, Glass, & Snyder, 1974; Steptoe, Melville, & Ross, 1984; Steptoe & Ross, 1981). An exception is a study performed by Lovallo and Pishkin (1980) who divided 80 male participants into equal numbers of type As and

---

[191] Recorded with 16 mm Ag/AgCl electrodes and 0.05 M NaCl in Unibase from the palms. Amplitude criterion: 100 Ω. Reaction scores were corrected for artifact-free baselines.

[192] Recorded as SR with Ag/AgCl electrodes from the medial phalanges of the index and middle fingers of the nondominant hand with 8 μA CC, transformed into SC, amplitude criterion 0.02 μS.

Bs by means of rating their behavior pattern through interviews. All participants underwent three tasks (serial pattern learning, anagram solving, and concept identification), while SC was measured with standard methodology. Under all three task conditions, type A participants showed higher SCLs and higher NS.SCR freq. (with 0.1 μS as an amplitude criterion). They also reacted with a higher SCL to success in the pattern learning task, a condition under which type B's SCL decreased.

In a multivariate study performed with 144 postinfarction patients, Langosch, Brodner, and Foerster (1983) analyzed 20 EDA parameters during 11 different task periods. In addition, cardiovascular, respiratory, performance, and subjective measures were used for stepwise multiple prediction of six diagnostic and prognostic criteria. The authors came to the overall conclusion that EDA was of minor importance as compared to the other predictors under investigation. Thus, EDA did not appear to be useful for selecting participants with coronary disease proneness, the link of which to type A has also to be generally questioned by Myrtek (1984) based on an extensive literature review and his own results.

Another personality construct that came into focus in differential psychophysiology in the 1970s is *sensation seeking*. The concept was originally extracted from a questionnaire developed by Zuckerman, Kolin, Price, and Zoob (1964) to measure long-lasting interindividual differences in the optimal arousal level (Sect. 3.2.1.1). Correlations could be established between the Sensation Seeking Scale (SSS) and, for example, variety of sexual partners, experience with drugs and preference for risky sports or more complex tasks (Zuckerman, 1983). As Feij (1984) pointed out, psychophysiological studies revealed close relationships of SSS to the "strength of the nervous system" which is the first basic property of higher nervous activity in Pavlov's biologically oriented personality concept (Nebylitsyn, 1972). According to this, individuals scoring high on the SSS are supposed to possess a stronger nervous system than those scoring low, which should result in elevated sensory thresholds as well as in lower reactivity. This had been demonstrated with cardiovascular measures by Ridgeway and Hare (1981) who found that sensation seekers responded to 60 dB 1 kHz tones with OR patterns, while individuals scoring low on the SSS showed patterns that resembled DRs (Sect. 3.1.1.2). No such results were obtained with EDA.

However, in several other studies, higher amplitudes of electrodermal ORs could be observed in individuals scoring high on the SSS. Neary and Zuckerman (1976) performed two experiments with extreme groups formed by the SSS (following approach (2) in Sect. 3.3.1.1). Their first experiment used two groups of 14 participants of both genders, one from the upper and one from the lower 15% of the SSS distribution. They measured the electrodermal OR[193] to ten presentations of a white rectangle followed by ten repeated presentations of a complex colored design. Sensation seekers showed significantly higher EDRs to the first stimulus of both series but did not differ in the habituation course from participants scoring low

---

[193] The authors performed unusual SR recordings with an active palmar and an inactive forearm electrode, Beckman standard electrodes and cream, and 20 μA constant current. SR scores were transformed to SC, and SCR amplitudes were square-root transformed.

on the SSS. In their second experiment, 20 participants of each SSS extreme group were chosen, half of whom were additionally classified as high or low anxious by means of the MAS (Sect. 3.3.1.2). After presenting ten white rectangles followed by one presentation of a complex colored design, ten tones (1 kHz with approximately 70 dB) were applied, and a 200 Hz tone terminated the series of stimuli. Sensation seekers showed an overall higher EDR amp. to the visual but not to the acoustic stimuli; however, they emerged similar responses to novel stimuli at the end of both series as participants scoring low on the SSS. No significant trait-anxiety effects were observed. Thus, differences between individuals scoring high and low on the SSS were not consistently seen in EDR patterns.

Smith, Perlstein, Davidson, and Michael (1986) reported relationships between sensation seeking and electrodermal reactivity to relevant, novel stimuli (tones, words, slides, and videotaped scenes) in 36 participants who belonged to extreme groups of scoring either high or low on the SSS. Sensation seekers showed larger initial EDRs under all types of stimulation and also showed higher SCLs for words.

By contrast, Stelmack, Plouffe, and Falkenberg (1983) could find only weak relationships between SSS scores and electrodermal ORs. Since there is a positive correlation between sensation seeking and the C-level personality dimension extraversion, while predictions concerning electrodermal reactivity of sensation seekers and extraverts were opposite (Sect. 3.3.1.1), the authors applied Eysenck's personality questionnaire in addition to the SSS. The correlation between extraversion and the total SSS score was $r = 0.60$ in their total sample of 93 female and 91 male participants, which is considerably higher than the usual correlation of $r = 0.40$ (Andresen, 1987). Out of the total sample, 118 participants received ten repeated presentations of a geometric figure, while 66 participants received ten verbal stimuli instead. Each series was followed by a novel stimulus. At the beginning of the verbal series, introverts showed higher SCR amp. (measured with standard methodology using K–Y gel) than extraverts, and participants scoring higher in two of the four SSS subscales yielded higher SCR amp. as compared to low sensation seekers. However, no appropriate effect could be found for the total SSS score, and no personality effects were obtained for visual stimulation.

In another study using visual stimulation (presentation of photographic slides), Plouffe and Stelmack (1986) also could not demonstrate a relationship between SSS and SCRs to the stimuli. Instead, they observed an age dependency of the correlation between SSS scores and the SRL. While a positive correlation appeared in 26 younger females (aged 17–24 years), no correlation was observed in 25 older females (aged 60–78 years).

In general, differences in OR between participants scoring high and low on the SSS were more prominent in HR and in ERPs than in EDA measures (Feij, 1984; Zuckerman, 1983). Zuckerman (1990) pointed to the possibility that inconsistent EDA results may have to do with the uniphasic nature of the (exosomatic) EDR which does not as univocally allow differentiating between ORs and DRs as does the biphasic HR response (Sect. 3.1.1.2; see also Turpin, 1986). More consistent relationships between EDA and need for sensation and novel stimulation might be expected if personality variables on a less general level than the SSS are investigated. In a study performed in Japan, Yoshino, Kimura, Yoshida, Takahashi, and Nomura (2005) obtained a personality dimension called "novelty seeking" from 70 male participants. Those being high in this variable showed significantly higher logarithmized SCR amp. (recorded with standard methodology) to a series of altogether 36 backward masked pictures of negative and positive valence but not to neutral pictures. Although correlations to sensation seeking were not provided, novelty seeking might constitute a subfactor with the property to better predict EDRs to emotional stimulation. Another investigation with such a scope was a study performed by De Pascalis, Valerio, Santoro, and Cacace (2007) with 61 participants (32 females, 29 males) who were median-split into those scoring high or low in an impulsive-sensation seeking scale. They were presented with standard, deviant, and novel auditory and somatosensory stimuli. Significant differences in SCLs and SCRs (recorded with standard methodology) revealed that participants scoring high in the personality measure yielded higher arousability and were less prone to DRs to novel or aversive stimulation as their low scoring counterparts.

Summarizing, the personality traits discussed in this section did not show a closer relationship to EDA than general traits (Sect. 3.3.1). It seems questionable whether psychophysiological measures such as certain EDA parameters may show some validity as universal indicators of personality dimensions obtained by questionnaire data. Therefore, it might be more promising to focus on measures of personality being closer to psychophysiological constructs in research into differential psychophysiology, an example of which is given in the next section.

3.3.2.2 Electrodermal Lability as a Trait

The rationale of using EDA to determine long-lasting individual differences in ANS reactivity dates back to the 1950s, when Mundy-Castle and McKiever (1953) reported that individuals showing a high rate of NS.EDRs under resting conditions also responded with a high frequency of EDRs elicited by subsequent repeated stimulation. Lacey and Lacey (1958) were the first to use the term "electrodermal labiles" for individuals showing a high NS.EDR freq. under resting conditions and/ or slow habituation to repeated stimulation, whereas they labeled individuals who produced few NS.EDRs or habituated rapidly "electrodermal stabiles." In several subsequently performed studies, the amount of spontaneous EDA observed under resting conditions had been consistently found to be related to electrodermal reactivity and to the course of habituation (Johnson, 1963; Koepke & Pribram, 1966; Wilson & Dykman, 1960).

A possible advantage of using ANS reactivity as measured by EDA during resting conditions over questionnaire-based personality dimensions has been demonstrated by Katkin and McCubbin (1969), who originally intended to establish differential courses of OR habituation as a function of anxiety as measured by the

MAS (Sect. 3.3.1.2). Their two groups of 24 median-separated high- and low-anxious male participants did not differ in the habituation course of the log SCR[194] to 15 presentations of 1 kHz tones of moderate and very low intensity. However, when they performed a different classification of their participants into electrodermal labiles and stabiles using the median of NS.EDR freq. during a 10 min resting period prior to stimulation to establish individual differences, their 25 electrodermal stabiles showed a steeper habituation rate in the moderate intensity series as compared to the 25 electrodermal labiles, who only habituated to the low-intensity tone. As this (nonsignificant) difference appeared to be related to the initial EDR amp. in the tone series, the authors concluded that the moderate tones may have elicited a DR in the electrodermal labile group, instead of an OR (Sect. 3.1.1.2) as in the group of electrodermal stabiles.

Crider and Lunn (1971) investigated whether the coherence between the spontaneous electrodermal fluctuation rate and habituation speed could be regarded as an expression of a common underlying personality dimension of electrodermal lability. The NS.SPR freq.[195] was recorded twice, 7 days apart, from 22 male students during a 5 min resting period and during 20 trials of 90 dB, 1,300 Hz tones with 2 s duration masked by 72 dB white noise. Retest reliabilities were $r = 0.54$ for the NS.SPR freq. and $r = 0.70$ for the habituation speed, which was determined as number of trials needed to fall below the habituation criterion of 0.1 mV within 3 s after stimulus offset (Sect. 3.1.1.3). The correlations between these measures were $r = 0.51$ in the first and $r = 0.73$ in the second sessions. Both measures revealed zero correlations with neuroticism, while correlations with extraversion and with different subfactors of impulsivity ranged from $r = -0.24$ to $r = -0.46$ for NS.SPR freq. and from $r = -0.40$ to $r = -0.57$ for habituation speed. Thus, reliability[196] and validity aspects yielded a slight superiority of habituation speed over the NS.EDR freq. as a measure of electrodermal lability.

Contrary to Crider and Lunn (1971), Cruz and Larsen (1995) obtained a significant correlation between electrodermal lability[197] and neuroticism ($r = 0.37$) in a study with 62 students (27 females, 35 males), using a test battery for obtaining major personality traits. This correlation was higher in females ($r = 0.45$) than in males ($r = 0.26$). However, the highest correlations of electrodermal lability with other personality dimensions were obtained in various second-order emotion-

---

[194] Recorded as SR with Ag/AgCl electrodes and NaCl electrode cream from Beckman, unipolar palmar against forearm, using 20 μA/cm^2 current, performing transformation to SC and logarithmization. The amplitude criterion for NS.EDRs during the resting condition was 100 Ω.

[195] Measured with nonpolarizing Ag/AgCl sponge electrodes between the palm and an alcohol-cleaned forearm site, AC-coupling (Sect. 2.1.3) with 0.45 s time constant, and an amplitude criterion of 0.1 mV. Several fluctuations within a 6 s window were regarded as a single SPR.

[196] For reliabilities of frequencies and mean amplitudes of NS.EDRs, see sections 2.5.2.1 under "Tonic Skin Conductance Measures" and 2.5.2.2 under "Tonic Skin Resistance Measures".

[197] NS.SCRs were recorded with standard methodology using a Wheatstone bridge (Sect. 2.1.3) during 40 s after a 5 min relaxation period, using an amplitude criterion of 0.05 μS (Sect. 2.3.1.2 "Choice of Amplitude Criteria").

related personality factors such as life satisfaction ($r = -0.62$), unhappiness ($r = 0.60$), and dominance of negative emotions in early family environment ($r = 0.52$), albeit only for females. Since males did not show equivalent correlations, the authors presumed that a differential social learning environment for females and males may contribute to observable gender differences in electrodermal lability.

Katkin (1975) recommended using electrodermal lability instead of questionnaire-recorded anxiety as a personality variable for predicting the reactivity to stressors of medium intensity levels. Based on a reanalysis of earlier experiments performed by his group, he hypothesized that a high rate of spontaneous electrodermal fluctuations would not only be an indicator of a defensive or perhaps anxious hyperreactivity to environmental stimuli; in addition, it should be regarded as a reliable indicator for state anxiety, whereas the direction of attention would be the critical mediating factor leading to an increase of EDA (Sect. 3.1.3.1). In agreement with this view, several authors suggested that electrodermal lability may reflect an individual's ability to allocate information processing capacity to stimuli that are to be attended (Dawson, Schell, & Filion, 1990; Katkin, 1975; Lacey & Lacey, 1958; Schell, Dawson, & Filion, 1988; Wilson & Graham, 1989).

This view is also supported by the well-established result that electrodermal labiles are likely to exhibit greater ability at keeping their attention focused to an ongoing task, thus avoiding decrements in vigilance and performance (Coles & Gale, 1971; Crider & Augenbraun, 1975; Hastrup, 1979; Munro, Dawson, Schell, & Sakai, 1987; Siddle, 1972; Vossel & Roßmann, 1984). This is also in accordance with the close relationship between electrodermal lability and introversion, which had been demonstrated by Crider and Lunn (1971), Mangan and O'Gorman (1969), Nielsen and Petersen (1976), and Coles et al. (1971), and with improved performance in vigilance tasks observed in introverts (Krupski et al., 1971). Conversely, Sostek (1978), using 66 male participants, found only nonsignificant correlations between electrodermal lability, as measured by the course of electrodermal habituation to 75 dB tones and by the NS.SRR freq.[198] on the one hand, and various personality dimensions like introversion, emotional lability (Sect. 3.3.1.2), and sensation seeking (Sect. 3.3.2.1) on the other hand. "Habituation lability" seemed to be a superior predictor of vigilance task performance than "spontaneous lability." Electrodermal labiles, as identified by either measure, showed the same response differences in a risky vs. cautious payoff instruction. This was not seen in electrodermal stabiles. Thus, the author suggested that electrodermal labiles may be more sensitive to environmental contingencies than their stabile counterparts. This could be related to the higher attention capacity of the former group (see also Hastrup, 1979).

Support for the treatment of electrodermal lability as an independent personality dimension came from a study performed by Hastrup and Katkin (1976) with 120 male students. They correlated a pool of 478 self-report items taken from various

---

[198] SR recorded palmar against a forearm site with 2 cm^2 Ag/AgCl electrodes, Beckman cream, and 10 μA/cm^2 constant current. Amplitude criterion: 100 Ω.

personality questionnaires with the NS.SRR freq. during a 15 min resting period and the habituation speed taken from a series of 20 tones (440 Hz, 93 dB, 2 s duration). Several correlational and discriminant function analyses did not yield any close relationship between electrodermal lability and traditional self-descriptive psychometrics. To test Katkin's (1975, p. 173) hypothesis, that electrodermal lability reflects differences in cognitive efficacy (i.e., a selective enhancement of effective central processes) rather than merely a generalized arousal mechanism, Solanto and Katkin (1979) performed a study on differential classical light-shock conditioning (Sect. 3.1.2.1), using the same kind of SR recordings transformed to log SC as Hastrup and Katkin (1976). Twenty electrodermal labiles and 21 stabiles were selected from 63 male students, according to their scoring above or below the medians of both the distribution of spontaneous EDRs during 10 min resting and of habituation scores. The latter were obtained as trials to habituation (three successive SRRs below 1 kΩ) in a series of 20 tones with 60 dB intensity. A major finding was that electrodermal labiles showed an overall higher SIR amp. than stabiles. However, the data did not provide support for possible differences in EDR conditioning between electrodermal labiles and stabiles, as had been suggested by Öhman and Bohlin (1973).

Siddle et al. (1979) investigated the differential influence of stimulus significance on ORs (Sect. 3.1.1.1) in electrodermal labiles and stabiles. In their initial study, they selected 28 participants of each group from a total of 230 male students for their first study, using the lower and upper 40% of the NS.SCR distribution.[199] Their participants were presented a series of 12 tones (1 kHz, 70 dB, 5 s), followed by a single presentation of a 500 Hz tone. Half of each group performed a RT task, responding as quickly as possible to each tone offset while the other half received no such instruction. Siddle et al. (1979) observed that electrodermal labiles were more responsive than stabiles, and RT groups displayed higher SCRs to the stimuli than non-RT groups, but the interaction was not statistically significant. Furthermore, group differences were not higher than the increase in SCR amp. produced by stimulus change alone. In a second experiment, 20 participants in each group were presented 12 slides with female names. On trial 13, half of the participants in each group received their own name, while the others were given a neutral male name. Again, higher SCRs were seen in electrodermal labiles if stimuli were significant. No interaction effects were observed, except that electrodermal labiles exhibited a considerably higher SCR amp. increase on presentation of their own names as compared to all other conditions. The observation that electrodermal reactivity to emotionally significant stimuli is higher in electrodermal labiles than in stabiles was confirmed by Waid and Orne (1980) within two experiments on the detection of deception (Sect. 3.5.2).

To date, there is no generally accepted theoretical framework for electrodermal lability. Crider (1993) pointed to a very simple possible explanation, according to which electrodermal lability might be an expression of heightened general arousal (Sect. 3.2.1.1). Crider (2008) mentioned a psychodynamic view, according to

---

[199] SCRs were recorded with standard methodology and an amplitude criterion of 0.02 µS during a 5 min period of no stimulation.

which electrodermal lability may reflect an internalized mode of processing emotional impulses as opposed to overt emotional expression. Buck et al. (1974) assumed a socially learned inhibition of overt affective responses as a possible explanation for the negative correlation between facial expressiveness and electrodermal responding to emotion-inducing stimuli.[200] In line with this, Crider (2008) proposed an *effortful control hypothesis* of electrodermal lability, assuming that a possible source of increased NS.EDR freq. among electrodermal labiles could be their effortful attempt to control their own emotional expression (Sect 3.2.2.1). Such an effort would require a certain amount of processing capacity, the request for which is accompanied by an EDR in the framework of Öhman's (1979) information processing model of the OR (Fig. 3.3, Sect. 3.1.2.1). Multiple requests will produce multiple EDRs, which appear as NS.EDRs if no specific stimuli can be determined (Sect. 2.3.2.2). This kind of view fits to the observation of reduced spare processing capacity among electrodermal labiles under cognitive challenge (Crider, 2008), which had also been demonstrated in a study of Schulter and Papousek (1992) described in Sect. 3.1.4.1. The authors found significant, albeit relatively low, correlations between verbal and spatial performance and electrodermal lability, which were positive for verbal speed in case of NS.SCR freq. ($r = 0.23$) but negative for accuracy, of both verbal and spatial and for NS.EDR freq. and mean NS.EDR. amp. ($r = -0.23$ to $r = -0.43$). In general, electrodermal labiles are clearly superior in sustaining attention to external stimuli and in rapid response execution, while stabiles are superior in tasks requiring STM and freedom from distraction (Crider, 1993). Finally, a neurophysiological view on electrodermal lability is that individuals showing predominance of BIS activity (Sect. 3.2.1.2) will be more likely to produce NS.EDRs than those who do not, which again brings electrodermal lability in close connection with manifest or state anxiety (Brenner et al., 2005).

In summary, electrodermal lability obtained either as high NS.EDR freq. during stimulus-free recording periods or as reduced habituation rate to relatively neutral stimuli seems at least feasible for predicting individual differences in EDRs under various conditions of stimulation.[201] However, this might be part of a general ANS reactivity instead of being an idiosyncrasy of the electrodermal system, since electrodermal labiles and stabiles show differences with respect to various psychophysiological measures, including cardiovascular responsiveness (e.g., O'Gorman & Lloyd, 1988; Schell et al., 1988). On the other hand, differential reactivity of cardiovascular and electrodermal measures has been reported quite consistently (Sect. 3.2.1.2), but there might not be enough empirical evidence for refuting the

---

[200] The possibility of electrodermal lability in adolescence being a protective factor against criminal behavior during adulthood since it prevents underarousal has been discussed by Raine, Venables, and Williams (1995); see also Sect. 3.4.1.2. As a possible explanation, Crider (2008) suggested an increased amount of self-control of emotional behavior in electrodermal labiles, which would be in line with his effortful control hypothesis.

[201] Crider (1993) stated that the temporal stability of electrodermal lability measures is somewhat lower than usually demanded of measures for individual differences.

hypothesis that electrodermal lability is an expression of a more general autonomic lability (see also Sect. 2.3.3.4 "Using Autonomic Lability Scores"). In addition, it is still debated how electrodermal lability should be embedded in a frame of personality dimensions as obtained by questionnaire data. As yet, there is not a specific area of validity being determined for electrodermal lability. For further discussion of the relationships between electrodermal lability and other personality variables see Crider (1993).

3.4 Psychopathology

One of the most important areas in the field of applied psychophysiology is the use of physiological measures in diagnosis and therapy of psychopathological disorders. Accordingly, a great deal of electrodermal research has been performed within the area of clinical psychophysiology. For getting an overview on the majority of applications of EDA in psychopathology, the reader is referred to Stern and Janes (1973), supplemented by the third volume of the book edited by Gale and Edwards (1983). The psychopathology section of the present book will be restricted to clinical areas in which the use of EDA is based upon certain aspects of electrodermal mechanism and/or hypotheses concerning the differential validity of EDA parameters. This section will focus on disorders of anxiety, psychopathy and depression (Sect. 3.4.1), schizophrenia (Sect. 3.4.2), and psychopharmacological treatment of anxiety disorders (Sect. 3.4.3).[202]

3.4.1 EDA in the Assessment of Anxiety, Psychopathy, and Depression

Symptoms of anxiety are very common in many psychiatric disorders. There are, however, certain disorders, the major characteristic of which is anxiety (Sect. 3.4.1.1). In depressive disorders (Sect. 3.4.1.3), anxious and depressed mood states are often not clearly distinguishable with respect to their phenomenology as well as to therapeutic aspects (Foulds & Bedford, 1976). This is also reflected by the action of antidepressive and antianxiety drugs (Sect. 3.4.3), which belong to different psychopharmacological classes, but act upon both primarily depressive as well as mainly anxious states (Derogatis, Klerman, & Lipman, 1972). Anxiety is also observed in schizophrenia (Sect. 3.4.2), being attributed at the beginning of the illness to the subjective experience of strange personality changes and in later stages to delusional contents.

---

[202] Typical applications of EDA within therapeutic techniques used in psychopathology can also be found in biofeedback (Sect. 3.1.2.3) and in systematic densitization (summarized by Katkin & Deitz, 1973).

3.4.1.1 EDA of Patients with Generalized Anxiety, Phobias, and Panic Disorders

According to the DSM IV-R (American Psychiatric Association, 2000), *generalized anxiety* that appears in neurotic patients is accompanied by symptoms of motor tension, autonomic hyperactivity, apprehensive expectations, and excessive vigilance and scanning. Clinical anxiety may be permanently present or appearing in form of attacks. Besides various subjective scales that were constructed for the diagnosis of general anxiety (e.g., Taylor's MAS; Sect. 3.3.1.2), various attempts have been made to objectively measure the actual anxiety level by recordings of its autonomic concomitants (e.g., using cardiovascular, electrodermal, or electromyographical measures). However, correlations between indicators of clinical anxiety stemming from the subjective and physiological realm were in general rather low (Lang, 1970; Hodges, 1976), which is also the case in other emotional states (Sect. 3.2.2.1).

The studies performed by Lader and Wing (1964, 1966) belong to the most frequently cited attempts to differentiate anxious patients from healthy controls by means of EDA.[203] Lader and Wing (1964) found both the SCL[204] and the NS.SCR freq. to be significantly higher in 20 patients suffering from anxiety states (17 of them showing "free floating" anxiety all the time), as compared to 20 matched normal controls. An elevated level of tonic EDA during resting conditions in anxiety patients, mostly confirmed by later studies (e.g., Chattopadhyay & Biswas, 1983; Raskin, 1975), had been interpreted as being due to a general "overarousal" in these patients, as already postulated by Malmo (1957).

In addition, Lader and Wing (1964) presented their participants 20 identical tones (1 kHz, 100 dB, 1 s duration). While the SCL showed a continuous decrease in normal individuals during resting as well as during the tone series (after an initial increase), anxiety patients showed a slight but continuous increase of SCL all the time. By contrast, the number of spontaneous EDRs yielded a steady decline, except for a small increase in response to the first few stimuli, which was very similar in both groups. Lader and Wing concluded that – other than in nonclinical individuals where SCL and NS.SCR freq. can be regarded as two equivalent measures of tonic EDA – both measures may reflect different aspects of arousal or vigilance in patients suffering from anxiety. A habituation regression analysis performed with log SCR amp. yielded significantly higher initial ORs and a steeper habituation gradient in the normal controls (Sect. 3.1.1). Lader and Wing (1964) as well as Lader (1975) interpreted the lower reactivity of anxiety patients as being due to ceiling effects or to functioning of the Law of Initial Values (Sect. 2.5.4.1).

---

[203] Lader and Wing's research had been continued by Chattopadhyay and co-workers Chattopadhyay, 1981; Chattopadhyay et al., 1975, 1980, 1982, 1983.

[204] Recorded with 10 µA CC using lead electrodes, filled with 0.05 M NaCl cream, from the distal phalanx of the right thumb against an inactive (rubbed) site on the lateral aspect of the arm above the elbow. SR was converted to log SC, and an SCR of 0.003 log µS was used as amplitude criterion (Sect. 2.3.1.2 "Choice of Amplitude Criteria").

This means that stimulation may have exerted little effect in addition to the already existing autonomic overarousal in patients. However, the lower initial reactivity did not determine the slowing down of habituation rate as well, since there was also a significant difference in H-scores between patients and normals (a habituation index independent of the size of the initial response; Sect. 3.1.1.3). Habituation being slowed down or even missing in anxiety patients is a result consistently found not only for SCRs (Lader 1967, 1975; Lader & Wing, 1964, 1966) but also for cardiovascular measures (Malmo & Smith, 1951; McGuinness, 1973), for EMG (Davis, Malmo, & Shagass, 1954), and for EEG parameters (Bond, James, & Lader, 1974; Ellingson, 1954).

Hart (1974) provided an alternative interpretation of the failure of anxious patients to habituate as rapidly as normal individuals. The 100 dB tones used by Lader and Wing could have well produced a DR in patients, which would have been more resistant to habituation than the OR observed in controls instead. The suggestion was that anxious individuals may have a lower threshold for exhibiting a DR than nonanxious ones. In his own study, Hart attempted to differentiate ORs from DRs in 18 psychiatric anxiety patients and 18 normal controls, presenting three intensities of signal and no-signal tones. He used an initial HR deceleration as an objective measure for an OR and an immediate HR acceleration as an indicator for DR (Sect. 3.1.1.2). The EDA parameters log SCL, SCR amp., and NS.SCR freq. were recorded with standard methodology as resistance measures and transformed to conductance units. The no-signal stimuli consisted of 30 tones (1 kHz, 2 s) with an intensity of 50, 75, or 100 dB, presented in series of triads, each triad containing one tone from each of the three intensities. Under signal conditions, tones were presented in pairs, 2 s apart, 12 trials for each level of stimulus intensity. The second tone of each pair was of a different frequency in eight trials of each series, and the participants' task was to judge whether the tones were the same or different in pitch.

In contrast to the results of Lader and Wing (1964), Hart (1974) did not find significant differences between anxious and nonanxious individuals in the SCR amp. following the first stimulus in the series. Furthermore, SCL also did not differentiate between the groups. In addition, the results of HR analyses were inconsistent with the hypothesis that anxious patients fail to habituate their OR as rapidly as nonanxious individuals. Instead, it seemed that, relative to normals, anxious individuals showed a deficit in orienting behavior, since they were more prone to respond with a DR pattern even when stimuli of low intensity were presented. There was also no significant difference in the slope of electrodermal habituation between the two groups. This was interpreted by Hart as being due to 50% nonhabituators in his control group, while Lader and Wing (1964) reported that their normal individuals were all habituators. In both studies, there had been a comparable percentage of habituators in the anxious group.

The contradictory results of studies comparing anxious and nonanxious individuals with respect to the slope of habituation may have been due to Hart's (1974) variations in signal values of the stimuli and also to the stimulus intensity changes used in his design. Both conditions may have reduced monotony in stimulus presentation, which, in turn, prevented habituation. Another difference between the two studies consisted in the presence of spontaneous EDA. Anxious patients in Hart's study only showed less than twice as much NS.SCRs in a 3 min period preceding the first no-signal tone as compared to normal controls, while Lader and Wing's patients showed more than three times as much spontaneous EDRs during resting as compared to the normals used in their studies.[205]

Differences in EDA between anxious and nonanxious individuals may also be influenced by the method of anxiety diagnosis. Neary and Zuckerman (1976) reported a negative correlation between the SCR amp. following 70 dB tones on the one hand and anxiety scores as obtained by the state-anxiety scale of the Multiple Affect Adjective Checklist (Zuckerman & Lubin, 1965) on the other hand. However, an additional classification of their participants according to trait-anxiety scores of the MAS (Taylor, 1953) did not yield any connection between EDA and anxiety level. It can be regarded as a consistent result that state anxiety is a better predictor of initial SCR amp. in stimulus series when compared to trait anxiety. According to Neary and Zuckerman (1976), a generalized increase in reactivity caused by increased levels of anxiety may reduce discriminability and hence the initial responses in stimulus series. However, there is strong evidence for an undoubtedly higher tonic EDA in anxious individuals facilitating ceiling effects during specific stimulation as mentioned above.

It has been demonstrated by Grillon (2002) that unpredictability of an aversive UCS can be an important factor that might facilitate the development of anxiety disorders via classical conditioning (Sect. 3.1.2.1). One hundred thirty-three healthy individuals (75 females, 58 males) were assessed by the trait portion of Spielberger's (1983) State-Trait Anxiety Inventory (STAI). They participated in two very similar experimental sessions, being either 1 week ($N = 72$) or 1 month ($N = 61$) apart. Each session consisted of two startle habituation phases, a pre acquisition, an acquisition, and a post acquisition (extinction) phase. Differential conditioning (Sect. 3.1.2.1) was realized with pictures of flowers and mushrooms as CSs and a 3.0 mA electric shock of 10 ms duration served as UCS, during which SCRs were recorded with standard methodology. At the end of the first session, participants were divided post hoc into those that have been aware of the CS+/UCS contingency ($N = 28$ in the 1-week group and $N = 25$ in the 1-month group) and those who had not been aware of such a contingency. Only the aware participants emerged significantly higher SCR amp. following the CS+ compared to the CS−. They also reported greater subjective fear elicited by the CS+ than the unaware participants. Interestingly, there was a significantly higher return rate for both second sessions (1 week, respectively, 1 month after the initial session) in the aware compared to the unaware participants. This was interpreted by Grillon as avoidance of an anxiety-evoking experimental context that had been associated with

---

[205] Possibly the small difference in amplitude criteria, 0.002 log μS used by Hart (1974) vs. 0.003 log μS used by Lader and Wing (1964), may also have contributed to that difference (Sect. 2.3.1.2 "Choice of Amplitude Criteria").

the occurrence of (by the unaware participants) unpredictable shocks. Furthermore, the unaware participants showed an increase of subjectively rated anxiety from the first to the second session, which constituted another hint for a possible facilitation of the development of anxiety disorders in case of perceived unpredictability.

As opposed to patients with generalized anxiety, *phobic* individuals are characterized by a defense-like overreaction to specific stimuli (or stimulus classes) being neutral or of mild threat for normal persons. Even symbolic representations of the feared stimuli may have the property to elicit such an overreaction in phobics. Potentially phobic stimuli were frequently used to investigate classical electrodermal conditioning and extinction, since conditioning has been regarded as a possible mechanism for acquisition of phobias (Sect. 3.1.2.1 "Recent Developments in EDR Conditioning"). In her summary of several studies on autonomic responses to phobic stimuli, Sartory (1983) concluded that the cardiovascular system shows a clear DR pattern in individuals with particular phobias, while EDR amp. are elevated as long as stimulus duration is below 5 s, whereas extended stimulus presentations fail to differentiate between phobic and nonphobic responses, which may be due to habituation effects.

Fredrikson (1981) used the supposed indicator function of a higher SCR amp. at palmar as compared to dorsal sites (Sect. 3.1.1.2) to distinguish between electrodermal DR and OR with respect to phobic vs. nonphobic responses. Twenty-four spider- or snake-phobic women were compared with 24 female controls who were conditioned to pictures of either snakes or spiders by means of electric shocks. Pictures of flowers and mushrooms served as neutral stimuli, and HR was recorded as an additional dependent variable. During the first session which served for conditioning, the phobic group received eight phobic and eight neutral stimuli and adjusted the electric shock level without further application of shocks, while the conditioning group watched 12 snake and 12 spider slides, one of which served as CS+, the other one as CS−, together with eight neutral stimuli. During the second session on another day, half of each group received either fear-relevant or neutral stimuli during the extinction phase. Palmar SCRs were recorded from the middle phalanges of the participants' left first and second fingers, while dorsal SCRs were taken from the middle phalanges of the left third and fourth fingers, using standard methodology with subsequent range correction (Sect. 2.3.3.4 "Range Corrections").

In the conditioning group, FIRs (Fig. 3.2, Sect. 3.1.2.1 "Components of EDR Conditioning") during acquisition tended to be higher at dorsal compared to palmar sites in response to the CS+, while the reverse was true for the CS−. This observed palmar/dorsal effect disappeared during extinction. When being confronted with their feared objects, phobics reacted with a palmar/dorsal pattern reflecting a DR, while nonfeared and neutral stimuli only elicited an OR. In addition, verbal-cognitive components of fear were positively correlated with palmar but not with dorsal SCRs, thus supporting Edelberg's (1973a) hypothesis of palmar EDRs reflecting aversiveness (Sect. 3.1.1.2). HR was accelerated following phobic and decelerated following neutral material. A similar tendency was observed during acquisition in the conditioning group.

Thus, besides the well-demonstrated HR acceleration, a difference in palmar/ dorsal SCR amp. may serve as a sensitive indicator for fear responses in phobics. The latter one can be interpreted as due to an active mechanism of coping with fear-relevant stimuli (Obrist, 1976), which is also in accordance with HR acceleration being an indicator of BAS activity (Sect. 3.2.1.2) as proposed by Fowles (1980). Similar response patterns can be elicited during acquisition of phobic responses in healthy individuals, especially when using "prepared" stimuli as CS+ (Sect. 3.1.2.1 "UCR Diminution, Preception and Preparedness"), while during extinction, the DR pattern switches to an OR pattern in both HR and EDA. As opposed to patients with generalized anxiety, phobic patients do not show a generally increased EDA but overrespond only to their specific fear-relevant stimuli.

With the advent of the possibility to combine EDA with fMRI recordings (Sect. 2.2.3.5), CNS structures being involved in classical conditioning of fear and phobias could be visualized. For example, Tabbert, Stark, Kirsch, and Vaitl (2006), using the methodology of Blecker, Kirsch, Schaefer, and Vaitl (2001) described in Sect. 2.2.3.5, investigated the effect of a contingency awareness manipulation in a differential conditioning paradigm with a total of 41 nonclinical participants (21 females, 20 males), using pictures of figures and numbers as CSs and an electric stimulus as UCS. While differential SCR conditioning was only observed in the aware group, enhanced responses in the amygdala and in the orbitofrontal cortex were seen in the unaware group, which pointed to the existence of an anxiety-generating CNS network being independent of cognitive factors (Sect. 3.1.2.1 "Cognitive vs. Noncognitive View of EDR Conditioning").

Wendt, Lotze, Weike, Hosten, and Hamm (2008) recorded SC[206] together with fMRI data in 13 spider phobics (above the 85th percentile of an appropriate questionnaire) and 13 controls (below the 15th percentile) while viewing pictures of spiders and mushrooms (control stimuli) as part of a more complex picture presentation. SCLs during viewing spider pictures increased significantly in the spider phobic group, while SCLs during viewing mushrooms rather decreased, as did the SCLs during both picture categories in nonphobic controls. The same picture emerged for HR. During the 30 s block of sustained presentation of phobic stimuli, the spider phobics' SCL continuously increased, reaching a plateau at 15 s, while the SCL measure habituated for sustained presentation of the control pictures and for both picture categories in the nonphobic controls. The fMRI recordings revealed that a sustained exposure of phobics to pictorial representations of material relevant for their particular phobia was associated with enhanced activation of the left midinsula. In contrast, an activation of the right amygdala seemed to be specific only during the first half of the sustained exposure, during which the SCL also continuously increased, but no longer during the second half.

---

[206] With standard methodology from two electrodes adjacently placed to the participant's right-hand hypothenar eminence, with a resolution of 0.001 μS, a sampling rate of 10 Hz, scored as SCL difference between the mean during the 3 s picture viewing and a baseline, log-transformed and range-corrected (Sects. 2.3.3.4 "Range Corrections" and "Transformation into Standard Values").

Under laboratory conditions, investigations into psychophysiological concomitants of phobic reactions were in most cases restricted to recordings during symbolic representations of phobic objects or situations. The use of ambulatory monitoring devices, however, enables such measurements under real-life conditions which elicit the original phobic response. In a placebo-treatment study with 14 female flight phobics, Wilhelm and Roth (1998) used the Vitaport system (Sect. 2.2.3.4) for collecting SC,[207] HR, respiratory activity, finger temperature, body movements, and barometric pressure. The participants rated their anxiety, tension, desire to leave the situation, and excitement on scales from 0 to 10 during the preflight baseline, 3 min after takeoff and during the postflight baseline. The participants boarded a commercial 12 min flight from an international airport and occupied a window seat. The 15 nonphobic participants (matched for gender and age) who served as controls showed significantly lower SCLs during flight but also during pre- and postflight baselines, while their NS.SCR freq. and HR were only during the flight significantly lower than those of the phobics. Stepwise discriminant analysis was used for post hoc reclassification of the participants. Other than cardiorespiratory measures, EDA parameters were not among the six most discriminating physiological variables. It is rather likely that phobic responses in real-life environments are predominantly accompanied by cardiovascular changes, whereas EDA plays a minor role for the differentiation between phobics and controls (Sect. 3.4.1.1).

However, a different picture can emerge when phobics are tested in virtual environments. In a laboratory study with nonclinical participants, Wilhelm et al. (2005) probed an exposure to virtual reality (a 14 min simulation of height environment, i.e., being on an open platform which was raised in 5 and lowered in two steps, by means of visual and auditory stimuli delivered through a head-mounted display, while being asked to move their heads) as a possible therapeutic tool for acrophobia. From a pool of 86 participants, the extreme 11 ones with highest and the 9 with lowest scores in an acrophobia questionnaire were selected. At the end of each step (every 2 min), participants rated their actual fear on a scale from 0 to 10. During the whole exposure and a previous baseline, SCL (recorded with standard methodology and artifact-cleaned), HR, and blood pressure were continuously recorded. The high-acrophobic group showed significantly greater electrodermal reactivity but only minimal HR increases. The low-acrophobic group revealed only small responses in both EDA and HR. The authors concluded that the BIS had been selectively activated in acrophobics during virtual exposure to the phobia-relevant situation (Sect. 3.2.1.2). Such a selective activation of EDA

---

[207] Recorded from the middle phalanges of digits 3 and 4 of the left hand with disposable Ag/AgCl electrodes of 2 cm^2 contact area and an isotonic electrode cream, using 0.5 V constant voltage and a 6 Hz sampling rate. The SCL was controlled for drift due to progressive skin moistening and/or maceration (Sect. 2.2.6.1) by simultaneous application of new electrodes after the flight. No adjustment was made since the SCL downward drift did not exceed 8.2% on average. Artifacts were removed during the interactive signal evaluation (Sect. 2.3.4.1).

can easily get lost during in vivo exposure to phobic stimuli, where both EDA and HR might be substantially increased.

A severe complication that may come with anxiety disorders is the occurrence of *panic attacks*, which can appear at any time, even when anxious individuals are explicitly trying to relax. Psychophysiological concomitants of panic attacks were first described by Lader and Mathews (1970), among others large HR increases (30–50 bpm) and smaller but distinct SCL increases (3–12 µS). Roth, Wilhelm, and Trabert (1998) compared 14 patients with panic disorders (8 females, 6 males) and 15 control patients (9 females, 6 males; matched for age) during a 10 min relaxation period between two 4-min talking periods. Besides SC,[208] HR, skin temperature, and room temperature were continuously recorded. Six out of the 14 panic patients but none of their control counterparts reported that they had at least one panic attack during the testing. The SCL decrease from the talking to the relaxation period was significantly smaller for panic patients than for control patients, pointing to their greater inability to relax. However, their skin temperature increased significantly more, which would be a sign of greater relaxation. No HR differences emerged. Deviant from the control patients, panickers did not show an SCL decline during relaxation while having a greater increase in skin temperature. A more detailed look at the NS.SCR freq. by means of spectral analysis revealed high mean coherences between SC and HR, which were highest in panickers (0.92), less high in panic patients who did not panick during the session (0.85) and lowest in control patients (0.80). Since SC appeared to be a more valid indicator of panic attacks than HR, the authors suggested that the type of attacks reported by their patients differed considerably from panic attacks described in the literature. However, SC constituted a very useful measure of autonomic instability during periods when panic patients attempted to sit quiet.[209]

Mayer, Merckelbach, de Jong, and Leeuw (1999) tested the hypothesis that a phobic fear response may occur in phobic patients, even if they will not be able to fully evaluate the phobic stimulus. They showed 47 spider-phobic individuals and 41 control participants (all females) backwardly masked slides of spiders and nonphobic slides (flowers, mushrooms, and snakes) to prevent conscious identification. No convincing evidence was found for masked spider slides eliciting higher SCR amp. (recorded with standard methodology) in spider phobics compared to neutral control slides. This result contradicts the notion of Öhman and Soares (1994) that an unconscious "preattentive" analysis of phobic stimuli would be sufficient for

---

[208] Recorded with standard methodology from the middle phalanges of digits 3 and 4 with 2 cm² disposable Ag/AgCl electrodes. Amplitude criterion 0.02 µS.

[209] SRL, NS.SCR amp., and mean habituation rate discriminated between patients having anxiety disorders with and without panic attacks (Birket-Smith, Hasle, & Jensen, 1993). During anticipation of delivering a speech and other stressors, patients with panic disorders showed substantially higher SCLs and NS.SCRs compared to healthy controls (Braune, Albus, Fröhler, Höhn, & Scheibe, 1994). Compared to healthy controls, panic patients yielded significantly higher NS.SCR freq. during a series of performance tests (Dratcu & Bond, 1998).

eliciting fear responses in humans. In a PET study, Carlsson et al. (2004) demonstrated that when awareness of spider- or snake-phobic stimuli was prevented by experimental manipulation, only the amygdala was involved, whereas an affective processing network, including prefrontal areas, was added when a more elaborated processing was enabled. For the present author, it looks as if investigating phobic responses by means of their psychophysiological concomitants is rather susceptible to even slight variations in experimental settings.[210]

3.4.1.2   EDA in Psychopathic or Antisocial/Conduct Disorders

The term *psychopathy* has been used for a variety of nonpsychotic personality disorders characterized by affective and social disturbances (Checkley, 1964). Their main characteristic is an increased appearance of social conflicts (Hare, 1975), which had been traced back by Eysenck (1967) to their general lack of conditionability. Thus, psychopaths were located in the extravert-neurotic quadrant of Eysenck's personality dimension system (Sect. 3.3.1.1). In addition, psychopaths were supposed having specific deficits in passive avoidance learning, which were discussed by Lykken (1957) and Trasler (1973) within the framework of Mowrer's (1960) theory. According to this theoretical background, the contingency between the appearance of a socially unwanted behavior and its negative consequences cannot be learned by psychopaths, since their reduced ANS reactivity prevents them from developing an unpleasant state of arousal which normally follows punishment (Sect. 3.1.3.1). One possible consequence of this lack could be that psychopaths are more prone to develop criminal behavior. Sometimes, research into psychopathy has been embedded in the broader category of antisocial behavior in general (Scarpa & Raine, 1997) or has been characterized as psychopathy/ sociopathy (Lorber, 2004).

Despite psychopathy being an interesting research field for the application of EDA in psychopathological research, results from different studies often cannot be easily compared because of problems existing within the diagnosis of psychopathy (Hare, 1978b; Siddle, 1977). Most investigators used questionnaires or rating scales, while several others relied on the appearance of delinquent and/or socially aggressive behavior, sometimes combined with imprisonment or hospitalization, to classify individuals as psychopaths, sociopaths, antisocials, or as individuals with conduct disorder. Furthermore, some authors proposed a differentiation between primary and secondary psychopaths, the latter ones having feelings of guilt or shame which the primary ones do not have (Blackburn, 1983). Such additional distinctions may further complicate the applicability of results obtained with this clinical group.

---

[210] Another anxiety-related disorder in which EDA has been used for probing conditioning is posttraumatic stress disease (e.g., Orr et al., 2006).

Observable Electrodermal Phenomena

A comprehensive review of earlier studies on EDA and psychopathy, which compared EDA in psychopaths with that of controls under various experimental conditions, had been performed by Hare (1978b). He concluded that there was a general tendency for *electrodermal hypoactivity* in psychopaths; an effect that appeared more clearly for the EDL than for the NS.EDR freq. However, under conditions of overstimulation (e.g., in situations with aversive elements) or understimulation (e.g., boring or monotonous situations), the difference between groups became more prominent. This was due to a further decrease of tonic EDA in psychopaths, whereas nonpsychopathic individuals showed an increase or no change in tonic EDA. Scarpa and Raine (1997) supplemented Hare's review by looking at more recent studies, confirming the evidence for electrodermal under-arousal in antisocial individuals, particularly in public offenders, conduct disorders, and nonviolent criminals. Low SCLs might be already present at early age in individuals who exert disruptive behavior as adolescents. This was shown by van Bokhoven, Matthys, van Goozen, and van Engeland (2005) in a follow-up study with 47 adolescents (5 girls, 42 boys; mean age about 17 years) who were diagnosed as disruptive behavior disorder children at the age of 7–12 years (mean age 10).[211] The resting SCL in childhood figured out to be an important predictor of poor adolescent outcome, rated either by participants or by their parents. The authors favor the so-called fearlessness theory, stating that low ANS activity as manifested in a low SCL counteracts the possible effect of social punishment, thus facilitating poor socialization and adolescent disruptive behavior.

In addition to hypoactivity, *electrodermal hyporeactivity* had also been observed in psychopaths. Borkovec (1970), who could not observe significantly lower SCLs[212] during resting and stimulation periods in 19 psychopathic compared to 21 neurotic and 26 normal juvenile delinquents, found instead significantly lowered SCR amp.[213] following the first stimulus of a series of 21 tones (1 kHz, with "moderate intensity") in psychopaths. Since no group differences were observed during the rest of the tone series, the electrodermal hyporeactivity of psychopaths seemed to be restricted to the first OR, not including a faster habituation. However, such a reduced OR to the first presentation of a nonsignaled stimulus could not be confirmed in 9 of 10 additional studies with psychopaths (summarized by Raine & Venables, 1984). Scarpa and Raine (1997) reported that only 2 out of 8 studies

---

[211] Since SCL data were not collected for 16 participants during their diagnosis and subsequent treatment, the results are based only on 31 participants. The recording method was not explicitly mentioned.

[212] Recorded with CV of about 0.5 V, using gold-plated dry electrodes attached by plastic tape to the first and third finger of the right hand. The volar finger sites were soap-washed, dried, and alcohol cleaned prior to attachment.

[213] SCR amp. was obtained as difference between the SCL at the peak and the SCL immediately before SCR onset.

using auditory stimuli ranging from 90 to 120 dB evidenced lower electrodermal reactivity in antisocial individuals. Some of the contradictory results in this field might have been partly due to the method of EDA parameter extraction. This had been demonstrated by Hare (1975) who compared two different procedures of range correction (Sect. 2.3.3.4), using results from one of his earlier studies. While applying (2.19a) did not yield significant results, (2.19b), which uses the maximum response given through the experiment, led to significantly lower range-corrected SCR amp. in psychopaths, both to the first tone and to a dishabituation tone within a series of 80 dB stimuli.

Other factors such as stimulus intensity and/or personality characteristics may also play an important role in this kind of research. In a study performed with 24 psychopathic and 40 nonpsychopathic delinquents, Hare (1978a) demonstrated that electrodermal hyporeactivity in psychopaths appeared only during high-intense, fast rise time stimulation, and only in a psychopathic subgroup scoring low in the socialization scale of the CPI (Gough, 1969). Six tones (1 kHz, 1 s) from each of five intensities (80–120 dB, in 10 dB steps) were presented in counterbalanced order, three with a fast rise time (10 μs) and three with a slow rise time (25 ms), while SC was recorded bilaterally with standard methodology, however, using hypertonic cream (5% NaCl). For the EDA measured at the right hand, the interaction of tone intensity with socialization was significant, whereas the interaction with psychopathy was not, which indicates that socialization has at least as important an influence on EDA hyporeactivity to aversive stimulation as psychopathy may exert. Scarpa and Raine (1997) came to the conclusion that a reduced ED-OR appears to be specific to a subgroup of antisocial psychopaths with schizoid or schizotypal features.

Raine, Venables, and Williams (1990a) reported data from a 15-year follow-up with the sample of Raine and Venables (1981). By this time, 17 of the 101 participants were found to possess a criminal record, differing from the noncriminals in school status and residential characteristics but not in occupations and only slightly in age. Fifteen years before, the criminals-to-become had shown a significantly lower resting HR, lower NS.SCR freq. taken from both hands, and more slow-frequency EEG activity than those who did not become criminals. The findings for the SCL were in the same direction but not significant. These results provided evidence for the role of both ANS and CNS underarousal in the development of criminal behavior. In addition, Raine, Venables, and Williams (1990b) presented data from a 9-year follow-up of the ANS reactivity data reported by Raine and Venables (1984). As compared to the 84 noncriminals, the 17 participants of the earlier study who later became criminals had shown significantly smaller SCRs and smaller HR acceleratory and deceleratory responses 9 years before. These results strengthen the evidence for ANS hyporeactivity, in addition to hypoactivity, being a possible marker for the development of criminal (antisocial) behavior.

Electrodermal hyporeactivity in psychopaths appears to be influenced to a great extent by motivational and activational states. In comparison to controls, psychopaths show lower EDA amp. during experimental procedures that are either monotonous or threatening (i.e., inducing either under- or overarousal), while moderately exciting situations (i.e., those that induce medium arousal levels) do not evoke such differences (Hare, 1978b). For example, Jutai and Hare (1983) could not find differences in SCL (recorded with standard methodology) between 11 psychopaths and 10 normal controls during video games. It is likely that psychopaths tend to be drowsiness-prone in boring situations, thus showing electrodermal hypoactivity as well as hyporeactivity, while their EDA is indistinguishable from normal individuals during motivating conditions which result in optimal arousal (Sect. 3.2.1.1). Under threatening conditions which induce high arousal, EDRs of psychopaths will decrease again, maybe due to their lower susceptibility to punishment. Another interpretation could be appearance of "sensory rejection" (Lacey & Lacey, 1974) as characterized by an increase in HR together with cortical deactivation. Indeed, cardiovascular activity has been observed to be markedly increased in psychopaths who anticipate aversive stimuli, while the anticipatory EDR is reduced (Blackburn, 1983; Hare, 1978a). This is also in accordance with the hypothetical BIS/BAS antagonism and its EDA/HR correlates (Sect. 3.2.1.2), which will be discussed in the next section.

Presumably, electrodermal hyporeactivity in psychopaths plays also a role in their *poor electrodermal conditionability*, which could be inferred from several studies using conditioning to electric shocks, as summarized by Hare (1975). Psychopaths do not readily develop conditioned EDRs, which is especially apparent in case of an aversive UCS (see Sect. 3.1.2.1). The question whether the poor conditionability of psychopaths, which had been predominantly shown in already delinquent individuals, is a cause or a consequence of the development of antisocial behavior has been investigated in a prospective study by Loeb and Mednick (1977). Sixty male and 44 female juveniles underwent a conditioning procedure prior to any observed delinquent behavior, using a 4.5 s 96 dB irritating noise as UCS that appeared 0.5 s after CS onset (a 1 kHz, 54 dB tone). A habituation phase with eight presentations of the CS was followed by 14 partial reinforcement trials (9 CS-UCS pairings and 5 CS alone trials), and a generalization testing with two tones of different frequencies terminated the session. Ten years later, 7 of the male participants had become delinquent. A parallel group of 7 nondelinquent participants from the original sample was used as control. Comparison of both groups yielded lower SCR amp.[214] in participants who became delinquent later during all phases of the testing procedure that was performed 10 years earlier, especially in the initial UCR, and delinquents showed a reduced amount of conditioning. In addition, stimulus generalization was observed in only one of the later delinquents. Therefore, the authors concluded that lowered autonomic reactivity, as measured by EDA, may have contributed to the development of an antisocial personality in their delinquents, instead of being a consequence of their antisocial behavior.

---

[214] Recorded with 7 mm diameter zinc electrodes and zinc sulfate electrolyte, using a Wheatstone bridge. The polarity of the 1.5 V reference was reversed every 1.2 s.

Raine and Venables (1981) investigated the possible role of poor socialization for a reduced conditionability of psychopaths in a correlational study with 101 fifteen-year-old male children. Besides teacher's ratings of refractory school behavior, several self-report measures of socialization, including the appropriate CPI scale, Eysenck's psychoticism scale, and the disinhibition scale of the SSS (Sect. 3.3.2.1), were obtained from each participant to form a factor-analytic socialization score. In a classical conditioning paradigm with partial reinforcement, 15 CSs (65 dB tones, 1 kHz, 10 s) were paired with 10 UCSs (105 dB tones, 1 kHz, 1 s) while SC was recorded.[215] For each presentation of CS without UCS, the mean magnitudes of FIR, SIR, and TOR (Sect. 3.1.2.1 "Components of EDR Conditioning") were correlated with the teacher's rating and the socialization score. Correlations were generally low, and a relationship between undersocialization and poor conditionability appeared only in higher-class children, whereas this relationship was reversed in lower-class children. However, the highest correlation obtained was $r = -0.27$ (between TOR and socialization score), which to some extent obscured the discussion of differential effects of the EDR components on socialization.

Raine and Venables (1984) reported correlations from the same sample between the first electrodermal OR obtained in a habituation series to nine of the above-mentioned CSs and their socialization score, all of them being negative and statistically significant, albeit low (up to $r = -0.41$). An additional analysis based on categories of electrodermal responding and habituating showed that 81% of the nonresponders were antisocials, while 80% of the nonhabituators were prosocials. In a second analysis, groups of prosocial nonresponders, antisocial responders, and antisocial nonresponders were formed, using the original SSS subscales and measures of "schizoid" tendency as personality measures, together with EDA results and an antisocial index. Antisocial nonresponders showed significantly more "schizoid" tendencies but not more sensation seeking. Therefore, Raine and Venables hypothesized that *electrodermal nonresponding* may be a biologically predisposition factor in antisocial personality, as it is supposed to be in schizophrenic disorders (Sect. 3.4.2.2).[216]

In addition to electrodermal hyporeactivity, as shown by reduced EDR amp., a *prolonged EDR recovery time* in psychopaths has been regarded as a consistent result in the literature (Hare, 1978b; Scarpa & Raine, 1997; Siddle, 1977). Such a prolonged recovery time had been observed in the prospective study performed by Loeb and Mednick (1977) described earlier. However, Hare (1978a) in his above-

---

[215] Bilateral recordings with Ag/AgCl electrodes of 4.5 mm diameter, filled with 0.5% KCl in agar-agar cream, using 0.5 V constant voltage. Amplitude criterion: 0.05 μS.

[216] Although schizophrenia has been the domain for electrodermal nonresponding, this phenomenon is clearly not specific to schizophrenia (Iacono, 1985; see Sect. 3.4.2.2). Raine, Bihrle, Venables, Mednick, and Pollock (1999) assessed SC-OR and schizotypy in 134 males during adolescence. Criminal offending and alcohol abuse were assessed 12 years later. Schizotypic individuals who became criminals had been characterized by deficits in ED-OR during adolescence.

mentioned study using stimuli between 80 and 120 dB could only find an increased SCR rec.t/2 following the 120 dB tones with short rise times, which can be characterized as aversive stimuli producing a startle response (Sect. 3.1.1.2). Two different explanations may be given for a prolonged EDR recovery time in psychopaths (Hare, 1978b):

1. It indicates a "tuning out" or attenuating of sensory input having aversive qualities (Hare, 1978a). This is in accordance with Edelberg (1970, 1972b) who suggested slow recovery being indicative of a DR. Furthermore, Venables (1975) hypothezised that a long SCR rec.t/2 is related to a "closed gate" state of attention, which is due to a predominance of the amygdala's excitatory influence on subcortical information processing (Table 3.1, Sect. 3.1.3.1). This in turn may point to psychopaths having deficits in their septo-hippocampal system (Sect. 3.2.1.2), preventing them from successful conditioning to punishment and from showing an appropriate ED-OR to novel stimuli.
2. It could be indicative of a delay in passive avoidance learning (Mednick, 1974). According to the two-process theory of Mowrer (1960), a reduction of anticipatory fear might act as reinforcer for an inhibition of antisocial behavior. Thus, a quick diminishing of anticipatory fear enables effective avoidance learning. Long SCR recoveries could be regarded as an indicator for a slow diminishing of anticipatory fear responses, thus indicating less successful learning to avoid antisocial behavior.

According to Hare (1978b), the observation that prolonged SCR rec.t/2 in psychopaths only appear during really aversive stimulation is in accordance with Mednick's hypothesis as formulated under (2). However, Hare questioned that the recovery rate to simple stimuli could be predictive of the recovery rate during avoidance learning.[217]

Since psychopaths also show lower EDR amp. in comparison with normal controls, the relationships found by Bundy and Fitzgerald (1975) between EDR rec.t/2 and amplitudes of preceding responses should be taken into account when discussing EDR recovery times in conditioning studies (Sect. 2.5.2.5). This was taken into consideration by Levander, Schalling, Lidberg, Bartfai, and Lidberg (1980) who studied the electrodermal habituation of 24 imprisoned delinquents during a series of 21 tones (1 kHz, 93 dB).[218] There was a significant correlation ($r = 0.47$) between

---

[217] The term "recovery rate" used in this context does not correspond to the same term used for recovery speed, which is the reciprocal of EDR recovery time (see sections 2.3.1.3 under "Recovery Parameters" and 2.3.3.3).

[218] EDA was recorded with Ag/AgCl electrodes of 9 mm diameter with 0.9% NaCl cream from sites of the left hand's second and third finger, prior cleaned with an ethanol (75%)/acetone (25%) mixture. The authors used a combined current density (9 µA/cm^2)/voltage (2.7 V) limiting system. If necessary, the SCR rec.t/2 values were extrapolated by the method of curve matching (Sect. 2.3.1.3 "Recovery Parameters"). Since the mean recovery time of the EDR to the first tone was conspicuously longer than those following the other tones, the latter ones were averaged, and analyses were performed separately for the first recovery and the mean of the others. The amplitude criterion for NS.SCRs was 0.0043 log µS.

inverted scores of the CPI socialization scale and the mean recovery time of trials 2–20. Since this recovery time showed a significant negative relationship to the mean NS.SCR amp. ($r = -0.65$), the Bundy effect (Sect. 2.5.2.5) was adopted by these authors as a possible alternative explanation to the DR interpretation which has been formulated under (1).

Electrodermal laterality effects (Sect. 3.1.4) have been also observed in psychopaths. In particular, the prolonged SCR rec.t/2 observed by Hare (1978a) did only appear at the left-hand sites. This was interpreted by Hare (1978b) as pointing to a dysfunction of the temporal-frontal limbic system of the left (i.e., dominant) hemisphere. However, this would only be a valid hypothesis in case of ipsilateral control of EDA, which is, however, still debated (Sect. 3.1.4.2).

A meta-analysis of 95 studies addressing the relationships between EDA and HR with aggression, psychopathy, and conduct disorders performed by Lorber (2004) highlighted the significance of ANS markers for the antisocial spectrum of psychopathology. Lower resting EDA was significantly associated with psychopathy/sociopathy. However, the effects were rather small. The same was true for EDRs to experimental conditions, whereas studies of adolescents yielded a (not significantly) smaller effect than those with adult psychopaths/sociopaths. The negative correlation between psychopathy/sociopathy and EDA during experimental tasks was evident only for stimuli with negative valence. Low resting EDA was reliably associated with conduct problems only in children but not in adolescents. A similar effect emerged when EDRs to experimental conditions were analyzed, but – contrarily to adult psychopaths – only when nonnegative stimuli were presented. The meta-analytic results confirmed the already described coherence between lower resting HR and conduct problems, both in children and in adults. No consistent association was found between psychopathy/sociopathy and HR, irrespective of the valence of experimental stimuli. Aggression appeared to be more tightly related to HR than to EDA. The strongest results concerned conduct problems in children, who had ANS patterns in common with adult aggressors (i.e., low resting HR) and psychopathic/sociopathic adults (i.e., low resting EDA).

In conclusion, Lorber (2004) pointed to the complexity of research in this area which requires further clarification. It is also still a matter of debate, what kind of theoretical modeling of ANS changes being observed in psychopaths would be most appropriate. Although psychophysiology offers unique possibilities not only for diagnosis but also for prognosis and treatment outcome control (Iacono, 1991), the pathology of the antisocial spectrum is still not fully anchored in neurophysiological modeling of psychophysiological changes.[219]

---

[219] Lower electrodermal activity/responsivity was also demonstrated in disruptive children (van Goozen, Matthys, Cohen-Kettenis, Buitelaar, & van Engeland, 2000) and for boys with conduct disorder (Herpertz et al., 2005).

Neurophysiological Considerations

In his review of the suggested biological bases of antisocial and aggressive behavior, Raine (2002) came to the conclusion that low resting HR constitutes the best replicated psychophysiological correlate of low autonomic functioning. However, as discussed in the previous section, certain EDA parameters may have a similar diagnostic value for psychopathy. This section will focus on explanations being anchored in neurophysiological considerations. Neurophysiological support for the relationships between psychopathic or antisocial behavior and EDA came from different sources. Hippocampal deficits, which may be caused by heredity, prenatal or perinatal factors (Mednick & Schulsinger, 1973), may account for a prolonged EDR recovery time (Table 3.1, Sect. 3.1.3.1) and also for a reduced NS.EDR freq. The latter can be regarded as being due to a malfunction of the septo-hippocampal BIS (Fig. 3.4, Sect. 3.2.1.2). According to Gray (1982), the BIS not only inhibits motor behavior but also increases attention as well as cognitive activity. Therefore, the supposed hippocampal dysfunction in psychopaths fits well into Eysenck's classification of that particular group into the extravert-neurotic quadrant (Fig. 3.4, Sect. 3.3.1.1), since extraverts are regarded by Eysenck to show a lowered cortical activation. Here, a vicious circle could be in action, since a reduced cognitive analysis of possible consequences of antisocial behavior may be a cause as well as a consequence of a BIS dysfunction.

Raine et al. (1995) recorded NS.SCR freq.[220] in a prospective study with 101 unselected 15-year-old male children. After 14 years, three groups of 17 participants each were formed: one group being registered for criminal offences; one group that had been juvenile offenders but did not perform crimes; and a control group that had been neither antisocial as adolescents nor criminal as adults. Criminals revealed significantly less NS.SCR freq. during resting conditions than both other groups and also showed less ED-ORs in a series of nine 1 kHz tones (10 s, 65 dB). Since low ANS arousal in adolescents seemed to be a predispositional factor for becoming an adult criminal, the authors concluded that high ANS arousal might be a protective factor against the development of criminal behavior.[221] Such an interpretation is in line with Eysenck's (1967) notion that low arousal may be a predisposition for antisocial and criminal behavior. Raine (2002) also pondered the possible role of stimulation seeking in the development of antisocial behavior, since low arousal might be experienced as an unpleasant state (Sect. 3.1.2.1). In addition, Raine (2002) discussed possible structural deficits in adult antisocial individuals in connection with failure to produce anticipatory autonomic responses in VMPFC damage patients (Sect. 3.1.3.3) and the suggested role of the prefrontal cortex in conditioning (Hugdahl, 1998). The underarousal hypothesis fits well to observations that methylphenidate which increases CNS arousal has been demonstrated

---

[220] Recorded bilaterally from the medial phalanges of the second and third fingers with 0.45 cm diameter Ag/AgCl electrodes and 0.5% potassium chloride in 2% agar-agar as electrolyte. Amplitude criterion 0.05 μS.

[221] The independence of this sample from the one used by Raine et al. (1990a) remains unclear.

to reduce conduct disorder (e.g., Klein et al., 1997). Thus, the suggested biological deficits that may underlie antisocial/conduct disorders might be effectively treated by means of procedures establishing an enduring increase of general arousal (Sect. 3.2.1.1) in adolescents.

As Fowles (1988) suggested, a weak BIS should result in an inability to inhibit responses which may be followed by punishment (Sect. 3.2.1.2). Furthermore, Checkley's (1964) characterization of psychopaths fits very well into the pattern one would expect from a weak aversive motivational system with appetitive motivation being quite normal.[222] The role of motivation in poorer conditionability of psychopaths was also stressed by Hare (1978b), pointing to the possible influence of cognitive factors on conditioning (Sect. 3.1.2.1 "Cognitive vs. Noncognitive View of EDR Conditioning" and 3.1.3.1). Accordingly, psychopaths may lack motivation for following the intention of a learning experiment, thus showing a deficit in awareness of the particular contingencies. Indeed, psychopaths especially have problems with differential electrodermal conditioning (i.e., learning to respond with a higher EDR amp. to a CS+ as compared to a CS−; see Sect. 3.1.2.1 "Components of EDR Conditioning"). A lack of general activation may also play a role, since cardiovascular and electrodermal ORs as well as habituation rates are increased in psychopaths (Table 3.1, Sect. 3.1.3.1), which goes with an increased amount of EEG-theta activity observed during drowsiness. Furthermore, conditionability of psychopaths may be increased by the introduction of unspecific stimulation (Hare, 1978b).

Electrodermal hyporeactivity in anticipation of aversive stimuli has been consistently found being a correlate of psychopathy and aggressive conduct disorder (for a summary, see Lykken, 1995).[223] If, as hypothesized above, such a hyporeactivity would reflect a weak BIS, psychopaths should score low in anxiety and high in behavioral disinhibition (Fowles, 2000). Fowles (2000) reviewed the literature on the connection between EDA, startle eyeblink (see Footnote 48 in Sect. 3.1.2.1 "Recent Developments in EDR Conditioning"), and two possible components of psychopathy, i.e., a primary psychopathy being characterized by a specific deficit in anxiety, and an antisocial disinhibitory behavioral component of psychopathy. His aim was addressing the nagging problem whether antisocial personality traits obtained by questionnaire data (Sect. 3.3.1) and psychophysiological concomitants of neurobehavioral processes such as determined by BIS activity could be reliably connected. Other than startle eyeblink, electrodermal hyporeactivity seemed to be related to both low anxiety and disinhibition, which constitute behavioral concomitants of the BIS. However, Fowles also discussed the

---

[222] Such a motivational imbalance was also mentioned as a key factor in psychopathy by Arnett (1997) in his review on ANS responsivity in psychopaths.

[223] Fung et al. (2005) observed reduced anticipatory SCRs in 65 psychopathy-prone 16-year-old males compared to 65 controls, demonstrating that the anticipatory electrodermal hyporesponsivity of psychopathic adults is an ANS impairment which may be already present in adolescents and could predispose individuals to adult psychopathy.

possibility that electrodermal hyporeactivity as observed in psychopaths might be a correlate of a broader executive function deficit. For example, there is a striking similarity between psychopaths and VMPFC patients[224] with respect to both a lack of anticipatory SCRs and normal SCRs to the actual occurrence of both reward and punishment (Fowles, 2000, p. 184). Such a possible connection between the theoretical concepts of BIS and somatic markers (Sect. 3.1.3.3) might open an interesting approach into neuropsychological deficits that may cause psychopathic, antisocial or conduct disorders, in addition to the already discussed closed attentional gate hypothesis as described in Sect. 3.1.3.1.

The relationship between electrodermal hyporeactivity and BIS-related personality characteristics may already be present at early age. In their follow-up study with 99 children (49 girls, 50 boys) described in Sect. 2.4.3.1, Fowles, Kochanska, and Murray (2000) found support for such a hypothesis. Correlations between low SCL on one side and lack of fearful temperament and poor inhibitory control on the other side, both assessed by observational test batteries, were significant, albeit modest, at the age of 4 years ($r = 0.21$ and $r = 0.25$, respectively), but not as early as in the toddler age of 2.

According to Fowles' (1980) BIS/BAS model, psychopaths should not only have a deficit in their BIS but also have an increased BAS activity, the psychophysiological concomitant of which is HR (Sect. 3.2.1.2). Indeed, when an unavoidable aversive stimulation is present, psychopaths have been demonstrated to not only show electrodermal hyporeactivity but also an increase in HR, while nonpsychopaths were more likely to respond with a marked increase of EDA but with only small HR changes (Hare, 1978b; Fowles, 1980). Arnett and Newman (2000), in an attempt to partly replicate the Gomez and McLaren (1997) study (Sect. 3.1.2.2), performed two experiments (i.e., a reward and an active avoidance experiment) with criminal offenders (Caucasian prison inmates) between age 18 and 40 ($N = 58$ in the first and $N = 64$ in the second study). In both experiments, EDA (recorded with standard methodology) and HR were recorded while participants performed a continuous performance task (Fowles et al., 1982). In the first experiment, the NS. SCR freq. increased significantly from the reward-only to the mixed-incentive phases, which was consistent with the BIS/BAS hypothesis. However, as in the Gomez and McLaren study, no correlation was found between these changes and anxiety measured by a questionnaire ($r = 0.05$). Also consistent with the BIS/BAS predictions, HR yielded a significant increase from the nonincentive to the reward-only phases, which was significantly correlated to an increase in RT ($r = 0.46$).

---

[224] Damasio, Tranel, and Damasio (1990) observed reduced EDA to social stimuli in 5 patients with sociopathic behavior who had lesions in the VMPFC (Sect. 3.1.3.3), in comparison to six brain-damaged and five normal controls who had no diagnosis of sociopathy. In a study combining fMRI with EDA, Raine, Lencz, Bihrle, LaCasse, and Colletti (2000) found both damage to gray and white matter in the prefrontal cortex plus lowered SC under stress compared to healthy controls in 21 male neurological patients who developed a pseudopsychopathic personality, thus relating subtle structural deficits in the prefrontal cortex to antisocial behavior and electrodermal hyporeactivity.

In experiment 2, participants showed a significant increase in SCR amp. to the punishment cues. However, there was no significant change in NS.SCR freq. from the active-avoidance to the mixed-incentive phases, which was contrary to the hypothesis. Anxiety was also not correlated to the change in NS.SCR freq. A significant increase of HR from the nonincentive practice phase to the active-avoidance phases was observed, which fits to the BIS/BAS hypothesis. In general, the BIS/BAS dichotomy may be a suitable theoretical background for a possible explanation of psychopathic behavior and its origin (see the end of Sect. 3.2.1.2). However, the model seems not being invariant to changes in experimental settings.

3.4.1.3 EDA in Depressive Patients

The clinical picture of major depression, as described by the DSM IV-R (American Psychiatric Association, 2000), is characterized by psychological symptoms (e.g., dysphoric mood, feelings of worthlessness or guilt, and thoughts of death, including suicidal ideation), major psychomotoric changes (agitation or retardation), and ANS disturbances (e.g., changes in sleep, weight, loss of energy, and various vegetative complaints). Major or unipolar depression is characterized by the absence of manic episodes which in turn appear in bipolar affective disorders. Stern and Janes (1973) reviewed several older studies that used EDA to differentiate depressed patients from normal controls, or subgroups of depressives from each other. Their conclusion was that spontaneous EDA as well as electrodermal responsivity may be reduced in depressive patients, except in those who are classified as agitated.

Electrodermal *hypoactivity* and *hyporeactivity* in depressed patients have been consistently found in subsequent studies (Carney, Hong, Kulkarni, & Kapila, 1981; Donat & McCullough, 1983; Lenhart, 1985; Williams, Iacono, & Remick, 1985). According to Iacono et al. (1983) as well as Iacono et al. (1984a), reductions of SCL, SCR amp., and NS.SCR freq. can be regarded as reliable signs of depressive disorders, since the appropriate differences between normals and depressive patients persist even after the patients having received clinical treatment. In their summary on the significance of electrodermal hypoactivity in depression, Sponheim, Allen, and Iacono (1995, p. 225) summarized the hitherto available results as follows: ". . . depressed patients, whether acutely ill or in remission, show electrodermal hypoactivation. This psychophysiological anomaly is present in both unipolar and bipolar disorders, is independent of changes in clinical state, is stable over time, and does not appear to depend on experimental conditions or stimulus characteristics. It is seen in subsyndromal individuals in nonclinical populations. Among depressed patients, low levels of electrodermal activity are evident in those with more severe disorders and with the type of phenomenology often associated with depressions believed to have a strong bipolar component."

Iacono et al. (1983) recorded SC bilaterally with standard methodology from 26 unipolar (20 males, 6 females) and 24 bipolar (8 females, 16 males) depressives as well as from 46 normal controls (8 females, 38 males) during a series of 17 tones

(1 kHz, 86 dB), including a dishabituation tone of 500 Hz at trial 16, together with an ignore instruction (as recommended by Iacono & Lykken, 1979). No lateral asymmetries were observed in any group (Sect. 3.1.4.3). Unipolar and bipolar depressives revealed 58 and 54% nonresponders, respectively, as compared to 24% in the normal group. In both patient groups, habituation rate (as assessed by the number of trials to three consecutive missing responses; Sect. 3.1.1.3) was faster, the maximum individual SCR amp. was lower and the dishabituation responses were smaller as compared to the control group. Furthermore, average SCLs preceding the tones as well as resting SCLs were significantly lower in patients. Using 6 µS as a cutoff value, 96 and 79% of the patients with unipolar and bipolar disorders, respectively, fell below that score, compared with only 54% of the normal control group. Twenty-nine of the depressives and 23 of the controls participated 1 year later in the study of Iacono et al. (1984a). They were exposed to eight 86 dB tones, twelve 105 dB tones, eight familiar sounds that reached a peak intensity of 105 dB, and a balloon burst test, while EDA was recorded as in the year before. The patients' electrodermal hypoacitivity and hyporeactivity could be fully confirmed, showing statistically significant reliabilities between $r = 0.45$ and $r = 0.69$ (Sect. 2.5.2.1).

No influence of an exposure to a series of electroconvulsive shocks for treatment purposes on EDA could be demonstrated by Dawson, Schell, and Catania (1977) in 20 hospitalized depressed patients (16 females, 4 males). Compared to an age- and gender-matched group of nondepressed controls, the patients showed lower SCLs and smaller SCRs with longer latencies[225] before and after the shocks. Unexpectedly, electroconvulsive treatment significantly lowered the SCL in depressives, but neither changes in EDA nor changes in HR were related to differences in subsequent clinical improvement. Storrie, Doerr, and Johnson (1981) could not demonstrate an influence of psychopharmacological treatment with antidepressants or antipsychotic medication on EDA in depressives. During resting and during performance of three valsalva maneuvers, both SCL and SCR amp. (recorded with standard methodology) yielded lower values in 13 male depressed patients as compared to 10 healthy male controls, irrespective of the treatment.

Two systematic investigations into the usefulness of SCL as a sensitive marker for depression were performed by Ward, Doerr, and Storrie (1983) with 12 female and 21 male patients, and by Ward and Doerr (1986) with 22 female and 15 male patients, meeting various criteria for unipolar depression. The control group in the 1983 study consisted of 33 female and 38 male participants, whereas in the 1986 study, 204 females and 201 males served as controls. SCL was recorded bilaterally with standard methodology and related to electrode area (Sect. 2.3.3.1). The mean log SCLs during the 15th and 16th min of the baseline resting period served as EDA

---

[225] Recorded as SR with a constant current of 6.4 µA/cm², using Beckman Ag/AgCl electrodes filled with K–Y gel. Recordings were performed during 5 min of resting, a free word-association test, stimulation with tones and bells of moderate intensity, a differential classical conditioning, and an RT task. EDA was expressed in terms of SC parameters.

measures. Since no significant laterality effects appeared, results were solely reported from the nondominant hand.

In both studies, SCLs were significantly lower in patients than in controls. In addition, there was a significant main effect of gender in the 1983 study, where females displayed lower SCLs than males (which is quite unusual; see Sect. 2.4.3.2). However, such a difference was observed in the 1986 study for patients only. Therefore, Ward and Doerr (1986) proposed the use of separate cutoff scores for classifying females (<3.0 $\mu S/cm^2$) and males (<4.8 $\mu S/cm^2$) as criteria for depression. Using these scores, 90% of patients and controls could be correctly classified. While the patient/nonpatient dichotomy had been confounded with age in the 1983 study, the 1986 study yielded neither main effects of nor interactions with age, which confirmed that results on EDA and depression cannot be generally attributed to age effecting EDA (Sect. 2.4.3.1). The additionally lowered SCL in patients who underwent repeated depressive episodes found in the 1983 study must be treated with caution, since the distribution of gender in that particular group was different compared to the rest of the patients. In accordance with earlier results, the 1986 study did not yield significant differences in mean SCLs between depressive subgroups (e.g., patients with or without dexamethasone suppression, being classified as endogenous or nonendogenous, and being medicated or nonmedicated).[226]

Marked differences between subgroups of depressed patients had been observed earlier by Lader and Wing (1969), comparing 17 agitated (10 females, 7 males) and 13 retarded depressives (9 females, 4 males) with 35 normal controls (matched to depressed participants of the same gender). As compared to controls, retarded depressives showed a lower SCL and fewer NS.SCRs,[227] while agitated depressives yielded higher scores in both tonic EDA measures. Furthermore, the habituation rate obtained from a series of 20 tones (100 dB, 1 kHz, 1 s) was much faster in agitated depressives than in controls. Slopes for retarded depressives were not calculated, since they gave only few responses. In contrast to Lader and Wing, Dawson et al. (1977), in their study described above, could not find differences in SCLs between 6 predominantly agitated and 6 retarded participants in their depressive patient sample. Ward and Doerr (1986) pointed to the possibility that the failure of confirming the results of Lader and Wing in subsequent reports could be partly due to the diagnosis of depression being more broadly defined in Britain than it is within DSM III-R.

---

[226] As an exception, EDA has also been found to be higher in depressive patients than in controls. In a study with 18 patients suffering from major depression (9 of each gender), who had not taken any medication for at least 10 days, and 18 controls (6 females, 12 males), Guinjoan, Bernabó, and Cardinali (1995) reported significantly higher NS.SPR amp. in patients while raising from lying to standing and during handgrip exercise, but not during other exercises such as hyperventilation, cold pressor test, and mental arithmetic. The authors interpreted their results being due to an altered sympathetic/parasympathetic balance in depressives.

[227] Recorded with 9.5 mm diameter double-element lead electrodes unipolarly (abraded arm site above the elbow vs. thumb), using a 0.05 M NaCl electrolyte and 14 $\mu A/cm^2$ constant current.

Differences in EDA between subtypes of depressive patients were investigated by Williams et al. (1985). Thirty-six patients were classified as unipolar (20 females, 7 males) or bipolar (5 females, 4 males) depressives using DSM III-R criteria. No differences between the subtypes were found in SCLs and in SCRs during presentation of stimuli series with low and high intensity.[228] This result was in accordance with Iacono et al. (1983), Iacono et al. (1984a) who observed that remitted unipolar depressives did not differ in EDA from bipolar patients. However, further classification of patients according to their psychomotor activity and dexamethasone suppression revealed that psychomotor normal (nonretarded, nonagitated) depressives had significantly higher SCLs than psychomotor retarded depressives. Diminished tonic EDA in retarded depressive patients, as observed also by Lapierre and Butter (1980), can be regarded as a reliable psychophysiological result with respect to subtypes of depression.

Furthermore, EDA may also be useful in determining vulnerability to depressive states in normal individuals. Lenhart (1985) selected 20 participants with risk and 20 participants without risk for depression by means of questionnaire data, an equal number of each gender, from a total of 278 undergraduates. SCLs during resting and SCRs following 20 presentations of 75 dB tones (1 kHz, 2 s) were recorded with standard methodology. No significant group differences emerged in any tonic or phasic EDA parameter. However, when SCR magnitudes were obtained by averaging every four trials, thus reducing the effect of no-response trials (Sect. 2.3.4.2), controls showed a significantly greater mean response than did the subsyndromal high-risk depressive group. Whether or not electrodermal hypoactivity may be used to identify individuals at risk for depression seems questionable, since it is not specific for depression and has not been observed in relatives of depressive patients (Sponheim et al., 1995).

In a series of studies performed in Germany, Heimann (1969, 1978, 1979, 1980) attempted to differentiate depressed from neurotic patients and healthy controls by means of their electrodermal response type. Based on an activation concept as proposed by Claridge (1967), Heimann regarded the EDL as an indicator for tonic activation, while EDR amp. and frequencies were supposed to be dependent on the action of an arousal modulation system (Sect. 3.2.1.1). According to Heimann, agitated depressives can be characterized by an increased tonic EDA (EDL as well as NS.EDR freq.), by responding more regularly to external stimulation, by showing delayed habituation, and by easier conditionability, in contrast to retarded depressives, as already observed by Lader and Wing (1969). However, as Heimann (1969) could show in a sample of 100 depressed patients, agitated and retarded syndromes are not completely independent, since patients classified as agitated also may express symptoms being characteristic of retarded depressives.

---

[228] 1 kHz, 1 s tones of either 85 or 105 dB; 10 and 12 stimuli, respectively; ISI 20–40 s. SC was recorded bilaterally with standard methodology; SCL measured immediately before each tone and averaged; SCR was obtained within 1–3 s after stimulus onset, with an amplitude criterion of 0.05 µS.

Heimann (1979) suggested that the report of subjective anxiety and psychomotor restlessness appearing in agitated depressives does not form a part of the original depressive syndrome, but is instead a reaction to the patient's general depressive state.

Heimann (1978) used factor analyses to obtain the above-mentioned group specific EDA patterns. As EDA parameters, SRL and NS.SRR freq. during resting and during different active and passive test situations (e.g., inspiration, habituation to ten 80 dB, 1 kHz tones, tone-noise conditioning, flash discrimination, RT-task, word association) were obtained from a total of 277 depressed and depressed-anxious patients, 55 of whom belonged to the category of primary affective disorders, and from 73 healthy age-matched controls. Factor analyses for each of these groups yielded a factor structure similar to the two above-mentioned activation factors explaining 70% of the total variance. A stepwise discriminant analysis yielded 84% correct separation of the normals from 73 matched subjects out of the patient group, when a set of ten variables including HR and respiration rate during resting was used. In another study, habituation to ten 80 dB tones had been used by Heimann (1979) to compare depressives with 24 nondepressed neurotics and 32 normals. Frequency distributions of a criterion measure for the end of habituation process (Sect. 3.1.1.3) were similar in the two latter groups, since most subjects did not show complete habituation after ten stimulus presentations, while the 297 depressed patients showed a completely different J-shaped distribution.

It seems questionable whether electrodermal hyporeactivity together with faster habituation can be regarded as being specific to depression, since subgroups of schizophrenics also show characteristic electrodermal hyporeactivity (Sect. 3.4.2.2). An interesting hypothesis on the difference between nonresponding in depressives and schizophrenics has been developed by Bernstein et al. (1988) who found similar patterns in SCR nonresponding but differences in finger pulse volume between both groups. Since depressives showed intact ORs in the finger pulse amplitude measure, their deficit in electrodermal responsivity may be due to their possible deficit in peripheral cholinergic mediation, thus having a different origin as in schizophrenics.

Heimann (1980) pointed to the general diagnostic value of electrodermal measures, not only for differentiating between subtypes of depressive and schizophrenic illnesses but also for possible specificity of the underlying neurophysiological disorders. With respect to this, inhibition of electrodermal reactivity in depressed patients as well as in schizophrenic nonresponders might be due to a similar inhibiting mechanism in CNS information processing (Sect. 3.1.3.1). Such a possibility could also be demonstrated by a reduction of the pre- and postimperative negative variation in the depressive patient's EEG (Giedke & Bolz, 1980). According to Akiskal and McKinney (1975), decreased arousability of depressives following external stimulation, which shows up in a reduction or even in a lack of electrodermal ORs and/or in an increased habituation rate, can be neurophysiologically attributed to a dysfunction of the "reward" system, or to an imbalance between "reward" and "punishment" systems in favor of the latter (Sect. 3.2.1.2). Instead, schizophrenic nonresponding may reflect a secondary adaptation of the organism to the psychotic flooding which results from stimulation (Heimann, 1979).

However, it would hardly be possible to test this kind of hypothesis by the sole use of psychophysiological measures in standard paradigms applied to patient samples.

Electrodermal measures have also been used as indicators for remission from depressive episodes. Thorell and d'Elia (1988) recorded SC[229] during 37 tones (1 kHz, 90 dB, ISIs 20–80 s) in 28 patients during their depressive state and during remission, as well as in 28 matched and 39 unmatched healthy controls. All EDA parameters (SCL, SCR amp. to the first stimulus, NS.SCR freq., and an index of SC nonresponding) were significantly elevated during the follow-up period which lasted between 3 and 37 months (with 24 months average duration) and did not differ from those of the matched healthy controls. However, in depressed patients showing extreme electrodermal hyporesponsivity during their depressed episode, EDA did not reach the same values as in the controls, except for the SCL. Similar results were obtained for patients with major depressive episode and a history of recurrent depression. According to the authors, these results point to the possibility that electrodermal hyporesponsivity may constitute a marker for vulnerability to relapse, and probably also for the probability to attempt suicide.

Recently, Bob, Susta, Glaslova, Pavlat, and Raboch (2007) investigated the hypothesis that electrodermal dysfunctions in both depressives and schizophrenics might be linked to certain hemispheric dysfunctions, as briefly discussed at the end of Sect. 3.1.4.3. They recorded EDA[230] bilaterally during 2 min of resting from 35 depressive inpatients (22 females, 13 males), 35 adult paranoid schizophrenic outpatients (19 females, 16 males), and 35 healthy controls (20 females, 15 males), finding significant hypoarousal in depressive patients and significant hyperarousal in paranoid schizophrenics compared to healthy controls. In addition, the left hemisphere revealed significantly more hypoarousal in depressives and more hyperarousal in schizophrenics. No such asymmetry was observed in the control group, thus confirming appropriate results of Freixa i Baqué et al. (1984). However, as reported above, EDA asymmetry does not constitute an unequivocal observation in depressives.

3.4.2   Electrodermal Indices in Schizophrenia Research

The term *schizophrenia* is used for a heterogeneous group of psychotic disorders having some typical symptoms in common (e.g., delusions, hallucinations, as well as disturbances of affect, cognition, and behavior). Despite the use of EDA in schizophrenia research starting as early as toward the end of the nineteenth century, results were rather inconsistent and inconclusive until the early 1970s (Stern & Janes, 1973).

---

[229] Recorded with 0.5 V CC and transformed to in $\mu S/cm^2$.

[230] The type of EDA was not specified; 8 mm diameter Ag/AgCl electrodes filled with conductive cream were attached to the medial phalanges of both index and middle fingers.

However, since then, studies using EDA in schizophrenia research have yielded more unequivocal results, due to the use of standardized EDA recording procedures and to the introduction of subgroups such as electrodermal responders vs. nonresponders on the other hand (Sect. 3.4.2.2). Öhman (1981) conducted a comprehensive literature review, as did Spohn and Patterson (1979) within their literature review of psychophysiology in schizophrenia. Venables (1983) provided a thorough discussion of methodological problems within this area of research. More recently, Dawson and Schell (2002) reviewed the evidence that various dysfunctions in EDA in schizophrenia may carry prognostic information for the development of symptoms as well as social and occupational outcome.

Several neurophysiological hypotheses were offered to explain the well-replicated psychophysiological abnormalities of schizophrenics. For example, Epstein and Coleman (1970) suggested an inadequately modulating inhibition system in schizophrenics, causing them either to over- or underreact. The following two hypotheses formed by Venables are more specifically related to abnormalities in EDA:

1. There is some evidence for disturbances in limbic structures (especially in the hippocampus and in the amygdala) or limbic transmitter systems (dopaminergic and cholinergic fibers) in schizophrenics (Venables, 1983). These structures are tightly connected to CNS sources of EDA (Sect. 1.3.4.1).
2. As a specific indicator of cognitive and attentional processes (Sect. 3.1.3.1), EDA is especially sensitive to disturbances of these functions, mainly indicated by changes in the electrodermal OR (Venables, 1975).

Furthermore, psychophysiological views of schizophrenic etiology like the vulnerability models proposed by Zubin and Spring (1977) or Nuechterlein and Dawson (1984) considered the EDA to be an especially suitable indicator of autonomic arousability in these patients (Nuechterlein, 1987). Since comprehensive reviews have been given elsewhere (e.g., Zahn, 1986), the following sections are restricted to some typical topics in schizophrenia research, in which EDA parameters play a predominant role, also centered on methodological aspects.

3.4.2.1 Electrodermal Recovery and Vulnerability for Schizophrenia

Various attempts have been made to find predictors for the risk of developing schizophrenia, including anomalies of the electrodermal system (for a summary, see Watt, Anthony, Wynne, & Rolf, 1984). One of the most serious methodological problems in this field is that psychophysiological differences between clinical groups and normal control groups are often obscured by factors arising from the circumstances of illness instead of those determining the disease in question. This is especially the case in schizophrenics, where long-lasting hospitalization and heavy medication are likely to be responsible for severe social, intellectual, and affective deficits. To avoid this kind of bias, Mednick and McNeil (1968) advocated the use of prospective studies with groups of individuals having an increased risk for schizophrenia, instead of cross-sectional comparisons between schizophrenics and nonschizophrenics.

Consequently, the Mednick group performed a longitudinal study (the so-called Copenhagen study), starting in 1962–1963 with 207 children (mean age of 15 years) who had chronically and severely schizophrenic mothers (the high-risk group) and 104 controls as a low-risk group, with a follow-up after 10 years and further reanalyses. Besides other psychophysiological variables, SCRs[231] were recorded during a series of eight 1 kHz tones, as well as during a tone-noise (96 dB, 4.5 s noise as UCS) conditioning procedure (Mednick, 1967). Mednick and Schulsinger (1968) reported that those 20 individuals who have suffered from a serious psychiatric breakdown during the first 5 years of the study showed substantially longer SCR recovery rates (see end of Sect. 2.3.1.3 "Recovery Parameters") and shorter SCR lat., as compared to a matched group of other high-risk participants without psychiatric problems as well as 20 participants from the low-risk group. EDR recovery, out of all psychophysiological variables, had been identified as the most suitable predictor for a later psychiatric illness (Mednick, 1974).[232]

The predictive value of SCR recovery rate for the appearance of schizophrenia in high-risk individuals was again demonstrated by Mednick (1978), reporting data from the 10-year follow-up of the Copenhagen study. Thirty-four high-risk participants had become schizophrenic by that time. Ten years before, the recovery rate of that group had been significantly faster than in stratified groups of high-risk participants without having developed an illness, and also compared to low-risk participants. Furthermore, electrodermal recovery rate could predict particular symptoms of hallucinations and delusions with a correlation of $r = 0.49$. In extending their previous view on the role of ANS factors in the development of schizophrenia, Mednick et al. (1978) suggested an "ANS construct" formed by the product of EDR recovery rate and electrodermal responsiveness. According to this concept, only in combination with high responsiveness, fast recovery could be a predisposition toward the development of schizophrenia which enables the learned evasion of life in those patients.

Erlenmeyer-Kimling (1975) tried to replicate the Mednick results in a prospective study performed with children of ages 7–12; 44 of whom had schizophrenic mothers, while 23 had schizophrenic fathers; and with 13 children from parents who were both diagnosed as schizophrenic, together with 100 control children from normal parents, and 25 children with parents having other psychiatric illnesses. From these data (the so-called New York study), obtained with a similar testing

---

[231] Recorded with 7 mm diameter zinc electrodes, sponges saturated in zinc sulfate solution used as electrolyte, sites washed and cleaned with alcohol.

[232] Venables (1983) mentioned several critical points in the investigations of the Mednick group. First, the ISIs in their classical conditioning paradigm may have been too short to allow separation of the different kinds of EDRs with respect to their latencies (Sect. 3.1.2.1). Second, the differences found in SCR lat. may have been confounded with different absolute auditory thresholds for different frequency ranges, as can be observed in schizophrenics.

procedure as in the Copenhagen study, Erlenmeyer-Kimling, Cornblatt, and Fleiss (1979) reported generally slower recovery rates in offspring of schizophrenic parents. The only exception was a slightly faster electrodermal recovery in the subgroup with schizophrenic mothers as compared to controls which, however, did not reach statistical significance. In addition, high schizophrenic risk children showed longer SCR lat. than the controls. In total, with respect to EDA, the results of the New York study were completely contradictory to those of the Copenhagen study (Erlenmeyer-Kimling et al., 1984, Table 3). A possibly important difference to the Mednick investigation was that no distinction had been made between individuals who developed a psychiatric illness later and those who stayed healthy. Other differences between the two studies may have been in the diagnostic criteria used, family histories,[233] and in motivational concomitants of taking part in the investigations, in addition to the apparent age differences of the individuals studied (Venables, 1983).

Another study that attempted to replicate the Mednick findings was performed by Salzman and Klein (1978) with twelve 10-year-old children having one schizophrenic parent, in comparison to 30 controls. Twenty habituation trials (1 kHz, 2 s tones, 75 dB) were followed by a tone-noise conditioning similar to the procedure used by Mednick (1967). The authors could only confirm higher SCR amp. to the UCS appearing in the high-risk group, while no differences in SCR lat. and SCR recovery appeared. Janes and Stern (1976), Janes, Hesselbrock, and Stern (1978), and Prentky, Salzman, and Klein (1981) also could not confirm Mednick's report of faster EDR recovery in children at risk for schizophrenia.[234]

The general conclusion of Mednick and Schulsinger (1974) that EDR recovery may be part of the genetic pattern transmitted from schizophrenic parents to their children has been seriously questioned by the failures of later studies to obtain clear-cut results. Furthermore, a much tougher test of possible genetic influences was performed by van Dyke, Rosenthal, and Rasmussen (1974), using the paradigm of Mednick and Schulsinger (1968). The results did not yield differences in electrodermal recovery between 47 participants (mean age 33 years), who were adopted-away offspring of schizophrenic parents, and 45 healthy controls. To gain additional predispositional factors besides the suggested genetic risk, Mednick and Schulsinger (1974) evaluated pregnancy and delivery complications and early separation from parents as additional determinants of EDA in their high-risk group. Response amplitudes were most heavily influenced by these complications

---

[233] Mednick (1978) pointed to different selection procedures: the New York study excluded individuals from nonintact families, while the Copenhagen study did not.

[234] Patterson (1976) detected 11 nonresponders (Sect. 3.4.2.2) among 31 male chronic schizophrenics. The remaining 20 participants showed a bimodal distribution with respect to SCR rec.t/2, and the fast recovery participants showed significantly slower pupillary constriction in the light/dark reflex as compared to the slow recovery participants, which was discussed by the author as possibly due to a greater adrenergic outflow in the first group. In addition, these results also question the generalizability of the results that shorter EDR recoveries appear in schizophrenics.

and by separation, and the latter was correlated with short EDR lat. in the high-risk group. On recovery rate, prenatal and delivery complications showed an effect which was additive to the influence of being an offspring of schizophrenic mothers.

The hypothesis that a short EDA recovery time is possibly a highly specific prognostic indicator for vulnerability of schizophrenia can be supported by connections between an "open gate" state of attentional processes and fast EDR recovery, as discussed in Sect. 3.1.3.1. According to this view, a reciprocal relationship between the duration of electrodermal recovery and the time needed to build up a neuronal model in a Sokolovian sense (Sect. 3.1.1) is suggested. Their "open attentional gate," which may be due to a predominance of hippocampal over amygdalar activity (Table 3.1, Sect. 3.1.3.1), will cause a permanent readiness for reorientation in schizophrenics, which also impedes habituation. As Zahn, Rosenthal, and Lawlor (1968) suggested, the slower habituation of schizophrenics to specific stimuli is partly due to constant yet partial dishabituation, which is a result of attentional shifts to novel, nonspecific stimuli. Accordingly, the rate of NS. EDRs is frequently increased in schizophrenics (Depue & Fowles, 1973), and children with high risk for schizophrenia show a generally increased tonic EDA (Öhman, 1981). Zahn et al. (1981a) could also find an increase of NS.SCR freq. together with faster SCR rec.t/2[235] in a sample of 46 acute schizophrenics as compared to 118 controls. Thus, as Mednick et al. (1978) suggested, a combination of electrodermal hyperresponsiveness and fast recovery may be more promising for utilization in early detection of populations at risk for schizophrenia.

Altogether, these considerations are in accordance with the hypothesis of hippocampal dysfunction in persons with risk for schizophrenia, since it may reflect a suppression of inhibitory influences of the hippocampus on EDA (Sect. 1.3.4.1 "Subcortical Control of EDA"), which is connected with typical attentional deficits observed in schizophrenic patients. Predominance of influences from the amygdala over hippocampal influences on attention and information processing as a possible factor in the vulnerability for schizophrenia may be due to genetic influences as well as to prenatal and perinatal complications. The latter causation is supported by Mednick (1970) who reported delivery complications in 70% of children that became schizophrenic.[236] More recently, Öhman and Hultman (1998) investigated birth records of 79 schizophrenic patients, from which EDA data were also available. They revealed a significant association between obstetric complications (combined frequency/number) and electrodermal nonresponsiveness. Hence, both genetic risk and obstetric complications may constitute predisposition factors for the development of schizophrenia.

---

[235] As can be inferred from other publications of the Zahn group, zinc/zinc sulfate electrodes with 0.79 cm^2 area were attached to palmar sites.

[236] It could be further speculated that different EDA parameters are related to different pathogenetic factors. Cannon et al. (1988), using a subsample from the Copenhagen study, found that individuals with enlarged third ventricles (which may point to hypothalamic and/or amygdalar deficits) showed significant overall reductions in EDR amp. and in percentage of EDRs observed during OR and conditioning trials (see also Sect. 3.4.2.2).

However, the role of electrodermal recovery in patients already suffering from schizophrenia remains unclear. Mednick and Schulsinger (1968), Ax and Bamford (1970), and Gruzelier and Venables (1972) found higher recovery rates in schizophrenics than in controls. These results could not be confirmed with drug-free schizophrenics. Maricq and Edelberg (1975) observed increased electrodermal recovery times in 28 hospitalized schizophrenics free of medication as compared to 27 controls under nonaversive conditions (i.e., resting, mild stimulation, or simple tasks), and no significant differences during an aversive cold pressor test. Furthermore, Gruzelier, Eves, Connolly, and Hirsch (1981) did not obtain differences between nonmedicated schizophrenics and controls in EDR recovery following 70 dB as well as 90 dB stimuli. Gruzelier and Hammond (1978) observed faster electrodermal recoveries after applying a 12 s, subjectively loud and unpleasant noise, to 18 schizophrenics under chlorpromazine medication as compared to drug-free intervals. Chlorpromazine, a phenothiazine which has been frequently applied in neuroleptic treatment of schizophrenia, exerts marked sympathicolytic properties and presumably exhibits its antipsychotic action by influencing monoaminergic pathways in the limbic system (Gruzelier and Connolly, 1979), where it may have a direct influence on the elicitation of electrodermal phenomena (Sect. 3.4.3.2). The effect of chlorpromazine on EDR recovery in normal individuals had been found by Kugler and Gruzelier (1980) who showed that a single dose of this neuroleptic drug markedly reduced SCR rec.t/2 to moderately intense stimuli. The problem of medication influencing EDA in schizophrenics supports again the need for prospective studies as pointed to at the beginning of this section.

In summary, the results on electrodermal recovery and risk for schizophrenia remain equivocal, since they are not consistent across samples and settings.[237] Nevertheless, there is some neurophysiological plausibility for the specific indicator function of parameters describing electrodermal response shape for possible genetic and prenatal or perinatal damages that could be related to the cause of schizophrenia. However, several approaches to vulnerability for schizophrenia prefer parameters like electrodermal responsivity in general, rather than of response shape. These models will be addressed in the next section.

---

[237] About 3 years after the Copenhagen study, an Israeli high-risk study started with 100 children at an average age of 11 years, half of them being offspring from schizophrenic parents, the other half not. All were subjected to an SC-OR paradigm. At about 26 years of age, 90 participants were reevaluated, 27 of whom (mostly from the high-risk group) were diagnosed as schizophrenic according to DSM-III. Results of the differences in SC-ORs between the groups and additional results from an investigation of the children at the age of 16 were reported by Kugelmass et al. (1995). To-become schizophrenics had significantly higher anxiety ratings at age 16 than the nondiagnosed participants. Unexpectedly, the children with the most pronounced electrodermal hyporesponsiveness at age 16 were especially prone to receive an affective disorder diagnosis with the age of 25, which confirms that electrodermal hyporesponsiveness is not specific for developing a schizophrenic disease (Sect. 3.4.1.3).

3.4.2.2 Electrodermal Nonresponding in Schizophrenics

As Dawson (1990) pointed out, there exists a consensus in the results from various research groups that a large subgroup of schizophrenic patients (between 40 and 50%) is electrodermally nonresponsive to innocuous stimulation, whereas the remaining patients show normal responsivity or even hyperresponsivity (for summaries, see Bernstein et al., 1982; Dawson & Nuechterlein, 1984; Öhman, 1981). Nonresponsivity concerns the failure to elicit any OR or – if an initial OR occurs – to emerge an unusually quick habituation to repeated stimulation (Sects. 3.1.1.1 and 3.1.1.3). In addition, these groups normally show differences in tonic EDA, since nonresponders also exhibit less NS.EDRs, while responders display an increased rate of nonspecific EDRs as compared to normals, despite their neuroleptic medication (Öhman, 1981). While Zahn et al. (1981a), in their study mentioned in the previous section, also observed a considerable increase of NS.SCR freq. in their schizophrenic sample during resting, SCL yielded a significant difference in the opposite direction. Accordingly, one-dimensional concepts of ANS hyperactivity and hyperreactivity to be existent in schizophrenic subsamples must be treated with caution (see also the discussion of phasic/tonic relationships in Sect. 2.5.4.2).

Since, as a rule, studies on electrodermal nonresponding were performed with participants that had already developed schizophrenia, several factors possibly having influenced the published results should be taken into account: the duration and severity of the illness, often confounded with the patient's age; the type and dosage of medication; and the patient's compliance as well as her/his ability to understand and follow instructions, the latter being largely dependent on the particular schizophrenic state. Furthermore, differences in intensity and frequency characteristics of the stimuli used, an induction or prevention of directing attention toward stimulation, as influenced by instructions, that may be controlled via subjective reactions (Venables, 1983), as well as interactions among all these factors, possibly exert influences on nonresponding.

The first authors who showed electrodermal hypo- and hyperresponsiveness in schizophrenics were Gruzelier and Venables (1972). Out of a total sample of 80 schizophrenic patients, both noninstitutionalized and institutionalized, 43 showed no EDRs to a series of 15 tones (1 kHz, 85 dB; EDA recorded with standard methodology, with the use of KCl cream). From the other 37 patients, only three reached the habituation criterion of three consecutive SCR amp. lower than 0.05 μS (Sect. 3.1.1.3). A group of nonpsychotic patients as well as a normal control group with 20 participants each showed normal EDRs and a normal habituation course. The result of a bimodal distribution of electrodermal reactivity in schizophrenics was later confirmed in several investigations, although contradictory results have also been obtained (Bernstein et al., 1982).

Öhman (1981, Table 1) summarized the results from more than 30 independent samples comprising nearly 1,000 schizophrenics taken from various studies. They included patients in different stages of illness as well as during remission, the proportion of nonresponders in the different samples ranging from 0 to 69% with a median close to 40%. However, these values have to be viewed in the context of a base rate of 5–10% electrodermal nonresponders in normal individuals and in nonschizophrenic psychiatric samples (Venables, 1978; Straube, 1979). Öhman (1981) outlined the following factors that influence the appearance of nonresponding:

1. Stimulus intensity and quality. There is an apparent tendency for a decrease in electrodermal nonresponding with higher stimulus intensities, although a substantial number of schizophrenics failed to respond even to the most intense stimuli. Several failures of schizophrenics to show EDRs may have been due to the use of tone frequencies below 1 kHz (e.g., Zahn, 1976), where schizophrenics show lower absolute thresholds than normals (Gruzelier & Hammond, 1976). In addition, stimulus rise time may have an important effect on EDR habituation in schizophrenics, as Bernstein et al. (1982, p. 192) showed, presenting a series of 15 tones (1 kHz, 90 dB) with rise times of 25 ms. The introduction of slow stimulus rise times reduced the proportion of nonhabituators within schizophrenics from 32% to 0, and within the controls from 72 to 10%. This suggests that schizophrenics are hyporeactive to OR-eliciting stimuli, while their DR or startle reflexes (Sect. 3.1.1.2) may remain intact (Dimitriev, Belyakova, Bondarenko, & Nikolaev, 1968).
2. Stimulus significance. Nonresponding mainly appears during the presentation of nonsignaling stimuli. Unfortunately, due to the cognitive disturbances present in schizophrenics, appropriate results are not always convincing. Venables (1975) suggested that schizophrenics show an extreme readiness for an uptake of irrelevant stimulation, while their shortened EDR recovery time following relevant stimulation (Sect. 3.4.2.1) may indicate their slow build up of a neuronal model in a Sokolovian sense (Table 3.1, Sect. 3.1.3.1). Bernstein, Schneider, Juni, Pope, and Starkey (1980) found that schizophrenics display electrodermal hyporesponsiveness essentially to verbal stimuli that were not given explicit attentional significance. Iacono and Lykken (1979) pointed to the possibility of interindividual differences in the significance that patients ascribe to stimuli which are facilitated by vague and uninformative instructions. For habituation experiments with schizophrenics, they recommended providing participants with an absorbing alternative task after being instructed to ignore the habituation stimuli.
3. Techniques of recording and scoring. There is a general tendency toward lower proportions of nonresponders in studies that used the constant current method as compared to studies using constant voltage (cf. Öhman, 1981, Table 1). This can be explained by the difference between both methods in amplification requirements (Sect. 2.6.2). In addition, the detection of EDRs is dependent on the time window used (Sect. 2.3.1.1). That means, the probability for including a spontaneous EDR in the evaluation of specific EDRs within a window of 1–5 s after stimulus onset (e.g., Gruzelier & Venables, 1972) is higher, compared to using a window of 1–2.4 s (e.g., Levinson & Edelberg, 1985).

4. Medication. Though responders and nonresponders in general did not differ in type or dose of neuroleptic medication (e.g., Gruzelier & Venables, 1972), subsamples of schizophrenics yielded differential electrodermal effects when given drugs (e.g., Stern, Surphlis, & Koff, 1965). Especially, as a rule, there was less nonresponding in medication-free intervals. However, in most instances the reported intraindividual differences were too small to infer a marked influence of medication on electrodermal responsivity. It can be assumed that neuroleptic treatment reduces EDL as well as NS.EDR freq. (Venables, 1975; see also Sect. 3.4.3.1). Results concerning the influence of these drugs on phasic EDA are less clear. Spohn, Thetford, and Cancro (1971) did not find an impact of phenothiazines on the SCR amp., while Magaro (1973) found SCR amp. to be considerably reduced under phenothiazine medication in schizophrenics and other hospitalized patients. However, SCR amp. were enhanced by drug influences in a schizophrenic subgroup having good prognostic values according to their premorbid adjustment. Whether EDR under medication may be used for prognosis of treatment outcome is yet to be investigated. In any case, the phenomenon of electrodermal nonresponding in schizophrenics can be observed in a considerable proportion including patients being not on medication (Öhman, 1981; Zahn et al., 1981a).

With respect to the conceptual/methodological orientation of the present book, the possible influences of measurement techniques as well as medication on the nonresponder phenomenon will be discussed in more detail here.

During the mid 1950s, there was a striking difference in the proportion of schizophrenic nonresponders found in studies performed in Britain (approximately 49%, as summarized by Venables, 1977), as compared to those performed in the United States (at most 14.8%, as summarized by Zahn, 1976). O'Gorman (1978) hypothesized this difference being due to the use of the constant voltage method in Britain, with an amplitude criterion of 0.05 µS for the detection of EDRs, while the US studies preferred the constant current method and an amplitude criterion of 0.4 kΩ (Sect. 2.3.1.2 "Choice of Amplitude Criteria"). However, Zahn (1978), in reanalyzing his data by eliminating EDRs with amplitudes lower than 0.05 µS as in the British studies, found only a small increase in proportion of nonresponders: from 13.5 to 15.3% in the schizophrenics and from 0 to 5% in normal individuals.[238] Instead of differences in measurement, Zahn suggested medication effects having produced the difference between results obtained in both countries, since he used acute and yet nonmedicated patients, while participants in the British samples were all taking neuroleptic drugs.

---

[238] Note that for purposes of transforming SCR amp. into SRR amp. and vice versa, SCLs and SRLs are required (Sect. 2.3.3.2).

Criteria which determine the occurrence of habituation, and hence the proportion of nonhabituators among patients, also influence results on electrodermal responsiveness. Frith, Stevens, Johnstone, and Crow (1982) used the habituation criterion of three consecutive trials with SCRs below 0.02 μS in a series of 14 tones (1 kHz, 85 dB) for the detection of habituators among their 41 acute schizophrenics before treatment. Therapeutic outcome was markedly better in 15 habituators as compared to 22 nonhabituators (4 patients were nonresponders). Comparing these schizophrenics with samples of 34 depressed and 51 anxiety patients, nonhabituation was most frequent in the anxiety patients and least frequent in the depressed ones, while the schizophrenics were intermediate. However, using form parameters of the habituation curve as a criterion (Sect. 3.1.1.3), schizophrenics showed significantly faster habituation than any other patient group. A reclassification of participants taking into account the amplitude of spontaneous fluctuations confirmed this result. Individuals being classified as habituators had to give two successive responses with amplitudes lower than the average NS.SCR amp. Using this criterion instead of zero responses for determining habituators, schizophrenics showed the lowest frequency of nonhabituation among all groups.

Levinson, Edelberg, and Bridger (1984, Table 1) summarized results from 19 schizophrenic samples with altogether more than 700 participants with respect to the time windows used by the different authors. They came to the conclusion that only studies using a long scoring window (4–5 s after stimulus onset) reported a considerable proportion of nonhabituators among patients. Since NS.EDRs can be expected already within 5 s after stimulus onset (see Fig. 2.21, Sect. 2.3.2.2), a distinction between stimulus-elicited and spontaneous EDRs cannot be made unambiguously. In their own study, Levinson et al. (1984) presented 36 male schizophrenic inpatients and 11 male controls two series of 1 kHz tones (1 s duration; 13 tones with 70 dB, and 12 tones with 90 dB), while recording SCRs with standard methodology, with KCl serving as electrolyte. Using a response window between 0.8 and 5 s, 56% of patients were classified as nonresponders, and 19% as slow habituators. When restricting the window to 1.0–4.2 s after stimulus onset, 75% of patients were scored as nonresponders and the remainder as faster habituators than normals. Since the narrower window led to a clear-cut subgrouping of schizophrenics and also avoided the danger of confounding spontaneous and OR-elicited EDA, these authors recommended its further use instead of the larger window which had been recommended by the Gruzelier group (e.g., Gruzelier, Eves, Connolly, & Hirsch, 1981).

As discussed above under (4), the general question arises whether or not electrodermal nonresponding in schizophrenics is dependent on medication. Since several neuroleptic drugs (e.g., the frequently applied chlorpromazine) have anticholinergic properties, it cannot be ruled out that they influence central as well as peripheral elicitation of electrodermal phenomena directly (Sect. 1.3.4). However, the electrodermal OR blocking effect of 50 mg chlorpromazine, as found by Patterson and Venables (1981) in their study with healthy participants described in Sect. 3.4.3.2, was considerably weaker compared to the application of 1 mg scopolamine, which is a potent anticholinergic drug. Furthermore, several studies yielded relative independence of the responder/nonresponder dichotomy from medication (e.g., Gruzelier, Eves, Connolly, and Hirsch (1981); Gruzelier & Hammond, 1978; Gruzelier & Venables, 1972; see Sect. 3.4.3.2). Straube (1979) was also not able to find differences in electrodermal reactivity between 21 drug-free schizophrenics and 29 patients tested under neuroleptic medication (including derivatives of butyrophenone, phenothiazine, and other tricyclic neuroleptics). Though medication effects on electrodermal nonresponding could not be ruled out, the general conclusion was that medication does not appear to account for nonresponding (Öhman, 1981; Zahn, 1986).

To test the robustness of the electrodermal nonresponder phenomenon, Bernstein et al. (1982) performed a joint evaluation of 14 studies drawn from six laboratories in the United States, Britain, and Germany. These studies included chronic and acute schizophrenics of both genders with and without drugs and normal as well as neurotic participants as controls. Data from habituation series with both auditory and visual stimuli of different intensities and rise time properties, obtained under differing instructions and conditions, were included. Electrodermal recordings were taken from palmar sites of one or both hands, with Ag/AgCl or zinc/zinc sulfate electrodes. The amplitude criteria were – according to the measurement technique used – either between 400 and 700 Ω or between 0.05 and 1 μS; the time windows for ORs were either 1–3, 1–4, or 0.8–5 s after stimulus onset. Frequency distributions of the number of nonresponsive individuals in each sample were obtained. For responsive individuals, the number of trials to habituation was evaluated, using a criterion of three consecutive trials without an OR.[239] Three different categories were formed:

1. Nonresponders, defined as those individuals who failed to elicit an OR on the first three trials.
2. Slow habituators, defined as those individuals who failed to habituate before trial number 10.
3. Percent at both extremes, combining both nonresponders and slow habituators, to test the bimodal hypothesis that schizophrenics are more likely to be on either extreme of the trials-to-habituation distribution.

Statistical tests of the distributions revealed that schizophrenics consistently displayed an abnormally high incidence of electrodermal nonresponsiveness (nearly 50% of the patient samples on average). In addition, schizophrenic responders were shown to be faster habituators as compared to nonschizophrenic

---

[239] Data for the two-trial habituation criterion were also analyzed, yielding similar results.

responders in most studies, though conflicting evidence existed in a minority of studies.[240] Only few of the papers analyzed by Bernstein et al. (1982) provided evidence for the bimodality hypothesis, as proposed by Gruzelier and Venables (1973) or by Rubens and Lapidus (1978).

In general, the distinction between responders and nonresponders in schizophrenics appeared to be reliable across studies and also of clinical utility, showing relationships to the distinction between positive vs. negative symptomatology (Dawson, Nuechterlein, & Adams, 1989; Fuentes, Merita, Miquel, & Rojo, 1993). For example, Straube (1979) observed that acute schizophrenic nonresponders as compared to responders committed more errors of omission in a dichotic listening and verbal shadowing task, suggesting an impaired selective attention capability in electrodermal responders (Sect. 3.1.3.1). Furthermore, that particular subgroup showed more symptoms of emotional withdrawal, conceptual disorganization, and lower spontaneous activity. Similar connections between electrodermal nonresponding and ratings of psychiatric symptoms were found by Bernstein et al. (1981) in chronic schizophrenics. Gruzelier (1976) reported that slow-habituating schizophrenic responders were rated as more manic, anxious, and attention demanding than nonresponders.

However, connections between electrodermal hypoactivity and patient outcome are not so straightforward. Schell et al. (2005) found that high levels of both tonic (SCL and NS.SCR freq.) and phasic EDA (number of SC-ORs) were predictive for negative symptomatology and poor social and occupational outcome. They investigated 78 (15% females) young recent-onset medicated schizophrenic outpatients together with 36 demographically matched controls (28% females) during resting, mild nonsignal tones (78 dB, 1 s, 12 tones of 1 kHz, followed by three tones of 1.2 kHz, ISIs 20–30 s), 12 task-significant 500 Hz tones of 1 s duration (the task was to move the head in the direction from which the tone was presented), and 12 loud white noise bursts (98 dB, 1 s). Since there was evidence that the group of schizophrenics investigated by Schell et al. (2005) had higher activation of the frontal cortex compared to the normal controls, the authors referred to a hypothesis suggested by Brekke, Raine, and Thomson (1995), stating that both disorganized symptoms and continued SC-OR responsiveness should be associated with excessive frontotemporal activation. In turn, the latter may interfere with effective cognitive processing in schizophrenics, the negative symptoms of whom might partially serve as their kind of coping with overarousal. The authors presumed that both hyperarousal/hyperresponsiveness and hypoarousal/hyporesponsiveness in relation to normal

---

[240] Results on habituation speed are largely dependent on the method used (Sect. 3.1.1.3). The trials-to-habituation criterion disregards initial amplitude differences, thus bearing the danger of misclassifying individuals showing a high amplitude to the first stimulus with subsequent borderline but not below-criterion EDRs as slow habituators. Zahn et al. (1968, 1981a) who defined habituation in terms of the EDR amp. decline relative to the trial block with the largest mean EDR amp. found schizophrenics to be slower habituators than normals.

controls may be predictive of negative symptoms and poor outcome, dependent on the groups of patients investigated.

A correspondence between extreme forms of electrodermal reactivity and the development of positive vs. negative symptomatology in schizophrenia had been revealed by Cannon, Mednick, and Parnas (1990) in a reanalysis of the Copenhagen high-risk study (Sect. 3.4.2.1). Using a decision-tree model of etiology in 138 schizophrenics, they found an increase from 35 to 86% in the rate of developing schizophrenia with predominantly negative symptoms, if these individuals had been ANS nonresponders 20 years before. All seven of the schizophrenics with predominantly negative symptoms had suffered severe delivery complications and were ANS nonresponders. This supports the hypothesis that perinatal complications could be a causative factor in third ventricle enlargement, which may contribute to electrodermal hyporesponsiveness (Cannon et al., 1988),[241] and is also a typical computer tomographic abnormality in schizophrenics (Cannon, Mednick, & Parnas, 1989). Contrarily, in another subsample of 160 schizophrenics from the Copenhagen study, 6 of the 8 patients with predominantly positive symptoms had suffered severely instable environments for growing up and evidenced high levels of ANS responsiveness. In a computer tomography study with 31 male chronic schizophrenics and 20 normal male controls, Kim, Shin, Kim, Cho, and Kim (1993) found the maximum diameter of the third ventricle related to lower SCL and reduced NS.SCR freq. (obtained with standard methodology from the palmar surface of the nonpreferred hand) during breathing exercise, relaxation, an OR stimulus, and a 1 kHz, 70 dB tone habituation series. Nonresponders also showed more severe thought disturbances and deficit symptoms than responders.

Katsanis and Iacono (1992) reported a relationship between electrodermal hyporesponsiveness and temporal lobe dysfunction assessed by neuropsychological tests in 63 chronic schizophrenics (7 females, 56 males). SC was recorded bilaterally with standard methodology from the first and second fingers during eight 85 dB and twelve 105 dB tones (1 kHz, 0.5 s) on a 55 dB noise background, separated by a 5-min break. SCRs were scored if they appeared 1–3 s after stimulus onset and exceeded 0.05 μS amplitude. SCL was recorded before each tone; the habituation rate was defined as the number of trials preceding three consecutive missing responses (Sect. 3.1.1.3) and evaluated separately for the two tone series. A frontal-horn-to-brain ratio was calculated from CT scans. None of the correlations between this ratio and SC variables reached significance. There were 70% nonresponders to the 85 dB tones, but only 54% to the 105 dB tones. All nonresponders performed worse on neuropsychological tests for temporal lobe functioning, which revealed impairment in verbal and figural memory processes, probably as a result of a temporal-limbic dysfunction.

---

[241] At variance with these results are those of Schnur et al. (1989) who found significantly wider third ventricles (by means of computer tomography) in nine schizophrenic responders as compared to 15 nonresponders (SCRs and fingerpulse responses to three 60 dB, 1 kHz tones).

Indirect support for frontal lobe impairment in electrodermal hyporesponsive schizophrenics has been provided by Perry, Felger, and Braff (1998), who compared 33 DSM-IV diagnosed schizophrenic patients (11 females, 22 males) with 31 normal controls (12 females, 19 males) during the presentation of complex and abstract stimuli (ten slides of Rorschach tables, presented for 5 s each). SC was recorded with standard methodology (however, from soap-washed sites). The same criteria as used by Katsanis and Iacono (1992) were used for obtaining SC-ORs. Schizophrenics had significantly lower SCLs and a significantly greater proportion of nonresponders (45 vs. 10% in controls). Hyporesponding was associated with increased stuck-in perseverations during answering the standard Rorschach questions, which were in turn correlated with negative symptoms as assessed by a neurocognitive measure. The authors suggested that hyperresponsive schizophrenics may constitute a specific subgroup, which is also less prone to a diagnosis of paranoia than electrodermal responders. [242]

Electrodermal habituation speed has also been demonstrated yielding some predictive value for short-term therapeutic outcome in schizophrenics. Frith, Stevens, Johnstone, and Crow (1979) found that habituation of SCRs to a series of 14 tones (1 kHz, 85 dB), as measured with standard methodology using K–Y gel, was a better predictor for improvement than treatment with neuroleptics. These results are consistent with the findings of Zahn, Carpenter, and McGlashan (1981b) that only schizophrenic patients who revealed EDRs to an RT task similar to those of normal, showed a marked decrease in their symptomatology.

To answer the question whether electrodermal nonresponsivity is purely a secondary effect of medication and other treatments or may reflect a long-term trait characteristic possibly associated with vulnerability to schizophrenia, several studies with acute vs. remitted patients were carried out. Iacono (1982), in his study described in the next section, observed that even in remitted schizophrenic outpatients, 46% were nonresponsive to 86 dB 1 kHz tones, while the remainder showed abnormally high tonic EDA. As a longitudinal follow-up of schizophrenics who had been studied in their early phase by Nuechterlein, Edell, Norris, and Dawson (1986), Dawson (1990) reported data from 22 patients and 22 matched normal controls. He found that the number of trials to habituation in a series of 12 tones (1 kHz, 78 dB) significantly increased in schizophrenics from a state of remission to a state of relapse. Olbrich (1990) could not find statistically significant differences in various EDA parameters, including tonic measures, initial SC-OR amp., and trials to habituation,[243] comparing data from 11

---

[242] In a pilot study with few participants, Hazlett, Dawson, Buchsbaum, and Nuechterlein (1993) found that EDA nonresponders had significantly lower metabolic rates in medial frontal areas, in the hippocampus, and in the amygdala, i.e., in areas that are suggested being involved in generating EDA (Sect. 1.3.4.1).

[243] Recorded in a series of 15 tones (1 kHz, 70 dB) with standard methodology, using a time window of 0.5–4 s after stimulus onset (Olbrich & Mussgay, 1987).

schizophrenics in an acute nonmedicated state and after remission, also without medication.

Dawson, Nuechterlein, Schell, Gitlin, and Ventura (1994) investigated whether ANS abnormalities in schizophrenics as recorded by EDA would constitute indicators of general vulnerability or episode. Twenty schizophrenic patients and 20 normal controls (4 females and 16 males in each group) were subjected to a 5-min resting period and three subsequent auditory stimulation phases, separated by 3 min (the same stimulus sequences as used by Schell et al., 2005). SC was recorded with standard methodology from the volar surfaces of the index and second fingers of each hand. Patients were drug-treated outpatients and did not have psychotic symptoms for longer than 2 years. EDA was collected on two occasions: during the psychotic state and during a state of symptomatic remission, with a median interval of 8 months in between. The NS.SCR freq. revealed a significant diagnosis main effect, a state main effect and a significant diagnosis-by-state interaction. Post hoc tests revealed that patients in remission did not differ from normal controls but had higher NS.SCR freq. during their psychotic episodes. Similarly, log SCL revealed a highly significant diagnosis-by-state interaction. The groups did not differ during remission, but SCLs were significantly higher in schizophrenics during their psychotic episodes. The authors concluded that the tonic EDA measures qualified as episode indicators. Contrarily, SC-ORs to innocuous stimuli figured out being a mediating vulnerability factor, but only if the NS.SCR freq. was taken into account and the SC-ORs of normal controls were used as predictors for those of the patients.[244]

Though the conclusion is only tentative, nonresponding (and possibly also hyperresponding) is likely to be the best candidate for a reliable electrodermal indicator for long-lasting diagnostic and prognostic characteristics in schizophrenics (Bernstein et al., 1982; Levinson et al., 1984; Zahn, 1986), while nonhabituating, probably together with an increased tonic EDA, may have properties of an "episode indicator" in these patients (Dawson, 1990). However, it has to be kept in mind that electrodermal nonresponding is not specific for schizophrenia, since a large number of patients with unipolar and bipolar affective disorders (Sect. 3.4.1.3) also show this characteristic, raising the possibility that electrodermal nonresponding reflects genetic liability for several forms of psychopathology (Iacono, 1985). Such a possibility had been investigated by Iacono, Ficken, and Beiser (1999) in an investigation with 135 first-episode psychiatric patients (schizophrenics and other

---

[244] A possible expansion of experimental possibilities for investigating electrodermal hypo- or hyperresponsivity in schizophrenics as compared to normal controls had been demonstrated by Lim et al. (1999b), using Lim et al.'s (1997) mathematical solution for evaluating overlapping EDRs during short-ISI paradigms, which also offers a possibility to combine EDA with ERP recordings (e.g., Roth, Goodale, & Pfefferbaum, 1991). In comparison with 50 normal controls, their 30 medicated schizophrenics showed a reduced SC-OR response rate, reduced proportion of responders, SCR amp., rise time, peak latency, and steady-state response amplitude during the presentation of 40 tones with ISIs down to about 2.5 s, but no group differences in SCR lat. or SCL emerged.

psychotic diagnoses), 104 non-psychiatric comparison participants, 178 biological first-degree relatives of individuals from both groups, and a comparison group of 61 chronic schizophrenics. They recorded SC with standard methodology during eight 85 dB tones, twelve 105 dB tones, and two tape-recorded sound effects with peaks of 95 dB. Electrodermal nonresponding was common to all patient groups but did not differentiate the relatives of psychotic patients from those of normal controls. However, first-degree relatives of electrodermal responders in both the first-episode and chronic schizophrenic patients also revealed an excessively high NS.SCR freq., which therefore may be a more suitable marker for risk of schizophrenia as EDA nonresponding.[245]

3.4.2.3 Other Issues in Schizophrenia Research Related to EDA

The aim of this section is to discuss additional results of psychophysiological research in schizophrenia directly related to issues of CNS elicitation of electrodermal phenomena. Based on neurological as well as neuropsychological evidence for left-hemisphere dysfunction in schizophrenics, a series of studies on bilateral EDA asymmetry (Sect. 3.1.4.3) in these patients have been conducted (for summaries, see Öhman, 1981; Zahn, 1986). In general, electrodermally responsive schizophrenics show higher right-hand than left-hand phasic and tonic EDA, while the tonic levels were elevated on the left hand of nonresponders.[246] This had been observed by Gruzelier (1973) in a study with 60 male schizophrenics and 15 healthy male controls, with an equal number of responders and nonresponders among the patients. Skin conductance was measured bilaterally with standard methodology, however, using KCl as electrolyte, during the presentation of 15 tones (1 kHz, 85 dB). Since phasic EDA is mainly contralaterally elicited (Sect. 1.3.4.1 "Three Different CNS Originating Pathways for EDA"), failure of contralateral inhibition in schizophrenics due to the left-hemisphere dysfunction of their limbic system had been suggested as a cause of the bilateral differences (Gruzelier, 1979). However, contralateral cortical inhibition of EDA cannot be distinguished clearly from ipsilateral excitation (Venables, 1983; Sect. 3.1.4.2).

An increase of tonic EDA in the left hand, which contrasted the results reported by Gruzelier (1983), had been observed by Bartfai, Edman, Levander, Schalling, and Sedvall (1984) in their study with 13 recently admitted nonmedicated

---

[245] Schell, Dawson, Nuechterlein, Subotnik, and Ventura (2002) investigated the 1-year temporal stability (reliability) of electrodermal measures in 71 young, recent-onset, drug-treated schizophrenics and 36 demographically matched controls (18 and 28% females, respectively) with the methodology used by Dawson et al. (1994). Reliabilities were significant for most EDA variables but generally lower in schizophrenics as in controls, which may be attributable to poorer general arousal regulation (Sect. 3.2.1.1) in patients.

[246] It had been discussed in Sect. 3.4.1.3 that depressive patients tend to show the reverse pattern (Venables, 1983). However, Iacono, and Tuason (1983) could not find consistent bilateral asymmetries in EDA in a 1-year follow-up with 26 unipolar and 24 bipolar depressives.

schizophrenics. The patients as well as a group of age- and gender-matched controls were presented a series of 21 tones (1 kHz, 85 dB), while SC was recorded bilaterally with standard methodology, however, using hypertonic (0.58 M) NaCl cream. During resting as well as during stimulation, the schizophrenics displayed significantly more NS.SCRs at their left as compared to their right hand, while the controls did not. Furthermore, Öhman (1981) questioned the specificity of elevated right-hand EDLs in schizophrenics, since normal controls may show even greater relative right-hand dominance than patients.

On the other hand, the right-hand superiority of phasic EDA in schizophrenics which had been regarded as a better confirmed finding possibly also lacks specificity for that group of patients (Zahn, 1986). Gruzelier and Venables (1974) recorded SC bilaterally during a habituation series (15 tones, 1 kHz, 75 dB), and during a discrimination task (1 vs. 2 kHz in a 24 tones series), using the methodology of their 1972 study (Sect. 3.4.2.2). Ten participants each were tested in subgroups of responders and nonresponders in hospitalized and noninstitutionalized schizophrenics under medication, in a group of unipolar depressives, and in a group with mixed personality disorders (including psychopathy and drug abuse). Right-hand SCL was elevated in schizophrenics but also in the group with personality disorders, mostly during the discrimination task (i.e., under highly arousing conditions), while the depressives revealed left-hand SCL dominance. The same lateralization effects as for SCL were obtained with SCR amp. In addition to the lack of specificity of laterality effects for schizophrenics, their direction was labile and related to arousal levels.

Neuroleptic medication also has to be regarded as an important factor influencing electrodermal laterality in schizophrenics. Gruzelier and Hammond (1977) recorded bilateral SC in 19 schizophrenic patients at the end of successive 4 week periods while being on chlorpromazine, on placebo, and again on chlorpromazine medication. The right-hand EDR dominance during an OR tone sequence (1 kHz, 80 dB) as found in earlier studies could be confirmed. Electrodermal asymmetry was markedly reduced during medication, which was interpreted by these authors as indicating the drug's therapeutic efficacy. In a further evaluation, Gruzelier and Hammond (1978) reported that chlorpromazine did not consistently influence bilateral differences in the number of EDRs to loud and unpleasant noise stimuli (75 dB, 12 s) serving as UCSs. However, there was a significant shift from right-hand dominance under placebo to higher left-hand EDR amp. under chlorpromazine. These data provided support for the existence of differential drug effects on signal and nonsignal stimuli, thus demonstrating the complex effects of anticholinergic neuroleptics, as will be outlined further at the end of Sect. 3.4.3.

Whether or not bilateral electrodermal asymmetry is related to diagnostic subgroups of schizophrenia and/or to therapeutic outcome cannot be answered sufficiently. Based on an analysis of EDA recordings[247] during the presentation of 15 tones (1 kHz, 90 dB) to a total sample of 44 nonmedicated hospital-admitted

---

[247] Measured as SCRs occurring between 0.8 and 5 s after stimulus onset, exceeding a 1 mm criterion with a maximum gain setting of 0.02 µS/cm.

patients, Gruzelier and Manchanda (1982) as well as Gruzelier (1983) reported evidence that larger left-hand EDRs were associated with "positive" symptoms (e.g., delusions and hallucinations), while higher right-hand responding appeared together with "negative" symptoms (e.g., emotional withdrawal; see also Sect. 3.4.2.2). Gruzelier (1979) suggested the prognosis being worse in schizophrenics who show right-hand EDR dominance as compared with those not showing that dominance.

No bilateral electrodermal asymmetry could be found by Iacono (1982) in 24 remitted schizophrenics who were compared to 22 medical outpatient controls during exposure to 17 tones (1 kHz, 86 dB; including a dishabituation trial at position 16 with an unusually long 500 Hz tone). None of the EDA parameters, recorded with standard methodology (NS.SCR freq., SCL, number of SCRs to tones, SCR amp. to the first tone and to the dishabituation tone), yielded differences between hands, neither in patients nor in controls. This result is in accordance with Tarrier, Cooke, and Lader (1978) who could not find evidence for bilateral EDA asymmetry in 18 partly remitted schizophrenics during 15 tone presentations (800 Hz, 85 dB). Additionally taking into account other conflicting results obtained with acute and chronic schizophrenic patients (summarized by Zahn, 1986), right-hand dominance of EDA cannot be regarded as a stable trait-like phenomenon in schizophrenia.

Another interesting line of research with respect to specificity of EDA parameters for schizophrenia focused on differences in NS.EDR freq. during the presence and absence of relatives rated as high or low in "*expressed emotion*" (for a summary, see Turpin, Tarrier, & Sturgeon, 1988). Tarrier, Vaughn, Lader, and Leff (1979) reported data from 21 schizophrenic outpatients and 21 age-and gender-matched normal participants, having been tested with Tarrier et al.'s (1978) method in the laboratory. In addition, electrodermal recordings were taken from the patients at their homes for 15 min under two conditions: with and without the presence of their key relative, who had been rated as either high or low on expressed emotion (EE) 2 years before. When compared to the controls, schizophrenics showed elevated levels of NS.SCR freq. during the presence of the experimenter alone. After the entry of their key relative, patients with high-EE relatives displayed a significantly greater amount of spontaneous EDA than those with low-EE relatives, which showed a decrease in NS.SCR freq.

Similar results were obtained by Sturgeon, Kuipers, Berkowitz, Turpin, and Leff (1981) with 20 acute schizophrenic patients during an interview conducted with the patient's key relative, whose EE had been measured earlier. Spontaneous SCRs (recorded with standard methodology, however, using K–Y gel; amplitude criterion = 0.02 μS) were significantly reduced in patients after the relative's entry in case of low-EE but not in case of high-EE relatives, as measured by individual regression slopes. The authors suggested that high-EE relatives may support the maintenance of a chronic state of high arousal in schizophrenics by stressful social interactions, while low-EE relatives might help the patients to adapt to stress by their supportive attitudes. Thus, the probability of relapse should be greater in the former group of patients compared to the latter one.

To test this hypothesis, Sturgeon, Turpin, Kuipers, Berkowitz, and Leff (1984) performed a follow-up study with 19 schizophrenics being at high risk for relapse (i.e., their relatives being high on EE), testing them with the methods used by Sturgeon et al. (1981) during acute illness and 9 months after discharge. During the initial testing, patients with high-EE relatives showed a significantly higher NS.SCR freq. than a control group of 11 patients with low-EE relatives, regardless of whether their key relative had been present or not. Patients with high-EE relatives were divided into a group that was offered a number of social interventions to reduce the relative's EE and/or contact with the patient, while the other group received no such training. This kind of intervention was highly successful in reducing relapse rates. However, its effects were not directly mediated via influences on spontaneous EDA, since patients whose relative changed during intervention from high- to low-EE did not reduce their rates of NS.SCRs to the level of the original patient group with low-EE relatives. Nevertheless, EDA seemed to be another independent indicator of the susceptibility to schizophrenic relapse, since NS.SCR freq. during initial testing was significantly higher for those patients who subsequently relapsed as compared to the patients who remained well.

It should be further investigated, in what respect and to what extent emotional expression as a social communication factor, which has shown close relationships to phasic electrodermal parameters (Sect. 3.2.2.1), and the rate of spontaneous EDA as a possible vulnerability indicator for schizophrenic relapse (Sect. 3.4.2.2) may depend on each other during the course of schizophrenic illness. Especially, as Olbrich (1989) pointed out, the different theoretical positions of a purely emotional arousal indicating the property of spontaneous EDA vs. its possible dependency on the schizophrenic's excessively allocating of central processing capacity to irrelevant stimuli (Sect. 3.1.3.1) should be focused on in future research.

3.4.3 EDA as an Indicator in the Psychopharmacological Treatment of Anxiety Disorders

Among the various kinds of drugs that have been used in the treatment of acute as well as chronic anxiety, the so-called *minor tranquilizers* are regarded as possessing the highest degree of specificity with respect to influencing anxiety. Despite having contributed considerably to the progress in anxiety treatment since the mid 1950s, and even labeled as anxiolytics or "anti-anxiety drugs" (Solomon & Hart, 1978; Rickels, 1978), the specificity of minor tranquilizers remained a matter of debate (Janke & Netter, 1986). This is due to both conceptual and methodological deficits in anxiolytic drug research with humans. However, since the 1950s, there has been a considerable progress in evaluating the neuropsychological background of anxiety and in linking psychophysiological measures to anxiety. EDA has been demonstrated as being a very sensitive indicator of anxiety both as trait and state (Sect. 3.3.1.2).

Anxiety is influenced not only by minor tranquilizers but also by other kinds of drugs such as hypnotics (e.g., barbiturates or alcohol) and small doses of neuroleptics (e.g., phenothiazines or butyrophenones), which are therefore labeled "major tranquilizers." Other drugs with different main action on CNS but anxiolytic side effects (e.g., MAO inhibitors, opiates, and tricyclic antidepressive agents like imipramine), as well as peripheral-acting agents like beta blockers (e.g., propanolol), or muscle-relaxing drugs (Janke & Netter, 1986; Lader & Petursson, 1983; Rickels, 1978) have also been used to treat anxiety.

Practically no therapeutic use can be made of opiates, barbiturates, or alcohol because of their addictive properties. MAO inhibitors and tricyclic antidepressants show considerable anxiolytic effects especially during phobic anxiety and panic attacks (Klein & Rabkin, 1981; see also Sect. 3.4.1.1), but do not generally influence anxiety states. Therefore, conceptual research on anxiolytic drugs should focus on the differentiation between minor tranquilizers as specific and neuroleptics or major tranquilizers as nonspecific anxiety-reducing agents. In addition, these classes of drugs acting centrally on anxiety should be conceptually separated from drugs like beta blockers, which act primarily on the adrenergic receptors in the periphery.

In a first approach, pharmacological effects on anxiety may be divided into primary and secondary ones. Benzodiazepines and hypnotics are drugs exerting their primary action on neurophysiological structures that are also regarded as anxiety evoking. During the late 1970s, specific benzodiazepine receptors were discovered at limbic and thalamic sites both in vitro (Squires & Braestrup, 1977) and in vivo (Williamson, Paul, & Skolnick, 1978). These receptors are linked to GABA receptors, thus increasing the inhibitory action of GABA via a specific postsynaptic receptor (Guidotti, Baraldi, Schwartz, & Costa, 1979). According to Gray (1982), benzodiazepines increase the GABA-ergic inhibition of noradrenergic activity stemming from the locus ceruleus as well as serotonergic fibers from raphé nuclei (Fig. 3.4, Sect. 3.2.1.2) because of the benzodiazepine receptors being located adjacent to the GABA receptors. Both monoamines are regarded as acting together in improving the analysis of stimuli within the basal hippocampal-stop circuit while influencing the gating process between the dentate gyrus and the hippocampal area CA3. The result is a more thorough analysis of the whole stimulus situation and is accompanied by an increased activity of the septo-hippocampal stop-system or BIS (Sect. 3.2.1.2), which had been demonstrated to cause inhibition of behavior in the rat during anxiety. Thus, the anxiolytic action of benzodiazepines can be labeled as primary, since they exert a direct influence on limbic neurotransmitter systems involved in the origin of anxiety.

The presumed specificity of benzodiazepine receptors for the pharmacopsychological influence on anxiety has been questioned by Janke and Netter (1986). First, those receptors also appear frequently in various systems that are not directly tied to anxiety (e.g., in motor systems or in the spinal cord) which gave rise to the conclusion that they are involved in anticonvulsive rather than in anxiolytic actions of benzodiazepines. Second, specific endogenous substances that are produced to counteract anxiety states (similar to endogenous opiates during pain) could not be detected until now. In addition, the development of experimental benzodiazepine antagonists like the beta-carbolines did not yield systematic results with respect to evoking anxiety (Rommelspacher, 1981). Despite the specificity of the benzodiazepine-GABA link as one mechanism underlying anxiolytic effects of those drugs, it needs further empirical support, from both human and animal studies. The theoretical approach provided by Gray (1982) may be included as one element of a general framework of tranquilizer action upon anxiety influencing information processing. Hypnotics like barbiturates as well as alcohol are also primary anxiolytic agents since they also enhance GABA-ergic inhibition of monoaminergic fibers which facilitate anxiety reactions in the limbic system. They do not directly increase the production of GABA; instead, they are indirect GABA-mimetics, because of their ability to bind to the picrotoxine receptors, thus preventing picrotoxine from acting as a GABA-antagonist. So GABA seems to be the common transmitter in the CNS for all primary anxiolytic agents. However, this could not be directly proved since the application of GABA did not show anxiolytic effects in animal studies (Koella, 1986).

The anxiolytic mechanism in the action of the so-called *major tranquilizers* is even less known. It had been assumed that they do not specifically influence anxiety but reduce general arousal via their sedating properties (Lader, 1979), together with a general reduction of muscular and emotional tension (Janke & Netter, 1986). Hence, their anxiety reducing mechanism is labeled as a secondary one.

Anxiety reduction not only is subjectively experienced but also can be measured objectively by means of physiological and behavioral parameters, the latter ones being predominantly used in animal research. Anxiety states are characterized by a markedly increased general arousal (Sect. 3.2.1.1). Hence, anxiolytic agents are expected to show at least some deactivating properties, both subjectively reported and objectively measured by various psychophysiological measures. However, reducing arousal is common in several classes of CNS drugs. Therefore, physiological measures to be used as indicators in the psychopharmacological treatment of anxiety should show at least some specificity with respect to the phenomenon in question.

The specific indicator function of tonic EDA with respect to BIS activity as suggested by Fowles (1980) relies on research in the field of conditioning and stress, mainly focusing on the appearance of stimulus dependent as well as spontaneous EDRs, and not on the EDL which is regarded as a rule being influenced more by peripheral physiological states (e.g., corneal hydration; Sect. 1.3.4.2) as compared to influences by fear-evoking stimuli. Therefore, the following section mainly focuses on the NS.EDR freq. as a specific indicator for anxiety reduction by classical anxiolytic drugs of the benzodiazepine type. There are two different approaches in the psychophysiological investigation of psychopharmacological actions:

1. The clinical approach, which compares a group of patients, mostly neurotics or persons with generalized anxiety syndrome, with a control group being as similar as possible, however showing no symptoms of anxiety. Using patients

as participants frequently yields the disadvantage of not allowing for placebo control, because often placebos cannot be used for ethical reasons.

2. The experimental approach, which uses only individuals without anxiety symptoms, who are assigned at random to either a group with or without an experimental induction of anxiety. Despite using normal individuals, personality traits like neuroticism or trait anxiety should be controlled (Sect. 3.3.1.2). The problem here is the external and ecologic validity of results, given the more severe forms of anxiety in patients and the myriad of potential anxiety provoking stimuli for truly anxious individuals.

Since both approaches show specific advantages as well as disadvantages, they have been used as complementary research strategies in psychopharmacological research.

3.4.3.1 Studies with Benzodiazepines

Unfortunately, clinical studies of the above-mentioned type (1) using physiological recordings are sparse, as most of them use global criteria of improvement following drug application obtained by the doctor's ratings or self-ratings (Giedke & Coenen, 1986). However, in case of physiological recordings being performed, specific drug actions with respect to anxiety reduction were more likely to be observed in EDA parameters as compared to other psychophysiological measures.

In a study using 30 neurotics of both genders who reported anxiety as their major symptom, Lapierre (1975) found acute, subacute, and chronic effects of diazepam in electrodermal but not in cardiovascular or respiratory measures. Following a 1-week wash-out period, subgroups of 10 patients each received three times a day either 5 mg diazepam, 7.5 mg chlorazepate (a benzodiazepine under investigation), or placebo following a double-blind schedule. Acute drug actions were recorded 3 h after the first application, the subacute ones 14 days, and the chronic ones 28 days later. As compared to placebo, diazepam yielded a significant reduction of the NS. EDR freq. under resting conditions and an increase of EDR lat. under stimulating conditions on all three occasions. Chlorazepate effects were present only during the 3 h postapplication recording period: a decrease in NS.EDR freq. together with an increase of the number of EDRs elicited by a nonspecific stimulation and no subacute and chronic effects on EDA. No significant chlorazepate-placebo differences were observed in HR, blood pressure, or respiration frequency.

The studies reported below assigned neurotic outpatients at random to four drug conditions, one of which was 5 mg diazepam twice a day, followed by a schedule three times a day together with another 5 mg during the night. The other schedule was 25 mg amitriptyline (an antidepressant) twice a day, followed by a schedule three times a day together with another 50 mg, and later on 75 mg during the night, a combination of both drugs not to be reported here as a third, and placebo as a fourth condition. In the first study (Johnstone et al., 1981) 181 patients of both genders, who showed either strong depressive or anxiety symptoms and were not previously drug treated, were subjected to a habituation procedure using 14 tones of 85 dB. As compared to the baseline recordings, the NS.SCR freq. and the SCL were reduced under all conditions. However, the NS.SCR freq. decreased to the greatest extent under diazepam, showing again its validity as a measure of anxiety reduction. The SCR rec.t/2, which was increased under placebo, decreased under diazepam and remained unchanged under amitriptyline. The plasma concentration of diazepam as measured by a benzodiazepine receptor binding technique yielded a highly significant correlation with the SCR recovery, while all other correlations of drug plasma concentrations with EDA measures were not significant. Johnstone et al. (1981) interpreted this result as pointing to a specific indicator function of EDR recovery for a drug-induced anxiety reduction. This would be in accordance with the hypothesis discussed earlier that EDR recovery is shorter during states of enhanced readiness for information uptake, together with distributed attention, which appears when hippocampal activity exceeds the amygdalar one (see Table 3.1; Sect. 3.1.3.1).

The second study (Frith, Stevens, Johnstone, & Owens, 1984) applied the same drug conditions as Johnstone et al. (1981) to 91 patients who were subjected to a habituation series of 17 tones (1 kHz, 85 dB) together with a 100 dB, 2 kHz tone interspersed after the 15th tone, which they should regard as irrelevant, and in addition to 71 patients who underwent 21 simple RT tasks using the same tones preceded by a warning signal (ISIs between 2 and 8 s). While amitriptyline showed a small reduction of tonic and phasic skin conductance under each experimental condition, there was a reduction of the SCR amp. following the irrelevant tones. Differential effects appeared during the RT paradigm. Participants who showed more than optimal arousal at the beginning yielded more errors together with higher SCR amp. under placebo, while patients with an increased error rate showed the lowest SCR amp. under diazepam. According to Frith and colleagues, this result indicates an influence of diazepam on the general arousal level as well as on attentional processes, both being indicated by electrodermal measures.

Further evidence for specific influences of benzodiazepines on EDA parameters stems from experimental psychopharmacological studies of the above-mentioned type (2). Boucsein and Wendt-Suhl (1976) investigated the action of 20 mg chlordiazepoxide as compared to placebo upon two different anxiety-evoking conditions and a control condition, using 90 healthy male participants in a double-blind schedule. Fifty minutes after application, the participants were instructed to expect an electric shock two times as strong under a weak-stress condition and five times as strong under a strong-stress condition in relation to an electric shock they had previously rated as unpleasant. During the anticipatory interval of 20 min duration, the course of which the participants pursued on a digital clock, NS.SRR freq., HR, respiration rate, and a rating of subjective emotional arousal were continuously recorded. In both electrodermal and subjective measures, significant main effects of the stress factor were only observed within the last 2 min of the anticipation interval (Sect. 3.2.2.2). However, interactions between drug and stress conditions reached significance for several minutes in an earlier phase of anticipation. In the middle of the interval, chlordiazepoxide reduced the NS.SRR freq., but only during the strong-stress condition and not during the weak-stress one. In the control group without stress, a so-called paradoxical effect of chlordiazepoxide appeared, yielding a higher NS.SRR freq. as compared to placebo. These results were paralleled by subjective ratings of emotional arousal, while the other physiological measures yielded no significant drug effects, except a general HR decrease under chlordiazepoxide previous to the stress-inducing instructions.

To compare the anxiety-reducing effects of 5 mg diazepam and 3 mg cloxazolam (a benzodiazepine that was under investigation), Boucsein and Wendt-Suhl (1982) applied three different stress conditions in counterbalanced order during a placebo-controlled, double-blind study with 144 male participants. The stress conditions were paralleled by appropriate neutral conditions in the control groups. The 30-min stress period, during which skin resistance, HR, and spontaneous EEG activity were continuously recorded, started 170 min after application of the drugs. One stress condition consisted of two successive 3-min anticipation periods of an unpleasant electric shock, the second of which had been announced as being twice as strong, which, however, was not the case. They were separated by a 2-min interval and pursued by the participants on a digital clock. Another stress condition used a speech anxiety paradigm[248] and the third stressor was the presentation of 12 anagrams, 10 of which were unsolvable for the experimental group but not for the control group (Boucsein & Frye, 1974). While cloxazolam showed heterogeneous results, the pattern of which was also not typical for tranquilizers, diazepam yielded differential effects, indicating its specificity to influence anxiety as well as the specific indicator function of EDA with respect to anxiety-reduction, since a decrease in the mean range-corrected amplitudes of NS.SRRs (Lykken, Rose, Luther, & Maley, 1966; Sect. 2.3.3.4 "Range Corrections") under diazepam as compared to placebo could only be observed when anxiety-evoking conditions like an anticipation of electric shocks or public speaking were applied, but not with an unspecific stress-evoking condition such as trying to solve unsolvable anagrams. No significant differences between diazepam and placebo appeared in HR.

Wilhelm and Roth (1997), in a double-blind study, randomly assigned 28 flight phobics to either a 1 mg alprazolam or a placebo condition ($N = 14$ in each group, matched for age and severity of phobia). Fifteen participants without flight phobia served as additional control group. Ambulatory monitoring of various psychophysiological measures including SC (as described by Wilhelm & Roth, 1998; see

---

[248] The speech anxiety paradigm used here was a very realistic extension of the one used by Boucsein and Wendt-Suhl (1980). A group of so-called speech experts was presented to the participant on a video screen, which was "joined" by the female experimenter (who could be seen from her back being in front of the group, which required her to always wear the same white collar and hair style throughout the whole study) who presented (over an auditory mixing device) the personal data of the actual participant who prepared the speech.

Sect. 3.4.1.1) was recorded during a 12 min flight in a commercial airplane. Alprazolam or placebo was given 1.5 h before the flight. The benzodiazepine reduced self-reported anxiety and symptoms more than placebo, but induced an increase in HR and respiratory rate. During a second flight without medication performed 1 week later, the group having received alprazolam before the first flight showed no extinction of subjective fear; instead, the participants' HR increased further and they revealed a significantly increased rate of panic attacks compared to the first flight. No effects of anxiety or drug were found in SCL or NS.SCR freq.

3.4.3.2 Studies with Beta-Blockers and Neuroleptics

During the 1980s, there was an increasing use of *beta-blockers* as anxiolytic agents (Netter, 1986). Their influence on anxiety may be exerted via two different mechanisms: (1) Mediated by blocking adrenergic beta-receptors in the periphery, thus preventing such anxiety-related ANS and humoral responses like HR increase, bronchial dilatation, and glycogenolysis in the liver, which are also typical ANS concomitants of stress (Sect. 3.2.2.2). (2) Since beta-blockers can normally easily pass the blood-brain barrier, at least a part of their anxiolytic capacity can be presumed to stem from their influences on beta-adrenergic synaptic transmissions within the CNS. As Gruzelier and Connolly (1979) pointed out, there is a direct influence of beta-blockers on the limbic system via impulses stemming from the amygdala, being characteristic for anxiety. These authors could show propanolol inducing a normal course of electrodermal habituation in schizophrenic slow habituators (Sect. 3.4.2.2). The particular deficit of habituation in this group of schizophrenia patients is supposedly due to a dysfunction of the amygdala, leading to hippocampal predominance during information processing (cf., Table 3.1; Sect. 3.1.3.1).

Besides the already mentioned neurophysiological influences of beta-blockers on EDRs, these agents may also influence EDA peripherally in a different way. Although sweat-gland innervation is now assumed being primarily cholinergic, there have always been discussions concerning a possible additional adrenergic supply (Sect. 1.3.3.1). Therefore, in addition to the widely used parasympathicolytics and parasympahicomimetics in the study of peripheral mechanisms of EDA (Muthny, 1984), direct actions of sympathicolytic and sympathomimetic substances on EDA in the periphery were also discussed (Edelberg, 1972b). Beta-blockers may exert indirect influences on EDA via their vasomotor effects (i.e., via reduction of skin blood flow), the possible influence and contribution of which on EDA remaining equivocal.

Experimentally controlled studies of the above-mentioned type (2) comparing the anxiolytic effects of beta-blockers with those of benzodiazepines using EDA are sparse, since most studies restricted themselves to cardiovascular measures. One study was performed by Farhoumand, Harrison, Pare, Turner, and Wynn (1979) who compared 480 mg of the beta-blocker oxprenolol with 2 mg of the tranquilizer lorazepam and placebo in a balanced within-subjects design using 6 male participants. Though in a considerably high dosage, the beta-blocker yielded less effects on EDA during stress induced by physical exercise as compared to the benzodiazepine.

Erdmann, Janke, Köchers, and Terschlüsen (1984), in a 3 × 3 factorial design with independent groups, assigned 108 male participants to either 40 mg oxprenolol, 5 mg diazepam, or placebo, following a double-blind design. Under each drug condition, two speech-anxiety groups and one control group were formed. Participants in the high speech-anxiety groups were allowed 5 min for preparing a talk to be held in front of experts being visible on a TV screen, while the low speech-anxiety groups were told that they would have to deliver their speech on tape for later analysis purposes. The control groups had to answer a questionnaire covering the same topic as the speech after the anticipatory period. Using measures from a 10 min baseline as covariates, NS.SRR freq., HR, and blood pressure were recorded and evaluated during 10 min following the 5 min preparation phase. Drug main effects were only significant for HR, due to the direct influence of the beta-blocker, whereas all physiological measures depicted the graded anxiety effects as attempted by the experimental design. Interactions between these and the drug effects reached significance for the NS.SRR freq., which was increased under oxprenolol in the neutral condition, showing in turn a tendency to be reduced under diazepam in the high speech-anxiety condition.

Since both studies did not yield anxiolytic effects of beta-blockers that are typically observed under benzodiazepines, a model of two classes of drugs influencing anxiety in a different manner can be proposed as a possible consequence: the centrally acting benzodiazepines which mainly influence EDA; and the beta-blockers, the action of which can be recorded most appropriately by HR, thus influencing only peripheral concomitants of anxiety. However, as Netter (1986) stated, subjective anxiety can be most effectively reduced by beta-blockers if one of its main causes is the irritating effect of an elevated HR.

Several studies compared the beta-blocker propanolol, which passes the blood-brain barrier more easily than oxprenolol, with different phenothiazines (i.e., neuroleptics). Gruzelier, Eves, Connolly, and Hirsch (1981) reported results from three habituation studies of the above-mentioned type (1) on the action of propanolol as compared with phenothiazine or chlorpromazine, performed with schizophrenics and normal controls. Besides the normalization of the habituation in one subgroup of patients, reported by Gruzelier and Connolly (1979) using the same data set (Sect. 3.4.2.1), an OR reinstatement in schizophrenic electrodermal nonresponders could be observed under propanolol. Since these effects appeared independently of tonic electrodermal changes in either SCL or NS.SCR freq., the authors concluded a specific influence of beta-blockers on the OR and its habituation without inducing changes in general arousal, as appeared under the influence of phenothiazines. On the other hand, the phenothiazines did not influence the patients' abnormal habituation when stimuli of medium intensity (70 dB) were used. Only in the third study, where 90 dB stimuli had been applied to 12 schizophrenics, an average dose of 320 mg chlorpromazine brought about a general reduction in SCR amp. Whether or not beta-blockers influence the OR, while phenothiazines act upon the DR (Sect. 3.1.1.2), as Gruzelier, Eves, Connolly, and Hirsch (1981) concluded, remains a testable hypothesis in psychopharmacological research.

In general, as already stated for beta-blockers, the influence of *neuroleptics* on EDA recordings as an indicator of anxiety reduction must be regarded with care, since neuroleptics also definitely exert anticholinergic properties. In addition, a different central mechanism acting directly on the elicitation of EDA may be involved when using neuroleptics, as evidenced by a study performed by Patterson and Venables (1981) with 12 healthy male participants. These authors used two different types of neuroleptics – 3 mg haldol, which blocks the dopaminergic fibers, and 50 mg chlorpromazine, which has both anticatecholaminergic and anticholinergic properties – together with 1 mg of scopolamine (an anticholinergic drug which easily passes the blood–brain barrier) and placebo in a within-subjects design. After 15 min of resting, the electrodermal OR following a 1 kHz 75 dB tone of 1 s duration and a short rise time of 15 ms was recorded under each drug condition. Four participants did not show any OR; therefore, they were classified as nonresponders. In the remaining participants, the SCR completely disappeared under scopolamine, while chlorpromazine reduced the SCR amp. and shortened the rise time as well as the SCR recovery time significantly. By contrast, haldol increased the SCR amp. together with a shortening of the SCR recovery time. This result shows that the influence of neuroleptics with anticholinergic properties such as chlorpromazine is not mediated via a general reduction of arousal, since haldol increased the ED-OR amp. Neuroleptics having anticholinergic properties presumably exert their influence on EDA via a depletion of central and possibly also peripheral acetylcholine reservoirs, thus invalidating the specific function of EDA as an indicator of anxiety reduction via a central neurophysiological mechanism, which has been demonstrated for benzodiazepines.

In summary, EDA can be used as a sensitive and valid indicator of anxiety-reducing properties of benzodiazepines (and for the other so-called minor tranquilizers as well). However, anxiety-evoking conditions must be carefully selected for application in this type of research. Especially when testing new drugs, it will be necessary to maintain the induced anxiety states over a certain period of time. This may be achieved by the successive introduction of different anxiety-evoking situations. Although electrodermal measures show a considerable specificity for indicating a successful anxiety treatment with anxiolytic drugs of the benzodiazepine type, the same cannot be stated for the anxiety reduction due to the pharmacological action of other types of drugs used in anxiety treatment such as beta-blockers or neuroleptics. Beta-blockers exert their anxiolytic capacity mainly via a reduction of typical adrenergic innervated concomitants of anxiety. Therefore, their effects on HR will be more prominent and probably more specific than their effects on EDA. Neuroleptics are likely to influence EDA mostly via their anticholinergic properties and do not act directly on the neurophysiological structures in which anxiety is supposed to originate.

3.5   The Use of EDA in Applied Psychology and in Medicine

Besides their clinical use, methods of electrodermal recording are present in several fields of applied psychology. In addition, the present section discusses the use of EDA in medicine. The main aim of this section is to stimulate inter-disciplinary cooperation in the development and application of electrodermal methodology, for example between psychophysiologists and dermatologists (Sect. 3.5.3).

Since EDA is one of the most sensitive psychophysiological indicators of stress (Sect. 3.2.2.2), it has also been applied in stress-strain research in the work place (Sect. 3.5.1.1). However, since the most specific sites for emotional recordings are at the palms and soles (Sects. 1.3.3.3 and 2.2.1.1), recording EDA during actual work may impede performance, and is likely to show increased artifact proneness as well (Sect. 2.2.5.1). Therefore, EDA as a stress indicator in this field has been less frequently used than HR, which is easier to record under working conditions in the field.

A widespread though controversial use of EDA in applied psychology consists in the detection of deception (Sect. 3.5.2). In this area, EDA as a sensitive and easy-to-evaluate method of detecting even small differences in emotional reactions to stimuli has revealed some superiority over various other psychophysiological indicators.

Other possible fields of application in which EDA has not been so frequently used are developmental and social psychology. With respect to the former one, the reader is referred to Sect. 2.4.3.1 and to a summary by Porges and Fox (1986). The use of EDA in social psychology has been summarized by Schwartz and Shapiro (1973) and by Cacioppo and Petty (1986).

The clinical use of EDA is not restricted to psychopathology (Sect. 3.4). In addition, several medical disciplines such as dermatology (Sect. 3.5.3) and neurology (Sect. 3.5.4) make specific use of electrodermal parameters for diagnostic purposes as well as in therapy evaluation. Furthermore, in various illnesses that are often classified as psychosomatic disorders, EDA has been used not only in diagnostics and therapy but also to establish models for explaining the psychophysiological nature of these disorders (Sect. 3.5.5).

3.5.1   EDA in Engineering Psychophysiology

The major use of EDA in the field of engineering psychology concerns its indicator function for altered levels of arousal and stress. Only a few studies that used EDA as an indicator of *job-related stress* have been performed at industrial sites. In an exploratory study performed with three female workers belonging to an assembly group in the electronic industry, Faber (1983) recorded SYL[249] and HR during several different subtasks. While HR increased with physical strain, an increase of SYL was found with increasing mental strain (work break-packing-soldering-assembling). Rakov and Fadeev (1986) provided results demonstrating that EDA may be used as an indicator for nonphysical workload. They measured SP[250] in 20 female workers in an electronic factory during resting and different production as well as during testing phases of work. As compared to resting, only small increases in NS.SPR freq. appeared during manufacturing. However, a marked increase in spontaneous EDA could be found during testing phases which were reported as especially prone to emotional strain. Rutenfranz and Wenzel (1958) investigated the dependence of skin impedance[251] on the load of physical strain at simulated work places. Data from 3 female participants showed a marked decrease of SZL and an increase of the capacitive component (Sect. 2.1.5) after 15 min work at a punch press as compared to an initial resting period. To further test the dependence of skin admittance on physical strain, Rutenfranz and Wenzel recorded EDA from one male participant while repeatedly performing a bicycle ergometer task with different workload (see Footnote 251). In conditions with 10 mkp/s performance and above, skin capacity steadily increased, starting 2.5 min after task onset, the gradient becoming steeper with increasing amount of strain, with no marked decreases during subsequent 10 min resting periods. The increase of skin capacitance was paralleled by a decrease of SZL, the gradients of which, however, showed no such clear-cut relationships to workload.

Strong support for differential influence of different kinds of strain (physical, mental, and emotional) on electrodermal and cardiovascular parameters stems from investigations at real and simulated office work places. Peters (1974) monitored HR, blood pressure, respiratory rate, frontalis EMG, skin temperature, and SR telemetrically in 11 female phonotypists. For each psychophysiological parameter, the different tasks to be performed during their work were ranked with respect to the amount of changes induced by that particular task. While HR increase was highest during tasks with predominantly physical strain (e.g., changing paper), and lowest during the most automated task of typewriting, electrodermal changes mainly appeared during mental tasks (e.g., thinking or reading).[252] Thus, HR appeared

---

[249] Measured with a 10 Hz and 0.5 V constant voltage system, using dry electrodes made from silver-plated nylon tissue (3.2 cm² area), taken from palmar finger sites, and monitored telemetrically.

[250] Recorded with nonpolarizing electrodes palmar/dorsal from the left hand, amplified by an EEG coupler. The number of SPRs was individually related to productivity, to reduce interindividual differences.

[251] Measured with 500 Hz, 1, and 10 kHz with constant voltage (1 V) (SYL transformed to SZL) using 3 × 4 cm V2A nets as electrodes at the backside of the lower legs while working at a punch press, and at the lower arm's inside during bicycle ergometer task (performed ten times each with 0, 5, 10, 15, and 20 mkp/s, and six times with 25 mkp/s, with 7.5 min duration).

[252] The highest amount of EDA was, however, recorded during speaking, which must be regarded as being mainly due to an artifact (Sect. 2.2.5.2).

more sensitive to physical strain, while mental (and/or emotional) strain was mainly reflected in EDA.

There have also been attempts to use EDA in shift-work research. Ficková (1983) took SRL[253] recordings, in addition to HR and oral temperature, from 21 operators at the beginning, in the middle, and at the end of morning, afternoon, and night shifts. The highest SRLs appeared during the morning shift, while the lowest SRLs were observed during the late afternoon. These results are in accordance with the results of Rutenfranz (1955). Intrashift correlational analysis yielded significant covariations between HR and SRL in the afternoon and night shifts, while HR was correlated with body temperature in the morning shift.

Boucsein and Ottmann (1996) recorded SC with standard methodology during 5 consecutive days and nights in the laboratory from 24 male participants. They performed a 10 h task daily at a simulated computer work place (vigilance tasks with additional STM strain). SC was recorded intermittently (for technical reasons) with standard methodology, during work and leisure time as well as during sleep. Half of the participants worked under either 80 or 50 dB white noise. EDA results with respect to shift paralleled those obtained with urine catecholamines, being higher during working at daytime as compared to night work. Differential effects of noise emerged for both kinds of variables. Noise of 80 dB (as compared to the 50 dB control condition) led to an increase of adrenaline excretion for night workers, while a decrease was observed under noise in day workers. No direct noise effects on SC were obtained during work. However, aftereffects of noise on SC appeared during the subsequent sleep (Sect. 3.2.1.3), yielding a significant increase in NS. SCR freq. after working under noise, together with increased excretion rates of noradrenaline. Thus, EDA can be regarded as a possible sensitive indicator of long-lasting emotional strain in the field of human engineering.

Boucsein and Backs (2000, Table. 1.4) summarized the hitherto published results from the use of EDA in engineering psychology. Most of the studies were performed in the laboratory or in simulated workplaces and generally confirmed the importance of NS.SCR freq. and EDR amp. as indicators for emotional load.

An adaption of the four arousal model shown in Fig. 3.4 (Sect. 3.2.1.2) for the field of engineering psychophysiology has been performed by Boucsein and Backs (2009). Table 3.2 lists the typical psychophysiological concomitants for each of the four arousal systems, based on an extensive literature review (see Boucsein & Backs, 2009, Table. 35.2). According to the underlying systems, the response groups are labeled 1 through 4 and they comprise both ANS- and CNS-elicited responses.

If a situation changes or certain stimulation occurs, *affect arousal* will show up in Group 1 measures as frequency or amplitude of the electrodermal response (EDA1) and phasic HR changes. Attention will be shifted toward the new stimulus, supported by involuntary somatomotor responses such as head or eye movements (not shown in Table 3.2). The *preparatory activation* system will provide an

---

[253] Measured five times successively at 2-s intervals with 10 mA constant current, from the first and second fingers of the left hand, using 1 cm² aluminium electrodes.

Table 3.2 Psychophysiological measures showing some specificity as indicators for the four types of arousal described in Fig. 3.4

Group 1 responses
  Affect arousal system and fight/
    flight system
	Increase of frequency and sum amplitude of the emotionally negatively tuned non-stimulus-specific electrodermal responses (EDA1)
	Phasic changes in heart rate
	  Heart rate decrease followed by an increase as components of an orienting response
	  Heart rate increase without previous decrease as component of a defensive response

Group 2 responses
  Effort system and behavioral
    inhibition system
	Decrease of heart rate variability
	Increase of recovery times of electrodermal responses
	Increase of P300 amplitude in the evoked potential calculated from the electroencephalogram
	Increase of theta activity in the spontaneous electroencephalogram

Group 3 responses
  Preparatory activation system
    and behavioral activation system
	Moderate increase of the tonic heart rate
	Increase of the amplitude of the preparatory non-stimulus-specific electrodermal responses (EDA2)
	Contingent negative variation and *Bereitschaftspotential* in the evoked potential calculated from the electroencephalogram

Group 4 responses
  General arousal system
    (reticular activation system)
	Increase of the sympathicus-driven responses of the autonomic nervous system
	  Marked increase of heart rate, blood pressure and tonic electrodermal activity
	Desynchronization in the electroencephalogram (alpha blockade)

From Boucsein & Backs (2009). Copyright 2009 by CRC Press/Taylor & Francis. Used by permission of the publisher

increased readiness of brain areas involved in eliciting intended somatomotor actions. This will increase brain negativity as can be seen in the CNV (McGuinness & Pribram, 1980, see Sect. 3.1.3.1) and the *Bereitschaftspotential* (readiness potential; Kornhuber & Deecke, 1965), but also other Group 3 responses such as a moderate increase of tonic HR (Fowles, 1980) and an increase of EDA2 amplitudes (Boucsein, 1992).

Dependent on novelty, stress or an increased emotional load, the normally straightforward chain of situation-response relationships can be modified by the *effort* system. It has the ability to disconnect Arousal Systems 1 and 3 to prevent immediate action and facilitate deliberate analysis performed by certain cortical-subcortical brain circuits (Gray, 1982), including the so-called Papez circuit (see Fig. 3.4, upper left). The ongoing central information processing will be reflected by a decrease in HRV, an increase of the P300 component of the ERP, enhanced frontal theta activity in the EEG, and an increase of EDR recovery time, shown as Group 2 responses in Table 3.2.

Group 4 responses indicate the amount of *general arousal*, which is seen in various measures of the ANS (HR, blood pressure, and tonic EDA) and in EEG desynchronization (beta replaces alpha activity, which is labeled alpha blockade). Dependent on the strength of stimulation or on the person's intentions, Group 4 responses may dominate the whole psychophysiological occurrence.

Although far from covering all possible psychophysiological relationships in arousal, emotion, and stress, the model proposed here may help providing a framework for generating refined hypotheses regarding the action of different arousal and emotional processes on physiological outcomes. It is crucial for such a neurophysiologically based approach to be supported with empirical results from the field. Boucsein and Backs (2009) have exemplified this with respect to workload and stress in the field of ergonomics, giving a summary of the sensitivity and reliability of all psychophysiological measures in their Table 35.2.

3.5.1.1 EDA in Human-Computer Interaction

When visual display terminals (VDTs) came into wider use during the 1960s, the application of psychophysiological methods in human-computer interaction (HCI) focused on ergonomic features of hardware and their implications for physical strain. Consequently, electromyographic and oculographic measures were predominantly used as physiological measures. About 20 years later, when computer tasks had become more and more sophisticated, mental and/or emotional stress during HCI became the focus of interest, and psychophysiologists started to use ANS measures such as HR and EDA.

However, increased caution must be exercised while studying real work places with respect to possible physiologically produced artifacts (Sect. 2.2.5.2), since ANS changes may result from movements and/or posture changes instead from psychological factors. For example, Springer, Müller, Langner, Luczak, and Beitz (1990) recorded various psychophysiological measures, including NS.SRRs[254] and their mean amplitude in 33 engineering students. They obtained significantly greater EDA during 120 min use of a drawing board, as compared to using computer aided-design software on a VDT for the same time. The difference turned out as being much more likely due to standing vs. sitting during work than to psychological strain.

Between 1982 and 2000, the present author's group performed a series of studies on psychophysiological stress reactions (Sect. 3.2.2.2) produced by system response times (SRTs) in HCI at simulated and real VDT work places, using electrodermal and cardiovascular measures among others as dependent variables (for summaries, see Boucsein, 2000, 2009). In a pilot study, Schaefer, Kuhmann, Boucsein, and Alexander (1986) continuously recorded HR and SC[255] during several hours of VDT work as well as during the interspersed rest breaks.

---

[254] Recorded from the left little finger with nonreported methodology.

[255] In all studies of the present author's group, SC was measured with standard methodology.

Twenty participants (16 females, 4 males) performed five blocks of 50 rather simple error detection tasks, while being subjected to intertask intervals of 2 or 8 s on average. Intertask intervals were either of constant or variable length. Short SRTs (i.e., higher work density) produced an increase in systolic blood pressure, as measured during the subsequent work breaks. This was interpreted by the authors as reflecting the greater amount of mental and/or physical strain. Contrarily, NS. SCR freq. showed a tendency to be higher under the condition of long SRTs, which was interpreted as due to emotional strain.

Kuhmann, Boucsein, Schaefer, and Alexander (1987) performed another experiment with 68 participants (22 females, 46 males), using a similar design. However, differing from the first study, trial blocks were of equal length, which implicated different number of tasks per block when varying intertask intervals (1,248 tasks in the 2 s system response time condition and 624 in the 8 s condition). Despite the differences in design, these authors replicated the main results of Schaefer et al. (1986), since higher systolic blood pressure levels emerged under short SRTs, and a significantly increased tonic EDA (NS.SCR freq. as well as SCL) was observed under long SRTs. The increase in EDA could not be attributed to artifacts (e.g., movements or an increased number of tasks per time), since it appeared under the condition of lower work density. Therefore, the authors confirmed that an increased EDA was reflecting emotional strain caused by involuntary breaks.

The ability of EDA to indicate emotional strain in HCI was directly shown in a third study by Kuhmann (1989), in which 48 participants (10 females, 38 males) performed the same kind of tasks with either 2, 4, 6, or 8 s SRTs during three training trials and five working trials of 20 min each. Though no general effects of the physiological variables recorded reached significance, an averaging procedure of phasic EDA across tasks, using the end of the intertask interval as a trigger point, revealed that EDA (in arbitrary units) within the 2-s interval was solely determined by the amount of EDA during the previous task. On the other hand, a complex pattern appeared in the course of the 8-s interval trials, where EDA was higher during task performance as compared to the time when waiting for the next task, both during training and during the first working trial. The reverse pattern emerged during the rest of the working trials, reflecting the development of an emotional tension while being interrupted in task performance by SRTs as artificial temporal delays, for which EDA appeared to be a sensitive psychophysiological measure.

The development of this kind of emotional strain as reflected by an increase of EDA could not be shown in short-term VDT work without time pressure which had been used in the studies reported above. Kuhmann, Schaefer, and Boucsein (1990) used SRTs of 2 or 8 s on average, being either constant or variable in length, in a within-subjects design with 24 participants (6 females, 18 males), who performed error-detection tasks in four trial blocks of 10 min length. While again an increased cardiovascular activity within the 2-s condition emerged as an elevated HR, a variable pattern of NS.SRR freq. appeared: spontaneous EDA was lowest under the 2-s-constant SRTs at the beginning, but even lower under the 8-s-variable condition at the end of the session.

Modern computer systems may allow the user to behave like a time-sharing system, thus providing the possibility to avoid adverse effects of SRTs by switching between different task windows. In a study with 48 participants (20 females, 28 males), Schaefer, Schäfer, and Boucsein (2000) systematically varied the virtual data transmission times in a mock power plant control task as between-subjects factor, together with the presence of feedback as a within-subjects factor. During short processing times of 10 s, both NS.SCR freq. and the sum of SCR amp. were significantly increased compared to 30 s processing times. The authors concluded that long waiting times in a multitasking system may be more convenient compared to short waiting times, since the delayed period can be better used for the performance of another task to be switched to. This enables optimal work scheduling, which might have attenuated emotional strain, thus reducing the amount of EDA under the long waiting times.

An optimal scheduling is also required for rest breaks during computer work. As in any kind of repetitive work, recovering from VDT work should be regularly scheduled to avoid adverse effects of accumulated mental and/or physical strain (e.g., neck muscle tension). Therefore, rest breaks of 10 min every hour have been introduced for data entry tasks in certain countries. However, such a predetermined work/rest schedule may not be appropriate for more complex HCI tasks. In a field study performed in a rather complex computerized environment, i.e., with 11 patent examiners (1 female, 10 males) who were members of a prototyping group which had access to patents on laser disks instead of patents stored in paper folders, Boucsein and Thum (1997) performed ambulatory monitoring (Sect. 2.2.3.4) of HR, SC (recorded from the right foot according to Fig. 2.7, Sect. 2.2.1.1), neck EMG, respiration, and gross body movement on 2 consecutive days with different rest break schedules in counterbalanced order: 15 min break after 100 min work on 1 day and 7.5 min break after 50 min work on the other day. The authors found frequently interspersed short breaks advantageous prior to the early afternoon, during which heart rate variability was increased as a sign of relaxation and NS. SCR freq. was diminished, compared to long breaks after a longer working time. The picture reversed in the afternoon, where the long rest break yielded a better recovery compared to the short breaks, as indicated by the same psychophysiological parameters.

To further investigate the differential psychophysiological effects of SRTs varying in length, Thum, Boucsein, Kuhmann, and Ray (1995) performed a study with 40 male participants, using intervals of 0.5, 1.5, or 4.5 s. The metabolic demands associated with mental workload were held constant by using an adaptive computer task, consisting of a randomly generated 6×6 matrices of 36 two-digit numbers. Participants had to decide whether one, both, or none of two target numbers was present. A special algorithm continuously varied the presentation time of the matrices, becoming shorter after a correct response and longer after two subsequent errors, thereby ensuring that all participants achieved the same percentage of correct responses. After each single task, feedback was given to the participant. The first of three 7-min trials was performed with 1.5 s SRTs and the two following ones with 0.5 or 4.5 s in a counterbalanced order. Half of the participants were given monetary incentive for exceeding a certain performance level. In short, the Thum et al. (1995) study showed that SRTs being shorter and longer than a certain medium range may induce considerable psychophysiological strain. Compared to the medium SRT of 1.5 s, both rather long (4.5 s) and rather short (0.5 s) SRTs yielded typical psychophysiological patterns: long SRTs increased NS.EDR amp. and reduced blood pressure, while short SRTs increased cardiovascular activity. The latter could be ascribed to mental workload, since it no longer appeared when the amount of workload was controlled, while the increase of EDA during long SRTs corresponded to negative self-reported emotional states, thus indicating emotional strain (Sect. 3.5.1).

In summary, the general findings of the present author's group were that negative physiological, behavioral, and subjective consequences resulted not only from rather long but also from rather short SRTs. The results support a concept of an optimal SRT, which is in accordance with the notion of Shneiderman (1992, p. 277) that there is a preferred SRT for a given user and task, and that both shorter and longer SRTs may generate debilitating effects on the effectiveness of HCI. As already suggested by Boucsein, Greif, and Wittekamp (1984), the use of EDA parameters opens the possibility to gain information on emotional strain at the VDT work place that goes beyond the largely metabolically determined physical and/or mental strain as measured by the frequently used cardiovascular parameters.[256]

EDA parameters have also been used for probing the influence of changes in VDT technical features on the user's psychophysiological responses. Reeves, Lang, Kim, and Tatar (1999) compared three different screen sizes (56-, 13,- and 2-in. vertical pictures height), presenting 60 different video segments of 6 s duration each to 38 participants while measuring HR and SC with standard methodology. EDA was evaluated as mean SCL and as the highest SCR amp. during the interval. The largest screen elicited greater HR deceleration compared to medium and small screens, which was interpreted as larger OR and hence more attention directed to the content of the video segment. The same result was obtained for the SCL, whereas no significant SCL differences were found between small and medium size screens. A significant interaction between screen size and the emotional content, rated by the participants after each video segment, emerged for SCR amp.: the most emotionally arousing videos (e.g., sex and violence scenes) elicited the EDRs with the highest amplitudes on the large screen compared to the two others, while there were no significant differences in SCR amp. elicited by different screen sizes for the subjectively nonarousing video-segments. The authors' interpretation that an increased excitability induced by extra large pictures as indicated by SCR amp. is in line with its indicator function for the BAS (see Table 3.2).

---

[256] However, caution has to be expressed with artifacts stemming from gross body movements. Goldstein and Shapiro (1988) found that cardiovascular parameters are more sensitive to postural changes during laboratory performance tests (mental arithmetic and isometric handgrip) than EDA. In addition, there was a marked increase in SCL as a transient response during standing up.

A special application of psychophysiological measures in HCI is their use for adapting computer behavior to human emotions. Because of its presumed specificity for indicating negatively tuned emotional states (Sect. 3.2.2.1), NS.EDR freq. is especially suitable to determine adverse emotional states during HCI that might be counteracted by appropriate computer actions. An "emotional mouse" (Whang, 2008) or other recording device such as "affective wearables" (Picard & Healy, 1997) can be used for continuously providing physiological data, which can be analyzed online and fed into an algorithm with the capability of determining certain emotional states.

Based on results of an earlier study (Whang, Lim & Boucsein, 2003), in which, among other psychophysiological measures, SC was recorded[257] during four emotional states that might be relevant for HCI, Whang (2008) obtained SC from 5 participants with dry electrodes, together with skin temperature and photo plethysmographic activity, by means of a computer mouse equipped with appropriate sensors. Recording was blocked during movements of the "emotional mouse" to avoid artifacts. An additional computer was used for parameterization and for detecting the user's current emotional state according to an individually determined rule base. As a first step in adapting the computer to the user for interacting with the user's current emotional state, the detected emotional state was displayed by means of an icon in the working display. The user was asked to validate the detected emotion and was offered a choice of stimuli to support her/him in recovering from negative emotional states.

A continuous online recording of EDA may also play a key role in the interaction of users with virtual agents (Backs & Boucsein, 2009). So far, psychophysiological measures have only been used for determining the user's emotional state, with the aim of adapting an avatar's behavior accordingly. The current standard for modeling emotional behavior of a virtual human is using facial expressions and gestures together with expressive speech (e.g., Pelachaud & Bilvi, 2003). However, if the interaction between avatar and user is aimed at approaching an interaction between humans, psychophysiological responses may have to be added to this very special kind of HCI.

3.5.1.2   EDA in Traffic and Automation

Traffic research is another field of engineering psychology where EDA recording has been systematically applied. Michaels (1960) conducted SR recordings from the left hand's first and third finger (with unreported methodology) of ten urban drivers, who used streets that differed in traffic volume. Spontaneous SRRs were detected, and a time window between 5 s before and 1 s after their onset was evaluated with respect to an event in traffic serving as trigger. Sixty percent of

---

[257] With stainless steel electrodes, covered with isotonic cream made from Unibase and attached to the right index and the middle finger.

SRRs could be related to unpredictable events like vehicles exiting their lane or crossing the road. In addition, mean SRR freq. was 40% lower on an individually preferred road, as compared to an alternative route.

In another study, Michaels (1962) used EDA to differentiate among the stress inducing characteristics of different expressway designs combined with traffic volume. Six male participants drove an 8–10 miles section of each highway four to eight times during off-peak hours while events causing a speed- or lane-change were recorded. The relation between the mean NS.SRR amp. and traffic volume was statistically significant, showing a linear increase up to 1,400 vehicles per lane per hour. For greater volumes, nonspecific EDA rose exponentially up to the maximum of 1,800 vehicles per lane per hour. When data were corrected for volume, significant differences between types of routes could be demonstrated, depending on the frequency of occurrence of conflicts with merging and exiting vehicles. These results indicate that the mean NS.SRR amp. may be used as a valid measure of driver stress, which is directly related to frequency and predictability of interferences with driving. Though this result parallels other results obtained in laboratory stress research (Sect. 3.2.2.2), it should be treated with more caution because of uncontrolled environmental influences on EDA.

The effect of rural intersection illumination on stress in four male drivers was investigated by Cleveland (1961). Each driver performed 12 runs through an intersection, twice on each of six paths, once with illumination and once without, while EDA was continuously recorded.[258] NS.EDR freq. and mean EDR amp. were 20% lower when the intersection was illuminated than without illumination.

Taylor (1964) reported data on EDA, driving behavior, and accident rate of drivers from two studies performed with 12 participants (5 females, 7 males) and 8 participants (4 of each gender). NS.EDR freq.[259] was recorded while driving standard routes during different times of day and night (which implies differences in traffic density and illumination) in counterbalanced order. No covariation of EDA with traffic density and illumination was observed. NS.EDR freq. showed a positive correlation to the number of turns per mile ($r = 0.67$) while correlating negatively with the average driving speed ($r = -0.75$). Furthermore, in the first experiment, a positive correlation ($r = 0.61$) was obtained between NS.EDR freq. and the average number of personal-injury accidents (taken from police records) per estimated vehicle-mile (by using calculations of traffic flow). Taylor interpreted his correlational data as being possibly dependent on the number of curves encountered per mile as the determining factor for an increased number of EDRs, but also for more accidents and for lower speed. Another result was that the mean number of NS.EDRs per minute exponentially decreased with driving experience, a factor however being confounded with age (Sect. 2.4.3.1).

To investigate possible connections between EDA and accident rate, Preston (1969), working in Britain, used the insurance classifications of her participants

---

[258] Measured with AC from the left hand's fingers, using a Wheatstone bridge.

[259] Recorded with AC (65 Hz), using 10 μA/cm^2 average current density, from the participant's fingers, data transformed into conductance changes.

(reflecting increasing premiums with number of accidents). In two studies, 17 and 21 participants of both genders drove over routes including narrow country roads as well as town roads. The dependent variable was the SRR amp.[260] summed up per mile driven. No general effects of age, gender, and insurance classifications appeared. However, separate evaluations for different types of roads yielded a significantly higher rate and intensity of EDA in participants with higher accident rates while driving on the country roads but not in town. Preston's interpretation was that driving in town is more limited, while rural driving allows a participant to demonstrate risky behavior, where EDA is a very sensitive measure of emotional strain when drivers are not absolutely certain of exerting full control.

In Sweden, Helander (1974) continuously recorded SR[261] from 60 participants with a wide range of age and experience in driving, on four different routes. In addition, HR, EMG from two muscle groups of the right leg (indicating release of accelerator and lifting of the leg for braking), and various vehicle variables (velocity, acceleration in three directions, steering wheel angle, and brake pressure) were recorded, and up to 25 traffic events were encoded by the experimenter. Readings from all variables, calculated for each 10 m, were rank-correlated. While Helander could not interpret a correlation of $r = 0.56$ between SRL and steering wheel angle, he revealed that EDRs were largely dependent on braking activity, since the covariation between the latter and SRR amp. was as high as $r = 0.89$. Since no such correlation was obtained during pressing the brake in the unmoving car, the EDR while braking was more likely to be psychologically determined than a motor artifact.

In a reanalysis of these data, Helander (1978) excluded situations of passing or being passed by another car and then obtained a rank correlation of $r = 0.95$ between SRR amp. and brake pressure. A detailed evaluation using cross-correlations of EDR and EMG data showed that the EDR was not a concomitant or consequence but an antecedent of braking. A comparison of EDRs and HR changes during steering yielded a much tighter covariation of the electrodermal system with the preparation of steering than for the cardiovascular system. Therefore, Helander concluded that EDR is a sensitive measure for detecting increases in task demand during driving.

In a study performed in Germany, Zeier (1979) recorded SYR[262] together with frontalis EMG, HR, and information from braking as well as from gear lever

---

[260] Recorded volar/dorsal from the left foot with 1 cm diameter electrodes filled with a cream from bentonite, glycerine, and Ringer's salt solution, using a constant current of 5 μA/cm^2 and a Wheatstone bridge.

[261] Beckman Ag/AgCl electrodes and electrode cream with 0.1N chloride concentration were used to record from the dorsal side of the hand with 12 μA/cm^2 constant current. For evaluation, psychophysiological responses were time-shifted 1 s earlier, in to compensate for the time delay associated with EDRs.

[262] AC recordings with a 5.25 Hz constant voltage (1 V) source between two Ag/AgCl electrodes, filled with Hellige isotonic electrode cream, attached according to Fig. 2.7 (Sect. 2.2.1.1) to the medial side of the left foot. EDA was recorded on tape with PCM (pulse code modulation) electronics. EDRs were classified into four groups: more than 10, 8–10, 5–7, and 2–4% change with respect to EDL, forming arbitrary units that were averaged per minute.

(or selector lever) activity continuously from 12 male participants driving a manual-gear or an automatic car in counterbalanced order with 1 week interval between driving experiences. Urine catecholamines, which were additionally recorded, were higher for driving a manual-gear car, as were NS.EDR freq. and HR, while no effects were found in EDL. Hence, in this study the frequency of nonspecific EDRs served as an indicator of general arousal (Group 4 response in Table 3.2) rather than of specific emotional strain. Additionally, EDA and HR were also elevated in passengers (who also took part in the study) while sitting in the manual-gear as compared to the automatic car, showing that even passive participation in the driving situation may cause considerable arousal.

Also in Germany, Richter, Wagner, Heger, and Weise (1998) continuously recorded SCR,[263] HR, HRV, eyeblink rate, movement activity, and car speed from 31 drivers (4 of them female), who drove in a quasi-randomized sequence on six roads, which differed in their curvature change rates. While the eyeblink rate decreased almost steadily with the increase in curvature change rate as an indicator for an increased information uptake requirement and HRV decreased as an indicator of increasing mental strain, NS.SCR freq. significantly increased from easy to very complicated curve driving, reflecting an increase in affect arousal (Group 1 response in Table 3.2). However, EDA did not differentiate between levels of intermediate difficulty, presumably because other variables such as oncoming traffic might have been more influential here.

The usability of EDA for detecting the level of driver's tension was demonstrated by Tanaka, Ishida, Kawagoe, and Kondo (2000) in Japan. Three experienced male drivers followed a vehicle on a test track, 5 times with and 11 times without a driver assistance system for lane keeping and adaptive cruise control. EDA was recorded from the left foot, which was not used for driving, as SP,[264] together with EMG from the right upper arm, for measuring steering movement strength. Driving assistance considerably reduced both physical workload as measured by EMG and the total amount of SPRs. Individual SPRs were related to speed changes in the leading vehicle, thus being indicative of mental and/or emotional workload.

Recordings of SC,[265] HR, HRV, EMG from the trapezius muscle (as a measure of general tension) and respiration from 24 drives of at least 50 min duration in the greater Boston area were analyzed by Healey and Picard (2005) in relation to a stress measure obtained from video recordings of situations and driver's gaze. For each of the 5 min driving segments, the total number of SCRs, plus the sums of their amplitudes, ascents, and estimated areas under the curve were calculated for both

---

[263] Recorded with standard methodology from the left foot according to Fig. 2.7 with a sampling rate of 20 Hz, evaluated as SCL and as NS.SCR freq. by means of a spline curve for detecting single responses, using an amplitude criterion of 0.05 μS.

[264] With Ag/AgCl electrodes, low-pass filtering of 3 and 10 Hz sampling frequency. The amplitude criterion was set to 1 mV.

[265] Measured at two sites: At the first and middle finger of the left hand and at the arch of the left foot, with unreported methodology, sampled at 31 Hz.

hand and foot recordings. A multivariate analysis of these parameters together with those from the other physiological measures revealed an almost perfect reclassification of situations having different predetermined stress levels. An additional analysis of continuous correlations, based on 1 s intervals, determined SC as the best real time correlate of the drivers' stress, followed by HR and HRV.

As compared with its use in vehicle driving research, EDA has not been used very often in the aviation environment. Lindholm and Cheatham (1983) continuously recorded SCR amp.[266] and HR from six air force reserve officer pilots while performing a landing task ten times in a simulator. Toward the end of the landing procedure, both measures showed a marked increase, which became less steep during practice in HR but not in EDA. Despite that result which showed some superiority of electrodermal over cardiovascular variables with respect to persistent emotional strain, these authors decided not to further record EDA in their studies with pilots.[267]

Kahabka, Oppelt, Rohmert, and Müller (1986) performed a field study with 3 participants, an inexperienced and an experienced pilot as well as an inexperienced passenger in a small plane. Monitoring of SCL,[268] HR, and EMG during five flight phases yielded differential effects on electrodermal and cardiovascular parameters: while HR and SCL were correlated in the inexperienced, they were not in the experienced pilot, where HR reflected the difficulties of flight, thus indicating mental strain. SCL showed a steep decline in the passenger during flight, being also uncorrelated with HR, which was interpreted by the authors as being due to the specific indicator function of EDA for emotional strain.

Wilson (2002) investigated 10 male general aviation pilots during a 90-min scenario, containing flight maneuvers under both visual and simulated instrument conditions, flown twice in a small single-engine aircraft. Besides ECG, EEG, and EOG, EDA was continuously recorded[269] together with an EMG from the calf of the right foot to control for movement artifacts resulting from steering the aircraft. SCL, NS.SCR freq., mean NS.SCR amp. and mean rise times and recovery times of NS.SCRs were analyzed. After each of the 22 flight segments, pilots gave their subjective estimates of mental workload on a scale from 0 to 100. Responses during the two flights did not differ considerably. Peaks in NS.SCR freq. during takeoff, touch-and-go, and landing were paralleled by peaks in HR and subjective mental workload, constituting a more or less general task determined arousal pattern. HRV was less sensitive than HR. Blink rates decreased during highly visually demanding flight segments.

---

[266] Measured with Beckman Ag/AgCl electrodes and Beckman cream from palmar/dorsal sites with 0.5 V constant voltage. The highest SCR amp. within every 5-s section was evaluated.

[267] In fact, the attachment of EDA electrodes being visible for everyone raises problems of compliance in pilots, which may explain some of its infrequent use in that field.

[268] Recorded with AC from the ankle, using the methodology of Faber (1983).

[269] Ag/AgCl electrodes placed on the arch of the right foot, 3.2 cm apart, filled with Grass EC33 electrode cream. EDA was recorded as SC with the Vitaport 2 ambulatory monitoring device (Sect. 2.2.3.4), together with the other measures.

Wright and McGown (2001) performed multiple psychophysiological recordings with 12 commercial pilots (1 female, 11 males) during transatlantic flights of approximately 9 h duration in each direction, flying westerly during daytime and easterly during night time. By means of ambulatory monitoring (Sect. 2.2.3.4), EEG, EOG, EMG, ECG, and EDA[270] were continuously recorded, together with various pilot movements and inputs given to the controls of the aircraft. Ten pilots either slept for short periods during their flight or showed evidence of sleepiness as assessed by EEG and EOG, partly during periods shorter than 20 s (microsleep), which were unnoticed by the pilots. Electrodermal parameters reflected more global changes in psychophysiological states such as a significant SRL increases from the first hour of cruise over sleepiness until after going to sleep, and also during the last 3 h of the night flight, which was interpreted by the authors as indicating a decrease of general arousal (Sect. 3.2.1.1).

Koglbauer, Kallus, Braunstingl, and Boucsein (2011) evaluated an anticipation-oriented training for general aviation pilots to recover from stalls, spins, and unusual attitudes by using ambulatory monitoring (Sect. 2.2.3.4) of EDA,[271] HR, and HRV during test flights in an aerobatic plane and in the simulator. Thirty-three active male pilots rated for flying under visual conditions only, 29 of whom could be completely evaluated, flew with an instructor in a two-place tandem biplane certified for aerobatics, performing full stalls, spins, overbank, and extreme pitch maneuvers. Seventeen of the participants received training of these maneuvers in a highly realistic, albeit fixed base, simulator, while 12 pilots served as control group and executed approaches and radio navigation tasks instead. On the next day, the training was followed by a simulator test with performing recoveries from the flight maneuvers that were trained. Finally, a test flight with each maneuver flown twice was performed in the aircraft for determining the amount of transfer of training from the simulator to real piloting. Performance of pilots who received simulator training of the maneuvers in question was superior to that of the control group. A marginally significant increase in SCR amp. in the training group compared to the control group was interpreted as indicating an increased preparatory activation (see Fig. 3.4, Sect. 3.2.1.2), which was in line with the anticipation-oriented nature of the simulator training. The control group, on the other hand, showed an increased NS.SCR freq. during the simulator and the final real flight tests, indicating higher affect arousal compared to the training group. Therefore, it is possible that the anticipation-oriented simulator training of the recovery maneuvers did not only improve performance but also contributed to the prevention of stress-related panic or "freezing" responses (Sect. 3.2.1.2) which could be fatal during dangerous real flight maneuvers (Boucsein & Backs, 2009). However, the groups also differed in

---

[270] Measured with a custom-made digital recorder with constant voltage across a pair of nickel electrodes attached to the volar surface of the third digit, with the output transformed to SR and recorded as mean SRL for 1 s intervals.

[271] Recorded as SC by the Varioport System with standard methodology from the left foot (Fig. 2.7) with a special fixation technique described at the end of Sect. 2.2.2.1.

HRV, being higher in the training group during real flights but higher in the control group during the simulator test. This result points to greater relaxation of the pilots in the training group during real flight but higher amount of mental strain during performance in the simulator, pointing to differences in mental workload between the groups.

A very special application of electrodermal measures in the domain of air traffic has been performed in the laboratory by Haarmann, Boucsein, and Schaefer (2009). Since automation has taken over much of the pilots' tasks especially during long haul operations, hypovigilance has become a threat during unexpected changes in situational demands. Attempts to keep pilots in an optimal state of vigilance and avoiding excessive amounts of workload at the same time have been made by means of adaptive automation. Besides EEG measures, which have been used in laboratory flight simulations (e.g., Scerbo, Freeman, & Mikulka, 2000) but might not be practicable in the real cockpit, HRV has been used as a psychophysiological measure of the pilot's workload, from which algorithms for an automated change of the degree of automation were derived. Recording of HRV was successfully combined with NS.SCR freq. recordings (measured with standard methodology) by Haarmann et al. (2009), the effect of which for adaptive automation was superior to NS.SCR freq. alone or in combination with HR. Their study was performed in a fixed-base flight simulator for general aviation aircraft with 48 nonpilot students (24 females, 24 males), using the degree of turbulence as a model for different automation modes. Although the transferability of results from laboratory simulations to the real cockpit might be challenged, the use of psychophysiological measures, including EDA, for an adaptive control of any operator's vigilance can be regarded as promising for further research into adaptive automation.

3.5.1.3   EDA in Marketing and Product Evaluation

Because of its indicator function in the domains of arousal and emotion (Sects. 3.2.1 and 3.2.2), EDA has for decades played an important role in psychophysiological recordings of consumer behavior for marketing purposes, since the EDR is a fast and sensitive indicator with sufficient reliability and validity (Kroeber-Riel & Weinberg, 2003). An advantage of using psychophysiological measures in marketing research is that consumers may not be willing to disclose their motives for buying a product if the rational appears not to be socially acceptable. More recently, EDA recordings were also used as core measures in the evaluation of products during the designing process (Boucsein & Schaefer, 2008).

An early attempt to relate EDRs[272] elicited by advertisements to subjective emotional responses was made by Caffyn (1964), who demonstrated that

---

[272] Recorded from the dorsal side of one hand by small suction cap electrodes, using a nonspecified psychogalvanometer.

advertisements that produced higher EDRs than control stimuli could be accompanied by either positive or negative emotions. In total, there was a considerable, but not significant, relationship between the amount of EDA and emotional responses. More recently, Groeppel-Klein, Domke, and Bartmann (2006) observed that individuals who showed high responses to television spots in SCR amp. and NS.SCR freq.[273] rendered significantly more positive judgments compared to individuals with low EDA responses. An additional research question addressed in this study with 126 female and 59 male participants was that television spots with "archetypal" content (e.g., sleeping beauty) elicited higher motivational arousal according to the multidimensional model described in Sect. 3.2.1.2. Compared with a pure informational spot, the "archetypal" spot elicited significantly higher SCR amp., which is in accordance with its indicator function as a "Group 3 response" (see Table 3.2).

Based on unitary arousal theories (Sect. 3.2.1.1), Kroeber-Riel (1979) made use of EDA as an indicator of consumer arousal elicited by various components of advertising. The rationale behind this approach was that the advertisement-induced phasic arousal is related to the efficiency of processing its information and that advertisement needs to trigger positive emotional arousal in the target person. In particular, the EDA amp. was considered a fast responding- easy-to-evaluate, and sensitive indicator of such processes. Advertisements that fail to induce arousal may have no effect on the consumer's purchasing behavior. In one study performed by the Kroeber-Riel group, SR was recorded with unreported methodology from two fingers of 20 participants watching colored vs. black-and-white commercials. Peaks of SRRs occurred significantly more often at times when the commercials tried to catch the viewer's attention (e.g., a sudden voice during a relatively silent period). Another study took EDA[274] from 60 students viewing a total of eight advertisements for 6 s each. With respect to brand names, slogans, as well as copy and kind of illustrations, four basic advertisements with a similar design were used. As an experimental manipulation, a mild and an intense version of each advertisement, was created by means of the persons shown wearing more or less clothing, thus varying their erotic attraction. As a result, three of the four more intense versions elicited significantly higher changes in SRL than their "mild" counterparts.

A field study using ambulatory monitoring (Sect. 2.2.3.4) of SC with nonspecified methodology in 180 participants of both genders, being divided in five age groups, was performed in their own home by von Dultzig (1997). Three different 30-min video clips were interrupted by a block of four 30-s advertisements, presented approximately in the middle of each film in counterbalanced order. The correlation between arousal and memory values of the hitherto unknown

---

[273] Obtained with standard methodology, 0.01 μS amplitude criterion; overlapping SCRs treated according to evaluation method B, Fig. 2.16, Sect. 2.3.1.2 "Amplitudes of Exosomatic Responses Recorded with Direct Current".

[274] Measured as SR with "a small electric current of constant intensity" from nonspecified palmar electrodes.

advertisements was low but significant ($r = 0.19$). A more fine-grained analysis revealed that such a relationship between arousal and memory held only for individuals below 45 years but not for the elder groups. For advertisements already viewed earlier, a long-term habituation effect occurred, i.e., the arousal measured by SCR amp. diminished with the number of times the participants had seen the video clips.

It is, however, critical for marketing research that advertisement and/or product-and-package design do not only raise interest but also elicit purchasing behavior. Advertisements which induce arousal and are perceived as entertaining without being followed by a purchasing act are called "Fools Good." Therefore, EDA recordings should be validated in field studies where real money is spent. Such a study has been performed by LaBarbera & Tucciarone (1995). In preparation for a fundraising telethon, they presented 35 appeals in counterbalanced order to a panel of 33 donors that were representative of the target group. Using the appeals and key words that elicited the highest EDR amp. (recorded by a psychogalvanometer with nonreported methodology) resulted in the best telethon in recent years, thus reversing a prior existing downward trend. The procedure was repeated the following year, leading to an even greater success. Unfortunately, no control group was included. Therefore, the value of the study for EDA validation is limited.

Groeppel-Klein (2005) used a telemetric device for ambulatory recording of SC[275] during shopping behavior at the point of sale in the fruit and vegetable department of two grocery stores. One store served as experimental, designed according to principles of environmental psychology, while the other store served as control. Fifteen, respectively, 12 participants were recorded during their normal shopping. Results showed that the experimental store evoked significantly higher mean SCR amp. and NS.SCR freq. than the control store. Correlations with subjective measures which were taken after shopping revealed that both measures were significantly related to "joy" ($r = 0.464$ and $r = 0.420$, respectively). Furthermore, the participants bought significantly more fruit and vegetables in the experimental store where they had shown considerably higher EDA. Similar results were obtained in a second study, comparing EDA and buying behavior during confrontation with three differently equipped bookstands in front of a book store located in a mall. The NS.SCR freq. recorded with the same methodology as in the first study was significantly greater while interacting with the two bookstands equipped with holiday items, one of which also announced special bargains, in comparison with a long table piled with books, which served as control condition. The amount of money spent in the stores was also significantly different, being correlated with the NS.SCR freq. In another study performed in a department store with the same methodology, buyers yielded highly significant higher mean SCR amp. and NS.SCR freq. compared to nonbuyers. Groeppel-Klein (2005) interpreted her results as EDA being a valid indicator of arousal and/or positive emotion, which is associated with actual purchasing behavior.

---

[275] With Ag/AgCl electrodes filled with 0.5% NaCl electrode cream and 0.4 V constant voltage from the nondominant hand's palmar sites.

Groeppel-Klein, Germelmann, and Woratschek (2007) videotaped female shoppers in two supermarkets and performed synchronized SC recording with the same methodology as used by Groeppel-Klein (2005). Their participants received a certain amount of money for buying products in three departments and completed a questionnaire about their buying behavior after each purchase. After excluding artifacts from the data sets, SCR amp. and NS.SCR freq. could be analyzed for 269 buying decisions. Using the questionnaire results, the buying behavior acts were assigned to three different behavior categories by means of a cluster analysis: 159 routine, 86 impulsive, and 23 cognitively controlled buying acts. Both EDA parameters yielded significantly higher values during the latter category compared to the other two ones, which was interpreted as cognitively controlled decisions needing a series of phasic arousal responses for information processing (Sect. 3.1.3.1). An additional comparison with 15 data sets from nonbuying situations revealed that the latter resulted in significantly lower total EDA compared to any form of buying, which was probably partly due to less general arousal if no items were selected (Sect. 3.2.1.1). Regression analyses showed that the relationship between the amount of money spent and arousal measured by EDA was logarithmic rather than linear, the correlation coefficients not exceeding $r = 0.45$.

Based on the East-Asian concept of "kansei engineering" (cf., Yagi, 2000), a psychophysiological approach for product evaluation has been developed by Boucsein, Schaefer, Schwerdtfeger, Busch, and Eisfeld (1999), labeled "objective emotional assessment" (OEA). Newly developed industrial products are presented to prospective consumers to be touched and manipulated, while physiological recordings are performed, comprising ANS measures and facial EMG. One of the core ANS measures is SCR, recorded from left thenar/hypothenar sites. For the 30 s up to 90 s recording intervals, NS.SCR freq. and averages of phasic parameters such as mean SCR amp. are obtained. In addition to univariate analyses, psychophysiological and subjective measures are subjected to discriminant function analytic procedures together, to obtain centroids for the products under investigation, allowing them to be discriminated from each other.

The first study (Boucsein et al., 1999) applied the OEA technique to industrial foams (tensides), which were brought automatically into contact with the participant's hand that was free of EDA electrodes.[276] Four test foams and a reference tenside were presented in counterbalanced order to each of the 12 participating highly trained female panelists. After 25 s passive contact with the foam, participants were asked to handle the foams freely for another 30 s. The experiment was repeated after a 2-week home use test. All studies were performed double-blind, the tensides were nonscented, and the participants were barred from seeing them by means of a camouflage. One of the test foams elicited marked ORs during the first contact, indicated by an increase of SCR amp. and HR deceleration (Sect. 3.1.1.1), while the NS.SCR freq. diminished during the handling period. By using facial EMG

---

[276] In this and the following studies, EDA was recorded with standard methodology.

parameters, this could be interpreted as an initial unpleasant surprise, followed by a more pleasant experience of the product. A different foam elicited an increase of NS. SCR freq. after an initial OR. The tenside given the most negative subjective rating elicited a rather small OR, as reflected in the SCR amp., but a continuing OR generation during handling, together with negative emotion inferred from facial EMG activities. Interestingly, the foam rated most favorably elicited the smallest amount of tonic EDA, which points to the utility of EDA as a specific indicator for negatively toned emotions in the context of product evaluation (Sect. 3.2.2.1).

In a second study (Boucsein, Schaefer, Kefel, Busch, & Eisfeld, 2002) performed with 12 female and 12 male participants, half of each group composed of laymen and experts in using a technique called sensory assessment (describing sensory-perception related product properties). They were presented with three hair tresses, two of them treated with different shampoos and one left untreated. Presentation was preceded by two different video clips, representing either a technically oriented or a positively toned emotional context for hair care products. A multivariate analysis with ten physiological measures, including the sum of SCR amp. and NS.SCR freq., produced three discriminant functions which, amongst others, revealed differences between treated and untreated hair tresses that could not be detected by the standard technique of sensory assessment. Under all six experimental conditions, laymen showed more arousal than experts during a manipulation phase, especially in the emotional "product world," which was clearly reflected in the NS.SCR freq.

Eisfeld, Schaefer, Boucsein, and Stolz (2005) investigated the intersensory effects of visual and olfactory stimulation on perception. Transparent gel formulations were produced with two different colors (red or green) combined with two different fragrances (strawberry or green apple). Two of the four resulting combinations matched (red and strawberry; green and "green apple"), the two others did not. A prime-probe concept was applied, presenting either the scent or the color first, followed by the other stimulus quality after 15 s. The four resulting stimulus combinations were presented to 6 female participants each, resulting in a total of 24 participants. Each participant received two combinations in counterbalanced order. In general, a stronger OR was observed for the "green apple" fragrance than for strawberry, being reflected in the SCR amp., and color primes induced stronger ORs than scent primes. From the first to the second presentation, habituation of the SCR occurred. Discriminant analyses yielded functions that primarily separated colors or fragrances, but also congruencies and incongruencies between vision and olfaction. The NS.SCR freq. contributed mainly to the congruency function, while the maximum SCR amp. during the 15 s interval contributed considerably to the discriminant function that separated the two different scent primes. Fine-grained analyses of the psychophysiological patterns revealed that ANS measures including EDA were rather strongly linked to the probably more subconscious detection of congruencies, while separating scents from colors is more likely reflected in facial EMG changes. These are more likely associated with information processing.

In another study probing fragrances by means of OEA, Boucsein and Schaefer (2008) presented lavender as a relaxing odor and jasmine as an activating fragrance to 24 female participants. Each fragrance was given twice to each participant in counterbalanced order. The initiation point for psychophysiological recording was determined by presenting the scent to the nostrils very exactly, so that stimulus-dependent SCRs could be separated from NS.SCRs. One discriminant function which separated the two trials yielded a high load in SCR amp. and NS.SCR freq., whereas the latter parameter additionally showed the highest load in a function that contrasted the two fragrances by their centroids moving in opposite directions in the discriminant space from trial 1 to trial 2.

The OEA methodology was also applied to evaluate textile samples that had previously been treated with two different fabric care formulations, compared to a fabric washed only in water, by Eisfeld, Wachter, Schaefer, and Boucsein (2007). First, a rectangular cotton sample was automatically pulled over the participant's bare forearm for 30 s. During the next 30 s, the 54 female participants were asked to actively manipulate the fabric with their hand. After 1 week, during which a cloak-like textile was tailored for each participant, 48 of the participants volunteered for removing their outer clothing in preparation for donning the cloak. After an initial contact during the cloak being pulled over the head, the participants walked on a treadmill for 9 min. The two EDA parameters contributed to differences in the first phase of the study but not much in the second one, presumably because of the too high a skin moisture produced by sweating under the cloak during the treadmill walk (Sect. 2.4.2.2).

In total, the use of EDA in marketing has a rather long tradition. Unfortunately, in the earlier studies the experimental designs and measurement techniques were not controlled thoroughly enough to meet current scientific standards. More recently, a boost was given to the field by the development of distinct techniques which successfully use EDA in the area of product evaluation.

3.5.2   EDA in the Detection of Deception

Detection of deception, which is more popularly known as "lie detection" or the "polygraph," is an emotional topic, both in scientific and in practical use (e.g., Furedy, 1986). As Lykken (1981) reported, by the 1980s there were between one and four million American citizens being confronted with a lie detector test every year, not only in case of criminal investigations but also in a variety of other contexts, including employee screening.[277]

---

[277] The US Congress enacted the 1988 Employee Polygraph Protection Act (EPPA) to curtail among other things, abuses reported as a result of the widespread use of the polygraph. Problems observed prior to EPPA included poorly standardized and unregulated field practices, and inadequately standardized training for field practitioners, and included cost-cutting and other competitive marketing efforts that led to the proliferation of "chart-rolling" practices which included the conduct of numerous short and unreliable examinations. Foremost among those problems was the selection of examination targets with unproven contribution to the desired outcomes of employee training success and employee integrity. Despite the restriction imposed by EPPA, there are remaining provisions that allow for government and public safety pre-employment polygraph screening, in addition to potential screening for employees in pharmaceutical and nuclear energy industries.

The largest user of the polygraph is arguably the United States government (National Research Council, 2003). Polygraph screening programs have steadily increased over time, and there are presently in excess of 20 federal U.S. polygraph programs dedicated to screening applicants, employees, and contractors for initial and continued access to sensitive information. Barland (1999) estimated at that time there were 69 countries around the world using the polygraph and that number is likely larger today. Polygraph screening programs are in place in both private and public sectors in the United States, Mexico, Israel, Japan, South Africa, Bulgaria, Russia, and Canada.[278]

Contrarily, in Europe there is little use of these techniques, and in Germany, the Supreme Court decided repeatedly not to accept the polygraph test as evidence, although this was moderately advocated by several German psychologists during the 1980s (Steller, 1987; Undeutsch, 1983; Wegner, 1981). In particular, the use of detection of deception for security checking or in employment settings is regarded as rather dubious in Europe (Gudjonsson, 1986), though quite a few countries use the polygraph for screening and diagnostic testing.

Polygraph techniques can be divided into two major categories, *knowledge-based tests* and *deception-based tests*.[279] The knowledge-based tests are sometimes called recognition tests and attempt to determine if the examinee has some knowledge that should only be available to persons directly involved in an incident of concern. These tests are also commonly known as guilty knowledge tests (GKT), or as concealed information tests (CIT).

Polygraph examiners generally rely on deception-based methods for the criminal testing and screening examinations. These methods ask directly about the matter to be assessed and are putatively capable of addressing multiple behavioral issues of concern. Circumstances and case facts of a criminal investigation drive the selection of specific polygraph questions in a very straightforward manner for diagnostic polygraph examinations. Unfortunately, the issues for preemployment screening polygraphs are often driven by agency policies instead by empirically derived predictors. Ideally, personnel hiring policies and polygraph targets would be informed by actuarial data concerning successful training and job performance outcomes.

There are two broad categories of deception tests, the historically older Relevant-Irrelevant and the Comparison Question Tests (CQT).[280] The Relevant-Irrelevant (RI) test involves asking direct questions, known as relevant questions, about the matters to be assessed (e.g., "Did you ever use illegal drugs?"). The RI test

---

[278] A comparison of the estimated number of polygraph examiners was provided by Barland (1988, Table 7.1).

[279] The author thanks Mark Handler for his contributions to this section, especially to its polygraph-related part.

[280] The abbreviation CQT was introduced initially for "Control Question Test." However, the term "control" has been replaced by "comparison" in modern polygraph use, since the term control as used in the original CQT did not meet its standard scientific sense. Control questions could only be accepted as an experimental control if they were comparable to the critical questions in all respects except for the process of deception that is under investigation (for more details, see Furedy & Ben-Shakhar, 1991).

also contains several simple, known-truth questions that are usually answered truthfully (e.g., "Is this the month of September?") labeled as irrelevant questions. The questions are repeated several times while the examinee's psychophysiology is monitored. The rationale of the RI test assumes that deceptive individuals will respond with the largest, most consistent, and most significant physiological response to those questions to which they are deceptive, whereas the truthful examinee will not show such responses. Often, this "global" evaluation of RI polygraph exams calls for the examiner to make an interpretation of what the terms *consistent* and *significant* mean while evaluating the test data. The introduction of this subjectivity undoubtedly has the potential to degrade interrater reliability and criterion validity.

Raskin and Honts (2002) concluded that the rationale of the RI technique is naïve, and that the approach does not presently satisfy the basic requirements of a psychological test and thus should not be used in forensic/investigative settings. There is, however, some evidence that shows the RI approach to screening may have some validity (Correa & Adams, 1981; Honts & Amato, 2007; Krapohl, Senter, & Stern, 2005). In the screening context, the RI test may be suitable as an early "screening in" tool in which the objective is to investigate multiple relevant topics rather than a "screening out" tool. More data are needed to make strong statements in support of the validity of the RI test in the screening setting.

The second family of deception tests is the CQT, which uses relevant and irrelevant questions similar to those used in the RI test, but also includes a third type of question, the comparison question. Comparison questions are designed to evoke responses from innocent individuals providing a place to focus one's emotionality and attention. In the CQT an interaction is expected between the physiological responses to question type (relevant and comparison) and guilt status. Theoretically, guilty examinees are expected to produce larger physiological responses to relevant questions than to comparison questions and innocent examinees are expected to produce larger physiological responses to the comparison questions than to the relevant questions (Raskin & Podlesny, 1979).

Within the CQT category, an additional distinction is that there are two approaches to the preparation and presentation of the comparison questions: the probable lie comparison (PLC) and the directed lie comparison (DLC). With PLCs, the examinee is maneuvered into denying transgressions generally related to those addressed by the relevant questions. For example, if the relevant questions address a bank robbery, a PLC question might be: "Have you ever stolen anything from a store?" The examiner discourages the examinee from admitting any transgressions by implying that the person who robbed the bank would have a similar pattern of theft in their life. This social dynamic persuades the examinee to lie to the PLC question to avoid presenting the appearance of the kind of person who would rob a bank. The rationale is that the innocent examinee will be more focused on, and hence more physiologically aroused, when lying to the PLC questions than when being truthful to the relevant questions (Offe & Offe, 2007; Raskin & Honts, 2002). It is further theorized that the actual robber will be more aroused physiologically by the relevant questions than by the PLC questions to which she/he is also lying. There is a substantial body of laboratory and field research in the forensic setting that supports this rationale and the validity of the PLC version of the CQT in a diagnostic setting (see the reviews by Honts, 2004; Raskin & Honts, 2002).

The DLC approach is a simpler and less manipulative approach in which the examiner instructs the examinee to lie to questions similar in form to PLC questions (Raskin & Honts, 2002). The examinee is told that it is important for the examiner to observe appropriate physiological responses from the examinee whenever lying to the DLC questions during the test, otherwise they will not pass the examination. DLC questions offer advantages over PLC questions, such as standardization of test questions and avoidance of the manipulative processes of the PLC variant. Examinees with prior polygraph experience or those who have researched polygraph techniques may be aware of the PLC procedures which would serve to reduce any potential face validity imparted on the PLC questions to the examinee by the examiner. The rationale underlying the DLC approach is similar to that of the PLC and the same interaction of question type and guilt is expected. Although there is less scientific research on the DLC test, the existing data suggest it is of equivalent or higher validity as compared to the PLC test.

Knowledge-based tests are an alternative to these so-called *direct techniques*. The GKT or CIT had been developed by Lykken (1959b) as a so-called *indirect technique*. The rationale of the GKT is that a guilty examinee should react stronger to certain facts that only she/he would recognize as relevant (e.g., details of a crime). These facts are embedded in a set of for example five alternatives that would seem equally plausible for an innocent examinee. The examinee has simply to answer "no" to each item or repeat it. Sometimes, verbalization is not requested at all, which is the most suitable method with respect to avoiding artifacts from speech (Sect. 2.2.5.2). False positive errors can be practically excluded when using the GKT, since it is highly improbable that an examinee will consistently show her/his highest response to the critical items within several series of stimuli (normally consisting of about ten questions).[281]

The advantages and disadvantages of direct and indirect techniques were discussed in details by Gudjonsson (1986) and Furedy (1986), and have been also summarized by Ben-Shakhar and Furedy (1990) as well as Iacono (2007). According to Gudjonsson (1986), interrater- as well as retest-reliabilities of polygraph tests are rather high (from $r = 0.71$ to $r = 0.96$), while aspects of validity, obtained from laboratory and field studies, are less convincing: 68–86% hits for guilty examinees, and 49–76% for innocent examinees.[282] Furthermore, a major

---

[281] Despite this putative superiority of the GKT over the CQT, the practical problem arises that the GKT requires the details of the crime to be used in the test having to be kept secret in the public, which may run counter to normal police procedures; this is regarded as a major reason for its infrequent use by polygraphers (Furedy & Heslegrave, 1988).

[282] Taken from an U.S. Congress Office of Technology Assessment Report in 1983. Steller (1987) summarized results from laboratory studies, 11 performed with the CQT, and seven with the GKT. According to these, the CQT correctly classified 15.8–90% of the innocent examinees, with false positives ranging from 4.2 to 31.6%. On the other hand, five of the GKT studies made 100% correct classifications, the remaining two studies yielding 88% correct innocents and 12% false positives. With respect to correct classifications of guilty examinees, both methods did not differ considerably (between 60 and 100% correct classifications).

problem with the direct techniques could be their particular proneness to false positive errors (Gudjonsson, 1986; Lykken, 1981).[283]

The rationale behind the use of ANS measures for the detection of deception is that stimuli elicit ANS responses commensurate with the degree of salience, be it orienting or emotionally based (Sects. 3.1.1.1 and 3.2.2.1). Among the various psychophysiological parameters used in the detection of deception, EDA can be regarded as the most sensitive one, followed by the vasomotor response (Barland & Raskin, 1973; Furedy & Heslegrave, 1988; Thackray & Orne, 1968; Waid & Orne, 1981). Therefore, electrodermal recordings are often used as the gold standard against which other candidate measures are compared. One reason is that a clear-cut EDR is elicited by any change in stimulation, the amplitude of which increases as a function of its salience or significance (Sect. 3.1.1.1).[284] In addition, the EDR amp. is easy to evaluate quantitatively by visual inspection, not only by the examiner but also by the examinee herself/himself (Fig. 3.6). This may be used to convince guilty examinees (and, unfortunately at times, to convince false positive innocents), thus leading to a breakdown and confession in about 25% of the examinees (Lykken, 1981).[285]

One of the most intriguing problems in the use of ANS measures for the detection of deception is the availability of so-called *countermeasures*, used by some examinees to appear truthful during a polygraph examination (i.e., to "beat the polygraph"). These can be divided into three broad categories: mental, physical, and chemical/pharmaceutical (Ben-Shakhar & Dolev, 1996; Gudjonsson, 1986). The most effective method is to voluntarily produce ANS responses to the irrelevant items to reduce the discriminative power of the relevant ones. Attempts to augment one's response to the irrelevant stimuli can be made by eliciting somatomotor responses which produce artifacts in EDA and other polygraphy measures, like deep inspirations, covert muscle contractions, pain (e.g., thumbtacks in the examinee's sock), or tongue-biting (Sect. 2.2.5.2). Lykken (1981) pointed to the advantage that an innocent suspect could not systematically self-stimulate on the control items of the GKT, since she/he would not know which of the alternatives could be relevant.

---

[283] In pre- or postemployment screening situations, a slightly different question format is employed, labeled the Relevant Control Test by Lykken (1981).

[284] In addition to various proofs of EDA being the most sensitive measure for the detection of deception in comparison with others, as found for example by Dawson (1980) in his study described below (comparing EDA with cardiovascular and respiratory measures), a comparison of an univariate with a multivariate statistical evaluation of CQT data performed by Kircher and Raskin (1988) also yielded a superiority of SCR amp. over blood pressure, respiratory, and vasomotor responses with both methods of evaluation.

[285] The ease of detecting psychophysiological correlates of emotion-relevant thoughts by phasic EDA is also used in obscure religious practice, where then so-called E-meters (simple SR monitoring devices) are used as a "scientific" tool to uncover hidden information in participants.

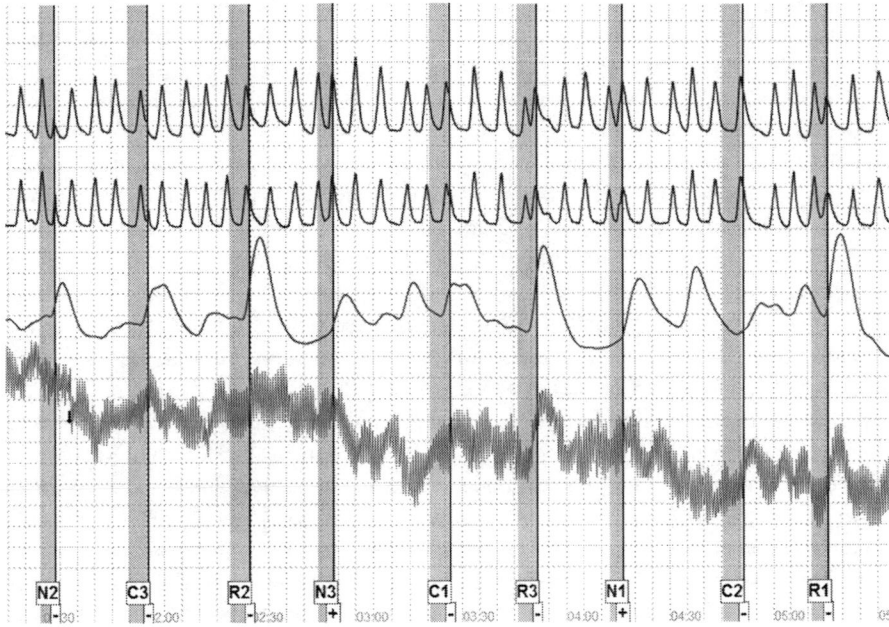

Fig. 3.6 Polygraph recording during CQT performance with comparison questions labeled C3, C1 and C2, and relevant questions labeled R2, R3 and R1. The following pairs of questions are compared against one another: C3 and R2, C1 and R3, and C2 and R1. The R2, R3 and R1 questions had been the critical ones asked of this examinee who was confirmed deceptive to the issue under investigation. Amongst all four parameters, i.e., respiration (*upper two tracings*), EDA (*third* from the *top*), and relative blood pressure/HR (*lower channel*); the EDR amp. displayed the most clear-cut differentiation. The questions labeled N2, N3 and N1 are non-evocative "neutral" questions which allow sufficient time to elapse to ensure the waveforms are stable prior to presenting a potentially evocative comparison question. The *plus* and *minus* signs are indicative of an examinee answering "yes" and "no" (courtesy of Mark Handler)

For the purpose of testing the lie detector's susceptibility to the use of countermeasures, the so-called *mock-crime paradigm* has been used in laboratory experiments. In this kind of studies, the experimental group receives the instruction to commit a specific mock crime, like stealing a purse from a desk drawer, whereas the control group receives instructions with details of that particular crime.[286]

---

[286] The GKT mock-crime paradigm has been used quite a lot by Ben-Shakar and his group for making stimuli significant in their OR studies (Sect. 3.1.1.1). In some cases, the experimental group only imagined having committed a mock-crime, the details of which are given to the participants by instruction, which constitutes a weaker experimental manipulation. The details given to the control group serve the purpose of making the circumstances of the mock crime known to them, to restrict group differences to having committed the mock crime or not.

An additional payment may be promised to the participants if they manage to "beat the polygraph," to provide an incentive that may increase the validity of the setting for real life polygraphy.[287]

The mock-crime technique has been used by Honts, Raskin, and Kircher (1987) for testing the effect of physical countermeasures on the outcome of the CQT. Fifteen female and 15 male participants were divided into three groups: two guilty groups that received tape-recorded instructions to enact a mock crime and an innocent group that listened to a tape describing the crime but being instructed not to enact it. One of the guilty groups received training in the use of countermeasures, i.e., tongue-biting and pressing the toes to the floor during the comparison questions. All participants were given a field polygraph test by an experienced field examiner, and they were offered money if they would produce an innocent outcome. SC was recorded with standard methodology from the left hand, and amplitudes as well as duration of SCRs which started within a time window between 0.5 s following the question and 5 s after the participant's answer were evaluated.[288] In addition, respiratory and vasomotor activity and blood pressure were taken as additional measures, and EMG recordings from gastrocnemius and temporalis muscles were recorded to detect physical countermeasures. As in standard field practice, each pair of comparison and relevant questions was assigned a score between −3 and +3 for each of the physiological systems, according to the largeness of the difference in the corresponding responses, positive scores indicating that responses to comparison questions were stronger. Total scores exceeding +5 were considered innocent, those being lower than −5 were considered deceptive, the remainder being regarded as inconclusive. In the innocent group, two false positives and 1 inconclusive participant appeared, while no false negatives and two inconclusives emerged in the guilty group without countermeasures. However, countermeasures completely distorted the detection of deception, leading to seven false negatives (guilty participants classified as innocent) and three remaining inconclusives. Comparison of these results with an earlier study performed by the Raskin group implied that the countermeasures were dependent on the presence of high motivation, which is surely present in real life polygraphy. Though EMG recordings have been demonstrated to be useful as countermeasure detectors in 90% of the trained users, their effectiveness in the field has been regarded by the authors as possibly limited.

Bradley and Warfield (1984) used the mock-crime paradigm to test the robustness of the GKT against innocent participants having crime-relevant information. Forty participants of both genders were randomly assigned to five groups: a guilty group; a control group which had no crime-relevant information; and three groups of innocent participants, who were given the same crime-relevant information but with different instructions. These scenarios were either witness to a fictitious murder;

---

[287] On the other hand, validity criteria of being guilty or innocent are not easy to obtain in field studies, since in the U.S. justice practice false admissions of guilt are common to reduce the amount of penalty.

[288] Such a time window for EDR evaluation was recommended by Raskin (1979, p. 597).

or be an innocent suspect; or carry out innocent activities involving crime-relevant information. All groups except the last one were promised a monetary incentive, should they be successfully judged innocent. Participants had to answer "no" to all items. SRRs, recorded with standard methodology (however, using as much as 50 μA current), were evaluated in mm deflection[289] for each item in ten sets of the GKT within 10 s following the beginning of the question. The first item of each set served as a buffer item for ORs, while the other four items were scored as follows: if the response to the critical item was largest, it received a score of 2; if it was the second largest, a score of 1; and zero was scored for any other response. Guilty participants were judged significantly guiltier than members of the other groups, showing that guilty knowledge is necessary but not sufficient for the detection of deception.

Alcohol and certain drugs may have the capacity to obscure results of the detection of deception. The possible effects of alcohol intake during the commitment of a mock crime and during the polygraph test on the detection of deception were investigated by Bradley and Ainsworth (1984) in a study using 40 male participants. Eight of them were "innocent," while the other 32 participants were informed of being guilty of a mock crime and were provided appropriate information. Half of the "guilty" participants were intoxicated with alcohol while the remainders were sober when committing the mock crime. In addition, half of each group was intoxicated with alcohol for the polygraph test performed on the subsequent day, while the other half was not. All participants were given both the CQT and the GKT. SRRs were recorded and scored for the GKT as performed by Bradley and Warfield (1984), while scores of +1, 0, or −1 were given in the CQT, depending on whether the SRR amp. to the comparison question was higher than, the same as, or lower than the response to the crime-relevant question. The same kind of scoring was also performed for HR and respiration cycle time, and for a composite score that had been formed using all three measures. By means of this score, 28 participants were correctly classified in total by the CQT, while seven judgments were incorrect and five remained inconclusive. In the GKT condition, 38 participants were correctly classified and two were not. In both tests, significantly better than chance classifications were obtained with both EDA and HR but not with respiration. Intoxication with alcohol during commitment of the mock crime markedly reduced detectability by means of the composite scores as well as by the SRR in both tests, regardless of alcohol consumption during the test. The intoxicated participants were more likely to be classified incorrectly as innocent or inconclusive in the GKT and also appeared more innocent in the CQT. A simple explanation following an impairment of learning by alcohol intoxication could not be applied, since an additional memory test did not yield appropriate differences. Interestingly, if the mock crime had been committed while being intoxicated, alcohol did not influence the EDA but did so with HR deceleration.

---

[289] Raskin (1979) recommended that the EDR amp. should be expressed in terms of mm of chart deflection, which had been regarded by him as producing more reliable results as compared to changes in μS.

No such effect of alcohol intoxication on the results of both CQT and GKT has been found in a mock-crime study involving 80 male participants conducted by O'Toole, Yuille, Patrick, and Iacono (1994). Sixty-four participants committed a mock crime (stealing the key for a cash-box and taking money from it), during which half of them were intoxicated with alcohol (approximately 1 mg/mL blood). The remaining 16 participants served as innocent controls. After 2 days, all participants returned for a test administration closely following the procedure previously described by Bradley and Ainsworth (1984) with the examiner being blind to the conditions under which the mock crime was committed. SC was recorded with standard methodology, together with blood pressure, respiration, and finger pulse volume amplitude (Sect. 3.1.1.2). Alcohol intoxication at the time of committing the mock crime had no significant effects on the outcome of either lie detection test. It would seem that alcohol only reduced anticipatory arousal before the crime and subsequent memory for the crime details. Additional manipulations for influencing arousal and memory for crime details had differential effects on the two polygraph tests. On the GKT, primed participants who rehearsed specific details following the crime were more easily detectable than unprimed counterparts. On the CQT, primed participants were only more detectable if their arousal during the crime was increased by making the situation appear more threatening to them.

Waid, Orne, Cook, and Orne (1981) demonstrated the effectiveness of a tranquilizer (400 mg meprobamate) given 30 min prior to the GKT in reducing the detection of deception. Eleven male participants took part in each of the following four groups: innocent; "guilty" with no medication; "guilty" with placebo; and "guilty" with meprobamate. The latter two groups were told they would receive a tranquilizer that would help them avoid detection. The question list consisted of 24 words, four in each of six semantic categories, one of the four being a word the "guilty" participants had memorized before. While all innocent participants, 9 of the nondrug participants, and eight ones under placebo were correctly classified by their SRR amp.[290] under meprobamate, only 3 "guilty" participants were classified correctly, leaving eight false negatives. The cardiovascular and respiratory measures did not discriminate between "guilty" and innocent participants at all. Since the EDA results were not due to lack of electrodermal responsiveness among drug participants – there were no differences between groups in the mean number of critical words that evoked a measureable EDR – the authors attributed their results as being due to the anxiety reducing properties of meprobamate, for which EDA was regarded as a sensitive indicator (Sect. 3.4.3).

By contrast, Iacono, Boisvenu, and Fleming (1984b) could not find significant influences of either a tranquilizer (10 mg diazepam) or a stimulant (20 mg methylphenidate) on the validity of the GKT. Sixty male participants were randomly assigned to three guilty groups receiving either one of these drugs or placebo or

---

[290] Recorded with Beckman Ag/AgCl electrodes thenar/hypothenar from the right hand with a current density of 3.8 $\mu A/cm^2$, using AC coupling with 0.3 s time constant.

to an innocent nondrug group. Participants of the guilty groups watched a videotaped burglary of an apartment through the eyes of the thief, while the control group viewed the interior of another apartment. Drugs were administered prior to the 12 or 10 min videotaping. As a result, the drugs reached their peak action during the subsequently performed 10-item GKT. Participants were promised a reward if appearing innocent. SC was measured bilaterally with standard methodology during the test. SCR amp. were scored as the difference of the participant's SCL during the maximum response and the SCL prior to the GKT item, and ranked within each question (except the first alternative to each question serving as buffer item). If the SCR amp. following the critical alternative was the highest of the four responses, a score of 2 was assigned, while a 1 was scored if being the second highest. An amplitude criterion (Sect. 2.3.1.2 "Choice of Amplitude Criteria") of 0.03 μS was used which had to be exceeded by the response to at least one alternative (other than the buffer item) to consider a question scorable. The actual guilt score was formed by summing up all 20 individual rank scores (10 from each hand's record) and by dividing this total by the number of scorable questions. Six participants had to be excluded from the analysis because they did not meet the criterion of 10 or more scorable responses out of 20. Participants scoring below 1 were classified as innocent and those with 1 or above were labeled guilty. The hit rates were 100% in the innocent group and 88% in the guilty groups, not considerably differing between drug conditions. However, the ability to remember critical facts recorded by a questionnaire correlated significantly ($r = 0.53$) with the likelihood of being found guilty, showing the susceptibility of the GKT to memory influences.

A more fundamental issue in detection of deception concerns the suggested psychophysiological mechanisms underlying the observed increase in EDR amp. following relevant as compared to irrelevant items. Several hypotheses were discussed here: an increased arousal being due to greater emotional involvement (Sects. 3.2.1.1 and 3.2.2.1); the acquisition of a conditioned EDR to details of the crime, which were connected with unconditioned fear stimuli (Sect. 3.1.2.1); and various cognitive influences on the EDR as outlined in Sect. 3.1.3 (Waid & Orne, 1981). Raskin (1979) discussed these differences in terms of OR and information processing (Sect. 3.1.1.1). He suggested that the introduction of irrelevant stimuli might lead to a general habituation effect of EDRs to that particular kind of stimuli, and that only the crime-relevant stimuli having a special signal value for guilty examinees elicit marked ORs in them. Comparing direct and indirect techniques in detection of deception, Raskin found some support in HR response patterns for his hypothesis that ORs would be predominantly obtained in the GKT, while the CQT would be more likely to produce DRs. He assumed a generally higher level of emotional arousal produced by indirect techniques being responsible for this, because of the overall more threatening and personal nature of the CQT questions.

However, a discussion of EDRs that appear in response to CQT items within the concepts of OR and DR is obscured by the necessity to immediately respond verbally to the question (Sect. 3.1.1.2). To allow a separate measurement of EDRs to questions and answers, Dawson (1980) performed an experiment with two versions of the CQT: one in which participants verbally responded immediately;

the other one in which they waited 8 s before giving their verbal answer. Twenty-four student actors of both genders, being trained in using personal memories of sensory experiences to recreate emotional states, were randomly assigned to a "guilty" and an "innocent" group, all of them were promised doubling of their payment if they managed to appear innocent in the polygraph test. After having received the instructions (to imagine having stolen money vs. to merely wait for the research assistant to return), participants were given each of the two forms of the CQT twice in counterbalanced order. Quantitative analyses of the mean SRR magnitudes (Sect. 2.3.4.2)[291] yielded significantly larger EDRs to the relevant questions than to the comparison questions for the "guilty" group, while the reverse was true for the "innocent" group for the response in the immediate answer CQT and the OR to the question in the delayed answer CQT. No such difference could be found for the SRRs following the verbal response in the delayed answer CQT. Thus, the SRR magnitudes were more likely indicators of differential ORs to relevant vs. irrelevant stimuli than being influenced by verbal activities of the participants.

With the goal of investigating whether CIT results would be based on ORs or DRs, Verschuere, Crombez, De Clercq, and Koster (2004) subjected 36 participants (29 females, 7 males) to a mock crime procedure, during which 18 participants "committed" one of two mock crimes, being unaware of the other mock-crime (a theft or an exam fraud). A secondary auditory RT probe was introduced for testing resource allocation during the CIT procedure. Participants were told that their primary task was beating the polygraph by trying to conceal recognition of details from their crime. The examination started with the presentation of four emotion-evoking visual stimuli and one auditory stimulus (71 dB white noise) for optimizing SC[292] and HR measurement. Thereafter, all pictures to be used in the CIT were presented for 2.5 s in random order to diminish novelty-elicited ORs to the control stimuli during the CIT. The test consisted of presenting 24 pictures in semirandom order to all participants, 12 related to each crime, with ISIs from 15 to 25 s. The auditory RT probe stimuli (1 kHz, 500 ms, 71 dB) were presented over headphones on half of the pictures, either 250, 500, or 750 ms after the picture stimulus onset. Twelve additional probes were randomly presented during the ISIs, but not within 5 s before or after a picture. Physiological recordings were evaluated only during probe free trials. Probe detection was practiced in 30 trials just prior to the CIT. Crime pictures elicited significantly higher SCR amp. and HR decelerations compared to control pictures, but there was no

---

[291] Recorded with 2.5 × 2.5 cm stainless steel electrodes from the palmar fingertips of the left hand, using 10 μA constant current. For the CQT form with immediate response, the largest decrease in SR which occurred between 1 s following the question onset and 5 s following the verbal answer was evaluated. For the delayed response CQT form, a time window between 1 s following the question onset and 1 s following completion of the question was used to obtain the question SRR, while the largest deflection within 1 and 5 s following the verbal answer was taken as the answer SRR.

[292] Recorded with 0.5 V and Ag/AgCl electrodes filled with K–Y jelly, attached to thenar/hypothenar sites of the left hand. The maximum SCR (minimal amplitude criterion 0.05 μS) between 1 and 5 s after stimulus onset was scored and square-root transformed.

significant difference in probe RTs. The authors' conclusion was that presentation of concealed information has the property to interrupt ongoing behavior and allocate attention to the significant stimulus, being accompanied by an OR (Sect. 3.1.3.2). However, the authors point to the likelihood that with increasing levels of threat, as to be expected during real crime investigations, the physiological response patterns to concealed information stimuli might shift from OR to DR. In conclusion, the GKT or CIT which have been extensively probed in laboratory settings may have to use mock-crime procedures under monetary incentives or under motivational instructions as in the Verschuere et al. (2004) and other studies, to resemble the interrogation situation in the field close enough (Ben-Shakhar & Elaad, 2003).

Going beyond an interpretation of mere differential ORs or DRs, Pennebaker and Chew (1985) hypothesized the suggested connection between EDA and the BIS (Sect. 3.2.1.2) as a neurophysiological basis for the electrodermal detection of deception. Thirty predominantly female participants were instructed to deceive the experimenter in a GKT on two separate occasions. They selected one of five code words printed on cards but had to answer "no" if asked for any word during the test. In the second GKT run, participants were assigned either to a group ($N = 20$) being observed by the experimenter, who tried to find out by viewing the participant's behavior what card she/he had selected, or to a control group ($N = 10$). Mean SCL[293] did not differentiate truth from lie words in the first GKT, while there was a significantly higher SCL when participants were observed, in addition to a marked increase of SCL from 2 to 4 s after deception (as compared to truth items) under both experimental conditions. For the 20 participants in the observed condition, changes in eye movement and facial expression (Sect. 3.2.2.1) were continuously coded during the second GKT and were summed during 2-s intervals following the questions. During seconds 2–4 and 4–6, the mean number of behavioral measures revealed the reverse pattern of SCL, indicating a behavior decrease following deceptive responses where the increase of SCL was most pronounced. Thus, an increase in EDA during deception may be at least partly due to its specific indicator function for behavioral inhibition as suggested by Fowles (1980), a theoretical line which requires further research.

Possible individual differences in electrodermal lability (Sect. 3.3.2.2) should also be considered when using EDA as a dependent measure in the detection of deception. Waid and Orne (1980) reported appropriate results from two experiments, using the GKT in the first one with 28 male participants and the CQT in the second one with 30 participants. In both studies, the deception of critical code words had been used, while SR was recorded in the first and SC was measured in the second one (both times with standard methodology except the use of K–Y jelly). For each participant, NS.EDR freq. was scored during the ISI, starting from 4.5 s following each word until the end of the ISI. Both studies confirmed a less

---

[293] Recorded as SRL with 10 mA constant current using Beckman Ag/AgCl electrodes from palmar finger sites, converted into SC units. SCL data were reported from 2 s after the question (where the participant answered "no") to 14 s after the question.

frequent detection of deception by participants showing lower spontaneous rates of EDRs (i.e., electrodermal stabiles) as compared to electrodermal labiles. Furthermore, among truthful participants, those being more electrodermal labile were falsely detected as deceptive on more questions than the stabiles.

In another study, Waid, Wilson, and Orne (1981) confirmed the effect of electrodermal lability on the detection of deception not only for electrodermal but also for cardiovascular and respiratory measures. Seventy-four male participants were classified, using the median of their NS.SCR freq.[294] during a 3-min baseline period, into labiles and stabiles, and randomly assigned to the "guilty" or "innocent" condition of a code word deception test. They were subjected to both a GKT and a professional CQT 1 week later, while measuring EDR, HR, blood pressure, and respiratory changes. Again, deception by electrodermal stabile participants was detected less frequently than was deception by labile participants, and the rate of false positives among truthful participants was greater for electrodermal labiles. Although accuracy of detection was highest with the EDR, the effects of electrodermal lability on the detection of deception were similar for the other ANS measures. Whether these individual differences should be interpreted in terms of (emotional) hyperreactivity, or as being due to differences in attention or conditionability, remains to be investigated (Sect. 3.3.2.2).

Despite the fact that the use of EDA is well established as a standard measure in the detection of deception, various methodological problems with the technique in general remain debatable. The following critical points in using the polygraph are mainly based on Furedy's (1986, 1987) remarks from a standpoint of scientific experimental psychophysiology:

1. Results are highly susceptible to examiner's influence (e.g., expectations or various examiner-examinee interactions), since blind procedures have been used only in a few research projects but are not part of practical polygraphy.
2. Some methods of scoring are subjective, at least to some degree. In the CQT, differences between responses to relevant and comparison stimuli are normally not specified in physical units (such as $k\Omega$ for SRR amp.), but in qualitative categories (e.g., scoring 1, 2, or 3 for slight, clear, and marked differences using a magnitude ranging from +3 to −3). Some scoring models use a "visibly discernable difference" approach and forego any assumption about the degree of difference in responses. This "bigger is better" transformation foregoes assumptions of linearity and assigns a score to the larger of the comparative responses. Other models use a ratio of difference in the size of the responses by comparing changes using the chart divisions as a metric.

---

[294] Recorded with standard methodology, however, using K–Y jelly and 0.74 V constant voltage. The amplitude criterion was 0.05 μS. For detection of deception, the amplitude criterion was lowered to 0.025 μS. The time windows started 1.5 s, ending 9 s for the CQT and 5 s for the GKT, after stimulus onset.

3. It is debatable whether the GKT detects deception itself. Rather, there might be simply a differentially greater OR associated with the identification of the relevant alternative, because of its greater significance. Indeed, a stimulus might gain significance simply by experimental manipulations (Sect. 3.1.1.1).

However, numerous attempts have been made to demonstrate the psychophysiological deception phenomenon in a controlled experimental setting. For example, Furedy, Davis, and Gurevich (1988) presented 16 participants of each gender with two lists of ten questions, to one of which they should respond honestly, while deceptive but plausible answers were trained for the other one. For interrogation, the items of both lists were randomly allocated to a 20-question list, the first and second ten items of which were presented under immediate and delayed (10 s waiting) response conditions. The major finding was that SCRs[295] in the interval immediately following the question were significantly larger when the question was answered deceptively, which could not be attributed to other factors than to the difference between deceptive and honest conditions. Other laboratory experiments of the Furedy/Ben-Shakhar group were performed with the so-called differentiation-of-deception paradigm, in which various factors that might influence the deception process were experimentally manipulated (e.g., Furedy, Gigliotti, & Ben-Shakhar, 1994; Furedy, Posner, & Vincent, 1991), which will not be reported in detail here.

In general, although EDA has been successfully used as a psychophysiological measure for the detection of deception in both laboratory and field contexts, further theoretical and methodological clarifications of the phenomenon are required, and attempts need to be made to avoid misuses of the so-called lie detection in practice.

3.5.3   EDA in Dermatology

Diseases of the skin should be a self-evident field of application for recording of electrodermal phenomena. Although some standard volumes in dermatology discuss EDA (e.g., Keller, 1963; Jarrett, 1978; Schliack & Schiffter, 1979; Thiele, 1981a, 1981b), clinical dermatology continues to prefer the use of more qualitative measurements of sweat rather than quantitative EDA recordings (Sect. 2.4.2.2).

Pathological changes of skin do not only influence its resistive or conductive properties but also skin capacity. This was already shown by Gougerot (1947) using AC measurement of EDA.[296] In individuals with normal skin, the SZLs always exceeded 200 Ω, and phase angles were greater than 45°, while SZLs in patients with

---

[295] Recorded as the highest deflection from prestimulus level with standard methodology (using Beckman NaCl cream) from the palmar finger sites of the left hand (previously cleaned with soap and water), within 1–5 s following question onset. SCR amp. were expressed in mm (using 0.5 mm as amplitude criterion) and converted to μS response magnitudes.

[296] Recorded with 4 kHz AC using lead electrodes.

active eczema were as low as 90 Ω, and phase angles decreased to 26°. Patients with psoriasis showed lower SZLs at affected dry sites, while SZLs at unaffected skin sites were abnormally elevated. A possible explanation for the latter result could be an increased rate of mitosis in the stratum germinativum (Sect. 1.2.1.1) as observed by Wright (1983) in psoriatic patients. Edelberg (1971), summarizing several studies on EDA and skin pathology, pointed to the specific value of AC recordings for differential diagnoses of epidermal changes, though the findings were also dependent on electrode size and frequency of the applied current, which both have the potentiality to influence capacitive properties of the skin (Sect.1.4.3.2).

Salter (1979) recommended AC measurement of EDA for quantifying the amount of healing in dermatological illnesses, reflecting mainly the degree of corneal hydration (Sect. 1.4.2.3) which may be a critical factor in various diseases. As compared to chemical measurement procedures, recording of EDA has the advantage of being truly noninvasive, quick and painless applied, and also quantitatively evaluated. Besides the predominantly used tonic measures in dermatology, phasic changes in capacitive properties of skin, which have only been of minor importance in normal individuals (Sect. 2.3.1.2 "Amplitudes of Exosomatic Responses Recorded with Alternating Current"), could be of considerable value in deliberately following up epidermal changes during the course of developing skin diseases or during the healing process.

Cambrai, Clar, Grosshans, and Altermatt (1979) used skin impedance recordings[297] to quantitatively compare the healing process from *psoriasis* in patients treated with dioxyanthranol, difluprednate, or photochemotherapy associated with 8-methoxypsoralen. Each of these treatments was applied to 4 participants over 13 days. As compared to healthy skin sites, SZL and the phase angle φ (Sect. 2.3.1.2 "Amplitudes of Exosomatic Responses Recorded with Alternating Current") were markedly reduced at affected sites up to measurement frequencies of 10 kHz, whereas these differences disappeared with higher frequencies. Values returned to normal within 1–2 days with difluprednate and within 5–10 days with dioxythranol, but took considerably longer with photochemotherapy. Changes in skin impedance were in good accordance with clinical data and exemplified the usefulness of electrodermal AC recording in quantifying pharmacokinetic effects during treatment of skin diseases.

An application of EDA which is in close relationship to the electrodermal phenomenon itself is its use in the quantitative diagnosis and therapy of *hyperhidrosis*. Apart from excessive sweat secretion being a diagnostic indicator of specific neurological damage (Sect. 3.5.4), hyperhidrosis as a systemic illness may appear mainly on palms, and a vicious cycle is likely to be included in its origin as follows: persons who respond to emotional strain with an increased sweat secretion will notice their visible palmar sweating. In turn, the unpleasant feelings produced by discerning the hyperhidrotic response will elicit emotional excitement, thus forming a positive feedback loop for further sweating.

---

[297] Measured with liquid electrolytes made from polyethylene glycol with 0.9% NaCl (Sect. 2.2.6.3), the active electrode made from platinum, and the reference electrode made from Ag/AgCl. A frequency range from 5 Hz to 500 kHz was used.

Since medical treatment of hyperhidrosis remains unsatisfactory (e.g., application of anticholinergics, bathing with salt or metal ingredients, or electrophysical therapy), the use of EDA biofeedback training should be regarded as more promising (Sect. 3.1.2.3). Electrodermal biofeedback was successfully used by Miller and Coger (1979) in 33 patients (19 females, 14 males; aged 15–61 years) with dishydrotic eczema. This particular disease is characterized by increased epidermal hydration (i.e., intercellular and/or intracellular edema). Twenty-two of the participants were trained for decreased SYL, while 11 participants were trained to increase their SYL by means of optical EDA biofeedback.[298] Participants who trained for 15 min twice a day during a period of 2 weeks were seen in the laboratory before and after their training for a 10 min resting phase, during which EDA was recorded. Participants being trained to decrease their SYL showed significantly lower SYLs during their second laboratory recording, while the SYL-increase group showed no change. These results were paralleled by a significant decrease of state anxiety in the SYL-decrease group and by no change of state anxiety in SYL-increase group, respectively. Furthermore, participants of the SYL-decrease training group showed overall improvement in their disease, while the others' became slightly worse.[299]

EDA has also proved to be a valid indicator for the severeness of *epidermal damage* produced by stripping techniques (Sect. 1.4.2.1) or skin drilling (Sect. 2.2.1.2). Edelberg (1971), in summarizing results from human and from animal research, reported that puncturing the epidermis reduced its resistance to 10–20% of its original value. A similar decrease was caused by skin drilling in rats, taking 3 days for half recovery, and 5 days to recover entirely. Treating human skin with sandpaper (Sect. 2.2.1.2) to the point of bleeding caused the surface negative SP to drop from -10 to -40 mV, requiring an average of 43 h to recover. Lykken (1971) found only very little recovery of SP during the first 100 h after performing 30 strips with cellophane-tape (Sect. 1.3.4.2 "The Role of the Epidermal Barrier Layer") at the lateral surface of the upper arm in two individuals. Thereafter, SP rapidly returned between the fourth and the sixth day, while the SR in the parallel branch as well as polarization capacity (see Fig. 1.18, Sect. 1.4.3.3) as measured with pulsed DC (Sect. 2.5.3.2) recovered more slowly. Pinkus (1952) observed numerous epidermal keratinocytes in all stages of mitosis (Sect. 1.2.1.1) 72 h after skin stripping.[300] Therefore, it can be suggested that getting off the stratum corneum will

---

[298] EDA was recorded in the laboratory with 100 Hz constant current less than 8 μA, using 0.5 cm^2 gold cup electrodes with standard NaCl Unibase cream, from alcohol-scrubbed left-hand sites. In the field part of the study, finger tip electrodes which consisted of silver fibers applied to Velcro pads were used for EDA biofeedback. SZLs were transformed to log SYLs for evaluation.

[299] A single case study of successful EDA biofeedback was published by Moan (1979), training a 28-year-old female urticaria patient 8 weeks with acoustic/optic EDA biofeedback combined with a relaxation training. Her mean SCL could be reduced from 12 to 7 μS (during the relaxation even to 4 μS), and the skin disease disappeared. There was no relapse seen in an 8 month follow-up.

[300] Klaschka (1979) reported an increase in the mitotic index by a factor of 20, 2 days after 30 cellophane-tape stripping, returning slowly to baseline from the third day on.

remove an electrical barrier, thus shunting the sweat gland potential (Sect. 1.4.2.3). This is in agreement with results of Takagi and Nakayama (1959) who investigated the effect of removal of the epidermis by inducing a blistering agent on the left little finger, after which the epidermis was taken off by scissors, leaving only the stratum Malpighii (Table 1.2, Sect. 1.2.1.1). Doing this, the negative SPR component (Sect. 1.4.3.2) totally disappeared but recovered after 2 days. Thus, the measurement of SP may be used to quantitatively determine the process of wound healing (Foulds & Barker, 1983).

Skin damage caused by buffered and unbuffered solutions of alkali and sodium phosphate was investigated by means of skin impedance by Malten and Thiele (1973). They found that SZL could be abolished almost completely by a 15–30 min exposure to NaOH (pH 12) solution, whereas exposure up to 60 min to NaOH (pH 10) solution hardly influenced SZL. Similar effects were observed with appropriate concentrations of sodium phosphate solutions. Furthermore, the changes produced by the application of pH 10 solutions on 5 successive days decreased, quantitatively showing adaptation of skin to less severe chemical damage, in contrast to severe damage.

Kiss (1979) quantitatively investigated the relationship between the concentration of NaOH applied to the skin on filter paper for 30 min and the SZL.[301] Up to concentrations of $1/40$-n NaOH, there was only a slight decrease in SZL, which became rapid (from 19 to 8 kΩ) when the concentration was increased to $1/10$-n NaOH. With a further increase of NaOH concentration, the SZL showed no considerable changes, which may have been due to a severe damage of the epidermal barrier at that time so that ions could pass without impedance (Sect. 1.3.4.2). With another 10 participants, Kiss continuously registered SZL during the application of $1/40$-n NaOH. He found an immediate decrease of SZL, reaching its new level about 3 min afterwards. Hence, AC measurements of EDA may be of great value for quantifying chemical damage of the skin.

Woodrough, Canti, and Watson (1975) used the recording of SP[302] to quantify differences between affected and normal skin sites on the face in 36 patients with basal cell *carcinoma* and in 19 participants with inflammatory lesions serving as a control group. Using the contralateral side of the face as reference (which is not fully justified, see Sect. 3.1.4.2), they observed a significant average increase of 14.4 mV in carcinoma-affected as compared to healthy skin, while the appropriate difference for inflammatory lesions failed to reach significance. However, the standard deviations were too large to allow differential diagnoses of skin diseases by the sole use of SP recordings. Kiss, Horvath, and Hajdu (1975) recorded SZL[303]

---

[301] Recorded with 1.6 kHz and 1 mA current density, using metal electrodes of 6 mm diameter, and a 5 mm diameter filter paper soaked with 0.9% NaCl solution, from the inner aspect of the forearm.

[302] Measured with a liquid electrode made from a syringe, combining Ag/AgCl with physiological saline in sodium methylcellulose; the inactive electrode placed in the mouth.

[303] Measured with 1.6 kHz, using 3 mm steel electrodes together with 4 mm diameter filter paper, soaked with 0.9% NaCl solution.

for determining differences between affected sites in 92 patients having malignant epidermoids and unaffected sites of these patients. They took recordings from 254 patients with benign skin deformations as an additional control, finding that SZLs in 86.9% of the malignant tumor sites were lower as compared to control sites, thus proposing the measurement of skin impedance as a diagnostic tool for skin tumors.

The validity of EDA for preliminary *cystic fibrosis* screening has been demonstrated by Williamson, Fowles, and Weinberger (1985), comparing 37 established cystic fibrosis patients with 45 asthmatic patients and ten normal controls. SP and SC were recorded with standard methodology[304] from palmar finger sites during voluntarily produced fast deep breaths serving as physiological stimuli for the elicitation of EDRs (Sect. 2.2.5.2). The deep breaths were repeated until five clear positive SPRs had been observed. Twelve parameters for endosomatic and exosomatic EDA were obtained including baseline values and responding to a balloon test (blowing a balloon until it bursts). All these electrodermal measures were highly significant in distinguishing between the cystic fibrosis patients and the normal or asthmatic control groups. Discriminant analysis using the two best EDA measures (the mean of five preresponse SPLs and the mean of five preresponse SCLs for each participant) for assignment of experimental group membership yielded 92.7% correct classification of the actual group membership. However, both SP and SC recordings were necessary to obtain such accuracy, since reclassifications of participants by discriminant analysis using only the six potential or the six conductance measures lowered the percentage of correct classifications to 86% for SP and 77% for SC.

Koehler and Weber (1992) exposed 20 female patients with *atopic dermatitis* and 20 controls to two stress situations (a stress film and mental arithmetic), while SC was recorded with standard methodology from the hypothenar eminence of the left hand. Unexpectedly, the patients' SCLs and NS.SCL freq. were lower than those of the controls throughout the whole experiment, though the differences did not reach significance, invalidating the hypothesis of an electrodermal hyperreactivity in atopic dermatitis.

The use of EDA in dermatology also includes the investigation of *cosmetics'* effects on the skin. Within this field of study, the Yamamoto group in Japan developed standardized procedures for AC measurement (for description of methodology, see Sect. 2.5.3.1). Using the generalized electrical model of skin as depicted in Fig. 1.18 (Sect. 1.4.3.3), these authors quantitatively determined the conductance values G_2 and G, being equivalent to the parallel resistances R_2 and R, as well as the capacity C, while neglecting the series resistance R_1. By matrix transformation (cf., Yamamoto et al., 1978. p. 625 f.), three parameters were obtained:

$\overline{C}_N$ as a quantity related to the dielectric constant due to polarization; $\overline{g}_N$ as the part of conductivity due to polarization; and $\overline{G}_N$ as the part of conductivity due to

---

[304] From isopropyl alcohol cleaned sites. The electrolyte for SP consisted of 0.05 M NaCl in a mixture of 50% Unibase and 50% polyethylene glycol, to keep the stratum corneum minimally hydrated (Sect. 2.2.6.1).

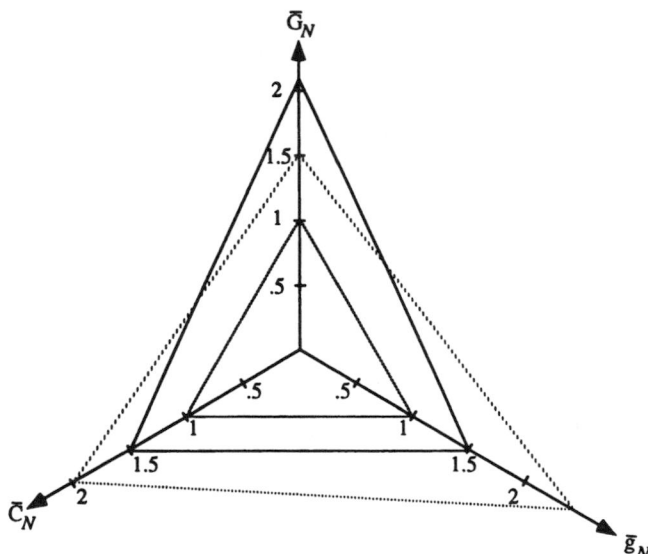

Fig. 3.7 Changes in the dielectric constant $\overline{C}_N$, the ionic conductivity $\overline{G}_N$, and the conductivity of the polarized material $\overline{g}_N$ from baseline (*inner triangle*) over 30 min (*dotted line*) until 3 h (*solid line*) after application of 50% sodium-pyrrolidone-carboxylic acid. Redrawn from Yamamoto et al. (1978), Fig. 7. Copyright 1978 by Peter Peregrinus. Used by permission of the publisher

ionic conduction. $\overline{G}_N$ decreases if the ion conduction in the epidermal stratum corneum decreases, while an increase of $\overline{C}_N$ reflects an increase in the dielectric constant in the corneum. The changes in these parameters were depicted in a plane coordinate system with angles of 120° between each of the three axes, being visualized by triangles.

Figure 3.7 depicts the mean changes in these parameters obtained by Yamamoto et al. (1978) at forearm sites of 3 participants under controlled conditions (with the participant's forearm in a climate chamber), after the application of a 50% solution of sodium-pyrrolidone-carboxylic acid (a natural moisturizing factor in the skin) being used in cosmetics to increase skin moisture. Thirty minutes after its application, the corneal ion conductivity $\overline{G}_N$ was markedly increased, with a further increase during the next 2.5 h. The polarization conductivity $\overline{g}_N$ and the dielectric constant $\overline{C}_N$ were also increased after 30 min, showing a decrease in the subsequent recording period. On the other hand, applications of emulsions of the type oil-in-water or water-in-oil yielded only small changes in these parameters. Though the mathematical rationale of their measurement technique looks complicated, the Yamamoto group provided a method of applying electrodermal AC recording in dermatology that goes far beyond the usual conductance-plus-phase-angle measures, by showing a close relationship to moisture-related bioelectric changes in skin.

Recently, Birgersson, Birgersson, Aberg, Nicander, and Ollmar (2011) refined the AC-recording technique as used by the Yamamoto group by using electrical impedance spectroscopy (see Footnote 50, Sect. 1.4.3.3). They presumed that tissue alterations that can be seen in the microscope during histology might be related to an "imprint" in the SZ spectrum measured at different AC frequencies, which Aberg et al. (2005) showed differentiating benign from malign skin tumors.

3.5.4   EDA in Neurology

Electrodermal and sweat secretion measures are used in neurology to draw inferences about the type and extent of damage in the peripheral and central nervous systems. The particular use of EDA for this area is not only in providing additional information because of slight differences in sensory and sudomotor dermatomes (see Table 1.3, Sect. 1.3.2.1); EDA measures also have an objectivity advantage over subjective reports of patients, since electrodermal phenomena can produce fine-graded responses, which correspond to the extent of damage being subjectively not represented.

Neurologists generally prefer endosomatic over exosomatic EDA measurement, mainly because of the availability of appropriate recording devices (e.g., EMG recorders) in their laboratories. Unfortunately, with few exceptions, they also adhere to their own terminology for the SPR, which they call "sympathetic skin response (SSR)" (for an overview, see Vetrugno, Liguori, Cortelli, & Montagna, 2003). The present author considers it desirable for the future that neurologists may switch to the standard terminology used in psychophysiology (see Table 1.1, Sect. 1.1.1). Therefore and for the sake of clarity, standard terms will be used throughout this section. It is also considered desirable for future research into the application of EDA to brain-related neurological disorders following a more theory driven approach than usual. Appropriate hypotheses can be derived from models of brain function which connect CNS structures to the elicitation of electrodermal concomitants of arousal, emotion, and information processing, as outlined in Sects. 3.1.3.1 and 3.2.1.2.

In neurology, EDA cannot only be applied to brain-related CNS diseases but also be used as a tool in the diagnosis of peripheral disorders, such as lesions of peripheral nerves, of spinal nerve roots, and of the sympathetic trunk. Therefore, three examples of nerve injuries outside the brain will be given, before the use of EDA in brain-related neurological disorders will be reviewed in three sections.

Egyed, Eory, Veres, and Manninger (1980) compared the sensory map, the sweating map (by ninhydrine test), and the SRL map[305] in 47 patients with injuries of the median nerve, in 33 patients with ulnaris nerve injuries, and in 19 patients having both nerves damaged. SRL has been found to be significantly higher in the areas of sensory loss than in corresponding normal skin surfaces, yielding also the advantage of better quantifiability as compared to the colorimetric ninhydrine test. Wilson (1985) used measures of SRL[306] for preoperative assessment of hand

---

[305] Recorded with 3 mm^2 electrodes from skin washed with soap and water, followed by rubbing with alcohol.

[306] Recorded with lead-coated stainless steel electrodes by the use of a digital ohmmeter.

injuries and to monitor the recovery of nerve function in several cases, finding a good concordance between measures of tactile sensitivity and SRL during the healing process.

The usability of SPRs for differential diagnosis in the peripheral nervous system has been demonstrated by Shahani, Halperin, Boulu, and Cohen (1984), who recorded SP[307] from 33 patients with peripheral neuropathies (aged 24–79 years), as well as from 30 normal controls (aged 13–62 years) during deep breaths and electrical stimulation. In 16 of the patients, no SPRs could be obtained. Correlations with clinical, pathological, and EMG observations showed that the SPR was usually absent in axonal neuropathies but present in demyelinating disorders. (For an overview of SPRs in different forms of peripheral neuropathy, see Vetrugno et al., 2003, Table 1).

Curt, Weinhardt, and Dietz (1996) recorded SPRs[308] in 70 patients (15 females, 55 males; mean age 38 years) who suffered from chronic traumatic ($N = 61$) or nontraumatic ($N = 9$) spinal cord injuries, as response to electric contralateral median nerve and transcranial magnetic stimulation (to control for lesions in afferent nerve fibers). Patients with complete paraplegia and those with thoracic lesions from levels T4-T8 showed SPRs in hands but not in feet, while patients with lesions below T8 responded in hand and feet. No patients with preserved SPRs developed symptoms of autonomic dysreflexia, which is in accordance with the assumption this clinical state is related to the disconnection of spinal sympathetic centers from supraspinal control.

3.5.4.1 Brain Lesions

In addition to the use of patients with brain-related CNS lesions for modeling the cortical control of EDA (Sect. 1.3.4.1 "Cortical Control of EDA"), recording of electrodermal phenomena has been applied for diagnostic and prognostic purposes in a diversity of neurological diseases resulting from brain damage. In several studies by Schuri and von Cramon (1979, 1980, 1981, 1982), EDA has been recorded to establish an objective measure of vigilance loss in patients with CNS damages. An attempt was made in their 1979 study to measure differences in responses to meaningful vs. meaningless acoustic stimulation in 8 severely poisoned patients who were in a *coma*. There were slightly though not significantly more SRRs[309] to the patients' first names presented repeatedly forward with 90 dB intensity as compared to backward presentation. In 27 patients with different levels

---

[307] With 10 mm diameter stainless steel electrodes and commercial electrode cream from palmar vs. dorsal hand as well as foot sites, from anterior vs. posterior surfaces of the upper arm, and from patella vs. popliteal fossa sites.

[308] With gold cup EMG disc electrodes from the ventral and dorsal surface of the right hand, using a bandpass filter of 0.3 Hz–3 kHz.

[309] Recorded with standard methodology, using Hellige isotonic electrode cream; time window 1–5 s after stimulus onset; amplitude criterion 500 Ω.

of coma due to drug overdose, Schuri and von Cramon (1980) recorded changes in HR, finger pulse volume amplitude (Sect. 3.1.1.2), and SRRs measured as in the 1979 study (except using an amplitude criterion of 1 kΩ) following optic, acoustic, tactile, and electrical stimulation. Increases of HR were closely related to behavioral changes (e.g., movements of the trunk, turning of the head, frowning) only in the more severe cases, while the finger pulse amplitude invariably increased with behavioral responses at all coma levels. Of all measures applied, the sensitivity to stimulation and correlation with behavioral reactivity was lowest for SRRs (evaluated with a dichotomous criterion response vs. no response).

In their 1981 study, Schuri and von Cramon again used presentations of the name forward and backward to differentiate SCRs (recorded with standard methodology) to meaningful vs. meaningless stimulation in 16 neurological patients (8 with cerebral vascular diseases and 8 comatose patients), compared with a control group of 16 healthy persons. Only in the most severely impaired patients, no differences were found between the two stimulus conditions, as had been the case in the 1979 study. In less severe cases, significantly higher SCR amp. to the patients' names presented forward were found as compared to their names presented backward, however, only during the first two of ten trials. In normal controls, the differences persisted throughout the trials. Habituation appeared as an overall effect in all groups.

The dependence of appropriate results on the amplitude criterion used (Sect. 2.3.1.2 "Choice of Amplitude Criteria") has been demonstrated by Schuri and von Cramon (1982) in a study with 18 neurological patients with severely disturbed vigilance and 18 healthy controls using a similar design. When SCR amp. below 0.025 μS were excluded, patients showed significantly less SCRs as compared to controls, and 5 patients were complete nonresponders (Sect. 3.4.2.2). Lowering the amplitude criterion to 0.005 μS abolished the significance of the group difference, with only one patient remaining nonresponsive.

The usability of spontaneous and/or elicited SRRs as prognostic indicators for survival in comatose patients has been shown by Bjornaes, Smith-Meyer, Valen, Kristiansen, and Ursin (1977). From a total of 40 patients, electrodermal recording was possible with 22, but only 15 met the criterion of showing any SRR[310] either spontaneously or following an electric shock. From these, all seven being below 50 years of age survived the next 1.5 years, and five from those over 50 also survived. All but one of the patients that had not shown EDA died during that period of time. However, Bjornaes et al. (1977) failed to establish electrodermal conditioning using a tone-shock pairing.[311]

---

[310] Recorded with 9 mm diameter Ag/AgCl electrodes filled with commercial electrode cream from palmar/dorsal sites previously washed with acetone. When laterality of the damage was known, recording was performed at the ipsilateral hand.

[311] There were also attempts using NS.EDR freq. and areas under the curve (Sect. 2.3.1.4) to predict awakening from total intravenous anesthesia. However, these parameters had considerably lower predictabilities compared to the "bispectral index"; based on a complex EEG evaluation (Ledowski et al., 2007).

Turkstra (1995) investigated SPRs[312] of 15 brain-injured patients in posttraumatic vegetative states (6 females, 9 males; aged 16–56 years) on their "best day" (determined by their arousal level regardless of EDA) following the presentation of startle stimuli consisting of a loud but not painful tone OR/habituation paradigm, and famous faces. In comparison to five control subjects (2 females, 3 males; age matched), patients showed significantly reduced values in all EDR measures. Patients who had already recovered from the vegetative state showed much better results than those who remained in it a year posttrauma. Although the database for this particular result was narrow, EDRs obtained in the first few months after the brain injury appeared to be predictive of recovery outcome.

EDA has also been used as a correlate of emotional changes in patients with CNS lesions. Zoccolotti, Scabini, and Violani (1982) observed significant differences between SCR amp.[313] following emotional (e.g., sexual stimulation) and those following neutral (e.g., landscape) slides in 16 patients with left unilateral *brain damage*, which did not appear in 16 right unilateral brain damaged patients, thus confirming results of Morrow, Vrtunski, Kim, and Boller (1981) that were obtained with a similar setting using 14 patients of either hemisphere damage. Zoccolotti et al. (1982) interpreted these results as being in accordance with the right hemisphere's role in the organization of adequate emotional behavior (Sect. 3.1.4.2) and claimed their experimental setting to be useful to objectively state emotional indifference in right brain-damaged neurological patients.[314]

Andersson and Finset (1998) recorded SC bilaterally with standard methodology from the middle phalanges of the second and third fingers (Fig. 2.6) as responses to two different problem-solving tasks used as mental stressors, in 27 patients with cerebrovascular lesions, 33 traumatic brain-injured patients and 14 patients with hypoxic brain injury (aged between 16 and 60 years). The cerebrovascular and traumatic patients with focal right-hemisphere injury showed a significantly reduced NS.SCR freq. compared to patients with focal left-hemisphere injury, indicating that lateralization of the lesion rather than diagnosis was the critical factor in electrodermal hyporeactivity to stress in brain-injured patients. In another study using similar samples, Andersson and Finset (1999) investigated electrodermal nonresponding to 1,000 Hz tones (80 dB, 1 s, ISIs 10–20 s) in 82 patients with various brain injuries compared to 28 normal controls. Similar to what has been observed with

---

[312] Recorded with Ag/AgCl electrodes from the hypothenar eminence or from the palmar side of the little finger as active electrode, with the dorsal forearm as inactive and the ventral forearm as ground electrode. SPR amp. was detected as peak-to-trough measure between 1 and 5 s after stimulus presentation.

[313] Recorded with 10 mm^2 gold-plated electrodes from palmar finger sites. SCR amp. was calculated as the square-root of the difference between previous SCL and the maximum SCL within 5 s following stimulus onset.

[314] Based on the results of an experiment with 20 healthy participants, Tranel, Fowles, and Damasio (1985) advocated the usability of EDRs in the detection of the ability to discriminate between familiar and unfamiliar faces of prosopagnosic patients, who have lost the ability to recognize faces.

schizophrenics (Sect. 3.4.2.2), nonresponders showed more negative symptoms and apathy compared to those who responded with EDRs. Thus, the association between electrodermal nonresponsiveness and negative symptoms might be regarded as being independent of the diagnostic group, may it be organic or psychogenic.

Andersson, Gundersen, and Finset (1999) classified 30 severe brain injured patients (8 females, 22 males; aged 16–64 years) into 20 apathetic and 10 nonapathetic individuals, according to a psychiatric rating scale of apathy. In addition to several cardiovascular measures, SC was recorded with the same method as used by Andersson and Finset (1998) during baseline, neutral speech, and therapeutic interaction, with an amplitude criterion of 0.01 μS for SCR detection. While the nonapathetic group showed significant increases from neutral speech to therapeutic interaction in all EDA measures and blood pressure but not in HR, apathetic patients emerged only increases in systolic and mean arterial blood pressure as well as in SCL. This was interpreted by the authors as a correlate to the lack of emotional responsivity, disengagement, lack of insight, and concern of patients about their own situation. As a consequence, psychophysiological recording including EDA during therapeutic intervention may serve as a method for monitoring emotional involvement of brain-injured patients and thus shed light on the possible therapeutic outcome.

Probing the influence of frontal lobe lesions on EDR attenuation to significant stimuli including emotional significance, Zahn, Grafman, and Tranel (1999) compared SCRs (recorded with standard methodology but using 0.5% KCl cream) in 32 patients with frontal lobe damage (2 females, 30 males; mean age 48 years) and 45 healthy controls (19 females, 26 males; mean age 39 years) during resting, presentation of 10 pure 1,000 Hz tones (80 dB, 1.5 s, ISIs 30–50 s), simple warned RT and presentation of emotion eliciting pictures. Patients showed a generally lower NS. SCR freq. in response to significant stimuli and situations compared to controls, but less prominent or absent differences emerged in ORs and during resting conditions. Furthermore, patients with left-hemisphere lesions were less affected in EDA than those with right hemisphere and bilateral lesions, which is in accordance with the results of Davidson et al. (1992) described in Sect. 3.1.4.2. In particular, patients with lateral prefrontal and paraventricular lesions were especially low in NS.SCR freq. during the RT task, and right and bilateral cingulate gyrus lesions figured to be important sources of attenuated SCR amp. in response to psychologically significant stimuli (Sect. 1.3.4.1 "Cortical Control of EDA").

A sophisticated approach to the consequences of selective unilateral amygdala-hippocampectomy for emotional learning has been performed by Peper, Karcher, Wohlfart, Reinshagen, and LeDoux (2001) with 14 left-hemisphere and 12 right-hemisphere medial temporal lobe excision patients, verified by brain imaging (CT or MRT), compared to 13 healthy controls (mean age 30–34 years). In a differential conditioning paradigm (Sect. 3.1.2.1), ten faces from the Ekman et al. (1972) series expressing negative emotions (Sect. 3.2.1.1), being presented by the VHF technique (Sect. 3.1.4.1), served as CS+, a 95 dB baby cry was used as UCS, and 14 facial expressions with positive valence served as CS−. Skin conductance was recorded bilaterally from thenar/hypothenar sites with standard methodology, with an interval of 1–4 s for the FIR (Sect. 3.1.2.1), using the correction method B from Fig. 2.16, Sect. 2.3.1.2 "Amplitudes of Exosomatic Responses Recorded with Direct Current", for correcting the amplitudes of superimposed SCRs. During extinction, the face stimuli were presented laterally and preattentively, using a backward masking procedure. In contrast to the healthy controls, both left and right temporal lobectomy patients failed to show an autonomic conditioning effect during extinction when the masked negative CS+ were presented in the left visual half field, pointing to a deficit in differential responding independent of the resection side. On the other hand, unconditioned and spontaneous SCRs remained intact, suggesting that these responses are independent of amygdalar influences. The authors presumed that these responses might have been elicited by the systems controlling EDA concomitants of motor and premotor activation (see Fig. 3.4, Sect. 3.2.1.2).

Korpelainen, Tolonen, Sotaniemi, and Myllylä (1993) recorded SPRs palmar/dorsal with disc electrodes (and otherwise unspecified technique) from both hands simultaneously in 58 *brain infarction* patients (17 females, 41 males; aged 30–71 years) and 36 healthy controls (16 females, 20 males; aged 31–65 years) during the repeated presentation of auditory click stimuli and electric stimulation of the median nerve at irregular ISIs (with a minimum of 60 s to prevent habituation). SPR amp. were significantly diminished and latencies prolonged in all patients compared to controls. However, prolonged SPR lat. were only seen in the acute phase (within 14 days) but not in the late phase (6–12 months) of the disease. The authors concluded that ANS dysfunction in brain infarction could be more extensive and complex as previously thought.

In an investigation with 29 patients (aged 31–78 years) suffering from brainstem stroke or infarction in the region of the middle cerebral artery, Linden and Berlit (1995) showed that contralateral SPR[315] abnormalities were more pronounced in cerebral artery than in brainstem patients, which evidences that EDRs predominantly originate in the contralateral hemisphere (Sect. 3.1.4.2). On the other hand, no significant lateralization of SPRs[316] could be observed by Schwalen, Altermann, Jörg, Berg, and Cramer (1996) in 24 patients (11 females, 13 males; aged 43–87 years) with infarction in the region of the middle cerebral artery, recorded from both hands and feet as responses to median and tibial nerve stimulation.

In six well-recovered stroke patients, MacIntosh et al. (2008) probed the usefulness of EDA as physiological marker for differences in effort required during movements of the hemiparetic compared with the unaffected limb. They recorded EDA (presumably EDL sampled at 100 Hz) concurrently with fMRI data (Sect. 2.2.3.5) during bilateral hand and ankle tasks, finding that EDA amplitudes were

---

[315] Recorded with 0.9 cm diameter Ag electrodes palmar/dorsal simultaneously from both hands and feet.

[316] Recorded from palmar and plantar surfaces simultaneously with indifferent electrodes attached to the volar side of the forearm (Fig. 2.6) and the lower part of the shinbone (Fig. 2.7), respectively, with otherwise unreported methodology.

more variable in tasks involving the hemiparetic limb. The authors concluded that stroke patients may require higher order motor processing for the performance of simple tasks in the affected limbs, for which EDA could serve as marker.

3.5.4.2 Degenerative Diseases

Electrodermal measures have also been used to determine deficits in various neurological diseases with degenerative CNS origin. Oscar-Berman and Gade (1979) observed the course of habituation of the electrodermal OR to 20 buzzer tones (100 dB, 1 s) in 10 aphasic patients, 8 Korsakoff patients, 15 parkinsonians, 7 Huntington's chorea patients, and 18 normal controls. SCR amp.[317] following the first stimulus, a regression measure of habituation rate (Sect. 3.1.2.1), and the NS. SCR freq. as well as the SCL during an initial 10 min resting period were evaluated. There were no significant differences in measures of EDL, but patients with Korsakoff's and Huntington's disease were significantly less responsive than normals and aphasics on the first stimulus presentation, and patients with Huntington's disease were also less responsive than Korsakoff patients. These results which were paralleled by those obtained from the habituation rate supported the view of Stern and Janes (1973) that no generalized changes in ANS reactivity are to be expected following brain lesions. Instead, differential effects are likely to appear being related to the specificity of the particular damage.

Such a group of neurological patients with specific relation to central origins of EDA are the *parkinsonians*. That particular neurological disorder is characterized by the degeneration of dopaminergic neurons connecting the compact part of the substantia nigra to the striatal part of the basal ganglia, causing a dopamine deficit in the latter. Besides the well-known motor symptoms (rigor, tremor, and hypokinesia), cognitive deficits were also observed in those patients (Canavan et al., 1989), which may be due to the basal ganglia's role in providing information on operant conditioning for frontal cortical areas (see Fig. 3.4; Sect. 3.2.1.2). Since the basal ganglia are also suggested to be the source of preparatory EDRs (i.e., EDA2, see Fig. 1.6; Sect. 1.3.4.1), this kind of EDA should be impaired together with cognitive deficits in parkinsonians while electrodermal OR and habituation should not. The latter ones are more likely to be controlled by amygdalar and hippocampal structures (i.e., EDA1, see Fig. 1.6).

An attempt to show this hypothetical connection between cognitive deficits in parkinsonians and specific electrodermal parameters has been performed in the present author's laboratory. Boucsein, Valentin, and Furedy (1993) contrasted 15 parkinsonians (5 females, 10 males; mean age 63 years) with 15 age-matched controls, and 15 healthy students (mean age 25 years). As predicted, SCR amp. recorded with

---

[317] Recorded as SR with 10 μA constant current unipolarly (thumb vs. upper arm), using 15 mm diameter Ag/AgCl electrodes, transformed to log SC values. Amplitude criterion for NS.SCRs = 0.003 log μS.

standard methodology during a habituation series of 20 tones (1 kHz, 60 dB) yielded no differences between patients and their matched controls. In a subsequent classical conditioning paradigm (light-noise pairings), both parkinsonians and age-matched controls failed to elicit considerable SIRs or TORs (Sect. 3.1.2.1) which the younger controls did, supposedly dependent on the generally lower electrodermal reactivity of old-aged participants (Sect. 2.4.3.1). Thus, in this investigation, age-related electrodermal effects may have simply bypassed possible neurological damage-related effects. Therefore, further research in this area should carefully select appropriate stimulus conditions for the old-age groups (e.g., by increasing stimulus intensities) to see if the loss of EDRs is due to age or due to CNS degeneration.

To reveal the nature of autonomic dysfunctions in parkinsonians, Wang et al. (1993) compared SPRs, recorded with palmar vs. dorsal electrodes from the right hand and foot, in 62 idiopathic parkinsonians (7 females, 55 males; aged 45–86 years) and 62 age-matched normal participants during electrical stimulation of the left wrist. In addition, ECG was recorded during resting and deep breathing to obtain average IBIs. Visual inspection of the EDA signal revealed no SPR abnormalities in controls and stage I parkinsonians, while altogether 14.5% of patients in stages II–IV did not show observable SPRs. Also, the duration of illness was significantly longer in patients without SPRs. Abnormalities in IBIs were correlated with age, while lack of SPRs was not, pointing to a differential indicator function of cardiovascular and electrodermal activity in parkinsonians.

No such correlation of SPR impairment with the duration of Parkinson's disease was found by Denislic and Meh (1996) in 23 idiopathic parkinsonians (12 females, 11 males; aged 20–81 years) with a similar methodology as used by Wang et al. (1993). However, SPR lat. was significantly prolonged and SPR amp. decreased compared to 41 healthy controls within the same age range, which gives evidence for ANS dysfunction in Parkinson's disease.

Esen, Celebi, Ertekin, and Colakoglu (1997) used the EDA1/EDA2 differentiation proposed by Boucsein (1992; see Sect. 1.3.4.1) to reveal the nature of ANS impairment in 25 parkinsonians (46–72 years) who used L-dopa for at least 1–4 years, compared to 27 healthy controls (45–68 years). They recorded skin resistance[318] during auditory (click) and mechanical (patella tendon tapping) stimulation. Almost all parkinsonians showed an SPR to the auditory stimuli, but 30% of them did not respond to mechanical stimulation. Furthermore, mean SPR lat. to tendon stimulation was significantly longer in the patient group than in the healthy controls. The authors concluded that EDA1 was intact in parkinsonians, while the EDA2 system, which originates in the premotor cortex and the basal ganglia (see Fig. 1.6), was impaired. Hence, the ANS impairment in patients with Parkinson's disease seems to be rather specific and restricted to the areas that produce the premotor EDA2 component.

---

[318] Recorded with 10 μA/cm² CC via Ag/AgCl electrodes from the thenar region of the hand. The skin was abraded with sand paper and cleaned with alcohol before electrode attachment.

In general, increases of EDR lat. compared to healthy controls are typical for parkinsonians and the body side which is clinically most affected shows greater EDR impairment than the contralateral side, but there is no unequivocal relationship between EDR abnormalities and duration or stages of Parkinson's disease (Jörg & Boucsein, 1998). SPR amp. being much lower in patients than in controls was demonstrated by Haapaniemi et al. (2000). They compared SPRs recorded palmar/ dorsal from hands and feet of 60 untreated idiopathic parkinsonians (23 females, 37 males) and from 20 age-matched healthy controls (7 females, 13 males). Administration of drugs such as L-dopa did not evoke a considerable change in SPR amp. in patients within a 6 month follow-up. However, patients having symptoms for more than 1 year showed significantly reduced SPR amp. compared to patients with a shorter symptom history. In conclusion, EDR amp. could be a valuable tool in diagnosing the progress of Parkinson's disease, independent of drug administration.

Patients with Parkinson's disease, especially those being treated for a considerable time with L-dopa, frequently show a phenomenon labeled freezing, an inability to move the legs especially when starting to walk, facing the need to step over an obstacle, or making a 360° turn. Jörg, Jock, Boucsein, and Schäfer (2004) recorded SCL, using standard methodology, together with skin temperature, ECG, respiration, and leg movements, by means of ambulatory monitoring with the Vitaport system (Sect. 2.2.3.4) from 14 parkinsonians having exhibited freezing in the past (4 females, 10 males) and from 14 parkinsonians without prior freezing experience (7 of each gender). Eleven patients in the freezing-experienced group exhibited freezing while walking on a predetermined course with standardized obstacles (carpets, turning around poles, etc.), producing altogether 26 freezing events. No freezing emerged in the other group of patients. Recordings between 5 s before and 15 s after the beginning of a freezing episode were used for evaluation and compared to similar periods from patients without freezing. There was a consistently observed, albeit nonsignificant, SCL increase about 1 s before the onset of the freezing phenomenon, being especially large in patients who reported having been afraid of freezing during the study. These results point to the possibility that freezing in patients with Parkinson's disease could be related to the BIS coupled motor inhibition (Sect. 3.2.1.2), for which an increased EDA can be regarded as specific ANS indicator. The other physiological measures did not show such a consistent pattern before the onset of freezing. The phenomenon itself elicited an OR as indicated by a significant HR deceleration (Sect. 3.1.1).

EDA can also be used to indicate the impairment of emotional processing in parkinsonians. Using the IGT (Sect. 3.1.3.3) in 21 nondemented idiopathic Parkinson patients with L-dopa and 23 healthy controls, comparable with respect to age, gender, and years of school education, Euteneuer et al. (2009) recorded skin conductance with standard methodology to determine anticipatory and feedback SCR amp. Although IGT performance was not significantly impaired in parkinsonians, they seemed to be impaired in learning from negative stimulation, since EDR amp. were significantly reduced after losses compared to healthy controls, but relatively unimpaired after gains. Thus, Parkinson patients may be impaired not only in the motor and cognitive loops (Fig. 3.4, Sect. 3.2.1.2) but also in an additional limbic loop (DeLong & Wichmann, 2007; see also Footnote 115 in Sect. 3.2.1.2).

Huntington's chorea can also be suggested to be related to the CNS elicitation of electrodermal phenomena, since cell damage in the striatal part of basal ganglia precedes cortical atrophy in the development of that particular illness. Establishing electrodermal markers for choreatic risk, as has been performed for schizophrenia (Sect. 3.4.2.1), would be of high value for eugenic counseling in the offspring of Huntington's patients, carrying 50% risk for developing the disease during midlife because of its autosomal dominant heritability. The marked deficit in electrodermal reactivity observed by Oscar-Berman and Gade (1979) in choreatic patients as described above stimulated Lawson (1981) to compare electrodermal ORs[319] to 24 sounds ranging from 75 to 90 dB (including pure tones, white noise, and synthetic speech phonemes) taken from 52 symptom-free patients suffering from Huntington's chorea (36 females, 16 males), with those taken from 26 controls (9 females and 15 males among the responders), being tested at their homes. Seventeen participants (13 females, 4 males) in the risk group were found to be nonresponders, while only 2 of the participants serving as controls showed electro-dermal nonresponding, the difference being statistically significant.

In addition to these deficits in OR, Leonard, Podoll, Weiler, and Lange (1984) observed an increased habituation rate in 27 patients with Huntington's chorea (13 females, 14 males) and in 32 persons at risk for the disease (symptom-free offspring of patients; 18 females, 14 males) as compared to 26 normal controls (13 of each gender). Habituation of SRR amp.[320] to 16 stimuli serving as UCSs in a classical conditioning paradigm (100 dB white noise) was terminated within the first eight presentations in 44% of the Huntington patients, and in 16% of the persons at risk, but in only one of the controls.

By contrast, Iacono, Roshi, and Lacoste (1987) could not find significant differences in SCRs[321] between 7 male patients in the early stages of Huntington's disease and 29 offspring of these patients (22 females, 7 males) on the one hand, and age and gender matched normal control samples on the other hand. Neither showed the at-risk group electrodermal abnormalities, nor could the patients them-selves be differentiated from their controls by means of EDR.

A demyelinating disease which results in SPR loss in about 50% of the patients (Jörg & Boucsein, 1998) is *multiple sclerosis* (MS). The diagnostic value of EDA impairment for ANS dysfunctions in MS patients has been investigated by several authors. Gutrecht, Suarez, and Denny (1993) recorded SPRs[322] during repeated

---

[319] Recorded bilaterally as SCRs with standard methodology, but using 0.5 KCl-agar cream. Time window: 3 s after stimulus onset; amplitude criterion $= 0.05$ μS.

[320] Recorded with standard methodology, however, using hypertonic cream. Time window: 1–5 s after stimulus onset. Habituation criterion: three consecutive SRRs below 500 Ω (Sect. 3.1.1.3).

[321] Recorded bilaterally with standard methodology during three series of acoustic stimuli (eight 85 dB tones, twelve 105 dB tones, and two familiar sounds).

[322] From the hand and foot opposite to stimulation by gold-plated disc electrodes, using the tip of the fifth finger and the thenar eminence, or the tip of the great toe and the anterior plantar area, respectively, as recording sites.

median nerve stimulation at the wrist with a brief electrical pulse (with minimum ISIs of 60 s to avoid habituation) in 29 MS patients (21 females, 8 males; aged 20–61 years) and in 26 healthy controls. There was a good correlation between delayed or absent SPRs and the severity of the illness in patients, but no correlation to MRI images of the hypothalamus and brain stem. The authors concluded that MS probably affected the sudomotor fibers located in the lateral columns of the spinal cord (see Fig. 1.3), which may be fragile and thus be disrupted in an early stage of MS.

De Seze et al. (2001) confirmed the role of spinal cord atrophy in autonomic dysfunctions of MS patients. They recorded SPR palmar/dorsal from all four limbs with EMG electrodes during repeated electrical stimulation (ISIs greater than 30 s) of the right median nerve at the wrist in 75 MS patients (46 females, 29 males; aged 30–60 years) and 15 controls matched for age and gender. Spinal cord MRI revealed that SPR impairment appeared to be more closely related to axonal loss, as shown by atrophy, than to demyelinating lesions. In addition, SPR dysfunction appeared more frequently in the 25 patients with primary progressive MS than in the other 50 MS patients. No such coherence between severity of illness and SPR abnormalities was found by McDougall and McLeod (2003) in 63 MS patients above 18 years. In this study, SPR was recorded palmar/dorsal from hand and feet with AgCl electrodes as response to an electric stimulation of the opposite median nerve at the wrist. Altogether, abnormalities of SPRs were present in 45% of the patients.

A study reporting good coherence between SPR abnormalities and severity of MS was performed by Saari et al. (2008). They recorded SPRs with Ag/AgCl electrodes palmar/dorsal from both hands and both feet in 27 patients with MS without specific drug treatment and 27 healthy controls (13 females, 14 males; mean age of 39 years in both groups). Normal SPRs could be elicited in controls from hands and feet with both auditory (click) and electrical stimulation, whereas SPRs in MS patients were disturbed or even absent. Patients who did not show SPRs had a more severe MS than those who did. The existence of sudomotor regulation failure in severe MS patients with focal lesions in various brain areas (e.g., temporal lobe, cerebellum, and pons) was confirmed by lesion volumetric MRI results.

A sophisticated approach into the nature of cognitive and emotional deficits in MS patients was performed by Kleeberg et al. (2004) who assessed decision making and impaired emotional reactivity by subjecting 20 MS patients (18 females, 2 males; aged 25–57 years) and 16 healthy controls (14 females, 2 males; aged 19–60 years) to the IGT (Sect. 3.1.3.3). Anticipatory and punishment SCRs were recorded with flat-surface electrodes and otherwise unreported methodology. Electrodermal equivalence of both groups was confirmed by comparable baseline SCR activity obtained at resting, in response to a loud noise, and after taking a deep breath. MS patients persisted longer than the controls in making disadvantageous choices in the IGT, suggesting that MS is associated with delayed learning of decision making. Their slower learning was associated with lower anticipatory and lower postchoice SCR amp. which pointed to an impaired emotional reactivity. Deficits in decision making together with altered emotional experience were identified by the authors as possible contributing factors to the altered quality of life in MS patients. Summarizing, SPRs can serve as a valuable tool to detect ANS irregularities in MS patients, since sudomotor regulation is often impaired. However, a relationship of ANS impairment to severity of MS could not always be confirmed.

EDA has also been used for investigating impaired fear conditioning in *Alzheimer's disease*. Hamann, Monarch, and Goldstein (2002) probed classical fear conditioning in 10 participants with probable Alzheimer's disease (6 females, 4 males; aged 56–81 years) and in 14 demographically matched healthy controls (11 females, 3 males), using 2-s presentations of green and red rectangles as CS+ and CS− equally often across participants. A 100 dB, 1 s white noise stimulus served as UCS. Patients yielded no differences in square-root transformed SCR amp. (recorded with standard methodology from the nondominant hand) between CS habituation, acquisition, and extinction, whereas the controls showed the to-be-expected higher SCR amp. to the CS+ compared to the CS− in the acquisition phase. The authors interpreted their results as demonstrating an impairment of nondeclarative emotional memory in Alzheimer patients, in addition to previously reported impairments in declarative emotional memory. Hoefer et al. (2008) studied electrodermal fear conditioning in 25 Alzheimer patients (12 females, 13 males; aged 50–77 years), 25 patients with frontotemporal lobe degeneration (8 females, 17 males; aged 49–83 years) and 25 controls (15 females, 10 males; aged 51–79 years). Blue and orange rectangles (2 s) were used as CS+ and CS−, counterbalanced across participants within the diagnostic groups, and a 100 dB, 1 s white noise stimulus served as UCS. SC was recorded by means of Ag/AgCl electrodes from the middle phalanges of the middle and index fingers of the nondominant hand. Both groups of patients did not show the square-root transformed SCR amp. difference between CS+ and CS− in the acquisition phase as did the control participants. Although the Alzheimer patients showed an initial response to the UCS which was almost as high as in the controls, indicating a normal EDR to aversive stimulation, their fear conditioning was severely impaired. Since the initial SCR amp. to the UCS was not half as high in the frontotemporal patients compared to the two other groups, the authors concluded that these patients yield a more serious deficit in emotional responding than patients with Alzheimer's disease.

3.5.4.3   Disorders with Primary Psychological Relevance

This section will review several neurological disorders having severe consequences in the psychological domain, the most striking one is failure to recognize faces that should be known by the patient. The most prevalent face recognition disorder is *prosopagnosia*. It refers to a neurological disease which is characterized by the inability to recognize previously familiar faces. Patients usually recognize a face as a face, but cannot recognize whose face it is. Autopsy and MRI studies in prosopagnosics revealed bilateral damage of the ventral visual stream from occipital to temporal cortical areas (Gross & Sergent, 1992), which is held responsible for overt face recognition. Interestingly, prosopagnosics may still show covert face recognition in absence of overtly recognizing a face, for which Bauer (1986) suggested an additional pathway besides the ventral route, i.e., the dorsal visual stream from the occipital cortex via the inferior parietal lobe to limbic structures. Patients with prosopagnosia may suffer from ventral stream damage, while the dorsal stream is still functioning. In this case, covert recognition of an overtly non-recognized familiar face may be indicated by a limbic-system elicited EDR in some prosopagnosics.

This has been demonstrated by Tranel and Damasio (1988) who recorded SCRs with standard methodology from 4 patients with prosopagnosia during three successive experimental settings with different sets of faces (family, politicians, therapists). All participants showed EDRs elicited by faces which had been familiar to them but were now rated as definitely unfamiliar. However, an attempt to reveal the nature of covert face recognition performed by Tranel and Damasio (1993) by means of a face learning paradigm with a severely amnestic patient did not confirm these results. Skin conductance was recorded with the same methodology as in the previous study during the presentation of 38 faces, containing 16 target faces (professionals and caregivers). No differences in SCR amp. emerged. However, the patient was able to covertly discriminate between faces which had been assigned to the categories "good" and "bad" by the patient herself/himself. The authors concluded that affective valence was the critical factor in the patient's face recognition but not familiarity.

In their critical review on the two-route model of face recognition, Breen, Caine, and Coltheart (2000) denied the necessity for adopting a dorsal visual pathway. Instead, they proposed a face recognition unit within the ventral system which connects to a person identity node and to a path being responsible for affective responses to familiar stimuli. The latter one being identified as the amygdala was suggested having the ability to elicit an EDR, together with influences from arousal and OR generating structures. By means of this path, prosopagnosics may generate an EDR even if they do not overtly recognize a previously familiar face.

Another face recognition disorder which has been regarded as to some extent mirror imaging prosopagnosia is *Capgras delusion* (Ellis & Lewis, 2001). It is characterized by the belief that persons who are familiar to the patient have been replaced by doubles, imposters, robots, or aliens (Ellis & de Pauw, 1994). According to Ellis and Young (1990), Capgras delusion might emerge if conscious face recognition is intact, whereas the covert face recognition system is malfunctioning, thus not providing confirmation to what is overtly recognized. Consequently, Capgras patients should not show SCRs to faces overtly recognized as familiar.

Hirstein and Ramachandran (1997) described the failure of a Capgras delusion patient to produce higher SCR amp.[323] in response to familiar persons, including his parents whom he called imposters, compared to unfamiliar faces. The authors

---

[323] Measured with Ag/AgCl electrodes affixed with Velcro straps to the middle phalanges of the left hand, voltage unreported.

suggested damage of the connection between the face processing areas in the temporal lobe to the limbic system as an explanation.

Ellis, Young, Quayle, and de Pauw (1997) recorded SCRs with standard methodology (however, nonreported voltage) from 5 Capgras delusion patients, 5 other psychiatric patients, and five normal controls during the presentation of 29 predominantly unfamiliar face stimuli, with occasionally familiar faces interspersed. To allow for interindividual comparisons, famous faces were used rather than personally familiar ones. The normal controls and the psychiatric controls revealed significantly higher mean SCR amp. to familiar compared to unfamiliar faces, while the Capgras delusion patients did not. Since their ORs to auditory stimuli were normal in magnitude and habituation rate, their failure to produce SCRs to familiar faces could be considered a face recognition deficit and not a sign of general autonomic hyporesponsiveness.

Ellis, Lewis, Moselhy, and Young (2000) tested a female Capgras delusion patient for both electrodermal and behavioral discrimination between famous and unfamiliar faces. The tests were also completed by six female controls of about the same age. While the latter ones showed significantly higher SCR amp. (recorded with unreported methodology) to famous compared to unfamiliar faces, the Capgras patient did not. However, her performance in a face/name priming task and in a test of face/name interference was comparable to that of the normal controls. Such dissociation between autonomic and behavioral concomitants of covert face recognition could be explained in the framework of Breen et al.'s (2000) model, which suggested that patients with Capgras delusion yield intact visual recognition structures for faces, but a disrupted connection between the proposed face recognition unit and the path being responsible for affective responses to familiar faces.

Another topic in neurology of primary psychological significance is *pain*. Riley and Richter (1975) mapped SRL[324] for 20 patients who had neck or upper extremity pain without clinical or radiographic evidence of spinal cord or nerve root irritation. They could show that areas of low SRL corresponded well to areas of subjective pain, thus providing some evidence for an unknown degenerative lesion process within the CNS underlying the reported pain in these patients.[325]

Jamner and Tursky (1987) recorded SCRs with standard methodology from 14 *migraine* sufferers (12 females, 2 males) and ten pain free controls (9 females, 1 male) during the visual presentation of 20 pain descriptors being shown twice for 12 s each with ISIs from 10 to 30 s. Participants' evaluations of the pain descriptors did not differ between the groups, but the migraine patients produced significantly higher SCR amp. than the pain-free participants, thus pointing to the feasibility of EDRs as objective indicator for migraine diagnostics.

---

[324] Recorded with an active roller electrode without cream and an ECG electrode with hypertonic cream as reference at the leg or arm, by use of a dermohmeter.

[325] Janssen, Arntz, and Bouts (1998) used SCL recordings in an investigation into the effect of epinephrine on heat pain threshold in 24 participants (12 of each gender). Focusing of attention exerted a much stronger influence on pain responses than epinephrine infusions.

One potential reason for the sustained electrodermal reactivity in migraine patients compared to healthy individuals could be their reduced EDR habituation. Siniatchkin, Gerber, Kropp, Voznesenskaya, and Vein (2000) probed the habituation of the CNV using an S1–S2 paradigm with 40 trials, which combined auditory warning and imperative stimuli, in 20 females with migraine 1–4 days before and 4 days after an attack, in comparison to 12 age- and gender-matched controls. In addition, all participants took part in a habituation session with 20 tones (1,000 Hz, 70 dB, 5 s) separated by ISIs between 5 and 15 s, during which SCRs were recorded.[326] Migraine patients showed significantly reduced habituation of the CNV and alpha blocking, but no differences in SCR habituation emerged in comparison with the controls. This might have been due to the use of tone stimuli alone in the SCR habituation procedure, since Huber, Henrich and Gündel (2005) found an impairment of SCR[327] habituation in 30 female migraine patients compared to 30 controls matched for gender, age, and social status in an achievement test (20 calculation tasks with ISIs of 20–30 s) but not in simple auditory stimuli (20 sinus tones, 1,000 Hz, 70 dB, 400 ms, same ISIs). The achievement tests were characterized by high cognitive demands under time pressure.

Flor, Knost, and Birbaumer (1997) presented 40 pain- and 40 body-related words plus 40 neutral words for 4 s each (ISIs 6–18 s) in pseudorandomized order to 12 chronic patients suffering from upper back pain daily for at least 6 months and to 12 healthy controls. SCL recorded with standard methodology was enhanced following pain-related words only in pain patients, which was paralleled by enhanced early ERP components to the same category of words. Thus, both CNS and ANS responses, including the electrodermal system, may be used as indicators for specific pain-related cognitive and emotional processing in patients suffering from various kinds of pain.

Recently, EDA has been successfully used as an objective index of the sympathetic ANS response to painful stimulation in an fMRI/EEG evaluation of appropriate CNS responses. Mobascher et al. (2009) delivered laser stimuli to the dorsum of the left hand of 12 healthy male right-handed participants, while concomitantly recording SC[328] and EEG in an fMRI (Sect. 2.2.3.5). Stimulus intensity was individually adjusted prior to the application of 60 laser stimuli to ensure its painfulness. Individual trials were classified according to the height of their SCR amp. Significantly higher BOLD responses emerged predominantly in the somatosensory cortex and in the insula during trials with high SCR amp. compared to those with low SCR amp.

---

[326] With Ag/AgCl electrodes filled with 0.5% potassium chloride in 2% agar-agar as electrolyte. SCRs were identified as ORs if being greater than 0.05 µS and occurring 1–3 s after tone onset.

[327] Recorded from volar finger sites with Ag/AgCl electrodes and otherwise unreported methodology.

[328] Recorded with standard methodology, using an MR capable sensor (Brain Products GmbH, Gilching, Germany). After applying MR artifact correction procedures and a bandpass filter of 0.016–5 Hz to the SC signal, SCR amp. was determined as the peak-to-peak difference between the minimum and the maximum SCL within the 1–8 s poststimulus interval.

Attention-deficit/hyperactivity disorder (ADHD) is a psychopathological condition prevalent in childhood with the ability to persist in adults. It is characterized by age-inappropriate inattention, impulsivity, low frustration tolerance, and hyperactivity. Besides their typical behavioral deficits, ADHD children exhibit an attenuated EDA. This had been demonstrated by Satterfield and Dawson (1971) in two experimental sessions with tone presentations (1,000 and 500 Hz, 5 s, ISIs 15–20 s), comparing 24 male hyperactive children aged 6–12 years with 12 normal controls, matched for age and gender. EDA was recorded as skin resistance[329] and converted to skin conductance. Hyperkinetic children showed a lower SCL, a lower NS.EDR freq., and a lower EDR amp. following the auditory stimuli compared to the control group. The authors offered a tentative hypothesis of a lower excitability of the RAS (Sect. 1.3.4.1 "Three Different CNS Originating Pathways for EDA"), which is in accordance with the calming effect of amphetamines in ADHD children, since stimulants are thought to raise RAS excitability.

Iaboni, Douglas, and Ditto (1997) attempted to use the differential validity of EDA and HR as indicators for BIS and BAS (Sect. 3.2.1.2) to reveal the brain mechanisms in ADHD children. They subjected 18 boys aged 8–13 years who were diagnosed as having ADHD and 18 normal boys matched in age, IQ, and socioeconomic status to the repetitive motor task developed by Fowles et al. (1982) and recorded SC with standard methodology as well as HR. As proposed by Fowles (1980), the normal boys responded to being rewarded with an increase of HR and to extinction with an increase in SCL. The ADHD boys showed also an HR increase during the first reward condition but habituated quickly. This may point to a somewhat stronger BAS in ADHD children compared to normals. However, an alternative explanation could be the generally decreasing attention in ADHD children during the course of the experiment. No increase in SCL during extinction was found in ADHD boys, thus providing support for a weak BIS in ADHD, which is similar in adult psychopaths (Sect. 3.4.1.2).

Beauchaine, Katkin, Strassberg, and Snarr (2001) compared 17 ADHD, 20 aggressive conduct disorder (CD), and 22 control male adolescents (12–17 years) during two phases of an experiment. The first phase consisted of a 5 min baseline plus a computerized repetitive response task which allowed for an isolated evaluation of BAS activity during reward and BIS activity during punishment. During the second phase, participants viewed an escalating conflict between peers. NS.SCRs were recorded with standard methodology from the thenar eminence and scored if they exceeded 0.05 μS. In addition, ECG and impedance cardiogram were recorded to assess the sympathetic nervous system influences on HR via preejection period. The expected attenuation of EDA as a sign of attenuated BIS activity in ADHD was observed during baseline but not for punishment during the response task. Furthermore, excessive BAS activity in ADHD which should have been reflected in shorter preejection periods during reward did not occur, but a lengthened preejection period

---

[329] Recorded with 50 μA CC from the first and third fingertip of the right hand through 4 mm diameter Ag/AgCl electrodes with Cambridge electrode cream.

instead, thus challenging the notion of a general opposed function of BIS and BAS (Sect. 3.2.1.2).

Lazzaro et al. (1999) found EDA attenuation and increased EEG theta and alpha1 (8–9 Hz) and reduced beta activity in 54 adolescent ADHD males (11–17 years) compared to 54 age- and gender-matched normal controls during a 2-min resting condition with eyes open. Skin conductance was recorded with standard methodology and evaluated as SCL and NS.SCR freq. The latter correlated significantly negative ($r = -0.31$ to $r = -0.38$) with absolute theta power not only in anterior cortical regions but also all over the brain, thus indicating a connection between electrodermal hypoarousal and an increased slow brain wave activity. This could be seen as at least partly confirming the Satterfield and Dawson (1971) hypothesis of reduced general arousal (Sect. 3.2.1.1) in ADHD individuals, providing at least an alternative to the BIS/BAS hypothesis.

Crowell et al. (2006) demonstrated that attenuated EDRs in ADHD children may be present as early as in preschoolers. They compared 18 children with either ADHD or oppositional defiant disorder (ODD) aged 4–6 years (7 girls, 11 boys) with 20 age-matched controls (9 girls, 11 boys) while performing a computer game, after which a previously chosen toy was given to the participants. NS.SCRs[330] exceeding 0.05 µS, ECG, and impedance cardiogram were recorded. During the task, ADHD and ODD children displayed a lower NS.SCR freq., which was, however, already the case during baseline recording. Together with an attenuated cardiac preejection period, the EDA results generally supported the hypothesis of reward insensitivity, but the possible inattention of ADHD children could have a reason for the group differences as well.

In general, EDA has been demonstrated to be valuable tool for investigating ADHD children. However, to date there is no generally accepted theory available to explain autonomic deficits in this disorder.

3.5.5   EDA in Other Medical and Psychological Applications

Despite their specific use in dermatology and neurology as described in previous sections, electrodermal measures can be useful in various medical contexts where either the skin itself or the sympathetic branch of the ANS are involved. In this section, examples will be provided mainly, where EDA is an indicator being used in internal and psychosomatic medicine.

Lawler, Davis, and Griffith (1960) summarized the results from several studies on SZ and *thyroid dysfunctions* that were performed during the 1930s, reporting that skin impedance and basic metabolic rates were correlated in hyperthyroidism but showed no relations to each other in hypothyroidism. Dolu, Süer, Özesmi,

---

[330] Recorded through standard Ag/AgCl electrodes, filled with Parker Labs Signa Gel, by a Grass Physiodata Amplifier System with a DC amplifier.

Kelestimur, and Esel (1997) compared SC[331] in 24 nonmedicated hyperthyroid patients (14 females, 10 males) with 35 healthy controls (18 females, 17 males). They observed significantly higher SCLs and shorter SCR lat. as well as longer SCR durations to 15 tones (1 kHz, 90 dB, 1 s) in hyperthyroid patients. The authors consider the relationship between thyroid dysfunctions and EDA being complex.

Knezevic and Bajada (1985) investigated the biphasic SPR following the electrical stimulation of the median nerve in 10 *diabetic* patients (see Sect. 2.5.1.1 for methodological details). SPR amp. were significantly lower as compared to those taken from 30 controls. The differences was 300 μV at palmar and 84 μV at plantar sites, while mean SPR lat. did not differ at either site. Macleod, Smith, Cowell, Richardson, and Sonksen (1991) used SR (recorded with constant current of nonreported density and silver-coated electrodes fixed with Velcro band to the first and third digits of the hand and foot) in 55 diabetic patients. Significant correlations of the toe/finger ratio with the tibial nerve conduction velocity (about $r = 0.50$) pointed to the possibility that impairment of sudomotor functioning parallels the impairment of the large myelinated motor and sensory fibers in the group of diabetic patients. Chassande, Charpentier, Budy, Willer, and Lille (1996) found that ANS tests (HR and endosomatic EDR recordings) in diabetic patients were severely impaired in those patients having peripheral neuropathies (Sect. 3.5.4). The SPR amp. was decreased in all 53 diabetic patients in comparison with 32 controls. Abnormalities in SPRs were reported in 66–83% of diabetic patients, their frequency increasing with disease progress (Vetrugno et al., 2003).

Stocksmeier and Langosch (1973) recorded SR twice over a period of 3 weeks during olfactory, acoustic, and optical stimulation from 57 male *rheumatic* patients and 24 controls, using dry silver electrodes. As compared to the controls, the patients showed significantly lower SRLs and SRR amp. during the first session, while after 3 weeks SRLs were higher in the rheumatics, and the SRR amp. did not differ between the two groups. The amplitude results were paralleled by an area measure (Sect. 2.3.1.4). Since during that short period no specific effect of anti-rheumatic treatment could be expected, the authors attributed the increase in tonic and phasic EDA to the general arousing effect of the treatment. No differences in SP or SC between *asthmatic* patients and the normal controls were observed by Williamson et al. (1985) in their study described in Sect. 3.5.3.

Doerr, Follette, Scribner, and Eisdorfer (1980) recorded SC with standard methodology during three valsalva maneuvers following each other with 4 min distance. Both the SCL and the highest SCR amp. during each maneuver were significantly lower in 25 *dialysis* patients (16 females, 9 males) compared to an age- and gender-matched control group of equal size. Furthermore, they obtained a significant correlation of $r = 0.52$ between the SCL and the residual creatine clearance. As there were also positive correlations between EDA and peroneal nerve conduction velocity ($r = 0.43$

---

[331] Recorded from the distal phalanges of the first and second fingers of the dominant hand with standard Ag/AgCl electrodes, using physiological NaCl in agar-agar paste as electrolyte. SC was expressed in $μS/cm^2$.

for SCL and $r = 0.41$ for SCR amp.) the most suitable interpretation for the relationship between EDA and the amount of residual kidney function might be a reduction in ANS nerve conduction velocity in these patients (Muthny, 1984).

Attempts to establish differences in EDA between patients with tension *headache* or migraine and normal controls were not successful. Chattopadhyay, Mazumdar and Basu (1982) as well as Thompson and Adams (1984) could not find appropriate electrodermal differences between these groups, neither in habituation to a series of light flashes nor during the induction of stressful imageries.

Kopp (1984) compared two groups of *psychosomatic* patients (50 male hypertensives and 47 male duodenal ulcer patients, both in the early mild reversible stage of the disease) with 65 male controls, with respect to their EDA during a sequence of different kinds of stimuli,[332] plus three tones (1 kHz, 93 dB) and eight colored stimuli. EDA was recorded as SR using standard methodology. Both patient groups displayed opposite electrodermal behavior in comparison with controls: NS. SRR freq. and EDR amp. were significantly reduced in hypertensives but increased in ulcer patients (in whom, however, the SRL was also increased). In the latter patient group, a significant prolongation of SRR rec.t/2 following the emotional disturbing words had been obtained, which was interpreted by the authors as being due to a DR (Sect. 3.1.1.2), and not to more intense information processing (Sect. 3.1.3.1), an interpretation which they used for the prolonged EDR recovery in the normal controls following unexpected stimulation.

Some specificity in EDA of *ulcer* patients during stress-inducing situations (Sect. 3.2.2.2) was also found by Koller, Zidek, and Haider (1986). They recorded NS.SCR freq. as well as mean SCR amp. in 30 patients during rehabilitation from a recent ulcer as compared to 30 patients recovering from their first myocardial infarction. The groups were matched for age and job status, in an experimental setting with different stressors (intermittent white noise, 90–92 dB; arithmetic with false negative feedback; a written anonymous personality report; and recall of negative live events). Maximum SCR amp. did not differ between the groups, but the ulcer patients showed a significantly higher NS.SCR freq. as compared to the myocardial infarction patients in the stress-inducing situation with the written personality report.

Fredrikson, Dimberg, and Frisk-Holmberg (1980) compared cardiovascular and electrodermal activity in 14 patients (5 females, 9 males) suffering from essential *hypertension* and 14 normotensive controls (4 females, 10 males) during two different tasks (i.e., letter identification and mental arithmetic). In both conditions, NS.SCR freq.[333] tended to correlate negatively with systolic and diastolic blood pressure in hypertensives ($r = -0.32$ to $r = -0.48$), while the reverse interrelationship was observed in normotensives ($r = 0.23$ to $r = 0.52$). This result could

---

[332] The stimulus conditions were listening to classic music and a word association task (five neutral words and five with high emotional content).

[333] Recorded with 8 mm diameter Ag/AgCl electrodes filled with isotonic KCl cream from palmar finger sites. The amplitude criterion was 0.05 μS.

not be confirmed in a second study (Fredrikson, Dimberg, Frisk-Holmberg, & Ström, 1982) with another five female and nine male hypertensives as compared to 15 age- and gender-matched normotensives, using the same kind of tasks. No significant correlation between NS.SCR freq. and systolic blood pressure was obtained, despite the negative correlations for the hypertensives were of the same magnitude as in the 1980 study and the tendency toward positive correlations also appeared in the group of normotensives. Though this could only be observed during the arithmetic task (counting backward silently from 1,070 in steps of seven), which was regarded as a typical case for "sensory rejection" in Lacey and Lacey's (1974) sense (Sect. 3.4.1.2 "Observable Electrodermal Phenomena"), the data did not support the hypothesis of differential electrodermal and cardiovascular reactivity being typical for hypertensives during the performance of rejection-type tasks.[334]

Van Doornen, Orlebeke, and Somsen (1980) used a variation of the predictability of an aversive stimulus (Sect. 3.1.2.1 "UCR Diminution, Preception and Preparedness") as a method to compare cardiovascular and electrodermal reactivity in 30 male *infarction* patients (35–50 years), 16 male controls with high risk, and 18 male controls with low risk for infarction. SCRs and HR were recorded following 10 aversive tones (1 kHz, 115 dB), half of which, in random order, were announced by a 60 dB, 1 kHz warning tone given 12 s prior to the aversive tone, while the warning interval was monitored by a clock (Sect. 3.2.2.2). A "preception" index (Sect. 3.1.2.1 "UCR Diminution, Preception and Preparedness"), being defined as percentage of the mean SCR amp. following warned in comparison with unwarned aversive tones, yielded a significantly higher benefit of prewarning for the low-risk group as compared to both other groups. This difference was paralleled by a differential accelerative HR response component within 2–5 s after the warning tone onset, in which no significant group differences in SCR amp. appeared. The authors interpreted the HR acceleration following the warning stimulus as reflecting anticipation of an effective attenuating preception process (Lykken & Tellegen, 1974), leading to the attenuation of the EDR following the aversive stimulus (Sect. 3.1.2.1 "UCR Diminution, Preception and Preparedness"), a mechanism which was not present in infarction patients or in coronary-prone individuals.

Gruzelier, Nixon, Liddiard, Pugh, and Baxter (1986) used bilateral recordings of EDA in 40 patients with mixed *cardiovascular disorders* (e.g., chest pain, angina, hypertension, ischemia, and infarction) as compared to age- and gender-matched controls (10 females, 30 males) to establish abnormalities in CNS control of ANS functions in this group of patients. SC, recorded with standard methodology, but using KCl cream, was chosen instead of cardiovascular measures because of its pure mediation by the sympathetic branch of the ANS, thus being unconfounded by peripheral parasympathetic influences, for measuring habituation in a series of 13

---

[334] In another study with normotensives, established and borderline hypertensives ($N = 12$ in each of the three groups), Fredrikson and Engel (1985) observed higher SCLs in borderline cases compared with the other groups. SC results paralleled cardiovascular results only in normotensives and did not yield hyperreactivity in hypertensives as did HR.

tones (1 kHz, 70 dB). When a habituation criterion of three successive trials without eliciting an SCR amp. higher than 0.02 µS was applied (Sect. 3.1.1.3), the patients showed a significantly slower habituation as compared to controls. The authors interpreted this result as suggesting an involvement of the limbic system in the development of cardiovascular disorders, since a slow habituation process indicates an over-wide range of attention, increased effort, and overresponsiveness, leading to information overload (Sect. 3.1.3.1), which may be a possible causative factor in the development of cardiovascular illness. Such a view is in accordance with the observation that the SRR amp. to the first stimulus has been significantly higher in patients than in controls. NS.SCR freq. during the ISIs and temporal measures of EDRs did not differentiate between the groups. In addition, electrodermal lateralization effects appeared, with the patients showing significantly higher right-hand SCLs (75% of patients as compared to 33% of controls), and ORs were also larger in the patient's right hands, which was statistically supported by computing a laterality coefficient ((3.2a), Sect. 3.1.4.1). The obtained laterality effects were interpreted by the authors as reflecting the loss of contralateral inhibition of EDA from the left hemisphere (Sect. 3.1.4.2), which could have been possibly due to the left hemisphere's vulnerability to fatigue in cardiovascular patients.

EDA has been applied as a tool for quantifying emotional reactivity in individuals suffering from *alexithymia*, which had been originally regarded as a psychosomatic disorder but is now more broadly identified as an individual's difficulty identifying and describing emotions which she/he might have. Rabavilas (1987) diagnosed 19 out of 105 patients (56 females, 49 males) with generalized anxiety (Sect. 3.4.1.1) as high alexithymic and 19 as low alexithymic. SC was bilaterally recorded with unreported methodology during the presentation of a series of OR-inducing stimuli (Sect. 3.1.1). No group differences emerged for the patients' rating of their subjective anxiety at the end of stimulation. However, SC-OR amp., SCR rec.t/2, and NS.SCR freq. were significantly enlarged in alexithymic patients, pointing to an increased sympathetic arousal which has no subjective representation.

Roedema and Simons (1999) recorded SC (with standard methodology, however, using K–Y jelly, from thenar/hypothenar sites of the nondominant hand), HR, and facial EMG (zygomatic and corrugator) from 34 individuals (19 females, 15 males) diagnosed by a questionnaire as alexithymic and 31 controls (16 females, 15 males) during the presentation of 21 IAPS pictures (Sect. 3.2.1.3), being classified as yielding positive, neutral, and negative valence or high, medium, and low arousing properties. Individuals with alexithymia generated less emotion-related words describing their own emotional response than controls. However, they also yielded fewer SCRs and showed less HR deceleration in response to all kinds of slides. Since no valence-related differences between alexithymics and controls could be observed, the suggested deficit of this group of individuals in processing the valence aspect of emotions did not emerge.

A different result was obtained by Franz et al. (1999) who investigated 12 high alexithymics (5 females, 7 males) and 14 low alexithymics (8 females, 6 males) during two performance tests and two 6-min film sequences (a destructive group therapy session, and an aggressive argument of a couple) with SC (recorded thenar/hypothenar with Ag/AgCl electrodes but otherwise unreported methodology), after which subjective emotional state measures were applied. Both groups did not differ in NS.SCR freq. during the performance tests and the first film, but alexithymics showed a significantly diminished NS.SCR freq. during the second film, which was, however, not paralleled by any subjective rating of emotions. The authors concluded that their results supported the hypothesis of "decoupling" physiological and subjective emotional responses in alexithymics. The "decoupling" hypothesis was also supported by Stone and Nielson (2001) who compared SC (with unreported methodology), HR, and subjective emotional intensity recorded before and after an arousing (10 high vs. 10 low alexithymics) and a neutral film (11 high vs. 10 low alexithymics). No significant group effects were found in the subjective reports, but high alexithymics emerged significantly higher SCLs induced by the arousing film.

Pollatos, Schubö, Herbert, Matthias, and Schandry (2008) demonstrated that deficits in emotional reactivity of alexithymic individuals are likely being already present at a very early stage in the processing of emotion-relevant stimuli. They compared 30 high alexithymics (18 females, 12 males) with 30 age- and gender-matched low alexithymic controls during the presentation of 60 IAPS pictures (20 neutral, 20 pleasant, and 20 unpleasant). Pictures were shown for 500 ms and backward masked by a flower picture, which was presented immediately after the first picture for 1,500 ms. The presentation was followed by a forced-choice recognition task and – after a break of 1 h – by a rating task. SCRs (recorded with standard methodology) to the masked emotional stimuli were evaluated as FIRs, i.e., the SCR with maximum amplitude between 1 and 4 s after stimulus onset (Sect. 3.1.2.1 "Components of EDR Conditioning"). Significant group differences in SCR amp. emerged, whereas high alexithymics yielded lower SCR amp. to negatively valenced pictures than their low-alexithymic counterparts. The differences in ratings also confirmed a general deficit of alexithymics in emotional reactivity during rather early stimulus processing, thus grossly confirming the alexithymia concept.

EDA has further been used in research into *anorexia* by Léonard, Pepinà, Bond, and Treasure (1998), who observed an increase of the SCL during the meal in anorectics, while premeal SCLs were lower in bulimics than in anorectics and controls. Female binge eaters maintained higher SCLs during exposure to and consume of food compared to controls (Vögele & Florin, 1997). EDA has been applied in research on smoking (Morris & Gale, 1993), caffeine (Barry, Clarke, Johnstone, & Rushby, 2008; Davidson & Smith, 1991; Lyvers & Miyata, 1993), chocolate craving (Rodriguez, Fernandez, Cependa-Benito, & Vila, 2005), and other substance-dependence research (Taylor, Carlson, Iacono, Lykken, & McGue, 1999) in surgical patients (Vögele & Steptoe, 1986), for monitoring perioperative stress (Storm et al., 2002), in sexual dysfunctions (Dettmers, van Ahlen, Faust, Fatepour, & Tackmann, 1994; Fowler, 1993), for detecting hot flushes (Sect. 2.4.3.2) in prostate cancer survivors (Hanisch, Palmer, Donahue, & Coyne, 2007), in the investigation of motion sickness (Hu et al., 1999) and in persons who attribute their symptoms to electric and/or magnetic field exposure (Lyskov, Sandström, & Mild, 2001).[335]

Finally, EDA has been used as an indicator in *acupuncture* which is regarded as belonging to the so-called alternative medicine. There have been serious attempts using EDA to verify the specificity of acupuncture points for some of the phenomena in question, and even a special EDA recording device has been set up for detecting acupuncture points.

Wang and Kain (2001) probed the effectiveness of bilateral auricular acupuncture for diminishing anxiety, with the goal of anxiety relief in patients prior to surgery. Fifty-five operating room staff members were randomly divided in three groups that were treated with acupuncture at different points (a "relaxation" point, the "shenmen" point, and a "sham" point as control). Thirty minutes, 24, and 48 h after insertion of the needles, HR, SC (recorded with CC from Ag/AgCl electrodes filled with a Bio-gel from the volar surfaces of the second and third finger of the nondominant hand), blood pressure, and state anxiety were assessed, but only subjective anxiety differed between the three acupuncture points. In none of the psychophysiological measures, time by

---

[335] EDA has also been applied in parapsychology – an area which is clearly outside scientific research. In their review of the hitherto published 25 investigations using EDA in "direct mental interaction with living systems" or "remote staring," Schmidt and Walach (2000) came to the conclusion that not even one of the studies referred to the standards mentioned at the beginning of the third chapter of the present book. Therefore, they highly recommended further experimenters in this area to adhere to these standards. Maybe parapsychology is not the most suitable candidate for demonstrating the negative effects of methodological pitfalls, but adhering to standard methodology as recommended here can be regarded as a minimum requirement in all kinds of applied electrodermal research. Stevens (2000) reanalyzed SC data from two previously conducted studies with altogether 123 participants, collected during periods in which a nonpresent "sender" tried to activate or calm the participants. A resting condition served as control. For better interindividual comparability, SC data were transformed to standardized z-scores according to (2.20a) in Sect. 2.3.3.4 "Transformation into Standard Values". Several individuals showed an occasional increase in SC shortly after a presumed stimulus onset, i.e., the start of a period during which they were assumed being mentally influenced by the "sender," but no clear pattern emerged that could have allowed a distinction between these changes and spontaneous EDRs. Some of the changes were also in the opposite direction as intended. Interestingly, SC emerged significantly more variability during the two "influence" periods as compared to the resting condition. Schmidt, Schneider, Binder, Bürkle, and Walach (2001) analyzed SC data (recorded with standard methodology from thenar/hypothenar eminences) from 26 sessions with a total of 52 participants (24 females, 28 males). The room temperature was set to either 23 or 26°C to enhance electrodermal reactivity (Sect. 2.4.1.1). In addition to SC, respiration was recorded, not so much for the control of artifacts but as a mediator for explaining some of the variance in phasic EDA (Sect. 2.2.5.2). Each session consisted of ten activate and ten calm epochs. The "sender" viewed the other participant's SC curve, trying to activate or deactivate the participant by means of mentality or intentionality. The randomized influence epochs were interspersed by 15-s resting periods. The authors applied five different procedures for evaluating their data, four of which yielded approximately the same results. Besides the SCL, NS.SCR freq., and mean NS.SCR amp. were evaluated. All three parameters showed a marked effect of the "activate" condition. However, since EDA substantially covaried with respiratory activity, the authors interpreted their results as demonstrating a sort of global effect of their "mental interaction" condition on the psychophysiological arousal of their participants.

group interactions reached significance. However, the question could be raised as to whether healthy volunteers with no specific anxiety symptoms were suitable for testing hypotheses about preoperative anxiety.

Colbert, Hammerschlag, Aickin, and McNames (2004) developed an electrodermal screening device for acupuncture points. Its rationale was that the respective skin sites were observed showing lower SRLs or SZLs compared to the surrounding sites. The device resembles a thick ball-point pen and is used together with a forearm Velcro strap containing a reference electrode (6 × 3.5 cm). The authors obtained 288 measurements from 31 participants (17 females, 14 males) at 24 "Jing-well" acupuncture points that were marked for a second testing, yielding a retest reliability of $r = 0.758$.

Vickland, Rogers, Craig, and Tran (2008) assigned half of their 60 female participants to a group receiving acupuncture at two unilateral points (LU7 and KD6) during three consecutive sessions being one week apart, while the other half served as control group who attended one session without acupuncture. SP was recorded bilaterally with Ag/AgCl electrodes, the active electrodes being attached to the palmar and the reference electrodes fixed to the dorsal surface of the hand. A rather long time constant (equivalent to 100 s) was applied to capture very slow phasic changes in SP. Compared to the control group, the acupuncture group yielded significantly more SPRs with a similar pattern on both hands. A decline of SPR amp. during the consecutive sessions indicated habituation of the response to acupuncture. The authors suggest their results showing that EDA recorded during acupuncture would not be just a local somatic response, but a complex response probably involving CNS structures. (Unfortunately, they did not have an independent measure for the possible mediating function of sensory stimulation induced by inserting the needles such as sham acupuncture.) Furthermore, EDRs appearing in parallel at both hands whereas acupuncture was performed unilaterally was interpreted as EDRs being not due to artifacts. Since about 20% of their participants emerged diminished EDA to the insertion of the needles, the authors speculated that the needles might not have been placed right in these cases. Thus, EDA could probably be used both as a tool for verifying suggested acupuncture points and as dependent variable for the success of acupuncture needle insertion.

3.6 Summary and Outlook

As seen in the manifold applications of EDA described in this chapter, its widespread use is fully justified by both theoretical and practical reasons. However, different aspects of the validity of electrodermal measures emerged which will be shortly summarized here.

Without question, the domain for using phasic EDA parameters is in stimulus-related basic psychophysiological research (Sect. 3.1). The early use of electrodermal recording in this field focused mainly on its indicator function in orienting and defensive responses and their habituation (Sect. 3.1.1). EDA is also one of the most frequently used indicators in autonomic conditioning of the classical and the instrumental kind (Sect. 3.1.2).

Recording of various EDR parameters, including electrodermal recovery, has been used to deliberately analyze autonomic concomitants of information processing, such as uptake, comparison, and storage (Sect. 3.1.3). In this context, the electrodermal system's high sensitivity for small changes in the external world as well as in CNS functions determined the specific value of EDA recording for this kind of basic research. As a consequence, several theoretical concepts in this area have been developed based on, or with specific respect to, electrodermal recording. A prominent example is the role of the EDA amp. in the somatic marker hypothesis (Sect. 3.1.3.3). However, using a peripheral indicator gives rise to some precautions, as the effector organs can be located rather far from the central processes under investigation. Properties of the peripheral system itself may obscure results, for example, response interferences appearing in case of high stimulus frequencies, when EDR amp. are high and/or EDR recovery times are long. Furthermore, dependencies of different EDA parameters on each other should be considered here, such as amplitude/shape or phasic/tonic relationships (see Sects. 2.5.2.5 and 2.5.4.2).

By contrast, different parameters which can be obtained from EDRs may reflect specific aspects of the underlying psychophysiological processes. For example, the height of the EDR amp. clearly increases with stimulus intensity, while an increase in EDR recovery time may reflect attention becoming more focused (Sect. 3.1.3.1). Another example is the investigation of electrodermal lateralization effects and hemispheric specialization, where different excitatory and inhibitory processes of phasic and tonic EDA have to be taken into account (Sect. 3.1.4). Furthermore, electrodermal measures play an important role within the general context of a multivariate psychophysiological approach, which can be seen in various attempts to determine the physiological concomitants of generalized psychological states like levels of arousal, motivation, emotion, and stress (Sect. 3.2). Here, electrodermal parameters have been especially useful in their contribution toward obtaining fine-grained analyses during states of rather low arousal.

The suggested different areas of validity for electrodermal and cardiovascular measures, being frequently pointed to throughout the chapter, can be at least partly explained on the theoretical background given by neurophysiological modeling as outlined in Sect. 3.2.1.2 (see Fig. 3.4). Although complicated models like this one are not easily testable, the available empirical evidence is encouraging and converging. Another domain of EDA is emotion and stress research (Sect. 3.2.2). The major reason for its importance lies in the fact that EDA is solely mediated by the sympathetic branch of the ANS (see Sect. 1.3.2), thus being not subjected to peripheral parasympathetic influences as most of the other autonomic measures. Especially, the NS.EDR freq. can be regarded as a valid indicator for the strength of – mostly negative – emotions, for observing the course of psychological stress, and for objectively determining coping efficacy. In addition, regard should be taken of the possibility to use different psychophysiological parameters as markers for various emotional states, as for example in research on emotional expression, where EDR amp. is correlated with the inner emotional involvement, while HR is more likely to reflect overt emotions.

A field of application where EDA had been used more frequently in the past than in the last few decades is personality and individual differences (Sect. 3.3). Although several theoretical attempts have been made to relate questionnaire-based general personality trait characteristics to psychophysiological indicators including EDA parameters, the hypothesized individual differences could not be demonstrated unambiguously enough (Sect. 3.3.1). The primary reason for this is that elaborative multitrait-multimethod studies in this field, which include psychophysiological measures, are lacking. With respect to electrodermal lability as a trait-like individual characteristic, it remains open how it is to be embedded in a framework of other personality dimensions being mostly obtained by questionnaire data (Sect. 3.3.2.2).

Besides these areas of basic research, one major application of EDA is in clinical psychophysiology (Sect. 3.4). Since EDA has been demonstrated as being a most viable indicator in emotion and stress research, its recording for purposes of assessment and treatment evaluation in anxiety-related psychopathological states is of special value (Sect. 3.4.1). Here, the predominant indicator function of EDA is being highly sensitive for minimal changes in generalized anxiety states, whereas cardiovascular measures have their domain in high arousal states of anxiety such as phobias (Sect. 3.4.1.1). EDA has also shown some properties of being a marker for predicting the occurrence of psychopathic and antisocial/conduct disorders (Sect. 3.4.1.2).

Prospective studies of persons at risk for schizophrenic illness (Sect. 3.4.2.1) is another area of research where electrodermal parameters have been successfully used as predictors for the development of psychopathological behavior. Here, recovery characteristics of the EDR have gained a specific quality as a potential marker for schizophrenia. Theoretical support comes from suggested deficits in subcortical information processing appearing in schizophrenics, being opposite to deficits assumed for psychopaths (see Table 3.1, Sect. 3.1.3.1). The most wide-spread use of EDA in schizophrenia research has, however, been trying to establish causes and consequences of electrodermal nonresponding in a large fraction of that clinical group (Sect. 3.4.2.2). In this field, impressive transcultural conjoint research has been performed, yielding differential diagnostic and prognostic values of both electrodermal nonresponding and nonhabituating. Furthermore, it will be of theoretical and practical interest to systematically investigate phenomena such as electrodermal hyporeactivity, which are not only observed in schizophrenics but also in other clinical groups as well, such as in psychopaths and depressives (Sects. 3.4.1.2 and 3.4.1.3).

In accordance with its specific value for objectively determining small changes in anxiety levels, EDA has been used as a major dependent variable in the psychopharmacological treatment of anxiety (Sect. 3.4.3). However, in this field precaution has to be taken with respect to possible central and peripheral influences of drugs on the elicitation of electrodermal phenomena itself, as this is especially the case when using neuroleptics with anticholinergic properties. The therapeutic use of EDA biofeedback (Sect. 3.1.2.3), which emerged from instrumental conditioning during the 1970s, has more recently been regarded with only moderate optimism.

In contrast to their widespread use in clinical applications, electrodermal measures have been less frequently taken into account as research tools in other fields of applied psychology, except in the detection of deception (Sect. 3.5.2). However, this particular application remains controversial, especially in Europe. The use of EDA in engineering psychophysiology (Sect. 3.5.1), including applications in traffic, industrial, and in office research, is of particular practical value, because of the differential validity of EDA as an indicator for emotional and/ or mental strain as opposed to physical strain, which in turn is more closely reflected in cardiovascular changes. A recently emerging area of application for EDA recordings is in marketing and product evaluation (Sect. 3.5.1.3). In this area, available systems for ambulatory EDA monitoring (Sect. 2.2.3.4) constitute a valuable tool. As theoretical background for applied research, the neurophysiological model evolved in Sect. 3.2.1.2 has been adapted for the area of engineering psychophysiology as four arousal model (see Table 3.2, Sect. 3.5.1), replacing the unitary arousal models as used earlier.

In addition to various applications of EDA in psychology, there are several fields in medicine for which electrodermal measures have proved to be of specific value for diagnostic and therapeutic evaluation purposes. Among these, neurology (Sect. 3.5.3) and dermatology (Sect. 3.5.4) can make use of the exact quantification of skin processes and of changes in the central and peripheral nervous system by means of EDA, as opposed to the more qualitative evaluation of sweating rate. At the intersection of medicine and clinical psychology, diseases such as psychosomatic disorders can be regarded as another specific area of application for electrodermal recordings (Sect. 3.5.5).

In summary, the third chapter of the present book being dedicated to various applications did not aim at uncritically recommending the use of electrodermal methods in all basic and applied areas of psychophysiological research. Instead, the focus was on critically discussing specific aspects of validity with respect to related methodological issues and appropriate neurophysiological modeling. To avoid misinterpretations or even misuses of EDA, methodological aspects should be carefully considered, including recommendations for standardization as outlined in Chap. 2. Furthermore, basic as well as applied electrodermal research could be much improved by establishing a common theoretical background. The model presented here could be refined by combining the various psychophysiological approaches (outlined in this chapter) with knowledge about the central origins of electrodermal activity (described in Chap. 1), for which methods of recording EDA concomitantly with brain imaging will certainly play a key role (Sect. 2.2.3.5). Finally, other recently emerging techniques for EDA recording and evaluation (Sect. 2.6.6) should have the property of facilitating developments of improved research designs, thus leading to progress in various fields of applications.

Appendix
EDR_PARA: A Computer Program for Interactive Evaluation of Electrodermal Recordings (Version 3.7)

Florian Schaefer

Wuppertal, Germany © 2011

Program Description

The program EDR_PARA reads binary or ASCII data files containing digitized skin resistance (SC) or skin conductance (SR) data. Electrodermal responses (EDRs) are detected and then subjected to parameterization. The results are written to an ASCII file. For control purposes, the original EDA curves as well as the parameterization results are graphically displayed.

Initial Control Input

After starting EDR_PARA, a window as shown below will appear asking for two files. For each file, the name that has been used in the last session is proposed as default. The names of the two default files are read from a file named EDR_PARA. PRE. These default file names can either be overwritten by new file names or accepted by pressing the ENTER key. The window will be closed after the lower most entry or by pressing the ESC key.

```
- Files used for evaluation -
Setup file: <lastSetup>
EDR file: <lastEDA-raw-data File>
```

Setup File

The Setup file contains the information about the data format and the evaluation control settings to be used for initiating the program. The evaluation settings may be changed during the interactive data processing. The appropriate changes can be saved at the end of a session (see below).

W. Boucsein, *Electrodermal Activity*, DOI 10.1007/978-1-4614-1126-0,
© Springer Science+Business Media, LLC 2012

EDR File

The EDR file contains the A/D converted raw data of the skin conductance or skin resistance curve. These data must be stored either as unsigned binary 16-bit integers or as ASCII digits. If only one data file is to be analyzed, the name of this file may be directly typed in the EDR file. If several EDR files are to be analyzed, which are equivalent in recording structure and sampling rate, the program can read the names of the raw-data files from an ASCII list file. In this case, the name of the list file will be typed in the field for the EDR file. This list file must have the extension .LST to make the program detecting the list mode.

Examples:

>   EDR file: SCR _S01.BIN
>   → Only the file SCR_S01.BIN will be analyzed.

>   EDR file: STUDY01.LST
>   The content of this file is:

| SCR_S01.BIN |
| SCR_S02.BIN |
| SCR_S03.BIN |

>   → All EDR files which are listed in the ASCII file STUDY01.LST will be analyzed.

Additional Channel Display

In addition to the EDA curve, a second channel may be displayed for control purposes. Such a channel may contain information about stimulus onsets (e.g., in habituation studies, Sect. 3.1.1.3, Chap. 3) or other psychophysiological recordings such as respiration (e.g., for artifact control, Sect. 2.2.5.2, Chap. 2). The filename of the control channel is to be given after the EDR filename, separated by a comma:

Example:

>   EDR file: SCR_S01.bin, RES_S01.bin

In this case, the content of the RES_S01.bin control channel is displayed in a separate window below the EDR curve. The setup file may also contain additional information about the control file data structure (see below).

Interactive Display

After the initial window is closed, the EDR curve of the first recording period is displayed on the screen together with the EDR parameters which are automatically detected by the program.

The bottom of the screen displays the *function keys F1 to F10*, each followed by a short label. These functions may be selected by mouse click or by pressing the appropriate function key:

F1: Info

displays the author's name, purchasing information, and the name of the person or institution for which the program is licensed.

If "(Demo)" appears as the license name, a valid license file EDR_PARA.USR is missing. In this case, the program works with all features but without producing any output files with EDR parameters.

F2: Setup

displays the control parameters read from the setup file. The settings may be changed (see below). The window is closed after the lower most entry or by pressing ESC (see initial control input).

F3: Value/Curve

toggles display between the graph of the EDR curve and a table containing the response parameters.

F4: Edit

starts the edit mode during which the automatically detected parameters may be manually changed (see below under "EDR editor").

F5: Reset

restarts the evaluation procedure from the beginning of the first recording period of the first EDR file. All of the response parameters already written on the output file .EDP will be overwritten.

F6: Filt.

displays a window with the actual setting of the low pass filter given in Hertz. The setting may be changed by overwriting. This does not affect the filter presetting in the setup procedure.

F7: Ampl−

by using the F7 and F8 keys, the display range of the curve

F8: Ampl+

amplification may be adjusted.

The display range is defined in bits of resolution. The actual value is displayed in the center legend below the graph, along with its µS (µmho) equivalent. This adjustment does not affect the display range presetting in the setup procedure. By pressing an uppercase O (<shift> o) the graph mode may be

	toggled between displaying with or without a μS or kΩ grid.
F9: Auto/Halt	toggles between interactive mode and the automatic mode. During the latter mode, the EDR curves are automatically displayed and analyzed according to the presetting in the setup without any halt.
F10: Quit	cancels further evaluation and exits the program. The output files are closed, keeping the parameters written into the files until this point of time. If the setup was changed during the session, a window is displayed asking whether the setup should be saved and which file name is to be used for it.
<ENTER>	if the parameterization of the recording period which is actual displayed shall be accepted, the ENTER key is to be pressed. Thereafter, the parameters are written to the output file .EDP and the next recording period is displayed.
<PAGEUP/PAGEDOWN>	shifts the graphical display vertically across the curve.
<SHIFT O>	toggles the display of μS- and s-units by means of a dashed line grid.
	The mean EDA level (offset) is displayed as a grey dashed line.

Setup Information

After the program is started, the control presetting values will be read from the setup file (default: EDR_PARA.DEF) and used for evaluation. These can be changed during the session by editing the setup (F2) or temporarily overwritten by pressing F6, F7, F8, or F9 (see above).

By pressing F2, the following *presetting values* are displayed:

--- **Setup EDR_PARA.DEF** ----
recording period(s): 10*20
sampling rate: 20
μS or kOhm/unit: 0.01
graphic display: y
user interaction: y
low pass frequency: .5
display range [bit]: 12

Recording Period(s)

The temporal structure of the recordings in s needs to be specified here. There is a direct and an indirect input mode. When using the direct mode, the total length of the period has to be given and will be analyzed as one continuous recording.

Example:

> **Recording period(s): 120**
> →One period of 120 s will be analyzed.

As there is always one complete recording period displayed on the screen, the visual control of the evaluation may become difficult when this period exceeds approximately 120 s. In this case, it is recommended to split up the recording into segments of equal length. The number of segments and their duration in s are divided by an asterisk.

Example:

> **Recording period(s): 120, 10*20**
> → The data file will be divided and analyzed as one period of 120 s and 10 subsequent periods of 20 s each.

Such a treatment of data is suitable when records are taken over subsequent experimental trials (e.g., data recorded during habituation studies).

For the indirect mode, an ASCII file containing information about the recording has to be specified. This file must have the extension .P?? or .R?? (? signifies any character). In this file, recording periods may be specified using subsequent lines, according to the direct input syntax. Evaluation of recording periods may also be *skipped* by specifying a *negative duration* for a period.

Example:

> **Recording period(s): TRIAL.REC**
> The content of TRIAL.PAR is:

```
120
-60
3*60
```

> →First, a period of 120 s will be analyzed; thereafter a 60 s period will be skipped followed by the evaluation of three trials of 20 s each.

In some studies, each participant will have an *individual structure of recording periods*, i.e., when recordings are triggered by task performance. In order to provide automatic evaluation in this case, the wildcard * may be used in front of the .P?? or

.R?? extension. By this, the missing file name information in front of the extension is imported from the .LST file.

Example:

Recording period(s): .REC
When the STUDY01.LST file from the example for the EDR file given above is used, the program will expect three REC files corresponding to the raw data file names:

> SCR_S01.REC
> SCR_S02.REC
> SCR_S03.REC

When the wildcard option is used, an individual file with recording period information must exist for each raw data file.

In some cases it may be more convenient to use the *absolute time of day* (real time) for specifying the recording periods. This may be specified in the following notation: hh:mm:ss>hh:mm:ss, either in the direct or in the indirect mode.

Example:

Recording period(s): 10:15:00>10:15:45, 10:20:15>10:22:05

→First a period of 45 s is analyzed, starting at 10:15:00 real time. The following four minutes and 30 s between the specified periods are skipped. The next period of one minute and 50 s is analyzed again.

It is also possible to mix the time of day information with fixed period definitions. The beginning of a period may be specified as real time in the notation hh:mm:ss, followed by the character > and the duration of one or several equidistant periods.

Example:

Recording period(s): 10:15:00>10*120
→ The data file will be divided and analyzed as 10 periods with a duration of 120 s each, starting at 10:15 real time. The periods are displayed as
> First period: 10:15:00–10:17:00
> Second period: 10:17:00–10:19:00
> etc.

Recording periods specified in the direct mode may be written on a file by appending a slash followed by a valid DOS file name. By using the wildcard * the filename is derived from the raw data file name with either the user defined extension or the default extension .REC.

Example:

Recording period(s): 120, 10*20 /time.p01

→ the specified recording periods are written to the file TIME.P01.

Recording period(s): 120, 10*20 / *.par

→ if the EDR file name is SCR S01.BIN (from the example given for the initial control input), the specified recording periods are written to the file SCR_S01.PAR.

Recording period(s): 120, 10*20 /*

→ if the EDR file name is SCR S01.BIN (from the example given for the initial control input), the specified recording periods are written to the file SCR_S01.REC.

Sampling Rate

The number of digitized data points per second must be specified here. For EDA recordings, this value is usually between 10 and 40/s. In addition, the raw data format may be specified. Default data format is binary 16-bit integer for each scanning point. If the raw data differs from this, specific characters need to be appended:

If ASCII numbers are used instead of binary integers, the letter "A" must be placed after the specification of the sampling rate:

Example:

Sampling rate: 20 A

→ The program expects 20 data points per s as ASCII numbers separated by blanks, commas or line feeds.

If the raw data are stored as 8-bit bytes, the letter "B" must be appended after the scanning rate.

For evaluation of ASCII-transformed Varioport©-Data (see Footnote 31, Sect. 2.2.3.4), a "V" is to be entered in addition to an "A" after the sampling rate to make the program read sensitivity information from the file header (see below).

Example:

Sampling rate: 16 AV (or: 16 ASCI Varioport)

For evaluation of ASCII-transformed Neuroscan©-Data, a "N" is to be entered in addition to an "A" after the sampling rate to make the program read information from the file header (see below).

Example:

Sampling rate: 16 AN (or: 16 ASCI Neuroscan)

μS or $k\Omega/AD$ Units

The transformation factor of the analog data acquisition system has to be specified here. The input defines the amount of skin resistance or conductance which is equal to one A/D-converting unit. This is important to adjust the EDR amp. in μS or $k\Omega$ units. The default value is 1, resulting in amplitudes equal to the units of the A/D-converter. The program expects EDR amp. being always positive. If the EDA recordings show responses in a negative direction, which may be the case for skin resistance recordings, the transformation factor must have a negative sign to obtain a correct parameterization.

For Varioport©-data, the sensitivity entry may be skipped if the "V"-option after the sampling information is set. Sensitivity will be automatically adjusted.

Graphic Display

This switch specifies whether the program will start using graphic or numerical display mode. Default is "y" for graphic display. By specifying "n," only the numerical parameters which are also written to the output file will be displayed. During the interactive mode, the display mode may be toggled by using the F3 key (Fig. A.1).

User Interaction

By accepting the default display mode "y", the program will stop after each graphic presentation of a trial until the ENTER key is pressed. During the halt, settings may be changed by the F-keys and the EDR parameters detected by the program may be edited. The interaction mode can be switched off by pressing F9 instead of the ENTER key. Then, subsequent periods will be analyzed without any halt. By specifying "n," the evaluation will run automatically but may be stopped again by pressing the F9 key.

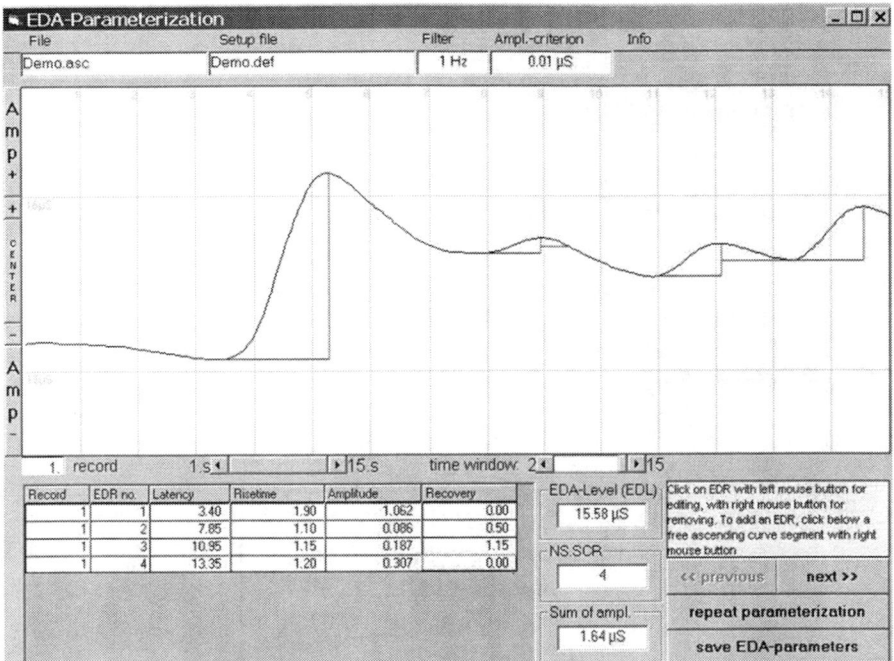

Fig. A.1 Screenshot of an example for the interactive graphical evaluation with EDR_PARA. The record comprises 15 s. Horizontal lines from the point of deflection to the peak of an SCR indicates the duration of SCR ris.t.; the other horizontal lines refer to SCR rec.t/2 (Fig. 2.15, Sect. 2.3.1.2 "Amplitudes of Exosomatic Responses Recorded with Direct Current" Chap. 2). There is no recovery parameter for the large SCR on the left, since the second SCR occurred before the criterion of half recovery, i.e., falling beyond half SCR amp., was not reached. In this case, Edelberg's (1967) evaluation method (method B in Fig. 2.16, Sect. 2.3.1.2, Chap. 2) will be applied. On the right margin of the screen shot, two overlapping SCRs can be seen, in case of which SCR rec.t/2 for the first SCR could be obtained. Ampl.-criterion (Sect. 2.3.1.2 "Choice of Amplitude Criteria," Chap. 2); EDA no. = number of SCR within the evaluation window; Sum of ampl. = all single SCR amp. in the window summarized

Low-Pass Frequency

The upper frequency limit in Hertz of the software low-pass filter is to be specified here. If the given value exceeds half of the sampling rate, filter processing is skipped.

Display Range

The graphical display resolution of the y-axis is specified by this parameter. The resolution is defined in bits. Therefore, if a 12 bit A/D converter was used during

EDA recording and the display range parameter is set to 12, the y axis of the display will be identical with the recording range of the converter. The equivalent range expressed in μS units is computed from the μS/bit parameter and displayed in the center legend below the graph.

Additional Channel Display

If a further channel is displayed in addition to the EDA curve, sampling rate, sensitivity factor (μS/bit), low pass filtering, and display range (when deviating from the EDA channel) may be defined by appending the appropriate parameters. These are separated by a comma.

Example:

```
--- Setup EDR_PARA.DEF ---
recording period(s): 10*20
     sampling rate: 20, 10
µS or kOhm/unit: 0.01, 1
    graphic display: y
    user interaction: y
low pass frequency: .5, .2
 display range [bit]: 12, 8
```

If only one value is given for these parameters, this value will be taken for both the EDA and the control channel.

EDR Editor

In some cases it may be necessary to modify the EDR parameters which were automatically computed by the program. This can be performed with ease by activating the EDR editor. After pressing F4, editing is initiated with the leftmost EDR displayed on the screen. The EDR under evaluation is indicated by changing the lines for rise time and amplitude from solid to dashed lines. In addition, the conjunction point of these lines is marked by two white dashes (which is important for very small EDRs). The conjunction point may be moved by the four arrow keys, using either the arrow keys on the keyboard or by performing a mouse-click on the arrow-key images displayed on the screen. By applying the horizontal moving keys, the peak of the EDR will be shifted along the curve. By application of the vertical moving keys, the point of deflection is shifted. Rise time and amplitude are continuously readjusted.

(When the point of deflection has reached a minimum of the curve and the arrow down key is pressed further on, the point will not move further down. This is because the point of deflection cannot fall below the curve. Instead, pressing the arrow down key will move the point of deflection further to the left, thereby following the curve even when it deflects up again. Vice versa, using the arrow up key after reaching the maximum will generally move the point of deflection to the right.)

When the adjustment on the displayed screen is completed, the new parameters are accepted either by pressing the ENTER key or by a mouse-click on the NEXT button. The adjusted rise time and amplitude lines become solid again and the recovery time is automatically recomputed. The editor switches to the next EDR.

To accept the proposed parameterization without changes, editing of an EDR can be skipped by pressing the ENTER key.

An EDR may be completely removed by pressing the F5 key or by mouse-click on the DEL button during editing.

After the uttermost right EDR on the screen was edited or skipped, the program returns to the normal interactive mode. The EDR parameters are not yet written to the output file. The editor may be invoked again or settings may be changed until an O.K. is given by pressing the ENTER key.

If the editor is started for a recording period without any automatically detected EDR, a dashed "default"-EDR will be displayed reaching from the leftmost point to the first maximum. This may be shifted to a curve segment where the automatic detection failed to detect an EDR. This may be the case when the point of deflection is outside the recording period or on an ascending curve segment.

Changing the low pass filter after editing will restart automatic parameterization, which will cancel prior changes performed by the editor.

Batch-Mode

The program can be run in batch-mode by specifying setup file and EDR file (or list file) as command line parameters. In this case, the initial control input window will be skipped and the program starts as specified in the setup file.

Example:

EDR_PARA STUDY01.DEF EDR_DATA.LST

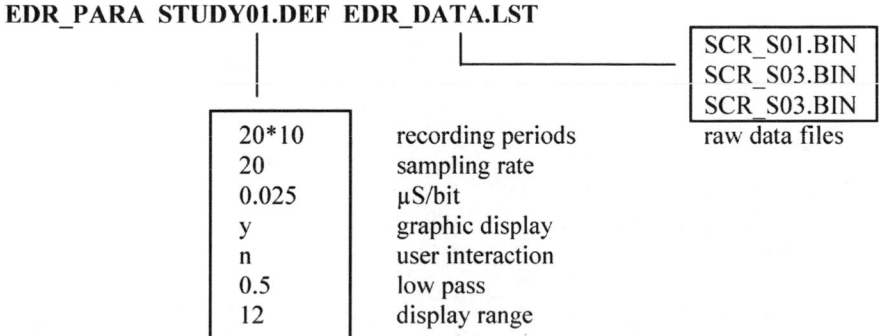

20*10	recording periods	SCR_S01.BIN
20	sampling rate	SCR_S03.BIN
0.025	µS/bit	SCR_S03.BIN
y	graphic display	raw data files
n	user interaction	
0.5	low pass	
12	display range	

Output Files

The program generates two output files: one file for the EDR parameters and a second file for the EDL information. The output in the EDL file only makes sense if EDA was recorded by a DC-amplifier without extracting the fluctuations by a time constant (Sect. 2.1.3, Chap. 2).

Output File Names

The names of the output files are derived from the name of the EDR file (or list file) by changing their extensions to .EDP for the response file and to .LEV for the level file. When a list of EDR files is analyzed, the results of all EDR files will be stored in the same output files. The results of each EDR file are preceded by its name.

Contents of the .EDP File

```
name of the EDA raw-data file
  number of recording period
     EDR number
       latency of the point of deflection since begin of trial
                rise time
                      amplitude (dependent on transform. factor)
                          1/2 recovery time
EDA_VP01.BIN

 1    1    13.20    1.95    0.58    0.00
 1    2    16.40    0.65    0.10    0.75
 1    3    26.20    2.30    0.49    2.35
 2    1    10.90    2.85    0.13    2.85
 2    2    19.75    3.15    0.29    2.95
 3    1    14.40    2.35    0.30    2.45
EDA_VP02.BIN
 1    1     1.85    3.00    0.25    3.95
 1    2    25.10    8.80    0.82    4.10
 2    1     5.40    2.00    0.07    0.00
 3    2    12.55    4.05    0.10    0.00
EOF
```

Contents of the .LEV File

```
                        name of the EDA raw-data file
                        number of recording period
                             EDA level

                    EDA_VP01.BIN
                      1    15.20
                      2    14.90
                      3    14.40
                    EDA_VP02.BIN
                      1    18.50
                      2    18.13
                      3    17.82
                    EOF
```

Purchasing Information

The Program EDR_PARA can be purchased at Psyrecon Ltd., Alte Freiheit 1, D-42103 Wuppertal, Germany, www.psyrecon.de, Email: stuermer@psyrecon.de. A demo-version can be downloaded from www.periphysys.com.

References

Aberg, P., Geladi, P., Nicander, I., Hansson, J., Holmgren, U., & Ollmar, S. (2005). Non-invasive and microinvasive electrical impedance spectra of skin cancer – A comparison between two techniques. *Skin Research and Technology, 11*, 281–286.

Adams, T. (1966). Characteristics of eccrine sweat gland activity in the footpad of the cat. *Journal of Applied Physiology, 21*, 1004–1012.

Adams, T., & Hunter, W. S. (1969). Modification of skin mechanical properties by eccrine sweat gland activity. *Journal of Applied Physiology, 26*, 417–419.

Ahlberg, J. H., Nilson, E. N., & Walsh, J. L. (1967). *The theories of splines and their applications.* New York: Academic.

Akiskal, H. S., & McKinney, W. T. (1975). Overview of recent research in depression. *Archives of General Psychiatry, 32*, 285–305.

Alexander, G. E., Crutcher, M. D., & DeLong, M. R. (1990). Basal ganglia-thalamocortical circuits: Parallel substrates for motor, oculomotor, "prefrontal" and "limbic" functions. *Progress in Brain Research, 85*, 119–146.

Alexander, D. M., Trengove, C., Johnston, P., Cooper, T., August, J. P., & Gordon, E. (2005). Separating individual skin conductance responses in a short interstimulus-interval paradigm. *Journal of Neuroscience Methods, 146*, 116–123.

Allen, J. A., Armstrong, J. E., & Roddie, I. C. (1973). The regional distribution of emotional sweating in man. *The Journal of Physiology, 235*, 749–759.

Almasi, J. J., & Schmitt, O. H. (1974). Automated measurement of bioelectrical impedance at very low frequencies. *Computers and Biomedical Research, 7*, 449–456.

American Psychiatric Association. (2000). *Diagnostic and statistical manual of mental disorders* (4th ed. revised (DSM IV-R)). Washington, DC: APA.

Anderson, R. K., & Kenney, W. L. (1987). Effect of age on heat-activated sweat gland density and flow during exercise in dry heat. *Journal of Applied Physiology, 63*, 1089–1094.

Andersson, S., & Finset, A. (1998). Heart rate and skin conductance reactivity to brief psychological stress in brain-injured patients. *Journal of Psychosomatic Research, 44*, 645–656.

Andersson, S., & Finset, A. (1999). Electrodermal responsiveness and negative symptoms in brain injured patients. *Journal of Psychophysiology, 13*, 109–116.

Andersson, S., Gundersen, P. M., & Finset, A. (1999). Emotional activation during therapeutic interaction in traumatic brain injury: Effect of apathy, self-awareness and implications for rehabilitation. *Brain Injury, 13*, 393–404.

Andresen, B. (1987). *Differentielle Psychophysiologie valenzkonträrer Aktivierungsdimensionen.* Frankfurt: Peter Lang.

Andrew, W., & Winston-Salem, N. C. (1966). Structural alternations with aging in the nervous system. *Journal of Chronic Disease, 3*, 575–596.

Annett, M. (1982). Handedness. In J. G. Beaumont (Ed.), *Divided visual field studies of cerebral organization* (pp. 195–215). New York: Academic.

Arena, J. G., Blanchard, E. B., Andrasik, F., Cotch, P. A., & Myers, P. E. (1983). Reliability of psychophysiological assessment. *Behavior Research and Therapy, 21*, 447–460.

Arnett, P. A. (1997). Autonomic responsivity in psychopaths: A critical review and theoretical proposal. *Clinical Psychology Review, 17*, 903–936.

Arnett, P. A., & Newman, J. P. (2000). Gray's three-arousal model: An empirical investigation. *Personality and Individual Differences, 28*, 1171–1189.

Arthur, R. P., & Shelley, W. B. (1959). The innervation of human epidermis. *The Journal of Investigative Dermatology, 32*, 397–411.

Asso, D., & Braier, J. R. (1982). Changes with the menstrual cycle in psychophysiological and self-report measures of activation. *Biological Psychology, 15*, 95–107.

Ax, A. F. (1953). The physiological differentiation between fear and anger in humans. *Psychosomatic Medicine, 15*, 433–442.

Ax, A. F., & Bamford, J. L. (1970). The GSR recovery limb in chronic schizophrenics. *Psychophysiology, 7*, 145–147.

Bach, D. R., Flandin, G., Friston, K. J., & Dolan, R. J. (2009). Time-series analysis for rapid event-related skin conductance responses. *Journal of Neuroscience Methods, 184*, 224–234.

Bach, D. R., Friston, K. J., & Dolan, R. J. (2010). Analytic measures for quantification of arousal from spontaneous skin conductance fluctuations. *International Journal of Psychophysiology, 76*, 52–55.

Backs, R. W., & Boucsein, W. (2009). Psychophysiology in digital human modeling. In V. G. Duffy (Ed.), *Handbook of digital human modeling* (pp. 16–1–16–14). Boca Raton: CRC.

Bagshaw, M. H., Kimble, D. P., & Pribram, K. H. (1965). The GSR of monkeys during orienting and habituation and after ablation of the amygdala, hippocampus and inferotemporal cortex. *Neuropsychologia, 3*, 111–119.

Balin, A. K., & Pratt, L. A. (1989). Physiological consequences of human skin aging. *Cutis, 43*, 431–436.

Baltissen, R., & Boucsein, W. (1986). Effects of a warning signal to aversive white noise stimulation: Does warning "short-circuit" habituation? *Psychophysiology, 23*, 224–231.

Baltissen, R. (1983). *Psychische und somatische Reaktionen auf affektive visuelle Reize bei jungen und alten Personen*. Unpublished Doctoral Dissertation, University of Düsseldorf, Germany.

Baltissen, R., & Weimann, C. (1989). Orienting reaction reinstatement or preception? Effects of predictability on reactions to pink noise stimulation of different intensities. *Psychophysiology, 26*, S12.

Ba-M'hamed-Bennis, S., Sequeira- Martinho, H., Freixa i Baqué, E., & Roy, J.-C. (1985). Skin potential responses elicited by reticular stimulation are not lateralized in the cat. *Biological Psychology, 21*, 250–251.

Bankart, C. P., & Elliot, R. (1974). Heart rate and skin conductance in anticipation of shocks with varying probability of occurrence. *Psychophysiology, 11*, 160–174.

Barabasz, A. F. (1970). Galvanic skin response and test anxiety among Negros and Caucasians. *Child Study Journal, 1*, 33–35.

Bard, P. (1960). Anatomical organization of the central nervous system in relation to control of the heart and blood vessels. *Physiological Reviews, 4*(Suppl. 4), 3–26.

Barland, G. H. (1988). The polygraph in practice. In A. Gale (Ed.), *The polygraph test: Lies, truth and science* (pp. 73–95). London: Sage.

Barland, G. H. (1999). The international scene. *American Polygraph Association Newsletter, 32*, 16–17.

Barland, G. H., & Raskin, D. C. (1973). Detection of deception. In W. F. Prokasy & D. C. Raskin (Eds.), *Electrodermal activity in psychological research* (pp. 417–477). New York: Academic.

Barry, R. J. (1975). Low-intensity auditory stimulation and the GSR orienting response. *Physiological Psychology, 3*, 98–100.

Barry, R. J. (1976). Failure to find the "local" EEG OR to low-level auditory stimulation. *Physiological Psychology, 4*, 171–174.

Barry, R. J. (1981). Comparability of EDA effects obtained with constant-current skin resistance and constant-voltage skin conductance methods. *Physiological Psychology, 9*, 325–328.

Barry, R. J. (1982). Novelty and significance effects in the fractionation of phasic OR measures: A synthesis with traditional OR theory. *Psychophysiology, 19*, 28–35.

Barry, R. J. (1987). Preliminary process in orienting response elicitation. In P. K. Ackles, J. R. Jennings, & M. G. H. Coles (Eds.), *Advances in Psychophysiology* (Vol. 2, pp. 131–195). Greenwich, CT: Jai.

Barry, R. J. (1990). Scoring criteria for response latency and habituation in electrodermal research: A study in the context of the orienting response. *Psychophysiology, 27*, 94–100.

Barry, R. J. (2004). Stimulus significance effects in habituation of the phasic and tonic orienting reflex. *Integrative Physiological and Behavioral Science, 39*, 166–179.

Barry, R. J., Clarke, A. R., Johnstone, S. J., & Rushby, J. A. (2008). Timing of caffeine's impact on autonomic and central nervous system measures: Clarification of arousal effects. *Biological Psychology, 77*, 304–316.

Barry, R. J., & O'Gorman, J. G. (1987). Stimulus omission and the orienting response: Latency differences suggest different mechanisms. *Biological Psychology, 25*, 261–276.

Barry, R. J., & Sokolov, E. N. (1993). Habituation of phasic and tonic components of the orienting reflex. *International Journal of Psychophysiology, 15*, 39–42.

Bartfai, A., Edman, G., Levander, S. E., Schalling, D., & Sedvall, G. (1984). Bilateral skin conductance activity, clinical symptoms and CSF monoamine metabolite levels in unmedicated schizophrenics, differing in rate of habituation. *Biological Psychology, 18*, 201–218.

Barontini, M., Lazzari, J. O., Levin, G., Armando, I., & Basso, S. J. (1997). Age-related changes in sympathetic activity: biochemical measurements and target organ responses. *Archives of Gerontology and Geriatrics, 25*, 175–186.

Bauer, R. M. (1986). The cognitive psychophysiology of prosopagnosia. In H. Ellis, M. Jeeves, F. Newcombe, & A. Young (Eds.), *Aspects of face processing* (pp. 253–267). Dordrecht: Nijhoff.

Beatty, J. (1983). Biofeedback in theory and practice. In A. Gale & J. A. Edwards (Eds.), *Physiological correlates of human behaviour* (Individual differences and psychopathology, Vol. 3, pp. 233–246). London: Academic.

Beatty, J., & Legewie, H. (Eds.). (1977). *Biofeedback and behavior*. New York: Plenum.

Beauchaine, T. P., Katkin, E. S., Strassberg, Z., & Snarr, J. (2001). Disinhibitory psychopathology in male adolescents: Discriminating conduct disorder from attention-deficit/hyperactivity disorder through concurrent assessment of multiple autonomic states. *Journal of Abnormal Psychology, 110*, 610–624.

Beaumont, J. G. (Ed.). (1982). *Divided visual field studies of cerebral organization*. New York: Academic.

Bechara, A., & Damasio, H. (2002). Decision-making and addiction (part I): Impaired activation of somatic states in substance dependent individuals when pondering decisions with negative future consequences. *Neuropsychologia, 40*, 1675–1689.

Bechara, A., & Damasio, A. R. (2005). The somatic marker hypothesis: A neural theory of economic decision. *Games and Economic Behavior, 52*, 336–372.

Bechara, A., Damasio, A. R., Damasio, H., & Anderson, S. W. (1994). Insensitivity to future consequences following damage to human prefrontal cortex. *Cognition, 50*, 7–15.

Bechara, A., Damasio, H., Damasio, A. R., & Lee, G. P. (1999). Different contributions of the human amygdala and ventromedial prefrontal cortex to decision-making. *The Journal of Neuroscience, 19*, 5473–5481.

Bechara, A., Damasio, H., Tranel, D., & Damasio, A. R. (2005). The Iowa Gambling Task and the somatic marker hypothesis: Some questions and answers. *Trends in Cognitive Sciences, 9*, 159–162.

Bechara, A., Dolan, S., Denburg, N., Hindes, A., Anderson, S. W., & Nathan, P. E. (2001). Decision making deficits, linked to a dysfunctional ventromedial prefrontal cortex, revealed in alcohol and stimulant abusers. *Neuropsychologia, 39*, 376–389.

Bechara, A., Dolan, S., & Hindes, A. (2002). Decision-making and addiction (part II): Myopia for the future or hypersensitivity to reward? *Neuropsychologia, 40*, 1690–1705.

Bechara, A., Tranel, D., & Damasio, H. (2000). Characterization of the decision-making deficit of patients with ventromedial prefrontal cortex lesion. *Brain, 123*, 2189–2202.

Bechara, A., Tranel, D., Damasio, H., & Damasio, A. R. (1996). Failure to respond automatically to anticipated future outcomes following damage to prefrontal cortex. *Cerebral Cortex, 6*, 215–225.

Becker-Carus, C., & Schwarz, E. (1981). Differentielle Unterschiede psychophysiologischer Aktivierungsverläufe und Kurzzeitgedächtnisleistungen in Abhängigkeit von Persönlichkeitskriterien. In W. Janke (Ed.), *Beiträge zur Methodik in der differentiellen, diagnostischen und klinischen Psychologie* (pp. 87–103). Königstein: Anton Hain.

Benedek, M., & Kaernbach, C. (2010). Decomposition of skin conductance data by means of nonnegative deconvolution. *Psychophysiology, 47*, 647–658.

Benjamin, L. S. (1967). Facts and artifacts in using analysis of covariance to "undo" the law of initial values. *Psychophysiology, 4*, 187–206.

Ben-Shakhar, G. (1980). Habituation of the orienting response to complex sequences of stimuli. *Psychophysiology, 17*, 524–534.

Ben-Shakhar, G. (1985). Standardization within individuals: A simple method to neutralize individual differences in skin conductance. *Psychophysiology, 22*, 292–299.

Ben-Shakhar, G. (1994). The roles of stimulus novelty and significance in determining the electrodermal orienting response: Interactive vs. additive approaches. *Psychophysiology, 31*, 402–411.

Ben-Shakhar, G., Asher, T., Poznansky-Levy, A., Asherowitz, R., & Lieblich, I. (1989). Stimulus novelty and significance as determinants of electrodermal responsivity: The serial position effect. *Psychophysiology, 26*, 29–38.

Ben-Shakhar, G., & Dolev, K. (1996). Psychophysiological detection through the guilty knowledge technique: The effects of mental countermeasures. *Journal of Applied Psychology, 81*, 273–281.

Ben-Shakhar, G., & Elaad, E. (2003). The validity of psychophysiological detection of information with the Guilty Knowledge Test: A meta-analytic review. *Journal of Applied Psychology, 88*, 131–151.

Ben-Shakhar, G., & Furedy, J. J. (1990). *Theories and applications in the detection of deception: A psychophysiological and international perspective.* New York: Springer.

Ben-Shakhar, G., & Gati, I. (2003). The effects of serial position and frequency of presentation of common stimulus features on orienting response reinstatement. *Psychophysiology, 40*, 139–145.

Ben-Shakhar, G., Gati, I., & Salamon, N. (1995). Generalization of the orienting response to significant stimuli: The roles of common and distinctive stimulus components. *Psychophysiology, 32*, 36–42.

Ben-Shakhar, G., & Lieblich, I. (1982). The dichotomization theory for differential autonomic responsivity reconsidered. *Psychophysiology, 12*, 277–281.

Ben-Shakhar, G., Lieblich, I., & Kugelmass, S. (1975). Detection of information and GSR habituation: An attempt to derive detection efficiency from two habituation curves. *Psychophysiology, 12*, 283–288.

Ben-Shakhar, G., Lieblich, I., & Kugelmass, S. (1982). Interactive effects of stimulus probability and significance on the skin conductance response. *Psychophysiology, 19*, 112–114.

Berardesca, E., de Rigal, J., Leveque, J. L., & Maibach, H. I. (1991). In vivo biophysical characterization of skin physiological differences in races. *Dermatologica, 182*, 89–93.

Berlyne, D. E. (1961). Conflict and the orientation reaction. *Journal of Experimental Psychology, 62*, 476–483.

Bernat, E., Patrick, C. J., Benning, S. D., & Tellegen, A. (2006). Effects of picture content and intensity on affective physiological response. *Psychophysiology, 43*, 93–103.

Bernstein, A. S. (1965). Race and examiner as significant influences on basal skin impedance. *Journal of Personality and Social Psychology, 1*, 346–349.

Bernstein, A. S. (1979). The orienting response as novelty and significance detector: Reply to O'Gorman. *Psychophysiology, 16*, 263–273.

Bernstein, A. S., Frith, C. D., Gruzelier, J. H., Patterson, T., Straube, E., Venables, P. H., & Zahn, T. P. (1982). An analysis of the skin conductance orienting response in samples of American, British, and German schizophrenics. *Biological Psychology, 14*, 155–211.

Bernstein, A. S., Riedel, J. A., Graae, F., Seidman, D., Steele, H., Connolly, J., & Lubowsky, J. (1988). Schizophrenia is associated with altered orienting activity; depression with electrodermal (cholinergic?) deficit and normal orienting response. *Journal of Abnormal Psychology, 97*, 3–12.

Bernstein, A. S., Schneider, S. J., Juni, S., Pope, A. T., & Starkey, P. (1980). The effect of stimulus significance on the electrodermal response in chronic schizophrenia. *Journal of Abnormal Psychology, 89*, 93–97.

Bernstein, A. S., Taylor, K. W., Starkey, P., Juni, S., Lubowski, J., & Paley, H. (1981). Bilateral skin conductance, finger pulse volume, and EEG orienting response to tones of differing intensities in chronic schizophrenics and controls. *The Journal of Nervous and Mental Disease, 169*, 513–528.

Besthorn, D., Schellberg, D., Pfleger, W., & Gasser, T. (1989). Using variance as a tonic SCR parameter. *Journal of Psychophysiology, 3*, 419–424.

Bijman, J. (1987). Transport processes in the eccrine sweat gland. *Kidney International. Supplement, 21*, S109–S112.

Bing, H. I., & Skouby, A. P. (1950). Sensitization of cold receptors by substances with acetylcholine effect. *Acta Physiologica Scandinavica, 21*, 286–302.

Birgersson, U., Birgersson, E., Aberg, P., Nicander, I., & Ollmar, S. (2011). Non-invasive bioimpedance of intact skin: Mathematical modeling and experiments. *Physiological Measurement, 32*, 1–18.

Birk, L., Crider, A., Shapiro, D., & Tursky, B. (1966). Operant electrodermal conditioning under partial curarization. *Journal of Comparative and Physiological Psychology, 62*, 165–166.

Birket-Smith, M., Hasle, N., & Jensen, H. H. (1993). Electrodermal activity in anxiety disorders. *Acta Psychiatrica Scandinavica, 88*, 350–355.

Biro, V., & Stukovsky, R. (1993). Components of the GSR curve in adult males. *Studia Psychologica, 35*, 111–117.

Bitterman, M. E., & Holtzman, W. H. (1952). Conditioning and extinction of the galvanic skin response as a function of anxiety. *Journal of Abnormal and Social Psychology, 47*, 615–623.

Bjornaes, H., Smith-Meyer, H., Valen, H., Kristiansen, K., & Ursin, H. (1977). Plasticity and reactivity in unconscious patients. *Neuropsychologia, 15*, 451–455.

Blackburn, R. (1983). Psychopathy, delinquency and crime. In A. Gale & J. A. Edwards (Eds.), *Physiological correlates of human behaviour* (Individual differences and psychopathology, Vol. 3, pp. 187–205). London: Academic.

Blank, I. H., & Finesinger, J. E. (1946). Electrical resistance of the skin. *Archives of Neurology and Psychiatry, 56*, 544–557.

Blecker, C. R., Kirsch, P., Schaefer, F., & Vaitl, D. (2001). Skin conductance measurement during fMRT scans: A methodology study. *Psychophysiology, 38*, S27.

Bloch, V. (1952). Nouveaux aspects de la méthode psychogalvanique ou électrodermographique (EDG) comme critère des tensions affectives. *L'Année Psychologique, 52*, 329–362.

Bloch, V. (1965). Le contrôle central de l'activité électrodermale. *Journal de Physiologie, 57*, 1–132.

Block, J. D., & Bridger, W. H. (1962). The law of initial value in psychophysiology: A reformulation in terms of experimental and theoretical considerations. *Annals of the New York Academy of Sciences, 98*, 1229–1241.

Bob, P., Susta, M., Glaslova, K., Pavlat, J., & Raboch, J. (2007). Lateralized electrodermal dysfunction and complexity in patients with schizophrenia and depression. *Neuroendocrinology Letters, 28*, 11–15.

Böhmelt, A. H., Vanman, E. J., Dawson, M. E., & Boucsein, W. (1983). Modification of the acoustic startle eyeblink reflex with complex visual prestimuli: Late effects of attention. *Journal of Psychophysiology, 9*, 261–262.

Bond, A. J., James, D. C., & Lader, M. H. (1974). Physiological and psychological measures in anxious patients. *Psychological Medicine, 4*, 364–373.

Borkovec, T. D. (1970). Autonomic reactivity to sensory stimulation in psychopathic, neurotic, and normal juvenile delinquents. *Journal of Consulting and Clinical Psychology, 35*, 217–222.

Botwinick, J., & Kornetsky, C. (1960). Age differences in the acquisition and extinction of the GSR. *Journal of Gerontology, 15*, 83–84.

Boucsein, W. (1973). *Analyse einiger psychologischer Testverfahren zur Erfassung von Persönlichkeitsmerkmalen.* Unpublished Report of the Psychological Institute, Düsseldorf.

Boucsein, W. (1988). *Elektrodermale Aktivität. Grundlagen, Methoden und Anwendungen.* Berlin: Springer.

Boucsein, W. (1992). *Electrodermal Activity.* New York: Plenum.

Boucsein, W. (2000). The use of psychophysiology for evaluating stress-strain processes in human-computer interaction. In R. W. Backs & W. Boucsein (Eds.), *Engineering psychology. Issues and applications* (pp. 289–309). Mahwah, NY: Lawrence Erlbaum.

Boucsein, W. (2001). Physiologische Grundlagen und Meßmethoden der dermalen Aktivität. In F. Rösler (Ed.), *Enzyklopädie der Psychologie, Bereich Psychophysiologie, Band 1: Grundlagen und Methoden der Psychophysiologie* (pp. 551–623). Göttingen: Hogrefe.

Boucsein, W. (2005). Electrodermal measurement. In N. Stanton, A. Hedge, K. Brookhuis, E. Salas, & H. Hendrick (Eds.), *Handbook of human factors and ergonomic methods* (pp. 18-1–18-8). CRC: Boca Raton.

Boucsein, W. (2009). Forty years of research on system response times – what did we learn from it? In C. M. Schlick (Ed.), *Methods and tools of industrial engineering and ergonomics* (pp. 575–593). Berlin: Springer.

Boucsein, W., & Backs, R. W. (2000). Engineering psychophysiology as a discipline: Historical and theoretical aspects. In R. W. Backs & W. Boucsein (Eds.), *Engineering psychophysiology. Issues and applications* (pp. 3–30). Mahwah, NJ: Lawrence Erlbaum.

Boucsein, W., & Backs, R. W. (2009). The psychophysiology of emotion, arousal, and personality: Methods and models. In V. G. Duffy (Ed.), *Handbook of digital human modeling* (pp. 35-1–35-18). CRC: Boca Raton.

Boucsein, W., Baltissen, R., & Euler, W. (1984). Dependence of skin conductance reactions and skin resistance reactions on previous level. *Psychophysiology, 21*, 212–218.

Boucsein, W., & Frye, M. (1974). Physiologische und psychische Wirkungen von Mißerfolgsstress unter Berücksichtigung des Merkmals Repression-Sensitization. *Zeitschrift für Experimentelle und Angewandte Psychologie, 21*, 339–366.

Boucsein, W., Greif, S., & Wittekamp, J. (1984). Systemresponsezeiten als Belastungsfaktor bei Bildschirm-Dialogtätigkeiten. *Zeitschrift für Arbeitswissenschaft., 38*(10 NF), 113–122.

Boucsein, W., & Hoffmann, G. (1979). A direct comparison of the skin conductance and skin resistance methods. *Psychophysiology, 16*, 66–70.

Boucsein, W., & Ottmann, W. (1996). Psychophysiological stress effects from the combination of night-shift work and noise. *Biological Psychology, 42*, 301–322.

Boucsein, W., & Schaefer, F. (2008). Objective emotional assessment of industrial products. In J. Westerink, M. Ouwerkerk, T. Overbeek, F. Pasveer, & B. de Ruyter (Eds.), *Probing experience: From assessment of user emotions and behaviour to development of products* (pp. 69–76). Dordrecht: Springer.

Boucsein, W., Schaefer, F., Kefel, M., Busch, P., & Eisfeld, W. (2002). Objective emotional assessment of tactile hair properties and their modulation by different product worlds. *International Journal of Cosmetic Science, 24*, 135–150.

Boucsein, W., Schaefer, F., & Neijenhuisen, H. (1989). Continuous recording of impedance and phase angle during electrodermal reactions and the locus of impedance change. *Psychophysiology, 26*, 369–376.

Boucsein, W., Schaefer, F., Schwerdtfeger, A., Busch, P., & Eisfeld, W. (1999). Objective emotional assessment of foam. *SÖFW-Journal, 125*, 2–17.

Boucsein, W., Schaefer, F., & Sommer, T. (2001). Electrodermal long-term monitoring in everyday life. In J. Fahrenberg & M. Myrtek (Eds.), *Progress in ambulatory assessment* (pp. 549–560). Göttingen: Hogrefe.

Boucsein, W., & Thum, M. (1996). Multivariate psychophysiological analysis of stress-strain processes under different break schedules during computer work. In J. Fahrenberg & M. Myrtek (Eds.), *Ambulatory assessment* (pp. 305–313). Seattle: Hogrefe & Huber.

Boucsein, W., & Thum, M. (1997). Design of work/rest schedules for computer work based on psychophysiological recovery measures. *International Journal of Industrial Ergonomics, 20*, 51–57.

Boucsein, W., Valentin, A., & Furedy, J. J. (1993). Psychophysiological and behavioral differences as a function of age and Parkinson's disease. *The Journal of Integrative Behavioral Science, 28*, 213–225.

Boucsein, W., & Wendt-Suhl, G. (1976). The effect of chlordiazepoxide on the anticipation of electric shocks. *Psychopharmacology, 48*, 303–306.

Boucsein, W., & Wendt-Suhl, G. (1980). An experimental investigation of elements involved in the anticipation of public speaking. *Archiv für Psychologie, 133*, 149–156.

Boucsein, W., & Wendt-Suhl, G. (1982). Experimentalpsychologische Untersuchung psychischer und psychophysiologischer Wirkungen von Cloxazolam und Diazepam unter angstinduzierenden und Normalbedingungen bei gesunden Probanden. *Pharmacopsychiatria, 15*, 48–56.

Boucsein, W., Fowles, D. C., Grimnes, S., Ben-Shakhar, G., Roth, W. T., Dawson, M., & Filion, D. L. (2012). Publication recommendations for electrodermal measurements. *Psychophysiology, 49* (in press).

Bowman, C. H., & Turnbull, O. H. (2003). Real versus facsimili reinforcers on the Iowa Gambling Task. *Brain and Cognition, 53*, 207–210.

Boyd, G. M., & Maltzman, I. (1983). Bilateral asymmetry of skin conductance responses during auditory and visual tasks. *Psychophysiology, 20*, 196–203.

Bradley, M. T., & Ainsworth, D. (1984). Alcohol and the psychophysiological detection of deception. *Psychophysiology, 21*, 63–71.

Bradley, M. M., Codispoti, M., Sabatinelli, D., & Lang, P. J. (2001). Emotion and motivation II: Sex differences in picture processing. *Emotion, 1*, 300–319.

Bradley, M. T., & Warfield, J. F. (1984). Innocence, information, and the guilty knowledge test in the detection of deception. *Psychophysiology, 21*, 683–689.

Bradshaw, J. L., & Nettleton, N. C. (1981). The nature of hemispheric specialization in man. *The Behavioral and Brain Sciences, 4*, 51–91.

Brand, G., Millot, J. L., Saffaux, M., & Morand-Villeneuve, N. (2002). Lateralization in human nasal chemoreception: Differences in bilateral electrodermal responses related to olfactory and trigeminal stimuli. *Behavioural Brain Research, 133*, 205–210.

Braune, S., Albus, M., Fröhler, M., Höhn, T., & Scheibe, G. (1994). Psychophysiological and biochemical changes in patients with panic attacks in a defined situational arousal. *European Archives of Psychiatry and Clinical Neuroscience, 244*, 86–92.

Braus, H., & Elze, C. (1960). *Anatomie des Menschen (Human anatomy)* (Vol. 3). Berlin: Springer.

Breen, N., Caine, D., & Coltheart, M. (2000). Models of face recognition and delusional misidentification: A critical review. *Cognitive Neuropsychology, 17*, 55–71.

Brekke, J. S., Raine, A., & Thomson, C. (1995). Cognitive and psychophysiological correlates of positive, negative and disorganized symptoms in the schizophrenia spectrum. *Psychiatry Research, 57*, 241–250.

Brenner, S. L., Beauchaine, T. P., & Sylvers, P. (2005). A comparison of psychophysiological and self-report measures of BAS and BIS activation. *Psychophysiology, 42*, 108–115.

Breska, A., Maoz, K., & Ben-Shakhar, G. (2011). Interstimulus intervals for skin conductance response measurement. *Psychophysiology, 48*, 437–440.

Broadbent, D. E. (1971). *Decision and stress*. London: Academic.

Broughton, R. J., Poire, R., & Tassinari, C. A. (1965). The electrodermogram (Tarchanoff effect) during sleep. *Electroencephalography and Clinical Neurophysiology, 18*, 691–708.

Brown, C. C. (1967). A proposed standard nomenclature for psychophysiological measures. *Psychophysiology, 4*, 260–264.

Brown, C. C. (1972). Instruments in psychophysiology. In N. S. Greenfield & R. A. Sternbach (Eds.), *Handbook of psychophysiology* (pp. 159–195). New York: Holt, Rinehart, & Winston.

Brown, B. H., Bygrave, C., Robinson, P., & Henderson, H. P. (1980). A critique of the use of a thermal clearance probe for the measurement of skin blood flow. *Clinical Physics and Physiological Measurement, 1*, 237.

Bryden, M. P. (1965). Tachistoscopic recognition, handedness and cerebral dominance. *Neuropsychologia, 3*, 1–8.

Bryden, M. P. (1979). Evidence for sex related differences in cerebral organization. In M. A. Wittig & A. C. Peterson (Eds.), *Sex-related differences in cognitive functioning* (pp. 121–143). New York: Academic.

Buck, R. (1977). Nonverbal communication of affect in preschool children: Relationships with personality and skin conductance. *Journal of Personality and Social Psychology, 35*, 225–236.

Buck, R. (1980). Nonverbal behavior and the theory of emotion: The facial feedback hypothesis. *Journal of Personality and Social Psychology, 38*, 811–824.

Buck, R., Miller, R. E., & Caul, W. F. (1974). Sex, personality, and physiological variables in the communication of affect via facial expression. *Journal of Personality and Social Psychology, 30*, 587–596.

Buck, R., Savin, V. J., Miller, R. E., & Caul, W. F. (1972). Communication of affect through facial expressions in humans. *Journal of Personality and Social Psychology, 23*, 362–371.

Bull, R. H. C., & Gale, A. (1971). The relationships between some measures of the galvanic skin response. *Psychonomic Science, 25*, 293–294.

Bull, R. H. C., & Gale, A. (1973). The reliability of and interrelationships between various measures of electrodermal activity. *Journal of Experimental Research in Personality, 6*, 300–306.

Bull, R., & Gale, A. (1974). Does the law of initial value apply to the galvanic skin response? *Biological Psychology, 1*, 213–227.

Bundy, R. S., & Fitzgerald, H. E. (1975). Stimulus specificity of electrodermal recovery time: An examination and reinterpretation of the evidence. *Psychophysiology, 12*, 406–411.

Burbank, D. P., & Webster, J. G. (1978). Reducing skin potential motion artifact by skin abrasion. *Medical & Biological Engineering & Computing, 16*, 31–38.

Burch, N. R., & Greiner, T. H. (1960). A bioelectric scale of human alertness: Concurrent recordings of the EEG and GSR. *Psychiatric Research Reports of the American Psychological Association, 12*, 183–193.

Burstein, K. R., Fenz, W. D., Bergeron, J., & Epstein, S. (1965). A comparison of skin potential and skin resistance responses as measures of emotional responsivity. *Psychophysiology, 2*, 14–24.

Burton, C. E., David, R. M., Portnoy, W. M., & Akers, L. A. (1974). The application of bode analysis to skin impedance. *Psychophysiology, 11*, 517–525.

Byrne, D. (1961). The repression-sensitization scale: Rationale, reliability, and validity. *Journal of Personality, 29*, 334–349.

Cacioppo, J. T., & Petty, R. E. (1986). Social processes. In M. G. H. Coles, E. Donchin, & S. W. Porges (Eds.), *Psychophysiology: Systems, processes, and applications* (pp. 646–679). Amsterdam: Elsevier.

Caffyn, J. M. (1964). Psychological laboratory techniques in copy research. *Journal of Advertising Research, 4*, 45–50.

Cahill, L., & McGaugh, J. L. (1998). Mechanisms of emotional arousal and lasting declarative memory. *Trends in Neurosciences, 21*, 294–299.

Cambrai, M., Clar, E. J., Grosshans, E., & Altermatt, C. (1979). Skin impedance and phoreographic index in psoriasis: Relationship with action kinetics of three treatments. *Archives of Dermatological Research, 264*, 197–211.

Campbell, S. D., Kraning, K. K., Schibli, E. G., & Momii, S. T. (1977). Hydration characteristics and electrical resistivity of stratum corneum using a noninvasive four-point microelectrode method. *The Journal of Investigative Dermatology, 69*, 290–295.

Campbell, M. C., Stout, J. C., & Finn, P. R. (2004). Reduced autonomic responsiveness to gambling task losses in Huntington's disease. *Journal of the International Neuropsychological Society, 10*, 239–245.

Campos, J. J., & Johnson, H. J. (1967). Affect, verbalization, and directional fractionation of autonomic responses. *Psychophysiology, 3*, 285–290.

Canavan, A. G. M., Passingham, R. E., Marsden, C. D., Quinn, N., Wyke, M., & Polkey, C. E. (1989). The performance on learning tasks of patients in the early stages of Parkinson's disease. *Neuropsychologica, 27*, 141–156.

Cannon, T. D., Fuhrmann, M., Mednick, S. A., Machon, R. A., Parnas, J., & Schulsinger, F. (1988). Third ventricle enlargement and reduced electrodermal responsiveness. *Psychophysiology, 25*, 153–156.

Cannon, T. D., Mednick, S. A., & Parnas, J. (1989). Genetic and perinatal determinants of structural brain deficits in schizophrenia. *Archives of General Psychiatry, 46*, 883–889.

Cannon, T. D., Mednick, S. A., & Parnas, J. (1990). Antecedents of predominantly negative- and predominantly positive-symptom schizophrenia in a high-risk population. *Archives of General Psychiatry, 47*, 622–632.

Carbonnell, L., Vidal, F., Sequeira, H., & Caverni, J.-P. (2006). A reasoning bias revealed by electrodermal activity. *Psychophysiology, 43*, 387–393.

Carlsson, K., Petersson, K. M., Lundqvist, D., Karlsson, A., Ingvar, M., & Öhman, A. (2004). Fear and the amygdala: Manipulation of awareness generates differential cerebral responses to phobic and fear-relevant (but nonfeared) stimuli. *Emotion, 4*, 340–353.

Carney, R. M., Hong, B. A., Kulkarni, S., & Kapila, A. (1981). A comparison of EMG and SCL in normal and depressed subjects. *The Pavlovian Journal of Biological Science, 16*, 212–216.

Carrillo, E., Moya-Albiol, L., González-Bono, E., Salvador, A., Ricarte, J., & Gómez-Amor, J. (2001). Gender differences in cardiovascular and electrodermal responses to public speaking task: The role of anxiety and mood states. *International Journal of Psychophysiology, 42*, 253–264.

Carstensen, L. L., Issacowitz, D. M., & Charles, S. T. (1999). Taking time seriously: A theory of socioemotional selectivity. *The American Psychologist, 54*, 165–181.

Carter, S., & Smith-Pasqualini, M. C. (2004). Stronger autonomic response accompanies better learning: A test of Damasio's somatic marker hypothesis. *Cognition & Emotion, 18*, 901–911.

Catania, J. J., Thompson, L. W., Michalewski, H. A., & Bowman, T. E. (1980). Comparisons of sweat gland counts, electrodermal activity, and habituation behavior in young and old groups of subjects. *Psychophysiology, 17*, 146–152.

Champion, R. A., & Jones, J. E. (1961). Forward, backward, and pseudoconditioning of the GSR. *Journal of Experimental Psychology, 62*, 58–61.

Charles, S. T., Reynolds, C. A., & Gatz, M. (2001). Age-related differences and change in positive and negative affect over 23 years. *Journal of Personality and Social Psychology, 80*, 136–151.

Chassande, B., Charpentier, G., Budy, I., Willer, J. C., & Lille, F. (1996). Sympathetic skin responses and heart rate variability in diabetic patients with different grades of polyneuropathy. *Revue Neurologique, 152*, 623–629.

Chattopadhyay, P. K. (1981). Bilateral skin resistance responses in anxiety. *Indian Journal of Clinical Psychology, 8*, 29–34.

Chattopadhyay, P. K., & Biswas, P. K. (1983). Characteristics of galvanic skin response in anxious patients and normal subjects. *Indian Journal of Clinical Psychology, 10*, 159–164.

Chattopadhyay, P. K., Bond, A. J., & Lader, M. H. (1975). Characteristics of galvanic skin response in anxiety states. *Journal of Psychiatric Research, 12*, 265–270.

Chattopadhyay, P. K., Cooke, E., Toone, B., & Lader, M. (1980). Habituation of physiological responses in anxiety. *Biological Psychiatry, 15*, 711–721.

Chattopadhyay, P. K., Mazumdar, P., & Basu, A. K. (1982). Habituation of electrodermal responses in tension-headache sufferers and non-tension headache controls. *Indian Journal of Psychiatry, 24*, 61–65.

Checkley, H. (1964). *The mask of sanity*. St. Louis: Mosby.

Chiu, Y.-C., Lin, C.-H., Huang, J.-T., Lin, S., Lee, P.-L., & Hsieh, J.-C. (2008). Immediate gain is long-term loss: Are there foresighted decision makers in the Iowa Gambling Task? *Behavioral and Brain Functions, 4*, 4–13.

Christie, M. J., & Venables, P. H. (1971). Basal palmar skin potential and the electrocardiogram T-wave. *Psychophysiology, 8*, 779–786.

Christie, M. J., & Venables, P. H. (1972). Site, state, and subject characteristics of palmar skin potential levels. *Psychophysiology, 9*, 645–649.

Claridge, G. S. (1967). *Personality and arousal.* Oxford: Pergamon.

Clements, K. (1989). The use of purpose-made electrode gels in the measurement of electrodermal activity: A correction to Grey and Smith (1984). *Psychophysiology, 26*, 495.

Cleveland, D. E. (1961). Driver tension and rural intersection illumination. *Traffic Engineering, 32*, 11–16.

Coan, J. A., & Allen, J. J. B. (2003). Frontal EEG asymmetry and the behavioural activation and inhibition systems. *Psychophysiology, 40*, 106–114.

Coan, J. A., & Allen, J. J. B. (2004). Frontal EEG asymmetry as a moderator and mediator of emotion. *Biological Psychology, 67*, 7–49.

Coan, J. A., Allen, J. J. B., & Harmon-Jones, E. (2001). Voluntary facial expression and hemispheric asymmetry over the frontal cortex. *Psychophysiology, 38*, 912–925.

Colbert, A. P., Hammerschlag, R., Aickin, M., & McNames, J. (2004). Reliability of the Prognos electrodermal device for measurement of electric skin resistance at acupuncture points. *Journal of Alternative and Complementary Medicine, 10*, 610–616.

Colby, C. Z., Lanzetta, J. T., & Kleck, R. E. (1977). Effects of the expression of pain on autonomic and pain tolerance responses to subject-controlled pain. *Psychophysiology, 14*, 537–540.

Coles, M. G. H., & Gale, A. (1971). Physiological reactivity as a predictor of performance in a vigilance task. *Psychophysiology, 8*, 594–599.

Coles, M. G. H., Gale, A., & Kline, P. (1971). Personality and habituation of the orienting reaction: Tonic and response measures of electrodermal activity. *Psychophysiology, 8*, 54–63.

Colombetti, G. (2008). The somatic marker hypotheses, and what the Iowa Gambling Task does and does not show. *The British Journal for the Philosophy of Sciences, 59*, 51–71.

Conklin, J. E. (1951). Three factors affecting the general level of electrical skin-resistance. *The American Journal of Psychology, 64*, 78–86.

Corah, N. L., & Stern, J. A. (1963). Stability and adaptation of some measures of electrodermal activity in children. *Journal of Experimental Psychology, 65*, 80–85.

Correa, E. J., & Adams, H. E. (1981). The validity of the pre-employment polygraph examination and the effects of motivation. *Polygraph, 10*, 143–155.

Cort, J., Hayworth, J., Little, B., Lobstein, T., McBrearty, E., Reszetniak, S., & Rowland, L. (1978). The relationship between the amplitude and the recovery half-time of the skin conductance response. *Biological Psychology, 6*, 309–311.

Corteen, R. S. (1969). Skin conductance changes and word recall. *British Journal of Psychology, 60*, 81–84.

Corteen, R. S., & Dunn, D. (1974). Shock-associated words in a nonattended message: A test for momentary awareness. *Journal of Experimental Psychology, 102*, 1143–1144.

Corteen, R. S., & Wood, B. (1972). Autonomic responses to shock-associated words in an unattended channel. *Journal of Experimental Psychology, 94*, 308–313.

Crider, A. (1993). Electrodermal response lability-stability: Individual difference correlates. In J.-C. Roy, W. Boucsein, D. C. Fowles, & J. H. Gruzelier (Eds.), *Progress in electrodermal research* (pp. 173–186). London: Plenum.

Crider, A. (2008). Personality and electrodermal response lability: An interpretation. *Applied Psychophysiology and Biofeedback, 33*, 141–148.

Crider, A., & Augenbraun, C. B. (1975). Auditory vigilance correlates of electrodermal response habituation speed. *Psychophysiology, 12*, 36–40.

Crider, A., & Lunn, R. (1971). Electrodermal lability as a personality dimension. *Journal of Experimental Research in Personality, 5*, 145–150.

Critchley, H. D. (2002). Electrodermal responses: What happens in the brain. *The Neuroscientist, 8*, 132–142.

Critchley, H. D., Elliott, R., Mathias, C. J., & Dolan, R. J. (2000). Neural activity relating to generation and representation of galvanic skin conductance responses: A functional magnetic resonance imaging study. *The Journal of Neuroscience, 20*, 3033–3040.

Critchley, H. D., Melmed, R. N., Featherstone, E., Mathias, C. J., & Dolan, R. J. (2001). Brain activity during biofeedback relaxation. *A functional neuroimaging investigation. Brain, 124*, 1003–1012.

Critchley, H. D., Melmed, R. N., Featherstone, E., Mathias, C. J., & Dolan, R. J. (2002). Volitional control of autonomic arousal: A functional magnetic resonance study. *NeuroImage, 16*, 909–919.

Crone, E. A., Somsen, R. J., van Beek, B., & van der Molen, M. W. (2004). Heart rate and skin conductance analysis of antecedents and consequences of decision-making. *Psychophysiology, 41*, 531–540.

Crowell, S. E., Beauchaine, T. P., Gatzke-Kopp, L., Sylvers, P., Mead, H., & Chipman-Chacon, J. (2006). Autonomic correlates of attention-deficit/hyperactivity and oppositional defiant disorder in preschool children. *Journal of Abnormal Psychology, 115*, 174–178.

Crowne, D. P., & Marlowe, D. (1960). A new scale of social desirability independent of psychopathology. *Journal of Consulting Psychology, 24*, 349–354.

Cruz, M. H., & Larsen, R. J. (1995). Personality correlates of individual differences in electrodermal lability. *Social Behavior and Personality, 23*, 93–104.

Culp, W. C., & Edelberg, R. (1966). Regional response specifity in the electrodermal reflex. *Perceptual and Motor Skills, 23*, 623–627.

Curt, A., Weinhardt, C., & Dietz, V. (1996). Significance of sympathetic skin response in the assessment of autonomic failure in patients with spinal cord injury. *Journal of the Autonomic Nervous System, 61*, 175–180.

Curzi-Dascalova, L., Pajot, N., & Dreyfus-Brisac, C. (1973). Spontaneous skin potential responses in sleeping infants between 24 and 41 weeks of conceptional age. *Psychophysiology, 10*, 478–487.

Cuthbert, B. N., Bradley, M. M., & Lang, P. J. (1996). Probing picture perception: Activation and emotion. *Psychophysiology, 33*, 103–111.

Damasio, A. R. (1994). *Descartes Error: Emotion, reason and the human brain*. New York: Avon.

Damasio, A. R., Tranel, D., & Damasio, H. (1990). Individuals with sociopathic behavior caused by frontal damage fail to respond autonomically to social stimuli. *Behavioural Brain Research, 41*, 81–94.

Damasio, A. R., Tranel, D., & Damasio, H. (1991). Somatic markers and the guidance of behavior: Theory and preliminary testing. In H. S. Levin, H. M. Eisenberg, & A. L. Benton (Eds.), *Frontal lobe function and dysfunction* (pp. 217–229). New York: Oxford University Press.

Darrow, C. W. (1933). The functional significance of the galvanic skin reflex and perspiration on the backs and palms of the hands. *Psychological Bulletin, 30*, 712.

Darrow, C. W. (1937a). Neural mechanisms controlling the palmar galvanic skin reflex and palmar sweating. *Archives of Neurology and Psychiatry, 37*, 641–663.

Darrow, C. W. (1937b). The equation of the galvanic skin reflex curve: I. The dynamics of reaction in relation to excitation-background. *Journal of General Psychology, 16*, 285–309.

Darrow, C. W. (1964). The rationale for treating the change in galvanic skin response as a change in conductance. *Psychophysiology, 1*, 31–38.

Darrow, C. W., & Gullickson, G. R. (1970). The peripheral mechanism of the galvanic skin response. *Psychophysiology, 6*, 597–600.

Davidson, R. J. (1993). Cerebral asymmetry and emotion: Conceptual and methodological conundrums. *Cognition and Emotion, 7*, 115–138.

Davidson, R. A., Fedio, P., Smith, B. S., Aureille, E., & Martin, A. (1992). Lateralized mediation of arousal and habituation: Differential bilateral electrodermal activity in unilateral temporal lobectomy patients. *Neuropsychologia, 30*, 1053–1063.

Davidson, R. A., & Smith, B. D. (1991). Caffeine and novelty: Effects on electrodermal activity and performance. *Physiology and Behavior, 49*, 1169–1175.

Davies, D. R. (1983). Attention, arousal and effort. In A. Gale & J. A. Edwards (Eds.), *Physiological correlates of human behaviour* (Attention and performance, Vol. 2, pp. 9–34). London: Academic.

Davis, M. (2000). The role of the amygdala in conditioned and unconditioned fear and anxiety. In J. P. Aggleton (Ed.), *The amygdala: A functional analysis* (2nd ed., pp. 213–287). Oxford: Oxford University Press.

Davis, T., Love, B. C., & Maddox, W. T. (2009). Anticipatory emotions in decision tasks: Covert markers of value or attentional processes? *Cognition, 112,* 195–200.

Davis, J. F., Malmo, R. B., & Shagass, C. (1954). Electromyographic reaction to strong auditory stimulation in psychiatric patients. *Canadian Journal of Psychology, 8,* 177–186.

Dawson, M. E. (1980). Physiological detection of deception: Measurement of responses to questions and answers during countermeasure maneuvers. *Psychophysiology, 17,* 8–17.

Dawson, M. E. (1990). Psychophysiology at the interface of clinical science, cognitive science, and neuroscience. *Psychophysiology, 27,* 243–255.

Dawson, M. E., Catania, J. J., Schell, A. M., & Grings, W. W. (1979). Autonomic classical conditioning as a function of awareness of stimulus contingencies. *Biological Psychology, 9,* 23–40.

Dawson, M. E., Filion, D. L., & Schell, A. M. (1989). Is elicitation of the autonomic orienting response associated with allocation of processing resources? *Psychophysiology, 26,* 560–572.

Dawson, M. E., & Furedy, J. J. (1976). The role of awareness in human differential autonomic classical conditioning: The necessary gate hypothesis. *Psychophysiology, 13,* 50–53.

Dawson, M. E., & Nuechterlein, K. H. (1984). Psychophysiological dysfunctions in the developmental course of schizophrenic disorders. *Schizophrenia Bulletin, 10,* 204–232.

Dawson, M. E., Nuechterlein, K. H., & Adams, R. M. (1989). Schizophrenic disorders. In G. Turpin (Ed.), *Handbook of clinical psychophysiology* (pp. 393–418). New York: Wiley.

Dawson, M. E., Nuechterlein, K. H., Schell, A. M., Gitlin, M., & Ventura, J. (1994). Autonomic abnormalities in schizophrenia. *Archives of General Psychology, 51,* 813–824.

Dawson, M. E., & Schell, A. M. (1982). Electrodermal responses to attended and nonattended significant stimuli during dichotic listening. *Journal of Experimental Psychology. Human Perception and Performance, 8,* 315–324.

Dawson, M. E., & Schell, A. M. (1985). Information processing and human autonomic classical conditioning. In P. K. Ackles, J. R. Jennings, & M. G. H. Coles (Eds.), *Advances in psychophysiology* (Vol. 1, pp. 89–165). Greenwich, CT: Jai.

Dawson, M. E., & Schell, A. M. (1987). Human autonomic and skeletal classical conditioning: The role of conscious cognitive factors. In G. Davey (Ed.), *Cognitive processes and Pavlovian conditioning in humans* (pp. 27–55). New York: Wiley.

Dawson, M. E., & Schell, A. M. (2002). What does electrodermal activity tell us about prognosis in the schizophrenia spectrum? *Schizophrenia Research, 54,* 87–93.

Dawson, M. E., Schell, A. M., Beers, J. R., & Kelly, A. (1982). Allocation of cognitive processing capacity during human autonomic classical conditioning. *Journal of Experimental Psychology: General, 111,* 272–295.

Dawson, M. E., Schell, A. M., & Catania, J. J. (1977). Autonomic correlates of depression and clinical improvement following electroconvulsive shock therapy. *Psychophysiology, 14,* 569–578.

Dawson, M. E., Schell, A. M., & Filion, D. L. (1990). The electrodermal system. In I. T. Cacioppo & L. G. Tassinary (Eds.), *Principles of psychophysiology* (pp. 295–324). Cambridge: Cambridge University Press.

Dawson, M. E., Schell, A. M., & Filion, D. L. (2007). The electrodermal system. In J. T. Cacioppo, L. G. Tassinary, & G. G. Berntson (Eds.), *Handbook of psychophysiology* (pp. 159–181). New York: Cambridge University Press.

De Bonis, M., & Freixa i Baqué, E. (1980). Stress, verbal cognitive activity and bilateral electrodermal responses. *Neuropsychobiology, 6,* 249–259.

De Jongh, G. J. (1981). Porosity of human skin in vivo assessed via water loss, carbon dioxide loss and electrical impedance for healthy volunteers, atopic and psoriatic patients. *Current Problems in Dermatology, 9,* 83–101.

De Pascalis, V., Valerio, E., Santoro, M., & Cacace, I. (2007). Neuroticism-anxiety, impulsive-sensation seeking and autonomic responses to somatosensory stimuli. *International Journal of Psychophysiology, 63,* 16–24.

De Seze, J., Stojkovic, T., Gauvrit, J.-Y., Devos, S., Ayachi, M., Cassim, F., Michel, T. S., Pruvo, J.-P., Guieu, J-D., & Vermersch, P. (2001). Autonomic dysfunction in multiple sclerosis: Cervical spinal cord atrophy correlates. *Journal of Neurology, 248,* 297–303.

Dean, R. S. (1981). Lateral preference patterns as a discriminator of learning difficulties. *Journal of Consulting and Clinical Psychology, 49,* 227–235.

DeLong, M. R., Georgopoulos, A. P., & Crutcher, M. D. (1983). Cortico-basal ganglia relations and coding of motor performance. *Experimental Brain Research, Supplement, 7,* 30–40.

DeLong, M. R., & Wichmann, T. (2007). Circuits and circuit disorders of the basal ganglia. *Archives of Neurology, 64,* 20–24.

Deltombe, T., Hanson, P., Jamart, J., & Clérin, M. (1998). The influence of skin temperature on latency and amplitude of the sympathetic skin response in normal subjects. *Muscle & Nerve, 21,* 34–39.

Dembroski, T. M., MacDougall, J. M., & Shields, J. L. (1977). Physiologic reactions to social challenge in persons evidencing the type A coronary-prone behavior pattern. *Journal of Human Stress, 3,* 2–10.

Dembroski, T. M., MacDougall, J. M., Shields, J. L., Petitto, J., & Lushene, R. (1978). Components of the type A coronary-prone behavior pattern and cardiovascular responses to psychomotor performance challenge. *Journal of Behavioral Medicine, 1,* 159–176.

Dembroski, T. M., Weiss, S. M., Shields, J. L., Haynes, S. G., & Feinleib, M. (Eds.). (1978). *Coronary prone behavior.* New York: Springer.

Denburg, N. L., Recknor, E. C., Bechara, A., & Tranel, D. (2006). Psychophysiological anticipation of positive outcomes promotes advantageous decision-making in normal older persons. *International Journal of Psychophysiology, 61,* 19–25.

Dengerink, H. A., & Taylor, S. P. (1971). Multiple responses with differential properties in delayed galvanic skin response conditioning: A review. *Psychophysiology, 8,* 348–360.

Denislic, M., & Meh, D. (1996). Sympathetic skin response in Parkinsonian patients. *Electromyography and Clinical Neurophysiology, 36,* 231–235.

Depue, R. A., & Fowles, D. C. (1973). Electrodermal activity as an index of arousal in schizophrenics. *Psychological Bulletin, 79,* 233–238.

Derogatis, L. R., Klerman, G. L., & Lipman, R. S. (1972). Anxiety states and depressive neuroses. *The Journal of Nervous and Mental Disease, 155,* 392–403.

Dettmers, C., Fatepour, D., Faust, H., & Jerusalem, F. (1993). Sympathetic skin response abnormalities in amyotrophic lateral sclerosis. *Muscle & Nerve, 16,* 930–934.

Dettmers, C., van Ahlen, H., Faust, H., Fatepour, D., & Tackmann, W. (1994). Evaluation of erectile dysfunction with the sympathetic skin response in comparison to bulbocavernosus reflex and somatosensory evoked potentials of the pudendal nerve. *Electromyography and Clinical Neurophysiology, 34,* 437–444.

DiCara, L. V., & Miller, N. E. (1968). Instrumental learning of vasomotor responses by rats: Learning to respond differentially in the two ears. *Science, 159,* 1485–1486.

Dimitriev, L., Belyakova, L., Bondarenko, T., & Nikolaev, G. (1968). Investigation of the orienting reaction and the defense reaction of schizophrenia in different stages of their illness. *Zhurnal Nevropatologie Psikhiatrii, 68,* 713–719.

Dimond, S. J., & Beaumont, J. G. (1974). Experimental studies of hemisphere function in the human brain. In S. J. Dimond & J. G. Beaumont (Eds.), *Hemisphere function in the human brain* (pp. 48–88). New York: Wiley.

Dimond, S. J., Farrington, L., & Johnson, P. (1976). Differing emotional response from right and left hemispheres. *Nature, 261,* 690–692.

Dindo, L., & Fowles, D. C. (2008). The skin conductance orienting response to semantic stimuli: Significance can be independent of arousal. *Psychophysiology, 45,* 111–118.

Doberenz, S., Roth, W. T., Wollburg, E., Maslowski, N. I., & Kim, S. (2011). Methodological considerations in ambulatory skin conductance monitoring. *International Journal of Psychophysiology, 80,* 87–95.

Docter, R., & Friedman, L. F. (1966). Thirty-day stability of spontaneous galvanic skin responses in man. *Psychophysiology, 2,* 311–315.

Doerr, H. O., Follette, W., Scribner, B. H., & Eisdorfer, C. (1980). Electrodermal response dysfunction in patients on maintenance renal dialysis. *Psychophysiology, 17*, 83–86.

Dolu, N., Süer, C., Özesmi, C., Kelestimur, F., & Esel, E. (1997). Electrodermal activity in nonmedicated hyperthyroid patients having no depressive symptoms. *Biological Psychiatry, 42*, 1024–1029.

Donat, D. C., & McCullough, J. P. (1983). Psychophysiological discriminants of depression at rest and in response to stress. *Journal of Clinical Psychology, 39*, 315–320.

Douglas, R. J., & Pribram, K. H. (1966). Learning and limbic lesions. *Neuropsychologia, 4*, 197–220.

Dratcu, L., & Bond, A. (1998). Panic patients in the non-panic state: Physiological and cognitive dysfunction. *European Psychiatry, 13*, 18–25.

Duffy, E. (1951). The concept of energy mobilization. *Psychological Review, 58*, 30–40.

Duffy, E. (1972). Activation. In N. S. Greenfield & R. A. Sternbach (Eds.), *Handbook of psychophysiology* (pp. 577–622). New York: Holt, Rinehart, & Winston.

Dunn, B. D., Dalgleish, T., & Lawrence, A. D. (2006). The somatic marker hypothesis: A critical evaluation. *Neuroscience and Biobehavioral Reviews, 30*, 239–271.

Dykman, R. A., Reese, W. G., Galbrecht, C. R., & Thomasson, P. J. (1959). Psychophysiological reactions to novel stimuli: Measurement, adaptation, and relationship of psychological and physiological variables in the normal human. *Annals of the New York Academy of Sciences, 79*, 45–107.

Ebbecke, U. (1951). Arbeitsweise der Schweißdrüsen und sudomotorische Reflexe bei unmittelbarer Beobachtung mit Lupenvergrößerung. *Pflügers Archiv für die gesamte Physiologie, 253*, 333–339.

Edelberg, R. (1961). The relationship between the galvanic skin response, vasoconstriction, and tactile sensitivity. *Journal of Experimental Psychology, 62*, 187–195.

Edelberg, R. (1964). Independence of galvanic skin response amplitude and sweat production. *The Journal of Investigative Dermatology, 42*, 443–448.

Edelberg, R. (1967). Electrical properties of the skin. In C. C. Brown (Ed.), *Methods in psychophysiology* (pp. 1–53). Baltimore: Williams & Wilkins.

Edelberg, R. (1968). Biopotentials from the skin surface: The hydration effect. *Annals of the New York Academy of Sciences, 148*, 252–262.

Edelberg, R. (1970). The information content of the recovery limb of the electrodermal response. *Psychophysiology, 6*, 527–539.

Edelberg, R. (1971). Electrical properties of skin. In H. R. Elden (Ed.), *A treatise of the skin* (Biophysical properties of the skin, Vol. 1, pp. 519–551). New York: Wiley.

Edelberg, R. (1972a). Electrical activity of the skin: Its measurement and uses in psychophysiology. In N. S. Greenfield & R. A. Sternbach (Eds.), *Handbook of psychophysiology* (pp. 367–418). New York: Holt, Rinehart, & Winston.

Edelberg, R. (1972b). Electrodermal recovery rate, goal-orientation, and aversion. *Psychophysiology, 9*, 512–520.

Edelberg, R. (1973a). Mechanisms of electrodermal adaptations for locomotion, manipulation, or defense. In E. Stellar & J. M. Sprague (Eds.), *Progress in physiological psychology* (Vol. 5, pp. 155–209). New York: Academic.

Edelberg, R. (1973b). The local electrical response of the skin to deformation. *Journal of Applied Physiology, 34*, 334–340.

Edelberg, R. (1983). The effects if initial levels of sweat duct filling and skin hydration on electrodermal response amplitude. *Psychophysiology, 20*, 550–557.

Edelberg, R. (1993). Electrodermal mechanisms: A critique of the two-effector hypothesis and a proposed replacement. In J.-C. Roy, W. Boucsein, D. C. Fowles, & J. H. Gruzelier (Eds.), *Progress in electrodermal research* (pp. 7–30). London: Plenum.

Edelberg, R., Greiner, T., & Burch, N. R. (1960). Some membrane properties of the effector in the galvanic skin response. *Journal of Applied Physiology, 15*, 691–696.

Edelberg, R., & Muller, M. (1981). Prior activity as a determinant of electrodermal recovery rate. *Psychophysiology, 18*, 17–25.

Edelberg, R., & Wright, D. J. (1964). Two GSR effector organs and their stimulus specifity. *Psychophysiology, 1*, 39–47.

Edwards, J. A., & Siddle, D. A. T. (1976). Dishabituation of the electrodermal orienting response following decay of sensitization. *Biological Psychology, 4*, 19–28.

Egyed, B., Eory, A., Veres, T., & Manninger, J. (1980). Measurement of electrical resistance after nerve injuries of the hand. *The Hand, 12*, 275–281.

Eisdorfer, C. (1978). Psychophysiological and cognitive studies in the aged. In G. Usdin & D. J. Hofling (Eds.), *Aging: The process and the people* (pp. 96–128). New York: Brunner/Mazel.

Eisdorfer, C., Doerr, H. O., & Follette, W. (1980). Electrodermal reactivity: An analysis by age and sex. *Journal of Human Stress, 6*, 39–42.

Eisenstein, E. M., Bonheim, P., & Eisenstein, D. (1995). Habituation of the galvanic skin response to tone as a function of age. *Brain Research Bulletin, 37*, 343–350.

Eisfeld, W., Schaefer, F., Boucsein, W., & Stolz, C. (2005). Tracking intersensory properties of cosmetic products via psycho-physiological assessment. *International Federation Societies of Cosmetic Chemists (IFSCC), 8*, 25–30.

Eisfeld, W., Wachter, R., Schaefer, F., & Boucsein, W. (2007). Objective emotional assessment of perceivable wellness effects. *Cosmetics & Toiletries, 122*, 63–72.

Ekman, P., Friesen, W. V., & Ellsworth, P. C. (1972). *Emotion in the human face: Guidelines for research and an integration of findings*. New York: Plenum.

Ekman, P., Friesen, W. V., & Simons, R. C. (1985). Is the startle reaction an emotion? *Journal of Personality and Social Psychology, 49*, 1416–1426.

Ellingson, R. J. (1954). The incidence of EEG abnormality among patients with mental disorders of apparently nonorganic origin: A critical review. *The American Journal of Psychology, 8*, 263–275.

Ellis, R. A. (1968). Eccrine sweat glands: Electron microscopy; cytochemistry and anatomy. In O. Gans & G. K. Steigleder (Eds.), *Handbuch der Haut- und Geschlechtskrankheiten* (Normale und pathologische Anatomie der Haut, Vol. 1/1, pp. 224–266). Berlin: Springer.

Ellis, H. D., & de Pauw, K. W. (1994). The cognitive neuropsychiatric origins of the Capgras delusion. In A. S. David & J. C. Cutting (Eds.), *The neuropsychology of schizophrenia* (pp. 317–335). Hove: Psychology.

Ellis, H. D., & Lewis, M. B. (2001). Capgras delusion: A window on face recognition. *Trends in Cognitive Sciences, 5*, 149–156.

Ellis, H. D., Lewis, M. B., Moselhy, H. F., & Young, A. W. (2000). Automatic without autonomic responses to familiar faces: Differential components of covert face recognition in a case of capgras delusion. *Cognitive Neuropsychiatry, 5*, 255–269.

Ellis, H. D., & Young, A. W. (1990). Accounting for delusional misidentifications. *The British Journal of Psychiatry, 157*, 239–248.

Ellis, H. D., Young, A. W., Quayle, A. H., & de Pauw, K. W. (1997). Reduced autonomic responses to faces in capgras delusion. *Proceedings of the Royal Society of London, 264*, 1085–1092.

El-Sheikh, M. (2007). Children's skin conductance level and reactivity: Are these measures stable over time and across tasks? *Developmental Psychobiology, 49*, 180–186.

Engel, B. T. (1972). Response specifity. In N. S. Greenfield & R. A. Sternbach (Eds.), *Handbook of psychophysiology* (pp. 571–576). New York: Holt, Rinehart, & Winston.

Epstein, S. (1972). The nature of anxiety with emphasis upon its relationship to expectancy. In C. Spielberger (Ed.), *Anxiety: Current trends in theory and research* (Vol. 2, pp. 291–337). New York: Academic.

Epstein, S., Boudreau, L., & Kling, S. (1975). Magnitude of the heart rate and electrodermal response as a function of stimulus input, motor output, and their interaction. *Psychophysiology, 12*, 15–24.

Epstein, S., & Coleman, M. (1970). Drive theories of schizophrenia. *Psychosomatic Medicine, 32*, 113–140.

Erdmann, G., & Baumann, S. (1996). Sind psychophysiologische Veränderungen im Paradigma "Öffentliches Sprechen" Ausdruck emotionaler Belastung? *Zeitschrift für Experimentelle Psychologie, 63*, 224–255.

Erdmann, G., Janke, W., & Bisping, R. (1984). Wirkungen und Vergleich der Wirkungen von vier experimentellen Belastungssituationen. *Zeitschrift für Experimentelle und Angewandte Psychologie, 31*, 521–543.

Erdmann, G., Janke, W., Köchers, S., & Terschlüsen, B. (1984). Comparison of the emotional effects of a beta-adrenergic blocking agent and a tranquilizer under different situational conditions. *I. Anxiety-arousing situations. Neuropsychobiology, 12*, 143–151.

Erlenmeyer-Kimling, L. (1975). A prospective study of children at risk for schizophrenia: Methodological considerations and some preliminary findings. In R. D. Wirt, G. Winokur, & M. Roff (Eds.), *Life history research in psychopathology* (Vol. 4, pp. 23–46). Minneapolis: University of Minnesota Press.

Erlenmeyer-Kimling, L., Cornblatt, B., & Fleiss, J. (1979). High-risk research in schizophrenia. *Psychiatric Annals, 9*, 79–99.

Erlenmeyer-Kimling, L., Marcuse, Y., Cornblatt, B., Friedman, D., Rainer, J. D., & Rutschmann, J. (1984). The New York high-risk project. In N. F. Watt, E. J. Anthony, L. C. Wynne, & J. E. Rolf (Eds.), *Children at risk for schizophrenia: A longitudinal perspective* (pp. 169–189). London: Cambridge University Press.

Esen, F., Celebi, G., Ertekin, C., & Colakoglu, Z. (1997). Electrodermal activity in patients with Parkinson's disease. *Clinical Autonomic Research, 7*, 35–40.

Euteneuer, F., Schaefer, F., Stuermer, R., Boucsein, W., Timmermann, L., Barbe, M. T., Ebersbach, G., Otto, J., Kessler, J., & Kalbe, E. (2009). Dissociation of decision-making under ambiguity and decision-making under risk in patients with Parkinson's disease: A neuropsychological and psychophysiological study. *Neuropsychologia, 47*, 2882–2890.

Eysenck, H. J. (1957). Drugs and personality: I. Theory and methodology. *Journal of Mental Science, 103*, 119–131.

Eysenck, H. J. (1967). *The biological basis of personality*. Springfield: Thomas.

Eysenck, M. W. (1982). *Attention and arousal*. Berlin: Springer.

Eysenck, H. J. (1983). Psychophysiology and personality: Extraversion, neuroticism and psychoticism. In A. Gale & J. A. Edwards (Eds.), *Physiological correlates of human behaviour* (Individual differences and psychopathology, Vol. 3, pp. 13–30). London: Academic.

Eysenck, H. J. (1994). Personality: Biological foundations. In P. A. Vernon (Ed.), *The neuropsychology of individual differences* (pp. 151–207). New York: Academic.

Eysenck, H. J., & Eysenck, M. W. (1985). *Personality and individual differences*. New York: Plenum.

Eysenck, S., & Zuckerman, M. (1978). The relationship between sensation-seeking and Eysenck's dimensions of personality. *British Journal of Psychology, 69*, 483–487.

Faber, S. (1977). Methodische Probleme bei Hautwiderstandsmessungen. *Biomedizinische Technik, 22*, 393–394.

Faber, S. (1980). *Hautleitfähigkeitsuntersuchungen als Methode in der Arbeitswissenschaft.* Düsseldorf: Fortschritt-Berichte der VDI-Zeitschriften.

Faber, S. (1983). Zur Auswertemethodik und Interpretation von Hautleitfähigkeitsmessungen bei arbeitswissenschaftlicher Beanspruchungsermittlung. *Zeitschrift für Arbeitswissenschaft, 37*(9 NF), 85–91.

Fahrenberg, J. (1987). Concepts of activation and arousal in the theory of emotionality (neuroticism): A multivariate conceptualization. In J. Strelau & H. J. Eysenck (Eds.), *Personality dimensions and arousal* (pp. 99–120). New York: Plenum.

Fahrenberg, J. (1988). Psychophysiological processes. In J. R. Nesselroade & R. B. Cattell (Eds.), *Handbook of multivariate experimental psychology* (pp. 867–914). New York: Plenum.

Fahrenberg, J., & Foerster, F. (1982). Covariation and consistency of activation parameters. *Biological Psychology, 15*, 151–169.

Fahrenberg, J., Foerster, F., Schneider, H. J., Müller, W., & Myrtek, M. (1984). *Aktivierungsforschung im Labor-Feld-Vergleich.* München: Minerva.

Fahrenberg, J., & Myrtek, M. (1967). Zur Methodik der Verlaufsanalyse: Ausgangswerte, Reaktionsgrößen (Reaktivität) und Verlaufswerte. *Psychologische Beiträge, 10*, 58–77.

Fahrenberg, J., & Myrtek, M. (Eds.). (1996). *Ambulatory assessment*. Seattle: Hogrefe & Huber.

Fahrenberg, J., & Myrtek, M. (Eds.). (2001). *Progress in ambulatory assessment*. Göttingen: Hogrefe.

Fahrenberg, J., Schneider, H.-J., & Safian, P. (1987). Psychophysiological assessments in a repeated-measurement design extending over a one-year interval: Trends and stability. *Biological Psychology, 24*, 49–66.

Fahrenberg, J., Walschburger, P., Foerster, F., Myrtek, M., & Müller, W. (1979). *Psychophysiologische Aktivierungsforschung: Ein Beitrag zu den Grundlagen der multivariaten Emotions- und Stress-Theorie*. München: Minerva.

Fahrenberg, J., Walschburger, P., Foerster, F., Myrtek, M., & Müller, W. (1983). An evaluation of trait, state, and reaction aspects of activation processes. *Psychophysiology, 20*, 188–195.

Falkowski, J., & Steptoe, A. (1983). Biofeedback-assisted relaxation in the control of reactions to a challenging task and anxiety-provoking film. *Behaviour Research and Therapy, 21*, 161–167.

Farhoumand, N., Harrison, J., Pare, C. M. B., Turner, P., & Wynn, S. (1979). The effect of high dose oxprenolol on stress-induced physical and psychophysiological variables. *Psychopharmacology, 64*, 365–369.

Feij, J. A. (1984). The psychophysiological and neurochemical bases of sensation seeking. In H. Bonarius, G. van Heck, & N. Smid (Eds.), *Personality psychology in Europe* (pp. 317–326). Lisse: Swets & Zeitlinger.

Fenske, N. A., & Lober, C. W. (1986). Structural and functional changes of normal aging skin. *Journal of the American Academy of Dermatology, 15*, 571–585.

Féré, C. (1888). Note sur les modifications de la résistance électrique sous l'influence des excitations sensorielles et des émotions. *Comptes Rendus des Séances de la Société de Biologie, 5*, 217–219.

Ficková, E. (1983). Dynamics of psychophysiological activation in shift-work operators. *Studia Psychologica, 25*, 105–113.

Filion, D. L., Dawson, M. E., & Schell, A. M. (1998). The psychological significance of human startle eyeblink modification: A review. *Biological Psychiatry, 47*, 1–43.

Filion, D. L., Dawson, M. E., Schell, A. M., & Hazlett, E. A. (1991). The relationship between skin conductance orienting and the allocation of processing resources. *Psychophysiology, 28*, 410–424.

Firth, H. (1973). Habituation during sleep. *Psychophysiology, 10*, 43–51.

Fishbein, D., Eldreth, D., Matochik, J., Isenberg, I., Hyde, C., & London, E. (2005). Cognitive performance and autonomic reactivity in abstinent drug abusers and nonusers. *Experimental and Clinical Psychopharmacology, 13*, 25–40.

Fisher, S. (1958). Body image and asymmetry of body reactivity. *Journal of Abnormal and Social Psychology, 57*, 292–298.

Fisher, L. E., & Kotses, H. (1973). Race differences and experimenter race effect in galvanic skin response. *Psychophysiology, 10*, 578–582.

Fisher, L. E., & Winkel, M. H. (1979). Time of quarter effect: An uncontrolled variable in electrodermal research. *Psychophysiology, 16*, 158–163.

Fitzgerald, M. J. T. (1961). Developmental changes in epidermal innervation. *Journal of Anatomy, 95*, 495–514.

Fletcher, R. P., Venables, P. H., & Mitchell, D. A. (1982). Estimation of half from quarter recovery time of SCR. *Psychophysiology, 19*, 115–116.

Flor, H., Knost, B., & Birbaumer, N. (1997). Processing of pain- and body-related verbal material in chronic pain patients: Central and peripheral correlates. *Pain, 73*, 413–421.

Flor-Henry, P. (1993). Electrodermal amplitude asymmetry and orienting response-non-response in psychopathology. In J.-C. Roy, W. Boucsein, C. D. Fowles, & J. H. Gruzelier (Eds.), *Progress in electrodermal research* (pp. 289–296). New York: Plenum.

Flykt, A., Esteves, F., & Öhman, A. (2007). Skin conductance response to masked conditioned stimuli: Phylogenetic/ontogenetic factors versus direction of threat? *Biological Psychology, 74*, 328–336.

Foerster, F. (1984). *Computerprogramme zur Biosignalanalyse*. Berlin: Springer.

Folkins, C. H. (1970). Temporal factors and the cognitive mediators of stress reaction. *Journal of Personality and Social Psychology, 14*, 173–184.

Forbes, T. W. (1964). Problems in measurement of electrodermal phenomena – Choice of method and phenomena – Potential, impedance, resistance. *Psychophysiology, 1*, 26–30.

Forbes, T. W., & Landis, C. (1935). The limiting A. C. frequency for the exhibition of the galvanic skin ("psychogalvanic") response. *The Journal of General Psychology, 13*, 188–193.

Foulds, I. S., & Barker, A. T. (1983). Human skin battery potentials and their possible role in wound healing. *British Journal of Dermatology, 109*, 515–522.

Foulds, G. A., & Bedford, A. (1976). The relationship between anxiety-depression and the neuroses. *The British Journal of Psychiatry, 128*, 166–168.

Fowler, C. J. (1993). Electrophysiologic evaluation of sexual dysfunction. In P. A. Low (Ed.), *Clinical Autonomic Disorders* (pp. 279–285). Boston: Little Brown.

Fowler, R. L., & Kimmel, H. D. (1962). Operant conditioning of the GSR. *Journal of Experimental Psychology, 63*, 563–567.

Fowles, D. C. (1974). Mechanisms of electrodermal activity. In R. F. Thompson & M. M. Patterson (Eds.), *Methods in physiological psychology* (Bioelectric recording techniques, Part C: Receptor and effector processes, Vol. 1, pp. 231–271). New York: Academic.

Fowles, D. C. (1980). The three arousal model: Implications of Gray's two-factor learning theory for heart rate, electrodermal activity, and psychopathy. *Psychophysiology, 17*, 87–104.

Fowles, D. C. (1986a). The eccrine system and electrodermal activity. In M. G. H. Coles, E. Donchin, & S. W. Porges (Eds.), *Psychophysiology: Systems, processes, and applications* (pp. 51–96). Amsterdam: Elsevier.

Fowles, D. C. (1986b). The psychophysiology of anxiety and hedonic affect: Motivational specificity. In B. F. Shaw, T. M. Segal, & T. M. Vallis (Eds.), *Anxiety disorders* (pp. 51–66). New York: Plenum.

Fowles, D. C. (1988). Psychophysiology and psychopathology: A motivational approach. *Psychophysiology, 25*, 373–391.

Fowles, D. C. (2000). Electrodermal hyporeactivity and antisocial behaviour: Does anxiety mediate the relationship? *Journal of Affective Disorders, 61*, 177–189.

Fowles, D. C., Christie, M. J., Edelberg, R., Grings, W. W., Lykken, D. T., & Venables, P. H. (1981). Publication recommendations for electrodermal measurements. *Psychophysiology, 18*, 232–239.

Fowles, D. C., Fisher, A. E., & Tranel, D. T. (1982). The heart beats to reward: The effect of monetary incentive on heart rate. *Psychophysiology, 19*, 506–513.

Fowles, D. C., & Johnson, G. (1973). The influence of variations in electrolyte concentration on skin potential level and response amplitude. *Biological Psychology, 1*, 151–160.

Fowles, D. C., Kochanska, G., & Murray, K. (2000). Electrodermal activity and temperament in preschool children. *Psychophysiology, 37*, 777–787.

Fowles, D. C., Roberts, R., & Nagel, K. E. (1977). The influence of introversion/extraversion on the skin conductance response to stress and stimulus intensity. *Journal of Research in Personality, 11*, 129–146.

Fowles, D. C., & Rosenberry, R. (1973). Effects of epidermal hydration on skin potential responses and levels. *Psychophysiology, 10*, 601–611.

Fowles, D. C., & Schneider, R. E. (1974). Effects of epidermal hydration on skin conductance responses and levels. *Biological Psychology, 2*, 67–77.

Fowles, D. C., & Schneider, R. E. (1978). Electrolyte medium effects on measurements of palmar skin potential. *Psychophysiology, 15*, 474–482.

Francini, F., Zoppi, M., Maresca, M., & Procacci, P. (1979). Skin potential and EMG changes induced by cutaneous electrical stimulation. *Applied Neurophysiology, 42*, 113–124.

Franz, M., Olbrich, R., Croissant, B., Kirsch, P., Schmitz, N., & Schneider, C. (1999). Gefühl ohne Sprache oder Sprache ohne Gefühl? Weitere Hinweise auf die Validität der Entkopplungshypothese der Alexithymie. *Nervenarzt, 70*, 216–224.

Fredrikson, M. (1981). Orienting and defensive reactions to phobic and conditioned fear stimuli in phobics and normals. *Psychophysiology, 18*, 456–465.

Fredrikson, M. (1986). Racial differences in cardiovascular reactivity to mental stress in essential hypertension. *Journal of Hypertension, 4*, 325–331.

Fredrikson, M., Annas, P., Georgiades, A., Hursti, T., & Tersman, Z. (1993). Internal consistency and temporal stability of classically conditioned skin conductance responses. *Biological Psychology, 35,* 153–163.

Fredrikson, M., Dimberg, U., & Frisk-Holmberg, M. (1980). Arterial blood pressure and electrodermal activity in hypertensive and normotensive subjects during inner- and outer- directed attention. *Acta Medica Scandinavica, 646,* 73–76.

Fredrikson, M., Dimberg, U., Frisk-Holmberg, M., & Ström, G. (1982). Haemodynamic and electrodermal correlates of psychogenic stimuli in hypertensive and normotensive subjects. *Biological Psychology, 15,* 63–73.

Fredrikson, M., & Engel, B. T. (1985). Cardiovascular and electrodermal adjustments during a vigilance task in patients with borderline and established hypertension. *Journal of Psychosomatic Research, 29,* 235–246.

Fredrikson, M., Furmark, T., Olsson, M. T., Fischer, H., Andersson, J., & Langström, B. (1998). Functional neuoranatomical correlates of electrodermal activity: A positron emission tomographic study. *Psychophysiology, 35,* 179–185.

Freedman, R. R., Woodward, S., & Norton, D. A. M. (1992). Laboratory and ambulatory monitoring of menopausal hot flushes: Comparison of symptomatic and asymptomatic women. *Journal of Psychophysiology, 6,* 162–166.

Freixa i Baqué, E. (1982). Reliability of electrodermal measures: A compilation. Biological Psychology, 14, 219–229.

Freixa i Baqué, E., Catteau, M.-C., Miossec, Y., & Roy, J.-C. (1984). Asymmetry of electrodermal activity: A review. Biological Psychology, 18, 219–239.

Freixa i Baqué, E., Chevalier, B., Grubar, J. C., Lambert, C., Lancry, A., Leconte, P., Meriaux, H., & Spreux, F. (1983). Spontaneous electrodermal activity during sleep in man: An intranight study. Sleep, 6, 77–81.

Freixa i Baqué, E., & de Bonis, M. (1983). Electrodermal asymmetry during human sleep. Biological Psychology, 17, 145–151.

Fricke, M. (1932). Theory of electrolytic polarization. *Philosophical Magazine and Journal of Science, 14,* 310–318.

Fried, R. (1982). On-line analysis of the GSR. *The Pavlovian Journal of Biological Science, 17,* 89–94.

Frith, C. D., & Allen, H. A. (1983). The skin conductance orienting response as an index of attention. *Biological Psychology, 17,* 27–39.

Frith, C. D., Stevens, M., Johnstone, E. C., & Crow, T. J. (1979). Skin conductance responsivity during acute episodes of schizophrenia as a predictor of symptomatic improvement. *Psychological Medicine, 9,* 101–106.

Frith, C. D., Stevens, M., Johnstone, E. C., & Crow, T. J. (1982). Skin conductance habituation during acute episodes of schizophrenia: Qualitative differences from anxious and depressed patients. *Psychological Medicine, 12,* 575–583.

Frith, C. D., Stevens, M., Johnstone, E. C., & Owens, D. G. C. (1984). The effects of chronic treatment with amitriptyline and diazepam on electrodermal activity in neurotic outpatients. *Physiological Psychology, 12,* 247–252.

Fuentes, I., Merita, M. G., Miquel, M., & Rojo, J. (1993). Relationships between electrodermal activity and symtomatology in schizophrenia. *Psychopathology, 26,* 47–52.

Fung, M. T., Raine, A., Loeber, R., Lynam, D. R., Steinhauer, S. R., Venables, P. H., & Stouthamer-Loeber, A. (2005). Reduced electrodermal activity in psychopathy-prone adolescents. *Journal of Abnormal Psychology, 114,* 187–196.

Furchtgott, E., & Busemeyer, J. K. (1979). Heart rate and skin conductance during cognitive processes as a function of age. *Journal of Gerontology, 34,* 183–190.

Furedy, J. J. (1967). Classical appetitive conditioning of the GSR with cool air as UCS, and the roles of UCS onset and offset as reinforcers of the CR. *Journal of Experimental Psychology, 75,* 73–80.

Furedy, J. J. (1968). Human orienting reaction as a function of electrodermal-versus plethysmographic response modes and single versus alternating stimulus series. *Journal of Experimental Psychology, 77,* 70–78.

Furedy, J. J. (1970). Test of the preparatory adaptive response interpretation of aversive classical autonomic conditioning. *Journal of Experimental Psychology, 84*, 301–307.

Furedy, J. J. (1972). Electrodermal recovery time as a supra sensitive autonomic index of anticipated intensity of threatened shock. *Psychophysiology, 9*, 281–282.

Furedy, J. J. (1975). An integrative progress report on informational control in humans: Some laboratory findings and methodological claims. *Australian Journal of Psychology, 27*, 61–83.

Furedy, J. J. (1986). Lie detection as psychophysiological differentiation: Some fine lines. In M. G. H. Coles, E. Donchin, & S. W. Porges (Eds.), *Psychophysiology: Systems, processes, and applications* (pp. 683–701). Amsterdam: Elsevier.

Furedy, J. J. (1987). Evaluating polygraphy from a psychophysiological perspective: A specific-effects analysis. *The Pavlovian Journal of Biological Science, 22*, 145–152.

Furedy, J. J., Arabian, J. M., Thiels, E., & George, L. (1982). Direct and continuous measurement of relational learning in human Pavlovian conditioning. *The Pavlovian Journal of Biological Science, 17*, 69–79.

Furedy, J. J., & Ben-Shakhar, G. (1991). The roles of deception, intention to deceive, and motivation to avoid detection in the psychophysiological detection of guilty knowledge. *Psychophysiology, 28*, 163–171.

Furedy, J. J., Damke, B., & Boucsein, W. (2000). Revisiting the learning-without-awareness question in human Pavlovian autonomic conditioning: Focus on extinction in a dichotic listening paradigm. *Integrative Physiological and Behavioral Science, 35*, 17–34.

Furedy, J. J., Davis, C., & Gurevich, M. (1988). Differentiation of deception as a psychological process: A psychophysiological approach. *Psychophysiology, 25*, 683–688.

Furedy, J. J., Gigliotti, F., & Ben-Shakhar, G. (1994). Electrodermal differentiation of deception: The effect of choice vs. no choice of deceptive items. *International Journal of Psychophysiology, 18*, 13–22.

Furedy, J. J., & Heslegrave, R. J. (1983). A consideration of recent criticisms of the t-wave amplitude index of myocardial sympathetic activity. *Psychophysiology, 20*, 204–211.

Furedy, J. J., & Heslegrave, R. J. (1988). Validity of the lie detector: A psychphysiology perspective. *Criminal Justice and Behavior, 15*, 219–246.

Furedy, J. J., & Klajner, F. (1972). Unconfounded autonomic indexes of the aversiveness of signaled and unsignaled shocks. *Journal of Experimental Psychology, 92*, 313–318.

Furedy, J. J., & Klajner, F. (1974). On evaluating autonomic and verbal indices of negative preception. *Psychophysiology, 11*, 121–124.

Furedy, J. J., Posner, R. T., & Vincent, A. (1991). Electrodermal differentiation of deception: Perceived accuracy and perceived memorial content manipulations. *International Journal of Psychophysiology, 11*, 91–97.

Furedy, J. J., & Poulos, C. X. (1977). Short-interval classical SCR conditioning and the stimulus-sequence-change-elicited OR: The case of the empirical red herring. *Psychophysiology, 14*, 351–359.

Furedy, J. J., Poulos, C. X., & Schiffman, K. (1975). Contingency theory and classical autonomic excitatory and inhibitory conditioning: Some problems of assessment and interpretation. *Psychophysiology, 12*, 98–105.

Furedy, J. J., & Riley, D. M. (1987). Human Pavlovian autonomic conditioning and the cognitive paradigm. In G. Davey (Ed.), *Cognitive processes and Pavlovian conditioning in humans* (pp. 1–25). New York: Wiley.

Furedy, J. J., & Schiffman, K. (1971). Test of the propriety of the traditional discriminative control procedure in Pavlovian electrodermal and plethysmographic conditioning. *Journal of Experimental Psychology, 91*, 161–164.

Furedy, J. J., & Schiffman, K. (1973). Concurrent measurement of autonomic and cognitive processes in a test of the traditional discriminative control procedure for Pavlovian electrodermal conditioning. *Journal of Experimental Psychology, 100*, 210–217.

Furedy, J. J., & Schiffmann, K. (1974). Interrelationships between human classical differential electrodermal conditioning, orienting reaction, responsivity, and awareness of stimulus contingencies. *Psychophysiology, 11*, 58–67.

Furedy, J. J., & Scull, J. (1971). Orienting-reaction theory and an increase in the human GSR following stimulus change which is unpredictable but not contrary to prediction. *Journal of Experimental Psychology, 88*, 292–294.

Gaebelein, J., Taylor, S. P., & Borden, R. (1974). Effects of an external cue on psychophysiological reactions to a noxious event. *Psychophysiology, 11*, 315–320.

Gainotti, G. (1979). The relationship between emotions and cerebral dominance: A review of clinical and experimental evidence. In J. H. Gruzelier & P. Flor-Henry (Eds.), *Hemisphere asymmetries of function in psychopathology* (pp. 21–34). Amsterdam: Elsevier.

Galbrecht, C. R., Dykman, R. A., Reese, W. G., & Suzuki, T. (1965). Intrasession adaptation and intersession extinction of the components of the orienting response. *Journal of Experimental Psychology, 70*, 585–597.

Gale, A., & Edwards, J. A. (Eds.). (1983). *Physiological correlates of human behaviour (Three volumes)*. London: Academic.

Gale, A., & Edwards, J. A. (1986). Individual differences. In M. G. H. Coles, E. Donchin, & W. Porges (Eds.), *Psychophysiology: Systems, processes, and applications* (pp. 431–507). Amsterdam: Elsevier.

Gao, Y., Raine, A., Dawson, M. E., Venables, P. H., & Mednick, S. A. (2007). Development of skin conductance orienting, habituation, and reorienting from ages 3 to 8 years: A longitudinal latent growth curve analysis. *Psychophysiology, 44*, 855–863.

Garwood, M., Engel, B. T., & Kusterer, J. P. (1981). Skin potential level: Age and epidermal hydration effects. *Journal of Gerontology, 36*, 7–13.

Garwood, M., Engel, B. T., & Quilter, R. E. (1979). Age differences in the effect of epidermal hydration on electrodermal activity. *Psychophysiology, 16*, 311–317.

Gatchel, R. J., McKinney, M. E., & Koebernick, L. F. (1977). Learned helplessness, depression, and physiological responding. *Psychophysiology, 14*, 25–31.

Gati, I., & Ben-Shakhar, G. (1990). Novelty and significance in orientation and habituation: A feature-matching approach. *Journal of Experimental Psychology. General, 119*, 251–263.

Gavazzeni, J., Wiens, S., & Fischer, H. (2008). Age effects to negative arousal differ for self-report and electrodermal activity. *Psychophysiology, 45*, 148–151.

Gaviria, B., Coyne, L., & Thetford, P. E. (1969). Correlation of skin potential and skin resistance measures. *Psychophysiology, 5*, 465–477.

Geer, J. H., & Davison, G. C. (1970). Reduction of stress in humans through nonveridical perceived control of aversive stimulation. *Journal of Personality and Social Psychology, 16*, 731–738.

Geer, J. H., & Maisel, E. (1972). Evaluating the effects of the prediction-control confound. *Journal of Personality and Social Psychology, 23*, 314–319.

Gellhorn, E. (1964). Motion and emotion: The role of proprioception in the physiology and pathology of the emotions. *Psychological Review, 71*, 457–472.

Germana, J. (1968). Rate of habituation and the law of initial values. *Psychophysiology, 5*, 31–36.

Giedke, H., & Bolz, J. (1980). Pre- and postimperative negative variation (CNV and PINV) under different conditions of controllability in depressed patients and healthy controls. In H. H. Kornhuber & L. Deecke (Eds.), *Motivation, motor and sensory processes of the brain. Electrical potentials, behavior and clinical use* (pp. 579–582). Amsterdam: Elsevier.

Giedke, H., & Coenen, T. (1986). Die medikamentöse Behandlung von Angstzuständen. In W. Janke & P. Netter (Eds.), *Angst und Psychopharmaka* (pp. 207–234). Stuttgart: Kohlhammer.

Goldberg, L. R. (1992). The development of markers for the Big-Five factor structure. *Psychological Assessment, 4*, 26–42.

Goldstein, J. M., Jerram, M., Abbs, B., Whitfield-Gabrieli, S., & Makris, N. (2010). Sex differences in stress response circuitry activation dependent on female hormonal cycle. *Journal of Neuroscience, 30*, 431–438.

Goldstein, J. M., Jerram, M., Poldrack, R., Ahern, T., Kennedy, D. N., Seidman, L. J., & Makris, N. (2005). Hormonal cycle modulates arousal circuitry in women using functional magnetic resonance imaging. *Journal of Neuroscience, 25*, 9309–9316.

Goldstein, I. B., & Shapiro, D. (1988). Cardiovascular responses to mental arithmetic and handgrip during different conditions of postural change. *Psychophysiology, 25*, 127–136.

Gomez, R., & McLaren, S. (1997). The effects of reward and punishment on response disinhibition, moods, heart rate and skin conductance level during instrumental learning. *Personality and Individual Differences, 23*, 305–316.

Gómez-Amor, J., Martínez-Selva, J. M., Román, F., Zamora, S., & Sastre, J. F. (1990). Electrodermal activity, hormonal levels and subjective experience during the menstrual cycle. *Biological Psychology, 30*, 125–139.

Gormezano, I., & Kehoe, E. J. (1975). Classical conditioning: Some methodological-conceptual issues. In W. K. Estes (Ed.), *Handbook of learning and cognitive processes* (Conditioning and behavior theory, Vol. 2, pp. 143–179). Hillsdale, NJ: Lawrence Erlbaum.

Gougerot, M. L. (1947). Recherches sur l'impédance cutanée en courant alternatif de basse fréquence au cours de differentes dermatoses. *Annales et Bulletin de Dermatologie, 8*, 101–111.

Gough, H. (1969). *Manual for the California psychological inventory*. Palo Alto: Consulting Psychologists Press.

Graham, F. K. (1973). Habituation and dishabituation of responses innervated by the autonomic nervous system. In H. V. S. Peeke & M. J. Herz (Eds.), *Habituation* (Behavioral studies, Vol. 1, pp. 163–218). New York: Academic.

Graham, F. K. (1979). Distinguishing among orienting, defense, and startle reflexes. In H. D. Kimmel, E. H. van Olst, & J. F. Orlebeke (Eds.), *The orienting reflex in humans* (pp. 137–167). Hillsdale, NJ: Erlbaum.

Gray, J. A. (1970). The psychophysiological basis of introversion-extraversion. *Behaviour Research and Therapy, 8*, 249–266.

Gray, J. A. (1973). Causal theories of personality and how to test them. In J. R. Royce (Ed.), *Multivariate analysis and psychological theory* (pp. 409–463). New York: Academic.

Gray, J. A. (1981). A critique of Eysenck's theory of personality. In H. J. Eysenck (Ed.), *A model for personality* (pp. 246–276). New York: Springer.

Gray, J. A. (1982). *The neuropsychology of anxiety: An inquiry into the functions of the septo-hippocampal system*. Oxford: Clarendon.

Gray, J. A. (1987). A conceptual nervous system for avoidance behaviour. In J. A. Gray (Ed.), *The psychology of fear and stress* (pp. 241–331). Cambridge: University Press.

Gray, J. A., & McNaughton, N. (2000). *The neuropsychology of anxiety* (2nd ed.). New York: Oxford University Press.

Gray, J. A., & Smith, P. T. (1969). An arousal-decision model for partial reinforcement and discrimination learning. In R. Gilbert & N. S. Sutherland (Eds.), *Animal discrimination learning* (pp. 243–272). New York: Academic.

Greenwald, M. K., Cook, E. W., & Lang, P. J. (1989). Affective judgement and psychophysiological response: Dimensional covariation in the evaluation of pictorial stimuli. *Journal of Psychophysiology, 3*, 51–64.

Grey, S. J., & Smith, B. L. (1984). A comparison between commercially available electrode gels and purpose-made gel, in the measurement of electrodermal activity. *Psychophysiology, 21*, 551–557.

Grice, K. A., & Verbov, J. (1977). Sweat glands and their disorders. In A. Rook (Ed.), *Recent advances in dermatology* (Vol. 4, pp. 155–198). New York: Churchill Livingstone.

Grillon, C. (2002). Associative learning deficits increase symptoms of anxiety in humans. *Biological Psychiatry, 51*, 851–858.

Grillon, C., & Davis, M. (1997). Fear-potentiated startle conditioning in humans: Explicit and contextual cue conditioning following paired vs. unpaired training. *Psychophysiology, 34*, 451–458.

Grimnes, S. (1982). Psychogalvanic reflex and changes in electrical parameters of dry skin. *Medical & Biological Engineering & Computing, 20*, 734–740.

Grimnes, S. (1983). Impedance measurement of individual skin surface electrodes. *Medical & Biological Engineering & Computing, 21*, 750–755.

Grimnes, S., & Martinsen, O. J. (2008). *Bioimpedance and bioelectricity basics* (2nd edition.). London: Academic Press.

Grimnes, S., Jabbari, A., Martinsen, O. G., & Tronstad, C. (2011). Electrodermal activity by DC potential and AC conductance measured simultaneously at the same skin site. *Skin Research and Technology, 17*, 26–34.

Grings, W. W. (1960). Preparatory set variables related to classical conditioning of autonomic responses. *Psychological Review, 67*, 243–252.

Grings, W. W. (1969). Anticipatory and preparatory electrodermal behavior in paired stimulation situations. *Psychopysiology, 5*, 597–611.

Grings, W. W. (1974). Recording of electrodermal phenomena. In R. F. Thompson & M. M. Patterson (Eds.), *Methods in physiological psychology* (Bioelectric recording techniques, Part C: Receptor and effector processes, Vol. 1, pp. 273–296). New York: Academic.

Grings, W. W., & Dawson, M. E. (1973). Complex variables in conditioning. In W. Prokasy & D. C. Raskin (Eds.), *Electrodermal activity in psychological research* (pp. 203–254). New York: Academic.

Grings, W. W., & Dawson, M. E. (1978). *Emotions and bodily responses: A psychophysiological approach*. New York: Academic.

Grings, W. W., Givens, M. C., & Carey, C. A. (1979). Contingency contrast effects in discrimination conditioning. *Journal of Experimental Psychology. General, 108*, 281–295.

Grings, W. W., & Schell, A. M. (1969). Magnitude of electrodermal response to a standard stimulus as a function of intensity and proximity of a prior stimulus. *Journal of Comparative and Physiological Psychology, 67*, 77–82.

Groeppel-Klein, A. (2005). Arousal and consumer in-store behavior. *Brain Research Bulletin, 67*, 428–437.

Groeppel-Klein, A., Domke, A., & Bartmann, B. (2006). Pretty woman or Erin Brokovich? Unconscious and conscious reactions to commercials and movies shaped by fairy tale archetypes – Results from two experimental studies. *Advances in Consumer Research, 33*, 163–174.

Groeppel-Klein, A., Germelmann, C., & Woratschek, H. (2007). Arousal and consumer decision-making. *Proceedings of the 36th European marketing academy conference*. Reykjavik, Iceland.

Gross, J. J. (1998). Antecedent- and response-focused emotion regulation: Divergent consequences for experience, expression, and physiology. *Journal of Personality and Social Psychology, 74*, 224–237.

Gross, J. J., Carstensen, L. L., Pasupathi, M., Tsai, J., Skorpen, C. G., & Hsu, A. Y. C. (1997). Emotion and aging: Experience, expression and control. *Psychology and Aging, 12*, 590–599.

Gross, J. J., & Levenson, R. W. (1993). Emotional suppression: Physiology, self-report, and expressive behavior. *Journal of Personality and Social Psychology, 64*, 970–986.

Gross, J. J., & Levenson, R. W. (1997). Hiding feelings: The acute effects of inhibiting negative and positive emotion. *Journal of Abnormal Psychology, 106*, 95–103.

Gross, C. G., & Sergent, J. (1992). Face recognition. *Current Opinion in Neurobiology, 2*, 156–161.

Groves, P. M., & Thompson, R. F. (1970). Habituation: A dual-process theory. *Psychological Review, 77*, 419–450.

Grueninger, W. E., Kimble, D. P., Grueninger, J., & Levine, S. (1965). GSR and corticosteroid response in monkeys with frontal ablations. *Neuropsychologia, 3*, 205–216.

Gruzelier, J. H. (1973). Bilateral asymmetry of skin conductance orienting activity and levels in schizophrenics. *Biological Psychology, 1*, 21–41.

Gruzelier, J. H. (1976). Clinical attributes of schizophrenic skin conductance responders and nonresponders. *Psychological Medicine, 6*, 245–249.

Gruzelier, J. H. (1979). Lateral asymmetries in electrodermal activity and psychosis. In J. H. Gruzelier & P. Flor-Henry (Eds.), *Hemisphere asymmetries of function in psychopathology* (pp. 701–713). Amsterdam: Elsevier.

Gruzelier, J. H. (1983). Disparate syndromes in psychosis delineated by direction of electrodermal response lateral asymmetry. In P. Flor-Henry & J. Gruzelier (Eds.), *Laterality and psychopathology* (pp. 525–538). Amsterdam: Elsevier.

Gruzelier, J. H. (1993). The laterality of electrodermal responses: A new perspective on individual differences in personality and psychopathology. In J.-C. Roy, W. Boucsein, C. D. Fowles, & J. H. Gruzelier (Eds.), *Progress in electrodermal research* (pp. 251–270). New York: Plenum.

Gruzelier, J. H., & Connolly, J. F. (1979). Differential drug action on electrodermal orienting responses as distinct from nonspecific responses and electrodermal levels. In H. D. Kimmel, E. H. van Olst, & J. F. Orlebeke (Eds.), *The orienting reflex in humans* (pp. 701–713). Hillsdale, NJ: Erlbaum.

Gruzelier, J. H., Eves, F., & Connolly, J. (1981a). Reciprocal hemispheric influences on response habituation in the electrodermal system. *Physiological Psychology, 9*, 313–317.

Gruzelier, J. H., Eves, F., Connolly, J. F., Eves, F., Hirsch, S. R., Zaki, S., Weller, M., & Yorkston, N. (1981b). Effect of propanolol and phenothiazines on electrodermal orienting and habituation in schizophrenia. *Psychological Medicine, 11*, 93–108.

Gruzelier, J. H., Eves, F., Connolly, J. F., & Hirsch, S. R. (1981c). Orienting, habituation, sensitization, and dishabituation in the electrodermal system of consecutive, drug-free admissions for schizophrenia. *Biological Psychology, 12*, 187–209.

Gruzelier, J. H., & Hammond, N. V. (1976). Schizophrenia: A dominant hemisphere temporal-limbic disorder? *Research Communications in Psychology, Psychiatry and Behavior, 1*, 32–72.

Gruzelier, J. H., & Hammond, N. V. (1977). The effect of chlorpromazine upon bilateral asymmetries in bioelectrical skin reactivity of schizophrenics. *Studia Psychologica, 19*, 40–51.

Gruzelier, J. H., & Hammond, N. V. (1978). The effect of chlorpromazine upon psychophysiological, endocrine and information processing measures in schizophrenia. *Journal of Psychiatric Research, 14*, 167–182.

Gruzelier, J. H., & Manchanda, R. (1982). The syndrome of schizophrenia: Relations between electrodermal response, lateral asymmetries and clinical ratings. *The British Journal of Psychiatry, 141*, 488–495.

Gruzelier, J. H., Nixon, P. G. F., Liddiard, D., Pugh, S., & Baxter, R. (1986). Retarded habituation and lateral asymmetries in electrodermal activity in cardiovascular disorders. *International Journal of Psychophysiology, 3*, 219–226.

Gruzelier, J., Sergeant, J., & Eves, F. (1988). The use of bilateral skin conductance measurement in elucidating stimulus versus response processing influences on the orienting reaction. *International Journal of Psychophysiology, 6*, 195–205.

Gruzelier, J. H., & Venables, P. H. (1972). Skin conductance orienting activity in a heterogeneous sample of schizophrenics: Possible evidence of limbic dysfunction. *The Journal of Nervous and Mental Disease, 155*, 277–287.

Gruzelier, J. H., & Venables, P. H. (1973). Skin conductance responses to tones with and without attentional significance in schizophrenic and nonschizophrenic psychiatric patients. *Neuropsychologia, 11*, 221–230.

Gruzelier, J. H., & Venables, P. H. (1974). Bimodality and lateral asymmetry of skin conductance orienting activity in schizophrenics: Replication and evidence of lateral asymmetry in patients with depression and disorders of personality. *Biological Psychiatry, 8*, 55–73.

Gudjonsson, G. H. (1981). Self-reported emotional disturbance and its relation to electrodermal reactivity; defensiveness and trait anxiety. *Personality and Individual Differences, 2*, 47–52.

Gudjonsson, G. H. (1986). The validity of polygraph techniques in lie detection. In D. Papakostopoulos, S. Butler, & I. Martin (Eds.), *Clinical and experimental neuropsychophysiology* (pp. 448–465). Dover: Croom Helm.

Guidotti, A., Baraldi, M., Schwartz, J. P., & Costa, E. (1979). Molecular mechanisms regulating the interaction between benzodiazepines and GABA receptors in the central nervous system. *Pharmacology Biochemistry and Behavior, 10*, 803–807.

Guinjoan, S. M., Bernabó, J. L., & Cardinali, D. P. (1995). Cardiovascular test of autonomic function and sympathetic skin responses in patients with major depression. *Journal of Neurology, Neuosurgery, and Psychiatry, 58*, 299–302.

Gutrecht, J. A., Suarez, G. A., & Denny, B. E. (1993). Sympathetic skin response in multiple sclerosis. *Journal of the Neurological Sciences, 118*, 88–91.

Haapaniemi, T. H., Korpelainen, J. T., Tolonen, U., Suominen, K., Sotaniemi, K. A., & Myllylä, V. V. (2000). Suppressed sympathetic skin response in Parkinson disease. *Clinical Autonomic Research, 10*, 337–342.

Haarmann, A., Boucsein, W., & Schaefer, F. (2009). Combining electrodermal responses and cardiovascular measures for probing adaptive automation during simulated flight. *Applied Ergonomics, 40*, 1026–1040.

Hagemann, T., Levenson, R. W., & Gross, J. J. (2006). Expressive suppression during an acoustic startle. *Psychophysiology, 43*, 104–112.

Hagfors, C. (1964). Beiträge zur Meßtheorie der hautgalvanischen Reaktion. *Psychologische Beiträge, 7*, 517–538.

Haider, M. (1969). Elektrophysiologische Indikatoren der Aktiviertheit. In W. Schönpflug (Ed.), *Methoden der Aktivierungsforschung* (pp. 125–156). Bern: Huber.

Haider, M. (1970). Neuropsychology of attention, expectation, and vigilance. In D. I. Mostofski (Ed.), *Attention: Contemporary theory and analysis* (pp. 419–432). New York: Appleton-Century-Crofts.

Hamann, S., Monarch, E. S., & Goldstein, F. C. (2002). Impaired fear conditioning in Alzheimer's disease. *Neuropsychologia, 40*, 1187–1195.

Hanisch, L. J., Palmer, S. C., Donahue, A., & Coyne, J. C. (2007). Validation of sternal skin conductance for detection of hot flashes in prostate cancer survivors. *Psychophysiology, 44*, 189–193.

Hare, R. D. (1975). Psychopathy. In P. H. Venables & M. J. Christie (Eds.), *Research in psychophysiology* (pp. 325–348). London: Wiley.

Hare, R. D. (1978a). Psychopathy and electrodermal responses to nonsignal stimulation. *Biological Psychology, 6*, 237–246.

Hare, R. D. (1978b). Electrodermal and cardiovascular correlates of psychopathy. In R. D. Hare & D. Schalling (Eds.), *Psychopathic behaviour: Approaches to research* (pp. 107–143). New York: Wiley.

Hare, R. D., Wood, K., Britain, S., & Frazelle, J. (1971). Autonomic responses to affective visual stimulation: Sex differences. *Journal of Experimental Research in Personality, 5*, 14–22.

Harris, M. D. (1943). Habituatory response decrement in the intact organism. *Psychological Bulletin, 40*, 385–422.

Hart, J. D. (1974). Physiological responses of anxious and normal subjects to simple signal and non-signal auditory stimuli. *Psychophysiology, 11*, 443–451.

Harten, H. U. (1980). *Physik für Mediziner*. Berlin: Springer.

Hashimoto, K. (1978). The eccrine gland. In A. Jarrett (Ed.), *The physiology and pathophysiology of the skin* (The sweat glands, skin permeation, lymphatics, and the nails, Vol. 5, pp. 1543–1573). New York: Academic.

Hastrup, J. L. (1979). Effects of electrodermal lability and introversion on vigilance decrement. *Psychophysiology, 16*, 302–310.

Hastrup, J. L., & Katkin, E. S. (1976). Electrodermal lability: An attempt to measure its psychological correlates. *Psychophysiology, 13*, 296–301.

Hazlett, E. A., Dawson, M. E., Buchsbaum, M. S., & Nuechterlein, K. H. (1993). Reduced regional brain metabolism assessed by positron emission tomography in electrodermal nonresponder schizophrenics: A pilot study. *Journal of Abnormal Psychology, 102*, 39–46.

Healey, J. A., & Picard, R. W. (2005). Detecting stress during real-world driving tasks using physiological sensors. *IEEE Transactions on Intelligent Transportation Systems*, 156–166.

Hécaen, H., & Sauguet, J. (1971). Cerebral dominance in left handed subjects. *Cortex, 7*, 19–48.

Heimann, H. (1969). Typologische und statistische Erfassung depressiver Syndrome. In H. Hippius & H. Selbach (Eds.), *Das depressive Syndrom: Internationales Symposium, Berlin 1968* (pp. 279–290). München: Urban & Schwarzenberg.

Heimann, H. (1978). Changes of psychophysiological reactivity in affective disorders. *Archiv für Psychiatrie und Nervenkrankheiten, 225*, 223–231.

Heimann, H. (1979). Auf dem Wege zu einer einheitlichen psychophysiologischen Theorie depressiver Syndrome. *Praxis der Psychotherapie und Psychosomatik, 24*, 281–297.

Heimann, H. (1980). Psychophysiologische Aspekte in der Depressionsforschung. In H. Heimann & H. Giedke (Eds.), *Neue Perspektiven in der Depressionsforschung* (pp. 85–87). Bern: Huber.

Heimer, L., Van Hoesen, G. W., Trimble, M., & Zahm, D. S. (2008). *Anatomy of neuropsychiatry: The new anatomy of the basal forebrain and its implications for neuropsychiatric illness.* London: Academic.

Helander, M. (1974). Drivers' physiological reactions and control operations as influenced by traffic events. *Zeitschrift für Verkehrssicherheit, 20,* 174–187.

Helander, M. (1978). Applicability of drivers' electrodermal response to the design of the traffic environment. *Journal of Applied Psychology, 63,* 481–488.

Helmer, J. E., & Furedy, J. J. (1968). Operant conditioning of GSR amplitude. *Journal of Experimental Psychology, 78,* 463–467.

Hermann, L., & Luchsinger, B. (1878). Über die Secretionsströme der Haut bei der Katze. *Pflügers Archiv für die gesamte Physiologie, 19,* 300–319.

Herpertz, S. C., Mueller, B., Qunaibi, M., Lichterfeld, C., Konrad, K., & Herpertz-Dahlmann, B. (2005). Response to emotional stimuli in boys with conduct disorder. *The American Journal of Psychiatry, 162,* 1100–1107.

Herrmann, F., Ippen, H., Schaefer, H., & Stüttgen, G. (1973). *Biochemie der Haut.* Stuttgart: Thieme.

Hettema, J. M., Annas, P., Neale, M. C., Kendler, K. S., & Fredrikson, M. (2003). A twin study of the genetics of fear conditioning. *Archives of General Psychiatry, 60,* 702–708.

Hinton, J., O'Neill, M., Dishman, J., & Webster, S. (1979). Electrodermal indices of public offending and recidivism. *Biological Psychology, 9,* 297–309.

Hiroshige, Y., & Iwahara, S. (1978). Digital and cephalic vasomotor orienting responses to indifferent, signal, and verbal stimuli. *Psychophysiology, 15,* 226–232.

Hirstein, W., & Ramachandran, V. S. (1997). Capgras syndrome: A novel probe for understanding the neural representation of the identity and familiarity of persons. *Proceedings of the Royal Society of London, 264,* 437–444.

Hodges, W. E. (1976). The psychophysiology of anxiety. In M. Zuckerman & C. D. Spielberger (Eds.), *Emotions and anxiety: New concepts, methods, and applications* (pp. 175–194). Hillsdale, NJ: Erlbaum.

Hoefer, M., Allison, S. C., Schauer, G. G., Neuhaus, J. M., Hall, J., Dang, J. N., Weiner, M. W., Miller, B. L., & Rosen, H. J. (2008). Fear conditioning in Alzheimer's disease. *Brain, 131,* 1646–1657.

Holloway, F. A., & Parsons, O. A. (1969). Unilateral brain damage and bilateral skin conductance levels in humans. *Psychophysiology, 6,* 138–148.

Holmes, D. S., Frost, D. O., Bennett, D. H., Nielsen, D. H., & Lutz, D. J. (1981). Effectiveness of skin resistance biofeedback for controlling arousal in non-stressful and stressful situations: Two experiments. *Journal of Psychosomatic Research, 25,* 205–211.

Holmes, D. S., McGilley, B. M., & Houston, B. K. (1984). Task-related arousal of type A and type B persons: Level of challenge and response specifity. *Journal of Personality and Social Psychology, 46,* 1322–1327.

Hölzl, R., Wilhelm, H., Lutzenberger, W., & Schandry, R. (1975). Galvanic skin response: Some methodological considerations on measurement, habituation, and classical conditioning. *Archiv für Psychologie (Archives of Psychology), 127,* 1–22.

Honts, C. R. (2004). The psychophysiological detection of deception. In P. Granhag & L. Strömwall (Eds.), *Detection of deception in forensic contexts* (pp. 103–123). London: Cambridge University Press.

Honts, C. R., & Amato, S. (2007). Automation of a screening polygraph test increases accuracy. *Psychology, Crime and Law, 13,* 187–199.

Honts, C. R., Raskin, D. C., & Kircher, J. C. (1987). Effects of physical countermeasures and their electromyographic detection during polygraph tests for deception. *Journal of Psychophysiology, 1,* 241–247.

Hord, D. J., Johnson, L. C., & Lubin, A. (1964). Differential effect of the law of initial value (LIV) on autonomic variables. *Psychophysiology, 1,* 79–87.

Hori, T. (1982). Electrodermal and electro-oculographic activity in a hypnagogic state. *Psychophysiology, 19,* 668–672.

Hot, P., Leconte, P., & Sequeira, H. (2005). Diurnal autonomic variations and emotional reactivity. *Biological Psychology, 69*, 261–270.

Hot, P., Naveteur, J., Leconte, P., & Sequeira, H. (1999). Diurnal variations of tonic electrodermal activity. *International Journal of Psychophysiology, 33*, 223–230.

Houdas, Y., & Ring, E. F. J. (1982). *Human body temperature: Its measurement and regulation.* New York: Plenum.

Houston, B. K. (1983). Psychophysiological responsivity and the type A behavior pattern. *Journal of Research in Personality, 17*, 22–39.

Hoyt, C. J. (1941). Note on a simplified method of computing test reliability. *Educational and Psychological Measurement, 1*, 93–95.

Hu, S., McChesney, K. A., Player, K. A., Bahl, A. M., Buchanan, J. B., & Scozzafava, J. E. (1999). Systematic investigation of physiological correlates of motion sickness induced by viewing an optokinetic rotating drum. *Aviation, Space, and Environmental Medicine, 70*, 759–765.

Huber, D., Henrich, G., & Gündel, H. (2005). Psychophysiological response patterns of migraine patients in two habituation tests. *Headache, 45*, 1375–1387.

Huck, S. W., & McLean, R. A. (1975). Using repeated measures ANOVA to analyse the data from pretest-posttest design: A potentially confusing task. *Psychological Bulletin, 82*, 511–518.

Hugdahl, K. (1984). Hemispheric asymmetry and bilateral electrodermal recordings: A review of the evidence. *Psychophysiology, 21*, 371–393.

Hugdahl, K. (1988). Bilateral electrodermal asymmetry: Past hopes and future prospects. *International Journal of Neuroscience, 39*, 33–44.

Hugdahl, K. (1995). *Psychophysiology. The mind-body perspective.* Cambridge, MA: Harvard University Press.

Hugdahl, K. (1998). Cortical control of human classical conditioning: Autonomic and positron emission tomography data. *Psychophysiology, 35*, 170–178.

Hugdahl, K., Broman, J.-E., & Franzon, M. (1983). Effects of stimulus content and brain lateralization on the habituation of the electrodermal orienting reaction (OR). *Biological Psychology, 17*, 153–168.

Hugdahl, K., & Öhman, A. (1980). Skin conductance conditioning to potentially phobic stimuli as a function of interstimulus interval and delay versus trace paradigm. *Psychophysiology, 17*, 348–355.

Humphrey, G. (1933). *The nature of learning.* New York: Harcourt Brace.

Hunt, D. P. (1977). A mathematical model of a simple human galvanic skin response upon its rate topography. *Bulletin of the Psychonomic Society, 10*, 149–151.

Hupka, R. B., & Levinger, G. (1967). Within subject correspondence between skin conductance and skin potential under conditions of activity and passivity. *Psychophysiology, 4*, 161–167.

Hustmyer, F. E., & Burdick, J. A. (1965). Consistency and test-retest reliability of spontaneous autonomic nervous system activity and eye movements. *Perceptual and Motor Skills, 20*, 1225–1228.

Hygge, S., & Hugdahl, K. (1985). Skin conductance recordings and the NaCl concentration of the electrolyte. *Psychophysiology, 22*, 365–367.

Iaboni, F., Douglas, V. I., & Ditto, B. (1997). Psychophysiological response of ADHD children to reward and extinction. *Psychophysiology, 34*, 116–123.

Iacono, W. G. (1982). Bilateral electrodermal habituation-dishabituation and resting EEG in remitted schizophrenics. *The Journal of Nervous and Mental Disease, 170*, 91–101.

Iacono, W. G. (1985). Psychophysiologic markers of psychopathology: A review. *Canadian Psychology, 26*, 96–112.

Iacono, W. G. (1991). Psychophysiological assessment of psychopathology. *Psychological Assessment, 3*, 309–320.

Iacono, W. G. (2007). Detection of deception. In J. T. Cacioppo, L. G. Tassinary, & G. Berntson (Eds.), *Handbook of psychophysiology* (pp. 688–703). New York: Cambridge University Press.

Iacono, W. G., Boisvenu, G. A., & Fleming, J. A. (1984b). Effects of diazepam and methylphenidate on the electrodermal detection of guilty knowledge. *Journal of Applied Psychology, 69*, 289–299.

Iacono, W. G., Ficken, J. W., & Beiser, M. (1999). Electrodermal activation in first-episode psychotic patients in their first-degree relatives. *Psychiatry Research, 88*, 25–39.

Iacono, W. G., & Lykken, D. T. (1979). The orienting response: Importance of instructions. *Schizophrenia Bulletin, 5*, 11–14.

Iacono, W. G., Lykken, D. T., Haroian, K. P., Peloquin, L. J., Valentine, R. H., & Tuason, V. B. (1984a). Electrodermal activity in euthymic patients with affective disorders: One-year retest stability and the effects of stimulus intensity and significance. *Journal of Abnormal Psychology, 93*, 304–311.

Iacono, W. G., Lykken, D. T., Peloquin, L. J., Lumry, A. E., Valentine, R. H., & Tuason, V. B. (1983). Electrodermal activity in euthymic unipolar and bipolar affective disorders: A possible marker for depression. *Archives of General Psychiatry, 40*, 557–565.

Iacono, W. G., Roshi, D., & Lacoste, D. (1987). Electrodermal activity in patients with Huntington's disease and their progeny. *Psychophysiology, 24*, 522–527.

Iacono, W. G., & Tuason, V. B. (1983). Bilateral electrodermal asymmetry in euthymic patients with unipolar and bipolar affective disorders. *Biological Psychiatry, 18*, 303–315.

Isamat, F. (1961). Galvanic skin responses from stimulation of limbic cortex. *Journal of Neurophysiology, 24*, 176–181.

Izard, C. E. (1971). *Face of emotion*. New York: Appleton.

Jackson, J. C. (1974). Amplitude and habituation of the orienting reflex as a function of stimulus intensity. *Psychophysiology, 11*, 647–658.

Jamner, L. D., & Tursky, B. (1987). Syndrome-specific descriptor profiling: A psychophysiological and psychophysical approach. *Health Psychology, 6*, 417–430.

Janes, C. L. (1982). Electrodermal recovery and stimulus significance. *Psychophysiology, 19*, 129–135.

Janes, C. L., Hesselbrock, V., & Stern, J. A. (1978). Parental psychopathology, age, and race as related to electrodermal activity of children. *Psychophysiology, 15*, 24–34.

Janes, C. L., & Stern, J. A. (1976). Electrodermal response configuration as a function of rated psychopathology in children. *The Journal of Nervous and Mental Disease, 162*, 184–194.

Janes, C. L., Strock, B. D., Weeks, D. G., & Worland, J. (1985). The effect of stimulus significance on skin conductance recovery. *Psychophysiology, 22*, 138–146.

Janes, C. L., Worland, J., & Stern, J. (1976). Skin potential and vasomotor responsiveness of black and white children. *Psychophysiology, 13*, 523–527.

Jänig, W. (1979). Reciprocal reaction patterns of sympathetic subsystems with respect to various afferent inputs. In C. M. Brooks, K. Koizumi, & A. Sato (Eds.), *Integrative functions of the autonomic nervous system*. Amsterdam: Elsevier.

Jänig, W. (1990). Functions of the sympathetic innervation of the skin. In A. D. Loewy & K. M. Spyer (Eds.), *Central regulation of autonomic functions* (pp. 334–347). New York: Oxford University Press.

Jänig, W., Sundlöf, G., & Wallin, B. G. (1983). Discharge patterns of sympathetic neurons supplying skeletal muscle and skin in man and cat. *Journal of the Autonomic Nervous System, 7*, 239–256.

Janke, W., & Netter, P. (1986). Angstbeeinflussung durch Psychopharmaka: Methodische Ansätze und Grundprobleme. In W. Janke & P. Netter (Eds.), *Angst und Psychopharmaka* (pp. 43–71). Stuttgart: Kohlhammer.

Janssen, S. A., Arntz, A., & Bouts, S. (1998). Anxiety and pain: Epinephrine-induced hyperalgesia and attentional influences. *Pain, 76*, 309–316.

Jarrett, A. (1973a). The epidermis and its relations with the dermis. In A. Jarrett (Ed.), *The physiology and pathophysiology of the skin* (1, Vol. The epidermis). New York: Academic.

Jarrett, A. (1973b). Normal epidermal keratinization. In A. Jarrett (Ed.), *The physiology and pathophysiology of the skin* (1, Vol. The epidermis). New York: Academic.

Jarrett, A. (Ed.). (1978). *The physiology and pathophysiology of the skin* (The sweat glands, skin permeation, lymphatics, and the nails, Vol. 5). New York: Academic.

Jarrett, A. (1980). Introduction: The permeability barrier. In A. Jarrett (Ed.), *The physiology and pathophysiology of the skin* (The mucous membranes, the action of vitamin A on the skin and mucous membranes, and transepidermal water loss, Vol. 6). New York: Academic.

Jeje, A., & Koon, D. (1989). An analysis on the rates and regulation of insensible water loss through the eccrine sweat glands. *Journal of Theoretical Biology, 141*, 303–324.

Jenkinson, P. M., Baker, S. R., Edelstyn, N. M. J., & Ellis, S. J. (2008). Does autonomic arousal distinguish good and bad decisions? *Journal of Psychophysiology, 22*, 141–149.

Johns, M. W., Cornell, B. A., & Masterton, J. P. (1969). Monitoring sleep of hospital patients by measurement of electrical resistance of skin. *Journal of Applied Psychology, 27*, 898–901.

Johnsen, B. H., Thayer, J. F., & Hugdahl, K. (1995). Affective judgment of the Ekman faces: A dimensional approach. *Journal of Psychophysiology, 9*, 193–202.

Johnson, L. C. (1963). Some attributes of spontaneous autonomic activity. *Journal of Comparative and Physiological Psychology, 56*, 415–422.

Johnson, L. C., & Corah, N. L. (1963). Racial differences in the skin. *Science, 139*, 766–767.

Johnson, L. C., & Landon, M. M. (1965). Eccrine sweat gland activity and racial differences in resting skin conductance. *Psychophysiology, 1*, 322–329.

Johnson, L. C., & Lubin, A. (1966). Spontaneous electrodermal activity during waking and sleeping. *Psychophysiology, 3*, 8–17.

Johnson, L. C., & Lubin, A. (1967). The orienting reflex during waking and sleeping. *Electroencephalography and Clinical Neurophysiology, 22*, 11–21.

Johnson, L. C., & Lubin, A. (1972). On planning psychophysiological experiments: Design, measurement, and analysis. In N. S. Greenfield & R. A. Sternbach (Eds.), *Handbook of psychophysiology* (pp. 125–158). New York: Holt, Rinehart, & Winston.

Johnson, H. J., & Schwartz, G. E. (1967). Suppression of GSR activity through operant reinforcement. *Journal of Experimental Psychology, 75*, 307–312.

Johnson, L. C., Townsend, R. E., & Wilson, M. R. (1975). Habituation during sleeping and waking. *Psychophysiology, 12*, 574–584.

Johnstone, E. C., Bourne, R. C., Crow, T. J., Frith, C. D., Gamble, S., Lofthouse, R., Owen, F., Owens, D. G. C., Robinson, J., & Stevens, M. (1981). The relationships between clinical response, psychophysiological variables and plasma levels of amitriptyline and diazepam in neurotic outpatients. *Psychopharmacology, 72*, 233–240.

Jones, J. E. (1962). Contiguity and reinforcement in relation to CS-UCS intervals in classical aversive conditioning. *Psychological Review, 69*, 176–186.

Jones, B. E., & Ayres, J. J. B. (1966). Significance and reliability of shock-induced changes in basal skin conductance. *Psychophysiology, 2*, 322–326.

Jörg, J., & Boucsein, W. (1998). Die sympathische Hautreaktion (SSR). *Klinische Neurophysiologie, 29*, 186–197.

Jörg, J., Jock, S., Boucsein, W., & Schäfer, F. (2004). Zur autonomen Dysregulation beim Freezing-Phänomen von Morbus-Parkinson-Patienten. *Ein ambulatorisches Monitoring und Videorecording. Aktuelle Neurologie, 31*, 338–346.

Jorgenson, R. J., Salinas, C. F., Dowben, J. S., & St. John, D. L. (1988). A population study on the density of palmar sweat pores. *Birth Defects, 24*, 51–63.

Jovanovic, U. J. (1971). *Normal sleep in man.* Stuttgart: Hippokrates.

Juniper, K., & Dykman, R. (1967). Skin resistance, sweat gland counts, salivary flow, and gastric secretion: Age, race, and sex differences, and intercorrelations. *Psychophysiology, 4*, 216–222.

Jutai, J. W., & Hare, R. D. (1983). Psychopathy and selective attention during performance of a complex perceptual-motor task. *Psychophysiology, 20*, 146–151.

Kaelbling, R., King, F. A., Achenbach, K., Branson, R., & Pasamanick, B. (1960). Reliability of autonomic responses. *Psychological Reports, 6*, 143–163.

Kahabka, G., Oppelt, W., Rohmert, W., & Müller, D. (1986). Geforderter Pilot – Gestreßter Fluggast. *Die Beanspruchung von Pilot und Passagier beim Motorflug. Aerokurier, 3*, 274–276.

Kahneman, D. (1973). *Attention and effort.* Englewood Cliffs: Prentice-Hall.

Katkin, E. S. (1965). Relationship between manifest anxiety and two indices of autonomic response to stress. *Journal of Personality and Social Psychology, 2*, 324–333.

Katkin, E. S. (1975). Electrodermal lability: A psychophysiological analysis of individual differences in response to stress. In C. D. Spielberger & I. G. Sarason (Eds.), *Stress and anxiety* (Vol. 2, pp. 141–176). New York: Wiley.

Katkin, E. S., & Deitz, S. R. (1973). Systematic desensitization. In W. F. Prokasy & D. C. Raskin (Eds.), *Electrodermal activity in psychological research* (pp. 347–376). New York: Academic.

Katkin, E. S., & McCubbin, R. J. (1969). Habituation of the orienting response as a function of individual differences in anxiety and autonomic lability. *Journal of Abnormal Psychology, 74*, 54–60.

Katkin, E. S., & Murray, E. N. (1968). Instrumental conditioning of autonomically mediated behavior: Theoretical and methodological issues. *Psychological Bulletin, 70*, 52–68.

Katsanis, J., & Iacono, W. G. (1992). Temporal lobe dysfunction and electrodermal nonresponding in schizophrenia. *Biological Psychiatry, 31*, 159–170.

Katz, R. (1984). Unconfounded electrodermal measures in assessing the aversiveness of predictable and unpredictable shocks. *Psychophysiology, 21*, 452–458.

Katz, R., & Wykes, T. (1985). The psychological difference between temporally predictable and unpredictable stressful events: Evidence for information control theories. *Journal of Personality and Social Psychology, 48*, 781–790.

Kaye, H. (1964). Skin conductance in the human neonate. *Child Development, 35*, 1297–1305.

Kayser, J. (1995). *Hemisphärenunterschiede, Emotion und bilaterale elektrodermale Aktivität.* Frankfurt am Main: Peter Lang.

Keller, P. (1963). Arbeitsphysiologie der Hornschicht in Grundzügen. In E. Schwarz, H. W. Spier, & G. Stüttgen (Eds.), *Handbuch der Haut- und Geschlechtskrankheiten* (Normale und pathologische Physiologie der Haut I, Vol. 1/3, pp. 36–89). Berlin: Springer.

Kendler, H. H. (1952). "What is learned?" – A theoretical blind alley. *Psychological Review, 59*, 269–277.

Kerassidis, S. (1994). Is palmar and plantar sweating thermoregulatory? *Acta Physiologica Scandinavica, 152*, 259–263.

Ketterer, M. W., & Smith, B. D. (1977). Bilateral electrodermal activity, lateralized cerebral processing and sex. *Psychophysiology, 14*, 513–516.

Ketterer, M. W., & Smith, B. D. (1982). Lateralized cortical/cognitive processing and electrodermal activity: Effects of subject and stimulus characteristics. *Psychophysiology, 19*, 328–329.

Kilpatrick, D. G. (1972). Differential responsiveness of two electrodermal indices to psychological stress and performance of a complex cognitive task. *Psychophysiology, 9*, 218–226.

Kim, K. H., Bang, S. W., & Kim, S. R. (2004). Emotion recognition system using short-term monitoring of physiological signals. *Medical & Biological Engineering & Computing, 42*, 419–427.

Kim, D. K. K., Shin, M. Y., Kim, C. E., Cho, H. S., & Kim, Y. S. (1993). Electrodermal responsiveness, clinical variables, and brain imaging in male chronic schizophrenics. *Biological Psychiatry, 33*, 786–793.

Kimble, G. A. (1961). *Hilgard and Marquis' conditioning and learning.* New York: Appleton-Century-Crofts.

Kimble, D. P., Bagshaw, M. H., & Pribram, K. H. (1965). The GSR of monkeys during orienting and habituation after selective partial ablations of the cingulate and frontal cortex. *Neuropsychologia, 3*, 121–128.

Kimmel, H. D. (1966). Inhibition of the unconditioned response in classical conditioning. *Psychological Review, 73*, 232–240.

Kimmel, H. D. (1967). Instrumental conditioning of autonomically mediated behavior. *Psychological Bulletin, 67*, 337–345.

Kimmel, H. D. (1973). Instrumental conditioning. In W. F. Prokasy & D. C. Raskin (Eds.), *Electrodermal activity in psychological research* (pp. 255–282). New York: Academic.

Kimmel, H. D., & Hill, F. A. (1961). A comparison of two electrodermal measures of response to stress. *Journal of Comparative and Physiological Psychology, 54*, 395–397.

Kimmel, H. D., & Kimmel, E. (1965). Sex differences in adaptation of the GSR under repeated applications of a visual stimulus. *Journal of Experimental Psychology, 70*, 536–537.

Kimmel, H. D., van Olst, E. H., & Orlebeke, J. F. (Eds.). (1979). *The orienting reflex in humans.* Hillsdale, NJ: Erlbaum.

Kimura, D. (1969). Spatial localization in left and right visual field. *Canadian Journal of Psychology, 23,* 445–458.

Kimura, D. (1973). The asymmetry of the human brain. *Scientific American, 228,* 70–78.

Kircher, J. C., & Raskin, D. C. (1988). Human versus computerized evaluations of polygraph data in a laboratory setting. *Journal of Applied Psychology, 73,* 291–302.

Kirsch, P., & Boucsein, W. (1997). Classical conditioning and information processing: Different mechanism for prepared and unprepared stimuli? *Integrative Physiological and Behavioral Science, 32,* 247–256.

Kirsch, P., Boucsein, W., & Baltissen, R. (1993). Electrodermal activity as an indicator of information processing in a nonaversive differential classical conditioning paradigm. *Integrative Physiological and Behavioral Science, 28,* 154–157.

Kiss, G. (1979). Messung der elektrischen Impedanz zur Bestimmung von durch Laugen bedingten Hautschädigungen. *Dermatologische Monatsschrift, 165,* 526–530.

Kiss, G., Horvath, I., & Hajdu, B. (1975). Elektrische Meßmethode und Gerät zum Nachweis bösartiger Wucherungen der Haut. *Dermatologische Monatsschrift, 161,* 374–378.

Klaschka, F. (1979). Arbeitsphysiologie der Hornschicht in Grundzügen. In E. Schwarz, H. W. Spier, & G. Stüttgen (Eds.), *Handbuch der Haut- und Geschlechtskrankheiten* (1/4A, Vol. Normale und pathologische Physiologie der Haut II, pp. 153–261). Berlin: Springer.

Kleck, R. E., Vaughan, R. C., Cartwright-Smith, J., Vaughan, K. B., Colby, C. Z., & Lanzetta, J. T. (1976). Effects of being observed on expressive, subjective, and physiological responses to painful stimuli. *Journal of Personality and Social Psychology, 34,* 1211–1218.

Kleeberg, J., Bruggimann, L., Annoni, J.-M., van Melle, G., Bogousslavsky, J., & Schluep, M. (2004). Altered decision-making in multiple sclerosis: A sign of impaired emotional reactivity? *Annals of Neurology, 56,* 787–795.

Klein, R. G., Abikoff, H., Klass, E., Ganeles, D., Seese, L. M., & Pollack, S. (1997). Clinical efficacy of methylphenidate in conduct disorder with and without attention deficit hyperactivity disorder. *Archives of General Psychiatry, 54,* 1073–1080.

Klein, D. F., & Rabkin, J. (Eds.). (1981). *Anxiety: New research and changing concepts.* New York: Raven.

Kleitman, N. (1963). *Sleep and wakefulness.* Chicago: University of Chicago Press.

Knezevic, W., & Bajada, S. (1985). Peripheral autonomic surface potential: A quantitative technique for recording sympathetic conduction in man. *Journal of the Neurological Sciences, 67,* 239–251.

Knygazev, G. G., Slobodskaya, H. R., & Wilson, G. D. (2002). Psychophysiological correlates of behavioural inhibition and activation. *Personality and Individual Differences, 33,* 647–660.

Koehler, T., & Weber, D. (1992). Psychophysiological reactions of patients with atopic dermatitis. *Journal of Psychosomatic Research, 36,* 391–394.

Koelega, H. S. (1990). Vigilance performance: A review of electrodermal predictors. *Perceptual and Motor Skills, 70,* 1011–1029.

Koella, W. P. (1986). Psycho-und neuropharmakologische Wirkungen und Wirkungsmechanismen von Anxiolytika vom Benzodiazepin-und Beta-Rezeptorenblocker-Typ. In W. Janke & P. Netter (Eds.), *Angst und Psychopharmaka* (pp. 73–90). Stuttgart: Kohlhammer.

Koepke, J. E., & Pribram, K. H. (1966). Habituation of GSR as a function of stimulus duration and spontaneous activity. *Journal of Comparative and Physiological Psychology, 61,* 442–448.

Koglbauer, I., Kallus K. W., Braunstingl, R., & Boucsein, W. (2011). Recovery training in simulator improves performance and psychophysiological state of pilots during simulated and real VFR flight. *The International Journal of Aviation Psychology, 21,* 307–324.

Köhler, T., Vögele, C., & Weber, D. (1989). Die Zahl der aktiven Schweißdrüsen (PSI, Palmar Sweat Index) als psychologischer Parameter. *Zeitschrift für Experimentelle und Angewandte Psychologie, 24,* 89–100.

Koller, M., Zidek, H., & Haider, M. (1986). Induced psychophysiological stress reactions in patients suffering from myocardial infarction and peptic ulcer. *Activitas Nervosa Superior, 28*, 123–128.

Kopacz, G. M., & Smith, B. D. (1971). Sex differences in skin conductance measures as a function of shock threat. *Psychophysiology, 8*, 293–303.

Kopp, M. S. (1984). Electrodermal characteristics in psychosomatic patients groups. *International Journal of Psychophysiology, 2*, 73–85.

Koriat, A., Averill, J. R., & Malmstrom, E. J. (1973). Individual differences in habituation: Some methodological and conceptual issues. *Journal of Research in Personality, 7*, 88–101.

Kornhuber, H. H., & Deecke, L. (1965). Hirnpotentialänderungen bei Willkürbewegungen und passiven Bewegungen des Menschen: Bereitschaftspotential und reafferente Potentiale. *Pflügers Archiv für die gesamte Physiologie, 284*, 1–17.

Korol, B., Bergfeld, G., & McLaughlin, L. J. (1975). Skin color and autonomic nervous system measures. *Psychology and Behavior, 14*, 575–578.

Korol, B., & Kane, R. (1978). An examination of the relationship between race, skin color and a series of autonomic nervous system measures. *The Pavlovian Journal of Biological Science, 13*, 121–132.

Korpelainen, J. T., Tolonen, U., Sotaniemi, K. A., & Myllylä, V. V. (1993). Suppressed sympathetic skin response in brain infarction. *Stroke, 24*, 1389–1392.

Kotses, H., Rapaport, I., & Glaus, K. D. (1978). Operant conditioning of skin resistance tonic levels. *Biofeedback and Self-Regulation, 3*, 43–50.

Koumans, A. J. R., Tursky, B., & Solomon, P. (1968). Electrodermal levels and fluctuations during normal sleep. *Psychophysiology, 5*, 300–306.

Krantz, D. S., Glass, D. C., & Snyder, M. L. (1974). Helplessness, stress level, and the coronary-prone behavior pattern. *Journal of Experimental Social Psychology, 10*, 284–300.

Krapohl, D. J., Senter, S. M., & Stern, B. A. (2005). An exploration of methods for analysis of multiple-issue relevant/irrelevant screening data. *Polygraph, 34*, 47–61.

Kreibig, S. D., Wilhelm, F. H., Roth, W. T., & Gross, J. J. (2007). Cardiovascular, electrodermal, and respiratory response patterns to fear- and sadness-inducing films. *Psychophysiology, 44*, 787–806.

Kring, A. M., & Gordon, A. H. (1998). Sex differences in emotion: Expression, experience, and physiology. *Journal of Personality and Social Psychology, 74*, 686–703.

Kroeber-Riel, W. (1979). Activation research: Psychobiological approaches in consumer research. *Journal of Consumer Research, 5*, 240–250.

Kroeber-Riel, W., & Weinberg, P. (2003). *Konsumentenverhalten*. München: Vahlen.

Krupski, A., Raskin, D. C., & Bakan, P. (1971). Physiological and personality correlates of commission errors in an auditory vigilance task. *Psychophysiology, 8*, 304–311.

Kryspin, J. (1965). The phoreographical determination of the electrical properties of human skin. *The Journal of Investigative Dermatology, 44*, 227–229.

Kubota, Y., Sato, W., Murai, T., Toichi, M., Ikeda, A., & Sengoku, A. (2000). Emotional cognition without awareness after unilateral temporal lobectomy in humans. *The Journal of Neuroscience, 97*(RC 97), 1–5.

Kugelmass, S., Faber, N., Ingraham, L. J., Frenkel, E., Nathan, M., Mirsky, A. F., & Ben-Shakhar, G. (1995). Reanalysis of SCOR and anxiety measures in the Israeli high-risk study. *Schizophrenia Bulletin, 21*, 205–217.

Kugelmass, S., & Lieblich, I. (1968). Relation between ethnic origin and GSR reactivity in psychophysiological detection. *Journal of Applied Psychology, 52*, 158–162.

Kugler, B. T., & Gruzelier, J. H. (1980). The influence of chlorpromazine and amylobarbitone on the recovery limb of the electrodermal response. *Psychiatry Research, 2*, 75–84.

Kuhmann, W. (1989). Experimental investigation of stress-inducing properties of system response times. *Ergonomics, 31*, 271–280.

Kuhmann, W., Boucsein, W., Schaefer, F., & Alexander, J. (1987). Experimental investigation of psychophysiological stress-reactions induced by different system response times in human-computer interaction. *Ergonomics, 30*, 933–943.

Kuhmann, W., Schaefer, F., & Boucsein, W. (1990). Effekte von Wartezeiten innerhalb einfacher Aufgaben: Eine Analogie zu Wartezeiten in der Mensch-Computer-Interaktion. *Zeitschrift für Experimentelle und Angewandte Psychologie, 37*, 242–265.

Kuno, Y. (1956). *Human perspiration*. Springfield: Thomas.

Kupfermann, J. (1985). Hypothalamus and limbic system II: Motivation. In E. R. Kandel & J. H. Schwartz (Eds.), *Principles of neural science*. Amsterdam: Elsevier.

Kushniruk, A., Rustenburg, J., & Ogilvie, R. (1985). Psychological correlates of electrodermal activity during REM sleep. *Sleep, 8*, 146–154.

LaBar, K. S., & Phelps, E. A. (1998). Arousal-mediated memory consolidation: Role of the medial temporal lobe in humans. *Psychological Science, 9*, 490–493.

LaBarbera, P. A., & Tucciarone, J. D. (1995). GSR reconsidered: A behavior-based approach to evaluating and improving the sales potency of advertising. *Journal of Advertising Research, 35*, 33–53.

Lacey, J. I. (1956). The evaluation of autonomic responses: Toward a general solution. *Annals of the New York Academy of Sciences, 67*, 125–163.

Lacey, J. I. (1967). Somatic response patterning and stress: Some revisions of activation theory. In M. H. Appley & R. Trumbull (Eds.), *Psychological stress: Issues in research* (pp. 14–37). New York: Appleton-Century-Crofts.

Lacey, J. I., & Lacey, B. C. (1958). The relationship of resting autonomic activity to motor impulsivity. *Research Publications – Association for Nervous and Mental Diseases, 36*, 144–209.

Lacey, J. I., & Lacey, B. C. (1970). Some autonomic-central nervous system interrelationships. In P. Black (Ed.), *Physiological correlates of emotion* (pp. 205–227). New York: Academic.

Lacey, B. C., & Lacey, J. I. (1974). Studies of heart rate and other bodily processes in sensorimotor behavior. In P. A. Obrist, A. H. Black, J. Brener, & L. V. DiCara (Eds.), *Cardiovascular psychophysiology* (pp. 538–564). Chicago: Aldine-Atherton.

Lacroix, J. M., & Comper, P. (1979). Lateralization in the electrodermal system as a function of cognitive/hemispheric manipulations. *Psychophysiology, 16*, 116–129.

Lademann, J., Jacobi, U., Surber, C., Weigmann, H. J., & Fluhr, J. W. (2008). The tape stripping procedure – Evaluation of some critical parameters. *European Journal of Pharmaceutics and Biopharmaceutics, 72*, 317–323.

Lader, M. H. (1964). The effect of cyclobarbitone on the habituation of the psychogalvanic reflex. *Brain, 87*, 321–340.

Lader, M. H. (1967). Palmar skin conductance measures in anxiety and phobic states. *Journal of Psychosomatic Research, 11*, 271–281.

Lader, M. H. (1970). The unit of quantification of the G.S.R. *Journal of Psychosomatic Research, 14*, 109–110.

Lader, M. H. (1975). *The psychophysiology of mental illness*. London: Routledge.

Lader, M. H. (1979). Anxiety reducing and sedation: A psychophysiological theory. *British Journal of Clinical Pharmacology, 7*, 91–105.

Lader, M. H., & Mathews, A. M. (1970). Physiological changes during spontaneous panic attacks. *Journal of Psychosomatic Research, 14*, 377–382.

Lader, M. H., & Petursson, H. (1983). Rational use of anxiolytic/sedative drugs. *Drugs, 25*, 514–528.

Lader, M. H., & Wing, L. (1964). Habituation of the psycho-galvanic reflex in patients with anxiety states and in normal subjects. *Journal of Neurology, Neurosurgery, and Psychiatry, 27*, 210–218.

Lader, M. H., & Wing, L. (1966). *Physiological measures, sedative drugs, and morbid anxiety*. London: Oxford University Press.

Lader, M. H., & Wing, L. (1969). Physiological measures in agitated and retarded depressed patients. *Journal of Psychiatric Research, 7*, 89–100.

Ladpli, R., & Wang, G. H. (1960). Spontaneous variations of skin potentials in footpads of normal striatal and spinal cats. *Journal of Neurophysiology, 23*, 448–452.

Landis, C., & Hunt, W. A. (1939). *The startle pattern*. New York: Farrar & Rinehart.

Lang, P. J. (1970). Stimulus control, response control and the desensitization of fear. In D. J. Lewis (Ed.), *Learning approaches to therapeutic behavior change* (pp. 148–173). Chicago: Aldine.

Lang, P. J., Bradley, M. M., & Cuthbert, B. N. (1990). Emotion, attention, and the startle reflex. *Psychological Review, 97*, 377–395.

Lang, P. J., Bradley, M. M., & Cuthbert, B. N. (1999). International Affective Picture System (IAPS): Digitized photographs, instruction manual and affective ratings. *Technical Report A-6*. Gainsville, FL: University of Florida.

Lang, H., Tuovinen, T., & Valleala, P. (1964). Amygdaloid afterdischarge and galvanic skin response. *Electroencephalography and Clinical Neurophysiology, 16*, 366–374.

Langosch, W., Brodner, G., & Foerster, F. (1983). Psychophysiological testing of postinfarction patients: A study determining the cardiological importance of psychophysiological variables. In T. M. Dembroski, T. H. Schmidt, & G. Blümchen (Eds.), *Biobehavioral bases of coronary heart disease* (pp. 197–227). Basel: Karger.

Langworthy, O. R., & Richter, C. P. (1930). The influence of efferent cerebral pathways upon the sympathetic nervous system. *Brain, 53*, 178–193.

Lanzetta, J. T., Cartwright-Smith, J., & Kleck, R. E. (1976). Effects of nonverbal dissimulation on emotional experience and autonomic arousal. *Journal of Personality and Social Psychology, 33*, 354–370.

Lapierre, Y. D. (1975). Clinical and physiological assessment of chlorazepate, diazepam and placebo in anxious neurotics. *International Journal of Clinical Pharmacology, 11*, 315–322.

Lapierre, Y. D., & Butter, H. J. (1980). Agitated and retarded depression: A clinical psychophysiological evaluation. *Neuropsychology, 6*, 217–223.

Lathrop, R. G. (1964). Measurement of analog sequential dependencies. *Human Factors, 6*, 233–239.

Latzman, R. D., Knutson, J. F., & Fowles, D. C. (2006). Schedule-induced electrodermal responding in children. *Psychophysiology, 43*, 623–632.

Lawler, K. (1980). Cardiovascular and electrodermal response patterns in heart rate reactive individuals during psychological stress. *Psychophysiology, 17*, 464–470.

Lawler, J. C., Davis, M. J., & Griffith, E. C. (1960). Electrical characteristics of the skin: The impedance of the surface sheath and deep tissues. *The Journal of Investigative Dermatology, 34*, 301–308.

Lawson, E. A. (1981). Skin conductance responses in Huntington's chorea progeny. *Psychophysiology, 18*, 32–35.

Lazarus, R. S. (1966). *Psychological stress and the coping process*. New York: McGraw-Hill.

Lazarus, R. S., & Opton, E. M. (1966). The study of psychological stress: A summary of theoretical formulations and empirical findings. In C. D. Spielberger (Ed.), *Anxiety and behavior* (pp. 225–262). New York: Academic.

Lazzaro, I., Gordon, E., Li, W., Lim, C. L., Plahn, M., Whitmont, S., Clarke, S., Barry, R. J., Dosen, A., & Meares, R. (1999). Simultaneous EEG and EDA measures in adolescent attention deficit hyperactivity disorder. *International Journal of Psychophysiology, 34*, 123–134.

LeDoux, J. (1996). *The emotional brain: The mysterious underpinnings of emotional life*. New York: Simon & Schuster.

Ledowski, T., Preuss, J., Ford, A., Paech, M. J., McTernan, C., Kapila, R., & Schug, S. A. (2007). New parameters of skin conductance compared with bispectral index® monitoring to assess emergence from total intravenous anaesthesia. *British Journal of Anaesthesia, 99*, 547–551.

Lenhart, R. E. (1985). Lowered skin conductance in a subsyndromal high-risk depressive sample: Response amplitudes versus tonic levels. *Journal of Abnormal Psychology, 94*, 649–652.

Léonard, T., Pepinà, C., Bond, A., & Treasure, J. (1998). Assessment of test-meal induced autonomic arousal in anorexic, bulimic and control females. *European Eating Disorders Review, 6*, 188–200.

Leonard, J. P., Podoll, K., Weiler, H.-T., & Lange, H. W. (1984). Habituation der elektrodermalen Orientierungsreaktion in der Diagnostik und Früherkennung der Chorea Huntington. *Zeitschrift für Experimentelle und Angewandte Psychologie, 31*, 447–463.

Lester, B. K., Burch, N. R., & Dossett, R. C. (1967). Nocturnal EEG-GSR profiles: The influence of presleep states. *Psychophysiology, 3*, 238–248.

Levander, S. E., Schalling, D. S., Lidberg, L., Bartfai, A., & Lidberg, Y. (1980). Skin conductance recovery time and personality in a group of criminals. *Psychophysiology, 17*, 105–111.

Levenson, R. W. (1988). Emotion and the autonomic nervous system: A prospectus for research on autonomic specificity. In H. L. Wagner (Ed.), *Social psychophysiology and emotion: Theory and clinical applications* (pp. 17–42). New York: Wiley.

Levenson, R. W., Carstensen, L. L., Friesen, W. V., & Ekman, P. (1991). Emotion, physiology, and expression in old age. *Physiology and Aging, 6*, 28–35.

Levenson, R. W., Ekman, P., & Friesen, W. V. (1990). Voluntary facial action generates emotion specific autonomic nervous system activity. *Psychophysiology, 27*, 363–384.

Leveque, J. L., Corcuff, P., de Rigal, J., & Agache, P. (1984). In vivo studies of the evolution of physical properties of the human skin with age. *International Journal of Dermatology, 23*, 322–329.

Levey, A. B. (1980). Measurement units in psychophysiology. In I. Martin & P. H. Venables (Eds.), *Techniques in psychophysiology* (pp. 597–628). New York: Wiley.

Levinson, D. F., & Edelberg, R. (1985). Scoring criteria for response latency and habituation in electrodermal research: A critique. *Psychophysiology, 22*, 417–426.

Levinson, D. F., Edelberg, R., & Bridger, W. H. (1984). The orienting response in schizophrenia: Proposed resolution of a controversy. *Biological Psychiatry, 19*, 489–507.

Levis, D. J., & Smith, J. E. (1987). Getting individual differences in autonomic reactivity to work for instead of against you: Determining the dominant "psychological" stress channel on the basis of a "biological" stress test. *Psychophysiology, 24*, 346–352.

Lieblich, I., Kugelmass, S., & Ben-Shakhar, G. (1973). Psychophysiological baselines as a function of race and ethnic origin. *Psychophysiology, 10*, 426–430.

Lim, C. L., Gordon, E., Harris, A., Bahramali, H., Li, W. M., Manor, B., & Rennie, C. (1999b). Electrodermal activity in schizophrenia: A quantitative study using a short interstimulus paradigm. *Biological Psychiatry, 45*, 127–135.

Lim, C. L., Gordon, E., Rennie, C., Wright, J. J., Bahramali, H., Li, W. M., Clouston, P., & Morris, J. G. L. (1999a). Dynamics of SCR, EEG, and ERP activity in an odball paradigm with short interstimulus intervals. *Psychophysiology, 36*, 543–551.

Lim, C. L., Rennie, C., Barry, J., Bahramali, H., Lazzaro, I., Manor, B., & Gordon, E. (1997). Decomposing skin conductance into tonic and phasic components. *International Journal of Psychophysiology, 25*, 97–109.

Linden, D., & Berlit, P. (1995). Sympathetic skin responses (SSRs) in monofocal brain lesions: Topographical aspects of central sympathetic pathways. *Acta Neurologica Scandinavica, 91*, 372–376.

Lindholm, E., & Cheatham, C. M. (1983). Autonomic activity and workload during learning of a simulated aircraft carrier landing task. *Aviation, Space, and Environmental Medicine, 54*, 435–439.

Lindsley, D. B. (1951). Emotion. In S. S. Stevens (Ed.), *Handbook of experimental psychology* (pp. 473–516). New York: Wiley.

Lindsley, D. B., Schreiner, L. H., Knowles, W. B., & Magoun, H. W. (1950). Behavioral and EEG changes following chronic brainstem lesions in the cat. *Electroencephalography and Clinical Neurophysiology, 2*, 483–498.

Lipp, O. V., Siddle, D. A. T., & Dall, P. J. (1997). The effect of emotional and attentional processes on blink startle modulation and on electrodermal responses. *Psychophysiology, 34*, 340–347.

Lloyd, D. C. (1961). Action potential and secretory potential of sweat glands. *Proceedings of the National Academy of Sciences USA, 47*, 351–358.

Lobstein, T., & Cort, J. (1978). The relationship between skin temperature and skin conductance activity: Indications of genetic and fitness determinants. *Biological Psychology, 7*, 139–143.

Lockhart, R. A. (1972). Interrelations between amplitude, latency, rise time, and the Edelberg recovery measure of the galvanic skin response. *Psychophysiology, 9*, 437–442.

Loeb, J., & Mednick, S. A. (1977). A prospective study of predictors of criminality: Electrodermal response patterns. In S. A. Mednick & K. O. Christiansen (Eds.), *Biosocial bases of criminal behavior* (pp. 245–254). New York: Gardener.

Lorber, M. F. (2004). Psychophysiology of aggression, psychopathy, and conduct problems: A meta-analysis. *Psychological Bulletin, 130,* 531–552.

Lovallo, W. R., & Pishkin, V. (1980). A psychophysiological comparison of Type A and B men exposed to failure and uncontrollable noise. *Psychophysiology, 17,* 29–36.

Love, T. J. (1980). Thermography as an indicator of blood perfusion. *Annals of the New York Academy of Sciences, 335,* 423–437.

Lovibond, P. F., Siddle, D. A. T., & Bond, N. W. (1993). Resistance to extinction of fear-relevant stimuli: Preparedness or selective sensitization? *Journal of Experimental Psychology, 122,* 449–461.

Löwenstein, W. R. (1956). Modulation of cutaneous receptors by sympathetic stimulation. *The Journal of Physiology, 132,* 40–60.

Lowry, R. (1977). Active circuits for direct linear measurement of skin resistance and conductance. *Psychophysiology, 14,* 329–331.

Lüer, G., & Neufeldt, B. (1967). Über Zeit- und Höhenmaße der galvanischen Hautreaktion. *Psychologische Forschung, 30,* 400–402.

Lüer, G., & Neufeldt, B. (1968). Über den Zusammenhang zwischen Maßen der galvanischen Hautreaktion und Beurteilungen von Reizen durch Versuchspersonen. *Zeitschrift für Experimentelle und Angewandte Psychologie, 15,* 619–648.

Luria, A. R., & Homskaya, E. D. (1970). Frontal lobes and the regulation of arousal processes. In D. Mostofsky (Ed.), *Attention: Contemporary theory and research* (pp. 303–330). New York: Appleton Century Crofts.

Lykken, D. T. (1957). A study of anxiety in the sociopathic personality. *Journal of Abnormal Psychology, 55,* 6–10.

Lykken, D. T. (1959a). Properties of electrodes used in electrodermal measurement. *Journal of Comparative and Physiological Psychology, 52,* 629–634.

Lykken, D. T. (1959b). The GSR in the detection of guilt. *The Journal of Applied Psychology, 43,* 385–388.

Lykken, D. T. (1968). Neuropsychology and psychophysiology in personality research. In E. F. Borgatta & W. W. Lambert (Eds.), *Handbook of personality theory and research: Part 2. Psychophysiological techniques and personality research* (pp. 413–509). Chicago: Rand McNally.

Lykken, D. T. (1971). Square-wave analysis of skin impedance. *Psychophysiology, 7,* 262–275.

Lykken, D. T. (1981). *A tremor in the blood: Uses and abuses of the lie detector.* New York: McGraw-Hill.

Lykken, D. T. (1982). Research with twins: The concept of emergenesis. *Psychophysiology, 19,* 361–373.

Lykken, D. T. (1995). *The antisocial personalities.* Hillsdale, NJ: Lawrence Erlbaum.

Lykken, D. T., Iacono, W. G., Haroian, K., McGue, M., & Bouchard, T. J. (1988). Habituation of the skin conductance response to strong stimuli: A twin study. *Psychophysiology, 25,* 4–15.

Lykken, D. T., Macindoe, I., & Tellegen, A. (1972). Preception: Autonomic response to shock as a function of predictability in time and locus. *Psychophysiology, 9,* 318–333.

Lykken, D. T., Miller, R. D., & Strahan, R. F. (1966). GSR and polarization capacity of skin. *Psychonomic Science, 4,* 355–356.

Lykken, D. T., Miller, R. D., & Strahan, R. F. (1968). Some properties of skin conductance and potential. *Psychophysiology, 5,* 253–268.

Lykken, D. T., & Rose, R. (1959). A rat-holder with electrodes for GSR measurement. *The American Journal of Psychology, 72,* 621–622.

Lykken, D. T., Rose, R., Luther, B., & Maley, M. (1966). Correcting psychophysiological measures for individual differences in range. *Psychological Bulletin, 66,* 481–484.

Lykken, D. T., & Tellegen, A. (1974). On the validity of the preception hypothesis. *Psychophysiology, 11*, 125–132.

Lykken, D. T., & Venables, P. H. (1971). Direct measurement of skin conductance: A proposal for standardization. *Psychophysiology, 8*, 656–672.

Lynn, R. (1966). *Attention, arousal and the orientation reaction.* Oxford: Pergamon.

Lyskov, E., Sandström, M., & Mild, K. H. (2001). Neurophysiological study of patients with perceived "electrical hypersensitivity". *International Journal of Psychophysiology, 42*, 233–241.

Lyvers, M., & Miyata, Y. (1993). Effects of cigarette smoking on electrodermal orienting reflexes to stimulus change and stimulus significance. *Psychophysiology, 30*, 231–236.

MacIntosh, B. J., McIlroy, W. E., Mraz, R., Staines, R., Black, S. E., & Graham, S. J. (2008). Electrodermal recording and fMRI to inform sensorimotor recovery in stroke patients. *Neurorehabilitation and Neural Repair, 22*, 728–736.

Macleod, A. F., Smith, S. A., Cowell, T., Richardson, P. R., & Sonksen, P. H. (1991). Non-cardiac autonomic test in diabetes: Use of the galvanic skin response. *Diabetic Medicine, 8 Symposium*, S67-S70.

Magaro, P. A. (1973). Skin conductance basal level and reactivity in schizophrenia as a function of chronicity, premorbid adjustment, diagnosis, and medication. *Journal of Abnormal Psychology, 81*, 270–281.

Magliero, A., Gatchel, R. J., & Lojewski, D. (1981). Skin conductance responses to stimulus "energy" decreases following habituation. *Psychophysiology, 18*, 549–558.

Mahon, M. L., & Iacono, W. G. (1987). Another look at the relationship of electrodermal activity to electrode contact area. *Psychophysiology, 24*, 216–222.

Maia, T. V., & McClelland, J. L. (2004). A reexamination of the evidence for the somatic marker hypothesis: What participants really know in the Iowa Gambling task. *Proceedings of the National Academy of Sciences USA, 101*, 16075–16080.

Malmo, R. B. (1957). Anxiety and behavioral arousal. *Psychological Review, 64*, 309–319.

Malmo, R. B. (1959). Activation: A neuropsychological dimension. *Psychological Review, 66*, 367–386.

Malmo, R. B. (1962). Activation. In A. J. Bachrach (Ed.), *Experimental foundations of clinical psychology* (pp. 386–422). New York: Basic Books.

Malmo, R. B. (1965). Finger-sweat prints in the differentiation of low and high incentive. *Psychophysiology, 1*, 231–240.

Malmo, R. B., & Smith, A. A. (1951). Responsiveness in chronic schizophrenia. *Journal of Personality, 18*, 359–375.

Malmstrom, E. J. (1968). The effect of prestimulus variability upon physiological reactivity scores. *Psychophysiology, 5*, 149–165.

Malten, K. E., & Thiele, F. A. J. (1973). Evaluation of skin damage. *The British Journal of Dermatology, 89*, 565–569.

Maltzman, I. (1977). Orienting in classical conditioning and generalization of the galvanic skin response to words: An overview. *Journal of Experimentel Psychology: General, 106*, 111–119.

Maltzman, I. (1979a). Orienting reflexes and significance: A reply to O'Gorman. *Psychophysiology, 16*, 274–282.

Maltzman, I. (1979b). Orienting reflexes and classical conditioning in humans. In H. D. Kimmel, E. H. van Oist, & J. F. Orlebeke (Eds.), *The orienting reflex in humans* (pp. 323–351). Hillsdale, NJ: Erlbaum.

Maltzman, I., Gould, J., Barnett, O. J., Raskin, D. C., & Wolff, C. (1979). Habituation of the GSR and digital vasomotor components of the orienting reflex as a consequence of task instructions and sex differences. *Physiological Psychology, 7*, 213–220.

Maltzman, I., & Langdon, B. (1982). Novelty and significance as determiners of the GSR index of the orienting reflex. *Physiological Psychology, 10*, 229–234.

Maltzman, I., Raskin, D. C., & Wolff, C. (1979). Latent inhibition of the GSR conditioned to words. *Physiological Psychology, 7*, 193–203.

Mangan, G. L., & O'Gorman, J. G. (1969). Initial amplitude and rate of habituation of orienting reaction in relation to extraversion and neuroticism. *Journal of Experimental Research in Personality, 3*, 275–282.

Mangina, C. A., & Beuzeron-Mangina, J. H. (1996). Direct electrical stimulation of specific human brain structures and bilateral electrodermal activity. *International Journal of Psychophysiology, 22*, 1–8.

Marchionini, A., & Spier, H. W. (Eds.). (1963). *Handbuch der Haut- und Geschlechtskrankheiten* (Normale und pathologische Physiologie der Haut I, Vol. I/3). Berlin: Springer.

Maricq, H. R., & Edelberg, R. (1975). Electrodermal recovery rate in a schizophrenic population. *Psychophysiology, 12*, 630–633.

Marsden, C. D. (1982). The mysterious motor function of the basal ganglia: The Robert Wartenberg Lecture. *Neurology, 32*, 514–539.

Martin, R. B., & Dean, S. J. (1970). Instrumental modification of the GSR. *Psychophysiology, 7*, 178–185.

Martin, A., & Rief, W. (2009). *Wie wirksam ist Biofeedback? Eine therapeutische Methode*. Bern: Hans Huber.

Martin, I., & Rust, J. (1976). Habituation and the structure of the electrodermal system. *Psychophysiology, 13*, 554–562.

Martin, I., & Venables, P. H. (1966). Mechanisms of palmar skin resistance and skin potential. *Psychological Bulletin, 65*, 347–357.

Martin, I., & Venables, P. H. (Eds.). (1980). *Techniques in psychophysiology*. Chicester: Wiley.

Martínez-Selva, J. M., Gómez-Amor, J., Olmos, E., Navarro, N., & Román, F. (1987). Sex and menstrual cycle differences in the habituation and spontaneous recovery of the electrodermal orienting reaction. *Personality and Individual Differences, 8*, 211–217.

Massaro, D. W. (1975). *Experimental psychology and information processing*. Chicago: Rand McNally.

Maulsby, R. L., & Edelberg, R. (1960). The interrelationship between the galvanic skin response, basal resistance, and temperature. *Journal of Comparative and Physiological Psychology, 53*, 475–479.

Mayer, B., Merckelbach, H., de Jong, P. J., & Leeuw, I. (1999). Skin conductance responses of spider phobics to backwardly masked phobic cues. *Journal of Psychophysiology, 13*, 152–159.

Maze, J. R. (1983). *The Meaning of Behaviour*. London: Allen & Unwin.

Mazurski, E. J., Bond, N. W., Siddle, D. A. T., & Lovibond, P. F. (1996). Conditioning with facial expressions of emotion: Effects of CS sex and age. *Psychophysiology, 33*, 416–425.

McClendon, J. F., & Hemingway, A. (1930). The psychogalvanic reflex as related to the polarization-capacity of the skin. *The American Journal of Psychology, 84*, 77–83.

McCubbin, R. J., & Katkin, E. S. (1971). Magnitude of the orienting response as a function of extent and quality of stimulus change. *Journal of Experimental Psychology, 88*, 182–188.

McDonald, D. G., & Carpenter, F. A. (1975). Habituation of the orienting response in sleep. *Psychophysiology, 12*, 618–623.

McDonald, D. G., Shallenberger, H. D., Koresko, R. L., & Kinzy, B. G. (1976). Studies of spontaneous electrodermal responses in sleep. *Psychophysiology, 13*, 128–134.

McDougall, A. J., & McLeod, J. G. (2003). Autonomic nervous system function in multiple sclerosis. *Journal of the Neurological Sciences, 215*, 79–85.

McDowd, J. M., & Filion, D. L. (1992). Aging, selective attention, and inhibitory processes: A psychophysiological approach. *Psychology and Aging, 7*, 65–71.

McFarland, R. A. (1981). *Physiological psychology: The biology of human behavior*. Palo Alto: Mayfield.

McGrath, J. E. (1982). Methodological problems in research on stress. In H. W. Krohne & L. Laux (Eds.), *Achievement, stress, and anxiety* (pp. 19–48). Washington: Hemisphere.

McGuinness, D. (1973). Cardiovascular responses during habituation and mental activity in anxious men and women. *Biological Psychology, 1*, 115–124.

McGuinness, D., & Pribram, K. (1980). The neuropsychology of attention: Emotional and motivational controls. In M. C. Wittrock (Ed.), *The brain and psychology* (pp. 95–139). New York: Academic.

McKeever, W. F., & Gill, K. M. (1972). Interhemispheric transfer time for visual stimulus information varies as a function of the retinal locus of stimulation. *Psychonomic Science, 26,* 308–310.

Mednick, S. A. (1967). The children of schizophrenics: Serious difficulties in current research methodologies which suggest the use of the "high-risk group" method. In J. Romano (Ed.), *Origins of schizophrenia* (pp. 179–200). Amsterdam: Excerpta Medica.

Mednick, S. A. (1970). Breakdown in individuals at high risk for schizophrenia: Possible predispositional perinatal factors. *Mental Hygiene, 54,* 50–63.

Mednick, S. A. (1974). Electrodermal recovery and psychopathology. In S. A. Mednick, F. Schulsinger, J. Higgins, & B. Bell (Eds.), *Genetics, environment and psychopathology* (pp. 135–146). Amsterdam: Elsevier.

Mednick, S. A. (1978). Berkson's fallacy and high-risk research. In L. C. Wynne, R. L. Cromwell, & S. Matthysse (Eds.), *The nature of schizophrenia: New approaches to research and treatment* (pp. 442–452). New York: Wiley.

Mednick, S. A., & McNeil, T. F. (1968). Current methodology in research on the etiology of schizophrenia: Serious difficulties which suggest the use of the high-risk-group method. *Psychological Bulletin, 70,* 681–693.

Mednick, S. A., & Schulsinger, F. (1968). Some premorbid characteristics related to breakdown in children with schizophrenic mothers. In S. Kety & D. Rosenthal (Eds.), *The transmission of schizophrenia* (pp. 267–291). Oxford: Pergamon.

Mednick, S. A., & Schulsinger, F. (1973). A learning theory of schizophrenia: Thirteen years later. In M. Hammer, K. Salzinger, & S. Sutton (Eds.), *Psychopathology* (pp. 343–360). New York: Wiley.

Mednick, S. A., & Schulsinger, F. (1974). Studies of children at high risk for schizophrenia. In S. A. Mednick, F. Schulsinger, J. Higgins, & B. Bell (Eds.), *Genetics, environment, and psychopathology* (pp. 109–116). Amsterdam: Elsevier.

Mednick, S. A., Schulsinger, F., Teasdale, T. W., Schulsinger, H., Venables, P. H., & Rock, D. R. (1978). Schizophrenia in high-risk children: Sex differences in predisposing factors. In G. Serban (Ed.), *Cognitive defects in the developement of mental illness* (pp. 169–197). New York: Brunner/Mazel.

Melis, C., & van Boxtel, A. (2001). Differences in autonomic physiological responses between good and poor inductive reasoners. *Biological Psychology, 58,* 121–146.

Meyers, M., & Smith, B. D. (1986). Hemispheric asymmetry and emotion: Effects of nonverbal affective stimuli. *Biological Psychology, 22,* 11–22.

Meyers, M. B., & Smith, B. D. (1987). Cerebral processing of nonverbal affective stimuli: Differential effects of cognitive and affective sets on hemispheric asymmetry. *Biological Psychology, 24,* 67–84.

Michaels, R. M. (1960). Tension responses of drivers generated on urban streets. *Highway Research Board Bulletin, 271,* 29–43.

Michaels, R. M. (1962). Effect of expressway design on driver tension responses. *Highway Research Board Bulletin, 330,* 16–26.

Miezejeski, C. M. (1978). Relationships between behavioral arousal and some components of autonomic arousal. *Psychophysiology, 15,* 417–421.

Miller, N. E. (1969). Learning of visceral and glandular responses. *Science, 163,* 434–445.

Miller, N. E. (1972). Learning of glandular and visceral responses: Postscript. In D. Singh & C. T. Morgan (Eds.), *Current status of physiological psychology: Readings* (pp. 228–250). Monterey: Brooks/Cole.

Miller, R. M., & Coger, R. W. (1979). Skin conductance conditioning with dyshidrotic eczema patients. *The British Journal of Dermatology, 101,* 435–440.

Miller, S., & Konorski, J. (1928). Sur une farme particulière des reflexes conditionels. *Comptes Rendues Sociétée Biologique Paris, 99*, 1155–1177.

Miller, L. H., & Shmavonian, B. H. (1965). Replicability of two GSR indices as a function of stress and cognitive activity. *Journal of Personality and Social Psychology, 2*, 753–756.

Millington, P. F., & Wilkinson, R. (1983). *Skin*. Cambridge: University Press.

Miossec, Y., Catteau, M. C., Freixa i Baqué, E., & Roy, J.-C. (1985). Methodological problems in bilateral electrodermal research. International Journal of Psychophysiology, 2, 247–256.

Mitchell, D. A., & Venables, P. H. (1980). The relationship of EDA to electrode size. *Psychophysiology, 17*, 408–412.

Mize, M. M., Vila-Coro, A. A., & Prager, T. C. (1989). The relationship between postnatal skin maturation and electrical skin impedance. *Archives of Dermatology, 125*, 647–650.

Moan, E. R. (1979). GSR biofeedback assisted relaxation training and psychosomatic hives. *Journal of Behavior Therapy and Experimental Psychiatry, 10*, 157–158.

Mobascher, A., Brinkmeyer, J., Warbrick, T., Musso, F., Wittsack, H. J., Stoermer, R., Saleh, A., Schnitzler, A. & Winterer, G. (2009). Fluctuations in electrodermal activity reveal variations in single trial brain responses to painful laser stimuli – A fMRI/EEG study. *NeuroImage, 44*, 1081–1092.

Monat, A., Averill, J. R., & Lazarus, R. S. (1972). Anticipatory stress and coping reactions under various conditions of uncertainty. *Journal of Personality and Social Psychology, 24*, 237–253.

Montagna, W., & Parakkal, P. F. (1974). *The structure and function of skin*. New York: Academic.

Montagu, J. D. (1958). The psycho-galvanic reflex: A comparison of AC skin resistance and skin potential changes. *Journal of Neurology, Neurosurgery, and Psychiatry, 21*, 119–128.

Montagu, J. D. (1963). Habituation of the psycho-galvanic reflex during serial tests. *Journal of Psychosomatic Research, 7*, 199–214.

Montagu, J. D. (1973). The measurement of electrodermal activity: An instrument for recording log skin admittance. *Biological Psychology, 1*, 161–166.

Montagu, J. D., & Coles, E. M. (1966). Mechanism and measurement of the galvanic skin response. *Psychological Bulletin, 65*, 261–279.

Montagu, J. D., & Coles, E. M. (1968). Mechanism and measurement of the galvanic skin response: An addendum. *Psychological Bulletin, 69*, 74–76.

Morimoto, T. (1978). Variations of sweating activity due to sex, age and race. In A. Jarrett (Ed.), *The physiology and pathophysiology of the skin* (The sweat glands, skin permeation, lymphatics, and the nails, Vol. 5, pp. 1655–1666). New York: Academic.

Morkrid, L., & Qiao, Z.-G. (1988). Continuous estimation of parameters in skin electrical admittance from simultaneous measurements at two different frequencies. *Medical & Biological Engineering & Computing, 26*, 633–640.

Morris, P. H., & Gale, A. (1993). Effects of situational demands on the direction of electrodermal activation during smoking. *Addictive Behaviors, 18*, 35–40.

Morrow, L., Vrtunski, P. B., Kim, Y., & Boller, F. (1981). Arousal responses to emotional stimuli and laterality of lesion. *Neuropsychologia, 19*, 65–71.

Mowrer, O. H. (1960). *Learning theory and behavior*. New York: Wiley.

Mundy-Castle, A. C., & McKiever, B. L. (1953). The psychophysiological significance of the galvanic skin response. *Journal of Experimental Psychology, 46*, 15–24.

Munro, L. L., Dawson, M. E., Schell, A. M., & Sakai, L. M. (1987). Electrodermal lability and rapid vigilance decrement in a degraded stimulus continuous performance task. *Journal of Psychophysiology, 1*, 249–257.

Muthny, F. A. (1984). *Elektrodermale Aktivität und palmare Schwitzaktivität als Biosignale der Haut in der psychophysiologischen Grundlagenforschung*. Freiburg: Dreisam.

Muthny, F. A., Foerster, F., Hoeppner, V., Mueller, W., & Walschburger, P. (1983). Skin evaporative water loss (SE) and skin conductance (SC) under various psychophysiological conditions. *Biological Psychology, 16*, 241–253.

Myrtek, M. (1984). *Constitutional psychophysiology. Research in review*. Orlando: Academic.

Myrtek, M., & Foerster, F. (1986). The law of initial value: A rare exception. *Biological Psychology, 22*, 227–237.

Myrtek, M., Foerster, F., & Wittmann, W. (1977). Das Ausgangswertproblem: Theoretische Überlegungen und empirische Untersuchungen. *Zeitschrift für Experimentelle und Angewandte Psychologie, 24*, 463–491.

Myslobodsky, M. S., & Rattok, J. (1975). Asymmetry of electrodermal activity in man. *Bulletin of the Psychonomic Society, 6*, 501–502.

Myslobodsky, M. S., & Rattok, J. (1977). Bilateral electrodermal activity in waking man. *Acta Psychologica, 41*, 273–282.

Nagai, Y., Critchley, H. D., Featherstone, E., Trimble, M. R., & Dolan, R. J. (2004). Activity in ventromedial prefrontal cortex covaries with sympathetic skin conductance level: A physiological account of a "default mode" of brain function. *NeuroImage, 22*, 243–251.

National Research Council (2003). *The polygraph and lie detection*. Committee to Review the Scientific Evidence on the Polygraph. Division of Behavioral and Social Sciences and Education. Washington, DC: The National Academies Press.

Naveteur, J., & Freixa i Baqué, E. (1987). Individual differences in electrodermal activity as a function of subjects' anxiety. *Personality and Individual Differences, 8*, 615–626.

Naveteur, J., Buisine, S., & Gruzelier, J. H. (2005). The influence of anxiety on electrodermal responses to distractors. *International Journal of Psychophysiology, 56*, 261–269.

Naveteur, J., & Sequeira-Martinho, H. (1990). Reliability of bilateral differences in electrodermal activity. *Biological Psychology, 31*, 47–56.

Neary, R. S., & Zuckerman, M. (1976). Sensation seeking, trait and state anxiety, and the electrodermal orienting response. *Psychophysiology, 13*, 205–211.

Nebylitsyn, V. D. (1972). *Fundamental properties of the human nervous system*. New York: Plenum.

Nebylitsyn, V. D. (1973). Current problems in differential psychophysiology. *Soviet Psychology, 11*, 47–70.

Neijenhuisen, H., & de Jongh, G. J. (1981). The phasevoltmeter. In G. Stüttgen, H. W. Spier, & E. Schwarz (Eds.), *Handbuch der Haut- und Geschlechtskrankheiten* (Normale und pathologische Physiologie der Haut III, Vol. I/4B, pp. 89–93). Berlin: Springer.

Neisser, U. (1967). *Cognitive psychology*. New York: Appleton.

Netter, P. (1986). Einflußfaktoren auf die zentral-nervöse Wirkung von Beta- Rezeptorenblockern. In W. Janke & P. Netter (Eds.), *Angst und Psychopharmaka* (pp. 169–204). Stuttgart: Kohlhammer.

Neufeld, R. W. J., & Davidson, P. O. (1974). Sex differences in stress response: A multivariate analysis. *Journal of Abnormal Psychology, 83*, 178–185.

Neumann, E. (1968). Thermal changes in palmar skin resistance patterns. *Psychophysiology, 5*, 103–111.

Neumann, E., & Blanton, R. (1970). The early history of electrodermal research. *Psychophysiology, 6*, 453–475.

Nicolaidis, S., & Sivadjian, J. (1972). High-frequency pulsatile discharge of human sweat glands: Myoepithelial mechanism. *Journal of Applied Physiology, 32*, 86–90.

Niebauer, G. (1957). Der Aufbau des peripheren neurovegetativen Systems im Epidermal-Dermalbereich. *Acta Neurovegetativa, 15*, 109–123.

Nielsen, T. C., & Petersen, K. E. (1976). Electrodermal correlates of extraversion, trait anxiety and schizophrenism. *Scandinavian Journal of Psychology, 17*, 73–80.

Niemelä, P. (1975). Effects of interrupting the process of preparation for film stress. *Scandinavian Journal of Psychology, 16*, 294–302.

Niepel, M. (2001). Independent manipulation of stimulus change and unexpectedness dissociates indices of the orienting response. *Psychophysiology, 38*, 84–91.

Nikula, R. (1991). Psychological correlates of nonspecific skin conductance responses. *Psychophysiology, 28*, 86–90.

Nishiyama, T., Sugenoya, J., Matsumoto, T., Iwase, S., & Mano, T. (2001). Irregular activation of individual sweat glands in human sole observed by a videomicroscopy. *Autonomic Neuroscience: Basic and Clinical, 88*, 117–126.

Nomikos, M. S., Opton, E., Averill, J. R., & Lazarus, R. S. (1968). Surprise versus suspense in the production of stress reaction. *Journal of Personality and Social Psychology, 8*, 204–208.

Norris, C. J., Larsen, J. T., & Cacioppo, J. T. (2007). Neuroticism is associated with larger and more prolonged electrodermal responses to emotionally evocative pictures. *Psychophysiology, 44*, 823–826.

Nuechterlein, K. H. (1987). Vulnerability models for schizophrenia: State of the art. In H. Häfner, W. F. Gattaz, & W. Janzarik (Eds.), *Search for the causes of schizophrenia* (pp. 297–316). Heidelberg: Springer.

Nuechterlein, K. H., & Dawson, M. E. (1984). A heuristic vulnerability/stress model of schizophrenic episodes. *Schizophrenia Bulletin, 10*, 300–312.

Nuechterlein, K. H., Edell, W. S., Norris, M., & Dawson, M. E. (1986). Attentional vulnerability indicators, thought disorders, and negative symptoms in schizophrenia. *Schizophrenia Bulletin, 12*, 408–426.

O'Connell, D. N., Tursky, B., & Evans, F. J. (1967). Normality of distribution of resting palmar skin potential. *Psychophysiology, 4*, 151–155.

O'Gorman, J. G. (1974). A comment on Koriat, Averill, and Malmstrom's "Individual differences in habituation". *Journal of Research in Personality, 8*, 198–202.

O'Gorman, J. G. (1977). Individual differences in habituation of human physiological responses: A review of theory, method, and findings in the study of personality correlates in non-clinical populations. *Biological Psychology, 5*, 257–319.

O'Gorman, J. G. (1978). Method of recording: A neglected factor in the controversy over the bimodality of electrodermal responsiveness in schizophrenic samples. *Schizophrenia Bulletin, 4*, 150–152.

O'Gorman, J. G. (1979). The orienting reflex: Novelty or significance detector? *Psychophysiology, 16*, 253–262.

O'Gorman, J. G., & Horneman, C. (1979). Consistency of individual differences in non-specific electrodermal activity. *Biological Psychology, 9*, 13–21.

O'Gorman, J. G., & Lloyd, J. E. M. (1988). Electrodermal lability and dichotic listening. *Psychophysiology, 25*, 538–546.

O'Toole, D., Yuille, J. C., Patrick, C. J., & Iacono, W. G. (1994). Alcohol and the physiological detection of deception: Arousal and memory influences. *Psychophysiology, 31*, 253–263.

Obrist, P. A. (1963). Skin resistance levels and galvanic skin response: Unilateral differences. *Science, 139*, 227–228.

Obrist, P. A. (1976). The cardiovascular-behavioral interaction – As it appears today. *Psychophysiology, 13*, 95–107.

Obrist, P. A., Black, F. W., Brener, J., & DiCara, L. W. (Eds.). (1974). *Cardiovascular psychophysiology*. Chicago: Aldine.

Odland, G. F. (1983). Structure of the skin. In L. A. Goldsmith (Ed.), *Biochemistry and physiology of the skin* (Vol. 1, pp. 3–63). New York: Oxford University Press.

Ödman, S. (1981). Potential and impedance variations following skin deformation. *Medical & Biological Engineering & Computing, 19*, 271–278.

Offe, H., & Offe, S. (2007). The comparison question test: Does it work and if so how? *Law and Human Behavior, 31*, 291–303.

Ogawa, T. (1984). Regional differences in sweating activity. In J. R. S. Hales (Ed.), *Thermal physiology* (pp. 229–234). New York: Raven.

Öhman, A. (1971). Differentiation of conditioned and orienting response components in electrodermal conditioning. *Psychophysiology, 8*, 7–22.

Öhman, A. (1979). The orienting response, attention, and learning: An information-processing perspective. In H. D. Kimmel, E. H. van Olst, & J. F. Orlebeke (Eds.), *The orienting reflex in humans* (pp. 443–471). Hillsdale, NJ: Erlbaum.

Öhman, A. (1981). Electrodermal activity and vulnerability to schizophrenia: A review. *Biological Psychology, 12*, 87–145.

Öhman, A. (1983). The orienting response during Pavlovian conditioning. In D. Siddle (Ed.), *Orienting and habituation: Perspectives in human research* (pp. 315–369). Chichester: Wiley.

Öhman, A. (1993). Stimulus prepotency and fear learning: Data and theory. In N. Birbaumer & A. Öhman (Eds.), *The structur of emotion* (pp. 218–239). Seattle: Hogrefe & Huber.

Öhman, A., & Bohlin, G. (1973). The relationship between spontaneous and stimulus-correlated electrodermal responses in simple and discriminative conditioning paradigms. *Psychophysiology, 10*, 589–600.

Öhman, A., Dimberg, U., & Esteves, F. (1989). Preattentive activation of aversive emotions. In T. Archer & L.-G. Nilsson (Eds.), *Aversion, avoidance, and anxiety* (pp. 169–193). Hillsdale, NJ: Erlbaum.

Öhman, A., Erikson, A., & Olofsson, C. (1975). One-trial learning and superior resistance to extinction of autonomic responses conditioned to potentially phobic stimuli. *Journal of Comparative and Physiological Psychology, 88*, 619–627.

Öhman, A., Eriksson, A., Fredrikson, M., Hugdahl, K., & Olofsson, C. (1974). Habituation of the electrodermal orienting reaction to potentially phobic and supposedly neutral stimuli in normal human subjects. *Biological Psychology, 2*, 85–93.

Öhman, A., Erixon, G., & Löfberg, G. (1975). Phobias and preparedness: Phobic versus neutral pictures as conditioned stimuli for human autonomic responses. *Journal of Abnormal Psychology, 84*, 41–45.

Öhman, A., & Hultman, C. M. (1998). Electrodermal activity and obstetric complications in schizophrenia. *Journal of Abnormal Psychology, 107*, 228–237.

Öhman, A., & Soares, J. J. (1994). "Unconscious anxiety": Phobic responses to masked stimuli. *Journal of Abnormal Psychology, 103*, 231–240.

Olbrich, R. (1989). Electrodermal activity and its relevance to vulnerability research in schizophrenics. *The British Journal of Psychiatry, 155*, 40–45.

Olbrich, R. (1990). The contributions of psychophysiology to vulnerability models. In H. Häfner & W. F. Gattaz (Eds.), *Search for the causes of schizophrenia* (Vol. 1, pp. 192–204). Berlin: Springer.

Olbrich, R., & Mussgay, L. (1987). Spontaneous fluctuations of electrical skin conductance and the actual clinical state in schizophrenics. *Psychopathology, 20*, 18–22.

Olds, J., & Olds, M. E. (1965). Drives, rewards, and the brain. In T. M. Newcomb (Ed.), *New directions in psychology II* (pp. 327–410). New York: Holt, Rinehart, & Winston.

Orfanos, C. E. (1972). *Feinstrukturelle Morphologie und Histopathologie der verhornenden Epidermis*. Stuttgart: Thieme.

Orlebeke, J. F., & van Olst, E. H. (1968). Learning and performance as a function of CS-intensity in a delayed GSR conditioning situation. *Journal of Experimental Psychology, 77*, 483–487.

Orr, S. P., & Lanzetta, J. T. (1980). Facial expressions of emotion as conditioned stimuli for human autonomic responses. *Journal of Personality and Social Psychology, 38*, 278–282.

Orr, S. P., Milad, M. R., Metzger, L. J., Lasko, N. B., Gilbertson, M. W., & Pitman, R. K. (2006). Effects of beta blockade, PTSD diagnosis, and explicit threat on the extinction and retention of an aversively conditioned response. *Biological Psychology, 73*, 262–271.

Oscar-Berman, M., & Gade, A. (1979). Electrodermal measures of arousal in humans with cortical or subcortical brain damage. In H. D. Kimmel, E. H. van Olst, & J. F. Orlebeke (Eds.), *The orienting reflex in humans* (pp. 665–676). Hillsdale, NJ: Erlbaum.

Overall, J. E., & Woodward, J. A. (1977). Nonrandom assignment and the analysis of covariance. *Psychological Bulletin, 84*, 588–594.

Overmier, J. B. (1985). Toward a reanalysis of the causal structure of the learned helplessness syndrome. In F. R. Brush & J. B. Overmier (Eds.), *Affect, conditioning, and cognition: Essays on the determinants of behavior* (pp. 211–227). Hillsdale, NJ: Erlbaum.

Packer, J. S., & Siddle, D. A. T. (1989). Stimulus miscuing, electrodermal activity, and the allocation of processing resources. *Psychophysiology, 26*, 192–200.

Page, M., & Robson, A. (2007). Galvanic skin responses from asking stressful questions. *The British Journal of Nursing, 16*, 622–627.

Paintal, A. S. (1951). A comparison of the galvanic skin responses of normals and psychotics. *Journal of Experimental Psychology, 41*, 425–428.

Panksepp, J. (1982). Toward a general psychobiological theory of emotions. *The Behavioral and Brain Sciences, 5*, 407–467.

Panksepp, J. (1986). The anatomy of emotions. In R. Plutchik & H. Kellermann (Eds.), *Emotion: Theory research and experience* (pp. 91–124). New York: Academic.

Papez, J. W. (1937). A proposed mechanism of emotion. *Archives of Neurology and Psychiatry, 38*, 725–743.

Pasquali, E., & Roveri, R. (1971). Measurement of the electrical skin resistance during skin drilling. *Psychophysiology, 8*, 236–238.

Patterson, T. (1976). Skin conductance recovery and pupillometrics in chronic schizophrenia. *Psychophysiology, 13*, 189–195.

Patterson, J. C., Ungerleider, L. G., & Bandettini, P. A. (2002). Task-independent functional brain activity correlation with skin conductance changes: An fMRI study. *NeuroImage, 17*, 1797–1806.

Patterson, T., & Venables, P. H. (1981). Bilateral skin conductance and the pupillary light-dark reflex: Manipulation by chlorpromazine, haloperidol, scopolamine, and placebo. *Psychopharmacology, 73*, 63–69.

Pavlov, I. P. (1927). *Conditioned reflexes. An investigation of the physiological activity of the cerebral cortex.* New York: Oxford University Press.

Peeke, S. C., & Grings, W. W. (1968). Magnitude of UCR as a function of variability in the CS-UCS relationship. *Journal of Experimental Psychology, 77*, 64–69.

Pelachaud, C., & Bilvi, M. (2003). Computational model of believable conversational agents. In M.-P. Huget (Ed.), *Communications in multiagent systems* (pp. 300–317). Berlin: Springer.

Pennebaker, J. W., & Chew, C. H. (1985). Behavioral inhibition and electrodermal activity during deception. *Journal of Personality and Social Psychology, 49*, 1427–1433.

Peper, M., & Karcher, S. (2001). Differential conditioning to facial emotional expressions: Effects of hemispheric asymmetries and CS identification. *Psychophysiology, 38*, 936–950.

Peper, M., Karcher, S., Wohlfart, R., Reinshagen, G., & LeDoux, J. E. (2001). Aversive learning in patients with unilateral lesions of the amygdala and hippocampus. *Biological Psychology, 58*, 1–23.

Perry, W., Felger, T., & Braff, D. (1998). The relationship between skin conductance hyporesponsivity and perseverations in schizophrenia patients. *Biological Psychiatry, 44*, 459–465.

Peters, T. (1974). Mentale Beanspruchung von Büroangestellten im Schreibdienst und bei Vorzimmertätigkeit. *Zentralblatt für Arbeitsmedizin und Arbeitsschutz, 24*, 197–207.

Petrinovich, L. (1973). A species-meaningful analysis of habituation. In H. V. S. Peeke & M. J. Herz (Eds.), *Habituation* (Behavioral studies, Vol. 1, pp. 141–162). New York: Academic.

Phillips, K. C., Evans, P. D., & Fearn, J. M. (1986). Heart rate and skin conductance correlates of monitoring or distraction as strategies for "coping". In D. Papakostopoulos, S. Butler, & I. Martin (Eds.), *Clinical and experimental neuropsychophysiology* (pp. 486–499). Dover: Croom Helm.

Picard, R. W., & Healy, J. (1997). Affective wearables. *Personal and Ubiquitous Computing, 1*, 231–240.

Pineles, S. L., Orr, M. R., & Orr, S. P. (2009). An alternative scoring method for skin conductance responding in a differential fear conditioning paradigm with a long-duration conditioned stimulus. *Psychophysiology, 46*, 984–995.

Pinkus, H. (1952). Examination of the epidermis by the strip method: II. Biometric data on regeneration of the human epidermis. *Journal of Investigative Dermatology, 19*, 431–447.

Pinkus, H. (1971). Embryology and anatomy of skin. In E. B. Helwig & F. K. Mostofi (Eds.), *The skin* (pp. 1–27). Baltimore: Williams & Wilkins.

Pivik, R. T. (1978). Tonic states and phasic events in relation to sleep mentation. In M. A. Arkin, J. S. Antrobus, & S. Ellman (Eds.), *The mind in sleep: Physiology and psychophysiology* (pp. 245–271). New York: Wiley.

Pivik, R. T. (2007). Sleep and dreaming. In J. T. Cacioppo, L. G. Tassinary, & G. Berntson (Eds.), *Handbook of psychophysiology* (pp. 633–662). New York: Cambridge University Press.

Plouffe, L., & Stelmack, R. M. (1984). The electrodermal orienting response and memory: An analysis of age differences in picture recall. *Psychophysiology, 21*, 191–198.

Plouffe, L., & Stelmack, R. M. (1986). Sensation-seeking and the electrodermal orienting response in young and elderly females. *Personality and Individual Differences, 7*, 119–120.

Plutchik, R. (1980). *Emotion – A psychoevolutionary synthesis*. New York: Harper & Row.

Plutchik, R., & Hirsch, H. R. (1963). Skin impedance and phase angle as a function of frequency and current. *Science, 141*, 927–928.

Poh, M. Z., Swenson, N. C., & Picard, R. W. (2010). A wearable sensor for unobtrusive, long-term assessment of electrodermal activity. *IEEE Transactions on Biomedical Engineering, 57*, 1243–1252.

Pollack, S. V. (1985). The aging skin. *The Journal of the Florida Medical Association, 72*, 245–248.

Pollatos, O., Schubö, A., Herbert, B. M., Matthias, E., & Schandry, R. (2008). Deficits in early emotional reactivity in alexithymia. *Psychophysiology, 45*, 839–846.

Porges, S. W., & Fox, N. A. (1986). Developmental psychophysiology. In M. G. H. Coles, E. Donchin, & S. W. Porges (Eds.), *Psychophysiology: Systems, processes, and applications* (pp. 611–625). Amsterdam: Elsevier.

Posner, M. I. (1975). Psychobiology of attention. In M. S. Gazzaniga & C. Blakemore (Eds.), *Handbook of psychobiology* (pp. 441–480). New York: Academic.

Potts, R. O., Buras, E. M., & Chrisman, D. A. (1984). Changes with age in the moisture content of human skin. *The Journal of Investigative Dermatology, 82*, 97–100.

Prentky, A., Salzman, L. F., & Klein, R. H. (1981). Habituation and conditioning of skin conductance responses in children at risk. *Schizophrenia Bulletin, 7*, 281–291.

Preston, B. (1969). Insurance classifications and drivers' galvanic skin response. *Ergonomics, 12*, 437–446.

Pribram, K. H. (1980). The biology of emotions and other feelings. In R. Plutchik & H. Kellerman (Eds.), *Emotion: Theory, research, and experience* (Theories of emotion, Vol. 1, pp. 245–269). New York: Academic.

Pribram, K. H., & McGuinness, D. (1975). Arousal, activation, and effort in the control of attention. *Psychological Review, 82*, 116–149.

Pribram, K. H., & McGuinness, D. (1976). Arousal, Aktivierung und Anstrengung: Gesonderte neurale Systeme. *Zeitschrift für Psychologie, 184*, 382–403.

Prinzel, L. J., Freeman, F. G., Scerbo, M. W., Mikulka, P. J., & Pope, A. T. (2003). The effects of a psychophysiological system for adaptive automation on performance, workload, and the event-related potential P300 component. *Human Factors, 45*, 601–613.

Prior, M. G., Cumming, G., & Hendy, J. (1984). Recognition of abstract and concrete words in a dichotic listening paradigm. *Cortex, 20*, 149–157.

Prokasy, W. F., & Ebel, H. C. (1967). Three components of the classically conditioned GSR in human subjects. *Journal of Experimental Psychology, 73*, 247–256.

Prokasy, W. F., & Kumpfer, K. L. (1973). Classical conditioning. In W. F. Prokasy & D. C. Raskin (Eds.), *Electrodermal activity in psychological research* (pp. 157–202). New York: Academic.

Prokasy, W. F., & Raskin, D. C. (Eds.). (1973). *Electrodermal activity in psychological research*. New York: Academic.

Pugh, L. A., Oldroyd, C. A., Ray, T. S., & Clark, M. L. (1966). Muscular effort and electrodermal responses. *Journal of Experimental Psychology, 71*, 241–248.

Purohit, A. P. (1966). Personality variables, sex differences, GSR responsiveness and GSR conditioning. *Journal of Experimental Research in Personality, 1*, 165–179.

Quiao, Z. G., Morkrid, L., & Grimnes, S. (1987). Simultaneous measurement of electrical admittance, blood flow and temperature at the same skin site with a specially designed probe. *Medical & Biological Engineering & Computing, 25*, 299–304.

Rabavilas, A. D. (1987). Electrodermal activity in low and high alexithymia neurotic patients. *Psychotherapy and Psychosomatics, 47*, 101–104.

Rachman, S. (1960). Reliability of galvanic skin response measures. *Psychological Reports, 6*, 326.

Raichle, M. E., MacLeod, A. M., Snyder, A. Z., Powers, W. J., Gusnard, D. A., & Shulman, G. L. (2001). A default mode of brain function. *Proceedings of the National Academy of Sciences USA, 98*, 676–682.

Raine, A. (2002). Annotation: The role of prefrontal deficits, low autonomic arousal, and early health factors in the development of antisocial and aggressive behavior in children. *Journal of Child Psychology and Psychiatry, 43*, 417–434.

Raine, A., Bihrle, S., Venables, P. H., Mednick, S. A., & Pollock, V. (1999). Skin-conductance orienting deficits and increased alcoholism in schizotypal criminals. *Journal of Abnormal Psychology, 108*, 299–306.

Raine, A., & Lencz, T. (1993). Brain imaging research on electrodermal activity in humans. In J.-C. Roy, W. Boucsein, D. C. Fowles, & J. H. Gruzelier (Eds.), *Progress in electrodermal research: From physiology to psychology* (pp. 115–135). London: Plenum.

Raine, A., Lencz, T., Bihrle, S., LaCasse, L., & Colletti, P. (2000). Reduced prefrontal gray matter volume and reduced autonomic activity in antisocial personality disorder. *Archives of General Psychiatry, 57*, 119–127.

Raine, A., Reynolds, G. P., & Sheard, C. (1991). Neuroanatomical correlates of skin conductance orienting in normal humans: A magnetic resonance imaging study. *Psychophysiology, 28*, 548–558.

Raine, A., & Venables, P. H. (1981). Classical conditioning and socialization – A biosocial interaction. *Personality and Individual Differences, 2*, 273–283.

Raine, A., & Venables, P. H. (1984). Electrodermal nonresponding, antisocial behavior, and schizoid tendencies in adolescents. *Psychophysiology, 21*, 424–433.

Raine, A., Venables, P. H., & Williams, M. (1990a). Relationship between central and autonomic measures of arousal at age 15 years and criminality at age 24 years. *Archives of General Psychiatry, 47*, 1003–1007.

Raine, A., Venables, P. H., & Williams, M. (1990b). Autonomic orienting responses in 15-year-old male subjects and criminal behavior at age 24. *The American Journal of Psychiatry, 147*, 933–937.

Raine, A., Venables, P. H., & Williams, M. (1995). High autonomic arousal and electrodermal orienting at age 15 years as protective factors against criminal behavior at age 29 years. *The American Journal of Psychiatry, 152*, 1595–1600.

Rajamanickam, M., & Gnanaguru, K. (1981). Physiological correlates of personality. *Psychological Studies, 26*, 41–43.

Rakov, G. V., & Fadeev, Y. A. (1986). Assessment of emotional stress during work activity by system analysis of the galvanic skin reflex. *Human Physiology, 11*, 215–220.

Rappaport, H., & Katkin, E. S. (1972). Relationships among manifest anxiety, response to stress, and the perception of autonomic activity. *Journal of Consulting and Clinical Psychology, 38*, 219–224.

Raskin, D. C. (1973). Attention and arousal. In W. F. Prokasy & D. C. Raskin (Eds.), *Electrodermal activity in psychological research* (pp. 125–155). New York: Academic.

Raskin, M. (1975). Decreased skin conductance response habituation in chronically anxious patients. *Biological Psychology, 2*, 309–319.

Raskin, D. C. (1979). Orienting and defensive reflexes in the detection of deception. In H. D. Kimmel, E. H. van Olst, & J. F. Orlebeke (Eds.), *The orienting reflex in humans* (pp. 587–605). Hillsdale, NJ: Erlbaum.

Raskin, D. C., & Honts, C. R. (2002). The Comparison Question Test. In M. Kleiner (Ed.), *Handbook of polygraph testing* (pp. 1–48). San Diego, CA: Academic.

Raskin, D. C., Kotses, H., & Bever, J. (1969). Autonomic indicators of orienting and defensive reflexes. *Journal of Experimental Psychology, 3*, 423–433.

Raskin, D. C., & Podlesny, J. A. (1979). Truth and deception: A reply to Lykken. *Psychological Bulletin, 86*, 54–59.

Reddy, M. M., & Quinton, P. M. (1994). Rapid regulation of electrolyte absorption in sweat duct. *Journal of Membrane Biology, 140*, 57–67.

Reeves, B., Lang, A., Kim, E. Y., & Tatar, D. (1999). The effects of screen size and message content on attention and arousal. *Media Psychology, 1*, 49–67.

Rescorla, R. A. (1967). Pavlovian conditioning and its proper control procedures. *Psychological Review, 74,* 71–80.

Rescorla, R. A. (1969). Pavlovian conditioned inhibition. *Psychological Bulletin, 72,* 77–94.

Rescorla, R. A. (1988). Pavlovian conditioning: It's not what you think it is. *American Psychologist, 43,* 151–160.

Rice, D. G. (1966). Operant conditioning and associated electromyogram responses. *Journal of Experimental Psychology, 71,* 908–912.

Richter, P., Wagner, T., Heger, R., & Weise, G. (1998). Psychophysiological analysis of mental load during driving on rural roads – A quasi-experimental field study. *Ergonomics, 41,* 593–609.

Rickels, K. (1978). Use of antianxiety agents in anxious outpatients. *Psychopharmacology, 58,* 1–17.

Rickles, W. H., & Day, J. L. (1968). Electrodermal activity in non-palmar skin sites. *Psychophysiology, 4,* 421–435.

Ridgeway, D., & Hare, R. D. (1981). Sensation seeking and psychophysiological responses to auditory stimulation. *Psychophysiology, 18,* 613–618.

Riley, L. H., & Richter, C. P. (1975). Uses of the electrical skin resistance method in the study of patients with neck and upper extremity pain. *The Johns Hopkins Medical Journal, 137,* 69–74.

Rippon, G. (1990). Individual differences in electrodermal and electroencephalographic asymmetries. *International Journal of Psychophysiology, 8,* 309–320.

Ritchie, B. H. (1953). The circumnavigation of cognition. *Psychological Review, 60,* 216–221.

Rizzolatti, G., & Buchtel, H. A. (1977). Hemispheric superiority in reaction time to faces: A sex difference. *Cortex, 13,* 300–305.

Roberts, L. E. (1974). Comparative psychophysiology of the electrodermal and cardiac control systems. In P. A. Obrist, A. H. Black, J. Brener, & L. V. DiCara (Eds.), *Cardiovascular psychophysiology* (pp. 163–189). Chicago: Aldine.

Roberts, L. E. (1977). The role of exteroceptive feedback in learned electrodermal and cardiac control: Some attractions of and problems with discrimination theory. In J. Beatty & H. Legewie (Eds.), *Biofeedback and behavior* (pp. 261–280). New York: Plenum.

Roberts, L. E., Lacroix, J. M., & Wright, M. (1974). Comparative studies of operant electrodermal and heart rate conditioning in curarized rats. In P. A. Obrist, A. H. Black, J. Brener, & L. V. DiCara (Eds.), *Cardiovascular psychophysiology* (pp. 332–352). Chicago: Aldine.

Roberts, L. E., & Young, R. (1971). Electrodermal responses are independent of movement during aversive conditioning in rats, but heart rate is not. *Journal of Comparative and Physiological Psychology, 77,* 495–512.

Rodriguez, S., Fernandez, M. C., Cependa-Benito, A., & Vila, J. (2005). Subjective and physiological reactivity to chocolate images in high and low chocolate cravers. *Biological Psychology, 70,* 9–18.

Roedema, T. M., & Simons, R. F. (1999). Emotion-processing deficit in alexithymia. *Psychophysiology, 36,* 279–387.

Román, F., García-Sánchez, F. A., Martínez-Selva, J. M., Gómez-Amor, J., & Carrillo, E. E. (1989). Sex differences and bilateral electrodermal activity: A replication. *The Pavlovian Journal of Biological Science, 24,* 150–155.

Rommelspacher, H. (1981). The beta-carbolines (harmanes): A new class of endogenous compounds: Their relevance for the pathogenesis and treatment of psychiatric and neurological diseases. *Pharmacopsychiatry, 14,* 117–125.

Rosenman, R. H., Friedman, M., Straus, R., Wurm, M., Jenkins, C. D., & Messinger, H. B. (1966). Coronary heart disease in the Western Collaborative Group Study. A follow-up experience of two years. *Journal of the American Medical Association, 195,* 130–136.

Rotenberg, V. S., & Vedenyapin, A. B. (1985). GSR as reflection of decision-making under conditions of delay. *The Pavlovian Journal of Biological Science, 20,* 11–14.

Roth, W. T., Goodale, J., & Pfefferbaum, A. (1991). Auditory event-related potentials and electrodermal activity in medicated and unmedicated schizophrenics. *Biological Psychiatry, 29,* 585–599.

Roth, W. T., Wilhelm, F. H., & Trabert, W. (1998). Autonomic instability during relaxation in panic disorder. *Psychiatry Research, 80,* 155–164.

Rothman, S. (1954). *Physiology and biochemistry of the skin*. Chicago: University of Chicago Press.

Routtenberg, A. (1968). The two-arousal hypothesis: Reticular formation and limbic system. *Psychological Review, 75*, 51–80.

Routtenberg, A. (1971). Stimulus processing and response execution: A neurobehavioral theory. *Physiology & Behavior, 6*, 589–596.

Roy, J.-C., Boucsein, W., Fowles, D. C., & Gruzelier, J. H. (1993). *Progress in electrodermal research: From physiology to psychology*. New York: Plenum.

Roy, J.-C., Delerm, B., & Granger, L. (1974). L'inhibition bulbaire de l'activité électrodermale chez le chat. *Electroencephalography and Clinical Neurophysiology, 37*, 621–632.

Roy, J.-C., Sequeira, H., & Delerm, B. (1993). Neural control of electrodermal activity: Spinal and reticular mechanisms. In J.-C. Roy, W. Boucsein, C. D. Fowles, & J. H. Gruzelier (Eds.), *Progress in electrodermal research* (pp. 73–92). New York: Plenum.

Roy, J.-C., Sequeira-Martinho, A. H., & Brochard, J. (1984). Pyramidal control of skin potential responses in the cat. *Experimental Brain Research, 54*, 283–288.

Rubens, R., & Lapidus, L. B. (1978). Schizophrenic patterns of arousal and stimulus barrier functioning. *Journal of Abnormal Psychology, 87*, 199–211.

Rushby, J. A., & Barry, R. J. (2007). Event-related potential correlates of phasic and tonic measures of the orienting reflex. *Biological Psychology, 75*, 248–259.

Rutenfranz, J. (1955). Zur Frage einer Tagesrhythmik des elektrischen Hautwiderstandes beim Menschen. *Internationale Zeitschrift für angewandte Physiologie einschließlich Arbeitsphysiologie, 16*, 152–172.

Rutenfranz, J. (1958). Der Widerstand der Haut gegenüber schwachen elektrischen Strömen. *Der Hautarzt, 9*, 289–299.

Rutenfranz, J., & Wenzel, H. G. (1958). Über quantitative Zusammenhänge zwischen Wasserabgabe, Wechselstromwiderstand und Kapazität der Haut bei körperlicher Arbeit und unter verschiedenen Raumtemperaturen. *Internationale Zeitschrift für angewandte Physiologie einschließlich Arbeitsphysiologie, 17*, 155–176.

Saari, A., Tolonen, U., Pääkkö, E., Suominen, K., Pyhtinen, J., Sotaniemi, K. A., Jauhiainen, J., & Myllylä, V. V. (2008). Sympathetic skin responses in multiple sclerosis. *Acta Neurologica Scandinavica, 118*, 226–231.

Sagberg, F. (1980). Dependence of EDR recovery times and other electrodermal measures on scale of measurement: A methodological clarification. *Psychophysiology, 17*, 506–509.

Salter, D. C. (1979). Quantifying skin disease and healing in vivo using electrical impedance measurements. In P. Rolfe (Ed.), *Non-invasive physiological measurements* (Vol. 1, pp. 21–64). London: Academic.

Salter, D. C. (1981). Alternating current electrical properties of human skin measured in vivo. In R. Marks & P. A. Payne (Eds.), *Bioengineering and the skin* (pp. 267–274). Lancaster: MTP.

Salzman, L. F., & Klein, R. H. (1978). Habituation and conditioning of electrodermal responses in high-risk children. *Schizophrenia Bulletin, 4*, 210–222.

Sargent, F. I. (1962). Depression of sweating in man: So-called "sweat gland fatigue". In W. Mortagra, R. A. Ellis, & F. Silver (Eds.), *Biology of the skin* (Vol. III, pp. 163–212). Oxford: Pergamon.

Sarkany, I., Shuster, S., & Stammers, M. C. (1965). Occlusion of the sweat pore by hydration. *The British Journal of Dermatology, 77*, 101–104.

Sartory, G. (1983). The orienting response and psychopathology: Anxiety and phobias. In D. Siddle (Ed.), *Orienting and habituation: Perspectives in human research* (pp. 449–474). Chichester: Wiley.

Sato, K. (1977). The physiology, pharmacology, and biochemistry of the eccrine sweat gland. *Reviews of Physiology, Biochemistry and Pharmacology, 79*, 51–131.

Sato, K. (1983). The physiology and pharmacology of the eccrine sweat gland. In L. A. Goldsmith (Ed.), *Biochemistry and physiology of the skin* (Vol. 1, pp. 596–641). New York: Oxford University Press.

Sato, K., Kang, W. H., Saga, K., & Sato, K. T. (1989). Biology of sweat glands and their disorders. I. Normal sweat gland function. *Journal of the American Academy of Dermatology, 20*, 537–563.

Sato, F., Owen, M., Matthes, R., Sato, K., & Gisolfi, C. V. (1990). Functional and morphological changes in the eccrine sweat gland with heat acclimation. *Journal of Applied Physiology, 69*, 232–236.

Sato, K., & Sato, F. (1981). Pharmacologic responsiveness of isolated single eccrine sweat glands. *The American Journal of Physiology, 240*, R44–R51.

Satterfield, J. H., & Dawson, M. E. (1971). Electrodermal correlates of hyperactivity in children. *Psychophysiology, 8*, 191–197.

Scarpa, A., & Raine, A. (1997). Psychophysiology of anger and violent behavior. *The Psychiatric Clinics of North America, 20*, 375–394.

Scerbo, A. S., Freedman, L. W., Raine, A., Dawson, M. E., & Venables, P. H. (1992). A major effect of recording site on measurement of electrodermal activity. *Psychophysiology, 29*, 241–246.

Scerbo, M. W., Freeman, F. G., & Mikulka, P. J. (2000). A biocybernetic system for adaptive automation. In R. W. Backs & W. Boucsein (Eds.), *Engineering psychophysiology. Issues and applications* (pp. 241–253). Mahwah, NY: Lawrence Erlbaum.

Schachter, S., & Singer, J. E. (1962). Cognitive, social and physiological determinants of emotional state. *Psychological Review, 69*, 379–399.

Schaefer, F. (1993). A new approach to circumventing the conductance-resistance choice: Phase angle between alternating-current and -voltage. In J. C. Roy, W. Boucsein, D. C. Fowles, & J. H. Gruzelier (Eds.), *Progress in electrodermal research* (pp. 43–48). London: Plenum.

Schaefer, F., & Boucsein, W. (2000). Comparison of electrodermal constant voltage and constant current recording techniques using phase angle between alternating voltage and current. *Psychophysiology, 37*, 85–91.

Schaefer, F., Kuhmann, W., Boucsein, W., & Alexander, J. (1986). Beanspruchung durch Bildschirmtätigkeit bei experimentell variierten Systemresponsezeiten. *Zeitschrift für Arbeitswissenschaft, 40*(12 NF), 31–38.

Schaefer, F., Schäfer, R., & Boucsein, W. (2000). Auswirkungen von Prozesslaufzeit und Prozessindikatoren beim Multi-Tasking auf Arbeitsstrategie und Beanspruchung des Benutzers. *Zeitschrift für Arbeitswissenschaft, 54*, 267–275.

Schandry, R. (1978). *Habituation psychophysiologischer Größen in Abhängigkeit von der Reizintensität*. München: Minerva.

Schell, A. M., Dawson, M. E., & Filion, D. I. (1988). Psychophysiological correlates of electrodermal lability. *Psychophysiology, 25*, 619–632.

Schell, A. M., Dawson, M. E., Nuechterlein, K. H., Subotnik, K. L., & Ventura, J. (2002). The temporal stability of electrodermal variables over a one-year period in patients with recent-onset schizophrenia and in normal subjects. *Psychophysiology, 39*, 124–132.

Schell, A. M., Dawson, M. E., Rissling, A., Ventura, J., Subotnik, K. L., Gitlin, M. J., & Nuechterlein, K. H. (2005). Electrodermal predictors of functional outcome and negative symptoms in schizophrenia. *Psychophysiology, 42*, 483–492.

Scheuplein, R. (1978). Site variations in diffusion and permeability. In A. Jarrett (Ed.), *The physiology and pathophysiology of the skin* (The sweat glands, skin permeation, lymphatics, and the nails, Vol. 5, pp. 1731–1752). New York: Academic.

Schiffmann, K., & Furedy, J. J. (1972). Failures of contingency and cognitive factors to affect long-interval differential Pavlovian autonomic conditioning. *Journal of Experimental Psychology, 96*, 215–218.

Schiffter, R., & Pohl, P. (1972). Zum Verlauf der absteigenden zentralen Sympathikusbahn. *Archiv für Psychiatrie und Nervenkrankheiten, 216*, 379–392.

Schiffter, R., & Schliack, H. (1968). Das sogenannte Geschmacksschwitzen. *Fortschritte der Neurologie-Psychiatrie, 36*, 262–274.

Schliack, H., & Schiffter, R. (1979). Neurophysiologie und Pathophysiologie der Schweißsekretion. In E. Schwarz, H. W. Spier, & G. Stüttgen (Eds.), *Handbuch der Haut- und Geschlechtskrankheiten* (1/4A, Vol. Normale und pathologische Physiologie der Haut II, pp. 349–458). Berlin: Springer.

Schmidt, S., Schneider, R., Binder, M., Bürkle, D., & Walach, H. (2001). Investigating methodological issues in EDA-DMILS: Results from a pilot study. *The Journal of Parapsychology, 65*, 59–82.

Schmidt, S., & Walach, H. (2000). Electrodermal activity (EDA) – State-of-the-art measurement and techniques for parapsychological purposes. *The Journal of Parapsychology, 64*, 139–164.

Schneider, R. L. (1987). A mathematical model of human skin conductance. *Psychophysiology, 24*, 610.

Schneider, R. E., & Fowles, D. C. (1978). A convenient, non-hydrating electrolyte medium for the measurement of electrodermal activity. *Psychophysiology, 15*, 483–486.

Schneider, R., Schmidt, S., Binder, M., Schaefer, F., & Walach, H. (2003). Respiration-related artifacts in EDA recordings: Introducing a standardized method to overcome multiple interpretations. *Psychological Reports, 93*, 907–920.

Schnur, D. B., Bernstein, A. S., Mukherjee, S., Loh, J., Degreef, G., & Reidel, J. (1989). The autonomic orienting response and CT scan findings in schizophrenia. *Schizophrenia Research, 2*, 449–455.

Schönpflug, W., Deusinger, I. M., & Nitsch, F. (1966). Höhen-und Zeitmaße der psychogalvanischen Reaktion. *Psychologische Forschung, 29*, 1–21.

Schulter, G., & Papousek, I. (1992). Bilateral electrodermal activity: Reliability, laterality and individual differences. *International Journal of Psychophysiology, 13*, 199–213.

Schulter, G., & Papousek, I. (1998). Bilateral electrodermal activity: Relationsships to state and trait characteristics of hemisphere asymmetry. *International Journal of Psychophysiology, 31*, 1–12.

Schulz, I., Ullrich, K. J., Frömter, E., Holzgreve, H., Frick, A., & Hegel, U. (1965). Mikropunktion und elektrische Potentialmessung an Schweissdrüsen des Menschen. *Pflügers Archiv für die gesamte Physiologie, 284*, 360–372.

Schuri, U., & von Cramon, D. (1979). Autonomic responses to meaningful and non-meaningful auditory stimuli in coma. *Archiv für Psychiatrie und Nervenkrankheiten, 227*, 143–149.

Schuri, U., & von Cramon, D. (1980). Autonomic and behavioral responses in coma due to drug overdose. *Psychophysiology, 17*, 253–258.

Schuri, U., & von Cramon, D. (1981). Electrodermal responses to auditory stimuli with different significance in neurological patients. *Psychophysiology, 18*, 248–251.

Schuri, U., & von Cramon, D. (1982). Electrodermal response patterns in neurological patients with disturbed vigilance. *Behavioural Brain Research, 4*, 95–102.

Schwalen, S., Altermann, A., Jörg, J., Berg, K., & Cramer, B. M. (1996). Bilateral suppression of the sympathetic nervous system in hemispheric brain infarction. *Journal of Neurology, 243*, 157–160.

Schwan, H. P. (1963). Determination of biological impedances. In W. L. Nastuk (Ed.), *Physical techniques in biological research* (Vol. 6, pp. 323–407). New York: Academic.

Schwartz, G. E. (1986). Emotion and psychophysiological organization: A systems approach. In M. G. H. Coles, E. Donchin, & S. W. Porges (Eds.), *Psychophysiology: Systems, processes, and applications* (pp. 354–377). Amsterdam: Elsevier.

Schwartz, G. E., & Shapiro, D. (1973). Social Psychophysiology. In W. F. Prokasy & D. C. Raskin (Eds.), *Electrodermal activity in psychological research* (pp. 377–416). New York: Academic.

Schwarz, E., Spier, H. W., & Stüttgen, G. (Eds.). (1979). *Handbuch der Haut- und Geschlechtskrankheiten* (Normale und pathologische Physiologie der Haut II, Vol. 1/4A). Berlin: Springer.

Segal, E. M., & Lachman, R. (1972). Complex behavior or higher mental process: Is there a paradigm shift? *American Psychologist, 27*, 45–55.

Seligman, M. E. P. (1969). Control group and conditioning: A comment on operationism. *Psychological Review, 76*, 484–491.

Seligman, M. E. P. (1971). Phobias and preparedness. *Behavior Therapy, 2*, 307–320.

Seligman, L. (1975). Skin potential as an indicator of emotion. *Journal of Counseling Psychology, 22*, 489–493.

Selye, H. (1976). *The stress of life*. New York: McGraw-Hill.

Sequeira, H., Hot, P., Silvert, L., & Delplanque, S. (2009). Electrical autonomic correlates of emotion. *International Journal of Psychophysiology, 71*, 50–56.

Sequeira, H., & Roy, J.-C. (1993). Cortical and hypothalamo-limbic control of electrodermal responses. In J.-C. Roy, W. Boucsein, C. D. Fowles, & J. H. Gruzelier (Eds.), *Progress in Electrodermal Research* (pp. 93–114). New York: Plenum.

Sequeira, H., & Roy, J. C. (1997). Neural control of electrodermal activity. In D. Jordan (Ed.), *Central nervous control of autonomic function* (pp. 259–293). Amsterdam: Harwood Academic.

Sequeira-Martinho, H., Roy, J.-C., & Ba-M'hamed, S. (1986). Cortical and pyramidal stimulation elicit nonlateralized skin potential responses in the cat. *Biological Psychology, 23*, 81.

Shackel, B. (1959). Skin-drilling: A method of diminishing galvanic skin potentials. *The American Journal of Psychology, 72*, 14–21.

Shahani, B., Halperin, J. J., Boulu, P., & Cohen, J. (1984). Sympathetic skin response – A method of assessing unmyelinated axon dysfunction in peripheral neuropathies. *Journal of Neurology, 47*, 536–542.

Shapiro, D. (1977). A monologue on biofeedback and psychophysiology. *Psychophysiology, 14*, 213–227.

Shapiro, D., & Leiderman, P. H. (1954). Studies on the galvanic skin potential level: Some statistical properties. *Journal of Psychosomatic Research, 7*, 269–275.

Sharpless, D., & Jasper, H. (1956). Habituation of the arousal reaction. *Brain, 79*, 655–681.

Shaver, B. A., Brusilow, S. W., & Cooke, R. E. (1965). Electrophysiology of the sweat gland: Intraductal potential changes during secretion. *Bulletin of the John Hopkins Hospital, 116*, 100–109.

Shields, S. A., MacDowell, K. A., Fairchild, S. B., & Campbell, M. L. (1987). Is mediation of sweating cholinergic, adrenergic, or both? A comment on the literature. *Psychophysiology, 24*, 312–319.

Shmavonian, B. M., & Busse, E. W. (1963). Psychophysiologic techniques in the study of the aged. In R. Williams, C. Tibbits, & W. Donahue (Eds.), *Processes of aging* (pp. 160–183). New York: Atherton.

Shmavonian, B. M., Miller, L. H., & Cohen, S. I. (1968). Differences among age and sex groups in electrodermal conditioning. *Psychophysiology, 5*, 119–131.

Shmavonian, B. M., Yarmat, A. J., & Cohen, S. I. (1965). Relationship between the autonomic nervous system and central nervous system in age differences in behavior. In A. T. Welford & J. E. Birren (Eds.), *Aging and the nervous system* (pp. 235–258). Springfield: Thomas.

Shneiderman, B. (1992). Response time and display rate. In B. Shneiderman (Ed.), *Designing the user interface* (pp. 277–301). Reading, MA: Addison-Wesley.

Siddle, D. A. T. (1972). Vigilance decrement and speed of habituation of the GSR component of the orienting response. *British Journal of Psychology, 63*, 191–194.

Siddle, D. A. T. (1977). Electrodermal activity and psychopathy. In S. A. Mednick & K. O. Christiansen (Eds.), *Biosocial bases of criminal behavior* (pp. 199–211). New York: Gardener.

Siddle, D. (Ed.). (1983). *Orienting and habituation: Perspectives in human research*. Chichester: Wiley.

Siddle, D. A. T. (1985). Effects of stimulus omission and stimulus change on dishabituation of the skin conductance response. *Journal of Experimental Psychology. Learning, Memory, and Cognition, 11*, 206–216.

Siddle, D. A. T. (1991). Orienting, habituation, and resource allocation: An associative analysis. *Psychophysiology, 28*, 245–259.

Siddle, D. A. T., & Heron, P. A. (1976). Reliability of electrodermal habituation measures under two conditions of stimulus intensity. *Journal of Research in Personality, 10*, 195–200.

Siddle, D. A. T., Lipp, O. V., & Dall, P. J. (1996). Effects of intermodality change and number of training trials on electodermal orienting and on the allocation of processing resources. *Biological Psychology, 43*, 57–67.

Siddle, D. A. T., O'Gorman, J. G., & Wood, L. (1979). Effects of electrodermal lability and stimulus significance on electrodermal response amplitude to stimulus change. *Psychophysiology, 16*, 520–527.

Siddle, D. A. T., & Packer, J. (1987). Stimulus omission and dishabituation of the electrodermal orienting response: The allocation of processing resources. *Psychophysiology, 24*, 181–190.

Siddle, D. A. T., & Remington, B. (1987). Latent inhibition and human Pavlovian conditioning: Research and relevance. In G. Davey (Ed.), *Conditioning in humans* (pp. 115–146). Chichester: Wiley.

Siddle, D. A. T., Remington, B., Kuiack, M., & Haines, E. (1983). Stimulus omission and dishabituation of the skin conductance response. *Psychophysiology, 20*, 136–145.

Siddle, D., Stephenson, D., & Spinks, J. A. (1983). Elicitation and habituation of the orienting response. In D. Siddle (Ed.), *Orienting and habituation: Perspectives in human research* (pp. 109–182). Chichester: Wiley.

Siddle, D. A. T., Turpin, G., Spinks, J. A., & Stephenson, D. (1980). Peripheral measures. In H. M. van Praag, M. H. Lader, O. J. Rafaelsen, & E. J. Sachar (Eds.), *Handbook of biological psychiatry: Part 2. Brain mechanisms and abnormal behavior – Psychophysiology* (pp. 45–78). New York: Dekker.

Silver, A., Montagna, W., & Karacan, I. (1965). The effect of age on human eccrine sweating. In W. Montagna (Ed.), *Advances in biology of skin* (Vol. 6, pp. 129–150). Oxford: Pergamon.

Silverman, A. J., Cohen, S. I., & Shmavonian, B. M. (1958). Psychophysiologic response specificity in the elderly. *Journal of Gerontology, 5*, 443.

Silverman, A. J., Cohen, S. I., & Shmavonian, B. M. (1959). Investigation of psychophysiological relationships with skin resistance measures. *Journal of Psychosomatic Research, 4*, 65–87.

Silverman, J. J., & Powell, V. E. (1944). Studies on palmar sweating: I. A technique for the study of palmar sweating. *American Journal of the Medical Sciences, 208*, 297–299.

Silvert, L., Delplanque, S., Bouwalerh, H., Verpoort, C., & Sequeira, H. (2004). Autonomic responding to aversive words without conscious valence discrimination. *International Journal of Psychophysiology, 53*, 135–145.

Silvestrini, N., & Gendolla, G. H. E. (2007). Mood effects on autonomic activity in mood regulation. *Psychophysiology, 44*, 650–659.

Simon, W. R., & Homoth, R. W. G. (1978). An automatic voltage suppressor for the measurement of electrodermal activity. *Psychophysiology, 15*, 502–505.

Simons, R. F., Detenber, B. H., Roedema, T. M., & Reiss, J. E. (1999). Emotion processing in three systems: The medium and the message. *Psychophysiology, 36*, 619–627.

Simpson, A., & Turpin, G. (1983). A device for ambulatory skin conductance monitoring. *Psychophysiology, 20*, 225–229.

Sinclair, D. (1973). Motor nerves and reflexes. In A. Jarrett (Ed.), *The physiology and pathophysiology of the skin* (The nerves and blood vessels, Vol. 2, pp. 475–508). New York: Academic.

Siniatchkin, M., Gerber, W.-D., Kropp, P., Voznesenskaya, T., & Vein, A. M. (2000). Are the periodic changes of neurophysiological parameters during the pain-free interval in migraine related to abnormal orienting activity? *Cephalalgia, 20*, 20–29.

Smith, B. D., Gatchel, R. J., Korman, M., & Satter, S. (1979). EEG and autonomic responding to verbal, spatial and emotionally arousing tasks: Differences among adults, adolescents and inhalant abusers. *Biological Psychology, 9*, 189–200.

Smith, B. D., Ketterer, M. W., & Concannon, M. (1981). Bilateral electrodermal activity as a function of hemispheric stimulation, hand preference, sex, and familial handedness. *Biological Psychology, 12*, 1–11.

Smith, B. D., Kline, R., & Meyers, M. (1990). The differential hemisphere processing of emotion: A comparative analysis in strongly-lateralized sinistrals and dextrals. *International Journal of Neuroscience, 50*, 59–71.

Smith, B. D., Perlstein, W. M., Davidson, R. A., & Michael, K. (1986). Sensation seeking: Differential effects of relevant, novel stimulation on electrodermal activity. *Personality and Individual Differences, 7*, 445–452.

Smith, B. D., Wilson, R. J., & Jones, B. E. (1983). Extraversion and multiple levels of caffeine-induced arousal: Effects on overhabituation and dishabituation. *Psychophysiology, 20*, 29–34.

Sokolov, E. N. (1960). Neuronal models in the orienting reflex. In M. A. Brazier (Ed.), *The central nervous system and behavior* (pp. 187–275). New York: Macy Foundation.

Sokolov, E. N. (1963a). Higher nervous functions: The orienting reflex. *Annual Review of Physiology, 25*, 545–580.

Sokolov, E. N. (1963b). *Perception and the conditioned reflex.* Oxford: Pergamon.

Sokolov, E. N. (1966). Orienting reflex as information regulator. In A. N. Leontiev, A. R. Luria, E. N. Sokolov, & O. S. Vinogradova (Eds.), *Psychological research in the USSR* (Vol. 1, pp. 334–359). Moscow: Progress.

Sokolov, E. N., & Boucsein, W. (2000). A psychophysiological model of emotion space. *Integrative Physiological and Behavioral Science, 35*, 81–119.

Solanto, M. V., & Katkin, E. S. (1979). Classical EDR conditioning using a truly random control and subjects differing in electrodermal lability level. *Bulletin of the Psychonomic Society, 14*, 49–52.

Solomon, K., & Hart, R. (1978). Pitfalls and prospects in clinical research on antianxiety drugs: Benzodiazepines and placebo: A research review. *The Journal of Clinical Psychiatry, 39*, 823–831.

Sorgatz, H. (1978). Components of skin impedance level. *Biological Psychology, 6*, 121–125.

Sorgatz, H., & Pufe, P. (1978). Die differentielle Reagibilität der elektrodermalen Aktivität für aversive Reize. *Zeitschrift für Experimentelle und Angewandte Psychologie, 3*, 465–473.

Sosnowski, T. (1988). Patterns of skin conductance and heart rate changes under anticipatory stress conditions. *Journal of Psychophysiology, 2*, 231–238.

Sosnowski, T., Nurzynska, M., & Polec, M. (1991). Active-passive coping and skin conductance and heart rate changes. *Psychophysiology, 28*, 665–672.

Sostek, A. J. (1978). Effects of electrodermal lability and payoff instructions on vigilance performance. *Psychophysiology, 15*, 561–568.

Spence, K. W., Haggard, D. F., & Ross, L. E. (1958). UCS intensity and the associative (habit) strength of the eyelid CR. *Journal of Experimental Psychology, 55*, 404–411.

Spiegel, E. A., & Hunsicker, W. C. (1936). The conduction of cortical impulses to the autonomic system. *The Journal of Nervous and Mental Disease, 83*, 252–274.

Spielberger, C. D. (1983). *Manual for the state-trait anxiety inventory*. Palo Alto, CA: Consulting Psychologist.

Spinks, J. A. (1977). *Information and the orientating response*. Unpublished Doctoral Dissertation, University of Southampton, Southampton

Spinks, J. A., Blowers, G. H., & Shek, D. T. L. (1985). The role of the orienting response in the anticipation of information: A skin conductance response study. *Psychophysiology, 22*, 385–394.

Spinks, J. A., Dow, R., & Chiu, L. W. (1983). A microcomputer package for real-time skin conductance response analysis. *Behavior Research Methods & Instrumentation, 15*, 591–593.

Spinks, J. A., & Siddle, D. (1983). The functional significance of the orienting response. In D. Siddle (Ed.), *Orienting and habituation: Perspectives in human research* (pp. 237–314). Chichester: Wiley.

Spohn, H. E., & Patterson, T. (1979). Recent studies of psychophysiology in schizophrenia. *Schizophrenia Bulletin, 5*, 581–611.

Spohn, H. E., Thetford, P. E., & Cancro, R. (1971). The effects of phenothiazine medication on skin conductance and heart rate in schizophrenic patients. *The Journal of Nervous and Mental Disease, 152*, 129–139.

Sponheim, S. R., Allen, J. J., & Iacono, W. G. (1995). Selected psychophysiological measures in depression: The significance of electrodermal Activity, electroencephalographic asymmetries, and contingent negative variation to behavioral and neurobiological aspects of depression. In G. A. Miller (Ed.), *The behavioral high risk paradigm in psychopathology* (pp. 222–249). New York: Springer.

Springer, S. P. (1977). Tachistoscopic and dichotic listening investigations of laterality in normal human subjects. In S. Harnad, R. W. Doty, L. Goldstein, J. Jaynes, & G. Krauthamer (Eds.), *Lateralization in the nervous system* (pp. 325–336). New York: Academic.

Springer, S. P., & Deutsch, G. (1981). *Left brain, right brain*. San Francisco: Freeman.

Springer, J., Müller, T., Langner, T., Luczak, H., & Beitz, W. (1990). Stress and strain caused by CAD-work – Results of a laboratory study. In L. Berlinguet & D. Berthelette (Eds.), *Work with Display Units 1989* (pp. 231–238). Amsterdam: Elsevier.

Squires, R. F., & Braestrup, C. (1977). Benzodiazepine receptors in rat brain. *Nature, 266*, 732–734.

Steigleder, G. K. (1983). *Dermatologie und Venerologie*. Stuttgart: Thieme.

Steinberg, E. P., & Schwartz, G. E. (1976). Biofeedback and electrodermal self-regulation in psychopathy. *Journal of Abnormal Psychology, 85*, 408–415.

Stellar, J. R., & Stellar, E. (1985). *The neurobiology of motivation and reward.* New York: Springer.

Steller, M. (1987). *Psychophysiologische Aussagebeurteilung. Wissenschaftliche Grundlagen und Anwendungsmöglichkeiten der "Lügendetektion.".* Göttingen: Hogrefe.

Stelmack, R. M. (1981). The psychophysiology of extraversion and neuroticism. In H. J. Eysenck (Ed.), *A model for personality* (pp. 38–64). New York: Springer.

Stelmack, R. M., Plouffe, L., & Falkenberg, W. (1983). Extraversion, sensation seeking and electrodermal response: Probing a paradox. *Personality and Individual Differences, 4*, 607–614.

Stelmack, R. M., Plouffe, L. M., & Winogron, H. W. (1983). Recognition memory and the orienting response: An analysis of the encoding of pictures and words. *Biological Psychology, 16*, 49–63.

Stemmler, G. (1984). *Psychophysiologische Emotionsmuster.* Frankfurt: Peter Lang.

Stemmler, G. (1987). Standardization within subjects: A critique of Ben-Shakhar's conclusions. *Psychophysiology, 24*, 243–246.

Stemmler, G. (1989). The autonomic differentiation of emotions revisited: Convergent and discriminant validation. *Psychophysiology, 26*, 617–631.

Stemmler, G. (2002). Methodological considerations in the psychophysiological study of emotion. In R. J. Davidson, H. H. Goldsmith, & K. R. Scherer (Eds.), *Handbook of affective science* (pp. 225–255). New York: Oxford University Press.

Stephens, W. G. S. (1963). The current-voltage relationship in human skin. *Medical, Electronics and Biological Engineering, 1*, 389–399.

Stephenson, D., & Siddle, D. A. T. (1976). Effects of "below-zero" habituation on the electrodermal orienting response to a test stimulus. *Psychophysiology, 13*, 10–15.

Stephenson, D., & Siddle, D. A. T. (1983). Theories of habituation. In D. Siddle (Ed.), *Orienting and habituation: Perspectives in human research* (pp. 183–236). Chichester: Wiley.

Steptoe, A., & Greer, K. (1980). Relaxation and skin conductance feedback in the control of reactions to cognitive tasks. *Biological Psychology, 10*, 127–138.

Steptoe, A., Melville, D., & Ross, A. (1984). Behavioral response demands, cardiovascular reactivity, and essential hypertension. *Pyschosomatic Medicine, 46*, 33–48.

Steptoe, A., & Ross, A. (1981). Psychophysiological reactivity and the prediction of cardiovascular disorders. *Journal of Psychosomatic Research, 25*, 23–31.

Stern, R. M. (1972). Detection of one's own spontaneous GSRs. *Psychonomic Science, 29*, 354–356.

Stern, R. M., & Anschel, C. (1968). Deep inspirations as stimuli for responses of the autonomic nervous system. *Psychophysiology, 5*, 132–141.

Stern, J. A., & Janes, C. L. (1973). Personality and psychopathology. In W. F. Prokasy & D. C. Raskin (Eds.), *Electrodermal activity in psychological research* (pp. 283–346). New York: Academic.

Stern, J. A., Surphlis, W., & Koff, E. (1965). Electrodermal responsiveness as related to psychiatric diagnosis and prognosis. *Psychophysiology, 2*, 51–61.

Stern, J. A., & Walrath, L. C. (1977). Orienting responses and conditioning of electrodermal responses. *Psychophysiology, 14*, 334–342.

Sternbach, R. A., & Tursky, B. (1965). Ethnic differences among housewives in psychophysical and skin potential responses to electric shock. *Psychophysiology, 1*, 241–246.

Stevens, P. (2000). Human electrodermal response to remote human monitoring: Classification and analysis of response characteristics. *The Journal of Parapsychology, 64*, 391–409.

Stewart, M. A., Stern, J. A., Winokur, G., & Fredman, S. (1961). An analysis of GSR conditioning. *Psychological Review, 68*, 60–67.

Stocksmeier, U., & Langosch, W. (1973). *Die Galvanische Hautreaktion bei inneren Erkrankungen.* Göttingen: Hogrefe.

Stone, L. A., & Nielson, K. A. (2001). Intact physiological response to arousal with impaired emotional recognition in alexithymia. *Psychotherapy and Psychosomatics, 70*, 92–102.

Storm, H., Myre, K., Rostrup, M., Stokland, O., Lien, M. D., & Raeder, J. C. (2002). Skin conductance correlates with perioperative stress. *Acta Anesthesiolologica Scandinavica, 46,* 887–895.

Storrie, M. C., Doerr, H. O., & Johnson, M. H. (1981). Skin conductance characteristics of depressed subjects before and after therapeutic intervention. *The Journal of Nervous and Mental Disease, 169,* 176–179.

Straube, E. R. (1979). On the meaning of electrodermal nonresponding in schizophrenia. *The Journal of Nervous and Mental Disease, 167,* 601–611.

Strelau, J. (1983). *Temperament, personality, activity* (pp. 141–166). New York: Academic.

Sturgeon, D., Kuipers, L., Berkowitz, R., Turpin, G., & Leff, J. (1981). Psychophysiological responses of schizophrenic patients to high and low expressed emotion relatives. *The British Journal of Psychiatry, 138,* 40–45.

Sturgeon, D., Turpin, G., Kuipers, L., Berkowitz, R., & Leff, J. (1984). Psychophysiological responses of schizophrenic patients to high and low expressed emotion relatives: A follow-up study. *The British Journal of Psychiatry, 145,* 62–69.

Stüttgen, G., & Forssmann, W. G. (1981). Pharmacology of the microvasculature of the skin. In G. Stüttgen, H. W. Spier, & E. Schwarz (Eds.), *Handbuch der Haut- und Geschlecht-skrankheiten* (Normale und pathologische Physiologie der Haut III, Vol. 1/4B, pp. 379–540). Berlin: Springer.

Surwillo, W. W. (1965). Level of skin potential in healthy males and the influence of age. *Journal of Gerontology, 20,* 519–521.

Surwillo, W. W. (1967). The influence of some psychological factors on latency of the galvanic skin reflex. *Psychophysiology, 4,* 223–228.

Surwillo, W. W. (1969). Statistical distribution of volar skin potential level in attention and the effects of age. *Psychophysiology, 6,* 13–16.

Surwillo, W. W., & Quilter, R. E. (1965). The relation of frequency of spontaneous skin potential responses to vigilance and to age. *Psychophysiology, 1,* 272–276.

Surwit, R. S., & Poser, E. G. (1974). Latent inhibition in the conditioned electrodermal response. *Journal of Comparative and Physiological Psychology, 86,* 543–548.

Sutton, S. K., & Davidson, R. J. (1997). Prefrontal brain asymmetry: A biological substrate of the behavioral approach and inhibition systems. *Psychological Science, 8,* 204–210.

Suzuki, A., Hirota, A., Takasawa, N., & Shigemasu, K. (2003). Application of the somatic marker hypothesis to individual differences in decision-making. *Biological Psychology, 65,* 81–88.

Swartzman, L. C., Edelberg, R., & Kemmann, E. (1990). The menopausal hot flush: Symptom reports and concomitant physiological changes. *Journal of Behavioral Medicine, 13,* 15–30.

Tabbert, K., Stark, R., Kirsch, P., & Vaitl, D. (2006). Dissociation of neural responses and skin conductance reactions during fear conditioning with and without awareness of stimulus contingencies. *NeuroImage, 32,* 761–770.

Takagi, K., & Nakayama, T. (1959). Peripheral effector mechanism of galvanic skin reflex. *The Japanese Journal of Physiology, 9,* 1–7.

Tanaka, J., Ishida, S., Kawagoe, H., & Kondo, S. (2000). Workload of using a driver assistance system. 2000 IEEE Intelligent Transportation Systems Conference Proceedings Dearborn, MI.

Tarchanoff, J. (1889). Decharges électriques dans la peau de l'homme sous l'influence de l'excitation des organes de sens et de differentes formes d'activité psychiqué. *Comptes Rendus des Séances de la Société de Biologie, 41,* 447–451.

Tarchanoff, J. (1890). Über die galvanischen Erscheinungen an der Haut des Menschen bei Reizung der Sinnesorgane und bei verschiedenen Formen der psychischen Tätigkeit. *Pflügers Archiv für die Gesamte Physiologie des Menschen und der Tiere, 46,* 46–55.

Tarrier, N., Cooke, E. C., & Lader, M. H. (1978). Electrodermal and heart-rate measurements in chronic and partially remitted schizophrenic patients. *Acta Psychiatrica Scandinavica, 57,* 369–376.

Tarrier, N., Vaughn, C., Lader, M. H., & Leff, J. P. (1979). Bodily reactions to people and events in schizophrenics. *Archives of General Psychiatry, 36,* 311–315.

Tassinary, L. G., Geen, T. R., Cacioppo, J. T., & Edelberg, R. (1990). Issues in biometrics: Offset potentials and the electrical stability of Ag/AgCl electrodes. *Psychophysiology, 27,* 236–242.

Taylor, J. A. (1953). A personality scale of manifest anxiety. *Journal of Abnormal and Social Psychology, 48*, 285–290.

Taylor, D. H. (1964). Drivers galvanic skin response and the risk of accident. *Ergonomics, 7*, 439–451.

Taylor, J., Carlson, S. R., Iacono, W. G., Lykken, D. T., & McGue, M. (1999). Individual differences in electrodermal responsivity to predictable aversive stimuli and substance dependence. *Psychophysiology, 36*, 193–198.

Tchanturia, K., Liao, P. C., Uher, R., Lawrence, N., Treasure, J., & Campbell, I. C. (2007). An investigation of decision making in anorexia nervosa using the Iowa Gambling Task and skin conductance measurements. *Journal of the International Neuropsychological Society, 13*, 635–641.

Thackray, R. I., & Orne, M. T. (1968). A comparison of physiological indices in detection of deception. *Psychophysiology, 4*, 329–339.

Tharp, M. D. (1983). Adrenergic receptors in the skin. In L. A. Goldsmith (Ed.), *Biochemistry and physiology of the skin* (Vol. 2, pp. 1210–1216). New York: Oxford University Press.

Thetford, P. E., Klemme, M. E., & Spohn, H. E. (1968). Skin potential, heart rate, and the span of immediate memory. *Psychophysiology, 5*, 166–177.

Thews, G., Mutschler, E., & Vaupel, P. (1985). *Human anatomy, physiology, and pathophysiology*. Amsterdam: Elsevier.

Thiele, F. A. J. (1981a). The functions of the atrichial (human) sweat gland. In G. Stüttgen, H. W. Spier, & E. Schwarz (Eds.), *Handbuch der Haut- und Geschlechtskrankheiten* (Normale und pathologische Physiologie der Haut III, Vol. 1/4B, pp. 2–121). Berlin: Springer.

Thiele, F. A. J. (1981b). The sweat gland and the stratum corneum. In G. Stüttgen, H. W. Spier, & E. Schwarz (Eds.), *Handbuch der Haut- und Geschlechtskrankheiten* (Normale und pathologische Physiologie der Haut III, Vol. 1/4B, pp. 501–514). Berlin: Springer.

Thom, E. (1988). Die Hamburger EDA-Auswertung. Appendix in W. Boucsein, *Elektrodermale Aktiviät. Grundlagen, Methoden und Anwendungen* (pp. 501–514). Berlin: Springer.

Thomas, P. E., & Korr, I. M. (1957). Relationship between sweat gland activity and electrical resistance of the skin. *Journal of Applied Physiology, 10*, 505–510.

Thompson, M. L. (1954). A comparison between the number and distribution of functioning eccrine sweat glands in Europeans and Africans. *The Journal of Physiology, 123*, 225–233.

Thompson, J. K., & Adams, H. E. (1984). Psychophysiological characteristics of headache patients. *Pain, 18*, 41–52.

Thompson, R. F., Groves, P. M., Teyler, T. J., & Roemer, R. A. (1973). A dual-process theory of habituation: Theory and behavior. In H. V. S. Peeke & M. J. Herz (Eds.), *habituation* (Behavioral studies, Vol. 1, pp. 239–271). New York: Academic.

Thompson, R. F., & Spencer, W. A. (1966). Habituation: A model phenomenon for the study of neuronal substrates of behavior. *Psychological Review, 73*, 16–43.

Thomson, S., & Thomson, M. L. A. (1952). A new technique for enumerating active sweat glands in man. Journal of Physiology, 117, 51–52.

Thorell, L.-H., & d'Elia, G. (1988). Electrodermal activity in depressive patients in remission and in matched healthy subjects. Acta Psychiatrica Scandinavica, 78, 247–253.

Thorpe, W. M. (1969). *Learning and instinct in animals*. London: Methuen.

Thum, M., Boucsein, W. J., Kuhmann, W., & Ray, W. J. (1995). Standardized task strain and system response times in human-computer interaction. *Ergonomics, 38*, 1342–1351.

Tomb, I., Hauser, M., Deldin, P., & Caramazza, A. (2002). Do somatic markers mediate decisions on the gambling task? *Nature Neuroscience, 5*, 1103–1104.

Toyokura, M. (1999). Waveform variation and size of sympathetic skin response: Regional difference between the sole and palm recordings. *Clinical Neurophysiology, 110*, 765–771.

Toyokura, M. (2006). Sympathetic skin responses: The influence of electrical stimulus intensity and habituation on the waveform. *Clinical Autonomic Research, 16*, 130–135.

Tranel, D. T. (1983). The effects of monetary incentive and frustrative nonreward on heart rate and electrodermal activity. *Psychophysiology, 20*, 652–657.

Tranel, D. (2000). Electrodermal activity in cognitive neuroscience: Neuroanatomical and neuro-psychological correlates. In R. D. Lane & L. Nadel (Eds.), *Cognitive neuroscience of emotion* (pp. 192–224). New York: Oxford University Press.

Tranel, D., & Damasio, A. R. (1988). Non-conscious face recognition in patients with face agnosia. *Behavioural Brain Research, 30*, 235–249.

Tranel, D., & Damasio, H. (1989). Intact electrodermal skin conductance responses after bilateral amygdala damage. *Neuropsychologia, 27*, 381–390.

Tranel, D., & Damasio, A. R. (1993). The covert learning of affective valence does not require structures in hippocampal system or amygdala. *Journal of Cognitive Neuroscience, 5*, 79–88.

Tranel, D., & Damasio, H. (1994). Neuroanatomical correlates of electrodermal skin conductance response. *Psychophysiology, 31*, 427–438.

Tranel, D. T., Fisher, A. E., & Fowles, D. C. (1982). Magnitude of incentive effects on heart rate. *Psychophysiology, 19*, 514–519.

Tranel, D., Fowles, D. C., & Damasio, A. R. (1985). Electrodermal discrimination of familiar and unfamiliar faces: A methodology. *Psychophysiology, 22*, 403–408.

Trasler, G. (1973). Criminal behaviour. In H. J. Eysenck (Ed.), *Handbook of abnormal psychology* (pp. 67–92). London: Pitman.

Traxel, W. (1957). Über das Zeitmaß der psychogalvanischen Reaktion. *Zeitschrift für Psychologie, 161*, 282–291.

Traxel, W. (1960). Die Möglichkeit einer objektiven Messung der Stärke von Gefühlen. *Psychologische Forschung, 26*, 75–90.

Tregear, R. T. (1966). *Physical functions of skin*. London: Academic.

Tronstad, C., Johnsen, G. K., Grimnes, S., & Martinsen, O. G. (2010). A study on electrode gels for skin conductance measurements. *Physiological Measurement, 31*, 1395–1410.

Tucker, D. M. (1981). Lateral brain function, emotion and conceptualization. *Psychological Bulletin, 89*, 19–46.

Turkstra, L. S. (1995). Electrodermal response and outcome from severe brain injury. *Brain Injury, 9*, 61–80.

Turpin, G. (1986). Effects of stimulus intensity on autonomic responding: The problem of differentiating orienting and defense reflexes. *Psychophysiology, 23*, 1–14.

Turpin, G., & Clements, K. (1993). Electrodermal activity and psychopathology: The development of the palmar sweat index (PSI) as an applied measure for use in clinical settings. In J.-C. Roy, W. Boucsein, D. C. Fowles, & J. H. Gruzelier (Eds.), *Progress in electrodermal research: From physiology to psychology* (pp. 49–60). London: Plenum.

Turpin, G., Schaefer, F., & Boucsein, W. (1999). Effects of stimulus intensity, risetime, and duration on autonomic and behavioral responding: Implications for the differentiation of orienting, startle, and defense responses. *Psychophysiology, 36*, 453–463.

Turpin, G., Shine, P., & Lader, H. (1983). Ambulatory electrodermal monitoring effects of ambient temperature, general activity, electrolyte media, and length of recording. *Psychophysiology, 20*, 219–224.

Turpin, G., & Siddle, D. A. T. (1979). Effects of stimulus intensity on electrodermal activity. *Psychophysiology, 16*, 582–591.

Turpin, G., Tarrier, N., & Sturgeon, D. (1988). Social psychophysiology and the study of biopsychosocial models of schizophrenia. In H. L. Wagner (Ed.), *Social psychophysiology and emotion: Theory and clinical applications* (pp. 251–272). Chichester: Wiley.

Uchiyama, I. (1992). Differentiation of fear, anger, and joy. *Perceptual and Motor Skills, 74*, 663–667.

Uncini, A., Pullman, S. L., Lovelace, R. E., & Gambi, D. (1988). The sympathetic skin response: Normal values, elucidation of afferent components and application limits. *Journal of the Neurological Sciences, 87*, 299–306.

Undeutsch, U. (1983). Die psychophysiologische Täterschaftsermittlung. In F. Lösel (Ed.), *Kriminalpsychologie* (pp. 191–206). Weinheim: Beltz.

Uno, H. (1977). Sympathetic innervation of the sweat glands and piloarrector muscles of macaques and human beings. *The Journal of Investigative Dermatology, 69*, 112–120.

Uno, T., & Grings, W. W. (1965). Autonomic components of orienting behavior. *Psychophysiology, 1*, 311–321.

Urry, H. L., van Reekum, C. M., Johnstone, T., & Davidson, R. J. (2009). Individual differences in some (but not all) medial prefrontal regions reflect cognitive demand while regulating unpleasant emotion. *Neuroimage, 47*, 852–863.

Van Bokhoven, I., Matthys, W., van Goozen, S. H. M., & van Engeland, H. (2005). Prediction of adolescent outcome in children with disruptive behaviour disorders. A study of neurobiological, psychological and family factors. *European Child and Adolescent Psychiatry, 14*, 153–163.

Van Boxtel, A. (1977). Skin resistance during square-wave electrical pulses of 1 to 10 mA. *Medical & Biological Engineering & Computing, 15*, 679–687.

Van de Staak, W. J. B. M. (1966). Experiences with the heated thermocouples method for measuring skin blood flow. *Dermatologica, 132*, 199–205.

Van der Valk, P. G. M., & Maibach, H. I. (1990). A functional study of the skin barrier to evaporative water loss by means of repeated cellophane-tape stripping. *Clinical and Experimental Dermatology, 15*, 180–182.

Van Doornen, L. J. P., Orlebeke, J. F., & Somsen, J. M. (1980). Coronary risk and coping with aversive stimuli. *Psychophysiology, 17*, 598–603.

Van Dyke, J. L., Rosenthal, D., & Rasmussen, P. V. (1974). Electrodermal functioning in adopted-away offspring of schizophrenics. *Journal of Psychiatric Research, 10*, 199–215.

Van Goozen, S. H. M., Matthys, W., Cohen-Kettenis, P. T., Buitelaar, J. K., & van Engeland, H. (2000). Hypothalamic-pituitary-adrenal axis and autonomic nervous system activity in disruptive children and matched controls. *Journal of the American Academy of Child and Adolescent Psychiatry, 39*, 1438–1445.

Van Twyver, H. B., & Kimmel, H. D. (1966). Operant conditioning of the GSR with concomitant measurement of two somatic variables. *Journal of Experimental Psychology, 72*, 841–846.

Vansteenwegen, D., Iberico, C., Vervliet, B., Marescau, V., & Hermans, D. (2008). Contextual fear induced by unpredictability in a human fear conditioning preparation is related to the chronic expectation of a threatening US. *Biological Psychology, 77*, 39–46.

Vaughan, K. B., & Lanzetta, J. T. (1981). The effect of modification of expressive displays on skin reflex. *Psychophysiology, 4*, 223–228.

Venables, P. H. (1955). The relationships between P.G.R. scores and temperature and humidity. *Quarterly Journal of Experimental Psychology, 7*, 12–18.

Venables, P. H. (1975). Psychophysiological studies of schizophrenic pathology. In P. H. Venables & M. J. Christie (Eds.), *Research in psychophysiology* (pp. 282–324). London: Wiley.

Venables, P. H. (1977). The electrodermal psychophysiology of schizophrenics and children at risk for schizophrenia: Controversies and developments. *Schizophrenia Bulletin, 3*, 28–48.

Venables, P. H. (1978). Psychophysiology and psychometrics. *Psychophysiology, 15*, 302–314.

Venables, P. H. (1983). Some problems and controversies in the psychophysiological investigation of schizophrenia. In A. Gale & J. A. Edwards (Eds.), *Physiological correlates of human behaviour* (Individual differences and psychopathology, Vol. 3, pp. 207–232). London: Academic.

Venables, P. H., & Christie, M. J. (1973). Mechanisms, instrumentation, recording techniques, and quantification of responses. In W. F. Prokasy & D. C. Raskin (Eds.), *Electrodermal activity in psychological research* (pp. 1–124). New York: Academic.

Venables, P. H., & Christie, M. J. (1980). Electrodermal activity. In I. Martin & P. H. Venables (Eds.), *Techniques in psychophysiology* (pp. 3–67). New York: Wiley.

Venables, P. H., & Fletcher, R. P. (1981). The status of skin conductance recovery time: An examination of the Bundy effect. *Psychophysiology, 18*, 10–16.

Venables, P. H., Gartshore, S. A., & O'Riordan, P. W. (1980). The function of skin conductance response recovery and rise time. *Biological Psychology, 10*, 1–6.

Venables, P. H., & Martin, I. (1967a). Skin resistance and skin potential. In P. H. Venables & I. Martin (Eds.), *A manual of psychophysiological methods* (pp. 53–102). Amsterdam: North Holland.

Venables, P. H., & Martin, I. (1967b). The relation of palmar sweat gland activity to level of skin potential and conductance. *Psychophysiology, 3*, 302–311.

Venables, P. H., & Mitchell, D. A. (1996). The effects of age, sex and time of testing on skin conductance activity. *Biological Psychology, 43,* 87–101.

Venables, P. H., & Sayer, E. (1963). On the measurement of the level of skin potential. *British Journal of Psychology, 54,* 251–260.

Veraguth, O. (1909). *Das psychogalvanische Reflexphänomen.* Berlin: Karger.

Verschuere, B., Crombez, G., De Clercq, A., & Koster, E. H. W. (2004). Autonomic and behavioral responding to concealed information: Differentiating orienting and defensive responses. *Psychophysiology, 41,* 461–466.

Vervliet, B., Vansteenwegen, D., Baeyens, F., Hermans, D., & Eelen, P. (2005). Return of fear in a human differential conditioning paradigm caused by a stimulus change after extinction. *Behavior Research and Therapy, 43,* 357–371.

Vetrugno, R., Liguori, R., Cortelli, P., & Montagna, P. (2003). Sympathetic skin response. Basic mechanisms and clinical applications. *Clinical Autonomic Research, 13,* 256–270.

Vickland, V., Rogers, C., Craig, A., & Tran, Y. (2008). Electrodermal activity as a possible physiological marker for acupuncture. *Complementary Therapies in Clinical Practice, 14,* 83–89.

Vigouroux, R. (1879). Sur le role de la résistance électrique de tissue dans l'électrodiagnostic. *Comptes Rendus des Seances de la Société de Biologie, 31,* 336–339.

Vögele, C., & Florin, I. (1997). Psychophysiological responses to food exposure: An experimental study in binge eaters. *International Journal of Eating Disorders, 21,* 147–157.

Vögele, C., & Steptoe, A. (1986). Physiological and subjective stress reponses in surgical patients. *Journal of Psychosomatic Research, 30,* 205–215.

Volow, M. R., Erwin, C. W., & Cipolat, A. L. (1979). Biofeedback control of skin potential level. *Biofeedback and Self-Regulation, 4,* 133–143.

von Dultzig, K. (1997). *Erfolgskontrolle von Fernsehwerbespots.* Köln: Josef Eul.

Vossel, G., & Roßmann, R. (1982). Interindividuelle Unterschiede in der Habituationsgeschwindigkeit der EDA: Eine systematische Analyse der Zusammenhänge verschiedener Habituationskennwerte. *Zeitschrift für Differentielle und Diagnostische Psychologie, 3,* 281–292.

Vossel, G., & Roßmann, R. (1984). Electrodermal habituation speed and visual monitor performance. *Psychophysiology, 21,* 97–100.

Wagner, A. R. (1969). Stimulus selection and a "modified continuity theory. In G. H. Bowers & J. T. Spence (Eds.), *The psychology of learning and motivation* (Vol. 3, pp. 1–41). New York: Academic.

Wagner, A. R. (1976). Priming in STM: An information-processing mechanism for self-generated or retrieval-generated depression in performance. In T. J. Tighe & R. N. Leaton (Eds.), *Habituation: Perspectives from child development, animal behavior, and neurophysiology* (pp. 95–128). Hillsdale, NJ: Erlbaum.

Wagner, A. R. (1978). Expectancies and the priming of STM. In S. H. Hulse, H. Fowler, & W. K. Honig (Eds.), *Cognitive process in animal behavior* (pp. 177–209). Hillsdale, NJ: Erlbaum.

Wagner, H. (1989). The peripheral physiological differentiation of emotions. In H. Wagner & A. Manstead (Eds.), *Handbook of social psychophysiology* (pp. 77–98). London: Wiley.

Waid, W. M. (1974). Degree of goal-orientation, level of cognitive activity and electrodermal recovery rate. *Perceptual and Motor Skills, 38,* 103–109.

Waid, W. M., & Orne, M. T. (1980). Individual differences in electrodermal lability and the detection of information and deception. *The Journal of Applied Psychology, 65,* 1–8.

Waid, W. M., & Orne, M. T. (1981). Cognitive, social, and personality processes in the physiological detection of deception. In L. Berkowitz (Ed.), *Advances in experimental social psychology* (pp. 61–106). New York: Academic.

Waid, W. M., Orne, E. C., Cook, M. R., & Orne, M. T. (1981). Meprobamate reduces accuracy of physiological detection of deception. *Science, 212,* 71–73.

Waid, W. M., Wilson, S. K., & Orne, M. T. (1981). Cross-modal physiological effects of electrodermal lability in the detection of deception. *Journal of Personality and Social Psychology, 40,* 1118–1125.

Wallin, B. G. (1981). Sympathetic nerve activity underlying electrodermal and cardiovascular reactions in man. *Psychophysiology, 18,* 470–476.

Wallin, B. G. (1992). Intraneural recordings of normal and abnormal sympathetic activity in man. In R. Bannister & C. J. Mathias (Eds.), *Autonomic failure* (pp. 359–377). Oxford: Medical.

Walrath, L. C., & Stern, J. A. (1980). General considerations. In H. M. van Praag, M. H. Lader, O. J. Rafaelsen, & E. J. Sachor (Eds.), *Handbook of biological psychiatry: Part 2. Brain mechanisms and abnormal behavior – Psychophysiology* (pp. 1–43). New York: Dekker.

Walschburger, P. (1975). Zur Standardisierung und Interpretation elektrodermaler Messwerte in psychologischen Experimenten. *Zeitschrift für Experimentelle und Angewandte Psychologie, 22*, 514–533.

Walschburger, P. (1976). Zur *Beschreibung von Aktivierungsprozessen: Eine Methodenstudie zur psychophysiologischen Diagnostik.* Freiburg: Unpublished Doctoral Dissertation, Albert-Ludwig-Universität.

Walschburger, P. (1986). Psychophysiological activation research. In J. Valsiner (Ed.), *The individual subject and scientific psychology* (pp. 311–345). London: Plenum.

Wang, G. H. (1964). *The neural control of sweating.* Madison: University of Wisconsin Press.

Wang, G. H., & Brown, V. W. (1956). Suprasegmental inhibition of an autonomic reflex. *Journal of Neurophysiology, 19*, 564–572.

Wang, S. J., Fuh, J. L., Shan, D. E., Liao, K. K., Lin, K. P., Tsai, C. P., & Wu, Z. A. (1993). Sympathetic skin response and R-R interval variation in Parkinson's disease. *Movement Disorders, 8*, 151–157.

Wang, S.-M., & Kain, Z. N. (2001). Auricular acupuncture: A potential treatment for anxiety. *Anasthesia & Analgesia, 92*, 548–553.

Wang, G. H., & Lu, T. W. (1930). Galvanic skin reflex induced in the cat by stimulation of the motor area of the cerebral cortex. *Chinese Journal of Physiology, 4*, 303–326.

Warburton, D. M. (1983). Exploration in the neurochemistry of behaviour. In G. Davey (Ed.), *Animal models of human behaviour* (pp. 339–353). London: Wiley.

Ward, N. G., & Doerr, H. O. (1986). Skin conductance: A potentially sensitive and specific marker for depression. *The Journal of Nervous and Mental Disease, 174*, 553–559.

Ward, N. G., Doerr, H. O., & Storrie, M. C. (1983). Skin conductance: A potentially sensitive test for depression. *Psychiatry Research, 10*, 295–302.

Waters, W. F., Koresko, R. L., Rossie, G. V., & Hackley, S. A. (1979). Short-, medium-, and long-term relationships among meteorological and electrodermal variables. *Psychophysiology, 16*, 445–451.

Watt, N. F., Anthony, E. J., Wynne, L. C., & Rolf, J. E. (Eds.). (1984). *Children at risk for schizophrenia: A longitudinal perspective.* London: Cambridge University Press.

Wechsler, D. (1925). The measurement of emotional reactions: Researches on the psychogalvanic reflexes. *Archives of Psychology, 12*, 1–181.

Wegner, W. (1981). *Täterschaftsermittlung durch Polygraphie.* Köln: Carl Heymanns.

Weigand, D. A., Haygood, C., & Gaylor, J. R. (1974). Cell layers and density of Negro and Caucasian stratum corneum. *The Journal of Investigative Dermatology, 62*, 563–568.

Weike, A. I., Schupp, H. T., & Hamm, A. O. (2007). Fear acquisition requires awareness in trace but not delay conditioning. *Psychophysiology, 44*, 170–180.

Weinberger, D. A., Schwartz, G. E., & Davidson, R. J. (1979). Low-anxious, high-anxious, and repressive coping styles: Psychometric patterns and behavioral and physiological responses to stress. *Journal of Abnormal Psychology, 88*, 369–380.

Weiner, J. S., & Hellmann, K. (1960). The sweat glands. *Biological Reviews, 35*, 141–186.

Weinstein, J., Averill, J. R., Opton, E. M., & Lazarus, R. S. (1968). Defensive style and discrepancy between self-report and physiological indexes of stress. *Journal of Personality and Social Psychology, 10*, 406–413.

Weisz, J., & Czigler, I. (2006). Age and novelty: Event-related brain potentials and autonomic activity. *Psychophysiology, 43*, 261–271.

Weitkunat, R., Bührer, M., & Sparrer, B. (1990). Cortical initiation of phasic electrodermal activity. *International Journal of Psychophysiology, 9*, 303–314.

Wendt, J., Lotze, M., Weike, A. I., Hosten, N., & Hamm, A. O. (2008). Brain activation and defensive response mobilization during sustained exposure to phobia-related and other affective pictures in spider phobia. *Psychophysiology, 45*, 205–215.

Wenger, M. A., & Cullen, T. D. (1962). Some problems in psychophysiological research: III. The effects of uncontrolled variables. In R. Roessler & N. S. Greenfield (Eds.), *Psychophysiological correlates of psychological disorder* (pp. 106–114). Madison: University of Wisconsin Press.

Westbury, H. R., & Neumann, D. L. (2008). Empathy-related responses to moving film stimuli depicting human and non-human animal targets in negative circumstances. *Biological Psychology, 78*, 66–74.

Westerink, J., Ouwerkerk, M., de Vries, G.-J., de Waele, S., van den Eerenbeemd, J., & van Boven, M. (2009, 10–12 Sept). Emotion measurement platform for daily life situations. *International Conference on Affective Computing and Intelligent Interaction (ACII)*, Amsterdam, The Netherlands.

Whang, M. C. (2008). The emotional computer adaptive to human emotion. In J. Westerink, M. Ouwerkerk, T. Overbeek, F. Pasveer, & B. de Ruyter (Eds.), *Probing experience: From academic research to commercial propositions* (pp. 209–219). Dordrecht: Springer.

Whang, M. C., Lim, J. S., & Boucsein, W. (2003). Preparing computers for affective communications: A psychophysiological concept and preliminary results. *Human Factors, 45*, 623–634.

Wieland, B. A., & Mefferd, R. B. (1970). Systematic changes in levels of physiological activity during a four-month period. *Psychophysiology, 6*, 669–689.

Wilcott, R. C. (1958). Correlation of skin resistance and potential. *Journal of Comparative and Physiological Psychology, 51*, 691–696.

Wilcott, R. C. (1963). Effects of high environmental temperature on sweating and skin resistance. *Journal of Comparative and Physiological Psychology, 56*, 778–782.

Wilcott, R. C. (1964). The partial independence of skin potential and skin resistance from sweating. *Psychophysiology, 1*, 55–66.

Wilcott, R. C. (1965). A comparative study of the skin potential, skin resistance and sweating of the cat's foot pad. *Psychophysiology, 2*, 62–71.

Wilcott, R. C. (1966). Adaptive value of arousal sweating and the epidermal mechanism related to skin potential and skin resistance. *Psychophysiology, 2*, 249–262.

Wilcott, R. C. (1969). Electrical stimulation of the anterior cortex and skin potential responses in the cat. *Journal of Comparative and Physiological Psychology, 69*, 465–472.

Wilcott, R. C., & Bradley, H. H. (1970). Low-frequency electrical stimulation of the cat's anterior cortex and inhibition of skin potential changes. *Journal of Comparative and Physiological Psychology, 72*, 351–355.

Wilcott, R. C., & Hammond, L. J. (1965). On the constancy-current error in skin resistance measurement. *Psychophysiology, 2*, 39–41.

Wilder, J. (1931). Das"Ausgangswert-Gesetz" – ein unbeachtetes biologisches Gesetz; seine Bedeutung für Forschung und Praxis. *Klinische Wochenschrift, 41*, 1889–1893.

Wilhelm, F. H., Pfaltz, M. C., Gross, J. J., Mauss, I. B., Kim, S. I., & Wiederhold, B. K. (2005). Mechanisms of virtual reality exposure therapy: The role of the behavioral activation and behavioral inhibition systems. *Applied Psychophysiology and Biofeedback, 30*, 271–284.

Wilhelm, F. H., & Roth, W. T. (1996). Ambulatory assessment of clinical anxiety. In J. Fahrenberg & M. Myrtek (Eds.), *Ambulatory assessment: Computer-assisted psychological and psychophysiological methods in monitoring and field studies* (pp. 317–345). Göttingen: Hogrefe.

Wilhelm, F. H., & Roth, W. T. (1997). Acute and delayed effects of Alprazolam on flight phobics during exposure. *Behaviour Research and Therapy, 35*, 831–841.

Wilhelm, F. H., & Roth, W. T. (1998). Taking the laboratory to the skies: Ambulatory assessment of self-report, autonomic, and the respiratory responses in flying phobia. *Psychophysiology, 35*, 596–606.

Wilhelm, F. H., Roth, W. T., & Sackner, M. (2003). The LifeShirt: An advanced system for ambulatory measurement of respiratory and cardiac function. *Behavior Modification, 27*, 671–691.

Wilken, J. A., Smith, B. D., Tola, K., & Mann, M. (2000). Trait anxiety and prior exposure to non-stressful stimuli: Effects on psychophysiological arousal and anxiety. *International Journal of Psychophysiology, 37*, 233–242.

Williams, L. M., Brammer, M. J., Skerrett, D., Lagopolous, J., Rennie, C., Kozek, K., Olivieri, G., Peduto, T., & Gordon, E. (2000). The neural correlates of orienting: An integration of fMRI and skin conductance orienting. *Neuroreport, 11*, 3011–3015.

Williams, L. M., Brown, K. J., Das, P., Boucsein, W., Sokolov, E. N., Brammer, M. J., Olivieri, G., Peduto, A., & Gordon, E. (2004). The dynamics of cortico-amygdala and automatic activity over the experimental time course of fear perception. *Brain Research. Cognitive Brain Research, 21*, 114–123.

Williams, K. M., Iacono, W. G., & Remick, R. A. (1985). Electrodermal activity among subtypes of depression. *Biological Psychiatry, 20*, 158–162.

Williams, W. C., Parsons, R. L., & Strayer, D. L. (1981). Classical discrimination conditioning using the solutions to verbal and spatial problems as CSs: Bilateral measures of electrodermal excitation and inhibition. *Psychophysiology, 18*, 148–149.

Williams, L. M., Phillips, M. L., Brammer, M. J., Skerrett, D., Lagopoulos, J., Rennie, C., Bahramali, H., Olivieri, G., David, A. S., Peduto, A., & Gordon, E. (2001). Arousal dissociates amygdala and hippocampal fear responses: Evidence from simultaneous fMRI and skin conductance recording. *NeuroImage, 14*, 1070–1079.

Williamson, P. S., Fowles, D. C., & Weinberger, M. (1985). Electrodermal potential and conductance measurements clinically discriminate between cystic fibrosis and control patients. *Pediatric Research, 19*, 810–814.

Williamson, M. J., Paul, S. M., & Skolnick, P. (1978). Labelling of benzodiazepine receptors in vivo. *Nature, 275*, 551–553.

Wilson, G. R. (1985). A simple device for the objective evaluation of peripheral nerve injuries. *The Journal of Hand Surgery, 10*, 324–330.

Wilson, G. D. (1990). Personality, time of day and arousal. *Personality and Individual Differences, 11*, 153–168.

Wilson, G. F. (2002). An analysis of mental workload in pilots during flight using multiple psychophysiological measures. *The International Journal of Aviation Psychology, 12*, 3–18.

Wilson, J. W. D., & Dykman, R. A. (1960). Background autonomic activity in medical students. *Journal of Comparative and Physiological Psychology, 53*, 405–411.

Wilson, K. G., & Graham, R. S. (1989). Electrodermal lability and visual information processing. *Psychophysiology, 26*, 321–328.

Winton, W. M., Putnam, L. E., & Krauss, R. M. (1984). Facial and autonomic manifestations of the dimensional structure of emotion. *Journal of Experimental Social Psychology, 20*, 195–216.

Woodrough, R. E., Canti, G., & Watson, B. W. (1975). Electrical potential difference between basal cell carcinoma, benign inflammatory lesions and normal tissue. *The British Journal of Dermatology, 92*, 1–7.

Woodworth, R. S. & Schlosberg, H. (1954). *Experimental psychology* (3rd revised edn) New York: Holt, Rinehart, & Winston.

Wright, N. A. (1983). The cell proliferation kinetics of the epidermis. In L. A. Goldsmith (Ed.), *Biochemistry and physiology of the skin* (Vol. 1, pp. 203–229). New York: Oxford University Press.

Wright, N., & McGown, A. (2001). Vigilance on the civil flight deck: Incidence of sleepiness and sleep during long-haul flights and associated changes in physiological parameters. *Ergonomics, 44*, 82–106.

Wundt, W. (1896). *Grundriß der Psychologie*. Leipzig: Engelmann.

Wyatt, R., & Tursky, B. (1969). Skin potential levels in right- and left-handed males. *Psychophysiology, 6*, 133–137.

Wynn, J. K., Dawson, M. E., & Schell, A. M. (2000). Discrete and continuous prepulses have differential effects on startle prepulse inhibition and skin conductance orienting. *Psychophysiology, 37*, 224–230.

Yagi, A. (2000). Engineering psychophysiology in Japan. In R. W. Backs & W. Boucsein (Eds.), *Engineering psychophysiology: Issues and applications* (pp. 361–368). Mahwah, NJ: Lawrence Erlbaum.

Yamamoto, T., & Yamamoto, Y. (1976). Dielectric constant and resistivity of epidermal stratum corneum. *Medical & Biological Engineering & Computing, 14*, 494–500.

Yamamoto, Y., & Yamamoto, T. (1978). Technical note: Dispersion and correlation of the parameters for skin impedance. *Medical & Biological Engineering & Computing, 16*, 592–594.

Yamamoto, Y., & Yamamoto, T. (1979). Technical note: Dynamic system for the measurement of electrical skin impedance. *Medical & Biological Engineering & Computing, 17*, 135–137.

Yamamoto, T., & Yamamoto, Y. (1981). Non-linear electrical properties of skin in the low frequency range. *Medical & Biological Engineering & Computing, 19*, 302–310.

Yamamoto, Y., Yamamoto, T., Ohta, S., Uehara, T., Tahara, S., & Ishizuka, Y. (1978). The measurement principle for evaluating the performance of drugs and cosmetics by skin impedance. *Medical & Biological Engineering & Computing, 16*, 623–632.

Yamazaki, K., Okamura, T., & Takasawa, N. (2001). Overt palmar surface sweating produces positive component of palmar skin potential responses. *Japanese Journal of Physiological Psychology and Psychophysiology, 19*, 1–6.

Yokota, T., & Fujimori, B. (1962). Impedance change of the skin during the galvanic skin reflex. *The Japanese Journal of Physiology, 12*, 200–209.

Yokota, T., & Fujimori, B. (1964). Effects of brain-stem stimulation upon hippocampal electrical activity, somatomotor reflexes and autonomic functions. *Electroencephalography and Clinical Neurophysiology, 16*, 375–382.

Yokota, T., Sato, A., & Fujimori, B. (1963). Inhibition of sympathetic activity by stimulation of limbic systems. *The Japanese Journal of Physiology, 13*, 138–154.

Yoshino, A., Kimura, Y., Yoshida, T., Takahashi, Y., & Nomura, S. (2005). Relationships between temperament dimensions in personality and unconscious emotional responses. *Biological Psychiatry, 57*, 1–6.

Zahn, T. P. (1976). On the bimodality of the distribution of electrodermal orienting responses in schizophrenic patients. *The Journal of Nervous and Mental Disease, 162*, 195–199.

Zahn, T. P. (1978). Sensitivity of measurement and electrodermal "nonresponding" in schizophrenic and normal subjects. *Schizophrenia Bulletin, 4*, 153.

Zahn, T. P. (1986). Psychophysiological approaches to psychopathology. In M. G. H. Coles, E. Donchin, & S. W. Porges (Eds.), *Psychophysiology: Systems, processes, applications* (pp. 508–610). Amsterdam: Elsevier.

Zahn, T. P., Carpenter, W. T., & McGlashan, T. H. (1981a). Autonomic nervous system activity in acute schizophrenia: I. Method and comparison with normal controls. *Archives of General Psychiatry, 38*, 251–258.

Zahn, T. P., Carpenter, W. T., & McGlashan, T. H. (1981b). Autonomic nervous system activity in acute schizophrenia: II. Relationships to short-term prognosis and clinical state. *Archives of General Psychiatry, 38*, 260–266.

Zahn, T. P., Grafman, J., & Tranel, D. (1999). Frontal lobe lesions and electrodermal activity: Effects of significance. *Neuropsychologia, 37*, 1227–1241.

Zahn, T. P., Rosenthal, D., & Lawlor, W. G. (1968). Electrodermal and heart rate orienting reactions in chronic schizophrenia. *Journal of Psychiatric Research, 6*, 117–134.

Zeier, H. (1979). Concurrent physiological activity of driver and passenger when driving with and without automatic transmission in heavy city traffic. *Ergonomics, 22*, 799–810.

Zeiner, A. R. (1970). Orienting response and discrimination conditioning. *Physiology and Behaviour, 5*, 641–646.

Zelinski, E. M., Walsh, D. A., & Thompson, L. W. (1978). Orienting task effects on EDR and free recall in three age groups. *Journal of Gerontology, 33*, 239–245.

Zimmer, H. (2000). Frequenz und mittlere Amplitude spontaner elektrodermaler Fluktuationen sind keine austauschbaren Indikatoren psychischer Prozesse. *Zeitschrift für Experimentelle Psychologie, 47*, 129–143.

Zipp, P. (1983). Impedance controlled skin drilling. *Medical & Biological Engineering & Computing, 21*, 382–384.

Zipp, P., & Faber, S. (1979). Rückwirkungsarme Ableitung bioelektrischer Signale bei arbeitswissenschaftlichen Langzeituntersuchungen am Arbeitsplatz. *European Journal of Applied Physiology and Occupational Physiology, 42*, 105–116.

Zipp, P., Hennemann, K., Grunwald, R., & Rohmert, W. (1980). Bewertung von Kontaktvermittlern für Bioelektroden bei Langzeituntersuchungen. *European Journal of Applied Physiology and Occupational Physiology, 45*, 131–145.

Zoccolotti, P., Caltagirone, C., Pecchinenda, A., & Troisi, E. (1993). Electrodermal activity in patients with unilateral brain damage. In J.-C. Roy, W. Boucsein, C. D. Fowles, & J. H. Gruzelier (Eds.), *Progress in electrodermal research* (pp. 311–326). New York: Plenum.

Zoccolotti, P., Scabini, D., & Violani, C. (1982). Electrodermal responses in patients with unilateral brain damage. *Journal of Clinical Neuropsychology, 4*, 143–150.

Zubin, J., & Spring, B. (1977). Vulnerability – A new view of schizophrenia. *Journal of Abnormal Psychology, 86*, 103–126.

Zuckerman, M. (1983). A biological theory of sensation seeking. In M. Zuckerman (Ed.), *Biological bases of sensation seeking, impulsivity, and anxiety* (pp. 37–76). Hillsdale, NJ: Erlbaum.

Zuckerman, M. (1990). The psychophysiology of sensation seeking. *Journal of Personality, 58*, 313–345.

Zuckerman, M., Kolin, E. A., Price, L., & Zoob, I. (1964). Development of a sensation-seeking-scale. *Journal of Consulting Psychology, 28*, 477–482.

Zuckerman, M., & Lubin, B. (Eds.). (1965). *Manual for the multiple affect adjective check list.* San Diego: Edits.

Index

CPSIA information can be obtained at www.ICGtesting.com
Printed in the USA
LVOW070326221211

260645LV00001B/1/P

9 781461 411253